Managing Health Services Organizations and Systems

SEVENTH EDITION

Managing Health Services Organizations and Systems

SEVENTH EDITION

by

Kurt Darr, J.D., Sc.D., LFACHE
The George Washington University

Michael Nowicki, Ed.D., FACHE, FHFMA
Texas State University, San Marcos

Baltimore • London • Sydney

Health Professions Press, Inc.
Post Office Box 10624
Baltimore, Maryland 21285-0624

www.healthpropress.com

Interior and cover designs by Erin Geoghegan. Typeset by ASI, Towson, Maryland.
Manufactured in the United States of America by Versa Press, East Peoria, Illinois.

The information provided in this book is in no way meant to substitute for the advice or opinion of a medical, legal, or other professional or expert. This book is sold without warranties of any kind, express or implied, and the publisher and authors disclaim any liability, loss, or damage caused by the contents of this book.

Library of Congress Cataloging-in-Publication Data

Names: Darr, Kurt, author. | Nowicki, Michael, 1952–author.
   Managing health services organizations and systems.
Title: Managing health services organizations and systems / by Kurt Darr, Michael Nowicki.
Description: Seventh edition. | Baltimore : Health Professions Press, [2021] | Preceded by
   Managing health services organizations and systems / by Beaufort B. Longest, Jr.,
   Kurt Darr. Sixth edition. [2014] | Includes bibliographical references and index. |
Identifiers: LCCN 2020054383 (print) | LCCN 2020054384 (ebook) | ISBN 9781938870903 (hard-
cover) |
   ISBN 9781938870910 (ebook)
Subjects: MESH: Health Facility Administration | Hospital Administration | United States
Classification: LCC RA971 (print) | LCC RA971 (ebook) | NLM WX 150 AA1 | DDC
362.11068—dc23
LC record available at https://lccn.loc.gov/2020054383
LC ebook record available at https://lccn.loc.gov/2020054384

British Cataloguing in Publication data are available from the British Library.

Contents

About the Authors

Kurt Darr, J.D., Sc.D., LFACHE, Professor Emeritus, The George Washington University, Washington, D.C.

Dr. Darr taught for 43 years in the Department of Health Services Management and Policy at The George Washington University. He became Professor Emeritus in 2015. He holds a Doctor of Science from The Johns Hopkins University and a Master of Hospital Administration and Juris Doctor from the University of Minnesota.

Professor Emeritus Darr completed his administrative residency at Rochester (Minnesota) Methodist Hospital and subsequently worked as an administrative associate at the Mayo Clinic. After being commissioned in the U.S. Navy, he served in administrative and educational assignments at St. Albans Naval Hospital and Bethesda Naval Hospital. He completed postdoctoral fellowships with the Department of Health and Human Services, the World Health Organization, and the Commission on Accreditation of Healthcare Management Education.

Dr. Darr is a Life Fellow of the American College of Healthcare Executives (ACHE) and a member of the District of Columbia and Minnesota Bars, and he served for 20 years as a mediator in the Superior Court of the District of Columbia. His service on commissions and committees of various professional organizations includes The Joint Commission on Accreditation of Healthcare Organizations, the ACHE, and the Commission on Accreditation of Healthcare Management Education. He volunteers as an educator and consultant on quality improvement and ethics at acute care hospitals in the Washington, D.C., metropolitan area. Professor Emeritus Darr is the author and editor of numerous articles, monographs, and books in the health services field.

Michael Nowicki, Ed.D., FACHE, FHFMA, Professor, Texas State University, San Marcos.

Dr. Nowicki has taught for 34 years in the School of Health Administration at Texas State University. He holds a Doctor of Education in Educational Policy Studies and Evaluation from the University of Kentucky and a Master of Arts in Health Care Administration from The George Washington University.

Professor Nowicki completed his administrative residency at Hutzel Hospital in Detroit and subsequently worked in a variety of administrative positions at Valley Medical Center of Fresno and the hospital division of Humana.

Dr. Nowicki is a Fellow of the ACHE, where he has served as founder of and advisor to student chapters, founder of and president of the Central Texas Chapter, chair of the national Book-of-the-Year Committee, Regent–Texas Central and South, and member of the Finance Committee of the national board. Dr. Nowicki is a Fellow of the Healthcare Financial Management Association (HFMA), where he has served as president of the South Texas

Chapter, regional executive for Region 9, national board member, and chair of the Chapter Services Council and the Council on Forums. He served on the HFMA Board of Examiners and chaired the board in 2001. Professor Nowicki has presented financial management seminars to audiences worldwide and is a frequent speaker at ACHE and HFMA events. He is the author of numerous articles and books on healthcare financial management.

Preface

Outstanding health services organizations (HSOs) and health systems (HSs) establish the benchmarks for best practices. They satisfy their customers and patients, achieve quality and safety goals, and meet cost objectives. Such levels of excellence are possible only with superior management, talented clinicians, and dedicated governing bodies.

The 7th edition of *Managing Health Services Organizations and Systems* (MHSOS) continues a more than 40-year effort to educate, stimulate, and support development of the health services management profession. This book is an important resource for health services management and the development of its managers in several ways. It can be used in programs of health services management education offered in traditional and nontraditional formats, and it can be used in nonformal education experiences such as seminars, webinars, and self-instruction. The wealth of information and encyclopedic development of numerous topics makes it an enduring professional resource and go-to reference that enriches the library of every practicing health services manager.

The focus is managing HSOs—the wide range of providers that includes acute care hospitals, nursing facilities, managed care organizations—and the HSs with which they are likely affiliated. Attention is also given to managing public health organizations and services. Whether HSOs are independent entities or are aligned in HSs, they function within a dynamic external environment—a mosaic of forces that include significant regulation and new technology, changing demographics, increased competition, public scrutiny, heightened consumer expectations, greater demands for accountability, and major constraints on resources. MHSOS is a resource to help managers understand and meet the challenges of those demands.

The 7th edition includes more than 25 new case studies; each chapter has at least one new case. Several cases have been moved from the text to the Instructor's Manual for supplemental use. Discussion questions have been deleted, added, or revised consistent with the needs of chapters. The sections on emergency preparedness, patient and staff safety, infection control, employee stress, hazardous materials, workplace violence, and project management have been revised and updated. New to this edition is a section on healthcare compliance.

The 7th edition has been reorganized to emphasize the basic functions of managers that were identified by the French mining engineer and management theorist, Henri Fayol: planning, organizing, staffing, directing, and controlling. This edition devotes a chapter to each, providing an emphasis synergistic to the learning experience of users. The content of the book's three parts is summarized in the next section, About This Edition.

Nascent managers cultivate professional sophistication by learning terms of art, accessing an enhanced and updated list of acronyms, and gaining insights into how the healthcare field came to be what it is. These basics are a vital foundation for lifelong learning and professional development.

In this book, experienced managers will find reinforcement of existing skills and experience, provision and application of new theory, and new ways of using traditional theory and concepts. Managing in the unique environment that is health services delivery requires attention to the essential managerial tools and techniques. The 14 chapters in this 7th edition of *Managing Health Services Organizations and Systems* are an integrated, comprehensive whole that covers the practice of management in HSOs and HSs. Updated and enhanced discussion questions and new cases will stimulate thought and dialogue about chapter content. This book will assist all who aspire to establish benchmarks of excellence in the extraordinarily complex and essential sector that is health services delivery.

About This Edition

The five chapters in Part I, "The Environment," describe the setting and provide a context for delivery of services.

Chapter 1, "Healthcare in the United States," identifies and describes public and private entities, knowledge about which is the grounding for understanding, organizing, and delivering health services. Organizations, regulators, educators, accreditors, and financing are discussed.

Chapter 2, "Ethical and Legal Environment," shows the pervasive role of ethics and law in health services. Ethical frameworks are described, ethical issues are identified, and organizational responses to them are suggested and analyzed. Law is the minimum level of performance for managing health services. The relationship of the law to the work of managers is highlighted.

Chapter 3, "Healthcare Economics," is new to this edition. Understanding macroeconomics is essential for the educated health services manager. The information here helps users comprehend effects of the economic environment on organizing, financing, and delivering health services.

Chapter 4, "The Quality Imperative: The Theory," highlights and analyzes the theoretical underpinnings of quality and performance improvement (Q/PI). It details the history of efforts to improve quality in clinical medicine. By comparison, applying Q/PI to managing health services delivery is in its infancy. This chapter is prelude to the Q/PI applications discussed in Chapter 8.

Chapter 5, "Healthcare Technology," describes the history, effects, and diffusion of health services technology and how HSOs/HSs acquire and manage it. American health services delivery is technology centric; a basic understanding is essential to managing health services effectively.

The four chapters in Part II, "The Tools," discuss the medium or adjunct skills needed to manage health services delivery.

Chapter 6, "Managerial Problem Solving and Decision Making," develops and applies a problem-solving model. Managers are problem solvers. Were there no problems to solve, managers would not be needed.

Chapter 7, "Financial Management," is new to the 7th edition. Any effective, successful manager must understand financial and quantitative data and have the ability to use data for problem solving and decision making.

Chapter 8, "The Quality Imperative: Implementation," applies Q/PI. It details how HSOs/HSs make continuous improvement of quality and productivity a reality. Improving processes improves quality. The result is enhanced productivity. Effective Q/PI requires a commitment from governance, management, clinicians, and staff to apply the methods and tools described.

Chapter 9, "Communicating," analyzes this essential skill and posits a process model that is applied to communicating in organizations and systems and between them and their external stakeholders.

The five chapters in Part III, "Application," are the culmination of the nine chapters in Parts I and II. Here, information about the environment and the tools are applied to Fayol's taxonomy of the five management functions. These functions encompass all that managers do. Separate chapters detailing the functions are new to the 7th edition and provide the orientation and skills set needed for effective and efficient management.

Chapter 10, "Planning," is the first of Fayol's management functions. The other four functions follow as a logical consequence of managing. Planning what is to be done is the essential framework for applying the other functions. Planning includes strategizing or identifying and addressing opportunities and threats.

Chapter 11, "Organizing," applies the second of the five management functions. Highlighted are the theory and ways to organize HSOs/HSs. As is typical, form follows function: The plan and what is to be done determine an organization's structure, content, and relationships.

Chapter 12, "Staffing," is new to this edition. The staffing function is commonly known as human resources management (HRM). Given that HSOs are labor-intensive, the importance and contribution of staffing to organizational success are difficult to overstate.

Chapter 13, "Directing," is the fourth management function. The work of managers and the work of leaders are differentiated. The extensive literature on functions, skills, roles and competencies, and leadership theories is reviewed. Motivation is defined and modeled. Power, influence, and motivation are analyzed in the context of understanding leadership and developing an integrative approach to leading as directing.

Chapter 14, "Controlling," presents a general model of control and focuses on controlling individual and organizational work results using management information systems, management and operations auditing, HRM, compliance, and budgeting. Control of healthcare quality using risk management and quality assessment and improvement are discussed. The chapter concludes with a comprehensive section on project management.

Book Features

Each chapter includes:

- A chapter outline

- Discussion questions

- Several case studies, each with discussion questions

- Extensive updated endnotes and sources

- Numerous exhibits to enhance instruction and ease learning

- URLs to Internet sources for further information and study

Additional resources in the book:

- Acronym list

- Detailed index

Instructor Resources

A rich array of downloadable materials is available to instructors by request to help with designing their courses when using the 7th edition of MHSOS. All materials are updated from the last edition and more have been added. Among these materials are:

- Instructor Manual containing supplemental materials for each chapter, including learning objectives and additional case studies not found in the book

- Customizable PowerPoint presentations for each chapter, totaling over 400 slides

- New to this edition: A test bank of multiple-choice and essay questions developed for each chapter

- PDF files of figures and tables for use in PowerPoint slides, tests, handouts, and the like

Please visit https://www.healthpropress.com/instructor-materials/.

Acknowledgments

Professor Emeritus Darr is grateful to Anne for her enthusiastic support of this latest edition and for never being impatient with its progress. She was my muse, unstintingly loyal supporter, friend, and life-partner for 52 years.

Professor Nowicki is grateful to Tracey and kids Hannah and David who have sacrificed time with me so I could pursue writing projects in addition to my teaching and service obligations. Professor Nowicki is also grateful to Professor Darr and the leadership of Health Professions Press for their confidence in selecting him as the coauthor for the seventh edition.

A book of this magnitude—even a revision—cannot be organized and written without help. Dr. Darr thanks Stephanie Spernak for asking insightful questions and for effective research and editorial assistance, all of which improved the content and presentation of his chapters. Dr. Nowicki thanks Dana Forgione, Ph.D., CPA, CMA, CFE, Professor of Accounting at the University of Texas at San Antonio, and Brian Conner, CPA, Partner, National Practice Leader, Hospitals, at Moss Adams, LLP, and Past Chair of the Healthcare Financial Management Association Principles & Practices Board, for their review of the financial statements in Chapter 7. Dr. Nowicki also thanks Dr. Kimberly Lee, Assistant Professor of Health Administration at Texas State University, for her in-depth review and comments on the chapter on directing. Drs. Darr and Nowicki thank Elizabeth Flores, graduate assistant at Texas State University, for assistance with instructional materials.

The authors wish to thank several people at Health Professions Press for their assistance with this book. Mary Magnus, Director of Publications; Kaitlin Konecke, Marketing and Textbook Manager; Erin Geoghegan, Graphic Design Manager; Diane Ersepke, copyeditor; and Carol Ersepke, proofreader; each made essential contributions. We are grateful to Linda G. Francis, Editorial & Production Manager, for her herculean efforts to make the book as good as it could be. Ms. Francis saw us through the project with good cheer and much assistance. We thank, too, the publishers and authors who granted permission to reprint material to which they hold the copyright. Finally, and by no means least, we thank users of the sixth edition whose comments and critiques helped improve the seventh edition.

The authors recognize the significant contributions of those who coauthored earlier editions, Beaufort B. Longest, Jr., Ph.D., and Jonathon S. Rakich, Ph.D. The authorship of the preceding six editions of this text was shared with Professor Emeritus Longest, and Professor Emeritus Rakich coauthored the first five. Their decades-long collaboration with Dr. Darr is acknowledged with thanks. The DNA contributed by them in earlier editions is palpable. This seventh edition was substantially enriched by their efforts.

Acronyms Used in Text

AA	associate of arts (degree)
AAAHC	Accreditation Association for Ambulatory Healthcare
AACN	American Association of Colleges of Nursing
AAHSA	American Association of Homes and Services for the Aging, also known as LeadingAge
AAMC	Association of American Medical Colleges
ABC	activity-based costing
ABMS	American Board of Medical Specialties
ACA	Affordable Care Act of 2010
ACEN	Accreditation Commission for Education in Nursing
ACHCA	American College of Health Care Administrators
ACHE	American College of Healthcare Executives
ACO	accountable care organization
ACS	American College of Surgeons
ADL	activities of daily living
ADR	alternative dispute resolution
AHA	American Hospital Association
AHCA	American Health Care Association
AHCPR	Agency for Health Care Policy and Research
AHIP	America's Health Insurance Plans
AHRQ	Agency for Healthcare Research and Quality
AI	artificial intelligence
AIDS	acquired immunodeficiency syndrome
ALOS	average length of stay
AMA	American Medical Association; American Marketing Association
AMD	advance medical directive
ANA	American Nurses Association
ANCC	American Nurses Credentialing Center
AND	allow natural death
AOA	American Osteopathic Association
APACHE	acute physiology and chronic health evaluation
APC	ambulatory payment category
APG	ambulatory patient group
APMA	American Podiatric Medical Association
APN	advanced practice nurse

AR	accounts receivable
ARRA	American Recovery and Reinvestment Act
AS	Auditing Standard 1001
ASC	ambulatory surgery center
ASQ	American Society for Quality
AUPHA	Association of University Programs in Health Administration
BBA	Balanced Budget Act
BCG	Boston Consulting Group
BEAM	brain electrical activity mapping
BFOQ	bona fide occupational qualifications
BIM	building information modeling
BLS	Bureau of Labor Statistics
BSC	balanced scorecard
BSN	bachelor of science in nursing (degree)
BYOD	bring your own device
CABG	coronary artery bypass grafting
CAD	computer-aided design
CAHME	Commission on Accreditation of Healthcare Management Education
CalRHIO	California Regional Health Information Organization
CAMH	Comprehensive Accreditation Manual for Hospitals
CAS	carotid artery stenting
CAUTI	catheter-associated urinary tract infection
CBO	Congressional Budget Office
CCNE	Commission on Collegiate Nursing Education
CCO	chief compliance officer
CDC	Centers for Disease Control and Prevention
CDI	Clostridium difficile infection
CDS	continuous deep sedation
CDSS	clinical decision support system
CEA	carotid endarterectomy
CEO	chief executive officer
CEPH	Council on Education for Public Health
CFO	chief financial officer
CGE	continuing governance education
CHA	Catholic Health Association of the United States
CHAP	Community Health Accreditation Program
CHC	community health center
CHIN	community health information network
CHIP	Children's Health Insurance Program
CIO	chief information officer
CLABSI	central line–associated bloodstream infection
CMO	chief medical officer
CMS	Centers for Medicare & Medicaid Services
CNA	certified nursing assistant
CNM	certified nurse midwife
CNO	chief nursing officer
CNS	clinical nurse specialist
COBRA	Consolidated Omnibus Budget Reconciliation Act of 1985
COE	Center for Outcomes and Evidence
CON	certificate of need

COO	chief operating officer
CoPs	conditions of participation
CPA	certified public accountant
CPG	clinical practice guideline
CPI	consumer price index
CPM	critical path method
CPME	Council on Podiatric Medical Education
CPR	cardiopulmonary resuscitation
CQI	continuous quality improvement
CQO	chief quality officer
CRA	consumer reporting agency
CRM	crew resource management
CRNA	certified registered nurse anesthetist
CSS	clinical support system
CT	computed tomography
CTO	chief technology officer
CUS	"I am Concerned. I am Uncomfortable. This is a Safety issue."
CUSP	comprehensive unit safety program
DBS	deep brain stimulation
DHHS	Department of Health and Human Services
DHS	designated healthcare service
DIC	diagnostic imaging center
DII	Defense Industry Initiative
DMAIC	Define, measure, analyze, improve, control
DNP	doctor of nursing practice
DNR	do not resuscitate
DNV GL Healthcare	Det Norske Veritas Germanischer Lloyd Healthcare
DO	doctor of osteopathy
DOJ	U.S. Department of Justice
DOL	U.S. Department of Labor
DPM	doctor of podiatric medicine
DRG	diagnosis-related group
DRII	Disaster Recovery Institute International
DVA	Department of Veterans Affairs
EAP	employee assistance program
ECHO	echocardiogram
ECRI	Emergency Care Research Institute
ECS	ethics consultation service
ECT	electroconvulsive therapy
ED	emergency department
EEOC	Equal Employment Opportunity Commission
EH	employee health
EHR	electronic health record
EMA	emergency management agency
EMR	electronic medical record
EMS	emergency medical services
EMT	emergency medical technician
EMTALA	Emergency Medical Treatment and Active Labor Act
EOC	environment of care
EOP	emergency operations plan
EPC	evidence-based practice center

ePHI	electronic protected health information
EPM	epidemiological planning model
ERG	existence, relatedness, and growth
EVM	earned value management
FAH	Federation of American Hospitals
FC	fixed costs
FASB	Financial Accounting Standards Board
FCRA	Fair Credit Reporting Act
FDA	Food and Drug Administration
FEMA	Federal Emergency Management Agency
FFM	Five Factor Model
FMCS	Federal Mediation and Conciliation Service
FMEA	failure mode effects analysis
fMRI	functional magnetic resonance imaging
FQHC	Federally Qualified Health Centers
FTC	Federal Trade Commission
FTE	full-time equivalent employee
GAAP	generally accepted accounting principles
GASB	Governmental Accounting Standards Board
GB	governing body
GDP	gross domestic product
GERT	graphical evaluation and review technique
GPO	group purchasing organization
GPS	Global Positioning System
GY	graduate year
HAI	healthcare-associated infection
HAPI	hospital-acquired pressure injuries
HCFA	Health Care Financing Administration
HCAPS	Hospital Consumer Assessment of Healthcare Providers and Systems
HCPCS	Healthcare Common Procedure Coding System
HCQIA	Health Care Quality Improvement Act of 1986
HDHP	high-deductible health plan
HEDIS	Health Plan Employer Data and Information Set
HFAP	Healthcare Facilities Accreditation Program
HFMA	Healthcare Financial Management Association
HHA	home health agency
HICS	hospital incident command system
HIE	health information exchange
HIPAA	Health Insurance Portability and Accountability Act
HIPDB	Healthcare Integrity and Protection Data Bank
HIT	health information technology
HIV	human immunodeficiency virus
HME	home medical equipment
HMO	health maintenance organization
HQI	hospital quality improvement
HR	human resources
HRET	Hospital Research and Educational Trust
HRM	human resources management
HRRP	Hospital Readmissions Reduction Program
HS	health system

HSA	health systems agency; also, health savings account
HSO	health services organization
HTA	healthcare technology assessment
HVA	hazard vulnerability analysis
ICD	International Classification of Diseases
ICRC	infant care review committee
ICS	incident command system
ICU	intensive care unit
IDN	integrated delivery network
IDS	integrated delivery system
IEC	institutional ethics committee
IG	inspector general
IHI	Institute for Healthcare Improvement
IHIE	Indiana Health Information Exchange
IHS	Indian Health Service
IOM	Institute of Medicine
IOR	interorganizational relationship
IPA	independent practice association
IRB	institutional review board
IRS	Internal Revenue Service
IS	information system
ISO	International Organization for Standardization
IT	information technology
IV	intravenous
JCAHO	Joint Commission on Accreditation of Healthcare Organizations (formerly, JCAH, Joint Commission on Accreditation of Hospitals; now known as The Joint Commission)
JCC	joint conference committee
JCRSB	Joint Committee on the Recognition of Specialty Boards
KQC	key quality characteristic
KPV	key process variable
LAN	local area network
LCL	lower control limit
LCME	Liaison Committee on Medical Education
LIP	licensed independent practitioner
LLC	limited liability company
LLP	limited liability partnership
LOS	length of stay
LPC	least preferred co-worker
LPN	licensed practical (vocational) nurse
LTC	long-term care
LTCH	long-term care (extended stay) hospital
M&M	morbidity and mortality
MBO	management by objectives
MBR	management by results
MCO	managed care organization
MD	medical doctor
MDSS	management decision support system
MEC	medical executive committee
MGMA	Medical Group Management Association
MICU	medical intensive care unit

MIS	management information systems
MRI	magnetic resonance imaging
MRSA	methicillin-resistant *Staphylococcus aureus*
MSD	musculoskeletal disorder
MS-DRG	medical severity diagnosis-related group
MSDS	material safety data sheets
MSI	magnetic source imaging
MSO	management services organization
M-TAC	multidisciplinary technology assessment committee
NA	nursing assistant
NAFTA	North American Free Trade Agreement
NAMSS	National Association Medical Staff Services
NASA	National Aeronautics and Space Administration
NaSH	National Surveillance System for Healthcare Workers
NCBI	National Center for Biotechnology Information
NCHSRHCTA	National Center for Health Services Research and Health Care Technology Assessment
NCHCT	National Center for Health Care Technology
NCHL	National Center for Healthcare Leadership
NCQA	National Committee for Quality Assurance
NCVL	noninvasive cardiovascular laboratory
NF	nursing facility
NGC	National Guideline Clearinghouse
NHE	national healthcare expenditure
NHS	National Health Service (U.K.)
NHSN	National Healthcare Safety Network (CDC)
NICU	neonatal intensive care unit
NIH	National Institutes of Health
NIMS	National Incident Management System
NIOSH	National Institute for Occupational Safety and Health
NLM	National Library of Medicine
NLN	National League for Nursing
NLNAC	National League for Nursing Accrediting Commission
NLRA	National Labor Relations Act
NLRB	National Labor Relations Board
NP	nurse practitioner
NPSG	National Patient Safety Goals
OBRA	Omnibus Budget Reconciliation Act of 1987
OCC	Osteopathic Continuous Certification
ODS	organized delivery system
OIG	office of the inspector general
OPG	ocular plethysmograph
OR	operating room
OSHA	Occupational Safety and Health Administration
OT	occupational therapy
OTA	Office of Technology Assessment
PA	physician assistant
PAC	political action committee
PAS	physician-assisted suicide
PBT	proton beam therapy
PCI	percutaneous coronary intervention

PCP	primary care physician
PDCA	plan, do, check, act
PDSA	plan, do, study, act
PERT	program evaluation and review technique
PET	positron emission tomography
PGY	postgraduate year
PHI	protected health information
PHO	physician-hospital organization
PI	productivity improvement; process improvement
PICU	pediatric intensive care unit
PIT	process improvement team
PKU	phenylketonuria
POA	power of attorney
POS	point of service
PPE	personal protective equipment
PPEC	professional practice evaluation committee
PPO	preferred provider organization
PRO	peer review organization
PSDA	Patient Self-Determination Act
PSO	professional staff organization
PSRO	professional standards review organization
PT	physical therapy
PTCA	percutaneous transluminal coronary angioplasty
PTO	paid time off
PVR	pulse volume recording plethysmograph
PVS	persistent vegetative state
Q/PI	quality/productivity improvement
QA	quality assurance
QA/I	quality assessment and improvement
QI	quality improvement
QIC	quality improvement council
QIO	quality improvement organization
QIT	quality improvement team
QMHCD	quality management for health care delivery
QMS	quality management system
QWL	quality-of-work life
RBRVS	resource-based relative value scale
RDE	rule of double effect
RDN	registered dietitian nutritionist
RHIO	regional health information organization
RM	risk management
RN	registered nurse
ROI	return on investment
RT	rehabilitation therapy
RUG	resource utilization group
RVU	relative value unit
SA	strategic alliance
SBAR	situation, background, assessment, recommendation
SBU	strategic business unit
SCAP	service, consideration, access, and promotion
SD	standard deviation

SEA	sentinel event alert
SEIU	Service Employees International Union
SHRM	strategic human resources management
SICU	surgical intensive care unit
SIM	strategic issues management
SNF	skilled nursing facility
SOX	Sarbanes-Oxley Act of 2002
SP	standard precaution
SPC	statistical process control
SPECT	single-photon emission computed tomography
SSU	strategic service unit
STEPPS	strategies to enhance performance and patient safety
SWOT	strengths/weaknesses/opportunities/threats
TB	tuberculosis
TC	total costs
TEAM	Technology Evaluation and Acquisition Methods
TEE	transesophageal echocardiography
TN	Trade NAFTA
tPA	tissue plasminogen activator
TQM	total quality management
UCL	upper control limit
UPMC	University of Pittsburgh Medical Center
UR	utilization review
USMCA	United States–Mexico–Canada Agreement
USPHS	United States Public Health Service
VA	U.S. Department of Veterans Affairs
VAP	ventilator-associated pneumonia
VC	variable costs
VNS	vagus nerve stimulation
VP	vice president
VP-HR	vice president–human resources
VP-MA	vice president–medical affairs
WAN	wide-area network

To those who manage health services organizations
and systems and to those who aspire

PART I

The Environment

Effective managers understand the world beyond the walls of their organization. That environment provides the wherewithal for health services organizations and health systems (HSOs/HSs) to do their work. The environment both constrains and facilitates HSOs/HSs. Successful managers monitor the environment and know how to use it for the organization's benefit.

Chapter 1 provides a general background and context for delivering health services. Knowing the forces that have shaped and continue to shape the healthcare field enables managers and leaders to perform the five management functions addressed in Part III.

Chapter 2 details the essential context provided by ethics and law. Ethics is a lodestar for healthcare managers and the organizations in which they work. The law reflects and affects ethics by setting societally enforced sanctions for managers and their organizations should they run afoul of it. The dynamic relationship of ethics and law is discussed.

The discussion of economics in Chapter 3 facilitates understanding the all-important role of sources and uses of funds for health services delivery. Health economics has a special place in the delivery and financing of healthcare. Its importance cannot be overstated.

Quality improvement (QI) has become a major focus as managers strive to gain efficiency and effectiveness in delivery of health services. The theory detailed in Chapter 4 is complemented by its applications in Chapter 8. It is critical to be conversant with the theory before undertaking applications because that enables managers to be more effective in applying QI.

Chapter 5 summarizes the history and current state of healthcare technology. American medical practice applies technology to diagnose, treat, and monitor healthcare delivery. Technology is expensive to purchase, operate, and maintain. This makes understanding evaluation, acquisition, and application of technology essential to its use.

In sum, the content of Part I, The Environment, prepares readers for discussion of The Tools in Part II and application of the five management functions as presented and analyzed in Part III. Users are advised to pay serious attention to the content of Part I; its content prepares them to gain the most from the remainder of this text.

1

Healthcare in the United States

Chapter Outline

Health and System Goals
Lack of Synchrony
Processes That Produce Health Policy
A Brief History of Health Services in the United States
Other Western Systems
Structure of the Health Services System
Classification and Types of HSOs
Local, State, and Federal Regulation of HSOs/HSs
Other Regulators of HSOs/HSs
Accreditation in Healthcare
Education and Regulation of Health Services Managers
Regulation and Education of Selected Health Occupations
Associations for Individuals and Organizations
Paying for Health Services
Government Payment Methodologies
System Trends

This first chapter describes the system of healthcare in the United States—the general environment in which managers of health services organizations (HSOs) and health systems (HSs) work. The chapter develops conceptual frameworks and presents information about healthcare resources describing their historical development, nature, and extent and the relationships among them. Resources include HSOs/HSs, programs, personnel, technology, and financing. Information about several types of HSOs—acute care hospitals, nursing facilities (NFs), managed care organizations (MCOs), and public health entities—is provided in Chapter 11.

Data and information presented here describe the manager's environment. Successful managers have a comprehensive and objective understanding of the world beyond their own organization; this includes a thorough understanding of trends and developments. The management model presented in the Introduction to Part III shows this relationship and should be referenced as necessary. It is important not only to understand individual presentations of data but to appreciate their interactions.

Table 1.1 shows that health expenditures in the United States in 2018 were about $3.65 trillion, which was 17.7% of gross domestic product (GDP), or $11,172 per capita.[1] Table 1.1 also shows that projections for 2019-2027 have a higher projected percent increase than in previous years (5.61% projected annual increase during 2019-2027 compared with the 4.49% actual annual increase during 2012-2018). Rates of growth for health expenditures are also a

Table 1.1 National Health Expenditure Amounts and Annual Percent Change by Type of Expenditure: Calendar Years 2011-2027[a]

Type of Expenditure (billions $)	Actual									Projected							
	2011	2012	2013	2014	2015	2016	2017	2018	2019	2020	2021	2022	2023	2024	2025	2026	2027
National health expenditures	$2,682.6	$2,791.1	$2,875.0	$3,025.4	$3,199.6	$3,347.4	$3,487.3	$3,649.4	$3,823.1	$4,031.1	$4,255.2	$4,501.5	$4,767.1	$5,048.7	$5,344.8	$5,650.8	$5,963.2
Health consumption expenditures	2,533.4	2,637.7	2,720.9	2,875.6	3,045.5	3,190.7	3,319.0	3,475.0	3,637.6	3,835.9	4,049.6	4,284.7	4,538.5	4,807.7	5,090.4	5,382.5	5,679.9
Personal health care	2,267.3	2,361.1	2,431.2	2,556.0	2,710.2	2,838.3	2,954.5	3,075.5	3,242.6	3,412.6	3,601.5	3,811.1	4,037.8	4,278.2	4,531.0	4,792.7	5,058.4
Hospital care	851.9	902.5	937.6	978.2	1,034.5	1,089.5	1,140.6	1,197.8	1,254.7	1,318.7	1,390.1	1,471.3	1,559.3	1,652.4	1,751.6	1,858.1	1,961.6
Professional services	716.6	743.2	759.6	792.5	837.9	883.2	924.0	965.1	1,013.6	1,067.1	1,125.6	1,186.9	1,253.2	1,324.1	1,397.5	1,468.2	1,541.2
Physician and clinical services	535.9	557.1	569.6	595.7	631.2	666.5	696.9	725.6	767.6	808.8	853.7	900.0	950.3	1,004.4	1,061.3	1,115.8	1,172.0
Other professional services	72.8	76.4	78.7	83.0	87.8	92.7	97.5	103.9	106.1	112.0	118.5	125.6	133.1	141.2	149.0	156.8	165.3
Dental services	108.0	109.7	111.2	113.8	118.9	124.9	129.6	135.6	139.9	146.4	153.3	161.3	169.8	178.5	187.2	195.6	203.9
Other health, residential, and personal care	131.7	139.1	144.3	151.5	164.5	173.6	183.2	191.6	196.9	207.8	220.3	234.5	249.5	265.4	282.0	299.7	318.6
Home health care	74.6	78.3	81.4	84.8	89.2	93.0	97.1	102.2	108.8	116.1	124.2	133.0	142.4	152.6	163.4	174.7	186.8
Nursing care facilities and continuing care retirement communities	145.4	147.4	149.0	152.4	158.1	163.0	166.3	168.5	178.0	186.3	195.5	206.2	217.8	230.2	243.2	256.7	270.7
Retail outlet sales of medical products	347.1	350.6	359.3	396.6	425.9	436.0	443.2	456.3	490.5	516.6	545.8	579.2	615.5	653.6	693.2	735.3	779.4
Prescription drugs	251.9	253.0	258.2	292.4	317.1	322.3	326.8	335.0	360.3	378.9	400.4	425.2	452.4	481.2	511.1	542.9	576.7
Durable medical equipment	42.3	43.7	45.1	46.7	48.6	51.0	52.4	54.9	60.9	64.6	68.6	72.8	77.5	82.2	87.2	92.4	97.8

(continued)

Table 1.1 (continued)

Other non-durable medical products	52.9	53.9	56.0	57.5	60.2	62.7	64.1	66.4	69.3	73.0	76.9	81.2	85.6	90.2	95.0	99.9	105.0
Government administration	32.9	34.2	37.5	42.3	42.8	44.9	44.8	47.5	49.4	52.0	54.9	58.5	62.5	66.6	70.9	75.8	81.0
Net cost of private health insurance	158.8	165.2	173.3	195.3	206.7	218.8	228.3	258.5	252.0	275.2	294.0	312.3	331.7	352.4	373.8	394.8	417.3
Government public health activities	74.4	77.2	79.0	82.0	85.8	88.7	91.4	93.5	93.6	96.2	99.1	102.8	106.5	110.4	114.7	119.2	123.2
Investment	149.4	153.3	154.1	149.8	154.1	156.7	168.3	174.4	185.5	195.1	205.6	216.9	228.6	241.1	254.3	268.3	283.3
Research[b]	49.6	48.4	46.7	46.0	46.4	47.4	50.1	52.6	56.2	59.0	62.0	65.2	68.4	71.8	75.3	79.0	83.3
Structures and equipment	99.6	105.0	107.5	103.7	107.7	109.3	118.2	121.8	129.3	136.1	143.6	151.7	160.2	169.3	179.0	189.2	200.0
Annual percent change by type of expenditure (%)																	
National health expenditures	—	4.0%	3.0%	5.2%	5.8%	4.6%	4.2%	4.6%	4.8%	5.4%	5.6%	5.8%	5.9%	5.9%	5.9%	5.7%	5.5%
Health consumption expenditures	—	4.1	3.2	5.7	5.9	4.8	4.0	4.7	4.8	5.5	5.6	5.8	5.9	5.9	5.9	5.7	5.5
Personal health care	—	4.1	3.0	5.1	6.0	4.7	4.1	4.1	5.1	5.2	5.5	5.8	5.9	6.0	5.9	5.8	5.5
Hospital care	—	6.0	3.9	4.3	5.8	5.3	4.7	4.5	5.1	5.1	5.4	5.8	6.0	6.0	6.0	6.1	5.6
Professional services	—	3.7	2.2	4.3	5.7	5.4	4.6	4.4	5.3	5.3	5.5	5.4	5.6	5.7	5.5	5.1	5.0
Physician and clinical services	—	4.0	2.2	4.6	6.0	5.4	4.7	4.1	5.4	5.4	5.6	5.4	5.6	5.7	5.7	5.1	5.0
Other professional services	—	5.0	3.0	5.4	5.9	5.5	5.2	6.5	5.3	5.5	5.9	5.9	6.0	6.1	5.5	5.2	5.4
Dental services	—	1.6	1.4	2.3	4.4	5.1	3.8	4.6	4.4	4.6	4.7	5.3	5.3	5.1	4.8	4.5	4.3
Other health, residential, and personal care	—	5.6	3.7	5.0	8.6	5.5	5.5	4.6	4.5	5.5	6.1	6.4	6.4	6.3	6.3	6.3	6.3

(continued)

Table 1.1 *(continued)*

Annual percent change by type of expenditure (%)	Actual										Projected						
	2011	2012	2013	2014	2015	2016	2017	2018	2019	2020	2021	2022	2023	2024	2025	2026	2027
Home health care	—	4.9	3.9	4.2	5.3	4.2	4.5	5.2	6.8	6.7	7.0	7.1	7.1	7.1	7.1	6.9	6.9
Nursing care facilities and continuing care retirement communities	—	1.4	1.1	2.3	3.8	3.1	2.0	1.4	4.2	4.7	4.9	5.4	5.7	5.7	5.7	5.5	5.4
Retail outlet sales of medical products	—	1.0	2.5	10.4	7.4	2.4	1.7	2.9	4.8	5.3	5.7	6.1	6.3	6.2	6.1	6.1	6.0
Prescription drugs	—	0.4	2.1	13.3	8.4	1.7	1.4	2.5	4.6	5.2	5.7	6.2	6.4	6.4	6.2	6.2	6.2
Durable medical equipment	—	3.4	3.2	3.6	4.1	4.9	2.9	4.7	6.1	6.1	6.2	6.1	6.4	6.2	6.0	6.0	5.8
Other non-durable medical products	—	2.0	3.9	2.7	4.7	4.1	2.2	3.6	4.7	5.3	5.2	5.6	5.5	5.3	5.3	5.2	5.1
Government administration	—	3.9	9.6	12.8	1.2	5.0	-0.2	6.0	5.7	5.2	5.7	6.6	6.7	6.7	6.4	7.0	6.7
Net cost of private health insurance	—	4.0	4.9	12.7	5.8	5.9	4.3	13.2	2.0	9.2	6.8	6.2	6.2	6.2	6.1	5.6	5.7
Government public health activities	—	3.7	2.3	3.8	4.6	3.4	3.0	2.4	2.8	2.8	3.0	3.7	3.7	3.6	3.9	3.9	3.4
Investment	—	2.8	0.0	-2.2	3.0	2.4	6.0	5.3	5.1	5.2	5.4	5.5	5.4	5.5	5.5	5.5	5.6
Research[b]	—	-2.4	-3.5	-1.3	1.1	2.3	6.5	5.4	5.1	5.0	5.1	5.0	5.0	4.9	4.9	5.0	5.3
Structures & equipment	—	5.4	2.4	-3.5	3.8	1.5	8.1	3.0	5.1	5.3	5.5	5.7	5.6	5.7	5.7	5.7	5.7

[a]*Source:* Centers for Medicare & Medicaid Services, Office of the Actuary, NHE Tables, Table 2, and NHE Projections, Table 2.

[b]Research and development expenditures of drug companies and other manufacturers and providers of medical equipment and supplies are excluded from research expenditures. These research expenditures are implicitly included in the expenditure class in which the product falls, in that they are covered by the payment received for that product.

Note: Numbers may not add to totals because of rounding.

function of changes in GDP because the denominator is affected. These changes have slowed the large upward trend of health expenditures as a percent of GDP that had been observed since the 1960s.[2] Table 1.1 shows that, from $3.65 trillion in 2018, health expenditures are projected to increase to $5.96 trillion in 2027, or 19.4% of GDP.[3] Note that the increase in health expenditures and the decrease in the GDP for 2020 due to the COVID-19 pandemic are not included in these projections. Expending larger sums suggests both the magnitude of the problems and the opportunities for HSO/HS managers. For instance, a 2018 review of contemporary research suggested that 30% of all health expenditures is the result of fraud, abuse, and waste.[4]

Health and System Goals

Distinguishing the healthcare system from the health services system may seem a pedantic exercise, but health services managers must understand the connections between them.

A model developed by Henrik Blum (American [1915–2006]), shown in Figure 1.1, identifies factors affecting health. The relative size of the arrows shows the degree of their effects—medical care services (prevention, cure, care, rehabilitation) are much less important than environment and somewhat less important than heredity and lifestyles in affecting health (well-being). In explaining the model, Blum stated that the "largest aggregate of forces resides in the person's environment. One's own behavior, in great part derived from one's experience with one's environment, is seen as the next largest force affecting health."[5] Effective managers understand the numerous influences on health status, both as factors that lead to episodes of illness and as affecting recovery and long-term absence of illness and minimization of disability. HSO/HS managers must have a broad view of illness and health. This requires looking beyond the organization. They must understand that, at best, the health services system has

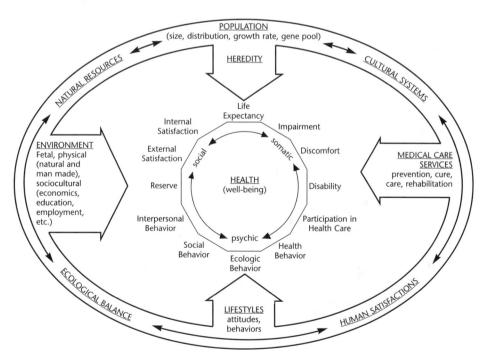

Figure 1.1. The force-field and well-being paradigms of health (From Blum, Henrik K. *Expanding Health Care Horizons: From General Systems Concept of Health to a National Health Policy*, 2nd ed., 37. Oakland, CA: Third Party Publishing, 1983; reprinted by permission.)

a limited effect and can provide only stopgap measures if negative influences on health undo what delivery of services has done.

Blum suggests several goals for a health services system:

- Prolonging life and preventing premature death

- Minimizing departures from physiological or functional norms by focusing attention on precursors of illness

- Minimizing discomfort (illness)

- Minimizing disability (incapacity)

- Promoting high-level wellness or self-fulfillment

- Promoting high-level satisfaction with the environment

- Extending resistance to ill health and creating reserve capacity

- Increasing opportunities for consumers to participate in health matters[6]

These goals are part of the conceptual framework underlying the use of this text.

The Precede–Proceed planning model in Figure 1.2 is a more applied conceptualization of the relationships among activities that are part of health promotion planning and evaluation and that should be part of efforts to deliver comprehensive healthcare.[7] Phase 1 is a social assessment that recognizes relationships among health and various social issues by identifying a target population's social, economic, cultural, and other nonmedical concerns and goals. The epidemiological assessment in Phase 2 has the initial goal of identifying specific health goals or problems that may contribute to, or interact with, the social goals or problems noted in the social assessment of Phase 1. Phase 2 uses vital indicators, such as morbidity, disability, mortality, and demographic patterns, as well as genetics and behavioral and environmental indicators

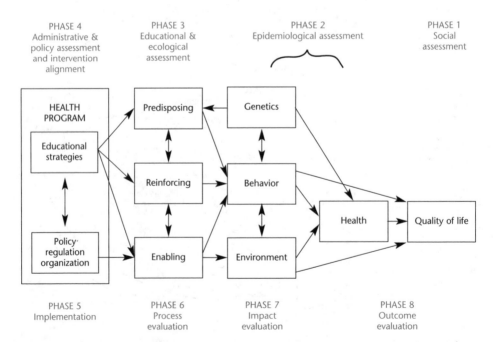

Figure 1.2.   The model for health promotion planning and evaluation Phases 1–4 make up the "Precede" stage; Phases 5–8, "Proceed." (From *Health Program Planning: An Educational and Ecological Approach*. 4th ed. Lawrence W. Green and Marshal W. Kreuter. New York: McGraw-Hill, 2005, 10.) With permission of the McGraw-Hill Companies, Inc.

of health problems. The health concerns needing amelioration are listed in rank order after the objectively appraised health problems identified in Phase 2 are compared with the subjectively appraised quality-of-life issues identified in Phase 1. The educational and ecological assessment in Phase 3 groups the factors associated with health concerns into predisposing factors, reinforcing factors, and enabling factors. The elements of these factors are sorted, categorized, and selected in terms of their greatest potential to change the behavioral and environmental targets generated in previous stages.

The administrative and policy assessment and intervention alignment in Phase 4 begin the interventions that lead to the Proceed portion of the model. This phase answers questions about what program components and interventions are needed and whether policy, organization, and resources are sufficient to make the program a reality. The result is the implementation in Phase 5. Phases 6, 7, and 8 are among the most important in the model. Here the program is evaluated in terms of process, impact, and outcome. The evaluation criteria are linked to objectives defined in the corresponding steps of the Precede portion of the model. The increasing emphasis on health promotion and prevention makes the Precede–Proceed model a useful tool in planning and delivering comprehensive healthcare, especially in integrated delivery systems that focus on population health.

Lack of Synchrony

The wide geographic variation in rates of hospitalization and lengths of hospital stay by diagnosis has been known for decades. Similar geographic variation occurs in use of NFs by Medicare beneficiaries.[8] The variation in hospital use is a true difference that cannot be explained by redefining or estimating the effect of variables such as age, sex, and climate. Even more puzzling are the large differences in rates of hospitalization and lengths of stay by diagnosis within geographic regions, and even within individual hospitals. The most plausible explanation is that physician practice patterns—physicians' clinical decisions—vary, sometimes widely. For instance, physician practice patterns can be affected by physician age, medical training, organizations (solo versus group practice), and Medicaid load.[9] It can be hypothesized that some rates of hospitalization and lengths of stay are more appropriate than others. This means that exceeding the appropriate level of resource use has significant implications for HSOs/HSs striving to use resources judiciously.

Other data have shown significant differences between morbidity and mortality caused by a disease and the amount of hospitalization for that disease.[10] The lack of synchrony can be explained in various ways: hospitals are constrained by available technology; hospitalization may be inappropriate to treat the medical condition that causes death or limits activity; and some medical conditions require more attention to prevention, which is historically a general deficit of acute care hospitals. Achieving synchrony suggests that services provided by HSOs and their use are in harmony with health needs.

There are important distinctions between need and demand for health services. Need is measured by morbidity and mortality data and by disability that limits activity. Need is more objective than demand, but value judgments invariably underpin conclusions about need. Demand occurs when need (or perceived need) is converted into demand for services. As suggested, need and demand do not have a one-to-one relationship. Providers such as hospitals and physicians have a role in demand, as does availability of third-party payment for services.

Demand for a service or treatment may be artificially low in a service area if, for instance, a hospital does not offer it and potential users must go elsewhere. Physicians' perspectives about whether a medical service is needed directly affect demand for it. From the consumers' perspective, need may not become demand because consumers lack knowledge about a disease or because social or cultural mores dissuade them from seeking treatment. In addition, demand may be less than need because people lack financial resources or there are other access barriers. Further, some demand, such as that for cosmetic surgery, is subjective and varies by individual consumers and their resources. The relationships between need and demand must be considered as health services are planned. The ethical dimensions of need and demand are addressed in Chapter 2.

Processes That Produce Health Policy

The federal Constitution is the basic law of the United States. The federal system that it established arose after the American Revolution when the several sovereign states relinquished specific powers to a central government. The enumerated powers of the federal government are found in the U.S. Constitution and are interpreted by the U.S. Supreme Court and its inferior courts. Important rights retained by the people are found in the first 10 amendments to the Constitution, called the Bill of Rights. Powers not delegated to the federal government by the Constitution are reserved to the states or the people. This is important because of the states' police power that allows states to pass and enforce quarantines during epidemics and pandemics. Each state has a constitution that establishes its form of government. The right to petition government is found in the First Amendment to the federal Constitution. This guarantee of access to government and its processes has produced various nonpublic efforts to affect the legislative, regulatory, and judicial processes.

Public Processes

Legislative Process
Statutes are enacted by state legislatures and the U.S. Congress. Comparable legislative activities are performed by local governments when ordinances are passed. The laws are binding, but they may be challenged in court if they violate constitutionally protected rights or were improperly enacted because of procedural irregularity. The legislative branch relies on the executive branch to implement and enforce the laws.

Paradigmatic of these processes is the process that occurs in the U.S. Congress. The basic legislative process in the Senate and House of Representatives is the same. The majority political party controls committees and subcommittees and determines legislative priorities. Bills related to healthcare introduced in either house are referred to committees or subcommittees and may be amended at various points, including in committee or subcommittee, on the floor, or in conference between the houses of Congress. During the legislative process, or to learn more about problems before drafting bills, committees or subcommittees may hold hearings to obtain testimony about a problem or issue. Individual managers or governing body members of HSOs/HSs rarely participate in the legislative process. Testimony, drafts of bills, and other input are provided by professional or trade associations, either by their staff or through lobbyists. A bill approved by the Senate and the House and signed by the president becomes law.

Implementing Law—Regulations
Laws are implemented by regulations issued by executive departments and agencies and independent regulatory bodies, such as the Federal Trade Commission (FTC). This process is governed by the Administrative Procedure Act of 1946, as amended.[11] Requirements include notice of proposed rulemaking, proposed regulations, and final regulations. The steps before final regulations are issued permit interested parties to comment on provisions. Interim regulations that test the effect of proposed regulations may be issued before final regulations are drafted and approved.

During the time for public comment, individual HSOs/HSs and their trade associations and lobbyists seek to affect the content of final regulations. It is most cost-effective to influence the process at this point. For example, lobbying by provider groups has moderated the Medicare fraud and abuse regulations. More recently, the American Medical Association lobbied to decrease the number of clinicians covered by the Medicare Access and CHIPs Reauthorization Act of 2015. In 2016, the Centers for Medicare and Medicaid Services (CMS) proposed regulations exempting clinicians who had less than $10,000 in Medicare Part B revenue or who saw fewer than 100 Medicare Part B patients per year. In 2017, CMS exempted clinicians who had less than $30,000 in Medicare Part B payments per year. In 2018, CMS exempted an additional 132,000 clinicians who had less than $90,000 in Medicare Part B payment or who saw fewer than 200 Medicare Part B patients per year.[12]

Results of the implementation process appear in the *Federal Register*, which is published each working day. Final regulations are compiled in the *Code of Federal Regulations*. It is important to note that regulations often do not have their desired effect or may have unintended consequences. For instance, the Hospital Readmissions Reduction Program (HRRP) initiated by CMS in 2012 financially penalized hospitals with higher-than-expected 30-day readmission rates for patients with specific diagnoses. While readmission rates have declined in response to the regulations, at least one study suggests mortality has increased, thus decreasing quality.[13]

Multiple Functions of the Regulatory Process

Implementation and enforcement of federal laws are accomplished by executive branch departments and agencies and by independent regulatory bodies, all of which were established by Congress. The regulatory process melds legislative, executive, and judicial functions.

Drafting and promulgating regulations (rulemaking) give executive departments and agencies and independent regulatory bodies quasi-legislative authority.[14] The basic law's specificity determines the latitude for interpretation in the rulemaking process. Regulations reflect the law and congressional intent and have general (prospective) application.

Executive departments and agencies and independent regulatory bodies have quasi-executive powers because they have authority to enforce the regulations. Compliance is achieved by bringing complaints, issuing directives such as cease-and-desist orders, and levying fines, all of which can occur pending a decision in the agency's hearing and review process or prior to a hearing in an emergency. Executive departments and agencies and independent regulatory bodies have quasi-judicial powers because they judge compliance in hearings and reviews held before their hearing officers or administrative law judges. Such officials have a degree of independence because they are appointed for specific terms by the president and can be removed only for cause.

Challenging a regulatory decision by engaging in the administrative hearing and review process is time-consuming and expensive. Legal counsel expert in the law being disputed, as well as in administrative law, are needed to work with retainer or in-house counsel. As a practical matter, small HSOs/HSs have little choice but to comply with a regulation or to simply accept an adverse administrative ruling without appeal to the courts. Legal challenges are costly and usually can be undertaken only by a large HSO/HS or association. This may change, however, because some federal laws permit successful challengers to recover costs.

An important development beginning in the late 20th century is the increasing complexity and significance of administrative law and rulemaking. Arguably, bureaucracies have become a de facto fourth branch of federal (and state) government. Generally, parties must exhaust the administrative review process before appeal to the federal courts is allowed.

Judicial Process

Space does not permit full discussion of various courts and their jurisdictions. Suffice it to say state and federal court systems are similar. Both have trial courts (county and district courts, respectively), intermediate courts (appeals courts), and supreme courts. Some states reverse use of the terms *supreme* and *appeals*. *Judge* is the title for jurists in courts other than the highest state and federal courts; *justice* is the title for members of state supreme courts and the U.S.

Supreme Court. Typically, governors nominate state judges and justices, who are ratified by the state senates. Some states elect judges and justices, although the election of judges is more common. Elected jurists typically serve terms of 10 or 15 years. Federal court judges and justices are nominated by the president and confirmed by the Senate. They serve for life and can be removed only for cause.

Appointment insulates the judiciary somewhat from politics. This results in more predictable and consistent court-made law. Judges and justices appointed by governors or presidents will likely have compatible political philosophies; the history of the U.S. Supreme Court shows notable exceptions, however. The need for legislative confirmation and the almost universal review of nominees by bar committees usually result in appointment of jurists who are competent and ethical.

The Courts

HSOs/HSs are often involved in state and federal courts as plaintiffs (those bringing civil legal action) or defendants (those against whom civil legal action is taken). In addition, when a case is heard by an appeals court, an individual or association may submit legal briefs as a friend of the court, or *amicus curiae*. The briefs bring to a court's attention legal precedents and other information from that group's perspective.

Stare Decisis and Res Judicata

Two legal doctrines make courts a source of formal law, as discussed in Chapter 2. *Stare decisis* is Latin, meaning courts will stand by precedent and not disturb a settled point.[15] Intrinsic to a stable society is that the law is fixed, definite, and known and that courts and litigants are guided by previous cases with similar facts. Whimsical changes and uncertainty must not result from judge-made law or legislative enactments. Nevertheless, precedents are sometimes overturned.

The second doctrine is reflected in the Latin phrase *res judicata,* which means that a matter has been judged or a thing has been judicially acted on or decided.[16] Thus, rehearing will occur only if there was a substantial problem in the original judgment because of factual error, misrepresentation, or fraud or if significant new information is available. *Res judicata* adds stability and predictability to the law because a case is rarely reopened after appeals are exhausted.

Executive Orders

Formal law results from executive orders issued by the president through the executive branch of the federal government. Authority for some executive orders, such as the president's role as commander-in-chief of the armed forces, is derived from the U.S. Constitution. Decisions arising from treaties result in executive orders. Another example is delegation of authority by Congress to the president to act in special circumstances, such as emergencies. An executive order that declares a disaster will enable an HSO/HS to qualify for federal assistance.

Private Processes

Influence of HSOs/HSs

Healthcare became highly politicized after massive federal financing of health services began in the mid-1960s with enactment of Medicare and Medicaid. The legislative and regulatory processes affecting health services were increasingly subject to the influence of lobbyists, political action committees (PACs), and other interest groups, all of whom sought to ensure their concerns were known. For HSOs/HSs and their trade associations, participating in federal and state government processes that affected them was a matter of survival.

In the management model in Part III, Figure 2, the change loop [6] suggests that HSOs/HSs affect their external environment, even as they are affected by it. This occurs when they advocate a position or support a trade association or PAC. Another effect results from bringing a lawsuit.

Trade Associations and Interested Parties

Washington, D.C., and environs are home to thousands of trade associations, many linked to healthcare. Physical proximity to policy makers and the bureaucrats who develop and enforce federal laws and regulations is considered an advantage. In addition to major trade associations there are hundreds of narrowly focused special interest groups. At best, trade associations and interested parties provide information that enhances the results of legislative and regulatory processes. HSOs/HSs and their associations seek to further their own interests, but their quasi-public role means their interests have much in common with the public's interests.

Associations and interested parties make their positions known at various points in the legislative and regulatory processes. Myriad bills and their often-complex subject matter minimize decision makers' understanding. An essential role of lobbyists is to provide decision makers with information that is otherwise unavailable, as well as identifying and analyzing intended and unintended consequences of proposed legislation. Interactions with lobbyists occur in private, which is not to suggest illegal or immoral acts. Legislators and their staffs know that lobbyists will present information most advantageously for the party they represent. A cardinal rule among lobbyists is truthfulness. Lobbyists found lying or purposefully misleading decision makers or staff will irretrievably lose credibility—their greatest asset. The obvious bears repeating: There will always be dishonest legislators whose vote can be bought and special interests who try to do more than express a viewpoint and make a convincing argument. Despite occasional publicity to the contrary, such ethical and legal lapses are the exception.

A Brief History of Health Services in the United States

Figure 1.3 shows trends in U.S. health services since 1945. It provides a useful context for understanding the evolution and current status of healthcare and health services.

Technology

The importance of ensuring the purity of food and water was shown during the "great sanitary awakening" in Western Europe in the mid-19th century. One result was the creation of local and state health departments. About the same time, the work of scientists such as Pasteur, Lister, and Koch resulted, first, in antisepsis and, later, asepsis. In addition, medical technology in the late 19th century, such as radiography, inhalation anesthesia, blood typing, and improved clinical laboratories, permitted efficacious surgical interventions with greatly reduced morbidity and mortality. Making these scientific advances available to the public required an organization, specialized staff, and effective systems. Hospitals were the answer.

It was common for hospitals to be sponsored by private, not-for-profit corporations formed by religious groups, concerned citizens, or wealthy benefactors; local governments sponsored others. In addition, many small "hospitals" were established as for-profit corporations, often by individual physicians who needed a place to care for their patients after surgery. Long-term care facilities were rare because extended families cared for one another. Persons with mental illnesses were isolated from society in facilities owned almost exclusively by state governments. Effective, large-scale treatment with psychoactive drugs became possible for these patients only after World War II. Another type of HSO sponsored by local and state governments was the public health department.

Advances in science and technology continue to transform contemporary health services and are detailed in Chapter 5.

Mortality and Morbidity

Except for tuberculosis, the incidence of which declined rapidly at the end of the 19th century with improvements in nutrition and housing, and leprosy, which has never been a major medical problem in the United States, there were few chronic diseases before the 20th century.

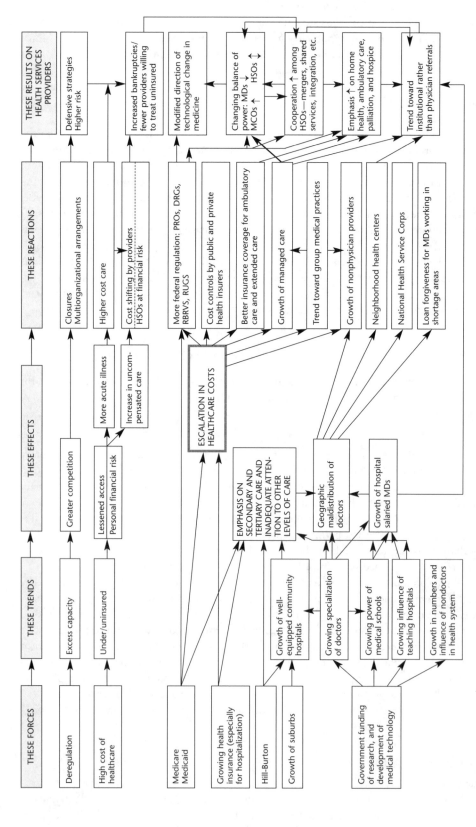

Figure 1.3. Trends in the U.S. healthcare system since 1945. (From Cambridge Research Institute. Trends Affecting the U.S. Health Care System, [Health Planning Information Series], 409. Washington, DC: Human Resources Administration, 1976. Revised and updated by the authors, 2013.)

Primarily, people died of acute gastrointestinal and respiratory tract infections, such as pneumonia, which usually occurred long before they could develop chronic diseases. Many communicable health problems common in the mid-19th century were solved through preventive measures taken by health departments. Pure food and water and improved sanitation were major contributors to decreased morbidity and mortality. The greatest influence on public health in the United States came from work done in England. Local public health departments were established in the early 19th century; those in Baltimore, MD, and Charleston, SC, were among the first.[17]

Causes of mortality and morbidity in the mid-20th century were, however, much less amenable to easy prevention or inexpensive treatment, and greater emphases on acute services increased costs greatly. As in the United States, the worldwide trend is that fewer illnesses are acute and result, for example, from water- and foodborne diseases that lead to premature death. Aging populations have more disability and will be afflicted by diseases such as Alzheimer's and Parkinson's. Such long-term conditions require significant resources.[18]

In 2017, life expectancy in the United States at birth was 78.6 years (up from 39 years a century ago but trending down recently largely because of increasing opioid-related deaths and suicides). The 10 leading causes of death in 2017 were the following:

1. Heart disease

2. Cancer

3. Unintentional injuries

4. Chronic lower respiratory diseases

5. Stroke

6. Alzheimer's disease

7. Diabetes

8. Influenza and pneumonia

9. Kidney disease

10. Suicide[19]

Figure 1.1 shows a link between lifestyle and medical problems. Several leading causes of death reinforce the seeming connection between lifestyle choices and medical conditions that result in death. Many types of prevention require changes in behavior. Efforts to effect these changes raise issues of individual choice and liberty rights, which are much more complex than purifying water and protecting food supplies. Modifying behavior raises questions such as: What are the limits of government efforts to force people to live healthy lives? What is society's obligation to those whose illnesses result from activities known to be unhealthy or to cause injury?

Social Welfare

A major shift in the locus of responsibility for social welfare occurred with the federal Social Security Act of 1935,[20] the enactment of which was a direct result of the Great Depression's catastrophic economic and social problems. To the extent government was involved in social welfare before 1935, it was provided at the local and state levels. City or county governments might own a "poor farm," for example, where needy persons could live and work until they regained their independence. Since 1935, there has been a massive shift of perceived and actual responsibility for social welfare from localities and states to the federal government. This accretion continued uninterrupted until revenue sharing and other federal programs were developed in the 1970s and 1980s.

Federal government–sponsored national health insurance programs, ranging in scope from all-encompassing to modest, were seriously considered in the late 1940s and late 1960s and again in the early 1990s. Various factors made them unattractive: lack of voter interest because of cost and fear of government control, widely available employer-provided health insurance, and the presence of Medicare and Medicaid that covered millions of Americans. Organized medicine's opposition is often cited, but its role is overstated. The experience with Medicare and Medicaid from 1966—especially rapidly rising costs—blunted the political will to universalize them. Passage of the Patient Protection and Affordable Care Act (ACA) (PL 111-148) marked a massive increase in federal government involvement in organizing, controlling, and financing delivery of health services.

In 2010, 13% of the population was age 65 or older, and by 2030 this proportion will grow to 20.6% (the first year all of the baby boomers will be 65+).[21] These data suggest that there will be greater demand for health services in general as well as specifically for services for the elderly: geriatrics, chronic diseases, rehabilitation, and institutional long-term care.

Federal Initiatives

Major beneficiaries of early federal programs were not-for-profit acute care hospitals, including those operated by local and state governments. From 1946 to 1981, the Hill-Burton Act (Hospital Survey and Construction Act of 1946, PL 79-725)[22] provided more than $4 billion in grants, loans, and guaranteed loans in a federal–state matching program and aided nearly 6,900 hospitals and other health services facilities in more than 4,000 communities. Initially, new inpatient facilities were constructed; later, outpatient facilities were constructed or remodeled. In return for Hill-Burton assistance, organizations provided uncompensated services for varying periods.[23] Legal processes that produced Hill-Burton and laws like it were discussed earlier in this chapter.

Another federal initiative provides generous funding for medical research. The National Institutes of Health (NIH) began with experimentation on cancer in the 1930s. In 2018, NIH included 27 institutes and centers that invested $39.2 billion annually in medical research: 80% of NIH funding is awarded in 50,000 competitive grants to more than 300,000 researchers at more than 2,500 universities.[24]

Significant federal programs to help educate physicians, nurses, technicians, and managers were established and funded in the 1960s. Congress recognized that knowledge produced by NIH and care delivered at hospitals built by Hill-Burton could improve health status only if enough health professionals were available.

The federal government has built large numbers of Department of Veterans Affairs (DVA) hospitals and other HSOs to serve former military personnel. The DVA system is separate from services provided to groups in special categories, including inmates in federal prisons, American Indians and Alaska Natives, and active-duty and retired military personnel and their dependents in the U.S. Army, U.S. Navy, and U.S. Air Force health facilities.

In 1965, amendments[25] to the Social Security Act of 1935 obligated federal government to pay for health services under the newly enacted Medicare and Medicaid programs. Medicare is exclusively federal and pays for medical services for persons with disabilities or who are 65 or older. Originally, Medicare included only Part A (hospital inpatient services), and Part B (physicians' services). The Balanced Budget Act of 1997 (PL 105-33)[26] added Part C, which allows Medicare beneficiaries to choose health plans, including fee-for-service, coordinated care plans, provider service organizations, and medical savings accounts.[27] Part D was added by the Medicare Prescription Drug, Improvement, and Modernization Act of 2003 (PL 108-173)[28] to provide a voluntary, outpatient prescription drug benefit program.

Medicaid is a state–federal cost-sharing program originally intended to give medical benefits to low-income people receiving cash assistance, with states determining eligibility.

Over time, a much larger group was covered: pregnant women, people of all ages with disabilities, and people who need long-term care. The Children's Health Insurance Program, created by the Balanced Budget Act of 1997 (PL105-33), provided health insurance and preventive care to children whose parents were uninsured but earned too much to be covered by Medicaid.[29] The federal government subsidizes a state's Medicaid program in varying ratios depending on per capita income; wealthy states receive less federal funding and poorer states receive more. Medicaid requires that participating states offer a minimum set of benefits: inpatient and outpatient hospital services; physician, midwife, and certified nurse practitioner services; laboratory and x-ray services; nursing homes and home healthcare for individuals age 21 or older; early and periodic screening, diagnosis, and treatment for children under age 21; family planning services and supplies; and rural health clinics or federally qualified health center services. In addition to basic benefits, states can receive federal matching funds for "optional" services, including prescription drugs, prosthetic devices, hearing aids, and dental care.[30] As part of the ACA, the federal government encouraged states to expand Medicaid eligibility from 100% to 138% of the federal poverty level by agreeing to pay 100% of the expansion costs for the first 7 years and 90% of expansion costs thereafter. The open-ended cost-sharing commitment by the federal government has proven largely uncontrollable because limiting or reducing benefits is politically infeasible. This has caused Medicaid to become very expensive for both state and federal governments. In many states, it is the largest budget item.

Meanwhile, Congress sought to rationalize health services.[31] The Comprehensive Health Planning and Public Health Service Amendments Act of 1966 (PL 89-749) was the first attempt. It enhanced the modest planning requirements in Hill-Burton by encouraging voluntary planning and use of planning processes and techniques. This legislation was amplified and expanded in the National Health Planning and Resources Development Act of 1974 (PL 93-641), which increased the control that planning agencies had over expansion of hospitals and services so as to regulate supply of services. Monitoring use and quality of services provided under Medicare and Medicaid programs was included in the Social Security Amendments of 1972 (PL 92-603) that established professional standards review organizations (PSROs). Political changes caused reassessment of planning and PSROs; federal support of planning ended. PSROs were replaced by peer review organizations (PROs), which are discussed later in this chapter.

Such regulatory controls were considered essential in slowing rapid increases in healthcare costs. Generally, they were ineffective. Except for 4 years between 1969 and 1996, the medical-care-items component of the consumer price index (CPI) had the highest rates of increase, usually by wide margins. In several years, the average annual percentage changes for hospital services were two to three times the annual percentage changes for all items measured by the CPI.[32] Healthcare costs are discussed later in this chapter.

The Tax Equity and Fiscal Responsibility Act of 1982 (PL 97-248) and the Social Security Amendments of 1983 (PL 98-21) established a prospective payment system to slow cost increases for hospital services.[33] Medicare reimbursement is determined prospectively for inpatients using diagnosis-related groups (DRGs), which tie federal government payment for Medicare patients to a hospital's case mix. The final important measure is the amount of annual deductibles and per visit copays (85% of covered workers with single coverage have an annual deductible with an average deductible of $1,350, and 66% of covered workers have a per visit copay).[34]

Other Western Systems

Western Europe, notably Germany and England, had government involvement in financing health services much earlier than did the United States. In 1883, Chancellor Otto von Bismarck achieved passage of a social insurance scheme, including a health services component, for some working-class Germans. In 1911, England adopted a national health insurance program, and in 1948, the United Kingdom established the National Health Service, which included government ownership of the health services system. Historically, Western European and Canadian healthcare systems have had more governmental control and financing than did those in the United States.

In the past, many of those countries had inflation in health services costs like that in the United States, despite greater government involvement in planning and financing. Since about 1985, however, the United States has had the highest growth rate in healthcare spending.[35] Countries whose public budgets allocate expenditures for health services prospectively spend much less than the United States. According to the Organisation for Economic Co-operation and Development, in 2018, as a percentage of GDP, the United States spent 16.9% ($10,586 per capita), Germany spent 11.2% ($5,986 per capita), Canada spent 10.7% ($4,974 per capita), and the United Kingdom spent 9.8% ($4,070 per capita).[36] One reason for this difference is that the United Kingdom and Canada spend much less on technology. Furthermore, elective and nonemergent procedures may be available only after long waiting periods, known as queues. Also, countries with national health insurance like the United Kingdom and Canada budget (limit) their health expenditures since the expenditures are government funded.

Structure of the Health Services System

Various types of HSOs are found in the private (owned by individuals or groups) and public (owned by government) sectors. HSOs may be institutions—the most important and numerous are hospitals and NFs—or they may be agencies and programs such as public health departments and visiting nurse associations. Information about select HSOs is found in Chapter 11. Various HSOs are aggregated into HSs for greater efficiency and to provide a network of services.

In this regard, HSOs are orienting their activities toward the health of populations and communities. HSOs depend on their environments (see Part III Introduction, Figure 2). The range of health services delivery and various providers is shown in Figure 1.4.

One way HSOs/HSs can improve their focus on populations and communities is to develop community care networks, with the following objectives: increasing access and coverage, enhancing accountability to the community, imbuing the healthcare system with a community health focus, improving coordination among the parts of the healthcare system, and using healthcare resources more efficiently. Participants include insurers, business alliances, schools, religious organizations, social services agencies, public health departments, local governments, and community-based organizations, in addition to HSs, hospitals, clinics, and physician groups.

Health departments can and should take a leading role in coordinating disparate providers and minimizing political and competitive issues to deliver integrated and comprehensive health services to the community.[37] Delivery of integrated services is discussed in Chapter 11, and community health information networks are discussed in Chapter 5.

Preventive care is an essential part of meeting the health needs of a population. It comprises two parts, education and prevention. Education about health is offered in K–12 schooling. It is increasingly important in health services delivery. Prevention is tripartite: primary, secondary, and tertiary. *Primary prevention* is preventing disease or injury. Examples include improved design of roadways, school education programs about tobacco use and substance abuse, and immunizing against poliomyelitis and measles. *Secondary prevention* slows or blocks progression of a disease or injury from impairment to disability. Using the Papanicolaou smear (Pap test) to identify early cellular changes that are precursors of cervical cancer is a type of secondary prevention. If impairment has already occurred, disability (or death) may be prevented through early intervention. Treating certain streptococcal infections with penicillin can prevent the

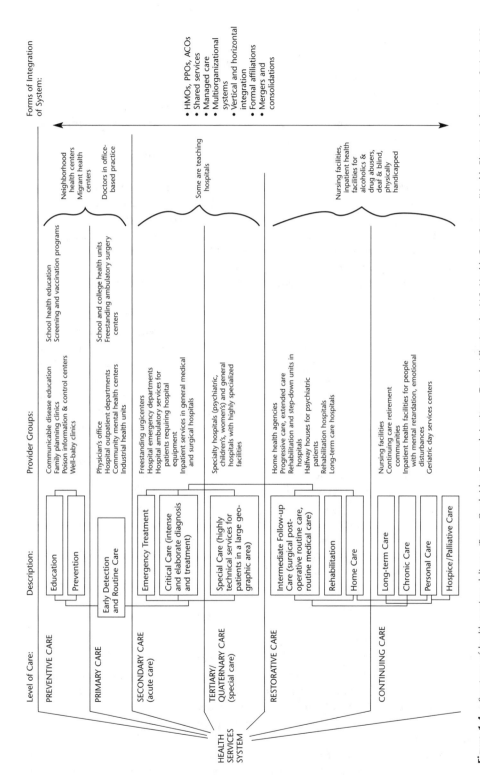

Figure 1.4. Spectrum of health services delivery. (From Cambridge Research Institute. *Trends Affecting the U.S. Health Care System*, [Health Planning Information Series], 262. Washington, DC: Human Resources Administration, 1976. Revised and updated by the authors, 2013.)

occasional development of rheumatic fever and serious heart disease. Early detection and treatment of high blood pressure reduces the probability of heart attack or stroke. *Tertiary prevention* blocks or retards the progression of disability to a state of dependence. Early detection and effective management of diabetes can prevent some dependencies, or at least slow or stop progression. Prompt medical care followed by rehabilitation can limit damage caused by a cerebrovascular accident (stroke); damage from heart attacks can be limited in the same way. Good vehicular design can reduce dependency that might otherwise result from an accident.[38] HSOs such as local and state health departments have programs at all three levels of prevention. Hospitals and NFs are more likely to engage in secondary and tertiary prevention than in primary prevention.

Figure 1.4 shows that primary care is provided in various settings—the most common being physicians' offices, clinics, and outpatient units of acute care hospitals. Primary care is routine care, a part of which is primary prevention. Primary care may also be part of secondary and tertiary prevention.[39] In addition, acute care hospitals provide secondary and tertiary acute care services through emergency treatment and inpatient services. Restorative care (rehabilitation) may be provided in acute care hospitals. It is also available in specialized hospitals, in NFs, and in the home through home health services. Continuing care is available in settings such as the home, NFs, and hospice.

Holistic, complementary, and alternative medicine are similar concepts that greatly broaden theories about disease prevention, causation, and treatment. They focus on nontraditional medicine, with special emphasis on self-help and on interventions less dramatic than chemicals and surgery, and they stress health promotion and prevention. Increasingly, such measures are adjuncts to allopathy—traditional Western medicine that emphasizes dramatic interventions, such as chemicals and surgery, to return the body to normal functioning.[40] The use of nontraditional medicine will significantly affect HSOs, physician (allopathic) practice, and healthcare financing. It is likely that the use of alternative sources will only shift where payment is made and not reduce costs to the system. In fact, costs may increase, at least in proportion to increases in alternate sources of care. Issues of third-party coverage and payment and effects on total costs and delivery of care are beginning to be addressed.

Most physician–patient interactions (visits) occur in physician offices. For 2017, Centers for Disease Control and Prevention (CDC) reported 990.8 million physician office visits, 136.9 million emergency department visits, and 125.7 million hospital outpatient visits.[41] Despite increasing numbers of physicians employed by HSOs, most are self-employed entrepreneurs who may share a receptionist, billing services, patient coverage, and perhaps diagnostic equipment with other physicians, or they may be in a partnership or may be "employees" of a physician (professional) corporation, such as a multi- or single-specialty group practice. A physician office practice is not considered an HSO unless it is part of a clinic or group practice.

⌐ Classification and Types of HSOs ⌐

Profit or Not for Profit

HSOs/HSs may be classified as profit seeking (for profit or investor owned) or not for profit. The former pay owners (investors) a return on investment. In the latter, any excess of income over expense is not available to any person or corporation and is used by the HSO/HS to enhance the content or quality of health services or to reduce charges. Government-sponsored HSOs/HSs are classified as not for profit, while privately owned corporations may be for profit or not for profit.

For-profit and not-for-profit HSOs/HSs may be converted to the opposite status. This is done for tax and other strategic reasons. Converting for-profit HSOs/HSs to not-for-profit status may result in provision of more uncompensated care in the service area, but it simultaneously decreases property and other tax revenue to local jurisdictions. Conversely, changing not-for-profit HSOs/HSs to for-profit status raises issues of valuing assets, private inurement, and the mission and activities of the charitable foundation usually established with proceeds of the sale.

Ownership

HSOs/HSs may be classified by ownership. Privately owned corporations are of two types: 1) sectarian (faith based) and nonsectarian that are organized as not-for-profit corporations, and 2) for-profit corporations that issue stock either to an identified group of investors (closely held corporations) or to the general public, in which case the stock is traded on stock exchanges. Government-owned HSO/HSs are owned by a public entity and classified as not for profit. All levels of government own and operate acute care hospitals and other types of HSOs or HSs. Cities and counties own acute care hospitals, some of which are financed by special tax districts. Cities and counties establish, fund, and control public health departments. HSOs/HSs owned by state government include health departments and psychiatric hospitals or HSOs for persons with mental disabilities. Many states own academic health (medical) centers, which may be university-affiliated teaching hospitals that treat acute illness, conduct research, and educate the health occupations.

The federal government has a long history of limited involvement in financing health services. To a lesser extent, it has delivered preventive, acute, and long-term health services to special groups. U.S. Public Health Service (USPHS) hospitals were established in the late 18th century to care for merchant seamen. USPHS hospitals serving general, acute care patients operated until 1981, when the few remaining hospitals closed or were converted to other uses. The only facility in the United States devoted to Hansen's disease (leprosy) is the National Hansen's Disease Clinical Center at the Ochsner Medical Center in Baton Rouge, LA.[42]

The federal government is responsible for the Indian Health Service (IHS), which provides healthcare to American Indians in 573 recognized tribes, and the DVA, which delivers healthcare to 9 million enrolled veterans annually. In 2018, the IHS, an agency of the Department of Health and Human Services (DHHS), operated 26 hospitals, 55 health centers, and 21 health stations. In addition, through self-determination contracts, American Indian and Alaska Native corporations administer 19 hospitals, 280 health centers, 62 health stations, and 134 Alaska village clinics.[43] In 2018, the DVA operated 172 medical centers (hospitals) and 1,069 outpatient clinics, nursing homes, residential rehabilitation treatment programs, and readjustment counseling centers and veterans benefits regional offices, and 128 national cemeteries.[44] In addition, the Military Health System operated by the Department of Defense includes over 50 hospitals and 600 clinics providing care to 9.6 million active-duty personnel, reservists, and some dependents.[45]

Length of Patient Stay

A third way to classify HSOs is by the length of time that care is provided. A general dichotomy divides HSOs by whether services are provided to inpatients—those treated 24 hours or longer—or to outpatients—those treated for less than 24 hours. Outpatient (ambulatory) services are provided in hospital emergency departments (EDs) and clinics, physicians' offices, and freestanding HSOs, such as surgery centers and imaging centers. Home health services are a unique blend of inpatient and outpatient services because care is provided in patients' homes over months or years. Hospice care is also a blend of inpatient care and care delivered in patients' homes. Hospice is available to the terminally ill—typically those with fewer than 6 months to live. Chapter 11 discusses several types of HSOs in detail.

HSOs that provide inpatient care are divided into short-term (acute) and long-term hospitals. The American Hospital Association (AHA) defines a short-term hospital as one in which the average length of stay (ALOS) is less than 30 days; a long-term hospital has patient stays that average 30 days or longer. The ALOS in community (short-term or acute care) hospitals has declined steadily from 9.1 days in 1946 to 5.4 days in 2017[46] due to changes in technology and reimbursement.

In the continuum of care measured by length of stay (LOS), long-term care hospitals (LTCHs) are sited between acute care hospitals and NFs. LTCHs provide extended medical and rehabilitative services to clinically complex patients who have multiple acute or chronic conditions. Federal regulations define LTCHs as hospitals whose ALOS is longer than 25 days.[47]

Further along the LOS continuum are NFs, which typically treat only inpatients, who are referred to as residents. Some rehabilitation services may be provided, but the level of care is custodial. LOS in an NF is measured in months or years.

Role in the Health Services System

A fourth way to classify HSOs/HSs is by their role in delivery of services. Health or health-related services may be provided in health department screening programs, in family planning and substance abuse treatment centers, or through sanitation efforts that protect food and water. There are thousands of privately and publicly owned and operated emergency medical units, such as rescue squads and ambulance services, often organized into emergency medical services systems. In addition, there are programs more oriented to social welfare; some only raise funds, others deliver services. Depending on their activities, they may or may not be defined as HSOs. The total number of HSOs in the United States is in the tens of thousands. Chapter 11 describes the history, numbers, functions, and organization of several types.

Unique Institutional Providers

In addition to inpatient HSOs, such as hospitals and NFs, many other types of inpatient facilities provide health and health-related services. Data about them are sparse. They include residential facilities or schools for special groups, such as persons who are blind or deaf, persons with emotional or physical disabilities, persons with mental disabilities, dependent children, pregnant women, alcoholics, drug abusers, and persons with various physical and mental disorders.

Community services may reduce the need for long-term inpatient care. Examples include diagnostic and evaluation clinics, day care centers, early childhood education facilities, rehabilitation programs, and summer camps and recreational facilities. All offer alternatives to institutional placement. Community-sponsored educational services are provided by local school districts directed by state special education programs. Programs for the developmentally disabled are typically operated at the local level and supported by state funding.

Mental Health Organizations

Mental health organizations are HSOs that provide services to persons with mental illness or emotional disturbances. Included are public or private psychiatric hospitals, psychiatric services in general acute care hospitals, outpatient psychiatric clinics, and mental health day/night facilities. Since 1955, the locus of delivering mental health services has changed markedly. In the mid-1950s, county and state mental hospitals accounted for 77% of inpatient services; 23% were outpatient. By 1975, a reversal had occurred, and 76% of mental health services were outpatient.[48] In 2018, there were 14,000 mental health facilities; 692 were classified as inpatient psychiatric hospitals and 1,066 as general hospitals with inpatient psychiatric capacity.[49] Many of these facilities also treat behavioral health disorders, behavioral health being a subset of mental health. For instance, mental health disorders can be caused by brain chemistry or genetics (e.g., bipolar disorder and schizophrenia), whereas behavioral disorders result from maladaptive behaviors (e.g., substance abuse and eating disorders). Both result in an inability to cope with the normal stress of life and are the most frequently diagnosed disorders.[50]

Teaching Hospitals

In 2018, 400 hospitals participated in graduate medical education as defined by the Council of Teaching Hospitals and Health Systems,[51] a dramatic decline of 914 since 1990. They fall under the general rubric of "teaching hospital" and offer a wide range of secondary, tertiary, and some quaternary medical services. These 400, plus many other hospitals, participate in training a wide variety of students in the health occupations. Many teaching hospitals are part of a medical center that includes a medical school. Those having no medical school are likely affiliated with one. Their prominence in medical education and their research and contributions to the medical and scientific literature make teaching hospitals a vital resource in healthcare.

A unique HSO that fits more than one of the categories described merits special mention. The premier institution among HSOs is the academic health (medical) center, which consists of a medical school, at least one other professional school or program, and one or more owned or affiliated teaching hospital or health system. According to the Association of Academic Health Centers, there were 89 U.S. member academic health centers in 2018.[52]

Rural Hospitals

Nearly 20% of Americans live in rural communities and are served by approximately 1,875 rural community hospitals listed by the AHA in 2019.[53] Of these, 1,343 have been designated critical access hospitals (hospitals with fewer than 25 beds that provide rural communities access to healthcare) by CMS, which allows them to receive lower-risk, cost-based reimbursement.[54] Even with higher reimbursement, however, 64 rural hospitals closed between 2013 and 2017 according to the Government Accountability Office. Financial distress caused by Medicare payment reductions and fewer patients seeking care typically cause the closures.[55]

⅄ Local, State, and Federal Regulation of HSOs/HSs

When the original colonies delegated specific powers to a national government and ratified the U.S. Constitution, they retained a wide range of authority traditionally held by the sovereign. These are known as the *police power*, generally defined as the authority to protect the public's health, safety, order, and welfare. State laws and regulations implement the police power, much of which may be delegated to, or shared with, local governments. It is common for state departments of health to regulate licensure of HSOs, for example. The typical regulatory authority delegated to local governments and reflected in city and county ordinances and exercised by local health departments includes food, fire, radiation, and environmental safety; air and water quality; waste and trash disposal; sanitation and pest control; and workplace hazards. These activities affect HSOs.

Licensure and Regulation

HSOs/HSs are subject to state laws and local ordinances, an important dimension of which is the group of inspections linked to licensure for specific types of HSOs. States may accept accreditation by a private organization in lieu of some types of regulation. For example, accreditation by the Joint Commission on Accreditation of Healthcare Organizations (The Joint Commission) is recognized for hospital licensure by 47 states and the District of Columbia.[56]

State and local government regulation focuses on the physical plant and safety. Scant attention is paid to the clinical quality of patient care. The *Fire Prevention Code, National*

Fuel Gas Code, National Electrical Code, and *Life Safety Code* published by the National Fire Protection Association, an international, not-for-profit organization, are prominent sources of environmental standards used by state and local government in regulating HSOs.[57]

Conditions of Participation

The 1965 Medicare law (1965 amendments to the Social Security Act of 1935) stated that Joint Commission–accredited hospitals were in "deemed" status (eligible) for purposes of reimbursement. In response to concerns about delegating government authority to a private group, the DHHS promulgated the "conditions of participation" (CoPs) in 1966.[58] Federal legislation in 1972 mandated oversight of Joint Commission accreditation and review of accredited hospitals based on random sampling or complaints. Originally, CoPs emphasized physical plant and safety (e.g., the *Life Safety Code*) and minimized attention to the content and processes of clinical practice and organization; Joint Commission emphases were the opposite. These private and public programs have evolved toward each other, with CoPs changing the most. Several other private accrediting organizations have been recognized by CMS as able to confer "deeming status." Among them are the Community Health Accreditation Program (CHAP), the American Osteopathic Association (AOA), and, more recently, Det Norske Veritas Germanischer Lloyd (DNV GL) Healthcare, which uses a combination of the CoPs and ISO 9001:2015 quality standards. HSOs not in "deemed" status must meet the applicable CoPs to receive payments from federal programs.

Planning, Rate Regulation, and Price Transparency

Much of what happens in the states is stimulated by the federal government, and because hospitals consume disproportionate resources, policy makers have given them disproportionate attention. The Hill-Burton Act of 1946 included statewide planning for hospital services. The Comprehensive Health Planning and Public Health Service Amendments Act of 1966[59] encouraged the use of planning methodologies to allocate resources, improve access, and contain costs. In the late 1960s, states began enacting laws to control health services costs. A special concern was Medicaid, the funding of which they shared. The laws used rate review to control capital expenditures and the costs of health services. New York and Maryland were among the first to enact capital expenditure review. Other states were prompted by the Social Security Amendments of 1972 (PL 92-603),[60] which established PSROs to review the quantity and quality of care for Medicare patients in hospitals. PSROs complemented planning laws by controlling the use of health services to reduce costs. Section 1122 required capital expenditure review to enhance planning agency control.

The National Health Planning and Resources Development Act of 1974 (PL 93-641)[61] required states to establish a health planning and development agency and a network of health systems agencies (HSAs). HSAs superseded the areawide health planning agencies ("b" agencies) required by the 1966 law. Planning laws sought to control costs by focusing on the supply of services. CON (certificate-of-need) laws required HSOs/HSs to have approval for a new service or construction or a renovation project exceeding a certain cost, usually several hundred thousand dollars. The purpose was to ration the supply of health services by controlling capital expenditures and preventing unneeded expansion. Critics of CON argued that this artificial limitation on the supply of services caused inflation. In the late 1970s, criticism about the usefulness of mandated planning grew. The antiregulatory mood in health services fit with the movement toward deregulation elsewhere in the economy. In 1987, the National Health Planning and Resources Development Act was repealed.[62] In the years since, states have reduced involvement in planning. In 2019, the District of Columbia and 35 states had CON laws or variations of them.[63]

In addition to CON, some states enacted health services rate review (cost review) laws. By 1983, mandatory programs had been enacted in six states,[64] and there were more than 20 voluntary programs. By regulating how much HSOs (primarily hospitals) charged or were paid, states were treating them as public utilities. States with rates of increase in health services costs below the national average were exempt from the federal DRG system for Medicare patients. In the mid-1980s, exempt states included New York, New Jersey, Maryland, and Massachusetts.[65] By 2008, only Maryland was exempt. This status has continued because Maryland has had a highly regulated, all-payer system to pay for hospital-based inpatient and outpatient care since 1971. The system allows only limited discounts; this inhibits the ability of Maryland hospitals to compete, especially in border areas.

The ACA required hospitals to make their prices transparent by publishing them for all services. Consumer knowledge of prices is essential in a competitive market and becomes increasingly important as high-deductible policies proliferate and the customer pays more out of pocket. As of January 1, 2019, hospitals must publish prices on their websites in a customer-friendly format. Hospitals have balked and argue this information is of little use to customers because hospital products and services are difficult to compare; prices are not relevant to customers because, overwhelmingly, they do not pay full price due to discounts; and quality information is difficult to discern and not inherent in price (an essential element of a competitive market).[66] In late 2019, several healthcare trade associations, including the AHA, filed suit to prevent implementation of the transparency regulations, citing that the regulations go well beyond the intent of the law, and the burden and cost of compliance are enormous.[67] Due to litigation, the deadline was delayed until January 1, 2021.

UR, PSROs, and PROs

Utilization review (UR) was a mandated part of hospital participation in the original Medicare law.[68] Hospitals had to certify the necessity of admission, continued stay, and professional services rendered to Medicare beneficiaries. Although UR was delegated to hospitals, rapid Medicare cost increases in the late 1960s showed that hospital-based UR was ineffective. Consequently, PSROs were mandated by the Social Security Amendments of 1972 (PL 92-603)[69] as federally funded physician organizations responsible for ensuring the appropriateness, medical necessity, and quality of care furnished to Medicare beneficiaries. As with UR, emphasis in the PSRO program was on hospital review. The three functions of PSRO were admission and continued-stay review, quality assurance, and profile analysis (patterns of care).

Ten years later, PSROs had proved neither cost-effective nor able to significantly improve quality. As a remedy and in response to prospective payment, Congress established professional review organizations (PROs) as part of the Tax Equity and Fiscal Responsibility Act of 1982 (P.L. 97–248).[70] PROs were outcome rather than process and structure oriented, and outcomes were measured against performance standards. The core PRO activities were to deny Medicare payment for medically unnecessary care, care rendered in an inappropriate setting, or care of substandard quality, while assuring that necessary care was provided within the prospective payment constraints. PROs also educated problem providers, reviewed 100% of problem cases, and exerted peer pressure. If correction was not achieved or if a gross and flagrant quality problem occurred, PROs recommended excluding the provider from Medicare.

Since the inception of PROs, their work expanded to include all federal payments for medical services, including those in physicians' offices. A major initiative in the early 1990s was implementing a uniform clinical data set that enabled PROs to consistently select cases that required review. This database allowed epidemiological studies and inter-PRO comparisons. Critics of PROs note few physicians and hospitals have been disciplined. The inspector general of DHHS estimated that, beyond the few sanctions against providers, far more hospital admissions were inappropriate than were found by PROs.[71]

n 2001, PROs were officially renamed quality improvement organizations (QIOs). Like
)s, QIOs provide services under contract with the CMS. The name change is largely sym-
ic, however, and although QIOs have been charged with quality improvement initiatives
.. numerous clinical areas and across healthcare settings, there are no published assessments
of whether hospitals believe QIO interventions are improving quality of care.[72] In 2019, there
were 53 QIOs operational in the United States.[73]

Other Regulators of HSOs/HSs

In addition to CMS, numerous federal regulators affect HSOs/HSs. Their activities are based
on authority in the U.S. Constitution, as interpreted by the U.S. Supreme Court, to regulate
interstate commerce and to provide for the general welfare. Regulators include independent
agencies and various other executive branch departments and bureaus. The Department of
Justice and the FTC enforce the Sherman Antitrust Act (1890)[74] and the Clayton Act (1914)[75]
and their various amendments prohibiting anticompetitive practices. The National Labor Relations Board applies provisions of the National Labor Relations Act (1935)[76] and its amendments to the process of union organizing and collective bargaining. The Occupational Safety
and Health Administration enforces provisions of the Occupational Safety and Health Act
(1970)[77] to safeguard the work environment. The Food and Drug Administration enforces
provisions of the Food, Drug, and Cosmetic Act of 1906[78] and its amendments and regulates
drugs and medical devices. The Securities and Exchange Commission enforces the Securities
Exchange Act of 1934, as amended,[79] and affects how investor-owned HSOs/HSs market,
sell, and trade stock. The Nuclear Regulatory Commission enforces provisions of the Atomic
Energy Act (1954)[80] and regulates and licenses the nuclear industry, thus regulating hazards
arising from storage, handling, and transportation of radioactive materials. The Equal Employment Opportunity Commission enforces the Equal Pay Act of 1963,[81] Title VII of the Civil
Rights Act of 1964,[82] and the Age Discrimination in Employment Act of 1967,[83] among others, and investigates complaints about treatment of employees and prospective employees. The
Bureau of Alcohol, Tobacco, Firearms, and Explosives of the Justice Department enforces the
alcohol and tobacco tax provisions of the Internal Revenue Code[84] and the Alcohol Administration Act of 1935[85] and regulates the use of tax-free alcohol. It is noteworthy that many federal regulatory, review, and control activities have applied to HSOs only since the early 1970s.
In addition, local and state governments may add to these regulatory requirements.

Accreditation in Healthcare

Accreditors of HSOs/HSs

The Joint Commission on Accreditation of Healthcare Organizations
No voluntary, private organization has affected HSOs, especially hospitals, as has The Joint
Commission. Its lineage can be traced to the "Hospital Standardization" program established
by the American College of Surgeons (ACS), which began surveying hospitals in 1918. ACS
single-handedly worked to improve hospital-based medical practice until 1951. Its director
during most of its formative period was Malcolm T. MacEachern, a Canadian-born physician
and health services leader, whose book, *Hospital Organization and Management*,[86] is a classic
in the field. The Joint Commission was formed in 1951 and began accrediting hospitals in
1953. As noted earlier, accreditation became much more important with the designation of
"deemed" status in the 1965 Medicare law.

Since 1951, The Joint Commission has expanded its accreditation services far beyond hospitals. It accredits eight types of providers: ambulatory care, behavioral healthcare, critical access
hospitals, home care, hospitals, laboratory services, nursing home care, and office-based surgery.[87]

Accreditation of networks (MCOs, managed behavioral healthcare organizations, and preferred provider organizations) ended in 2006.[88] Each accreditation program has a set of standards. Surveys of common standards such as physical plant, licensure, and corporate bylaws in multiprogram HSOs are combined to minimize duplication. In 2019, 4,487 hospitals, or about 77%, of the nation's hospitals were accredited by The Joint Commission, and more than 16,000 programs were certified by it.[89]

The Joint Commission accreditation has the following benefits:

- Strengthens community confidence in the quality and safety of care, treatment, and service

- Provides a competitive edge in the marketplace

- Improves risk management and risk reduction

- Helps organize and strengthen patient safety efforts

- Provides education on good practice to improve business operations

- Provides professional advice and counsel, enhancing staff education

- Provides a customized, intensive process of review grounded in the unique mission of the organization

- Enhances staff recruitment and development

- Provides deeming authority for Medicare certification

- Is recognized by insurers and other third parties

- May reduce liability insurance costs

- Provides a framework for organizational structure and management

- May fulfill regulatory requirements in select states[90]

Accreditation by The Joint Commission establishes the HSO's community and professional credibility because it meets standards for patient safety, provides education on good practice to improve business operations, and holds a competitive edge in the marketplace. Accredited HSOs maintain a framework for organizational structure and management that improves quality of care and patient safety.

The Joint Commission will continue to be a major force in developing performance expectations for HSOs. Even those HSOs that choose not to be accredited will benefit from considering its standards in developing and managing their programs. The Joint Commission emphasizes outcomes and continuous quality improvement, the theory and application of which are described in Chapters 4 and 8. The Joint Commission will remain viable only if its standards are state of the art, if HSOs and the public value accreditation, and if the survey is worth the thousands of dollars it costs. In their evolution, the CoPs developed by CMS pose an existential threat to the continued need for The Joint Commission. In addition, competing private specialty and programmatic accreditation efforts, several of which are described later, will challenge The Joint Commission's preeminence as "the" accrediting body.

Healthcare Facilities Accreditation Program

Begun by the AOA in 1945 to accredit osteopathic hospitals, the Healthcare Facilities Accreditation Program (HFAP) now accredits acute care hospitals, critical access hospitals, ambulatory surgery centers, clinical laboratories, behavioral health facilities, and ambulatory care/office-based surgery centers. CMS recognizes HFAP accreditation as granting "deemed" status. In 2019, HFAP accredited 157 acute care and critical access hospitals and 197 other healthcare facilities.[91]

DNV GL Healthcare

In 2008, after a 4-year application process, DNV GL Healthcare received authority from CMS to deem hospitals in compliance with the CMS Conditions of Participation for hospitals.[92] DNV GL Healthcare standards emphasize improvement and sustainability through integration with international standards (ISO 9001:2015).[93] The International Organization for Standardization is described later in the chapter. In 2019, DNV GL Healthcare accredited about 500 hospitals in the United States.[94]

Community Health Accreditation Partner

CHAP, which specializes in home care and community health, is an independent, not-for-profit accrediting body created by a joint venture between the American Public Health Association and the National League for Nursing. CHAP began accreditation activities in 1965, accrediting community nursing centers, home healthcare aide services, home health organizations, infusion therapy services, home medical equipment, hospice, private duty nursing, public health organizations, and supplemental staffing services. CHAP confers "deemed" status for home health care. CHAP standards emphasize organizational structure and function; quality of services and products; adequacy of human, financial, and physical resources; and long-term viability.[95]

International Organization for Standardization

The International Organization for Standardization (ISO) in Geneva is a nongovernmental organization established in 1947. ISO is a worldwide federation of national standards bodies from 164 countries.[96] Its work results in international agreements published as international standards—to the benefit of consumers. ISO registers the organizations that meet its standards. Although it does not "accredit," as that term is generally used, ISO registration has a similar effect.

ISO 9000 and ISO 14000 are families of generic management system standards that focus on processes and not directly on the results of process activities, even though what happens in the process affects the outcome. This means they can be applied to any organization in any sector of activity, including HSOs. ISO 9000 is concerned primarily with quality management, which means the features of a product or service conform to customer requirements. ISO 14000 is primarily concerned with environmental management, which is what an organization does to minimize harmful effects to the environment caused by its activities.[97] Organizations or components of organizations that seek certification or registration using ISO 9000 or ISO 14000 standards are surveyed by independent, ISO-qualified auditors, not by ISO representatives.[98] The certification or registration is not officially recognized by ISO, even though its standards are used. The ISO does not accredit organizations or components of organizations against its standards, as does The Joint Commission, for example. Increasingly, HSOs are using the ISO 9000 and ISO 14000 families of standards to certify departments; Chapter 8 discusses their application. ISO 9001:2015 is a Quality Management System standard including seven quality management principles to promote organizational improvement. As noted, the DNV GL Healthcare National Integrated Accreditation for Healthcare Organizations program uses a combination of CMS's CoPs and ISO 9001:2015 quality management standards to survey healthcare providers. This is the first healthcare accreditation program to combine CoPs and ISO 9001:2015 Quality Management Systems.

National Committee for Quality Assurance

The National Committee for Quality Assurance (NCQA) began accrediting health plans in 1991. More than 1,200 of the nation's MCOs are accredited by NCQA.[99] In 1992, NCQA began developing the Health Plan Employer Data and Information Set, which is widely used by employers and HMOs to judge and compare quality. As part of accreditation, NCQA requires health plans to submit audited results of clinical quality and consumer survey measures.

Clinical quality includes childhood and adolescent immunization status, breast cancer and cervical cancer screening, advice to smokers to quit, and postpartum checkups. Examples of consumer survey measures are giving care quickly, doctors who communicate, courteous and helpful office staff, getting needed care, claims processing, and consumer service. Most health plans offer several different products, such as a Medicare plan, a Medicaid plan, an HMO, and a point-of-service plan; NCQA reports on these products separately.[100]

Educational Accreditors

Various accreditors review the quality of didactic and clinical programs that educate health services professionals. Typically, accreditors have governing bodies composed of representatives from professional groups in their fields.

Managers

Programs for master's level education in health services management are accredited by the Commission on Accreditation of Healthcare Management Education (CAHME). CAHME is composed of professionals from the healthcare field. In 2019, CAHME accredited 104 graduate programs in North America, including programs in Canada (several universities offer more than one program accredited by CAHME).[101] The accreditation process includes a self-study, a site visit, and follow-up reports.

The Council on Education for Public Health (CEPH) accredits schools of public health and graduate public health programs. CEPH is composed of representatives from various groups in public health. In 2019, CEPH accredited 200 schools and programs in public health.[102]

Physicians

The Liaison Committee on Medical Education (LCME), jointly sponsored by the Association of American Medical Colleges (AAMC) and the American Medical Association (AMA), accredits medical programs leading to the MD degree. In 2019, LCME accredited 153 programs in the United States[103] and 17 programs in Canada.[104] The AOA accredits 35 osteopathic medical schools in the United States.[105]

Nurses

Two national organizations accredit nursing education: the Accreditation Commission for Education in Nursing accredits associate, diploma, baccalaureate, and master's programs, and the Commission on Collegiate Nursing Education accredits baccalaureate, master's, and doctor of nursing practice (DNP) programs.[106]

Since 1912, the National League for Nursing has been a leader in nursing education[107] and in 1996 established the Nursing League for Nursing Accrediting Commission to accredit all levels of nursing education. The Nursing League for Nursing Accrediting Commission changed its name in 2013 to the Accreditation Commission for Education in Nursing (ACEN).[108] In 2019, ACEN reported 1,239 accredited nursing programs: 33 diploma, 165 practical, 742 associate, 206 baccalaureate, 77 master's/post master's certificate, and 16 clinical doctorate.[109]

Since 1969, the American Association of Colleges of Nursing (AACN) has also maintained a leadership role in nursing education. In 1996, the AACN established the Commission on Collegiate Nursing Education (CCNE) to accredit baccalaureate and graduate nursing programs. In 2018, CCNE reported 1,754 accredited nursing programs: 769 baccalaureate, 490 master's, 277 DNP, 180 postgraduate certificate, 26 employee-based residency, and 12 federally funded residency.[110]

Medical Specialization

Medical specialization for allopathic physicians did not exist in the United States until the early 20th century. The American Board of Ophthalmology, incorporated in 1917, was the first certifying board; the American Board of Integrative Medicine was approved in 2013.[111]

Each board offers at least one general certification of specialization, and most have subspecializations. In 2019, there were 24 specialty boards in allopathic medicine and surgery that were members of the American Board of Medical Specialties (ABMS), in addition to 151 subspecialties.[112] Specialty boards are essential to certify training and monitor continued competence of physicians in specialties. Through member boards, the ABMS is significant in undergraduate, postgraduate, and continuing medical education. Specialty boards include representatives of the associations organized for that specialty.

Medical specialization for osteopathic physicians (doctors of osteopathy [DOs]) was begun by AOA in 1939. In 2019, AOA's 16 specialty certifying boards offered certifications in 29 primary certifications and 77 subspecialties.[113]

The Accreditation Council for Graduate Medical Education accredits residencies for both MDs and DOs, but the content of residency education is largely determined by each medical specialty board's residency review committee. The Accreditation Council for Continuing Medical Education accredits the continuing medical education required by specialty boards for continued certification. Medical specialty recertification is known as *maintenance of certification.* Developed by the ABMS and member boards, maintenance of certification is a program of continuous professional development used as a formal means of measuring a physician's continuing competency in a specialty or subspecialty. Continuing competency includes six core competencies: practice-based learning and improvement, patient care and procedural skills, systems-based practice, medical knowledge, interpersonal and communication skills, and professionalism.[114] Approximately 90% of all practicing physicians are board certified by an ABMS board.[115] The AOA initiated Osteopathic Continuous Certification (OCC) in 2013, recognizing an increased focus on competency-based versus knowledge-based assessment and outcomes. The OCC process to maintain AOA specialty and subspecialty certification has five components: licensure, continuing medical education, cognitive assessment, practice performance assessment, and AOA membership.[116]

HSOs/HSs must be vigilant about board certification. There are scores of self-designated medical "specialty boards" without ABMS recognition. Some states try to protect the public by regulating use of "board certification" and "board certified."[117] A proliferation of "boards" diminishes the public's ability to identify practitioners who have earned significant, accepted formal recognition of specialty skills.

Neither licensure nor board certification entitles a physician to clinical privileges in an HSO. Licensure is basic—lawful medical practice is impossible without it; specialty certification is, however, only one indicator of competence. The HSO has an independent ethical and legal duty to determine competence initially and to monitor care delivered to its patients by licensed independent practitioners (LIPs), whether or not they are board certified. The credentialing process is detailed in Chapter 11.

Education and Regulation of Health Services Managers

Hospital administration was identified as a distinct educational discipline when the University of Chicago established the first professional master's degree program in 1934. This followed founding of the American College of Hospital Administrators, now the American College of Healthcare Executives (ACHE) in 1933. Graduate and undergraduate programs exist or are being developed worldwide. Accredited graduate programs in health services administration can be found in different university settings: business, medicine, public health, public administration, and health professions. As a result, different university settings offer degrees in health services administration: MBA, MHA, MPH, MS, and MHSA.[118] In 2019, CAHME reported that 78 universities in North America offered accredited graduate programs in the discipline.[119]

To meet the demands of a complex environment, education for health services managers is eclectic, with emphasis on generic management education. Some programs offer specialty preparation in hospital, NF, or ambulatory services management. The didactic portion for ac-credited programs is at least one academic year. A required field experience is common to allow application of the academic preparation under the guidance of an on-site preceptor.

Curricula of accredited master's degree programs must include proof of competencies in the following areas: the health sector and healthcare management; communications and interpersonal effectiveness; critical thinking, analysis, and problem solving; management and leadership; and professionalism and ethics.[120]

As with graduate programs, rapid growth in the number of undergraduate programs that prepare health services management personnel occurred in the late 1960s and early 1970s. In 2018, there were 47 universities with fully certified baccalaureate programs in health ser-vices administration. Program certification, while similar to accreditation in standards and self-study, differs in that no site visit is required. Program faculty present their self-study to a review committee at the national meeting of the Association of University Programs in Health Administration (AUPHA).[121] In addition to scores of other healthcare management education programs in the United States, there are health services curricula of various types. The two levels have different foci. Master's programs educate graduates to become senior line or staff managers; baccalaureate programs train supervisors or department managers. Coordinating graduate and undergraduate programs is a continuing, unmet challenge.

In 2019, no state required licenses for hospital administrators; all states licensed NF ad-ministrators, and some license assisted-living facility administrators. NF administrators must pass the National Association of Long-Term Care Administrator Boards examination and obtain a state license.[122] Managers in other types of HSOs/HSs are rarely licensed. Regula-tion results when problems in an industry show self-regulation and self-discipline have been ineffective.

Health Services Workers

In 2018, 7,108,000 persons were employed by hospitals, and another 10,636,000 were employed by healthcare providers such as ambulatory healthcare services, physicians' of-fices, outpatient care centers, home health services, residential care facilities, and NFs.[123] Table 1.2 shows numbers in healthcare practitioner and technical occupations in the United States. Most workers listed are employed by healthcare providers and are included in the 17,744,000 already referenced. Many, however, such as physicians, dentists, optometrists, and podiatrists are predominantly self-employed or employed by organizations that they themselves own or control. To be meaningful, time series comparisons of numbers in various healthcare occupations should use ratios of their numbers compared with the U.S. popula-tion. Ratios do not consider maldistribution of providers, who tend to be concentrated in metropolitan and urban areas—to the point of surplus. This leaves rural and less populated areas underserved.

Physician and nonphysician clinicians licensed to treat patients independently are LIPs. Regulation and education of LIPs are discussed later in this chapter. Many types of LIPs compete (for instance, 16 states allow nurse practitioners [NPs] to practice without a physi-cian's supervision) because they provide similar or overlapping services—with largely un-known implications for healthcare costs. Quality and productivity are less an issue, however. For example, NPs and physician assistants (PAs) provide care of equivalent quality when they perform many tasks of a primary care physician.[124]

Most physicians and many other types of LIPs are self-employed entrepreneurs, even though employment may provide part of their income. In contrast, non-LIPs, or dependent caregivers, are employed in the practices of LIPs or in HSOs, such as NFs or hospitals. Physi-cians in residencies are usually employed by their residency sites; their training status makes them unique and unlike employed physicians, however. These relationships are part of the context for HSO staffing, which is discussed in Chapter 12.

Table 1.2 Selected numbers in healthcare practitioner and technical occupations, United States, May 2019[125]

	2019 No.	U.S. No./100,000 2020 Pop. 329,626,934
Health Diagnosing and Treating Practitioners		
Chiropractors	35,010	10.62
Dentists	127,200	38.58
Dietitians and nutritionists	67,670	20.53
Optometrists	39,420	11.96
Pharmacists	311,200	94.41
Physicians and surgeons	685,830	208.06
Physician assistants	120,090	36.43
Podiatrists	9,770	2.96
Occupational therapists	133,570	40.52
Physical therapists	233,350	70.79
Radiation therapists	17,860	5.42
Recreational therapists	19,070	5.79
Respiratory therapists	132,090	40.07
Speech-language pathologists	154,360	46.83
Exercise physiologists	7,280	2.21
Registered nurses	2,982,280	904.74
Nurse anesthetists	43,570	13.22
Nurse midwives	6,930	2.1
Nurse practitioners	200,600	60.86
Audiologists	13,590	4.12
Health Technologists and Technicians		
Clinical lab technologists	326,020	98.91
Dental hygienists	221,560	67.22
Radiologic technologists	207,360	62.91
Cardiovascular technologists	56,110	17.02
Diagnostic medical sonographers	72,790	22.08
Magnetic resonance imaging technologists	37,900	11.5
Nuclear medicine technologists	18,110	5.49
Emergency medical technicians & paramedics	260,600	79.06
Pharmacy technicians	417,780	126.74
Surgery technologist	109,000	33.07
Licensed practical/vocational nurses	697,510	211.61
Medical records & health information technicians	331,790	100.66
Healthcare Support Occupations		
Nursing assistants	1,419,920	430.77
Dental assistants	351,470	106.63
Medical assistants	712,430	216.13
Phlebotomists	128,290	38.92
Physical therapy assistants/aides	146,110	44.33

Physicians

Allopathic medicine—the profession of the medical doctor (MD)—traces its lineage to Hippocrates (460–377 B.C.). It emerged as the dominant theory of treating disease at the beginning of the 20th century. As noted, allopathy holds that interruptions of the body's normal functioning must be treated with significant interventions to restore normal bodily functioning (health). The germ theory of disease causation and increasingly efficacious surgery in the late 19th century gave allopathy a scientific basis, which secured its place and dominance in Western medicine. The increase in effective chemical therapies early in the 20th century enhanced its stature, as did the scientific knowledge developed during the 20th century.

Major competing theories of disease causation and cure in the mid- to late 19th century were naturopathy, homeopathy, osteopathy, and chiropractic. After being relegated to the fringe of medical practice, naturopathy and homeopathy have seen a revival of interest, though they remain far from medicine's mainstream. Osteopathy has largely merged with allopathy. Chiropractic is more accepted in the United States than at any time in its history; nevertheless, orthodox medicine still considers it a manipulative therapy with no clear scientific basis.

Osteopathy evolved from the bonesetters of England, who practiced the craft of repositioning dislocated collar bones, cartilages, and other skeletal structures—work spurned by orthodox medicine.[126] The philosophy and science of osteopathic medicine were first described in 1874 by Virginian Andrew Taylor Still, a physician who founded the American School of Osteopathy in 1892. Osteopaths are educated in osteopathic medical schools and earn the DO in an education that emphasizes structure and functioning of the musculoskeletal system and an appreciation for the body's ability to heal itself when it is in its normal functional relationship and has a favorable environment and nutrition.[127] Osteopathic healthcare emphasizes manipulative methods of detecting and correcting structural problems. It also utilizes generally accepted conventional medical and surgical treatment. Osteopathic medical training is like that for allopathic medicine; in most respects, osteopaths and allopaths are equivalent. Many osteopaths enter allopathic residency training programs and are licensed under the same state statutes.

Chiropractic, an offshoot of osteopathy, emphasizes manipulation to correct anatomical faults that cause functional disturbances in the body. It is uniquely American. Daniel David Palmer (American [1845-1913]) established the first school of chiropractic medicine in Iowa in 1895. Palmer's theories stressed the importance of minor spinal displacements, or subluxations, as chiropractors later called them. Subluxations are less severe than dislocations but cause nerve irritation that leads to disturbances of the nervous system and eventually to illness. Palmer asserted that medical orthodoxy is mistaken in its treatment of disorders without understanding their source—the spinal column—and that chiropractic treatment remedies the problem.[128]

Physician Numbers

Table 1.2 shows the physician and surgeon workforce in 2019. The U.S. population is projected to grow 7.4% from 2020 to 2030; however, growth for the under-65 age group increases only 2.6%, whereas the growth for the 65+ age group, which uses significantly more healthcare, increases 31.3% over the same time period.[129] According to the AAMC, the United States could see a shortage of up to 120,000 physicians by 2030. While most of the shortage is the result of increased demand by the 65+ age group, the AAMC also notes that one third of the supply of currently active physicians will turn 65 by 2030.[130] Previous AAMC reports explained that greater use of nonphysician providers, such as PAs and NPs, could reduce the effects of too few physicians. "Complex changes such as improving efficiency, reconfiguring the way some services are delivered and making better use of our physicians will also be needed."[131]

Predictions of physician shortages or surpluses have caused federal support of medical education to wax and wane for several decades. In addition to federal and state government support, income from hospitals and clinics, nongovernmental grants and contracts, and endowment and philanthropy have been important revenue sources for medical schools. In 2017, tuition and fees contributed only 3.7% of revenues in *both* public and private medical schools: practice plans contributed 41.8%; total grants and contracts contributed 22.3%; hospital-purchased services and investments contributed 19.8%; government and corporate parent contributed 5.0%; gifts contributed 1.9%; endowments contributed 1.8%; and miscellaneous (royalties, consulting) contributed 3.7%.[132] In 2018, there were more than 135,326 residents in Accreditation Council for Graduate Medical Education–accredited and combined special programs. Those residents included 83,923 U.S. medical graduates, 32,040 international medical graduates, 19,205 DOs, 157 Canadian medical graduates, and 1 unknown.[133]

Historically, it was believed that a ratio of two thirds primary care physicians to one third specialists was desirable. In 1970, 40.9% of physicians were in primary care, defined by the AMA to include the general specialties of family medicine, general practice, internal medicine, obstetrics and gynecology, and pediatrics.[134] Federal legislation in the 1970s sought to redress the imbalance between primary care physicians and specialists. Impetus was added to efforts to reduce the emphasis on specialization when specialty societies and boards reconsidered the number of specialty residencies that would be available. Third-party payers, including the federal government, MCOs, and HMOs, also decided to deemphasize specialists. The almost exclusive emphasis on primary care physicians subsided. Specialist physicians were once again in demand by the end of the 1990s.[135] Such cycles will recur as more private and public efforts are made to "manage" delivery of services and the uses and availability of various types of clinical providers.

By 1996, only 34.0% of physicians were classified as primary care practitioners,[136] and in 2010 the Agency for Healthcare Research and Quality (AHRQ) reported that, of the 624,434 physicians that spent the majority of their time in direct patient care, only 209,000 (33.5%) were primary care physicians as already defined.[137] Of the shortage of 120,000 physicians by 2030 mentioned earlier, AAMC projects 49,000 (40.8%) should be primary care physicians and 71,000 (59.2%) should be specialists, which begins to address the imbalance between primary care physicians and specialists.[138]

The focus on absolute numbers ignores the geographic maldistribution of physicians and nonphysician clinicians. Public and private efforts appear to be no more interested in underserved areas—usually inner city and rural communities—than are physicians.[139]

Nonphysician Clinicians

Of concern, too, is whether the numbers of nonphysician caregivers will increase to meet the needs. Advanced practice nurses (APNs), such as clinical nurse specialists, NPs, nurse midwives, and nurse anesthetists, have considerable freedom to make decisions and suggest treatment and care for patients, and many states allow APNs to practice independently. This trend is likely to continue. In 2019 the Bureau of Labor Statistics reported the following employment statistics for APNs: 200,600 NPs, 6,930 nurse midwives, and 43,570 nurse anesthetists.[140] In its report "Future of Nursing: Leading Change, Advancing Health," the Institute of Medicine (IOM) recommended higher levels of education in the nursing field. This recommendation was made to prepare nurses for the more complex care needed by sicker patients and sophisticated new technologies.[141]

Major growth is projected among nonphysician clinicians who provide primary care because of projected physician shortages. A physician shortage suggests potential problems for HSO/HS managers, while concomitantly creating opportunities.

Regulation and Education of Selected Health Occupations

Licensure, Certification, and Registration

Licensing of the healthcare occupations is ubiquitous. All states and the District of Columbia require physicians (MDs and DOs) and RNs, licensed practical (vocational) nurses (LPNs), and NPs to take licensing examinations after completing the appropriate educational programs at accredited educational institutions.[142] There is wide variation beyond these groups, however. The trend is toward greater regulation of the health occupations.[143] For example, the Omnibus Budget Reconciliation Act of 1987 (PL 100-203; commonly known as OBRA '87) required states to register nursing assistants (NAs).

Licensure, registration, and certification have important distinctions, as follows:

Licensure: Approval granted by government that allows someone to engage in an occupation after a finding that the applicant has achieved minimum competency. Licensing is a state function under the police power. Physicians and dentists are always licensed, for example. Physicians and osteopaths are the only LIPs granted an unlimited license.

Registration: Listing of qualified individuals on an official roster maintained by a governmental or nongovernmental body. States may require registration for someone to engage in a health occupation. If so, registration has the effect of licensure. Persons who are registered may use that designation. Registered nurses and registered dietitians are examples.

Certification: Process by which a nongovernmental agency or association grants recognition to someone who meets its qualifications. States may require certification for someone to engage in a health occupation, thus giving certification the effect of licensure. Nurse midwives are certified, for example.

In terms of regulation, nonphysicians may be divided into two groups: 1) LIPs, who are licensed to treat patients independently; and 2) those who may or may not be licensed, registered, or certified but are dependent on an LIP's orders before they deliver health services. Nonphysician LIPs have state licenses that limit their practice to certain parts of the body or specific medical problems; optometrists, podiatrists, dentists, and chiropractors are examples. In many states, nurse midwives and some types of NPs are LIPs with limits. Some states allow RNs without specialty training to perform *certain* examinations and procedures. Applying the general principle of independent versus dependent practice is complicated because acute care hospitals and other types of HSOs limit further the scope of practice of health services staff (even physicians) to clinical activities in which they have demonstrated current competence. Similarly, HSOs may limit the licenses of nonphysician LIPs to activities ordered or supervised by physicians.

Dependent caregivers may or may not be licensed, registered, or certified, but they provide services only after receiving an order from an LIP. Distinctions beyond this are blurred. Dependent caregivers include medical technologists, pharmacists, radiographers, LPNs, and NAs. RNs and pharmacists use *registered* as a synonym for *licensed*. Dietitians are registered by a private association and are licensed or statutorily certified or registered in several states.[144]

Certification is a process of approval involving a professional association and, oftentimes, the AMA. Certificates are issued on the person's passing an examination, the eligibility for which requires specific academic preparation. A confusing aspect of the process is that sometimes the certificate is issued by a body that uses the title *registry*. Often, a group of specialty physicians also certifies. For example, the American Society of Clinical Pathologists certifies medical technologists through its board of registry.[145] Those unable to meet the private certifying group's standards are likely to be unemployable in HSOs; this gives certification the effect of licensure. Concomitantly, someone certified who does not continue to meet the group's standards loses certification; employment is likely forfeited.

Education of Clinicians

Physicians

The most important modern effort to improve education of allopaths occurred in 1910 when Abraham Flexner's study of medical education in the United States detailed its weaknesses. As a result, the science curriculum was enhanced, the didactic portion was lengthened, and the clinical component was strengthened. Weak allopathic medical schools failed when they could not meet the more stringent standards.

In 1950 there were 79 U.S. allopathic medical schools, by 1970 there were 103. In 2018 there were 151 accredited allopathic medical schools with 91,391 students[146] and 19,553 graduates annually.[147] DOs are educated in 35 AOA-accredited colleges of osteopathic medicine, with nearly 31,000 students in 2018.[148]

Postgraduate Education

Following graduation from medical school with either a 4-year postbaccalaureate education or, less often, a 6- or 7-year combined baccalaureate/MD, the new allopathic physician begins a residency. Historically, *intern* was a designation for medical school graduates in the first year of post-MD clinical training. *Resident* is the correct title, however; *intern* has not been used officially for allopaths in training since 1975.[149] Residents are designated by postgraduate year (PGY) or graduate year (GY). For example, a PGY-2 has had 1 year of clinical experience after medical school and is in the second year. Clinical activities of residents are supervised by more senior residents, fellows (postresidency physicians in training), and teaching faculty (physicians) who have faculty appointments through a medical school or are active staff at the HSO, usually a hospital. Residencies are accredited by the Accreditation Council for Graduate Medical Education, which is composed of professional associations in the medical field.

Each specialty has a residency review committee that sets standards for specialty training and accredits the program. The specialty determines the number of PGYs needed and the specific clinical content so the program may be accredited and will provide the basis for certification in that specialty. For example, anesthesiology requires licensure, 1 year of general residency, completion of an accredited anesthesiology residency, and at least 2 years in private practice.[150]

In 2017, Veterans Administration (VA) medical centers had affiliations with 144 of 151 allopathic medical schools and all 35 osteopathic medical schools. About 70% of VA staff physicians have medical school faculty appointments, and the VA is the second-largest federal payer for medical training behind Medicare.[151] It has been estimated that more than half of practicing physicians have received some part of their professional training in a VA medical center.[152]

Licensure

U.S. and Canadian medical graduates are licensed in most states after passing the U.S. Medical Licensing Examination and completing 1 year of residency. Several states require 2 years; a few require 3.[153] In addition, all states and the District of Columbia require physicians to complete continuing medical education credits to remain licensed.[154] Licenses issued by the states are unlimited in terms of the medical activities physicians may undertake. Thus, physicians may legally prescribe all medications (except some narcotics and experimental drugs) and perform all medical and surgical activities. It is only in HSOs that the scope of this otherwise unlimited legal right to practice medicine is modified.

Limiting medical practice to that consistent with demonstrated current competence is essential in acute care hospitals because of the acuity of illnesses and the significant treatment provided. Protecting patients by ensuring the competence of physicians and LIPs, such as podiatrists and clinical psychologists, is vital in all HSOs, however. Protection is achieved with a credentialing process that includes a review of didactic and clinical experience, licensure, specialty certification, and health status, among other factors. Periodic review of clinical performance is part of the recredentialing process used to assure that the practitioner should continue to have privileges in the HSO. Credentialing and recredentialing are detailed in Chapter 11. Many state medical boards fail to discipline physicians with problems related to their professional activities.

Nonphysician Caregivers

Nowhere is there greater fragmentation and specialization of work than in HSOs. Apparently, each new technology requires a new category of technical expertise. In the early years of modern medicine, physicians usually worked with little need for other types of caregivers. Support became necessary, however, and some physician activities were performed by technicians. Nurses were the earliest example; sonographers are among the most recent.

Changes in staffing will continue as old technologies evolve and others are introduced. The use of roentgen rays (x-rays), discovered by Wilhelm Roentgen in 1895, is instructive. Roentgenology became radiology, which bifurcated into diagnostic radiology and therapeutic radiology. Diagnostic radiology has added computers, analysis of cellular emissions, and use of sound waves and has become known as diagnostic imaging. Similarly, therapeutic radiology now includes linear accelerators added to x-ray equipment, and the use of radioactive sources spawned the specialty of nuclear medicine. Specialized staff are needed to deliver this state-of-the-art, high-technology medicine.

Podiatrists

Podiatrists are LIPs who provide services in offices, clinics, and hospitals. Podiatrists employed by HSOs or who are members of their attending staffs should be subject to a credentialing process; credentialing is required in hospitals.

Podiatry is the branch of the healing arts and sciences that treats the foot and its related or governing structures by medical, surgical, or other means. Applicants to the nine colleges of podiatric medicine in the United States should hold a baccalaureate, but exceptions are made.[155] The first 2 years of instruction emphasize basic medical sciences, such as anatomy, physiology, microbiology, biochemistry, pharmacology, and pathology. The second 2 years emphasize clinical sciences, including general diagnosis, therapeutics, surgery, anesthesia, and operative podiatric medicine. Graduates are awarded the degree of doctor of podiatric medicine (DPM). Most graduates complete a residency of 1 to 4 years. Podiatrists are licensed in all states. The American Podiatric Medical Association (APMA) has assigned responsibility or specialty board recognition to the Council on Podiatric Medical Education (CPME), which established the Joint Committee on the Recognition of Specialty Boards (JCRSB). The JCRSB recognizes two specialty boards: the American Board of Podiatric Medicine, which certifies primary podiatric medicine, and the American Board of Foot and Ankle Surgery, which certifies podiatric orthopedics.[156]

Nurses

Early recognition and increased stature of nursing were achieved largely through the efforts of Florence Nightingale, an Englishwoman who worked to improve nursing in the mid-19th century. Until then, secular nursing had a poor reputation. Dorothea Dix was an early nursing leader and educator in the United States. As education and professional standards improved and licensing was introduced in the United States, RNs became second only to physicians in numbers and importance on the patient care team. Nurse licensing began in the early 1900s and was initially linked to state registration. In 1903, North Carolina was the first state to establish state registration for nurses, and only those found qualified by a board of examiners could be listed as RNs in a county and use the designation *RN*. Voluntary licensure (registration) has been superseded by mandatory licensure (registration).[157] RNs may be LIPs, depending on specialty preparation.

Of the 3.06 million licensed RNs in the United States in 2018, it was estimated that 2.95 million were employed in nursing.[158] In 2018, the largest sources of employment were general medical and surgical hospitals (57.5%), physician offices (6.7%), home health services (6.1%), NFs (5.2%), and outpatient facilities (4.8%).[159]

RNs are educated in programs of varying length in various educational settings: baccalaureate (4 years, university or college based, leading to a bachelor of science in nursing [BSN]), diploma (3 years, hospital based, leading to a diploma in nursing), and associate's degree (2 years, junior or community college based, leading to an associate of arts [AA]). Graduates of all three programs may be licensed (registered) as RNs. BSN preparation is the gold standard and is preferred by organized nursing. It is considered a superior preparation in the practice setting. LPNs, sometimes known as licensed vocational nurses, are another type of nurse and are found in all types of HSOs. Other nursing personnel widely found in NFs and hospitals are NAs, who are sometimes called nurse aides. NAs must be registered and may be certified. Certification is required by CMS for NAs working in NFs; they are then certified nursing assistants (CNAs). LPNs and NAs are clinically and usually administratively subordinate to the RN. Table 1.2 shows almost 697,510 employed LPNs in 2019.

In the late 1970s, the American Nurses Association (ANA) began an RN certification program that became the American Nurses Credentialing Center (ANCC). According to the ANCC, in 2018 RNs could take 52 ANCC certification examinations, depending on educational preparation, including 13 NP certifications; 10 clinical nurse specialist (CNS) certifications; 28 RN specialty nursing certifications; and 1 new interdisciplinary certification in national healthcare disaster [planning].[160] The 11,000 RNs certified by ANA in 1982[161] increased to 233,526 by 2018.[162] In addition to the ANCC, other organizations certify nurses.[163]

Most states have categories of caregivers who become RNs first and then prepare in a specialty. NPs, for example, have full independent practice authority in 21 states and the District of Columbia.[164] Some types of independent practice nurses are certified by private associations (e.g., certified registered nurse anesthetists [CRNAs], certified nurse midwives [CNMs]). In 2018, 17 states allowed CRNAs to administer anesthesia without a physician's supervision.[165] Use of CRNAs will increase because Medicare regulations no longer require an anesthesiologist's supervision.[166] CNMs are licensed as RNs and certified by the American College of Nurse-Midwives. In 2019, 28 states and the District of Columbia allowed CNMs to practice independently, 17 states required collaborative agreements with a physician, and 6 states required physician supervision of the overall practice.[167] Advanced practice nurses generally include NPs, CNSs, CRNAs, and CNMs, who are likely to be credentialed by HSOs, either as a group or individually. Such providers are LIPs. HSO managers will be challenged to recruit and retain RNs as well as to use RN resources effectively.[168] Productivity is addressed in Chapters 8.

Pharmacists

The pharmacist is a type of nonphysician caregiver commonly found in HSOs, and always in hospitals. The profession of pharmacy emerged later than nursing. Historically, the pharmacist's role in the spectrum of care was narrow and primarily limited to dispensing medications. Recently, hospital pharmacists have emerged as active members of the clinical care team. They monitor medication use and advise physicians in prescribing and nurses in administering medications. Pharmacists are educated in 129 accredited colleges of pharmacy in the United States.[169] The baccalaureate in pharmacy has been replaced by the doctor of pharmacy, which is earned in a 6-year program that includes 2 years of postsecondary education and 4 years in pharmacy college. State licensure requires candidates to graduate from an accredited program, complete a variety of experiences in practice settings under the supervision of licensed pharmacists, and pass a state board examination. Pharmacists are not LIPs and dispense medications only on the orders of LIPs, such as physicians, podiatrists, and dentists.[170] Table 1.2 shows that there were 311,200 pharmacists employed in the United States in 2019.

Dietitians

A type of nonphysician caregiver almost always found in hospitals and NFs is the registered dietitian nutritionist (RDN), who plans therapeutic menus in consultation with a physician. RDNs provide nutritional counseling as well. Like pharmacists, RDNs emerged later than nurses, and their role is narrower. Historically, RDNs have been registered by the American Dietetic Association, which changed its name to the Academy of Nutrition and Dietetics in 2012. In the mid-1980s, states began licensing or certifying RDNs. Minimum preparation to become an RDN includes a baccalaureate, a minimum of 1,200 supervised practice hours of professional experience, and passing a national, written exam administered by the Commission on Dietetic Registration.[171] Currently, 47 states, Puerto Rico, and the District of Columbia regulate the dietetics profession; 39 states require licensure.[172] Table 1.2 shows that there were 67,670 employed dietitians and nutritionists in 2019.

Technologists

Radiologic technologists include radiographers, cardiovascular-interventional technologists, sonographers, radiation therapists, mammographers, nuclear medicine technologists, computerized tomography technologists, magnetic resonance imaging technologists, dosimetrists, and quality management technologists. [173] The titles reflect job responsibilities and the extent of specialization. Radiologic technologists are trained in 2-year academic or nonacademic programs or 4-year programs leading to a baccalaureate. They become registered by passing one of several national certifying examinations. Forty-three states have specific licensing laws.[174] Table 1.2 shows that there were 207,360 employed radiologic technologists in 2019.

More than half of clinical laboratory or medical technologists are employed in hospitals. Typically, they hold a baccalaureate in medical technology or one of the life sciences. They perform various laboratory tests and may specialize in clinical chemistry, blood bank technology, cytotechnology, hematology, histology, microbiology, or immunology. Training is offered by colleges, universities, and hospitals. Technologists are certified by various groups, including the Board of Registry of the American Society of Clinical Pathologists and the American Medical Technologists. Many states require medical technologists to be licensed or registered.[175] Table 1.2 shows that there were 326,020 employed clinical laboratory technologists and technicians in 2019. Both radiologic technologists and medical technologists are dependent nonphysician caregivers because they have no independent access to patients and perform services only in response to the order of an LIP.

Physician Assistants

Another type of dependent caregiver common to HSOs is the PA, the concept for which originated in the 1960s and was based on the army medic or navy corpsman. Typically, students have a bachelor's degree and three years of healthcare clinical experience before entering a PA program. Most PA programs take 3 academic years and award a master's degree.[176] In 2019, 242 accredited programs educated PAs.[177] Historically, PAs were directed or supervised by a physician, who was accountable for their activities. The trend is for PAs to have greater independence, and more states are licensing, registering, or certifying PAs. The National Commission on Certification of Physician Assistants awards a certification used to regulate PAs. All 50 states and the District of Columbia license PAs.[178] Table 1.2 shows that 120,090 PAs were in active practice in the United States in 2019, with primary care the most frequently practiced specialty (27.3%), followed by surgical subspecialties (25.4%) and internal medicine subspecialties (11.7%). All states allow physicians to delegate authority to write prescriptions to the PAs they supervise. Most PAs practice in outpatient clinics or physician offices (51.5%), hospitals (31.5%), and urgent care centers (5.3%). In terms of primary employers, 35% work for a hospital, 19.9% work for a single-specialty group, 13.5% work for a multispecialty group, and 4.5% work for a solo practice.[179] The demand for PAs is expected to increase by 37% from 2016 to 2026: much faster than the average for all other health occupations.[180]

Associations for Individuals and Organizations

The health services field has numerous professional and trade associations for personal and institutional providers, both in generic groups and in an increasing number of subsets.

Professional Associations for Individual Managers

With more than 48,000 affiliates, the American College of Healthcare Executives ACHE is the leading professional association for HSO/HS managers. It was established in 1933 as the American College of Hospital Administrators. Important categories of affiliation are fellow, member, and student associate. Fellows are board certified in healthcare management and have mastered healthcare management competencies through education, examination, experience, and continuing education. With 78 local chapters, ACHE offers continuing education programs and opportunities to network, provide local volunteer service, and participate in leadership opportunities. ACHE publishes and enforces a code of ethics.[181]

The Medical Group Management Association (MGMA) was established in 1926 to provide education and networking opportunities to medical group executives. It has over 55,000 individual members, with organizational membership also available.[182] In 2011, MGMA merged with its standard-setting body, the American College of Medical Practice Executives, which had offered certification since 1956. Members who master medical group management competencies through examination, continuing education, and experience become board certified under the auspices of the American College of Medical Practice Executives.[183] To earn fellowship status, certified members must prepare a business plan, volunteer in their community, and maintain competencies through continuing education.[184] With its state chapters, MGMA offers networking, continuing education, and leadership opportunities.

Examples of other professional groups include those for specialized managerial personnel in HSOs: the American Academy of Medical Management, the American College of Mental Health Administrators, the American College of Health Care Administrators (of NFs), the National Association of Health Services Executives, the National Association of Latino Healthcare Executives, the American Organization of Nurse Executives, the Healthcare Financial Management Association, and the American College of Physician Executives. Some groups have levels of affiliation and advancement requirements. All provide a forum and educational activities to improve the content and quality of professional practice.

Physicians

Preeminent among physician groups is the AMA, established in 1847. While the AMA is a significant lobbying voice both nationally and in the states, its membership has declined steadily. In the 1950s, about 75% of physicians belonged to the AMA[185]; today only about 25% of practicing physicians are members.[186] The AMA is synonymous with "organized medicine"; it has been both a conservative and a progressive force in healthcare. Conservatism is exemplified by historical opposition to government-sponsored health insurance and by resistance to salaried physician arrangements and innovations such as HMOs, which were seen as infringing on professional independence and physicians' total commitment to their patients. The AMA has been a progressive force by embracing the ideas of universal access for patients, freedom of choice for patients, and freedom of practice for physicians, as well as federal laws, such as Medicare (once enacted) and the Affordable Care Act,[187] and by encouraging federal expenditures for basic and applied research and medical and paramedical education. Its involvement in establishing standards for medical education and licensure has contributed significantly to the unequaled quality of American medicine. The AMA publishes and enforces a code of ethics.

There are many other associations for physicians. The National Medical Association represents more than 50,000 African American physicians and has goals like the AMA's.[188] In addition, medicine has numerous professional associations called colleges or academies, whose memberships are based on medical and surgical specialties. Among the most prominent are the American College of Physicians and the American College of Surgeons. Affiliates are known as fellows or diplomates. These associations represent the interests of affiliates and assist them in continuing education.

Nonphysician Providers

The list of associations for members of the health professions is almost endless. Each new type of provider considers it necessary to have a professional association to focus common interests. Some have a long history; the American Nurses Association was established in 1896.[189] Other examples of nonphysician provider groups include the American Dental Association, the American Podiatry Association, the American Psychological Association, the Association of Operating Room Nurses, the National Association of Social Workers, the American Pharmaceutical Association, the National Federation of Licensed Practical Nurses, and the American Academy of Physician Assistants. The hundreds of professional associations for organizational and personal providers and managers reflect the high degree of specialization and fragmentation in the healthcare field.

Associations for HSOs/HSs

American Hospital Association

With approximately 5,000 institutional members, the AHA is the most prominent association for hospitals. Founded in 1898, AHA educates and represents its members. It is a focal point for hospital participation in the political process, a key element of which is lobbying the federal government. In 1991, AHA's executive offices moved to Washington, D.C. Other activities are based in Chicago.[190]

Federation of American Hospitals

The Federation of American Hospitals (FAH) is the investor-owned counterpart to AHA. Established in 1966, FAH is the national representative for more than 1,000 investor-owned or managed community hospitals and systems in the United States. It monitors health legislation, regulatory and reimbursement matters, and developments in the healthcare industry at the state and national levels. In addition, FAH compiles statistics on the investor-owned hospital industry.[191]

Other Hospital Associations

The Catholic Health Association of the United States (CHA) represents a subset of hospitals with sectarian ownership and interests. CHA represented more than 600 hospitals and 1,600 long-term care and other facilities in 2019.[192]

In addition to national hospital associations, there are regional and state hospital associations that link hospitals to geographical or state communities of interest. State hospital associations gained importance as states became more involved in regulating hospitals.

American Health Care Association

Founded in 1949, the American Health Care Association (AHCA) is a federation of more than 13,500 not-for-profit and for-profit nursing, assisted-living, developmentally disabled, and subacute care providers. AHCA's objectives are to improve standards of service and administration of member organizations; secure and merit public and official recognition and approval of the work of nursing homes; and adopt and promote programs of education, legislation, better understanding, and mutual cooperation.[193]

LeadingAge

LeadingAge, known as the American Association of Homes and Services for the Aging (AAHSA) until 2011, is the trade association for over 6,000 not-for-profit adult day services, home health services, community services, senior housing, assisted living residences, continuing care retirement communities, and nursing homes. LeadingAge lobbies Congress and federal agencies on members' behalf; certifies practitioners and facilities; and offers conferences, programs, and publications. Members may participate in group purchasing and insurance programs.[194]

America's Health Insurance Plans

America's Health Insurance Plans (AHIP) is the successor trade association to the American Association of Health Plans, which was established in 1996 when the Group Health Association of America and the American Managed Care and Review Association merged.[195] AHIP is a national trade association for organizations that provide health insurance coverage to Americans and is committed to market-based solutions and public–private partnerships that improve affordability, value, access, and well-being for consumers. AHIP represents members in state and federal legislative and regulatory matters and in matters involving the media, consumers, and employers. It provides information to stakeholders and conducts education, research, and quality assurance.[196]

Paying for Health Services

Expenditure Trends

As noted, the percentage of U.S. GDP devoted to health expenditures has increased steadily since the 1960s—an interesting juxtaposition to the passage of Medicare and Medicaid. National health expenditures in 2018 consumed 17.7% of GDP, or about $3.65 trillion. CMS projects that healthcare will consume $5.96 trillion, or 19.4% of GDP, by 2027.[197]

The period of rapid inflation occurred soon after the passage of Medicare and Medicaid in 1965; this demand–pull stimulation is a likely cause of the initial and continuing cost increases. In turn, these significant increases have been the stimulus for state and federal efforts to control healthcare costs, or at least limit what they will pay.

Table 1.1 shows that, except for professional services (a category with several elements), hospitals consume the largest amount of health expenditures. This has resulted in hospitals' bearing the brunt of state and federal efforts to control costs. The perspective of regulators and politicians seems to be that hospitals are badly managed, and excessive use of high technology, expensive tests, and treatments is a major source of the increases. Less time spent in hospitals has been posited as the best means of reducing costs; thus, there has been great emphasis on reducing both admission rates and ALOS. It has been suggested, however, that a policy of "single-mindedly emptying hospitals not only does not save any money, it might even add to total national health spending."[198] More recently, rapid increases in Medicaid costs, both general costs and costs for subacute and postacute services, such as NFs and home health, are likely to redirect and broaden cost-control efforts.

Sources and Uses of Funds in Healthcare

As shown in Table 1.1, personal healthcare expenditures follow a similar trend of dramatic annual increases. In 2018, these expenditures total over $3.0 trillion, compared with $2.3 trillion in 2011. It is forecast that by 2027, personal healthcare expenditures will total over $5.1 trillion.

Table 1.1 shows other uses of funds expended on health from 2011 to 2018, with projections to 2027. Private, nongovernmental sources continue to decline (47% of personal healthcare expenditures) as government's role in financing healthcare grows.[199] As noted, it is the willingness and ability of the American public (unlike those in systems in which private expenditures are illegal or purchasing power is limited) to spend personal funds on healthcare that makes expenditures high compared with other countries. Simultaneously, it shows the importance of freedom of choice in the United States.

Inflationary pressures in healthcare expenditures have moderated since 2000, although, with few exceptions, they continue to lead increases in the CPI.[200] Hospital services have had very significant cost increases since 1969. The contribution of physicians' services has been significant, but less than that of hospital services. Data such as these caught the attention of federal policy makers. DRGs, diagnosis related groups, and resource-based relative value scales, which are discussed in Chapter 3 and Chapter 7, have been their response.

Historically, much of the cost of health services has been borne by employers, and many have been instrumental in forming strategic alliances to control them. Strategic alliances join hospitals, physicians, employers, organized labor, insurers, and sometimes government to collect and exchange data and discuss how to finance and deliver health services in a community. Strategic alliances are discussed in Chapter 11. Large increases in healthcare costs to employers have caused some employers to stop providing health insurance (smaller employers); narrow the range and content of health insurance product choices; or require employees to pay a larger share of costs through higher premiums, copays, and deductibles.

Private Payment under the Insurance Principle

The first insurer to write "sickness" insurance did so in 1847, but the insurance industry paid little attention to health insurance until after World War I. Contributing to this lack of interest was a perception that sickness and paying for treatment were too unpredictable to fit traditional actuarial concepts.

It was not until 1929 that Blue Cross showed it could be done. Blue Cross began when a group of schoolteachers made an agreement with Baylor Hospital in Dallas to provide hospital room and board and certain diagnostic services for a monthly fee. In 1932, the first citywide plan was established with a group of hospitals in Sacramento. The comparable plan for physicians' services became known as Blue Shield and was established in California in 1939. Hospitals fostered development of Blue Cross to enhance their patients' ability to pay the costs of hospitalization. After several mergers and reorganizations during the 1990s, by 2012 there were 36 Blue Cross and Blue Shield plans insuring more than 110 million people.[201]

Private health insurance coverage grew rapidly during the 1940s and 1950s. It received a boost during World War II, when wages and salaries were subjected to federal government controls but fringe benefits were not. Commercial carriers began writing substantial amounts of health insurance. By 1955, they had more beneficiaries than Blue Cross, and in 1981 more than 1,000 commercial insurance companies were writing health insurance in the United States.[202] The number of commercial insurance carriers writing healthcare coverage has remained relatively stable since the 1980s. In 2017, 907 commercial carriers wrote health insurance. That number is predicted to decline due to consolidation and growth in public sector coverage.[203]

About 47% of Americans get health insurance through their employer.[204] The number of persons uninsured was estimated to be more than 27.5 million in 2018.[205] It is important to analyze the categories of uninsured persons. Some are self-pay; many choose not to pay for insurance through their employers or similar sources. Most of those uninsured would be medically indigent in a major illness. Estimates of how many people are uninsured do not indicate how many cannot get care as needed.

Historically, Blue Cross has been a community-rated service plan; all insured persons in the same geographic area paid the same rate. Blue Cross paid providers a negotiated fee pursuant to a contract. In contrast to service plans, indemnity insurance—the type usually written by commercial carriers—indemnifies (pays) the insured person a fixed amount for each different diagnosis or treatment. A variation of indemnification is assignment—the insured person assigns the payment to the provider, who is paid directly. Service plan limits are expressed in days of care and services covered. Blue Shield paid participating physicians according to a fee schedule, which was payment in full and which had the effect of assignment. Nonparticipating physicians billed the patient, who was reimbursed per the fee schedule. Another difference between Blue Cross/Blue Shield and commercial carriers is that, historically, the former were not-for-profit corporations that prided themselves on providing consumer-oriented coverage with low overhead costs for plan administration.

Government Payment Methodologies

As noted, until 1965 the federal government focused on providing the wherewithal to support private delivery of services. The advent of Medicare and Medicaid brought federal and state governments into direct financing of medical care. Historically and presently, federal programs provide services to veterans, military personnel, and Native Americans. State governments provide services for special health problems, such as mental illness, disabilities, and tuberculosis. States may operate general acute care hospitals that are part of academic health centers connected with state medical schools. Other HSOs, usually general acute care hospitals, are owned by local governments.

The federal government has sought to control the increase in healthcare expenditures through programs such as PROs. Also, states have used regulatory controls such as CON and rate review through rate-setting commissions to moderate the increase in healthcare costs. Most have sought to slow the growth of Medicaid costs by hospital preadmission screening, limiting hospital days, reducing payment for each day of care or each service, paying months (or years) after bills are submitted by HSOs and physicians, requiring beneficiaries to pay larger copays for optional services, increasing eligibility (income) restrictions, and decreasing the range of services available. Oregon uses a priority list of services (and a budget) for which its Medicaid program will pay.

For many services, Medicaid pays a fraction of the costs incurred by HSOs to provide them. Reducing what Medicaid pays has ripple effects. Other payers must make up the difference by cost shifting if the HSO is to be financially viable. Government programs do not pay charges (the nonnegotiated fee charged by the HSO), nor does Blue Cross. Commercial insurers are almost certain not to pay charges, and indemnity plans pay a fixed fee to the beneficiary regardless of what the beneficiary is charged or pays. Only self-pay patients pay charges. Their small number makes cross subsidies infeasible.

Cost shifting raises basic questions of fairness. Should any payer pay less than costs for services? Medicare is a case more politically difficult than Medicaid because Medicare is an exclusively federal program. Congress has been unwilling to cut benefits, although it has increased copayments and deductibles (e.g., Medicare Part A, hospitalization) and the insurance premium (e.g., Medicare Part B, physicians' services) several times since 1965. Medicare has been called uncontrollable because once beneficiaries are eligible, all services are available. Meaningful savings will occur only if benefit levels are controlled, which is politically unpalatable.

System Trends

Significant efforts by state and federal governments to control the costs of their health services programs will continue. Hospitals consume about one quarter of health expenditures.[206] Thus, they will continue to receive disproportionate attention from government and other third-party payers. The large component of fixed and semivariable costs will limit the savings HSOs can achieve. Case-mix cost control through DRGs will cause hospitals to treat patients with the most remunerative diagnoses. There will be economic pressure to discharge patients quickly, perhaps earlier than sound practice warrants. In addition, treating the less ill with alternative regimens and in nonhospital HSOs leaves only the most ill in acute care hospitals. The result will be that costs per day of care will increase, ultimately putting even greater financial pressure on hospitals. Unless hospitals close beds, discontinue services, and reduce the number of employees, the cost per case and the total cost per hospitalization will rise.

Regulation was the watchword in the late 1960s and early 1970s. The competitive environment that emerged in the late 1970s and early 1980s has continued, especially among hospitals. Public and private payment sources are unwilling to subsidize the inefficient. The bankruptcies, mergers, and joint activities among HSOs/HSs that began in the 1980s have continued. Increasingly, hospitals will be connected to one another as part of systems and through shared services, group purchasing, and strategic alliances. As with politics, all healthcare delivery is local. HSs tend to be local or regional rather than national, a reality that is likely to continue. Predictions that the 21st century would find U.S. healthcare provided by a few national HSs, some large unaffiliated facilities, and a few small, freestanding hospitals proved incorrect.

The widespread corporate restructuring undertaken by hospitals in the early 1980s was largely unsuccessful. Even as corporate restructuring protected and enhanced hospitals' assets and reimbursement and expanded their range of activities, it caused management to lose sight of the core business. Consequently, hospitals have divested themselves of noncore businesses and are again focusing on their original raison d'être. Restructuring is addressed in Chapter 11.

Increasingly, physicians are undertaking activities that compete with hospitals. As technology becomes portable and new medical interventions that do not require hospitalization are developed, hospitals will have sicker and sicker patients. The fragmentation and ultraspecialization of hospital clinical staff will continue. As a result, the problems of acquiring, retaining, and managing human resources and their appropriate roles in HSOs will be exacerbated.

Discussion Questions

1. What are the ramifications and implications for the health services system of the model developed by Blum? What are its strengths and weaknesses?

2. Select a disease and apply the Precede–Proceed model described in this chapter. How should HSO/HS governing bodies and managers use this model?

3. Describe and analyze the relationships among the various institutional and programmatic providers in the health services system.

4. Facilities and programs other than acute care hospitals are much more numerous and arguably have a greater effect on health status, but acute care hospitals remain the focus of attention. Why is this? What are the desirable and undesirable aspects of this attention from the standpoints of the acute care hospital *and* the consumer of health services?

5. Proliferation of the health professions continues unabated. What is desirable and undesirable about this fragmentation? If something should be done to slow or stop it, what should it be, and how can it be achieved?

6. Highlight changes in reimbursement to HSOs that have occurred since 1965. What forces in the general environment were most important in causing these changes? Sketch and defend a scenario that suggests the likely developments in reimbursement during the first part of the 21st century.

7. Federally supported state health planning has risen and fallen since the passage of Medicare and Medicaid. Identify the advantages and disadvantages of statewide or areawide health planning from the standpoints of providers *and* consumers.

8. Describe how licensure, registration, and certification are different. What are the advantages and disadvantages of each from the standpoint of providers and consumers? How do they facilitate *and* inhibit the availability of health services occupations?

9. Discuss how cost shifting works.

10. Discuss why health expenditures are increasing and discuss possible solutions to the increase.

Case Study 1   Gourmand and Food—a Fable[207]

The people of Gourmand loved good food. They ate in good restaurants, donated money for cooking research, and instructed their government to safeguard all matters having to do with food. Long ago, the food industry had been in total chaos. There were many restaurants, some very small. Anyone could call himself or herself a chef or open a restaurant. In choosing a restaurant, one could never be sure that the meal would be good. A commission of distinguished chefs studied the situation and recommended that no one be allowed to touch food except for qualified chefs. "Food is too important to be left to amateurs," they said. Qualified chefs were licensed by the state, and there were severe penalties for anyone else who engaged in cooking. Certain exceptions were made for food preparation in the home, but those meals could be served only to the family. Furthermore, a qualified chef had to complete at least 21 years of training (including 4 years of college, 4 years of cooking school, and a 1-year apprenticeship). All cooking schools had to be first class.

These reforms did succeed in raising the quality of cooking, but a restaurant meal became substantially more expensive. A second commission observed that not everyone could afford to eat out. "No one," they said, "should be denied a good meal because of income." Furthermore, they argued that chefs should work toward the goal of giving everyone "complete physical and psychological satisfaction." The government declared that those people who could not afford to eat out should be allowed to do so as often as they liked, and the government would pay. For others, it was recommended that they organize themselves into groups and pay part of their income into a pool that would be used to pay the costs incurred by members in dining out. To ensure the greatest satisfaction, the groups were set up so that members could eat out anywhere and as often as they liked, their meals could be as elaborate as they desired, and they would have to pay nothing or only a small percentage of the cost. The cost of joining such prepaid dining clubs rose sharply.

Long before this, most restaurants had employed only one chef to prepare the food. A few restaurants had been more elaborate, with chefs specializing in roasting, fish, salads, sauces, and many other things. People had rarely gone to these elaborate restaurants because they had been so expensive. With the establishment of prepaid dining clubs, everyone wanted to eat at these fancy restaurants. At the same time, young chefs in school disdained going to cook in a small restaurant where they would have to cook everything. Specializing and cooking at a very fancy restaurant paid much better, and it was much more prestigious. Soon there were not enough chefs to keep the small restaurants open.

With prepaid clubs and free meals for the poor, many people started eating three-course meals at the elaborate restaurants. Then restaurants began to increase the number of courses, directing the chefs to "serve the best with no thought for the bill." (Eventually, a meal was served that had 317 courses.)

The costs of eating out rose faster and faster. A new government commission reported as follows:

1. Noting that licensed chefs were being used to peel potatoes and wash lettuce, the commission recommended that these tasks be handed over to licensed dishwashers (whose 3 years of dishwashing training included simple cooking courses) or to some new category of personnel.

2. Concluding that many licensed chefs were overworked, the commission recommended that cooking schools be expanded, that the length of training be shortened, and that applicants with lesser qualifications be admitted.

3. The commission also observed that chefs were unhappy because people seemed to be more concerned about the decor and service than about the food. (In a recent taste test, not only could one patron not tell the difference between a 1930 and a 1970 vintage, but he also could not distinguish between white and red wines. He explained that he always ordered the 1930 vintage because he knew that only a very good restaurant would stock such an expensive wine.)

The commission agreed that weighty problems faced the nation. They recommended that a national prepayment group be established, which everyone must join. They recommended that chefs continue to be paid on the basis of the number of dishes they prepared. They recommended that the Gourmandese be given the right to eat anywhere they chose and as elaborately as they chose and pay nothing.

These recommendations were adopted. Large numbers of people spent all of their time ordering incredibly elaborate meals. Kitchens became marvels of new, expensive equipment. All those who were not consuming restaurant food were in the kitchen preparing it. Because no one in Gourmand did anything except prepare or eat meals, the country collapsed.

Questions

1. Read and analyze the fable of Gourmand. How well does the allegory fit delivery of healthcare in the United States?

2. What is, and what should be, the role of the consumer in healthcare?

Case Study 2   Normal Saline and Hurricane Maria[208]

Hurricane Maria made landfall on the island of Puerto Rico (PR) on September 20, 2017. Its effects were devastating: heavy loss of life and destruction of property, and dislocation of thousands of residents. Of great significance were the hurricane's effects on infrastructure, especially the island's fragile and inadequate electrical grid. Six months later a third of PR still had no electricity. The electrical problems had a profound effect on PR's pharmaceutical industry, which accounts for about a third of PR's gross domestic product. PR is a U.S. territory; its residents are citizens.

A significant part of PR's pharmaceutical industry is production of normal saline, a mixture of sodium chloride and sterile water. Normal saline is widely used in healthcare for rehydration, dilution of medications administered intravenously, renal dialysis, and cleansing wounds. The U.S. Food and Drug Administration (FDA) monitors production of normal saline. Producing a solution that is sterile and free of pyrogens and particulate matter requires a complex, time-intensive manufacturing process: 29 steps over 10 days for each batch, with 350 checks for quality mandated by the FDA. Baxter International sells a third of U.S. normal saline. It ships about one million units of normal saline throughout the United States daily.

By 2018, normal saline had been in short supply for 5 years. Several reasons caused demand to increase faster than manufacturing capacity could be added. To increase supply, the FDA agreed to import normal saline from Brazil, Norway, Spain, and Germany. In addition, the FDA encouraged new production; shortages persisted, however. Hurricane Maria's effects on the production of normal saline in PR greatly exacerbated the shortages.

Especially in short supply were the 250 mL or smaller bags of normal saline. These are used as a diluent to deliver parenteral medications to patients. Baxter's production in PR supplied 50% of the normal saline in smaller bags to U.S. hospitals.

The chronic shortage has caused several large healthcare systems to form a joint venture to manufacture normal saline in the United States.

Questions

1. Identify the steps an HSO that uses copious amounts of normal saline should take to plan in the short term for the type of shortage described here. Long term?

2. Identify the individuals and groups in a hospital that should be involved in planning the short-term and long-term response(s) to a shortage of normal saline.

3. Large-scale pharmaceutical manufacturing in PR is no accident. Section 936 of the U.S. Internal Revenue Service (IRS) Code provides for a tax credit equal to the federal tax liability on certain income earned in PR and some other U.S. possessions. The tax credit is equivalent to exempting completely from federal taxes the income of qualifying corporations in PR. Identify three positive and three negative aspects of the distortion in sources of pharmaceuticals caused by the tax credit described in Section 936 of the IRS code.

4. Describe the respective roles of private enterprise and government in 1) preventing, and 2) solving the types of shortages described in the case.

Case Study 3 — Bipartisan Policy Group Proposes Cuts to Hospital Spending[209]

An increasing refrain in Washington, D.C., is that too much of national healthcare spending goes to hospitals (about 30%). Lawmakers cite the following factors:

- Increasing mergers and acquisitions

- Increasing market dominance

- Increasing charges

- Lagging site-neutral payments

- Increasing purchases of physician practices

- Continuing opacity of prices

- Growing executive salaries

Republican lawmakers have introduced a 200-page proposal to cut hospital spending in the following areas:

- Tightening requirements on not-for-profit hospital spending on community benefits

- Preventing rural hospitals from bidding up labor costs for all hospitals

- Requiring pricing transparency for "shoppable services"

- Barring hospitals from setting contracting parameters with health plans

- Setting pay limits for not-for-profit hospital executives

- Requiring open health plan rate bidding by hospitals

Question

1. As the spokesperson for the American Hospital Association, what is your response to the legislative proposal? In your response, address both the factors contributing to increased hospital spending and the remedies offered by lawmakers.

Notes

1. Centers for Medicare & Medicaid Services. "CMS Office of the Actuary Releases 2018 National Health Expenditures." *https://www.cms.gov/newsroom/press-releases/cms-office-actuary-releases-2018-national-health-expenditures*, retrieved May 3, 2020.
2. Centers for Medicare and Medicaid Services. "National Health Expenditures Data, Historical, Table 2." *https://www.cms.gov/Research-Statistics-Data-and-Systems/Statistics-Trends-and-Reports/National-HealthExpendData NationalHealthAccountsHistorical.html*, retrieved December 10, 2019.
3. Centers for Medicare and Medicaid Services. "National Health Expenditures Data, Projected, Table 2." *https://www.cms.gov/research-statistics-data-and-systems/statistics-trends-and-reports/nationalhealthexpend-data/nationalhealthaccountsprojected.html*, retrieved December 10, 2019.
4. O'Neill, Daniel P., and David Scheinker. "Wasted Health Spending: Who's Picking Up the Tab?" *Health Affairs Blog.* May 31, 2018. *10.1377/hblog20180530.245587*, retrieved February 7, 2019; Brownlee, Shannon. *Overtreated: Why Too Much Medicine Is Making Us Sicker and Poorer.* New York: Bloomsbury, USA, 2007.
5. Blum, Henrik L. *Expanding Health Care Horizons: From a General Systems Concept of Health to a National Health Policy,* 2nd ed., 34. Oakland, CA: Third Party Publishing, 1983.
6. Blum, Henrik L. *Planning for Health: Development and Application of Social Change Theory,* 96–100. New York: Human Sciences Press, 1974.
7. The discussion of the Precede-Proceed model for health planning and evaluation is adapted from Green, Lawrence W., and Marshall W. Kreuter. *Health Program Planning: An Educational and Ecological Approach,* 4th ed., 9–17. New York: McGraw Hill, 2004.
8. Health Care Financing Administration. "Trends in Medicare Skilled Nursing Facility Utilization: CYs 1967–1994." *Health Care Financing Review,* Statistical Supplement (1996): 64.
9. O'Neill, Liam, and John Kuder. "Explaining Variation in Physician Practice Patterns and Their Propensities to Recommend Services." *Medical Care Research and Review* 62 (June 2005): 339–357.
10. Data from the National Center for Health Statistics, 1987 and 1988; Thompson-Hoffman, Susan, and Inez Fitzgerald Storck. *Disability in the United States: A Portrait from National Data,* 37. New York: Springer-Verlag, 1991.
11. Administrative Procedure Act of 1946, PL 79-404, 60 Stat. 993 (1946).
12. CMS. "How Do We Determine MIPS Eligibility?" *Quality Payment Program. https://qpp.cms.gov/participation-lookup/about,* retrieved March 18, 2019.
13. Wadhera, Risha K. "Association of the Hospital Readmission Reduction Program with Mortality among Medicare Beneficiaries Hospitalized for Heart Failure, Acute Myocardial Infarction, and Pneumonia." *Journal of the American Medical Association* 320 (December 25, 2018): 2542–2552.
14. U.S. Supreme Court held that the delegation of legislative authority by the Congress was unconstitutional. United States v. Shreveport Grain and Elevator Company, 287 U.S. 77 (1932).
15. *Black's Law Dictionary,* 6th ed., 1406. St. Paul, MN: West Publishing, 1990.
16. *Black's Law Dictionary,* 1305.
17. Pickett, George, and John J. Hanlon. *Public Health: Administration and Practice,* 9th ed., 28–32. St. Louis: Times Mirror/Mosby College Publishing, 1990.
18. Brown, David. "Longer Lives Shift Landscape of Disease." *Washington Post,* December 14, 2012, 1, reporting the results of the Global Burden of Disease Study.
19. Murphy, Sherry L., et. al. "Mortality in the United States, 2017." National Center for Statistics, Centers for Disease Control and Prevention. *http://www.cdc.gov/nchs/products/databriegs/db328.htm,* retrieved March 20, 2019.
20. The Social Security Act of 1935. Social Security Online. *http://www.ssa.gov/history/35act.html,* retrieved June 16, 2020.
21. United States Census Bureau. *Population Projections: 2017 National Population Projections Tables, Table 2. https://www.census.gov/data/tables/2017/demo/popproj/2017-summary-tables.html,* retrieved March 23, 2019.
22. Hospital Survey and Construction Act of 1946 (Hill-Burton Act), PL 79-725, 60 Stat. 1040 (1946).
23. Public Health Service. *Directory of Facilities Obligated to Provide Uncompensated Services, by State and City as of March 1, 1989,* I. Washington, DC: U.S. Department of Health and Human Services, 1989.

24. National Institutes of Health. Budget. *https://www.nih.gov/about-nih/what-we-do/budget,* retrieved March 23, 2019.
25. Social Security Act Amendments (1965). Our Documents. *http://www.ourdocuments.gov/doc.php?flash=true&doc=99,* retrieved June 16, 2020.
26. Balanced Budget Act of 1997, PL 105-33, 111 Stat. 251 (1997).
27. Grimaldi, Paul L. "Medicare Part C Means More Choices." *Nursing Management* 28 (November 1997): 30.
28. Medicare Prescription Drug, Improvement, and Modernization Act of 2003, PL108-173. CMS Legislative Summary. April 2004. *https://www.govinfo.gov/content/pkg/PLAW-108publ173/pdf/PLAW-108publ173.pdf,* retrieved June 16, 2020.
29. Centers for Medicare and Medicaid Services. "History." *https://www.cms.gov/About-CMS/Agency-information/History/,* retrieved March 23, 2019.
30. Kaiser Commission on Medicaid and the Uninsured. "The Medicaid Program at a Glance." March 2007. (Photocopy)
31. Comprehensive Health Planning and Public Health Service Amendments Act of 1966, PL 89-749, 80 Stat. 1180 (1966); National Health Planning and Resources Development Act of 1974, PL 93641, 88 Stat. 2225 (1974); Social Security Amendments of 1972, PL 92-603, 86 Stat. 1329 (1972).
32. CPI Detailed Report. *http://www.bls.gov/cpi/cpid1207.pdf,* retrieved September 23, 2012.
33. Tax Equity and Fiscal Responsibility Act of 1982, PL 97-248, 96 Stat. 324 (1982); Social Security Amendments of 1983, PL 98-21, 97 Stat. 65 (1983).
34. The Kaiser Family Foundation. "Employer Health Benefits: 2018 Summary of Findings." *http://files.kff.org/attachment/Summary-of-Findings-Employer-Health-Benefits-2018,* retrieved on July 19, 2019.
35. *The Guardian.* "Healthcare Spending around the World, Country by Country." *http://www.guardian.co.uk/news/datablog/2012/jun/30/healthcare-spending-world-country,* retrieved September 14, 2012.
36. OECD. *Health at a Glance 2019: OECD Indicators,* OECD Publishing, Paris. *http://www.oecd.org/health/health-systems/health-at-a-glance-19991312.htm* Tables 7.1 and 7.3, retrieved May 5, 2020.
37. Strenger, Ellen Weisman. "The Road to Wellville." *Trustee* 49 (May 1996): 20–25.
38. Pickett, George E., and John J. Hanlon. Pub*lic Health Administration and Practice,* 9th ed., 83. St. Louis: Times Mirror/Mosby College Publishing, 1990.
39. Adding to confusion about *primary* is that many small acute care hospitals are known as primary care hospitals. This means that they offer a limited range of services, including normal deliveries and routine medical and surgical treatment. Patients needing significant interventions are transferred to secondary, tertiary, or quaternary care hospitals.
40. Seebach, Linda. "Alternative Therapy Eruption." *Washington Times,* July 6, 1998, A14; Okie, Susan. "Widening the Medical Mainstream: More Americans Using 'Alternative' Therapies, Some Prove Effective." *Washington Post,* November 11, 1998, A1.
41. CDC. National Center for Health Statistics. "FastStats: Ambulatory Care Use and Physician Office Visits 2017," *https://www.cdc.gov/nchs/fastats/physician-visits.htm,* retrieved March 30, 2019.
42. "National Hansen's Disease Program." *https://www.hrsa.gov/hansens-disease/index.html,* retrieved June 18, 2020.
43. Indian Health Service. "Fact Sheet, HIS Profile." *https://www.ihs.gov/newsroom/factsheets/ihsprofile/,* retrieved March 30, 2019.
44. U.S. Department of Veterans Affairs. "About the VA." *https://www.va.gov/health/,* retrieved March 30, 2019.
45. Department of Defense. "Fact Sheet: Overview of the Department of Defense's Military Health System." *https://archive.defense.gov/home/features/2014/0614_healthreview/docs/Fact_Sheet_Overview.PDF,* retrieved March 31, 2019.
46. American Hospital Association. *AHA Hospital Statistics 2019.* Chicago: AHA Data & Insights, 2018.
47. Medicare. "What Are Long-term Care Hospitals?" *https://www.medicare.gov/pubs/pdf/11347-Long-Term-Care-Hospitals.pdf,* retrieved July 19, 2019.
48. Norback, Judith. *The Mental Health Yearbook/Directory 1979–80,* 200. New York: Van Nostrand Reinhold, 1979.
49. Statistica. "Number of Mental Health Facilities in the U.S. in 2018, by Facility Type." *https://www.statista.com/statistics/712614/mental-health-facilities-number-in-the-us-by-facility-type/,* retrieved May 7, 2020.
50. Alvarado Parkway Institute. "The Difference between Mental and Behavioral Health." *https://www.apibhs.com/blog/2018/5/17/the-difference-between-mental-and-behavioral-health,* retrieved April 1, 2019; National Institute of Mental Health. "U.S. Leading Categories of Diseases/Disorders." *https://www.nimh.nih.gov/health/statistics/disability/us-leading-categories-of-diseases-disorders.shtml,* retrieved April 1, 2019.

51. Association of American Medical Colleges. "Council of Teaching Hospitals and Health Systems (COTH)." *https://www.aamc.org/members/coth/*, retrieved April 1, 2019.

52. Association of Academic Health Centers. "Academic Health Centers: Defined and Members." *http://www.aahcdc.org/About/Academic-Health-Centers*, retrieved December 11, 2019.

53. The section "Rural Hospitals" is largely based on material in Rubin, Rita. "Declining Numbers of Rural US Hospitals." *Journal of the American Medical Association* 320, 20 (2018): 2067. *https://jamanetwork.com/journals/jama/fullarticle/2716542*, retrieved December 11, 2019.

54. American Hospital Association. "Fast Facts on U.S. Hospitals, 2019." *https://www.aha.org/statistics/fast-facts-us-hospitals*, retrieved December 11, 2019.

55. U.S. Government Accountability Office. "Rural Hospital Closures: Number and Characteristics of Affected Hospitals and Contributing Factors." August 29, 2018. *https://www.gao.gov/products/GAO-18-634*, retrieved December 11, 2019.

56. The Joint Commission. "State Recognition Details." *https://www.jointcommission.org/state_recognition/state_recognition_details.aspx?ps=100&b=39*, retrieved April 7, 2019.

57. National Fire Protection Association. "Fact Sheet." *https://www.nfpa.org/-/media/Files/Code-or-topic-fact-sheets/ReferencedStandardsFactSheet.ashx*, retrieved July 19, 2019.

58. "Hospital Conditions of Participation in Medicare." In *Medicare: A Strategy for Quality Assurance*, vol. 1, edited by Kathleen N. Lohr, 119–137. Washington, DC: Institute of Medicine, 1990. *http://books.nap.edu/openbook.php?record_id=1547&page=119*, retrieved June 16, 2016.

59. Hilleboe, H. E., A. Barkhuus, and W. C. Thomas. "Health Planning in the USA." In *Approaches to National Health Planning*, edited by H. E. Hilleboe, A. Barkhuus, and W. C. Thomas, 69–86. Geneva: World Health Organization, 1972. Public Health Paper No. 46. *http://www.popline.org/docs/0133/725576.html*, retrieved January 28, 2008.

60. Statement of Robert D. Reischauer, Deputy Director, Congressional Budget Office, before the Subcommittee on Oversight, Committee on Ways and Means, U.S. House of Representatives, June 27, 1979.

61. Werlin, S. H, A. Walcott, and M. Joroff. "Implementing Formative Health Planning under PL 93-641." *New England Journal of Medicine* 295, 3 (September 23, 1976): 698–703.

62. O'Donnell, James W. "The Rise and Fall of Federal Support." *Provider* 13 (December 1987): 6.

63. National Conference of State Legislatures. "CON-Certificate of Need State Laws." *http://www.ncsl.org/research/health/con-certificate-of-need-state-laws.aspx*, retrieved April 7, 2019.

64. Cohen, Harold A. *Health Services Cost Review Commission*. Baltimore: Health Services Cost Review Commission, 1983.

65. Kent, Christina. "Twenty Years of Maryland Rate Regulation." *Medicine & Health* 45 (August 19, 1991): Perspectives insert.

66. The Commonwealth Fund. "Hospital Price Transparency: Making It Useful for Patients." *https://www.commonwealthfund.org/blog/2019/hospital-price-transparency-making-it-useful-patients*, retrieved April 7, 2019.

67. Coleman, Justine. "Hospital Groups File Lawsuit to Stop Trump Price Transparency Rule." *The Hill*, December 4, 2019. *https://thehill.com/policy/healthcare/472944-hospital-groups-file-lawsuit-to-stop-trump-administrations-price*, retrieved December 17, 2019.

68. Parts of the section "UR, PSROs, and PROs" are adapted from *History of Peer Review*. Washington, DC: Health Care Financing Administration. (Undated, unpublished report received December 1991.)

69. Statement of Robert D. Reischauer, Deputy Director, Congressional Budget Office, before the Subcommittee on Oversight, Committee on Ways and Means, U.S. House of Representatives, June 27, 1979.

70. *Federal Register*. Medicare and Medicaid Programs; Utilization and Quality Control Peer Review Organization (PRO); Assumption of Responsibilities and Medicare Review Functions and Coordination of Medicaid With Peer Review organization—HCFA. Proposed Rule. July 17, 1984, 49 (138): 29026-41. *https://pubmed.ncbi.nlm.nih.gov/10299606/*, retrieved June 26, 2020.

71. Ready, Tinker. "PROs under Assault by Government, Consumers." *Healthweek* 4 (February 12, 1990): 6, 44–45.

72. Bradley, Elizabeth H. "From Adversary to Partner: Have Quality Improvement Organizations Made the Transition Look Smart?" *Health Services Research* (April 2005): 2. h*ttps://www.ncbi.nlm.nih.gov/pmc/articles/PMC1361151/*, retrieved June 16, 2020.

73. Centers for Medicare and Medicaid Services. "Quality Improvement Organizations" (2012). *http://www.cms.gov/Medicare/Quality-Initiatives-Patient-Assessment-Instruments/QualityImprovementOrgs/index.html?redirect=/QualityImprovementOrgs/*, retrieved July 21, 2013.

74. "The Sherman Antitrust Act." The Washington Post Company, 1998. *http://www.washingtonpost.com/wp-srv/washtech/longterm/antitrust/sherman.htm*, retrieved June 16, 2020.

75. Federal Trade Commission. The Antitrust Laws. *https://www.ftc.gov/tips-advice/competition-guidance/guide-antitrust-laws/antitrust-laws*, retrieved June 26, 2020.

76. National Labor Relations Act. National Labor Relations Board. *https://www.nlrb.gov/guidance/key-reference-materials/national-labor-relations-act*; retrieved June 16, 2020.

77. The Occupational Safety and Health Act (1970[0]). *https://www.osha.gov/laws-regs/oshact/completeoshact*, retrieved June 16, 2020.

78. *The 1906 Food and Drugs Act and Its Enforcement*. U.S. Food and Drug Administration. *https://www.fda.gov/about-fda/fdas-evolving-regulatory-powers/part-i-1906-food-and-drugs-act-and-its-enforcement*, retrieved June 16, 2020.

79. "Securities Exchange Act of 1934." U.S. Securities and Exchange Commission. *https://www.sec.gov/answers/about-lawsshtml.html#secexact1934*, retrieved June 16, 2020.

80. The Atomic Energy Act of 1954, PL 83-703, 68 Stat. 919 (1954). U.S. Nuclear Regulatory Commission. *https://www.nrc.gov/docs/ML1327/ML13274A489.pdf*, retrieved June 16, 2020.

81. The Equal Pay Act of 1963. U.S. Equal Employment Opportunity Commission. *https://www.eeoc.gov/statutes/equal-pay-act-1963*, retrieved June 16, 2020.

82. Title VII of the Civil Rights Act of 1964. U.S. Equal Employment Opportunity Commission. *https://www.eeoc.gov/statutes/title-vii-civil-rights-act-1964*, retrieved June 16, 2020.

83. The Age Discrimination in Employment Act of 1967. U.S. Equal Employment Opportunity Commission. *https://www.eeoc.gov/statutes/age-discrimination-employment-act-1967*, retrieved June 16, 2020.

84. *Tax Code, Regulations and Official Guidance*. U.S. Department of the Treasury. https://www.irs.gov/privacy-disclosure/tax-code-regulations-and-official-guidance, retrieved June 16, 2020.

85. *Trade Practices Laws and Regulations*. Alcohol and Tobacco Tax and Trade Bureau https://www.ttb.gov/trade-practices, retrieved June 16, 2020.

86. MacEachern, Malcolm T. *Hospital Organization and Management*, 3rd ed. Chicago: Physicians' Record Co., 1957.

87. The Joint Commission. "What Is Accreditation?" *https://www.jointcommission.org/accreditation/accreditation_main.aspx*, retrieved April 7, 2019.

88. Bryan, Steven W., and Patricia Pejakovich. *The JCAHO Survey Coordinator's Handbook*, 8th ed., 2006, *https://books.google.com/books?id=dNxG_vIIbugC&pg=PA3&lpg=PA3&dq=#v=onepage&q&f=false*, retrieved June 26, 2020.

89. The Joint Commission. "Facts about Joint Commission Accreditation and Certification." *https://www.jointcommission.org/facts_about_joint_commission_accreditation_and_certification/*, retrieved April 7, 2019.

90. The Joint Commission. "Benefits of Joint Commission Accreditation." December 11, 2018. *https://www.jointcommission.org/accreditation/accreditation_main.aspx*, retrieved April 28, 2019.

91. Healthcare Facilities Accreditation Program. "Overview" and "Accredited Facilities." *https://www.hfap.org/about/overview.aspx and https://www.hfap.org/AccreditedFacilities/index.aspx?FacilityType=HOSPN*, retrieved April 7, 2019.

92. Department of Health and Human Services, Centers for Medicare & Medicaid Services. "Policy and Requirements for an Application for Approval of an Accreditation Program." *https://www.cms.gov/Medicare/Provider-Enrollment-and-Certification/SurveyCertificationGenInfo/Downloads/applicationrequirements.pdf*, retrieved July 19, 2019.

93. Becker's Healthcare. "Understanding Det Norske Veritas Healthcare's National Integrated Accreditation for Healthcare Organizations Program." *https://www.beckershospitalreview.com/quality/understanding-det-norske-veritas-healthcare-s-national-integrated-accreditation-for-healthcare-organizations-program.html*, retrieved April 7, 2019.

94. DNV GL Healthcare. "DNV GL's Pioneering NIAHO Program Integrates ISO 9001 with the Medicare Conditions of Participation." *https://www.DNV GLhealthcare.com/accreditations/hospital-accreditation*, retrieved April 7, 2019.

95. Community Health Accreditation Partner. "CHAP Accreditation." *https://chapinc.org/accreditation-process/*, retrieved April 28, 2019.

96. International Organization for Standardization. "All about ISO." *https://www.iso.org/about-us.html*, retrieved April 28, 2019.

97. International Organization for Standardization. "Benefits of ISO Standards." *https://www.iso.org/benefits-of-standards.html*, retrieved April 18, 2019.

98. ISO. Certification. h*ttps://www.iso.org/certification.html*, retrieved June 26, 2020.

99. National Committee for Quality Assurance. "Health Plans." April 15, 2019. *https://reportcards.ncqa.org/#/health-plans/list?p=119*, retrieved April 28, 2019.

100. National Committee for Quality Assurance. "Health Plan Accreditation." *https://www.ncqa.org/programs/health-plans/health-plan-accreditation-hpa/*, retrieved April 28, 2019.

101. CAHME. "Search for an Accredited Program." *https://cahme.org/healthcare-management-education-accreditation/students/search-for-an-accredited-program/*, retrieved April 28, 2019.

102. Council on Education for Public Health. "Accreditation Statistics." *https://ceph.org/constituents/schools/faqs/general/accreditation-statistics/#1*, retrieved April 28, 2019.

103. Liaison Committee on Medical Education. "Accredited MD Programs in the United States." February 21, 2019. *http://lcme.org/directory/accredited-u-s-programs/*, retrieved on April 28, 2019.

104. Liaison Committee on Medical Education. "Accredited MD Programs in Canada." October 19, 2018. *http://lcme.org/directory/accredited-canadian-programs/*, retrieved April 28, 2019.

105. American Osteopathic Association. "About Us." *https://osteopathic.org/about/*, retrieved April 29, 2019.

106. All Nursing Schools. "Nursing School Accreditation." *https://www.allnursingschools.com/articles/nursing-school-accreditation/*, retrieved May 5, 2019.

107. National League for Nursing. "History of NLN." *http://www.nln.org/about/history-of-nln*, retrieved May 4, 2019.

108. National League for Nursing Commission for Nursing Education Accreditation. "Overview." *http://www.nln.org/accreditation-services/overview*, retrieved May 4, 2019.

109. Accreditation Commission for Education in Nursing. Personal correspondence from ACEN, May 26, 2019.

110. American Association of Colleges of Nursing. "Our History 1969–2019." *https://www.aacnnursing.org/aacn50th/Our-History*, retrieved May 5, 2019.

111. American Board of Physician Specialties. "American Board of Integrative Medicine." *http://www.abpsus.org/integrative-medicine*, retrieved June 22, 2013.

112. American Board of Medical Specialties. "ABMS Guide to Medical Specialties." *https://www.abms.org/media/194925/abms-guide-to-medical-specialties-2019.pdf*, retrieved May 27, 2019.

113. American Osteopathic Association. "AOA Board Certification." *https://certification.osteopathic.org/*, retrieved May 27, 2019.

114. American Board of Medical Specialties. "Steps Toward Initial Certification and MOC." *https://www.abms.org/board-certification/steps-toward-initial-certification-and-moc/*, retrieved July 19, 2019.

115. Torrey, Trisha. "What Is Medical Board Certification?" *Verywell Health. https://www.verywellhealth.com/what-is-medical-board-certification-2615005*, retrieved July 19, 2019.

116. American Osteopathic Association. "Osteopathic Continuous Certification." *https://certification.osteopathic.org/osteopathic-continuous-certification/*, retrieved May 27, 2019.

117. Farrell, Michael. L. "The Effect of State Medical Board Action on ABMS Specialty Board Certification." Journal of Medical Regulation 105(2), July, 2019: 33-41, *https://meridian.allenpress.com/jmr/article-abstract/105/2/33/430123/The-Effect-of-State-Medical-Board-Action-on-ABMS?redirectedFrom=fulltext*, retrieved June 26, 2020.

118. Commission on Accreditation of Healthcare Management Education. "Why CAHME Accreditation Is Important." *https://cahme.org/healthcare-management-education-accreditation/university-programs/accreditation-information/*, retrieved May 29, 2019.

119. Healthcare Administration EDU. "CAHME-Accredited Program." *https://www.healthcareadministrationedu.org/accredited-healthcare-administration-programs/*, retrieved May 29, 2019.

120. Commission on Accreditation of Healthcare Management Education. "CAHME Eligibility Requirements." *https://www.cahme.org/files/accreditation/FALL2017_CAHME_CRITERIA_FOR_ACCREDITATION_2018_06_01.pdf*, retrieved on May 30, 2019.

121. Association of University Programs in Health Administration. 2018/2019 Annual Report. *https://higherlogicdownload.s3.amazonaws.com/AUPHA/5c0a0c07-a7f7-413e-ad73-9b7133ca4c38/UploadedImages/governance%20docs/2018-2019_AUPHA_Annual_Report.pdf*, retrieved December 11, 2019.

122. U.S. Department of Labor, Bureau of Labor Statistics. "Occupational Outlook Handbook: Medical and Health Services Managers." *https://www.bls.gov/ooh/management/medical-and-health-services-managers.htm#tab-4*, retrieved May 31, 2019.

123. U.S. Department of Labor, Bureau of Labor Statistics. "Labor Force Statistics from the Current Population Survey, 2018." *https://www.bls.gov/cps/cpsaat18.htm*, retrieved May 31, 2019.

124. Barber, Michael. "What Is a Nurse Practitioner? Doctors vs. Nurse Practitioners." *https://www.solvhealth.com/blog/doctors-vs-nurse-practitioners-what-s-the-difference*, retrieved May 31, 2019.

125. U.S. Census Bureau. "US Population by Month." *https://www.multpl.com/united-states-population/table/by-month*, retrieved May 9, 2020; United State Department of Labor Statistics, Occupational Employment Statistics. "May 2019 National Occupational employment and Wage Estimates, United States." *https://www.bls.gov/oes/current/oes_nat.htm#29-0000*, retrieved May 9, 2020.

126. Inglis, Brian. *Fringe Medicine,* 94–102. London: Faber & Faber, 1964.

127. "AOA Fact Sheet." Chicago: American Osteopathic Association, January 1999.

128. Inglis, *Fringe Medicine,* 102–105, 111–113.

129. Colby, Sandra L., and Jennifer M. Ortman. "Projections of the Size and Composition of the U.S. Population: 2014 to 2060." U.S. Census Bureau Report P25-1143. *https://www.census.gov/content/dam/Census/library/publications/2015/demo/p25-1143.pdf,* retrieved June 2, 2019.

130. Association of American Medical Colleges. "New Research Shows Increasing Physician Shortages in Both Primary and Specialty Care." AAMCNEWS. April 11, 2018. *https://news.aamc.org/press-releases/article/workforce_report_shortage_04112018/,* retrieved June 2, 2019.

131. Dill, Michael J., and Edward S. Salsberg. *The Complexities of Physician Supply and Demand: Projections through 2025,* 5. Center for Workforce Studies, Association of American Medical Colleges. November 2008. *http://www.innovationlabs.com/pa_future/1/background_docs/AAMC%20Complexities%20of%20physician%20demand,%202008.pdf,* retrieved May 26, 2013.

132. Association of American Medical Colleges. "Tables and Graphs for Fiscal Year 2017." Table 1: Revenues Supporting Programs and Activities at Fully Accredited U.S. Medical Schools, 2017. *https://www.aamc.org/data/finance/2017-tables/,* retrieved June 2, 2019.

133. Accreditation Council for Graduate Medical Education. "2018 Annual Report." *https://www.acgme.org/Portals/0/PDFs/2017-18AnnualReport.pdf,* retrieved June 3, 2019.

134. Randolph, Lillian. *Physician Characteristics and Distribution in the U.S.: 1997–1998,* 9. Chicago: American Medical Association, 1998.

135. Weinstock, Matthew. "Specialists Are Back in Demand as 'Frenzy' for Primary Docs Subsides." *AHA News* 34 (September 7, 1998): 5.

136. Randolph, *Physician Characteristics and Distribution in the U.S.*

137. Agency for Healthcare Research and Quality. "The Number of Practicing Primary Care Physicians in the United States." *https://www.ahrq.gov/research/findings/factsheets/primary/pcwork1/index.html,* retrieved June 2, 2019.

138. Association of American Medical Colleges. "New Research Shows Increasing Physician Shortages."

139. Rural Health Information Hub. "Rural Healthcare Workforce." July 19, 2018. *https://www.ruralhealthinfo.org/topics/health-care-workforce,* retrieved December 11, 2019.

140. United State Department of Labor Statistics, Occupational Employment Statistics. "May 2019 National Occupational Employment and Wage Estimates, United States." *https://www.bls.gov/oes/current/oes_nat.htm#29-0000,* retrieved May 9, 2020.

141. Institute of Medicine. "The Future of Nursing: Leading Change, Advancing Health." *http://www.iom.edu/Reports/2010/The-Future-of-Nursing-Leading-Change-Advancing-Health.aspx,* retrieved June 29, 2013.

142. Richard A. Cooper. "Credentialing Complementary and Alternative Medical Procedures." *Annals of Internal Medicine* 136 (2002): 965–973.

143. Omnibus Budget Reconciliation Act of 1987, PL 100-203, 101 Stat. 1330 (1987); *Professional Credentialing Statutes,* 1. Chicago: American Hospital Association, 1990.

144. *Laws That Regulate Dietitians/Nutritionists.* Chicago: American Dietetic Association, 1999.

145. American Society of Clinical Pathologists. "ASCP Board of Certification." *https://www.ascp.org/content/board-of-certification,* retrieved December 11, 2019.

146. Association of American Medical Colleges. "Table B-1.2: Total Enrollment by U.S. Medical School and Sex." *https://www.aamc.org/download/321526/data/factstableb1-2.pdf,* retrieved June 8, 2019.

147. Association of American Medical Colleges. "Table B-2.2: Total Graduates by U.S. Medical School and Sex." *https://www.aamc.org/download/321532/data/factstableb2-2.pdf,* retrieved June 8, 2019.

148. American Association of Colleges of Osteopathic Medicine. "U.S. College of Osteopathic Medicine." *https://www.aacom.org/become-a-doctor/us-coms,* retrieved June 8, 2019.

149. *Health Care Almanac,* 2nd ed., edited by Lorri A. Zipperer, 305. Chicago: American Medical Association, 1998.

150. American Board of Physician Specialty. "Anesthesiology Board Certification Eligibility Requirements." *https://www.abpsus.org/anesthesiology-requirements,* retrieved June 8, 2019.

151. Heisler, Elaine, and Sidath Viranga Panangala. "The Veterans Health Administration and Medical Education: In Brief." Congressional Research Service. *https://fas.org/sgp/crs/misc/R43587.pdf,* retrieved June 8, 2019.

152. Logan, Jane, and Billie Jean Summers. "The 'New' VA." *Tennessee Nurse* 60 (June 1997): 14–15.

153. Federation of State Medical Boards. "State-Specific Requirements for Initial Licensure." *http://www.fsmb.org/step-3/state-licensure/,* June 16, 2020.

154. Federation of State Medical Boards. "Continuing Medical Education: Board-by-Board Overview." *http://www.fsmb.org/siteassets/advocacy/key-issues/continuing-medical-education-by-state.pdf*, retrieved June 26, 2020.

155. American Association of Colleges of Podiatric Medicine. "Admissions." *https://aacpm.org/becoming-a-podiatric-physician/admissions/*, retrieved June 26, 2020.

156. Council on Podiatric Medical Education. "Specialty Certifying Boards." *https://www.cpme.org/boards/content.cfm?ItemNumber=2423*, retrieved June 6, 2019.

157. Stanfield, Peggy S., and Y. H. Hui. *Introduction to the Health Professions,* 131. Boston: Jones & Bartlett, 1998.

158. United States Department of Labor, Bureau of Labor Statistics. "Occupational Employment Statistics. May 2017 National Occupational employment and Wage Estimates, United States." *https://www.bls.gov/oes/2017/may/oes_nat.htm#29-0000*, retrieved June 1, 2019.

159. United States Department of Labor Statistics, Bureau of Labor Statistics. "Occupational Employment and Wages, May, 2018: Registered Nurses." *https://www.bls.gov/oes/current/oes291141.htm*, retrieved June 8, 2019.

160. American Nurses Credentialing Center. "2018 ANCC Certification Data." *https://www.nursingworld.org/~499e5e/globalassets/docs/ancc/2017-certification-data-for-website.pdf*, retrieved June 24, 2019.

161. American Nurses Association. "ANA Certification Catalogue." Kansas City, MO: American Nurses Association, 1983.

162. American Nurses Credentialing Center. "2018 ANCC Certification Data."

163. Nurse.org. "Complete List of Common Nursing Certifications." *https://nurse.org/articles/nursing-certifications-credentials-list/*, retrieved on June 24, 2019.

164. American Association of Nurse Practitioners. "State Practice Environment." *https://www.aanp.org/advocacy/state/state-practice-environment*, retrieved June 24, 2019.

165. Verywell health. "States That Allow CRNAs to Practice without Physician Supervision." *https://www.verywellhealth.com/which-states-allow-crnas-to-practice-independently-1736102*, retrieved June 24, 2019.

166. Jacobson, Nadine M. "Rule on Physician Supervision for Certified Nurse Anesthetists." *Policy, Politics, & Nursing (May 2001). http://ppn.sagepub.com/cgi/reprint/2/2/157.pdf*, retrieved November 14, 2006.

167. American College of Nurse-Midwives, "2017 Annual Report." *http://midwife.org/acnm/files/ccLibraryFiles/Filename/000000006930/2017-ACNM-Annual-Report.pdf*, retrieved June 24, 2019.

168. Greene, J., and A. M. Nordhaus-Bike, "Nurse Shortage: Where Have All the RNs Gone?" *Hospital & Health Networks* 75, 15–18 (1998): 78, 80.

169. Accreditation Council for Pharmacy Education. *https://www.acpe-accredit.org/shared_info/programs Secure.asp*, retrieved September 23, 2012.

170. U.S. Department of Labor, Bureau of Labor Statistics. "Pharmacists." *Occupational Outlook Handbook. https://www.bls.gov/OOH/healthcare/pharmacists.htm*, retrieved June 16, 2020.

171. Academy of Nutrition and Dietetics. "Academy History." *https://www.eatrightpro.org/about-us/academy-vision-and-mission/academy-history*, retrieved July 10, 2019.

172. Commission on Dietetic Registration. "Licensure Information by State." *https://www.cdrnet.org/state-licensure*, retrieved July 10, 2019.

173. American Society of Radiologic Technologists. "Careers in Radiologic Technology." *https://www.asrt.org/main/career-center/careers-in-radiologic-technology*, retrieved July 10, 2019.

174. American Society of Radiologic Technologists. "Individual State Licensure Information." *https://www.asrt.org/main/standards-and-regulations/legislation-regulations-and-advocacy/individual-state-licensure*, retrieved July 10, 2019.

175. United States Department of Labor. Bureau of Labor Statistics. "Medical and Clinical Laboratory Technologists and Technicians." *https://www.bls.gov/ooh/healthcare/medical-and-clinical-laboratory-technologists-and-technicians.htm*, retrieved July 11, 2019.

176. American Academy of Physician Assistants. "Become a PA." *https://www.aapa.org/career-central/become-a-pa/*, retrieved on July 11, 2019.

177. Accreditation Review Commission on Education for the Physician Assistant. "Program Accreditation Status." *http://www.arc-pa.org/accreditation/accredited-programs/*, retrieved July 11, 2019.

178. American Academy of Physician Assistants. "List of Licensing Boards." *https://www.aapa.org/advocacy-central/state-advocacy/state-licensing/list-of-licensing-boards/*, retrieved July 11, 2019.

179. American Academy of Physician Assistants. "A Glimpse into the Aging PA Workforce: A Report from the AAPA PA Practice Survey, January 18, 2019." Tables, 6, 7, 8. *https://www.aapa.org/wp-content/uploads/2019/01/PARetirement_PAPrS.pdf*, retrieved on July 11, 2019.

180. United States Department of Labor. Bureau of Labor Statistics. "Physician Assistants." *https://www.bls.gov/ooh/healthcare/physician-assistants.htm*, retrieved on July 11, 2019.

181. American College of Healthcare Executives. "About ACHE." *https://www.ache.org/about-ache,* retrieved July 12, 2019.
182. Medical Group Management Association. "About MGMA." *https://www.mgma.com/about/organization,* retrieved July 12, 2019.
183. Medical Group Management Association. "Board Certification Requirements." *https://www.mgma.com/career-pathways/career-advancement/acmpe/acmpe-board-certification,* retrieved July 12, 2019.
184. Medical Group Management Association. "Fellowship Requirements." *https://www.mgma.com/career-pathways/career-advancement/fellowship/acmpe-fellowship,* retrieved July 12, 2019.
185. Collier, Roger. "American Medical Association Membership Woes Continue." *Canadian Medical Association Journal* 183, 11 (2011): 713–714. *https://www.ncbi.nlm.nih.gov/pmc/articles/PMC3153537/,* retrieved July 12, 2019.
186. Graham, Judith. "Like a Slap in the Face: Dissent Roils the AMA, the Nation's Largest Doctor's Group." *https://www.statnews.com/2016/12/22/american-medical-association-divisions/,* retrieved July 12, 2019; Campbell, Kevin. "Don't Believe AMA's Hype, Membership Still Declining." *https://www.youtube.com/watch?v=BoPdyOUSnSc,* retrieved July 12, 2019.
187. American Medical Association. "AMA Letter to Congressional Leaders on Reform of Health Care System." *https://www.ama-assn.org/press-center/press-releases/ama-letter-congressional-leaders-reform-health-care-system,* retrieved July 12, 2019.
188. National Medical Association. "About Us." *https://www.nmanet.org/page/About_Us, retrieved July 15, 2019.*
189. American Nurses Association. "About ANA." *https://www.nursingworld.org/ana/about-ana/,* retrieved July 15, 2019.
190. American Hospital Association. "About the AHA." *https://www.aha.org/about,* retrieved July 15, 2019.
191. Federation of American Hospitals. "About FAH." *https://www.fah.org/about-fah/mission-statement,* retrieved July 15, 2019.
192. Catholic Health Association. "Catholic Health Care in the United States: Updated January 2019." *https://www.chausa.org/about/about,* retrieved July 15, 2019.
193. American Health Care Association. "About AHCA." *https://www.ahcancal.org/about_ahca/Pages/default.aspx,* retrieved July 15, 2019.
194. LeadingAge. "Our Story." *https://www.leadingage.org/our-story,* retrieved July 15, 2019.
195. American Association of Health Plans. https://www.ahip.org/about-us/, retrieved June 16, 2020.
196. America's Health Insurance Plans. "About." *https://www.ahip.org/about-us/,* retrieved July 15, 2019.
197. U.S Department of Health and Human Services, Centers for Medicare and Medicaid Services. "NHE Fact Sheet, 2018." *https://www.cms.gov/Research-Statistics-Data-and-Systems/Statistics-Trends-and-Reports/NationalHealthExpendData/NHE-Fact-Sheet,* retrieved December 11, 2019.
198. Reinhardt, Uwe E. "Spending More through 'Cost Control': Our Obsessive Quest to Gut the Hospital." *Health Affairs* 15 (Summer 1996): 145–154. Reinhardt argues that the incremental cost of convalescent days in a hospital is much less expensive than care provided by alternative sources, such as home health. Thus, rather than reduce national healthcare costs, shifting care outside hospitals has actually added to the costs. It is noted that despite major reductions in inpatient stays from 1980 to 1995, total U.S. health spending increased by more than 50%.
199. U.S. Department of Health and Human Services, Centers for Medicare and Medicaid Services. "National Health Expenditures by Type of Service and Source of Funds: 1960–2018." *https://www.cms.gov/Research-Statistics-Data-and-Systems/Statistics-Trends-and-Reports/NationalHealthExpendData/NationalHealthAccountsHistorical,* retrieved December 11, 2019.
200. U.S. Department of Labor, Bureau of Labor Statistics. "Consumer Price Index." *https://www.bls.gov/cpi/,* retrieved December 11, 2019.
201. Blue Cross Blue Shield Association. *https://www.bcbs.com/bcbs-companies-and-licensees,* retrieved December 11, 2019.
202. Health Insurance Association of America. *Source Book of Health Insurance Data, 1982–83,* 7. Washington, DC: Health Insurance Association of America, 1982–1983.
203. Insurance Information Institute. "Facts + Statistics: Industry Overview." *https://www.iii.org/fact-statistic/facts-statistics-industry-overview,* retrieved December 11, 2019.
204. Kaiser Family Foundation. "What's the Role of Private Health Insurance Today and under Medicare-for-All and Other Public Option Proposals?" *https://www.kff.org/health-reform/issue-brief/whats-the-role-of-private-health-insurance-today-and-under-medicare-for-all-and-other-public-option-proposals/,* retrieved December 11, 2019.
205. Vox. "The Uninsured Rate Has Been Steadily Declining for a Decade. But Now It's Rising Again." September 10, 2019. *https://www.vox.com/policy-and-politics/2019/9/10/20858938/health-insurance-census-bureau-data-trump,* retrieved December 11, 2019.

206. U.S. Department of Health and Human Services, Centers for Medicare and Medicaid Services. "NHE Fact Sheet, 2018." *https://www.cms.gov/Research-Statistics-Data-and-Systems/Statistics-Trends-and-Reports/NationalHealthExpendData/NHE-Fact-Sheet,* retrieved December 11, 2019.

207. Lave, Judith R., and Lester B. Lave. "Health Care: Part I." *Law and Contemporary Problems* 35 (Spring 1970); reprinted by permission. Copyright 1970, 1971 by Duke University.

208. Fry, Erika. "There's a National Shortage of Saline Solution. Yeah, We're Talking Salt Water. Huh?" *Fortune,* February 5, 2015. *http://fortune.com/2015/02/05/theres-a-national-shortage-of-saline/,* retrieved August 28, 2018; Mazer-Amirshahi, Maryann, and Erin R. Fox. "Saline Shortages—Many Causes, No Simple Solution." *New England Journal of Medicine* (April 19, 2018). *https://www.nejm.org/doi/full/10.1056/NEJMp1800347,* retrieved August 28, 2018; Sacks, Chana A., Aaron S. Kesselheim, and Michael Fralick. "The Shortage of Normal Saline in the Wake of Hurricane Maria. *JAMA Internal Medicine* 178, 7 (2018): 885–886. *https://jamanetwork.com/journals/jamain-ternalmedicine/fullarticle/2681062,* retrieved August 1, 2018.

209. Daly, Rich. "Bipartisan Policy Group Aims to Slash Hospital Budgets." HFMA News, Payment Trends, December 13, 2019. *https://www.hfma.org/topics/news/2019/12/bipartisan-policy-group-aims-to-slash-hospital-budgets.html?MessageRunDetailID=1066688139&PostID=9947391&utm_medium=email&utm_source=rasa_io,* retrieved December 17, 2019.

2

Ethical and Legal Environment

This chapter considers the ethical and legal environment of health services management. The relationships between ethics and the law are numerous, varied, and dynamic.

The value system (moral framework) of a society is the context from which both its ethics and its body of law arise. Ethics is the organized study of standards of conduct and moral judgment. In this respect, ethics is both a source of law and a function of it. With respect to a profession, ethics is the group's principles or code. Law is a system of principles and rules for human conduct that arises from a society's value system, is prescribed or recognized by society, and is enforced by public authority. This definition applies to both criminal and civil law.

Criminal law has moral underpinnings because it reflects society's value system of right and wrong—its moral code, or ethic. This is also true for civil law, which governs organizational and individual relationships, such as contracts and malfeasance, including medical malpractice. Here, however, the underlying moral principles are more obscure.

Society and the Law

Some societies regarded law as a gift from the gods; Plato's Greece is an example. Plato considered written law an oversimplification that could not account for nuances, conditions, and differences among persons and circumstances in a dispute. He believed the best method to resolve a dispute used a philosopher who applied an unwritten law. His own experience proved this impossible in practice, however, and Plato later accepted a written form of law in which authorities become servants of the law and administer it without regard to parties in the dispute.[1] The principle of "a rule of law, not of men" is reflected in the Anglo-American legal system.

Beyond written law, which reflects the most significant concerns of society, are other considerations. There are times when orderliness and continuity must yield to justice or fairness. Aristotle recognized the importance of unwritten law that incorporates concepts of justice too elusive or varied in their application to be readily codified.[2] Known as chancery, this concept of justice was established in England. American legal practice uses a similar concept, called equity, in which courts seek to do justice to parties in a dispute that is unique and unlikely to recur. Such a principle of law permits the right (fair) result in a case in which blindly following the law would provide no remedy or one unsatisfactory or unfair.

Edgar Bodenheimer, a scholar of jurisprudence, divided sources of law into formal and nonformal. Examples of formal law affecting health services are constitutions, treaties, statutes, executive orders, regulations, judicial precedents, and charters and bylaws of autonomous or semiautonomous bodies. Nonformal law comprises standards of justice, principles of reason, individual equity, moral convictions, and customary law.[3] Especially important for health services organizations (HSOs) and health systems (HSs) are the charters and bylaws of autonomous or semiautonomous bodies as formal sources of law. Courts look to them to determine the rights and obligations of those affected. State governments issue charters that legally establish corporations and create other types of organizations sanctioned by law.

Bodenheimer's *formal sources of law* include professional associations' codes of ethics. Written codes with interpretations that guide application and decision making have the virtues of consistency and predictability. Professional codes of ethics set a standard higher than the law. They state the profession's mission and philosophy, its goals and strivings, and minimally acceptable behavior. Formal sources of law supersede nonformal sources, except when the former lack comprehensiveness or require interpretation. All types of formal law—even treaties between the United States and other countries—may affect HSOs/HSs. The processes that produce the law are described in Chapter 1. Law is the basic grounding for society. Aristotle stated it well over 2 millennia ago when he wrote "for law is order, and good law is good order."[4]

Relationship of Law to Ethics

Generally, democratically derived laws reflect the majority's views of justice and fairness. Some in society may consider a law unjust or immoral and risk or invite punishment by breaking it. Classic contemporary examples are the widespread recreational use of narcotics and engaging in civil disobedience to protest government or private actions deemed morally wrong.

It is not necessarily true that what is lawful is ethical and what is unlawful is unethical. The law is minimum performance. Professions expect members to obey the law, but simultaneously hold them to a higher standard. Thus, a profession's code of ethics requires members to act in ways different from members of society.

Henderson's models identify relationships of law and ethics.[5] Figure 2.1 shows the succession of events that results in public scrutiny of corporate decisions and a determination that they are legal, ethical, or both. This judgment is retrospective, despite management's efforts to predict the effects of their actions. The model suggests the difficulty of knowing if those (e.g., law enforcement officials) who eventually judge the decision will consider it legal and if those (e.g., members of the profession or the public) who eventually judge the decision will consider it ethical. This adds uncertainty to HSO/HS decisions. Predicting an action's legality is often easier than predicting if it will be judged ethical.

Figure 2.2 shows the combinations of legal, illegal, ethical, and unethical factors involved in corporate decision making. Decisions made in Quadrant I are ethical and legal and easily identified: managers who obey the law act ethically and legally. Quadrant II includes decisions

Figure 2.1.   The relationship between law and ethics.

that are ethical but illegal. The American College of Healthcare Executives (ACHE) code of ethics states that obeying the law is minimal ethical conduct. This blanket prohibition means that only compelling moral justification exculpates an illegal act by a health services manager. An example is to disregard a law because obeying it will cause significant injustice for a patient.

Quadrant III includes decisions that are unethical but legal. This quadrant is often reflected in a profession's code of ethics that requires performance more demanding than the law. Examples include failing to take all reasonable steps to protect patients from medical malpractice and managerial self-aggrandizement to the detriment of patients.

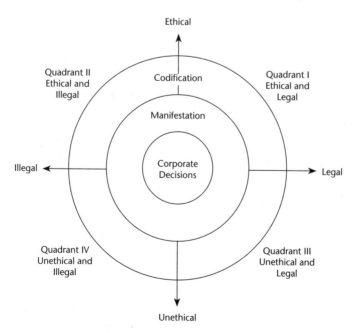

Figure 2.2.   A matrix of possible outcomes concerning the ethics and legality of corporate decisions. (From Henderson, Verne E. "The Ethical Side of Enterprise." *MIT Sloan Management Review* 23 [Spring 1982]: 37–47. Copyright © 1982 by Massachusetts Institute of Technology. All rights reserved.)

Quadrant IV includes actions that are both illegal and unethical. Examples are easy. Codes of ethics require obeying the law; actions that break the law are both illegal and unethical. Failing to meet life safety code requirements, embezzlement, or filing a false Medicare report lie in this quadrant.

Ethics Framework

Ethical issues arise in all HSOs and HSs. Until recently, the use of medical technology in acute care hospitals was the source of most biomedical ethical issues. In the 21st century, however, changes in the locus of care mean other types of HSOs increasingly have ethical issues. The complexity and unique role of HSOs and HSs result in ethical issues with legal dimensions and legal issues with ethical dimensions. Capable managers identify and understand both.

The dynamic relationship between ethics and law is sometimes synergistic, sometimes antagonistic. Each affects and is affected by the other. The law is the basic framework of society and is the context for application of ethics in health services.

Moral Philosophies

Teleology, deontology, and natural law have found extensive application in Western societies. Two other moral philosophies, casuistry and virtue ethics, have experienced a revival and are considered as well. These five moral philosophies provide a basis to study morals (ethics), provide a framework for a personal ethic and an organizational philosophy, and help determine the moral rightness or wrongness of an action.

Teleology

Teleology is derived from *telos,* Greek for *end*. The most prominent moral philosophy using this concept is utility theory; its adherents are utilitarians. The underlying premise is that the moral rightness or wrongness of an act or decision is judged by whether it brings into being more good (utility) or ungood (disutility) than alternative decisions. Classical utilitarianism's most prominent proponent was the English philosopher John Stuart Mill (1806–1873). Utilitarians have no independent right or wrong to guide them. They look at the consequences of an act— the "good" is independent of the "right." Utilitarians are sometimes called consequentialists because they judge actions by their consequences.

Utilitarianism is divided into act utility and rule utility. Act utility assesses each decision and determines its consequences when judging moral rightness or wrongness. Act utilitarians judge each action independently, without reference to preestablished guidelines (rules). They measure the amount of good, or (nonmoral) value, brought into being and the amount of evil, or (nonmoral) dis-value, brought into being *or* avoided by acting on a choice. Each person affected is counted equally. This suggests a strong sense of objectivity. Act utilitarianism receives no further attention here because it is episodic and incompatible with developing and deriving the ethical principles needed for codes of ethics and a personal ethic.

Rule utility is more formal. It assesses courses of action (or nonaction) and measures their consequences—the amount of (nonmoral) good or ungood produced. The morally superior course of action must be taken, even though it may not produce the most good (or least ungood) in a specific application. Utility theory is the basis for cost–benefit analysis. A crude summary statement describing utilitarianism is "the end justifies the means."

Deontology

Deontology is based on the presence of an independent right or wrong. It does not consider consequences. *Deontology* is derived from *deon,* Greek for *duty*. The best-known proponent of a duty-based moral philosophy was the German philosopher Immanuel Kant (1724–1804).

Briefly stated, Kantian deontology asserts the end (result) is unimportant because human be-ings have duties to one another as moral agents, and these duties take precedence over conse-quences. For Kant, an act is moral if it arises from good will and if, therefore, one acts from a sense of duty. The Kantian test of morality is whether the action meets the categorical impera-tive, which requires that we act in accordance with what we wish to become a universal law. The universal law is that what is right or wrong for one person is right or wrong for everyone, in all places and times. According to Kant, an action is right only if it can be universalized without violating the equality of human beings. For example, Kantians see it as logically inconsistent to argue that a terminally ill person should be euthanized (actively caused to die), because this is saying life can be improved by ending it. Deontology may be summarized as never treating human beings only as a means, but rather always as an end.[6] Another summary of deontology is to practice the Golden Rule, "Do unto others as you would have them do unto you."

The work of a contemporary American philosopher, John Rawls (1921–2002), extended Kantian deontology. In *A Theory of Justice,* Rawls used elaborate philosophical constructs to develop the elements of a social contract among free, equal, self-interested, and rational per-sons. He reasoned that such persons would reject utilitarianism and select instead the concepts of right and justice as necessary to the good.[7]

Natural Law

Natural law states that ethics (morality) must be grounded in a concern for human good and is, therefore, teleological (consequential). Natural law is based on Aristotelian thought as interpreted and synthesized with Christian dogma by St. Thomas Aquinas (1225–1274).[8] It assumes a natural order in relationships and a predisposition among rational persons to do, or refrain from doing, certain things. Human beings are rational. Therefore, we can discover what we should do, and in that attempt, we are guided by a partial notion of the eternal law that is linked to our capacity for rational thought. Because natural law guides what rational persons do, it is the basis for positive law, some of which is reflected in statutes. Natural law contends that the good *cannot* be defined only in terms of subjective inclinations; rather, there is a good for human beings that is objectively desirable, although not reducible to desire.[9] A summary statement of the basic precepts of natural law is that we should "do good and avoid evil."

Casuistry

Historical definitions of casuistry are disparaging. Critics argued it used evasive reasoning and encouraged rationalizations for desired ethical results. Regardless, contemporary advocates see casuistry as a pragmatic way to understand and solve ethical problems. Casuistry is case-based reasoning in historical context. It avoids excessive reliance on principles and rules, which may provide only partial answers and may not guide decision makers comprehensively. Casuistry al-lows problem solvers to use the concrete circumstances of actual cases and the specific maxims persons invoke in facing moral dilemmas.[10]

At base, casuistry is like the law; court cases and the precedents they establish guide deci-sion makers. "Cases in ethics are similar: Normative judgments emerge through majoritarian consensus in society and in institutions because careful attention has been paid to the details of problem cases. That consensus becomes authoritative and is extended to similar cases."[11] HSOs use casuistry as institutional ethics committees develop a body of experience with ethical issues.

Clinical medicine and management education rely on cases. This makes cases easy to use in health services, in which traditional ethics problem solving has applied moral principles to cases—from the general to the specific, or deductive reasoning. Modern casuists benefit from classical casuists' reliance on paradigm cases, reference to broad consensus, and using probable certitude—assent to a proposition but acknowledging its opposite might be true.[12] Large num-bers of cases in HSOs/HSs and a body of experience will lead to consensus and more certainty in charting moral direction.

Virtue Ethics

Western thought about the importance of virtue can be partially traced to Aristotle. Like natural law, virtue is based on theological ethics but without a primary focus on obligations or duties. Like casuistry, it has received more attention recently, some of which results from a perception that traditional rules, or principle-based moral philosophies, are inadequate for the realities of ethical decision making. This is to say that rules offer limited help in solving ethical problems. When there are competing ethical rules or situations to which no rules apply, something more than a coin toss is needed. Here, virtue ethicists claim to have a superior moral philosophy.

Contemporary authors argue that virtue ethics has three levels. The first two are observing laws and observing moral rights and fulfilling moral duties that go beyond the law. The third and highest level is the practice of virtue.[13]

> Virtue implies a character trait, an internal disposition habitually to seek moral perfection, to live one's life in accord with a moral law, and to attain a balance between noble intention and just action. In almost any view the virtuous person is someone we can trust to act habitually in a good way—courageously, honestly, justly, wisely, and temperately.[14]

In this view, virtuous physicians (and managers) are disposed to the right and good intrinsic to the practice of their professions and will work for the good of the patient.

Some virtue ethicists argue that, as with any skill or expertise, practice and constant striving to achieve virtuous traits (good works) improve one's ability to be virtuous. Others argue that accepting in one's heart the forgiveness and reconciliation offered by God (faith) "would lead to a new disposition toward God (trust) and the neighbor (love), much as a physician or patient might be judged to be a different (and better) person following changed dispositions toward those persons with whom . . . [they] are involved."[15]

All persons should live virtuous lives, but those in the professions have a special obligation to do so. Virtuous managers and physicians are not just virtuous persons practicing a profession; they are expected to work for the patient's good even at the expense of personal sacrifice and legitimate self-interest.[16] Virtuous physicians place the good of their patients above their own and seek that good, unless pursuing it imposes an injustice on them or their families or violates their conscience.[17] Similarly, virtuous managers put the good of the patient above their own.

Linking Theory and Action

Ethical theories and derivative principles guide development of rules for individuals and organizations. These rules determine specific judgments and the subsequent actions of organizations and individuals.[18] Moral theories do not necessarily conflict; they may reach the same conclusion about an action, albeit through different reasoning or use of varying philosophical constructs. Four principles should guide health services managers: respect for persons, beneficence, nonmaleficence, and justice. These principles should be reflected in the organization's philosophy, as well as the manager's personal ethic.[19]

Respect for Persons

The principle of respect for persons has four elements. The first, autonomy, requires that persons act toward others in a way that enables them to be self-governing. To choose and pursue a course of action, persons must be rational and uncoerced (unconstrained). Sometimes physical or mental conditions cause persons to become nonautonomous. They are owed respect, nonetheless, even though special means are needed for them to express autonomy. Autonomy underlies the need to obtain consent for treatment, as well as how HSOs view and interact with patients and staff.

Autonomy is in dynamic tension with paternalism. The Hippocratic oath is antecedent to paternalism in the patient–physician relationship and suggests that physicians should act in their patients' best interests—as physicians judge those interests. Giving autonomy primacy limits paternalism to specific circumstances.

The second element of respect for persons is truth telling, which requires managers to be honest in all they do. At its absolute, truth telling eliminates "white lies," even if knowing the truth causes harm to the person learning it.

Confidentiality, the third element of respect for persons, requires managers and clinicians to keep secret what they learn about patients and others in their work. Legal requirements necessitate morally justified exceptions to confidentiality.

The fourth element is fidelity, defined as doing one's duty or keeping one's word. Sometimes called promise keeping, fidelity, like the other three elements of respect for persons, requires managers to be respectful of everyone, whether they are patients, staff, or others.

Beneficence

The second principle, beneficence, is rooted in Hippocratic tradition and is defined as acting with charity and kindness. Contemporary health services applications of beneficence are broader, including a positive duty. Generally, beneficence anchors one end of a continuum, at the opposite end of which is the principle of nonmaleficence, defined as refraining from actions that aggravate a problem or cause other negative results.

Beneficence includes conferring benefits and balancing benefits and harms. Conferring benefits is well established in medicine; failing to provide benefits when one can violates an ethical obligation of clinicians. Modified consistent with their role, beneficence applies to managers. The positive duty suggested by beneficence requires HSOs to do all they can for patients. There is a lesser duty to aid potential rather than actual patients. Application of this distinction varies with the HSO's values, mission, and vision and with the population served.

The second dimension of beneficence is balancing the benefits and harms of an action. This is the principle of utility, the philosophical basis for cost–benefit and risk–benefit analyses. Utility is but one of several considerations in health services decision making. Its more limited application results from a positive duty to act in the patient's best interests because one cannot act with kindness and charity if risks outweigh benefits. Regardless, utility cannot morally justify overriding patients' interests and sacrificing them to the greater good.

Nonmaleficence

The third principle applicable to managing HSOs is nonmaleficence. It, too, is rooted in medicine. Nonmaleficence can be defined as *primum non nocere*—first, do no harm. This dictum to guide physicians applies to health services managers. Nonmaleficence gives rise to specific moral rules, but neither the principle nor derivative rules are absolute. For example, it is appropriate (with the patient's consent) to inflict harm (e.g., administer cancer chemotherapy) to avoid worse harm (e.g., a surgical procedure or fatal cancer), and it may be appropriate to compromise truth telling if telling the truth likely results in significant mental or physical harm.

Nonmaleficence most commonly applies to HSO relationships with patients. Its application means managers have duties to staff. Placing staff at unnecessary or extraordinary risk to their health and safety violates a manager's duty to them, even if the result meets the principle of beneficence to patients. Balancing benefits and harms is to apply the concept of utility.

Justice

The fourth principle, justice, is important in managerial decision making such as allocating the HSO's resources or developing and applying human resources policies. What is justice, and how does one know when it is achieved? Justice is defined variously. Some definitions require that all persons get their just desserts—what they are due. Rawls defined justice as fairness. But how are just desserts and fairness defined? Aristotle defined justice as equals being treated equally, unequals treated unequally—a concept common to public policy analysis. Equal treatment of equals is reflected in liberty rights, such as freedom of speech for all. Unequal treatment of persons unequally situated justifies redistribution of wealth using a progressive income tax. Aristotle's concept of justice is expressed in health services when greater resources are expended on those more ill. Such definitions of justice are helpful but do not solve the problems of definition and opinion so troublesome for managers. At a minimum, clinicians and managers act justly if they consistently apply clear and prospectively determined criteria in decision making.

Summary

Moral philosophies and the derivative principles are a framework to hone and apply a personal ethic. Like philosophers, managers are unlikely to adopt only one moral philosophy. Most will be eclectic in developing and reconsidering a personal ethic. The principles of respect for persons, beneficence, nonmaleficence, and justice help define relationships among patients, managers, and organizations. The principles may be weighted differently and take precedence over one another, depending on the issue. Justice requires, however, that they are consistently ordered and weighted as similar ethical issues are considered.

Personal Ethic and Professional Codes

The many written and unwritten "codes" that guide human behavior arise from family, religious training, professional affiliations and allegiances, and an often-ill-defined personal code of moral conduct—an amalgam of intellect, reasoning, experience, education, and relationships. Guidelines may be vague, even contradictory. Those solving ethical problems will find many difficult questions and choices but few easy answers. Such situations highlight the necessity of a well-developed, internalized personal ethic.

A personal ethic is a moral framework that guides decision making and allows one to assess and refine guidelines, judgments, and actions. Membership in a professional association with a code of ethics and employment in an HSO with an organizational philosophy (expressed values system) reflected in its mission and vision statements are not substitutes for a coherent, consistent, and comprehensive personal ethic. All persons are moral agents whose actions, inactions, and misactions have moral consequences for which they are responsible. Morally, one's conduct cannot be excused by claiming "I was following orders" or "That's not my area of responsibility." Orders from lawfully constituted public authorities pose special problems. Moral agents who judge them unjust disregard them at their peril and must bear the sanctions imposed. Ethical (moral) implications of acts must be considered independently of the acts.

One hallmark of a profession is a code of ethics that distinguishes acceptable from unacceptable behavior. Codes are common in health services, but general language and vague performance standards limit enforceability. Professional codes of ethics are best seen as guides for those seeking to do the right thing and needing help to know what that is. Those at the moral fringe of a profession are rarely dissuaded from questionable actions by a code of ethics.

Conflicts may arise between the HSO's ethic, as expressed in its values statement, and a manager's personal ethic. The concept of moral agency should cause managers to think carefully about the implications of acquiescing in specific expressions of an HSO's philosophy. It may seem easier to "go along to get along" than to risk one's position and economic association by speaking out. Failure to speak when one should, however, violates moral agency. State and federal "conscience clause" laws support individual and institutional values expressed by not providing certain types of treatment. The presence of such laws is a compelling reason for organizations to have clearly stated positions on value-laden medical treatment. For example, 45 states permit individual providers to refuse to participate in abortions; 42 allow religious, private, or, in some states, all institutions to refuse to provide abortions.[20] Several federal statutes have conscience clause protection for HSOs and their staffs if religious belief or moral conviction prevents them from performing sterilizations or abortions.[21]

Health Services Codes of Ethics

Managers

American College of Healthcare Executives

The ACHE first adopted a code of ethics in 1939, 6 years after its founding. Several iterations later the code is more specific. In 2018, it had five sections that detailed the healthcare executive's responsibilities to the profession, to patients or others served, to the organization, to employees, and to the community and society. The final section charged affiliates with a positive duty to communicate facts to the committee on ethics when they have reasonable grounds to believe an affiliate has violated the code.[22] Biomedical ethical issues receive very little attention. The 1987 revision used the concept of moral agent (since changed to *moral advocate*) and recognized a positive duty for affiliates to report violations. ACHE ethical policy statements guide affiliates on issues such as medical records confidentiality, decisions at the end of life, and professional impairment. The committee on ethics investigates allegations and makes recommendations regarding breaches of the code. Expulsion is the maximum disciplinary action.

American College of Health Care Administrators

The American College of Health Care Administrators (ACHCA) code guides managers of long-term care facilities. Expectations for managers are stated as prescriptions and proscriptions: 1) the welfare of those receiving care is paramount; 2) maintain professional competence; 3) maintain professional posture, holding paramount the interests of facility and residents; and 4) meet responsibilities to public, profession, and colleagues. Specific areas include quality of services; confidentiality of patient information; continuing education; conflicts of interest; and fostering increased knowledge, supporting research, and sharing expertise. Affiliates shall not defend, support, or ignore unethical conduct perpetrated by colleagues, peers, or students. No enforcement process is described.[23]

Clinicians

Physicians

The American Medical Association (AMA) is the preeminent professional association for allopathic physicians. The AMA's first "Principles of Medical Ethics," adopted at its founding in 1847, was based on a code of medical ethics developed by the English physician and philosopher Sir Thomas Percival (1740–1804) in 1803.[24] After several iterations, the 2001 principles emphasize providing competent medical care, honesty in all professional interactions, and safeguarding patient confidences. Members "shall . . . strive to report physicians deficient in character or competence, or engaging in fraud or deception, to appropriate entities."[25] Opinions of the AMA's Council on Ethical and Judicial Affairs interpret the principles. The 2001 principles recognize rights and responsibilities first noted in 1980; that iteration was "the opening to an ethics based on notions of rights and responsibilities rather than benefits and harms. It is the first document in the history of professional medical ethics in which a group of physicians is willing to use the language of responsibilities and rights."[26]

Nurses

The "Code for Nurses" was first adopted by the American Nurses Association (ANA) in 1950. The 2015 iteration has nine expectations: principles to guide practice, primary commitment to patients' interests, advocating for patients, individual accountability, duties to self and others, improving healthcare, advancing the profession, collaboration, and obligations to the profession. An interpretive statement follows each. Like the ACHE, ACHCA, and AMA, the ANA code obliges nurses to counter or expose problematic practice: "The nurse promotes, advocates for, and strives to protect the health, safety, and rights of the patient."[27]

Institutional Trade Associations

The American Hospital Association (AHA) is the leading trade association for hospitals. The AHA's "Patient Care Partnership" includes high-quality care, a clear and safe environment, involvement in the patient's care, protection of the patient's privacy, help when the patient is leaving the hospital, and help with billing claims.[28]

The American Health Care Association (AHCA) includes for-profit and not-for-profit long-term facilities. AHCA's code guides these organizations and is a model for state affiliates and their members. It includes taking moral responsibility, using good business practice, making difficult choices, acting responsibly, providing quality services, dealing with conflicting values, making use of information, practicing responsible advocacy, avoiding conflicts of interest, respecting others, and engaging in fair competition.[29]

The statement of commitment of America's Health Insurance Plans guides member health plans. Included are commitment to improve quality, to give all Americans access through public and private coverage and through support for the public health infrastructure, and to improve affordability.[30]

Bills of Rights

Patient bills of rights guide relationships between consumers and HSOs. Organizations with patient bills of rights (which have various names) include the AHA, The Joint Commission, the U.S. Department of Veterans Affairs, and the American Civil Liberties Union.[31] They reflect the law as to confidentiality and consent and meet Bodenheimer's definition of a formal source of law but have no legal effect. They set an ethical tone for HSO relationships with those served. Bills of rights are only as effective as the organization's willingness to make them known and to develop processes that encourage and monitor their use.

Ethical Issues Affecting Governance and Management

Fiduciary Duty

The concept of fiduciary arose in Roman law. Fiduciary means that in certain relationships, someone in a position of superior knowledge and authority and in whom trust is reposed has unique duties. This person is a fiduciary. Ethically (and legally), fiduciary duties arise in relationships such as physician–patient, priest–penitent, attorney–client, and professor–student. Fidelity (an element of respect for persons), beneficence, and nonmaleficence underpin the ethical aspects of fiduciary duty.

Governing body members of for-profit and not-for-profit corporations are fiduciaries and have special obligations.[32] Fiduciaries have primary duties of loyalty and responsibility:

> Loyalty means that the individuals must put the interest of the corporation above all self-interest, a principle based on the biblical doctrine that no man can serve two masters. Specifically, no trustee is permitted to gain any secret profits personally, to accept bribes, or to compete with the corporation.[33]

Fiduciary duty means that in governance activities, governing body members must exercise reasonable care, skill, and diligence in proportion to the circumstances, and can be held personally liable for gross negligence, which can result from acts of commission or omission.[34]

Trustees are fiduciaries responsible for assets held in trust. The law holds them to a very high standard. Trustees may not use their position for personal gain and must act only in the best interests of the beneficiary of the trust. Governing body members of not-for-profit HSOs/HSs may use the title *trustee,* though they are not true trustees. Unless they are fiduciaries of a trust, the technically correct legal term is *director* or *corporate director.*

Conflicts of Interest

General Considerations

Activities with potential for conflicts of interest are rife in HSOs/HSs. A conflict of interest occurs when someone has multiple obligations that demand loyalty, and decisions based on these loyalties are different or in conflict. The element of fidelity (promise keeping) assists in ethical analysis of conflicts of interest. The principles of beneficence and nonmaleficence provide an ethical framework to analyze conflicts of interest.

The ACHE code states only that the healthcare executive shall "avoid financial and other conflicts of interest," an admonition that provides little guidance. "Matter of degree" is useful guidance in determining that a duality of interests has devolved into a presumptive conflict of interest. No conflict of interest is likely if a vendor buys an inexpensive lunch for a manager. An expense-paid, 2-week vacation is presumptive of a conflict of interest. Large gifts are presumed to encourage or reward specific behavior. Extravagant gifts from vendors and self-dealing by executives are easily defined as conflicts of interest. Most are subtler, however.

Is it ethical for a manager to use a position of influence or power to gain personal aggrandizement of titles and position at the expense of patient care? Is it ethical for a manager to be lax in implementing an effective patient consent process? Is it ethical for an executive to keep negative information about management's performance from the governing body? Is it ethical for a manager who believes there are quality-of-care problems in a clinical department to ignore them? Is it ethical for managers who have concerns about their personal ability to meet the demands of their position to remain in it? The conflicts of interest suggested by such questions can be identified and understood through continued questioning and self-analysis.

Managing Care

The duality of interests when care is managed has an inherent potential for conflicts of interest. The goals, purposes, and objectives (the interests) of persons managing care likely differ from those of members. Both want a financially strong, well-functioning organization that meets member needs in a timely and effective manner. Beyond this congruence, divergence is likely.

Marketing and Operations

The tension among those managing care and members and potential members begins when benefit packages and market segments are identified. For example, is marketing that focuses on healthy, low-risk persons ethical?[35] As a bureaucracy, those managing the organization and its physicians and staff seek to maximize position, power, income, and other rewards with least disruption of homeostasis. Achieving those goals, especially maximizing income, may minimize service even if this is inconsistent with mission or contracts. Marketing must decide if it should "keep its light under a bushel." An organization known as a leader in treating certain medical conditions may be overwhelmed by adverse selection if large numbers of persons with, or at risk of, that medical condition enroll.

Utilization

Service use has the greatest potential for conflicts of interest. Here, enrollees may be divided into appropriate users and over users. The organization's interests and those of appropriate users are congruent. To be competitive, over users must be controlled. Even appropriate users may be a financial threat in a competitive environment. To trim costs, the organization may encourage underuse. This duality of interests may result in a conflict of interest.

Physician Incentives and Disincentives

Members must be concerned about subtle and possibly serious constraints affecting physicians. There are numerous dual interests among the organization and its members and physicians. The Hippocratic tradition directs physicians to act only in their patients' best interests. Physician treatment decisions are facilitated or inhibited by the organization's procedures.

Physicians face numerous behavior-modifying guidelines: limits on referrals (especially out of plan) and hospitalization, financial disincentives (and incentives), quotas on numbers of patients seen (used in staff-model health maintenance organizations), and peer review. Undesirable physician practice patterns may cause various actions. In order of increasing severity, they include data-based peer pressure, letters of warning or admonition, economic incentives or disincentives, nonrenewal, and dismissal. Positive constraints encourage judicious resource use.

Further, the organization may forgo purchase of high-technology diagnostic and treatment equipment, or it may contract with physicians or hospitals without such technology. Both strategies reduce costs. Lower costs that enhance financial integrity and support availability of services make the organization's and members' interests congruent. This strategy has no advantage for those who might benefit from an unavailable technology. To them it suggests a conflict of interest. When are constraints excessive and members deprived of *needed* services? How are *wanted* services to be paid? When do constraints infringe on the principles of nonmaleficence and beneficence? Such questions defy simple answers. Constraints are a function of the organization's willingness, prompted by its managers acting as moral agents, to use safeguards that balance competitiveness and financial viability with members' needs.

Minimizing Conflicts of Interest in Managed Care

A first step in preventing or minimizing conflicts of interest is to acknowledge the many dual interests present in relationships among the organization and its members and physicians. Awareness is key. In addition, verification is needed. An ombudsman or consumer relations specialist can assist members to receive services. Procedures to review members' concerns are needed. Utilization data and interorganizational comparisons will show appropriate use.[36] These types of activities help managers meet their ethical obligations to patients.

Confidential Information

HSOs/HSs are rife with confidential information about patients, staff, and the organization. Managers are ethically and legally bound to use this information properly. Conflicts of interest occur if confidential information is used to benefit a manager or others with whom the manager is associated or related, or to harass or injure. Examples of misusing confidential information include disclosing governing body decisions so advantageous sales or purchases can be made by the insider's associates; selling or giving patient information to the media or attorneys; and disclosing the organization's marketing strategy to competitors. An example with problems of conflicts of interest *and* confidential information is when a manager serves on the governing body of a planning agency or competing HSO/HS. Fidelity to one's HSO/HS conflicts with the duty to objectively consider another HSO's certificate of need, for example. Also, the manager becomes privy to information important to that manager's HSO/HS. Duality of interests and antitrust law make cooperating with other HSOs/HSs problematic.

Ethics and Marketing

HSOs/HSs are social enterprises with economic dimensions, not economic enterprises with social dimensions. Regardless, HSOs/HSs market—and did so long before "marketing" became acceptable. Marketing occurs in the physicians' hospital lounge, at health fairs, at new employee orientation, and in press releases. Applying the 4 *P*s of marketing—product, price, place, and promotion—to health services is easy; HSOs/HSs find service, consideration, access, and promotion (SCAP) more appropriate. Competition makes marketing a necessity.

Marketing and advertising raise questions as to how HSOs/HSs meet their ethical obligation to serve those potentially in need of a service while avoiding creating unnecessary demand. Previously, AHA's guidance on advertising stated that "healthcare organizations implement their advertising with fairness, honesty, accuracy, and sensitivity to the special trust that exists between patients and healthcare providers."[37] That guidance was replaced by a policy on use of social media by AHA's staff and member hospitals.[38]

Responsible marketing is a vital, if elusive, concept. HSOs/HSs whose focus is return on investment view marketing and competition differently from those with more charitable goals. To be responsible means tempering customers' desires and potential demand for a service with objective judgments of its value and usefulness. HSO/HS decision makers must determine which expenditures are of most benefit to population health consistent with the mission and their expertise as providers. This approach has a strong element of paternalism, however.

Biomedical Ethical Issues

Resource Allocation

Both macro and micro resource allocation embody the principle of justice. They necessitate decisions about who has access to what, when, and how. Value-laden criteria, such as worth, usefulness, merit, and need, are common. Government involvement portends political motives. HSOs/HSs use macroallocation criteria for equipment purchases and whether to offer a service line or program. Microallocation includes physicians' willingness to refer, patients' geographic access to services and technologies, and economic considerations. Often, micro-level decisions are guided (predetermined) by government policy, or by HSOs/HSs. Often, the "greatest good" (utility) principle of utilitarianism is used; this is only a partial answer. The principles of utility allow decision makers to diminish or ignore considerations of need, fairness, and justice.

Allocation theories vary. At one end of a continuum is egalitarianism. It posits that all persons must have equal health services. Hyperegalitarianism denies services unavailable to all to any. At the other end of that continuum is the theory that health services are not a right guaranteed by society but a privilege to be earned. This hyperindividualistic position holds that caregivers have no obligation to provide services but may choose to do so. Between the extremes is a view that society should encourage, develop, and provide health services in some situations. A macroallocation theory formulated by Charles Fried suggests that a "decent minimum" (routine services) should be available to all; high technology services are limited in several ways and are provided differently.[39] Microallocation—allocation to persons—theories of exotic lifesaving services were formulated by James Childress and Nicholas Rescher. They detail how (by what criteria) to make decisions about who gets what. Both start with medical criteria to determine need and appropriateness for treatment. Then they diverge.[40] It is rare that HSOs/HSs address ethical issues of resource allocation in an organized, prospective manner. Having criteria for decisions shows the public the system of allocation is fair. In 2020, the COVID-19 pandemic, later called severe acute respiratory syndrome coronavirus 2 (SARS-CoV-2), raised resource allocation questions regarding mechanical ventilators and ICU beds.[41]

Consent

Ethical Aspects

Ethics and law treat consent similarly. Ethics is more demanding. Consent began at law to protect the right to be free from nonconsensual touching. Ethicists expanded the legal concept of consent, named it autonomy, included it in the principle of respect for persons (and self-determination), and found it reflected in the special relationship of trust and confidence (fiduciary relationship) between physician and patient. Consent reflects Kant's views of the equality of human beings. Ethically and legally, consent must be voluntary, competent, and informed. Ethically, HSOs should independently determine that these criteria are met.

Legal Aspects

Failing to obtain consent can lead to legal action for battery, an intentional tort. In addition, an action for negligence can be brought if physicians breach the duty to communicate informa-tion the patient needs to decide.[42] Consent is implied when someone seeks treatment; consent is implied in emergencies. Elective, routine treatment requires general consent; special consent is needed for invasive, surgical, experimental, or unusual procedures. The law requires that consent is voluntary, competent, and informed.

> *Voluntary:* Consent is given without duress that substantially affects the decision. Prisoners are not independent; ethically they cannot give voluntary consent to participate in medi-cal research, for example. Voluntariness is lessened if inducements are so great a person is imprudent or incautious. Similarly, even small inducements may reduce voluntariness—starving persons will agree to risky medical experiments if offered food. Beyond obvious problems, "voluntariness" is elusive. A patient may feel duress to accept the physician's recommendations—they fear losing the physician's goodwill. Patients are influenced by family and friends and may be persuaded (coerced) to accept (or reject) treatment. One's freedom in medical decisions may be only that of refusing treatment.[43]

> *Competent:* The patient knows the nature and consequences of what is contemplated or the decision to be made. The law presumes an unemancipated minor is incompetent, as is an individual with a mental illness or a developmental disability.

> *Informed:* References to "informed consent" may suggest it is the only criterion. The legal standard for consent that is *informed* requires disclosing the condition to be treated, signifi-cant facts about it, and an explanation of likely consequences. This standard was based on the information a reasonable physician would give in the same or similar circumstances. By comparison, ethical criteria suggest more active patient participation. Criteria developed by the President's Commission for the Study of Ethical Problems in Medicine and Biomedical and Behavioral Research state patient sovereignty with complete participation in the pro-cess is preferred. It noted this goal is not easily achieved.[44] Most courts use a standard based on what a reasonable patient wants to know. A legal criterion reflecting patient sovereignty is used in some states: "What would *this* patient want to know?

End-of-Life Decisions

As technology advanced, the historical definition of death as cessation of blood circula-tion and circulation-dependent animal and vital functions, such as respiration and pulsation (heartbeat), became inadequate. A 1968 Harvard Medical School committee definition of irreversible coma was an important first step in redefining death.[45] The criteria were use-ful, but the President's Commission found them deficient.[46] Since the mid-1990s, all states have recognized alternate definitions of death: 1) irreversible cessation of circulatory and respiratory functions *or* 2) irreversible cessation of all functions of the entire brain, includ-ing the brain stem (brain death). At this writing, 37 states and the District of Columbia have enacted the Uniform Determination of Death Act, which incorporates these criteria for determining death.[47]

Life-Sustaining Treatment

Decisions about life-sustaining treatment are where ethics and law converge. Hospitals and nursing facilities (NFs) face ethical issues about withholding or withdrawing life-sustaining treatment. In the past, risk of legal liability made HSOs reluctant to withdraw life support absent court approval. In *Cruzan v. Director, Missouri Department of Health* (1990),[48] the

U.S. Supreme Court ruled on life-sustaining treatment. Nancy Cruzan had been in a persistent vegetative state (PVS) since a 1983 automobile accident. She was a patient in a Missouri state hospital, where a gastrostomy tube had been inserted for nutrition and hydration. Cruzan's parents sued after the facility refused to remove the tube. The Court held that the U.S. Constitution does not prevent Missouri from requiring "clear and convincing evidence" that an incompetent person in PVS would not wish to be kept alive artificially. The court distinguished competent persons, who have a constitutionally protected right to refuse life-sustaining hydration and nutrition, from incompetent persons. Adopting a "clear and convincing evidence" standard gave states broad latitude to protect and preserve life. At a hearing, Cruzan's parents offered new evidence as to their daughter's wishes. The feeding tube was removed; Cruzan died in a few days.

Advance Medical Directives

Patient participation in and control of healthcare decisions were enhanced when the federal Patient Self-Determination Act ([PSDA] PL 101-508) took effect in 1991. The PSDA requires that HSOs participating in Medicare and Medicaid give all patients written information as to their rights under state law to accept or refuse treatment and to formulate advance medical directives (AMDs).[49] Medical records must document a patient's AMD, and the HSO must educate staff and community about AMDs. The PSDA may have increased use of AMDs among NF residents. Despite PSDA and widespread state legislation, most patients do not have an AMD.[50] AMDs may be called advance care plans.

Living Wills

Since the 1960s living wills have allowed persons to communicate their wishes as to medical treatment before they reach a point at which they cannot do so. In theory, living wills allow patients to control what happens to them medically. Absent legislation or case law, however, living wills have no legal status; caregivers must be willing to follow their directives.

Natural Death Act Statutes

Interest in living wills and public reaction to seemingly excessive treatment led to state laws codifying the right of competent adults to control treatment. As a basic liberty right, competent adults may refuse any or all medical intervention. The "right to say no" should not be confused with demands to continue treatment absent hope of benefit; there is no such positive right. This is an instance in which ethics (autonomy) and law merge. Common titles for natural death act statutes are *living will laws, natural death acts,* or *death with dignity laws.* All states have laws recognizing AMDs.[51] Each state's AMD form is available online.[52]

Natural death act statutes codify a competent person's right to direct caregivers as to extent and types of treatment, including withholding or withdrawing life-sustaining treatment. If statutory requirements are met, caregivers must follow the AMD. Statutes may be narrow and apply only if a physician determines a patient is terminally ill with no prospect for recovery. Some states require reaffirmation of AMDs when persons are terminally ill. State courts interpret AMD laws as to control (autonomy); roles of proxies, patients, and families; and HSO and provider actions.

Problems with Use of AMDs

Data about use of AMDs are not encouraging. Only a third of patients complete AMDs; most do so only after a major hospital event.[53] Only 12% of patients with AMDs are asked about preferences for end-of-life care; 70% of physicians were unaware their patients had AMDs.[54] A meta-analysis of studies published 2011–2016 found advance care completion rates of about one third.[55] AMDs may be unused because caregivers are unaware of them or disagree with provisions, or because families intervene. Care in other HSOs complicates use; AMDs at an NF may be unavailable if a resident is hospitalized. HSOs must encourage completion of AMDs. Persons being hospitalized are more likely to complete an AMD if they receive information before admission.[56] Reminders, education, and feedback to attending physicians increase how many patients have AMDs.[57] Family physicians may be an unused resource to increase the number of persons with AMDs.[58] Limitations in the extent and depth of the physician–patient relationship appear to be the most frequent impediments to writing do-not-resuscitate (DNR) orders.[59]

Substituted Judgment

Surrogates make decisions for persons who lack decision-making capacity. By 2018, 42 states and the District of Columbia allowed surrogate decision making for a person without an AMD.[60] Powers of attorney (POAs) are another type of decision making by surrogates. These delegations of authority are prospective and may be general or limited. POAs are "durable" if the authority continues beyond the time the grantor becomes incompetent. By 2004, all states and the District of Columbia allowed appointment of healthcare agents using durable POAs.[61]

Do-Not-Resuscitate Orders

The DNR order is a type of AMD. Patients without a DNR order are presumed to want a "full code," or maximum cardiopulmonary resuscitation (CPR). Despite best efforts, CPR is rarely successful. Its violence may cause collateral damage, including broken ribs and internal injuries, especially in the frail elderly.[62] Patients may require surgery and anesthesia for palliation, to relieve pain or stress, or to improve quality of life. As noted, it is vital that physicians understand and support patient wishes about CPR.

Prehospital DNR orders allow persons to refuse resuscitation in medical emergencies. They are known as emergency medical services (EMS) DNR orders, EMS-DNRs, or durable DNRs. They give legal effect to the patient's decisions about treatment outside the hospital. By 2018, 50 states and the District of Columbia had authorized nonhospital DNR orders. Special forms, wristbands, and registries are used to document a person's wishes.[63]

Summary

Widespread use of AMDs may encourage rationing of healthcare, especially to the elderly. The right to decline treatment must not become a duty to die. Government attention to AMDs suggests a greater concern with economics than with autonomy. Managers must foster policies that respect patient wishes, consistent with organizational values.

Euthanasia

The Hippocratic tradition prohibited physicians from giving a deadly drug. *Euthanasia* (Greek for "good death" [*eu* and *thanatos*]) was care that made an inevitable death pain free. In contemporary use, however, *euthanasia* describes mercy killing—active steps to cause death. There is an important ethical distinction between intervening to hasten death and providing palliation that allows pain-free, dignified death as the natural course of a disease.

Ordinary versus Extraordinary Care

Ordinary and *extraordinary* do not mean usual and unusual, respectively. Instead, the measure is hope of benefit compared with excessive expense, pain, or other inconvenience. Absent hope of benefit, *any* medicine, treatment, or operation is extraordinary. If there is hope of benefit, using the same medicine, treatment, or operation is not excessive and is ordinary.

Comparing benefits and burdens is another way to judge treatment. *Proportionate* and *disproportionate*—may be more descriptive than *ordinary* and *extraordinary*. Proportionate and disproportionate care are measured like ordinary and extraordinary care. Type of treatment and its complexity or risk, cost, and appropriateness are studied and compared with the results expected, considering someone's health and physical and moral resources.[64] With this calculus, treatment is ethical if the benefit justifies the burden. These comparisons are qualitative. In sum, they ask, Does the benefit justify the burden?

Types of Euthanasia

Euthanasia has four permutations: voluntary active (consenting person is killed), voluntary passive (person consents to allow natural death [AND]), involuntary active (nonconsenting person is killed), and involuntary passive (nonconsenting person is AND). *Voluntary* means the person has consented freely. *Involuntary* means the person has not consented freely or cannot consent freely but is presumed to want to die. *Active* means steps are taken to cause death (killing). *Passive* means death is not hastened—the natural course of the disease causes death. Passive euthanasia always includes palliative care.

Physician-Assisted Suicide

Background

Also called "aid in dying," physician-assisted suicide (PAS) is not euthanasia. PAS is similar to voluntary, active euthanasia, but there is a critical difference. PAS occurs when a physician provides the means, medical advice, and (sometimes) assurance death will result. The person performs the act that causes death. Broadly defined, PAS is *eu thanatos;* it relieves suffering and is intended to be pain free. The physically disabled need help to perform PAS, which is then voluntary, active euthanasia. It was unethical in the Hippocratic tradition to deliberately cause death. Lacking further treatment, physicians were expected to "comfort always."

Dr. Death

The first widely publicized PAS occurred in 1990 when Janet Adkins, 54, who had Alzheimer's disease, was aided in her suicide by Jack Kevorkian, a retired Michigan pathologist. Known to critics as Dr. Death, Dr. Kevorkian gained prominence using a device that enabled persons wishing to commit suicide to self-administer chemicals, after initial help from a physician.[65] The case focused public attention on active, voluntary euthanasia and aid in dying. After assisting in over 100 suicides, Dr. Kevorkian was convicted of second-degree murder and served 8 years in prison. As context, a substantial proportion of physicians receive requests for aid in dying. About 6% have complied at least once.[66]

Legal Aspects of PAS

At this writing, PAS is legal in seven states and the District of Columbia.[67] Oregon legalized PAS in 1997; its law is paradigmatic. Physicians in these states may prescribe, but *not* administer, fatal doses of oral drugs to competent, terminally ill adults with fewer than 6 months to live. The physician's role is much less active than was Dr. Kevorkian's. The Blue Cross and Blue Shield plans of Oregon began covering PAS in early 1998.[68] In late 1998, the Oregon Health Plan (Medicaid patients) added PAS to end-of-life palliative care and hospice.[69] From 1998 to 2017, 1,275 Oregonians were assisted in suicides. In 2017, assisted suicides accounted for about 0.4% of all deaths in Oregon.[70]

Physicians and PAS

Many physicians regard providing active assistance in dying as turning medicine on its head—those who traditionally guarded life are asked to help end it. Historically, organized medicine has condemned physicians who provided aid in dying. Domestic survey findings suggest this reaction is overstated. In a 2016 survey, 57% of U.S. physicians responded that physician-assisted suicide or physician-assisted dying should be allowed for patients who are terminally ill. In 2010, 46% of physicians favored such actions. Support did not vary by sex of physician.[71] Aid in dying raises moral questions about reexamination of the physician–patient relationship. In addition, there is evidence that physician participation in assisted suicide or euthanasia may have profound, harmful effects on the physicians involved.[72]

International Comparisons

Assisted suicide has been available in parts of Switzerland since 1942; increasingly, it is a destination for "suicide tourists."[73] In 2002, Belgium legalized voluntary euthanasia and assisted suicide with a law similar to one in the Netherlands.[74] Soon after, Belgian lawmakers proposed expanding euthanasia to children under 18.[75] PAS and euthanasia are being debated elsewhere in Europe, notably Spain and France. A 2012 survey in France found that 89% favored or tolerated euthanasia.[76] In 2016, France began granting terminally ill persons a right to continuous deep sedation (CDS) until death. CDS is an alternative to euthanasia—the "French response" to end-of-life problems. The law distinguishes CDS from euthanasia and other end-of-life symptom control. France is the first country to enact CDS.[77]

The vanguard of assisted dying in Europe is the Netherlands. Despite being illegal, euthanasia and PAS have been practiced there since the 1980s; 92% of the population supports euthanasia.[78] Euthanasia and PAS were made legal in 1993; their use is expanding.[79] In 2011, euthanasia deaths in the Netherlands increased by 18%. This follows increases of 13% in 2009 and 19% in 2010.[80] In 2005, Dutch health ministry guidelines known as the Groningen (University Medical Center) Protocol allowed euthanasia of children (including newborns) when "a child is terminally ill with no prospect of recovery and suffering great pain, when two sets of doctors agree the situation is hopeless, and when parents give consent."[81] The Groningen protocol has been roundly criticized by disability rights groups[82] and others.[83] That a Western European democracy so willingly accepts active (voluntary *and* involuntary) euthanasia raises ethical questions. The Dutch experience shows active euthanasia, seemingly begun to enhance individual self-determination, is not limited to those requesting it. The number of persons involuntarily, actively euthanized highlights the slippery slope, defined as one exception leading to other, more easily accepted exceptions.

HSOs/HSs and Ethical Issues

None of Dr. Kevorkian's "work" occurred in an HSO. Similarly, the Oregon statute has no role for them. Regardless, HSOs often face ethical issues at the end of life and may be asked to provide aid in dying. An NF, for example, may have a resident in PVS or a terminally ill resident too sick to transfer. The "conscience clause" found in state and federal laws protects caregivers and HSOs who refuse to participate in activities that compromise their ethics. The organizational philosophy of HSOs should prospectively address both voluntary and involuntary active euthanasia.

New forms of payment and organizational arrangements will change economic incentives, even as HSOs become less able to cover costs of services. Hospitals have already experienced a form of capitation in diagnosis-related groups, with their incentive to limit services. The increasing difficulty of cost shifting means HSOs/HSs must reduce costs through better quality or greater productivity, or by changing the content of care. When physicians were less affected by cost reduction, they counterbalanced any organizational effort to limit services. Traditional relationships are changing, however, and economically linking physician and HSO raises myriad ethical issues.

Futile Treatment

Background

In many ways, futility theory is old wine in new bottles. Its origins lie in the distinction between ordinary and extraordinary care, which are distinguished by "hope of benefit" and "excessive expense, pain, or other inconvenience." These distinctions make it ethical to withhold any medicine, treatment, or operation that offers no reasonable hope of benefit or that cannot be obtained or used without excessive expense, pain, or inconvenience.

Futility theory has quantitative and qualitative aspects. *Quantitative* is concerned with the *probability of success* were a treatment continued or attempted. Probability of success means the likelihood that the treatment can be successfully performed and can achieve its intended purpose. For example, tube feeding maintains the life of a patient in PVS; it will not restore cognition. This example highlights the importance of viewing care as a continuum, not an isolated event.

Qualitative assumes successful treatment that achieves its intended purpose but asks if the result is such that treatment *ought* to be undertaken. The quantitative determination is made by clinical experts. The qualitative determination (judgment) must be made by the patient or surrogate. The concept of futility in its quantitative expression limits the qualitative decision.

Three basic variations of circumstances raise questions of futile treatment. The first is patients demand services that offer no hope of benefit. Absent supporting data, these situations may be urban myth or misperception. Generally, AMDs limit medical intervention, although they may request services clinicians deem futile.

The second type occurs when treatment is continued because surrogates demand it. An example is Helga Wanglie, a Minneapolis woman in PVS whose husband demanded all efforts to keep her alive, despite a prognosis that doing so offered no hope of benefit.

A third type of futile treatment occurs when HSOs insist on providing treatment that surrogates and physicians have determined offers no hope of benefit and should end.

Futile Treatment Guidelines
It is likely that acute care hospitals will have futile-treatment guidelines or policies. Their use has been stimulated by perceptions that patients and/or surrogates demand treatment clinicians deem to have little, if any, likelihood of benefiting the patient. Consent and autonomy drive the initial phases of decision making for patients able to participate. They should receive the information to make informed choices about treatment or nontreatment options. Patients bear the brunt of continuing treatment that is futile, a fact that likely makes them more willing than surrogate decision makers to limit what is done. Patients and surrogates may have unrealistic goals or expectations of medical science. If treatment is futile, clinicians have a moral obligation to withhold or withdraw it. Guidelines for withholding or withdrawing life-sustaining treatment usually require agreement of attending *and* consulting physicians that it is futile.

Decisions about appropriateness of continued medical treatment are made in the context of the purposes of medical care. Generally, the goals of treatment are to cure, restore, improve, or maintain some level of a person's ability to think, feel, and interact with others and the environment. Medical interventions with little likelihood of achieving any of these treatment goals can be considered futile.

Futile-treatment guidelines or policies should emphasize that physicians have no moral (or legal) obligation to provide treatment they judge inappropriate. Physicians' professional integrity is compromised, and they fail to meet their duty to their patients if they provide treatment that has neither benefit nor hope of benefit. Physicians fail, too, in their ethical obligation to use resources parsimoniously if futilely ill patients consume them.

Examples of futile treatment include ventilator support for a patient who meets brain death criteria, CPR for a patient with metastatic end-stage cancer or a patient with multiple organ failure, and aggressive therapies for a patient who is comatose or in PVS.

Common steps in futile treatment guidelines at the facility level include the following:

1. Attending physician determines current or proposed treatment is/will be futile.

2. Attending physician's determination is confirmed by consulting physician(s).

3. Patient/surrogate is told treatment is futile; will be stopped/will not be started.

4. If patient/surrogate agrees, suitable orders are written.

5. If patient/surrogate disagrees, ethics committee consult is requested.

6. Ethics committee determines futile treatment process has been followed.

7. Process okay—ethics committee negotiates with parties for an acceptable result.

8. If negotiation is unsuccessful an outside mediator tries to resolve the dispute.

9. If mediation fails, patient/surrogate is informed treatment will be stopped/will not be started.

10. Patient/surrogate given several days to find alternative facility for transfer.

11. Failing to find alternative facility, futile treatment is stopped or given a limited trial.

The ethics committee is significant here. Dialogue is emphasized. The mediator is a neutral who works with the parties, so they agree as to the course of treatment, or its discontinuation. A likely result of mediation is that the parties agree to a limited trial of continued treatment. This assures all involved that the patient has a chance to benefit from treatment that might have a good result. Comforting to all is that there is no abrupt discontinuation of treatment.

All but five states give physicians and hospitals latitude in refusing to provide end-of-life treatment that is futile.[84] In Virginia, for example, families have 14 days to find another facility that will accept the patient. Despite such laws, however, it is doubtful either physicians or hospitals will refuse to provide futile treatment, except after considerable continued treatment and when the prognosis is beyond challenge. The potential for accusations that passive, involuntary euthanasia is occurring or that patients are being treated cruelly or killed is too great.

Guidelines encourage physicians to address futile treatment. Frank discussions with patients or surrogates may allow futile treatment to be withheld or withdrawn. By informing patients or surrogates of their moral objection to continuing medically inappropriate (and harmful) treatment, physicians may gain assent without invoking futile treatment guidelines. The "transfer out" option is likely not viable but is useful to convince decision makers how seriously physicians view the problem. Practically, patients may be too ill to transfer; as likely, no facility will accept them. The concept of futile treatment has its critics, however.[85]

Organizational Responses to Ethical Problems

How do HSOs/HSs organize to solve administrative and biomedical ethical problems? The starting point is the organizational philosophy, which reflects the values of the HSO/HS. It establishes moral direction and a framework for the vision and mission. The personal ethic of the manager as a leader influences the organizational philosophy and is influenced by it. Ethical problem solving occurs in the context of the organizational philosophy, but it is affected by the manager's personal ethic, which is likely to be more specific and comprehensive. This dynamic reinforces the importance of the personal ethic of organizational leadership. The organization's philosophy is subject to the external constraints of civil and criminal laws and regulations that represent a minimum standard. External constraints, such as the "conscience clause" discussed earlier, support the values of HSOs and their staffs. Federal guidelines that protect human research subjects are the starting point for an HSO's relationship with persons who participate in research.

Means to Resolve Ethics Issues

From the 1970s, HSOs/HSs began to develop specific means to address ethical problems. Most common are institutional ethics committees (IECs), institutional review boards (IRBs), and infant care review committees (ICRCs). IECs provide a broad range of assistance on administrative and biomedical ethical issues. IRBs are specialized IECs that focus on preventing and solving ethical issues in research. ICRCs are specialized IECs that prevent and solve ethical issues that arise in caring for infants with profound impairment.

Institutional Ethics Committees

Before beginning work, the IEC should develop a statement of its ethic within the framework of the organizational philosophy (value system). Doing so identifies and minimizes differences in members' personal ethic and facilitates effectiveness. Understanding and enunciating its own ethic enables the IEC to appreciate how its values differ from the patient's. The IEC's ethic does not determine how ethical problems are solved. Rather, its general principles are a framework for deliberations and recommendations.

IECs perform generic activities, such as developing and reconsidering the organizational philosophy, policy development, education, and guidance for staff and patients. Specific activities include case consultation, reviewing consent procedures, considering macroallocation of resources, whistleblowing, developing DNR policies, and advising on futile treatment.

Membership of IECs

IECs should be, and typically are, interdisciplinary. Physicians and nurses are the most common members. Others are governing board and community members, risk managers, attorneys, clergy, and administrators. More than half of IEC members are women.[86]

Relationships of IECs

IECs are more effective if they wait to be consulted rather than interposing themselves. Consultation means making recommendations, not final decisions. IEC participation in biomedical and administrative decisions may be optional or mandatory. Whether IEC advice must be followed could be optional or mandatory too. Table 2.1 shows the combinations. Physicians are unlikely to accept mandatory involvement of IECs if the advice they give is mandatory (i.e., must be followed). Even physicians unwilling to share clinical decisions with an IEC will benefit from its analysis and recommendations.

The administrative location of the IEC is important. It may be a standing committee of the governing body, professional staff organization, or administration. Physician dominance of a clinical IEC may be avoided by making the committee part of governance or administration.

Summary

IECs are not without problems. Organizational interests, especially legal aspects and avoiding public embarrassment, may overwhelm patient goals.[87] At the extreme, it is suggested that IECs cannot be objective because they are part of the HSO/HS. This may cause them to fail as patient advocates because, when a dispute arises, they will take the side of management to avoid risk.[88] Management must ensure IECs are not subverted in this manner. Overall, an effective IEC will improve clinical and administrative decisions. It should not be assumed that the mere presence of an IEC means it is successful or useful. IECs must be evaluated to improve their performance.[89]

Table 2.1. Optional versus Mandatory Use of an Institutional Ethics Committee

Involvement of IEC in decision making	Acceptance and use of advice given by IEC
Optional	Optional
Optional	Mandatory
Mandatory	Optional
Mandatory	Mandatory

Institutional Review Boards

Background

To protect human subjects, HSOs conducting research should establish an IRB, which is an independent committee composed of scientific and nonscientific members that meets the requirements of federal law.[90] IRBs conduct initial and continued review of research involving human subjects. The Department of Health and Human Services (DHHS) and the U.S. Food and Drug Administration (FDA) are the most important federal entities that require an IRB to review, approve, and maintain oversight of research. DHHS requirements for IRBs and protection of human subjects are applicable to research funded by any of 17 federal agencies and departments that use the "common rule" or "federal policy" for the protection of human subjects (i.e., research supported or conducted by and regulated under a specific research statute).[91] Federal entities using DHHS rules include the Department of Defense, Veterans Affairs, the Environmental Protection Agency, the National Science Foundation, and the Consumer Product Safety Commission.

Membership and Purpose

Institutions may choose specific IRB members, but federal regulations (and perhaps state law) govern membership, nature of review, and IRB members' conflicts of interest.[92] IRBs review research proposals for conformance with the law, standards of professional conduct and practice, and institutional commitment and regulations. IRBs acceptable to DHHS have at least five members of varying backgrounds (one with scientific professional interests and one whose interests are nonscientific) and who can review research proposals and activities commonly performed by the organization.[93]

IRBs must apply specific requirements when reviewing research activities:[94]

• Risks to subjects are minimized.

• Risks to subjects are reasonable relative to anticipated benefit, if any.

• Selection of research subjects is equitable.

• Informed consent is sought from each prospective subject or the subject's representative.

• Informed consent is appropriately documented.

• Research plan has provisions to monitor data collected to ensure safety of subjects.

• Research plan has provisions to protect privacy of subjects and maintain confidentiality of data.

Safeguards are needed if subjects are vulnerable to coercion or undue influence. Examples are children, prisoners, pregnant women, persons with mental disabilities, or persons with economic or educational disadvantages. Information needed for informed consent is identified.

Summary

Regulations such as DHHS's focus responsibility on the organization and its IRB. Regardless of the law, managers have independent ethical duties to protect research subjects under the principles of respect for persons, beneficence, nonmaleficence, and justice (i.e., fair allocation of research support). The virtues of honesty, integrity, and trustworthiness are applicable. Managers must establish and maintain systems and procedures to prevent unauthorized research and to provide extra protection when innovative treatment or surgical research is proposed or undertaken. Staff awareness of acceptable practice *and* the courage to act are key.

Infant Care Review Committees

ICRCs are specialized IECs whose focus is biomedical ethical problems of infants with life-threatening conditions. The Child Abuse Amendments of 1984 directed the DHHS to encourage establishment of ICRCs in health facilities, especially those with tertiary-level neo-natal units. Guidelines include the following: 1) educate hospital personnel and families of disabled infants with life-threatening conditions, 2) recommend institutional policies and guidelines concerning withholding medically indicated treatment from infants with life-threatening conditions, and 3) offer counsel and review in cases of infants with life-threatening conditions.[95]

The DHHS considers it prudent to establish an ICRC; the HSO decides whether to do so. The ICRC should be interdisciplinary, so it has the expertise to supply and evaluate information. Membership should include a practicing physician (e.g., pediatrician, neonatologist, pediatric surgeon), practicing nurse, hospital executive, social worker, representative of a disability group, lay community member, and a physician member of the professional staff, who is the chair.[96] The DHHS suggests staff support, including legal counsel. Hospital staff and families should know of its existence and functions. Case summaries, deliberations, and disposition should be kept.[97]

Specialized Assistance

Ethics Consultation Service

An ethics consultation service (ECS) uses specialized personnel to advise and assist in solving biomedical ethics problems. It is staffed by ethicists with graduate degrees in philosophy, of-ten at the doctoral level, and by clinical personnel who may be physicians or other caregivers with preparation in ethics. The clinicians are a bridge between the ethicist and clinical staff attending the patient and a resource for the ethicists. An ethicist is on call; a clinical member is involved, as needed. The ECS reports to the IEC, which is a sounding board for problems during ethics consultation.[98]

Ethicists

A less formal approach than an ECS is common in larger HSOs and HSs, which may employ full- or part-time ethicists. Like ECSs, ethicists may be doctorly qualified. They may be univer-sity or medical school faculty who consult on biomedical ethical issues. Here, as with the ECS, an ethicist is the clinically oriented, problem-solving extension of an IEC.

Dispute Resolution

Treatment options and decisions regarding them often cause disputes among stakeholders such as clinicians, patients, and families. The various ethics committees—IECs, IRBs, and ICRCs—may resolve disputes, but their connection with the HSO raises questions as to ob-jectivity. If so, arbitration and mediation should be considered. Arbitration uses a neutral to whom the parties have delegated authority to make a decision. Mediators are neutrals who work with the parties to reach a result acceptable to them. Unlike arbitrators, mediators have no authority to impose a decision. Neutrals minimize the power imbalance in health services settings.[99] Mediators were discussed earlier in the context of futile care.

Ethics Officer

An ethics officer facilitates an organization's focus on ethics issues by managing internal report-ing systems, assessing ethics risk areas, developing and distributing ethics policies and publi-cations, investigating alleged violations, and designing training programs. This senior-level executive can manage corporate compliance programs as well.[100]

Managers and the Law

Almost everything done in the delivery of health services is affected by statutes, regulations, and court decisions. As with ethics, health services managers who have a basic understanding of the law and its effects on the HSO/HS will be more aware of potential problems and be more effective in avoiding them.

Contracts

A contract is an agreement between two or more parties that identifies rights and obligations. The parties agree to do or not do certain things. The definition of formal law includes understandings (contracts) between private parties or between private parties and government. Decision makers in contract disputes look first to the generally applicable law and then interpret the private agreement within this context.

Elements of a Contract

A valid contract has several elements: 1) It is an agreement reached after an offer and acceptance for which 2) there is consideration (something of value) that is 3) reached by parties who have the legal capacity to contract and 4) the objective of which is lawful. This seems simple enough, but applying the elements of contracts has resulted in a vast body of statutes, regulations, and case law.

Even small HSOs have scores of contracts for goods and services. Examples are collective bargaining agreements and contracts to buy supplies, equipment, and consulting services; sell maintenance, laundry, or clinical services; and employ staff. Many transactions are not and need not be in writing; for example, a food service manager asks a produce market to supply vegetables, with payment on delivery. Oral contracts are treated differently from written contracts, however. Oral contracts may not be legally binding if they exceed a certain dollar amount or if their duration exceeds a certain length of time. Managerial control of contracting is maintained by using purchase orders that, when sent to the seller, constitute an *offer* to buy or, if sent in response to a previous offer to sell, constitute the *acceptance*. Increasingly, HSOs/HSs sell services. Hospitals sell laboratory services to physicians or contract to provide hospital services to health plan members. Visiting nurse agencies sell therapists' services to NFs. Services are usually offered at predetermined prices, although cost-plus contracts may be used.

Breach of Contract

When compared with the total number of contracts that HSOs/HSs execute annually, breaches of contract are rare. A breach of contract occurs when one of the parties fails to perform as promised. There are defenses when a breach of contract occurs. The contract may be impossible to perform because of destruction or unavailability of the subject matter, death or illness, or legal prohibition. Three types of remedies are available when "impossibility" is not an issue and there is simply a breach of contract: rescission for a material breach, specific performance, or damages. Rescission means the contract is null and void, and the parties are put into their original positions relative to each other, as far as possible. Specific performance requires the party in breach to do what was agreed in the contract. If neither rescission nor specific performance is the appropriate remedy, the aggrieved party may seek money damages.

Breaches of contract usually involve lawyers, legal fees, and often a trial, even if one party is clearly right and the other clearly wrong. Consequently, breaches should be avoided. An excellent preventive measure is to involve competent legal counsel in negotiating and drafting contracts. Binding arbitration is a common, low-cost means to resolve contract disputes. It is standard in commercial contracts and should be included in other types, as well.

Torts

Breach of Contract and Tort Distinguished

A principle of Anglo-American legal tradition is that persons are responsible for the harm they cause, whether they act intentionally or unintentionally (negligently). Such responsibility falls into the domains of both contract and tort obligations. *Tort* is derived from the Latin *tortus,* or *twisted*. As its use in standard English faded, *tortus* acquired a technical meaning in the law.[101] A tort is a civil wrong, other than a breach of contract, for which courts provide a remedy in the form of an action for damages.[102] To be successful, the action must include certain elements: there must be a duty, a breach of that duty, and resulting harm that is causally linked to the defendant.

Defendants may be liable for punitive damages in addition to actual damages, depending on their intent and the circumstances. Contract liability is distinguished from tort liability primarily by what is protected:

> The distinction between tort and contract liability, as between parties to a contract, has become an increasingly difficult distinction to make. It would not be possible to reconcile the results of all cases. The availability of both kinds of liability for precisely the same kind of harm has brought about confusion and unnecessary complexity. . . . Tort obligations are in general obligations that are imposed by law—apart from and independent of promises made and therefore apart from the manifested intention of the parties—to avoid injury to others. By injury here is meant simply the interference with the individual's interest or an interest of some other legal entity that is deemed worthy of legal protection. . . . Contract obligations are created to enforce promises which are manifestations not only of a present intention to do or not to do something, but also a commitment to the future. They are, therefore, obligations based on the manifested intention of the parties to a bargaining transaction.[103]

This statement suggests that breach of contract and tort are more easily distinguished in theory than in application. This is especially true in the breach of an implied warranty, a hybrid of contract and tort. In general, there is an implied warranty that goods are fit (merchantable) for their usual and customarily intended purposes.

> The doctrine of (strict) liability imposes liability on those responsible for defective goods which pose an unreasonable risk of injury and which do in fact result in injury, regardless of how much care was taken to prevent the dangerous defect. An important distinction has been made between products and services, and the doctrine does not normally apply to the latter. For example, in attempts to hold hospitals strictly liable for injuries caused by blood transfusions, courts generally have held that hospitals are providing a service and not in the business of selling blood; therefore, strict liability does not apply.[104]

The legal concept of implied warranty is widely applied to medical products and devices. Clearly, the legal distinction between products and services is important to health services providers.

Intentional Torts

Some torts result from intentional rather than negligent conduct. The actor's intent need not be hostile or result from a desire to harm; rather, there is an intent to "bring about a result which will invade the interests of another in a way that the law will not sanction."[105] The intentional torts most likely to affect HSOs include battery, defamation, false imprisonment, invasion of privacy, tortious interference in contractual obligations, wrongful discharge of an employee, and wrongful disclosure of confidential information. Assault is often linked to battery in criminal proceedings, but rarely in civil law. Assault must raise a reasonable apprehension of harmful or offensive contact and can occur without the physical touching necessary for battery. As noted, to be ethically acceptable, consent for treatment must be informed, voluntary, and competent. Legal requirements are similar. Consent is discussed here in the context of intentional torts, but a legal action regarding consent can arise in negligence, as well.

Written consent is rarely obtained for routine outpatient visits if no invasive or potentially dangerous medical treatment is rendered. Consent is presumed when treatment is sought; this is sufficient for routine care. Because significant medical treatment is likely, hospitals obtain written general consent for routine services when patients are admitted.

Nonroutine diagnostic, surgical, or other invasive procedures require special consent. Usually, an HSO's role in special consent is secondary and limited to obtaining the patient's signature on a form that authorizes it to participate in treatment ordered or rendered by physicians. For example, before admitting a patient to the hospital for surgery, the attending physician provides information the patient needs to give informed consent. This consent is recorded in the physician's office. After admission but before treatment, the hospital determines that the medical record includes the special consent signed by the patient verifying that the patient received an explanation of the treatment and gave consent. HSOs concerned with the ethics of consent independently determine that patients whose treatment requires special consent understand the treatment's nature and consequences as it was explained by the physician. This is ethically appropriate, but doing so exceeds the legal standard of care.

Important to informed consent are how much the patient must be told and the judgment made by the physician as to the patient's understanding. States apply three different legal standards to how much information the patient should be given: 1) that given by a reasonable physician, 2) that given to a reasonable patient, and 3) as a minority view, what this patient wants. The legal concept of therapeutic privilege allows physicians to withhold information if they judge the patient might be harmed by or engage in harmful behavior because of having the information.

In the future, the consent process may oblige physicians to divulge their own mental and physical health status, clinical experience and competence, outcomes for the procedure being contemplated, and if they have been sued for malpractice or disciplined for poor clinical work. It is difficult to argue that such information is unimportant to informed decision making. The law is evolving in that direction. At the forefront of a duty to disclose are *Behringer v. The Medical Center at Princeton* and *Doe v. Noe,*[106] which held that HIV-positive physicians have a duty to disclose that fact to their patients.

The earlier discussion of the ethical issues of consent suggested that myriad factors, including education, intellect, emotional status, and general physical and psychological conditions, make it difficult or even impossible for patients to give truly informed consent. Many patients put themselves in their physicians' hands and accept their recommendations, thus minimizing the burden of consent for both.

Negligence

Background

Negligence is defined as not doing something that a reasonable person who is guided by reasonable considerations which ordinarily regulate human affairs would do or doing something that a reasonable and prudent person would not do.[107] The test in health services is the actions or nonactions of a reasonable and prudent physician, nurse, manager, or governing body. As with the law of contracts, this seems straightforward, but volumes have been written to define and apply the concept of reasonable person. What the reasonable person would do is called the "standard of care." The standard of care is used to measure performance of the acts (actions) in question—the alleged negligence. If the plaintiff—the party who brought the lawsuit and must prove the allegations (bears the burden of proof)—convinces the finder of fact (a jury or judge) by a preponderance of the evidence that the acts (actions) deviated from the standard of care, the finder of fact will find for the plaintiff. *Preponderance of the evidence* refers to evidence that produces the stronger effect or impression, has a greater weight, and is more convincing as to its truth—its effect is greater. If the burden of proof is not met by a preponderance of the evidence, the finder of fact must find for the defendant.

The person who commits a tort is always liable for damages. Commonly, however, HSOs/HSs are named as defendants because of legal theories discussed later in the chapter. To be successful, a lawsuit for negligent medical conduct must meet four elements:

1.　The caregiver(s)—physician(s) or other care provider(s)—must have had a duty to provide care of a certain quality (standard of care).

2.　There must have been a breach of that duty—the care provided must have been less than the established standard for a reasonable provider of that type of care.

3. The breach of duty must have been a substantial factor in causing the harm (proximate cause).

4. The patient must have been injured.

Absent any element, the plaintiff cannot recover damages on a theory of negligence.

Duty

With few exceptions, laws in the United States place no positive duty on one person to aid another. This is true for physicians and other caregivers as well. Once a duty is established, however, care may be discontinued only if alternate provisions have been made and the patient is protected from harm. Abandonment is an intentional tort that supports a lawsuit.

Standard of Care

How is the standard that providers have a duty to provide services of a certain quality determined? The standard of care has evolved from a locality rule that used the provider's geographic location, to a broader standard using the practice in communities of similar size and medical resources, to the current expectation that providers must meet a national standard. In general, providers are held to the standard of care that could be reasonably expected of a minimally competent member of their specialty under similar circumstances, delivered with the same reasonable and ordinary care, skill, and diligence as those in good standing would ordinarily exercise in like cases. This "minimally competent test"[108] is a national standard. Because providers are of different types, using various theories about disease causation and cure, practitioners must meet the standards for their types of practice.

Breach

The breach of the standard of care is shown by testimony from persons able to testify as to what is normally expected of that type of practitioner delivering care with ordinary and reasonable care, skill, and diligence. This is done through expert witnesses. In addition, breach of the standard of care may be established by citing the treating physician's own statements, calling that physician as a hostile or adverse witness, using standard medical textbooks or similar sources, or invoking a doctrine known as *res ipsa loquitur* (the thing speaks for itself), which is a legal theory limited to specific circumstances. Sometimes the negligence is a matter of common knowledge, and expert testimony is not needed.

Proximate Cause

The third element necessary for negligent medical conduct—causation—has several aspects:

> In addition to proving that a physician was negligent, that is, failed to meet the standard of care, and that the patient was injured, a malpractice plaintiff must also prove that the injury resulted from the negligence. Although this element of proof is called "causation," the term has a different sense from that used in medicine. The law considers an injury to be caused by a negligent act if the injury would not have occurred but for the defendant's act, or if the injury was a foreseeable result of the negligent conduct. The legal cause of an injury is often termed the proximate cause. Note that the plaintiff need not prove that the negligent act caused the result, but only the strong likelihood that it did. Also, the negligence need not be the sole cause, but only a significant factor in the injury. It must be remembered that the purpose of a malpractice trial is not to convict the defendants of malpractice, but to decide whether the loss caused by the injury should be allocated to the defendants. The standards of proof are thus lower than for a criminal trial, for example.[109]

To solve questions of liability when two causes act together to bring about an event and either one of them alone would have brought the same result, some courts use the concept of substantial factor. Was the defendant's conduct a substantial factor in bringing about the injury? An example of substantial factor occurs when two physicians treat a patient essentially simultaneously in an emergency and both are negligent, so either could have caused the injury.

This concept was applied by the California Supreme Court in *Landeros v. Flood,* a medical malpractice case in which the defendant negligently failed to diagnose and report battered child syndrome to authorities. The plaintiff child was returned to the same environment, where continued battering caused further injuries. The court ruled that actors may be liable if their negligence is a substantial factor in causing injury and that they are not relieved of liability because of the intervening act of a third person if such act was reasonably foreseeable at the time of their negligent conduct.[110]

Injury

The finder of fact (a judge or a jury) must determine that the plaintiff was injured, the extent to which the injuries diminish quality of life or economic opportunities, and the costs the plaintiff will incur to meet the special needs that resulted from the injuries. Damages awarded to the plaintiff can be nominal, actual, and/or punitive. Nominal damages are paid when the plaintiff proves the case but cannot prove the extent of damages. Actual damages are awarded for past and future medical expenses and loss of income, as well as for physical pain and mental suffering. Plaintiffs are awarded punitive damages when the finder of fact determines the defendant should be punished. Punitive damages may be called exemplary damages. They are like a fine levied against a defendant in a criminal case. Punitive damages are appropriate when conduct has been reckless, willful, malicious, or grossly negligent.

TORTS AND HSOs/HSs

The previous discussion about torts emphasized the roles of persons who commit the civil wrong, intentionally or unintentionally (negligently). This section identifies and analyzes legal theories used to find liability against HSOs/HSs when there is an employment relationship or when physicians or other licensed independent practitioners (LIPs) are independent contractors. Two legal doctrines result in liability for HSOs/HSs: agency, and the general concept that organizations owe a duty to patients and others. The legal risk for HSOs/HSs has expanded greatly since the 1960s.

Historically, the legal doctrines of governmental immunity and charitable immunity allowed HSOs to avoid liability for employees' negligent acts. Governmental immunity derived from the sovereign power of a monarch to be free from civil actions. The doctrine of charitable immunity arose from the concept that assets of a charitable HSO were unacceptably threatened if actions for medical malpractice could be brought against them. Court decisions and statutes such as the Federal Tort Claims Act[111] have eroded the doctrines of charitable and governmental immunity; in some jurisdictions or circumstances, they have disappeared completely.

Agency and Corporate Liability

Agency

The master's responsibility for a servant's negligence was established in English common law. It is the basis for the law of agency and is embodied in the Latin phrase *respondeat superior* (let the master answer). Though not masters per se, principals are responsible for their agents' acts. The negligence of a servant or agent is imputed (vicarious liability) to the person best able to exercise control—the master or principal. An important pragmatic consideration underlying *respondeat superior* is that courts may search for a "deep pocket"; employers usually have one. This doctrine applies to HSO/HS employees acting within the scope of their employment. It has limited applicability to caregivers who are independent contractors—they exercise control over the means and methods of performing their tasks, rather than being controlled by the HSO/HS. Therefore, the legal theory of agency cannot be used to hold the HSO/HS liable for the negligent acts of independent contractors. Physicians are the most common type of independent contractor in HSOs. The legal doctrine of apparent or ostensible agency is applied if a patient wittingly or unwittingly believes the organization employs a caregiver who would otherwise be defined as an independent contractor. A reasonable person standard is used.

Corporate Liability

The other legal basis for liability of HSOs/HSs is the general theory that the HSO/HS owes a duty to patients (as well as to others, such as visitors) to protect them from harm. This is known as corporate liability, an area of tort law that expanded rapidly in the last third of the 20th century. In the past, this legal doctrine allowed recovery by patients and visitors who were injured because the HSO failed to keep buildings, grounds, and equipment in a safe condition. Further, the organization has a duty to take reasonable steps in selecting and retaining those who provide services as independent contractors. HSOs may be found liable for the negligence of their independent contractor physicians using legal theories, such as nondelegable duties by contract, or by statute, joint venture, agency, or apparent or ostensible agency.[112]

Merged Concepts

Southwick has concluded that the two concepts of organizational liability for malpractice found in agency and corporate liability have almost become one:

> It should . . . be acknowledged that in the hospital setting there is no longer a viable distinction between the rules of *respondeat superior,* on one hand, and corporate or independent negligence, on the other. Essentially, the two theories have become one. In the delivery of healthcare services in an institutional setting it is increasingly difficult to determine factually who is in control of whom. As allied healthcare professionals proliferate and are accorded a greater degree of independence from the direct supervision and control of the attending physician, the matter of the right to control another's actions becomes a very difficult question both as a matter of fact and of law. It therefore becomes necessary to place either sole or joint liability upon the institution which, in the final analysis, is ultimately responsible for arranging, providing, and coordinating the activities of a host of professional individuals, all of whom must work together in the care of patients.[113]

The evolution of this legal doctrine has major implications for HSOs/HSs. They are not yet guarantors of the results of medical treatment, but the law is moving toward unequivocal accountability for activities that fall below the standard of care. HSOs use quality assessment, continuous quality improvement, and risk management to establish and maintain quality. These concepts are considered in Chapters 4, 8, and 14.

Enterprise Liability

Enterprise liability is not new. It includes strict liability and corporate liability discussed earlier, and no-fault liability yet to be discussed. Also known as organizational liability, enterprise liability changes the locus of liability for patient injuries with no significant changes in rules of proof and damages.[114] Channeling liability to HSOs/HSs has been justified on several grounds:

> First, insurers would have an improved ability to price insurance, since difficulties in pricing for individual physicians in high-risk specialties would be eliminated; in most other areas of tort law, from environmental to products risk, business enterprises bear the cost of insuring against liability. Second, by eliminating the insurance problems inherent in the fragmented malpractice market, specialties such as obstetrics would no longer face onerous burdens, nor will physicians have to face premiums that fluctuate excessively from year to year. Third, physicians would be freed from the psychological stress inflicted by being named defendants in malpractice suits. Fourth, administrative and litigation costs would be reduced by having only one defendant, rather than the multiplicity of providers named in the typical malpractice suit. Fifth, and most important, patterns of poor medical practice would be deterred by placing liability on institutions rather than individuals, since organizations have superior data collection abilities and management tools for managing risks.[115]

Proponents argue that a compensation system that rewards more claimants, especially small ones, more evenhandedly and rapidly than the current tort system will be an improvement, even if it is not cheaper.[116] Opponents of enterprise liability argue that persons rather than HSOs should be accountable for medical care, excessive power will accrue to HSOs, and physicians will be pitted against HSOs.[117] Changes in how medicine is practiced may make the transition to enterprise liability inevitable.

> Economic and societal forces are shifting the nature of health care from the individual physician to a system of healthcare professionals, characterized by accountable care organizations. In particular, more physicians are employed, quality and outcomes are routinely measured, and reimbursement is moving to value-based purchasing. Medical malpractice likewise needs to transition to a new model that is consistent with the modern era of patient-centered care. Collective accountability, the concept that patient care is the responsibility of all the members of the healthcare organization, requires malpractice reform that reflects a systems-based practice of medicine. Enterprise liability, coupled with medical error communication and resolution programs, provides the legal framework necessary for the patient-centered practice of medicine in today's environment.[118]

Enterprise liability is a logical extension of the evolution of vicarious liability and corporate negligence, both of which have moved the locus of much medical liability from independent contractor physicians to HSOs. Enterprise liability may be adopted by court decision and become (common) law even absent legislative enactment.

The discussion of quality and process improvement in Chapters 4 and 8 posits that processes, not persons, are the most likely sources of problems in medical care, and by extension, medical malpractice. This is further support for the concept of enterprise liability.

Reforms of the Medical Malpractice System

The cost of medical malpractice can only be estimated, but it adds tens of billions of dollars annually to the healthcare system. Another cost is defensive medicine, which is defined as physicians ordering tests and procedures not clinically indicated because they fear being sued if there is a bad outcome and the patient has not received them. Physician self-assessment found 20% of overall care is unneeded, and 85% of that results from fear of being sued.[119] The costs of medical malpractice and defensive medicine are huge, even though accurate calculations may be impossible.

Early state efforts at tort reform included limiting noneconomic damages, primarily recovery for pain and suffering; capping plaintiffs' legal fees; and allowing juries to learn how much money plaintiffs received from other sources (modifying the collateral source rule). State supreme courts have found such limitations constitutional.[120] Other legislative proposals include modifying the joint liability doctrine, allowing defendants to pay in installments, establishing malpractice screening panels, establishing patient compensation funds, granting immunity, and implementing a no-fault scheme.[121] Such reforms do not address the root of malpractice; the basic system is unchanged. Caps on damages and attorneys' fees reduce insurance premiums, but "patients with the most serious injuries are the ones who pay the price for the strategy."[122] Tort reform has had mixed results.[123] It is estimated that healthcare expenditures in the 28 states that limited malpractice payments were reduced only 3%–4%.[124] Later studies found little or no effect on Medicare and Medicaid costs.[125]

It is argued that reforms such as no-fault, which compensate injured persons without litigation or assigning liability, are key to reducing medical malpractice costs. Workers' compensation, which pays medical expenses and lost income to workers injured on the job, is an example of no-fault. No-fault malpractice systems in Virginia and Florida apply to newborns who suffer neurological damage caused by medical treatment during delivery. Both states allow recovery for medical and rehabilitation expenses, as well as compensation to replace lost future wages and noneconomic losses.[126] Because all those injured may file claims, no-fault may increase rather than decrease costs. There is evidence that (primary care) physicians who communicate well with patients are sued less often, and physicians who admit errors and apologize for them are less likely to be sued.[127]

Nonjudicial Means of Resolving Disputes

Most lawsuits are settled before trial; some are settled after trial begins. Settlement occurs at the behest of counsel, or the parties may perceive the advantages of avoiding a trial, such as uncertainty of outcome, desire to control the result, and avoiding a trial's negative publicity. State law may require settlement efforts; many courts have mandatory procedures to settle cases.

Resolving disputes in court is expensive and time consuming. Since the mid-1980s, much attention has been given to alternative dispute resolution (ADR). ADR includes binding and nonbinding arbitration (which may be voluntary or nonvoluntary), mediation, minitrials, neutral fact finding, and variations of these techniques. ADR is private, inexpensive, and efficient, aspects especially useful for HSOs/HSs. Each type of ADR has attributes that make it the best choice for certain disputes. For example, mediation is most effective when the parties want a continuing relationship. Professional staff should be aware of ADR's advantages; their bylaws should reflect its use. Several private organizations provide mediators, arbitrators, and others expert in ADR.

Mediation is common in court-annexed programs. For example, the Superior Court of the District of Columbia requires mediation of all cases in its small claims division (for monetary compensation claims under $5,000).[128] Judges may order mediation or case evaluation, which is like neutral fact finding, for cases in the civil division. Medical malpractice cases may be mediated in the civil division. In both divisions, cases that do not settle are scheduled for trial.[129]

Arbitration is common in managed care and health plans. It is increasingly common elsewhere in healthcare.[130] The U.S. Supreme Court has ruled that state arbitration laws must be consistent with the Federal Arbitration Act of 1925.[131] States have considerable latitude, however. Courts dislike contracts of adhesion (contracts in which one party offers unalterable terms [take them or leave them]) and may rule that provisions such as mandatory arbitration are unenforceable.[132] This view is buttressed by strong constitutional safeguards of the right to a jury trial.[133] There is a broad trend to arbitrate disputes in business-to-consumer transactions. Applying these concepts in health services means disputes such as tort claims for medical negligence, loss of a chance, and other allegations of medical malpractice resulting in physical and psychological injury will be decided by arbitration.[134] Physicians and hospitals are including pretreatment, mandatory arbitration clauses in patient intake contracts. Patients are unlikely to be aware of these clauses—especially that arbitration is mandatory—until a dispute arises. It is fundamentally unfair if vulnerable patients unknowingly lose their right to a civil action for damages if there is medical malpractice.[135] It is fairer to use mediation or voluntary binding arbitration to resolve malpractice claims. *Voluntary* means the parties agree to arbitrate and the arbitrator's award is binding. Choosing voluntary, binding arbitration precludes judicial remedies.

This discussion of ADR has focused on medical malpractice. Numerous other types of problems with legal dimensions occur in HSOs/HSs, including professional staff appointment and credentialing; disputes regarding sales, employment, and construction contracts; debt collection; and zoning matters. ADR is common outside health services; it has significant potential for greater use in HSOs/HSs.

Select Legal Areas Affecting HSOs/HSs

Peer Review

Historically, antitrust lawsuits against physicians and HSOs arose in hospitals in which members of the professional staff organization (PSO) conducted peer review of other physicians' clinical work. When peer decisions caused PSO members to lose or be denied clinical privileges, the actions were alleged to be anticompetitive because they were based on economics, not efforts to improve quality. In *Patrick v. Burget,* a physician alleged federal antitrust violations when a peer review action ended his clinic practice and caused suspension of his hospital privileges.[136]

The chilling effect of such lawsuits on peer review and other efforts to improve quality resulted in passage of the Health Care Quality Improvement Act (HCQIA) of 1986 (PL 99-660).[137] HCQIA grants limited immunity from paying damages in private lawsuits under federal or state law (except civil rights laws) for any "professional review action" (including peer review) if the professional review follows requirements in the law. These include a reasonable belief that the action was justified in furthering the quality of healthcare, there was a reasonable effort to obtain the facts, and the physician (or dentist) was given adequate notice and a fair hearing or such other procedures considered fair under the circumstances. *Austin v. McNamara* and *Egan v. Athol Memorial Hospital* show that HCQIA's peer review protections are achieving their purpose.[138]

Emergency Medical Treatment and Active Labor Act

The federal Emergency Medical Treatment and Active Labor Act (EMTALA) (PL 99-272) was passed in 1985.[139] This unfunded mandate requires hospitals participating in Medicare to provide screening examinations to persons who seek treatment at their emergency departments, regardless of ability to pay. If an emergency condition exists, the hospital must treat and stabilize the patient unless the patient requests a transfer in writing with knowledge of the hospital's obligation under EMTALA, or unless a physician certifies that the benefits to the patient of an unstabilized transfer outweigh the risks. The means of transportation must meet statutory requirements as to adequacy of equipment and personnel, the receiving facility must agree to accept the transfer, and medical records must be provided to the receiving facility. In 1989, EMTALA was amended to apply to women in any stage of labor, rather than merely active labor.[140] Women in labor are an emergency if transfer cannot occur before delivery or if transfer presents a health threat to the woman or unborn child.[141]

Medicare and Medicaid Fraud and Abuse

Since Medicare and Medicaid were enacted in 1965, a large body of law has developed from the amendments, regulations, and court decisions that followed. A special focus of Congress has been fraud and abuse, which is defined to include lying, stealing, providing too few or too many services, improperly coding services, bribes and kickbacks, and self-referrals.[142] Congress has assisted providers by identifying exceptions and by authorizing the DHHS "to issue 'safe harbor' regulations delineating conduct DHHS determined would not be subject to prosecution or exclusion under the anti-kickback statute."[143] Of the many actions defined by Medicare and Medicaid as fraud and abuse, only fraudulent billing and self-referral are addressed here.

Fraudulent Billing

In addition to *qui tam* actions described below, there are civil and criminal penalties for false claims made to Medicare and Medicaid. Fraudulent billing is a common type of false claim. Some infractions are presumed fraudulent; for example, a psychiatrist billed Medicaid for 4,800 hours in a year (40 hours/week = 2,080 hours/year). Other cases are less clear. A court upheld a $258,000 fine against anesthesiologists whose defense was that, at most, they were guilty of "unartfully" describing services rendered. The court found the applicable standard of care was exacting; "unartful descriptions" were descriptions of services not rendered as claimed.[144] A troubling dimension of "fraudulent billing" occurs if physicians who review angiograms used to justify placement of a cardiac stent disagree with the diagnosis of the cardiologist who placed the stent. In *U.S. v. Paulus* a cardiologist's conviction for fraudulent billing was set aside by the trial court because "the evidence in this case established that degree of stenosis is a *subjective medical opinion,* incapable of confirmation or contradiction," and thus a "reasonable jury could not conclude, beyond a reasonable doubt, that Dr. Paulus had made a false statement." An appeals court reversed when it determined evidence was sufficient to support a conviction for fraud.[145]

Physician Self-Referral

Another example of fraud and abuse is physician self-referral.[146] Amendments to Medicare in 1989 and 1993 to restrict self-referral are known as Stark I and Stark II, respectively, after the congressman instrumental in their passage. Stark I restricted referral of Medicare patients for clinical laboratory services by physicians who had financial relationships with the laboratory.[147] Stark II expanded restrictions on self-referral to services such as physical and occupational therapy; radiology services; radiation therapy; durable medical equipment and supplies; parenteral and enteral nutritional services; prosthetics, orthotics, and prostheses; home health; outpatient prescription drugs; and inpatient and outpatient hospital services.[148] Penalties are substantial. Civil penalties of thousands of dollars *per item or service,* plus assessments of two or three times the amount claimed, can be imposed. Some infractions result in criminal sanctions. Providers can be excluded from participating in Medicare and Medicaid, a penalty likely harshest of all.[149]

Healthcare Integrity and Protection Data Bank

Section 221 of the Health Insurance Portability and Accountability Act of 1996 (PL 104-191)[150] created the Healthcare Integrity and Protection Data Bank (HIPDB), the purpose of which is to record adverse actions against healthcare providers, suppliers, or practitioners. Included are civil judgments against a healthcare provider, supplier, or practitioner; criminal convictions from delivery of a healthcare item or service; adverse actions by federal or state agencies responsible for licensing and certification; exclusion of a provider, supplier, or practitioner from federal or state healthcare programs; and any other adjudicated actions or decisions the secretary of DHHS may establish by regulations.[151] This legislation highlights the need for HSOs/HSs to have legal advice. HIPDB may achieve far less than its intended results, and at considerable cost to providers.

Qui Tam Actions

The vast amounts of money spent by federal programs allow significant potential for fraud, abuse, and waste. In 1986, Congress enacted the False Claims Act Amendments (PL 99-562) to strengthen Civil War–era legislation that protected whistle-blowers who report fraud, abuse, and waste in federally funded programs.[152] One provision allows whistle-blowers, whom the law calls relators, to sue in the name of the federal government, with the incentive that they may receive 15%–30% of triple damages and fines imposed. Such suits are known as *qui tam,* from the Latin for "who as well." Estimated annual healthcare fraud costs in the United States are $98 billion.[153] In 2017, 64% of fraud recoveries resulted from *qui tam* actions that totaled over $3 billion.[154] A 2005 federal law encouraged states to pass their own *qui tam* statutes by increasing their share of Medicaid fraud recoveries.[155]

Tax-Exempt Status of HSOs/HSs

Federal tax law has long recognized the special role of organizations performing charitable work. HSOs/HSs organized as not-for-profit corporations may apply to the Internal Revenue Service (IRS) to become tax-exempt organizations under Section 501(c)(3) of the Internal Revenue Code. If approved, the HSO/HS is exempt from federal income and excise taxes, and donors may deduct gifts to them in calculating federal income tax. If local and state governments accept the IRS determination, the HSO avoids property, inventory, excise, sales, and other taxes levied on for-profit businesses. Being tax exempt provides significant economic benefits.

From 1956 to 1969, the IRS required a tax-exempt hospital to "be operated to the extent of its financial ability for those not able to pay for the services rendered and not exclusively for those who are able and expected to pay."[156] A 1969 IRS revenue ruling removed the requirement to render service to those unable to pay and stated that promoting health was a sufficient charitable purpose that benefited the community as a whole. By operating an emergency room open to all and providing care for community members unable to pay, a hospital was promoting the health of a class of persons broad enough to benefit the community. The IRS position was upheld in the legal challenge that followed.[157] Thus, less emphasis on treating those unable to pay did not cause loss of tax-exempt status. The 1969 IRS revenue ruling criteria are reflected in the "community benefit" standard of Section 501(c)(3). Other indicators of charitable purpose and community benefit include a mission to provide community benefit: providing essential services, educating the public, and serving unmet human needs.[158] The Affordable Care Act, enacted in 2010, added new requirements for tax-exempt hospitals regarding community health needs assessment and planning, financial assistance, charges, and billing and collections.[159] The AHA's definition of uncompensated care is instructive.[160] Further attention to community benefit and charity care is given in Chapter 7.

Despite a consistent approach by the IRS, the issue is unresolved at other levels of government. The stakes are high. The value of hospitals' exemption from taxes is elusive; it was estimated at $24.6 billion in 2011.[161] Historically, state and local governments accepted the IRS determination; this has changed. Some cases argued hospitals provided too little public service and charity care to justify tax-exempt status. Some tax-exempt hospitals paid, others fought, some won.[162] Seemingly politically motivated challenges to tax-exempt status were successful in Urbana, IL. Local authorities alleged two hospitals were overly aggressive in their collections, some properties were used in for-profit businesses, and the hospitals did not provide charity care to all needing it.[163] The value, appropriateness, and effects of tax-exempt status for not-for-profit HSOs are matters of continuing interest to the healthcare industry and policy makers.[164]

Adding political impetus to review of tax-exempt status by state and local jurisdictions is that many hospitals and other HSOs are involved in service integration, diversification, reorganization, mergers, and joint ventures, all of which suggest for-profit businesses, not charitable activities worthy of tax-exempt status. Highly compensated executives have also stirred political interest. Such developments diminish the public perception of "community benefit" that previously distinguished not-for-profit HSOs/HSs. A public that believes not-for-profit HSOs/HSs are like other businesses will not support tax-exempt status. Further clouding issues of tax-exempt status and charitable purpose are data from a Congressional Budget Office report that found tax-exempt hospitals provided only slightly more uncompensated care as a percentage of operating expenses than for-profit hospitals, which receive none of the tax benefits given not-for-profit hospitals.[165]

A tax-exempt organization may participate in activities unrelated to its exempt purpose if the activities are insubstantial parts of operations. Beyond that proviso, Congress has imposed an unrelated business income tax to eliminate unfair competition from tax-exempt entities.[166]

Overall, the trend is to narrow tax-exempt status, with Congress tying continued tax exemption to minimum levels of charity care likely to be a percentage of the benefit of being tax exempt.

Telemedicine

The law of contract, negligence, malpractice, and strict liability apply to telemedicine, but like the technology, the law of telemedicine is evolving and is unlikely to achieve stability soon. Problematic are confidentiality, data compression, artificial intelligence, licensure, credentialing, consent, and quality. No uniform physician standard-of-care has been developed for telemedicine.[167]

The American Telemedicine Association defines telemedicine as "the remote delivery of health care services and clinical information using telecommunications technology. This includes a wide array of clinical services using internet, wireless, satellite, and telephone media."[168]

Telemedicine uses three main types of technologies:

- *Store-and-forward telemedicine.* Transmits data such as medical images to an LIP for assessment. The patient and LIP need *not* be present at the same time.

- *Remote monitoring or self-monitoring.* The LIP monitors patients remotely to manage chronic diseases or conditions with devices patients use to obtain health indicators.

- *Interactive telemedicine services.* Provide real-time, face-to-face interaction between the patient and LIP as an alternative to in-person care delivery. The LIP can diagnose, consult, and treat patients.[169]

Confidentiality

Electronic patient records with multiple users and distributed computer systems make information security problematic. Confidentiality issues include improper disclosure, such as by leaving visible or easily retrievable data on a screen; unauthorized access, such as by hackers; aggregating data to identify individual patients; and data integrity and authenticity.[170] Providers' liability for failing to maintain the confidentiality of patient information is well established; largely undetermined, however, is the legal duty of organizations that provide telemedical support.[171]

Data Compression

The large amount of data in health services requires special handling so systems are not overwhelmed. Compressing files makes the data stream more manageable, but greater compression ratios increase the risk of image degradation. This means, for example, that teleradiology may be unable to achieve the reliability of in-person readings.[172] Most physician malpractice claims from 2007 to 2014 resulted from remote reading of x-rays and other films.[173]

Artificial Intelligence

Telemedicine includes aids to decision making, one of which is artificial intelligence (AI). Expert systems are a type of AI that help practitioners solve problems by asking questions, discarding irrelevant information, and producing an explained, reasoned conclusion.[174] An example of applying expert systems is the Acute Physiology and Chronic Health Evaluation that helps manage intensive care unit patients by monitoring various indicators and calculating the probability of death.[175] Studies comparing the conclusions of expert physicians with AI diagnostic systems found the systems provided useful but potentially misleading information. In addition, AI could lead to information overload that distracts physicians, or it may be used to unfairly question physician treatment when, in fact, it is the technology that is limited.[176] AI's contribution to health services will increase but bring potential legal problems.

Credentialing

LIPs who provide telemedicine consultation or support must have clinical privileges at the HSO in which it is provided. HSOs that request consultation must modify their PSO bylaws, rules and regulations accordingly to fit telemedicine. Medicare modified its telemedicine encounter rules so rural hospitals may accept the credentialing process of the HSO at which the specialist has clinical privileges.[177] More complex and unresolved is the situation in which a consulting LIP is unaffiliated with an HSO, which means there was no credentialing process on which to rely.

Licensure

States regulate LIPs and many non-LIP providers. Those not licensed in a state in which they consult have engaged in unauthorized practice in that state. Concomitantly, if they were not practicing in the state (e.g., because no professional relationship has been established with the patient), reimbursement may be denied. Such barriers limit wider use of telemedicine. States are addressing aspects of telemedicine as they apply to Medicaid.[178] An AMA ethical guideline advises members to "adhere to applicable law governing the practice of telemedicine."[179] The American College of Radiology recommends that physicians who interpret teleradiology images be familiar with licensing requirements at both the transmitting and receiving sites and obtain licensure as appropriate. "Under current law, that typically involves licensure in the transmitting state, but not necessarily the receiving state."[180] The College of American Pathologists position is that a physician must be licensed in the state in which the patient is located.[181] The American College of Physicians supports licensure for physicians who provide telemedicine services.[182]

Consent

Telemedicine makes the legal aspects of consent more complex. Disclosing that treatment is being provided via telemedicine becomes more important legally as "direct" participation increases—for example, when robotic surgery is managed remotely. Ethically and legally, it is prudent to obtain consent that informs patients about all providers treating them. As noted, consent for treatment in emergencies is presumed. Elective treatment allows enough time to obtain consent that is voluntary, competent, and informed.

Quality

Well-managed, telemedicine is generally equal to the quality of conventional healthcare delivery. Managing heart failure using telemedicine produced health outcomes like those of face-to-face or telephone delivery of care. Telemedicine can improve the control of blood glucose for diabetics.[183]

Inevitably, use of telemedicine will show poor quality too. In one instance, researchers posing as patients with skin problems were misdiagnosed, and medications were prescribed without a medical history or warnings about adverse effects. Two telemedicine sites linked users with overseas physicians who were not, as required by law, licensed in the states where the patients were.[184] Another aspect of telemedicine with potential quality of care issues is reduced continuity of care. Continuity is lost when patients use on-demand telemedicine services that randomly connect them with a provider. The patient's primary care provider may not have access to records from other visits, will have an incomplete medical history, or will not have information about care routines.[185]

Conclusion

The environment for telemedicine continues to improve. An important reason telemedicine has not expanded into routine care is stringent regulation of Medicare reimbursement for such services. Some federal-level barriers were removed with passage of the 2000 Omnibus Budget Bill.[186] States vary as to telehealth services covered by their Medicaid programs.[187] Telemedicine offers a cost-efficient way to improve access and quality of medical services everywhere; impediments and the resulting uncertainty are limiting wider use. With its world-wide mission, the U.S. military has been a leader in telemedicine. It is, however, not bound by constraints that affect civilian sector providers.

The two major drivers of contemporary telemedicine development are high-volume demand for a clinical service, and high criticality of the need for clinical expertise to deliver the service. Both offer promise to study and enhance applicable telemedicine methods and have potential for large-scale deployment internationally, which will contribute significantly to advancing healthcare.[188]

The increased use of telemedicine during the COVID-19 (SARS-CoV-2) pandemic of 2020 receives further attention in Chapter 5.

Legal Process of a Civil Lawsuit

This discussion of the legal process of a civil lawsuit is based on a tort, not a breach of contract. A civil lawsuit begins when a plaintiff files a complaint in a court with jurisdiction to hear the case. This filing makes the complaint an official document and a matter of public record. It is served on (delivered to) a defendant by a process server, who is often a marshal or a sheriff's deputy. The defendant's response to the complaint is known as an answer, and it must be filed within a limited time. The answer may deny the allegations in the complaint in whole or in part, or it may assert specific affirmative defenses, such as that the complaint is barred by the statute of limitations and the suit may not be brought, the plaintiff assumed the risk, or the plaintiff was partly to blame for the injury (contributory negligence). The defendant may also make certain motions before the court—for example, a motion to dismiss because the complaint fails to state a cause of action or a motion to dismiss because the complaint was filed in a court that lacks jurisdiction. Few cases are dismissed at this stage. The next phase is discovery, which allows the parties to learn about the opponent's case. The plaintiff seeks information to support the allegations of tortious conduct; the defendant seeks to determine the strength of the plaintiff's case, and vice versa.

During discovery, the plaintiff will make motions that ask the court to require the defendant(s) to produce documents (production) needed to prepare its case. The defendant may ask the court to deny the motions for reasons such as statutory privilege, relevance, and reasonableness of demands. In addition, the parties obtain information through written interrogatories (questions) and by taking depositions (sworn statements) of the parties, other persons with knowledge of the alleged injuries, or those who will testify as expert witnesses. With rare exceptions, all states protect the results of peer review by health services providers from discovery. The discovery phase may take months or years; statutes determine the time. Procedural maneuvering to prevent a party (usually the plaintiff) from obtaining documents and information adds time and expense to the process.

Many cases are settled during discovery or when discovery is complete, primarily because the parties have learned enough about the accuracy of the allegations and the strength of the case to make an informed decision whether to proceed with litigation or attempt settlement. States have various requirements to determine the merits of a medical malpractice claim, as well as alternative means of settling cases.

If the case has merit but is not settled, a trial date is set. The trial begins with opening statements by counsel, in which they outline their cases and suggest what they will attempt to show. The plaintiff's case is presented first, and the elements of a tort must be proven by a preponderance of the evidence. This is done by introducing evidence consisting of documents and testimony by persons who may have observed the event or can offer other information, and by expert witnesses. If there is no direct evidence as to the cause of the tort, the plaintiff must use circumstantial evidence from which inferences can be drawn that convince the finder of fact (the jury, or judge sitting without a jury) as to causation. Both parties will object to introduction of evidence that may damage their cases. The judge rules on the admissibility of evidence and any motions that are made by counsel during the trial. If present, a jury hears and sees the evidence and makes findings of fact.

Witnesses are questioned in several steps. The party calling the witness asks questions first; this is called direct examination. After direct examination, opposing counsel asks questions to cross-examine the witness. Cross-examination permits counsel to impeach the witness by raising questions about the accuracy of the witness's memory, veracity, reputation, and the like. This tests the witness's testimony and allows the finder of fact to give it the weight that it considers appropriate. After cross-examination, redirect examination allows counsel to rehabilitate the witness—to minimize undesirable impressions left by cross-examination. The last round of questions is called re-cross-examination. A major theory of the law is that truth will emerge from this adversarial process and the finder of fact can determine the reliability of the witnesses.

The defendant's case is presented following the plaintiff's and follows the same steps. When the evidence has been heard (and seen), the jury is charged (given instructions) by the judge. This means that the judge instructs the jury in writing that if it determines certain facts are present, the law requires it to find in specific ways. Jury instructions are very important, and both sides submit proposed instructions from which the judge chooses. Proposed instructions are cast by each party in the light most favorable to its case. If there is no jury, the judge considers the evidence and renders a decision. In some jurisdictions, the decision to find for the plaintiff or defendant is separate from a decision on damages, if the finding is for the plaintiff.

At various times during the trial, the parties make motions for the judge to consider and on which the judge rules. For example, the defendant usually moves for a directed verdict after the plaintiff's case has been presented. This motion asks the judge to rule that the plaintiff has not presented enough evidence to support the claim—that it is not a *prima facie* case—and as a matter of law, the plaintiff is not entitled to damages. If the motion is granted, which is rare, the trial ends because the judge has found for the defendant. Both parties may move for a directed verdict after all the evidence has been presented. When the jury finds for one of the parties, the other may ask for a judgment notwithstanding the verdict or, alternatively, for a new trial. If the judge grants the former, which is rare, the jury verdict is overturned, and judgment is entered for the other party. If the latter is granted, a new trial is set. Motions are supported or opposed by briefs from the parties that cite legal precedents and arguments as to why their motions should be granted or their opponents denied.

If the defendant loses and the jury awards damages the defendant believes are excessive as a matter of law, the defendant can petition the court for *remittitur,* which allows the judge to decrease the award, if granted. Again, the defendant's brief will argue that the evidence and/or the law does not support the verdict. The plaintiff submits a brief in opposition. Similarly, the doctrine of *additur* allows the court to increase a jury award that the judge finds inadequate.

The losing party may appeal the verdict. Appeals are based on alleged errors made by the trial court and that show misapplication of the law by the judge. These appeals are entered in the appeals court (the intermediate level) or, on further appeal, in the highest court of a state. Typical errors alleged by the losing party are admitting (or not admitting) evidence, granting (or not granting) a motion, content of jury instructions, and the judge's decision to qualify or refuse to qualify expert witnesses.

Trial and appeals court proceedings are very expensive. Discovery before trial requires paying fees for documents, deposing parties and witnesses, and paying the costs of expert witnesses. Usually, such costs must be paid as they are incurred. There are major costs to defendants who must answer interrogatories, produce documents, and cope with the disruption and other aspects of defending the suit. Trial appearances by attorneys command higher fees than those charged for other work. In addition, court costs must be paid. An appeal requires a transcript of the stenographic record of the trial. This record is several thousand pages long, even for a short trial, and costs thousands of dollars to prepare. High stakes, however, warrant such costs. Contingency fees for attorneys are suggested as a cause of the large number of medical malpractice suits. However, contingency fee arrangements allow injured patients to seek redress even if they cannot pay for an attorney to prepare and try the case.

Special Considerations for the Manager

Managers face a range of problems in effectively handling legal and quasi-legal matters. These run the gamut from patients with a grievance and who are potential litigants to instructing staff on the maintenance and confidentiality of medical records. It must be remembered that HSOs/HSs have an independent ethical obligation to the patient and community that is separate from and more demanding than that arising from their legal obligations.

Recordkeeping

Lacking adequate medical records, healthcare providers have great difficulty proving their actions comported with the standard of care. Medical records hold no legal magic. The information contained in medical records is admissible only under an exception to the hearsay rule of evidence. They are used to refresh the recollection of caregivers who participated in treatment and made entries in the record. In addition, the record is the basis for opinions by expert witnesses. The complexity and extent of events and treatment, the mobility of caregivers, and fading memories necessitate that medical records are complete, accurate, and legible. EHRs eliminate problems of legibility.

Persons who fear that information in a medical record may lead to embarrassment, dismissal, or a lawsuit may alter the medical record. Doing so violates a basic ethical duty *and* breaks the law. Alterations are likely to be discovered, however, and not only make juries more willing to award damages but may persuade a judge to punish the defendant by awarding punitive damages. Effective risk management requires that a responsible person obtain custody of the medical record at the first indication of a potentially compensable event. This control should be exercised continuously until the dispute has been resolved, including any appeal.

A problem with paper medical records was handwritten entries were hard to read or illegible. An electronic health record (EHR) eliminates legibility issues. The HSO's medical records committee or its equivalent must work to monitor and improve quality of the medical record. It must ensure records are organized, authenticated, completed properly and in a timely fashion, and available as needed. Chapter 5 discusses advantages and disadvantages of EHRs.

Effective Use of Retainer and House Counsel

HSOs/HSs obtain legal advice in two basic ways. Smaller HSOs pay a retainer to an attorney to guarantee consultation as needed. Considering the law's importance in managing HSOs/HSs and the need for ongoing advice and counsel, this may be the best option. Usually, larger HSOs/HSs employ in-house counsel. In this arrangement, the attorney is a staff assistant to management and the governing body. Access to either retainer counsel or in-house counsel is essential because HSOs/HSs can no longer rely on free advice from an attorney-member of the governing body, for example. Health services law is so specialized and frequently applied that casual or informal relationships are insufficient. Effective use of legal counsel has the same problems for management as interacting with other technical staff. Specifics vary depending on whether in-house or retainer counsel is used. A major advantage of in-house counsel is that they are integrated into systems such as risk management that alert managers to legal problems or prevent their occurrence. Further, greater contact with in-house counsel enhances managers' knowledge of the law and potential legal problems, and they are more likely to seek timely guidance. In-house counsel is committed to one organization and not distracted by other clients. Finally, in-house counsel will be expert in the HSO's/HS's unique characteristics and special problems. In sum, these considerations offer enhanced effectiveness. Legal expertise can be obtained in other ways too. Law school graduates with dual degrees—management or a clinical area—allow HSOs/HSs to hire managers and program directors with legal training, thus enhancing their ability to comply with the law.

Having in-house counsel does not eliminate the need for outside counsel, however. Specialized areas of the law and litigation are referred to outside attorneys. Like medicine, the practice of law has become highly segmented. Appropriate skills will optimize outcomes.

Testifying

During their careers, health services managers are likely to testify in legal proceedings. Common is testimony to provide information about how the HSO/HS is organized or how it functioned in a specific circumstance. Less common is providing information as to an incident about which the manager may have firsthand knowledge.

Written interrogatories ask managers and staff to answer questions about the organization, staffing, functions, and similar topics. The answers are prepared with assistance of legal counsel. Interrogatories aid counsel in requesting documents and information and are the first step in the discovery process. Managers may be deposed by counsel for the opposing party. The deponent (manager) swears (or affirms) to answer questions truthfully. The HSO's/HS's attorney is present and may object to questions, but they are usually answered. A verbatim record is made. If the deposition is used in court, the judge rules on the objections counsel made during the deposition. The finder of fact weighs the testimony of witnesses, who are expected to testify in an honest and forthright manner.

Expert witnesses are ubiquitous in legal proceedings involving HSOs/HSs. The experience and education of health services managers qualify them to be expert witnesses regarding the organization and management of HSOs/HSs, about which they are knowledgeable. Once qualified by the court, the expert renders an opinion as to whether the organization, management, and performance of an HSO/HS or its staff met the standard of care. Hypothetical questions may be used to establish the standard of care, but they are less common than in the past. Questions are as likely to be formulated in terms of whether performance conformed with the standard of care. Being an expert witness requires no special skills beyond knowledge of one's field and a clear understanding of how it applies to the case.

Discussion Questions

1. Describe the relationship between law and ethics. Which is more demanding? Why? Identify and be prepared to explain examples other than those used in the chapter.

2. Identify health services laws or regulations based on 1) a utilitarian philosophy, 2) a deontological philosophy, and 3) elements of both. How compatible are these philosophies when included in the same law or regulation?

3. What does a professional code of ethics reflect? How can enforcement be made meaningful? Must a profession "police" its standards? Why or why not?

4. Describe uses and limitations of codes of ethics that apply to HSOs/HSs. Should they be communicated to patients who are served by the organization? If so, how?

5. What is the HSO's/HS's role regarding patient rights? Are some duties or obligations surpassed by the organization's duty to patients? If so, give examples of how this occurs.

6. Define *fiduciary*. State some examples in and out of health services. Are HSOs/HSs and their services unique in terms of this concept? If so, how?

7. Define *conflict of interest*. Give examples in HSOs or HSs. How can they be minimized? What is the manager's role in minimizing them?

8. What should be the role of managers in allocating resources at the micro- and macro-levels? What can be done to reduce the likelihood that ethical problems will arise?

9. What types of experimentation might occur in HSOs/HSs? In terms of safeguards, distinguish surgical experimentation from that involving drugs and devices. How can patients be protected?

10. Identify the types of advance medical directives (AMDs). What are their effects on HSOs? How can managers ensure that HSOs interact effectively with patients in terms of AMDs?

11. What is euthanasia? What are the types of euthanasia? Distinguish euthanasia from physician-assisted suicide (PAS). Develop brief scenarios that highlight the differences between the various types of euthanasia and PAS.

12. Some research indicates most patients are willing and able to participate in end-of-life decisions by communicating about their preferences for care. Do such findings diminish hospitals' need to develop a futile treatment policy? Explain how futility theory is compatible with PAS.

Case Study 1   Understanding[189]

The department of public health of Alplex County offers many health promotion and disease prevention services. Patients who require medical or surgical intervention are referred to hospital-affiliated clinics or physicians' offices, as appropriate. These providers contract with the health department and receive reimbursement on a sliding scale, according to a prearranged fee schedule.

Eighteen-year-old Shirley Brown was seen by a nurse practitioner (NP) at a health department clinic. She was referred to a private practice gynecologist, who diagnosed severe dysmenorrhea. Ms. Brown was treated with a regimen of medications. Several months later, she returned to the health department clinic complaining of the same problem. The NP explained that surgery might be necessary to correct her problem. Ms. Brown returned to the gynecologist, telling him that the NP had discussed the surgical option. The gynecologist told her surgery was a last resort. She was so distressed by the severe dysmenorrhea she told the gynecologist to do whatever was necessary to make her feel better.

Ms. Brown was admitted to the hospital and underwent a hysterectomy. Only after recovering from the surgery did she grasp the meaning of the procedure and that, as a result, she was unable to bear children. The realization caused her to become very distraught. She went back to the NP, with whom she had developed a good rapport, to complain about her lack of understanding of the implications of the surgical option.

Questions

1. Describe the role of each provider involved, including the hospital, regarding patient consent.

2. Describe how the roles are complementary. How are they different?

3. Identify how a patient's age is important in the consent process.

4. Outline a process by which situations like Ms. Brown's could have been prevented.

Case Study 2   Viral Pandemic

In late 2019, a coronavirus outbreak occurred in Wuhan, a city of 12 million in east central China. The Communist central government isolated the city from the rest of China. International flights from and to Wuhan were allowed to continue, however, thus enabling spread of the virus. The virus caused a worldwide pandemic. It was labeled the novel 2019 coronavirus (COVID-19). Later, the name changed to the severe acute respiratory syndrome coronavirus 2 (SARS-CoV-2).[190]

The initial benign reaction by U.S. officials gave way to serious concern in early 2020. Some epidemiologic models of the spread of SARS-CoV-2 showed a U.S. death toll of a million, or more. Government leaders and medical experts feared hospitals would be overwhelmed by the influx of patients. Policymakers decided that the curve of new SARS-CoV-2 infections had to be flattened to spread likely demand for medical services over several months. Hospitals were ordered to stop elective admissions to make more beds available. Nonessential services and businesses were closed by order of state and local governments. Those who could teleworked. Wearing masks was suggested or, in some instances, mandated; social distancing was implemented as people were told to remain at least six feet apart to slow spread of the virus.

Symptoms of SARS-CoV-2 are high fever, dry cough, and difficulty breathing. Most at risk are persons over 65 and those with co-morbid medical conditions that compromise their immune systems and diminish pulmonary function. Medical experts feared demand for ventilators and ICU beds would exceed capacity. Commonly, patients in ICUs require respiratory support from a mechanical ventilator that breathes for the patient.

Several ethical, legal, and constitutional issues arise during a pandemic. The police power of the states (and as delegated by states to local governments) to protect the health, safety, order, and welfare of their citizens is well established. This is especially true for public health. In matters of state police power, federal government has only a supporting role, which allows guidance from agencies such as the Centers for Disease Control and Prevention and financial assistance and distribution of other resources to help states perform their police functions, as, for example, during a public health emergency.

Flattening the curve also allows development of herd immunity, which occurs when 60-80% of the at-risk population has antibodies to a disease. Herd immunity means the probability of a person with no antibodies to the disease encountering someone with an active case of the disease is greatly diminished. Thus, unprotected persons are less likely to contract the disease.

Questions

1. Develop guidelines that allocate ventilators to hospitalized patients. Use the theories of James Childress and Nicholas Rescher to support your guidelines for distribution of scarce, life-saving medical resources.

2. Describe the roles of hospital executives *and* members of the professional staff–especially physicians–in developing guidelines to allocate ventilators.

3. Research the concept of medical triage. What is the effect of applying triage in allocating scarce, life-saving medical resources such as ventilators?

4. List three implications for hospital nursing and support staff when the guidelines you developed are implemented.

Case Study 3	Concerned Physicians, Unconcerned Managers

Disheartened, the three hospital intensivists left their one-hour-long meeting with the hospital CEO, medical director, and chief nursing officer. They had hoped for a much better result.

As they discussed why the meeting hadn't had a better outcome, they tried to determine what to do next. The intensivists are convinced that problems in the hospital's two intensive care units (ICUs) would neither be solved, nor would the clinical functioning in the ICUs become more effective until several problems with nurse staffing were resolved. The intensivists had anecdotal evidence about the problems but had neither systematic nor comprehensive data. Even with better data and documentation, however, they were pessimistic that the negative attitudes expressed by hospital management in the meeting would improve. Worst of all, no managers in the meeting wanted to learn more about the problems the intensivists had described. The CEO seemed least interested in their concerns; she mentioned the hospital's contract with them in a way that suggested their continued relationship with the hospital might be at risk if they pressed their concerns.

As they talked, they listed their concerns: 1) inadequately trained nursing staff assigned to the ICUs, 2) RN staffing ratio in the ICUs inadequate to assure patient safety, 3) capricious disciplinary actions against nursing staff in the ICUs, and 4) timely availability of medications and pharmacist support for effective ICU clinical decision making and delivery of care.

The intensivists pondered their next steps. They agreed they could not ignore the matter—something had to be done. But what? How? And by whom?

Questions

1. Identify three reasons that might account for hospital management's seeming disinterest in the intensivists' concerns.

2. Identify the ethical dimensions for the intensivists. Identify the legal aspects. How can these be used to convince hospital management to act?

3. The literature suggests a link between physicians' interest in improving clinical and patient care quality and the likelihood of success. Why is physicians' involvement essential?

4. Outline a strategy the intensivists can use to convince managers about problems in the ICUs and gain a commitment from them to improve.

Case Study 4	Which Hurts More: The Truth or the Lie?

By all appearances they were a normal mid-1980s American family—happily married parents with two daughters born three years apart. When the elder daughter was 14, she began to have what were later diagnosed as significant psychiatric problems. The primary manifestation was her belief and accusation that father had repeatedly abused her sexually. Father vehemently denied the accusations; there was no proof of daughter's allegations. The focus became treating her.

Daughter's treatment included psychotherapy, psychoactive drugs, and, eventually, electroconvulsive therapy (ECT). Although common historically, ECT is used now only for some mental illnesses and in a more limited, controlled way. The result of the therapies and interventions is a young woman whose mental abilities are highly compromised. Now 40, daughter lives in a group home and can neither hold a job nor maintain meaningful relationships. It is unknown if her condition will or can be improved.

About this time father dies unexpectedly. As wife and sister sort through his papers, they find photographs proving daughter's claims of sexual abuse by father. Mother argues forcefully that: "What's done is done; there's no way to go back and recover what daughter had or might have had." Sister is torn as to what to do. She thinks it is only honest and right to tell her sister they have found photographs proving she told the truth about father. Sister believes that knowing she was abused might give daughter comfort. Further, the knowledge might help her achieve a state of mind that improves her quality of life. Conversely, there may be little to no benefit. Or, sister may get worse.

Sister does not want to go against mother's wishes, but she feels she must do what is right. Sister is desperate to help her sister who has suffered so much pain and anguish and had a normal life taken from her.

Questions

1. Suggest other reasons why mother is reluctant to tell daughter about the photographs.

2. What arguments can sister make to convince mother that telling daughter is the honest and right thing to do?

3. Does honesty have limits? How is it known when honesty is not the best thing to do?

4. Outline a plan of action(s) the concerned sister can use to help her abused sister.

Notes

1. Bodenheimer, Edgar. *Jurisprudence: The Philosophy and Method of the Law,* 6. Cambridge, MA: Harvard University Press, 1974.
2. Bodenheimer, *Jurisprudence,* 6.
3. Bodenheimer, *Jurisprudence,* 325.
4. Aristotle. *Politics,* 287. Translated by Benjamin Jowett. New York: The Modern Library, 1943.
5. Henderson, Verne E. The Ethical Side of Enterprise. *Sloan Management Review* 23 (Spring 1982): 41–42; Can a Corporation Know the Difference Between Right and Wrong? In *State v. Christy-Pontiac, GMC, Inc.* (354 N.W.2d 17), the Minnesota Supreme Court held that a corporation could form the specific intent necessary to commit theft and forgery and thus be subject to criminal fines. The irony of the case lies in the fact that corporate officers were found not guilty when tried separately on the same charges. Simonett, John E. "A Corporation's Soul." *Minnesota Bench & Bar* (September 1997): 34–35.
6. Kant, Immanuel. Fundamental Principles of the Metaphysics of Morals. Translated by Thomas K. Abbott. In *Knowledge and Value,* edited by Elmer Sprague and Paul W. Taylor, 535–558. New York: Harcourt, Brace, 1959.
7. Rawls, John. *A Theory of Justice,* 60. Cambridge, MA: Belknap Press, 1971.
8. Bodenheimer, *Jurisprudence,* 23.
9. Arras, John, and Nancy Rhoden. *Ethical Issues in Modern Medicine,* 3rd ed. Mountain View, CA: Mayfield Publishing, 1989.
10. Jonsen, Albert R., and Stephen Toulmin. *The Abuse of Casuistry: A History of Moral Reasoning,* 13. Berkeley, CA: University of California Press, 1988.
11. Beauchamp, Tom L., and LeRoy Walters. *Contemporary Issues in Bioethics,* 4th ed., 21. Belmont, CA: Wadsworth, 1994.
12. Jonsen, Albert R. "Casuistry and Clinical Ethics." *Theoretical Medicine* 7 (1986): 71.
13. Pellegrino, Edmund D., and David C. Thomasma. *For the Patient's Good: The Restoration of Beneficence in Health Care,* 121. New York: Oxford University Press, 1988.
14. Pellegrino and Thomasma, *For the Patient's Good,* 116.

15. Carney, Frederick S. "Theological Ethics." In *Encyclopedia of Bioethics,* vol. 1, edited by Warren T. Reich, 435–436. New York: The Free Press, 1978.

16. Pellegrino and Thomasma, *For the Patient's Good,* 121.

17. Pellegrino, Edmund D. The Virtuous Physician and the Ethics of Medicine. In *Contemporary Issues in Bioethics,* 4th ed., edited by Tom L. Beauchamp and LeRoy Walters, 53. Belmont, CA: Wadsworth, 1994.

18. Beauchamp and Walters. *Contemporary Issues in Bioethics.*

19. This section is adapted from Kurt Darr. Linking Theory and Action. In *Ethics in Health Services Management,* 6th ed., pp. 26–30. Baltimore: Health Professions Press, 2019; used with permission.

20. Guttmacher Institute. "An Overview of Abortion Laws." (October 1, 2018) *https://www.guttmacher. org/state-policy/explore/overview-abortion-laws,* retrieved November 2, 2018.

21. The first federal conscience clause enacted in 1973 was named after its sponsor, U.S. Senator Frank Church. The Church Amendment relieved from adverse consequences HSOs and their staffs if religious beliefs or moral convictions prohibited performing sterilizations or abortions. Similarly, it protected staff who refused to participate in those activities even if organizational values permitted them. An overview of "Conscience Protections for Healthcare Providers" is available through the Health and Human Services website. *https://www.hhs.gov/conscience/conscience-protections/index.html,* retrieved December 3, 2018.

22. American College of Healthcare Executives. "ACHE Code of Ethics. Amended by the Board of Governors on November 13, 2017." *https://www.ache.org/abt_ache/code.cfm,* retrieved November 2, 2018.

23. American College of Health Care Administrators. "Code of Ethics." Available at *https://achca. memberclicks.net/assets/docs/code%20of%20ethics_achca%20non-member_140430.pdf,* retrieved November 2, 2018.

24. "Thomas Percival (1740–1804) Codifier of Medical Ethics." *JAMA* 194, 12 (1965): 1319–1320. doi:10.1001/jama.1965.03090250053021.

25. American Medical Association. "Principles of Medical Ethics." *https://www.ama-assn.org/delivering-care/ama-principles-medical-ethics,* retrieved November 2, 2018.

26. Veatch, Robert M. "Professional Ethics: New Principles for Physicians?" *Hastings Center Report* (June 1980): 17.

27. *Code of Ethics for Nurses.* Washington, DC: American Nurses Association, 2015. *https://www. nursingworld.org/coe-view-only,* retrieved November 2, 2018.

28. American Hospital Association. "The Patient Care Partnership: Understanding Expectations, Rights, and Responsibilities." © 2003. Available at *https://www.aha.org/system/files/2018-01/ aha-patient-care-partnership.pdf,* retrieved November 2, 2018.

29. S. Langmead, personal communication, July 12, 2013.

30. "A Commitment to Improve Health Care Quality, Access, and Affordability." Board of Directors Statement. Washington, DC: America's Health Insurance Plans, 2004.

31. Annas, George J. *The Rights of Patients: The Basic ACLU Guide to Patient Rights,* 2nd ed. Totowa, NJ: Humana Press, 1992.

32. Bryant, L. Edward, Jr. "Ethical and Legal Duties for Healthcare Boards." *Healthcare Executive* 20, 4 (July/August 2005): 46, 48.

33. Showalter, J. Stuart. *The Law of Healthcare Administration,* 4th ed., 91. Chicago: Health Administration Press, 2004.

34. Showalter, *The Law of Healthcare,* 93.

35. A furor resulted from a report that some Medicare HMOs' advertising targeted healthy seniors. Hilzenrath, David S. "Study: HMOs Target Healthiest Seniors." *Washington Post,* July 14, 1998, C3.

36. Some physicians are "gaming" MCO constraints—sometimes through fraud and deception— so their patients get the medical treatment needed, but the MCO will not authorize. Such actions go well beyond the physician-as-advocate role and raise several ethical issues. Hilzenrath, David S. "Healing vs. Honesty? For Doctors, Managed Care's Cost Controls Pose Moral Dilemma." *Washington Post,* March 15, 1998, H1.

37. American Hospital Association. "American Hospital Association Guidelines: Advertising by Health Care Facilities." *http://www.100tophospitals.com/exclusives/guidelines/,* retrieved January 4, 2007.

38. American Hospital Association, *Social Media Policy. https://www.aha.org/standardsguidelines/2018-04-02-american-hospital-association-social-media-policy,* retrieved December 4, 2018.

39. Harron, Frank, John Burnside, and Tom Beauchamp. *Health and Human Values: A Guide to Making Your Own Decisions,* 148. New Haven, CT: Yale University Press, 1983.

40. Childress rejects subjective criteria (utilitarianism) because these comparisons demean persons and run counter to the inherent dignity of human beings. He argues that the only ethical system of allocation is one that views all persons needing a specific treatment as equals. To properly recognize human beings, we should provide treatment on a first-come, first-served basis or, alternatively, through random selection, as by a lottery. (Childress, James F. "Who Shall Live When Not All Can Live?" *Soundings, An Interdisciplinary Journal* 53 [Winter 1970]: 339–355.) Rescher uses a two-tiered approach. The first tier includes basic screening for factors such as constituency served (service area), progress of science (benefit of advancing science), and prospect of success by type of treatment or recipient, such as denying dialysis to the very young or very old. The second tier considers individual patients and judges biomedical factors, including relative likelihood of success for the patient and life expectancy, as well as social aspects, including family role, potential future contributions, and past services rendered. When all factors are equal for two persons, Rescher uses random selection to make a final choice. (Rescher, Nicholas. "The Allocation of Exotic Medical Lifesaving Therapy." In *Unpopular Essays on Technological Progress,* 30–44. Pittsburgh: University of Pittsburgh Press, 1980.) Because they result from value judgments, the social aspects are the most difficult. Rescher considered it irrational, however, to base choice on chance (after meeting medical criteria), as Childress advocated. Each of these microallocation theories has advantages (and disadvantages); the resulting decisions will not satisfy everyone. The decision frameworks address issues and problems in an organized fashion, however. The choices as to which persons will receive extraordinary lifesaving treatment may be unpredictable, in the case of random allocation (Childress), or rational and almost totally predictable (Rescher). It may be left to chance and, in that sense, be fair to all needing treatment (Childress). Or, it may be a matter of primarily subjective criteria (Rescher). Kantian principles of respect for persons and not using persons as means to ends are reflected in Childress's theory. Conversely, Rescher's criteria are predominantly utilitarian.

41. Maragakis, Lisa Lockerd. Coronavirus disease 2019 vs. the flu. *Health.* Johns Hopkins Medicine. *https://www.hopkinsmedicine.org/health/conditions-and-diseases/coronavirus/coronavirus-disease-2019-vs-the-flu,* retrieved May 8, 2020.

42. Contrast this view with a case in Japan, in which a physician told a patient that she had gallstones rather than frighten her by telling her that she had gallbladder cancer. She delayed surgery. The cancer spread, and she died. Her family sued. The court said that the patient herself was to blame because she had not followed the physician's advice to have the surgery and that the physician had no obligation to inform her of the true condition. Hiatt, Fred. "Japan Court Ruling Backs Doctors." *Washington Post,* May 30, 1989, A9.

43. Katz, Jay. "Informed Consent—a Fairy Tale." *University of Pittsburgh Law Review* 39 (Winter 1977): 137–174.

44. President's Commission for the Study of Ethical Problems in Medicine and Biomedical and Behavioral Research. *Making Health Care Decisions,* vol. 1. Washington, DC: President's Commission, 1982.

45. Harvard Medical School. "A Definition of Irreversible Coma." *Journal of the American Medical Association* 205 (August 5, 1968): 337–338.

46. President's Commission for the Study of Ethical Problems in Medicine and Biomedical and Behavioral Research. *Defining Death: Medical, Legal, and Ethical Issues in the Determination of Death,* 25. Washington, DC: President's Commission, 1981.

47. Uniform Law Commission. "Determination of Death Act." *https://www.uniformlaws.org/committees/community-home?CommunityKey=155faf5d-03c2-4027-99ba-ee4c99019d6c,* retrieved September 16, 2020.

48. *Cruzan v. Director,* Missouri Department of Health, 110 S. Ct. 2841 (1990).

49. Patient Self Determination Act of 1989, PL 101-508, 104 Stat. 1388-27 (November 5, 1990).

50. Yadav, K. N., et al. "Approximately One in Three US Adults Completes Any Type of Advance Directive for End-of-Life Care." *Health Affairs* (Millwood) 36, 7 (July 1, 2017): 1244–1251. doi: 10.1377/hlthaff.2017.0175. *https://www.ncbi.nlm.nih.gov/pubmed/28679811.*

51. DeMartino, E. S., et al. "Who Decides When a Patient Can't? Statutes on Alternate Decision Makers." *New England Journal of Medicine* 376, 15 (2017): 1478–1482.

52. States' AMDs are found at *http://www.caringinfo.org/i4a/pages/index.cfm?pageid=3289,* retrieved November 3, 2018.

53. Yadav, K. N., et al., "Approximately One in Three US Adults."

54. Agency for Healthcare Research and Quality. "Advance Care Planning: References for Care at the End of Life." *http://www.ahrq.gov/research/endliferia/endria.htm,* retrieved February 7, 2013.

55. Yadav, K. N., et al. "Approximately One in Three US Adults."

56. Brown, Jonathan Betz, Arne Beck, Myde Boles, and Paul Barrett. Practical Methods to Increase Use of Advance Medical Directives. *Journal of General Internal Medicine* 14 (1999): 21–26. Mailing written materials to older adults with a substantial baseline placement rate increased the placement of AMDs in the medical record.

57. Reilly, Brendan M., Michael Wagner, C. Richard Magnussen, James Ross, Louis Papa, and Jeffrey Ash. "Promoting Inpatient Directives about Life-Sustaining Treatments in a Community Hospital." *Archives of Internal Medicine* 155 (November 27, 1995): 2317–2323

58. Crane, Monica K., Marsha Wittink, and David J. Doukas. "Respecting End-of-Life Treatment Preferences." *American Family Physician* 72, 7 (October 1, 2005): 1263–1268.

59. Eliasson, Arn H., Joseph M. Parker, Andrew F. Shorr, Katherine A. Babb, Roy Harris, Barry A. Aaronson, and Margaretta Diemer. "Impediments to Writing Do-Not-Resuscitate Orders." *Archives of Internal Medicine* 159, 18 (1999): 2213–2218.

60. DeMartino, E. S., et al. "Who Decides When a Patient Can't?"

61. Health Care Power of Attorney and Combined Advance Directive Legislation. Chicago: American Bar Association, Commission on Legal Problems of the Elderly, September 1, 2004. (Photocopy)

62. Shmerling, Robert H. "CPR: Less Effective than You Might Think." *InteliHealth.* Last updated and revised on November 29, 2005. *http://www.intelihealth.com/IH/ihtIh/WSIHW000/35320/35323/372221.html?d=dmtHMS,* retrieved March 30, 2007. The article cites success rates of CPR in several settings: 2% to 30% effectiveness when administered outside the hospital; 6% to 15% for hospitalized patients; and less than 5% for elderly patients with multiple medical problems.

63. "EMS Legal Update: DNR Tattoos, Are They Legal and Is EMS Bound to Comply?" EMS1.com, January 11, 2018. *https://www.ems1.com/paramedic-chief/articles/372711048-DNR-tattoos-Are-they-legal-and-is-EMS-bound-to-comply/,* retrieved November 4, 2018.

64. "Declaration on Euthanasia." Rome: Vatican Congregation for the Doctrine of the Faith, June 26, 1980.

65. Gibbs, Nancy. "Dr. Death's Suicide Machine." *Time,* June 18, 1990, 69–70.

66. Meier, Diane E., Carol-Ann Emmons, Sylvan Wallenstein, Timothy Quill, R. Sean Morrison, and Christine K. Cassel. "A National Survey of Physician-Assisted Suicide and Euthanasia in the United States." *New England Journal of Medicine* 338 (April 23, 1998): 1193–1201.

67. https://euthanasia.procon.org/view.resource.php?resourceID=000132. Retrieved September 16, 2020.

68. "Oregon Health Plans Proceed with Caution on Suicide Coverage." *AHA News* 34, 10 (March 16, 1998): 5.

69. "Assisted-Suicide Coverage Could Be Expanded." *AHA News* 34, 43 (November 2, 1998): 6.

70. Oregon Death with Dignity Act 2017 Data Summary. Available at *https://www.oregon.gov/oha/PH/PROVIDERPARTNERRESOURCES/EVALUATIONRESEARCH/DEATHWITHDIGNITYACT/Documents/year20.pdf,* retrieved November 3, 2018.

71. Reese, Shelly. "Medscape Ethics Report 2016: Life, Death, and Pain." December 23, 2016. *https://www.medscape.com/features/slideshow/ethics2016-part2#page=2,* retrieved December 5, 2018.

72. Stevens, Kenneth R., Jr. "Emotional and Psychological Effects of Physician-Assisted Suicide and Euthanasia on Participating Physicians." *Issues in Law & Medicine* 21, 3 (Spring 2006): 187–200.

73. Langley, Alison. "'Suicide Tourists' Go to the Swiss for Help in Dying." *New York Times,* February 4, 2003, A3.

74. Humphry, Derek. "A Twentieth Century Chronology of Voluntary Euthanasia and Physician Assisted Suicide." (March 9, 2003). *ERGO. http://www.finalexit.org/chronframe.html,* retrieved January 1, 2004.

75. "Belgian Lawmakers Propose Euthanasia for Children." WorldNetDaily, June 21, 2003. *http://worldnetdaily.com/news/article.asp?ARTICLE_ID=33199,* retrieved November 17, 2003.

76. Alexander, Victoria. "Digital Journal. France to Legalize Euthanasia." (December 21, 2012.) *http://www.digitaljournal.com/article/339542,* retrieved February 6, 2013.

77. Horn, R. "The 'French Exception': The Right to Continuous Deep Sedation at the End of Life." *Journal of Medical Ethics* 44 (2018): 204–205.

78. Truehart, Charles. "Holland Prepares Bill Legalizing Euthanasia." *Washington Post,* August 15, 1999, A19.

79. Simons, Marlise. "Dutch Parliament Approves Law Permitting Euthanasia." *New York Times,* February 10, 1993, A10.

80. Saunders, Peter. "Dutch Euthanasia Preys on Mentally Ill, Psychiatric Patients." Lifenews.com. (September 27, 2012.) *https://www.lifenews.com/2012/09/27/dutch-euthanasia-preys-on-mentally-ill-psychiatric-patients/,* retrieved February 6, 2013.

81. Sterling, Toby. "Dutch Target Terminally Ill Newborns." *Washington Times,* September 30, 2005, A18.

82. Drake, Stephen. "Euthanasia Is Out of Control in the Netherlands." *Hastings Center Report* 35, 3 (May/June 2005): 3.

83. Vizcarrondo, Felipe E. "Neonatal Euthanasia: The Groningen Protocol." *Linacre Quarterly* 81, 4 (November 2014): 388-392. *https://www.ncbi.nlm.nih.gov/pmc/articles/PMC4240050/,* retrieved February 7, 2019.

84. Pope, Thaddeus Mason. "Dispute Resolution Mechanisms for Intractable Medical Futility Disputes." *New York Law School Law Review* 347 (2013–2014); Robert Powell Center for Medical Ethics at the National Right to Life Committee. "Will Your Advance Directive Be Followed?" 2012. *http://www.nrlc.org/euthanasia/AdvancedDirectives/WillYour AdvanceDirectiveBeFollowed.pdf*, retrieved July 23, 2013.

85. Valko, Nancy. "Futility Policies and the Duty to Die." *Voices* (online edition) (2003). *www.wf-f. org/03-1-Futility.html*, retrieved November 13, 2013.

86. Bernt, Francis, Peter Clark, Josita Starrs, and Patricia Talone. "Ethics Committees in Catholic Hospitals: A New Study Assesses Their Role, Impact, and Future in CHA-Member Hospitals." *Health Progress* 87, 2 (March–April 2006): 22.

87. Mannisto, Marilyn M. "Orchestrating an Ethics Committee: Who Should Be on It, Where Does It Best Fit?" *Trustee* 38 (April 1985): 17–20.

88. Annas, George, and Amy Haddad. "Do Ethics Committees Work?" *Trustee* 47 (July 1994): 17.

89. Scheirton, Linda S. "Measuring Hospital Ethics Committee Success." *Cambridge Quarterly of Health-care Ethics* 2 (1993): 495–504.

90. Section 46.107—IRB Membership. *Code of Federal Regulations.* Title 45, Department of Health and Human Services, Part 46, Protection of Human Subjects, and Title 21, Part 56.

91. Department of Health and Human Services, Office for Human Research Protections, Revised Common Rule Educational Materials. *https://www.hhs.gov/ohrp/education-and-outreach/revised-common-rule*, retrieved November 3, 2018.

92. "Institutional Review Boards: Purpose and Challenges." *Chest* 148, 5 (2015): 1148–1155.

93. Section 46.107—IRB Membership. *Code of Federal Regulations.* Title 45, Department of Health and Human Services, Part 46, Protection of Human Subjects, and Title 21, Part 56, effective July, 2018. *https://www.ecfr.gov/cgi-bin/retrieveECFR?gp=&SID=83cd09e1c0f5c6937cd9d7513160fc3f&pitd=20180719&n=pt45.1.46&r=PART&ty=HTML#se45.1.46_1107*, retrieved November 4, 2018.

94. Section 46.111—Criteria for IRB Approval of Research. *Code of Federal Regulations*, Title 45, Department of Health and Human Services, Part 46, Protection of Human Subjects, effective July 2018. *https://www.ecfr.gov/cgi-bin/retrieveECFR?gp=&SID=83cd09e1c0f5c6937cd9d7513160fc3f&pitd=20180719&n=pt45.1.46&r=PART&ty=HTML#se45.1.46_1107*, retrieved November 4, 2018.

95. Department of Health and Human Services, Office of Human Development Services. "Final Rule, Child Abuse and Neglect Prevention and Treatment Program." *Code of Federal Regulations*, Title 45 §1340. Washington, DC: Office of the Federal Register, 1985.

96. Department of Health and Human Services, Office of Human Development Services. "Services and Treatment for Disabled Infants; Model Guidelines for Health Care Providers to Establish Infant Care Review Committees." 50 *Federal Register* 14893. Washington, DC: Office of the Federal Register, 1985.

97. Department of Health and Human Services, Office of Human Development Services. "Services and Treatment for Disabled Infants."

98. Fletcher, John C., Margo L. White, and Philip J. Foubert. "Biomedical Ethics and an Ethics Consultation Service at the University of Virginia." *HEC Forum* 2, 2 (1990): 89–99.

99. Roscoe, Jerry P., and Deirdre McCarthy Gallagher. "Mediating Bioethical Disputes: Time to Check the Patient's Pulse?" *Dispute Resolution Magazine* 9, 3 (Spring 2003): 21–23.

100. Petry, Edward. "Appointing an Ethics Officer." *Healthcare Executive* 13 (November/December 1998): 35.

101. Keeton, W. Page, ed. *Prosser and Keeton on the Law of Torts*, 5th ed., 2. St. Paul, MN: West Publishing, 1984.

102. Keeton, *Prosser and Keeton*, 2.

103. Keeton, *Prosser and Keeton*, 655–656.

104. Southwick, Arthur F. *The Law of Hospital and Health Care Administration*, 2nd ed., 67–68. Ann Arbor, MI: Health Administration Press, 1988.

105. Prosser, William L. *Handbook of the Law of Torts*, 4th ed., 31. St. Paul, MN: West Publishing, 1971.

106. *Behringer v. The Medical Center at Princeton*, 249 N.J. Super. 597, 592 A.2d 1251 (1991); *Doe v. Noe*, Ill. App. Ct. December 26, 1997.

107. *Black's Law Dictionary*, 5th ed., 930. St. Paul, MN: West Publishing, 1979.

108. Moffett, Peter, and Gregory Moore. "The Standard of Care: Legal History and Definitions: The Bad and Good News." *Western Journal of Emergency Medicine* 12, 1 (February 2011):109–112.

109. Southwick, *The Law of Hospital*, 69.

110. *Landeros v. Flood*, 17 Cal. 3d 399 (1976).

111. Federal Tort Claims Act of 1946, 60 Stat. 842 (August 2, 1946).

112. Baumberger, Charles H. "Vicarious Liability Claims against HMOs." *Trial* 34 (May 1998): 30–33, 35.

113. Southwick, *The Law of Hospital*, 580.

114. Furrow, Barry R., Thomas L. Greaney, Sandra H. Johnson, Timothy S. Jost, and Robert L. Schwartz. *Health Law: Cases Materials and Problems,* 3rd ed., 353. St. Paul, MN: West Publishing, 1997.

115. Furrow, et al., *Health Law,* 353.

116. Furrow, et al., *Health Law,* 354.

117. Thornhill, Michael C., and William H. Ginsburg. "Enterprise Liability: Cure or Curse." *Whittier Law Review* 16 (Spring 1995): 143–156.

118. Stamm, Jason A., Karen A. Korzick, Kirsten Beech, and Kenneth E. Wood. "Medical Malpractice: Reform for Today's Patients and Clinicians." *American Journal of Medicine* 129, 1 (January 2016). *https://www.sciencedirect.com/science/article/pii/S0002934315008566,* retrieved February 7, 2019.

119. Carroll, Aaron E. "The High Costs of Unnecessary Care." *JAMA* 318, 18 (2017): 1748–1749. doi:10.1001/jama.2017.16193. *https://jamanetwork.com/journals/jama/fullarticle/2662877,* retrieved February 17, 2019.

120. Goldstein, Avram. "Va. High Court Upholds Malpractice Cap." *Washington Post,* January 9, 1999, B3. The unanimous opinion upheld the constitutionality of Virginia's $1 million cap on medical malpractice damage awards, including punitive damages, lost wages, future medical costs, and interest on unpaid judgments against doctors and hospitals. Supporters argue that the cap has stabilized the physicians' malpractice insurance market and eased their ability to get malpractice insurance.

121. Wencl, Annette, and Margaret Brizzolara. "Medical Negligence: Survey of the States." *Trial* 32 (May 1996): 21.

122. Grant, Ruth Ann. "Tinkering on Tort Reform Not Enough to Solve Problem: Experts." *AHA News* 27 (March 18, 1991): 2.

123. Grant, "Tinkering on Tort Reform," 5; *Health Care Statistics and the Effect of Caps on Noneconomic Damages,* 17–18. Washington, DC: Citizen Action, 1996; *Best v. Taylor Machine Works* 179 Ill.2d 367, 689 N.E.2d 1057 (1997); Smith, William C. "Prying Off Tort Reform Caps: States Striking Down Limits on Liability and Damages, and Statutes of Limitations." *ABA Journal* 85 (October 1999): 28–29.

124. Hellinger, Fred J., and William E. Encinosa. "The Impact of State Laws Limiting Malpractice Damage Awards on Health Care Expenditures." *American Journal of Public Health* 98, 6 (August 2006): 1375–1381.

125. Paik, Myungho, Bernard Black, and David A. Hyman. "Damage Caps and Defensive Medicine, Revisited." *Journal of Health Economics* 51 (January 2017): 84–97. *https://www.sciencedirect.com/science/article/abs/pii/S0167629616304106,* retrieved February 7, 2019.

126. Stein, Alex. "The Scope of Virginia's Birth-Related Neurological Injury Compensation Program." Harvard Law, Petrie-Flom Center–Bill of Health (March 2015). *http://blog.petrieflom.law.harvard.edu/2015/03/08/the-scope-of-virginias-birth-related-neurological-injury-compensation-program/,* retrieved November 2, 2018.

127. Darr, Kurt. "Communication: The Key to Reducing Malpractice Claims." *Hospital Topics* 75 (Spring 1997): 4–6.

128. "District of Columbia Courts, Mediation in Small Claims." *https://www.dccourts.gov/services/mediation-matters/small-claims,* retrieved November 3, 2018.

129. "District of Columbia Courts, Mediation in Medical Malpractice Cases." *https://www.dccourts.gov/services/civil-matters/mediation-in-medical-malpractice-cases,* retrieved November 3, 2018.

130. Sachs, Sara. "The Jury Is Out: Mandating Pre-treatment Arbitration Clauses in Patient Intake Contracts." *Journal of Dispute Resolution* 2 (2018), Article 16.

131. Sachs. "Jury Is Out"; United States Arbitration Act, Ch. 392, 61 Stat. 883 (1925) (current version at 9 U.S.C.)

132. "Arbitration Accepted as a Means for Resolution of Medical Malpractice Disputes." *American Journal of Orthodontics and Dentofacial Orthopedics* 3 (March 1997): 349–351. This reference includes a form to contract for arbitration of medical malpractice disputes.

133. White, Jeffrey Robert. "Mandatory Arbitration: A Growing Threat." *Trial* 35 (July 1999): 32–34, 36.

134. Gilles, Myriam. "Operation Arbitration: Privatizing Medical Malpractice Claims." *Theoretical Inquiries in Law* 15, 2 (2014): 671–696, I. Published online June 6, 2014. DOI: https://doi.org/10.1515/til-2014-0215

135. Sachs. "Jury Is Out."

136. Patrick v. Burget, 800 F.2d 1498 (9th Cir. 1986), reversed, 486 U.S. 94 (1988), rehearing denied 487 U.S. 1243 (1988). Dr. Patrick prevailed in the antitrust claims in the trial court. The court of appeals reversed the decision because the peer review activity that was established by Oregon was determined to be state action, which is exempt from federal law. The Supreme Court reversed the appeals court on a finding that the state judiciary did not supply active supervision and raised the question of whether state court review could constitute state action.

137. Health Care Quality Improvement Act of 1986, PL 99-660, 100 Stat. 3784.

138. Austin v. McNamara, 731 F.Supp. 934 (C.D. Cal. 1990), affirmed 979 (F.2d) 726 (9th Cir. 1992); Egan v. Athol Memorial Hospital, 971 F.Supp. 37 (D. Mass. 1997), affirmed *per curiam* 134 F.3d 361 (1st Cir. 1998), *certiorari* denied, 119 S.Ct. 409 (1998).

139. Emergency Medical Treatment and Active Labor Act of 1985, PL 99-272, 100 Stat. 174.

140. Furrow, et al., *Health Law,* 547.

141. Furrow, et al., *Health Law,* 539.

142. Furrow, et al., *Health Law,* 638.

143. Furrow, et al., *Health Law,* 648.

144. Furrow, et al., *Health Law,* 641–642.

145. United States v. Paulus, No. 17-5410 (6th Cir. 2018). *https://law.justia.com/cases/federal/appellate-courts/ca6/17-5410/17-5410-2018-06-25.html,* retrieved September 4, 2019.

146. Centers for Medicare and Medicaid Services. Physician Self Referral. *https://www.cms.gov/Medicare/Fraud-and-Abuse/PhysicianSelfReferral,* retrieved May 6, 2020.

147. Crane, Thomas S., Richard G. Cowart, Robert G. Homchick, Ellen P. Pesch, Sanford V. Teplitzky, and Harvey Yampolsky. "Stark II Proposed Regulations." *Health Law Digest* 26 (February 1998): 3–4.

148. "Spotlight on the Stark II Regulations." *Health Lawyers News* 2 (February 1998): 6.

149. Furrow, et al., *Health Law,* 643.

150. Health Insurance Portability and Accountability Act of 1996, PL 104-191, 110 Stat. 1936 (August 2, 1996).

151. U.S. Health and Human Services. "National Provider Data Bank," HIPDB Archives. *https://www.npdb.hrsa.gov/resources/hipdbArchive.jsp,* retrieved November 3, 2018.

152. False Claims Act Amendments of 1986, PL 99-562, 100 Stat. 3153 (October 17, 1986).

153. *The Economist.* "Health-Care Fraud: The $272 Billion Swindle, Why Thieves Love America's Health-Care System." *https://www.economist.com/united-states/2014/05/31/the-272-billion-swindle,* retrieved November 3, 2018.

154. U.S. Department of Justice. "Justice Department Recovers Over $3.7 Billion from False Claims Act Cases in Fiscal Year 2017." *https://www.justice.gov/opa/pr/justice-department-recovers-over-37-billion-false-claims-act-cases-fiscal-year-2017,* retrieved November 3, 2018.

155. Gibeaut, John. "Seeking the Cure." *ABA Journal* 92 (October 2006): 46.

156. Havighurst, Clark C. *Health Care Law and Policy: Readings, Notes, and Questions,* 204. Westbury, NY: Foundation Press, 1988.

157. Havighurst, *Health Care Law,* 204–205.

158. Clarke, Richard L. "Consumerism: A Matter of Trust." *Trustee* 60, 6 (June 2007): 27.

159. Catholic Hospital Association. *Community Benefit.* St. Louis. *https://www.chausa.org/communitybenefit/resources/defining-community-benefit,* retrieved December 8, 2018.

160. Uncompensated care is an overall measure of hospital care provided for which no payment was received from the patient or insurer. It is the sum of a hospital's bad debt and the financial assistance it provides. Financial assistance includes care for which hospitals never expected to be reimbursed and care provided at a reduced cost for those in need. A hospital incurs bad debt when it cannot obtain reimbursement for care provided; this happens when patients are unable to pay their bills, but do not apply for financial assistance, or are unwilling to pay their bills. Uncompensated care excludes other unfunded costs of care, such as underpayment from Medicaid and Medicare. AHA. "Uncompensated Care Cost Fact Sheet." December 2017. Chicago: AHA. *https://www.aha.org/system/files/2018-01/2017-uncompensated-care-factsheet.pdf,* retrieved December 7, 2018.

161. Rosenbaum, Sara, David A. Kindig, J. Bao, M. K. Byrnes, and C. O'Laughlin. "The Value of the Nonprofit Hospital Tax Exemption Was $24.6 Billion in 2011." *Health Affairs* (Millwood). 34, 7 (July 2015): 1225–1233.

162. Warraich, Haider. "Hospitals Need to Earn Their Tax-Exempt Status." *StatNews.* November 27, 2017. *https://www.statnews.com/2017/11/27/hospitals-tax-exempt-status/,* retrieved November 3, 2018.

163. Monson, Mike. "Ruling: Provena Not Tax-Exempt Entity." *News-Gazette Online.* February 18, 2004. *https://www.news-gazette.com/news/ruling-provena-not-tax-exempt-entity/article_7a82e740-075c-531e-858b-0171eb12b48c.html.* Retrieved September 16, 2020. The opportunity for Urbana officials to review Provena's tax status occurred because in Illinois the new owner of a charitable organization must reapply for tax-exempt status. Provena was formed in 1997 by consolidation of the health activities of three religious orders of sisters, but reapplication for tax-exempt status did not occur until 2002. Lagnado, Lucette. "Hospital Found "Not Charitable" Loses Its Status as Tax Exempt." *Wall Street Journal,* February 19, 2004, B1.

164. Herring, Bradley, Darrell Gaskin, Hossein Zare, and Gerard Anderson. "Comparing the Value of Nonprofit Hospitals' Tax Exemption to Their Community Benefits." *Inquiry* 55 (January–December 2018). Published online February 13, 2018. *https://www.ncbi.nlm.nih.gov/pmc/articles/PMC5813653/,* retrieved December 7, 2018.

165. Francis, Theo. "Lawmakers Question If Nonprofit Hospitals Help Poor Enough." *Wall Street Journal.* July 20, 2007. *https://www.wsj.com/articles/SB118489137586972426,* retrieved September 16, 2020.

166. Stanley, J. Mark, and David R. Ward. "UBIT May Hit Common Transactions." *Tax Advisor* 25 (September 1994): 557.

167. Gallegos, Alicia. "Telemedicine Poses Novel Legal Risks for Doctors." *Chest Physician.* October 6, 2015. *https://www.mdedge.com/chestphysician/article/103362/health-policy/telemedicine-poses-novel-legal-risks-doctors,* retrieved February 8, 2019.

168. American Telemedicine Association. FAQ. *http://www.americantelemed.org/about/telehealth-faqs-,* retrieved February 17, 2019.

169. American Medical Association. "Your Questions about Telemedicine Answered." April 30, 2015. *https://www.ama-assn.org/practice-management/digital/your-questions-about-telemedicine-answered,* retrieved February 18, 2019.

170. McMenamin, Joseph P. "Telemedicine: Technology and the Law." *For the Defense* 39 (July 1997): 11.

171. McMenamin, "Telemedicine," 11.

172. McMenamin, "Telemedicine," 13.

173. Gallegos, "Telemedicine Poses."

174. McMenamin, "Telemedicine," 13.

175. McMenamin, "Telemedicine," 13.

176. McMenamin, "Telemedicine," 14.

177. Gallegos, "Telemedicine Poses."

178. Kelly, Beckie. "Telemedicine Begins to Make Progress." *Health Data Management* 10, 1 (January 2002): 73.

179. American Medical Association. "Ethical Practice in Telemedicine." Code of Medical Ethics Opinion 1.2.12. Chicago. *https://www.ama-assn.org/delivering-care/ethics/ethical-practice-tele-medicine,* retrieved February 19, 2019.

180. "ACR White Paper on Teleradiology Practice: A Report from the Task Force on Teleradiology Practice." *Journal of the American College of Radiologists*10 (2013): 575–585. Available at *https://www.acr.org/-/media/ACR/Files/Legal-and-Business-Practices/ACR_White_Paper_on_Teleradiology_Practice1.pdf,* retrieved February 19, 2019.

181. American Medical Association. "Physician Licensure: An Update of Trends," 6. August 11, 2005. *http://www.ama-assn.org/ama/pub/category/print2378.html,* retrieved February 15, 2007.

182. Daniel, Hilary, and Lois Snyder Sulmasy. "Policy Recommendations to Guide the Use of Tele-medicine in Primary Care Settings: An American College of Physicians Position Paper." *Annals of Internal Medicine* (November 17, 2015). *https://annals.org/aim/fullarticle/2434625/policy-recommendations-guide-use-telemedicine-primary-care-settings-american-college,* retrieved February 18, 2019.

183. Flodgren, G., et al. "Interactive Telemedicine: Effects on Professional Practice and Health-care Outcomes." *Cochrane Database of Systematic Reviews* 5, 9 (September 7):CD002098. doi: 10.1002/14651858.CD002098.pub2. *https://www.ncbi.nlm.nih.gov/pubmed/26343551,* retrieved February 18, 2019

184. Beck, Melinda. "Study of Telemedicine Finds Misdiagnoses of Skin Problems." *Wall Street Journal,* May 15, 2016. *https://www.wsj.com/articles/study-of-telemedicine-finds-misdiagnoses-of-skin-problems-1463344200,* retrieved February 18, 2019.

185. "10 Pros and Cons of Telemedicine." *eVisit.* May 25, 2018. *https://evisit.com/resources/10-pros-and-cons-of-telemedicine/,* retrieved February 18, 2019.

186. Kelly, "Telemedicine Begins to Make Progress," 72; Omnibus Budget Bill of 2000, PL 106-554, 114 Stat. 2763 (2000).

187. Center for Connected Health Policy. "State Telehealth Laws and Medicaid Program Policies." 2018. Available at *https://www.cchpca.org/sites/default/files/2018-10/CCHP_50_State_Report_Fall_2018.pdf,* retrieved February 18, 2019.

188. Wilson, Laurence S., and Anthony J. Maeder. "Recent Directions in Telemedicine: Review of Trends in Research and Practice." *Healthcare Informatics Research* 21, 4 (October 2015): 213–222. Published online October 31, 2015. doi: 10.4258/hir.2015.21.4.213. *https://www.ncbi.nlm.nih.gov/pmc/articles/PMC4659877/,* retrieved February 18, 2019.

189. Written by Gary E. Crum, Ph.D., M.P.H., District Director of Health (retired), Northern Kentucky Independent District Health Department. Used with permission.

190. Maragakis, Lisa Lockerd. Corona virus disease 2019 vs. the flu. *Health.* Johns Hopkins Medicine. https://www.hopkinsmedicine.org/health/conditions-and-diseases/coronavirus/coronavirus-disease-2019-vs-the-flu. Retrieved May 8, 2020.

3

Healthcare Economics

Chapter Outline

Economic Growth in Healthcare
Special Characteristics of the Healthcare Economy
Healthcare Demand
Healthcare Supply
Economic Solutions for Healthcare

Currently, the United States spends at least a third more on healthcare (measured per person or per gross domestic product [GDP]) than other first-world countries, yet many health outcomes are no better; some are worse. For example, life expectancy is in the bottom third among first-world countries. However, the data across different healthcare outcomes reveal delicate variations: The United States performs well on 30-day in-hospital mortality rates after heart attacks and stroke and on breast cancer 5-year survival rates.[1] Observers must look beyond broad categories for a true appreciation of how well U.S. healthcare is doing compared to healthcare in other countries.

Our healthcare sector has systemic problems that keep costs high and drive costs up at a pace much faster than the rate of inflation, including, but not limited to, the following:

- Fee-for-service payments that incentivize doctors to perform procedures rather than focus on the outcome of patient health and that encourage development and proliferation of cost-increasing medical technology

- Tax incentives that subsidize employer-provided insurance and dull employees' awareness of healthcare's full cost

- Some new technologies in healthcare that may drive costs up instead of down and lead to little or no improvement in health outcomes

- Fragmented and unusable data about healthcare costs and outcomes

- Lack of price transparency that makes it hard for patients to know the price of their treatment or to comparison shop

- Concern about lawsuits that may cause physicians to practice expensive defensive medicine

- Inefficient and excessive administrative costs[2]

The U.S. healthcare system is, however, often described as the envy of the world.

- Most preemptive cancer screening

- Highest rate of cancer survival

- Best treatment of chronic disease

- Most identification and treatment of psychological disease

- Most advanced equipment per capita

- High pay that attracts the best doctors

- Most advanced research

- Best legal environment for patients to recover financially for negligence[3]

In addition, the U.S. system provides unparalleled access to specialist referrals (especially surgery), and diagnostic tests, such as computed tomographic (CT) scans and magnetic resonance imaging (MRI). Physician and resource maldistribution is a problem whether or not the system is centrally planned and controlled. In addition, amenities such as healthcare facilities' physical plant, home health, and support services are without peer worldwide. The absence of a budgeted maximum expenditure level, as is the case in most centrally planned single-payer health systems, means few constraints on access, with or without insurance.

Economic Growth in Healthcare

National healthcare expenditures (NHEs) have shown phenomenal growth during the last 60 years, tripling in the 1970s, 1980s, and 1990s and doubling in the 2000s (see Figure 3.1).

Over the last 60 years, U.S. health expenditures increased much more rapidly than all other spending as a percentage of GDP, demonstrating the increased importance that society places on healthcare relative to non-health goods and services (see Figure 3.2). In 1972,

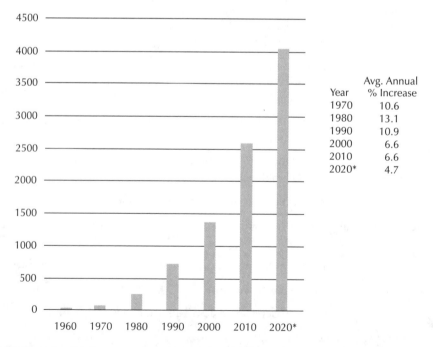

Year	Avg. Annual % Increase
1970	10.6
1980	13.1
1990	10.9
2000	6.6
2010	6.6
2020*	4.7

Figure 3.1.   National healthcare expenditures by year (amount in billions and average annual percent increase). Source: CMS. National Health Expenditures, Historical Table 1 and Projected Table 1. https://www.cms.gov/Research-Statistics-Data-and-Systems/Statistics-Trends-and-Reports/NationalHealthExpendData/index, retrieved on January 2, 2020. *Projected.

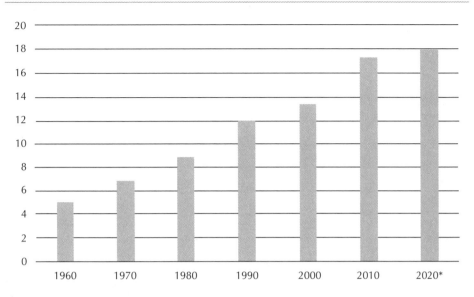

Figure 3.2. National healthcare expenditures as a percent of GDP by year. Source: CMS. National Health Expenditures, Historical Table 1 and Projected Table 1. https://www.cms.gov/Research-Statistics-Data-and-Systems/Statistics-Trends-and-Reports/NationalHealthExpendData/index, retrieved on January 2, 2020.
*Projected.

Senator Ted Kennedy (D-MA) predicted the effects of the increased importance that society placed on healthcare.

> Even though we are a nation that places a high value on health, we have done very little to ensure that quality healthcare is available to all of us at a price we can afford. We have allowed rural and inner-city areas to be slowly abandoned by doctors. We have allowed hundreds of insurance companies to create thousands of complicated policies that trap Americans in gaps, limitations, and exclusions in coverage, and that offer disastrously low benefits . . . We have allowed doctor and hospital charges to skyrocket out of control through wasteful and inefficient practices to the point where more and more Americans are finding it difficult to pay for health care and health insurance. We have also allowed physicians and hospitals to practice with little or no review of the quality of their work, and with few requirements to keep their knowledge up to date or to limit themselves to the areas where they are qualified. In our concern not to infringe on doctors' and hospitals' rights as entrepreneurs, we have allowed them to offer care in ways, at times, places, and at prices designed more for their convenience and profit than for the good of the American people.
>
> When I say "we have allowed," I mean that the American people have not done anything about it through their government, that the medical societies and hospital associations have done far too little about it, and that the insurance companies have done little or nothing about it.[4]

A great deal has changed since Senator Kennedy made that statement a half century ago. These changes are reflected in significant private and public efforts to improve quality, rein in costs and cost increases, and provide access. Numerous examples of these efforts were provided in Chapter 1 and are discussed in this chapter. It must be emphasized that healthcare insurance neither guarantees nor prevents access to care.

From 1960 through 2018, the average annual growth for NHEs was 8.8% compared to an average annual growth in GDP of 6.5%. NHEs as a percentage of GPD can be affected by two factors: changes in NHEs or changes in GDP caused by inflation. After accounting for inflationary effects, personal healthcare spending (excluding investment, public health,

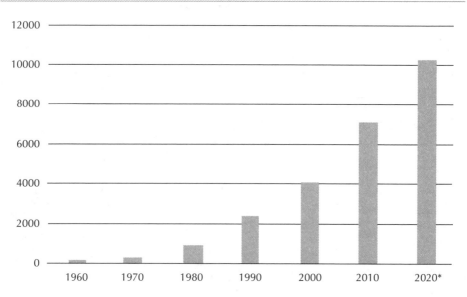

Figure 3.3. Personal healthcare expenditures per person by year. Source: CMS. National Health Expenditures, Historical Table 1 and Projected Table 5. https://www.cms.gov/Research-Statistics-Data-and-Systems/Statistics-Trends-and-Reports/NationalHealthExpendData/index, retrieved on January 2, 2020.
*Projected.

government administration, and net cost of insurance) increased at a faster rate than the general economy due to technology, population, use, and intensity (the number of procedures per patient).[5]

From 1960 through 2018, personal healthcare spending (healthcare goods and services) increased from $125 to $9,415 per person, an average annual increase of 7.8%. In comparison, per person personal income increased from $2,267 to $54,446, reflecting an average annual percent increase of 5.5%, lagging significantly behind personal healthcare spending.[6]

The material that follows in this section is based on a paper by Catlin and Cowan (CMS), who reviewed health expenditures in five distinct eras from 1960 through 2013.[7]

Pre-Medicare and Medicaid Era (1960–1965)

In this era, average annual NHE growth was 8.9%, whereas average annual GDP growth was 6.5%. Before implementation of Medicare and Medicaid, health expenditures were financed largely by private payers, with both private insurance and out-of-pocket spending accounting for over 66% of all healthcare expenditures. Most expenditures were out-of-pocket healthcare expenditures, accounting for 48% of all healthcare expenditures.

Coverage Expansion and Rapid Price Growth Era (1966–1982)

Between 1966 and 1982, average annual NHE growth was 13.0% while average annual GDP growth was 9.2%. NHE growth was largely driven by expanded insurance coverage due to Medicare and Medicaid and strong price inflation due in part to high inflation during the period. During 1967 to 1973, Medicare expenditures grew an average of 28.6% per year reaching $10.7 billion in 1973 largely as a result of increase demand for physician services, hospital services, and skilled nursing care and a ready supply of financing from federal government.

Amendments to the Social Security Act (PL 92-603) in 1972 included limited reimbursement for dialysis services by Medicare regardless of age. By 1973, Medicaid expenditures had reached $9.4 billion. Amendments to the Social Security Act in 1971 (PL 92-223) expanded Medicaid eligibility to the mentally retarded (now the intellectually disabled) and inpatient psychiatric care. The implementation of Medicare and Medicaid also initiated a substantial shift in sponsors of care (private sponsors of care including businesses, households (out-of-pocket spending, contributions to private health insurance premiums, and contributions to Medicare through payroll taxes and Medicare premiums, and other private revenues and public sponsors of care including the federal government and state and local governments). Private sponsor expenditures declined as a share of NHE from 76% in 1966 to 71% in 1967 and public sponsor expenditures increased as a share of NHE from 24% in 1966 to 29% in 1967.

Payment Change and Moderate Price Growth Era (1983–1992)

Average annual NHE growth was 9.9%, whereas average annual GDP growth was 6.9% between 1983 and 1992. Lower growth in both NHEs and GDP was largely attributable to lower economy-wide and medical-specific price inflation. Significant changes in how healthcare was reimbursed and delivered contributed to lower growth. In 1983, Medicare initiated prospective payment (PL 98-21), ended cost-based reimbursement for most Medicare hospital inpatients, and began reimbursing hospitals for Medicare inpatients based on a predetermined, fixed amount based on a diagnosis classification system, or diagnosis-related group (DRG). The new payment system had an immediate impact on hospital utilization, such as length of stay, and moved some patient care to an outpatient basis. In 1984, after years of double-digit growth in physician payments by Medicare, Congress froze physician reimbursement for Medicare patients through 1986[8] (PL 98-369) and in 1992, implemented a prospective payment system based on resource-based relative value scale (PL 101-239).

Cost Containment Followed by Backlash Era (1993–2002)

Between 1993 and 2002, average annual NHE growth was 6.7%, whereas average annual GDP growth was 5.3%. Most of the slower growth in NHEs resulted from cost-containment efforts by businesses that offered lower-premium healthcare plans with tightly controlled access to care through managed care. During the 1990s, managed care plans slowed the rate of increase in health spending by negotiating lower prices with tighter networks of providers and by slowing the growth in utilization.

However, in 2002, NHE growth was 9.6%, reflecting a consumer backlash against managed care and tightly controlled networks. Slower growth in the public sector was the result of federal legislation designed to slow the growth of Medicare and Medicaid. For instance, the Balanced Budget Act of 1997 (BBA of 1997 [PL 105-33]) reduced Medicare spending by $112 billion from 1998 through 2002 by reducing planned updates (increased reimbursement intended to keep up with inflation), moving more providers to prospective payment,[9] and capping[10] payments per Medicare beneficiary for home health visits. The BBA of 1997 also allowed states to move Medicaid beneficiaries into cost-saving managed care plans.

The actual economic impact of the BBA of 1997 was greater than expected. For instance, capping payments for home health visits contributed to 3,500 home health agencies closing.[11] With expanding federal budget surpluses (one of the goals of the BBA of 1997), Congress attempted to ease the economic impact of the BBA of 1997 by passing the Balanced Budget Refinement Act of 1999 (PL 106-113) and the Benefits Improvement and Protection Act of 2000 (PL 106-554), both of which halted or delayed some of the payment reductions mandated in the BBA of 1997.

Recent Slower Growth Era (2003–2013)

In this era, the average annual NHE growth was 5.4%, whereas the average annual GDP growth was 3.9%. Continued slower growth in NHEs during this period was the result of two notable factors: the increase in high-volume prescription medications going generic and the most severe economic recession since 1929. In 2002, 39% of dispensed drugs were generic, with an increase to 80% in 2013. The decreased spending due to generic drugs offset the increased utilization of all drugs caused by the Medicare Prescription Drug, Improvement, and Modernization Act of 2003 (MMA of 2003 [PL 108-173]), which provided a voluntary outpatient drug benefit (Part D) to Medicare beneficiaries.

Fully implemented in 2006, prescription drug spending increased 9.3% due partly to the increased utilization caused by the expanded drug coverage. This law also shifted outpatient drug spending from private sponsors (private health insurance and out-of-pocket spending) to the public sector (Medicare). For instance, the share of prescription drug expenditures paid by Medicare in 2005 was 2%; the share of prescription drug expenditures paid for by Medicare in 2006 was 18%.

During the 2007–2009 recession and modest recovery from 2010 through 2013, growth in healthcare expenditures slowed substantially to 4.8% in 2008 and 3.8% in 2009. To help stimulate the economy, the federal government passed the $787 billion American Recovery and Reinvestment Act of 2009 (ARRA of 2009[PL 111-5]). ARRA provided $87 billion in matching funds to help the states pay for the spending associated with increased Medicaid enrollments due to the recession, and $17 billion to hospitals and physicians to modernize health information technology systems.[12]

The passage of the $940 billion Patient Protection and Affordable Care Act of 2010 (ACA of 2010 [PL 111-148]), to be implemented over 8 years, had a negligible effect on healthcare spending during this period. Provisions implemented in 2010 included rebates on Part D drug costs as well as the following: young adults could stay on their parents' policies until age 26, private plans were required to provide preventive services to patients with no copayments or deductibles, and insurance companies could not deny coverage due to pre-existing illness or drop coverage due to illness. The 2011 provisions required insurance companies to prove that they spent at least 80% of premiums on the provision of medical services. There were no required provisions in 2013.[13]

Beyond 2013

Between 2014 and 2018, average annual NHE growth was 4.9%, whereas average annual GDP growth was 4.2%.[14] The year-by-year trajectory was as follows:

- 2014—NHEs increased 5.3% due to coverage expansions in both Medicaid and private health under the ACA of 2010 and a 12.2% increase in prescription drug costs partly due to the introduction of hepatitis C drugs.[15]

- 2015—NHEs increased 5.8% due to increased intensity as millions gained and used coverage under the ACA of 2010, and prescription drug costs continued to increase at 9.0%.[16]

- 2016—NHEs slowed to 4.3%, with across-the-board deceleration.[17]

- 2017—NHEs slowed to 3.9%, with slow growth in the three largest categories of expenditures: hospital spending (33% of total healthcare expenditures) slowed to 4.6%; physician and clinical service spending (20% of total healthcare expenditures) slowed to 4.2%; and prescription drug spending (10% of total healthcare expenditures) slowed to 0.4%.[18]

- 2018—NHEs increased to 4.6%, which was slower than the 5.4% rate of increase for the GDP, causing NHEs as a percentage of GDP to decrease from 17.9% in 2017 to 17.7% in 2018. Part of the growth in healthcare expenditures was attributed to the reinstatement of the health insurance tax (part of ACA funding) in 2018 after a 1-year moratorium on the tax in 2017. As a result, private health insurance spending (34% of total healthcare spending) increased 5.8%.[19]

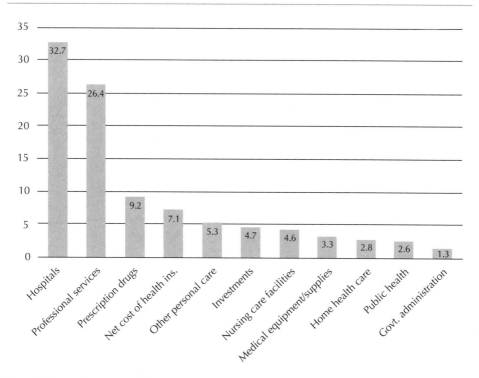

Figure 3.4. NHE by spending category, percent of total, 2018. Source: CMS. National Health Expenditures, Historical Table 1. https://www.cms.gov/Research-Statistics-Data-and-Systems/Statistics-Trends-and-Reports/NationalHealthExpend Data/index, retrieved on January 2, 2020.

It should be noted that the spending bill passed by Congress and signed by the president in December 2019 repeals the health insurance tax beginning in 2021.[20]

At the end of 2019, NHEs were projected to increase by an average rate of 5.5% per year through 2027, reaching nearly $6.0 trillion. NHEs are projected to grow 0.8% per year faster than growth in the GDP; as a result, NHEs as a percentage of GDP are projected to increase from 17.7% in 2018 to 19.4% in 2027. Largely due to a comparatively higher projected enrollment growth, Medicare spending is projected to increase 7.4% per year compared to Medicaid at 5.5% and private health insurance at 4.8%.[21] Also, due to enrollment growth in Medicare and Medicaid, the public sector as a sponsor of healthcare expenditures will increase from 44.8% of NHEs in 2018 to 47.4% of NHEs in 2027.[22]

Figure 3.4 shows the services on which $3.65 trillion was spent during 2018. Hospitals, professional services, and prescription drugs accounted for almost 70% of all healthcare spending. Figure 3.5 shows sources of payment for the $3.65 trillion during 2018. Private health insurance continues to be the largest single source of payment. Health spending by sponsor (the entity that is ultimately responsible for paying the healthcare bill, however, tells a different story (see Figure 3.6):[23]

- Households accounted for 28.4% of payments and includes employee contributions to employer-sponsored private health insurance premiums, directly purchased health insurance, the medical portion of property and casualty insurance premiums, employee and self-employment payroll taxes and premiums paid to Part A, premiums paid by individuals to Part B and Part D, and out-of-pocket spending.

- Federal government accounted for 28.3% of payments and includes federal contributions to employer-sponsored private health insurance premiums, employer Medicare Part A contributions, federal general revenue contributions to Medicare Part B and Part C, the federal

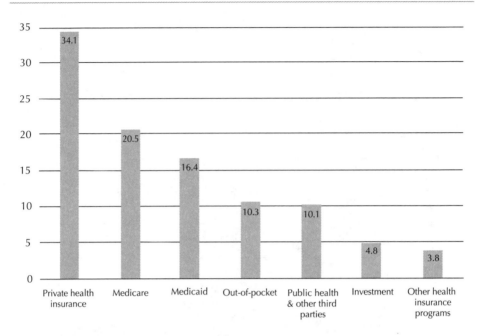

Figure 3.5. NHE by source, percent of total, 2018. Source: CMS. National Health Expenditures, Historical Table 1. https://www.cms.gov/Research-Statistics-Data-and-Systems/Statistics-Trends-and-Reports/NationalHealthExpendData/index, retrieved on January 2, 2020.

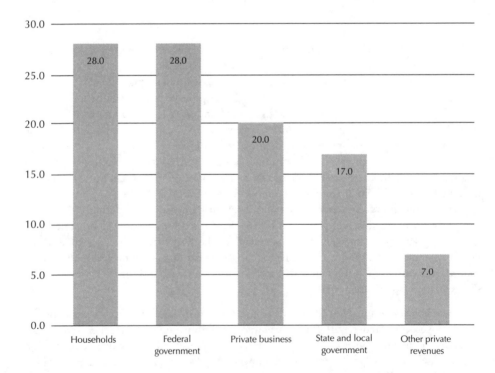

Figure 3.6. NHE by sponsor, percent of total, 2018. Source: CMS. National Health Expenditures, Historical Table 5. https://www.cms.gov/Research-Statistics-Data-and-Systems/Statistics-Trends-and-Reports/NationalHealthExpendData/index, retrieved on January 2, 2020.

portion of Medicaid payments, the federal portion of Medicare buy-in premiums, retiree drug subsidy payments, and marketplace tax credits and subsidies.

• Private business accounted for 19.9% of payments and includes employer-sponsored private health insurance premiums, employer Part A payroll taxes, workers' compensation, temporary disability insurance, and worksite healthcare.

• State and local government accounted for 16.5% of payments and includes state contributions to employer-sponsored private health insurance premiums, the state portion of Medicaid payments, and the state portion of Medicare buy-in premiums.

• Other private revenues accounted for 6.9% of payments and include health-related philanthropic support, nonoperating revenue, investment income, and privately funded structures and equipment.

Special Characteristics of the Healthcare Economy

Is healthcare a right? As a senator, Barack Obama campaigned on the notion that healthcare should be a "right" for every American. The ACA of 2010 improved access to that "right" for approximately 20 million uninsured Americans. Most would agree with the World Health Organization that accessible healthcare for all is a moral right[24]; however, fewer would agree that healthcare is or should be a legal right and therefore should be provided to all Americans. In the United States, this issue splits along party lines, with 70% of Democrats supporting a national health plan that covers all Americans and only 30% of Republicans supporting such a plan.[25] Proponents of a national health plan argue for a system that distributes healthcare evenly, on the basis of need, regardless of financial means. Opponents argue increasing access will lead to overutilization of healthcare resources, increasing costs, and eventually a budgeted maximum national expenditure for health services, the result of which will be to diminish access and referrals, which is seen in other centrally planned systems. Therefore, implementing this right will be dependent on the resources available in and allocated to healthcare by society through government action.[26]

What is the role of the consumer-patient? In most purchases, consumers are reasonably knowledgeable as to the quality of products and services, as well as the alternatives, and can choose based on price and quality. In healthcare, patients have far less information for making decisions, although this is beginning to change with pricing transparency laws and quality reporting and public disclosure requirements by the Centers for Medicare and Medicaid Services (CMS).[27] Historically, once persons select a physician, the physician, as an agent, helps them make decisions about their health and their healthcare. Agency arises from the physician's knowledge about patient needs (and sometimes wants), and patients trust and accept the physician's decisions about their care.[28]

What is the role of the physician? There seems to be a consensus among economists that an agency relationship exists. However, such an agency relationship does not necessarily mean that physicians act as perfect agents. A perfect agent would make decisions that are in the best interest of the patient or would make decisions the patient would make if fully knowledgeable.[29] In fact it does not seem realistic to expect perfect agency in almost any human interactions. Nonetheless, physicians have a moral and legal obligation to educate their patients and involve them in decision making. Questions that should be asked include the following: What level and type of services are medically and ethically necessary? How does a physician know what a patient would want if fully knowledgeable? Should the physician act on what the patient wants or on what the physician determines is medically best?[30]

Fee-for-service linked with third-party payment is another special characteristic of the healthcare economy. In fee-for-service, providers are paid for the volume of healthcare services performed regardless of outcomes. Even though fee-for-service as a payment method is declining, as fee-for-service providers perform more services, their incomes increase and the costs are passed on to insurers or government who, in turn, increase premiums or taxes. Because the connection between services received and who pays for them is indirect with third-party payment by insurers and the government, there is little incentive for patients or providers to limit services that may not be needed.[31] In a 2017 survey physicians responded that 20% of overall medical care was unnecessary.[32] In 2013, the Institute of Medicine reported that unnecessary services added $210 billion to healthcare spending.[33] For the worried well, more healthcare when unnecessary increases the chance of medical error as well as cost.[34] Most patients are, however, not just worried well. It must be remembered that physicians and other licensed independent practitioners must order referrals, testing, and treatment. The review of services consumed has a dampening effect on any tendency to order unnecessary use of resources. In addition, managed care organization (MCO) providers, such as health maintenance organizations (HMOs) and preferred provider organizations (PPOs) are very attentive to resource utilization.

For decades, price discrimination and cost shifting have been discussed as problems in policy for hospital payment from public sources. Shortly after the implementation of Medicare and Medicaid in the mid-1960s, Paul Starr (American [1949–]) gave the following warning: "Commercial insurance companies worried that if the government tried to solve its fiscal problems simply by tightening up cost-based reimbursement, the hospitals might simply shift the costs to patients who pay charges [or a portion of a charge increase]."[35] While providers charge every payer the same amount for a procedure during a given time period, what payers actually pay can be very different. This difference can be based on contracts between providers and payers that discount from charges based on volumes, or bad debt or charity care, both of which pay less than the charge. So, price discrimination, or different payers paying different amounts for the same service, occurs in healthcare as it does in other industries. While economists agree there is substantial price discrimination in healthcare in the United States, associating a cost-shifting theory with price discrimination is not universally accepted. According to Uwe Reinhardt (American [1937–2017]), providers attempt to shift unreimbursed costs to private payers who have no choice but to pay what healthcare providers charge.[36] Some economists argue that cost shifting occurs even when private payers have some choice in compensating healthcare providers.[37] The American Hospital Association (AHA) publishes hospitals' underpayment and payment-to-cost ratios annually. In 2017, AHA analyses showed that payments from Medicare and Medicaid were well below hospitals' costs for providing services, with underpayments of $53.9 billion or 86.8% of costs and $22.9 billion or 88.1% of cost, respectively. Payment from private insurance was substantially above cost (144.8% of cost).[38] Hospitals also provided $38.4 billion in uncompensated care.[39]

Healthcare Demand

The law of demand states that the quantity of goods or services demanded falls as the price rises and increases as the price falls. Demand, or the services and goods purchased at different prices, is a core concept in healthcare economics. For instance, demand forecasts by managers are essential to projecting revenues. Demand for healthcare is different from that in other industries, however, for the following reasons:[40]

- The price of care to the patient is often distorted by health insurance. "Moral hazard" describes how people change their behavior when they have insurance.[41] Insured patients often demand higher quantity and higher quality of healthcare than they could otherwise afford.

- Healthcare decisions are complex and have economic effects in several different contexts at the personal level.

- Patients are poorly informed about costs, benefits, and substitutes for healthcare services needed or wanted. Such "rational ignorance" is natural and requires that healthcare providers make recommendations to the patient.

Demand can be elastic, meaning that small changes in price affect the amount demanded, or demand can be inelastic, meaning that even large changes in price will not affect the amount demanded. Most demand for healthcare is inelastic[42] because of rational ignorance, emergency and essential treatment, and the emotional impact of some decisions. However, research such as the Rand Study[43] shows that substantial moral hazard exists for medical care and that cost-sharing mechanisms such as copays and deductibles could reduce moral hazard utilization without eroding quality. Rather than limit incentives of patients demanding healthcare of marginal value, HMOs limit incentives of providers to order services of marginal value, thereby reducing both moral hazard and induced demand. Many believe health savings accounts (HSAs) that rely more heavily on deductibles can reduce demand for services even more than HMOs. With HSAs, patients must use as much as several thousand dollars from their HSA to pay for medical services before coverage begins (often referred to as high deductible health plans).[44]

Physicians diagnose, treat, and bill for their work. This situation puts them in a position to induce demand for financial gain. Nobel Prize–winning economist Kenneth Arrow (American [1921–2017]) argued that even though "advice given by physicians as to further treatment by himself or others is supposed to be completely divorced from self-interest,"[45] there is little doubt that physicians induce demand for various reasons—some justifiable, some not. After more than 60 years of research dating to Milton Roemer (American [1916–2001]), who said, "In an insured population, a hospital bed built is a filled bed,"[46] there is no consensus as to the extent of physician-induced demand.

Healthcare Supply

According to the law of supply, the supply of goods or services rises as the price rises and falls as the price falls. In the traditional competition-based economic model, demand is prerequisite to supply in that supply is always reacting to changes in demand. In healthcare, however, partly due to demand induced by providers, incentives to influence provider behavior can alter demand. Examples of incentives to influence provider behavior include payment systems that reimburse providers on a fixed fee, such as per diem, per diagnosis, or per head (capitation). In these payment systems, if providers provide care at less cost than the payment, they can make a profit. This calls into question whether unnecessary utilization should be addressed on the demand side, the supply side, or both. Supply-side solutions to reducing unnecessary utilization include the following:[47]

- Reimbursement systems that reduce retrospective reimbursement and move to prospective reimbursement in which providers know the amount of reimbursement before they diagnose and treat the patient (and presumably keep costs below the amount of reimbursement). Here, the risk is undertreatment.

- Reimbursement systems that reduce fee-for-service that encourages volume and move to fixed-payment arrangements in which providers share in both utilization and cost risk. Fixed-payment arrangements include per head (capitation), per diagnosis, and per day. Here, the risk is undertreatment.

- Value-based reimbursement systems that pay providers based on efficiency and quality.

- Evidence-based practice guidelines that recommend the best way to diagnose and treat patients with specific symptoms or illness.

- Utilization management that reviews utilization within the HSO. Utilization management can be prospective, concurrent, or retrospective.

- Patient-centered care that attempts to make physicians better agents for the patient by improving relationships between them and improving coordination among physicians treating a patient. Patient-centered medical homes extend patient-centered care and give patients an ongoing relationship with a primary care provider who coordinates care among providers.

MCOs use many of these solutions to manage utilization and costs, with specific emphasis on financing and delivery. Since the late 1980s, MCOs have evolved from HMOs (the most aggressive form of MCO, which requires patients to stay in the network, see the HMO's primary care physician first, and pays physicians on salary or capitation) to PPOs, which have a wider network of affiliated providers from which patients choose and which pay physicians a discounted fee-for-service), and point-of-service (POS) plans, which allow patients to see physicians out of network. If patients receive care out of network they pay any difference in cost. POSs were created in the early 2000s to solve concerns about limited access (freedom of choice) and quality of in-network providers.

The law of supply as applied to labor states that the labor supply rises as the price (or reimbursement) rises and falls as the price (or reimbursement) falls. This has been true in the supply of nurses. In times of declining reimbursement (introduction of prospective pricing [DRGs] in the early 1980s) and passage of the Balanced Budget Act (PL 105-33), supply of nurses in hospitals as measured by staffing levels declined.[48] Other factors determining the supply of nurses include the following:[49]

- Income and return on educational investment

- Migration and emigration of the workforce

- Education system capacity, curriculum, and culture

- Employment conditions, including job location

- Demographics of the workforce

- Local economic conditions

- Global economic and political stability that affects net migration

Research shows both a current physician shortage and a predicted future shortage; recently, however, physician-to-population ratios have been stable. Since there is no consensus on desirable physician-to-population ratios, the need for more physicians is usually based on gaining better access to care. Research findings on the current physician supply show the following:

- Twenty-five percent of U.S. physicians are international medical school graduates.[50]

- The physician workforce is smaller and younger than previously thought.[51]

- There is a shortage of primary care physicians.

- There may be a shortage of allopathic physicians, but osteopathic physicians and nonphysician providers will provide a buffer.[52]

- A substantial body of research shows that physicians are maldistributed nationwide (excess physicians in cities, shortages in rural areas).

Factors determining the supply of physicians include the following:[53]

- Income and return on educational investments including student loan debt

- Interest in serving people

- Job opportunities

- Location opportunities

- Prestige of the medical profession

Economic Solutions for Healthcare

Overall goals for reforming the healthcare system to make high quality healthcare affordable to all include reducing the rate of growth in healthcare spending, promoting prevention and wellness, implementing Medicare reforms, and implementing private sector reforms. The material that follows in the first three sections below is based on the documentary *I.O.U.S.A. Solutions: Part 4 of 5*.[54]

Reducing the Rate of Growth in Healthcare Spending

A number of strategies should be implemented to reduce the rate of growth in healthcare spending:

- Replace fee-for-service with payment methods that transfer both utilization and cost risk to providers.

- Improve interprovider communication and coordination to reduce duplication.

- Continue to implement electronic medical records so providers can easily obtain patient care information from the system.

- Increase physician and hospital accountability for quality, cost, and access.

- Support malpractice reform in states that have not reformed their malpractice laws to reduce defensive medicine costs.

- Reduce administrative processes and costs associated with a fragmented system.

- Reduce medical errors and their associated costs.

- Educate healthcare consumers so they are better informed about prices and costs.

- Make better decisions about end-of-life care (approximately 30% of all Medicare reimbursement is for care in the last year of life). Families should have discussions, supported by medical professionals, regarding end-of-life scenarios, as well as advance medical directives.[55]

Promoting Prevention and Wellness

Strategies for promoting disease prevention and wellness include the following:

- Engage the public in healthier lifestyle decisions (over half of all healthcare problems and related costs are preventable; patients with multiple chronic conditions spend most of the Medicare dollars).[56]

- Consider monetary incentives (tax credits and reduced insurance premiums) for patients who adopt healthier lifestyles.

Implementing Medicare Reforms

Medicare reforms that could be implemented include the following:

- Establish a federal budget for healthcare, including caps on federal spending.

- Raise premiums on voluntary parts of Medicare (Part B covering physician and outpatient payments and Part D covering outpatient prescription drug benefits) to make them self-sustaining (both are heavily subsidized by the federal government now).

- Gradually raise the Medicare eligibility age to be consistent with changes in eligibility for Social Security that have already been made.

Implementing Reforms in the Private Sector

Private sector reforms include the following:

- Consolidation by both payers and providers. In *Health Care 2020: Part 3 on Consolidation,* the Healthcare Financial Management Association analyzed the potential antitrust threat of higher prices and reduced competition and the potential value to consumers from more coordination and better quality of care.[57]

- Direct contracting involves large, self-insured employers working directly with an accountable care organization (ACO [hospitals, physicians, and other providers organized for coordinated care]) to care for the medical needs of employees. In some cases, the employer has an insurance company or claims administrator to process claims using fee for service. In others, the employer pays the ACO a capitated amount per employee and eliminates the insurance company relationship. In the second case, it serves both the ACO and the employer to lower costs by improving employee health. Examples of direct contracting include Whole Foods and Adventist Health in Southern California, Intel Corporation and Presbyterian Healthcare in Albuquerque, and Boeing Corporation and Providence-Swedish Health Alliance in Seattle.[58]

The discussion on healthcare reform tends to address two extremes: do nothing and let healthcare bankrupt the country or reform the system to reduce demand which to some would look like rationing care. A third option is to redesign healthcare to reduce costs by addressing fraud, abuse, error, and waste and then to use the savings to make higher quality healthcare available to more people.[59]

Discussion Questions

1. Identify several reasons healthcare expenditures have increased at a faster rate than other expenditures in the economy.

2. Review Figure 3.4 showing NHEs by spending category. In which categories is most money spent? Suggest why this is true.

3. Review Figure 3.5. Identify the largest sources of healthcare dollars and what those sources can do to control healthcare spending.

4. Discuss why the healthcare sector of the economy is different from other sectors, such as the automobile sector.

5. If healthcare is a right, what are the ramifications for health policy in the United States? Are there ramifications for citizens (potential patients)?

6. According to Uwe Reinhardt, what is the difference between price discrimination and cost shifting?

7. Why is demand for healthcare different from demand for other services in the economy?

8. Define the concept of "moral hazard." Discuss ways patients with health insurance behave differently than those without it.

9. Explain the differences among HMO, PPO, and POS health plans.

10. If the physician workforce is smaller and younger than previously thought, what are the advantages and disadvantages of such a finding?

11. Explain the differences between Medicare reforms and private sector reform.

 Case Study 1   Price and Discount Transparency[60]

President Donald J. Trump's first round of hospital reforms, effective January 2019, required hospitals to make public their full list of charges for services, called a charge-master, so patients and potential patients and their insurers could make better decisions regarding the cost of care.[60] Opponents argue that there is a difference between the price, the price after a negotiated discount by an insurer, and what amount the patient is responsible for paying. In November 2019, the administration announced a proposed regulatory rule, effective January 2021, that renews efforts to bring pricing transparency to hospital and physician services. The proposed rule would force health insurance companies to release confidential details of negotiated discounts with both hospitals and physicians, or essentially, what part of the prices released in January 2019 insurance companies pay.

Questions

1. Why would providers not want to release prices?

2. Why would providers not want to release discounts?

3. What do patients need for them to compare healthcare products and services based on price?

Case Study 2   Comparing Healthcare in High-Income Countries[61]

In 2016, using per capita spending and health spending as a percentage of GDP, the United States spent nearly twice as much on healthcare as 10 other high-income countries. Contrary to some explanations for high healthcare spending, social spending and healthcare utilization do not differ between the United States and the 10 other high-income countries. What does differ is the prices for labor and goods, including pharmaceuticals and medical devices, and administrative costs. Relative to the comparison countries, the United States fared better on access measures, including wait times to see both primary care and specialist physicians, but especially the latter. Relative to population health outcomes, the United States consistently has the poorest health outcomes in life expectancy (78.8 years compared with a mean of 81.7 years for the comparison countries), infant mortality (5.8 deaths per 1,000 live births compared with a mean of 3.6 for comparison countries), and maternal mortality (26.4 deaths per 100,000 live births compared with a mean of 8.4 for comparison countries). Researchers concluded that while the United States spends approximately twice as much as other high-income countries and while utilization rates are similar, population health outcomes are often worse.

Questions

1. Discuss the reasons the U.S. healthcare system is considerably more expensive while producing worse population *health outcomes* than other high-income countries.

2. Distinguishing between health outcomes and healthcare outcomes, discuss reasons the U.S. healthcare system produces better *healthcare outcomes* for individuals. Answering this question may require additional reading.

Case Study 3 | The Role of Insurance in Guaranteeing Access to Healthcare

The discussion noted, "It must be emphasized that healthcare insurance neither guarantees access to care nor prevents it."

Questions

1. Analyze this statement based on your own experience or an experience known to you.

2. Identify laws and regulations that enhance access to healthcare in the United States.

Case Study 4 | Physician Consolidation[62]

Privia Medical Group, with more than 1,400 physicians in six states, is one of the fastest growing physician group practices. Formed in 2013, Privia seeks markets in which health plans engage providers with at-risk contracts (contracts that transfer cost risk and utilization risk to the providers). Physicians in Privia own and manage their individual practices but assign their revenues to Privia's management company, which provides population health management technology, resources, and operational strategies. Privia's management company negotiates performance-based contracts on behalf of the physicians. "Our goal is to build medical groups that are provider-owned and provider-managed and are being rewarded for lowering the cost of healthcare by making the appropriate choices and educating patients about the appropriate choices," says Privia's COO.[63]

Questions

1. If you were a physician, would you be attracted to contracting with a group like Privia? If so, why?

2. What are the advantages and disadvantages for physicians to contract with groups like Privia?

Notes

1. Schneider, Eric C., et. al. *Mirror, Mirror 2017: International Comparison Reflect Flaws and Opportunities for Better U.S. Health Care.* Commonwealth Fund. *https://interactives.commonwealthfund.org/2017/july/mirror-mirror/*, retrieved January 29, 2020.
2. Peterson, Peter G. *Steering Clear: How to Avoid a Debt Crisis and Secure Our Economic Future.* New York: Penguin Group, 2015, 11–12.
3. Lubin, Gus. "10 Reasons Why the US Healthcare System Is the Envy of the World." *Business Insider*, March 10, 2010. *https://www.businessinsider.com/10-reasons-why-the-us-health-care-system-is-the-envy-of-the-world-2010-3*, retrieved January 29, 2020.
4. Kennedy, Edward M. *In Critical Condition: The Crisis in America's Health Care.* New York: Simon & Schuster, 1972, 16–17.

5. Catlin, Aaron E., and Cathy A. Cowan. *History of Health Spending in the United States, 1960–2013.* November 19, 2015. *https://www.cms.gov/Research-Statistics-Data-and-Systems/Statistics-Trends-and-Reports/NationalHealthExpendData/Downloads/HistoricalNHEPaper.pdf,* retrieved January 18, 2020; CMS. National Health Expenditures, Historical Table 1. *https://www.cms.gov/Research-Statistics-Data-and-Systems/Statistics-Trends-and-Reports/NationalHealthExpendData/index,* retrieved January 2, 2020.

6. CMS. National Health Expenditures, Historical Table 1 and Projected Table 5. *https://www.cms.gov/Research-Statistics-Data-and-Systems/Statistics-Trends-and-Reports/NationalHealthExpendData/index,* retrieved on January 2, 2020; U.S. Regional Economic Analysis Project. United States Comparative Trend Analysis: Per Capita Personal Income Growth and Change, 1958–2018. *https://united-states.reaproject.org/analysis/comparative-trends-analysis/per_capita_personal_income/tools/0/0/,* retrieved January 18, 2020.

7. Adapted from Catlin, Aaron C., and Cathy A. Cowan, *History of Health Spending in the United States, 1960–2013,* 7–25. Centers for Medicare & Medicaid Services. *https://www.cms.gov/Research-Statistics-Data-and-Systems/Statistics-Trends-and-Reports/NationalHealthExpendData/Downloads/HistoricalNHEPaper.pdf,* retrieved January 18, 2020.

8. Mitchell, Janet B., Gerard Wedig, and Jerry Cromwell. "The Medicare Physician Fee Freeze: What Really Happened?" *Health Affairs,* January 1989. *https://www.healthaffairs.org/doi/full/10.1377/hlthaff.8.1.21,* retrieved January 19, 2020.

9. Guterman, Stuart. "The Balanced Budget Act of 1997: Will Hospitals Take a Hit on Their PPS Margins?" *Health Affairs,* January/February 1998. *https://www.healthaffairs.org/doi/pdf/10.1377/hlthaff.17.1.159,* retrieved January 20, 2020.

10. Komisar, Harriet. *The Balanced Budget Act of 1997: Effects on Medicare's Home Health Benefit and Beneficiaries Who Need Long-Term Care,* December 1997. The Commonwealth Fund. *https://www.commonwealthfund.org/publications/fund-reports/1997/dec/balanced-budget-act-1997-effects-medicares-home-health-benefit,* retrieved January 20, 2020.

11. Levit, Katharine, Cynthia Smith, Cathy Cowan, Helen Lazenby, and Anne Martin. "Inflation Spurs Health Spending in 2000." *Health Affairs,* January 2001. *http://content.healthaffairs.org/content/21/1/172.full,* retrieved January 20, 2020.

12. Amadeo, Kimberly. "ARRA, Its Details, with Pros and Cons." *The Balance,* July 30, 2019. *https://www.thebalance.com/arra-details-3306299,* retrieved January 20, 2020.

13. Amadeo, Kimberly. "2010 Patient Protection & Affordable Care Act Summary." *The Balance,* June 20, 2019. *https://www.thebalance.com/2010-patient-protection-affordable-care-act-3306063,* retrieved January 20, 2020.

14. CMS. National Health Expenditures, Historical Table 1. *https://www.cms.gov/Research-Statistics-Data-and-Systems/Statistics-Trends-and-Reports/NationalHealthExpendData/index,* retrieved January 20, 2020.

15. CMS Press Release. "CMS Releases 2014 National Health Expenditures," December 2, 2015. *https://www.cms.gov/newsroom/press-releases/cms-releases-2014-national-health-expenditures,* retrieved January 20, 2020.

16. CMS Press Release. "CMS Releases 2015 National Health Expenditures," December 2, 2016. *https://www.cms.gov/newsroom/press-releases/cms-releases-2015-national-health-expenditures,* retrieved January 20, 2020.

17. CMS Press Release. "CMS Office of the Actuary Releases 2016 National Health Expenditures," December 6, 2017. *https://www.cms.gov/newsroom/press-releases/cms-office-actuary-releases-2016-national-health-expenditures,* retrieved January 20, 2020.

18. CMS Press Release. "CMS Office of the Actuary Releases 2017 National Health Expenditures," December 6, 2018. *https://www.cms.gov/newsroom/press-releases/cms-office-actuary-releases-2017-national-health-expenditures,* retrieved January 20, 2020.

19. CMS Press Release. "CMS Office of the Actuary Releases 2018 National Health Expenditures," December 5, 2019. *https://www.cms.gov/newsroom/press-releases/cms-office-actuary-releases-2018-national-health-expenditures,* retrieved January 20, 2020.

20. Moyler, Hunter. "Here Are All the Affordable Care Act Taxes Disappearing in 2020." *Newsweek,* December 19, 2019. *https://www.newsweek.com/affordable-care-act-taxes-repealed-1478323,* retrieved January 20, 2020; As part of the $1.4 trillion spending package approved by Congress and signed by the President Trump in December, 2019, the following three ACA taxes were repealed effective 2021 with a loss of tax revenue to federal government projected at $373.3 billion over ten years: the "Cadillac tax" imposed a 40% excise tax on employer-sponsored plans that exceeded $10,000 in premiums per year for a single person and $27,500 per year for a family; the health insurance tax paid by insurance companies often cited as a cause of rising premiums to consumers; and the medical device tax, a 2.3% excise tax on gross sales of medical devices for human beings.

21. CMS. "NHE Fact Sheet, Projected NHE, 2018-2027." *https://www.cms.gov/Research-Statistics-Data-and-Systems/Statistics-Trends-and-Reports/NationalHealthExpendData/NHE-Fact-Sheet*, retrieved December 20, 2020.

22. CMS. National Health Expenditures, Historical Table 1 and Projected Table 16. *https://www.cms.gov/Research-Statistics-Data-and-Systems/Statistics-Trends-and-Reports/NationalHealthExpendData/index*, retrieved January 20, 2020.

23. CMS. "National Health Expenditures 2018 Highlights." *https://www.cms.gov/files/document/highlights.pdf*, retrieved December 20, 2019; CMS. "National Health Expenditures, Historical Table 5." *https://www.cms.gov/Research-Statistics-Data-and-Systems/Statistics-Trends-and-Reports/NationalHealthExpendData/index*, retrieved January 2, 2020.

24. Braverman, Paul, and Sofia Gruskin. "Poverty, Equity, Human Rights and Health." *Bulletin of the World Health Organization*, 2003, 539–545. *https://www.ncbi.nlm.nih.gov/pmc/articles/PMC2572503/*, retrieved January 20, 2020.

25. Kaiser Family Foundation. Public Opinion on Single-Payer, National Health Plans, and Expanding Access to Medicare Coverage, November 26, 2019. *https://www.kff.org/slideshow/public-opinion-on-single-payer-national-health-plans-and-expanding-access-to-medicare-coverage/*, retrieved January 20, 2020.

26. Maruthappu, Mahiben, Rele Ologunde, and Ayinkeran Gunarajasingam. "Is Health Care a Right? Health Reforms in the USA and Their Impact upon the Concept of Care." *Annals of Medicine and Surgery* (February 5, 2012). *https://www.ncbi.nlm.nih.gov/pmc/articles/PMC4326121/*, retrieved January 20, 2020.

27. CMS. "SNF Quality Reporting Program Public Reporting." Last updated October 24, 2019. *https://www.cms.gov/Medicare/Quality-Initiatives-Patient-Assessment-Instruments/NursingHomeQualityInits/Skilled-Nursing-Facility-Quality-Reporting-Program/SNF-Quality-Reporting-Program-Public-Reporting*, retrieved January 20, 2020.

28. Richardson, Jeff, and S. J. Peacock. "Supplier-Induced Demand: Reconsidering the Theories and New Australian Evidence." *Applied Health Economics and Health Policy* 5, 2 (2006): 87–98.

29. Rice, Thomas, and Lynn Unruh. *The Economics of Health Reconsidered*, 4th ed., 182. Chicago: Health Administration Press, 2016.

30. Richardson and Peacock. "Supplier-Induced Demand."

31. Peterson, Peter G. *Steering Clear*, 97–98.

32. Carroll, Aaron E. "The High Costs of Unnecessary Care." *JAMA Forum* (November 14, 2017). *https://jamanetwork.com/journals/jama/fullarticle/2662877*, retrieved January 21, 2020.

33. Smith, Mark, Robert Saunders, Leigh Stuckhardt, and J. Michael McGinnis, eds. *Best Care at Lower Cost: The Path to Continuously Learning Health Care in America*. Washington, DC: National Academies Press, 2013. *https://books.google.com/books?hl=en&lr=&id=_wUw6XCFqGwC&oi=fnd&pg=PR1&ots=0KpGw7mkws&sig=Gl-iPrrSQEpnYkoJKecz2jEPzMA#v=onepage&q&f=false*, retrieved January 21, 2020.

34. Brownlee, Shannon. *Overtreated: Why Too Much Medicine Is Making Us Sicker and Poorer*. New York: Bloomsbury Publishers, 2007.

35. Starr, Paul. *The Social Transformation of American Medicine*. New York: Basic Books, 1982, 388.

36. Reinhardt, Uwe E. "The Many Different Prices Paid to Providers and the Flawed Theory of Cost Shifting: Is It Time for a More Rational All-Payer System?" *Health Affairs*, November 2011.

37. Dobson, Allen, Joan DaVanzo, and Namrata Sen. The Cost-Shift Payment 'Hydraulic': Foundation, History, and Implications. *Health Affairs*, January/February 2006. *https://www.healthaffairs.org/doi/full/10.1377/hlthaff.25.1.22*, retrieved January 25, 2020.

38. American Hospital Association. Table 4.4: Aggregate Hospital Payment-to-cost Ratios for Private Payers, Medicare, and Medicaid, 1995-2016. *Trendwatch Chartbook 2018*. *https://www.aha.org/system/files/2018-05/2018-chartbook-table-4-4.pdf*, retrieved January 25, 2020.

39. Sanborn, Beth Jones. "Medicare, Medicaid Underpaid U.S. Hospitals by $76.8 Billion in 2017, American Hospital Association Says." Healthcare Finance, January 4, 2019, *https://www.healthcarefinancenews.com/news/medicare-medicaid-underpaid-us-hospitals-768-billion-2017-american-hospital-association-says*, retrieved January 25, 2020.

40. Lee, Robert H. *Economics for Healthcare Managers*, 3rd ed. Chicago: Health Administration Press, 2015, 112.

41. Dranove, David. *The Economic Evolution of American Healthcare*. Princeton: Princeton University Press, 2000, 29.

42. Ellis, Randall P., Bruno Martins, and Wenjia Zhu. "Health Care Demand Elasticities by Type of Service." *Journal of Health Economics* (July 29, 2017). *https://www.ncbi.nim.nih.gov/pmc/articles/PMC5600717/*, retrieved January 26, 2020.

43. Powell, David, and Dana P. Goldman. "Moral Hazard and Adverse Selection in Private Health Insurance." Rand Corporation, 2014. *https://www.rand.org/pubs/working_papers/WR1032.html*, retrieved January 29, 2020.

44. Dranove, David. *The Economic Evolution of American Healthcare*, 30–31.

45. Arrow, Ken. "Uncertainty and the Welfare Economics of Medical Care." *American Economic Review*, December 1963, 949–950.

46. Now known as Roemer's Law and attributed to him in his obituary, University of California, Los Angeles School of Public Health, January 8, 2001.

47. Rice and Unruh. *The Economics of Health Reconsidered*, 4th ed., 192–205.

48. Mobley, Lee Rivers, and Jon Magnussen. "The Impact of Managed Care Penetration and Hospital Quality on Efficiency in Hospital Staffing." *Journal of Health Care Finance* (Summer 2002): 24–42; Lindrooth, Richard C., Gloria J. Bazzoli, Jack Needleman, and Romana Hasnain-Wynia. "The Effect of Changes in Hospital Reimbursement on Nurse Staffing Decisions at Safety Net and Non-safety Net Hospitals." *Health Services Research* (June 2006): 701–720.

49. Rice and Unruh. *The Economics of Health Reconsidered*, 4th ed., 318.

50. Goodman, David C., and Elliott Fisher. "Physician Workforce Crisis? Wrong Diagnosis, Wrong Prescription." *New England Journal of Medicine* 368 (April 17, 2008): 1658–1661.

51. Staiger, Douglas, David I. Auerbach, and Peter I. Buerhaus. "Comparison of Physician Workforce Estimates and Supply Projections." *Journal of the American Medical Association* 302 (October 21, 2009): 1674–1680.

52. Auerbach, David I., et al. "Nurse-Managed Health Centers and Patient-Centered Medical Homes Could Mitigate Expected Primary Care Physician Shortage." *Health Affairs* 32 (November 2013): 1933–1941.

53. Rice and Unruh. *The Economics of Health Reconsidered*, 4th ed., 318–319.

54. Fisher, Elliot. I.O.U.S.A. Part 4—The Healthcare Economy. *https://www.youtube.com/watch?v=9ain_VXnUhs&list=PL72876526757E649D&index=5&t=0s*, retrieved January 26, 2020.

55. Leland, John. "She Is 96 and Does Not Fear Her Death. But Do Her Children?" *New York Times*, January 3, 2020. *https://www.nytimes.com/2020/01/03/nyregion/ruth-willig-oldest-death.html?utm_source=pocket-newtab*, retrieved January 5, 2020.

56. Erdem, Erkan, Sergio I. Prada, Samuel C. Haffer. "Medicare Payments: How Much Do Chronic Conditions Matter?" *Medicare and Medicaid Research Review*, a publication of the Centers for Medicare & Medicaid Services, 3, 2 (2013): E1–E15. *https://www.cms.gov/mmrr/Downloads/MMRR2013_003_02_b02.pdf*, retrieved January 29, 2020.

57. HFMA. *Health Care 2020, Part 3: Consolidation*, Fall 2016. *https://www.hfma.org/content/dam/hfma/document/research_reports/PDF/51087.pdf*, retrieved February 1, 2020; Gooch, Kelly. "What Does Consolidation Mean for the Future of Healthcare? 6 Things to Know." *Becker's Hospital Review*, November 29, 2016, *https://www.beckershospitalreview.com/hospital-transactions-and-valuation/what-does-consolidation-mean-for-the-future-of-healthcare-6-things-to-know.html*, retrieved February 1, 2020; Oliver, Eric. "3 Experts Break Down the Past, Present & Future of Consolidation." *Becker's Hospital Review*, April 17, 2019. *https://www.beckershospitalreview.com/hospital-transactions-and-valuation/3-experts-breakdown-the-past-present-future-of-consolidation.html*, retrieved February 1, 2020.

58. Livingston, Shelby. "Left Out of the Game: Health Systems Offer Direct-to-Employer Contracting to Eliminate Insurer." *Modern Healthcare*, January 27, 2018. *https://www.modernhealthcare.com/article/20180127/NEWS/180129919/left-out-of-the-game-health-systems-offer-direct-to-employer-contracting-to-eliminate-insurers*, retrieved February 1, 2020.

59. Fisher, Elliott. I.O.U.S.A. Part 4—The Healthcare Economy.

60. Ryder, Brett. "Diagnosis: Opaque—Donald Trump wants hospitals to be more upfront about pricing." *Economist*, Business Section, November 23, 2019.

61. Papanicolas, Irene, Liana R. Woskie, and Ashish K. Jha. "Health Care Spending in the United States and Other High-Income Countries." *Journal of the American Medical Association* 319 (March 13, 2018), *https://jamanetwork.com/journals/jama/fullarticle/2674671?guestAccessKey=29ae801c-a8a6-4f8b-9889-b9f0ef4345f4&utm_source=silverchair&utm_campaign=jama_network&utm_content=weekly_highlights&cmp=1&utm_medium=email#188507855*, retrieved January 26, 2020.

62. HFMA. *Health Care 2020, Part 3: Consolidation*, Fall 2016.

63. HFMA, *Health Care 2020*, 9.

4

The Quality Imperative: The Theory

Chapter Outline

Improving Quality and Performance
Importance of QI
Background to the Present Focus on Quality Improvement
Taking a CQI Approach
CQI, PI, and Competitive Position
Theory of CQI
Strategic Quality Planning: Hoshin Planning
Two Models to Improve Processes
Organizing for Improvement
The Next Iteration of CQI: A Community Focus

The management model that appears in the Part III introduction of this text (Figure III.2) shows how health services organizations (HSOs) and health systems (HSs) convert inputs into outputs. The inputs of structure, tasks and technology, and people are integrated to achieve individual and organizational outputs (productivity). The type and nature of inputs and the conversion process determine quality of output. This chapter details the conceptual framework of quality improvement; Chapter 8 shows the applications.

The conceptual framework discussed here is the first dimension of quality improvement (QI). The framework is drawn from QI theorists and pioneers. Prominent among them are Florence Nightingale (English, 1820–1910), Ernest A. Codman (American, 1869–1940), Walter A. Shewhart (American, 1891–1967), W. Edwards Deming (American, 1900–1993), and Avedis Donabedian (Lebanese American, 1919–2000). All made important contributions to the theory of QI, applying theory to performance improvement (PI), and measuring results. Deming was the most important modern-day QI theorist. Deming's contemporaries, Joseph M. Juran (Romanian American, 1904–2008), and Philip B. Crosby (American, 1926–2001), developed applications of QI in the workplace. Hoshin planning is a methodology used to align the HSO's quality efforts. "Performance improvement" and "productivity improvement" are treated as synonyms here, even though logically sequencing their relationship would have improved productivity following improved performance.

Process improvement is the second dimension of quality. Chapter 8 describes how to organize for quality and provides a primer of methodologies, techniques, and tools to make continuous quality improvement (CQI) a reality. Application of CQI in the operating units is also discussed in Chapter 8. HSOs and HSs that use CQI to become more productive and cost-effective have a significant competitive advantage.

Improving Quality and Performance

Attention was first paid to the quality of clinical practice in HSOs in the late 19th century. At that time, technology and efficacious surgery were centralizing clinical services in the acute care hospital. Peer review was the methodology used to measure quality and was defined as physician review of the care provided by physicians and other categories of caregivers. In 1912, the American College of Surgeons (ACS) began to develop the concept of peer review. By 1918, it published *The Minimum Standard*, part of which addressed peer review of medical treatment in hospitals: "The [medical] staff [shall] review and analyze at regular intervals their clinical experience in the various departments of the hospital."[1] The first survey using *The Minimum Standard* showed how inadequate 150 hospitals were; the results were burned in the furnace of the Waldorf Astoria Hotel in New York City. The role of Dr. Ernest A. Codman in developing *The Minimum Standard* and establishing the American College of Surgeons' Hospital Standardization Program is discussed later in the chapter. Chapter 1 noted that The Joint Commission continued the work of the ACS upon its establishment as the Joint Commission on Accreditation of Hospitals (JCAH) in 1951. JCAH is now known as The Joint Commission.

The process of peer review was called medical audit, terminology that continued into the 1960s. Enactment of Medicare codified utilization review (UR), which focused on appropriate use of services. UR did not directly affect the quality of care in hospitals, except that reviewing appropriateness of admission, use of ancillary services, and length of stay may have helped reduce nosocomial (institution-caused) and iatrogenic (physician-caused) problems. The focus of UR in Medicare was discussed in Chapter 1. A major shortcoming of medical audit and UR was that they made no attempt to solve the problem(s) identified.

Efforts to measure quality continued to evolve. In the early 1970s, The JCAH required quality assessment activities, a variation on medical audit. In the mid-1970s, the words were changed to *medical care evaluation*, but it remained essentially medical audit. By 1980, the concept of quality assurance (QA) had become a JCAH standard. QA meant that JCAH standards had evolved from finding and describing problems (as in medical audit) to be more proactive and dynamic by stressing problem solving to improve clinical quality. As noted earlier, PI is now the umbrella concept for all quality-related Joint Commission standards.

Historically, quality was defined as the degree of adherence to standards or criteria. As applied in health services, ensuring quality means using criteria that are determined prospectively to measure performance, with measurement done retrospectively. Newer definitions of quality are discussed here in the context of CQI. These include conformance to requirements and fitness for use, or fitness for need. They are customer driven because they focus on customer expectations and do not exclusively reflect criteria or standards developed using professional expertise. It is suggested that quality should be defined as meeting latent needs—identifying "needs" customers may not even know they have but will be pleased to have identified for them and met by the provider. CQI defines *customer* broadly to include all who receive goods or services.

Measuring quality using the concepts of QA required that the HSO/HS establish standards (criteria), typically through peer judgments. Developing criteria was only the first step. Two other elements were necessary: 1) a means of surveillance to identify deviations requiring action and 2) a corrective action to stop the deviation or minimize its recurrence. These steps are simple in theory and may be simple in practice as well, depending on what is being measured. Much of the conceptual framework used to measure quality was developed by Avedis Donabedian, a physician whose construct of *structure*, *process*, and *outcome* became standard in health services. Structure and process were the major foci of the JCAH's QA standards in the 1980s.

Donabedian recognized the difficulties of defining quality of medical care and measuring the quality of interpersonal relationships between physicians and patients—a relationship essential to the process of medical care, as reflected in the outcome. Technical aspects of medical care are more definable and measurable than are interpersonal relationships.[2]

Regardless, measuring quality under traditional QA began with criteria developed internally, externally imposed, or both.

Structure, Process, and Outcome in Quality Theory

Donabedian defined *structure* as the tools and resources that providers of medical care have at their disposal and the physical and organizational settings in which they work.[3] *Process* comprises the activities that occur within HSOs and between practitioners and patients. Here, judgments of quality may be made either by direct observation or by reviewing recorded information. Donabedian considered this means of measuring quality to be largely normative, in that the norms come either from the science of medicine or from the ethics and values of society.[4] *Outcome* is a change in a patient's current and future health status that can be attributed to antecedent healthcare.[5] Donabedian defined *outcome* broadly to include improvement of social and psychological function, in addition to physical and physiological aspects. Also included were patient attitudes, health-related knowledge acquired by the patient, and health-related behavioral change.[6]

Donabedian concluded that "good structure, that is, a sufficiency of resources and proper system design, is probably the most important means of protecting and promoting the quality of care."[7] He added that assessing structure is a good deal less important than assessing process and outcome. In comparing process and outcome, Donabedian concluded neither is clearly preferable. Either may be superior, depending on the situation and what is being measured. He emphasized it is critical, however, to know the link between the content of the process *and* the outcome. Only by knowing this link (preferably at the level of a causal relationship) can what is done or not done in the process be modified to improve the outcome. Not knowing how a desirable outcome was achieved makes replication only a matter of chance. Table 4.1 shows advantages and disadvantages of focusing on process and outcome to measure quality. Outcome indicators in Donabedian's taxonomy focus on overall outcomes of medical care, such as health status and disability. Donabedian's emphases on system (structure of care) and process (of care) are emblematic of how QI is presently conceptualized and applied.

Development and application of QA peaked in the late 1980s with adoption of a 10-step QA process. From then to the present, The Joint Commission began its evolution to the use of outcome indicators (measures). In 1987, its Agenda for Change initiated a major shift to adopting CQI. These activities were subsumed into what became known as the ORYX® initiative.[8] It was generally conceded that the QA implemented in the 1980s did little to improve quality of care. "On the whole, to the extent that quality measurement tools have been developed at all, they tend to unveil the fact of flaw, not its cause."[9]

The first clinical indicators developed were hospital-wide care, obstetrical care, and anesthesia care.[10] In early 1989, 12 key principles of organizational and management effectiveness were announced by The Joint Commission, and pilot testing began. The purpose was to characterize an acute care hospital's commitment to continuously improving its quality of care by identifying and monitoring clinical outcomes. By 1991, indicators had been developed for anesthesia, obstetrics, cardiovascular medicine, oncology, and trauma care.[11] These indicators focused on the high-risk, high-volume, and problem-prone aspects of care. Hospitals could choose from among hundreds of performance measurement systems and thousands of performance measures. A major goal of ORYX® was to develop standardized, evidence-based measures.[12] In 2019, the 14 core performance measures from which hospitals could choose included stroke, acute myocardial infarction, venous thromboembolism, perinatal care, children's asthma care, immunizations, and emergency department (ED) care.[13] A major initiative of the Centers for Medicare & Medicaid Services (CMS) is to reduce hospital readmissions after an inpatient stay. Hospitals with excess readmissions risk lesser Medicare payments.[14] The number and range of evidence-based performance measures by which hospital outcomes can be compared will increase and are strongly supported by CMS.[15]

Table 4.1 Advantages and disadvantages of process and outcome measures of quality

Process		Outcome	
Advantages	**Disadvantages**	**Advantages**	**Disadvantages**
Practitioners have no great difficulty specifying technical criteria for standards of care. Even not fully validated standards and criteria can serve as interim measures of acceptable practice. Information about technical aspects of care is documented in the medical record and usually is accessible as well as timely—it can be used for prevention and intervention. Use of this information permits specific attribution of responsibility so that credit or blame can be more easily ascertained and specific corrective action can be taken.	Great weakness in the scientific basis for much of accepted practice and use of prevalent norms as the basis for judging quality may encourage dogmatism and perpetuate error. Because practitioners prefer to err on the side of doing more than is necessary, there is a tendency toward overly elaborate and costly care; this is reflected in the norms. Although technical aspects are overemphasized, the management of the interpersonal process tends to be ignored, partly because the usual sources of data give little information about the physician–patient relationship.	When the scientific basis for accepted practice is in doubt, emphasis on outcome tends to discourage dogmatism and helps maintain a more open and flexible approach to management. An open and flexible approach may help in the development of less costly but no less effective strategies of care. Outcomes reflect all of the contributions of all of the practitioners to the care of the patient and thus provide an inclusive, integrative measure of the quality of care. Also reflected in the outcome is the patient's contribution to the care that may have been influenced by the relationship between patient and practitioners; a more direct assessment of the patient–physician relationship can be obtained by including aspects of patient satisfaction among measures of care.	Even expert practitioners are unable to specify the outcomes of optimal care, as to their magnitude, timing, and duration. When indicators of health status are obtained, it is difficult to know how much of the observed effect can be attributed to medical care. Choosing outcomes that have marginal relevance to the objectives of prior care is an ever-present pitfall; even when relevant outcomes are selected, information about many outcomes often is not available in time to make it useful for certain types of monitoring. Waiting for a pattern of adverse outcomes can be questioned on ethical grounds. Examining outcomes without examining means of attaining them may result in a lack of attention to the presence of redundant or overly costly care.

Adapted from Donabedian, Avedis. *Explorations in Quality Assessment and Monitoring. Vol. 1, The Definition of Quality and Approaches to its Assessment*, 119–122. Chicago: Health Administration Press, 1980.

Importance of QI

The importance of evaluating and improving quality was suggested in Chapter 1 and is expanded here. The Joint Commission and other accreditors, such as the Community Health Accreditation Program, American Osteopathic Association, and Det Norske Veritas Healthcare, Inc., require organized, effective QI activities. HSOs not accredited by a CMS-approved accreditor are not in "deemed" status and can be reimbursed for services to federal beneficiaries only by meeting the conditions of participation promulgated by the Department of Health and Human Services (DHHS). Accreditors of medical education programs require the HSO to be accredited, but not necessarily by The Joint Commission. Insurers of all types expect HSOs to be accredited. Lending institutions and organizations that rate bond offerings consider accreditation in their decisions. Chapter 11 details the importance of credentialing licensed independent practitioners, an activity indispensable to QI. In addition, failing to assess quality increases the likelihood of adverse malpractice judgments because the HSO may be seen as failing to meet the legal standard of care.

QI is considered important by managerial, clinical, and support staff who strive to do their best because they have internalized the motivation to provide high-quality care and achieve excellence in their HSO. This necessitates learning what is being done well and what is not, and closing the gap.

QI and QA Compared

HSOs that immerse themselves in the philosophy and techniques of CQI have achieved a paradigm shift away from traditional approaches to quality, such as QA. As will be described, QI uses powerful tools that result from a radically different philosophy about relationships between managers and staff. Table 4.2 suggests differences between QI and QA; several are highlighted here.

QA is negatives. It focuses on the "who" and seeks to identify those who caused the problem. Focusing on persons as the cause of problems is a human tendency and can be found even in HSOs trying to apply CQI concepts. QI seeks the "why." Workers are not the focus. QI implements the philosophy of W. Edwards Deming, whose theories are detailed later in the chapter, that 85%–94% of problems result from a process; few are caused by those who work in a process.

Commonly, QA measures only the quality of clinical practice, which was The Joint Commission's focus until the 1990s. QI measures clinical outcomes but is more concerned with myriad processes and systems that support delivery of clinical services, as well as those that are administrative, such as admitting and patient accounts. The clinical and administrative aspects of many processes cannot be separated easily, and QI seeks to improve integrated or cross-functional processes as well as those that are intradepartmental. Improving quality in support and administrative processes positively affects clinical processes and, thus, delivery of care, because there is greater organization-wide quality consciousness and because, without exception, these areas affect clinical services. For example, inefficient intradepartmental or interdepartmental admitting processes directly and indirectly affect patient care. It is certain they affect patient satisfaction.

Another important difference is that QI focuses on *improving* processes, whereas QA focuses on solving the problems that *result* from a faulty process. QA addresses the unusual or unique—what Deming called special causes of variation—and investigates results that exceed thresholds. Similarly, the QA philosophy causes managers to spend their time "fighting fires."

Table 4.2   Characteristics of QI versus QA

QI	QA
"Why" focused (positive)	"Who" focused (negative)
Prospective	Retrospective
Internally directed	Externally directed
Follows patients	Follows organizational structure
Involves the many	Delegated to the few
Integrated analysis	Divided analysis
Bottom up	Top down
Proactive	Reactive
Employee focused	Management focused (directing)
Full staff involvement	Limited staff involvement
Process based	Event based
Process approach	Inspection approach
Quality is integral activity	Quality is separate activity
Focus on all processes to improve fitness for use	Focus on meeting clinical criteria
Focus on improving processes	Focus on solving problems
Makes no assumption about irreducibility of problems	Assumes problems/numbers of problems reach irreducible number

Putting out fires is necessary but doing so neither improves processes nor increases their efficiency or effectiveness. Putting out a fire only returns the process, more or less, to its state before the fire. QI asserts that unique and unusual results or outcomes should be ignored unless they pose a significant risk or danger; instead, attention should focus on improving the process(es). HSO managers cannot ignore unusual or unique events that affect patients, but the effort spent on them should be minimized; the real gain will come from improving processes to reduce variation, error rates, and other causes of poor process performance.

Finally, the assumptions made about the irreducibility of problems were the most insidious part of the QA philosophy and contributed to delays in improving the quality of care. Psychologically, it is essential that "good enough" is no longer acceptable; the QI philosophy rejects it. An element of "good enough" is suggested when HSOs/HSs compare outcome indicators or other performance measures with internal or external criteria. Criteria and indicators are important starting points and provide a macro-level understanding of outcomes produced by an HSO/HS, generally, or by a specific process. In fact, organizations that implement CQI improve quality by reducing waste, rework, and redundancy, not by accepting a place within the herd. Until a systematic search for the root causes of medication errors has been performed using QI tools, for example, no one knows what the irreducible level of medication errors in an HSO is.

In the final analysis, improving clinical (and managerial) quality requires change. If Deming is correct that only 6%–15% of problems result from causes within worker control, management must enlist staff to improve quality. Managers must shed the old view that poor quality occurs because staff choose to perform poorly. Given the increased emphasis on outcome indicators, it is essential to understand the link between process and outcome. Here, Donabedian's dictum must be restated: Unless it is known how a result was produced, desired outcomes cannot be purposefully replicated, nor can a process be changed to prevent undesired outcomes.

Background to the Present Focus on Quality Improvement

The 1980s saw a shift in the health services paradigm with respect to quality:[16] "It represent(ed) a 'new order of things' in the provision of healthcare."[17] This shift occurred at two levels: the definition of quality output and the means of achieving it. First, the newly adopted definition of quality of care and service (i.e., output) went beyond meeting specifications or standards and incorporated conformance to requirements and fitness for use, both of which include meeting or exceeding patient (customer) expectations. Second, it recognized a need to focus on improving inputs and processes that generate outputs of product and service.[18] This expanded definition of quality output and the focus on improving inputs and processes are the twin pillars of CQI. Adopting the philosophy and methods of CQI will positively affect HSO/HS management and organizational arrangements; resource allocation, utilization, cost-effectiveness, and PI; the quality of services provided (i.e., conformance to requirements and customer satisfaction); and the HSO's/HS's competitive position.

International competition and increased consumer demands and expectations for quality products and services profoundly affected American industry in the last decades of the 20th century. Industry was found wanting. The quality awakening in the 1980s and 1990s increased awareness of the importance of quality and the need to satisfy customers; stimulated initiatives to improve the quality of outputs to be globally competitive; and, as described by Deming, began the transformation of American business[19] that has continued.

Like industry, the health services system is undergoing profound change. The last 2 decades of the 20th century were tumultuous for HSOs/HSs. The effects of environmental forces and the changes that occurred have continued into the 21st century. Changes include revenue and cost pressures from private and government payers; competition from alternate forms of delivery, such as managed care; and restructuring because of closures, mergers, consolidations, and other actions of HSs.[20] The turbulent health services environment and increasing demands from, and account-ability to, customers for lower-cost care with improved quality put HSOs/HSs at risk. The concept of customers has expanded beyond patients to include all third-party payers.[21] To survive and thrive, HSOs/HSs must respond effectively to the expectations of these customers and stakeholders.

Quality—Two Dimensions

Traditionally, quality in HSOs focused on product or service content[22] and meeting specifica-tions or standards. Quality was evaluated retrospectively; the product or service was assessed using predetermined criteria. Examples are accuracy of diagnosis, physiological change and improvement in patients at discharge, mortality and morbidity rates, and the efficacy of medi-cal procedures and drugs. Methods of quality evaluation included inspection, peer review, and QA, as well as tracking indicators such as infection rates, unplanned readmissions after dis-charge from inpatient treatment, and accuracy and timeliness of diagnostic testing.

The contemporary view of health services quality includes conformance to requirements and fitness for use—both of which incorporate satisfying customer needs and meeting or exceeding expectations. The American Society for Quality (ASQ) defines quality as "1. the characteristics of a product or service that bear on its ability to satisfy stated or implied needs; 2. a product or service free of deficiencies."[23]

Quality judgments occur when the HSO or individuals within it generate outputs.[24] Judg-ing quality includes asking questions such as Are there defects? Does the product work? Was the service appropriate? Is treatment reliable? Was the service on time? Was it delivered in a friendly manner? Was it the right service? Did it meet the customer's needs? Was the customer delighted? Did product or service attributes exceed customer expectations?[25] The answers to such questions about customers' expectations are influenced by customers' experiences, perceptions, and values.

The American Hospital Association's Hospital Research and Educational Trust (HRET) Quality Management for Health Care Delivery (QMHCD) report termed this *delivery quality*. Delivery quality covers all aspects of the customer's satisfaction with the HSO.[26] Conformance and expectation quality monitoring and improvement must be directed at every level and every process.[27] Customers include patients as well as physicians and other internal customers (downstream users of a unit's output) and external customers, such as payers and the com-munity. For example, nursing is a customer of pharmacy for medications and a customer of dietary services for patients' dietary needs; physicians are customers of diagnostic testing; the intensive care unit is a customer of the ED when trauma patients are admitted; third-party payers are customers of patient billing; and all HSO departments and units are customers of administration. Depending on the transaction, the process, department, unit, or staff member changes from customer to processor to supplier.[28] It is essential that persons in a process understand their roles as customer, processor (person who adds value), and supplier. They must know how their activity in a given role contributes to the aim of the organiza-tion and its efforts to optimize performance. Figure 4.1 is a simplified representation of a

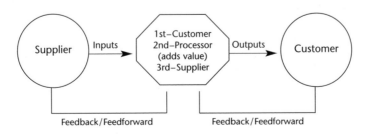

Figure 4.1.   The customer–processor–supplier relationship.

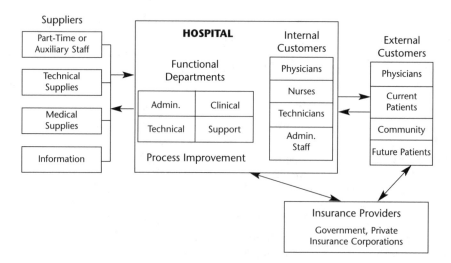

Figure 4.2. Internal and external customers of hospital functional departments. (From Carol Greebler, *TQM Plus*, San Diego, CA, 1989; reprinted by permission.)

customer–processor–supplier relationship. In vertically integrated HSs, the skilled nursing facility is the customer of the acute care hospital. Figure 4.2 shows the internal and external customers of a hospital's functional departments.

Taking a CQI Approach

Background

The philosophy now pervasive about quality in healthcare began to gain wide acceptance in the late 1980s. It draws on the work of industrial quality experts W. Edwards Deming,[29] Joseph M. Juran,[30] and Philip B. Crosby.[31] The CQI philosophy has four attributes. First, output quality includes meeting or exceeding customer needs and expectations. Second, monitoring and evaluating quality are retrospective; they are prospective in that poor quality can be prevented. Third, "quality is not the responsibility of just one department or individual,"[32] it is organization-wide and involves everyone. Fourth, quality and CQI focus on both process (and inputs) and outcomes, not just outcomes.[33]

The Joint Commission publishes standards manuals and quality measures specifications manuals for the types of HSOs it accredits. The *Specifications Manual for Joint Commission National Quality Measures (v2020A)*, addresses the need for inpatient outcome and process quality. A CQI philosophy and applications are clear in this manual, which references control charts, care processes, quality improvement, data-driven decisions, quality and safety of patient care, performance assessment and improvement, and achieving continuous improvement in key areas of safety and quality.[34]

The *Specifications Manual for National Hospital Inpatient Quality Measures* resulted from collaboration between the Centers for Medicare & Medicaid Services and The Joint Commission that resulted in a uniform set of national hospital quality measures.[35] There is little evidence, however, that patients who chose a hospital accredited by The Joint Commission received greater healthcare benefits than those who chose a hospital accredited by another independent accrediting organization.[36]

Improving quality may use several names: *quality management*,[37] *total quality management (TQM)*,[38] *total quality care*,[39] or *QI*.[40] *CQI* is preferred because it reflects the major break from previous efforts to achieve quality, states the concept positively, and minimizes any suggestion that quality is the job of only one group in an organization. CQI is defined as an ongoing, organization-wide framework in which HSOs and their employees and clinical staff are committed to and involved in monitoring and evaluating all aspects of the organization's activities (inputs and processes) and outputs for the purpose of continuously improving them.[41] The essential elements of this definition are as follows:

- *CQI is organization-wide.* CQI can be successful only if the organization is transformed to seek quality in all that it does. CQI requires a total commitment to quality—a philosophical transformation—by the governing body and senior-level management; involves all HSO/HS employees, including the clinical staff[42]; and is rooted in a cultural setting that supports quality initiatives, teamwork, adaptability, and flexibility.[43]

- *CQI is process focused.* CQI seeks to understand processes, identify process characteristics that should be measured, and monitor processes as changes are made to determine the effects of those changes. The result is improved processes that enhance productivity through more efficient and effective use of resources. In sum, CQI improves conversion processes, thus generating higher quality products and service (outputs).

- *CQI is staff focused.* Process understanding and improvement require a team-based approach that involves and empowers employees to effect change.

- *CQI uses output measures.* Outcomes of care (indicators) provide macro-level data to determine how well groups of processes and the organization as a whole are performing. Indicators allow time-series as well as inter-HSO/HS comparisons. These crude arrows may point to a need for specific foci to achieve process improvement.

- *CQI is customer driven.* The goal is to meet or exceed the expectations of customers, who are defined broadly and include internal and external customers.

The literature is replete with CQI applications in HSOs,[44] hospitals,[45] and integrated health systems.[46] Success stories come from disparate areas: clinical medicine,[47,48] laboratory,[49] radiology,[50] medical records,[51] EDs,[52] trauma centers,[53] pharmacy,[54] and adverse drug events.[55] CQI is being used internationally: small general medical practices (Netherlands),[56] multidisciplinary teams in cancer care (Australia),[57] multisite teaching hospital (Canada),[58] and high-risk cardiovascular patients (Brazil).[59] A survey of U.S. and Canadian hospitals found approximately 90% of respondents had implemented CQI, and 65% had undertaken six or more CQI projects. The study found that larger teaching hospitals were more likely to be involved in CQI than smaller, nonteaching hospitals.[60]

CQI Model

CQI fundamentally shifts organizational thinking because it is customer driven and focuses on internal and external customers. CQI is systematic and organization-wide, with top management commitment to improving processes (and inputs) through employee empowerment. The result is improved quality and customer satisfaction, PI, and enhanced competitive position.

The HRET QMHCD describes the CQI challenge: "Continuous Quality Improvement demands that healthcare providers answer three questions. Are we doing the right things? Are we doing things right? How can we be certain that we do things right the first time, every time?"[61] Figure 4.3 answers these questions in the context of a CQI model. The following discussion references the numbers in the CQI model [1], whose goal is, "How can we be certain that we do things right the first time, every time?"

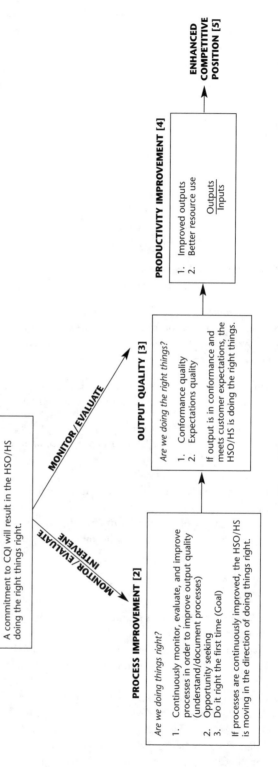

CONTINUOUS QUALITY IMPROVEMENT [1]

GOAL: How can we be certain we do things right the first time, every time?

1. Organizational philosophy (organizationwide, all levels)
2. Governing body, management, staff, and clinical staff commitment and involvement
3. Prospective, ongoing
   —focus on two dimensions of quality
   —focus on improving processes (and inputs)
4. Leadership and organizational change

A commitment to CQI will result in the HSO/HS doing the right things right.

MONITOR/EVALUATE

MONITOR/EVALUATE/INTERVENE

PROCESS IMPROVEMENT [2]

Are we doing things right?

1. Continuously monitor, evaluate, and improve processes in order to improve output quality (understand/document processes)
2. Opportunity seeking
3. Do it right the first time (Goal)

If processes are continuously improved, the HSO/HS is moving in the direction of doing things right.

OUTPUT QUALITY [3]

Are we doing the right things?

1. Conformance quality
2. Expectations quality

If output is in conformance and meets customer expectations, the HSO/HS is doing the right things.

PRODUCTIVITY IMPROVEMENT [4]

1. Improved outputs
2. Better resource use

$$\frac{\text{Outputs}}{\text{Inputs}}$$

ENHANCED COMPETITIVE POSITION [5]

Figure 4.3. Continuous quality improvement model.

Are We Doing the Right Things?

The first pillar of CQI, output quality [3], determines if the HSO is doing the right things. Products and services that are in conformance and that meet or exceed customer expectations mean the organization is doing the right things. From the CQI perspective, the concept of customers is all encompassing. CQI defines customers not only as patients and external stakeholders but also as internal users of a department, a unit, or the outputs produced by an individual. In CQI, a customer is the person or process that relies on another person or process for inputs. Output that is in conformance and meets the needs and expectations of customers is a quality product or service and means the HSO is doing the right things.

Are We Doing Things Right?

Process improvement [2] is the second pillar of CQI. Output quality can be improved only by improving the processes that produce it. All processes can be improved. Improving processes in health services delivery is daunting because they are technical, complex, and often intense, and they are necessarily personal, intimate, and focused on individuals. These challenges have been and can be met, however, and their high degree of dependence on human action does not preclude patient care systems from being improved.[62] CQI means that even a well-functioning process can be improved.[63] "If it isn't perfect, make it better."[64]

Finally, "doing things right" requires continuous monitoring, evaluating, and intervening to improve processes. Requisite to continuous improvement is developing a systematic understanding and documentation of processes. All staff must be trained in process improvement and encouraged to seek opportunities to improve work results by improving the way results are produced. The outcome is not only improved output quality [3] but also improved productivity [4], in which there is more effective resource use, and enhanced competitive position [5]. Crosby urged organizations to establish a goal of "do it right the first time."[65] This goal may be unattainable in an absolute sense, but HSOs that continuously improve processes are moving in the "right" direction.

How Can We Be Certain That We Do Things Right the First Time, Every Time?

CQI has the goal of doing things right the first time, every time. If there is quality output (the right things) and process improvement (doing things right) with CQI, the HSO will move in the direction of doing things right the first time, every time (goal).[66] The essential attributes of CQI [1] are as follows (see Figure 4.3):

- CQI is an organizational philosophy that becomes pervasive in the culture—the ingrained beliefs and values of the HSO/HS. It is customer driven and requires transforming existing beliefs and values regarding quality.

- CQI requires the total commitment and involvement of everyone in the HSO/HS. Management must nurture the value system and commit the resources that support continuous improvement as integral to the work of everyone in the organization.[67] Staff must participate in, and be committed to, continuously improving their work results and the way those results are achieved. This requires collaboration and cross-functional coordination among work units and departments.[68] All staff must be involved in problem solving, especially to seek and identify opportunities for improvement.

- CQI is prospective and ongoing. The focus on output quality must be prospective, not just retrospective; it must be continuous, not intermittent.[69] The aim is to prevent poor quality before it happens and to seek opportunities to improve processes in an organized fashion.

- CQI requires that management meet its leadership responsibility to train employees; encourage innovation, worker participation, and empowerment; build teams so employees can contribute to process improvement problem solving; and facilitate organizational change that leads to improvement.

CQI, PI, and Competitive Position

The CQI paradigm is the opposite of the conventional cost-containment initiatives prevalent during the 1970s and 1980s. In the context of the management model in the Part III introduction (Figure III.2), the emphasis then was to increase ratios of outputs to inputs. The resulting initiatives were narrowly applied, episodic, and short term. Typically, those initiatives had little worker involvement and commitment and focused on reducing input costs rather than enhancing output quality. By contrast, rather than simply cutting costs, CQI initiatives are broad based, long term, and ongoing; have extensive management and employee involvement and commitment; are customer driven; and focus on improving both process and output quality.

Figure 4.3 depicts how CQI improves quality and performance [4] and leads to enhanced competitive position [5]. Deming asserted that improving productivity does not improve output quality. Instead, improving quality results in greater productivity. The Deming Chain Reaction in Figure 4.4 suggests the relationship: Better quality decreases costs, which improves productivity. In turn, this leads to decreased prices and increased market share; thus, the organization stays in business, provides jobs, and yields greater returns. As a consequence, competitive position is enhanced. Deming argued that improved quality results in better resource use (lower costs) because improved processes mean less rework (readmissions), fewer mistakes (repeats of tests), and fewer delays (waiting for service). These results occur because the prospective and continuous assessment of, and changes made to, work processes and inputs yield both improved quality and improved productivity.[70]

The Malcolm Baldrige National Quality Award, named for a U.S. secretary of commerce who died while in office, was created in 1987 and has been awarded since 1988. The application process is rigorous; the award prestigious. Its purpose is to promote quality excellence; recognize organizations that have made significant improvements in product, service, and competitive position; and foster information sharing among organizations. Categories of criteria for the Baldrige award in healthcare include leadership, strategic planning, customer focus, workforce focus, operations focus, and results, as well as measurement, analysis, and knowledge management.[71]

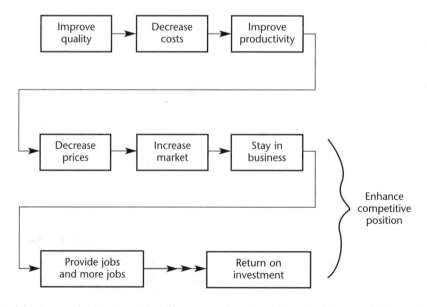

Figure 4.4. Deming Chain Reaction. (Adapted from Joiner, Brian L. *Fourth Generation Management: The New Business Consciousness*, 23. New York: McGraw-Hill, 1994; reprinted by permission of the McGraw-Hill Companies, Inc.)

Theory of CQI

The Pioneers

Sir Thomas Percival (1740–1804)

Modern history is replete with those who sought to improve the quality of care. The eminent English physician, Thomas Percival, lived and worked in Manchester, where he was active in improving clinical practice and public health. Percival's experiences prompted him to write two pamphlets with the goal of stimulating reform: "Internal Regulation of Hospitals 1771" and "A Scheme of Professional Conduct Relative to Hospitals and Other Medical Charities 1772."[72] In 1803, Percival presented the idea of a hospital register to help physicians improve the quality of their care.[73] The concept must have been startling (and perhaps alarming) to his medical colleagues; little interest resulted. Chapter 2 notes that the AMA's "Principles of Medical Ethics" reflect Percival's influence.

Ignaz Semmelweis (1818–1865)

In 1847, the Austro-Hungarian physician, Ignaz Semmelweis, sought to reduce the incidence of puerperal (childbed) fever, an often-fatal bacterial infection rampant among newly delivered women at the Vienna General Hospital. Semmelweis used mortality data to show that washing hands and instruments in carbolic acid (a solution of chlorinated lime) stopped the causative bacterium from spreading and virtually eliminated childbed fever from his ward. Medical colleagues rejected his findings and ridiculed him such that he left Vienna.[74] Only after the French bacteriologist, Louis Pasteur (1822–1895), demonstrated the germ theory of disease causation in 1862 was Semmelweis vindicated.

Joseph Lister (1828–1912)

In 1877, the English surgeon, Joseph Lister, visited New York City and reported on the benefits of antisepsis in preventing the spread of microorganisms by disinfecting surgical instruments (as had Semmelweis), gowns, and drapes with carbolic acid, as well as using it copiously throughout the operating theater. William S. Halsted, who later became an eminent surgeon at The Johns Hopkins Hospital, was beginning his career and sought to introduce antisepsis at Bellevue Hospital in New York City. Most surgeons opposed the concept, and there was such resistance to his use of antisepsis that he was forced to perform surgery in a tent outside the main hospital building. Halsted's results were so startling, however, that surgeons throughout New York City soon followed his example.[75]

Reformers such as these were vindicated—some sooner, some later. Their struggles against medical orthodoxy, however, reflect the difficulties of changing a profession's trajectory, even after the evidence clearly shows a better way and a need for change. Their like-minded successors fared somewhat better.

Florence E. Nightingale (1820–1910)

Florence Nightingale first became famous when she demonstrated the value of good organization, cleanliness, and properly trained nurses in treating British soldiers during the Crimean War (1854–1856). Tireless work there earned her the title of "The Lady with the Lamp," which she carried as she tended the wounded and those ill from disease.

Nightingale was named for Florence, Italy, where she was born while her parents vacationed there. She became interested in nursing, which her parents actively discouraged because nursing had a very poor reputation at the time. Her parents relented; in 1851 she went to Kaiserswerth, Germany, where she trained as a nurse. This training enabled her to become superintendent of a hospital for gentlewomen in Harley Street, London, in 1853. The following year the Crimean War found Great Britain, France, and Turkey allied against Russia. One result was large numbers of British casualties. The desperate lack of proper facilities and care for the wounded caused the British war ministry to send Nightingale and a team of nurses to

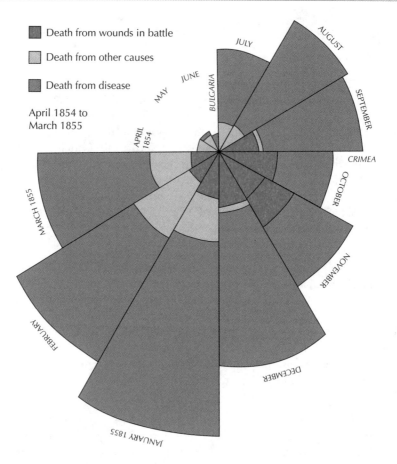

Figure 4.5. Florence Nightingale's original polar-area diagram. (From J. J. Connor and E. F. Robertson, "Florence Nightingale Biography," 2003. Retrieved February 12, 2013, from https://mathshistory.st-andrews.ac.uk/Biographies/Nightingale/)

military hospitals in Turkey. She and her nurses greatly improved conditions and substantially reduced the mortality rate.[76]

Nightingale used data to significantly improve clinical outcomes, including development of a "model hospital statistical form" to collect and organize consistent data and statistics.[77] Nightingale applied epidemiological principles to develop the "polar-area diagram," later known as the pie chart and shown here as Figure 4.5. This visual display facilitated understanding the morbidity and mortality of soldiers who had been wounded or were ill from disease.[78]

Following her return to England, Nightingale established the Nightingale Training School for nurses at St. Thomas's Hospital in London in 1860. This was the first professional training school for nurses. After training, the nurses were sent to hospitals throughout Britain, at which they introduced what they had learned, and established nurse training on the Nightingale model. Nightingale's theories, published in "Notes on Nursing" (1860), were influential, and her concerns for sanitation, military health, and hospital planning established practices used today.[79]

Nightingale's contributions to health services and public health are legion. In addition to founding the first professional training school for nurses, she published over 200 books, reports, and pamphlets on nursing and healthcare; invented the pie chart; inspired the founding of the Red Cross; and was the first woman to be elected to the Royal Statistical Society. Her accomplishments are even more noteworthy because she contracted brucellosis while serving in the Crimea. Brucellosis is a painful and debilitating bacterial infection that causes constant fevers, sweating, and weakness. In much of her later life Nightingale was bedridden, but she continued her work despite her malady.[80] Nightingale's efforts to organize and improve hospital-based care qualify her to be known as the first hospital administrator.[81]

Ernest A. Codman (1869–1940)

Ernest A. Codman, a surgeon, was an advocate of hospital reform and is the acknowledged founder of what is known today as outcomes management in patient care. It was his lifelong pursuit to establish an "end results system" that tracked outcomes of patient treatment and identified clinical misadventures that would provide a foundation to improve care for future patients.[82] Codman is credited with several firsts in medical care. As a prominent surgeon on staff at Massachusetts General Hospital in the early 1900s, he organized morbidity and mortality (M&M) conferences at which physicians discussed cases openly to learn about the care received by patients and whether it contributed to good results. M&M conferences became ubiquitous and are required in hospitals with an accredited graduate medical education program. Codman was one of several leading American surgeons who organized the American College of Surgeons (ACS) in 1913.[83] The "end result system of hospital standardization" became the stated objective of the ACS in its *Minimum Standard*. The Hospital Standardization Program became the Joint Commission on Accreditation of Hospitals in 1951 (now known as The Joint Commission). In 1920, Codman established the first bone tumor (cancer) registry in the United States, which was the precedent for a national exchange of information about bone tumor cases.[84]

The failure of Massachusetts General Hospital to adopt outcomes evaluation, or end results, led to Codman's resignation. In 1911, he established his own private hospital, the Codman Hospital, at which he instituted a program of monitoring surgical performance. He tracked patients after hospital treatment to understand the long-term benefits—the "end results"—of care and to learn how physician and hospital care could be improved. The data, both negative and positive, were made public, and Codman challenged hospitals everywhere to do the same. Codman's review of his own clinical outcomes found that one error occurred for every three patients treated.[85]

It is useful to recall that in the late 19th century, the modern hospital was only just emerging from the darkness of scientific ignorance. Supported by technologies such as asepsis, laboratory and x-ray services, and inhalation anesthesia, hospitals became temples of healing that was based largely on efficacious surgery. Codman's proposal must have been startling and intimidating to clinicians and administrators alike. Making outcome evaluations public could be embarrassing and even politically and economically dangerous for hospitals and their physicians; it is easy to understand the reluctance to publicize results of the care provided. Codman's reforming efforts brought him ridicule, poverty, and censure, but he never stopped his efforts to link care, errors, and end results and to measure, report, and improve.[86] Except for the ACS and its Hospital Standardization Program, Codman's end results system died with him.

Public reporting of hospital outcomes has become commonplace because of intense pressure from public interest groups, third-party payers, and government. Although Percival's idea to establish a hospital register of end results predated Codman's work by almost a century, Codman must be credited with beginning the long, often-interrupted, 100-year journey to the current emphasis on quality and PI in health services delivery. Codman's application of elements of classic CQI methodology occurred well before the work of Walter A. Shewhart and his successors.

Walter A. Shewhart (1891–1967)

Walter A. Shewhart and Ernest A. Codman were contemporaries, although there is no evidence they met—regrettably. Dr. Shewhart was the trail-blazing American statistician who developed the basic theory and application of statistical process control (SPC) and the precursor to the plan, do, study, act (PDSA) cycle that provide the methodological underpinnings for CQI.

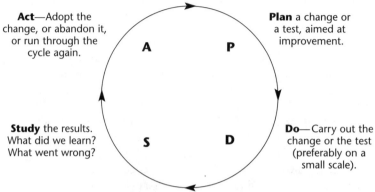

Figure 4.6. The PDSA cycle. (From Deming, W. Edwards. *The New Economics for Industry, Government, Education,* 2nd ed., 132. Shewhart Cycle. © 2000 W. Edwards Deming Institute, by permission of MIT Press.)

Shewhart's theories of SPC were applied in the 1920s at the Hawthorne Works of Western Electric, a facility near Chicago that manufactured telephones. W. Edwards Deming was one of Shewhart's students and a colleague during the 1920s and 1930s. Shewhart's book *Statistical Method from the Viewpoint of Quality Control,* published in 1939, was edited by Deming and contained the first version of the "Shewhart cycle." The Shewhart cycle evolved during the next 4 decades and is known as the PDSA cycle (as Shewhart and Deming developed it) and the plan, do, check, act (PDCA) cycle in Japan, primarily because of a misunderstanding in translation.[87]

The success of Shewhart's efforts is reflected in the slogan "alike as two telephones," which suggests that quality can be improved by reducing variation to the point that products are indistinguishable. His monumental work, *Economic Control of Quality of Manufactured Products,* published in 1931, is regarded as a complete and thorough exposition of the basic principles of quality control.[88] Shewhart's SPC and PDSA cycle were applied extensively and very successfully to military production during World War II. The PDSA cycle is also known as the Shewhart cycle.[89] Figure 4.6 shows the PDSA cycle, with a description for each step. When World War II ended in 1945, the American industrial base was undamaged; Germany's and Japan's lay in ruins. This fact, plus the pent-up demand for consumer goods after almost 4 years of total focus on war production, allowed American manufacturers to be less concerned about quality—there were buyers for everything they could produce, regardless of quality. Thus, quantity became ascendant over quality. It was not until the 1980s that the focus returned to quality, prompted by declining markets for American products. Attention to service quality soon followed.

The Builders

Deming, Juran, and Crosby

Three theorists, educators, and practitioners of quality who were contemporaries—W. Edwards Deming, Joseph M. Juran, and Philip B. Crosby—advocated CQI and greatly influenced its philosophy and practice. Their work provides thinking and methodologies for establishing a quality culture.

To varying degrees and in a variety of forms, their principles have been adopted by HSOs/HSs.[90] The three were not of one mind on some specifics of how to achieve quality, however.

The emphasis here is on Deming, who developed a philosophy applicable to life *and* to management that applies to improving quality in both product and service. His theory of "profound knowledge" is a conceptualization of what is necessary for quality to be improved. Juran developed numerous models and statistical methods that support the managerial and applications perspectives. Crosby was more an organizational behaviorist and motivator and less a philosopher or technician. Their routes differed, but they had the same destination: improved quality.[91]

W. Edwards Deming (1900–1993)

W. Edwards Deming earned his doctorate in mathematical physics and was Shewhart's protégé at the Hawthorne Works. Deming made extensive use of Shewhart's theories of SPC and PDSA in his approach to improving quality.[92] Deming went to Japan in 1947 to assist in taking a census. Because of his work in QI, he was invited to Japan in 1950 to lecture to Japanese manufacturers about how to improve their consumer products, which had inferior quality and were poorly regarded before and after World War II. Deming's lectures were widely attended by leaders of Japanese industry and were highly influential as Japan rebuilt an industrial base that transformed it into the major economic power it became. Dr. Deming's work is considered so important that Japan's highest award for quality is the Deming Prize. Because Deming introduced Shewhart's PDSA cycle to Japan, it is known there as the Deming cycle. It was only in the 1980s that Deming's work began to be appreciated in the United States.[93] Deming's most significant book, *Out of the Crisis*, was published in 1986. He was 86 years of age.

Deming defined *quality* broadly: "A product or service possesses quality if it helps somebody and enjoys a good and sustainable market."[94] Key to understanding how to improve quality is his view that poor quality results from badly designed or malfunctioning processes—not worker actions. Workers work in processes over which they have little or no control and are, therefore, able to do only what the process allows them to do. The process, not the worker, produces good or poor quality. Thus, better quality can be achieved only by improving the process. Management controls processes; therefore, it must lead in QI. This view is reflected in Deming's emphasis on monitoring and evaluating processes through SPC and searching for ways to improve them. The Deming Chain Reaction in Figure 4.4 shows how improving quality will decrease costs, increase productivity, and enhance competitive position. This sequence is incorporated in the CQI model in Figure 4.3.

The Deming method has two distinct components. The first is critical: Managers must establish and maintain an environment in which quality is integral to all work. This means a transformation—a major philosophical shift and commitment that HSOs/HSs will improve quality. This philosophy is reflected in Deming's 14 points (see the list that follows). The second, concurrent component is that efforts to improve quality must be supported by SPC—management must have data that show what processes are doing and how well they are doing it. Analyses of these data enable managers to identify and correct problems. More importantly, the data support efforts to improve the process.

Deming's theory of profound knowledge includes four elements: appreciation for a system, knowledge about variation, theory of knowledge, and psychology.[95] *Appreciation for a system* means that management must understand the need for interdependent components to work together to try to accomplish the aim of a system. The greater the interdependence among components, the greater is the need for cooperation and communication. Some components of the system may have to suboptimize if doing so allows optimization of the system. *Knowledge about variation* means that management must understand there is variation in every activity and in every process. Management must collect data to know if a process is in statistical control; a process "in control" has a definable capability and can be improved. Deming's *theory of knowledge* teaches that a statement, if it contains knowledge, predicts future outcome. Rational prediction requires theory and builds knowledge through systematic revision and extension of theory based on comparison of prediction with observation. In this regard, management is prediction. The fourth element, *psychology*, helps us understand people, interactions of people and circumstances, and interactions between manager and staff in any system of management. Managers must be aware that people are different and learn differently and that there are intrinsic and extrinsic sources of motivation. In total, Deming's system of profound knowledge challenges managers to understand themselves and their jobs and staff in ways that will enhance effectiveness of staff.

Deming's 14 points for improvement of management are complementary to CQI and its application; they are essential to creating an environment in which quality can be achieved. The 14 points for quality[96] have been discussed extensively[97] and have been applied to HSOs by Batalden and Vorlicky, as cited in Deming[98] and Darr.[99]

1. *Create constancy of purpose toward improvement of product and service with the aim to become competitive, to stay in business, and to provide jobs.*[100] This means identifying customers, giving them good-quality service, and ensuring organizational survival through innovation and constant improvement.

2. *Adopt the new philosophy.* Commonly accepted levels of nonquality are unacceptable.

3. *Cease dependence on inspection to achieve quality.* Health services should require statistical evidence of quality of incoming materials, such as pharmaceuticals, serums, and equipment. Inspection is not the answer. Inspection is too late and unreliable. Inspection does not produce quality. . . . Require corrective action, where needed, for all tasks that are performed in the hospital or other facility, ranging all the way from bills that are produced to processes of registration. Institute a rigid program of feedback from patients in regard to their satisfaction with services.[101]

4. *End the practice of awarding business on the basis of price tag.* The intent is to develop long-term relations with suppliers so that they can improve the quality of the products (and services) they provide as an input to the HSO/HS.

5. *Improve constantly and forever the system of production and service, to improve quality and productivity, and thus constantly decrease costs.* Improvement is not a one-time effort. Management is obligated to continually look for ways to reduce waste and improve quality.

6. *Institute training on the job.* Too often, workers learn their job from other workers who were never trained properly. They cannot do their job well because no one tells them how.

7. *Institute leadership.* A supervisor's job is not to tell people what to do or to punish them, but to lead. Supervisors need time to help people on the job; they need to find ways to translate the constancy of purpose to the individual employee. "Supervisors must be trained in simple statistical methods for aid to employees, with the aim to detect and eliminate special causes of mistakes and rework."[102]

8. *Drive out fear so that everyone may work effectively for the company.* Many workers are afraid to take a position or ask questions, even when they do not understand the job or what is right or wrong. We must break down the class distinctions between types of workers within the organization—physicians, nonphysicians, clinical providers versus nonclinical providers, physician to physician. Stop blaming employees for system problems. Management should be held responsible for faults of the system. People must feel secure to make suggestions.[103]

9. *Break down barriers between departments.* Often, areas compete with one another or have conflicting goals. They do not work as a team to solve or foresee problems. Worse, one department's goals may cause trouble for another department.

10. *Eliminate slogans, exhortations, and targets for the workforce asking for zero defects and new levels of productivity.* "Instead, display accomplishments of the management in respect to assistance to employees to improve their performance."[104]

11. *Eliminate work standards (quotas) on the factory floor.* Quotas that represent measured day work or output alone without regard to quality should be eliminated. "It is better to take aim at rework, error, and defects [all measures of quality], and to focus on [helping] people to do a better job."[105]

12. *Remove barriers that rob the hourly worker of the right to pride of workmanship.* People are eager to do a good job and distressed when they cannot. Too often, misguided supervisors, faulty equipment, and defective materials are in the way. These barriers must be removed.

13. *Institute a vigorous program of education and self-improvement.* "Institute a massive training program in statistical techniques. Bring statistical techniques down to the level of the individual employee's job and help him to gather information in a systematic way about the nature of his job."[106] Also, the training "program should keep up with changes in model, style, materials, methods, and if advantageous, new machinery."[107]

14. *Put everyone in the company to work to accomplish the transformation.* As noted by Darr, "Taking action to accomplish the transformation will take a special top management team with a plan of action to carry out the quality mission. Workers can't do it on their own, nor can managers."[108]

An interpretation of Deming is useful:

> Quality must become a central focus of the corporation. The emphasis must shift from inspection to prevention. Preventing defects before they occur and improving the process so that defects do not occur are goals for which a company should strive.

> Training and retraining of employees [are] critical to the success of the organization. Deming believes that it is management's job to coach employees. Education and training are investments in people. They help to avoid employee burnout, [reenergize] employees, and give a clear message to employees that management considers employees to be a valuable resource. Finally, Deming also believes that management must pay attention to variability within processes. He advocates systematic understanding of variation and reduction of variation as a strategy to improve processes.

> Deming believes that the road to enhanced productivity is through continuous quality improvement called the Deming Chain Reaction. Improving quality through improving processes leads to a reduction of waste, rework, delays, and scrap. This reduction causes productivity as well as quality to improve.[109]

Even in the last years of his life, Deming worked with an intensity improbable for someone his age. He continued his worldwide consulting practice and writing until he died at age 93. At his death, he was working on his last book, *The New Economics for Industry, Government, Education*, second edition, which was published posthumously. Deming was impatient to see his philosophy and methods implemented in the United States, where, until very late in life, he was, as the aphorism states, "a prophet without honor in his own country."

Joseph M. Juran (1905–2008)

Joseph M. Juran, consultant and founder and chairman emeritus of the Juran Institute, was an advocate of total quality management (TQM). During his career, he was an engineer, industrial executive, government administrator, university professor, corporate director, and management consultant.[110] Juran worked at the Hawthorne Works of Western Electric in the mid-1920s,[111] making him a contemporary of Deming. Juran, too, worked with the Japanese after the war, but did so several years later and did not achieve the prominence in Japan that Deming had.

Juran defined quality as fitness for use, which includes being free from deficiencies and meeting customer needs.[112] Juran's Quality Trilogy is a generic way to think about quality. It is applicable to all functions, levels, and product lines.[113] The components of the quality trilogy are quality planning, quality control, and quality improvement.

Quality Planning: At the initial stage, products and services that will meet customers' needs are developed as follows:

1. Determine who the customers are.

2. Determine the needs of customers.

3. Develop product features that respond to customers' needs.

4. Develop the processes that are able to produce those product features.

5. Transfer the resulting plans to the operating forces.

Quality Control: This activity has three steps:

1. Evaluate actual quality performance.

2. Compare actual performance with quality goals.

3. Act on the differences.

Quality Improvement: This is a means of raising quality performance to unprecedented levels ("breakthrough"). The methodology includes four steps:

1. Establish the infrastructure that is needed to secure annual QI.

2. Identify the specific needs for improvement—the improvement projects.

3. Establish a team for each project with clear responsibility for bringing the project to a successful conclusion.

4. Provide the resources, motivation, and training that are needed by teams to diagnose the causes, stimulate the establishment of a remedy, and establish controls to hold the gains.[114]

Juran asserted that there is a cost to nonquality, including reworking defective products, scrap, liability from lawsuits, and lost sales from dissatisfied previous customers or customers who purchase competitors' products or services because their quality is better.[115] Figure 4.7 depicts the trilogy, which Juran described as follows:

> The Juran Trilogy diagram is a graph with time on the horizontal axis and cost of poor quality (quality deficiencies) on the vertical axis. The initial activity is quality planning. The planners determine who the customers are and identify customers' needs. The planners then develop product and process designs that are able to respond to those needs. Finally, the planners turn the plans over to the operating forces.

> The job of the operating forces is to run the processes and produce the products. As operations proceed it soon emerges that the process is unable to produce 100 percent good work. Figure 4.7 shows that 20 percent of the work must be redone as a result of quality deficiencies. This waste then becomes chronic because the operating process was designed that way.

> Under conventional responsibility patterns, operating forces are unable to get rid of that planned chronic waste. What they do instead is carry out quality control—to prevent things from getting worse. Control includes putting out the fires, such as that sporadic spike.

> The chart also shows that in due course the chronic waste is driven down to a level far below the level that was planned originally. That gain is achieved by the third process of the trilogy: quality improvement. In effect, it is realized that chronic waste is also an opportunity for improvement, and steps are taken to seize that opportunity.[116]

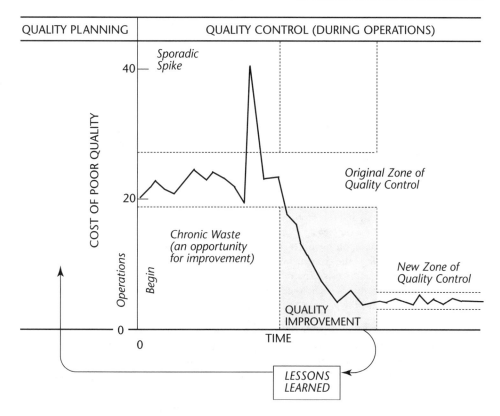

Figure 4.7. Juran Quality Trilogy. (From Juran, Joseph M. "The Quality Trilogy." *Quality Progress* 19 [August 1986]: 20.) Adapted and reprinted with permission from Quality Progress © 2020 ASQ, www.asq.org. All rights reserved. No further distribution allowed without permission.

The third part of the Juran Trilogy uses CQI to improve an existing process (redesigned, if necessary) so that the chronic waste associated with the "original zone of quality control" can be reduced and quality increased. The result is the "new zone of quality control" shown in Figure 4.7. Juran viewed CQI as seeking and finding opportunities for improvement that result in achieving the new zone. In earlier writings, Juran called this the "breakthrough" zone, consisting of a new and better level of performance and quality. A breakthrough necessitates accepting the premise that current performance is not good enough and can be improved, as well as making an attitudinal change about quality that becomes part of the organization's culture.[117] Juran described the triple role of the worker shown in Figure 4.1. Workers in a process have three basic functions: being customers by receiving work products that come to them, being processors who add value to the input supplied, and in turn, being suppliers to the customers in the next step in the process. Juran also formulated the criteria that must be present for workers to be in a state of self-control, which allows management to hold the worker, rather than the process, responsible for quality: workers must have 1) knowledge of what they are supposed to do, 2) knowledge of what they are doing, and 3) the means to regulate what they are doing if they fail to meet goals.[118] Juran guided managers to apply quality control principles in the workplace. Juran's seminal work is the *Quality Handbook*, first published in 1951 and now in its seventh edition.

Philip B. Crosby (1926–2001)

Philip B. Crosby was a former vice president of quality at International Telephone and Telegraph and a consultant to many industrial organizations. Crosby emphasized understanding nonquality: "Quality is free. It's not a gift, but it is free. What costs money are the nonquality things—all the actions that involve not doing jobs right the first time."[119] Crosby defined quality as "conformance to requirements" and said that an organization's goal should be to "satisfy the customer first, last, and always."[120]

> Crosby strongly advocates a system of quality improvement that focuses on prevention rather than appraisal. Prevention involves careful understanding of the process and identification of problem areas, followed by improvement of the process.
>
> Crosby strongly advocates the ultimate goal of quality as "Zero Defects" and that a company should constantly strive to achieve this goal. He believes that the best measure of quality is "cost of quality" and that this cost can be divided into two components: the price of nonconformance, and the price of conformance. The price of nonconformance includes the cost of internal failures (i.e., the cost of reinspection, retesting, scrap, rework, repairs, and lost production) and external failures (i.e., legal services, liability, damage claims, replacement, and lost customers). Crosby estimates that an organization's *cost of nonconformance can be as high as 25 to 30 percent of operating costs* [emphasis added]. The price of conformance, on the other hand, includes the cost of education, training, and prevention as well as the costs of inspection and testing. An organization must minimize the sum of both costs. The focus on process improvement, error-cause removal, employee training, management leadership, and worker awareness of quality problems are all important tenets.[121]

Crosby emphasized that organizations must identify the hidden costs of poor quality. In health services, malpractice is one such cost. Seven-eighths of an iceberg is below the waterline, and Figure 4.8 uses this simile to suggest the visible and hidden costs of poor quality for an HSO/ HS. Crosby's goals were "do it right the first time" and the derivative concept of "zero defects."[122] These ultimate quality goals may be unattainable, but they give important direction to the organization, nevertheless.[123] To move toward improved quality, the HSO/HS must go through a maturation process with respect to a philosophy about quality and then use Crosby's 14 steps of CQI (see the following list).

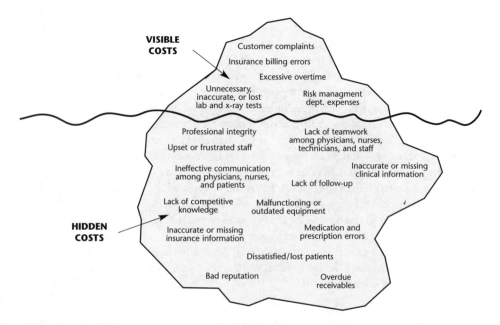

Figure 4.8. The iceberg of visible and hidden costs of poor quality. (From Carol Greebler, *TQM Plus*, San Diego, CA, 1989; reprinted by permission.)

Crosby's organizational maturity model includes the stages of uncertainty, awakening, enlightenment, wisdom, and certainty.[124] Enlightenment occurs when management's understanding and attitude about CQI are heightened and it is supportive of and accepts CQI; problems are faced openly and resolved in an orderly manner; and there is implementation of Crosby's 14 steps to quality. Crosby stated that in the last stage, certainty, CQI is ingrained in the organization's culture.

Crosby's 14 steps of CQI are not necessarily sequential; many are concurrent:

1. Management commitment to and involvement in quality

2. Use of QI teams composed of people with process knowledge and a commitment to action

3. Quality measurement so that areas for improvement can be identified and action can be taken

4. Measuring the cost of quality, meaning the cost of nonquality

5. Quality awareness by all organization members

6. Corrective actions—seek opportunities for improvement

7. Zero defects planning—striving to "do it right the first time"

8. Employee education, with formal orientation at all levels of management (and employees), about the 14 steps

9. Zero Defect Day, which is management's demonstration of its commitment to quality

10. Goal setting—the ultimate is zero defects, but "intermediate goals move in that direction"

11. Error-cause removal, in which people describe problems that prevent error-free work

12. Recognition of those who meet their goals

13. Quality councils composed of quality professionals assisting others in QI

14. Doing it all (steps 1–13) over again[125]

Crosby stated that his 14-step program is "a systematic way of guaranteeing that organized activities happen the way they are planned."[126] It results in doing the right things the right way and doing them right the first time.

Table 4.3 shows the differences and similarities among Deming, Juran, and Crosby, including their definitions of quality, objectives for CQI, general approaches to quality, methods for CQI, and views of management responsibilities. For Crosby, the journey toward zero defects is attaining and surpassing the enlightenment stages of his organizational maturity model and moving to the certainty stage. Of Crosby's several books, *Quality Is Free*, published in 1979, is among his most important.

Strategic Quality Planning: Hoshin Planning

In Japanese, *hoshin* means "shining metal compass" or "pointing direction."[127] Some literature adds *kanri* (administration), to hoshin, producing the combination of direction (hoshin) and administration (kanri).[128] Hoshin planning is a strategic approach to quality also known as focused planning, policy deployment, or strategic quality planning. Hoshin planning is customer oriented, is externally focused, and seeks to achieve breakthroughs in performance, quality, and competitive position. It is a way of linking quality planning, such as that in CQI and reengineering (discussed in Chapter 8), to the overall strategic planning

Table 4.3 Differences and similarities in the approaches to quality of Deming, Juran, and Crosby

Dimension	Deming	Juran	Crosby
Definition of quality	A product or service that helps someone and has a good and sustainable market	Fitness for use—free of deficiencies and meeting customer needs	Conformance to requirements, including "satisfy the customer"
Poor quality	Overwhelmingly caused by process, not workers; common cause variation	Caused by poor planning/design (chronic) and sporadic spike (see Figure 4.7)	Nonconformance; there are (hidden) costs of nonquality (see Figure 4.8)—quality is free
Quality objective	Error-free (reduce common cause variation); hit target every time	Reduce chronic poor quality and sporadic spike; move to "new zone" of quality control	Zero defects (objective); "do it right the first time"
Customer orientation	Yes, transformation— improve quality (so customers buy products) to improve competitive position (see Figure 4.4)	Yes, meet customer needs	Yes, satisfy the customer
General approach to quality	Prospective prevention in all processes, not retrospective inspection; understand and reduce variation through statistical process control; transform organization (change culture)	General management approach; find opportunities for improvement; "breakthrough"; change culture regarding quality	Managerial approach: QI teams, project basis for improvements, move to "certainty" stage, prevention and error-cause removal
Method for quality improvement	14 points for QI	Trilogy (quality planning, quality control, QI)	14 steps to QI
Management responsibility	Commitment to quality control (central focus); cause transformation; establish and perpetuate environment in which quality is integral to work of all employees; don't blame employees; drive out fear; break down barriers; and train, coach, and teach statistical methods to employees	Commitment to quality, especially design; instill quality culture; support operating forces and QI project teams	Commitment, leadership, and involvement in QI; worker training; promote quality awareness by all employees and management

process discussed in Chapter 9. Hoshin planning identifies and focuses improvement activities on a few key areas that are strategic priorities to meet customer needs and enhance competitive position.[129] Philosophically, hoshin draws heavily on Deming's plan, do, check, act (PDCA) cycle.

Hoshin planning has six attributes:

1. *A focus for the organization* in the form of a few breakthrough goals that are vital to the organization's success

2. *A commitment to customers,* including targets and means at every level of the organization that are based on meeting the needs and expectations that customers rank as most important

3. *Deployment of the organization's focus* so that employees understand their specific contributions to it (referred to as the "golden thread" that links employees to what is important to customers and to one another)

4. *Collective wisdom to develop the plan* through a top-down, bottom-up communication process called catch-ball

5. *Tools and techniques* that make the hoshin planning process and the plan helpful, clear, and easy to use

6. *Ongoing evaluation of progress* to facilitate learning and continuous improvement, that emphasizes both results and the processes that are used to achieve results[130]

An example of hoshin kanri is found in the Henry Ford Health System,[131] a leader in applying quality improvement in a large, integrated health services delivery system.[132]

Hoshin planning is vertical (compared with the horizontal planning of CQI), is based on the strategic vision of the organization in conjunction with its values and mission, and is a systematic way of prioritizing and integrating key success factor process improvement initiatives.[133] It allocates resources and aligns or restructures the organization so "all units attempt to achieve or contribute to the same few key organizational goals or objectives."[134]

As delivery of health services evolves from focusing on illness to supporting wellness and from independent organizations to aggregations of HSOs in systems, managers must address critical questions:

- How do we plan a successful integrated system?

- What are the right things for people to focus on to ensure long-term success of the system?

- How do we align many different people, departments, and organizations to work together toward the success of the whole system?

- How can we increase employee understanding of the system's priorities and plans?

- How can we balance the need for organizational direction with opportunities for employee initiative and creativity?

- How can we promote breakthrough thinking and results?[135]

Strategic quality planning, or hoshin planning, answers these questions.

Hoshin planning is summarized in Figure 4.9. Components include 1) choosing the focus (defining the future organization), 2) aligning the organization to review and improve performance, 3) finalizing and implementing the plan and monitoring performance against the plan, and 4) reviewing the plan and making improvements in it to enhance competitive position.

Customers and Focus

Choosing the focus includes the tasks inherent in strategic planning discussed in Chapter 9: integrating mission and objectives into the plan; analyzing external environment opportunities and threats, including customers, markets, and competitive position; and assessing the HSO's/ HS's internal environment to identify strengths and weaknesses. Hoshin planning focuses on strategic vision—identifying and articulating what the HSO/HS seeks to do, for example, become the highest value provider in the service area, integrate delivery to enhance community health, expand delivery capacity and capability, and provide information on demand for customers.[136]

Align the Organization

The alignment component of Figure 4.9 identifies the performance targets for key success factors that meet customers' needs. Gap analysis using survey data from customers and management will reveal discrepancies between expectations and actual performance

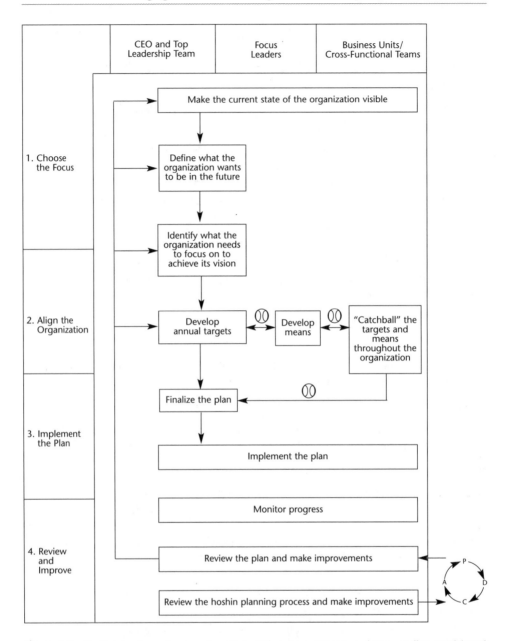

Figure 4.9. Hoshin planning system overview. (From Melum, Mara Minerva, and Casey Collett. *Breakthrough Leadership: Achieving Organizational Alignment through Hoshin Planning*, 127. Chicago: American Hospital Publishing, 1995; reprinted by permission.)

in service delivery.[137] An organization-wide iterative process known as catch-ball develops, negotiates, and communicates targets for key process performance.[138]

> In the catch-ball process, one level of management throws the ball—the tasks to be accomplished—to the next level of management or another planning team. [There is] input to the development of means to achieve the targets. Dialogue about targets and means proceeds within and across departments, down to the next level of the people closest to the relevant customers and work processes, until the plan is developed in sufficient detail. Then, the process is reversed. As the plan is finalized, it is rolled back up the organization and checked for gaps, overlaps, and feasibility.[139]

The staff's collective wisdom is applied as the iterative process develops specific targets at all organizational levels and the plans to achieve them. The process includes top-down, horizontal, and bottom-up cascades throughout the HSO/HS. Important outcomes are an understanding of how targets and plans relate to other organizational processes and how they are interconnected. Including employees in planning and implementation enhances acceptance of the strategic plan and their commitment and motivation to succeed. Furthermore, catch-ball and the resulting understanding of interrelationships facilitate teamwork. The "golden thread" is the concept that interconnected performance targets from all levels tie the organization together.

Implement the Plan and Review and Improve

Steps 3 and 4 in Figure 4.9 show that implementation of the plan and reviewing and improving it involve the same steps as those in the PDSA (PDCA) cycle. Implementation is based on targets for the processes critical to success and the resulting plan(s). Data are used to track performance for each target. Reviewing and improving the plan are concurrent and interactive with implementation. The process is essentially a problem-solving and control activity. If desired results are not attained in key processes, assessment will determine how deviations can be corrected. Assessment may also indicate no deviation, but that further improvement is possible. As in the PDSA cycle, lessons learned can be communicated. This can be done with reviews by quality improvement teams (QITs), the next level of management, and senior management. These activities will facilitate achieving the vision developed in the focus stage.

Two Models to Improve Processes

CQI uses data to understand the performance of processes. Monitoring data allows managers to identify the parts of a process that will benefit most from improvement efforts. There are many variations on Shewhart's PDSA cycle, but it remains the methodological core of quality/productivity improvement (Q/PI).

Model 1 One widely used variation is FOCUS-PDCA, developed in the 1980s by for-profit Columbia/HCA (formerly Hospital Corporation of America):

(F)ind a process to improve.

(O)rganize a team that knows the process.

(C)larify current knowledge of the process.

(U)nderstand sources of process variation.

(S)elect the process improvement.

(P)lan the improvement.

(D)o the improvement.

(C)heck the effect of the change.

(A)ct to hold the gain.

Data allow managers to monitor and evaluate, to determine if an opportunity for improvement is present, to clarify current knowledge about a process to be improved, to uncover causes of variation, to determine effects of improvement, and to continue monitoring.

Model 2 In 2005, HRET published Quality Management for Health Care Delivery (QMHCD), an evolution of the 1989 Quality Measurement and Management Project research initiative that connected CQI and HSOs. QMHCD is a CQI model like the FOCUS-PDCA model.[140] QMHCD emphasizes the need to achieve quality through a structured approach that affects competition, quality, and cost and system synergy.[141]

HRET's QMHCD model includes the following:[142]

1. *Find a process that needs improvement.*

2. *Assemble a team that knows the process.* In general, those who understand it best are the employees involved in it. "Through its members, the team must also have an understanding of continuous quality improvement principles, statistical quality control, the use of data management systems, and access to management so that organizational roadblocks to improvement can be overcome."

3. *Identify customers and process outputs, and measure customer expectations regarding outputs.* Different processes have different outputs, and "the team's first task is therefore to list the outputs of the process, identify its customers, and measure expectations of outputs." Customers may be patients, external stakeholders, or an internal downstream process.

4. *Document the process.* A process consists of a series of steps that convert inputs into outputs. They are usually hierarchical; that is, the main process may be broken down into subprocesses, each with sub inputs and sub outputs. The hierarchical chain may be followed to that level of detail necessary to understand the process.

5. *Generate output and process specifications.* "A specification is an explicit, measurable statement regarding an important attribute of an output (a customer expectation) or the (sub) process that produces it."

6. *Eliminate inappropriate variation (implement).*

7. *Document continuous improvement (innovate).* The team can select those ideas that seem most promising and then apply them on a test basis within their process. The proposed change can then be discarded, implemented, or modified and tried again, based on the results of the test.

As noted, QMHCD credits Deming with providing the framework and inspiration for improving quality in health services.[143]

Organizing for Improvement

Role of Governance and Senior Managers

The governing body (GB) sets the overall direction of the HSO/HS. In this leadership position, the GB, through senior management, determines the organization's level of commitment to quality and QI. The GB's decisions regarding strategic direction, selection of the chief executive officer (CEO) and approval of other senior leadership, and expectations regarding QI are key. The GB must support its commitment to quality with resources sufficient to ensure success. In addition, the GB sets a moral tone that ultimately affects the organization's culture and its focus on quality. Thus, in Dr. Deming's words, the transformation of the HSO/HS begins at the top, which is where the constancy of purpose and adoption of the new philosophy toward improvement of product and service that are hallmarks of CQI must be found.

Typically, GB members are unlikely to be conversant with Q/PI theory and applications in health services delivery. It rests with the CEO and other senior leadership to educate GB members and instill and nurture a dedication to CQI. Failure to educate them as to the long-term commitment needed to transform the organization will cause quality efforts to falter long before they are integral to the organization's culture and are the focus of all that is done. The need to nurture and reinforce the GB's commitment cannot be overstated. Common shortcomings are that governance is unwilling to commit the resources for training of staff and the staff members and consultants who ensure the success of the Q/PI effort; in addition, there is a tendency to be impatient. A culture that focuses on quality cannot be achieved easily; constancy of purpose and a long-term commitment to achieving this paradigm shift are essential.

Special attention must be directed to educating and involving members of the GB's quality committee because it will be most closely linked to operationalizing CQI. GB members whose experience is focused on performance in the next quarter must understand that transforming a culture to put quality at the forefront of all that is done may take a decade or more. Becoming a quality-focused HSO/HS is neither easy nor quickly accomplished.

Quality Improvement Council

Reporting to the GB's quality committee is the quality improvement council (QIC). The QIC is the implementation and monitoring arm for Q/PI. The QIC's core membership is typically 12 to 15 and includes senior managers (including nursing and professional staff organization leadership), various middle managers, and specialists and consultants in CQI. Ad hoc participants are those reporting on QI activities, including service line managers, "owners" of cross-functional processes, department heads, and staff such as those monitoring infectious disease, those doing UR, and patient educators.

The QIC's important roles include using customer satisfaction, quality, and performance data to set priorities for improvement efforts; sanctioning and monitoring cross-functional QITs; reviewing measures of clinical and administrative performance, and patient satisfaction data; and setting education and staff involvement goals.

Quality Improvement Teams

There are several types of QITs. The simplest and most common are those in functional areas or departments, each of which should have several QITs undertaking internal improvement efforts at any one time. These teams improve processes that are almost entirely internal to the department or functional area and over which the responsible manager has more or less exclusive authority. Typically, the process improvements these teams recommend can be approved and implemented by the department head or functional area manager without review by more senior management. Only when other areas are affected or additional resources are required must higher authority be consulted. Such efforts are the grassroots of Q/PI.

QITs for processes that cross functional area lines or are interdepartmental must be sanctioned by the QIC. This is done because 1) it is likely that resource consumption will be greater; 2) it is almost certain that more than one department or process will be investigated for improvement, and the cooperation of all managers is needed; and 3) the changes that will be recommended by the cross-functional team will have to be judged and possibly implemented. Thus, there is need for the QIC imprimatur.

Complex HSOs such as hospitals have scores of cross-functional processes; improving them will provide the greatest gain of higher quality and lower costs. The QIC sanctioning process must identify a process owner, who is usually the manager whose work most depends on the performance of the process being studied. Although the process owner will lead the team in its quest to improve quality, the QIC must be sure that team members are educated to participate effectively. Often, cross-functional QITs include a facilitator who is a member of the HSO's/HS's quality resources department. Facilitators meet with the team but are not team members. They assist with group process, application of QI tools, and efficient use of meeting time.

The Next Iteration of CQI: A Community Focus

What is the future of CQI? Its next iteration will be a quantum leap to involve multiple independent HSOs or HSs in a community. Acceptance of CQI by all health services providers in a community, including those in public health, will be difficult to achieve, and their arrangements will be complex.[144] Essential features will be 1) data sharing among participating provider organizations, which may be threatening to them and a possible barrier to cooperation; 2) accommodating different organizational cultures and answering questions of control; and 3) the shift in quality activities from independent providers to a collection within the community that represents "a transformation from hierarchies to markets."[145] CQI initiatives beyond the HSO or HS will likely use a public health model that relies on health status indicators, community satisfaction, and overall community benefit.[146] The Precede-Proceed model in Figure 1.2 reflects these elements.

CQI in the context of a community-wide model will require application of CQI principles, perhaps reengineering, and, certainly, strategic quality planning. However, it will be necessary to manage the changed leadership patterns among participating HSOs/HSs, lessen threats to them, and gain the cooperation of providers that have traditionally competed. Achieving this will be problematic. The following steps will facilitate the transformation from traditional organization-based to community-oriented quality initiatives:[147]

1. *Be cautious in implementing a conventional QI infrastructure that may have worked in intraorganizational initiatives.* All organizations may not have the same experience with quality initiatives; they may have different agendas and different priorities.

2. *Achieve the commitment of top management to community-based needs assessment.* Community-based indicators of need and quality must be developed, with HSO/HS leaders focusing on the needs of the community, not their individual organizations.

3. *Develop long-run objectives, but also set short-run measurable objectives.* Because of variability in commitment among different organizations, short-run objectives, perhaps involving modest initiatives, are necessary to demonstrate that community-wide quality initiatives can work.

4. *Select topics to utilize network participants who are ready for a common QI approach to specific objectives, capitalizing on small wins.* Build consensus by selecting issues and areas for cooperation that the majority of key participants is ready to implement.

5. *Emphasize data feedback and improved insight.* Use feedback to lessen the concerns of HSOs/HSs, as well as autonomous professionals who may be conceding some sovereignty.

6. *Avoid "religious" wars.* One organization should not proselytize its concept of quality as the one and only.

7. *Build the network of organizations carefully.* Elicit the cooperation of community stakeholders who are critical to success.

8. *Recognize initial efforts as a coalition arrangement.* Indicate to potential participants how the community quality initiatives will benefit them and help to achieve their organization's objectives. Also, permit them to participate or not participate in initiatives; in a confederation, it is necessary to allow some freedom.

Efforts to improve the community's health will only be successful through interorganizational cooperation, a goal that all health services executives should strive to achieve.

Discussion Questions

1. What important changes occurred in health services delivery in the 1980s and 1990s that stimulated HSOs/HSs to adopt the philosophy of CQI?

2. Define CQI. Why is it an organizational philosophy? What are its attributes? How can CQI lead to an enhanced HSO/HS competitive position?

3. Throughout history, reformers have sought to improve the quality of medical care. What common threads connect them? Why did some fail?

4. Think about the nursing service in a hospital. Who or what are its customers? If the nursing service is the customer, who or what provides inputs (is the supplier)?

5. Identify the similarities and differences in the approaches to quality taken by Deming, Juran, and Crosby.

6. Discuss the elements of the PDSA cycle. Apply it in a health services setting using a hypothetical example.

7. Discuss the application(s) of the Deming Chain Reaction in health services delivery.

8. Figure 4.8 identifies visible and hidden costs of poor quality. Add several types to each category.

9. Discuss the role and activities of quality improvement teams (QITs). Identify the attributes of their members.

10. Identify the ways HSOs interact with their communities. Discuss the importance of CQI in those interactions.

Case Study 1   Extent of Obligation

You are a physician who is the managing director of a 100-member, multispecialty group practice. There are 290 employees, exclusive of the physicians and other licensed independent practitioners (LIPs). The small human resources department is responsible for non-LIP staff. Your job requires significant involvement in recruiting physicians, credentialing them, and monitoring performance during their first year of associate membership in the group.

About 12 months ago you successfully recruited a surgeon, Dr. F. W. Nieren, who had had a fellowship that included significant experience using the DaVinci robotic surgical system. The DaVinci robot is a programmable device that can perform intricate surgical procedures with results consistent with those achieved by surgeons unaided by the robot. The group had sought to add a surgeon qualified with the DaVinci system for several years, partially because of competitive pressures, but also because having the robot would provide prestige and marketing potential. The $3 million device was installed and available soon after Dr. Nieren joined the staff.

Now, after almost 12 months to observe, monitor, and interact with Dr. Nieren you are very disappointed with the mixed quality of outcomes for her patients, the negative reactions of trusted non-LIP members of the staff to working with Dr. Nieren, and her unpleasant affect and often disruptive behavior. The number of incidents, especially the quality of clinical outcomes, has given you great concern. About a month ago, you asked several senior members of the surgical staff to conduct a full review of Dr. Nieren's clinical work, including the behavioral problems that had been documented. The probationary period of 12 months will end in 2 weeks. The report of the review committee supported your judgment about Dr. Nieren.

After consulting with members of the practice's executive management committee to which you report, you conclude that Dr. Nieren should not become a member of the group and should be asked to leave.

Your conversation with Dr. Nieren did not go well. She reacted angrily to the points you made, and alleged that she had been treated unfairly by LIP and non-LIP staff members and the review committee. She stated that she would leave without protest only if she received a laudatory letter of recommendation. Dr. Nieren stated that she was prepared to retain legal counsel and make life for the group "a living hell." Your response to Dr. Nieren's demand for a laudatory letter was that the best you can do is to write a letter that offers only the dates of her employment, but that provides no information as to her clinical or collegial performance.

Questions

1. Identify the ethical, legal, and quality issues present in the case.

2. What should you do regarding the letter that Dr. Nieren is demanding?

3. Identify and discuss your obligations to Dr. Nieren's future patients and the sites at which she might seek clinical privileges.

4. Draft a letter that could be sent in response to inquiries from sites of potential employment or clinical affiliation for Dr. Nieren.

Case Study 2 Surgical Safety—Retained Foreign Objects

Your hospital established a safety program to track surgical sponges several years ago when The Joint Commission and the CMS identified retained sponges as a "never event." A never event is something that should never occur—sponges should never be left inside a patient after a procedure. Unfortunately, there was a recent incident in which a patient had to be taken back to the OR. The cause of her pain was a retained sponge. The surgical count in the medical record showed no discrepancy in the sponge count.

Questions

1. After reading the documentation of the process being used, what resources are there to compare your program to national best practices?

2. Your patient safety department decided it should organize a group to perform the root cause analysis required by The Joint Commission. Use titles to identify those who should be included.

3. The root cause analysis found there is a process to keep track of surgical sponges, but there are other places to put used sponges that blood has colored red. This can conceal the fact that a sponge was misplaced. How should this fact be included in the best practice?

4. Comment on the possibility that an OR staff member miscounted or deliberately reported a correct count when it was actually incorrect.

Case Study 3 Which Team's Fastest?[148]

In early 2015, the Philadelphia Veterans Administration Medical Center (PVAMC) announced a new incentive program to reward employees with cash and food if they processed veterans' disability determination cases more quickly. As proposed, the team that processed the most claims at the end of every second week would be rewarded with breakfast, lunch, or a snack.

In addition, the team meeting its target before a specific date would receive a bonus of $15,000. Teams had different goals. The range was 400 to 1,000 claims every 2 weeks.

PVAMC employees were concerned the program would lead to the same kind of "cooked books" that had caused major problems at the Phoenix VA Hospital, including a secret list of 40 veterans who allegedly died waiting for care, data manipulation about waiting times for appointments, and putting interests of VA staff ahead of veterans' care. Employees at the PVAMC asserted it can take months to process a disability claim properly. Conversely, it takes little time to deny a claim. Thus, the incentive plan encouraged staff to deny disability claims to close cases quickly and receive rewards under the incentive program.

When the incentive program was proposed, the PVAMC was being investigated by the VA inspector general for data manipulation, including hiding or shredding returned mail that was undeliverable and processing easy claims first to misrepresent performance.

The incentive program was canceled only two days after it began. This required PVAMC staff to work mandatory overtime to process the backlog of disability claims. The goal is to process a claim in 125 days; the PVAMC average is 164. The PVAMC director said she is at a loss as to how to improve performance. She said she would use a suggestion box for ideas from the staff. An audit of disability claim determinations at the PVAMC found an accuracy rate of 92.8%.

Questions

1. Apply the principles of quality and performance improvement to critique the incentive program developed by the PVAMC. Identify three likely results if this incentive program is used for several years.

2. Develop an opportunity statement for process improvement that could be used in the PVAMC's disability determination process.

3. Identify three problems for employees and the organization when mandatory overtime is used to process disability claims. Identify detriments to veterans if mandatory overtime is used.

4. Write a suggestion for the director's suggestion box describing how to improve processing of disability claims. Use a maximum of 200 words.

Notes

1. American College of Surgeons. *The Minimum Standard*. Chicago: American College of Surgeons, 1918.
2. Donabedian, Avedis. *Explorations in Quality Assessment and Monitoring*, vol. II, *The Criteria and Standards of Quality*. Ann Arbor, MI: Health Administration Press, 1982.
3. Donabedian, Avedis. *Explorations in Quality Assessment and Monitoring*, vol. I, *The Definition of Quality and Approaches to Its Assessment*, 81. Ann Arbor, MI: Health Administration Press, 1980.
4. Donabedian, *Explorations*, vol. I, 79–89.
5. Donabedian, *Explorations*, vol. I, 8.
6. Donabedian, *Explorations*, vol. I, 83.
7. Donabedian, *Explorations*, vol. I, 82.
8. The Joint Commission. *A Comprehensive Review of Development and Testing for National Implementation of Hospital Core Measures*, 2. Oak Brook Terrace, IL: Joint Commission on Accreditation of Healthcare Organizations, 2007.
9. Berwick, Donald M., A. Blanton Godfrey, and Jane Roessner. *Curing Health: New Strategies for Quality Improvement*, 11. San Francisco: Jossey-Bass, 1990.
10. The Joint Commission. *Agenda for Change*, 3–4. Oak Brook Terrace, IL: The Joint Commission on Accreditation of Healthcare Organizations, June 1988.
11. The Joint Commission. *Accreditation Manual for Hospitals*, Appendix D, 225–232. Oakbrook Terrace, IL: The Joint Commission on Accreditation of Healthcare Organizations, 1992.
12. The Joint Commission. *A Comprehensive Review of Development and Testing for National Implementation of Hospital Core Measures*, 2. Oak Brook Terrace, IL: Joint Commission on Accreditation of Healthcare Organizations, 2007.

13. The Joint Commission. *Specifications Manual for Joint Commission National Quality Measures* (v2018B1) Discharges 01-01-19 (1Q19) through 06-30-19 (2Q19). 2019. *https://www.joint·commission.org/specifications_manual_joint_commission_national_quality_core_measures.aspx,* retrieved February 3, 2019, and *https://www.jointcommission.org/assets/1/18/5_Joint_Commission_Measures_Effective_January_1_2019.pdf,* retrieved May 5, 2020.

14. Centers for Medicare & Medicaid Services. "Readmissions Reduction Program." *http://www.cms.gov/Medicare/Medicare-Fee-for-Service-Payment/AcuteInpatientPPS/Readmissions-ReductionProgram.html,* retrieved August 22, 2013.

15. Centers for Medicare & Medicaid Services. Core Measures. *https://www.cms.gov/Medicare/Quality-Initiatives-Patient-Assessment-Instruments/QualityMeasures/Core-Measures.html,* retrieved February 3, 2019.

16. Laffel, Glenn, and David Blumenthal. "The Case for Using Industrial Management Science in Health Care Organizations." *Journal of the American Medical Association* 262 (November 24, 1989): 2870; Merry, Martin D. "Total Quality Management for Physicians: Translating the New Paradigm." *Quality Review Bulletin* 16 (March 1990): 104; McLaughlin, Curtis P., and Arnold D. Kaluzny. "Total Quality Management in Health: Making It Work." *Health Care Management Review* 15 (Summer 1990): 7.

17. Kaluzny, Arnold D., and Curtis P. McLaughlin. "Managing Transitions: Assuring the Adoption and Impact of TQM." *Quality Review Bulletin* 37, 4 (November 1992): 380.

18. *Quality Management: A Management Advisory,* 1. Chicago: American Hospital Association, 1990; James, Brent C. *Quality Management for Health Care Delivery—Quality Measurement and Management Project,* 10. Chicago: Hospital Research and Educational Trust, 1989; Laffel and Blumenthal, "The Case for Using," 2870; O'Connor, Stephen J. "Service Quality: Understanding and Implementing the Concept in the Clinical Laboratory." *Clinical Laboratory Management Review* 3 (November/December 1989): 330; Schumacher, Dale N. "Organizing for Quality Competition: The Coming Paradigm Shift." *Frontiers of Health Services Management* 5 (Summer 1989): 113. For a useful model of quality, see Lanning, Joyce A., and Stephen J. O'Connor. "The Health Care Quality Quagmire: Some Signposts." *Hospital & Health Services Administration* 35 (Spring 1990): 42.

19. Deming, W. Edwards. *Out of the Crisis,* 18. Boston: Massachusetts Institute of Technology, 1986.

20. Milakovich, Michael E. "Creating a Total Quality Health Care Environment." *Health Care Management Review* 16 (Spring 1991): 9.

21. Casurella, Joe. "Managing a 'Total Quality' Program." *Federation of American Health Systems Review* 22 (July/August 1989): 31.

22. James, *Quality Management,* 11.

23. American Society of Quality. "Quality Glossary." 2013. *http://asq.org/glossary/q.html,* retrieved February 12, 2013.

24. James, *Quality Management,* 10.

25. McLaughlin, Curtis P., and Arnold D. Kaluzny. *Continuous Quality Improvement in Healthcare: Theory, Implementation, and Applications,* 12. Gaithersburg, MD: Aspen Publishers, 1994.

26. James, Brent. *Quality Management for Health Care Delivery.* HRET and the TRUST Award. July 25, 2005. *http://www.hret.org/hret/about/content/monograph.pdf,* retrieved January 9, 2007.

27. Re, Richard N., and Marie A. Krousel-Wood. "How to Use Continuous Quality Improvement Theory and Statistical Quality Control Tools in a Multispecialty Clinic." *Quality Review Bulletin* 16 (November 1990): 392.

28. Marszalek-Gaucher, Ellen, and Richard J. Coffey. *Transforming Healthcare Organizations: How to Achieve and Sustain Organizational Excellence,* 85. San Francisco: Jossey-Bass, 1990; Arndt, Margarete, and Barbara Bigelow. "The Implementation of Total Quality Management in Hospitals: How Good Is the Fit?" *Health Care Management Review* 20 (Fall 1995): 9.

29. Deming, W. Edwards. "Improvement of Quality and Productivity through Action by Management." *National Productivity Review* 1 (Winter 1981–1982): 12–22; Deming, W. Edwards. *Quality, Productivity, and Competitive Position.* Boston: The MIT Press, 1982; Deming, W. Edwards. "Transformation of Western Style Management." *Interfaces* 15 (May/June 1985): 6–11; Deming, *Out of the Crisis.*

30. Juran, Joseph M. *Managerial Breakthrough: A New Concept of the Manager's Job.* New York: McGraw-Hill, 1964; Juran, Joseph M. "The Quality Trilogy." *Quality Progress* 19 (August 1986): 19–24; Juran, Joseph M. *Juran on Leadership for Quality.* New York: The Free Press, 1989; Juran, Joseph M. *Juran on Planning for Quality.* New York: The Free Press, 1988.

31. Crosby, Philip B. *Quality Is Free.* New York: McGraw-Hill, 1979; Crosby, Philip B. *Let's Talk Quality.* New York: McGraw-Hill, 1989; Crosby, Philip B. *Quality without Tears.* New York: McGraw-Hill, 1984.

32. *Quality Management: A Management Advisory,* 2.

33. For ease of reading, when reference is made in this chapter to process improvement, it also includes input improvement.

34. The Joint Commission. *Specifications Manual for Joint Commission National Quality Measures* (v2020A). *https://manual.jointcommission.org/releases/TJC2020A/*. Retrieved May 1, 2020.

35. The Joint Commission. *Specifications Manual for National Hospital Inpatient Quality Measures Discharges* 07-01-19 (3Q19) through 12-31-19 (4Q19) Version 5.6. *https://www.jointcommission. org/-/media/tjc/documents/measurement/specification-manuals/hiqr_specsman_july2019_v5_6.pdf* Retrieved May 1, 2020.

36. Lam, Miranda B., Jose F. Figueroa, et al. "Association between Patient Outcomes and Accreditation in U.S. Hospitals: Observational Study." *BMJ* (2018):363; k4011. Published October 18, 2018. "US hospital accreditation by independent organizations is not associated with lower mortality and is only slightly associated with reduced readmission rates for the 15 common medical conditions selected in this study. There was no evidence in this study to indicate that patients choosing a hospital accredited by The Joint Commission confer any healthcare benefits over choosing a hospital accredited by another independent accrediting organization." *https://www.bmj.com/content/363/bmj.k4011*, retrieved February 13, 2019.

37. James, *Quality Management*, 1.

38. Anderson, Craig A., and Robin D. Daigh. "Quality Mind-Set Overcomes Barriers to Success." *Health-care Financial Management* 45 (February 1991): 21; Kroenberg, Philip S., and Renee G. Loeffler. "Quality Management Theory: Historical Context and Future Prospect." *Journal of Management Science & Policy Analysis* 8 (Spring/Summer 1991): 204; McLaughlin and Kaluzny, "Total Quality Management," 7; Sahney, Vinod K., and Gail L. Warden. "The Quest for Quality and Productivity in Health Services." *Frontiers of Health Services Management* 7 (Summer 1991): 2.

39. Milakovich, "Creating a Total," 9.

40. McEachern, J. Edward, and Duncan Neuhauser. "The Continuous Improvement of Quality at the Hospital Corporation of America." *Health Matrix* 7 (Fall 1989): 7; Postal, Susan Nelson. "Using the Deming Quality Improvement Method to Manage Medical Records Department Product Lines." *Topics in Health Records Management* 10 (June 1990): 34.

41. *Quality Management: A Management Advisory*, 2; James, *Quality Management*, 1; Lynn, Monty L., and David P. Osborn. "Deming's Quality Principles: A Health Care Application." *Hospital & Health Services Administration* 36 (Spring 1991): 113.

42. Berwick, Donald M. "Managing Quality: The Next Five Years." *Quality Letter for Healthcare Leaders* 6, 6 (July/August 1994): 3.

43. Boerstler, Heidi, Richard W. Foster, Edward J. O'Connor, James L. O'Brien, Stephen M. Shortell, James M. Carman, and Edward F.X. Hughes. "Implementation of Total Quality Management: Conventional Wisdom Versus Reality." *Hospital & Health Services Administration* 41 (Summer 1996): 143.

44. Taylor, Mark. "Quality as Gospel." *Modern Healthcare* 35, 18 (May 2, 2005): 32, 6 pages. *https://www.modernhealthcare.com/article/20050502/NEWS/505020335/quality-as-gospel*, retrieved June 24, 2020. A good review of CQI, including barriers, can be found in Barbara Bigelow and Margarete Arndt, "Total Quality Management: Field of Dreams?" *Health Care Management Review* 20 (Fall 1995): 15–25 and in Gustafson, David H., and Ann Schoofs Hundt. "Findings of Innovation Research Applied to Quality Management Principles for Health Care." *Health Care Management Review* 20 (Spring 1995): 16–33.

45. Lynn and Osborn, "Deming's Quality Principles"; Taylor, Mark. "Quality as Gospel."

46. Towne, Jennifer. "Going 'Lean' Streamlines Processes, Empowers Staff and Enhances Care." *Hospitals & Health Networks Management* 80, 10 (October 2006): 34; Postal, "Using the Deming"; McEachern and Neuhauser, "The Continuous Improvement"; Sahney and Warden, "The Quest for Quality"; Walton, Mary. *Deming Management at Work*. New York: Putnam, 1990.

47. Ferguson, T. Bruce, Jr., Eric D. Peterson, Laura P. Coombs, Mary C. Eiken, Meghan L. Carey, Frederick L. Grover, and Elizabeth R. DeLong. "Use of Continuous Quality Improvement to Increase Use of Process Measures in Patients Undergoing Coronary Artery Bypass Graft Surgery: A Randomized Controlled Trial." *Journal of the American Medical Association* 290, 1 (July 2, 2003): 49–56; James, Brent C. "TQM and Clinical Medicine." *Frontiers of Health Services Management* 7 (Summer 1991): 42–46.

48. Kronick, Steven L., et al. Part 4: Systems of Care and Continuous Quality Improvement. *Circulation* 132, 18 (suppl 2). Originally published November 3, 2015. *Circulation* 132 (2015): S397–S413. *https://www.ahajournals.org/doi/full/10.1161/CIR.0000000000000258.* retrieved February 14, 2019.

49. Haugh, Richard. "The Demand for More Exacting Test Results—Fast!—Reformulates Hospital Labs." *Hospital & Health Networks* 80, 1 (January 2006): 46–48, 50, 52.

50. Benedetto, Anthony R. "Adapting Manufacturing-Based Six Sigma Methodology to the Service Environment of a Radiology Film Library." *Journal of Healthcare Management* 48, 4 (July/August 2003): 263–280; Cascade, Philip N. "Quality Improvement in Diagnostic Radiology." *American Journal of Radiology* 154 (May 1990): 1,117–1,120.

51. Postal, "Using the Deming."

52. Zimmerman, Rosanne, Rhonda Smith, Christopher M.B. Fernandes, Teresa Smith, and Ayad Al Darrab. "A Quest for Quality." *Quality Progress* 39, 3 (March 2006): 41–46.
53. Harvin, John A., Susan H. Wootton, Charles C. Miller. Using Quality Improvement to Promote Clinical Trials of Emergency Trauma Therapies. *JAMA* 320, 18 (October 2018). *https://www.researchgate.net/publication/328211304*, retrieved June 24, 2020.
54. Peterson, Charles D. "Quality Improvement in Pharmacy: A Prescription for Change." *Quality Review Bulletin* 16 (March 1990): 106–108.
55. Esimai, Grace. "Lean-Six Sigma Reduces Medication Errors." *Quality Progress* 38, 4 (April 2005): 51–57.
56. Geboers, Harrie, Henk Mokkink, Pauline van Montfort, Henk van den Hoogen, Wil van den Bosch, and Richard Grol. "Continuous Quality Improvement in Small General Medical Practices: The Attitudes of General Practitioners and Other Practice Staff." *International Journal for Quality in Health Care* 13, 5 (October 1, 2001): 391–397.
57. Robinson, Tracy E., et al. Embedding Continuous Quality Improvement Processes in Multidisciplinary Teams in Cancer Care: Exploring the Boundaries between Quality and Implementation Science. *Australian Health Review* 41, 3 (July 4, 2016): 291–296. *https://doi.org/10.1071/AH16052. http://www.publish.csiro.au/ah/ah16052*, retrieved February 14, 2019.
58. Zimmerman, Rosanne, Rhonda Smith, Christopher M.B. Fernandes, Teresa Smith, and Ayad Al Darrab. "A Quest for Quality." *Quality Progress* 39, 3 (March 2006): 41–46.
59. Machline-Carrion, M. Julia; Rafael Marques Soares; et al. Effect of a Multifaceted Quality Improvement Intervention on the Prescription of Evidence-Based Treatment in Patients of High Cardiovascular Risk in Brazil: The BRIDGE Cardiovascular Presentation Cluster Randomized Clinical Trial. *JAMA Cardiology*. Published online April 3, 2019. *https://jamanetwork.com/journals/jamacardiology/fullarticle/2729583?guestAccessKey=761c523a-519c-4e44-887a-49e03ac9db7d&utm*, retrieved April 6, 2019.
60. Chan, Yee-Ching Lilian, and Shih-Jen Kathy Ho. "Continuous Quality Improvement: A Survey of American and Canadian Healthcare Executives." *Hospital & Health Services Administration* 42 (Winter 1997): 529–534.
61. James, *Quality Management for Health Care Delivery*, 7.
62. O'Leary, Dennis S. "CQI—a Step beyond QA." *Joint Commission Perspectives* 10 (March/April 1990): 2.
63. President of The Joint Commission, cited in Patterson, Pat. "JCAHO Shifts Its Emphasis to QI—Quality Improvement." *OR Manager* 6 (May 1990): 1.
64. Everett, Michael, and Brent C. James. "Continuous Quality Improvement in Healthcare: A Natural Fit." *Journal for Quality and Participation* (January/February 1991): 10.
65. Crosby, *Let's Talk Quality*, 63.
66. See also Berwick, Donald M., A. Blanton Godfrey, and Jane Roessner. *Curing Health Care: New Strategies for Quality Improvement*, 32–43. San Francisco: Jossey-Bass, 1990.
67. Darr, Kurt. "Applying the Deming Method in Hospitals: Part 1." *Hospital Topics* 67 (November/December 1989): 4.
68. Milakovich, "Creating a Total," 12.
69. Kaluzny, Arnold D., Curtis P. McLaughlin, and B. Jon Jaeger. "TQM as a Managerial Innovation: Research Issues and Implications." *Health Services Management Research* 6 (May 1993): 79.
70. Deming, *Out of the Crisis*, 3; Walton, Mary. *The Deming Management Method*, 25. New York: Perigee Books, 1986.
71. Baldrige Performance Excellence Program. *https://www.nist.gov/baldrige*, retrieved June 27, 2020.
72. "Thomas Percival, 1740–1804." *http://www.thornber.net/cheshire/ideasmen/percival.html*, retrieved June 24, 2020.
73. "Ernest Amory Codman." *http://www.whonamedit.com/doctor.cfm/2558.html*, retrieved June 24, 2020.
74. "Ignaz Semmelweis." Wikipedia. *http://en.wikipedia.org/wiki/Ignaz_Semmelweis*, retrieved June 24, 2020.
75. Holleb, Arthur I. "Halsted Revisited." *American College of Surgeons Bulletin* 71, 9: 20–21.
76. BBC. "Florence Nightingale (1820–1910)." *https://www.bbc.co.uk/teach/florence-nightingale-saving-lives-with-statistics/zjksmfr*, retrieved June 24, 2020.
77. Audain, Cynthia. "Biographies of Women Mathematicians: Florence Nightingale." *https://www.agnesscott.edu/lriddle/women/nitegale.htm*, retrieved June 24, 2020.
78. Riddle, Larry. "Biographies of Women Mathematicians: Polar-Area Diagram." *http://www.agnesscott.edu/lriddle/women/nightpiechart.htm*, retrieved June 24, 2020.
79. BBC. "Florence Nightingale."
80. Bostridge, Mark. *Florence Nightingale: The Woman and Her Legend*. London: Viking Books, 2008.
81. MacEachern, Malcolm T. *Hospital Organization and Management*, 17. Berwyn, IL: Physicians' Record Company, 1962.
82. Pellegrini, Carlos A. "Ernest Amory Codman Award honoree furthers quality improvement mission." *Bulletin of the American College of Surgeons*, November 1, 2016. *https://bulletin.facs.org/2016/11/ernest-amory-codman-award-honoree-furthers-quality-improvement-mission/*, retrieved September 16, 2020.

83. American College of Surgeons. "Public Information: What Is the American College of Surgeons?" *http://www.facs.org/about/corppro.html*, retrieved June 24, 2020.

84. "Ernest Armory [sic] Codman." *http://www.whonamedit.com/doctor.cfm/2558.html*, retrieved June 25, 2020.

85. Neuhauser, Duncan. "Heroes and Martyrs of Quality and Safety: Ernest Amory Codman, MD." *https://qualitysafety.bmj.com/content/qhc/11/1/104.full.pdf*, retrieved June 25, 2020.

86. Neuhauser, Duncan. "Heroes and Martyrs of Quality and Safety."

87. Moen, Ron and Cliff Norman. "Evolution of the PDSA Cycle." No date. *http://www.cologic.nu/files/evolution_of_the_pdsa_cycle.pdf*, retrieved June 27, 2020. This reference includes valuable background on the PDSA cycle and persons important in its evolution.

88. ASQ. About Walter A. Shewhart. *asq.org/about-asq/who-we-are/bio_shewhart.html*, retrieved June 25, 2020.

89. Moen, Ron, and Cliff Norman. "Evolution of the PDSA Cycle."

90. Lowe, Ted A., and Joseph M. Mazzeo. "Crosby, Deming, Juran: Three Preachers, One Religion." *Quality* 25 (September 1986): 22–25; Sahney and Warden, "The Quest for Quality," 4–7.

91. Lowe and Mazzeo, "Crosby, Deming, Juran," 22.

92. Deming, W. Edwards. "Walter A. Shewhart, 1891–1967." *The American Statistician* 21, 2 (April 1967): 39–40.

93. Darr, Kurt. "Eulogy to the Master: W. Edwards Deming." *Hospital Topics* 72 (Winter 1994): 4.

94. Deming, W. Edwards. *The New Economics for Industry, Government, Education*, 2nd ed., 2. Cambridge, MA: MIT-CAES, 2000.

95. Deming, *The New Economics for Industry, Government, Education*, 2nd ed., chap. 4, 92–115.

96. Deming, "Improvement of Quality"; Deming, *Quality, Productivity*; Deming, "Transformation of Western"; Deming, *Out of the Crisis*.

97. Darr, "Applying the Deming Method: Part 1"; Darr, Kurt. "Applying the Deming Method in Hospitals: Part 2." *Hospital Topics* 68 (Winter 1990): 4–6; Gabor, Andrea. *The Man Who Discovered Quality: How W. Edwards Deming Brought the Quality Revolution to America—the Stories of Ford, Xerox, and GM*. New York: Random House, 1990; Gitlow, Howard S., and Shelly J. Gitlow. *The Deming Guide to Quality and Competitive Position*. Englewood Cliffs, NJ: Prentice-Hall, 1987; Neuhauser, Duncan. "The Quality of Medical Care and the 14 Points of Edwards Deming." *Health Matrix* 6 (Summer 1986): 7–10; Scherkenbach, William W. *The Deming Route to Quality and Productivity*. Washington, DC: CEEP Press, 1986; Walton, *The Deming Management Method*.

98. Deming, *Out of the Crisis*, 199–203.

99. Darr, "Applying the Deming Method: Part 1," 4.

100. Deming's 14 points (in italics) are drawn from Deming, *Out of the Crisis*, 22–24.

101. Deming, *Out of the Crisis*, 200.

102. Deming, *Out of the Crisis*, 201.

103. Deming, *Out of the Crisis*, 202.

104. Deming, *Out of the Crisis*, 202.

105. Deming, *Out of the Crisis*, 202.

106. Deming, *Out of the Crisis*, 203.

107. Deming, "Improvement of Quality," 22.

108. Darr, "Applying the Deming Method: Part 1," 5.

109. Sahney and Warden, "The Quest for Quality," 4–5.

110. Personal communication, Juran Institute, January 1999.

111. "Joseph M. Juran." Wikipedia. *http://en.wikipedia.org/wiki/Dr._Joseph_Moses_Juran*, retrieved June 25, 2020.

112. Juran, *Managerial Breakthrough*; Juran, "Quality Trilogy"; Juran, *Juran on Planning*; Juran, *Juran on Leadership*, 361.

113. Sahney and Warden, "The Quest for Quality," 6–7.

114. Adapted with permission of The Free Press, a Division of Simon & Schuster Adult Publishing Group, from *Juran on Leadership for Quality: An Executive Handbook* by Joseph M. Juran. Copyright © 1989 by Juran Institute, Inc. All rights reserved.

115. Juran, *Juran on Planning*, 1.

116. Adapted with permission of The Free Press, a Division of Simon & Schuster Adult Publishing Group, from *Juran on Leadership for Quality: An Executive Handbook* by Joseph M. Juran. Copyright © 1989 by Juran Institute, Inc. All rights reserved.

117. Juran, *Managerial Breakthrough*, 7.

118. Juran, J. M., and Frank M. Gryna, eds. *Juran's Quality Control Handbook*, 4th ed., 6.19. New York: McGraw-Hill Book Company, 1988.

119. Crosby, *Quality Is Free*, 1.

120. Crosby, *Let's Talk Quality*, 104.
121. Sahney and Warden, "The Quest for Quality," 6.
122. The industrial concept of zero defects means conformance to standards or specifications. For example, size is allowed to vary by ±3 millimeters. *Zero defects* does not mean that the product is perfect, although *zero defects* has been used in industry as a slogan—an exhortation directed at workers. Deming opposed setting specifications except as general guides. He argued that efforts to seek perfection are thwarted if the goal is only to meet specifications. Point 10 of Deming's 14 points for improvement of management expressed his opposition to slogans. In his judgment, management has been unwilling to accept blame for poor processes and, instead, has blamed the workers, an attitude that has caused management to substitute slogans for process improvement. Deming believed slogans alone only cause worker anger and frustration. His reaction to slogans and exhortations was to ask, "By what means?"
123. Crosby, *Let's Talk Quality*, 9.
124. Crosby, *Quality Is Free*, 38–39.
125. Crosby, *Quality Is Free*, 132–138; Crosby, *Quality without Tears*, 101–124; Crosby, *Let's Talk Quality*, 106–107. The quotation in Point 10 is from Crosby, *Quality without Tears*, 117.
126. Crosby, *Quality Is Free*, 22.
127. The section on Hoshin planning is adapted and updated from Rakich, Jonathon S. "Strategic Quality Planning." *Hospital Topics* 78, 2 (Winter 2000): 5–11. Used with permission from Helen Dwight Reid Education Foundation. Published by Heldref Publications, 1319 18th St. NW, Washington, DC 20036-1802. Copyright © 2000.
128. Wikipedia. Hoshin Kanri. *https://en.wikipedia.org/wiki/Hoshin_Kanri*, retrieved February 15, 2019.
129. See O'Brien, James L., Stephen M. Shortell, Edward F. X. Hughes, Richard W. Foster, James M. Carman, Heidi Boerstler, and Edward J. O'Connor. "An Integrative Model for Organization-Wide Quality Improvement: Lessons from the Field." *Quality Management in Health Care* 3, 4 (1995): 21; Hyde, Rebecca S., and Joan M. Vermillion. "Driving Quality through Hoshin Planning." *Joint Commission Journal on Quality Improvement* 22 (January 1996): 28; Horak, Bernard J. *Strategic Planning in Healthcare: Building a Quality-Based Plan Step by Step*, 2–4. New York: Quality Resources, 1997.
130. Boisvert, Lisa. "Strategic Planning Using Hoshin Kanri." White paper. May 2012. *https://goalqpc.com/cms/docs/whitepapers/GOALQPCHoshinWhitepaper.pdf*, retrieved June 25, 2020.
131. "Hoshin Kanri Strategic Planning." *https://www.henryford.com/hcp/academic/pathology/production-system/wednesdays-words/2011-articles/march-9-2011*, retrieved February 16, 2019.
132. "Henry Ford's Commitment to Quality and Safety." *https://www.henryford.com/about/quality*, retrieved February 16, 2019.
133. Shortell, Stephen M., Daniel Z. Levin, James L. O'Brien, and Edward F. X. Hughes. "Assessing the Evidence on CQI: Is the Glass Half Empty or Half Full?" *Hospital & Health Services Administration* 40 (Spring 1995): 6.
134. Kennedy, Maggie. "Using Hoshin Planning in Total Quality Management: An Interview with Gerry Kaminski and Casey Collett." *Journal on Quality Improvement* 20 (October 1994): 577.
135. Melum, Mara Minerva, and Casey Collett, *Breakthrough Leadership: Achieving Organizational Alignment through Hoshin Planning*, 4. Chicago: American Hospital Publishing, 1995.
136. Melum and Collett, *Breakthrough Leadership*, 17.
137. Hyde and Vermillion, "Driving Quality," 30.
138. Plsek, Paul E. "Techniques for Managing Quality." *Hospital & Health Services Administration* 40 (Spring 1995, Special CQI Issue): 68–69.
139. Melum and Collett, *Breakthrough Leadership*, 21.
140. James, *Quality Management*, iii.
141. Readers interested in HRET research projects can find information on the American Hospital Association website at *https://www.aha.org/aha-search?search_api_fulltext=hret*.
142. James, *Quality Management*, 26–28, 32.
143. James, *Quality Management for Health Care Delivery*.
144. Kaluzny, Arnold D., Curtis P. McLaughlin, and David C. Kibbe. "Quality Improvement: Beyond the Institution." *Hospital & Health Services Administration* 40 (Spring 1995, Special CQI Issue): 176.
145. Kaluzny, McLaughlin, and Kibbe, "Quality Improvement," 175.
146. Kaluzny, McLaughlin, and Kibbe, "Quality Improvement," 178–180.
147. Adapted from Kaluzny, McLaughlin, and Kibbe, "Quality Improvement," 181–185.
148. Sources for this case were Klimas, Jacqueline. "VA Gets Incentives to Speed Up Claims: Bonuses for Hitting Benchmarks." *Washington Times*, January 13, 2015, A1; Klimas, Jacqueline. "VA Cancels Employee Incentive to Rush Claims: Plan Unfair to Veterans, Workers Say." *Washington Times*, January 15, 2015, A1.

5

Healthcare Technology

Advancement and diffusion of technology are among the most complex and controversial aspects of health services. Technological innovation has given health services providers the means to diagnose and treat an ever-increasing range of conditions and illnesses. The same advances have been criticized, however, for their effect on the practice of medicine and on national healthcare expenditures, which are projected to be $4.3 trillion in 2021 and $5.7 trillion by 2026 or about 19.7% of the gross domestic product.[1]

Analyzing the effects of technology on health services and their costs is complex, especially in terms of costs. Some technologies increase costs. Some technologies decrease costs. And some technologies do both. Some raise costs in the short run but save money over the full course of treatment. Others lower costs by moving care to nonhospital settings but increase costs overall because care is more accessible and used more often. How technology affects costs depends on the technology, where it is used, and—above all—on how the concepts of costs and benefits are defined. Indeed, that is the challenge.[2]

Medical technology includes the procedures, equipment, and processes by which medical services are delivered. "Medical technology can be defined as the application of science to develop solutions to health problems or issues such as the prevention or delay of onset of diseases or the promotion and monitoring of good health."[3] This broad definition includes biologicals and pharmaceuticals; high technology, such as positron emission tomography (PET) scanners and implantable defibrillators; low technology, such as laboratory tests and nutrition services; specific facilities, such as intensive care units; specific procedures, such as endoscopy, laparoscopy, organ transplantation, angioplasty, joint replacement, and coronary artery bypass; clinical and management information and control systems, such as electronic health records (EHRs), clinical and management decision support systems, and telemedicine; and managerial and clinical technologies, including those that organize and provide care, such as home health, and the use of physician extenders, such as physician assistants and nurse practitioners.

The dramatic rise in healthcare costs since 1950 is partly a function of proliferation of new technologies, increased use of existing tests and procedures (including attendant, specialized staff), and use of technology. The cost of *acquiring* technology is significant, but its overall effect on national healthcare expenditures is minimal. Estimates of national expenditures to *purchase* healthcare technology, which ran the gamut from routine medical supplies to advanced diagnostic products and implantable devices to major *capital* equipment, ranged from 5.1% of healthcare spending in the mid-1990s[4] to 10% (about $200 billion) in 2004.[5] In 2011, *capital* medical equipment accounted for $200 billion in sales.[6] In 2017, hospitals, research institutes, and other buyers of medical instrumentation spent $500 million to $1 billion on equipment; the figure varies depending on whether items such as computers, hearing aids, or x-ray units are included. Recently, expenditures increased 15% to 20% annually. Hospital spending for instrumentation, equipment, accessories, and supplies was $500 to $1,000 per bed per year.[7]

The part of increased healthcare costs attributable to *application* of technology is less certain. Estimates from the 1980s were as high as 70%.[8] More recent estimates of the rise in healthcare costs attributable to application of new technology range from 24% to 50%.[9,10] In the 1990s it was estimated that approximately 50% of the rise in total healthcare expenditures resulted from *use* of new technologies and *overuse* of existing ones.[11] More recent analyses showed a range of 25% to 33%.[12] The wide variation is caused by differences in definitions of *technology*: using the concepts of *application* of technology versus its actual *use*; and methods of cost estimation, measurement time frames, and types of expenditures analyzed. Increases in the amount of technology tend to be related to higher rates of use and spending for that technology (e.g., greater availability of diagnostic imaging appears to be associated with incremental use rather than substitution for other technologies).[13] Concerns are being raised that ready availability of diagnostic imaging is causing overuse while producing marginal results. The findings from such imaging, called incidentalomas, lead to more testing, thus adding further to costs.[14] This economic analysis fails to consider benefits for patients whose incidentaloma was an early-stage cancer. Suffice it to say: Technology affects costs.

Health economists conceptualize the issues variously. One theory examines the effect of technology on acute care hospital costs as measured by discrete units, such as labor and nonlabor inputs for use of technology. A second theory analyzes costs associated with specific acute care hospital-based technologies. A third examines the effect of technology on treating specific conditions and types of illnesses over time. A fourth measures the effect of technology on total healthcare expenditures. It is generally agreed that technology increases how intensively resources are used to treat individual cases, and this increases costs. Increased intensity also results from introduction of new technologies used on new diseases and categories of patients, in addition to using existing technologies in new ways. The exact contribution of technology *use*—new procedures, capabilities, and products—to healthcare costs is unknown; it is assuredly major.

The typology in Table 5.1 categorizes medical technologies by their characteristics. Historically, these technologies were found primarily in acute care hospitals. Increasing portability of technology, however, allows its delivery in nonhospital and outpatient settings and even in the patient's home. Such portability has a significant economic effect on acute care hospitals. Portability does not lower *total* costs, however. On the contrary, home health services, once seen as a lower-cost alternative in healthcare delivery, have grown rapidly. This supports the view that demand for health services is almost limitless—only the site of delivery changes.

Another way to describe medical technology is based on the charge or cost of each use. Laboratory tests, imaging, and other ancillary services that cost less than $100 are low-cost

Table 5.1 Types of Medical Technologies

Type	Examples
Diagnostic	CT scanner
	Fetal monitor
	Computerized electrocardiography
	Automated clinical labs
	MRI
	Ambulatory blood pressure monitor
Survival (lifesaving)	Intensive care unit
	Cardiopulmonary resuscitation
	Liver transplant
	Autologous bone marrow transplant
Illness management	Renal dialysis
	Pacemaker
	PTCA (angioplasty)
	Stereotactic cingulotomy (psychosurgery)
Cure	Hip joint replacement
	Organ transplant
	Lithotripter
Prevention	Implantable automatic cardioverter-defibrillator
	Pediatric orthopedic repair
	Diet control for phenylketonuria
	Vaccines for immunization
System management	Medical information systems
	Telemedicine

From Rosenthal, Gerald. "Anticipating the Costs and Benefits of New Technology: A Typology for Policy." In Medical Technology: The Culprit Behind Health Care Costs? (Publication No. [PHS] 79-3216), 79. Washington, DC: Department of Health and Human Services, 1979, as updated.

or "small-ticket" technologies compared with high-cost or "big-ticket" technologies, such as magnetic resonance imaging (MRI) scans costing about $1,500,[15] and organ transplantation, which ranges from $200,000 to $900,000, or higher.[16] The controversy over increasing costs focuses on high-cost technologies, but inexpensive technologies raise similar concerns because they are used in high volume and may be labor intensive. Data from the 1950s and 1960s show that a primary reason for higher costs was a rapid increase in the use of large numbers of low-cost ancillary services, such as laboratories and x-rays. Data from the 1970s and 1980s, however, show that the use of small-ticket technologies hardly changed, but several new, expensive technologies came into common use, raising costs considerably.[17] In terms of costs, new technology may be a hybrid—its use reduces the costs of treatment or diagnosis, but resulting higher volume increases total costs. Laparoscopic cholecystectomy is an example.[18]

Rather than classify technologies by cost, it is more useful to focus on the value obtained by using them. This is done by emphasizing cost-effectiveness and using clinical guidelines to reduce variation.[19] Despite differences in how technologies are described, research, development, and application of technology will continue. It is useful to examine factors behind this trend and its effects on the healthcare system and on individual health services organizations (HSOs) and health systems (HSs).

Background

The technology of modern allopathic (Western) medicine can be traced to the end of the 19th century and the advent of efficacious surgery. The most significant advances in diagnosing, treating, and managing disease, however, date from the 1950s, concomitant with the increasing prominence of the National Institutes of Health (NIH). Growth of NIH was sparked by a renewed interest in curing disease, which was supported by new knowledge in the basic sciences. By the 1950s, immunizations to prevent infectious diseases, such as polio and influenza, as well as drug therapies to treat noninfectious conditions, such as pernicious anemia, diabetes, gout, and hyperthyroidism, were readily available. It was hoped that new technologies would prevent or cure chronic and life-threatening diseases, such as heart disease, cancer, chronic lower respiratory diseases, and stroke, which are leading causes of death.

Acute care hospitals adopt the latest technologies to provide state-of-the-art services and remain competitive. Physicians in training use state-of-the-art technology; they expect to have it when they practice. HSOs/HSs lacking advanced technologies are at a competitive disadvantage for attracting licensed independent practitioners (LIPs) and marketing their capabilities to the general public.

Acute care hospitals are especially quick to add technology. No acute care hospital reported having an MRI scanner in 1984; by 1988, 10.6% had MRI scanners.[20] The speed of generalizing this technology was astounding—in the late 1980s, an MRI unit cost $1.5 million to buy and $200,000 to install.[21] In 2012, the cost of MRI scanners varied by the weight and capacity of the magnet: A 3-tesla unit cost $2.4 million, a 1.5-tesla unit cost $1.5 million, a sub-1-tesla open MRI unit cost $1.4 million, and an extremity MRI unit cost $1 million.[22] To the cost of the machine must be added the costs of site preparation and installation. In the early 1990s, the ability to measure and map sources of electrical activity in the heart, the neuromuscular system, and especially the brain was substantially enhanced with the introduction of magnetic source imaging (MSI). Computed tomography (CT) and MRI scans diagnose pathologies that leave brain lesions, but MSI provides important supplemental information.[23]

Laparoscopic surgery had extraordinarily rapid diffusion—almost 100% of hospitals and surgeons adopted it the first year it was available.[24] Other examples early in the 21st century are bariatric surgery for the morbidly obese and liposuction as an appearance-enhancing cosmetic procedure. Cosmetic surgery to correct various perceived or real natural defects in appearance is increasingly common and is being performed on children.

New technology may have few, if any, advantages over established technology. It is adopted because it is seen as state-of-the-art; its inability to advance the art becomes known only later. The da Vinci robot for laparoscopic surgery approved by the U.S. Food and Drug Administration (FDA) in 2000 is an example. Each robot costs about $2 million. Using da Vinci costs $3,000 to $6,000 more than conventional laparoscopic surgery, but results are no better. A major source of demand for robotic surgery is the public, which thinks new technology means better results. This perception is reinforced by providers' marketing.[25]

Acute care hospitals are slow to abandon established diagnostic technology when newer technology could replace it,[26] or to substitute a newer, lower-cost treatment for an older one.[27] Such inertia is explained largely by the practice patterns and preferences of physicians and other clinical treatment and support staff. Hence, acute care hospitals have a large financial investment in newly acquired equipment and in the high maintenance costs of established equipment that may be used less and less but is not abandoned. Physician expectations and competitive pressures are major reasons acute care hospitals acquire technology.

Not to be underestimated is the consumer's role in diffusing technology. The public is stimulated by the media and perceptions that procedures are safe, efficacious, available, and, as with liposuction, fashionable. The pervasiveness of direct-to-consumer marketing of prescription drugs shows how pharmaceutical companies try to involve patients in physician prescribing decisions.

Types of Technologies

Definitive (Curative, Preventive) Technologies

Technologies are definitive when they cure or prevent a central disease agent or mechanism.[28] Some, such as vaccines and antibiotics, are relatively inexpensive, even considering the cost of research and development. Others, such as surgical intervention for acute appendicitis, are more expensive, but curative. Definitive technologies, such as monitoring and screening programs, may or may not be expensive, depending on the cost of finding a true positive. Figure 5.1 shows the availability of management methods and definitive technologies for several conditions. Progress in providing effective therapy differs widely. For example, prevention, cure, and control have been attained for many infections. Congenital malformations can be corrected by surgery, and high blood pressure can be controlled with weight loss and medication.

Absent a definitive therapy, technologies are available to replace, or supplement, affected organs. Pseudo-solutions assist current patients but do not affect underlying causes or effect cures that benefit future generations. Development of two definitive technologies was stimulated by the risk of blood-borne diseases, such as human immunodeficiency virus (HIV) and hepatitis B and C. At the end of 2018, no blood substitute was approved by the FDA; research in the area spans 7 decades.[29] The other, a blood plasma–scrubbing technology that removes viruses, has received FDA approval.[30,31] The benefits of avoiding blood-borne diseases are obvious.

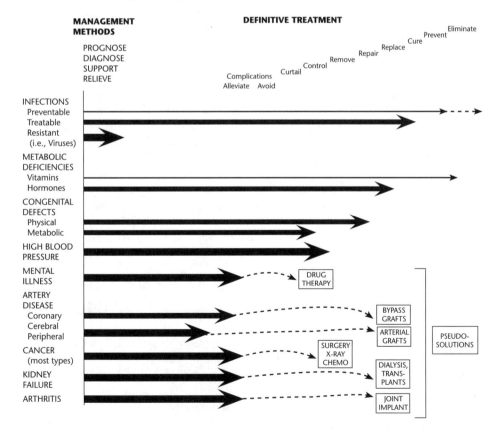

Figure 5.1. Advances in medical technology. From Stephen J. Williams, ed., *Introduction to Health Services*, 3rd edition. Delmar Publishing, 1989. Reprinted with permission.

Halfway (Add-On) Technologies

New medical technologies usually add to cost or generate new costs while achieving something not previously possible. Overwhelmingly, they are "halfway" or "add-on" technologies that range from inexpensive interventions, such as feeding tubes, to treatment costing several hundred thousand dollars, such as the iron lung used in the 1940s and 1950s for polio victims. The halfway technology improves a clinician's ability to diagnose and/or treat, but the technologies are used in addition to, not instead of, others.

Primarily, research in heart disease, cancer, and stroke has yielded halfway technologies to diagnose and manage, but not prevent or cure. Therapies produced by the "war" on cancer declared in the 1970s have been disappointing; lower mortality largely reflects the effects of changes in incidence or early detection.[32] Regardless of reasons, *deaths* from cancer have declined 27% since the late 1990s. At this writing, the focus is melanoma and endometrial, liver, thyroid, uterine, and pancreatic cancers. Some appear linked to the obesity epidemic.[33]

The historical trend suggests cancer *incidence rates* will increase because of improved screening, earlier detection, and effective treatment, all of which should lead to lower mortality rates.[34] The metaphors of a war on cancer and magic bullets to kill cancers are useful, if not very meaningful. Recent, extraordinary advances in cancer science and medicine have occurred. An integrative, refined approach to cancer must consider the spectrum of its types and subtypes, organize specialized approaches for cancer patients, and consider patient individuality in treatment regimens.[35] Among advances fitting these criteria is gene therapy. In 2017, the FDA approved a cancer therapy using genetically engineered immune cells to treat a blood and bone marrow cancer affecting children and young adults. CAR-T therapy extracts a patient's T cells, which are genetically altered to include a new protein that causes T cells to kill leukemia cells. The genetically modified cells are infused into the patient. The cost of a half million dollars will likely decline as use increases.[36] Gene therapy gives hope that a curative technology for some cancers is close.

Transplants are another halfway technology that improves the health status of a few but adds greatly to healthcare costs. In 2017, there were 19,849 kidney, 8,082 liver, 3,244 heart, 213 pancreas, 2,449 lung, 29 heart/lung,[37] and about 50,000 corneal transplants.[38]

Halfway technologies have improved diagnoses of brain disease. CT and MRI scans show the brain's structure. Brain electrical activity mapping enhances the study of brain waves. Blood circulation, energy consumption, and chemical neurotransmitter systems are measured with single photon emission computed tomography, positron emission tomography (PET) scans, and functional MRI.[39] An example of applying neuroimaging is its use to understand the neuropsychiatric side effects of interferon in hepatitis C.[40] Other halfway technologies are transesophageal echocardiography (TEE), deep brain stimulation (DBS), and vagus nerve stimulation (VNS). TEE improves diagnostic ability; DBS and VNS offer symptomatic relief of disease. All are obtained at significant cost.

Deferral Technologies

Some technologies slow progression of disease and may even dramatically improve a patient's condition, but improvement is short lived and repeat treatments are usually needed. Surgical treatment of coronary artery disease is an example. Coronary artery bypass grafting (CABG) is an expensive surgical procedure that must be repeated for many patients every 5 to 7 years. Development of percutaneous transluminal coronary angioplasty (PTCA) provided a simple, less invasive procedure that costs far less than bypass surgery. These attributes caused its rapid diffusion. CABG surgery did not decline, however. It is thought that after repeat angioplasties bypass surgery is needed. Thus, angioplasty defers the need for bypass surgery but does not eliminate it, while adding considerable costs.[41] Even after a technology is widely used, its safety may be questioned, as happened with drug-coated carotid artery stenting.[42]

Competing Technologies

Technologies that compete may have similar results but very different costs. One historic example involved the thrombolytic (blood clot–dissolving) agents streptokinase and tissue plasminogen activator (tPA [Genentech's Activase]). In 2012 streptokinase cost about $200.[43] per dose; tPA cost $2,200. The average cost-effectiveness of tPA was $8,000 per quality-adjusted life-year (QALY) gained.[44] Analysis showed that, compared with the pattern of thrombolytic agent choice observed, targeting tPA to the half of patients *most likely to benefit* could save 247 lives and $174 million nationally per year. It is difficult for clinicians to determine which thrombolytic agent to administer, however. Some patients fare much better with streptokinase than tPA; others may be harmed by tPA.[45] Use of streptokinase and tPA has been superseded by a new technology. Primary percutaneous coronary intervention (PCI) has better results, combined with thrombolytics as needed. PCI is also called angioplasty or stenting.[46]

As noted, CABG and PTCA treat the same condition, but average costs of CABG are 53% higher than PTCA. Costs reflect geographic location and supplies used during the procedure.

Technologies that compete to treat stenosis (narrowing) of the carotid artery are carotid endarterectomy (CEA) and carotid artery stenting (CAS). One study found the cost of CAS was 40% higher than that of CEA for asymptomatic patients and 37% higher for symptomatic patients. Hospitalization costs for CAS patients were much higher than for CEA patients.[47]

Proton-beam therapy (PBT) for prostate cancer is a high-technology treatment that may not offer advantages over less expensive interventions, such as surgery or conventional radiation. Proton radiotherapy uses atomic particles rather than x-rays to treat cancer. PBT was approved by the FDA in 1988 and approved for reimbursement by the Centers for Medicare & Medicaid Services (CMS) in 1997.[48] Its greater precision minimizes damage to normal cells. The cost of the first units ($120–$180 million) and space needed (football-field size) meant PBT was limited to major providers. New units, however, are a fifth the cost and the size of an x-ray machine. Such innovation will allow many HSOs/HSs to offer PBT.[49]

Cost-Saving Technologies

Few new technologies prevent disease for either individuals or populations (as vaccines protect future generations). Nonetheless, many reduce costs, especially when compared with old technologies used to treat the same diseases. Examples include arthroscopy, implantable infusion pumps, laparoscopic and endoscopic procedures, and lasers. These technologies may be halfway or deferral therapies, but if they replace more costly treatment or those of lesser quality in terms of efficaciousness, the result will be lower costs and better outcomes for patients and the healthcare system. Costs and benefits are defined broadly and include hospitalization, sick days avoided, early return to work, reduced pain and discomfort, and short- and long-term quality of life. Assessing a technology must include all these dimensions.[50] A laparoscopic technology that increased quality while reducing total costs is the port access system that enables surgeons to perform heart surgery without "cracking" the patient's sternum (breastbone). Specially designed catheters, surgical instruments, and imaging equipment are used. Patients avoid the trauma and pain of having their chest opened and are hospitalized only 3–5 days, compared with 8–12 days using open techniques; also, they can return to work within 2 weeks, compared with 8–12 weeks after open-heart surgery. In addition, the risk of infection and other complications is greatly reduced.[51] The potential savings in costs, pain, and discomfort, as well as the increase in quality, are obvious. Improved diagnostic technologies can reduce the costs of diagnosis and improve the quality of care, but they may increase overall costs because of a higher rate of use. Elasticity imaging of breast tissue using ultrasonography allows radiologists to distinguish benign from malignant breast tissue with almost 100% accuracy. Malignant tissue is harder than normal tissue. By gauging movement (elasticity) when tissue is pushed, radiologists can distinguish the two types. The technique greatly reduces need for needle biopsies,

thus minimizing patient pain, discomfort, and anxiety.[52] Thermographic imaging offers another advance in diagnosis of tumors in breast and other soft tissue. This technology measures
heat from tissue. Tumors have a higher temperature than normal tissue and are identifiable on
the scan. Thermographic imaging has the further advantage of not exposing patients to radiation and harsh manipulation of breast tissue.[53]

Effects of Technology on Health Status

Halfway and deferral technologies improve diagnosis and management of disease. For example, a CT scan may prevent or shorten hospitalization and save resources such as exploratory
surgery. The effect of halfway and deferral technologies on health status is uncertain, however.
The modest increase in life expectancy from 1965 (at enactment of Medicare and Medicaid)
to 1999 of only 2.7 years at age 65 and 1 year at age 85 suggest that advances in medical technology to that point had had little effect on longevity. Early in the third millennium, however,
projections of average life expectancy at 2080 were for an additional 23.6 years at age 65 and
9.6 years at age 85.[54] These projections may have been optimistic. Data from 2017 show a
decline (by one-tenth of a year) in American life expectancy to 78.6 years, which resulted from
a sharp increase in suicides and a continuing rise in deaths from opioid abuse.[55] The role of
HSOs/HSs in preventing suicide and opioid abuse is ill-defined. If not reversed, the obesity
epidemic with its major health implications of hypertension, fatty liver, orthopedic problems,
sleep apnea, and Type 2 diabetes will cause further decline in life expectancy.[56]

One way to understand longevity is *health expectancy,* a construct that measures more than
years of life. Health expectancy analyzes healthy and unhealthy years of life. It may be a better
way to measure population health for both morbidity and mortality. Unresolved is lack of a
standard definition of "healthy years."[57] An expression of health expectancy is quality-adjusted
life years (QALYs), which are the years of life subsequent to a healthcare intervention weighted
to adjust for a patient's expected quality of life during those years. Healthcare outcome variables measure the safety, efficacy, and effectiveness of health technologies. Major categories
include mortality (death rate), morbidity (disease rate), adverse healthcare events (e.g., harmful
side effects), quality of life, functional status, and patient satisfaction.[58]

Since 1968, death rates from coronary artery disease have declined by 68%; death rates
from strokes by 75%. These declines are attributed to technology and better understanding
of risk factors and prevention.[59] Improving health status by reducing morbidity and disability
will likely cause unintended consequences. Paradoxically, saving a life or preventing disease
increases the likelihood of future morbidity and disability. Similarly, health promotion such as
smoking cessation may increase healthcare costs long term.[60] In sum, the results of technology
and prevention are double-edged; quality of life may be improved by reducing morbidity and
mortality, but costs for long-term, debilitating diseases may increase as people live longer. Data
suggest, however, that persons with lower health risks because of better health habits have less
lifetime disability, as well as less disability at every age.[61] This may diminish a need for long-
term, labor-intensive services for debilitating physical and mental impairment.

Forces Affecting Development and Diffusion of Technology

Medical Education and Medical Practice

Among the most important factors encouraging development and diffusion of technology after
World War II (1941–1945) were changes in medical training and the practice of medicine.
Biomedical research funded by the NIH stimulated medical schools to investigate special-
ized areas of medicine, which led to the growth of specialty departments within academic

medical centers. Increasingly, medical school graduates received postgraduate training and practiced in a specialty.

Historically, specializing meant physicians trained with technology. Not surprisingly, they expected to use the same technologies in their practice. The desire to have state-of-the-art technology and use it as necessary—despite its cost—is called the technological imperative. The technological imperative is apparent in acute care hospitals and explains the proliferation of highly specialized technology in them. Chapter 1 includes data on physicians in primary care and in specialties.

In 2016, the healthcare and social assistance sector had $93.6 billion in capital expenditures. Of this amount, 51% was spent on structure projects and 49% on equipment. Total capital expenditures by acute care hospitals were $55.4 billion. Outpatient centers and other ambulatory healthcare services spent $7.1 billion in capital expenditures, while nursing and residential care facilities spent $8.9 billion on capital expenditures in 2016.[62]

Acute care hospitals must have state-of-the-art physical plants and acquire leading-edge technology to be competitive. In addition, decreasing the number of staffed beds and increasing average patient acuity by earlier discharge means a higher ratio of plant assets per bed. Thus, hospitals will become more expensive to operate and maintain. The almost universal presence of technology should not suggest it is applied evenly. Historically, there was wide geographic variation in treating patients with the same diagnoses.[63] The variation includes hospitalization rates and lengths of stay for treatment regimens. For example, patients with coronary artery disease may be treated with risk factor modification (diet, exercise) and medication to reduce the frequency and severity of angina (chest pain), or with an intervention such as PTCA or CABG.[64] The *Dartmouth Atlas of Health Care* (*www.dartmouthatlas.org/*) shows this variation.

Patient safety and costs are adversely affected by overtreatment and overuse of technology. It is estimated that unneeded scans, blood tests, and procedures cost the nation's healthcare system $210 billion annually.[65] For decades a "sacred cow" of medicine has been the annual checkup. Questions are being asked as to its benefit for healthy people; instead, attention should focus on specific screening. Curbing tests thought to be ineffective has been controversial.[66] It is estimated that the U.S. health care system spends $300 million a year on unneeded tests ordered during annual physicals. Billions more are spent on follow-up tests and treatments.[67]

Routine mammograms to screen for breast cancer are an example of preventive screening that may result in unnecessary treatment. It has been estimated that since the early 1980s false-positive diagnoses of breast cancer following mammograms have caused more than 1 million women to have unnecessary treatment for cancer, including surgery, radiation therapy, hormonal therapy, and chemotherapy.[68]

Despite extensive testing, there are problems diagnosing medical conditions. A study of diagnostic errors in primary care that resulted in medical malpractice claims found that missed, wrong, or delayed diagnoses accounted for almost 29% of claims. Reasons for errors included breakdown in communication during the patient's initial visit, physicians failing to refer patients to a specialist, patients failing to provide an adequate medical history, physicians failing to follow up with the patient after a diagnosis, and diagnostic tests interpreted incorrectly. Pneumonia, worsening congestive heart failure, acute renal failure, cancer, and urinary tract or kidney infection were the top five diagnoses missed.[69] Such errors diminish quality of medical care, risk patient safety, and add to healthcare costs.

Wide variation in practice patterns raises doubts about medicine's scientific certainty and whether low-technology, less interventionist, and less expensive treatment might not be as effective as high-technology, more interventionist, and more costly treatment. Understanding the factors that influence physician practice patterns and variation, as well as determining efficacy, will enable HSOs/HSs to deliver effective medical services more efficiently.

Third-Party Reimbursement for Services

Central to diffusing technological advances into medical practice and presence of the technological imperative has been third-party reimbursement. In traditional fee-for-service medical practice, decisions to use new technologies are usually made by individual physicians based on a judgment that the technology has benefit with low probability of harm. Unlike other industries, innovations in medical technology have not been judged primarily based on performing some function better or more efficiently, but rather on if they will yield a benefit to individual patients. Similarly, decisions to reimburse for new technologies have been based on acceptance and use of the technology by physicians. Manufacturers' prices for new technologies, particularly medications and devices, tend to be high to recover research and development costs. Provider charges are high to pay for the skill and expertise in learning and offering a technology as well, and to recover capital costs of its acquisition. Historically, once in the reimbursement system, the charges tend to remain high even after initial costs have been recovered.[70]

Assurance of payment for tests and procedures under cost-based reimbursement allowed HSOs to acquire technology knowing that costs of capital investment and operation would be met. Historically, there were few incentives to evaluate cost-effectiveness of new technologies, and acquisition of technology was stimulated by a need for providers to attract physicians and patients. Changed government funding, efforts to manage care, and a focus on disease prevention and population health reduce assurance that reimbursement for new technology will be adequate or even available. If true for access to technology generally, such trends have major effects on diffusing technology and, possibly, costs of health services.

Diagnosis-Related Groups

ICD-10-CM is the official system of assigning codes to diagnoses and procedures associated with hospital utilization in the United States. Initially, the International Classification of Diseases (ICD) was designed to promote international comparability in collecting, processing, classifying, and presenting mortality statistics. This included a format for reporting causes of death on death certificates. The reported conditions are converted into medical codes using the classification structure and the selection and modification rules contained in the applicable ICD, which is published by the World Health Organization. The ICD is revised to incorporate developments in the medical field. To date, there have been nine revisions of the ICD beginning in 1900. ICD-10 was implemented on October 1, 2015.[71]

In late 1983, payment for Medicare patients in acute care hospitals changed from cost-based reimbursement to a prospective payment system based on diagnosis-related groups (DRGs), which are discussed in Chapter 1. As noted, the incentive for hospitals under DRGs is to do less, not more—the opposite of retrospective, cost-based reimbursement. Reimbursement is based on average cost per case for each DRG, a method that will cause careful evaluation of a technology, its more efficient use, and when possible, selection of cost-saving technologies.

When DRGs were implemented it was thought hospitals providing a service infrequently would be unable to compete with those providing it frequently. In theory, the latter group has lower average unit costs. It was also thought that because costs of using technology were not reimbursed separately, hospitals would have few incentives to adopt new technologies that increase per-case cost by adding new operating expenses. It seems, however, that acquisition and use of technology by hospitals have not changed and may even have accelerated. Possibly, only with further reduction in payments will the full effect of DRGs on technology be felt.

Congress has continued trying to reduce Medicare costs—primarily by reducing DRG payments. Apparently, those who feared DRGs would stifle diffusion of new technology and adversely affect patient care were wrong, and those who said a need for acute care hospitals to be competitive and maintain admissions levels would necessitate acquiring technology were correct. Regardless, the long-term influence of DRGs on acute care hospitals and their use of technology is unknown. The real effects of DRGs may not comport with those intended; unintended consequences are rarely fully appreciated prospectively.

Centers for Medicare & Medicaid Services

In the late 1980s, the Health Care Financing Administration (HCFA), now CMS, began applying more uniform and stringent standards to judge appropriate use of technology. It was not until 1989—23 years after Medicare took effect—that HCFA issued proposed regulations to define *reasonable* and *necessary*—the criteria used in Medicare to describe technology and procedures for which it would pay.[72] In defining *reasonable* and *necessary*, the final regulations rely heavily on FDA categorizations by requiring that technology and procedures are safe, effective, and noninvestigatory.

Typically, states underfund Medicaid; thus, it is notable that considerable funds are spent on transplants. The federal Early and Periodic Screening, Diagnosis, and Treatment Program requires participating states to provide "medically necessary" services. These are interpreted to include bone marrow, liver, heart, and lung transplants for persons younger than 21 years of age. Historically, services available in Medicaid have been comprehensive. Most provided bone marrow, liver, and heart transplants for adults; almost half provided lung transplants. Some states put monetary limits on each type of transplant covered.[73]

The Public

A third force influencing diffusion of technology is the public. The practice of highly technical and specialty-oriented medicine, coupled with widely publicized advances in medical care, fostered consumers' expectations that a technology is available to diagnose and treat every medical problem and that quality medical care necessarily involves extensive use of technology. Historically, Americans have expressed a willingness to pay the costs of health services and to spend what is needed to improve and protect their health.[74] More recently, however, the rapid increases in costs reflected in health insurance premiums, copays, and deductibles have given the public pause and may cause a reconsideration of their open-ended willingness to pay for whatever services are needed. People not protected by third-party coverage are likely to be less willing to share their physicians' expectations that all possible technologies should be available. Payment systems that limit use of technology threaten the traditional autonomy of patients and providers, an issue very near the surface in managed care and implicit in proposals for government-sponsored universal healthcare coverage.

Competitive Environment

Competition is an important fourth force in diffusion of technology. There is competition among HSOs/HSs, between physicians and HSOs/HSs, among physician specialties, and between physicians and nonphysician LIPs. One way acute care hospitals, and to a lesser extent other types of HSOs, compete is to acquire and offer advanced technology and shift services to outpatient settings, which have lower costs and offer greater convenience to users.

Historically, hospitals were the repository of medical technology because they had the capital, staff, and medical backup to support it. Increasingly, medical technology is *portable*, which allows it to be applied outside acute care hospitals in nontraditional HSOs. Portability is creating a "medical arms race" between hospitals and physicians, as physicians deliver technically advanced services in their own specialty hospitals, freestanding ambulatory surgery centers, and their offices.[75] Finally, technology is disrupting traditional lines among medical specialties, which necessarily causes them to compete for patients and healthcare dollars.

Technologies that enable health services to be safely moved from inpatient to outpatient settings include improved anesthesia that allows quicker return to consciousness with few aftereffects; better analgesics for pain control; and minimally invasive procedures, such as laser surgery, endoscopy, and laparoscopy.[76] In 1987, the number of outpatient visits first surpassed the number of inpatient days.[77] Of the 58 million combined total outpatient and inpatient surgical and nonsurgical procedures performed annually, 31% (14.9 million) were performed in freestanding ambulatory surgery centers (ASCs). The number of freestanding ASCs increased by almost 20% from 2005 to 2009.[78] The minimally invasive surgical techniques that are revolutionizing cardiovascular surgery enable surgeons to operate on a beating heart. In the future, they may allow outpatient cardiovascular surgery.[79] The major shift into home health services is well under way and is likely to continue.

New technology, much of it more portable and less costly to buy (or lease) and operate, coupled with efforts to limit the use of specialists, is blurring the traditional fiefdoms of physician specialties and causing fierce competition among them, as well as with nonphysician LIPs. Prominent among the specialists that have become more interventional in their treatment of patients are gastroenterologists, cardiologists, and radiologists. Medical imaging is a prime example of the increasing use of ambulatory testing performed outside the hospital, much of which may be done by nonradiologists.[80] These developments have major implications for the specialties involved, as well as for HSOs/HSs and, if the volume of procedures increases, have the potential to increase overall costs to the system. Generally, physicians are unconstrained by regulations such as certificates of need (CONs), which means that establishing an imaging center, for example, is a matter of raising capital and finding a location. Abuses resulting from physician ownership of HSOs that provide diagnosis and treatment caused state and federal governments to regulate self-referrals, which are defined as physicians sending patients to providers in which they have an ownership interest. The controversy over physician-owned cardiac specialty hospitals is only the most recent example of hospitals competing with their own physicians.[81] Risk-adjusted mortality rates for patients treated in specialty cardiac hospitals were significantly lower than mortality rates in all hospitals; however, the rate was significantly higher when physicians who owned cardiac specialty hospitals treated patients in general hospitals.[82] Such comparisons should give pause to those critical of the quality of care in cardiac specialty hospitals.

Responses to Diffusion and Use of Technology

As HSOs/HSs acquired technology, issues of cost, benefit, and safety emerged. It became clear that diffusion and use of technology were only partially based on cost–benefit or cost-effectiveness considerations. Existing technological capabilities were often ignored or discounted, despite their proven efficacy. In addition, the hazards associated with a technology were inadequately understood. These concerns were the focus of federal laws to improve premarket evaluation of medical devices (e.g., amendments to the Food, Drug, and Cosmetic Act) and to influence acquisition and use of technologies, especially in acute care hospitals (i.e., professional standards review organizations [PSROs] were followed by peer review organizations [PROs], quality improvement organizations [QIOs], and CONs). Another result was establishment of the congressional Office of Technology Assessment (OTA) and the Department of Health and Human Services' (DHHS's) National Center for Health Care Technology (NCHCT), both of which were later defunded.

Table 5.2 shows several of the public and private organizations that ensure the safety and efficacy of technology. Amendments to the federal Food, Drug, and Cosmetic Act in 1976 and 1990 gave the FDA a greatly expanded role in monitoring manufacturers and investigating devices linked to patient death or serious injury or illness.[83] State authorities are

Table 5.2　Biomedical Equipment Regulation

Authority	Federal	State	Profession
	Food and Drug Administration (FDA)	Department of public safety/public health	JCAHO, NFPA, etc.[a]
Objectives	Manufacturer quality	Personal safety	Hospital quality
Standards	FDA specifications	National testing laboratory	JCAHO accreditation manual, NFPA codes, etc.

[a]JCAHO, Joint Commission on Accreditation of Healthcare Organizations; NFPA, National Fire Protection Association.

concerned with staff and patient safety—a traditional police power of the state described in Chapter 1—and may require the licensure of practitioners who use the equipment, approval of types of equipment by a national testing laboratory, and regular inspections, especially of radiation sources, such as x-ray equipment. Private organizations have been important in producing consensus standards. Among them are the National Fire Protection Association, which has developed standards on design and use of facilities and some biomedical equipment, and The Joint Commission on Accreditation of Healthcare Organizations (The Joint Commission), whose standards govern equipment management and maintenance. Some standards affecting technology in HSOs have been stimulated by court decisions. CMS does not regulate medical technology directly. Its decisions as to technologies for which it will pay—as in the case of durable medical equipment—do, however, have an indirect effect on furthering or impeding use of a technology.[84]

Public Sector Activities

Food and Drug Administration

Although the FDA has been involved in premarket approval of drugs since 1962, evidence of the safety and efficacy of other medical technologies was not required. The Medical Device Amendments of 1976[85] to the Food, Drug, and Cosmetic Act extended the FDA's premarket approval process to medical devices, divided into three classes. The most stringent regulation is for Class III—devices that support or sustain human life, are of substantial importance in preventing impairment of human health, or present a potential and unreasonable risk of illness or injury. Manufacturers must obtain approval from the FDA before such devices may be marketed, a procedure that requires evidence of safety and efficacy.[86] FDA control of marketing new drugs and devices has been criticized as unnecessarily impeding introduction of technological innovations because of the time and money that are required to conduct clinical trials and obtain approval. In the late 1980s, pressure on the FDA from those wanting rapid access to new drugs to treat acquired immunodeficiency syndrome (AIDS) caused reconsideration of review processes, especially for drugs that might help treat fatal illnesses.

　　Legal liability for HSOs/HSs increased when the Safe Medical Device Act of 1990[87] codified the need to report device-related serious injuries and death to the manufacturer and, in the case of death, to the FDA. The FDA defines *medical device* broadly; there are significant penalties for failing to report. A checklist form is recommended to guide the incident investigation.[88] Medical devices range from simple tongue depressors and bedpans to complex programmable pacemakers with microchip technology to laser surgical devices. The lengthy official definition distinguishes between a medical device and other FDA-regulated products, such as drugs. If its primary intended use is achieved through chemical action or being metabolized by the body, the product is usually considered a drug.[89]

　　Following FDA approval of the medical device, the organization developing the medical device must continue to evaluate and periodically report on the safety, effectiveness, and reliability of the device for its intended use. The organization must maintain specific records.[90] The FDA does not license technicians.[91] Absent licensure, voluntary certification programs such as those of the International Certification Commission and the Association for the Advancement of Medical Instrumentation ensure technicians' competence.[92]

PSROs, PROs, and QIOs

A history of PSROs and how they were replaced by PROs beginning in 1984 is included in Chapter 1. In terms of medical technology, PSROs were established in 1972 as part of federal and state efforts to control healthcare costs by regulating the acquisition of new technology and reducing its use through review of utilization. PSROs sought to ensure that Medicare (and later Medicaid) services were "medically necessary, met professional standards of care, and were provided in the most economical setting possible consistent with quality care."[93] Initially, review focused on appropriateness of acute care hospital admission and length of stay. Later, services provided were also reviewed.

PSRO effectiveness was hampered by Medicare's interpretation of "reasonable and necessary." This concept meant that a procedure that is no longer experimental and that is accepted by the local community is deemed reasonable and may be necessary. PSROs determined indications for use.[94]

PROs replaced PSROs and had a similar role regarding technology. They reviewed validity of diagnostic and procedural information provided by hospitals; completeness, adequacy, and quality of care provided; and appropriateness of admissions patterns, discharges, lengths of stay, transfers, and services furnished in outlier cases.[95] Decisions of the PRO were usually binding as to reimbursement.

Chapter 1 noted that PROs were renamed QIOs in 2001. QIOs are charged with quality improvement initiatives in numerous clinical areas and across healthcare settings. By evaluating quality of outcomes, QIOs will effect more appropriate application of technology, as did PROs.[96] The effect is indirect and realized only in the long term. In 2018, there were 53 QIOs.[97]

Certificate of Need (CON)

States enacted CONs and Section 1122 laws pursuant to the National Health Planning and Resources Development Act of 1974 (PL 93-641),[98] which require approval of technology acquisition and construction by acute care hospitals. Amendments in 1981 and regulations in 1984 increased dollar limits. In the 1980s, a philosophical shift at the federal level toward increased competition reduced support for regulation such as CONs. Diminished federal support reduced state interest. As Chapter 1 noted, 38 states and the District of Columbia had CON laws in 2019.[99]

CON and health planning legislation assumed that the availability of technology invites use and potential abuse and that its cost is paid by all healthcare system users. CT scanners became controversial because of their wide availability and alleged overuse. In the 1990s, MRI and caesarean sections became a focus. These examples illustrate the problem inherent in one of the primary assumptions underlying CON legislation: Quality healthcare can be provided without extensive use of technology. This assumption conflicted with professional and societal expectations that appropriate technology would be available and used, as needed.

CON laws were criticized in five general areas because they

1. Gave no attention to low-cost technologies, whose high-volume use can significantly affect costs (e.g., electronic fetal monitoring, a widely used, low-cost technology whose capital cost excluded it from CON review)[100];

2. Did not consider operating costs of installing and using technology, which typically exceed capital costs in a few years;

3. Decreased competition by regulating acute care hospital services and types of technology, which eliminated a major incentive to compete;

4. Focused on acute care hospitals, even as increasingly portable technology allowed free-standing HSOs to become ubiquitous; and

5. Did not consider the role of professional staff in acquiring and using technology, as well as its importance in attracting and retaining physicians.

Underutilization of high technology can be avoided by requiring that certain levels of use are met before the regulatory process will approve new units.[101] The number of MRI scanners and their use vary considerably by country. Worldwide, in 2017 Japan and the United States had the highest number of MRI scanners per million population—51.6 and 37.6, respectively; Canada had fewer than 10. Compared with Canada, the United States performed more than two times the number of MRI scans, with 111 per 1,000 population in 2017, compared with 51 in Canada.[102] The U.S.–Canada disparities suggest several interpretations: In the United States, too many MRI scans are performed; in Canada, too few MRI scans are performed, or access to MRI is limited, or both.

Tort Law

Concomitant with greater regulation of medical technology has been the application of more demanding liability standards. Strict liability (discussed in Chapter 2) has been applied to HSOs; they may be liable for defects in devices unknown to the manufacturer. HSOs may be responsible for going beyond the maintenance recommendations of the manufacturer, if necessary. As noted, they must inform the FDA about experience contrary to that reported by the manufacturer. This area of the law will evolve, almost certainly toward more demanding and costly standards for HSOs.

Private Sector Activities

Accreditors

As noted in Chapter 1, several private organizations have "deeming authority," which means HSOs accredited by them may receive payment for services provided to beneficiaries of federal programs. The Joint Commission was granted deeming authority in the original Medicare and Medicaid law (1965) and is the most significant private sector accreditor. Standards for managing hospital biomedical equipment are found in its *Comprehensive Accreditation Manual for Hospitals*. Chapter 1 noted that some hospitals and other types of HSOs use the federal "conditions of participation (CoPs)" promulgated by CMS.[103] CMS has granted deeming authority to several private accreditors that have met its criteria. DNV GL Healthcare surveys hospitals using CMS's CoPs as integrated with standards developed by the International Organization for Standardization (ISO), specifically ISO 9001. Other organizations with deeming authority include the Community Health Accreditation Program, the American Osteopathic Association, the Accreditation Association for Ambulatory Health Care, and the Commission on Accreditation of Rehabilitation Facilities.

ISO 9000

The ISO has developed a series, or family, of standards, known as ISO 9000, which includes ISO 9001. Organizations voluntarily adopt ISO standards to help them meet or exceed their customers' needs and expectations. Distilled to their essence, the principles of ISO 9000 state that high-quality service results only from a well-planned, well-documented, and well-executed quality management system. ISO 9000 is not quality control, but a quality management program based on continuous improvement.[104] The history of ISO is discussed in Chapter 1; applying ISO standards is addressed in Chapter 8.

Health Technology Assessment

Health technology assessment (HTA) evaluates the safety, efficacy, cost, and cost-effectiveness of technology and identifies ethical and legal implications, both in absolute terms and by comparison with competing technologies.[105] The Institute of Medicine of the National Academy of Sciences estimated that in 1983 only 2.9% of national health expenditures was spent for HTA.[106] In the late 1990s, the United States had 53 HTA programs and activities, most in the private sector.[107] Private and public organizations involved in HTA assessment include private insurers, managed care organizations, professional and specialty societies, provider associations, group purchasing organizations, technology industry groups, disease-specific interest groups, private research groups (including academic medical centers, universities, and not-for-profit and for-profit research organizations), and various units of state and federal government.[108] This list suggests how decentralized HTA is in the United States. Decentralizing HTA and related activities widens the expertise available to the process, broadens perspectives, and diminishes or balances potential conflicts of interest. In all, these benefits add credibility to HTA processes and findings, and they lessen charges that assessments reflect narrow or self-serving interests of agencies or organizations.[109] Figure 5.2 uses an input–process–outcome sequence to show the typical flow of HTA. These general methods include randomized clinical trials, evaluating diagnostic technologies, series of consecutive cases, case studies, registers and databases, sample surveys, epidemiological methods, surveillance, quantitative synthesis methods (meta-analysis), group judgment methods,[110] cost-effectiveness and cost–benefit analyses, and mathematical modeling. Important, too, are the social and ethical issues of HTA.[111,112]

Public Sector

In the 1990s, public sector HTA included seven federal agencies (including OTA) and units in Minnesota, New York, and Oregon. From 1974 to 1995, OTA helped Congress understand and plan for policy implications of technology by studying efficacy of medical procedures, health education, and quality of care.[113] OTA was disestablished in 1995.[114]

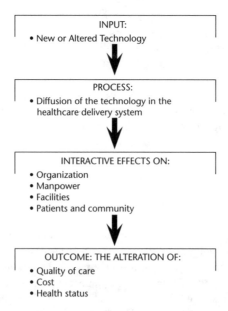

Figure 5.2. Technology assessment methods measure the impact on healthcare in an input-process-outcome sequence. (From Glasser, Jay H., and Richard S. Chrzanowski, "Medical Technology Assessment: Adequate Questions, Appropriate Methods, Valuable Answers," *Health Policy, 9,* 267–276 [1988] with permission from Elsevier Science.)

Concern about proliferation of medical technology and its benefits, costs, and risks caused Congress to pass the Health Services Research, Health Statistics, and Health Care Technology Act of 1978 (PL 95-623),[115] which established the National Center for Health Care Technology (NCHCT) in the U.S. Public Health Service of DHHS as a clearinghouse for information on medical technology, the safety and efficacy of new technologies, and their cost-effectiveness. NCHCT advised HCFA, now CMS, as to cost-effectiveness, appropriateness, and medical validity of technologies reimbursed by Medicare and Medicaid.[116] NCHCT was defunded in 1981 and its role transferred to the Office of Health Technology Assessment. After more reorganizations the Agency for Healthcare Research and Quality (AHRQ) became the lead federal agency for quality research and the primary source of federal government–sponsored HTA. AHRQ's mission is "to produce evidence to make healthcare safer, higher quality, more accessible, equitable, and affordable, and to work within the U.S. Department of Health and Human Services and with other partners to make sure that the evidence is understood and used."[117] AHRQ's Center for Practice and Technology Assessment conducts HTA internally and by contract and collaboration with 12 evidence-based practice centers (EPCs).[118] The EPCs are in academic health centers and research institutions in the United States; one is in Canada. They prepare "evidence reports" and HTA to support clinical guidelines, coverage policies, and other practices and policies.[119]

AHRQ's effort to develop clinical practice guidelines in the mid-1990s ultimately failed. Physicians seemed threatened by them.[120] AHRQ had collaborated with the American Medical Association and the American Association of Health Plans (now America's Health Insurance Plans) to establish a National Guideline Clearinghouse (NGC) to aid clinical management. The NGC Internet site became operational in 1998 and provided access to guidelines from public and private organizations.[121] By 2012, the NGC had over 2,500 practice guidelines. When NGC was disestablished in 2018,[122] the effort went to the private sector. The Emergency Care Research Institute (ECRI), an independent, not-for-profit patient safety organization, established the ECRI Guidelines Trust™, a repository of evidence-based practice guidelines. Healthcare providers have no-cost access to the website. The guidelines come from guideline developers, medical specialty societies, and healthcare organizations.[123] There is significant evidence, however, of poor adherence to clinical guidelines even after they are adopted.[124]

Other parts of the federal government perform HTA. FDA determines the efficacy and safety of drugs and medical devices. NIH conducts and sponsors research on medical technology. The National Center for Biotechnology Information (NCBI) is part of the National Library of Medicine (NLM). NCBI databases support biotechnology and biomedicine and are a resource for bioinformatics tools and services. Several states conduct HTA.

The history of the federal government shows a lack of focus and a limited role for HTA in policy development. The lack of leadership in HTA supports the conclusion that "the United States is thus out-of-step with much of the developed world where government-linked agencies have been established with responsibility for providing advice to policy-makers at the national or regional level."[125] Over two decades later, this observation remains true.

Private Sector

The majority of the 53 HTA programs and activities in the late 1990s were private initiatives. They included academic health centers, health insurance companies (including managed care entities), health professional societies, hospitals or hospital chains, consulting firms, and medical industry manufacturers. In addition, an unknown number of private sector efforts assessed technology or aided potential users and purchasers in decision making.[126]

Data on private sector HTA activities are elusive. Examples are the Medical Technology and Practice Patterns Institute (MTPPI) and ECRI. MTPPI, a not-for-profit research institute, specializes in analyzing health outcomes, healthcare services, and policies using staff and collaborations with 28 health services providers and academic institutions.[127] ECRI conducts evidence-based assessments of medical technologies and practices for 5,000 healthcare institutions and systems worldwide to guide their operational and strategic decisions and protect patients from unsafe and ineffective medical technologies and practices.[128]

As noted, medical specialty groups perform HTA. Examples include the American Academy of Pediatrics, American College of Obstetricians and Gynecologists, American College of Radiology, American Dental Association, and American Gastroenterological Association.

Summary

It is easy to conclude that both the private and public sectors are equivocal about giving HTA a high priority. That seems unlikely, however, given that hundreds of billions of dollars are spent annually in a health services system driven significantly by technology. The lack of a focused, organized approach is consistent with the pluralistic approach to decision making in the United States. Most intermittent have been the efforts of the federal government, whose HTA has waxed and waned for decades. The private sector provides a rich source of data about health technology. The lack of a technology information clearinghouse and limited assistance in understanding and assessing technology must be decried, however. Developing a generic prototype for HTA by communities and HSOs/HSs should be a national priority.

HSO/HS Technology Decision Making

Assessing technology at the operating level is different from that done by public or private HTA groups. Among the most important differences is that, when machine- and chemical-based technologies have become generally available to HSOs/HSs, questions of safety and efficacy have been answered by the FDA. At the operating level, however, the safety and efficacy of new surgical techniques or innovative uses of already approved machine- and chemical-based technologies are evaluated almost exclusively by the HSO or HS. It is less than reassuring to find that, even into the new millennium, few HSOs or HSs have a formal HTA program.[129] Lack of operating-level HTA in the United States is even starker if compared with other countries.

Criteria useful to assess technology include its appropriateness for the service area or community; financial feasibility, cost-effectiveness, useful life, and operating costs; availability of technical personnel to staff it, expert physicians, and support services; availability of backup technologies, such as open-heart surgery if angioplasty fails; and adequacy of reimbursement.[130] Nonexotic technologies and replacement equipment should be scrutinized similarly. New technology should be evaluated 6–12 months after its introduction to determine its performance level and effect on the quality of care.[131] Generally, physicians are considered technically qualified to decide about acquiring technology and are given great deference in decisions. Technology is essential to attracting and retaining top physicians.

Review and Planning

Cost-containment pressure, increased legal liability, and competition have caused HSOs/HSs to reassess how they make decisions to acquire and use technology and to ensure its safe operation and maintenance. One approach establishes annual review and financial planning processes for medical technologies that are separate from other capital expenditure decision making. This is necessary for financial planning in terms of depreciation, because many expensive technologies are obsolete before the end of their useful life. As a result, depreciation and replacement allowances rarely meet the costs of newer technology. If the rate of technological innovation and diffusion increases, this problem will become even more pressing. The transition to noninvasive diagnosis of the heart is a prime example of changing and improved treatment options that will increase the quality (and cost) of healthcare as HSOs/HSs invest in this technology.

HSOs/HSs should develop strategic technology plans to guide technology acquisition, professional staff development, and market strategies. The plans should assess emerging technology in near- and longer-term time frames and identify niches where they should focus staff development and market strategies.[132]

Financing Technology

On average, acute care hospitals have the most capital- and technology-intensive physical plants of any type of HSO. Historically, acute care hospitals had annual capital equipment budgets of several million dollars; technology was financed internally or from gifts and was relatively inexpensive.[133]

In the era of diminished reimbursement, however, successful healthcare executives must be creative to meet the costs of technology. Technology may be financed from current revenue, reserves, donations, debt, joint ventures, or venture capital. Other strategies have been suggested: 1) merge interests with physicians and other HSOs and develop complementary plans to reduce duplication of high-cost technology; 2) obtain manufacturer support to develop, train for, and maintain technology; 3) become a demonstration site for manufacturers; and 4) become a service center for other providers.[134]

Evaluating and Acquiring Technology—TEAM

A methodology to improve decision making about technology was developed by the American Hospital Association (AHA) and the Center for Health Services Research at the University of California, Los Angeles, in the late 1970s. TEAM (Technology Evaluation and Acquisition Methods) organized a review process, determined participation, and developed criteria. It addressed four common problems acute care hospitals faced in evaluating and acquiring technology: 1) treating requests for medical technology in the same way as requests for other capital expenditures, 2) absence of multidisciplinary staff participation in planning and evaluation of technology requests, 3) sporadic and unorganized physician participation in acquisition decisions, and 4) relying on staff members who requested technology to also assess its need and feasibility.[135] In TEAM, the governing board (GB) and CEO established a policy to ensure that requests for technology were compatible with the HSO's mission, vision, and strategic plan. TEAM used an interdisciplinary standing committee to conduct mini assessments and make recommendations for each proposed technology as to need and use; effect on staffing, space, and supply; effect on patient care; vendor and product evaluation; and financial impact.[136] Despite its potential, AHA did not develop TEAM further.

Alternatives to TEAM

Chief Technology Officer

A chief technology officer (CTO) may manage the HSO's/HS's technology and translate vision and planning into programs.[137] Meeting this goal is eased if line managers of technology, such as chiefs of clinical pharmacy, clinical engineering, and information systems, report to the CTO.[138] The CTO differs from a chief information officer (CIO). The CTO is the organization's senior technology architect who uses technology to improve services, engages users and customers, and works with vendors to enhance services. The CIO manages the organization's technology infrastructure and is responsible for internal information technology (IT) operations.[139] Like TEAM, appointing a CTO gained limited acceptance, perhaps because both affect or disrupt established roles of senior managers, and because technical support information

flows up the organization only when solicited. An additional difficulty is finding suitably qualified candidates.

Technical Support Committee
An alternative to TEAM and a CTO with less effect on common modi operandi is a standing committee that provides recommendations to senior management and resolves day-to-
day technical problems.[140] The committee's strength lies in making decisions about acquiring
technology, which requires answering questions about costs of acquisition, maintenance, and
replacement. A senior manager is the chair; members include managers of plant operations,
biomedical engineering, medical physics, information systems, and risk management and
safety. The committee performs the following five functions:

- Coordinates and maintains strategic technology planning compatible with the strategic
  plan

- Coordinates Joint Commission–mandated "environment of care" plans and programs

- Provides technical recommendations for HTA and equipment acquisition

- Ensures equipment effectiveness

- Identifies and secures funding for purchase, and monitors problem reporting and correction

Notably, and by design, the committee has no clinical members. It recommends technologically acceptable options. As users, clinicians choose equipment from these options. This
committee goes far to maintain continuity of purpose and improve communication about
biomedical equipment at the operating level.

Multidisciplinary HTA Committee
The multidisciplinary technology assessment committee (M-TAC) approach is the broadest of
the options discussed. M-TAC draws on the organization's strengths and has three phases.[141] In
Phase I, the capital planning process is modified to include the elements of HTA. The committee established in Phase I is multidisciplinary, emphasizes physician participation, and applies
assessment criteria to technology in the context of the organization's mission, vision, and strategic plan. Phase II includes a technology inventory and post-acquisition evaluation of technology. In Phase III, M-TAC develops a strategic technology plan that includes identifying
new technologies that meet service area and competitive needs. In all three phases, the committee can function as decision maker or advisory body. If technology meets predetermined
criteria, the committee performs an in-depth analysis and asks, Does it work? Is it safe? Is
it an improvement over existing technology? Will it have organization-wide impact? What
is its cost? Is it cost-effective? What are its potential effects on patient and community? Are
there risk management and legal liability issues? Are there regulatory requirements? Will it
assist in a managed care environment? What are its potential ethical, social, and political
effects? Is it needed urgently?[142] The flow diagram in Figure 5.3 shows the capital planning
and HTA process.

International Comparisons of HTA
International comparisons about HSO-level HTA are insightful. Greater focus on HTA at
the operational level outside the United States may reflect less availability of technical advice and assistance from non-HSO sources, as well as fewer resources to acquire technology.
Four models are suggested:[143]

1. *Ambassador model*—Clinicians recognized as opinion leaders are ambassadors of the HTA
   message in the organization and are a key part of diffusing results of HTA.

2. *Mini HTA*—Individual professionals are part of HTA and collect data to inform decision
   makers.

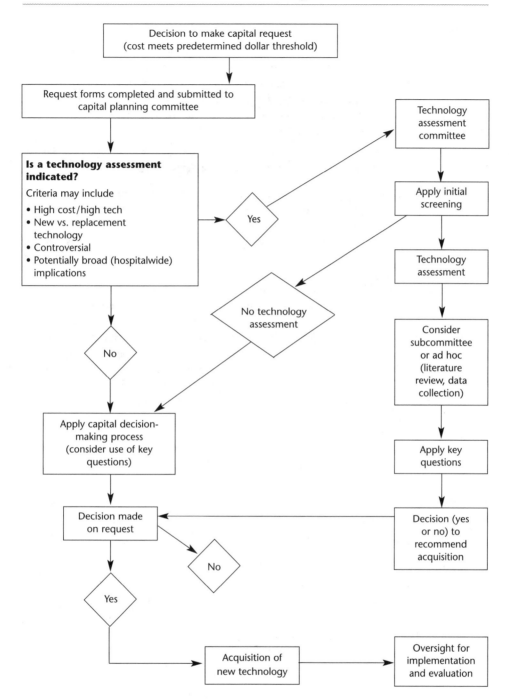

Figure 5.3. Flowchart for capital planning and technology assessment. From Uphoff, Mary Ellen, Thomas Ratko, and Karl Matuszewski, "Making Technology Assessment Count." *Health Measures 2* (March 1997): 22.

3. *Internal committee*—Evidence from multidisciplinary groups (internal committee) represents different perspectives, reviews evidence, and makes recommendations.

4. *HTA unit*—Specialized staff in the hospital work on HTA.

Meta-analysis of HTA determined that decision makers most frequently used clinical, economic, and political/strategic information. Legal, social, and ethical aspects were rarely the most important in decision making.[144]

Summary

Assisted or not, HSOs/HSs must make decisions about technology. In addition to the literature and public sources, private for-profit HTA services and not-for-profit groups provide information about technology. HSs have more resources for HTA than HSOs. The generic process for HTA is to set priorities; assess clinical efficacy, safety, and costs; synthesize information; provide assessments to users who make recommendations; initiate acquisition; and monitor after-purchase performance to assess its benefits.[145]

Managing Biomedical Equipment

Equipment used in delivering health services is called biomedical equipment. Table 5.3 suggests how biomedical equipment diagnoses, treats, monitors, and supports patient treatment. Some equipment, such as an MRI scanner, is very expensive; most biomedical equipment is small, portable, and relatively low cost, however. In total, biomedical equipment is a major economic asset of the HSO/HS and has significant potential to consume resources in terms of acquisition and operating costs, training of staff, and maintenance. In the late 1990s, acute care hospitals carried an inventory of 5,000 to 15,000 pieces of equipment.[146]

As noted, the staggering increases in the amount and complexity of biomedical equipment, coupled with increased legal liability for defects and malfunctions, necessitate considering biomedical equipment as one element in a complicated system that includes staff, internal environment, technology, organization, and external relations.[147] The categories of equipment shown in Table 5.3 are likely to affect one another. For instance, certain equipment supports a surgical process, even as the surgical process requires the equipment. Effective biomedical equipment use depends on internal factors, such as the availability of trained staff, standard operating procedures, staff credentialing, and staff's willingness to accept and use new technology. Equipment use is also a function of external factors, such as availability and receptiveness of patients, certification of staff by professional societies, and governmental regulation that governs the technology's safety and efficacy.

Systems Engineering

Important to selecting biomedical equipment is whether the equipment being considered can be integrated with existing equipment, people, processes, and environment to provide a safe and effective system under both normal and contingency conditions. Figure 5.4 suggests these relationships. This integration requires technical expertise, especially when it involves multiple units of programmable equipment from several manufacturers or when facility modifications are necessary. This "systems engineering" may be completed by HSO staff with appropriate skills, by consultants from the HS or elsewhere, or by equipment manufacturers.

Managing computerized biomedical equipment is much more complex because it is likely to be part of the HSO's/HS's information system. As a result, more elements of the organization are affected; among the most important are clinicians, managers, and the governing body.

Table 5.3 Biomedical equipment categories with examples

Diagnostic	Therapeutic	Monitoring	Support
Body potentials	Resuscitation	Patient	Communication
Blood flow	Prosthetic and orthotic	Environment	Management
Chemical composition	Surgical support		Maintenance and testing
Radiant energy	Special treatment		Teaching
	Radiant energy		Records and statistics

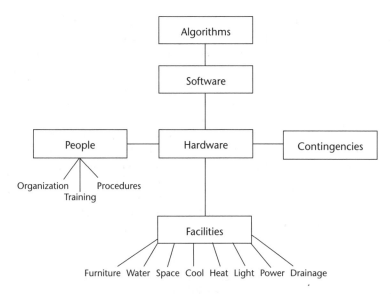

Figure 5.4.　Systems engineering components.

Other areas that may be affected are fiscal affairs, plant maintenance and operations, biomedical engineering, risk management and safety, quality assessment and improvement, supply chain, and information systems.

Organization

External Standards

The two most prominent external organizations affecting technology in HSOs are The Joint Commission and CMS. Each has a set of standards that requires attention to the safety and quality of the HSO's equipment. Non-equipment technology is not affected by the standards, except indirectly as to how use affects the quality and outcomes of patient care.

The Joint Commission requires hospitals to manage biomedical equipment safely and effectively. Its standards are in the *Comprehensive Accreditation Manual for Hospitals* and are paradigmatic of those used for other types of HSOs. Surveys determine if equipment management is appropriate and followed.

The CoPs for hospitals promulgated by CMS parallel The Joint Commission's but are less specific. The CoPs are found in 42 CFR Part 482—Conditions of Participation for Hospitals at section 482.41, Condition of participation: Physical environment: "Facilities, supplies, and equipment must be maintained to ensure an acceptable level of safety and quality."

Maintaining and Servicing Biomedical Equipment

HSOs/HSs have four basic options for maintaining and servicing biomedical equipment: 1) having a facility-based biomedical engineering and management information system (MIS) support and service department; 2) having a combination of facility-based service and subcontracted service from equipment manufacturers or independent service companies; 3) expanding facility-based biomedical and MIS service departments to provide service to other HSOs/HSs to achieve economies of scale; and 4) outsourcing maintenance, repair, and technical support.[148]

It is common for large HSOs, especially acute care hospitals, to have biomedical or clinical engineering departments with biomedical equipment technicians to perform equipment maintenance and management. Historically, biomedical engineering included equipment research and development, maintenance, and management support. As equipment proliferated and manufacturers became more active in research and development, *biomedical engineering* became the umbrella term for three subspecialties—bioengineering for research, medical engineering for development, and clinical engineering for integrating and servicing equipment. Many HSOs have kept the umbrella title *biomedical engineering* for their clinical engineering activities. In HSOs with large equipment inventories, biomedical engineers may be added to provide systems engineering and a higher level of equipment management.

Clinical engineering has several functions: 1) development and integration of new biomedical equipment systems through *planning* (e.g., system concept and design; cost estimates), *purchasing* (e.g., buying decisions), *new installation* (e.g., contractor liaison), *training* (e.g., education seminars), and *evaluation* (e.g., system performance; cost effectiveness); 2) operation, maintenance, and calibration of biomedical equipment (e.g., preoperation preparation and checkout; repairs); and 3) medical research and development support (e.g., proposal development; evaluation testing).[149]

Responsibility for some biomedical equipment may be vested in other departments. For instance, central supply may inspect and repair devices used throughout the HSO—intravenous pumps and suction equipment are examples. Similarly, clinical departments such as anesthesiology, respiratory therapy, or radiology may prefer to manage their own equipment because it is so specialized.

Organizationally, biomedical engineering likely reports to a midlevel executive or to the director of plant operations or supply chain, a structure that may create a communication gap between biomedical engineering and equipment users. Rarely does biomedical engineering report to senior management or the professional staff organization. Clinical departments perform setup and checkout and use their own equipment; administrative departments manage, inspect, and repair it. For example, critical care technicians may store, provide, and check equipment used by clinical departments to conserve equipment and ensure procedural consistency. This helps bridge gaps between clinical departments and biomedical engineering.

Fiscal constraints and increasing cost pressures from third party payers may force HSOs to downsize their biomedical engineering departments or to use external sources, such as independent or manufacturer service organizations. Outsourced biomedical equipment maintenance and repair are often cheaper than repair by manufacturers, the contractor may provide an on-site biomedical engineer, and there are fewer external organizations to manage.[150] Acute care hospital CEOs may be outsourcing as much as two thirds of biomedical engineering services, with pest management the most common (85%), with very high levels of satisfaction. One in five acute care hospitals will expand their overall outsourcing within the next few years,[151] a trend likely to continue.[152] Service providers are also moving from basic reactive repair and maintenance to value-added services, such as consultation and customized, project-oriented services. This change has resulted in multivendor servicing—one company services another manufacturer's equipment. This consolidates contracts, reduces costs, and has one source of accountability.

In addition, service workloads have been reduced by improved equipment reliability, troubleshooting by substituting circuit boards, and eliminating preventive maintenance that has little effect on failure rates.[153] In many cases, it may be impossible to significantly change average times between failures. Such equipment is replaced before failure,[154] These factors, in conjunction with manufacturer offerings, such as corrective maintenance contracts that range from complete to partial after-sales support, built-in diagnostics, and manufacturer-provided remote online failure diagnosis, enable HSOs/HSs to employ less-skilled technician and engineering staff. As a result, more experienced technician and engineer staff believe their future opportunities lie in consulting, manufacturing, and independent service organizations.[155]

This may render them a vanishing resource in HSOs. Indeed, there has been a change from data dominance, which provides information for reasoning and calculation, to knowledge dominance that is based on practical experience and learning. These clinical information systems may increase the need for systems engineering in the HSO/HS. Shaffer suggested that survival of biomedical engineering in hospitals will depend primarily on how well it supports clinical information systems and only secondarily on its ability to support the equipment–management interface for administration.[156]

Another approach to maintaining and servicing biomedical equipment is to broaden biomedical engineering to become directly involved in patient care activities. Part of this expanded role is to proactively provide HSO management and clinical staff with comprehensive information about potential equipment purchases through an ongoing process of HTA.[157]

Beyond the purchase, resale and recycling of medical equipment are affected at the federal level by the Health Information Portability and Accountability Act, Health Information Technology for Economic and Clinical Health, the FDA, and the Environmental Protection Agency. There are firms that buy and resell medical equipment after it has been purged of patient-identifiable information.[158] The importance of properly disposing of medical equipment was highlighted when a cancer radiation device stolen from a warehouse was opened in a metal salvage yard in Juarez, Mexico. The resulting spill of 6,010 cobalt-60 (gamma rays) pellets exposed at least 200 persons to unsafe levels of radiation. Radioactive scrap metal from that yard was processed into steel reinforcing rods used to construct houses, which were ruled uninhabitable.[159] Equipment recycling and resale require HSO managers to know and follow state and federal environmental laws.

HSOs may not track medical devices and supplies effectively. This results in waste when unexpired items are discarded, for example. It is estimated approximately 25% of spending in the U.S. healthcare system, or between $760 billion and $935 billion, is waste.[160] Likely, a significant part comes from waste of medical devices and supplies. A California hospital estimated its neurosurgery department wasted about $3 million in supplies in 1 year.[161]

Health Information Technology

Historically, most IT applications in health services have been business related, with finance and administration first among them. Clinical applications became more common with the growth of computing power and storage capacity. Like other technical areas, healthcare executives need not be expert in IT, but they need help from those who are. IT assists in four areas:[162]

1. *Process management:* Redesigning processes to make them seamless and more efficient

2. *Care management:* Expert systems and other ways to assist clinicians, some of which will be described here

3. *Demand management:* Especially useful in integrated systems to attract physicians, employers, health plans, and enrollees, as well as to direct patients to the least intensive setting able to meet their needs

4. *Health management:* Essential to store and retrieve risk assessment information, genetic profiles, family health histories, and similar data that predict and prevent disease, a use especially important in a capitated payment system

Of all IT applications in HSOs/HSs, the subset used for clinical purposes is the focus here. IT applications in HSOs receive further attention in Chapter 14. Electronic applications in health (clinical) information have developed at the national, regional (community), and enterprise levels. This discussion addresses the latter two, which have the most direct effect on HSOs/HSs. Enterprise information networks, or corporate intranets, emphasize the internal applications of the electronic health record (EHR) but also link delivery sites in an HS. This discussion uses the EHR as a generic concept to describe IT as applied to interaction with various health-care providers that run a gamut from acute care to prevention and wellness care and holistic medicine. The literature may use EHR. It is common, however, to see *electronic medical record, personal health record,* or *patient record,* which tend to reflect a narrower, episodic, and more acute care focus. Health information networks date from the 1960s, when the NLM offered an online bibliography, academic medical centers experimented with telemedicine, and the first internal patient information networks were established. Later developments included comput-erized links among pharmaceutical manufacturers, wholesalers, retail stores, and payers; hos-pitals and suppliers; and hospitals and fiscal intermediaries who processed Medicare claims.[163]

In the late 1990s, it was estimated there were 10,000 medical-based websites.[164] Ten years later, it was estimated there were over 100,000; in addition, the Internet connects service providers for clinical information interchange.[165] Health websites are an important source of health information for consumers who perform millions of web-based searches daily. Growth of Internet use by consumers seeking health information seems exponential: 80% of Internet users, or about 93 million Americans, have searched for a health-related topic online.[166]

A subset of IT applications in health services is health information technology (HIT), de-fined as application of information processing involving both computer hardware and software that deals with storage, retrieval, sharing, and use of healthcare information, data, and knowledge for communication and decision making.[167] National expenditures for HIT were estimated at more than $90 billion in 2015. It is estimated the U.S. HIT market will be $1.7 trillion by 2025.[168] The cost of software rose from $6.8 billion in 2010 to over $8.2 billion in 2012.[169] De-spite these ever larger expenditures, there are significant deficiencies and inadequacies technology could help remedy; it has been estimated healthcare lags behind other industries in adopting IT by at least 5–7 or as many as 10–15 years.[170] Wide application of HIT promises to improve pa-tient safety, reduce hospital lengths of stay, increase appropriate medication use, facilitate chronic disease management, and reduce healthcare costs, generally. It has been estimated only about 35% of hospitals and 55% of physicians' offices[171] have an HIT system; small hospitals are even less likely to have HIT. The cost of purchasing and installing an HIT system ranges from $15,000 to $70,000 per provider, with an estimated yearly maintenance cost of $8,000 per provider.[172]

Regional Health Information Organizations

From the late 1980s to the early 1990s, community health information networks (CHINs) were established to share health information among patients, providers, and the community for the mutual benefit of all involved, but especially the patient. The few CHINs surviving into the new millennium focus more on reimbursement transactions than on sharing clini-cal information.[173] The successors to CHINs are regional health information organizations (RHIOs), with a goal of forming a national health information network. RHIOs comprise hospitals, physicians, government agencies, insurers, laboratories, employers, and consumers. Other important stakeholders include schools, community agencies, and patients. Figure 5.5 shows healthcare data links like those in a RHIO. By 2011, over 200 RHIOs had been formed. Many were in the formative stage, 20 more were exchanging information. The federal govern-ment has encouraged development of RHIOs but has provided little funding.[174]

Some RHIOs are informal collaborations among participating healthcare entities; others are formally organized as for-profit or not-for-profit corporations. Means of sharing informa-tion vary, but there are four general types that connect participating entities in a RHIO: 1) point-to-point systems (patient information is shared as needed); 2) federated systems (each entity [doctor's office, hospital, etc.] stores patient information electronically and is linked to others through a wide area network [WAN]); 3) centralized systems (all patient information is stored in a central database); and 4) hybrid systems (elements of federated and centralized systems are combined).[175] Figure 5.6 shows a RHIO that uses a federated system.

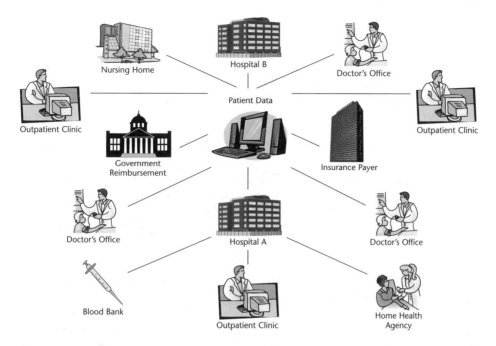

Figure 5.5.   Example of healthcare data links. Copyright © Sheldon I. Dorenfest and Associates. Used with permission.

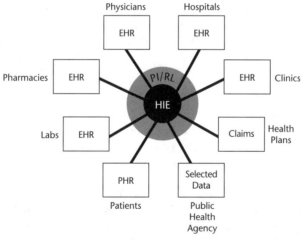

EHR	Electronic health record. Data are stored at each provider location, not in a central location.
PHR	Personal health record. Enables individuals to access their health records.
PI/RL	"Patient Index" and "Record Locator" software. These tools guide data requests through the network to the relevant information about the correct patient.
HIE	Health information exchange network. Information technology structure that enables health data transfer.

Figure 5.6.   Regional health information organization: federated system example. (From Legislative Analyst's Office, "A State Approach: Promoting Health Information Technology in California," February 2007, https://www.lao.ca.gov/2007/health_info_tech/health_info_tech_021307.aspx.

RHIO—Case Examples

Indiana

The Indiana Health Information Exchange (IHIE) is a not-for-profit corporation with roots in the late 1980s. IHIE has the largest and broadest participant community in the nation, which enables hospitals, physicians, laboratories, payers, and other health services providers to avoid redundancy and deliver faster, more efficient, higher quality healthcare to patients in Indiana. IHIE makes information available to approximately 50,000 healthcare providers in Indiana and neighboring states. In addition, IHIE's EHR system connects 117 hospitals representing 38 HSs, 16,592 physician practices, 46,408 individual providers, and almost 15 million patients. Its data system has over 12 billion clinical elements. The EHR system allows ED physicians to gain immediate electronic access to the medical records of persons who present for treatment. IHIE has connections with more than 30 EHR systems, and it has clinical messaging services for laboratory and radiology, electronic order entry, public health reporting and surveillance, and privacy and security features.[176]

Rochester, New York

The Rochester RHIO is a not-for-profit, community-run organization founded in 2006 using state funds and matching grants from organizations in greater Rochester. It is a secure electronic health information exchange (HIE) serving authorized medical providers and over 1.4 million patients in 13 counties in upstate New York. It was developed by and for doctors, hospital systems, health insurers, and privacy officers. Its mission is to provide the greater Rochester medical service area with a system of HIE that allows timely access to clinical information to improve decision making. The primary goal is to improve patient care and reduce system inefficiencies. The HIE allows providers to instantly access lab results, radiology reports and images, clinical documents, hospital discharge summaries, and admission/discharge notifications from its 13-county service area. Rochester's HIE includes over 142 million clinical documents for 1.4 million residents; 89% of physicians benefit from one or more of its services. For example, the RHIO helps physicians manage their EHR systems. The RHIO's Regional Account team supports hospitals and physician practices in their efforts to achieve CMS "Meaningful Use" certification.[177]

Problems of Implementing RHIOs

In seeking to maximize health in their regions, RHIOs go well beyond the financial aspects of healthcare and use information for clinical, educational, research, and management purposes. Health information networks have long faced formidable barriers because they are complex and costly, are believed to threaten privacy, and have been resisted by professional groups and institutions.

Further impeding progress of RHIOs is that the health information community has not developed standards, such as those for data definitions, computer coding, and interfaces. These impediments greatly diminish the ability of RHIOs to have interoperable systems that facilitate data exchange.[178] RHIOs continue to have no formal standards.

Sharing patient information is incompatible with a competitive environment, which is increasingly true for HSOs/HSs. Information about encounters and episodes of illness is usually fragmented; persons receive care from different providers at various times. Each provider has pieces of the whole. Unless all providers participate, the value of interoperability in a RHIO is greatly diminished.

RHIOs may encounter some of the same issues of regulation and licensure as telemedicine. Avoiding them will require that a RHIO limit itself to one state, whereas the natural boundaries of a region may cross one or more state lines. The resulting legal issues are, for example, likely to compromise the ability of a physician to provide consultation and coordination of care to a patient in another state. Legal issues of telemedicine are addressed in Chapter 2.

Regardless of the many impediments and difficulties RHIOs will encounter, there is reason to believe RHIOs will increase in number and importance. Service boundaries of HSOs/HSs are ambiguous and constantly changing, but all of them must communicate if healthcare is to be comprehensive, effective, and oriented to population health. The market is likely to favor enterprise information networks that offer wider connections (including services on the Internet), and, absent monopolistic control, the broader networks will prevail.[179]

Enterprise-Level EHRs

Despite several decades of effort and tens of billions of dollars spent by hospitals and other HSOs/HSs, the goal of a comprehensive, enterprise-wide EHR remains elusive for most providers. The promise is enormous. An enterprise-level EHR system is the computer hardware and software used to organize and manage health information.

The electronic medical (health) record system at the Mayo Clinic, Rochester, MN, was initiated in the mid-1990s. By 2011, this massive enterprise-level system had 16,000 active users, 298 million laboratory and procedure results, 44 million radiology reports, 344 million stored lab results, 30,400 EHR terminals, and 4.6 million clinical notes per year.[180] The system covered all inpatient and outpatient services from admission or patient appointment through examination and consultation, test results, consultation and diagnosis, and treatment (including surgery and postoperative treatment) and discharge. Authorized users may access information from anywhere in the organization. The system's goals are to improve patient safety and quality; improve clinical processes of care; enhance compliance with regulations and accreditation; improve operational efficiency and reduce costs; enhance revenue recognition; and provide data for reporting, analysis, and research.[181] A major advantage of an enterprise-level EHR system is its use to monitor and improve population health. Mayo's system includes one million patient EHRs from 27 counties in southeastern Minnesota and southwestern Wisconsin. Known as the epidemiology project, information from the EHRs identifies causes of disease; patients' responses to surgery, medication, or other interventions, and helps predict trajectories of specific diseases or medical conditions.[182] This system has significant potential to monitor and improve population health and is a significant step in operationalizing Codman's concept of end results as discussed in Chapter 4.

A contemporary extension of the information explosion is medical informatics, a generic term for the application of computing and communication technology in health services. Medical informatics may be defined as "the interdisciplinary study of the design, development, adoption, and application of IT-based innovations in healthcare delivery, management, and planning.[183] This definition is broad enough to incorporate management and health network applications, such as WANs and RHIOs.

Despite significant applications of HIT, much remains to be done. Development of electronic health information systems in hospitals faces problems that include standardization to achieve systems' interoperability, obtaining necessary funding, excessive regulation, privacy and information security issues, and a uniform approach to matching patients to their records.[184]

Advantages of Enterprise-Level EHRs

There are numerous advantages to maintaining medical information in an electronic format. EHRs facilitate use of medical and health information. Internally, the need to create, file, move, and store paper records is eliminated, and information is readily available throughout the HSO. Externally, delivery of services at multiple sites is facilitated because all providers can access the same medical and health information, which is almost impossible with paper records. A second advantage of EHRs is reduced offline storage and retrieval costs. Paper records require significant space and are costly to store. Third, EHRs improve quality and coherence of the care process. For example, the logistics problems of paper records—loss or unavailability when needed, difficulty of finding information in them, and illegibility—are largely solved.[185] A fourth advantage is that clinical guidelines can be automated to positively affect physician decisions and care processes. Computer-assisted decision support program reminders using local clinician-derived clinical guidelines can, for example, improve antibiotic use, reduce associated costs, and reduce emergence of antibiotic-resistant pathogens.[186] Fifth, EHRs support research and quality improvement. Both are data driven, and ready access to medical and health information facilitates them. Integrated EHR systems can be used to reduce variation in clinical processes and outcomes, thereby lowering costs.[187] A sixth benefit of EHRs is that readily available data facilitate reporting of all types.

Disadvantages of Enterprise-Level EHRs

A major problem with making EHRs operational is that the typical HSO has scores of electronic data sources—most complex are those in acute care hospitals. The number of sources grew considerably with ready availability of personal computers and increasingly powerful, inexpensive memory chips. Internal clinical information systems, such as those in laboratories, pharmacies, EDs, and imaging may be unable to "talk" to one another; neither can they interface with administrative and support areas, such as admissions and discharge, patient billing, scheduling, risk management, and medical transcription. External systems such as those in physicians' offices, commercial pharmacies, freestanding affiliated outpatient units and surgical centers, home health agencies, and RHIOs store information that would facilitate effective and efficient delivery of services were it available as needed. Both internal and external systems are rife with duplicative information, all of it obtained and stored at high cost and with inconvenience and frustration to the consumer.

Obtaining an interface among these various clinical systems, especially those internal to the HSO/HS, is key to realizing the advantages of an EHR. The interface problems are solvable with the standards available. "Standards provide the bridges to the many islands of electronic patient data so that the data can be inexpensively combined into an electronic (health) record."[188] A remaining challenge is to obtain physician information inexpensively in a coded or structured format compatible with electronic storage. Use of electronic documentation (dictation) into the EHR reduces the time a physician needs for dictation, as well as the time needed to access medical information, because most dictation occurs within the patient's medical (health) record. Also, electronic documentation requires fewer transcriptionists in the medical records department, an additional saving to the HSO.[189]

Confidentiality, privacy, and consent raise significant issues regarding EHRs. Confidentiality concerns may cause HSOs/HSs to control patient information so tightly that some or all advantages of EHRs are lost. For example, administration may determine that only the ordering physician may access test results. This will be problematic when nurses or on-call colleagues need test results, or in an emergency.[190] "Family charts" combine health records of family members. This makes family practice more efficacious but raises issues of privacy and consent.[191]

For most patients, electronically linking internal health record information is unlikely to raise confidentiality concerns. Paper records are subject to the same issues of misuse as are electronic records. In fact, paper records are potentially more subject to inappropriate use than are EHRs, for which access codes and audit trails can be established. For some patients, however, the mysteries of electronic formats may create a greater psychological issue than do paper records.

The efficiencies achieved by linking external data sources assist providers and insurers, but they ultimately benefit consumers. Consumers will be more concerned about confidentiality and privacy issues as health information and data sets from external sources are linked. Beyond the reality is the psychological discomfort of knowing that comprehensive data banks contain personal, perhaps embarrassing, information and that there is potential for misuse. Witness the frequency with which websites, databases, and computers are hacked. Confidentiality and privacy concerns, as well as legal issues of consent and wrongful release of information, may cause so many restrictions on use of information in EHRs that their advantages are lost.[192] In addition to using dedicated electronic or hardwired links, providers can communicate over the Internet, which has security tools to alleviate confidentiality concerns.[193]

The previous discussion noted the elusiveness of cost-savings with EHRs. Some efficiencies may result from reductions in staff, but implementing an electronic medical record in family practice residency programs did not decrease the need for support staff.[194] More recent analysis suggests caution in claiming EHRs will reduce healthcare costs. One study concluded that "use of these health information technologies, whatever their other benefits, remains unproven as an effective cost-control strategy with respect to reducing the ordering of unnecessary tests. . . . History suggests caution in assuming advances in medical technology will result in cost savings. In fact, the opposite is more often the case."[195] As noted, these findings are consistent with other clinical and nonclinical applications of HIT.

Gauging patient reaction to increased computer use by physicians must occur in the context that computers are ubiquitous. Concerns that patients may have less confidence in physicians who use computers to enter and retrieve patient-specific clinical information, gain access to decision support or an expert system, or search for reference information regarding diagnosis and treatment during a consultation are probably unfounded.[196] Similarly, patients do not seem to believe that physicians who use computers are paying inadequate attention to them; apparently, patients support physicians' use of computers.[197] Patients may interpret failure to use computers in consultations and treatment as less than state-of-the-art medicine.

EHRs were highly touted to achieve major cost reductions in health services. To date, however, there is scant evidence of cost savings. In fact, some studies of HIT implementation show higher costs.[198] Beyond a lack of savings is the failure to achieve the productivity and quality benefits that were expected. One unanticipated consequence is that applying HIT has *increased* healthcare costs by making it easier to bill for some services.[199]

Many physicians are equivocal that EHRs help them deliver high-quality patient care. Time used typing notes into a computer is time not interacting with patients. The clinical notes generated lack the richness and detail of handwritten notes.[200] Diminishing richness further is the likelihood that sloth will prompt physicians to choose standard phrases from the EHR system for their entries. That said, EHRs do make service delivery more efficient by improving accessibility, interoperability, analyses, billing, and supply chain. Most are financial and economic dimensions. Yet to be seen is if EHRs will improve the quality of clinical services. Legal aspects of EHRs are discussed in Chapter 2.

Summary

Development and use of EHRs will continue and at great financial cost. The ultimate EHR promises to use patient data to perform outcomes analyses, utilization review, profiling, and costing, which are features of special interest to policy makers, researchers, and health services managers.[201] Integrating EHRs with IT that supports diagnosis and treatment is essential.

Telemedicine

Telemedicine is defined as medical information sent electronically from one site to another. Examples include videoconferencing, transmitting still images, e-health (including patient portals), remote monitoring of vital signs, continuing medical education, and nursing call centers. In 2018, about 200 telemedicine networks connected 3,500 medical institutions; half of U.S. hospitals use telemedicine.[202] Clinical applications include radiology, dermatology, ophthalmology, cardiology, psychiatry, emergency medicine, pathology, obstetrics/gynecology, and orthopedics. Telemedicine visits grew rapidly from 2005 to 2017 in a large, commercially insured population, with most increases in tele-mental health (56%) and primary care (36%).[203]

Several types of interactions occur in telemedicine. These range from medical education to diagnostic or therapeutic consultation and case management. Medical education and training are typically provided by one- or two-way real-time or delayed video. Diagnostic or therapeutic consultation is done in real time but may use data acquired, transmitted, and reviewed later. Specialist consultations via satellite links with physicians or non–licensed independent practitioner providers in remote locations are increasingly common. The third area of telemedicine interactions is more long term and involves transfer of electronic text, images, or other data. The importance of CHINs and the EHR increases considerably when there is long-term patient management via telemedicine.[204] The prototype of telemedicine was the telephone consultation between physicians; facsimile (fax) machines transmitted electrocardiograms and medical records. Telemedicine enables various interactions. Digitized images of patients' retinas can be sent to diagnose retinal disorders.[205] Teleradiology gives providers in remote areas access to consultations at tertiary care hospitals and gives radiology residents experience treating a wider variety of cases.[206] Digitized wound photography allows surgeons to diagnose surgical site infections using online monitoring.[207]

Beyond clinical consultation, telemedicine is significant for administrative support and education. Many applications do not require two-way, full-motion video. Still images are used for radiology and pathology in which "store and forward" technologies transmit static images or video clips to any computer in the world for later retrieval, review, and consultation.[208] Telemedicine benefits both patients and providers by giving greater access to patients.[209] Monitoring patients at home is an important example.

Managed care organizations were early users of telemedicine, but as telemedicine becomes ubiquitous, its advantages for marketplace differentiation will diminish. Military hospitals are at the forefront of using telemedicine to serve personnel in remote locations where it is impossible to provide advanced technology, physician specialists, and other highly trained clinical staff.[210] Telemedicine offers opportunities for providers in the United States to consult and assist in providing healthcare worldwide.

Five issues in telemedicine remain unresolved:[211]

1. *Clinical expectations and medical effectiveness:* Much of the information about the clinical effectiveness of telemedicine is anecdotal.

2. *Matching technology to medical needs:* The inconvenience of interactive technology is a major obstacle to widespread use. Rural practitioners may lack support technologies to use it.

3. *Economics of telemedicine:* It is costly to acquire and maintain telemedicine equipment. Health plans may not pay for telemedicine. State telemedicine reimbursement policies may significantly affect the viability of billing Medicare for telemedicine services.[212] The cost-effectiveness of telemedicine is an open question.[213]

4. *Legal and social issues:* Remote licensure and liability must be addressed, as must the social and political issues relating to access to telemedicine. (Chapter 2 discusses legal aspects of telemedicine.)

5. *Organizational factors:* Organizations must consider the issues surrounding telemedicine prospectively and specifically.

Unresolved issues aside, telemedicine continues to be an essential element in health services delivery in the 21st century, and significant growth is certain. Managers must enable their HSOs/HSs to participate fully.

One aspect of telemedicine is both good news and bad news. Increased access will increase costs. One study found "12% of direct-to-consumer telehealth visits replaced visits to other providers, and 88% represented new utilization. Net annual spending on acute respiratory illness increased $45 per telehealth user."[214] This does not measure improvement in users' quality of life. Telehealth's convenience may tap into unmet demand for services. Important for researchers is whether this new demand reflects true healthcare needs. More growth in telemedicine is likely. By 2016, 32 states had enacted telemedicine "parity" laws mandating coverage and reimbursement for telemedicine.[215] Federal government mandates that Medicare Advantage plans offer telemedicine as a core benefit.[216]

The COVID-19 (SARS-CoV-2) pandemic of 2020 stimulated a sudden, significant increase in use of telemedicine. Persons were homebound; many feared traveling to and being in clinics or physicians' offices. As a matter of medical necessity, physicians and other clinicians used telemedicine to monitor, diagnose, and treat patients remotely. The pandemic prompted CMS to reconsider its policies on accepting and reimbursing treatment by telemedicine.

Future Developments

Biomedical Equipment

Cost containment may slow biomedical equipment development, manufacture, and use. Conversely, competition among HSOs/HSs encourages having advanced equipment and using new procedures. Free-standing HSOs are likely to have state-of-the-art biomedical equipment, but with little standby equipment and few spare parts. This necessitates increased reliability and speed of repair to minimize downtime. There will be greater emphasis on preventive maintenance and reliability too.

Technologies in general—especially medical technologies—are transformative. To ensure the safety and effectiveness of technology, its potential and associated management methods and tools must be known. Without that, technology function and patient outcomes will be impaired. Well-designed medical technology management methods and tools include objectives and protocols for efficient practice and decision making in a technology's life cycle. These include the following:

- Strategic technology planning

- Technology assessment

- Technology acquisition and implementation

- Technology risk management and quality improvement

- Technology utilization and servicing

- Technology value or cost/benefit analysis.[217]

As technology advances, HSO/HS managers must ensure that biomedical equipment is appropriate, complies with regulations, performs correctly, and is used properly. A major challenge will be achieving an interface among all elements. Maximum benefit can be realized only if various technologies can communicate. In addition, organizations expect to get more from their equipment; this means portability and a good fit with the environment are important.[218]

Clinical Support and Information Systems

Computer and communication technologies support development of artificial intelligence; microprocessor and computer- and robot-assisted diagnosis and treatment; general applications of expert systems to integrate computers and machines; the Internet and intranets; and local area networks (LANs), WANs, and RHIOs, all of which give providers direct access to data and information. In addition to the NGC noted earlier, current operational and experimental uses of the Internet include online patient registration, interactive question-and-answer services for disease management, dissemination of managed care organization guidelines to member physicians, and e-mail. Thousands of Internet sites provide information on consumer health, support groups, physician specialties, disease tracking and reporting, physician recruitment, and long-term care facilities. As mentioned previously, it is estimated 80% of U.S. Internet users seek health information online; they are more likely to get health information from the Internet than from family, friends, healthcare professionals, or traditional media.[219] The risk in using the Internet is information may have no basis in medical fact or science.[220] Thus misled, users may ignore to their detriment what medical science can offer.

A new generation of mobile computing devices has the public's attention and will likely become important in telehealth. These computers are considered "mobile" devices because they are small, lightweight, and portable. Most popular is the smartphone, so called because it provides the voice and text communication of a cell phone but allows access to resources of the Internet. Smartphone market penetration has reached almost 80% among U.S. adults.[221] Designing mobile devices for healthcare applications such as monitoring cardiac rhythm and transmitting real-time data to clinicians for diagnosis and treatment is big business.[222,223] Analysts project the market for a wide range of wearable medical monitoring devices will grow to $30 billion by 2024.[224] Some experts predict digital mobile computer technology will profoundly alter traditional delivery of face-to-face healthcare and increase access, lower costs per unit of treatment, and enhance personalized medicine.[225]

Increasingly, expert systems will guide physicians. One in use is a computerized scoring system that determines the statistical effectiveness of treatment for critical care patients. It uses a point system for age, seven morbid conditions that affect short-term mortality, and 16 physiologic variables that reflect values for vital signs, laboratory tests, and neurologic status.[226] Another suggests the optimum location for an HSO by using demographic data and factors such as anticipated financial, operational, and clinical performance; competing institutions; access roads; and ambulance support.[227] Most important, standards have been developed to transfer medical images and patient information, which brings medicine closer to the ultimate goal of a universal electronic patient record.[228] On the horizon is use of models, the power behind artificial intelligence and big data. A model is a decision framework whose logic is derived by algorithm from data, rather than explicitly programmed by the developer or implicitly conveyed by a person's intuition. The output is a prediction on which to make decisions. Models can learn from successes and failures with speed and sophistication human beings cannot usually match.[229] The clinical applications of models seem almost limitless.

The Internet has great potential to centralize medical information in a patient-managed website with controlled access, including read-only protection. Providers can view and download information in the record, and entries can be made following treatment. Giving all providers access to the same database may greatly improve efficiency and efficaciousness, to the great benefit of the patient.

Technology and the Future of Medicine

Advances in tissue and genetic engineering, gene therapy, artificial organs and tissues, implantable computer chips and "smart" wafers, nanotechnology (microscopic machines and molecular-level tools), robotic "caterpillars" to deliver medication and treat internal organs, and minimally invasive, keyhole, and bloodless surgery are affecting medicine in a cascade of change. Advances in pharmaceutical research, including robotic chemistry—the science of applying computers on a large scale to drug molecule research—will speed basic research and development of medications.[230] Potentially new antibiotics are being found in soil samples using genetic sequencing techniques.[231]

Increasingly, surgeons are using the body's natural openings—nose, mouth, rectum, and vagina—to pass instruments into the body to perform surgery and provide other treatment. As with laparoscopic surgery, this procedure is less traumatic; recovery time is greatly reduced.

The FDA defines gene therapy as a medicine that "introduces genetic material into a person's DNA to replace faulty or missing genetic material to treat a disease or medical condition." At this writing, a promising gene therapy for children not yet approved by the FDA will treat phenylketonuria (PKU), a rare disease that prevents the body from breaking down the amino acid, phenylalanine. The result is delayed development, intellectual disability, and psychiatric disorders. A better understanding of the human microbiome allows scientists to genetically engineer bacteria that are ingested to treat PKU.[232] Major research is under way to manipulate the human microbiome to prevent or treat a broad range of disease.[233]

Similarly, gene therapy, including immunotherapy, oncolytic virotherapy, and gene transfer, is being used to treat various types of cancer.

> Immunotherapy uses genetically modified cells and viral particles to stimulate the immune system to destroy cancer cells. Recent clinical trials of second and third generation vaccines have shown encouraging results with a wide range of cancers, including lung cancer, pancreatic cancer, prostate cancer and malignant melanoma. Oncolytic virotherapy, which uses viral particles that replicate within the cancer cell to cause cell death, is an emerging treatment modality that shows great promise, particularly with metastatic cancers. . . . Gene transfer is a new treatment modality that introduces new genes into a cancerous cell or the surrounding tissue to cause cell death or slow the growth of the cancer. This treatment technique is very flexible, and a wide range of genes and vectors is being used in clinical trials with successful outcomes.[234]

In 2017, the FDA approved a revolutionary cancer therapy. CAR-T uses genetically engineered human immune cells to treat an often-lethal blood and bone marrow cancer affecting children and young adults. The therapy has shown remarkable results, but the one-time treatment costs $475,000. The manufacturer will not charge if a patient fails to respond within a month.[235] Bacteriophages (genetically engineered viruses) are being used to treat antibiotic-resistant infections.[236]

Increasingly, allopathic (Western medicine) is being supplemented by holistic and nontraditional medicine. Complementary and alternative medicine includes chiropractic, homeopathy, and naturopathy; aroma, music, and massage therapies; biofeedback and visualization techniques; therapeutic touch; and Eastern medical theories, prominent among which are acupuncture, Chinese herbal remedies, and ayurvedic medicine. The mind–body connection is yet to be fully explored.[237] The sum of these modalities—as well as technologies yet to be developed—promises to revolutionize health and medicine, including the sites at which the "technology" is available.

The aggregate financial effect of wholesale use of an increasing array of technologies is that healthcare costs will increase, perhaps significantly. HSOs/HSs must identify, acquire, and manage the support systems needed as the range of interventions broadens. Effective managers are boundary scanners; medical technology is a critical part of boundary scanning. Effective managers will have a basic understanding of health technology.

Society is experiencing an epidemic of diagnoses. One aspect is medicalization of everyday life—the physical or emotional sensations previously seen as a normal part of living have become symptoms of dis-ease. Thus, they require a diagnosis and, more important for healthcare, a treatment. The other aspect of this epidemic is the drive to find disease early—to diagnose illness in persons without symptoms, those with so-called pre-disease or those "at risk." The epidemic of diagnoses leads to a pandemic of treatment. For those severely ill, potential harm from treatment pales when compared with potential benefit. For others, it must be remembered that not all treatment has important benefits, but almost all may cause harm, and some of the harm may be apparent only years into the future.[238,239] Because they raise important considerations of ethics and costs, the implications of overdiagnosing and overtreatment lie within the purview of managers even as they attract the attention of third-party payers.

Discussion Questions

1. Describe the effects of medical technology on HSOs/HSs and costs of health services. Link the theories of distribution of scarce lifesaving technology described in Chapter 2 with problems HSOs/HSs experience in managing medical technology.

2. Identify the effects of various types of payment mechanisms on development of new medical technology. What are the likely effects on use? Identify four implications for patient care.

3. Portability of technology allows it to be available elsewhere than in traditional HSOs. Acute care hospitals have been greatly affected by portability. Identify advantages and disadvantages from the standpoint of the acute care hospital *and* the patient.

4. Trends suggest significant consumer interest in alternatives to traditional Western medicine. These include the low- or no-technology treatment found in holistic medicine, wellness care, and disease prevention. Identify the implications for society *and* HSOs, such as hospitals.

5. Control of development and generalization of medical technology is fragmented. Identify control points and suggest ways to improve them. Distinguish the private and public sectors.

6. Technology is present in HSOs/HSs for two reasons: physicians demand it and patients expect it. Describe changes in the external environment that affect availability and application of technology. What is management's role in assessing technology?

7. Electronic health records promise to revolutionize delivery of healthcare. Identify advantages and disadvantages for patients *and* providers.

8. Management of biomedical equipment poses several problems for managers. How do managers involve clinical staff to solve these problems? Identify types of equipment that managers can purchase without involving clinical staff.

9. Competition is a major force in health services. Marketing is critical to HSO/HS success. Identify relationships between marketing and acquisition and use of medical technology. Give examples from your experience or the literature.

10. Usually, scant attention is paid to nonclinical technology, such as financial or management systems. Such technology can affect HSO/HS costs and effectiveness, however. Identify types of nonclinical equipment and their effects on managing HSOs/HSs. What are the connections between clinical and nonclinical technologies?

Is Cleansing Your Hands in My Room a Problem, Doctor?

Stefanie was hospitalized after surgery. She has several days of in-hospital recovery and reha-bilitation before she can be discharged. Stefanie is an avid reader of the print media, blogs, and the Internet. She knows the importance of caregivers cleansing their hands with soap and water or an alcohol rub before putting on fresh examination gloves when they care for her. Stefanie is concerned that caregivers are not cleansing their hands before gloving and treating her. When her stay began Stefanie visited with the unit's supervisor to confirm the hospital policy: All caregivers must wash their hands with soap and water or use hand sanitizer before gloving and having physical contact with a patient.

Stefanie is alert and interacts amicably with caregivers who enter her private room. To be sure caregivers wash or cleanse their hands thoroughly, Stefanie asks each to do so in her sight. She does this in a friendly manner and uses "please" and "thank you" in her interactions. The caregivers' reactions are usually a demurral and either an apology that they forgot or a sheep-ish smile and compliance. Some protest that they just washed their hands or used hand sani-tizer. When she insists, they wash or cleanse their hands in her sight. They usually comply. If not, Stefanie tells them they cannot examine or treat her. This has caused awkward situations.

Some caregivers become hostile when asked to follow hospital protocol. Stefanie notes that physicians are those most often hostile to her request. She asked her mother to put a note on the whiteboard in her room to remind caregivers about washing or cleansing their hands. Her mother taped a handwritten sign on the door to her room with the same request. Regard-less, she must monitor caregivers to assure compliance.

Stefanie knows she may be seen by some caregivers as a difficult patient. She fears mak-ing her caregivers—especially the physicians—angry and losing their goodwill because it may reduce the number and effectiveness of their interactions with her.

To support her concerns about compliance, Stefanie begins to keep a written record of the problems she's encountering. Caregivers know she's keeping track; some become even more vocal about their anger with what she's doing.

Questions

1. Is Stefanie being unreasonable? Is there anything she might have done differently to pre-vent the staff's anger?

2. What is the role of the unit supervisor in this matter? The role of the hospital office respon-sible for patient safety and compliance with hospital protocol?

3. Hospitals may use secret shoppers to check compliance in these situations. Is asking for patients' help a good way to improve compliance? Why? Why not?

4. The case highlights a major problem in minimizing spread of microorganisms among hospitalized patients. Outline a program to enhance compliance.

"Who Does What?"

When she purchased, installed, and staffed the single-photon emission computed tomography (SPECT) camera at a cost of more than $500,000, Andrea Berson thought it was one of the most difficult things she had done as chief operating officer at Sinai Hospital. Looking back, however, it could pale in comparison with the problem looming on the horizon. The SPECT camera's three-dimensional visualization of the heart makes it an exquisite diagnostic tool. Cardiologists commonly perform biplanar (two-dimensional) nuclear cardiology studies in their offices, but SPECT's high cost virtually precludes its use in physicians' offices.

Sinai has an exclusive contract with a radiology group to perform all inpatient radiology services. Four members of the group are board certified in nuclear medicine and credentialed for SPECT. Several cardiologists who refer patients to Sinai have expressed grave concerns about the quality of the readings of SPECT scans done by two of these four radiologists. When SPECT scans are done on their patients, these cardiologists want privileges to read the scans at Sinai. They threaten to refer patients for SPECT scans and other diagnostic radiology workups to a competing hospital if their request is denied.

The radiologists learned of the cardiologists' request and sent Berson a letter stating they expect her to meet the terms of their exclusive contract. The letter stated that the radiologists board certified in nuclear medicine do high-quality work and have the training, experience, and proven ability to read SPECT scans. The letter emphasized that the change contemplated would adversely affect the quality of patient care because the technologies involved in two- and three-dimensional scans are very different and reading SPECT scans requires unique skills. In addition, granting these privileges to cardiologists would violate established relationships and cause other, unspecified disruptions. Berson suspected there might be an economic reason too.

The problem in radiology reminded Berson of the turf war between interventional radiologists and surgeons about using lasers and the turf war over which specialties should perform laparoscopic surgery. As she reread the letter, Berson mused about the course of modern medicine. Many conditions can now be diagnosed and treated without a scalpel. She thought briefly about Dr. McCoy, the *Star Trek* physician who had only to pass a small, handheld device over someone to make a diagnosis. Is that where we're headed? She wondered.

"But, enough of science fiction," she said to herself. "How do I solve yet another turf battle without too many casualties, not the least of whom could be me?"

Questions

1. Identify the quality-of-care issues. How are they similar to, and how are they different from, the economic issues?

2. What information should Berson possess to understand the facts and issues? To whom should Berson turn for advice?

3. Develop three options that Berson could use. Identify and justify your choice of the best.

4. Identify three other quality/economic controversies that occur among institutional or personal health services providers.

Case Study 3   "Let's 'Do' a Joint Venture"

In 1990, a consortium of churches established Arcadia Continuing Care Community as a not-for-profit, tax-exempt corporation. Located in the tidewater region of eastern Virginia near a major naval base, Arcadia had 200 apartments for independent and assisted living and a 30-bed skilled nursing facility. Arcadia featured indoor and outdoor recreational activities and emphasized maximum independence for residents in a supportive, caring environment.

By 2000, poor management had brought Arcadia to the brink of bankruptcy. It was rescued by a large loan from the consortium and put under professional management. Arcadia was soon on firm financial footing, and the board of directors determined that its services should be diversified. Arcadia developed a respite care program to provide weekend and day services for dependent older adults and give relief to family members. It also established a home hospice program.

The board hired a consultant to assist in strategic planning. Based on market analyses and community assessments, the consultant suggested several new programs. First on the list was a rehabilitation center. The consultant noted the absence of outpatient rehabilitation services in the area, that rehabilitation logically extended existing services (including respite care and residential services), and that reimbursement was adequate. Start-up costs, including leasing space and equipping and staffing a rehabilitation center, were estimated at $500,000. The board was enthusiastic, but it had less than $100,000 for a new venture. Arcadia was leveraged (mortgaged) to the maximum, and there was no ready source of new capital.

As the board grappled with this question, the consultant suggested a joint venture with a physiatry group located 35 miles away. The consultant proposed that they pool their capital and establish a for-profit subsidiary to offer rehabilitation services. A telephone call to the physiatrists revealed that they were interested.

Questions

1. Critique what Arcadia is doing in terms of the technology that it has considered and is considering. Include both the positive and negative aspects.

2. Identify additional compatible activities that Arcadia could undertake. Be specific as to how they fit with its current activities and implied mission.

3. Identify the benefits and risks of forming a joint venture with the physiatry group.

4. What is the role of Arcadia's managers, especially the CEO, in these activities?

Notes

1. CMS National Health Expenditures and Selected Economic Indicators Levels and Annual Percentage Change: Years 2010–2026. *https://www.cms.gov/research-statistics-data-and-systems/statistics-trends-and-reports/nationalhealthexpenddata/nhe-fact-sheet.html*, retrieved October 28, 2018.

2. Samuel, Frank E., Jr. "Technology and Costs: Complex Relationship." *Hospitals* 62 (December 5, 1988): 72.

3. "Health, United States, 2009: With Special Feature on Medical Technology." Hyattsville, MD: National Center for Health Statistics (US), 2010 Jan. *http://www.ncbi.nlm.nih.gov/books/NBK44737/*, retrieved July 6, 2020.

4. Littell, Candace L., and Robin J. Strongin. "The Truth about Technology and Health Care Costs." *IEEE Technology and Society Magazine* 15 (Fall 1996): 11.

5. Beever, Charles, Heather Burns, and Melanie Karbe. "U.S. Health Care's Technology Cost Crisis." March 31, 2004. Booz Allen Hamilton, Inc., *strategy+business enews. https://www.strategy-business.com/article/enews033104?gko=0ec2d*, retrieved July 6, 2020.

6. Weiss, Joshua. "Medical Marketing in the United States: A Prescription for Reform." *http://www.gwlr.org/wp-content/uploads/2012/08/79-1-Weiss.pdf*, retrieved July 6, 2020.

7. Abele, John E., and Harry E. Barnett. "Administration of Medical Electronics." *Biomedical Instrumentation & Technology* 15, 3 (May/June 2017): 189–192. *https://search.proquest.com/openview/66713cf3dffb388782c56cdd12c9b490/1?pq-origsite=gscholar&cbl=38199*, retrieved March 21, 2019.

8. Stevens, William K. "High Medical Costs Under Attack as Drain on the Nation's Economy." *New York Times*, March 28, 1982, 50.

9. Congressional Budget Office. "Technological Change and the Growth of Healthcare Spending." *http://www.cbo.gov/sites/default/files/cbofiles/ftpdocs/89xx/doc8947/01-31-techhealth.pdf*, retrieved July 21, 2013.

10. Smith, S., J. P. Newhouse, and M. S. Freeland. "Income, Insurance, and Technology: Why Does Health Spending Outpace Economic Growth? " *Health Affairs* 28, 5 (September–October, 2009): 1276–1284.

11. Newhouse, John P. "An Iconoclastic View of Health Cost Containment." *Health Affairs* (12, suppl. 1993): 152; Bucy, Bill. "'Star Trek' Medical Devices Not So Far Out in the Future." *Business Journal* 13 (January 29, 1996): 23.

12. Cohen, Alan B., and Ruth S. Hanft. *Technology in American Health Care: Policy Directions for Effective Evaluation and Management*, 18–20. Ann Arbor: University of Michigan Press, 2004.

13. Baker, Laurence, Howard Birnbaum, Jeffrey Geppert, David Mishol, and Erick Moyneur. "The Relationship between Technology Availability and Health Care Spending." *Health Affairs* Web Exclusive, November 5, 2003. *https://www.healthaffairs.org/doi/10.1377/hlthaff.W3.537*, retrieved July 6, 2020.

14. Oren, Ohad, Electron Kebebew, and John P. S. Ioannidis. "Curbing Unnecessary and Wasted Diagnostic Imaging." *Journal of the American Medical Association*. Published online January 7, 2019. *doi:10.1001/jama.2018.20295*, retrieved February 3, 2019.

15. "New Choice Health: Medical Cost Comparison. MRI Cost & MRI Procedure Introduction." *http://www.newchoicehealth.com/MRI-Cost,* retrieved January 15, 2013.

16. Transplant Living. Costs. *http://www.transplantliving.org/before-the-transplant/financing-a-transplant/the-costs/,* retrieved January 15, 2013.

17. Scitovsky, Anne A. "Changes in the Costs of Treatment of Selected Illnesses, 1971–1981." *Medical Care* 23 (December 1985): 1345–1357; Showstack, Jonathan A., Mary Hughes Stone, and Steven A. Schroeder. "The Role of Changing Clinical Practices in the Rising Costs of Hospital Care." *New England Journal of Medicine* 313 (November 7, 1985): 1201–1207.

18. Chernew, Michael, A., Mark Fendrick, and Richard A. Hirth. "Managed Care and Medical Technology: Implications for Cost Growth." *Health Affairs* 16 (March/April 1997): 196–206.

19. Shine, Kenneth I. "Low-Cost Technologies and Public Policy." *International Journal of Technology Assessment in Health Care* 13 (1997): 562–571.

20. Souhrada, Laura. "Biotechnology, Cost Concerns Dominate in 1989." *Hospitals* 63 (December 20, 1989): 32.

21. Russell, Louise B., and Jane E. Sisk. "Medical Technology in the United States: The Last Decade." *International Journal of Technology Assessment in Health Care* 4 (1988): 275. By way of context, the most rapid generalization of new technology is almost certainly the diagnostic x-ray (radiograph). Discovered by German physicist Wilhelm Roentgen in 1895, it was only months before radiographs were in general use. Such rapid generalization was possible because scientists worldwide had similar apparatuses and made them available to clinicians. The chest x-ray continues to be the most common radiological procedure. *MedlinePlus.* Imaging and Radiology. *http://www.nlm.nih.gov/medlineplus/ency/article/007451.htm,* retrieved July 6, 2020.

22. Nafziger, Brendon. "FDA Clears Siemans' Low Cost of Ownership 3T MRI." July 24, 2012. DOTmed news. *http://www.dotmed.com/news/story/19206,* retrieved July 6, 2020.

23. Ray, Amit, and Susan Bowyer. "Clinical Applications of Magnetoencephalography in Epilepsy." *Annals of Indian Academy of Neurology* Jan-Mar; 13(1):14–22. (2010). *http://www.ncbi.nlm.nih.gov/pmc/articles/PMC2859582/,* Retrieved May 2, 2020.

24. Chernew, Fendrick, and Hirth. "Managed Care and Medical Technology."

25. Scott, Cameron. "Is da Vinci Robotic Surgery a Revolution or a Rip-Off?" *Healthline.* August 10, 2016. *https://www.healthline.com/health-news/is-da-vinci-robotic-surgery-revolution-or-ripoff-021215#7,* retrieved January 23, 2019.

26. Eisenberg, John M., J. Sanford Schwartz, F. Catherine McCaslin, Rachel Kaufman, Henry Glick, and Eugene Kroch. "Substituting Diagnostic Services: New Tests Only Partly Replace Older Ones." *Journal of the American Medical Association* 262 (September 1, 1989): 1196–1200.

27. Ubel, Peter A., and David A. Asch. "Creating Value in Health by Understanding and Overcoming Resistance to De-Innovation." *Health Affairs* 34, 2 (2015): 239–244.

28. Kennedy, Donald. "Health Care Costs and Technologies." *Western Journal of Medicine* 161 (October 1994): 424–425.

29. Grethlein, Sara J., Emmanuel C. Besa, and Arun Rajan. "Blood Substitutes." *Medscape.* December 11, 2018. *https://emedicine.medscape.com/article/207801-overview,* retrieved March 20, 2019.

30. Hellstern, P., and B. G. Solheim. "The Use of Solvent/Detergent Treatment in Pathogen Reduction of Plasma." *Transfusion Medicine and Hemotherapy* 38, 1 (2011): 65–70.

31. FDA. "FDA Approves Octaplas to Treat Patients with Blood Clotting Disorders." 2013. *https://www.healio.com/news/hematology-oncology/20130117/hot0113octaplas_10_3928_1081_597x_20130101_01_999120,* retrieved July 6, 2020.

32. Hanahan, Douglas. "Rethinking the War on Cancer." *The Lancet* 383, 9916 (February 8, 2014): 558–563.

33. Marcus, Amy Dockser. "Cancer Deaths Decline Sharply." *Wall Street Journal,* January 9, 2019, A1.

34. Vittayarukskul, Lily. *Cancer Fundamentals.* Research to the People. *https://svai.gitbook.io/research-to-the-people/specialized-biological-domains/untitled,* retrieved July 8, 2020.

35. Hanahan, Douglas. Rethinking the war on cancer. *The Lancet* 2014; 383:558-63. Published online December 16, 2013. *http://dx.doi.org/10.1016/S0140-6736(13)62226-6.* Retrieved November 29, 2018.

36. Mullin, Emily. "FDA Approves Groundbreaking Gene Therapy for Cancer." *MIT Technology Review Insider.* August 30, 2017. *https://www.technologyreview.com/s/608771/the-fda-has-approved-the-first-gene-therapy-for-cancer/,* retrieved November 29, 2018.

37. Health Resources and Services Administration. "Organ Procurement and Transplantation Network." 2017. *https://optn.transplant.hrsa.gov/data/view-data-reports/national-data/,* retrieved October 20, 2018.

38. 2017 EyeBanking Statistical Report form the Eyebank Association of America. *https://restoresight.org/what-we-do/publications/statistical-report/,* retrieved October 20, 2018.

39. "Schizophrenia Update—Part I." *Harvard Mental Health Letter* 12 (June 1995). Because fMRI allows imaging of soft tissue and concentrations of substances, scientists have been able to track human thought and emotion. "Mapping Thought Patterns." *Biomedical Instrumentation & Technology* 31 (March/April 1997): 111–112.

40. Matthews, Scott C., Martin P. Paulus, and Joel E. Dimsdale. "Contribution of Functional Neuroimaging to Understanding Neuropsychiatric Side Effects of Interferon in Hepatitis C." *Psychosomatics* 45 (July/ August 2004): 4.

41. Kennedy, Donald. "Health Care Costs."

42. Edelson, Ed. "Death Rate High in Drug-Coated Stent Trial." *Washington Post,* July 10, 2007. *http://www.washingtonpost.com/wp-dyn/content/article/2007/07/10/AR2007071000740.html*, retrieved July 6, 2020.

43. BioPharm International. "A 25-Year Retrospective on the Biotech of Business." *http://www.biopharminternational.com/biopharm/article/articleDetail.jsp?id=771926,* retrieved July 6, 2020.

44. Jarou, Zach, Juan Rango, Nate Harris, Samantha Shaw, et al. "Acute Ischemic Stroke (AIS) & IV tPA." *http://www.slideshare.net/zachjarou/health-policy-use-of-iv-tpa-for-acute-ischemic-strokes,* retrieved January 15, 2012.

45. Kent, David M., Sandeep Vijan, Rodney A. Hayward, John L. Griffith, Joni R. Beshansky, and Harry P. Selker. "Tissue Plasminogen Activator Was Cost-Effective Compared to Streptokinase in Only Selected Patients with Acute Myocardial Infarction." *Journal of Clinical Epidemiology* 57 (2004): 843–852.

46. Bryan, Jenny. "The Rise and Fall of the Clot Buster." *Pharmaceutical Journal* (July 18, 2014). *https://www.pharmaceutical-journal.com/news-and-analysis/features/the-rise-and-fall-of-the-clot-buster-a-review-on-the-history-of-streptokinase/20065679.article?firstPass=false,* retrieved January 23, 2019. The article noted: "However, tPA has been given a new lease on life thanks to its fibrinolytic effects on ischemic stroke; NICE (National Institute for Health and Care Excellence [Department of Health, United Kingdom]), recommends that it should be started not more than 4.5 hours after the onset of stroke symptoms. But streptokinase does not have this indication."

47. Obeid, Tammam, Husain Alshaikh, Besma Nejim, Isibor Arhuidese, Satinderjit Locham, and Mahmoud Malas. "Fixed and Variable Cost of Carotid Endarterectomy and Stenting in the United States: A Comparative Study." *Journal of Vascular Surgery* 65, 5 (May 2017): 1398–1406.

48. Vittayarukskul, Lily. *Cancer Fundamentals.*

49. Beck, Melinda. "Costly Cancer Treatment Dinged." *Wall Street Journal,* December 13, 2012, A3.

50. A continuing useful discussion of the technology assessment process is found in Glasser, Jay H., and Richard S. Chrzanowski. "Medical Technology Assessment: Adequate Questions, Appropriate Methods, Valuable Answers." *Health Policy* 9 (1988): 267–276.

51. Ramage, Michelle. "New Devices Emphasize Less Trauma to Body and Billfold." *Business Journal* 41 (January 20, 1997): 59.

52. Radiological Society of North America. "Elasticity Imaging Identifies Cancers and Reduces Breast Biopsies." Press Release, November 27, 2006. *https://press.rsna.org/timssnet/media/pressreleases/pr_target.cfm?ID=293*, retrieved July 8, 2020.

53. Thermographic Diagnostic Imaging. "About Thermography." 2013. *http://www.tdinj.com/about-thermography.html,* retrieved June 7, 2013.

54. Manton, Kenneth G., XiLiang Gu, and Vicki L. Lamb. "Long-Term Trends in Life Expectancy and Active Life Expectancy in the United States." *Population and Development Review* 32, 1 (March 2006): 94.

55. McKay, Betsy. "U.S. Life Expectancy Declines Further." *Wall Street Journal,* November 29, 2018, A1.

56. Ludwig, David S., and Kenneth S. Rogoff. "The Toll of America's Obesity: Beyond the Human Suffering, Diet-Related Diseases Impose Massive Economic Costs." *New York Times,* August 9, 2018.

57. Saito, Yasuhiko, Jean-Marie Robine, and Eileen M. Crimmins. "The Methods and Materials of Health Expectancy." *Statistical Journal of the International Association for Official Statistics. https://www.ncbi.nlm.nih.gov/pmc/articles/PMC6178833/,* retrieved December 1, 2018.

58. Goodman, Clifford S. *HTA 101—Introduction to Health Technology Assessment,* II-11. Falls Church, VA: The Lewin Group, 2014.

59. National Institutes of Health. Research Portfolio Online Reporting Tools. "Heart Disease." *http://report.nih.gov/nihfactsheets/ViewFactSheet.aspx?csid=96,* retrieved January 23, 2013.

60. Healthcare costs for smokers at a given age are as much as 40% higher than those of nonsmokers. In a population in which no one smoked, the (health care) costs would be 7% higher for men and 4% higher for women. If all smokers quit, healthcare costs would be lower at first, but after 15 years, they would be higher. Over the long term, complete smoking cessation would cause a net increase in health care costs. Barendregt, Jan J., Luc Bonneux, and Paul J. van der Maas. "The Health Care Costs of Smoking." *New England Journal of Medicine* 337 (October 9, 1997): 1052–1057.

61. Vita, Anthony J., Richard B. Terry, Helen B. Hubert, and James F. Fries. "Aging, Health Risks, and Cumulative Disability." *New England Journal of Medicine* 338 (April 9, 1998): 1035–1041.

62. U.S. Census Bureau. "Capital Expenditures for Structures and Equipment for Companies with Employees: 2016 and 2015 Revised." *https://www2.census.gov/programs-surveys/aces/visualizations/2016/healthcare.pdf,* retrieved October 20, 2018.

63. Skinner, Jonathan, James N. Weinstein, Scott M. Sporer, and John E. Wennberg. "Racial, Ethnic, and Geographic Disparities in Rates of Knee Arthroplasty among Medicare Patients." *New England Journal of Medicine* 349 (2003): 1350–1359.

64. The Dartmouth Institute of Health Policy & Clinical Practice, Variation in the Care of Surgical Conditions Dartmouth-Hitchcock (2015). Hanover, NH: The Center for Evaluative Clinical Services, Dartmouth Medical School. *Dartmouth Atlas of Health Care in the United States,* 115. Chicago: American Hospital Publishing.

65. "Unnecessary Medical Tests, Treatments Cost $200 Billion Annually, Cause Harm." *Healthcare Finance,* May 24, 2017. *https://www.healthcarefinancenews.com/news/unnecessary-medical-tests-treatments-cost-200-billion-annually-cause-harm,* retrieved November 14, 2018.

66. Wang, Shirley S. "Value of Medical Checkups Doubted." *Wall Street Journal,* October 17, 2012, A2

67. American Board of Internal Medicine Foundation and Consumer Reports. "Choosing Wisely: Health Checkups: When You Need Them—and When You Don't." *http://www.choosingwisely.org/patient-resources/health-checkups/,* retrieved November 11, 2018.

68. Aizenman, N. C. "Breast Screens' Value Is Disputed." *Washington Post,* November 22, 2012, A1.

69. Tehrani, Saber A. S., H. Lee, S. C. Mathews, et al. "25-Year Summary of US Malpractice Claims for Diagnostic Errors 1986–2010: An Analysis from the National Practitioner Data Bank." *BMJ Quality & Safety* 22 (2013): 672–680.

70. Bunker, John P., Jinnet Fowles, and Ralph Schaffarzick. "Evaluation of Medical Technology Strategies: Effects of Coverage and Reimbursement." *New England Journal of Medicine* 306 (March 11, 1982): 622–623.

71. Centers for Medicare and Medicaid Services. Official CMS Industry Resource for the ICD-10 Transition. *https://www.cms.gov/Medicare/Coding/ICD10/index.html,* retrieved November 11, 2018.

72. "Medicare Program: Criteria and Procedures for Making Medical Services Coverage Decisions That Relate to Health Care Technology. Proposed Rule. 42 CFR Parts 400 and 405." *Federal Register* 54 (January 30, 1989): 4302–4318.

73. Transplant Administrative Rule Book, 2015. Oregon Health Authority Health Systems Division Integrated Health Programs. *https://www.oregon.gov/oha/HSD/OHP/Policies/124rb100115.pdf,* retrieved October 27, 2018.

74. Newhouse, John P. "An Iconoclastic View of Health Cost Containment." *Health Affairs* (12, suppl. 1993): 164–165. A 1982 survey found that 51% of respondents were unwilling "to limit the opportunities for people to use expensive modern technology"; another 14% were uncertain. Most respondents were willing, however, to consider a change in the health care system that might reduce costs, such as having routine illnesses treated by a nurse or a physician assistant rather than by a doctor, and going to a clinic that assigned a patient to any available doctor rather than the patient's own private doctor. Reinhold, Robert. "Majority in Survey on Health Care Are Open to Changes to Cut Costs." *New York Times,* March 29, 1982, A2, D11.

75. "Report Says Physicians, Hospitals Locked in 'Medical Arms Race.'" *Hospitals & Health Networks* 81, 1 (January 2007): 71–72.

76. Kozak, Lola Jean, Margaret Jean Hall, Robert Pokras, and Linda Lawrence. "Ambulatory Surgery in the United States, 1994." *Advance Data* 283 (March 14, 1997): 3. National Center for Health Statistics, Centers for Disease Control and Prevention, U.S. Department of Health and Human Services.

77. Robinson, Michele L. "Turf Battle Rocks Radiology." *Hospitals* 63 (November 5, 1989): 47.

78. American Hospital Association Resource Center Blog. "Growth in Ambulatory Surgery Centers Slows in 09." March 16, 2011. *http://www.aharesourcecenter.wordpress.com/2011/03/16/growth-inambulatory-surgery-centers-slows-in-09/,* retrieved January 23, 2013.

79. Carrington, Catherine. "Finding a Gentler Way to Mend the Heart." *Health Measures* 2 (March 1997): 35–36, 41.

80. Robinson, Michele L. "Turf Battle Rocks Radiology," 47. A 1988 study by the American College of Radiology found that 60% of imaging studies were done outside the acute care hospital by nonradiologists.

81. Darr, Kurt. "Physician Entrepreneurs and General Acute-Care Hospitals—Part I." *Hospital Topics* 83, 3 (Summer 2005): 33–35; Darr, Kurt. "Physician Entrepreneurs and General Acute-Care Hospitals—Part II." *Hospital Topics* 83, 4 (Fall 2005): 29–31.

82. O'Neill, Liam, and Arthur Hartz. "Lower Mortality Rates at Cardiac Specialty Hospitals Traceable to Healthier Patients and to Doctors' Performing More Procedures." *Health Affairs.* 2012. *https://www.healthaffairs.org/doi/full/10.1377/hlthaff.2011.0624,* retrieved July 6, 2020.

83. Medical Device Amendments of 1976, PL 94-295, 90 Stat. 539 (1976); Safe Medical Device Act of 1990, PL 101-629, 104 Stat. 4511 (1990).

84. Medicare Interactive. Durable Medical Equipment. *https://www.medicareinteractive.org/get-answers/medicare-covered-services/durable-medical-equipment-dme/dme-overview,* retrieved March 20, 2019.

85. U.S. Food and Drug Administration. *A History of Medical Device Regulation & Oversight in the United States. https://www.fda.gov/medical-devices/overview-device-regulation/history-medical-device-regulation-oversight-united-states,* retrieved July 8, 2020.

86. U.S. Food and Drug Administration. *Overview of Medical Device Classification and Reclassification. https://www.fda.gov/about-fda/cdrh-transparency/overview-medical-device-classification-and-reclassification,* retrieved July 8, 2020.

87. U.S. Food and Drug Administration. *Overview of Medical Device Classification and Reclassification.*

88. Sloane, Elliot B. "Subacute: New Equipment, New Maintenance Concerns." *Nursing Homes* 44 (October 1995): 27.

89. U.S. Food and Drug Administration. "How to Determine if Your Product is a Medical Device." *https://www.fda.gov/medical-devices/classify-your-medical-device/how-determine-if-your-product-medical-device,* retrieved September 17, 2020.

90. U.S. Food and Drug Administration. Drugs@FDA: FDA-Approved Drugs. *https://www.accessdata.fda.gov/scripts/cder/daf/,* retrieved July 8, 2020.

91. U.S. Food and Drug Administration. Drugs@FDA.

92. Association for the Advancement of Medical Instrumentation. *https://www.aami.org/training/about-aci,* retrieved July 6, 2020; Association for the Advancement of Medical Instrumentation. "About AAMI." *https://www.aami.org/about-aami,* retrieved July 6, 2020.

93. Lashof, Joyce C. "Government Approaches to the Management of Medical Technology." *Bulletin of the New York Academy of Medicine* 57 (January/February 1981): 40–41.

94. Lashof, "Government Approaches," 41.

95. Committee on Ways and Means, U.S. House of Representatives. *1998 Green Book Appendix D. Medicare Reimbursement to Hospitals.* Washington, DC: U.S. House of Representatives, 1998.

96. Bradley, Elizabeth H. "From Adversary to Partner: Have Quality Improvement Organizations Made the Transition?" *Health Services Research.* April 2005, 2. *https://www.ncbi.nlm.nih.gov/pmc/articles/PMC1361151/,* retrieved July 6, 2020.

97. U.S. Department of Health and Human Services. Office of the Assistant Secretary for Legislation. Report to the Congress on the Administration, Cost, and Impact of the Quality Improvement Organization Program for Medicare Beneficiaries for Fiscal Year (FY) 2017. *https://www.cms.gov/Medicare/Quality-Initiatives-Patient-Assessment-Instruments/QualityImprovementOrgs/Downloads/Annual-Report-to-Congress-QIO-Program-Fiscal-Year-2017.pdf,* retrieved January 24, 2019.

98. National Health Planning and Resources Development Act of 1974, PL 93-641, 88 Stat. 2225 (1974).

99. National Conference of State Legislators. "Certificate of Need State Laws." *http://www.ncsl.org/research/health/con-certificate-of-need-state-laws.aspx,* retrieved May 12, 2019.

100. Cohen, Alan B., and Donald R. Cohodes. "Certificate of Need and Low Capital-Cost Medical Technology." *Milbank Memorial Fund Quarterly* 60 (Spring 1982): 307–328.

101. Brice, Cindy L., and Kathryn Ellen Cline. "The Supply and Use of Selected Medical Technologies." *Health Affairs* 17 (January/February 1998): 17. An example is Pennsylvania, where the number of MRI scanners more than doubled between 1988 and 1993, to a total of 187 machines. Many were underused; now MRI scanners must operate at 85% of capacity before additional units are approved.

102. OECD. Data: Magnetic Resonance Imaging (MRI) Exams. *https://data.oecd.org/healthcare/magnetic-resonance-imaging-mri-exams.htm,* and Magnetic Resonance Imaging (MRI) Exams. *https://data.oecd.org/healthcare/magnetic-resonance-imaging-mri-exams.htm,* retrieved October 20, 2018.

103. Centers for Medicare & Medicaid Services. Conditions for Coverage (CfCs) & Conditions of Participation (CoPs). *https://www.cms.gov/Medicare/Provider-Enrollment-and-Certification/CertificationandComplianc/Hospitals.ht,* retrieved January 24, 2019.

104. International Organization for Standardization, ISO 9001-2015 PowerPoint. *https://www.iso.org/iso-9001-quality-management.html,* retrieved November 27, 2018.

105. Perry, Seymour. "Technology Assessment in Health Care: The U.S. Perspective." *Health Policy* 9 (1988): 318.

106. Institute of Medicine, Committee for Evaluating Medical Technologies in Clinical Use. *Assessing Medical Technologies,* 9, 37. Washington, DC: National Academies Press, 1985.

107. Perry, Seymour, and Mae Thamer. "Health Technology Assessment: Decentralized and Fragmented in the U.S. Compared to Other Countries." *Health Policy* 40 (1997): 181.

108. Cohen, Alan B., and Ruth S. Hanft. *Technology in American Health Care.*

109. National Library of Medicine. National Information Center on Health Services Research and Health Care Technology (NICHSR). HTA 101: X. Selected Issues in HTA. *https://www.nlm.nih.gov/nichsr/hta101/ta101012.html*, retrieved July 8, 2020.

110. A concise discussion of consensus development conferences is found in Jacoby, Itzhak. "Update on Assessment Activities: United States Perspective." *International Journal of Technology Assessment in Health Care* 4 (1988): 100–101.

111. Institute of Medicine, Committee for Evaluating Medical Technologies in Clinical Use. *Assessing Medical Technologies*, 9, 70–175. Washington, DC: National Academies Press, 1985.

112. Goodman, Clifford S. *HTA 101: Introduction to Health Technology Assessment.* Bethesda, MD: National Library of Medicine, 2014.

113. Office of Technology Assessment, U.S. Congress. *OTA Health Program.* Washington, DC: Office of Technology Assessment, 1989.

114. Bimber, Bruce. *The Politics of Expertise in Congress,* 69. Albany: State University of New York Press, 1996.

115. Health Services Research, Health Statistics, and Health Care Technology Act of 1978, PL 95-623, 92 Stat. 334 (1978).

116. Perry, "Technology Assessment," 320.

117. Agency for Healthcare Research and Quality: Advancing Excellence in Healthcare. *https://www.ahrq.gov/*, retrieved January 27, 2019.

118. Department of Health and Human Services, Agency for Healthcare Research and Quality. "AHRQ Plays an Important Role in Health Technology Assessment." *Research Activities* 264 (August 2002). *http://www.ahrq.gov/research/aug02/*, retrieved August 1, 2007.

119. National Library of Medicine. National Information Center on Health Services Research and Health Care Technology (NICHSR). HTA 101: X. Selected Issues in HTA. *https://www.nlm.nih.gov/nichsr/hta101/ta101012.html*, retrieved July 8, 2020.

120. Greene, Jan. "An Agency for Change." *Hospitals & Health Networks* 71 (October 20, 1997): 68, 70.

121. Department of Health and Human Services, Agency for Health Care Policy and Research. "AHCPR to Collaborate with AMA and AAHP to Develop a National Guideline Clearinghouse." *Research Activities* 205 (June 1997): 16.

122. U.S. Department of Health and Human Services, Agency for Healthcare Research and Quality, *Guidelines and Measures Updates, Information about the National Guideline Clearinghouse (NGC)*. *https://www.ahrq.gov/gam/updates/index.html*, retrieved November 27, 2018.

123. ECRI Institute Opens Access to Clinical Practice Guidelines. News Release, November 18, 2018. *https://www.ecri.org/press/ecri-institute-opens-access-to-clinical-practice-guidelines*, retrieved January 17, 2019.

124. Silow-Carroll, Sharon, Jennifer Edwards, and Diana Rodin. The Commonwealth Fund. "Using Electronic Health Records to Improve Quality and Efficiency." July 2012. *https://www.commonwealthfund.org/publications/issue-briefs/2012/jul/using-electronic-health-records-improve-quality-and-efficiency*, retrieved July 6, 2020.

125. Perry and Thamer, "Health Technology Assessment," 196.

126. Perry and Thamer, "Health Technology Assessment," 181.

127. Medical Technology and Practice Patterns Institute. *http://mtppiorg.ipage.com/v1/about*, retrieved January 28, 2019.

128. ECRI. *https://www.ecri.org/about/*, retrieved January 28, 2019.

129. Rogers, T. Lynn, Jr. "Hospital Based Technology Assessment." *Journal of Clinical Engineering* 27, 4 (Fall 2002): 277.

130. Perry, "Technology Assessment," 323.

131. Carrington, Catherine. "Community Hospitals Balance Progress and Costs." *Health Measures* 2 (March 1997): 9.

132. Coile, Russell C., Jr. "The 'Racer's Edge' in Hospital Competition: Strategic Technology Plan." *Healthcare Executive* 5 (January/February 1990): 22.

133. Anderson, Howard J. "Survey Identifies Technology Trends." *Medical Staff Leader* (October 1990): 30–33.

134. Miccio, Joseph A. "The Migration of Medical Technology." *Healthcare Forum Journal* (September/October 1989): 24.

135. McKee, Michael, and L. Rita Fritz. "TEAM Up for Technology Assessment." *Hospitals* 53 (June 1, 1979): 119–122.

136. American Hospital Association. "Trustee Development Program: The Board's Role in the Planning and Acquisition of Clinical Technology." *Trustee* 32 (June 1979): 47–55.

137. Lodge, Denver A. "Someone Must Guide Technology Acquisition." *Modern Healthcare* 22 (December 7, 1992): 21.

138. Heller, Ori. "The New Role of Chief Technology Officer in U.S. Hospitals." *International Journal of Technology Management* 7 (Special Issue on the Strategic Management of Information and Telecommunications Technology, 1992): 455–461.

139. Singh, Rahul. "The Differences between a CIO and a CTO." March 12, 2015. *https://www.linkedin.com/pulse/difference-between-cio-cto-rahul-singh,* retrieved July 6, 2020.

140. Shaffer, Michael D., and Michael J. Shaffer. "Technical Support for Biomedical Equipment and Decision Making." *Hospital Topics* 73 (Spring 1995): 35–41.

141. Uphoff, Mary Ellen, Thomas Ratko, and Karl Matuszewski, "Making Technology Assessment Count." *Health Measures* 2 (March 1997): 22.

142. Uphoff, Ratko, and Matuszewski, "Making Technology Assessment Count," 24.

143. Metz, Laurent. "Hospital-Based Health Technology Assessment: A Promising Approach to Evaluate New Technologies for Healthcare Providers." *Asian Hospital Healthcare Management,* 31 (2015). *https://www.asianhhm.com/information-technology/hospital-based-health-technology-assessment,* retrieved January 29, 2019.

144. Olholm, Anne Mette, Kristian Kidholm, Mette Birk-Olsen, and Janne Buck Christensen. "Hospital Managers' Need for Information on Health Technology Investments." *International Journal of Technology Assessment in Health Care* 31,6 (2015): 414–425. *https://www.ncbi.nlm.nih.gov/pmc/articles/PMC4824957/,* retrieved January 29, 2019.

145. Rogers, T. Lynn. "Hospital-Based Technology Assessment." *Journal of Clinical Engineering* 27, 4 (Fall 2002): 278–279.

146. Blumberg, Donald F. "Evaluating Technology Service Options: Technology Services for Healthcare Organizations." *Healthcare Financial Management* 51 (May 1997): 72.

147. Heller, "The New Role of Chief Technology Officer."

148. Blumberg, "Evaluating Technology Service Options," 72–74, 76, 78–79.

149. Shaffer, Michael J., Joseph J. Carr, and Marian Gordon. "Clinical Engineering—an Enigma in Health Care Facilities." *Hospital & Health Services Administration* 24 (Summer 1979): 81.

150. DeVivo, L., P. Derrico, D. Tomaiuolo, C. Capussotto, and A. Reali. "Evaluating Alternative Service Contracts for Medical Equipment." In *Proceedings of the 26th Annual International Conference of the IEEE EMBS.* San Francisco, September 1–5, 2004. *https://ieeexplore.ieee.org/document/1403978,* retrieved July 6, 2020.

151. Sunseri, Reid. *Hospitals and Health Networks.* "Outsourcing on the Outs." *https://pubmed.ncbi.nlm.nih.gov/10555494/,* retrieved July 6, 2020

152. Lagasse, Jeff. "Hospital Costs Should Be Cut 24 Percent by 2022 to Break Even, Outsourcing May Help, Survey Says." *Healthcare Finance.* May 8, 2018. *https://www.healthcarefinancenews.com/news/hospital-costs-should-be-cut-24-percent-2022-break-even-outsourcing-may-help-survey-says,* retrieved January 30, 2019.

153. Keil, Ode R. "Accreditation and Clinical Engineering." *Journal of Clinical Engineering* (July/August 1996): 258–260.

154. Keil, Ode R. "Is Preventive Maintenance Still a Core Element of Clinical Engineering?" *Biomedical Instrumentation & Technology* 29 (July/August 1997): 408–409.

155. Ridgeway, Malcolm. "Changes in Industry Bring Opportunity." *Health Technology Management* 7 (October 1996): 48.

156. Shaffer, Michael J. "The Reengineering of Clinical Engineering." *Biomedical Instrumentation & Technology* 31 (March/April 1997): 178.

157. Rogers, T. Lynn. "Hospital Based Technology Assessment," 279.

158. Advanced Technology Recycling. Medical Equipment Disposal. *https://www.atrecycle.com/medical-equipment-disposal/,* retrieved September 12, 2019.

159. Marshall, Elizabeth. "Juarez: An Unprecedented Radiation Accident." *Science* 223, 4641 (March 16, 1984): 1152–1154. *https://science.sciencemag.org/content/223/4641/1152,* retrieved September 12, 2019.

160. Shrank, William H., Teresa L. Rogstad, and Natasha Parekh. Waste in the US Health Care System: Estimated Costs and Potential for Savings. *JAMA.* October 7, 2019, 322:15, pp.1501-1509. *https://jamanetwork.com/journals/jama/article-abstract/2752664.* retrieved May 3, 2020.

161. White, Jess. "Hospitals Wasting Millions due to Unused Supplies." *Hospital Management,* March 10, 2017. *http://www.healthcarebusinesstech.com/hospital-unused-supplies/,* retrieved September 12, 2019.

162. Lando, MaryAnn. "Information Technology 101: What Every CEO Needs to Know." *Healthcare Executive* 13 (May/June 1998): 16–20.

163. Starr, Paul. "Smart Technology, Stunted Policy: Developing Health Information Networks." *Health Affairs* 16 (May/June 1997): 94.

164. Menduno, Michael. "Prognosis: Wired." *Hospitals & Health Networks* 72 (November 5, 1998): 2–30, 32–35.

165. Illman, John. "WHO's Plan to Police Health Websites Rejected." *British Medical Journal* (2000). *http://www.ncbi.nlm.nih.gov/pmc/articles/PMC1173488/*, retrieved January 23, 2013.

166. Weaver, Jane. "More People Search for Health Online." 2013. Telemedicine online. *http://www.nbcnews.com/id/3077086/t/more-people-search-health-online#.XFIKfc1OmUk,* retrieved January 30, 2019.

167. The Lewin Group. "Health Information Technology Leadership Panel Final Report." March 2005, 2. *http://www.providersedge.com/ehdocs/ehr_articles/HIT_Leadership_Panel-Final_Report.pdf,* retrieved July 6, 2020.

168. Deltek Federal Health Information Technology Market, 2018–2023, April 5, 2018. *https://iq.govwin.com/neo/marketAnalysis/view/40062?researchTypeId=2,* retrieved October 27, 2018.

169. Mearian, Lucas. Benton Foundation. "Healthcare IT Spending to Hit $40 Billion This Year." May 26, 2011. *https://www.computerworld.com/article/2508583/healthcare-it-spending-to-hit—40b-this-year.html,* retrieved July 6, 2020.

170. The Lewin Group. "Health Information Technology Leadership Panel Final Report," 26.

171. Hedges, Lisa. "Do EMRs Improve Patient Care? Most Patients Say Yes." *Software Advice.* July 11, 2018. *https://www.softwareadvice.com/resources/emrs-improve-patient-care/,* retrieved September 17, 2020.

172. HealthIT.gov. "How Much Is This Going to Cost Me?" The Basics. *https://www.healthit.gov/faq/how-much-going-cost-me,* retrieved July 6, 2020.

173. Cohen, Michael R., and Margret Amatayakul. "A Noble Concept." Advance Online Editions for Health Information Executives. *http://www.mrccg.com/published-works/,* April 2005.

174. Vest, Joshua, and Larry Gamm. "Health Information Exchange: Persistent Challenges and New Strategies." *Journal of the American Medical Informatics Association* (May 2010). *http://www.ncbi.nlm.nih.gov/pmc/articles/PMC2995716/,* retrieved July 6, 2020.

175. "A State Policy Approach: Promoting Health Information Technology in California." February 2007. *http://www.lao.ca.gov/2007/health_info_tech/health_info_tech_021307.aspx,* retrieved July 6, 2020.

176. Indiana Health Information Exchange. *Better Outcomes. Delivered. https://www.ihie.org/,* retrieved January 30, 2019.

177. Rochester RHIO. Better Information for Better Healthcare. *https://rochesterrhio.org/,* retrieved March 21, 2019.

178. Ferris, Nancy. "Regional Health Information Networks Gain Traction." June 9, 2005. *https://www.healthcareitnews.com/news/regional-health-information-networks-gain-traction,* retrieved July 6, 2020.

179. Starr, Paul. "Smart Technology, Stunted Policy: Developing Health Information Networks." *Health Affairs* 16 (May/June 1997): 102–103.

180. Mayo Clinic. "The Electronic Medical Record at Mayo Clinic." *http://www.mayoclinic.org/emr/,* retrieved November 28, 2012.

181. Mohr, David. "The Mayo Clinic EMR: What, When, How, Why?" PowerPoint presentation at the 2007 MN e-Health Summit: Lessons Learned Breakout Session; Brooklyn Park, MN; June 28, 2007.

182. Rochester Epidemiology Project. Mayo Clinic. *http://rochesterproject.org/,* retrieved December 3, 2018.

183. Health Information and Management Systems Society: Medical Informatics. *https://www.himss.org/clinical-informatics/medical-informatics,* retrieved October 27, 2018.

184. Gaille, Louise. 12 Advantages and Disadvantages of Electronic Health Records. *Vittanna. https://vittana.org/12-advantages-and-disadvantages-of-electronic-health-records,* retrieved September 17, 2020.

185. McDonald, Clement J. "The Barriers to Electronic Medical Record Systems and How to Overcome Them." *Journal of the American Medical Informatics Association* 4 (May/June 1997): 213–221.

186. Pestotnik, Stanley L., David C. Classen, R. Scott Evans, and John P. Burke. "Implementing Antibiotic Practice Guidelines through Computer-Assisted Decision Support: Clinical and Financial Outcomes." *Annals of Internal Medicine* 124 (May 15, 1996): 884–890.

187. Tierney, William M., J. Marc Overhage, and Clement J. McDonald. "Demonstrating the Effects of an IAIMS on Health Care Quality and Cost." *Journal of the American Medical Informatics Association* 4 (March/April 1997 [suppl.]): S41–S46.

188. McDonald, Clement J. "The Barriers to Electronic Medical Record Systems and How to Overcome Them," 218.

189. Sangster, William M., and Robert H. Hodge. "Electronic Documentation vs. Dictation: How Do They Compare?" *Physician Executive* (March/April 2003).

190. Potts, Jerry F. "Electronic Medical Records: More Information but Less Access?" *Postgraduate Medicine* 101 (February 1997): 31–32.

191. Potts, "Electronic Medical Records," 35.

192. Potts, "Electronic Medical Records," 36.

193. McDonald, Clement J. "The Barriers to Electronic Medical Record Systems," 218.

194. Swanson, Todd, Julie Dostal, Brad Eichhorst, Clarence Jernigan, Mark Knox, and Kevin Roper. "Recent Implementations of Electronic Medical Records in Four Family Practice Residency Programs." *Academic Medicine* 72 (July 1997): 611.

195. McCormick, Danny, David H. Bor, Stephanie Woolhandler, and David U. Himmelstein. "Giving Office-Based Physicians Electronic Access to Patients' Prior Imaging and Lab Results Did Not Deter Ordering of Tests. *Health Affairs* 31, 3 (March 2012). *https://www.healthaffairs.org/doi/full/10.1377/hlthaff.2011.0876*, retrieved March 21, 2019.

196. Gardner, Martin. "Information Retrieval for Patient Care." *British Medical Journal* 314 (March 29, 1997): 350–353.

197. Swanson, Dostal, Eichhorst, Jernigan, Knox, and Roper, "Recent Implementations."

198. Soumerai, Stephen, and Ross Koppel. "A Major Glitch for Digitized Health-Care Records." *Wall Street Journal*, September 18, 2012, A17.

199. Abelson, Reed, and Julie Creswell. "In 2nd Look, Few Savings from Digital Care Records." *New York Times*, January 11, 2013, B1.

200. Kommer, Curtis G. "Good Documentation." *Journal of the American Medical Association* 320, 9 (2018): 875–876. *http://jamanetwork.com/journals/jama/article-abstract/2698930*, retrieved September 12, 2018.

201. Weng, Chunhua, Paul Appelbaum, George Hripcsak, Ian Kronish, Linda Busacca, Karina W Davidson, and J. Thomas Bigger. "Using EHRs to Integrate Research with Patient Care: Promises and Challenges." *Journal of the American Medical Informatics Association* 19, 5 (April 29, 2012): 684–687. *https://doi.org/10.1136/amiajnl-2012-000878*, retrieved December 3, 2018.

202. American Telehealth Association. *Telehealth Basics. https://www.americantelemed.org/resource/why-telemedicine/*, retrieved July 8, 2020.

203. Barnett, Michael L., Kristin N. Ray, Jeff Souza, et al. "Trends in Telemedicine Use in a Large Commercially Insured Population, 2005–2017." *Research Letter*, November 27, 2018. *https://jamanetwork.com/journals/jama/article-abstract/2716547*, retrieved December 4, 2018.

204. Perednia, Douglas A., and Ace Allen. "Telemedicine Technology and Clinical Applications." *Journal of the American Medical Association* 273 (February 8, 1995): 484.

205. American Telehealth Association. *Telehealth Basics. https://www.americantelemed.org/resource/why-telemedicine/*, retrieved July 8, 2020.

206. eVisit. "What is teleradiology? A definition. *https://evisit.com/resources/what-is-teleradiology/*, retrieved July 8, 2020.

207. Broman, Kristy Kummerow, Cameron E. Gaskill, Ado Faqih, et al. "Evaluation of Wound Photography for Remote Postoperative Assessment of Surgical Site Infections." *Journal of the American Medical Association Surgery.* Published online October 24, 2018. *doi:10.1001/jamasurg.2018.3861.*

208. University of Illinois at Chicago. Health Informatics and Health Information Management. *http://healthinformatics.uic.edu/future-of-telemedicine/*, retrieved November 28, 2012.

209. University of Illinois at Chicago. Health Informatics and Health Information Management. *http://healthinformatics.uic.edu/future-of-telemedicine/.*

210. "Balancing Hospital Productivity, Health Care Utilization and Medical Expenditures." *Health Care Strategic Management* 15 (March 1997): 12.

211. "Telemedicine in Healthcare 1: Exploring Its Uses, Benefits, and Disadvantages." *Nursing Times. https://www.nursingtimes.net/roles/nurse-managers/telemedicine-in-healthcare-1-exploring-its-uses-benefits-and-disadvantages-26-10-2009/*, retrieved May 2, 2020.

212. Neufeld, Jonathan D., Charles R. Doarn, and Reem Aly. "State Policies Influence Medicare Telemedicine Utilization." *Telemedicine and e-Health* 22: 1. Published online January 13, 2016. *https://doi.org/10.1089/tmj.2015.0044*, retrieved October 22, 2018.

213. de la Torre-Diez, Isabel, Miguel López-Coronado, Cesar Vaca, Jesús Saez Aguado, and Carlos de Castro. "Cost-Utility and Cost-Effectiveness Studies of Telemedicine, Electronic, and Mobile Health Systems in the Literature: A Systematic Review." *Telemedicine and e-Health.* 21: 2. Published online January 30, 2015. *https://doi.org/10.1089/tmj.2014.0053*, retrieved October 31, 2018.

214. Ashwood, J. Scott, Ateev Mehrotra, David Cowling, and Lori Uscher-Pines. "Direct-to-Consumer Telehealth May Increase Access to Care But Does Not Decrease Spending." *Health Affairs* 36: 3. March 2017. *https://doi.org/10.1377/hlthaff.2016.1130*, retrieved November 1, 2018.

215. Barnett, Michael L., Kristin N. Ray, Jeff Souza, et al. "Trends in Telemedicine Use in a Large Commercially Insured Population, 2005–2017."

216. Terry, Ken. "New Rule Provides Telemedicine Opportunity." *Medical Economics* 96, 9 (May 10, 2019): 33–36.

217. Yadin, David, Thomas M. Judd, and Raymond P. Zambuto. "Introduction to Medical Technology Management Practices." In *Clinical Engineering Handbook,* edited by Joseph F. Dyro, 101. San Diego, CA: Academic Press, 2004. *https://www.sciencedirect.com/book/9780122265709/clinical-engineering-handbook#book-description*, retrieved January 31, 2019.

218. Sandrick, Karen. "Interview with John E. Abele." *Hospitals & Health Networks* 70 (January 5, 1996): 28–30.

219. Jacobs, Wura, Ann O. Amuta, Kwon Chan Jeon, and Claudia Alvares. "Health Information Seeking in the Digital Age: An Analysis of Health Information-Seeking Behavior among U.S. Adults." *Cogent Social Sciences* 3, 1 (2017). *doi: 10.1080/23311886.2017.1302785,* retrieved November 13, 2018.

220. Brody, Jane E. "There's a Good Chance Dr. Google Doesn't Know Best." *New York Times,* January 22, 2019, D5.

221. Pew Research Center. Mobile Fact Sheet. February 5, 2018. *https://www.pewinternet.org/fact-sheet/mobile/,* retrieved March 20, 2019.

222. *Wearable Medical.* ECG/Cardiac Monitors. *https://wearablemedical.com/ecgcardiac-monitors/,* retrieved March 20, 2019.

223. *ScienceDaily.* "ECG on Smartwatch Accurately Detects AFib, Study Suggests: Real-Time Display of Heart Rhythm May Help Avoid Procedures, Save Costs." February 28, 2018. *https://www.sciencedaily.com/releases/2018/02/180228085250.htm,* retrieved March 20, 2019.

224. BCC Research. Wearable Medical Devices: Technologies and Global Markets. March 2019. *https://www.bccresearch.com/market-research/healthcare/wearable-medical-devices-hlc192b.html,* retrieved March 20, 2019.

225. Steinhubl, Steven R., Evan D. Muse, and Eric J. Topol. "Can Mobile Health Technologies Transform Healthcare? *JAMA* (2013). *doi: 310.10.1001/jama.2013.281078.*

226. Higgins, Thomas L. "Severity of Illness Indices and Outcome Prediction: Development and Evaluation." In *Textbook of Critical Care,* 4th ed., edited by Ake Grenvik, Stephen M. Ayres, Peter R. Holbrook, and William C. Shoemaker, 2069–2083. Philadelphia: W.B. Saunders, 2000.

227. "Inforum" brochure, Nashville, TN, 1994.

228. Steven, Peter. "All Roads Lead to the Electronic Patient Record." *Healthcare Technology Management* 7 (December 1996): 33–35.

229. Cohen, Steven A., and Matthew W. Granade. "Models Will Run the World." *Wall Street Journal,* August 20, 2018, A17.

230. Moukheiber, Zina. "A Hail of Silver Bullets." *Forbes* 161 (January 26, 1998): 76–81.

231. Hotz, Robert Lee. "Scientists Unearth Hope for New Antibiotics: Researchers Identified New Compounds by Sifting through Genetic Material from Soil Samples. *Wall Street Journal.* February 12, 2108. *https://www.wsj.com/articles/genetic-sequencing-unearths-hope-for-new-antibiotics-1518451201,* retrieved August 7, 2019.

232. Zimmer, Carl. "Retooling Bacteria to Cure Disease." *New York Times,* September 4, 2018, D1.

233. Detwiler, Jacqueline. "The Biggest Thing Since Penicillin." *Popular Mechanics* 196, 4, June 2019, 32.

234. Cross, Deanna, and James K. Burmester. "Gene Therapy for Cancer Treatment: Past, Present and Future." *Clinical Medicine & Research* 4, 3 (September 2006): 218–227. *https://www.ncbi.nlm.nih.gov/pmc/articles/PMC1570487/,* retrieved January 31, 2019.

235. Mullin, Emily. "FDA Approves Groundbreaking Gene Therapy for Cancer: The Treatment Will Be Sold by Novartis for $475,000. *MIT Technology Review.* August 30, 2017. *https://www.technologyreview.com/s/608771/the-fda-has-approved-the-first-gene-therapy-for-cancer/,* retrieved January 31, 2019.

236. Brianna Abbott. "Virus Therapy Saves Patient with an Antibiotic-Resistant Infection. *Wall Street Journal,* May 9, 2019, A3.

237. Warner, Melanie. *The Magic Feather Effect: The Science of Alternative Medicine and the Surprising Power of Belief.* New York, NY: Scribner, 2019.

238. Welch, H. Gilbert, Lisa Schwartz, and Steven Woloshin. "What's Making Us Sick Is an Epidemic of Diagnoses." *New York Times,* January 2, 2007, F1.

239. Treadwell, Julian, and Margaret McCartney. "Overdiagnosis and Overtreatment: Generalists—It's Time for a Grassroots Revolution." *British Journal of General Practice* 66, 644 (March 2016): 116–117. *https://www.ncbi.nlm.nih.gov/pmc/articles/PMC4758471/,* retrieved December 3, 2018.

PART II

The Tools

The second part of this text discusses the tools necessary to manage HSOs and HSs: problem solving and decision making, financial management including quantitative analysis, improving quality, and communicating. After understanding the complexities of the healthcare environment introduced in Part I and before applying the management functions in Part III, managers must master the above-referenced tools.

Anticipating and preventing problems before they occur is the mark of a great manager, as discussed in Chapter 6. Solving problems when prevention fails is a traditional and essential management task. The new healthcare environment emphasizes patient safety and relies on continuous improvement of quality and performance, a proactive approach that assumes all processes can be improved and that managers must create the environment and give employees the tools to make improvement possible. One of these tools, problem analysis, includes recognizing and defining circumstances that require action (a decision) and implementing and evaluating the alternative that is chosen. Decision making is a collateral but supportive management tool defined as choosing among alternatives. Simply put, decision making has two steps: identifying and evaluating alternatives and choosing an alternative. Problem solving and decision making are integral to all management functions, activities, and roles.

The purpose of financial management, discussed in Chapter 7, is to provide financial accounting and managerial accounting information that helps management to make better decisions regarding the organizational purpose established by the governing body (GB). Financial accounting information includes the financial statements. Managers and the GB use a variety of tools such as ratio analysis to assess past performance and to make decisions to improve future performance. Managerial accounting information includes cost accounting information, reimbursement information, working capital information, and resource allocation information. Managers and the GB improve decision making with managerial accounting tools such as break-even analysis, revenue cycle analysis, cash flow analysis, and capital investment analysis.

The purpose of quality improvement is to not only do the right thing but also to do the right things right. Chapter 8 builds on the theory of quality/productivity improvement discussed in Chapter 4 and introduces a continuous quality improvement process improvement tool. The chapter also discusses the relationship between problem solving and use of teams in process improvement: benchmarking, six sigma, lean manufacturing, and reengineering. Productivity improvement tools to improve work systems and job design; capacity and facilities layout; and production control, scheduling, and materials handling are described.

Management functions in all settings rely on effective communication, which is the creation or exchange of understanding between senders and receivers. In Chapter 9, a communication process model is introduced with several tools to improve communications with both external and internal stakeholders. Barriers to effective communication are introduced with tools to manage those barriers.

6

Managerial Problem Solving and Decision Making

Health services organizations and health systems (HSOs/HSs) are vibrant entities in a fluid environment. The management model shown in the introduction to Part III (Figure III.2) reflects this dynamism. HSOs/HSs convert inputs (e.g., human resources, material and supplies, technology, information, and capital) into outputs (individual and organizational work results) to achieve objectives—work results such as delivering health services, educating, and researching. HSO/HS managers produce that conversion when they integrate structure, tasks/technology, and people. In doing so, they are accountable for allocating and using resources and for the outcomes.

Anticipating and preventing problems, and solving them when prevention fails, are traditional and essential management tasks. The new paradigm emphasizes patient safety and relies on permutations of continuous improvement of quality and performance, a proactive approach that assumes all processes can be improved and that managers must create the environment and give employees the tools to make improvement possible.

This chapter distinguishes problem solving, problem analysis, and decision making. A problem-solving model is developed, and the factors influencing managerial problem solving and decision making are discussed. The benefits of group problem-solving strategies are identified. A model assists in determining when group, rather than individual, problem solving is more effective.

Problem Analysis and Decision Making

Managers' work revolves around the two parts of problem solving—problem analysis and decision making. Problem analysis includes recognizing and defining circumstances that require action (a decision) and implementing and evaluating the alternative that is chosen. Decision making is a collateral, but supportive, management function defined as choosing among alternatives.[1] *Choosing* is key and defines decision making. Simply put, decision making has two steps: identifying and evaluating alternatives and choosing an alternative.

Decision making is integral to all management functions, activities, and roles. For example, planning involves making decisions (choosing), whether senior managers are formulating strategy or middle managers are implementing programs. Decisions about the management function of organizing range from establishing authority–responsibility relationships to designing work systems, procedures, and flows, and from establishing structure–task–people relationships to job assignments. In the staffing function, managers decide about number of staff and qualifications, their pay and training, and performance appraisal. In leading, managers choose the most effective management style and when, where, and to whom information is imparted. When managers control, they compare individual and organizational work results with predetermined expectations and standards and decide if results can be improved or standards raised. This means making decisions about what information to collect and report and which monitoring systems to use to measure and compare HSO/HS conversion activities and output with expectations and standards. Managers decide, too, which managerial roles to adopt by choosing among interpersonal, informational, and decisional roles. Managerial roles are detailed in Chapter 13. The speed and reduced cost of communication in the digital age have brought many more staff members into the flow of decision making through e-mail, Slack (team messaging), and internal knowledge-sharing platforms. Major problems result from unclear decision-making authority.[2] Figure 6.1 shows the relationship of problem solving and decision making with the five management functions.

Types of Decisions

Three types describe most managers' decisions: 1) ends–means, 2) administrative–operational, and 3) nonprogrammable–programmable.

Ends–Means

Ends decisions determine the individual or organizational objectives and results to be achieved. Means decisions choose the strategies or programs and activities to accomplish desired results. For example, a decision to emphasize quality and productivity improvement (means)

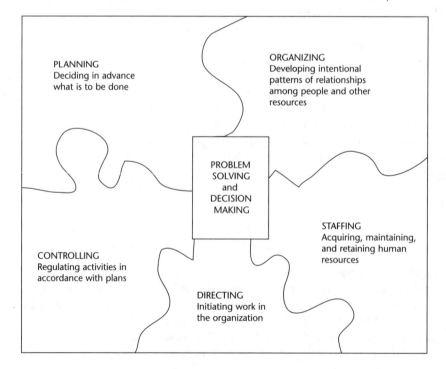

Figure 6.1.   The management functions are interrelated like the pieces of a puzzle.

accomplishes the organizational objectives of enhancing care and service, higher patient or customer satisfaction, and better resource use (ends). Ends are shown as the output component of the management model in Figure 2 of the Part III introduction. Decisions about ends are inherent in strategic planning, which includes formulating objectives. Health systems may make these decisions at the corporate level. Greater specificity is found in a department's ends–means decision making, which reflects its objectives and the operational programs that contribute to the HSO's/HS's overall mission.

Administrative–Operational

Many administrative decisions made by senior executives significantly affect the HSO/HS and have major implications for resource allocation and utilization. Here, *policy decision* is a synonym for *administrative decision*. Examples include deciding whether to use deficit financing for facility construction or renovation, recognize a union without demanding a certification election, hire hospital-based physicians, contract for laundry services, reduce the capital equipment budget, or participate in an integrated system of HSOs. In contrast, operational decisions are made about day-to-day activities by middle- and first-level managers. Operational decisions include deciding whether to purchase noncapital equipment, reassign staff, modify work systems, and change job content.

Nonprogrammable–Programmable

Nonprogrammable decisions are novel, unstructured, and significant.[3] Examples are whether to expand facilities; add, close, or share services; seek Medicare certification of skilled beds; restructure the organization or align with a network of HSOs; acquire a clinical information system; or add a family practice residency program. Such decisions occur infrequently. Programmable decisions are repetitive and routine; procedures and rules are used to guide them.[4] Patient admitting, scheduling, and billing, and inventory and supply chain procedures are examples.

Overlap of Decision Types

The Venn diagram in Figure 6.2 shows that the three decision types overlap—decisions may include parts of each. For example, merging with another HSO or establishing a satellite urgent care center or primary care preferred provider organization is a means decision because it is a strategy to achieve the organization's objectives. Furthermore, it is an administrative decision because it involves a major commitment of resources, compared with a primarily operational decision about day-to-day activities. This decision is nonprogrammable because it is unique and occurs infrequently.

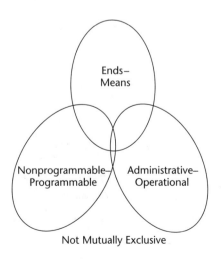

Figure 6.2.   Types of decisions.

Problem Solving

Managers are problem solvers. Problems may be unstructured or structured; complex or simple; major or minor; urgent or nonurgent; and they may involve varying degrees of cost, risk, and uncertainty. Problem solving involves several steps "characterized by intentional reasoning about what the problem is and what the solution should be,"[5] the result of which is to make the current state of an organization more closely match the desired state.[6] Using terminology from the management model, problem solving causes change so actual HSO/HS results or outputs more closely align with those desired. The process by which managers solve problems includes the following:

- Selecting and analyzing a situation that requires a decision

- Developing and evaluating alternative solutions to address the situation

- Choosing an alternative (sometimes called decision analysis)

- Implementing the alternative

- Evaluating the results after implementation

Figure 6.3 shows the relationships among problem solving, problem analysis, and decision making. Often, the terms *problem solving* and *decision making* are used interchangeably. They are not synonymous. All problem solving involves decision making (i.e., choosing among alternatives), but not all decision making involves problem solving.[7] The distinction is that problem solving includes problem analysis—predecision situation assessment and postdecision implementation and evaluation. The discussion that follows is relevant for both problem solving and decision making; they are distinguished, as necessary.

Managers perform several steps when undertaking either problem analysis or decision making. As with all processes, there are variables, conditions, and situations that influence the approach, manner, and style used. Problem-solving skills are crucial to managerial success; there are situations in which being an effective problem solver is more important than are communication or interpersonal relationship skills, which is not to diminish their importance, generally. Problem solving is fundamental to everything a manager does and to effective managerial performance.

In brief, managers are problem solvers and decision makers. The importance of problem solving and decision making in managerial effectiveness was shown by surveys of health

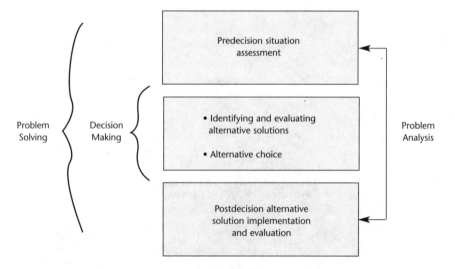

Figure 6.3. Problem solving and decision making.

services managers.[8,9] These survey findings on the importance of problem solving are reinforced by academic literature.[10,11] "A leader must never view a problem as a distraction, but rather as a strategic enabler for continuous improvement and opportunities previously unseen."[12]

Process and Model

Problem solving is the process by which managers analyze situations and make decisions that cause organizational results to be more like those desired. Prospective problem solving anticipates organizational results that are desirable. Retrospective problem solving identifies and corrects previous causes of deviation from desired results. Concurrent problem solving occurs in HSOs/ HSs that are committed to a philosophy of continuously improving quality and performance.

Conditions That Initiate Problem Solving

Another way to classify problem solving is by the conditions that initiate it.[13] Figure 6.4 shows the following conditions and corresponding approaches to problem solving:

* *Prospective*—Opportunity/threat (prospective, might)

* *Immediate*—Crisis (immediate, will)

* *Retrospective*—Deviation (retrospective, has/is)

* *Concurrent*—Improvement (concurrent, seek)

Opportunity problem solving is prospective and anticipatory. It occurs when a favorable internal or external circumstance enables the HSO/HS to achieve or enhance desired results.[14] For example, technology and consumer expectations permit an acute care hospital to offer obstetrics services at a birth center. Developing the birthing center program involves problem analysis, which consists of predecision assessment and postdecision evaluation. The outcome is organizational results (new service) that align more closely with desired results, including improved patient service and satisfaction and increased revenue.

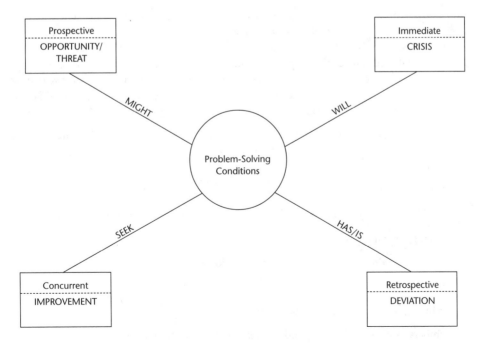

Figure 6.4. Problem-solving conditions.

Threat problem solving is also prospective and anticipatory but is the converse of opportunity problem solving. Threats may be internal or external and, if left unaddressed, may cause future results to be less than desired. For example, not responding to a competitor's aggressive marketing program may cause loss of market share.

Crisis problem solving is immediate. It responds to a current or predictable threat. Failing to act promptly will cause untoward results, such as a decline in near-term performance. Examples of crisis problem solving are a local natural disaster, a wildcat strike by unionized employees, bypass equipment malfunction during surgery, or a sudden reduction in Medicaid payments. Loss of an essential employee may be a crisis.

Deviation problem solving is retrospective and occurs when actual and desired results differ. Even small deviations may indicate large problems that must be identified and solved.

Improvement problem solving reduces the need for future deviation problem solving or improves performance. The perspective and process of continuous improvement differ from other problem-solving conditions in two important ways. First, continuous improvement is rooted in the philosophy that improvement is always possible; management's job is to support those efforts. This leads to continuously monitoring processes and seeking ways to improve them. Second, analysis is concurrent, broad-based, and organization-wide and focuses on inputs and the conversion process. The management model in the introduction to Part III (Figure III.2) shows this relationship. Improvement problem solving involves managers and staff as *problem seekers* who systematically seek opportunities for improvement.[15]

The condition of deviation is used to illustrate application of the problem-solving process model shown in Figure 6.5. The model is generic and applicable to all problem solving except that conducted under the condition of improvement, in which problem analysis differs. Historically, managers have engaged most frequently in problem solving under conditions of deviation.[16] The contemporary emphasis on quality and performance improvement, which is undertaken without a condition of deviation, will likely make improvement problem solving the most common type of problem solving. Chapters 4 and 8 detail improvement problem solving.

Problem-Solving Activities

Middle- and senior-level managers spend most of their time solving problems. The results of these efforts affect allocation and use of resources as well as work product. The circumstances surrounding problem solving are often complex, unstructured, and nonroutine, thus making the task difficult and time consuming. Sometimes the situation is beyond the manager's direct control. Except for the condition of improvement, the process is essentially the same regardless of problem type, scope, time involved, intensity of analysis, or the conditions that initiate it. Basic problem solving includes the following seven steps, as shown in Figure 6.5:

1. Problem recognition and definition—recognizing the presence of a problem that requires solution (including gathering and analyzing information); developing the problem statement

2. Developing assumptions

3. Identifying tentative alternative solutions and selecting those to be considered in depth

4. Developing and applying decision criteria

5. Selecting the alternative that best meets the criteria

6. Implementing the solution

7. Evaluating the solution and actual results

The numbers in Figure 6.5 correspond to those used in the following discussion.

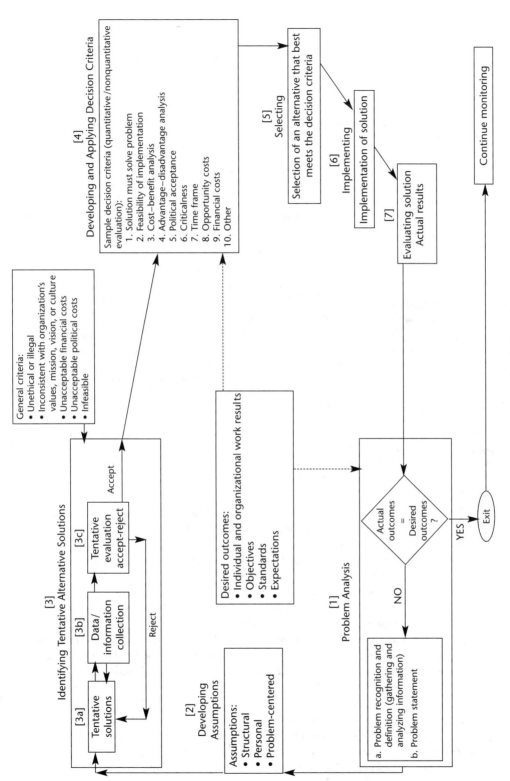

Figure 6.5. Problem-solving process model under the condition of deviation.

225

Problem Analysis [1]

Problem analysis is divided into problem recognition and definition and developing a problem statement. The product of problem analysis is the problem statement. It is the problem statement about which assumptions are made in Step [2].

Problem Recognition and Definition

Problem solving under the condition of deviation begins when actual results are inconsistent with desired results and the manager determines this is a problem that needs a solution. Examples of desired results are 1) organization-wide objectives, such as quality of patient care, better client services, and financial solvency; 2) departmental objectives, such as increasing customer satisfaction, reducing staff turnover, decreasing surgical infection rates, eliminating mislabeled laboratory specimens and imaging retakes, and minimizing budget variances; and 3) improving the work of an individual employee. Whether negative deviation indicates the presence of a problem depends on if it is "common cause" variation or "special cause" variation, a statistical process control concept discussed in Chapters 4 and 8. Similarly, positive special cause variation (deviation) should be studied so it can be incorporated into the process.

Applying the theory of problem recognition is not easy. Problem recognition:

> rarely occurs as a completely discrete event. In practice the process occurs through various time intervals (from seconds to years), amidst a variety of ongoing activities and in different ways depending on both situational and individual factors. At times, the process of problem recognition is automatic; at other times, it involves conscious effort. Often, it is a highly objective phenomenon resulting in problem descriptions that most anyone would agree on. At other times it is definitely a subjective process, where the nature of a problem description varies from individual to individual.[17]

Problem recognition occurs in three stages. The first is gestation/latency, in which some cue or triggering event indicates a potential problem. The second is categorization, in which managers become aware that something is wrong but cannot fully or clearly describe it. The third is diagnosis, which involves efforts to obtain the information that will provide greater certainty in problem definition.[18]

Often, symptoms clutter and confuse and make it difficult to recognize a problem and define its parameters. More experienced and expert managers tend to be better problem solvers because they have developed superior problem recognition and definition skills. Asking the right questions, recognizing limits, and being able to identify and interpret clues are skills gained only with experience.

Problem recognition and definition include gathering, systematically evaluating, and judging the importance of information from sources, such as routine reports and data, interviews and observation, information from workgroups, and customer feedback.[19] In this process, it is difficult to overestimate the importance of facts—information derived from consistently applied operational definitions.[20] An essential and difficult job for the problem solver is to distinguish facts from other types of information—again, a learned and honed ability that enables better problem solving.

In unstructured or complex situations, circumstantial evidence (evidence that requires reasoning or inference to prove a fact) and deductive reasoning (arguing from a general to a specific) are helpful. Exclusionary thinking may be used to "rule out" problems. Once conclusions are reached, the problem is classified by type, nature, and scope. The stage of problem recognition and definition is formative because subsequent actions, especially developing alternatives, are derived from it.[21] Ending the problem definition stage too soon is likely to result in a low-quality solution or solving the wrong problem.[22]

Problem Statement

The problem statement puts what is learned during the definition stage into a brief description of the problem to be solved and sets a direction. Almost always, one sentence is sufficient. Good problem statements have four parts: 1) an invitational stem, 2) an ownership component, 3) an action component, and 4) a goal component.[23] The following example of a problem statement has the four parts: In what ways can we improve system response time to reduce how long marketing analysts must wait for an answer to an inquiry?

- In what ways can (stem)

- we (ownership)

- improve system response time (action)

- to reduce how long marketing analysts must wait for an answer to an inquiry? (goal)[24]

The management position and responsibilities of the problem solver must be known if problem statements are to be understood. The same problem seen from the perspective of a chief nursing officer will be stated differently than if viewed from the perspective of a nursing unit supervisor, or that of a staff nurse. A problem-solving team must understand how views differ; care must be taken to resolve these differences before problem solving is undertaken. This reinforces the importance of the problem statement.

The invitational stem, "In what ways can," encourages a divergent response, unlike the more narrow "How can." *Divergent* means thinking in different directions or searching for a variety of answers to a question (problem) that may have many right answers.[25]

The problem statement should have other attributes too. Ideally, the problem definition phase has identified the root cause, which is reflected in the problem statement. If the problem statement reflects only a symptom, the problem must be "solved" repeatedly. A clinical simile is the symptomatic relief that aspirin gives flu sufferers; they feel better, but the cause is uncured. Sometimes the root cause of a problem cannot be determined, or even if the root cause is known, resources may be insufficient to solve it. Occasionally, it is politically infeasible to solve the root cause. There may be many reasons why addressing symptoms is the only realistic choice. Doing so, however, must be seen for what it is—a temporary, expedient solution.

The problem statement should be narrow enough that solving it is within the problem solver's authority, resource limits, and the like, but not so narrow that only symptoms are "treated." For example, some employees are taking too many coffee breaks. A narrow problem statement focuses on the employees. A somewhat broader problem statement addresses coffee breaks or breaks in general. An even broader problem statement, but one that is not too broad, identifies the efficient use of time or the quantity and assignment of work as the focus for action. Focusing on employees addresses only a symptom, not the root cause.

The breadth of the problem statement also determines the clarity of direction that is given the problem solver. A narrow problem statement identifies what problem must be solved, but risks addressing only a symptom. Overly broad problem statements may leave the problem solver without clear direction—no understanding of the first step. Sometimes problems are amorphous or lack specificity, especially as to knowing where to start. Organizational malaise or morale problems are amorphous. Here, problem solvers must cast their nets widely as they gather information and engage in several iterations of problem solving—from the broad to the narrower and specific—before the problem is identified and the correct focus is achieved. Iterative problem solving is also known as heuristic problem solving.

The psychological stimulus provided by an action-oriented problem statement must not be underestimated. Problem statements include positive goals but may also include limitations. The problem statement regarding coffee breaks described earlier could be stated as follows: In what ways can I (we) solve the problem of excessive coffee breaks by staff to maximize use of staff resources, but without damaging morale? Here, a limitation in selecting a solution is to not damage morale.

There is more than one correct way to state a problem, but doing it well requires thought and the patience to prepare more than one iteration. The importance of developing a problem statement lies in the discipline of reducing thoughts to writing and the advantages of a written document in communicating to others working to solve the problem. As the American educator John Dewey stated, "A question well put is half answered."[26] The admonition to "Stand there, don't just do something" until a suitable problem statement has been developed has more application than first blush might suggest.

Facts and Reasoning

A fact is defined as an actuality, certainty, reality, or truth. Facts are highly prized and provide the firmest grounding for problem solving and decision making. Some facts are objectively verifiable. Many "facts" are subject to dispute, however, unless they result from an operational definition. Deming stressed the critical importance of operational definitions.[27] Objectively verifiable facts, or facts based on the same operational definition, take precedence over all other types of information.

Once facts are identified, two other issues arise. One is the weight to be given to each. Some facts are more important than others, and those sharing problem-solving responsibilities must understand how the facts are weighted. A second issue is that facts are subject to judgment and interpretation. For example, a tape measure will gauge a room's dimensions. Whether the room is large enough for a certain activity or job is a matter of opinion. The fact that a room has seating does not answer the question of how comfortable the seating is. Decision makers must separate fact from conclusion (judgment), interpretation, and opinion. These *must* be kept separate.

Rarely are facts enough to solve a problem. Obtaining facts is necessarily constrained by time and resources. Problem solvers can partly overcome this deficit through inductive and deductive reasoning. *Inductive* reasoning moves from a single event or fact to a conclusion or generalization based on that event or fact. Inductive reasoning allows one to conclude that the fact of a painted wall means there was a painter. *Deductive* reasoning uses the facts of related or similar events to reach a conclusion. Deductive reasoning is employed in a criminal prosecution when circumstantial evidence is used to prove guilt, despite the lack of direct evidence, such as fingerprints or the testimony of a witness. Circumstantial evidence is based on inferences (deductions [deductive reasoning]) drawn from facts. A deduction from finding room after room with half-painted walls is that the work of the painter(s) is unfinished. Inductive and deductive reasoning are the logical processes used by problem solvers to make assumption(s) about a circumstance or situation. Because inductive reasoning is based on only one fact, it is less reliable than deductive reasoning and should carry less weight.

Often, problem solvers and decision makers must consider the weight, if any, to give information that is hearsay, rumor, or assertion. Hearsay is words (or writings) attributed to a third party. With some exceptions, hearsay is not admissible in court proceedings. Similarly, decision makers should learn to identify hearsay and give it little or no weight. As in all organizations, rumors abound in HSOs/HSs; many will come to the notice of decision makers. Rumors, too, should be given little weight. Assertions may be based on fact, hearsay, or rumor. Assertions may be stated forcefully and with a degree of authority that makes them seem credible. Only assertions, or preferably put, conclusions, based on facts are credible.

Hearsay and rumor may have an element of truth and, thus, are important to the extent they suggest potential problems that warrant further investigation. In themselves, hearsay and rumor should never be a basis for decision making. Persons who make assertions must be asked to show how the assertions are supported by facts. Absent facts, assertions should be given little or no weight by decision makers or problem solvers.

Developing Assumptions [2]

The problem statement developed in problem analysis [1] is the focus of the next step, developing assumptions [2]. Assumptions do not take the place of facts. When facts are insufficient, however, problem solvers use the logic of inductive and deductive reasoning to make assumptions. Only in the most unusual circumstances should problem solvers make assumptions unsupported by logic, because doing so means the assumptions were selected capriciously—certainly not a basis for good management. Assumptions are based on extending what is known. For example, if every time a nurse is disciplined, flyers are distributed that urge nurses to unionize, deductive reasoning tells us that the same thing is likely to happen next time a nurse is disciplined. This, then, is a fact-based, logical assumption.

Assumptions have a significant effect on the choice and quality of the solution and, as a result, on the quality of problem solving. There are three types of assumptions: structural, personal, and problem centered.[28] Table 6.1 summarizes their attributes.

Structural assumptions relate to the context of the problem—they are boundary assumptions: The problem lies within (or outside) a manager's authority, additional resources are (or are not) available to solve the problem, other departments cause the problem, or the problem is caused by uncontrollable external factors (for example, high unemployment in the service area means fewer people have employer-based health insurance to pay for elective procedures).

Personal assumptions are about the decision maker—conclusions and biases the decision maker bring to the problem. Often, they are based on experience. Managers may have a high or low tolerance for risk and the uncertainty inherent in changes that invariably result from problem solving. A manager's experience of being blamed for problems caused by changes after problem solving may cause an aversion to risk—this may lead to making assumptions about the problem or alternatives that cause selection of low-risk solutions. Assumptions may be made about the likely reactions of superiors, subordinates, or stakeholders to potential solutions.

Table 6.1.   Attributes of the three types of assumptions

Assumptions	Attributes
Structural	Relate to context of problem—boundary assumptions
	Within (outside) manager's authority
	Additional resources are (are not) available
	Other departments cause problem
	Problem caused by uncontrollable external factor(s)
Personal	Conclusions and biases decision makers bring to problem
	Risk taker; risk averse
	Likely reactions of superiors, subordinates, stakeholders
	Anchoring—adjustments from past starting point
	Escalating commitment—unwilling to admit past mistakes
	Confirmation bias—notice more, give greater weight, or seek evidence that confirms a claim/position
Problem Centered	Perceived relative importance of problem
	Degree of risk from problem
	How urgently solution is needed
	Economic cost and benefit
	Political cost and benefit
	Degree to which subordinates or superiors will accept solution
	Likelihood of success if solution implemented

In addition to risk taking and other types of experiences that cause bias in the decision maker, the personal assumptions identified as "anchoring" and "escalating commitment" can affect problem solving. Anchoring occurs when the individual "chooses a starting point (an 'anchor'), perhaps from past data, and then adjusts from the anchor based on new information."[29] Using last year's budget as a starting point for this year's budget is an example of anchoring—it assumes expenditures last year were appropriate, and the budget for this year simply adds to them. Contrast this with zero-base budgeting, which starts at zero, and all elements of the new budget must be justified. An inaccurate anchor causes flawed analysis. Regardless, "decision makers display a strong bias toward alternatives that perpetuate the status quo."[30]

Escalating commitment occurs when a manager is unwilling to admit earlier mistakes. A manager whose decisions have become a problem will "tend to be locked into a previously chosen course of action."[31] The tendency of decision makers to make decisions that justify past choices has also been described as the "sunk-cost trap," meaning previous investments of time and resources cannot be recovered, but further commitments are made because managers cannot admit past mistakes.[32] Decision makers must be aware of confirmation bias—the inclination to "notice more, assign more weight to, and actively seek out evidence that confirms their claims."[33] Confirmation bias tends to ignore or avoid seeking evidence that might dispute the decision maker's position. Confirmation bias affects physicians[34]; it is a continuing problem in corporate decision making.[35]

Problem-centered assumptions cover a wide range, including perceived relative importance of the problem, degree of risk posed by the problem, and how urgently a solution is needed. Other problem-centered assumptions include economic and political costs and benefits, the degree to which subordinates or superiors will accept solutions, and the likelihood of success if a solution is implemented.

It is important to emphasize that the three types of assumptions affect the decision maker and the problem-solving process differently. The three types of assumptions differ in at least two ways: qualitatively, and in the amount of control decision makers have over them. For example, a structural assumption that no funds are available to solve a problem will profoundly affect solutions that can be considered; there may be little or nothing the decision maker can do to remedy the lack of funds. A personal assumption that the decision maker is averse to risk can be overcome to some extent, even though the decision maker remains less willing to accept certain solutions or may continue to be reluctant to experience higher levels of discomfort. Problem-centered assumptions likely involve more judgment, which is often based on the decision maker's experience, hunch, or intuition, than are structural assumptions.

In summary, making assumptions is necessary for almost all problem solving. Decision makers must be cautious in formulating and accepting assumptions. Poorly formulated assumptions limit the scope of problem solving or may even preclude identifying the best solution.[36]

Identifying Tentative Alternative Solutions [3]

After the manager has recognized, defined, and analyzed the problem; established its cause(s) and parameters; prepared a problem statement [1]; and made assumptions [2], tentative alternative solutions are developed [3]. In Figure 6.5, this step includes identifying tentative alternative solutions [3a], collecting data/information, if necessary [3b], and evaluating the merits of each tentative alternative [3c] for an initial accept–reject decision. The initial accept–reject decision uses general criteria, such as whether the tentative solution is unethical or illegal; is inconsistent with organizational values, mission, vision, and culture; has unacceptable financial or political costs; or is infeasible. If a tentative alternative meets any of these general negative criteria, it must be discarded. Unique, nontraditional, and creative tentative solutions are identified more readily if structural, personal, and problem-centered assumptions are not overly restrictive.

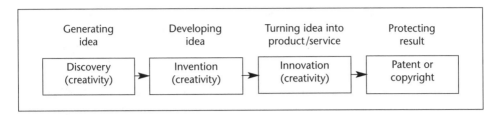

Figure 6.6. Differentiation of discovery/invention/innovation. (Adapted from Cougar, Daniel J. *Creative Problem Solving and Opportunity Finding*, 18. Danvers, MA: Boyd & Fraser, 1995; reprinted by permission.)

Identifying tentative solutions is important. It consumes more resources than other parts of problem solving. If creativity is to occur, it must occur here[37]; creativity is desirable.[38] Although often used synonymously, *creativity*—defined as imagination and ingenuity—should be distinguished from the narrower concept of *innovation*—defined as changing or altering to develop something new.[39] Figure 6.6 shows this distinction.

Several categories or tactics that can be used to identify ideas for solutions have been described.[40] Most do not suggest creativity. "Ready-made" tactics assume organizations have a store of ready-made solutions—solutions waiting for problems. "Search" tactics develop solutions from available ideas. Proposals are elicited and compared to select solutions that seem viable. A "design" tactic seeks a custom-made solution—an opportunity for creativity.

Several factors influence the time and resources devoted to the tentative alternative solution loop. Most important are the quality and precision of the initial problem definition and the restrictiveness of assumptions. Others include sophistication of the HSO's/HS's information systems, availability of data, and the degree to which the problem is structured. Unstructured problems are more complex, involve many variables, and take longer to solve than problems that are straightforward, relatively obvious, or narrowly defined. Typically, unstructured problems require several iterations of problem solving.

The tentative alternative solution loop has two hazards. Some managers spend excessive time and resources seeking optimal solutions when other solutions are acceptable—the best becomes the enemy of the good. In addition, extensive attention to activities in the loop and reiteration may be excuses for not acting. "I need more information" may be an excuse to procrastinate and make no decision.[41]

Developing and Applying Decision Criteria [4]

Alternatives that meet the general criteria applied in the tentative alternative solution loop [3] are ready for formal assessment. To select the best alternative solution, managers must develop decision criteria that allow solutions to be evaluated and compared [4]. Decision criteria include those in the desired outcomes cell in the center of Figure 6.5: individual and organizational work results, objectives, standards, and expectations. At least three other decision criteria are usually applied: effectiveness of the alternative in solving the problem, feasibility of implementation, and acceptability of the alternative based on objective and subjective analyses.[42]

Alternatives that do not solve the problem are rejected. Examples are those that solve only part of a problem, address only symptoms, or are not permanent. Exceptions may be necessary, however. For example, if need for action is critical, it may be appropriate to select and implement a less-than-optimal solution because the consequences of doing nothing or waiting for a better solution are worse.

The feasibility of implementing an alternative is the second common decision criterion. Infeasible alternatives should have been rejected in the tentative alternative solution loop. Those that survive may be implemented to varying degrees in terms of effort; structural boundaries and constraints; dependence on other people, departments, or both; and costs. Managers are less likely to select an alternative that depends on people and departments beyond their control. This is especially true if high political costs are associated with forcing implementation.

The third common criterion judges the effective use of resources through quantitative (objective) cost–benefit analysis and assessment of nonquantitative (subjective) advantages and disadvantages. Lowest cost should be but one criterion—costs and benefits of alternatives must be considered, as should the opportunity costs of doing nothing. *Objective evaluation* means quantifying costs and benefits; it should be attempted despite the difficulty of estimating some data. *Subjective evaluation* means understanding advantages and disadvantages that may be very difficult to quantify but cannot be ignored. Both types should be considered when evaluating and comparing alternatives. If an alternative is costly, but the problem solver concludes that subjective considerations are more important, a rational decision has been made. Here, it might be useful to list nonquantitative advantages and disadvantages, which will add the useful dimension of subjective judgment to the decision-making process.

Some decision criteria are likely to be more important than others; several methods may be used to differentiate them. One method ranks decision criteria using decision-maker judgments. Another method divides criteria into "mandatory" (must be met) and "wanted." A solution that does not meet a mandatory criterion is discarded. Wanted criteria are weighted by degree of desirability. The resulting weighted scores determine which solution is selected.[43] A third method assumes all decision criteria are equally important (which is unlikely) and judges how closely or well each alternative meets them and assigns a numerical value. The alternative chosen has the highest total. A decision matrix, as shown in Table 6.2, is a tool to array and compare decision criteria and solutions. The virtues of numerically weighting decision criteria include forcing decision makers to compare and evaluate the criteria and providing a basis for discussion in group decision making. It is important that the numbers are understood to result from judgments by decision makers—judgments that could be challenged. This subjectivity means the numbers are approximations. This must be borne in mind during analysis.

As noted earlier, this step is sometimes called decision analysis. Most often, decision makers have several alternative solutions that can be used; it is a matter of determining which

Table 6.2. Decision matrix from evaluating alternative solution[a]

Decision criteria	Alternative solution 1	Alternative solution 2	Alternative solution 3
Must meet these requirements			
1. Solution effectively solves the problem	3	5	5
2. Feasibility of implementation	5	3	5
3. Cost–benefit analysis	5	5	3
4. Advantage–disadvantage analysis	3	3	5
Want to meet these requirements			
5. Political acceptability	1	3	3
6. Criticalness	1	3	5
7. Time frame	1	3	5
8. Opportunity costs	5	1	3
9. Monetary costs	3	5	5
Total score	27	31	39

Conclusion: Alternative solution 3 accepted.

[a]Key: 5 = Solution *fully* meets decision criterion. 3 = Solution *partially* meets decision criterion. 1 = Solution *fails* to meet decision criterion.

Adapted from Arnold, John D. *The Complete Problem Solver: A Total System for Competitive Decision Making*, 62. New York: John Wiley & Sons, 1992.

one best (fully or partially) meets the decision criteria. There are, however, other variations of decision analysis. Sometimes, there is only one solution, and a yes/no, accept/reject decision must be made. Here, the analysis compares the proposed solution to a reasonable (perhaps idealized) model of what could or should be done, to determine if the solution is acceptable. At other times, there are no alternatives, and the decision maker must decide how to accomplish a desired result. Here, the first step is to define objectives and then select components that will most feasibly and effectively meet those objectives.[44]

Selecting, Implementing, and Evaluating the Alternative Solution [5, 6, and 7]

Almost always, a manager selects an alternative (makes a decision) [5]. This does not end the problem-solving process, however. Implementation [6] and evaluation [7] must be planned. Implementation [6] usually requires resources. The effects of the intervention (change) that was implemented must be evaluated (monitored) [7] to determine if they are consistent with the desired results [1]—the problem has been solved. Effective implementation and evaluation require prospectively determining who will do what, how, and in what time frame. It is desirable for evaluation to be integral (built into) implementation. Data collection must be specific, especially as to where in the organization intervention will occur and with whom responsibility lies.

Evaluation is an often-neglected part of problem solving—busy managers assume that the solution selected and implemented will be effective, and they turn to solving other problems. The solution, however, may solve the problem completely, partially, or not at all. A solution's effectiveness can only be known if data are collected.

If the problem is not solved, the problem-solving process begins again, perhaps by fine tuning the alternative implemented, reconsidering alternatives previously rejected, or developing new alternatives. Furthermore, solving one problem often causes others. For example, increased average length of stay in an acute care hospital paid by diagnosis-related groups may reduce total revenue, inefficiently use nurse resources, and unnecessarily use support services for patients who could have been discharged to post–acute care services, such as home health. This ripple effect will lead to new rounds of problem solving.

Implications for the Health Services Manager

Health services managers are responsible for problem solving. When problem solving is done well, allocation of resources and their efficient consumption are superior, and results are more consistent with those desired. Managers' skills in problem solving, including decision making, are directly reflected in the quality of solutions and interventions.

Influencing Problem Solving and Decision Making

Problem solving and decision making do not occur in a vacuum; many factors shape how they are performed, the style that is used, and the outcome. Figure 6.7 shows three sets of factors: 1) attributes of the problem solver, 2) nature of the situation, and 3) characteristics of the environment.[45] These affect all steps of problem solving and decision making.

Attributes of the Problem Solver

Experience, Knowledge, and Judgment

Among the most important attributes affecting problem solving are the decision maker's experience, knowledge, and judgment. A trained and experienced clinical staff is essential to high-quality patient care, and these attributes are recognized by licensing and certification. Health services managers are formally educated in graduate programs and informally educated through continuing education and in-service training. Their education is tempered and tested

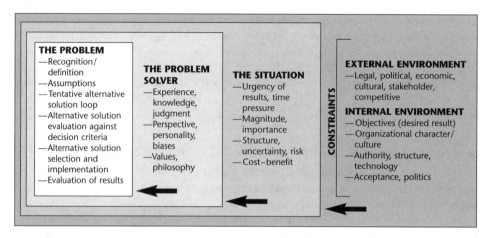

Figure 6.7. Factors influencing problem solving and decision making.

in administrative residencies and by the experience gained, especially in the first several years of work. Knowledge and experience are insufficient, however. Sound judgment must be added to achieve effective problem solving. Sometimes, intuition and hunch are important.[46]

Perspective, Personality, and Biases

The problem solver's perspective and personality influence problem solving and decision making. Decision-maker biases were discussed in the section on assumptions, but they warrant further attention.

Perspective determines how the problem solver views a problem or situation. Problem solvers with narrow perspectives (tunnel vision) and those who think vertically rather than horizontally approach problems differently and are likely to make lower-quality decisions.[47] Vertical thinking is logical and seeks solutions using existing knowledge or ideas. It is unlikely to involve much risk. Horizontal thinking is creative and generates ideas in new directions. The best results combine vertical and horizontal thinking.[48] The conclusions and biases discussed earlier in the section on personal assumptions are extensions of perspective, which is the manager's general outlook or worldview—their *Weltanschauung*. Similarly, biases affect problem solving, and making assumptions allows decision makers to understand their effect on specific situations.

Individual qualities, such as humor, aggressiveness, self-centeredness, self-assurance, and self-confidence, as well as someone's demeanor (introvert or extrovert) and tolerance for risk, change, uncertainty, or instability all influence how managers solve problems and the quality of their decisions. Nonassertive, procrastinating people who are risk averse and fear change will likely make assumptions or select solutions that limit the range of problem solving.

Such managers are less creative in the tentative alternative solution loop, stay in it longer as they search for the best solution (or implicitly hope the problem will dissipate), and compromise or choose less bold solutions. Often, they are reactive and must be forced to act. Conversely, proactive people take the initiative, anticipate problems, manage events rather than being managed by them, and get the job done. This type of manager is more inclined to make difficult, bold, progressive, or nontraditional decisions that include higher levels of risk.

Values and Philosophy

One's value system and personal ethic influence problem solving by affecting problem definition, formulation of assumptions, and selection of acceptable alternatives. For example, solutions inconsistent with the problem solver's value system will likely be excluded. Managers whose value system is ego centered are likely to select solutions that are short-term and self-serving, but may be inconsistent with, or even detrimental to, the long-term goals of the HSO/HS. A manager's value system includes views on politics and policy issues, as well as leadership and motivation. Effective problem solvers have a clear understanding of their personal ethic and the values from which that ethic is derived. Chapter 2 discusses the personal ethic.

Nature of the Situation

The circumstances and facts of a problem influence the problem-solving process and outcome. Those identified in Figure 6.7 are the urgency of results and time pressure; magnitude and importance of the problem; degree of structure, uncertainty, and risk; and costs versus benefits.

Urgency of Results and Time Pressure

Sometimes, immediate decisions are required. Trauma or medical crises are examples. Another clinical example was the sudden surge in demand for acute care services in 2020 from the COVID-19 (severe acute respiratory syndrome coronavirus 2 [SARS-CoV-2]) pandemic. An impending work stoppage, a major initiative by a competitor, or too little cash to meet payroll require quick action because such problems have major negative consequences. They necessitate rapid use of the tentative alternative solution loop and a less thorough evaluation process. In situations with little time pressure, such as problem solving under conditions of opportunity, noncrisis deviation, or improvement, problem solvers use a decision style that involves consultation, collecting more information, and thoroughly evaluating alternatives.

Magnitude and Importance

The problem's magnitude and importance directly affect the time, energy, and resources spent in assessing it and making a decision. For example, because of their greater effect administrative decisions warrant greater attention and more intense evaluation than operational decisions. Major resource commitment and opportunity costs of delay are other measures of importance.

Problems with high cost or resource commitment (e.g., those addressed under conditions of opportunity or improvement) justify spending more time and collecting more information in the tentative alternative solution loop than do low-cost problems. The same is true for unstructured problems. A potential hazard for managers is that resources such as time consumed to find the best solution may approach or exceed the cost consequences of the problem. It is senseless to spend $15,000 of staff time for feasibility studies and collection of nonroutine data to solve an equipment storage problem when unneeded equipment can be sold or stored off-site. Obviously, the cost of developing alternatives must not exceed the benefits of the one selected. Conversely, a freestanding HSO in financial distress would appropriately spend more time and resources evaluating an acquisition offer by an HS.

Structure, Uncertainty, and Risk

From a problem-solving perspective, structure is the clarity of the situation—the degree to which the scope and nature of the problem and alternatives are precise.[49] Ends–means, administrative, and nonprogrammable decision situations are less structured than are operational or programmable situations. Problems regarding equipment and supplies, job design, and process flow are more structured than are those with behavioral dynamics or with external stakeholders and competitors. Risk is a function of certainty. A problem that is certain is one for which the manager has complete information and can predict the outcomes of alternative solutions. Less information means greater risk because even carefully derived estimates have some uncertainty. For example, the likelihood of negative results is almost 100% if mismatched blood is transfused. Certainty is less than 100% if the problem-solving process finds that establishing a freestanding family practice center will provide inpatient referrals to a hospital. Unstructured and uncertain situations require more time and resources, and it is likely that a participative problem-solving and decision-making process will be used.

Cost–Benefit

Ultimately, problem solving means choosing an alternative derived from quantitative cost–benefit or nonquantitative advantage–disadvantage criteria, or both. Many problems are suited to cost–benefit analysis: What equipment most improves productivity and decreases patient waiting time? Which new service will enhance revenue? Will more nursing staff (cost) decrease length of stay (benefit)? Sometimes costs and benefits cannot be measured, or nonquantitative criteria may be more important. An alternative should be chosen only after using both quantitative and nonquantitative decision criteria. Excluding either diminishes the quality of the decision.

Characteristics of the Environment

The HSO/HS environment influences problem solving by imposing variables management is unable to control. This affects the feasibility of alternatives and constrains implementation of the solution.

External

Policy, political, economic, cultural, stakeholder, competitive, and similar external forces are ubiquitous. A requirement to obtain a certificate-of-need for facility expansion or a new service constrains alternatives. High local unemployment with loss of employer-paid health insurance diminishes revenue and increases bad debt. Unfunded federal mandates and regulations constrain HSs with a managed care component or a hospital with an emergency department. Changes in Medicare and Medicaid reimbursement limit acquisition of technology and equipment.

Internal

The HSO's/HS's internal environment affects problem solving. Organizational objectives restrict which alternatives can be considered. Influential but less precise is the organization's character/culture—embedded and permeating values and beliefs. An organization's culture may be creative or traditional, assertive or restrained, proactive or reactive, friendly or distant. Such characteristics influence problem solving. Managers in a reactive, tradition-bound culture are less likely to select bold solutions. Similarly, managers in an action-oriented culture tend to act more quickly, with less preparation. Solutions inconsistent with the organization's character and culture are almost certain to fail.

As managers apply decision criteria, they must consider implementation, which is affected by factors ranging from resource availability to organizational commitment. Notable factors are authority, structure, and technology. An alternative whose implementation is beyond the scope of the manager's authority is likely infeasible. The president of the professional staff organization has no authority to change the HSO/HS electronic health records system; the CEO cannot discharge a patient.

Organizational configuration (structure) may make implementing an alternative infeasible; absence of a technology may eliminate others. Physical plant layout may preclude changing patient flow, changing the supply chain may be constrained by union contracts, or the inpatient health records software may be incompatible with the system in the emergency department.

Another factor necessary to successfully implementing an alternative is acceptance by superiors, peers, and subordinates. A decision to decrease inpatient length of stay by reducing turnaround time for diagnostic testing will be difficult to implement if those interpreting tests are resistant. Involving others in problem solving is influenced by how important their acceptance to implementation is. Organizational politics affect problem solving. The informal influence, conflict, and competition among factions may cause a manager to negotiate, collaborate, compromise, or "satisfice" (find a workable, if imperfect, solution) when solving problems.

Implications for the Health Services Manager

Problem-solver attributes, the nature of the situation, and the environment influence how problem solving is done, the time and resources used, and the quality of the decision. These influences are not mutually exclusive; one may supersede or preempt others. A crisis can force the manager who usually seeks input, develops a range of alternatives, and does extensive evaluation to act quickly and unilaterally.

Health services managers should be sensitive to factors that affect problem solving, change methods as needed, modify and mitigate detrimental influences if possible, and learn to cope with factors that cannot be changed. Doing so will improve their problem solving.

Unilateral and Group Problem Solving

In meeting their accountability for resource allocation and utilization, managers may solve problems and make decisions unilaterally, or they may involve superiors, peers, or subordinates on a continuum from minimal or consultative to group participation. Both have advantages and disadvantages. Consultative problem solving is intraorganizational in a freestanding HSO and interorganizational in an HS. Chapter 2 discusses ethical aspects of problem solving and decision making.

Unilateral problem solving is efficient; group problem solving increases overhead costs.[50] Unilateral action avoids "groupthink" and "risky shift," which are negative aspects of group problem solving. Anchoring, escalating commitment, and confirmation bias are more likely in unilateral than group decision making, however.

Groups exert social pressure to conform and concur with decisions; this can result in group conformity. Groupthink occurs when team members discount warnings about what others (competitors) may do, fail to examine critical and underlying assumptions, stereotype others, put heavy pressure on dissenters, self-censor, share an illusion of unanimity, and stop the flow of information contrary to the group's position through self-appointed "mind-guards."[51] Others have observed that "groupthink has been a primary cause of major corporate and public-policy debacles. Although it may seem counterintuitive . . . the teams that engaged in healthy conflict over issues not only made better decisions but moved more quickly, as well."[52] The Watergate political scandal of the 1970s is a classic example of political groupthink.[53]

A hazard of group problem solving is risky shift, which occurs because the diffused responsibility of a group encourages accepting riskier decisions than would be acceptable if one person were responsible for a decision.[54]

Generally, group problem solving produces better-quality solutions. The reasons are numerous. Multiple perspectives and more information and experience are brought to bear. Knowledgeable staff, especially subordinates, can help define a problem and identify tentative alternative solutions. Involving staff with process knowledge is essential to successful quality improvement (QI). Group problem solving results in consideration of more alternatives because overly restrictive assumptions will be challenged. Further, involving others enhances acceptance and facilitates implementation because those involved take ownership and are usually more committed to implementation. Finally, group problem solving improves communication and coordination because those involved in implementation have greater knowledge about the solution and the process that produced it.

The benefits of employee participation in problem solving and decision making are well documented in the behavioral science literature. Involved employees identify with HSOs/HSs and their actions. Kaluzny's model of involvement and commitment has two foci useful in QI.[55] First, senior managers must rethink problem solving to increase the role, responsibility, and authority of middle managers. Second, middle managers must rethink superior–subordinate relationships because more staff participation in complex decisions adds expertise, facilitates work unit performance, and enhances commitment to the organization.[56]

Group Problem Solving and Quality Improvement

Certain conditions must exist if group problem solving in QI is to be effective. First, a climate of openness must permit free expression of ideas; the focus must be finding solutions, not finding fault.[57] Second, participation must be legitimate—subordinates involved in problem solving must believe managers are interested in the group's reasonable recommendations. This is called empowering—subordinates influence decisions.[58] Problem solving based on staff expertise about their work will produce better solutions; greater employee involvement and commitment to the HSO/HS will lead to higher motivation, morale, and job satisfaction.[59] Given the opportunity, employees can and do contribute significantly to solving problems.

Quality Circles

A failed group problem-solving method with significant promise for improving productivity and quality in health services delivery was quality circles, which were common in hospital nursing services. A quality circle is an informal, parallel structure established to involve staff in problem solving. Parallel structures are separate from an organization's normal activities and operate in a unique way. In quality circle programs, groups are composed of volunteers from a work area who meet with a leader and/or facilitator to examine productivity and quality problems.[60]

An effective quality circle program requires that senior management is committed to the process and its outcomes. Staff time and training in problem solving are needed; management must act on suitable recommendations. Quality circles failed because management made no commitment to them, which suggested that staff efforts were unimportant and a waste of time.

Other Group Formats

Ad hoc task forces may be formed to solve major organization-wide problems or unstructured problems under conditions of opportunity or threat. Focus group teams[61] or QI teams can be used too. QI teams may be departmental or cross-functional. As their name suggests, departmental teams improve intradepartmental processes. Cross-functional teams improve processes or undertake other QI initiatives that may span the organization and hierarchical levels. Chapter 8 details QI teams. Finally, managers should encourage ad hoc problem solving by subordinates and assist them, as needed. This may involve one or more managerial subordinates in a group, but it need not be formalized, as are QI teams.

Problem-Solving and Decision-Making Styles

The manager's problem-solving and decision-making styles may involve individuals or groups. The style used is influenced by the problem's nature and importance, how clearly it can be defined, and if acceptance by organization members is key to implementation.

Involving Others—a Conceptual Model

A conceptual model of problem-solving and decision-making styles developed by Vroom helps determine the degree and conditions of subordinate involvement.[62] The five problem-solving and decision-making styles in Table 6.3 specify subordinate involvement; they are applicable to peers and superiors too. Each uses a different degree of involvement.[63] Style AI is unilateral (autocratic)—subordinates are not involved in predecision assessment or choosing the solution. AII is a variant of AI—subordinates only provide information. Managers using consultative styles CI or CII elicit and consider subordinates' opinions. GII is a group style that involves subordinates; the manager accepts the group's decision. Managers must decide if the quality of a decision and its acceptance by subordinates will be enhanced by group problem solving.

Table 6.3. Management problem-solving and decision-making styles

AI	The manager solves the problem or makes the decision unilaterally, using information available at that time.
AII	The manager obtains necessary information from subordinate(s), then develops and selects the solution unilaterally. Subordinates may or may not be told what the problem is when the manager gets information from them. Subordinates provide necessary information rather than generating or evaluating alternative solutions.
CI	The manager shares the problem with relevant subordinates individually, getting their ideas and suggestions without bringing them together. The manager's decision may or may not reflect the subordinates' contribution.
CII	The manager shares the problem with subordinates as a group, obtains their ideas and suggestions, and then makes the decision that may or may not reflect the subordinates' contribution.
GII	The manager shares the problem with subordinates as a group. Together they generate and evaluate alternatives and attempt to reach agreement (consensus) on a solution. The manager's role is much like that of chairperson—not trying to influence the group to adopt a particular solution. The manager is willing to accept and implement any solution supported by the group.

Situational Variables (Problem Attributes)

The situational variables influencing style are characterized by the seven different problem attributes (a–g) at the top of Figure 6.8. The problem-solving style outcomes in Figure 6.8 are identified by capital letters: AI, AII, CI, CII, and GII. The first four problem attributes, a–d, denote the importance of decision quality and acceptance by subordinates. The last three attributes, e–g, moderate the effects of subordinates' participation on quality and acceptance (a–d). The seven problem attributes in Figure 6.8 are used in Table 6.4, with diagnostic questions using yes-or-no answers.

Situations and Styles

Answers to diagnostic questions for the seven problem attributes in Table 6.4 produce 14 possible situations shown as 1–14 in Figure 6.8. Each is linked to the appropriate problem-solving/decision-making style, AI–GII. Vroom assumes managers wish to minimize the time needed to solve a problem; thus, each style is the most restrictive for that set of problem attributes. For example, a manager with Situation 1 could use Styles AII, CI, CII, or GII, but they require more time. Therefore, the problem attributes suggest AI is appropriate; it saves time compared with less restrictive styles.

Using the Model

A manager assesses the situation using problem attributes a–g and answering yes or no to the questions. The model identifies the most appropriate decision style (AI–GII). The following discussion analyzes the branching for Situations 1, 2, 3, 11, 12, 13, and 14 to show how managers could use the model.

Situations 1, 2, and 3

Situations 1, 2, and 3 assume there is no decision quality requirement [a]. The presence of several obvious, relatively meritorious alternatives suggests the decision maker has enough information [b] to solve the problem unilaterally. Thus, the problem must be structured [c]. If subordinates' acceptance of the decision is not critical to implementation [d], the manager is correct to use unilateral Style AI for Situation 1 (1-AI in Figure 6.8). If subordinate acceptance is critical to implementation, Attribute e is evaluated. If subordinates are likely to accept the unilateral decision, the manager can use Style AI for Situation 2 (2-AI in Figure 6.8).

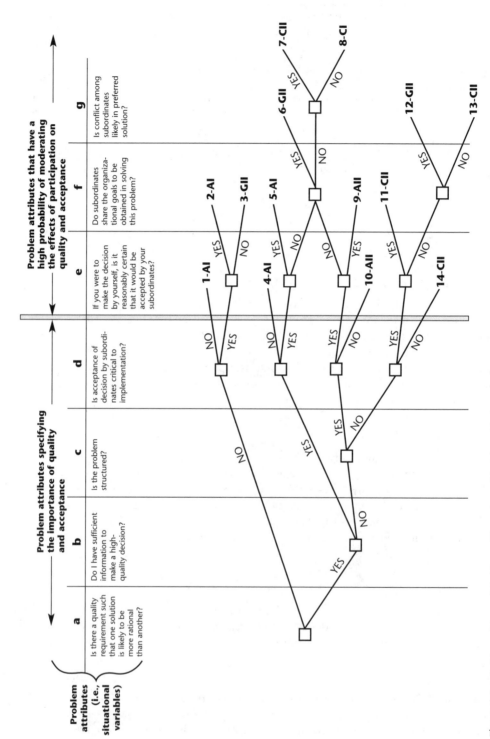

Figure 6.8. Problem-solving and decision-making style model. (Adapted from Vroom, Victor H. "A New Look at Managerial Decision Making." *Organizational Dynamics* 1 [Spring 1973]: 66–80; reprinted by permission from Elsevier. © 1973. American Management Association, New York. All rights reserved.)

Table 6.4. Problem attributes used in the problem-solving and decision-making style model (Figure 6.7)

Problem attributes	Diagnostic questions
a. Importance of the quality of the decision	Is quality requirement such that one solution is likely to be more rational (better) than another? (Another way of discerning the quality is: If the alternatives are *not* equally meritorious—some are or can be much better than others—there is a quality requirement.)
b. Extent to which the decision maker possesses sufficient information/expertise to make a high-quality decision unilaterally	Do I have sufficient information to make a high-quality decision?
c. Extent to which problem is structured	Is problem structured? (Does decision maker know what information is needed and where to find it?)
d. Extent to which acceptance or commitment of subordinates is critical to effective implementation	Is acceptance of decision by subordinates critical to effective implementation?
e. Prior probability that a unilateral decision will receive acceptance by subordinates	If decision is made unilaterally, will it probably be accepted by subordinates?
f. Extent to which subordinates are motivated to attain organizational goals as represented in objectives explicit in statement of problem	Do subordinates share organizational goals to be obtained in solving problems?
g. Extent to which subordinates are likely to be in conflict over preferred solutions	Is conflict among subordinates likely to occur in preferred solutions?

Adapted from Vroom, Victor H. "A New Look at Managerial Decision Making." *Organizational Dynamics* 1 (Spring 1973): 66–80; reprinted by permission from Elsevier. © 1973. American Management Association, New York. All rights reserved.

If subordinates are unlikely to accept the manager's decision, as in Situation 3, Style GII is appropriate (3-GII in Figure 6.8) because participation increases acceptance. Also, the manager is indifferent as to which alternative solution is chosen. There is no quality requirement; all are relatively meritorious [a].

Situations 11, 12, 13, and 14
Situations 11, 12, 13, and 14 assume there is a quality requirement [a]; alternatives are not equally acceptable because one is more rational. Situations 11, 12, 13, and 14 assume the manager has insufficient information to make a high-quality decision [b], and the problem is not structured [c].

If the attribute of subordinate acceptance [d] is critical to implementation, the manager determines if subordinates would be likely to accept a unilateral decision [e]. If subordinates would accept a unilateral decision, Style CII is appropriate for Situation 11 (11-CII in Figure 6.8). If subordinates are unlikely to accept a unilateral decision (i.e., the answer to Attribute e is no), the manager assesses whether subordinates share the organizational goals met by solving the problem—Attribute f. If the answer is yes, Style GII is appropriate (12-GII in Figure 6.8). Group involvement is appropriate because the acceptance critical to implementing the alternative is enhanced. Because all participants have the same goal, the group cannot make a decision that is different from the decision the manager would have made. However, if the answer to Attribute f is no (i.e., subordinates do not share the organizational goals met by solving the problem), Style CII is appropriate for Situation 13 (13-CII in Figure 6.8).

If the attribute of subordinate acceptance [d] is not critical to implementation, the consultative Style CII is appropriate for Situation 14 (14-CII in Figure 6.8). Here, sharing the problem with subordinates and obtaining their ideas and suggestions provide information the manager needs, yet the decision made need not reflect subordinates' influence.

Implications for the Health Services Manager

The problem-solving and decision-making style model in Figure 6.8 is an algorithm to assist in selecting the decision style appropriate for different conditions. Although linked here to the degree of subordinates' involvement in problem solving, the same model can be used in analyses of peer or superior involvement. In addition, it is important to remember that individual, situational, and environmental variables influence decision style. Vroom's model is a systematic way to determine the involvement of others in decision making and how that involvement affects the quality of the solution and the success of implementation.

Discussion Questions

1. Explain why decision making is integral to the management functions. Identify the three managerial decision classifications; give examples of each.

2. What conditions initiate problem solving? Discuss how problem solving under the condition of improvement is related to problem solving under the condition of opportunity.

3. How are problem solving and decision making related? What predecision and postdecision activities are inherent in problem solving? What are the steps of problem solving?

4. Using the problem-solving process model in Figure 6.4, discuss and give examples of the following: How assumptions affect problem solving. Positive and negative results that can occur in the tentative alternative solution loop. The importance of quantitative *and* nonquantitative criteria when evaluating and choosing an alternative.

5. Distinguish facts from assumptions. Give examples of inductive and deductive reasoning in making assumptions.

6. Identify factors that influence problem solving. Describe three situations; indicate which factors were influential in shaping the outcomes.

7. Identify advantages of group problem solving. List reasons why it is critical to the success of organization-wide QI. Describe a situation from your experience in which groupthink occurred.

8. Identify types of problem-solving and decision-making styles. Use Figure 6.8 and Table 6.4 to describe situations that show the following decision-making styles: AI, CI, and GII.

Case Study 1   The Nursing Assistant

You are the supervisor on the day shift at a 100-bed nursing facility. In one 20-bed unit, the workload relative to other units has been very heavy for the past month. In that unit, you observed family members of a bed-bound resident turning the resident. When you asked why they were doing that, one family member said, "Nursing assistant Johnson told us the staff is too busy. If we want our father turned, we have to do it ourselves or wait 3 or 4 hours before the staff can help." On several occasions in the past week, you saw nursing assistant Johnson sitting in the utility room for what seemed to be long periods of time.

Questions

1. Identify the facts in this case.

2. State the problem.

3. Make assumptions of the three types described in the chapter. List them in order of declining certainty.

4. Develop five solutions that should be considered. Which one should be chosen? Why?

Case Study 2   The New Charge Nurse

You are a third-shift (11:00 p.m. to 7:00 a.m.) nurse supervisor to whom several charge nurses report. Each charge nurse is responsible for a nursing unit. Six months ago, you promoted Sally Besnick to be one of the charge nurses. Six months before she was promoted, Besnick had earned a bachelor of science in nursing (B.S.N.) from an out-of-state university. She is the same age as the five registered nurses (RNs) she supervises, all of whom graduated from a two-year associate of arts (A.A.) nursing degree program at a local technical college. B.S.N. programs are generally considered the "gold standard" of nursing preparation. Sally is the only charge nurse with a B.S.N. who reports to you.

Besnick received the same in-service training in supervision as the other charge nurses, but there are major problems on her unit. Morale among her nursing staff is low, absenteeism is high, and not all administrative work on her unit is getting done. There are no indications that the quality of care on her unit is below acceptable levels, however. You think Besnick's main difficulty is that she cannot control, lead, discipline, or correct her subordinates. She seems easygoing; her subordinates call her Soft Sally behind her back. Given their hands-on training and greater experience, they feel they can deliver technically better patient care than she can.

Besnick is personable and well-liked by you and by the other charge nurses. She socializes with them after hours and, like them, Besnick participates in American Nurses Association professional activities. Besnick and her husband recently bought a new home in town after renting for the year she has worked at the hospital. They adopted a baby 2 months ago.

You are concerned that if you demote Besnick, her pride will be hurt, and she will quit. You do not want to lose a good RN, especially one with a B.S.N.

Questions

1. Describe the education and training received by nursing assistants, licensed practical (licensed vocational) nurses, and RNs. Refer to the discussion of nursing in Chapter 1, as needed.

2. Develop a problem statement. Identify several tentative alternative solutions.

3. Which solution is best? Why?

4. Describe how to implement the solution chosen. How would it be evaluated?

Case Study 3   Chris's New Baby

Chris was about to have her first baby. Her family practice physician referred her to an obstetrician-gynecologist (OB-GYN) at a regional hospital, and Chris was scheduled for an elective caesarean section (C-section). Chris and her husband live in rural Arizona. She is the only daughter of a board-certified OB-GYN, Dr. Ned, who retired recently after 35 years of practice.

Chris wanted her father, Dr. Ned, and her mother to be with her during the surgery. Chris told her family practice physician she would feel reassured if her father was with her during the C-section. When she met the OB-GYN the day of surgery, Chris told her she wanted her father to be in the surgical suite and that Dr. Ned is a retired physician. Chris did not mention his specialty or that he is a board-certified OB-GYN. Chris's OB-GYN agreed reluctantly, saying, "I prefer family members are not present during surgery. They can be a distraction and may be fearful—they don't understand what's happening. But he's a doctor so it's okay."

On the day of surgery Dr. Ned arrived with Chris. Chris's husband and her mother stayed in a family waiting area. While Chris was prepped for the C-section, Dr. Ned donned a gown and mask. Out of habit he scrubbed and put on surgical gloves. As the procedure started, Dr. Ned stood to one side, observing intently. After the initial incision Dr. Ned moved closer. Chris's OB-GYN seemed to hesitate. A few minutes later, Dr. Ned became more concerned; Chris showed signs that she was in pain. Apparently, her spinal block wasn't fully effective. The nurse anesthetist saw Chris grimacing and asked if she had pain; she said, "Yes." This information was unnerving to the OB-GYN; she seemed uncertain how to proceed. Dr. Ned was increasingly concerned. He made some comments under his breath. Then he spoke: "I should tell you I'm a recently retired board-certified OB-GYN and qualified to perform C-sections. You're the surgeon, but there seems to be a problem. Would you like me to assist?"

Questions

1. State the problem from the hospital CEO's perspective when the information from this case becomes known to the CEO.

2. State the problem from Dr. Ned's perspective at this point in the C-section.

3. Develop three alternative solutions for the CEO's problem statement.

4. What should Dr. Ned do if Chris's surgery becomes an emergency?

Notes

1. Drucker, Peter F. *An Introductory View of Management*, 396. New York: Harper's College Press, 1977; Pearce, John A., III, and Richard B. Robinson, Jr. *Management*, 62. New York: Random House, 1989.

2. DeSmet, Aaron, Gerald Lackey, and Leigh M. Weiss. Untangling your organization's decision making. *McKinsey Quarterly*, June 2017. *https://www.mckinsey.com/business-functions/organization/our-insights/untangling-your-organizations-decision-making*, retrieved February 11, 2019.

3. Simon, Herbert A. *The New Science of Management Decision*, rev. ed., 46. Englewood Cliffs, NJ: Prentice-Hall, 1977.

4. Pearce, John A., III, and Richard B. Robinson, Jr. *Management*, 63–64. New York: Random House, 1989.

5. Gallagher, Thomas J. *Problem Solving with People: The Cycle Process*, 9. New York: University of America Press, 1987.

6. Vroom, Victor H., and Arthur G. Jago. *The New Leadership: Managing Participation in Organizations*, 56. Englewood Cliffs, NJ: Prentice-Hall, 1988.

7. Higgins, James M. *The Management Challenge: An Introduction to Management*, 70–71. New York: Macmillan, 1991.

8. Hastings, John E. F., William R. Mindell, John W. Browne, and Janet M. Barnsley. "Canadian Health Administrator Study." *Canadian Journal of Public Health* 72 (March/April 1981, suppl. 1): 46–47.

9. American College of Hospital Administrators. *The Evolving Role of the Hospital Chief Executive Officer*. Chicago: The Foundation of the American College of Hospital Administrators, 1984.

10. Gary, Loren. "Want Better Results? Boost Your Problem-Solving Power." *Harvard Management Update* (October 2004): 3–6.

11. Spradlin, Dwayne. "Are You Solving the Right Problem?" *Harvard Business Review* 90, 9 (September 2012): 85–93.

12. Llopis, Glenn. "The Four Most Effective Ways Leaders Solve Problems." *Forbes.com*, November 4, 2013. *https://www.forbes.com/sites/glennllopis/2013/11/04/the-4-most-effective-ways-leaders-solve-problems/#3f201e354f97*, retrieved February 11, 2019.

13. Cowan, David A. "Developing a Process Model of Problem Recognition." *Academy of Management Review* 11 (Spring 1986): 763–764.

14. Gallagher, *Problem Solving*, 77; Pearce and Robinson, *Management*, 65.

15. Postal, Susan Nelson. "Using the Deming Quality Improvement Method to Manage Medical Record Department Product Lines." *Topics in Health Record Management* 10 (June 1990): 36.

16. Cowan, "Developing a Process," 764.

17. Cowan, "Developing a Process," 764.

18. Cowan, "Developing a Process," 766.

19. Andriole, Stephen J. *Handbook of Problem Solving: An Analytical Methodology*, 25. New York: Petrocelli Books, 1983.

20. An operational definition defines something to determine its existence, duration, or quantity.

21. Nutt, Paul C. "How Top Managers in Health Organizations Set Directions That Guide Decision Making." *Hospital & Health Services Administration* 36 (Spring 1991): 59.

22. For a discussion on problem definition, see Chow, Chee W., Kamal M. Haddad, and Adrian Wong-Boren. "Improving Subjective Decision Making in Health Care Administration." *Hospital & Health Services Administration* 36 (Summer 1991): 192–193.

23. Evans, James R. *Creative Thinking in the Decision and Management Sciences*, 104. Cincinnati: SouthWestern, 1991.

24. Couger, Daniel J. *Creative Problem Solving and Opportunity Finding*, 184. Danvers, MA: Boyd & Fraser, 1995.

25. Couger, *Creative Problem Solving*, 113.

26. Dewey, John. *How We Think: A Restatement of the Relation of Reflective Thinking to the Educative Process*, 108. Boston: D.C. Heath, 1933.

27. "There is no true value of any characteristic, state, or condition that is defined in terms of measurement or observation. Change of procedure for measurement (change in operational definition) or observation produces a new number. There is no true value for the number of people in a room. Whom do you count? Do we count someone that was here in this room, but is now outside on the telephone or drinking coffee? Do we count the people that work for the hotel? Do we count the people on the stage? The people managing the audio-visual equipment? If you change the rule for counting people, you come up with a new number. There is no such thing as a fact concerning an empirical observation. Any two people may have different ideas about what is important to know about any event. Get the facts! Is there any meaning to this exhortation?" (Deming, W. Edwards. *The New Economics for Industry, Government, Education*, 2nd ed., 104–105. Cambridge, MA: MIT-CAES, 2000.)

28. A useful discussion of problem-solving constraints, including assumptions, is found in Chapter 3 of Brightman, Harvey J. *Problem Solving: A Logical and Creative Approach*. Atlanta, GA: Business Publication Division, College of Business Administration, Georgia State University, 1980.

29. Chow, Haddad, and Wong-Boren, "Improving Subjective Decision Making," 194.

30. Hammond, John S., Ralph L. Keeney, and Howard Raiffa. "The Hidden Traps in Decision Making." *Harvard Business Review* 84, 1 (January 2006): 120.

31. Chow, Haddad, and Wong-Boren, "Improving Subjective Decision Making," 202.

32. Hammond, Keeney, and Raiffa. "The Hidden Traps in Decision Making," 122.

33. "Confirmation bias—definition." *wordiQ.com*, retrieved September 10, 2012.

34. Ridley, Matt. "When Bad Theories Happen to Good Scientists." *Wall Street Journal*, July 21–22, 2012, C4. The discussion states: "One of the alarming things about confirmation bias is that it seems to get worse with greater expertise. Lawyers and doctors (but not weather forecasters who get regularly mugged by reality) become more confident in their judgment as they become more senior, requiring less positive evidence to support their views than they need negative evidence to drop them."

35. Meissner, Philip, Olivier Sibony, and Torsten Wulf. "Are You Ready to Decide?" *McKinsey Quarterly*, April 2015. *https://www.mckinsey.com/business-functions/strategy-and-corporate-finance/our-insights/are-you-ready-to-decide*, retrieved February 10, 2019.

36. Chow, Haddad, and Wong-Boren, "Improving Subjective Decision Making," 192.

37. Nutt, Paul C. "The Identification of Solution Ideas during Organizational Decision Making." *Management Science* 39 (September 1993): 1071.

38. An excellent discussion of techniques for generating solutions is found in Chapter 8 of Couger, *Creative Problem Solving*.

39. Couger, *Creative Problem Solving,* 18.
40. Nutt, "The Identification of Solution Ideas," 1,072.
41. Etzioni, Amitai. "Humble Decision Making." *Harvard Business Review* 67 (July/August 1989): 125.
42. Pearce and Robinson (*Management,* 75) describe these criteria as follows: Will the alternative be effective? Can the alternative be implemented? What are the organization consequences?
43. Kepner, Charles H., and Benjamin B. Tregoe. *The New Rational Manager,* 94–99. Princeton, NJ: Kepner-Tregoe, 1981.
44. Kepner and Tregoe, *The New Rational Manager,* 103–137.
45. Good discussions of problem solving and factors influencing problem solving are found in Ackoff, Russell L. *The Art of Problem Solving.* New York: John Wiley & Sons, 1978; Ivancevich, John M., James H. Donnelly, Jr., and James L. Gibson. *Management Principles and Functions,* 4th ed. Homewood, IL: Irwin, 1989; Kepner and Tregoe, *The New Rational Manager;* and Nutt, "How Top Managers."
46. "Decision Making: Better; Faster; Smarter." *Harvard Business Review* 84, 1 (January 2006, Special Issue).
47. Brightman, *Problem Solving,* 83–84.
48. Hernandez, J. S., and P. Varkey. "Vertical versus Lateral Thinking." *Physician Executive* 34, 3 (2008): 26–28.
49. Vroom and Jago, *The New Leadership,* 56.
50. Vroom and Jago, *The New Leadership,* 28.
51. Brightman, Harvey J. *Group Problem Solving: An Improved Managerial Approach,* 51. Atlanta, GA: Business Publishing Division, College of Business Administration, Georgia State University, 1988. Pages 63–69 discuss techniques for overcoming groupthink.
52. Eisenhardt, Kathleen M., Jean L. Kahwajy, and L. J. Bourgeois III. "How Management Teams Can Have a Good Fight." *Harvard Business Review* 75, 4 (July/August 1997): 85.
53. Ways, Max. "Watergate as a Case Study in Management." *Fortune* 88 (November 1973): 196–201. Watergate is the residential and commercial complex in Washington, D.C., that housed the Democratic National Committee during the 1972 presidential election campaign. Operatives of the (Republican) Committee to Reelect the President (Richard M. Nixon) were arrested there during a failed burglary. The political stonewalling, resulting scandal, and Nixon's resignation are collectively called Watergate. The problem-solving process and mindset of the people who were involved in the aftermath of the break-in exemplify groupthink.
54. Higgins, *The Management Challenge,* 87.
55. Kaluzny, Arnold D. "Revitalizing Decision Making at the Middle Management Level." *Hospital & Health Services Administration* 34 (Spring 1989): 42.
56. Kaluzny, "Revitalizing Decision Making," 45.
57. Crosby, Bob. "Why Employee Involvement Often Fails and What It Takes to Succeed." In *The 1987 Annual: Developing Human Resources,* edited by J. William Pfeiffer, 179. San Diego: University Associates, 1987.
58. Crosby, "Why Employee Involvement," 181.
59. Kahn, Susan. "Creating Opportunities for Employee Participation in Problem Solving." *Health Care Supervisor* 7 (October 1988): 39.
60. Lawler, Edward E., III, and Susan A. Mohrman. "Quality Circles: After the Honeymoon." In *The 1988 Annual: Developing Human Resources,* edited by J. William Pfeiffer, 201. San Diego: University Associates, 1988.
61. Dailey, Robert, Frederick Young, and Cameron Barr. "Empowering Middle Managers in Hospitals with Team-Based Problem Solving." *Health Care Management Review* 16 (Spring 1991): 55.
62. Vroom, Victor H. "A New Look at Managerial Decision-Making." *Organizational Dynamics* 1 (Spring 1973): 66–80.
63. See also Vroom, Victor H., and Philip W. Yetton. *Leadership and Decision-Making.* Pittsburgh: University of Pittsburgh Press, 1973, and Vroom and Jago, *The New Leadership.*

7

Financial Management

Financial management provides financial and managerial accounting information that managers use to make decisions in keeping with the organization's mission, as established by the governing body (GB). The GB, with its finance and audit committees, approves and oversees policy implementation and plan adoption to ensure the organization's financial success and sustainability. The GB also evaluates and selects a competent chief executive officer (CEO).[1] (Chapter 11 provides more information on the GB–CEO relationship). The CEO delegates authority for day-to-day financial matters to the chief financial officer (CFO).

Organization of Financial Management

The CFO is responsible for day-to-day financial matters. Two major functions report directly to most CFOs: the controller function, including financial accounting, managerial accounting, tax accounting, patient accounting, and internal auditing; and the treasurer function, including working capital, investments, and capital expenditure financing.

Chief Financial Officer

Much has been written about the expanding role of the healthcare CFO over the last 25 years. In 1994, the Financial Executives Institute provided the following classic definition of CFO duties:

1. Establish, coordinate, and maintain, through authorized management, an integrated plan for the control of financial operations, including cost standards, expense budgets, revenue forecasts, profit planning, and programs for capital investments/financing.

2. Measure performance against approved operating plans and standards, and report and interpret the financial results of operations to all levels of management.

Contributions to the section on budgeting and other financial control methods were made by Joy Volarich, M.B.A., M.H.A., FHFMA, Adjunct Instructor, The George Washington University.

3. Measure and report on the validity of business objectives and the effectiveness of policies, organizational structure, and procedures in attaining those objectives.

4. Report to government agencies as required and supervise all matters related to taxes.

5. Interpret and report on the effects of external influences on the attainment of business objectives, including a continuous appraisal of political, economic, and social forces.

6. Provide protection for the assets of the organization, including the development and maintenance of internal controls, internal audits, risk management standards, and insurance protection.[2]

In 2002, the federal government passed corporate accountability legislation in response to the Enron and WorldCom bankruptcies. The Sarbanes-Oxley Act of 2002 (PL 107-204), commonly referred to as SOX, was the first major government influence on the CFO's duties. SOX only applies to publicly traded, for-profit corporations, but the law has become best governance and accounting practice; therefore, many not-for-profit HSOs/HSs voluntarily adopted SOX standards. In addition, states such as New York and California have adopted similar legislation.[3] The most notable SOX standards for HSOs/HSs include the following:

- Section 302, "Corporate Responsibility for Financial Reports," requires that principal officers and financial officers sign the financial report certifying that it is materially correct and contains no false statements. This section also states that officers are responsible for

  - establishing and maintaining internal controls,

  - designing controls so material is known to officers,

  - evaluating effectiveness of internal controls, and

  - presenting conclusions about the effectiveness of controls.

- Section 404, "Management Assessment of Internal Controls," requires that annual financial reports include an Internal Control Report stating management is responsible for

  - an adequate internal control structure,

  - an assessment by management of effectiveness of the control structure, including any shortcomings, and

  - external auditor certification of management's assertion that internal controls are in place, operational, and effective.

- Section 406, "Code of Ethics for Senior Financial Officers," requires

  - ethical handling of actual or apparent conflicts of interest,

  - full disclosure in the financial reports, and

  - compliance with government rules and regulations.[4]

- Sections 201–206, "Auditor Independence," describe

  - general conditions of auditor independence,

  - specific prohibited non-audit services like consulting to clients, and

  - prohibited relationships like clients hiring auditor employees within 1 year of working on the audit.[5]

It is important to note that the first prosecution under SOX (Sections 302 and 404) was a healthcare organization—HealthSouth in 2004. HealthSouth, a publicly held for-profit chain of rehabilitation facilities, fraudulently reported $2.7 billion in income to inflate HealthSouth's earnings. Several senior executives pleaded guilty for their involvement, but HealthSouth's CEO was found not guilty after a trial in 2005.[6,7]

Table 7.1 Competency-Based Model for Healthcare CFOs

	Time frame		
	Past		
	Present		
	Future		
Roles	Financial expert	Business adviser	Enterprise leader
Competencies	Technical expertise	Decision support	Strategic leadership
	Results oriented	Compliance oversight	System influencer
	Supervisor	Coach/Teacher	Mentor
	Internal focus	Internal/external	External focus
	Risk minimizer	Risk quantifier	Risk acceptor

Source: Clarke, Dick. "Healthcare Financial Competency Model." Paper presented at HFMA's 2003 CFO Exchange, San Francisco.

The Healthcare Financial Management Association (HFMA) has proposed a healthcare CFO competency model that demands new roles and competencies.

The 2005 HFMA Compensation Survey added the following competencies to the list in Table 7.1:

- Case management—fixed reimbursements will drive CFOs to look at new ways to lower costs in operations.

- Sales—Lowering costs will require CFOs to sell efficiency to managers and professional staff organizations (PSOs).

- Education—new ways of doing things will lead CFOs into educational roles with managers and PSOs.[8]

> Of all the changes to the CFO role in recent years, the most significant is that it's become much more strategic. . . . Having eyes on the future requires CFOs to work in partnership more closely with other members of the C-suite. . . . In many ways, the CFO is almost becoming a coach to help clinical and operational leaders use their financial data [to make better decisions].[9]

There are no licensure, certification, or educational requirements for CFOs. In the past, most had earned accounting degrees and were certified public accountants (CPAs). The most frequent progression is from controller, as described in the next section. Table 7.2 provides a CFO profile over the last 10 years.

Table 7.2 Hospital CFO Profile

	2011	2013	2015	2017
Average annual compensation	$224,500	$236,600	$266,000	$258,000
Average age	51	53	53	53
Percent female	29	28	30	33
Percent with master's degree	51	51	55	47
Percent certified public accountants	50	47	52	48
Percent certified as healthcare financial professionals	27	28	28	36
Years of healthcare experience				25

Source: HFMA Compensation Surveys. https://www.hfma.org/topics/research_reports/54960.html, retrieved December 24, 2019.

Controller

The controller is the chief accounting officer and is responsible for all matters related to accounting: financial, managerial, tax, and patient accounting, and internal auditing.[10] While not required to be an accountant by licensure or certification, it would be difficult for the controller to maintain credibility compared with accountants having those credentials. Titles vary and can include vice president/director of accounting. Controller duties include the following and related specific activities:

1. Financial accounting

   • Prepare periodic financial statements and analyses

   • Prepare recurring and one-time financial reports

   • Prepare financial transaction reports, including timing and appropriate authorization

2. Managerial accounting

   • Coordinate the budgeting process

   • Monitor budgets and provide feedback

   • Audit fixed assets

   • Analyze and allocate costs

3. Tax accounting

   • Supervise all matters related to taxes

   • Prepare and file tax returns

4. Patient accounting

   • Supervise the patient billing process

   • Ensure billing timeliness and accuracy

5. Auditing

   • Establish and monitor controls to ensure transactions are processed appropriately

   • Establish and monitor controls to safeguard assets

   • Monitor controls to ensure compliance with government regulations

   • Schedule and manage periodic internal audits and communicate results to management and GB

   • Prepare work papers and assist as required by independent auditors.

For additional information on compliance, see Chapter 14. The work of internal auditors is described later in the chapter.

Treasurer

The treasurer is responsible for matters related to cash management: information aggregation, liquidity management, and risk management.[11] The most appropriate educational background for a treasurer is finance, neither licensure nor a degree is required. Titles vary and can include vice president/director of finance. The treasurer's duties include the following:

1. Related to information aggregation

   • Forecast cash needs

   • Reconcile the bank statement

2. Related to liquidity management

  • Manage cash receipts

  • Manage cash disbursements

  • Manage cash investments

  • Obtain debt and equity financing

  • Maintain credit rating agency relationships

3. Related to risk management

  • Manage risk "posed by the types of investments used, the stability of lenders, legal restriction on cash flows, and the inherent variability of interest rates"[12]

Independent Auditors

Independent auditors, sometimes called external auditors, are auditing firms retained by HSOs/HSs to ensure that financial reports required by external agencies are correct as to accounting format.[13] Examples of external agencies are Medicare and Medicaid, insurance companies, and lenders. "Correct accounting format" refers to generally accepted accounting principles (GAAP) developed by the Financial Accounting Standards Board (FASB) used by the private sector and the Governmental Accounting Standards Board (GASB) used by state and local governments. The Securities and Exchange Commission has legal oversight for the private sector that is for-profit and publicly traded.

Independent auditors typically audit the client HSO/HS once each year. The audit begins with an audit engagement letter prepared by the auditor. The audit engagement letter specifies audit arrangements between the auditor and client, and when signed by the parties it is a contract. The duration of the audit depends on the size of the organization. When the audit is completed, the independent auditor submits to the client's GB an audit report that includes the following:

• Report on financial statements

• Management's responsibility for financial statements

• Auditor's responsibility

• Auditor's opinion[14]

The opinion is the heart of the audit report. Independent auditors use four types of opinions:

1. *Unqualified opinion* means that, in all material (significant) respects, the financial statements fairly present the financial position, results of operations, and cash flows of the organization in conformance with GAAP.

2. *Qualified opinion* means that, in all material (significant) respects, the financial statements fairly present the financial position, results of operations, and cash flows of the organization in conformance with GAAP, except for matters identified in additional paragraphs of the report. Auditors issue a qualified opinion when there is insufficient evidentiary matter, when the organization has placed restrictions on the scope of the audit, or when the financial statements depart in a material way. *Material way* means impact of an omission or misstatement that requires following accounting standards, though not substantial (the impact would not, in the aggregate, change the interpretation), manner from GAAP.[15]

3. *Adverse opinion* means the financial statements do not fairly present the financial position, results of operations, and/or cash flows of the organization in conformance with GAAP. Auditors use additional paragraphs after the opinion to describe the reasons for the adverse opinion.

4. *Disclaimer of opinion* means the auditor does not express an opinion, usually because the scope of the audit was insufficient for the auditor to render one.

What is the role of the independent auditor in the detection of fraud? What was the role of the independent auditor in the detection of fraud at HealthSouth? While the independent auditor has no responsibility to detect *all* fraud (meaning the detection of fraud is not a purpose of the independent audit), the independent auditor has a responsibility to detect fraud that materially (significantly) misstates the financial statements. Auditing Standard (AS) 1001, Responsibilities and Functions of the Independent Auditor, states that "the auditor has a responsibility to plan and perform the audit to obtain reasonable assurance about whether the financial statements are free of material misstatement, whether caused by error or fraud."[16]

Internal Auditors

Internal auditors are employees of the HSO/HS with significant independence.[17] Their primary task is to protect the organization from fraud, error, and financial loss by reviewing accounting and operating policies, procedures, and practices to assure compliance and to ensure that internal controls are effective. They use a continuous, systematic, and disciplined approach in audits and subsequent recommendations for improvement in effectiveness of risk management and control (see Chapter 14) and governance processes (see Chapter 11). To ensure independence, the internal audit function reports to the audit committee of the GB for audit activities (what is audited) and to the CEO (required by law for publicly traded companies), chief operating officer (COO), CFO, or controller for day-to-day operations (schedules). The scope of internal auditing includes ensuring compliance with federal and state law (see compliance in Chapter 14); accounting and financial reporting of risk; assessing internal controls at all levels; evaluating operations, including key performance indicators; evaluating independent audits; assessing accounting and financial reporting processes; evaluating computer systems, including security; and reviewing effectiveness of codes of conduct policies.[18] Because internal audits involve accounting and operating policies, educational backgrounds of auditors vary. Licensure or certification is not required.[19]

Healthcare Financial Accounting

The primary purpose of healthcare financial accounting is to produce the five financial statements required by GAAP for private hospitals, both not-for-profit and for-profit: statement of operations, balance sheet, state of changes in net assets, statement of cash flows, and notes to the financial statements. Some accounting terminology differs between not-for-profits and for-profits. Because most hospitals are not-for-profit, this discussion uses not-for-profit terminology. Government hospitals use GAAP promulgated by GASB, which can differ from the FASB rules that not-for-profit and private hospitals use: GASB standards are not covered in this discussion.

Balance Sheet

The balance sheet shows the organization's financial position at a point in time. It presents the organization's assets, liabilities, and net assets, and their relationships, which are expressed in the following accounting equation:

$$Assets = Liabilities + Net\ Assets$$

Assets are economic resources that benefit the organization. They are classified as *current assets* (provide benefit for 1 year or less) and *noncurrent assets* (provide benefit for more than 1 year). Current assets are listed in order of liquidity (easily convertible to cash or to meet current liabilities): *cash, temporary investments,* net *receivables* (net of allowances for price concessions and bad debt), *inventory,* and *prepaid expenses.* Noncurrent assets include *net plant and equipment* (net of accumulated depreciation) and *long-term investments. Liabilities* are economic obligations of the organization. Liabilities are classified as *current liabilities* (obligations due in 1 year or less) and *long-term liabilities* (obligations due in more than 1 year). *Net assets* is the difference between total assets and total liabilities and is the owner's financial interest in the organization. Current GAAP requires net assets to be classified in two ways: *net assets without donor restrictions* and *net assets with donor restrictions.* Table 7.3 shows a sample balance sheet.

Table 7.3   Colonial Medical Center Balance Sheet as of December 31, 2020 (in thousands)

		2020	2019
ASSETS			
Current assets	Cash	$124	$280
	Temporary investments	45	30
	Receivables, net	3,536	2,860
	Inventory	175	140
	Prepaid expense	32	40
Total current assets		3,912	3,350
Noncurrent assets	Land, plant, and equipment	6,980	6,580
	Less accumulated depreciation	(1,730)	(1,259)
	Land, plant, and equipment, net	5,250	5,321
	Long-term investments	609	790
	Other noncurrent assets	113	109
Total noncurrent assets		5,972	6,220
TOTAL ASSETS		9,884	9,570
LIABILITIES AND NET ASSETS			
Current liabilities	Accounts payable	302	370
	Notes payable	345	335
	Accrued expenses payable	871	606
	Deferred revenues	10	15
	Estimated third-party settlements	137	224
	Current portion of long-term debt	184	178
Total current liabilities		1,849	1,728
Noncurrent liabilities	Long-term debt, net of current portion	3,600	3,500
TOTAL LIABILITIES		5,449	5,228
NET ASSETS			
Net assets without donor restrictions		3,283	3,190
Net assets with donor restrictions		1,152	1,152
Total net assets		4,435	4,342
TOTAL LIABILITIES AND NET ASSETS		$9,884	$9,570

Reprinted with permission from Nowicki, Michael. *Introduction to the Financial Management of Healthcare Organizations,* 7th ed. Chicago: Health Administration Press, 2018.

Statement of Operations

The statement of operations summarizes the organization's net revenues, expenses, and excess of revenues over expenses, at a point in time. While accounts on the balance sheet are permanent (balances carry forward to the subsequent accounting period), the accounts on the statement of operations are temporary and their balances are transferred to the balance sheet at the end of the accounting period. This relationship is best described by the expanded accounting equation:

$$Assets = Liabilities + Net\ Assets + (Net\ Revenues - Expenses)$$

Net patient services revenue is generated by providing patient care services (*gross patient services revenue*) minus *explicit price concessions* (discount to patients or insurance companies based on an agreement), *implicit price concessions* (discounts to patients not based on an agreement), and *charity care* if a charge had been generated (charity care is defined as a patient unable to pay based on the organization's charity care policy). The cost of charity care, the method of arriving at the cost of charity care, and the organization's charity care policy are a required note to the financial statements. Net patient services revenue is the amount the HIO/HS expects to collect. *Premium revenue* is money generated from capitated agreements that must be reported separately because premium revenue is earned by agreeing to provide care to an enrolled population, regardless of whether the care has been delivered. Other operating revenue is money generated from services that are not healthcare to patients and enrollees and may include operating revenue from rental equipment and office space, cafeteria and gift shops, and the like.

Operating expenses are the resources used by the organization to provide patient care and other operations related to the HSO's/HS's mission. These expenses can be listed by function (organizational unit) or by natural classification (salaries, supplies, etc.). GAAP currently classifies bad debt (bad debt is defined as a patient unable to pay based on an unexpected adverse event) as an operating expense based on charges. Under the previous standard, hospitals reported bad debt as the difference between what was billed and what was collected for patients where a negotiated contract for payment was in place (contractual allowance). Under the current standard, hospitals can report this difference as bad debt only for patients who have an adverse event like bankruptcy or loss of employment. For patients without an adverse event, the difference would be recorded as an implicit price concession if the hospital continues to care for the patient even if the patient is unlikely to pay or the hospital does not perform a credit assessment on the patient before delivering care.[20] Under the current standard, hospitals will report less bad debt in the future and more implicit price concessions. Not-for-profit hospitals argue the current standard will reduce a benefit they give to their communities.[21]

Operating income is money earned by providing patient care services and the promise to provide patient care services to enrolled populations minus total operating expenses. *Nonoperating income* is the money earned from nonpatient care, such as interest income. *Excess of revenues over expenses* is the operating income plus the nonoperating income. GAAP allows not-for-profit organizations to report a performance indicator (report the financial results of the organization); excess of revenue over expense is often used as the performance indicator. GAAP also requires not-for-profit hospitals to include changes in net assets without donor restrictions to be included on the statement of operations. GAAP allows not-for-profit hospitals to also include changes in net assets with donor restrictions on the statement of operations, thus negating the need for a separate statement of changes in net assets.[22] See Table 7.4 for an example of a statement of operations.

Statement of Cash Flows

The statement of cash flows shows the organization's cash receipts and where they came from and cash disbursements and where they went during a specific period of time. In a not-for-profit organization, the statement is divided into three sections: cash flow from operations,

Table 7.4 Colonial Medical Center[a,b] Statement of Operations and Changes in Net Assets, through December 31, 2020 (in thousands)

	2020	2019
REVENUES		
Net patient service revenue[c]	$8,402	$8,119
Premium revenue	400	0
Other operating revenue	440	447
Total operating revenue	9,242	8,566
EXPENSES		
Salaries, wages, and benefits	4,980	4,278
Supplies, drugs, and purchased services	3,080	2,956
Bad debt expense[d]	600	500
Depreciation expense	471	443
Interest expense	113	109
Total operating expenses	9,244	8,286
OPERATING INCOME	(2)	280
NONOPERATING INCOME		
Investment income	95	85
EXCESS OF REVENUES OVER EXPENSES	$93	$365
CHANGES IN NET ASSETS		
Net assets without donor restrictions Jan 1	$3,190	$2,285
Net assets without donor restrictions Dec 31	3,283	3,190
Net assets with donor restrictions Jan 1	1,152	1,152
Net assets with donor restrictions Dec 31	1,152	1,152
Total net assets Jan 1	4,342	3,977
Total net assets Dec 31	4,435	4,342

[a,b,c,d]See Table 7.6, "Notes to Financial Statements."
Reprinted with permission from Nowicki, Michael. *Introduction to the Financial Management of Healthcare Organizations*, 7th ed. Chicago: Health Administration Press, 2018.

cash flow from investments, and cash flow from financing. *Cash flow from operating activities* begins with the excess of revenues over expenses for the year and then includes the changes in cash between statement periods for providing patient care services. Since revenues and expenses do not represent cash in accrual accounting, they must be adjusted as well as noncash events, such as depreciation. *Cash flow from investing activities* includes changes in cash between statement periods for investing in fixed assets, such as property and equipment, and for selling fixed assets. *Cash flow from financing activities* includes changes in cash between statement periods for financing activities such as debts, endowments, and grants. See Table 7.5 for an example of a statement of cash flows.

Notes to the Financial Statements

In addition to the four required financial statements, GAAP requires the following notes to financial statements (see Table 7.6).

Ratio Analysis

A language common to all organizations is numerical data. For example, HSOs/HSs are described by number and types of beds, number and types of employees, and size and specialty

Table 7.5 Colonial Medical Center Statement of Cash Flows, as of December 31, 2020 (in thousands)

		2020	
CASH FLOW FROM OPERATING ACTIVITIES			
Excess of revenues over expenses for the year		$93	
Adjustments to reconcile change in net assets to net cash	Add:		
	Depreciation expense	471	
	Decrease in prepaid expense	8	
	Increase in notes payable	10	
	Increase in accrued expenses payable	265	
	Increase in current portion of long-term debt	6	
	Less:		
	Increase in temporary investments	(15)	
	Increase in net receivables	(676)	
	Increase in inventory	(35)	
	Decrease in accounts payable	(68)	
	Decrease in deferred revenues	(5)	
	Decrease in estimated third-party adjustments	(87)	
	Net cash flow from operating activities		(33)
CASH FLOW FROM INVESTING ACTIVITIES			
	Purchasing of property, plant, and equipment	(400)	
	Proceeds from sale of long-term investments	181	
	Purchase of noncurrent assets	(4)	
	Net cash flow from investing activities		(223)
CASH FLOW FROM FINANCING ACTIVITIES			
	Proceeds from issuance of long-term debt	100	
	Net cash flow from financing activities		100
Net increase (decrease) in cash for the year			(156)
	Add: Cash balance at Jan. 1		280
Cash balance at Dec. 31			$124

Reprinted with permission from Nowicki, Michael. *Introduction to the Financial Management of Healthcare Organizations*, 7th ed. Chicago: Health Administration Press, 2018.

mix of their PSOs. HSOs/HSs are partly evaluated by numbers of patients admitted, procedures performed, and expenditures. Managers use similar data to monitor and control the HSO's/HS's functioning and how well it is accomplished. This may be done by comparing an activity with predetermined standards or by ratio analysis, which involves evaluating a relationship expressed as an index or percentage. These analyses are simple measures and are typically expressed in two modes: point specific and longitudinal. These analyses are applied to operational activity and financial status.[23]

Operational activity analysis is control by evaluating input, process, or output variables. Control charts are one type of analysis. Run charts record performance over time and are the basis for control charts. Run chart data are used to calculate upper and lower control limits; this changes the run chart into a control chart (see Figure 8.2). Control charts allow managers to distinguish common cause variation from special cause variation, which they must do before

Table 7.6   Colonial Medical Center Notes to Financial Statements, 2020

a	**Organization and Nature of Operations**
	Colonial Medical Center is a 120-bed, not-for-profit medical center offering the following services: inpatient, outpatient, emergency, long-term care, rehab, and home care.
b	**Community Benefit and Charity Care**
	Colonial Medical Center provides healthcare services through various programs that are designed to enhance the health of the community. Colonial Medical Center provides emergent and urgent care to persons who cannot afford health insurance because of inadequate financial resources. Colonial Medical Center's financial assistance policy provides care to patients regardless of their ability to pay, and all uninsured patients are eligible for discounts based on their income up to 400% of the federal poverty level. The amount of charity care provided is based on this policy, and the cost of charity care is calculated based on the charges for such services multiplied by the medical center's cost-to-charges ratio. The cost of charity care provided in 2020 was $420,000, and the amount for 2019 was $408,000. Not included in this amount, but still considered a community benefit by the medical center, is the loss to the Medicaid program.
c	**Net Patient Services Revenue**
	Patient services revenue is reported at estimated net realizable amounts for services rendered. The amount is net of provisions for explicit price concessions of $3,703,200 for 2020 and $3,592,800 for 2019. Provisions for explicit price concessions recognized discounts provided based on agreements with Medicare, Medicaid, other government programs, insurance companies, and individual patients. Net patient service revenue is also net of implicit price concessions of $925,800 for 2020 and $898,200 for 2019. Provisions for implicit price concessions recognized discounts provided to patient without an agreement with the medical center and were most likely classified as bad debt in previous accounting periods.
d	**Bad debt**
	The amount of bad debt expense is based on the current GAAP on revenue recognition that recognized bad debt only if the medical center expected to collect the amount billed to the patient and only for patients who have an adverse event like bankruptcy or loss of employment. The amount recognized as bad debt in 2020 was $600,000 based on charges and the amount recognized as bad debt in 2019 was $500,000 based on charges.

Reprinted with permission from Nowicki, Michael. *Introduction to the Financial Management of Healthcare Organizations*, 7th ed. Chicago: Health Administration Press, 2018.

undertaking process improvement. The control chart in Figure 8.3 shows performance of the process from the time noon meal trays leave the kitchen until the first patient receives a tray on a nursing unit. Control charts can be developed for the performance of any process.

Another method for operational activity analysis is using and evaluating nonfinancial indices expressed in ratios or percentages. Managers can design operational activity ratios (or percentage indices) to meet specific control needs if they can be expressed numerically. Ratios are flexible and can be used as point-specific input, conversion, and output standards. Table 7.7 shows a sample of common operational ratios and their definitions.

Table 7.7   Sample of Common Operational Ratios

	Definition	Preferred Direction
Average length of stay (ALOS) (days)	Patient days divided by discharges; used as an indicator of inpatient efficiency	Lower
Occupancy rate (%)	Patient days divided by licensed beds × 365; used as an indicator of inpatient volume and utilization	Higher
Maintained occupancy rate (%)	Patient days divided by maintained (staffed) beds × 365; used as an indicator of inpatient volume and utilization	Higher
Preregistration rate	Number of preregistered patient encounters divided by total patient encounters; used as an indicator that patient access is timely, accurate, and efficient.	Higher
Point-of-service (POS) cash collections	POS cash collections from patients divided by total cash collections from patients	Higher

Ratios can be derived by comparing any two relevant numbers. They should be tracked and compared longitudinally to show trends. When used in control, ratio trend analysis should address two issues. First, does the ratio provide meaningful information? Some do not; for example, the ratio of maintenance expenditures per Medicare patient-day is meaningless. Managers must evaluate the underlying derivation of the ratio, what it measures, and its meaning. Second, judgment must be used when interpreting results. Particularly important is assessing the many causes of single-point deviation (i.e., deviation occurring at one point) or longitudinal deviation (i.e., change over time). Ratios are only one of many types of indicators that show how actual results deviate from those desired. The cause of the deviation must be investigated, understood, and corrected, if necessary. Blindly using ratios will result in inappropriate conclusions and intervention and undesirable consequences. An example of an operational ratio is preregistration rate (see Table 7.7 for definition). It has been shown that preregistering a patient by collecting pertinent demographic information and verifying the patient's insurance eligibility, coverage, and limitations before the patient arrives on site decreases patient wait time, increases patient satisfaction, and increases billing accuracy and revenue collection. Therefore, the chief revenue cycle officer (or comparable manager) could track this ratio over time to monitor trends. If the ratio is lower than desired, the manager could analyze the preregistration process for improvement opportunities, one of which could be training for staff. After these changes are implemented, the ratio should be tracked to determine if the desired result (increased preregistration) has occurred.

If numeric data are the common language of organizations, their lifeblood is finance. Financial ratio analysis calculates and evaluates various indices that measure HSO/HS profitability, liquidity, capital structure, and efficiency.[24]

1. *Profitability ratios* are indicators of the ability of an HSO/HS to generate revenue that is greater than its expenses over a period of time. Few organizations could remain financially viable without profit (or without excess of revenues over expenses in a not-for-profit organization). Cash flow would be insufficient to meet cash requirements. Sister Irene Kraus of the Daughters of Charity is credited with the phrase "No margin, no mission."[25]

2. *Liquidity ratios* are indicators of the organization's ability to meet short-term obligations.

3. *Capital structure ratios* are indicators of the organization's ability to meet long-term obligations. Long-term creditors and bond rating agencies evaluate capital structure ratios to determine the organization's ability to increase its amount of debt financing.

4. *Asset efficiency ratios* are indicators of the organization's ability to operate efficiently and will increase in importance as HSOs/HSs are asked to do more with fewer resources. Asset efficiency ratios measure the relationship between revenue and assets. The numerator is always revenue as an output and the denominator is investment in a category of assets as an input.

   An example of a financial ratio is collection period (days)(see Table 7.8 for the formula). Cash tied up in accounts receivable (AR) is unavailable to pay operating expenses, purchase assets, or earn investment income. Therefore, the CFO, or comparable manager, could track this ratio to monitor trends. If the ratio is higher than desired, the CFO and business office manager could analyze the process(es) to find opportunities for improvement (e.g., decreasing time to submit final bills, decreasing claim rejections from payers, initiating a staff training program). After these changes are implemented, the ratio should be tracked to determine if AR have been reduced.

Benchmarking

For control purposes, benchmarking provides standards against which comparisons can be made. Benchmarking is also discussed in Chapter 8. External benchmarking compares the HSO's/HS's performance in various operational and financial measures to reference standards and industry best practices. The comparison should be against data from organizations of similar type and

Table 7.8　Sample of Common Financial Ratios

	Formula	Optum 2016 Median*	Preferred Direction
Profitability			
Operating margin	$\dfrac{Operating\ income}{Total\ operating\ revenue} \times 100$	.46	Higher
Total margin	$\dfrac{Excess\ of\ revenues\ over\ expenses}{Net\ assets} \times 100$	3.72	Higher
Return on net assets	$\dfrac{Excess\ of\ revenues\ over\ expenses}{Net\ assets} \times 100$	5.00	Higher
Liquidity			
Current ratio	$\dfrac{Total\ current\ assets}{Total\ current\ liabilities}$	2.17	Depends[a]
Collection period (days)	$\dfrac{Net\ receivables}{Net\ patient\ services\ revenue\ /\ 365}$	47.5	Lower
Payment period (days)	$\dfrac{Total\ current\ liabilities}{(Total\ expenses - depreciation\ expense)\ /\ 365}$	56.4	Lower
Days cash-on-hand (days)	$\dfrac{Cash + temporary\ investments}{(Total\ expenses - depreciation\ expense)\ /\ 365}$	42.6	Higher
Capital structure			
Net asset financing	$\dfrac{Net\ assets}{Total\ assets} \times 100$	51.7	Higher
Debt to capitalization	$\dfrac{Long\text{-}term\ debt}{(Long\text{-}term\ debt + net\ assets)} \times 100$	27.8	Lower
Asset efficiency			
Age of plant	$\dfrac{Accumulated\ depreciation}{Depreciation\ expense}$	11.79	Lower
Fixed asset turnover	$\dfrac{Total\ operating\ revenues}{Net\ plant\ \&\ equipment}$	2.50	Higher
Inventory turnover	$\dfrac{Total\ operating\ revenues}{Inventory}$	59.53	Higher

Source: Information taken from audited financial statements as reported by Optum360, LLC. *2018 Almanac of Hospital Financial and Operating Indicators*.

[a]Related to the current ratio, which lacks direction; a ratio that is too low means the organization has poor short-term debt paying capacity, whereas a ratio that is too high means the organization has too much invested in current assets and is losing the opportunity for a larger return in a long-term investment.

with similar service activities. Most major health-related associations (e.g., American Hospital Association [AHA], Medical Group Management Association, and HFMA. provide benchmarking data for members, and many government (e.g., Centers for Medicare & Medicaid Services, Centers for Disease Control and Prevention), nonprofit organizations (e.g., Kaiser Family Foundation), and vendors (e.g., Truven Health Analytics and Premier, Inc.) provide benchmark data and best practices reference information. Many benchmarks are available internally. They are specific to the organization and cannot be compared externally (e.g., a health system that tracks referral rates from each system hospital to the system's nursing facility). In these cases, internal benchmarks should be established by the GB or senior management and tracked over time to monitor current data against historical data and the internal benchmark. Both external and internal benchmarks must be used with caution. Benchmarks suggest results that could be obtained if the benchmarking HSO/HS (or constituent unit) had systems and processes identical to those used in achieving the benchmark. Lacking those, the benchmarking entity can, at best, only be aware of results it is possible to achieve, even as it strives to achieve them.

Cost Accounting

Cost accounting is the analysis of costs, including methods for classifying costs and allocating costs.[26] The objective of cost accounting is to determine the actual cost of products and services (e.g., determining what it costs for imaging to produce a computed tomographic scan). With the advent of prospective payment based on diagnosis-related groups (DRGs) in 1983, hospitals knew what they would be paid for each DRG, but few hospitals knew what the DRG cost to produce. With increased discounting to managed care plans in the late 1980s, some hospitals discounted rates below what it cost to produce the product or service. As a result of these two trends and without sophisticated cost accounting systems to support decision making, hospitals struggled during the 1980s[27] and the AHA reported 698 hospital closures during the decade.[28] A 2018 study found only 10% of executives responsible for patient care knew the cost of that care.[29]

Classifying Costs

The first part of cost accounting is to understand that costs can be classified by the following:

- Accounting function, including financial accounting costs and managerial accounting costs

- Management function, including operating costs and nonoperating costs

- Traceability to products and services, including direct costs, indirect costs, full costs, and average costs

- Behavior in relation to volume of products and services, including variable costs, fixed costs, semivariable costs, and marginal costs

- Relevance to decision making, including true costs, controllable costs, uncontrollable costs, differential costs, sunk costs, opportunity costs, and relevant costs

Allocating Costs

The second part of cost accounting is to understand the various ways costs are allocated from the non–revenue-producing departments to the revenue-producing departments and, ultimately, to the patient in the form of a bill. Ways to allocate costs are listed from the least to the most sophisticated.

- Direct allocation is the easiest way to allocate costs and involves a one-time allocation from the non–revenue-producing departments to the revenue-producing departments. While it is easy, direct allocation does not consider non–revenue-producing departments doing work (and allocating costs) for non–revenue-producing departments before the final allocation to the revenue-producing departments. While the total costs will be the same, it is more accurate for non–revenue-producing departments to allocate costs first. Because of limited accuracy, some third-party payers, including Medicare, do not allow direct allocation.

- Step-down allocation corrects the problem with direct allocation. Step-down allocation involves a two-time allocation: the first allocation among non–revenue-producing departments and the second allocation from non–revenue-producing departments to revenue-producing departments. The advantage of step-down is that it can be done manually or with little computer support. This makes it attractive to smaller facilities. The disadvantage is step-down does not consider revenue-producing departments doing work (and allocating costs) for other revenue-producing departments. This can be remedied by an interdepartmental charge system or double allocation.

- Double allocation also involves a two-time allocation: the first allocation among non–revenue-producing departments and simultaneously an allocation among revenue-producing departments and the second allocation from non–revenue-producing to revenue-producing departments. The advantage of double allocation is accuracy—most systems use a version of double allocation—while the disadvantage is cost of computer time required which has declines over time.

- Multiple allocation involves allocations among non–revenue-producing departments and multiple allocations between revenue-producing departments to refine the accuracy of costs allocated to each. While used for research, multiple allocation has limited practical use.

Once costs have been allocated, the information is reported to management. For instance, controllable cost information is assembled by department so department managers can control costs. Full cost information is assembled for profitability and rate-setting analyses.

Product Costs

Full cost information can be used to determine cost per unit (product or service). The four methods of determining unit costs range from least accurate to most accurate: ratio of costs to charges, process costing, job order costing, and activity-based costing (ABC).

Ratio of cost to charges takes a relationship in the working papers of the statement of operations, total patient care expenses divided by gross patient care revenues, and then applies that percentage to any product or service charge—the resulting answer is the cost for that product or service. While accurate in the aggregate, the application at the procedural level can vary greatly because charges vary widely (e.g., charges for some products may be set at 25% over cost, whereas charges for other products in the same department may be set at 75% over cost).

Process costing divides total costs of the department, after allocation, by the gross number of products or services produced by the department, to get an average cost per product or service. For departments with a homogeneous product or service line (all products or services are the same), this method is accurate.

Job order costing is used for departments that have a heterogeneous product or service line. Job order costing divides the total costs of the department, after allocation, by an established relative value unit (RVU). The RVU is used to show variability among products or services, and each product or service has a different RVU based on resource consumption. Cost accounting systems of most large healthcare organizations are based on job order costing.

For HSOs/HSs to become more efficient, better cost accounting systems are required. Other industries adopted ABC decades ago, but the healthcare field has been slow to adopt it because of cost and lack of senior management commitment.[30] ABC is a bottom-up method of assigning costs "because it finds the costs of each service at the lowest level, the point where resources are used, and aggregates them upward into products or services. ABC is based on the paradigm that activities consume resources and processes consume activities."[31] ABC allocates indirect costs much more accurately than job order costing, which tends to allocate indirect costs in the same relationship as direct costs. Cost accounting systems that use ABC must do the following:

- Identify potential cost efficiencies

- Allow the organization to maximize its resources

- Highlight opportunities for continuous process improvement[32]

Break-Even Analysis

Volume analysis with revenue as a variable is often called *break-even analysis*. It is one of the simplest analytical techniques to evaluate the economic viability of a proposed alternative involving resource allocation. The following are important components of volume analysis with revenue as a variable:

- Identifiable revenue measured by price/reimbursement per unit of output or service (x)— (e.g., average or payer-specific reimbursement per outpatient visit, laboratory test, electrocardiogram, or imaging study performed or per MS-DRG (medical severity DRG or the newest classification of DRGs) of inpatient hospital stay. It should be noted that type of reimbursement (per procedure, such as HCPCS [Healthcare Common Procedure Coding System]); fixed, such as MS-DRG or APC (ambulatory payment classification); capitated; and/or other contractual arrangements and payer mix may complicate use of volume analysis. Calculating reimbursement across payer mix produces the best results.

- Identifiable fixed costs—costs that do not vary with output or volume (e.g., associated capital costs for facility and equipment lease or depreciation, and pay for minimum staffing levels)

- Identifiable variable costs—costs that vary with output or volume (e.g., supplies, materials, medications, staff beyond minimum levels, and overtime)

Variants of volume analysis yield different results depending on which variables are known. The break-even formula determines the economic viability of an alternative. If fixed costs, variable costs per unit, and price per unit of output/service are known, the break-even formula determines the volume of output/service needed to break even.

$$Breakeven\ point\ (volume) = \frac{Fixed\ cost}{Price\ per\ unit - Variable\ cost\ per\ unit}$$

For example, Figure 7.1 shows an acute care hospital that proposes to open a freestanding satellite urgent care center. Fixed costs (building and equipment depreciation, minimum staffing levels) are $600,000/year. Variable costs (supplies and materials) per patient visit are assumed to

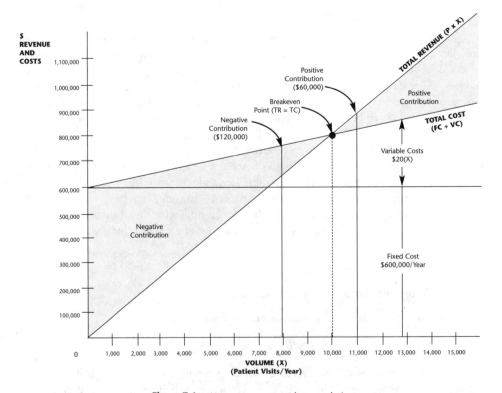

Figure 7.1. Urgent care center volume analysis.

be $20. The average price per patient visit is $80. Breakeven analysis can be used to determine the number of patient visits per year necessary to break even. This is determined as follows:

$$Breakeven = \frac{\$600,000}{\$(80 - 20)}$$

$$Breakeven = 10,000 \; visits \; per \; year$$

If other information (competition, population in the service area) is available, the decision maker can judge if it is reasonable to expect 10,000 patient visits per year (28/business day) and determine the economic viability of the project. If only 8,000 patient visits can be expected each year, profit (loss) would be –$120,000, as indicated using a more complex formula:

$$Profit = Revenue - (Fixed \; cost + [Variable \; cost \; per \; visit \times Volume])$$

$$Profit = 640,000 - (600,000 + [20 \times 8,000])$$

$$Profit = -120,000$$

Similarly, if volume were 11,000 patient visits per year, profit would be $60,000. Freestanding satellite urgent care centers often see patients whose needs are greater than they can meet. Estimates must be made as to the profit (or loss) that might result from referring these cases to the acute care hospital's emergency department (ED) or its other services. Hospital management must see the system (hospital and urgent care center) as a whole. It may be necessary (or desirable) that the urgent care center suboptimize its financial performance so performance of the entire system is optimized, whether in terms of community service, referrals, and/or revenue.

Volume Analysis without Revenue

Often, HSOs/HSs have alternate situations that do not have identifiable revenue attributes but do have volume and fixed and variable cost attributes. Volume analysis without revenue evaluates and compares the cost consequences of alternatives. It may be used if there is no revenue or when revenue is difficult to predict or determine. Because revenue is not a variable, the analysis focuses on fixed and variable cost trade-offs among volume alternatives.

For example, and as illustrated in Figure 7.2, leasing one of two copying machines is being considered. Machine A is slow (10 copies per minute) and leases for $200/month (fixed cost). Machine B is faster (30 copies per minute) and leases for $600/a month (fixed cost). Machine A has a lower fixed cost than Machine B ($FC_a < FC_b$); however, the variable cost of staff waiting at the machine while photocopying is higher ($VC_a > VC_b$). Given the different fixed and variable cost attributes, the preferred alternative is different at various volume levels. If volume is $x1$, then Machine A is preferred because total costs are lower ($TC_a1 < TC_b1$). If volume is $x2$, then Machine B is preferred ($TC_b2 < TC_a2$). Thus, alternative preference depends on the extent of fixed and variable cost trade-offs relative to volume.

Volume analysis without revenue is powerful because it focuses on the relationship of cost components to volume alternatives. Applications include equipment replacement and machine/technology–people substitution. As larger percentages of HSO/HS revenues are prospectively determined by case (i.e., DRGs, or capitated), alternative evaluation from a cost trade-off perspective becomes more important.

Table 7.9 presents additional quantitative techniques for decision making that also apply to Chapter 6.

Reimbursement

A major objective of healthcare financial management is ensuring that the organization is reimbursed for the products and services it provides.[33] Because of the nature of healthcare, services are often provided without either the patient or the provider knowing the cost, charges, or

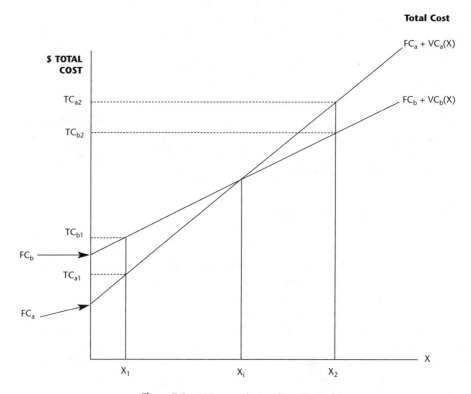

Figure 7.2.   Volume analysis without revenue.

reimbursement. In addition, over 85% of all personal healthcare expenditures are reimbursed to providers by third parties. In 2018, 40.4% was reimbursed by private health insurance; 24.4% by Medicare; 19.4% by Medicaid, and 1.2% by other third-party payers.[34]

The reimbursement due providers can either be determined after delivery of products and services, called retrospective reimbursement, or before delivery of products and services, called prospective reimbursement. In retrospective reimbursement, providers incur little cost risk by providing care because the cost of providing it is likely to be less than the payment. In prospective reimbursement, third-party payers shift substantial cost risk to providers, and sometimes utilization risk because reimbursement is established before delivery of products and services, and excess costs incurred by the provider are not reimbursed.

Payment Methodologies

Payers use several different payment methodologies to reimburse providers.[35] Common methodologies include the following:

- Fee-for-service—Providers establish a fee or charge for their services, and reimbursement by third parties and patients is based on that established fee or may be based on a predetermined discount from established fees. Predetermined discounts may be based on volume, prompt payment, or cash transactions.

- Per diem—Providers are paid a flat rate for each day of inpatient care regardless of costs associated with a day of care. Providers have substantial cost risk in per diem payment.

- Per case—Providers are paid a predetermined amount based on the patient's discharge category, condition, or diagnosis. DRGs are an example of per case reimbursement. Providers have substantial cost risk in per case payment methodologies.

Table 7.9 Quantitative Techniques for Decision Analysis

Technique	Description
Linear programming	This technique attempts to optimize the distribution of scarce resources among competing activities. This is accomplished by the maximization or minimization of a dependent variable, which is a function of several independent variables that are subject to a set of restraints, i.e., limited resources. This method is capable of being executed manually but is very adaptable to solution by a computer.
Queuing theory	Queuing theory is the study of the probabilities associated with the length of a waiting line and the time an individual must wait in the queuing system. This information is used to achieve a balance between the cost of waiting for a service and the cost associated with providing this service. "Cost in a medical setting invariably includes elements defined by 'good medical care,' which are, at best, difficult to quantify but must be included with monetary cost to obtain the proper solution." In queuing theory, the waiting line may be organized on a first-in–first-out basis, a random basis, or by some other priority technique. The waiting line can have a finite or infinite calling population, and it is assumed that the average service rate is greater than the average arrival rate for a single-channel–single-server queuing model.
Network analysis	Network analysis is characterized by a network of events and activities. Activities are defined as the actual performance of tasks, whereas events represent the start or completion of an activity. Events do not consume time. This technique allows the determination of probabilities of meeting specified deadlines; identifies bottlenecks in the project; evaluates the effect of shifting resources from a noncritical activity to a critical activity and vice versa; and enables the manager to evaluate the effect of a deviation of the actual time requirement for an activity from what had been predicted. Specific network analysis models include critical path methods (CPMs), program evaluation and review techniques (PERTs), and graphical evaluation and review techniques (GERTs). The difference between these systems lies in their different abilities to analyze complex network systems.
Regression analysis	This is a technique that derives a mathematical equation to describe or express the relationship between the data of two or more variables over a period of time. The variable to predict in this equation is referred to as the dependent variable. The other variables in the equation are called independent variables or predicting variables. The basic measure of the relationship between the dependent variable and the independent variable(s) is depicted by a regression line, which is computed by the method of least squares. This will result in an equation, based on historical data, that will predict the future behavior of the dependent variable. This technique is used primarily for the purpose of forecasting and control.

Excerpted from Helmer, F. Theodore, William H. Kucheman, Edward B. Oppermann, and James D. Suver. "Basic Management Science Techniques for Decision Analysis." *Hospital & Health Service Administration 27* (March/April 1982): 68–69. © 1982 Foundation of the American College of Healthcare Executives, Ann Arbor, MI: Health Administration Press.

- Per episode—Providers are paid a predetermined single amount based on an episode of care over a specific time. For instance, a bundled payment is a single payment to providers for all products and services necessary to treat a given condition over a specific time. Providers have substantial cost risk in per episode payment methodologies.

- Per head, or capitation—Providers are paid a premium each month per subscriber, which obligates the provider to accept a subscriber as a patient if the patient wants/needs care. In capitation, or per head, payment methodologies, providers have both cost risk (keeping the cost of care below the capitated amount) and utilization risk (predicting and keeping the number of times the patient seeks care and the type of care they seek within clinical protocols determined by physicians).

- Risk-based contracts—Providers furnish specific healthcare services for a negotiated price, which may be an amount per day, per case, or per episode. As an alternative, providers contract to provide all defined healthcare services to a specific group of subscribers in return for a predetermined premium. A risk-based contract may provide for shared risk between providers and third-party payers to improve quality and control costs.

Fee-for-service reimbursement was part of the volume-based business model that put the provider at risk only for controlling costs within the fee the provider set but had *no* limit on number of services provided or their quality. Per diem, per case, per episode, and per head solve a major problem with fee-for-service: the number of services provided. Risk-based contracts with incentive and/or penalties to improve quality and efficiency address the problem of quality of service provided.[36]

Working Capital

Every manager in an HSO/HS affects working capital directly or indirectly.[37] Working capital is total current assets: cash, temporary investments or marketable securities, accounts receivable, inventory, and prepaid expenses. Current assets are classified by liquidity, or how easily and quickly they can be converted to cash. *Working capital* and *net working capital* are often used synonymously. Either describes the difference between current assets and current liabilities (also listed and measured by their liquidity): accounts payable, notes payable, accrued expenses payable, deferred revenues, estimated third-party settlements (estimated money due to or from third parties because of underpayments or overpayments), and the current portion of long-term debt.

Working capital is a catalyst to make long-term assets productive. For example, hospitals and capital equipment (long-term assets) cannot produce revenue without current assets of labor as accrued expenses payable and supplies as inventory. The sources and methods to finance working capital, as well as working capital kept on hand, are the working capital policy. Sources of working capital include owner, debt, and trade credit. The owner (usually the community or religious order in not-for-profit HSOs/HSs) establishes the permanent working capital, or the minimum amount needed to establish the organization. Debt or trade credit is used to cover temporary working capital needs. Trade credit is "borrowing" from a vendor to which the HSO/HS owes money by not paying on time. The treasurer compares the late fee for delinquent payment to the amount of interest owed in debt and chooses the least costly alternative.

Managing Cash Flow

Cash flow is the difference between cash receipts and cash disbursements for an accounting period. Managing cash flow involves managing the cash conversion cycle and is typically the responsibility of the treasurer. The cash conversion cycle is the process of converting cash outflows from payroll and vendor payments into products and services and cash inflows from collections for products and services provided. A predetermined amount of cash should be maintained for transactions, precautions (emergencies), and speculations (taking advantage of a good offer by a vendor). To maintain a predetermined amount of cash on hand, the treasurer uses a cash budget that predicts the timing and amounts of cash inflows and cash outflows and examines the implications of cash management decisions. Should the HSO/HS have excess cash on hand, the GB-approved investment policy guides the treasurer's investment decisions.

Managing the Revenue Cycle

In HSOs/HSs, accounts receivable is the largest current asset because of the nature of services provided (often urgent or emergent), cost of services provided (very expensive giving the patient little time to save for the expenditure, even if covered in part by third parties), and the method of payment through third parties (extend credit to patients recognized as accounts receivable because the patient is covered in part by a third party). Revenue cycle is a multidisciplinary effort to reduce accounts receivable by managing production and payment cycles (see Table 7.10).

The revenue cycle is important because performance as measured by the collection period ratio can vary significantly among organizations. Variance results from the financial class of

Table 7.10.　Revenue Cycle

	Patient Activity	**Revenue Cycle Activity**
Production cycle	Precare	Obtain demographics
		Obtain insurance
		Verify insurance
		Obtain authorizations
		Obtain deductibles
		Obtain copays
	Care	Record charges
		Maintain medical record
		Review utilization
	Discharge	Transfer medical record
		Analyze medical record
		Abstract medical record
		Code medical record
		Transcribe dictation
Payment cycle		Print bill
		Submit bill
		Follow up on bill
		Collect or resolve bill

Reprinted with permission from Nowicki, Michael. *Introduction to the Financial Management of Healthcare Organizations*, 7th ed. Chicago: Health Administration Press, 2018.

patients—often beyond management's control, the GB's credit and collection policy, and management efforts to reduce accounts receivable. Costs associated with the revenue cycle include carrying costs of the patient account, credit and collection costs of the patient account, and delinquency costs of a patient account not paid on time, or at all.

Managing the Supply Chain

Effective supply chain management is a multidisciplinary effort to provide the right kind and right amount of consumable and reusable inventory to meet the needs of patient care. Meeting patient needs involves the uncertainty of demand for most inventory, understanding the time needed to receive an order, and planning for discontinuities in products. Effective supply chain management reduces costs by determining how much inventory to order and how much it will cost per year. The lack of secondary vendors became a major concern during the COVID-19 pandemic. The following formulas determine the ideal order quantity and unit cost per year.

$$Qe = \sqrt{\frac{2DO}{IP + 2H}}$$

where Qe is the economic order quantity or the ideal amount to order each time,

D is the annual demand,

O is the ordering cost per order,

I is the prevailing interest rate,

P is the price per unit, and

H is the holding cost per unit.

$$TC = PD + \frac{D}{Q}O + \left(HQe + IP\left[\frac{Qe}{2}\right]\right)$$

where TC is the total cost of placing an item in inventory for 1 year

where $IP\dfrac{Qe}{2}$ is the opportunity cost,

where HQe is the holding cost, and

where $HQe + IP\dfrac{Qe}{2}$ is the carrying cost.

Resource Allocation

HSO/HS resource allocation has four parts: strategic planning, operational planning, budgeting, and capital investment analysis. Two distinct but related types of planning are strategic and operational. Strategic planning is performed by the GB and senior managers with input from other parts of the organization, including leaders of the PSO. Strategic planning determines the intended outputs for an HSO/HS. The GB may not originate strategy, although it ensures that strategic proposals brought to it by senior managers are prepared and consistent with mission and responsibilities to stakeholders.

Managers use operational planning to determine how to produce planned outputs. Operational planning is derived from and must harmonize with strategic planning. It establishes objectives and programs, policies, and procedures in organizational units, such as individual or groups of departments and smaller units and programs. While strategic planning is multiyear, operational planning is short term, with time frames of 1 year or less. Middle managers undertake operational planning, and design and implement programs, policies, and procedures for their areas of responsibility. Finally, first-level managers plan specific operations or activities, such as estimating workload, scheduling work activity, allocating resources, and designing and implementing programs, policies, and procedures for their areas of responsibility. Planning is covered in more depth in Chapter 10.

Budgeting

Budgets have several purposes.[38] First, they convert operating plans into revenues and expenses. Second, they become control standards against which results are compared. And third, budgets educate managers on financial matters. Types of budgets and time frames vary. Operating budgets usually span 1 year and may be updated annually (a fixed budget), or more frequently (a rolling budget) to reflect changes in business plans. Likely, capital budgets are continuously updated and span multiple years.

Budgeting depends on planning and forecasting. Expense centers forecast the volume of services they expect to deliver, the workload demand, and the resources needed in the next budget period. Expense centers are organizational units with a well-defined relationship between inputs and outputs. Examples are surgical services, nursing service (inpatient [care] units), EDs, outpatient clinics, laboratories, pharmacy, diagnostic testing, dietary, patient billing, medical records, information technology, and maintenance.

HSOs/HSs calculate and track revenue budgets differently. Patient care revenues are generated at the procedure level and are recorded in the revenue center for the department where generated. Examples include outpatient clinics, outpatient diagnostic testing, and physician office services. As reimbursement for multiple patient care services using capitated and bundled payments increases through use of per member per month, MS-DRGs, APCs, accountable care organizations, and shared savings plan payments, it becomes more difficult to attribute revenues to revenue centers in specific departments. Some HSOs/HSs choose to record these revenues in total, others use an allocation methodology to record them at the individual expense center.

HSOs/HSs typically control resource consumption and conversion through the operating budget process at the level of cost center or department. Operating expense budgets include two types of expenses: direct and indirect, which have limitations. Direct expenses are those incurred by an expense center or a department that can be attributed to it and include labor and nonlabor. Labor expenses include salary, wages, and fringe benefit expenses. Direct nonlabor expenses include supplies, services (e.g., maintenance agreements), and equipment as rental or depreciation expense. Usually, expense centers can control only their direct expenses.

Indirect expenses are not attributable to a specific expense center or department and include expenses such as facility maintenance, building depreciation, utilities, and management staff not identified with an expense center. Indirect expenses are usually allocated among expense centers on bases such as square feet occupied (for building-related expenses), number of employees (for management staff expenses), or volume of output. The goal of allocating expenses is to present a more complete financial picture of the total expenses of treating individual patients and providing specific services.

For all departments, operating budgets reflect the amount and types of resources necessary to perform the projected workload. Managers who insist that all departments and functional areas "pay their own way" are thinking in boxes—they do not see the organization as a system in which all parts must work together to try to achieve the aim of the system. Managers must understand that some units may have to suboptimize their performance if the performance of the entire system is to be optimized.

Operating budgets can be based on volumes that are fixed, variable, or fixed-variable. Fixed budgets are a resource commitment to an expense center or department for the budget period based on expected workload. Variable budgets recognize that resource needs change as volume, workload, or service demands change; they project various scenarios over the budget period.[39] Hybrid fixed-variable operating budgets separate fixed and variable components, with the latter changing as workload increases or decreases.

Budgets force managers to be aware of inputs used and the expenses for staff, materials, equipment, or supplies. Preparing an operating budget requires a manager to project the resources that will be used to achieve outputs (conversion). For optimal control, managers should receive monthly financial reports that compare actual expenditures for the month, and year to date, with the amount budgeted. Variances showing deviation of actual from budgeted amounts should be used for control. Revenue budgets/projections are part of comprehensive HSO/HS financial management and not part of the control function. They are not addressed here.

A sample ED budget for a 100-bed hospital is shown in Table 7.11. The top section reports operating revenue and direct operating expenses; it does not include allocated indirect expenses. The bottom section includes allocated indirect expenses. Before cost allocation procedures were widely adopted by HSOs/HSs, managers had difficulty defining end products (services) and the expenses associated with producing them; there were few incentives to do so. Excluding indirect expenses makes the ED look very profitable. This could mislead managers who are not aware of the distinction. The data allow several types of comparisons of ED performance with budget. This type of report enables managers to exercise greater control over resource use and allows them to determine if revenue and expenses are lower than, equal to, or exceed expectations. Managers should determine the root cause of these variances and correct them, as necessary.

Capital Investment Analysis

Capital investment analysis refers to techniques that evaluate, compare, and rank multiple capital investment alternatives or compare single alternatives to a given criterion, such as rate

Table 7.11 Community Hospital Emergency Department Revenues and Expenses (a)

	A Current month actual	B Current month budget	C Current month variance (A–B)	D Year-to-date actual	E Year-to-date budget	F Year-to-date variance (D–E)	G Year-to-date prior year
Example A (direct expenses only)							
Operating revenue							
Inpatient	50,632	66,288	(15,656)	448,093	596,592	(148,499)	442,524
Outpatient	562,020	526,036	35,984	4,973,877	4,734,324	239,553	4,912,055
Total net revenue	612,652	592,324	20,328	5,421,970	5,330,916	91,054	5,354,578
Operating expenses							
Salaries and wages	268,176	245,276	22,900	2,373,358	2,207,484	165,874	2,333,131
Supplies	60,944	50,504	10,440	539,354	454,536	84,818	512,369
Purchased services	0	464	(464)	0	4,176	(4,176)	925
Repair, maintenance, rent, lease	3,948	8,460	(4,512)	34,940	76,140	(41,200)	30,819
Other direct expenses	784	1,128	(344)	6,938	10,152	(3,214)	3,041
Total operating expenses	333,852	305,832	28,020	2,954,590	2,752,488	202,102	2,880,285
Department profit (loss)	278,800	286,492	(7,692)	2,467,380	2,578,428	(111,048)	2,474,293
Example B (direct and indirect allocated expenses)							
Operating revenue							
Inpatient	50,632	66,288	(15,656)	448,093	596,592	(148,499)	442,524
Outpatient	562,020	526,036	35,984	4,973,877	4,734,324	239,553	4,912,055
Total net patient revenue	612,652	592,324	20,328	5,421,970	5,330,916	91,054	5,354,578
Operating expenses							
Salaries and wages	268,176	245,276	22,900	2,373,358	2,207,484	165,874	2,333,131
Supplies	60,944	50,504	10,440	539,354	454,536	84,818	512,369
Purchased services	0	464	(464)	0	4,176	(4,176)	925
Repair, maintenance, rent, lease	3,948	8,460	(4,512)	34,940	76,140	(41,200)	30,819
Other direct expenses	784	1,128	(344)	6,938	10,152	(3,214)	3,041
Allocated ancillary department expenses (b)	32,496	36,940	(4,444)	287,590	332,460	(44,870)	277,892
Allocated overhead department expenses (c)	92,796	86,632	6,164	821,245	779,688	41,557	801,256
Allocated facility and utility expenses (d)	72,940	73,840	(900)	645,519	664,560	(19,041)	650,896
Total operating expenses	532,084	503,244	28,840	4,708,943	4,529,196	179,747	4,610,329
Department profit (loss)	80,568	89,080	(8,512)	713,027	801,720	(88,693)	744,249

(a) All amounts in U.S. dollars.
(b) Includes dietary, housekeeping, security, central sterile, transport, etc.
(c) Includes business office, IT, human resources, medical records, executive suite, accounting, marketing, legal, contracting, etc.
(d) Includes building cost and maintenance, electric, gas, phone, Internet, etc.

of return. The degree of sophistication ranges from simply determining payback period to complex evaluations of revenue and expense streams that are discounted to net present value.[40]

Payback period is an uncomplicated capital investment analysis technique because it does not consider the net present value of revenue and expense streams for investment alternatives under consideration. It simply determines the number of years needed to recoup an initial investment. In payback period analysis, necessary components for each alternative are as follows:

- Initial investment and salvage value

- Annual operating revenue generated

- Annual cash expenses (includes both fixed and variable expenses, but typically excludes depreciation expenses, which are a noncash expense)

Dividing net investment by net benefit determines the number of years to return the cost of the investment. The general formula for the payback period is

$$Payback\ period = \frac{(Initial\ investment) - (Salvage\ value)}{(Operating\ revenue\ generated) - (Operating\ cash\ expenses)}$$

For example, a satellite ambulatory care center is considering purchasing a magnetic resonance imaging (MRI) scanner for diagnostic imaging. The MRI scanner's capital cost is $1,300,000; salvage value is $100,000 after 7 years. Anticipated volumes will result in revenue of $6,000 per operating day, or $1,680,000/year. Anticipated cost of salaries, supplies, and other cash expenses (excluding depreciation) is $1,380,000/year. Payback period analysis can be used to determine the number of years to recoup the initial investment as follows:

$$Payback\ period = \frac{\$(1,300,000 - \$100,000)}{\$(1,680,000 - 1,380,000)}$$

$$Payback\ period = \frac{\$1,200,000}{\$300,000}$$

$$Payback\ period = 4\ years$$

Management can use this information to determine if 4 years is an acceptable payback period. Payback period ranks and compares multiple capital investment alternatives. Results are distorted, however, if revenue and expense streams are dissimilar and useful lives of alternatives differ appreciably. Type of provider payment and payer mix affect analysis.

A more precise ranking index is the present value of alternatives, which produces a dollar answer. If net cash flows (revenues minus expenses) are discounted to present value (and assuming a given rate of interest), a new present value index like the payback index can be used to rank alternatives. Uses usually involve adding or replacing equipment, facility expansion, or alternatives such as building a parking deck or medical office building.

Alternative present value = Present value of the cash flows – Original investment

Another analytical technique for capital investment analysis is return on investment (ROI), which produces a percent answer. This methodology uses information in the alternative's net present value and converts it to a percent return over the life of the alternative. Most investments have lower revenues and higher expenses in the first year, and revenue increases each year as services are initiated and volume increases. Therefore, it is advisable to look at net cash flows over the life of the alternative.

This technique allows management to compare alternatives against a GB-approved hurdle rate. For example, most HSs have a fixed amount of cash/borrowing capacity for capital investment, and that cash is invested at a guaranteed return of 5%. Management might announce that requested alternatives must exceed a rate of 5% or have additional justification. The right answer depends on current cash position, borrowing capacity, and other competing needs for capital.

Discussion Questions

1. Explain the roles and responsibilities of the GB, CEO, CFO, controller, and treasurer as they relate to financial matters of the organization.

2. Explain the differences between an internal auditor and an independent auditor.

3. Briefly describe the uses of a balance sheet, statement of operations, and statement of cash flows.

4. Briefly describe the difference between direct allocation, step-down allocation, and double allocation.

5. Identify the pros and cons of the four methods of identifying product costs: ratio of costs to charges, process costing, job order costing, and activity-based costing.

6. What are the differences between operational planning and strategic planning?

7. Table 7.10 shows a departmental budget with and without indirect expense allocations. Prepare a written variance analysis of the two budgets. As the department manager, which variances would you investigate first and what steps would you take to control them?

8. Identify the pros and cons of the three methods of analyzing capital investments.

Case Study 1   Calculating Net Patient Services Revenue[41]

Assume a patient with commercial insurance is discharged from a hospital with incurred charges of $24,000. The hospital records an explicit price concession (as defined by the agreement with the insurance company) of $13,000, collects $10,000 from the insurance company, and sends a $1,000 bill to the patient. The hospital historically has collected 30% of the amount billed to patients in this portfolio (a group of patients with similar financial condition like a group of insured patients with a $1,000 copay), and thus records an estimated $700 implicit price concession when revenue is recorded.

Question

1. Provide the following missing information in the hospital's financial records:

    Charges for services rendered

    Explicit price concession

    Billed to and paid by insurance

    Billed to patient

    Implicit price concession

    Estimated amount to be collected from patient

Case Study 2   Calculating Bad Debt Expense[42]

Using the previous case, 1) assume the patient pays nothing with no reasonable explanation, and then 2) assume the patient pays nothing because of a documented bankruptcy.

Question

1. Fill in the missing blanks in the hospital's financial records:

	Assumption 1	Assumption 2
Charges for services rendered		
Explicit price concession		
Billed to and paid by insurance		
Billed to patient		
Implicit price concession		
Amount to be collected from patient		
Implicit price concession		
Bad debt expense		

Case Study 3   Analyzing Financial Statements

You are a financial consultant. Your first client, Colonial Medical Center, has asked you to analyze its financial statements (shown in Tables 7.3, 7.4, 7.5, and 7.6).

Question

1. Use ratio analysis to calculate the ratios and determine if each ratio is acceptable or unacceptable.

Case Study 4   Break-Even Analysis for a Capitated Contract[43]

Bend-Me Straight (BMS), an orthopedic surgical practice, is considering signing a capitated agreement with Comprehensive Care (CC), an HMO, for joint replacement surgery. CC would pay $200 per enrollee per year for 100 enrollees.

Question

1. If BMS wants to make a $2,000 profit on the program and if fixed costs are $5,000, BMS must keep variable costs per patient under what amount to make the desired profit?

Case Study 5   Your Organization's Path to the Second Curve: Integration and Transformation[44]

"Environmental pressures are driving hospitals and care systems toward greater clinical integration, more financial risk and increased accountability. To provide high-quality, efficient and integrated care, hospitals and care systems must explore and pursue transformational paths that align with the organization's mission and vision and cater to patients and communities. Hospital leaders need to develop strategies that move their organizations from the first curve, or volume-based environment, to the second curve, in which they will be building value-based systems and business models."

Question

1. You are the CFO of your HSO. Based on the above quote, how are you and the departments that report to you going to change to be ready for the second curve? Be specific.

Case Study 6   Economic Order Quantity and Total Cost

You are the director of supply chain for your HSO. See the information provided below about a needed item.

Price per unit is $5.

Annual demand is 20,000 units.

Cost of placing a single order is $10.

Interest rate is 10%.

Holding cost per unit is $.75/month, year?

Questions

1. Find the economic order quantity and the total cost associated with the above information.

2. Assuming you have only $90,000 budgeted for the item for the year, what price must you negotiate with the vendor to make budget?

Notes

1. In *Reserve Life Insurance Company v. Salter* (1957) 152 F. Supp. 868, the court found that the GB had failed in its duty to select a competent administrator: "Failing to appreciate their duties and responsibilities led these trustees to feel, according to their testimony, that they had discharged their duties by picking as an administrator, Salter, a former school teacher, apparently as ignorant of operating a hospital as they themselves were."

2. Berman, Howard J., Steven F. Kukla, and Lewis E. Weeks. *The Financial Management of Hospitals*, 8th ed., 38. Ann Arbor: Health Administration Press, 1994.

3. Cohen, Rick. "Sarbanes-Oxley: Ten Years Later. *Nonprofit Quarterly* 19 (2012): 46–50. *https://nonprofitquarterly.org/sarbanes-oxley-ten-years-later/,* retrieved December 22, 2019.

4. Ginn, Gregory O., Hope Rachel Hetico. "Sarbanes-Oxley and the Healthcare Industry." *Medical-Executive Post*, January 9, 2008. *https://medicalexecutivepost.com/2008/01/09/sarbanes-oxley-and-the-healthcare-industry/,* retrieved December 22, 2019.

5. U.S. Securities and Exchange Commission. "Audit Committees and Auditor Independence." *https://www.sec.gov/info/accountants/audit042707.htm,* retrieved December 22, 2019.

6. Carlson, R. Loring, John M. Coulter, and Thomas J. Vogel. "HealthSouth Corp.: The First Test of Sarbanes-Oxley." *Journal of Forensic & Investigative Accounting* 1, 2 (2009): 1–27. *http://web.nacva.com/JFIA/Issues/JFIA-2009-2_8.pdf,* retrieved on December 25, 2019.

7. Beam, Aaron and Chris Warner. *HealthSouth: The Wagon to Disaster.* Fairhope, AL: Wagon Publishing, 2009.

8. Healthcare Financial Management Association. "HFMA's Biennial Career and Compensation Guide, 2005." *hfm* (July 2005, suppl.): CS12–CS254.

9. Hegwer, Laura Ramos, and Nick Hut. "The Healthcare CFO of the Future." *hfm* (September 2019): 32–37.

10. The information in the "Controller" section is largely from Bragg, Steven M. *The Controller's Function: The Work of the Managerial Accountant*, 4th ed. Hoboken: John Wiley & Sons, 2011.

11. The information in the "Treasurer" section is largely from Bragg, Steven M. *Corporate Cash Management*, 3rd ed. Centennial, CO: Accounting Tools, Inc., 2017.

12. Bragg, *Corporate Cash Management*, 3.

13. The information in the "Independent Auditors" section is largely from Nowicki, Michael. *Introduction to the Financial Management of Healthcare Organizations*, 7th ed., 42–44. Chicago: Health Administration Press, 2018.

14. See *AICPA Audit & Accounting Guide for Health Care Entities, 2019*, for an example of the audit report, Exhibit 2-1, 46–47.

15. Securities and Exchange Commission. SEC Staff Accounting Bulletin 99—Materiality. August 12, 1999. *https://www.sec.gov/interps/account/sab99.htm*, retrieved January 11, 2020.

16. Carmichael, Doug. "Audit vs. Fraud Examination: What's the Real Difference?" *CPA Journal* (February 2018). *https://www.cpajournal.com/2018/03/05/audit-vs-fraud-examination/*, retrieved December 27, 2019

17. The information in the "Internal Auditors" section is largely from The Institute of Internal Auditors: North America. *Standards and Guidance*. *https://na.theiia.org/standards-guidance/Pages/Standards-and-Guidance-IPPF.aspx*, retrieved January11, 2020.

18. The Institute of Internal Auditors. *Internal Audit Reporting Relationships: Serving Two Masters*. March 2003. *https://na.theiia.org/iiarf/Public%20Documents/Internal%20Audit%20Reporting%20Relationships%20Serving%20Two%20Masters.pdf*, retrieved January12, 2020.

19. Nowicki, Michael. *Introduction to the Financial Management of Healthcare Organizations*, 44.

20. Advisory Board. "The Definition of 'Bad Debt' Just Changed. Here's What You Need to Know." March 23, 2018. *https://www.advisory.com/daily-briefing/2018/03/23/bad-debt*, retrieved December 27, 2019.

21. Bannow, Tara. "Implicit Price Disguises." *Modern Healthcare*, October 28, 2019.

22. AICPA. *Audit & Accounting Guide for Health Care Entities, 2019*, 54, 59. New York: Author, 2019.

23. Those interested in more information about this subject may refer to Zelman, William N., Michael J. McCue, Noah D. Glick, and Marci S. Thomas. *Financial Management of Health Care Organizations: An Introduction to Fundamental Tools, Concepts, and Applications*, 4th ed., chap. 4. San Francisco: Jossey-Bass, 2014.

24. Optum 360°. *2018 Almanac of Hospital Financial and Operating Indicators*. USA: Author.

25. Bellandi, Deanna. "Daughters Founder Dies: Sister Irene Kraus Was One of Healthcare's Leading Lights." *Modern Healthcare* (August 31, 1998). *https://www.modernhealthcare.com/article/19980831/PREMIUM/808310328/daughters-founder-dies-sister-irene-kraus-was-one-of-healthcare-s-leading-lights*, retrieved December 31, 2019.

26. The "Cost Accounting" section is adapted from Nowicki, *Introduction to the Financial Management of Healthcare Organizations*, 7th ed., chap. 8.

27. Schwartz, William B., and Daniel N. Mendelson. "Hospital Cost Containment in the 1980s—Hard Lessons Learned and Prospects for the 1990s." *New England Journal of Medicine*, 324, 15 (April 11, 1991). *https://www.nejm.org/doi/full/10.1056/NEJM199104113241506*, retrieved December 31, 2019.

28. American Hospital Association. "Total Hospital Closures in the 1980s Hit 698." *Hospitals*, June 20, 1990.

29. Strata Decision Technology and Becker's Healthcare. "CFOs' Fatal Flaw: Survey Finds 9 out of 10 Hospital Executives Don't Know Their Cost." *https://go.beckershospitalreview.com/cfos-fatal-flaw-survey-finds-9-of-10-hospital-executives-dont-know-their-cost*, retrieved December 21, 2019.

30. Lawson, Raef. "Costing Practices in Healthcare Organizations: A Look at Adoption of ABC." HFMA featured on-line article, December 5, 2017, *https://www.hfma.org/topics/article/57198.html*, retrieved January 3, 2020.

31. Zelman et al. *Financial Management of Health Care Organizations*, 560.

32. Lawson, Raef. "Costing Practices in Healthcare Organizations."

33. The information in the "Reimbursement" section is largely from Zeiler, Kevin D. "Managing Costs and Revenues." In *Introduction to Health Care Management*, 4th ed., edited by Sharon B. Buchbinder, Nancy H. Shanks, and Bobbie J. Kite, 223-250. Burlington: Jones & Bartlett Learning, 2021.

34. Centers for Medicare and Medicaid Studies, Office of the Actuary, National Health Statistics Group, and Department of Commerce, Census Bureau. "National Health Expenditures and Health Insurance Enrollment, Aggregate and Per Enrollee Amounts, and Annual Growth, by Source of Funds, Calendar Years 2012–2018." NHE Tables, Table 4. *https://www.cms.gov/Research-Statistics-Data-and-Systems/Statistics-Trends-and-Reports/NationalHealthExpendData/NationalHealthAccountsHistorical*, retrieved January 1, 2020.

35. The information in the "Payment Methodologies" section is largely from AICPA. *Audit & Accounting Guide for Health Care Entities, 2019*, 214–215. New York: Author, 2019.

36. Miller, Harold. "From Volume to Value: Better Ways to Pay For Health Care." *Health Affairs*, September/October 2009. *https://www.healthaffairs.org/doi/full/10.1377/hlthaff.28.5.1418*, retrieved January 2, 2020.

37. The information in the "Working Capital" section is largely from Nowicki, *Introduction to the Financial Management of Healthcare Organizations,* 7th ed., chap. 10.

38. Contributions to the section on budgeting and other financial control methods were made by Joy Volarich, MBA, MHA, CHFP. Ms. Volarich is an adjunct instructor at The George Washington University.

39. Finkler, Steven A. "Flexible Budgeting Allows for Better Management of Resources as Needs Change." *Hospital Cost Management and Accounting* 8 (June 1996): 1.

40. Further reading about the capital budgeting analytical technique in HSOs can be found in Baker, Judith J., R. W. Baker., and Neil R. Dworkin. *Health Care Finance: Basic Tools for Non-financial Managers,* 5th ed., chap. 17. Sudbury, MA: Jones and Bartlett Publishers, 2018; Zelman et al. *Financial Management of Health Care Organizations,* chaps. 7 and 8; Pink, George H., and Paula H. Song, *Gapenski's Understanding Healthcare Financial Management,* 8th ed., chaps. 6–12. Chicago: Health Administration Press, 2020.

41. Thomas, Karen. Healthcare Financial Management Association. "Healthcare Financial Management Association Releases Revenue Recognition Guidance," January 2019. *https://www.globenewswire.com/news-release/2019/01/18/1702024/0/en/Healthcare-Financial-Management-Association-Releases-Revenue-Recognition-Guidance.html,* retrieved September 6, 2019, with personal correspondence to author on September 7, 2019, from Brian Conner.

42. Thomas, Healthcare Financial Management Association.

43. Nowicki, *Introduction to the Financial Management of Healthcare Organizations,* 7th ed., 197.

44. AHA. "Your Hospital's Path to the Second Curve: Integration and Transformation." January 1, 2014. *https://www.aha.org/ahahret-guides/2014-01-01-your-hospitals-path-second-curve-integration-and-transformation,* retrieved January 2, 2020.

8

The Quality Imperative: Implementation

Chapter Outline

Undertaking Process Improvement
Other Improvement Methodologies
Improvement and Problem Solving
Statistical Process Control
Tools for Improvement
Productivity and Productivity Improvement
LIPs and CQI
Patient and Staff Safety in Healthcare
QI Methods Useful in Patient and Staff Safety
Overlap of Patient and Staff Safety
Sustainability

Efforts toward quality improvement (QI) focus on doing the right things and doing the right things right. This chapter builds on the theory of quality/productivity improvement (Q/PI) discussed in Chapter 4 and introduces a continuous quality improvement (CQI) process improvement (PI) model. The chapter also discusses the relationship between problem solving and use of teams in PI, and it addresses benchmarking, six sigma, lean manufacturing, and reengineering. Accreditation and registration by The Joint Commission and the International Organization for Standardization (ISO), respectively, are noted. The chapter describes productivity improvement[1] methods to improve work systems and job design; capacity and facilities layout; and production control, scheduling, and materials handling. It also considers the necessity for and means of achieving LIP involvement in Q/PI. The chapter concludes with a discussion of patient and staff safety. As Chapter 4 noted, performance improvement and productivity improvement are treated as synonyms even though logically sequencing their relationship would have improved productivity following improved performance.

Typically, health services organizations (HSOs) and health systems (HSs) have a chief quality officer (CQO), who is a member of senior management and responsible for Q/PI. The Institute for Healthcare Improvement (IHI) identified five primary activities for CQOs in HSs, which also apply to HSOs: 1) develop the infrastructure to support quality; 2) create a culture that enables and motivates people; 3) plan; 4) improve; and 5) sustain improvement.[2] The last three suggest the Juran Quality Trilogy, as discussed in Chapter 4. Educating staff about Q/PI is key to success.

The section on Patient and Staff Safety in Healthcare was written by Mary Mohyla, RN, CIC, Senior Director, Quality and Accreditation, Holy Cross Health, Silver Spring, Maryland.

Undertaking Process Improvement

Q/PI begins by selecting a process to improve and choosing the members of the quality improvement team (QIT). Improving quality takes significant staff time, both for team members and for those supporting it. Thus, the HSO is best served if high-value processes are improved first. Success in improving simple, important processes—picking the "low-hanging fruit"—will produce results quickly, show CQI's value, and convince staff of its usefulness.

Figure 8.1 shows the flow of QI activities. Data sources (many of them outcome indicators) focus the attention of the quality improvement council (QIC), which is the coordinating body. As Chapter 4 noted, the QIC approves (sanctions) formation of cross-functional QITs to analyze processes and recommend changes to improve them. Intradepartmental and functional QITs are established by departments and/or managers who are part of the functional area(s) that are monitored locally. In addition, departments or functional areas may assign staff who may be the process owner(s) (controls/responsible for a process) to monitor and improve processes. QICs may have authority to approve changes and expenditures based on QIT recommendations. More likely a senior manager must approve changes.

QITs

The basic component for undertaking quality improvement is the QIT, sometimes known as a PI team (PIT), despite the latter's unfortunate acronym. As noted, QITs may be internal to a function or department or may be cross-functional. The plan, do, study, act (PDSA) cycle described in Chapter 4 is the basic methodology used by QITs.

QITs are composed of persons who have process knowledge and who can document the process as it functions *currently*. Understanding the process in its current state is essential. Processes tend to entropy—they devolve to a lower level of performance than that intended in the quality planning phase described by Juran. The QIT identifies the key quality characteristics (KQCs) of the process—a process outcome that measures quality: patient satisfaction, waiting time, or accuracy of medication. There may be several KQCs. Next, the QIT develops an understanding of the process. Flowcharts, also known as flow diagrams or process maps, are used to visualize and understand the process in its current state. The most useful visualization of a process will show its complexity in detail. Process complexity and handoffs from one step to the next are common sources of delay, error, and rework. Only by understanding everything about the process can improvement be effected.

QITs for processes that are cross-functional or interdepartmental must be sanctioned by the QIC. This is done because 1) it is likely that more resources will be needed to effect improvement, 2) it is likely that more than one department or process will be studied, and 3) changes recommended by cross-functional teams must be judged and possibly implemented. Thus, it is necessary to obtain the QIC's imprimatur.

After the process is fully understood, data can be collected to learn if the process is in control (i.e., only common cause variation [within 3 standard deviations]) is present. A process not in control must be brought into control before it can be improved. Bringing a process into control means eliminating special cause variation, which is variation beyond 3 standard deviations. Walter A. Shewhart termed variation beyond 3 standard deviations assignable variation. Once a process is in control, key process variables (KPVs) can be identified and measured, and the data can be used to determine the points in the process at which to make change(s) to help the process meet the KQC(s). The process should be changed in only one way at a time so that effects of a change can be measured. Data collected after the change measure effects of the change. Understanding cause and effect is key to further improvement. A pilot project or experimental design should be used so that change(s) in processes used elsewhere in the HSO can be understood before they are widely implemented. For example, changes in a nursing care process should be piloted (tested) in one unit before being more widely implemented.

Figures 8.2 and 8.3 show monitoring and evaluating a process, respectively. Both are key to successful PI. Formal data sources include routine reports, run charts, control charts, and

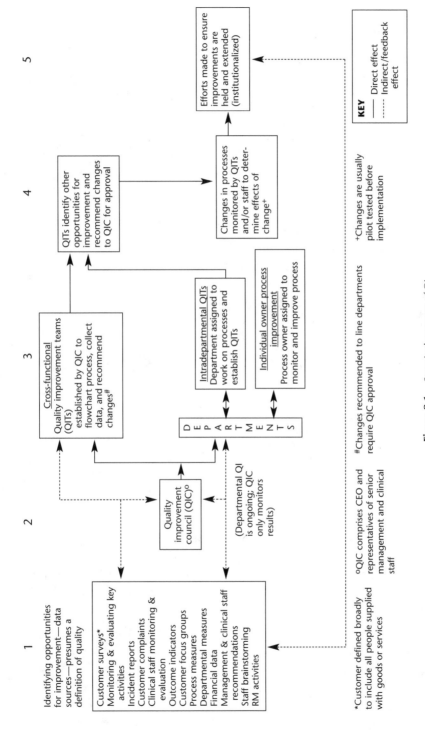

1

Identifying opportunities for improvement—data sources—presumes a definition of quality

Customer surveys*
Monitoring & evaluating key activities
Incident reports
Customer complaints
Clinical staff monitoring & evaluation
Outcome indicators
Customer focus groups
Process measures
Departmental measures
Financial data
Management & clinical staff recommendations
Staff brainstorming
RM activities

2

Quality improvement council (QIC)°

(Departmental QI is ongoing; QIC only monitors results)

3

Cross-functional Quality improvement teams (QITs) established by QIC to flowchart process, collect data, and recommend changes#

D E P A R T M E N T S

Intradepartmental QITs
Department assigned to work on processes and establish QITs

Individual owner process improvement
Process owner assigned to monitor and improve process

4

QITs identify other opportunities for improvement and recommend changes to QIC for approval

Changes in processes monitored by QITs and/or staff to determine effects of change+

5

Efforts made to ensure improvements are held and extended (institutionalized)

KEY
—— Direct effect
- - - Indirect/feedback effect

*Customer defined broadly to include all people supplied with goods or services

°QIC comprises CEO and representatives of senior management and clinical staff

#Changes recommended to line departments require QIC approval

+Changes are usually pilot tested before implementation

Figure 8.1. Steps in the process of QI.

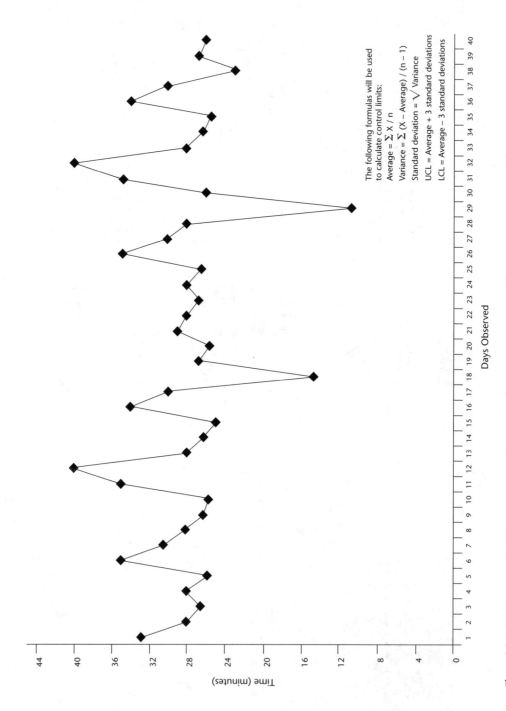

Figure 8.2. Run Chart: Time elapsed between noon meal food trays leaving kitchen and first patient receiving tray on unit 2W, by day, in minutes. UCL, upper control limit; LCL, lower control limit. Source for formulas: Dunn, Oliver Jean. *Basic Statistics: A Primer for the Biomedical Sciences.* New York City: John Wiley & Sons, Inc., 1964, 38.

The following formulas will be used
to calculate control limits:

Average = $\sum x / n$

Variance = $\sum (X - \text{Average}) / (n - 1)$

Standard deviation = $\sqrt{\text{Variance}}$

UCL = Average + 3 standard deviations

LCL = Average − 3 standard deviations

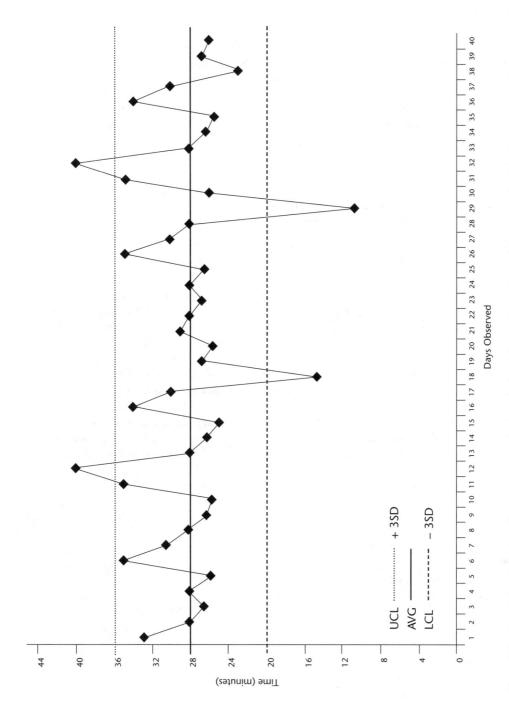

Figure 8.3. Control Chart: Time elapsed between noon meal food trays leaving kitchen and first patient receiving tray on unit 2W, by day, in minutes. UCL, upper control limit; LCL, lower control limit.

customer and staff surveys. Informal, anecdotal data sources include customer complaints and staff suggestions. Both types must be organized to be usable in decision making.

Other Improvement Methodologies

Since the concepts of CQI, including the PDSA cycle, were first applied to health services in the 1980s, there have been many permutations. Some, such as the ISO standards, predate health services applications but do not predate concepts such as statistical process control (SPC), developed in the 1920s. Others are "old wine in new bottles"; they are posited as more useful or effective than CQI but are primarily repackaged variations of it. This does not denigrate their usefulness, but it suggests that basic CQI and its corollaries are intrinsic to them. Anyone versed in the fundamentals of CQI will find a familiar landscape.

Lean and Six Sigma

Lean reduces waste and eliminates unnecessary steps to increase throughput speed and productivity. Six sigma reduces variation to improve quality.[3] Typically, lean and six sigma are used complementarily.

Lean

Lean is derived from the Toyota production system, or just-in-time production. Its antecedents are Eli Whitney (American [1765–1825]), who developed interchangeable parts to manufacture muskets in 1799, and Henry Ford (American [1863–1947]), who developed the assembly line to manufacture the Ford Model T in 1910. Ford may be considered the first user of just-in-time and lean manufacturing, although those terms were not known at the time. After World War II, Taiichi Ohno (Japanese [1912–1990]) and Shigeo Shingo (Japanese [1909–1990]) applied Ford production, SPC, and quality circles at Toyota in Japan.[4]

The benefits of lean come only after strategic planning. A lack of governing body (GB) and senior management knowledge and commitment is often blamed for failure of a transformation to lean. Short-term solutions are not the answer,[5] a theme repeatedly sounded by Deming. In health services delivery, theories of lean can be applied as lean processes.[6]

Lean's goal is to eliminate activities that add no value. Customers will pay for value. Lean relies on various methods and tools, including problem-solving diagrams and statistical techniques, to find waste.[7] Common sources of waste include processing, correction, overproduction, needless motion, material movement, waiting, and inventory. A typical example in healthcare is the work-around that occurs when nursing staff must obtain supplies from another nursing unit if the supply chain does not or cannot meet the needs of their unit. Preventive error proofing is needed because lean implementation often results in *reduction* of automation and an increase in manual labor (for some processes automation is less flexible than an operator). The possibility that manual labor may be more effective than automation for a specific use is counterintuitive and requires adaptive thinking. It must be borne in mind that reducing automation may increase the opportunity for error even if work is standardized.[8] Fewer errors using automation assumes that devices are calibrated properly and in good repair. Deming noted that devices (he called them gadgets) may increase variation in a process if they are constantly adjusting for the previous result, which renders them a mechanical form of tampering.[9]

Staff empowerment is integral to lean because as the number of staff decreases, those remaining must find ways to overcome the deficiency. This approach allows staff intellect to be applied in problem solving, encourages buy-in, and enables self-actualization.

Six Sigma

Lean often precedes use of six sigma, a statistical description of performance. Some literature combines the two as "lean–six sigma." Six sigma originated with the work of mathematician Carl Frederick Gauss (German [1777–1855]), who developed the concept of the normal curve.

Shewhart (and Deming) used *three sigma* to distinguish nonassignable from assignable variation and guide decisions about the actions to be taken. *Six sigma* as applied to QI was first used by Motorola engineer Bill Smith (American [1929–1993]) and has been refined since the 1970s into a change-management and data-driven methodology focusing on business excellence.[10] The objective of six sigma is to reduce process output variation so that over time there are no more than 3.4 defects per million opportunities (for defects). For example, a healthcare process with a sigma level between 5 and 6 is 5.4 deaths caused by anesthesia per million surgeries. A sigma level between 3 and 4 is 1% of a million hospitalized patients (10,000) injured by negligence.[11] As the sigma value of a process increases from 0 to 6, the variation of the process around the mean value decreases. With a high enough sigma value, the process approaches zero variation and is known as having zero defects. Decreasing process variation increases the sigma of the process, resulting in higher customer satisfaction and lower costs.[12] A framework within which to apply six sigma to reduce variation uses a methodology with a long history in health services quality and performance improvement—define, measure, analyze, improve, control (DMAIC).[13]

ISO 9000 and ISO 14000

In 1947, the ISO (Geneva, Switzerland), began developing voluntary technical standards for almost all sectors of business, industry, and technology. ISO 9000 and ISO 14000 are two families of generic management systems standards applicable in health services. *Generic* means the standards can be applied to any activity, whether product or service based; *management system* means what the organization does to manage its processes or activities. ISO 9000 is concerned with *quality management*, that is, what the organization is doing to enhance customer satisfaction by meeting customer and applicable regulatory requirements and to continuously improve performance.[14] ISO 14000 is concerned with environmental management and what the organization does to minimize its activities' harmful effects on the environment and to continuously improve its environmental performance.[15]

Once standards are implemented, the organization seeks certification and is audited by an independent auditor who determines if the quality management system (QMS) conforms to the ISO standard. If so, certification is recorded by the auditing body, which is registration of the QMS.[16] Like accreditation by The Joint Commission, ISO 9000–compliant organizations have met the minimum standards for a QMS. Unlike The Joint Commission, which employs surveyors and manages the accreditation process, ISO neither conducts certification to its standards nor controls the business aspects of certification activities.[17]

ISO standards do not define quality—the organization does. The guidelines in the standards provide the *structure* for developing and maintaining a QMS. Customers know the organization is structured to produce consistent results. The organization may extend its QMS requirements up the supply chain and require ISO registration of suppliers to ensure conformance to requirements. ISO registration by suppliers helps ensure the inputs HSOs receive have few or no defects. Higher-quality inputs enable HSOs to perform with fewer quality problems.

There are seven quality management principles (QMP) of ISO 9000:

QMP 1. *Customer focus*—The primary focus of quality management is to meet customer requirements and to strive to exceed customer expectations.

QMP 2. *Leadership*—Leaders at all levels establish unity of purpose and direction and create conditions in which people are engaged in achieving the organization's quality objectives.

QMP 3. *Engagement of people*—Competent, empowered, and engaged people at all levels throughout the organization are essential to enhance its capability to create and deliver value.

QMP 4. *Process approach*—Consistent and predictable results are achieved more effectively and efficiently when activities are understood and managed as interrelated processes that function as a coherent system.

QMP 5. *Improvement*—Successful organizations have an ongoing focus on improvement.

QMP 6. *Evidence-based decision making*—Decisions based on the analysis and evaluation of data and information are more likely to produce desired results.

QMP 7. *Relationship management*—For sustained success, an organization manages its relationships with interested parties, such as suppliers.[18]

By the late 1990s, registration to ISO 9000 standards had made few inroads into the dominant positions in health services accreditation held by The Joint Commission and accreditors such as the Community Health Accreditation Program and the National Committee for Quality Assurance. By 2012, only 40 U.S. hospitals were ISO registered.[19] Det Norske Veritas Germanischer Lloyd (DNV GL) Healthcare was discussed in Chapter 1. DNV GL Healthcare was granted "deeming authority" by the Centers for Medicare & Medicaid Services (CMS) in 2009. Deeming authority means providers accredited by DNV GL Healthcare can be reimbursed for services provided to federal healthcare program beneficiaries. DNV GL Healthcare uses a combination of National Integrated Accreditation for Healthcare Organizations standards, which are based on the CMS conditions of participation, and ISO 9000-2000 quality standards. The survey process is described at https://www.isheweb.org/documents/ASHEPresentation DN.pdf. At this writing, over 500 hospitals were in deemed status using DNV GL Healthcare accreditation.[20] Most affected by growth of DNV GL Healthcare accreditation will be The Joint Commission, which has been the preeminent accrediting body for over 100 years.

Reengineering

Reengineering is more technique and less philosophy, and it complements CQI. It is "plan" in the PDSA cycle, and quality planning in the Juran Quality Trilogy, as described in Chapter 4. CQI and reengineering are process oriented and dedicated to improvement; they begin with the customer.[21] Reengineering is an approach in the continuum of improvement that builds on CQI principles and tools.[22] It adds features of radical change and process redesign.

Michael Hammer (American [1948–2008]) and James Champy (American [1942–]) defined reengineering as "the fundamental rethinking and radical redesign of business processes to achieve dramatic improvement in critical, contemporary measures of performance such as costs, quality, service, and speed."[23] Sometimes termed process innovation or core process redesign,[24] reengineering as applied to health services seeks fundamental and radical change in processes and how healthcare is arranged and delivered, including time and place.[25]

Outward-In, Right to Left

Creating quality and enhancing competitive position require an outward-in orientation. To obtain the high-quality service that enhances competitive position, reengineering directs HSOs/HSs to work backward—thinking right to left—to improve processes. The CQI model in Figure 4.3 focuses meeting customer needs to gain a competitive advantage [5]. This is done through quality outcomes that conform to requirements and meet or exceed customer expectations [4]. CQI changes existing processes incrementally to improve quality.[26] Changes in customers' needs or competition may cause a performance gap.

> If the world has changed dramatically since the process was (or most recently [was]) redesigned, the current design may be fundamentally flawed and incapable of delivering the required performance. Reengineering is then called for. Reengineering does not merely enhance the individual steps of the process but entirely reconsiders how they are put together.[27]

The transition from inpatient to outpatient care in HSOs,[28] including support mechanisms, apparatus, facilities, and staffing, is an example of a radical change in the process of delivering care. Formation of HSs is an example of redesigning integration and delivery of care among entities. The shift toward prospective pricing and managed care increased the bargaining power of payers and required rethinking how HSOs and HSs do business.

Elements

The following are eight critical elements of reengineering:

1. Outside-in, customer focus, putting the organization in the shoes of the customers to understand and meet their needs

2. Focusing on cross-functional, end-to-end processes, versus intradepartmental processes

3. Understanding processes and customer requirements, leading to recognition of the weaknesses of the existing process and the performance requirements of the new one[29]

4. Articulating a vision of where the HSO/HS wants to be in the future, with that vision communicated and understood by all organization members

5. Practicing top-down rather than bottom-up leadership initiated with committed senior-level management who elicit and obtain acceptance by process owners

6. Identifying and questioning underlying assumptions about processes

7. Designing new processes, including piloting (small-scale use) to see if they work, and redesigning and rolling out the new processes in rapid fashion

8. Supporting reengineering with an organizational environment that includes communication throughout the organization, supportive leader personal behavior, measurements, rewards, and "selling the new way of working and living to the organization as a whole"[30]

Additional elements to be implemented are senior management's commitment to and championing of reengineering; identification of process owners—those with direct interest in and responsibility for processes—and empowering them to initiate change; formation of reengineering teams to diagnose existing processes, oversee redesign, and implement new processes; and use of a steering committee, "a policy-making body of senior managers who develop the organization's overall reengineering strategy and monitor its progress."[31]

What Reengineering Is Not (Reengineering and CQI)

A major criticism of reengineering is that it is an excuse to justify downsizing, which includes cost-reduction strategies to reduce labor costs, outsource work previously done in house, replace permanent with temporary employees,[32] or discontinue programs or services. Reengineering can be differentiated by what it is not. It is not automating, restructuring, or downsizing, nor is it reorganizing, de-layering, or flattening the organization. These results do occur, however, with the "clean sheet of paper" radical, cross-functional redesign with a customer focus. Further, reengineering is not CQI. "Quality improvement seeks steady incremental improvement to process performance. Reengineering . . . seeks breakthroughs, not by enhancing existing processes, but by discarding and replacing them with entirely new ones."[33] CQI improves processes and performance on a consistent upward slope. At some point performance gaps, such as diminished competitive position and changed customer needs and demands, necessitate replacing some processes using reengineering, which is a stepwise change, rather than a slope. After reengineering, CQI—improvement of new, redesigned processes—continues until external forces require another breakthrough change. This relationship is like the Juran Quality Trilogy (described in Chapter 4) of quality planning (reengineering), quality control (preparatory to CQI), and quality improvement (CQI).

The drivers of reengineering include a strategy of retrenchment because the HSO/HS no longer has a competitive advantage or market position for a program or service; because of limited resources that can be allocated more effectively to other existing or new services; or because of changing needs of patients, including shifts in market demand or composition. Examples include exiting a product or service line, based on assessment of external threats and opportunities and internal strengths and weaknesses, or a situation in which the HSO/HS cannot maintain or attain a comparative advantage. Reengineering as the organization's response to a changing marketplace can be viewed as *strategic* in nature, whereas CQI is *tactical*.[34]

Applications

Reengineering solves problems about service decentralization, clinical resource management, patient aggregation, skill-mix changes, and modifying noncore processes. Service decentralization occurs when ancillary services, such as respiratory therapy, physical therapy, dietary, laboratory, and radiology are separate departments in hospitals. Multiple patient handoffs and "throwing services over the wall" to the next department cause scheduling problems, increased patient waiting times, and decreased patient satisfaction. Reengineering connects departments to improve efficiency. Similarly, support services, such as phlebotomy and respiratory services, were initiated on the nursing units. "Housekeeping, dietary, and EKGs were often combined into new patient services positions titled patient care associates, patient care partners, or support partners."[35] Clinical resource management initiatives involved creating clinical protocols to lessen treatment variation and provide a day-to-day schedule for each type of patient by diagnosis using licensed independent practitioner (LIP) "best practices." Only modest success was reported here, however.[36]

Patient aggregation and process redesign involves grouping patients who need similar clinical skills and resources. Homogeneous patient populations allow dedicated delivery teams to enhance their skills, improve coordination and continuity of care, decrease unnecessary clinical variation, enhance outcomes of quality, and increase patient satisfaction.[37] Skill-mix changes used nursing assistants instead of licensed practical nurses and lessened primary nursing. Examples of reengineering in nonpatient care include increased charge capture, improved materials contracts, and modified employee benefits.[38]

Although advocates of reengineering state that downsizing and de-layering are not a focus, it was reported that "downsizing through layoffs was specifically a focus of many executives,"[39] in part because of lower inpatient census and diminished competitive position. Those critical of reengineering cite its use to absolve HSOs of blame if layoffs are perceived negatively.[40]

Reengineering: Barriers and Facilitators

Change is threatening. Successful CQI and performance improvement require it. Changes for improvement can occur only if managers are willing to make them. Resistance to change may be political, or it may arise if those affected adversely are resistant, have low tolerance for change and prefer the status quo, or are unconvinced change is needed. Resistance may be overt or covert. Managers must identify resistance to change, understand what causes it, offer incentives to those affected and disincentives to those not accepting it, and address concerns of those affected.[41] Table 8.1 summarizes facilitators and barriers to reengineering.

Vision, organizational values, senior management commitment, LIP participation, process design and implementation, and performance measures help ensure its success. Complete and open communication lessens fear and dispels uncertainty; employee involvement may lead to their co-optation and accepting ownership of the change. Chapter 12 discusses resistance as a natural reaction to change. Chapter 13 discusses overcoming resistance to change.

Reengineering can be especially effective in hospitals because of the "silos" that have traditionally separated departments and functions from one another. Reengineering systems and processes can be the basis for higher quality and improved performance.[42]

Improvement and Problem Solving

Problem solving for PI uses the problem-solving model shown in Figure 6.3. Conditions that initiate problem solving are deviation (actual results are inconsistent with those desired), crisis, opportunity or threat, and improvement (see Figure 6.4). As with other categories, problem solving under the condition of improvement involves 1) problem analysis, including stating the problem, 2) developing assumptions, 3) identifying tentative alternative solutions, 4) developing and applying decision criteria, 5) selecting the alternative that fits the criteria best, 6) implementing the solution chosen, and 7) evaluating the solution. Postchange performance is compared with the results desired.

Table 8.1 Reengineering facilitators and barriers

Facilitators	Barriers
Establish and maintain a constant, consistent vision	Lack of continuity of vision/purpose
	Disconnection of vision from environment
Prepare smooth transitions for the reengineering effort	Poor transition between project phases
	Planning to implementation
	Implementation to a continued process
Prepare and train for reengineering changes	Inadequate administrative skills
	Inadequate clinical/technical skills
Establish continual, multiple communication methods	Historical practices
	Lack of continuity of communication
	Little or inadequate feedback
	Perceived dishonest communication
Establish strong support and involvement	Inconsistent support and involvement
	Lack of consistent and even administrative support
	Lack of equitable departmental participation
Establish mechanisms to measure reengineering's progress and outcomes	Inability to measure progress
	Complexity of changes without understanding causal mechanisms
Effectively establish both new authority and responsibility relationships	Inadequate authority/responsibilities assigned
Find methods to involve physicians	Lack of time and interest

From Walston, Stephen L., and John R. Kimberly. "Reengineering Hospitals: Evidence from the Field." *Hospital & Health Services Administration* 42 (Summer 1997): 153; reprinted by permission from Wolters Kluwer Health.

The PDSA cycle is conceptually like the steps of problem solving. CQI also involves problem solving under the condition of deviation, as when special cause variation is investigated. CQI, however, enhances performance by improving processes. The situation analysis step is different when the problem-solving model is applied to opportunities for improvement. It involves collecting and evaluating data about a process that is "in control" so opportunities for improvement can be identified. The purpose is to make the acceptable better. Improvement problem solving for Deming is reducing common cause variation in processes; for Juran, it is moving a process to the new zone of quality control; and for Philip B. Crosby, it is moving toward the goal of doing it right the first time.

The discussion of making assumptions in Chapter 6 states that narrow, overly restrictive structural, personal, and problem-centered assumptions produce lower-quality solutions, which are less adequate because restrictive assumptions limit the range of alternatives. The same concern arises in PI.

The advantages of group problem solving discussed in Chapter 6 are even more applicable to PI. Participation of persons with process knowledge is essential for a QIT to be effective.[43] In addition, QIT members learn new tasks, become aware of others' problems, and are more attuned to the triple role of customer, processor, and supplier. Figure 4.1 in Chapter 4 shows Juran's triple role of the worker. Team members will be more eager to assist in solving problems, team spirit will develop, and motivation and a sense of worth will be enhanced.[44] An important benefit, especially for cross-functional QITs, is that staff will see more clearly how their work fits into the whole system of delivering services and how what they do can help optimize the system.

Management must show its commitment to CQI by allocating resources for education, staff, and computer software, implementing a participative philosophy, and encouraging employee team building. Deming, Juran, and Crosby advocated giving employees the authority to act. Others call it empowerment.[45] The knowledge of QIT team members allows systematic dissection of a process so it can be fully understood, as requisite to improvement.

Statistical Process Control

Life teaches there is variation in everything, everywhere. Examples are the time it takes to travel to work and return home, or the time needed to perform a repetitive task. It takes but a bit of imagination to apply that same concept of variation to any workplace process. This allows one to understand how variation in a process contributes to output of lesser quality. Managers must ask a basic question: To whom (or what) are quality issues in process output to be attributed? Historically, the answer has been that workers are responsible for what they produce. The process is fine; it was planned and implemented by management. It is the worker in the process who causes poor quality. That perception began changing in the 1980s.

Deming and Juran asserted that poor quality is almost always caused by processes, not workers. They emphasized use of statistical methods for quality control and the need to identify sources of process variation.[46] Deming was adamant that variation in processes causes poor quality. Ample empirical evidence shows he was correct. Many consider the world's finest violins to be those crafted by Antonio Stradivari in the 17th and 18th centuries. These instruments were made to a perfect thickness in all parts; the result, even centuries later, is an incomparable quality of sound. The seven-time world champion Formula One driver, Michael Schumacher, best known as a driver for Ferrari, determined the fastest line around a racetrack at practice. During the race, he deviated from that line as little as possible, thereby earning the best time and, ultimately, 91 victories.

For purposes of SPC, Deming defined variation as "performance within three standard deviations of the mean—a generous amount of variation, although management can set more stringent limits."[47] Depending on the process and amount of variation in it, HSOs/HSs may set control limits at two standard deviations. Narrowing control limits risks increasing the number of false positives—common cause variation (caused by unknown factors in the process) that appears to be special cause variation (caused by known factors) but is not. Thus, management may try to find the source of what appears to be special cause variation, an exercise in futility because the false positive is common cause variation, which cannot be assigned to a source.

Variation within control limits is common cause variation and is produced by the process. Variation beyond the control limits is special cause variation. Shewhart called special cause variation assignable because, usually, it could be attributed to a cause from outside the process. Special cause variation may be negative or positive. Reasons for negative special cause variation must be identified and prevented, if possible.[48] Examples include an act of nature, such as a hurricane, or delays in service because of an unanticipated surge in arrivals in the emergency department (ED). Special cause variation for Juran is the "sporadic spike," which causes the process to not be "in control." Deming and Juran asserted that only processes "in control," meaning those affected only by common cause variation, can be improved. Juran referred to this performance improvement as moving to the "new zone of quality control." Deming termed this improving the process by decreasing common cause variation around the mean. For Crosby, it meant moving through the organizational maturity stages toward certainty and striving for the goal of "do it right the first time." Deming used control charts to determine if a process is stable (in statistical control). If so, its performance is predictable; improvement can begin.

The most important reason for performance improvement is to reduce common cause variation around the mean in a process that is in statistical control. To be in statistical control means that in a control chart with control limits of ±3 standard deviations, there is a 99.74%

probability the next data point (process output being measured) will be within control limits, even though it is impossible to know where within the control limits that data point will fall.

Deming asserted all processes in (statistical) control can be improved, and initiatives to reduce variation will result in higher quality, which in turn means improved productivity. Juran called this moving to the new zone of quality control. For Crosby, this is moving toward the goal of zero defects.

Tools for Improvement

Control Charts

Control charts are essential to SPC and successful Q/PI. Chapter 4 discusses the theoretical bases for control charts. Control charts are essential to distinguishing common cause variation from special cause variation, an ability indispensable to managing effectively. Special cause variation *cannot* be identified only by looking at a set of numbers, even if they are arrayed on a run chart. Control limits *must* be calculated.

Run charts are a simple data collection tool. Figure 8.2 is a run chart of data that show performance of one aspect of inpatient food service on a nursing unit. Run chart data are used to calculate the standard deviation. As already noted, 3 standard deviations are commonly used in SPC. Drawn on the run chart, the upper and lower control limits of 3 standard deviations transform it into a control chart as in Figure 8.3. Thus, the process itself sets the limits that distinguish common cause from special cause variation. As a corollary, it is wrong to set an arbitrary number that the process (and its workers) is expected to produce. Process capability—the capacity of the process—is inherent in it and necessarily limits performance of the process.

Both run charts and control charts array data on two axes. The vertical axis is the performance being measured; the horizontal axis shows time. Control charts can be used to monitor any process, such as customer waiting time in patient admitting, units of laboratory output, or utilization of diagnostic equipment.

The control chart in Figure 8.3 shows an average time of 28 minutes between when noon meal trays leave the kitchen and when a tray is delivered to the first patient on nursing unit 2W. There is wide common cause variation around the mean, however, with a range of 23 to 35 minutes. This process is not "in control," because there are four special cause variation data points—two well below the lower control limit (LCL) and two well above the upper control limit (UCL). As a first step, SPC requires that the process is brought into control by investigating special causes of variation to determine their sources. Delivery times of 40 minutes will almost certainly diminish customer satisfaction. Negative special causes should be identified and eliminated, if possible, or if not, their effects on the process must be minimized. Positive special cause variation is present in delivery times that were much shorter than the mean of 28 minutes. Early delivery times are not necessarily better; nursing staff and patients may not be ready for the meal. They do, however, show faster delivery is possible. Reasons for the positive special cause variation should be identified and, if possible, incorporated into the process because it is almost certain that food delivered sooner will be more palatable, of higher quality, and, thus, more likely to meet the patient's (customer's) expectations. Once the process is in control, PI can be used to reduce variation around the mean and, if desirable, move the mean toward a shorter delivery time.

Because nursing staff is involved in delivering trays to patients, one KPV will be predictability. If the staff members on a nursing unit know trays will arrive within a narrow range of variation, they can be ready to serve meals to patients. This will invariably lead to greater customer satisfaction. In this process, both nursing staff and patients are customers.

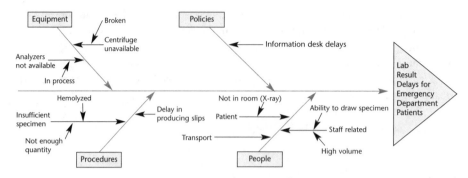

Figure 8.4. A fishbone, or cause-and-effect, diagram examining reasons for delays in laboratory test results for emergency department patients. The fishbone diagram is drawn after a brainstorming session. The central problem is visualized as the head of the fish, with the skeleton divided into branches showing contributing causes of different parts of the problem. (From Merry, Martin D. "Total Quality Management for Physicians: Translating the New Paradigm." *Quality Review Bulletin* 16 [March 1990]: 102; reprinted by permission. Copyright 1990 by Joint Commission Resources.)

Fishbone, or Ishikawa, Diagram

Often, a QIT's first step is to brainstorm perceived causes of problems in a process and develop a cause-and-effect diagram like that shown in Figure 8.4. The cause-and-effect diagram is also known as the fishbone diagram, because of its shape, or the Ishikawa diagram, after its originator Kaoru Ishikawa. An effect is a desirable or undesirable situation, condition, or event produced by a system of causes. Figure 8.4 shows reasons for laboratory test delays for patients in an ED. Primary process variables (components) are shown by the long arrows; minor process variables are shown by the short arrows and are elements of the primary variables. Brainstorming to identify problems thought to be present in a process suggests the focus of confirmatory data collection. In turn, these data suggest solutions to the problem(s).

Pareto Analysis

Another contribution of Juran was discovering the work of an Italian economist, Vilfredo Pareto. Often cited as separating the "vital few" from the "trivial many," Juran realized that the many are still QI methods useful in patient and staff safety and cannot be ignored.[49] Also known as the 80/20 rule, the Pareto principle is commonly applied in marketing where, for example, 80% of sales are derived from 20% of products or services. In QI, it means 80% of defects—errors, delays, rework, and the like—are typically caused by 20% of variables in a process. Applied to a hospital operating room (OR) schedule, Pareto analysis might find 80% of delays are caused by 20% of surgeons. The 80/20 ratio is neither fixed nor magical; rather, it helps decision makers understand relationships. Pareto analysis can show the relative importance of variables in a process and their contributions to a result, thus assisting to develop priorities in CQI. The Pareto diagram in Figure 8.5 shows that physicians' untimed routine and discharge orders are two areas in which most improvement can occur. QITs should focus there.

Scatter Diagrams

Scatter diagrams, also called scatter plots, show the relationship between two variables. Figure 8.6 depicts the relationship between the number of coronary artery bypass grafting (CABG) surgeries per year on the horizontal axis and the percent of operated patients who died (mortality)—an indication of quality—on the vertical axis. The data show an inverse relationship between mortality and the number of CABG procedures. The learning, or experience, curve for surgeons and staff is often cited as the reason for this relationship.

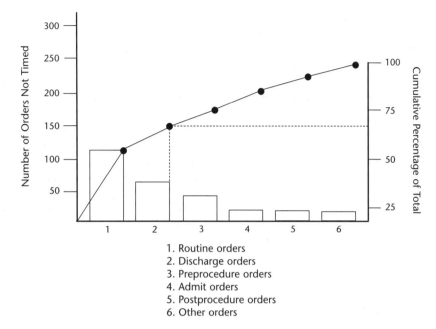

1. Routine orders
2. Discharge orders
3. Preprocedure orders
4. Admit orders
5. Postprocedure orders
6. Other orders

Figure 8.5.   Pareto diagram showing the rank order of untimed physicians' orders in a major hospital. This diagram ranks classes of orders that failed to be timed with a plot line showing that the correction of the first two classes of orders would lead to a greater than 50% improvement in all untimed orders. (From Re, Richard N., and Marie A. Krousel-Wood. "How to Use Continuous Quality Improvement Theory and Statistical Quality Control Tools in a Multispecialty Clinic." *Quality Review Bulletin* 16 [November 1990]: 394; reprinted by permission. Copyright 1990 by Joint Commission Resources.)

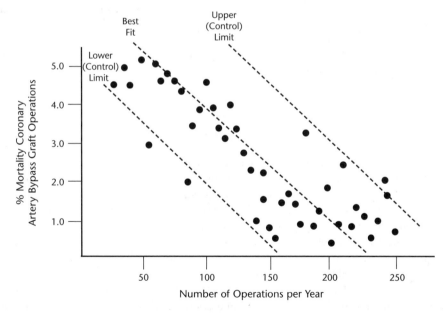

Figure 8.6.   Scatter diagram used to determine a possible relationship between two variables: the mortality rate for a surgical procedure and the number of times the procedure is performed during a 12-month period. (From Merry, Martin D. "Total Quality Management for Physicians: Translating the New Paradigm." *Quality Review Bulletin* 16 [March 1990]: 103; reprinted by permission. Copyright 1990 by Joint Commission Resources.)

The statistical technique of least squares linear regression can be applied to scatter diagrams to show a "best fit line." UCLs and LCLs are calculated using the variation of data points from the best fit line. Control limits of 3 standard deviations mean there is a 99.74% confidence level that a data point beyond the UCL or LCL is *not* due to chance alone. Figure 8.6 shows one data point above the UCL and two below the LCL. These points are Deming's special cause variation, Juran's sporadic spike, and Shewhart's assignable cause. All three data points showing special cause variation are of interest. The cause of the data point above the UCL should be determined so recurrence of this undesirable result can be prevented. Data points below the LCL should be investigated to understand why these positive results occurred so they can be studied and replicated, if possible. For example, a surgical team with superior results (positive special cause variation) should be studied and the lessons applied to other surgical teams. Positive special cause variation may result from input differences, such as surgeons' skills and training, or the acuity levels of patients on whom surgery was performed. Or, the process of performing the surgery may be the cause of positive special cause variation.

Failure Mode Effects Analysis

Failure mode effects analysis (FMEA) was developed by the National Aeronautics and Space Administration (NASA), the civilian agency of the federal government responsible for space travel. The complexities of NASA's systems required a technique to identify root causes of potential problems so they could be designed out of processes or processes could be modified to prevent them from occurring. FMEA is proactive. It prevents problems—the failure mode—from occurring when the process becomes operational. This makes FMEA part of Juran's quality planning. FMEA can be applied after problems arise, as well.

FMEA is applicable to HSOs. It uses a template that enables team members to work through the failure mode and its effect. After identifying a service feature or a process, the team brainstorms to identify potential failure modes, the potential effect of each failure, the severity rating for each potential failure, the potential causes of failure, the likelihood of the failure occurring, and the likelihood of detection by current process controls. Finally, the team assigns priority numbers to identify issues that should receive the most attention. The second half of the template addresses how the potential problems will be prevented.[50] Applications of FMEA in health services have included the blood product transfusion process.

Crew Resource Management

Crew resource management (CRM) is a generalized application of cockpit resource management, a concept developed jointly by the Federal Aeronautics Administration and the airline industry in the 1980s to enhance the quality of responses to emergencies involving the crews of commercial aircraft. The study of human factors in aviation emphasizes the role of human beings in high-stress, high-risk environments. An estimated 80% of airplane accidents are caused by human factors. The purpose of CRM is to develop techniques and procedures to catch mistakes before they cause problems.[51] There are striking similarities between the cockpit of a commercial aircraft and a hospital's OR ED. CRM can be applied to any area in which a team provides care.[52] Since the late 1990s, CRM has been applied in hospital EDs, ORs, and intensive care units. Unlike CQI, however, CRM is *not* data driven.

CRM seeks to enhance patient safety and quality of care by improving teamwork with better cooperation, coordination, and communication. Techniques include presurgical briefings, preoperative assessments, and methods to ensure effective handoffs from one part of the process or staff member to another. These safety measures (tools) ensure the staff's daily use of teamwork and communication skills acquired in training classes. The purpose is to achieve a permanent change in behavior.[53] Specific examples of applying safety tools in the OR include the OR time out, which requires confirming vital information about a patient, and surgical

site verification, which confirms the surgical site before surgery begins and may
a patient to state what procedure is to be performed.

Hospitals that have applied CRM report significant positive results,
costs of malpractice, higher staff satisfaction levels and less turnover, and {.
surgeries—wrong patient, wrong site, wrong device.[54] Wrong surgeries are known .
events—they should never happen. The evidence of CRM's value is anecdotal, however. CRm
warrants more investigation in health services; it is premature to conclude it can reduce medical errors.[55] Questions have been raised about the extent of behavior change[56] and the link
between attitudes about teamwork and patient outcomes.[57]

Benchmarking

Organization-wide or macro-level data collection permits management to prioritize the order
in which processes will be improved. Micro- or PI-level data collection allows QITs to measure
process variables, which is requisite to improvement. Benchmarking allows comparisons by
providing norms, standards, and measures for various processes and outcomes, such as patient
admitting, customer satisfaction, quality of care, and financial performance.

There are several types of benchmarking. Internal benchmarking compares similar activities or processes within the HSO/HS. External benchmarking compares HSO/HS performance with similar activities and processes in comparable organizations in- and outside
health services. Competitive benchmarking involves comparisons with competitors who provide the same service in similar markets. Its most aggressive application identifies the "best
patient outcomes for each service measured by factors such as mortality rates, nosocomial
(HSO-acquired) infections, [and] patient mobility" as well as practice patterns and resource
consumption profiles of competitors.[58] World-class benchmarking compares the HSO/HS to
organizations in- or outside health services that excel in using similar processes. Examples common to a wide variety of organizations are order fulfillment, supplier relations, and billing and
collection processes.[59]

Benchmarks are only guidelines. Achieving the same results as a world-class performance
benchmark, for example, requires that the HSO/HS have an exact replica of everything in
the benchmark organization, including its culture. Regardless, knowing what can be accomplished might stimulate the HSO/HS to achieve higher quality or even to achieve at a level
higher than the benchmark.

Benchmarking includes determining what to benchmark, collecting internal and external
data, and applying the conclusions reached to improve existing processes. Admitting, billing,
patient transport, surgical scheduling, and OR use are examples of HSOs/HSs benchmark
processes. Control is another application of data obtained about other HSOs/HSs. Chapter 14
includes sources for peer organization performance and financial outcomes and resource consumption data. The data provide comparative benchmarks for "best in class" performance
and allow HSOs/HSs to know the extent to which they can improve their competitive position—if resources are adequate. Chapter 10 discusses external environmental analysis that
enables HSOs/HSs to attain and sustain their competitive position by knowing competitors'
performance.

Productivity and Productivity Improvement

Cost-efficiency and PI result from CQI. Figure 4.3 suggests PI [2] leads to higher quality outputs [3], which lead to PI and better resource use [4] and, thus, enhanced competitive position
[5]. The Deming Chain Reaction shown in Figure 4.4 connects improved quality, decreased
costs, improved productivity, and the organization's ability to decrease prices, increase market
share, and stay in business. CQI and PI are integral and inseparable. Similarly, input resource

costs and quality are conjoined with output quality; neither can be considered in isolation from the other.

Productivity is the index of outputs relative to inputs.[60] Alternatively, productivity is the results achieved relative to resources consumed:[61]

$$Productivity = \frac{Outputs}{Inputs} = \frac{Results\ achieved}{Resources\ consumed}$$

Productivity is improved by any change that increases the ratio of outputs to inputs, which is achieved by altering either the conversion process (structure, tasks/technology, people) or the inputs (see Figure III.2 in the introduction to Part III). For example, fewer nurses caring for the same number of patients increases productivity: fewer inputs (lower costs), but the same output. More radiographic procedures per day with the same staff and equipment increases productivity. If, however, productivity (output) is increased without maintaining or enhancing quality (defined as conformance to requirements and patient satisfaction) a lower quality of higher output will diminish productivity because there are errors, rework, and dissatisfaction among customers and staff. Producing poor-quality radiographs or performing unnecessary radiographic procedures (nonconformance output) is not productivity improvement. Neither is decreasing the number of surgical assistants so patient and physician wait times are increased; this lessens customer satisfaction. Productivity improvement occurs only when the index ratio of outputs to inputs increases, and conformance and expectation quality is maintained or enhanced. This is shown in the following formula:[62]

$$Productivity = improvement \frac{Outputs}{Inputs} = \frac{Quantity}{Inputs} + Quality = \frac{Results\ achieved}{Resources\ consumed}$$

CQI and PI

Figure 8.7 shows the relationship of the PI triangle to CQI. PI occurs only when lowest costs (inputs) are consistent with appropriate quality (outputs). This is the value of healthcare.[63] Because PI focuses on the relationship of inputs and costs to outputs and quality, both inputs and processes are analyzed in PI, as in CQI.

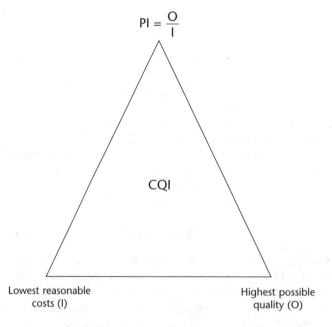

Figure 8.7.   Productivity improvement (PI) triangle.

HSOs/HSs are service organizations with high levels of customer interaction. Some, such as acute care hospitals, need flexible capacity to meet surges in demand. Conversely, nursing facilities have little need for flexible capacity. Their customers are long-term residents; demand is stable.

CQI focuses on improving processes (see Figure 4.3), which necessitates evaluating inputs. For example, the QIT may determine that a process will be higher quality if staff is more skilled (and likely more expensive) or if staff is cross-trained so work assignments are more flexible as workloads change. Enhancing technology inputs may improve work systems by substituting equipment for people. Magnetic resonance imaging improves clinical diagnosis, and personal computers enhance accuracy and productivity in billing and admitting. Other techniques may add efficiency to inputs: increasing quality of materials and supplies by working with suppliers (Deming advocated developing long-term relationships with suppliers and suggested sole-source suppliers will improve quality); using a just-in-time inventory system to eliminate inventory other than that needed for safety stock; and using ABC inventory analysis,[64] which is similar to Pareto analysis, to identify supplies that are most expensive or critical and require special attention. Management information systems provide data for control and utilization evaluation; successful forecasting enables managers to anticipate demand and alter capacity. Work measurement monitors employee utilization and workloads; a patient acuity classification system permits efficient staffing patterns.

Productivity may be improved in ways other than analyzing inputs. Examination of a process or work system in a CQI framework should ask questions such as the following: Is what we do necessary? Are we doing the right things? Can the work be done another way with the same or better quality? How are the results of one job interdependent with other jobs, materials, or processes? Can we improve the process with a different mix of resources that will improve quality, decrease costs, or both? These questions can be answered using methods such as 1) analysis and improvement of work systems and job design; 2) capacity planning and facilities layout; and 3) production control, scheduling, and supply chain. Inputs are integral to each.

Work Systems (Processes) and Job Design

Analyzing and improving work systems and job design are integral to quality and lead to PI. The objectives are to find better ways to work in general, improve jobs, and increase the ratio of quality to costs—with the same, fewer, or a less costly mix of inputs.

Work systems (processes) are interrelated jobs that form a whole. Hospitals have thousands of systems and subsystems. Nonpatient care systems include admitting, discharge, accounts receivable and payable, transportation, inventorying and distributing materials, patient food delivery, and medication order fulfillment. Direct patient care systems include nursing service, clinical support services (e.g., laboratory, radiology, and respiratory therapy), and therapeutic activities, such as perioperative services. Analysis of a system can be exclusive (how it functions) or inclusive (how it interrelates with other systems). The purpose is to improve systems to enhance output quality and productivity. Process and methods analyses evaluate systems. Health services processes are operations, steps, or activities by which patients, materials, or information flow. Documenting this flow allows each step to be evaluated. This allows a determination if altering flow, combining or eliminating operations, or methods redesign will result in higher-quality outputs and PI. As noted, one of the first activities of a QIT is to prepare a flow diagram (process map) of the process.

Figure 8.8 is a flowchart (flow diagram) that outlines the process for implementing physicians' orders. Knowing the steps in a process shows where improvements will eliminate bottlenecks, delays, rework, or steps. Flow analysis is used for processes with high customer interaction to find where and how interactions may be enhanced or lessened, whichever will result in higher patient satisfaction.

HSO work systems are interdependent; multisystem process flow analysis is needed to identify areas for improvement. For example, timely reading and reporting of test results (e.g., imaging, electrocardiography, electroencephalography, and laboratory) positively affect patient care and shorten lengths of stay; delayed reading or reporting negatively affects patient care and

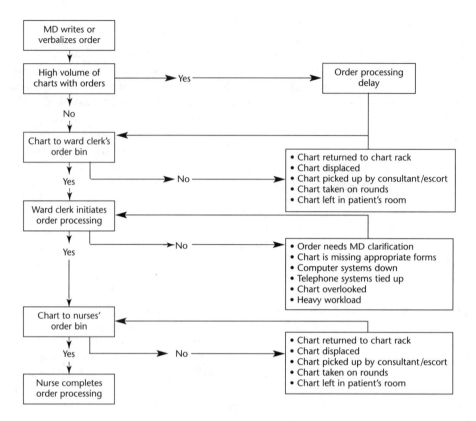

Figure 8.8. Flow diagram outlining initial steps in implementing physicians' orders, clearly identifying points of supplier (physician)–consumer (ward clerk) interchange and sites of possible system failure or delay. (Note: this figure is an example of a flow diagram; some points are outdated with use of electronic health records.) From Re, Richard N., and Marie A. Krousel-Wood. "How to Use Continuous Quality Improvement Theory and Statistical Quality Control Tools in a Multispecialty Clinic." *Quality Review Bulletin* 16 (November 1990): 393; reprinted by permission. Copyright 1990 by Joint Commission Resources.

increases lengths of stay. Staff knowledge about and improvement of system or process outputs that become inputs elsewhere in the HSO positively affect productivity.

Methods analysis involves evaluating how work is done—the specific operations, steps, or activities performed. Analyses include evaluating need for and content of the operation, step, or activity; considering alternate inputs, such as substituting staff and equipment or redesigning jobs; or evaluating information flow and media used.

At a micro-level, job design improvement evaluates the tasks in a job or cluster of jobs that constitute a step in a process. Included is the sequence of job tasks, design of physical layout, and person–machine relationships (ergonomics), as well as equipment, material, and supplies used. Job design improvement or a variant, work simplification (organizing work into specific tasks to make it easier), eliminates unneeded tasks, reduces time between tasks, reallocates tasks among jobs, combines jobs, or centralizes common tasks into one job.

Finally, work simplification evaluates and improves jobs and enhances work results. User-friendly, menu-driven information systems in admissions enable staff to admit patients more quickly and more accurately, both of which increase quality, productivity, and customer satisfaction.

Capacity Planning and Facilities Layout

Facilities analysis is an important dimension of performance improvement. It focuses on physical aspects of a process, need for flexibility in meeting variable demands, and balance of timeliness of service and idle resources. Facility layout is how equipment and work areas are arranged. Facilities, process flow, equipment, and workstations may be rearranged to improve sequence and flow, decrease unneeded worker movement and materials transportation, and eliminate bottlenecks and congestion. The result is faster patient throughput. Layout analysis is achieved by using drawings, proximity charts, templates, or three-dimensional models. Computer simulation is used to design physical layout within predetermined constraints and assumptions.

Analysis of traffic patterns and materials flow is used to observe and record movement to decrease travel, eliminate or reduce delays, or substitute alternate materials handling or delivery methods. For example, analysis of traffic patterns may find that restricting use of some elevators to patients, staff, and movement of equipment reduces delays in clinical activities. Similarly, materials and supplies flow analysis may justify an exchange cart system to improve logistics, decrease inventory and staffing, and ensure that patient care supplies and medications are on units when needed.

Production Control, Scheduling, and Supply Chain

Production control in HSOs involves matching workload with capacity through work scheduling. Examples are admitting, ORs, diagnostic testing, clinics, LIP offices, and outpatient services. Production-smoothing spreads workload throughout a shift. For example, if all inpatients are brought to radiology at about the same time, or all outpatients arrive at 9:00 a.m., waiting lines build, staff is overloaded, and longer waiting times lessen patient satisfaction. By comparison, the afternoon staff is underutilized. Workload spread throughout a day minimizes patient waiting time and staff is productive during an entire shift. If demand cannot be controlled by scheduling, part-time staff can be used, or other adjustments made to meet demands of peak load.

Workload balancing by scheduling demand or capacity ensures that staff, equipment, and facilities are used efficiently and customer waiting time is lessened. Manual and computerized scheduling techniques are available, including short-interval scheduling, multiple-activity charts, and work distribution analysis. Another technique, simulation, is discussed in Chapter 14.

Effective supply chain management and timely distribution of materials and supplies are essential to downstream processes. Improvement techniques may be as simple as using exchange carts to deliver supplies to nursing units. On alternate days, one cart is filled, the other is used. Carts are exchanged daily. A case cart system may be used in ORs. Each surgeon has a list of instruments, devices, and supplies used by type of procedure. Before surgery, the case cart for that procedure is packed and delivered to the OR. The unit dose system is used to distribute drugs. Medications are purchased individually packaged or are packaged in the pharmacy and distributed to nursing units. Costs are higher, but the risk of medication errors is reduced because each dose is available as needed.

LIPs and CQI

HSOs/HSs are unique because they are structural blends of administrative and patient care activities in which LIPs have significant autonomy. Historically, the blended structure created conflict between the two. Adopting a quality philosophy changed this relationship. It expects more shared managerial and clinical accountability for quality, collaboration in quality initiatives, and a mutual interest in both retrospective and concurrent process performance.[65] HSO/HS managers and LIPs realize they must respect each other's competencies and collaborate to succeed in providing quality services and making changes, such as improving processes, reengineering, or strategic quality planning. One such change is more widespread use of practice guidelines.

Clinical Practice Guidelines

Public and private entities have developed clinical practice guidelines (CPGs), which establish standards of patient care supported by strong scientific evidence (evidence based). Intended to optimize care, CPGs result from systematic review of evidence and assess benefits and costs of alternative care options.[66] Various names are used: critical paths, practice parameters, clinical guidelines, clinical protocols or algorithms, care maps or target tracks, case management, and clinical pathways. All assist LIPs in making clinical decisions. HSOs/HSs may define CPGs differently and with varying precision. Implementing them is stimulated by a commitment to improve quality and lessen costs by reducing *unnecessary* variation in clinical decision making. This is not "cookbook medicine," as opponents of CPGs have alleged. Deviations can and must be made, *if* clinically justified by the LIP. CPGs are not the same as clinical indicators; they *lead to* indicators. CPGs describe what *should be* done; indicators measure what *was* done.

The American Academy of Pediatrics developed the first CPGs in 1938. In 1990, 26 physician specialties had CPGs.[67] Early in the 21st century, 87% of hospitals used CPGs; many others planned to do so.[68] In 2012, the National Guideline Clearinghouse (NGC) had over 2,500 CPGs. Chapter 5 noted that after NGC was disestablished in 2018, development of CPGs went to the private sector. The Emergency Care Research Institute (ECRI), an independent, not-for-profit patient safety organization, established the ECRI Guidelines Trust™, a repository of evidence-based CPGs. Healthcare providers have no-cost access to the website. Adherence to CPGs may be poor even after they are adopted, however.[69]

Clinical CQI initiatives such as CPGs improve quality even as they reduce costs. Both dimensions are important in a provider-at-risk environment with capitated budgets, per case revenue, and managed care cost limits. CPGs are also an analytical tool to identify optimal timing for clinical interventions by diagnosis and achieve more effective resource use and better outcomes.[70] CPGs reduce variation around the mean and result in more consistent clinical decisions. Better clinical decisions and less unneeded variability in diagnosis and treatment enhance the quality of inputs and outcomes.

Sample CPGs can be reviewed on the federal Agency for Healthcare Research and Quality (AHRQ) website (https://www.ahrq.gov/professionals/clinicians-providers/guidelines-recommendations/guide/section2.html#brprev). HSs with multiple units providing services on the same part of the care continuum should monitor CPGs for "best practices" consistency.[71] CPGs have proven their value; for example, CPGs for congestive heart failure have resulted in fewer readmissions and decreased costs and length of stay by increasing use of recommended post-hospital medications.[72] CPGs for intraoperative monitoring (monitoring during surgery) developed by the American Society of Anesthesiologists have almost eliminated hypoxic (insufficient oxygen) injury lawsuits and greatly reduced medical malpractice insurance premiums.[73] Another important potential benefit of CPGs is major reductions in losses per malpractice claim in high-risk areas, such as EDs, obstetrics, and ORs. One study found a 96% reduction when CPGs were used in all three.[74] Clearly, CPGs have value.[75]

Beyond guidance for LIPs, CPGs help establish the legal standard of care. During litigation, LIPs can explain deviations from a CPG, if any. Deviations are likely because CPGs assist LIPs; they do not eliminate the need for individualized patient treatment plans.[76] CPGs may become presumptive of the legal standard of care. This shifts the burden of proof to the LIP to show that deviation(s) were justified.

Involving LIPs

LIPs include physicians and all other licensed independent practitioners of the medical arts. LIPs are likely to support clinical CQI if they are involved and have ownership.[77] LIP champions are needed; they must be convinced such initiatives will enhance quality without inappropriately jeopardizing professional autonomy or the needs of individual patients.[78]

Three general categories of HSO work have been identified: 1) support services, such as admission/discharge, billing, medical records, and scheduling; 2) medical infrastructure for direct patient care, such as blood bank, laboratory, radiology, and other ancillary services; and 3) clinical products, "the diagnostic and treatment processes that hospitals provide to patients. For example, normal obstetrical delivery, medical treatment of acute myocardial infarction (heart attack), and surgical treatment of appendicitis are all clinical products."[79]

The ways to increase LIP involvement in CQI initiatives apply to reengineering and strategic quality planning, as well.[80] First, CQI principles are not foreign to them. They are trained in scientific, numbers-oriented investigation and reasoning. Management must educate LIPs about the philosophy of CQI and train them to use CQI tools. "Quality improvement theory should be presented as a direct extension of the principles that the medical profession has always espoused."[81] Clinical quality initiatives seek improved medical outcomes; LIPs will be comfortable with their data-driven scientific approaches and process orientation. These initiatives will result in better mobilization and use of resources to meet the needs of patients and LIPs.[82]

Second, LIPs will likely distrust clinical measurement efforts unilaterally initiated by management.[83] Management must reassure clinicians and dispel any perception that quality projects are "thinly disguised efforts to reduce healthcare resource utilization, seemingly without regard for the potential impact of such actions on patients' health."[84] If trust is established, LIPs and managers can work toward common goals in delivery of high-quality and cost-effective services.[85]

Third, quality teams develop clinical products and can participate in other quality initiatives. Quality assurance (see Chapter 4) includes peer review "typically organized through sub-specialty medical staff groups and reports through an independent medical staff organization."[86] CQI should be part of this process. To use LIPs' time well, clinical improvement projects can occur during staff meetings and be allocated to salaried LIPs' work time.[87] Management "should consider physicians' (and LIPS') self-perceived role as customers or providers as they plan physician (and LIP) involvement on quality improvement teams."[88]

Fourth, LIPs should be encouraged to be involved in clinical product quality initiatives with other organization members and be given administrative support.[89] Support can include staff to collect and analyze data, assist clinical QITs in other ways, and invest in real-time clinical and management information systems.[90]

Fifth, clinical CQI requires stable diagnostic and treatment processes. LIPs determine when these processes are used. This means management must be vitally interested in improving processes and ensuring that LIPs participate in Q/PI initiatives and understand how they are both customer *and* supplier in a process. "It is more important how you [managers] implement than what you implement. The aim is to manage clinical processes, not to manage the physicians (and LIPs)."[91]

Sixth, a 2-year study to identify and assess attributes of successful CQI initiatives in acute care hospitals concluded that LIP involvement on clinical QITs early in the CQI program is essential for success.[92] Similarly, CQI will stimulate LIPs' use of process measures.[93] Management must train a nucleus of LIPs at the outset of a CQI initiative to generate a sense of ownership.[94]

Seventh, the focus should be strategically important clinical issues and procedures—high cost, high volume, and with readily available data and improvement opportunities.[95] It has been suggested that management identification of these conditions will be an important motivating factor and reinforces the HSO's commitment to improving areas of concern to LIPs.[96] The champions should be LIP leaders who have administrative appointments, as well as those who are highly respected by their peers.[97]

Eighth, management must be both persevering and opportunistic[98] and be prepared to respond to the "neutral" majority of LIPs who identify a clinical problem or concern.[99] When they do, management should show how CQI relates to those LIPs or their practices, orient them to CQI methods, and arrange for them to interact with LIP champions committed to CQI.[100]

Results of Involving LIPs

The rise of managed care has given impetus to improving consistency of clinical practice and development of evidence-based "best practice" guidelines. Data from implementing clinical guidelines and improving clinical performance in 25 integrated delivery systems and managed healthcare plans that provided healthcare to 40 million people are instructive. The most frequently cited method for improving clinical practice was feedback on clinical profiles of individual clinicians using audits of medical records and comparing their practice with their peers or other benchmarks. Second most cited was clinician feedback from clinical department or administrative heads at regular meetings. Third was involvement of local LIPs in developing practice guidelines; the same number of organizations also used or considered using financial incentives by "tying a small percentage of income to factors such as patient satisfaction, rates of preventive services, and efforts to improve quality."[101] Other efforts to improve quality of care include linking patient satisfaction to incomes of three-quarters of employed physicians. Quality of practice is factored into incomes of 72% of employed physicians. The rate affected only 3%–5% of total compensation but is predicted to rise to 7%–10% in the next several years.[102]

Failed approaches to achieving improvement in clinical performance include sending information to LIPs or increasing their knowledge alone, feedback with group data alone, and developing practice guidelines outside the managed care plan or practice unit without local LIP involvement.[103] The success of clinical improvement was based on HSO/HS leadership's promoting a CQI culture, respect for LIPs, involvement of LIPs and other staff, a customer perspective, organizational support, and "viewing physicians (LIPs) as important participants but not necessarily the focus of a system whose performance is to be improved."[104] The latter point paraphrases Deming—blame problems with quality on the process, not the workers.

Regardless of skills or professional eminence, LIPs are vital to HSO processes and reify Juran's triple role of the worker. They are vital to processes such as admitting, medication, therapeutic dietetics, laboratory, radiology, and discharge. They are "suppliers" by writing orders and providing information; they are "processors" by reviewing test results and judging appropriateness of treatment; they are "customers" by receiving information from various sources and using it in clinical decisions. LIPs are part of processes in various ways, and their work will be enhanced or diminished by the quality of processes that support them and of which they are a part. If they ever existed in history, the days of the Lone Ranger are gone.[105] Modern medicine cannot be practiced in isolation.

Patient and Staff Safety in Healthcare

Although patients and healthcare staff have a separate history of how safety was incorporated into their realms, the work being done with high-reliability organizations (organizations adept at achieving goals and avoiding errors[106]) and safety cultures in healthcare has introduced a new paradigm of safety in healthcare. This paradigm focuses on dissolving the distinct silos of patient and staff safety and captures the synergy of the work for both groups on the many issues they share.[107]

The essence of the Hippocratic oath is embodied in the phrase "First, do no harm," and patient safety has been a core value of medicine since its beginning. However, it was not until the 1999 report from the Institute of Medicine (IOM), *To Err Is Human: Building a Safer Health System*, that the harm being done was described and quantified.[108] The view that the human beings delivering care were fallible and sometimes made fatal mistakes had been accepted for generations. This attitude was challenged by comparing service organizations such as airlines and credit card issuers that also function in high-risk environments but have a process reliability of over 99%. HSOs began to consider utilizing the same tools and processes to produce that level of quality. The IOM report stated six aims of healthcare—to be effective, safe, patient centered, timely, efficient, and equitable.[109] Importantly, the IOM stated errors resulted from faulty systems or processes, not individuals.

The IOM report spawned several new organizations that focus on patient safety. The Agency for Healthcare Research and Quality (AHRQ), established in 2000 by the U.S. Congress, became the largest funding source for patient safety research.[110] In addition to the federal government, the private sector became involved. The Leapfrog Group, a collaboration of *Fortune 500* companies, was launched in November 2000. Its goal is to assure quality healthcare for employees of member companies by rewarding hospitals that significantly improve quality and safety.

When the federal government and the insurance industry announced they would not pay (or would decrease reimbursement) for inferior patient outcomes, the healthcare industry began to view patient safety differently. The National Quality Forum defined a never event in 2002 as a serious reportable event, such as surgery on the wrong body part. The Center for Medicare & Medicaid Services (CMS) went further and defined a serious hospital-acquired condition as a nonreimbursible never event. Since the original list debuted, other never events have been added (see Table 8.2). CMS no longer pays for surgery on a wrong body part. It is a "universal protocol" that the surgeon and surgical team will pause and confirm that preprocedure site verification, site marking, and the time out have occurred and are correct before surgery begins.

The Joint Commission, which was discussed in Chapter 1, developed National Patient Safety Goals (NPSGs) in 2003 as updated and shown in Table 8.3. These are the NPSGs for hospitals.[111] In addition, The Joint Commission has NPSGs for ambulatory healthcare, behavioral healthcare, critical access hospitals, and home care. The NPSGs are reassessed annually with input from clinicians, purchasers, consumer groups, and other stakeholders. Items removed are usually added to Joint Commission standards.

Instead of never events, The Joint Commission uses *sentinel event*, which it defines as "an event that is an unexpected occurrence involving death or serious physical or psychological injury, or the risk thereof."[112] These events are sentinel because they signal a need for immediate response and investigation and because they evidence underlying process problems. The Joint Commission also releases "sentinel event alerts" (SEAs) based on data from organizations that have had sentinel events related to patient and staff safety. As of December 2018, there have been 60 SEAs on topics such as workplace violence and developing a reporting culture. SEAs summarize current knowledge on the topic and recommend how to reduce the risk of that type of event occurring.

In 2015 (15 years after *To Err Is Human* was released), an expert panel convened by the National Patient Safety Foundation evaluated the state of patient safety and outlined work needed for the next 15 years. The panel recognized that some patient safety goals had been achieved, but many were unaddressed or showed no improvement. The most recent report, titled "Free from Harm: Accelerating Patient Safety Improvement Fifteen Years after *To Err Is Human*" is a call to action. Eight recommendations span work for GBs, leadership, government agencies, public–private partnerships, healthcare organizations, ambulatory care practices and settings, researchers, professional associations, regulators, educators, the healthcare workforce, and patients and their families:[113]

1. Ensure that leaders establish and sustain a safety culture.

2. Create centralized and coordinated oversight of patient safety.

3. Create a common set of safety metrics that reflect meaningful outcomes.

4. Increase funding for research in patient safety and implementation science.

5. Address safety across the entire care continuum.

6. Support the healthcare workforce.

7. Partner with patients and families for the safest care.

8. Ensure that technology is safe and optimized to improve patient safety.

Table 8.2   Never Events: National Quality Forum List of Serious Reportable Events, 2016

Surgical events
Surgery or other invasive procedure performed on the wrong body part
Surgery or other invasive procedure performed on the wrong patient
Wrong surgical or other invasive procedure performed on a patient
Unintended retention of a foreign object in a patient after surgery or other procedure
Intraoperative or immediately postoperative/postprocedure death in an American Society of Anesthesiologists Class I patient
Product or device events
Patient death or serious injury associated with the use of contaminated drugs, devices, or biologics provided by the healthcare setting
Patient death or serious injury associated with the use or function of a device in patient care, in which the device is used for functions other than as intended
Patient death or serious injury associated with intravascular air embolism that occurs while being cared for in a healthcare setting
Patient protection events
Discharge or release of a patient/resident of any age, who is unable to make decisions, to other than an authorized person
Patient death or serious disability associated with patient elopement (disappearance)
Patient suicide, attempted suicide, or self-harm resulting in serious disability, while being cared for in a healthcare facility
Care management events
Patient death or serious injury associated with a medication error (e.g., errors involving the wrong drug, wrong dose, wrong patient, wrong time, wrong rate, wrong preparation, or wrong route of administration)
Patient death or serious injury associated with unsafe administration of blood products
Maternal death or serious injury associated with labor or delivery in a low-risk pregnancy while being cared for in a healthcare setting
Death or serious injury of a neonate associated with labor or delivery in a low-risk pregnancy
Artificial insemination with the wrong donor sperm or wrong egg
Patient death or serious injury associated with a fall while being cared for in a healthcare setting
Any stage 3, stage 4, or unstageable pressure ulcers acquired after admission/presentation to a healthcare facility
Patient death or serious disability resulting from the irretrievable loss of an irreplaceable biological specimen
Patient death or serious injury resulting from failure to follow up or communicate laboratory, pathology, or radiology test results
Environmental events
Patient or staff death or serious disability associated with an electric shock in the course of a patient care process in a healthcare setting
Any incident in which a line designated for oxygen or other gas to be delivered to a patient contains no gas, the wrong gas, or is contaminated by toxic substances
Patient or staff death or serious injury associated with a burn incurred from any source in the course of a patient care process in a healthcare setting
Patient death or serious injury associated with the use of restraints or bedrails while being cared for in a healthcare setting
Radiologic events
Death or serious injury of a patient or staff associated with introduction of a metallic object into the MRI area
Criminal events
Any instance of care ordered by or provided by someone impersonating a physician, nurse, pharmacist, or other licensed healthcare provider
Abduction of a patient/resident of any age
Sexual abuse/assault on a patient within or on the grounds of a healthcare setting
Death or significant injury of a patient or staff member resulting from a physical assault (i.e., battery) that occurs within or on the grounds of a healthcare setting

Source: Adapted from National Quality Forum List of SREs (http://www.qualityforum.org/Topics/SREs/List_of_SREs. aspx), retrieved from Agency for Healthcare Research and Quality: Advancing Excellence in Healthcare. Patient Safety Network. https://psnet.ahrq.gov/primers/primer/3.

Table 8.3   National Patient Safety Goals for Hospitals (2019)

Identify patients correctly	Use at least two ways to identify patients. For example, use the patient's name and date of birth. This is done to make sure that each patient gets the correct medicine and treatment.
	Make sure that the correct patient gets the correct blood when they get a blood transfusion.
Improve staff communication	Get important test results to the right staff person on time.
Use medicines safely	Before a procedure, label medicines that are not labeled. For example, medicines in syringes, cups, and basins. Do this in the area where medicines and supplies are set up.
	Take extra care with patients who take medicines to thin their blood.
	Record and pass along correct information about a patient's medicines. Find out what medicines the patient is taking. Compare those medicines to new medicines given to the patient. Make sure the patient knows which medicines to take when they are at home. Tell the patient it is important to bring their up-to-date list of medicines every time they visit a doctor.
Use alarms safely	Make improvements to ensure that alarms on medical equipment are heard and responded to on time.
Prevent infection	Use the hand cleaning guidelines from the Centers for Disease Control and Prevention or the World Health Organization. Set goals for improving hand cleaning. Use the goals to improve hand cleaning.
	Use proven guidelines to prevent infections that are difficult to treat.
	Use proven guidelines to prevent infection of the blood from central lines.
	Use proven guidelines to prevent infection after surgery.
	Use proven guidelines to prevent infections of the urinary tract that are caused by catheters.
Identify patient safety risks	Find out which patients are at risk for suicide.
Prevent mistakes in surgery	Make sure that the correct surgery is done on the correct patient and at the correct place on the patient's body.
	Mark the correct place on the patient's body where the surgery is to be done.
	Pause before the surgery to make sure that a mistake is not being made.

The purpose of the National Patient Safety Goals is to improve patient safety. The goals focus on problems in healthcare safety and how to solve them. Adapted from The Joint Commission, 2019. Hospital National Patient Safety Goals. https://www.jointcommission.org/assets/1/6/2019_HAP_NPSGs_final2.pdf, retrieved August 13, 2019.

Concern for safety of healthcare staff is more recent than patient safety. Florence Nightingale (British [1820–1910]) worked to reform nursing education and improve conditions in hospitals. Growth of organized labor in the early 20th century focused attention on workers' rights.[114] Only in 1958 did the American Medical Association and the American Hospital Association issue a joint statement supporting staff health programs in hospitals. In 1971, the federal Occupational and Safety Health Administration (OSHA) was established to protect the safety and health of American workers. The law includes the "general duty clause" that requires employers to provide a safe working environment. The "right to know" about hazards in the workplace was covered in the 1983 hazard communications standard. It requires employers to label chemicals and provide material safety data sheets and worker training.[115] The standard was updated in 2012 to comply with the United Nations classification and labeling system for chemicals (Globally Harmonized System of Classification and Labeling of Chemicals). Employers must provide information about chemicals that workers can understand. Pictograms and symbols are required for all chemicals, and staff must be trained to recognize them.[116]

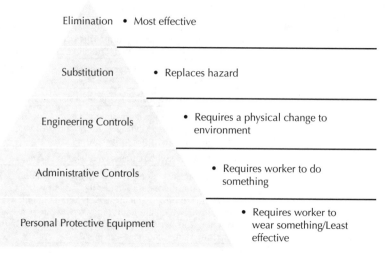

Elimination • Most effective

Substitution • Replaces hazard

Engineering Controls • Requires a physical change to environment

Administrative Controls • Requires worker to do something

Personal Protective Equipment • Requires worker to wear something/Least effective

Figure 8.9.   Hierarchy of Controls. (Adapted from the Occupational Safety and Health Administration, "Hierarchy of Controls.")

OSHA inspects only a small percentage of the more than 8 million U.S. worksites. Its priorities during inspections are imminent danger, fatality/catastrophe, complaints/referrals, and programmed inspections. Organizations with over 10 employees must use a process to document and report injuries (OSHA 300 Log). Log data are used to direct prevention efforts.

OSHA has developed a hierarchy for addressing safety problems, which is shown in Figure 8.9. Most effective is eliminating the hazard. Next is substituting a less hazardous material or procedure. Engineering controls are a physical change that makes the workplace safer. Administrative or work practice changes require staff to follow a policy or procedure that limits exposure to the hazard. Least effective is using personal protective equipment (PPE), which requires workers to wear gloves, gowns, and masks, and to use other protective gear to prevent contact with the hazardous substance.

In addition to the National Institute for Occupational Safety and Health (NIOSH) established by OSHA, the *Criteria for an Effective Occupational Health Program in Hospitals*, and the 1982 Centers for Disease Control and Prevention (CDC) *Guidelines for Infection Control in Hospital Personnel*, the most significant legislation was the 1991 blood-borne pathogen standard. The regulations and the 2001 safe sharps legislation require HSOs to assess their practices and initiate a hierarchy of controls to mitigate and possibly eliminate blood-borne pathogen hazards. Sharps injuries decreased significantly in nonsurgical hospital settings between 2001 and 2006. During the same period, however, the injury rate in surgical settings increased.[117]

Despite these efforts, healthcare is a high-hazard industry. The U.S. Department of Labor reported healthcare support staff has an incidence rate of nonfatal occupational injuries and illnesses requiring days away from work almost two and one-half times that of other industries.[118] Numerous risks in HSOs remain to be ameliorated.

QI Methods Useful in Patient and Staff Safety

The data are clear: Both patient and staff safety need attention, but HSOs likely deal with them separately. Most HSOs address staff safety using an environment of care (EOC) safety committee that focuses on physical plant. The patient safety committee is an extension of hospital risk management (risk management is discussed in Chapter 14), which involves members of the professional staff and focuses on events that harm patients. These committees often compete for resources even though both focus on safety. The study of high-reliability organizations offers a new paradigm to improve safety for patients and staff. Because they use similar tools to enhance safety, coordinating their improvement efforts will benefit the entire HSO.

In addition to technical details for preventing injuries to patients and staff, management determines how to organize for safety. This applies to HSOs of all types and includes staff members to address the issues and nurture a culture of safety.

A culture of safety is present when the focus is on a system or process as the cause of a failure. In such a culture staff consider all underlying reasons why an event occurred, and there is rigorous attention to operational processes and staff resilience. High-reliability organizations were the models for reducing errors and improving performance in HSOs. Management must understand that establishing and nurturing a culture of safety requires resources. Failing to nurture a culture of safety increases economic and other costs of patient and staff injuries, as well as causing negative publicity for the HSO.

Human factors is the study of interactions among human beings and other elements of a system. It was first used in the early 1940s during World War II to fit machines to human beings, rather than, as previously, to fit human beings to machines.[119] It has been used to improve aviation safety for decades.[120] More recently, health services began to apply human factors engineering to assess relationships of human beings and elements of a system to improve results, safety, and quality.[121] Work processes are being reengineered to make it harder to do the wrong thing and easier to do the right thing. Beginning in 2012, The Joint Commission identified human factors such as staffing levels and skills mix, staff orientation, in-service education, competency assessment, supervision, medical resident supervision, LIP credentialing and privileging, professional staff peer review, and factors such as rushing, fatigue, distraction, complacency, and bias as among the most common root causes of sentinel events.[122]

Management strategies to support a culture of safety and science of human factors and systems engineering include mapping work processes, training, recognizing and rewarding performance, using area-based safety coaches and champions, and surveying staff about the culture. Among the most important strategies is increasing communication among the parties. In addition to giving staff an opportunity and structure to continually update each other on what needs to be done and where risks are (use of situation, background, assessment, recommendation [SBAR] reports, daily huddles, and staff meetings), staff must be empowered to communicate so everyone knows there is a safety concern. Some HSOs are successful using the phrase *CUS words*: "I am *C*oncerned. I am *U*ncomfortable. This is a *S*afety issue." Key to success is that everyone knows what it means when these phrases are used. Another communication tactic uses methodologies that allow staff to close the communication loop and assure a message was correct and understood as received. Repeating back verbal orders and recording them and asking patients to repeat back teaching by staff are examples of this tactic. Management must reinforce these communication methods as the norm and intervene when staff deviate from them. Communication is discussed in Chapter 9.

There are multiple ways HSOs can assess their safety landscape and resolve safety and cultural issues. The following sections describe others.

Team STEPPS (Team *Strategies* to *Enhance Performance* and *Patient Safety*)

Developed by the U.S. Department of Defense, Team STEPPS is an evidence-based teamwork system to improve communication and teamwork skills among healthcare staff. There are three phases of Team STEPPS:

1. Assessing need

2. Planning, training, and implementation

3. Sustainment[123]

The methodology is based on lessons learned, master trainer or change agent experience, literature on quality and patient safety, and culture change. A successful Team STEPPS initiative requires thorough assessment of the HSO and its processes and a carefully prepared implementation and sustainment plan.

IHI Bundles

The IHI has identified interventions and treatment that are considered best practice and are generally recognized by clinicians. The parts of the bundle must be used completely or not at all. For example, the bundle for central line care has five elements. An audit of compliance must show the team performed *all* five if it is to get credit. The first bundles were developed to prevent infections when central lines and ventilators were used.[124]

Johns Hopkins University CUSP (Comprehensive Unit Safety Program) Initiative.

CUSP is a five-step process to change the culture of a unit by empowering staff to assume responsibility for safety in their environment.[125] AHRQ has partnered to use this process nationwide for central line–associated bloodstream infection (CLABSI) prevention projects.

The modules of the core CUSP toolkit help clinicians by using these seven steps:[126]

1. Learn about CUSP
2. Assemble the team
3. Engage senior executives
4. Understand the science of safety
5. Identify defects through "sensemaking"
6. Implement teamwork and communications
7. Apply CUSP

Overlap of Patient and Staff Safety

Safe Patient Handling

Staff injuries from moving a patient are usually musculoskeletal disorders, which include back, neck, shoulder, arm, wrist, and knee injuries. The rate of injuries incurred by nursing and patient care staff is among the highest of any occupation.

Safe patient handling has finally become an issue discussed, studied, and addressed by most HSOs. The healthcare workforce is aging, and the U.S. patient population is getting heavier. The injuries to staff from unassisted lifting are costly in time, money, and pain. Best practice dictates adopting a safe lifting program that requires staff to use equipment to move or lift any patient. Some states have enacted laws that require organizations to adopt a safe lifting program. Its success depends on how willing the staff is to use new the processes and equipment. Patients, too, can be injured from inappropriate or ineffective attempts to lift them; these injuries are often overlooked or miscategorized as to cause. Falls or skin ulcers can begin as failed attempts to move patients. In the old paradigm, two groups analyzed the injuries—the EOC safety committee and the patient safety committee. Many EOC requests for solutions to patient movement issues are subordinated to projects the patient safety committee has in its queue. A combined patient safety/EOC safety committee review means these projects can be considered together.

Lift equipment can be portable or installed in patient rooms. Portable equipment stored near the point of need is key to staff use. Hanging roll boards in hallways or patient rooms keeps them top of mind for staff. Easy access to cleaning materials to sanitize equipment after each use is key to success of staff using the right equipment. With training, patients can use many types of lift equipment. This has the further advantage of giving patients a sense of control over their movement. This requires that staff assess the risk to patients.

Historically, lifting injuries were managed by employee or occupational health and reported to the EOC committee. Often, the economic cost of lifting injuries is hidden; calculations for a specific employee or HSO/HS-wide data will show management the financial effect of lifting injuries.

Combining patient and staff lifting-related injuries includes all aspects of the problem. Initial assessment of the HSO's quantifiable injuries is required. This allows the work plan to identify which actions are most problematic—lateral transfers, wheelchair transfers to automobiles, or patient transfers from stretcher to bed. These data will show which equipment and training are needed. Another advantage is that care teams must discuss their assessment of patients' mobility needs and how that information is communicated among team members and with the patient and family.

Slips, Trips, and Falls

Injuries from slips, trips, and falls in hospitals are the second most common reason for staff to lose days away from work. Falls from the same level are more common than falls from a higher elevation.[127] Staff falls are caused by wet floors, tripping over cords or objects on the floor, and, often for reasons the injured employee cannot explain.

Solutions to this type of hazard include floor mats at building entrances, umbrella bags to prevent water on floors near entrances, spill clean-up centers in hallways adjacent to high-risk spill areas (cafeterias, etc.), use of wet floor signs by environmental services staff, and cord-control equipment in offices and patient care areas. Requiring or providing nonskid shoes for staff with the highest fall rates can decrease falls substantially.

Slips, trips, and falls outside the HSO require assessing external conditions. Handrails along changes in elevation, easy access to snow-melting chemicals, monitoring conditions of sidewalks and curbs, and adequate lighting in walkways and parking areas are helpful. HSOs in northern climates have been successful by supplying ice cleats for staff members' shoes.

Overall, falls are a leading cause of death for people 65 and older. In hospitals, 3%–20% of inpatients fall at least once. Patient falls are one of the top sentinel events reportable to The Joint Commission. Patient falls require different analyses than staff falls. Patients are affected by medications and are in new physical surroundings and highly emotional states. CMS defines patient falls in HSOs as a never event and will not reimburse for treating resulting injuries. Various interventions have received mixed results. Universal fall precautions mean assessing on admission a patient's risk of falling, signage or bright bracelets to identify patients at risk, low-rise beds, bed or chair alarms, and nonskid socks.[128]

Employee injury data are reported to the EOC; patient and volunteer falls are reported to the patient safety committee. Management is paying more attention to staff falls; older women are more likely to fall.[129] In addition to employer-paid workers' compensation insurance costs, falls are significant because of lost time on the job. Hazard assessment prioritizes HSO interventions.

QI methodologies can be used to ask questions about patient and staff safety and develop creative and realistic solutions to reduce injuries. Incident reports by staff for injuries that occurred or almost occurred (near misses) focus priorities. Root cause analysis should be done on each fall to pinpoint the cause. Sharing this information with committees and staff will make the injury tangible and highlight prevention.

Sharps Injury Prevention

Blood-borne pathogen exposures of healthcare staff from needlesticks and other sharp objects such as scalpels and broken glass (from test tubes, etc.) are a significant problem. Infection with hepatitis B, hepatitis C, and HIV can result from these injuries. In 2008, there were almost 400,000 sharps injuries.[130] Laws in 1990 (blood-borne pathogen standard [universal precautions] and 2000 [safe sharps]) addressed blood-borne pathogens. Laws, however, cannot eliminate sharps injuries. Data on numbers of needlestick and other sharps injuries to healthcare staff are not readily available; and staff may underreport sharps injuries. "It has been estimated about half or more of sharps injuries go unreported, so the numbers and frequencies that we do have access to are only the tip of the proverbial iceberg."[131] The economic cost of a blood-borne pathogen *exposure* varies but may be as high as $5,000.[132] Other estimates of direct and indirect costs per exposure range from $199 to $1,691.[133] Economic costs, however, ignore the significant stress to staff who will not know if they have contracted a disease from the injury until after the incubation period.

A sharps safety program has multiple components, not the least of which is that staff must participate *and* apply what they learn. There are many ways to circumvent safety systems designed to minimize exposure. The federal mandate to offer the hepatitis B vaccine to at-risk staff, the long incubation period of hepatitis C, and the low numbers of healthcare staff with occupationally acquired HIV make some staff think they have little cause for concern. Nurses are the group most likely to be exposed to blood-borne pathogens. From 2009 to 2013, nurses incurred 40.1% of all sharps injuries in hospitals.[134] Others frequently exposed are OR and laboratory staff.

The CDC's National Healthcare Safety Network database on sharps injuries, last updated in 2011, is the National Surveillance System for Healthcare Workers (NaSH). It showed that most injuries are on inpatient units (40%) or ORs (29%) and involve hollow-bore needles (56%).[135] Each HSO must review its injuries and identify operational issues to be addressed. The hierarchy of controls for blood-borne pathogen injuries starts by eliminating as many sharps as possible from daily operations. Using needleless intravenous systems or replacing glass with plastic are examples of first-level prevention. Engineering controls include a sharps disposal system to help prevent injuries when staff dispose of needles and syringes, as well as injection equipment with immediate retraction to prevent staff from sticking themselves after use. Work practice controls need staff cooperation (e.g., OR teams using no-touch passing of instruments or blunted sutures to prevent staff from sticking each other accidently).

Although uncommon, patients are exposed to blood-borne pathogens. For example, a patient may be exposed to body fluids of a staff member. In 2009, CDC reported finding 33 outbreaks of hepatitis B from 1998 to 2008 resulting from deficient practices using injection equipment. In 2014, CDC and others supported the One and Only One Campaign, whose focus is to assure that new equipment is used for each injection. Each HSO must work to prevent exposures and have a policy showing how it complies with state and federal law. A culture of safety that reports and analyzes all injuries *and* near misses and involves staff who are injured in this effort will reduce potentially serious events.

Healthcare-Associated Infections

HAIs are categorized in several ways: infections patients bring into the HSO and spread to staff and others, infections associated with devices, procedures, or the environment to which patients are exposed during treatment, or infections transmitted to patients from ill or infected healthcare staff.

Transmitting diseases in healthcare is unintended. Data show a continuing problem in HSOs because best practices were not followed. In 2014, a nurse in Texas contracted Ebola after exposure to an infected patient from Liberia. The infection may have occurred because the nurse did not use PPE correctly when treating the patient. A recurring example of noncompliance is seasonal flu vaccination rates for healthcare staff. For many years the compliance rate was about 40%. Since the flu virus can be spread when someone is asymptomatic, HSOs began to mandate flu shots. Because the shots are mandatory, many hospitals have influenza vaccination rates of 90%–100%. Some healthcare staff contend that they have medical and/or religious reasons for not being vaccinated. Mandating vaccinations requires following state laws and labor union contracts, developing a process to judge requests for exemptions, and determining how to handle exempted staff who want to work during flu season. The measles (rubeola) outbreak in 2019 challenged HSOs as to patients and visitors with no immunity to this highly communicable disease and who will be near others who are unprotected and may be immunocompromised.

In late 2019, the World Health Organization (WHO) reported that an "unknown viral pneumonia" had been identified in Wuhan, China.[136] After the severe acute respiratory syndrome (SARS [also a coronavirus]) pandemic in 2003, The Joint Commission required accredited hospitals to develop a Respiratory Epidemic plan to respond to an influx of infectious patients.[137] The U.S. mobilized to prevent the spread and minimize the impact of what became known as the COVID-19 (later SARS-CoV-2) virus. In March 2020 WHO declared a worldwide pandemic of COVID-19.[138] Cases from infected travelers to the United States caused community spread. Increasingly, patients needed hospital care.

Once there is community spread, it is difficult to determine if a staff member's case came from contact at work or contact in the community. This is also true for patients whose COVID-19 is diagnosed while hospitalized. Critical infection control measures are required to protect all persons.[139] Other challenges for HSOs included a worldwide shortage of raw materials used to make PPE, which put great pressure on supply chains. As of this writing, healthcare staff in all countries have contracted COVID-19 (SARS-CoV-2).

The wide range of settings in healthcare means staff have jobs such as registered nurse, physical therapist, physician, and pharmacist. The work of each type of provider carries a different risk of exposure to healthcare-associated communicable diseases. Management must assess risks of potential harms and institute appropriate controls (administrative, engineering, work practice, and PPE) to safeguard patients and staff.

Various interventions address risks of infection. They are categorized in a hierarchy of controls. Administrative controls include policies and procedures based on national and best practice guidelines. These include screening patients for multiresistant organisms on admission, requiring mandatory vaccination against seasonal flu for staff, and annual screening of staff for tuberculosis. Engineering controls cover interventions such as providing negative-pressure rooms for patients whose diseases require airborne isolation (tuberculosis, rubeola, varicella [chicken pox]), as well as using safe sharps and needle boxes to protect staff from contaminated equipment. PPE, including gloves, gowns, masks, and eye protection, is basic in healthcare and has specific uses. According to the 1991 OSHA blood-borne pathogen standard and use of universal precautions (now called standard precautions), gloves must be worn whenever staff may be in contact with body fluids or other potentially infectious materials. Finally, work practices include hand hygiene as a basic underpinning of infection prevention and control. Cleaning one's hands is expected before and after a patient interaction. Physicians' stethoscopes may be heavily contaminated with bacteria, including methicillin-resistant *Staphylococcus aureus* (MRSA), which can cause fatal antibiotic-resistant infections.[140] Patients and visitors help prevent the spread of organisms by sanitizing their hands after touching surfaces and before touching themselves or others.

Diseases healthcare staff are potentially exposed to during patient care are divided into three basic modes of transmission—contact, droplet, and airborne. Contact transmission can be subdivided into direct contact and indirect contact. Direct contact includes situations in which disease can be spread through skin-to-skin contact with the patient. Indirect contact occurs if someone comes into contact with the contaminated environment or equipment used by the infected person. Infectious diseases that require contact isolation are multidrug-resistant organisms such as MRSA and *Clostridium difficile* infection (CDI).

Droplet transmission occurs when air someone exhales contains organisms that can travel 3–6 feet and may reach someone's eyes or respiratory tract, causing diseases such as pertussis (whooping cough) or *Neisseria meningitidis* meningitis (a bacterial meningitis).

Airborne transmission occurs when air a person exhales contains organisms that can travel long distances for a considerable time. The causative organisms of diseases such as tuberculosis (TB), varicella, and rubeola can float for hours in the right environment. There are vaccines for some, but no vaccine is 100% effective. Exposure to some of these diseases requires antibiotic prophylaxis or monitoring over time.

The highest risk for patients is infections related to devices used in their care or procedures performed on them. Device-related infections include CLABSI, catheter-associated urinary tract infections (CAUTIs), and ventilator-associated pneumonias (VAPs). Much work has been done to identify best practices and develop them into "bundles" of preventive measures for staff to use. Device-related infection rate data are collected by many organizations. The outcome data are public; patients can use them to choose an HSO. States may require hospitals to participate in CDC's NHSN database. CMS requires collection of data on specific surgical procedures and device-related events if they are to be reimbursed by Medicare. The data are available on the CMS website, Hospital Compare (https://www.medicare.gov/hospitalcompare/search.html). CDC's 2017 National and State Healthcare-Associated Infections Progress Report on hospital-associated infections shows good progress in decreasing them. Despite this, however, *each day* about 1 in 31 patients contracts at least one infection associated with hospital care.[141]

Healthcare is provided in various settings; all have different risks of infection. CDC has developed minimum guidelines for outpatient settings, which have many outbreaks of communicable diseases because of failure to standardize the environment of care and work practices.[142] Substandard injection practices are especially problematic. This is true even though some providers are highly regulated to make their services safer. Dialysis centers are in this category. Surgicenters have received more attention to assure their standards are the same as those of the hospital. Nursing facilities (NFs) are high risk for residents, as shown by the disproportionately large number of deaths in NFs during the 2020 COVID-19 (SARS-CoV-2) pandemic. Multiple factors in NFs cause this problem. Usually, residents are elderly and more susceptible to communicable diseases. Many are cognitively impaired and cannot follow basic hygiene practices. Residents meet in public places in the NF, including dining rooms and day rooms, which increases exposure to communicable diseases. Caregivers may not be trained to prevent infections acquired in the facility. Such factors coalesce for problems such as urinary tract infections, skin and soft tissue infections, diarrhea—possibly from *C. difficile*—multidrug-resistant organisms, and influenza.

Exposure to Hazardous Materials

Hazards for patients and staff in the environment of care or healthcare workplace have been noted. Even simple day-to-day activities carry risks, such as chemicals to clean the environment, drugs used for treatment, and chemicals needed for diagnosis. Patients and staff have different risk-to-benefit ratios. Patients want to get better so potential benefits usually outweigh potential risks. Staff have potential unintentional, frequent exposure with no personal benefit, except for the employment relationship.

Many substances must be considered: chemicals, pharmaceuticals, and radioactive materials are primary categories. Methods of exposure include inhaling a substance, skin contact, ingestion, and injection.

The public expects HSOs to be clean, an expectation that must be added to the growing number of drug-resistant organisms in HSOs. This means hospital-grade disinfectants must be strong and may cause irritation in various ways. For example, there is an association between use of cleaning products and asthma in female hospital staff.[143] This causes tension between those cleaning the environment and patients and staff in the environment. It is critical to consider how to clean carpeting, furniture, and curtains before they are purchased and installed. If furniture in a patient area cannot withstand strong disinfectants, it is wasteful to buy it.

In addition to cleaning the environment, reusable equipment must be cleaned, disinfected, and sterilized. Likely, chemicals used to clean and disinfect it are toxic, and specific rules and processes must be used to minimize errors. Also, staff may be hurt by the high temperatures of sterilization. It is likely patients will be harmed by equipment that is inadequately sterilized. In 2015, CDC reported an outbreak from a multiresistant organism that infected patients during a procedure using an inadequately sterilized duodenoscope. Despite redesign of the scope and new cleaning instructions, a second outbreak of the same organism was reported in 2017.[144]

Pharmacies, laboratories, morgues, and dialysis units are HSO work areas that use harmful substances. Pharmacies have many hazardous drugs. Laboratories and morgues use chemicals such as formalin and xylene to preserve and fix specimens. Dialysis employs chemicals to make the water used to dialyze the patient safe. NIOSH estimates about 8 million U.S. healthcare workers are exposed to hazardous chemicals at their worksites.[145] There was a twofold increase in the rate of spontaneous abortion for women who handled chemotherapeutic agents for more than 1 hour per day during their first trimester of pregnancy.[146] NIOSH recommends a comprehensive safety program to protect healthcare workers, including medical surveillance. The program includes collecting information on employees' potential exposures and periodic communication concerning reproductive and general health. A comprehensive prevention program includes engineering controls, policies and procedures that delineate high-quality work practices, PPE, and educating and training staff.[147]

Exposure to radiation is another environmental risk in HSOs, where many forms of radiation are used to diagnose and treat. As noted, patient exposure to radiation has a different risk–benefit ratio than for staff. Both groups have specific risks and ways to reduce them. Since the mid-1980s, exposure to ionizing radiation in the United States has doubled.[148] New technology may require staff to be physically closer to patients than previously. Such changes require review of the effect radiation exposure has on staff and patients. HSOs must inform staff as to the cumulative radiation a patient has received if tests or treatment are done in different settings in a short time period. Patients must be told about risks of repetitive radiological testing if patients request it. The Joint Commission Sentinel Event Alert on risks of radiation exposure in diagnostic imaging describes issues, risks, and actions to mitigate them.[149]

Violence in the Workplace

Media reports about workplace violence are common. Most alarming are incidents involving active shooters at hospitals.[150] NIOSH defines workplace violence as "violent acts (including physical assaults and threats of assaults) directed toward persons at work or on duty." This definition covers the gamut from bullying to terrorism. It might seem the healthcare workplace will be less violent than elsewhere, but the U.S. Merit Systems Protection Board reported in *Employee Perceptions of Federal Workplace Violence* that employees in medical, hospital, and police/security occupations experience higher rates of workplace violence than other occupations.[151] Patients are the most common source of violence, but a third of the time other staff is responsible.[152] Of the fatal occupational injuries reported to the U.S. Bureau of Labor Statistics in 2011, 30% were violence against healthcare and education staff. This compares with only 17% for *all* types of workers.[153] Between 2002 and 2013, healthcare workers sustained four times the number of serious incidents of workplace violence (those requiring time off for recovery) than did workers, on average, in *all* other private sector occupations. Analysis of violence against healthcare workers in 2013 found that 80% of incidents were attributed to patient aggression.[154] The economic and psychological costs for staff and HSOs are obvious. Violence in the healthcare workplace is not limited to the United States. Hospitals in Ontario, Canada, reported 68% of nurses and personal support staff in the province experienced physical violence on the job at least once during the past year.[155]

Several factors put healthcare and social service staff at risk of work-related assaults:

- Prevalence of handguns and other weapons among patients, families, or friends

- Increasing use of hospitals by police and the criminal justice system for criminal holds and the care of acutely disturbed, violent individuals

- Increasing number of acute and chronic mentally ill patients released from hospitals without follow-up care (these patients have the right to refuse medicine and can no longer be hospitalized involuntarily unless they pose an immediate threat to themselves or others)

- Availability of drugs or money at hospitals, clinics, and pharmacies, making them likely robbery targets

- Factors such as unrestricted movement of the public in clinics and hospitals and long waits in emergency or clinic areas that lead to client frustration over an inability to obtain services promptly

- Increasing presence of gang members, drug or alcohol abusers, trauma patients, or distraught family members

- Low staffing levels during times of increased activity, such as mealtimes, visiting times, and when staff are transporting patients

- Isolated work with clients during examinations or treatment

- Solo work, often in remote locations with no backup or way to get assistance, such as communication devices or alarms (particularly true in high-crime settings)

- Lack of staff training in recognizing and managing escalating hostile and assaultive behavior

- Poorly lit parking areas[156]

As with any organizational risk, prevention and mitigation of workplace violence depend on how well a safety and health program is used. Management commitment, staff involvement, engineering and administrative controls, workplace practices, staff training, recordkeeping, and analysis are required. HSOs/HSs recognize the risk to staff and are acting to diminish the risk.[157]

Stress in the Healthcare Setting

It is important to understand that workplace stress in healthcare has an effect well beyond the staff member. Issues of staffing (too many/too few staff), rotating schedules, no scheduled breaks, excessive assignments, and overtime affect staff. These factors are associated with more staff errors to the detriment of patients. Data suggest high levels of registered nurse staffing decrease patient mortality.[158] Long before HSOs addressed staff schedules, the aviation industry tried to increase safety by rules protecting rest periods of pilots. This is not a simple issue with one solution. Often what has been proved safer (e.g., shorter shifts) may not be what staff want. Longer shifts that permit fewer working days with more days off may appeal to parents. Rotating shifts may appeal to students or those with multiple positions. The prohibition against napping on the job is being reviewed, considering research showing that short, planned rest periods are beneficial to fatigue management.[159]

Another aspect of workplace stress is organizational response to errors. Does staff feel supported and not blamed when a system or process fails? Is there a "just culture" that distinguishes between human error, at-risk behavior, and reckless behavior?[160] Can staff report errors or near misses without fear of retaliation? If staff becomes the "second victim" or "second patient" after a poor patient outcome, is there a process that allows the staff member to recover, thrive, and move on?[161] Such questions reflect Deming's concept of the workplace as discussed in Chapter 4.

How is the patient informed and supported when an error occurs? Historically, HSOs allowed physicians to decide whether to tell a patient and/or family about an untoward event—regardless of the cause or outcome. Following The Joint Commission's lead on sentinel events, the Leapfrog Group's never events policy requires apologies to the patient and family, who must also be informed about the hospital's actions to prevent recurrences using findings from the root cause analysis.[162] Doing both is key in the follow-up to a never event. How an HSO supports patients who may feel anger, sorrow, or fear after a never event varies, but it must be addressed.

Other Issues

Safety in HSOs almost always affects patients *and* staff; solutions for one reduce risk for the other. No healthcare staff member or patient chooses to put another at risk. The system and processes must be evaluated for potential failure points, and they must be improved or reengineered to make it easy to do the right thing. Many HSOs include patient–family advisory groups when planning for quality and safety, which, if done from the unique perspectives of patients and staff will make the healthcare setting safer for all.

Sustainability

Improving quality is complex, multifaceted, and demanding. HSO/HS managers and staff have seen management fads and "new" theories come and go for decades. Only a long-term, clear, and persistent effort to embed Q/PI in the organization's culture and nurture its application will convince doubters of the organization's commitment. Sustaining Q/PI is a challenge for GBs and senior management. The benefits of Q/PI are clear; making them the context for the organization's culture requires a continuing, clear commitment by its leaders. This commitment must be palpable inside and outside the organization. To sustain the focus on quality and performance improvement, the GB and senior managers must 1) communicate how the Q/PI aligns with the organization's mission, 2) direct improvement efforts at problems that benefit staff (and patients), and 3) ensure that managers are coaches who enable small wins and thereby increase staff motivation and engagement.[163]

Discussion Questions

1. What is the purpose of QITs? Distinguish between those that are intradepartmental and those that are cross functional.

2. Define common cause variation. Distinguish it from special cause variation. Why must managers be able to distinguish the two types of variation?

3. What is the purpose of ISO standards? Why should HSOs consider their use? Identify other ways to use ISO registration in addition to the entire organization.

4. Define benchmarking. What are its benefits? Identify some risks of benchmarking.

5. What is the relationship between quality improvement and productivity improvement?

6. Identify and discuss briefly three quality improvement tools.

7. How does the PDSA cycle relate to the problem-solving model in Figure 6.4?

8. Define *reengineering*. What are its attributes? What is common to both CQI and reengineering?

9. What are the four steps in strategic quality planning? How is it related to strategic planning as described in Chapter 10?

10. Why must LIPs be involved in CQI? What are the benefits and difficulties? What steps should be used to increase their involvement?

11. Patient and staff safety have different histories. What do they have in common?

12. Use the concept of the hierarchy of controls when considering the patient/staff safety issue of slips, trips, and falls. Give an example of each tier of the controls.

13. What is the most important category of management strategies that supports the culture of safety in an HSO?

14. If an HSO continues to struggle with a safety issue, what is the best course for senior leadership?

Case Study 1   The Carbondale Clinic[164]

The Carbondale Clinic, located in Carbondale, Illinois, is a large group practice of about 30 physicians. The clinic employs about 100 people and serves a regional population of about 100,000. Specialties ranging from pediatrics to psychiatry are offered by the clinic, which also operates its own laboratory, basic imaging services, and outpatient surgical center.

For some years, the clinic has been receiving complaints from its patients that appointment times are not being met. For instance, a patient with an appointment for 2 p.m. might not get in to see the physician until 4 p.m. However, the clinic has felt that such delays are unavoidable due to the uncertainty involved in the time it takes to adequately examine each patient and the possibility of emergency cases that must be inserted into the schedule.

Several criteria are used for scheduling. For instance, many patients are scheduled for annual physical exams. These are usually scheduled at least several weeks in advance because they require coordination of laboratory services and physician time. However, some physicians begin examining a patient and then decide the patient needs a physical immediately. The physicians believe this does not really cause problems because they can send the patient down to the laboratory while they continue to see other patients.

Some patients also phone the clinic for an appointment when they have nonemergency, routine problems, such as a mild fever or sore throat. Such patients are scheduled into available time slots as soon as possible—usually a day or two from the time they call. The objective here is to fit such patients in as quickly as possible without overloading the schedule with more patients than can reasonably be examined in a given time period. Usually the plan is to schedule four patients per hour.

However, each day, various emergencies occur. These can range from a splinter in the eye to a heart attack, and these cases cannot wait. For an emergency that is not life threatening, the approach is to try to squeeze the person into a time slot that is not too heavily scheduled. However, a case of life or death—such as a heart attack—means that the schedule must be disrupted and the patient treated immediately.

Currently, all scheduling of appointments is done centrally. However, this frequently causes problems because the people making appointments often do not know how long it should take to examine a patient with a complaint. On the other hand, the nurses in each department are usually too busy to do the scheduling themselves. Generally, if there is a doubt about whether a patient can be fitted into a time slot, the preference is to go ahead and schedule the patient. This is because the physicians prefer not to have any empty times in their schedules. At times, if it looks as if there might be an available opening, the clinic even calls patients who were originally scheduled for a later time and asks them to come in early.

Questions

1. "For some years, the clinic has received complaints from patients that appointment times are not being met." Why has no action been taken to correct the situation?

2. You are a member of a QIT asked to evaluate the appointment/scheduling process. Are there "assumptions" in the narrative that you question? If data were sufficient for a Pareto diagram of problems with the appointment/scheduling process, what do you think the items would be? Please list them.

3. Draw a cause-and-effect (Ishikawa) diagram of causes for patient complaints.

4. What recommendations would you make to decrease patient waiting time?

Case Study 2   Respiratory Pandemic and the Hospital

Tens of thousands of cases of a respiratory viral illness have been reported abroad; infected travelers bring it to the United States. Soon, there are confirmed cases of community spread. Initially, only your ED is screening and testing patients with the viral infection, using guidance from the state health department and the CDC. As the pandemic matures, however, patients must be admitted to the hospital for critical care. Staff safety becomes a major concern.

Questions

1. How do you use OSHA's "Hierarchy of Controls" to manage the hospital's response?

2. When PPE becomes scarce worldwide, what can be done to protect the clinical staff in the hospital?

Case Study 3   Infections—CLABSI

Your state quality improvement organization has asked all hospitals to participate in an initiative to prevent central line–associated bloodstream infections (CLABSIs). You have agreed to form a team and work on the CLABSI prevention bundle.

Questions

1. Which staff members should be on your unit-specific team?

2. What is the response if staff ask for equipment to assist in complying with the prevention bundle, but supply chain says it is too expensive?

3. How do you educate staff on the components of the quality improvement process?

4. How do you keep this project top of mind for all staff on a daily basis?

Case Study 4   Sharps Injuries

While reviewing the quarterly sharps injury statistics, the employee health manager notices a significant increase in sharps injuries over the past 90 days. After review, it is found that the OR had most injuries. In addition, the OR had 50% more sharps injuries than in any quarter for the past 3 years. One of the OR injuries occurred when a medical student stuck himself just before the needle he was holding stuck a patient. The employee health manager reported this incident to the patient safety committee.

Questions

1. Which types of staff should be included in an investigation of the increase in sharps injuries in the OR?

2. What safety measures can be taken in the OR to protect staff and patients from sharps injuries?

3. How likely is it that the sharps injury reports from employee health are accurate?

4. If an employee complains to OSHA about the increase in sharps injuries, what document will the surveyor ask to see at the hospital?

Case Study 5   Violence in the Workplace

At the monthly environment of care safety meeting, the security office reports data on disruptive patients and visitors. The number of incidents has been increasing, especially in the ED. To date, however, senior management has not agreed to station a security guard in the ED 24/7.

Questions

1. How can the problem be quantified?

2. What can be done to address the problem of angry, emotional patients, families, and visitors?

3. Should a security guard be present in the ED? Should the guard be armed?

Notes

1. Productivity improvement and performance improvement are similar concepts, although not synonymous. The quality improvement literature uses the former, The Joint Commission the latter.
2. McGrath, Petrina, Angela A. Shippy, and David M. Williams. Leading quality across a system. *Healthcare Executive* 33, 6 (November/December 2018): 66–68.
3. "Lean Six Sigma Training in Full Swing at USMA." *U.S. Federal News Service*, February 2, 2007. *https://www.army.mil/article/1667/lean_six_sigma_training_in_full_swing_at_usma*, retrieved July 16, 2020.
4. Strategos, Inc. "Just in Time, Toyota Production & Lean Manufacturing: Origins & History of Lean Manufacturing." Kansas City, MO. *http://www.strategosinc.com/just_in_time.htm*, , retrieved July 21, 2020.
5. Lean Manufacturing Updates Some Lean Manufacturing Tools. *https://www.tpslean.com/leantools/leantoolsmenu.htm*, retrieved July 21, 2020.
6. Leslie, Marshall, Charles Hagood, Adam Royer, Charles P. Reece, Jr., and Sara Maloney. "Using Lean Methods to Improve OR Turnover Times." *AORN Journal* 84, 5 (2005): 849–855; Jennifer Town. "Going 'Lean' Streamlines Processes, Empowers Staff and Enhances Care." *Hospitals and Health Networks* 80, 10 (October 2006): 34–35.
7. Thilmany, Jean. "Thinking Lean." *Mechanical Engineering* 127, 7 (July 2005): 5.

8. Bukowski, Eugene R., Jr., and Mary Litteral. "Produce Perfect Products." *Quality* 45, 11 (November 2006): 40–43.
9. W. Edwards Deming. *The New Economics for Industry, Government, Education,* 2nd ed., 219–220. Cambridge, MA: MITCAES, 1994.
10. Laux, Daniel T. "Six Sigma Evolution Clarified—Letter to the Editor." *Six Sigma Healthcare. https://www.isixsigma.com/new-to-six-sigma/roles-responsibilities/six-sigma-evolution-clarified-letter-editor/,* retrieved July 16, 2020.
11. Chassin, Mark R. Is Health Care Ready for Six Sigma Quality? *The Milbank Quarterly,* 76, 4 (1998). *http://www.milbank.org/uploads/documents/featured-articles/html/Milbank_Quarterly_Vol-76_No-4_1998_Chassin.htm,* retrieved July 16, 2020.
12. "Statistical Six Sigma Definition." iSix Sigma. *https://www.isixsigma.com/new-to-six-sigma/statistical-six-sigma-definition/,* retrieved July 16, 2020.
13. Brown, Lewis, and Denise Taylor. "Reducing Delayed Starts in Specials Lab with Six Sigma." iSixSigma. *https://www.isixsigma.com/new-to-six-sigma/dmaic/reducing-delayed-starts-specials-lab-six-sigma/,* retrieved July 16, 2020.
14. International Organization for Standardization. ISO 9000:2015: Quality Management Systems— Fundamentals and Vocabulary. *https://www.iso.org/standard/45481.html,* retrieved June 28, 2019.
15. International Organization for Standardization. ISO 14000 Family– Environmental Management. *https://www.iso.org/iso-14001-environmental-management.html,* retrieved June 28, 2019.
16. "The Art of Service. The importance of ISO 9000 and ISO 14000. *https://theartofservice.com/the-importance-of-iso-9000-and-iso-14000.html,* retrieved July 21, 2020.
17. International Organization for Standardization. "What We Do." *https://www.iso.org/about-us.html,* retrieved July 21, 2020.
18. International Organization for Standardization. Quality Management Principles. *https://www.iso.org/files/live/sites/isoorg/files/archive/pdf/en/pub100080.pdf,* retrieved June 28, 2019.
19. UNC Health Care. Pardee. *https://www.pardeehospital.org/about-us/quality-safety/,* retrieved July 21, 2020.
20. DNV GL Healthcare. *https://www.dnvglhealthcare.com/hospitals?search_type=and&q=&c=&c=&c=26279&c=&prSubmit=Search&page=51,* retrieved August 12, 2019.
21. Hammer, Michael. *Beyond Reengineering: How the Process-Centered Organization Is Changing Our Work and Our Lives,* 81–82. New York: HarperBusiness, 1996.
22. Kennedy, Maggie. "Reengineering in Healthcare." *Quality Letter for Healthcare Leaders* 6 (September 1994): 2–3.
23. Hammer, Michael, and James Champy. *Reengineering the Corporation: A Manifesto for Business Revolution,* 32. New York: HarperBusiness, 1993.
24. Stewart, Thomas A. "Reengineering: The Hot New Management Tool." *Fortune* 128 (August 1993): 41.
25. Bergman, Rhonda. "Reengineering Health Care." *Hospitals & Health Networks* 68 (February 5, 1994): 30.
26. Hammer. *Beyond Reengineering,* 80.
27. Hammer. *Beyond Reengineering,* 82.
28. Leatt, Peggy G., Ross Baker, Paul K. Halverson, and Catherine Aird. "Downsizing, Reengineering, and Restructuring: Long-Term Implications for Healthcare Organizations." *Frontiers of Health Services Management* 13 (June 1997): 17.
29. Hammer, Michael, and Steven A. Stanton. *The Reengineering Revolution: A Handbook,* 56. New York: HarperBusiness, 1995.
30. Hammer and Stanton. *The Reengineering Revolution,* 57.
31. Hammer and Champy. *Reengineering the Corporation,* 102.
32. Leatt, Baker, Halverson, and Aird. "Downsizing, Reengineering," 5–6.
33. Hammer and Champy. *Reengineering the Corporation,* 49.
34. Patrick McHughand A. John Pendlebury. *Business Process Reengineering: Breakpoint Strategies for Market Dominance,* 15. New York: John Wiley & Sons, 1993; Griffith, John R., Vinod K. Sahney, and Ruth A. Mohr. *Reengineering Health Care: Building on CQI,* 14. Ann Arbor, MI: Health Administration Press, 1995.
35. Walston, Stephen L., and John R. Kimberly. "Reengineering Hospitals: Evidence from the Field." *Hospital & Health Services Administration* 42 (Summer 1997): 150.
36. Walston and Kimberly. "Reengineering Hospitals," 151.
37. Schweikhart, Sharon Bergman, and Vicki Smith-Daniels. "Reengineering the Work of Caregivers: Role Redefinition, Team Structures, and Organizational Redesign." *Hospital & Health Services Administration* 41 (Spring 1996): 22.
38. Walston and Kimberly, "Reengineering Hospitals," 151–152.

39. Walston and Kimberly, "Reengineering Hospitals," 151–152.
40. Arndt, Margarete, and Barbara Bigelow. "Reengineering: Déjà Vu All Over Again." *Health Care Management Review* 23 (Summer 1998): 63.
41. Hammer and Champy. *Reengineering the Corporation*, 128–133.
42. Carter, Tony. "Hospitals and Reengineering." *Journal of Hospital Marketing & Public Relations* 14, 1 (2002): 59–78. Republished online September 22, 2008. *https://www.tandfonline.com/doi/abs/10.1300/J375v14n01_06,* retrieved June 30, 2019; Walston, S. L., L. D. Urden, and P. Sullivan. "Hospital Reengineering: An Evolving Management Innovation: History, Current Status, and Future Direction." *Journal of Health and Human Services Administration* 23, 4 (Spring 2001): 388–415.
43. James, Brent C. "Implementing Continuous Quality Improvement." *Trustee* 43 (April 1990): 16.
44. Goldense, Robert A. "Attaining TQM Through Employee Involvement: Imperatives for Implementation." *Journal of Management Science & Policy Analysis* 8 (Spring/Summer 1991): 268.
45. Kazemek, Edward A., and Rosemary M. Charny. "Quality Enhancement Means Total Organizational Involvement." *Healthcare Financial Management* 45 (February 1991): 15; Kronenberg, Philip S., and Renee G. Loeffler, "Quality Management Theory: Historical Context and Future Prospect." *Journal of Management Science and Policy Analysis* 8 (Spring/Summer 1991): 211–212.
46. Lowe, Ted A., and Joseph M. Mazzeo. "Crosby, Deming, Juran: Three Preachers, One Religion." *Quality* 25 (September 1986): 23.
47. Darr, Kurt. "Applying the Deming Method in Hospitals: Part 2." *Hospital Topics* 68 (Winter 1990): 4.
48. Darr, "Applying the Deming Method: Part 2," 4.
49. "Joseph M. Juran." Wikipedia. *https://en.wikipedia.org/wiki/Joseph_M._Juran,* retrieved July 16, 2020.
50. McCain, Cecelia. "Using an FMEA in a Service Setting." *Quality Progress* 39, 9 (September 2006): 24–29.
51. "Most Airplane Crashes Caused by Human Error." *Quality Progress* 39, 11 (November 2006): 12.
52. Meyers, Susan. "Standardizing Safety: Borrowing Lessons Learned from the Airline Industry, Hospitals See the Results of Teamwork and Clear Communication." *Trustee* 59, 7 (July/August 2006): 12.
53. Meyers. "Standardizing Safety," 14.
54. Meyers. "Standardizing Safety," 21.
55. Pizzi, Laura, Neil I. Goldfarb, and David B. Nash. "Chapter 44. Crew Resource Management and Its Applications in Medicine," 7. *http://www.ahrq.gov/clinic/ptsafety/chap44.htm,* retrieved June 11, 2007.
56. Harris, Karen T., Catharine M. Treanor, and Mary L. Salisbury. "Improving Patient Safety with Team Coordination: Challenges and Strategies of Implementation." *Journal of Obstetrics, Gynecology, and Neonatal Nursing* 35, 4 (July/August 2006): 557.
57. Dunn, Edward J. "Effects of Teamwork Training on Adverse Outcomes and Process of Care in Labor and Delivery: A Randomized Controlled Trial." Letter to the Editor. *Journal of Obstetrics and Gynecology* 109, 5 (June 2007): 1457.
58. Anderson, Craig, and Peggy A. Rivenburgh. "Benchmarking." In *Total Quality Management: The Health Care Pioneers,* edited by Mara Minerva Melum and Marie Kuchuris Sinioris, 326. Chicago: American Hospital Publishing, 1992.
59. Anderson and Rivenburgh. "Benchmarking," 226.
60. Eastaugh, Steven R. *Financing Health Care: Economics, Efficiency, and Equity,* 258. Dover, MA: Auburn House, 1987.
61. Fogarty, Donald W., Thomas R. Hoffmann, and Peter W. Stonebraker. *Production and Operations Management,* 18. Cincinnati, OH: South-Western Publishing, 1989.
62. Selbst, Paul L. "A More Total Approach to Productivity Improvement." *Hospital & Health Services Administration* 30 (July/August 1985): 86.
63. James, Brent C. *Quality Management for Health Care Delivery—Quality Measurement and Management Project,* 10. Chicago: Hospital Research and Educational Trust, 1989.
64. In ABC inventory analysis, items are classified into A, B, or C groups based on volume, criticalness, or dollar value. A is high; C is low. The A group should have the highest priority.
65. McLaughlin, Curtis P., and Arnold D. Kaluzny, "Total Quality Management in Health: Making It Work." *Healthcare Management Review* 15 (Summer 1990): 8.
66. Graham, Robin, Michelle Mancher, Dianne Miller Wolman, Sheldon Greenfield, and Earl Steinberg, eds.; Institute of Medicine (US), Committee on Standards for Developing Trustworthy Clinical Practice Guidelines. *Clinical Practice Guidelines We Can Trust.* Washington, DC: The National Academies Press, 2011.
67. Kelly and Swartwout. "Development of Practice Parameters," 55.

68. Holmer, Haley, Lauren Ogden, Shelley Selph, and Rongwei Fu. "Conflict of Interest Disclosures for Clinical Practice Guidelines in the National Guideline Clearinghouse." *PLOS ONE* (November 7, 2012). *http://www.plosone.org/article/info%3Adoi%2F10.1371%2Fjournal.pone.0047343*, retrieved July 16, 2020.

69. Silow-Carroll, Sharon, Jennifer Edwards, and Diana Rodin. "Using Electronic Health Records to Improve Quality and Efficiency." *The Commonwealth Fund.* July 2012. *https://www.common wealthfund.org/publications/issue-briefs/2012/jul/using-electronic-health-records-improve-quality-and -efficiency*, retrieved July 16, 2020.

70. Coffey, Richard J., Janet S. Richards, Carl S. Remmert, Sarah S. LeRoy, Rhonda R. Schoville, and Phyllis J. Baldwin. "An Introduction to Critical Paths." *Quality Management in Health Care* 1 (Fall 1992): 46.

71. Gillies, Robin P., Stephen M. Shortell, and Gary J. Young. "Best Practices in Managing Organized Delivery Systems." *Hospital & Health Services Administration* 42 (Fall 1997): 303.

72. "Good News on Guidelines." *Hospitals & Health Networks* 72 (January 5, 1998): 13.

73. Kelly and Swartwout. "Development of Practice," 55.

74. "Risk Management: Guideline Payoff." *Trustee* 51 (October 1998): 7.

75. Clinical Guidelines and Standardization of Practice to Improve Outcomes. Committee on Patient Safety and Quality Improvement; Committee on Professional Liability. American College of Obstetricians and Gynecologists. Committee Opinion, Number 629, October 2019. *https://www .acog.org/Clinical-Guidance-and-Publications/Committee-Opinions/Committee-on-Patient-Safety-and -Quality-Improvement/Clinical-Guidelines-and-Standardization-of-Practice-to-Improve-Outcomes*, retrieved June 29, 2019.

76. Larsen-Denning, Laurie, Catherine Rommal, and Annie Stoekmann. "Clinical Practice Guidelines." In *Risk Management Handbook for Health Care Organizations*, 2nd ed., edited by Roberta Carrol, 579. Chicago: American Hospital Publishing, 1997.

77. Bigelow, Barbara, and Margarete Arndt. "Total Quality Management: Field of Dreams?" *Healthcare Management Review* 20 (Fall 1995): 21.

78. Weiner, B. J., S. M. Shortell, and J. Alexander. Tulane University Medical Center. "Promoting Clinical Involvement in Hospital Quality Improvement Efforts: The Effects of Top Management, Board, and Physician Leadership." October 2007. *http://www.ncbi.nlm.nih.gov/pubmed/9327815*, retrieved February 14, 2013.

79. James, Brent C. "How Do You Involve Physicians in TQM?" *Journal for Quality and Participation* (January/February 1991): 43.

80. See also Kaluzny, Arnold D., Curtis P. McLaughlin, and David C. Kibbe. "Continuous Quality Improvement in the Clinical Setting: Enhancing Adoption." *Quality Management in Health Care* 1 (Fall 1992): 37–44; Berwick, Donald M. "The Clinical Process and Quality Process." *Quality Management in Health Care* 1 (Fall 1992): 1–8, for ways to enhance physician involvement in CQI; and Caverzagie, K. J., E. C. Bernabeo, S. G. Reddy, and E. S. Holmboe. "The Role of Physician Engagement on the Impact of the Hospital-Based Practice Improvement Module (PIM). *Journal of Hospital Medicine* 4, 8 (October 2009): 466–470. *https://www.ncbi.nlm.nih.gov/pubmed/19824089*, retrieved June 30, 2019.

81. James, Brent C. "Implementing Practice Guidelines through Clinical Quality Improvement." *Frontiers of Health Services Management* 10 (November 1993): 44.

82. Laffel, Glenn, and David Blumenthal, "The Case for Using Industrial Management Science in Health Care Organizations." *Journal of the American Medical Association* 262 (November 24, 1989): 2870.

83. Lagoe, Ronald J., and Deborah L. Aspling. "Enlisting Physician Support for Practice Guidelines in Hospitals." *Health Care Management Review* 21 (Fall 1996): 61–67.

84. James. "How Do You Involve," 44.

85. Succi, Melissa J., Shou-Yih Lee, and Jeffrey A. Alexander. "Trust between Managers and Physicians in Community Hospitals: The Effects of Power over Hospital Decisions." *Journal of Healthcare Management* 43 (September/October 1998): 398.

86. James. "How Do You Involve," 44.

87. James. "How Do You Involve," 44.

88. James. "How Do You Involve," 47.

89. James. "How Do You Involve," 47.

90. Shortell, Stephen M., James L. O'Brien, Edward F. X. Hughes, James M. Carman, Richard W. Foster, Heidi Boerstler, and Edward J. O'Connor. "Assessing the Progress of TQM in U.S. Hospitals: Findings from Two Studies." *Quality Letter for Healthcare Leaders* 6 (April 1994): 15–16.

91. James. "Implementing Practice Guidelines," 7.

92. Carman, James M., Stephen M. Shortell, Richard W. Foster, Edward F. X. Hughes, Heidi Boerstler, James L. O'Brien, and Edward J. O'Connor. "Keys for Successful Implementation of Total Quality Management in Hospitals." *Health Care Management Review* 21 (Winter 1996): 58.

93. Ferguson, T. Bruce, Eric D. Peterson, Laura P. Coombs, Mary C. Eiken, Meghan L. Carey, Frederick L. Grover, and Elizabeth R. DeLong. "Use of Continuous Quality Improvement to Increase Use of Process Measures in Patients Undergoing Coronary Artery Bypass Graft Surgery." *Journal of the American Medical Association* 290, 1 (July 2, 2003): 49–56.

94. Shortell et al. "Assessing the Progress," 15.

95. Lagoe and Aspling. "Enlisting Physician Support," 61.

96. Shortell et al. "Assessing the Progress," 15.

97. Berwick. "The Clinical Process," 3.

98. Kaluzny et al. "Continuous Quality Improvement," 40.

99. Shortell et al. "Assessing the Progress," 16.

100. Shortell et al. "Assessing the Progress," 16; Carman et al. "Keys for Successful," 50.

101. Sisk, Jane. "How Are Health Care Organizations Using Clinical Guidelines?" *Health Affairs* 17 (September/October 1998): 97.

102. Herman, Bob. "74% of Healthcare Organizations Tie Physician Pay to Patient Satisfaction." *Becker's Hospital Review*. January 20, 2012. *https://www.beckershospitalreview.com/compensation-issues/74-of-healthcare-organizations-tie-physician-pay-to-patient-satisfaction.html*, retrieved July 16, 2020.

103. Sisk. "How Are Health Care," 99–100.

104. Sisk. "How Are Health Care," 106.

105. The Lone Ranger is a fictional comic book and movie character who fought evil and brought justice in the American West, aided only by his Native American companion, Tonto. Characterizing persons as a "lone ranger" suggests they alone, or with little assistance, will solve a problem.

106. Hines, S., K. Luna, J. Lofthus, et al. *Becoming a High Reliability Organization: Operational Advice for Hospital Leaders.* (Prepared by the Lewin Group under Contract No. 290-04-0011.) AHRQ Publication No. 08-0022. Rockville, MD: Agency for Healthcare Research and Quality, April 2008.

107. The Joint Commission. *Improving Patient and Worker Safety: Opportunities for Synergy, Collaboration and Innovation.* Oakbrook Terrace, IL: The Joint Commission, November 2012. *http://www.jointcommission.org/assets/1/18/TJC-ImprovingPatientAndWorkerSafety-Monograph.pdf*, retrieved July 16, 2020.

108. Institute of Medicine. *To Err Is Human: Building a Safer Health System.* Washington, DC: National Academy Press, 1999.

109. Institute of Medicine. *To Err Is Human.*

110. The Agency for Healthcare Research and Quality. *http://www.ahrq.gov/*, retrieved November 20, 2013.

111. The Joint Commission. "National Patient Safety Goals." *https://www.jointcommission.org/standards/national-patient-safety-goals/*, retrieved July 16, 2020.

112. The Joint Commission. "Sentinel Event Policy and Procedures," June 10, 2013. *https://www.jointcommission.org/resources/patient-safety-topics/sentinel-event/sentinel-event-policy-and-procedures/*, retrieved July 16, 2020.

113. Institute for Healthcare Improvement. "Free from Harm: Accelerating Patient Safety Improvement Fifteen Years after *To Err Is Human*." *http://www.ihi.org/resources/Pages/Publications/Free-from-Harm-Accelerating-Patient-Safety-Improvement.aspx*, retrieved August 13, 2019.

114. *New York Times.* "Labor—the New American Job." *http://topics.nytimes.com/top/reference/timestopics/subjects/l/labor/index.html*, retrieved November 20, 2013.

115. OSHA. "Hazard Communication in the 21st Century Workplace," March 2004. *https://www.osha.gov/dsg/hazcom/finalmsdsreport.html*, retrieved May 22, 2020.

116. United Nations. "Globally Harmonized System of Classification and Labeling of Chemicals (GHS), 2011." *https://www.osha.gov/dsg/hazcom/ghsguideoct05.pdf*, retrieved May 22, 2020.

117. Phillips, E., et al. "Percutaneous Injuries before and after the Needlestick Safety and Prevention Act (Correspondence)." *New England Journal of Medicine* 366 (February 16, 2012): 670–671.

118. The Joint Commission. *Improving Patient and Worker Safety: Opportunities for Synergy, Collaboration and Innovation,* 26. Oakbrook Terrace, IL: The Joint Commission, November 2012. *http://www.jointcommission.org/assets/1/18/TJC-ImprovingPatientAndWorkerSafety-Monograph.pdf*, retrieved July 16, 2020.

119. Savage-Knepshield, Pamela. "Human Factors." *DocsBay Explore. https://docsbay.net/Human-Factors*, retrieved August 14, 2019.

120. U.S. Department of Transportation. Federal Aviation Administration. "Human Factors in Aviation Safety (AVS)." *https://www.faa.gov/aircraft/air_cert/design_approvals/human_factors/*, retrieved August 14, 2019.

121. *Human Factors in Healthcare. A Systems-Based Approach to Improve Safety, Efficiency and Quality.* Washington, DC: MedStar Health. National Center for Human Factors in Healthcare. *https://ct1. medstarhealth.org/content/uploads/sites/130/2019/04/HF_booklet.pdf,* retrieved August 14, 2019.

122. The Joint Commission. *Sentinel Event Data: Root Causes by Event Type, 2004–2012. http://www. jointcommission.org/assets/1/18/Root_Causes_Event_Type_04_4Q2012.pdf,* retrieved November 20, 2013.

123. Agency for Healthcare Research and Quality. "TeamSTEPPS: National Implementation." *http:// teamstepps.ahrq.gov/,* retrieved November 20, 2013.

124. Resar, R., F. A. Griffin, C. Haraden, and T. W. Nolan. "Using Care Bundles to Improve Health Care Quality." IHI Innovation Series white paper. Cambridge, MA: Institute for Healthcare Improvement, 2012. *http://www.ihi.org/resources/Pages/IHIWhitePapers/UsingCareBundles.aspx,* retrieved May 17, 2020.

125. Johns Hopkins Medicine. Armstrong Institute for Patient Safety and Quality. "The Comprehensive Unit-Based Safety Program." *https://www.hopkinsmedicine.org/armstrong_institute/training_services/ workshops/cusp_implementation_training/cusp_guidance.html,* retrieved August 14, 2019.

126. McGinley, Patton. "AHRQ: CUSP–Scaling Up a Safety Framework, June 3, 2013." *https://www. psqh.com/analysis/cusp-scaling-up-a-safety-framework/,* retrieved August 14, 2019.

127. U.S. Department of Labor. Bureau of Labor Statistics. "Employer-Reported Workplace Injury and Illnesses, 2017." *https://www.bls.gov/news.release/osh.nr0.htm,* retrieved August 15, 2019.

128. Bonshon, B., G. Nielsen, P. Quigley, P. Rutherford, J. Taylor, D. Shannon, and S. Rita. *How-to Guide: Reducing Patient Injuries from Falls.* Cambridge, MA: Institute for Healthcare Improvement, 2012. *http://www.ihi.org/resources/Pages/Tools/TCABHowToGuideReducingPatientInjuriesfromFalls.aspx,* retrieved July 21, 2019.

129. Collins J. W., and J. L. Bell. "Prevention of Slip, Trip, and Fall Hazards for Workers in Hospital Settings." In *Handbook of Modern Hospital Safety,* edited by W. Charney. Boca Raton, FL: CRC Press, 2009.

130. Centers for Disease Control and Prevention. *Workbook for Designing, Implementing, and Evaluating a Sharps Injury Prevention Program.* Last reviewed February 11, 2015. *https://www.cdc.gov/sharpssafety /resources.html,* retrieved August 15, 2019.

131. Centers for Disease Control and Prevention. National Occupational Research Agenda. "Stop Sticks Campaign: Sharps Injuries." *https://www.cdc.gov/nora/councils/hcsa/stopsticks/sharpsinjuries.html,* retrieved August 15, 2019.

132. Bureau of Labor Statistics. "May 2011 Employment and Wage Estimates." Washington, DC: Bureau of Labor Statistics. *http//www.bls.gov/oes.home.htm,* retrieved November 19, 2013.

133. Mannocci, Alice, Gabriella De Carli, Virginia Di Bari, Rosella Saulle, Brigid Unim, Nicola Nicolotti, Lorenzo Carbonari, Vincenzo Puro, and Giuseppe La Torre. "How Much Do Needlestick Injuries Cost? A Systematic Review of the Economic Evaluations of Needlestick and Sharps Injuries among Healthcare Personnel." *Infection Control and Hospital Epidemiology* 37, 6 (June 2016): 635–646. *https://www.ncbi.nlm.nih.gov/pmc/articles/PMC4890345/,* retrieved August 15, 2019.

134. Mitchell, Amber Hogan, and Ginger B. Parker. "Preventing Needlestick and Sharps Injuries." *American Nurse Today* 10, 9 (September 2015). *https://www.americannursetoday.com/preventing -needlestick-sharps-injuries/,* retrieved August 16, 2019.

135. Centers for Disease Control and Prevention. "The National Surveillance System for Healthcare Workers (NaSH)." *www.cdc.gov/nhsn/PDFs/NaSH/NaSH-Report-6-2011.pdf,* retrieved November 19, 2013.

136. World Health Organization. *Novel Coronavirus(2019-nCoV) Situation Report -121.* January 2020. *https://www.who.int/docs/default-source/coronaviruse/situation-reports/20200121-sitrep-1-2019-ncov. pdf?sfvrsn=2a99c10_4,* retrieved May 23, 2020.

137. The Joint Commission. *Comprehensive Accreditation Manual for Hospitals.* Infection Control 01.06.01 EP4. Oakbrook Terrace, Illinois, 2020.

138. World Health Organization. *Coronavirus disease 2019 (COVID-19) Situation Report –51.* March 11, 2020. *https://www.who.int/docs/default-source/coronaviruse/situation-reports/20200311-sitrep-51 -covid-19.pdf?sfvrsn=1ba62e57_10,* retrieved May 23, 2020. As of May 19, 2020, there were 4,881,619 confirmed cases worldwide and 322,457 deaths. The United States had 1,524,107 cases and 91,661 deaths. The COVID-19 Dashboard, Center for Systems Science and Engineering, Johns Hopkins University. *https://systems.jhu.edu/,* retrieved May 23, 2020.

139. Centers for Disease Control and Prevention. Coronavirus (COVID-19). *https://www.cdc.gov /coronavirus/2019-ncov/index.html,* retrieved May 23, 2020.

140. Lagnado, Lucette. "Hospitals Step Up the War on Superbugs." *Wall Street Journal,* September 10, 2018, A11.

141. Centers for Disease Control and Prevention. Current HAI Progress Report. 2017 National and State Healthcare-Associated Infections Progress Report. *https://www.cdc.gov/hai/data/portal/progress-report.html,* retrieved August 16, 2019.

142. Centers for Disease Control and Prevention. *Guide to Infection Prevention for Outpatient Settings: Minimum Expectations for Safe Care. https://www.cdc.gov/infectioncontrol/pdf/outpatient/guide.pdf,* retrieved August 15, 2019.

143. Dumas, O., et al. "Occupational Exposure to Cleaning Products and Asthma in Hospital Workers." *Occupational and Environmental Medicine* 69, 12 (December 2012): 883–889.

144. Petersen, Melody. Olympus' Redesigned Scope Is Linked to Infection Outbreak." *Los Angeles Times,* March 22, 2017. *https://www.latimes.com/business/la-fi-olympus-scope-outbreak-20170322-story.html,* retrieved August 15, 2019.

145. Centers for Disease Control and Prevention. "Personal Protective Equipment for Health Care Workers Who Work with Hazardous Drugs." *http://www.cdc.gov/niosh/docs/wp-solutions/2009-106/,* retrieved November 19, 2013.

146. Lawson, C. C., C. M. Rocheleau, E. A. Whelan, E. N. Lividoti Hibert, B. Grajewski, D. Spiegelman, and J. W. Rich-Edwards. "Occupational Exposures among Nurses and Risk of Spontaneous Abortions." *American Journal of Obstetrics and Gynecology* 206 (2012): 327.e1–8.

147. Centers for Disease Control and Prevention. "Workplace Solutions: Medical Surveillance for Healthcare Workers Exposed to Hazardous Drugs." 2012. *http://www.cdc.gov/niosh/docs/wp-solutions/2013-103/pdfs/2013-103.pdf,* retrieved November 19, 2013.

148. The Joint Commission. "Improving Patient and Worker Safety." 2012. *http://www.jointcommission.org/improving_Patient_Worker_Safety/,* retrieved November 19, 2013.

149. The Joint Commission. "Sentinel Event Alert 47: Radiation Risks of Diagnostic Imaging and Fluoroscopy." Revised February 2019. *https://www.jointcommission.org/resources/patient-safety-topics/sentinel-event/sentinel-event-alert-newsletters/sentinel-event-alert-issue-47-radiation-risks-of-diagnostic-imaging-and-fluoroscopy/,* retrieved May 24, 2020.

150. Rege, Alyssa. "Hospital Shootings: How Common Are They? 8 Things to Know." *Becker's Hospital Review.* February 10, 2017. *https://www.beckershospitalreview.com/population-health/hospital-shootings-how-common-are-they-8-things-to-know.html,* retrieved August 15, 2019.

151. US Merit Systems Protection Board. "Employee Perceptions of Federal Workplace Violence." September 2012. *http://www.mspb.gov,* retrieved November 19, 2013.

152. US Merit Systems Protection Board. "Employee Perceptions."

153. "Fatalities among Health Care Workers." *OSHA Guide for Health Care Facilities* 19, 4 (November 2012): 5.

154. Occupational Safety and Health Administration. Workplace violence in healthcare: Understanding the challenge, 2015. *https://www.osha.gov/Publications/OSHA3826.pdf,* retrieved May 24, 2020.

155. Mojtehedzadeh, Sara. "Violence against Health-Care Workers 'Out of Control,' Survey Finds." *The Star,* November 5, 2017. *https://www.thestar.com/news/gta/2017/11/05/violence-against-health-care-workers-out-of-control-survey-finds.html,* retrieved July 16, 2019.

156. Occupational Safety and Health Administration. "Guidelines for Preventing Work Place Violence for Healthcare & Social Service Workers." *https://www.osha.gov/Publications/osha3148.pdf,* retrieved July 16, 2020.

157. Coutré, Lydia. "Healthcare Workers Face Violence 'Epidemic.'" *Modern Healthcare,* March 11, 2019. *https://www.modernhealthcare.com/providers/healthcare-workers-face-violence-epidemic,* retrieved August 15, 2019.

158. Needleman, J., P. Buerhaus, V. S. Pankratz, C. L. Leibson, S. R. Stevens, and M. Harris. "Nurse Staffing and Inpatient Hospital Mortality." *New England Journal of Medicine* 364, 11 (March 17, 2011): 1037–1045. PubMed PMID:21410372.

159. Clavreul, Genevieve M. "Why Power Napping Might be Right for the Nurses at Your Hospital: Research Shows the Benefits of Catching 40 Winks during a Long Shift." *Working Nurse. https://www.workingnurse.com/articles/Why-Power-Napping-Might-be-Right-for-the-Nurses-at-Your-Hospital,* retrieved August 15, 2019.

160. American Nursing Association. "Position Statement: Just Culture." (January 28, 2010) *https://www.nursingworld.org/practice-policy/nursing-excellence/official-position-statements/id/just-culture/,* retrieved July 16, 2020.

161. Lane, M. A., B. M. Newman, M. Z. Taylor, M. O'Neill, C. Ghetti, R. M. Woltman, and A. D. Waterman. "Supporting Clinicians after Adverse Events: Development of a Clinician Peer Support Program." *Journal of Patient Safety* 14, 3 (September 2018). *https://www.ncbi.nlm.nih.gov/pubmed/29878948,* retrieved August 15, 2019.

162. The Leapfrog Group. "When Hospitals Say, 'I'm Sorry.'" *https://www.leapfroggroup.org/influencing/ never-events,* retrieved August 15, 2019.

163. Holweg, Matthias, Bradley Staats, and David M. Upton. "Making Process Improvements Stick." *Harvard Business Review,* November–December 2018, 16–19. *https://hbr.org/2018/11/making-process -improvements-stick,* retrieved October 12, 2019.

164. From Vonderembse, Mark A., and Gregory P. White. *Operations Management: Concepts, Methods, and Strategies,* 2nd ed., 549–550. St. Paul, MN: West Publishing, 1991; reprinted by permission. Copyright © 1991 by West Publishing Company. All rights reserved.

165. Case studies 3 through 5 were written by Mary Mohyla, RN, CIC, Senior Director, Quality and Accreditation, Holy Cross Health, Silver Spring, Maryland.

9

Communicating

Management activities in all settings rely on effective communication, which is the creation or exchange of understanding between senders and receivers. Communication is not restricted to words alone. It includes all verbal and nonverbal means to achieve understanding among those involved in communicating.

Absent good communication in health services organizations (HSOs) and health systems (HSs), decision making would take place in an information vacuum; mission, objectives, and strategies and plans to achieve them would be understood only by those who originate them; entities would be organized and staffed only as a conglomeration of isolated people and departments or organizations; leading people as to what, when, how, or why to do their work would be impossible; and control and evaluation would be meaningless without communication about performance results to affect future performance.

Communicating Is Key to Effective Stakeholder Relations

All HSOs/HSs have various stakeholders, individuals or groups with a *stake*, or significant interest, in performance and results.[1] Managers must communicate effectively with the *internal* stakeholders in their domains and ensure effective communication between their organizations and systems and various *external* stakeholders. Internal stakeholders are the participants in an entity, including employees, volunteers, and clinicians. External stakeholders include current and potential patients or customers, as well as accrediting agencies, competitors, government (as payer and regulator), insurance plans, media, and suppliers, among many others. In a commentary on the role of the manager, McAlearney and Kovner[2] note that managers must identify key stakeholders and ask themselves questions as to what these stakeholders expect and how satisfied they are with current performance. Maintaining effective relationships with stakeholders requires that managers successfully communicate with them.

Figure 9.1 is an external stakeholder map for a health program operating within an HSO/HS. Such a map can be customized for any HSO/HS or its units and programs.

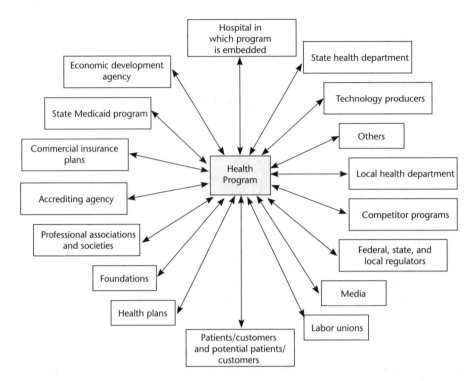

Figure 9.1. External stakeholder map for a health program.

Typically, relationships and interactions in which managers in HSOs/HSs are involved with internal and external stakeholders are information dependent and thus depend on good communication. The degree to which understanding is transmitted and received effectively through communication is critical to successful managing. People communicate facts, ideas, feelings, and attitudes while working. If communication is adequate, work is done more effectively. Poor communication leads to medical errors, such as hospital-acquired infections, surgical errors or wrong-site surgeries, medication errors, in-hospital injuries, and misdiagnoses. The Agency for Healthcare Research and Quality (AHRQ) has identified communication problems as the leading cause of medical errors, closely followed by inadequate information flow.[3] In 1999, the Institute of Medicine Report, *To Err Is Human*, estimated that between 46,000 and 98,000 patients die each year due to medical errors.[4] A more recent study at Johns Hopkins estimated annual deaths from medical error to be 250,000 nationally.[5] The loss of lives is tragic; the economic impact is staggering, taking into account additional medical expenses associated with these errors, costs of litigation, and loss of worker productivity.[6] The Cisco Internet Business Solutions Group developed an economic model to predict losses in nursing productivity resulting from communication delays. They found more than $3.4 billion lost across the United States or about $1.7 million per 500-bed hospital.[7]

Some communication provides information that people need to understand what they are to do. Information about an HSO's/HS's mission and objectives, operating plans and activities, resources, and alternatives is necessary for people to contribute to organizational performance. Managers must provide information to external stakeholders, especially potential customers, third-party payers, and regulators, if their organizations are to function effectively.

Although motivation is a process internal to the person (see Chapter 13), managers can affect motivation by informing others about rewards based on performance, providing information that builds commitment to the HSO/HS and its objectives, and helping employees to understand and fulfill their personal needs. Managers also communicate with external stakeholders to influence them to act in ways that benefit the organization. Examples include motivating consumers to use the organization for health services, motivating health plans to pay adequate rates for services, and influencing public policy makers to regulate them fairly.

Many kinds of communications facilitate controlling performance. Activity reports, policies to establish standard operating procedures, budgets, and verbal directives are examples. Such communication increases control (see Chapter 14) when it clarifies duties, authority, and responsibilities.

Communication Process Model

Managers communicate with internal or external stakeholders using the process shown in Figure 9.2. Communicating with internal stakeholders depends on formal channels and networks to transmit understandable information in the HSO or HS. These channels and networks communicate multidirectionally—downward, upward, horizontally, and diagonally.

In addition to communicating in the organization, managers—especially senior executives—must communicate with external stakeholders.[8] Examples include marketing services and products, maintaining community relations, influencing (lobbying) political constituencies, and building alliances. An important aspect of communicating with external stakeholders, which will be discussed more fully in this chapter, is receiving information from them. To manage effectively, managers must relate to and understand the external environment.

Because communicating with internal and external stakeholders involves creation or exchange of understanding between the sender and receivers, both types use the mechanisms shown in Figure 9.2. Usually, communications are meant to be understood; sometimes they intend to obfuscate. Unfortunately, complete understanding seldom results, because of the many environmental and personal barriers to effective communication. These barriers and how to overcome them are discussed in the following section.

Sender and Receivers

In Figure 9.2, the sender—which may be an individual, a department, a unit of an HSO, an HSO, an HS, or a group of them—has ideas, intentions, and information it wants to convey. The sender uses words and symbols to encode ideas and information into a message for an intended receiver.

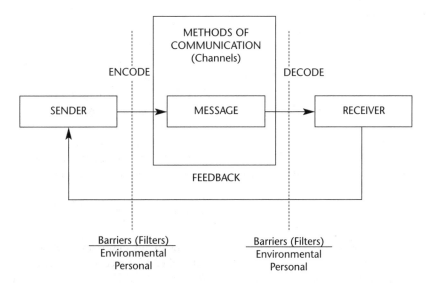

Figure 9.2. The basic mechanism of communication.

Words alone may be insufficient to ensure that the message is understood. Because words may have different meanings for people, or people may not understand certain words, it is often useful to augment the message with symbols. In HSOs/HSs, symbols such as objects, pictures, or actions play a role in communicating. For example, uniforms permit easy identification of staff. Pictures or visual representations are another type of symbol and helpful in communication. Consider how many words would be needed to explain an HSO's/HS's organizational structure in lieu of the information depicted in a chart. Or imagine the difficulty of communicating the information in a magnetic resonance image using only words. Finally, action or inaction communicates. A smile or a hearty greeting has meaning. A promotion or pay increase conveys a great deal to the recipient and to others. Lack of action has symbolic meaning too. Managers who miss opportunities to praise participants for good performance or fail to provide promised support are sending messages.[9]

Actions or inactions inconsistent with words or other symbols transmit contradictory messages. The manager who tells an employee, "I have confidence in your ability, your performance is excellent, and I want to expand your duties by delegating more to you," acts inconsistently by showing anger if a small error occurs. The receiver who says "I am listening" to the sender and then looks at the clock impatiently or starts to walk away during the conversation sends a mixed message. And it is well documented that patients (as receivers) listening to information provided by physicians (as senders) recalled less than 50% of the information, and about half of the information recalled was incorrect.[10]

Channels of Communication

The channels or methods of communicating are the means to transmit messages as shown in the communication process in Figure 9.2.[11] Channels include face-to-face and telephone conversations, e-mail, faxes, letters and memoranda, policy statements, operating room schedules, reports, electronic message boards, videoconferences, newspapers, television and radio commercials, and written or intranet newsletters for internal or external distribution. An important dimension of channels is whether they are synchronous or asynchronous. Synchronous channels, such as face-to-face conversations or meetings and telephones, allow parties to communicate at the same time. Information can move freely in real time. Synchronous channels are preferable for communicating about time-sensitive or dense information. Asynchronous channels, such as letters, e-mails, and texts, are preferable for communicating when a record of the communication is necessary.

Selecting channels is important in communicating. Effective communication often involves multiple channels to transmit a message. For example, a major change in human resource (HR) policy, such as modifying the benefit package, may be announced in an e-mail from the vice president of HR to all employees, graphically illustrated by posters in key locations, and then reinforced at group meetings in which managers explain the policy and answer questions. A decision to lobby a state legislature for higher Medicaid reimbursement might result in messages transmitted through channels such as letters (more formal than e-mail) to legislators, direct contact between managers or trustees and legislators, and newspaper advertisements stating the organization's position. Other HSOs/HSs might participate through an association to produce and distribute television commercials or use other channels to increase support for their position.

Messages Encoded and Decoded

Messages transmitted must be decoded by the receiver. Decoding means interpreting the words and symbols in the message. Decoding involves the receiver's perceptual assessment of the content of the message, the sender, and the context in which the message was transmitted. Messages must be decoded (interpreted) by the receiver. This raises the possibility that the message the sender intends is not the message the receiver receives. The closer the decoded message is to that intended by the sender, the more effective the communication.

The most effective way to determine if messages are received as intended is through feedback. Feedback is a two-way communication process between senders and receivers by which information can be shared, recycled, and clarified until an unambiguous mutual understanding is achieved. In intraorganizational communication, in which interdependencies between individuals and units of an HSO/HS are significant, the feedback loop is very important in ensuring that enough information is exchanged to effectively manage these interdependencies. Similarly, communication with external stakeholders is improved greatly by feedback to senders, who can adjust the message if it is not received as intended. When a sender encodes and transmits a message to a receiver, who decodes the message and shows understanding by giving feedback, effective two-way communication has occurred.

Feedback can be direct or indirect. Direct feedback is the receiver's response to the sender regarding a message. Indirect feedback is more subtle and involves the consequences of a message. Internally, indirect feedback on a policy to change the benefits package might include higher levels of employee satisfaction if the change is liked, or increased turnover and lower morale if the change is disliked. Externally, indirect feedback on attempts to change Medicaid reimbursement might include an increase in rates if the legislature agrees with the HSO/HS, no action if the legislature disagrees, or even hostile action if the legislature disagrees with the message or is upset by the method(s) used to communicate it.

Barriers to Effective Communication

There are always barriers to effective communication. The environmental and personal barriers illustrated in Figure 9.2 are ubiquitous in the communication process within HSOs/HSs and between them and external stakeholders. These barriers can block, filter, or distort messages as they are encoded, sent, decoded, and received.

Environmental (or Contextual) Barriers

Environmental barriers are created by certain characteristics of an organization and its environment. Two are competition for attention and competition for time on the part of senders and receivers. Multiple and simultaneous demands requiring attention may cause the sender to inappropriately package a message, or they may cause the message to be incorrectly decoded by a receiver not giving the message complete attention. Similarly, time constraints may be a barrier to effective communication, prohibiting the sender from thinking through and properly structuring the message to be conveyed or giving the receiver too little time to determine its meaning.

Other environmental barriers that can filter, distort, or block a message include the HSO's/HS's managerial philosophy, multiplicity of hierarchical levels, and power or status relationships between senders and receivers. Managerial philosophy can inhibit or promote effective communication. Managers uninterested in promoting intraorganizational communication upward or disseminating information downward will establish procedural and organizational blockages. Requirements that all communication "flow through channels"; inaccessibility; lack of interest in employees' frustrations, complaints, or feelings; and insufficient time allotted to receiving information are symptoms of a philosophy that retards communication. Furthermore, managers who fail to act on complaints, ideas, and problems signal to those wanting to communicate upward that the effort is unlikely to have much effect, so they discourage information flow.

Managerial philosophy also has a significant impact on an HSO's/HS's communication with external stakeholders. This topic is addressed more fully in a later section but suffice it to say here that philosophy leads managers to react in particular ways of communicating with external stakeholders in a crisis. For example, if there is a chance that patients could have been exposed to a dangerous infection while hospitalized because of improper handling of contaminated material, managers might react by covering up the incident or, conversely, by contacting all who may have been exposed so they can be tested. Varying reactions to events reflect different managerial philosophies and ethical values about communicating.

Multiple levels in an HSO's/HS's hierarchy and other organizational complexities, such as size or scope of activity, raise barriers that inhibit communicating and cause message distortion. As messages are transmitted, people interpret them according to their own personal frame of reference and vantage point. When the communication chain has multiple links, information can be filtered, dropped, or added, and emphasis can be rearranged as the message is retransmitted, distorting or even blocking the message. For example, a message sent from the chief executive officer (CEO) to employees through several layers of an organization is received in a different form than originally sent. Or a report prepared for the CEO that passes through the hierarchy may not reach its destination because it is lying on a desk or is a blocked e-mail that has not been read.

Power or status relationships can present barriers to effective communication by distorting or inhibiting transmission of messages. A discordant superior–subordinate relationship can dampen the flow and content of information. Furthermore, experiences may inhibit an employee's communication because reprisal, sanctions, or ridicule are feared. For example, a subordinate may not inform a superior that something is wrong or that a plan will not work because of poor superior–subordinate rapport. Power or status communication barriers are prevalent in healthcare settings in which professionals interact and status relationships create a complex situation. Does the nurse practitioner with 20 years of experience tell a new medical resident that a procedure or treatment about to be ordered is not efficacious? Is the nurse practitioner's message encoded bluntly or obliquely?

A final environmental or contextual barrier arises when messages require the use of terminology unfamiliar to the receiver or when messages are especially complex. Each profession has its jargon. Managers and those responsible for direct care may use the same words in different ways. Both may use words that are unfamiliar to external stakeholders. Communications between people who use words differently can be ineffective simply because people attribute different meanings to the same words. Misunderstanding is more likely when a message is complex and contains terminology that is unfamiliar to the receiver. This barrier is widespread in communication within HSOs/HSs, as well as between them and many external stakeholders.

Personal Barriers

Personal barriers to communication can arise from people's nature, both in their interactions with others and in communication within HSOs/HSs and between them and external stakeholders. When people encode and send messages or decode and receive them, they do so according to their own frame of reference or beliefs. They may consciously or unconsciously engage in selective perception, and communications may be influenced by emotions such as fear or jealousy.

Socioeconomic background and experiences constitute an individual's frame of reference and shape how messages are encoded and decoded, or even if communication is attempted. For example, someone whose cultural background includes admonitions such as "don't speak unless spoken to" or "never question elders" may be inhibited in communicating. Naive people tend to accept communication at face value without filtering out erroneous information or observing gaps in information they receive. Self-aggrandizing people may disseminate information, so the message is distorted for personal gain. Furthermore, unless people have experience with the subject of a message, they may not completely understand it. People who have health insurance may have difficulty understanding the concerns of people without it. Those who have never experienced pain or childbirth or witnessed death may be unable to understand messages about these experiences.

Closely related to one's experience are beliefs, values, and prejudices that can cause messages to be distorted or blocked in transmission or reception. This occurs because people have different personalities and backgrounds; they have opinions and prejudices in politics, ethics, religion, equity in the workplace, and lifestyle. These biases, beliefs, and values filter and may distort communication.

Selective perception is one of the most difficult personal barriers for sender and receiver to overcome. People tend to screen out derogatory information. Selective perception can be conscious or subconscious. It is conscious when one fears the consequences and intentionally distorts the truth. This can happen when patients receive bad news about their condition; it also occurs in management situations. For example, supervisors whose units have high staff turnover may fear the consequences of their superiors' noticing it. They might amplify the argument that turnover is the result of low wages over which they have no control (or responsibility), or they might delete, alter, or minimize the importance of this information in reports to their superiors.

Sometimes jealousy, especially when coupled with selective perception, results in filtering and distorting incoming information, transmitting misinformation, or both. For example, managers with able assistants who make them look good may block or distort information that reveals the truth to superiors. Sometimes petty personality differences, the feeling of professional inferiority, or greed leads to jealousy resulting in distorted communication.

Two additional personal barriers to communication arise because those receiving messages evaluate the source (the sender) and because they prefer the status quo. These personal barriers to effective communication are common in HSOs/HSs. Receivers often evaluate the source to decide whether to filter out or discount some of the message. However, this can bias communicators. For example, a hostile union–management environment or one in which employees do not trust management may cause employees to ignore messages from management. Or managers may ignore messages from physicians with whom they frequently disagree. Evaluating sources may be necessary to cope with the barrage of communication, but one must recognize the risk that messages may be misunderstood.

Preference for the status quo can be a barrier if it results in a conscious effort by the sender or receiver to filter out information—in sending, receiving, or retransmitting—that would upset the present situation. Internally, conditions that cause fear of sending bad news, or a lack of candor among participants, can create this barrier. When communicating with external stakeholders, communicators in an HSO/HS may want to protect the status quo by not sending upsetting information.

A final personal barrier to effective communication is a lack of empathy: being insensitive to the frames of reference or emotional states of others in the communication relationship. Sensitivity promotes understanding. Empathy helps the sender encode a message for maximum understanding and helps the receiver correctly interpret it. For example, subordinates who empathize with superiors may discount an angry message because they are aware that extreme pressure and frustration can cause such messages to be sent, even when they are not warranted.

Similarly, a sender sensitive to the receiver's circumstance may decide how best to encode a message or whether it is better left unsent. For example, if the receiver is having a difficult day, a reprimand may be interpreted as stronger than intended. Or, if a receiver has just had a traumatic experience, such as a family illness or financial setback, the empathetic sender may delay bad news until later. Managers concerned about an entity's community image might delay announcing a generous across-the-board wage increase or a large price increase just after a major local employer announces a plant closing because of adverse economic conditions.

Managing Barriers to Effective Communication

Awareness of environmental and personal barriers to effective communication is the first step in minimizing their impact. Positive actions will overcome the barriers, and, depending on circumstances, several general guidelines can be suggested.

Environmental barriers are reduced if receivers and senders ensure that attention is given to their messages and adequate time is devoted to listening. In addition, a management philosophy that encourages the free flow of communications is constructive. Reducing the number of links (levels in the organizational hierarchy or steps between the HSO/HS as a sender and external stakeholders as receivers) reduces opportunities for distortion. The power or status barrier is more difficult to eliminate because it is affected by interpersonal and interprofessional relationships. However, consciously tailoring words and symbols so messages are understandable and reinforcing words with actions significantly improve communication between different power or status levels. Finally, using multiple channels to reinforce complex messages decreases the likelihood of misunderstanding.

Personal barriers to effective communication are reduced by conscious efforts to understand another's frame of reference and beliefs. Recognizing that people engage in selective perception and may be prone to jealousy and fear is a first step toward eliminating or at least diminishing these barriers. Empathy may be the surest way to increase the likelihood that the messages will be received and understood as intended.

Effectively communicating between entities in an HS can be demanding because barriers resulting from organizational complexity can be formidable. Adapting Porter's approach to achieving effective linkages between business units in complex organizations suggests ways in which managers can overcome some of these barriers:[12]

- Use devices or techniques that cross organizational lines, such as partial centralization and interorganization task forces or committees, to actively facilitate communication. At the governance level, HSs can enhance communication through interlocking boards, defined as boards with overlapping membership. Interlocking boards can improve communication between components in an HS.

- Use management processes that are cross-organizational to improve communication in areas such as planning, control, incentives, capital budgeting, and management information systems.

- Use human resource practices that facilitate cooperation between the HSOs in an HS, such as cross-organizational job rotation, management forums, and training, because these increase the likelihood that managers in one part of the HS will understand their counterparts elsewhere in the system and that they will communicate more effectively.

- Use management processes that effectively and fairly resolve conflicts between HSOs in an HS to improve communication. The key to such processes is that corporate management installs and operates a process that fairly settles disputes between component organizations in the system. Equitable settlement of disputes facilitates effective communication.

Both environmental and personal barriers can be overcome or minimized by effective *listening* within the communication process. The following enhance listening: Clear away physical distractions (e.g., noise or interruptions), express your interest in listening, empathize with the speaker, maintain your focus while listening, ask questions as you listen but don't interrupt, listen with your mind as well as your ears, take notes, and listen early and often.[13]

Flows of Intraorganizational Communication

Intraorganizational communication flows downward, upward, horizontally, and diagonally. Each direction has its appropriate uses and unique characteristics, as illustrated in Figure 9.3. Typically, downward flow is communication from superiors to subordinates; upward flow uses the same channels but in the opposite direction. Horizontal flow is manager to manager or staff member to staff member. Diagonal flow cuts across functions and levels. Although this violates an organization's chain of command, it may be permitted in situations in which speed and efficiency of communication are important.

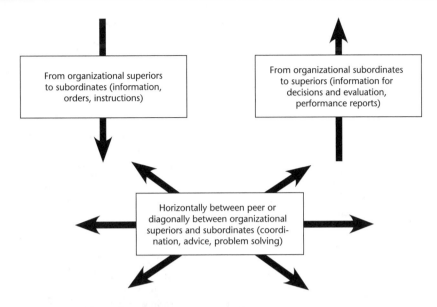

Figure 9.3. Communication flows in organizations.

Downward Flow

Downward communication in HSOs/HSs primarily involves passing on information from superiors to subordinates through verbal orders, one-to-one instructions, speeches to employee groups, meetings, e-mails, test messages, and websites. Myriad written methods, such as handbooks, procedure manuals, newsletters, bulletin boards, the ubiquitous memorandum, and computerized information systems contribute greatly to downward flow in HSOs/HSs.

Upward Flow

Objectives of upward communication include providing managers with decision-making information, revealing problem areas, providing data for performance evaluation, indicating the status of morale, and, in general, underscoring the thinking of subordinates. Upward communication in HSOs becomes more important with increased organizational complexity and scale and especially with participation in HSs. Managers rely on effective upward communication and encourage it by creating a climate of trust and respect as integral to the organizational culture.[14]

In addition to its direct value to managers, upward communication satisfies employees' personal needs. It permits those with lesser authority to transmit information to those with greater authority; as a result, they feel a heightened sense of participation. The hierarchical chain of command is the main channel for upward communication in HSOs/HSs, but this may be supplemented by grievance procedures, open-door policies, counseling, employee questionnaires, exit interviews, participative decision-making techniques, and ombudsmen.

Horizontal and Diagonal Flows

In HSOs/HSs, which frequently have abrupt demands for action and reaction, horizontal flow must occur, as in the coordinated work of patient care units. The matrix designs described in Chapter 11 illustrate the value of horizontal communication and coordination in organizations and systems. Committees, task forces, and cross-functional project teams are all useful for horizontal communication.

Diagonal flows are the least common communications in HSOs/HSs. However, diagonal flows are growing in importance. For example, diagonal communication occurs when the clinical pharmacist alerts a nurse in medical intensive care about a potential adverse reaction between two medications when the ordering physician is unavailable. Diagonal flows violate the usual pattern of upward and downward communication flows by cutting across departments, and they violate the usual pattern of horizontal communication because the communicators are at different levels in the organization. Yet, such communication is essential.

While committees, task forces, quality improvement teams, and cross-functional project teams are established to perform tasks or solve problems, they all serve as subsidiary means of diagonal communication as well as vertical and horizontal communications. They encourage representatives of different organizational units to discuss common concerns and potential problems face-to-face and coordinate activities. Committees and other groups of participants are useful boundary-spanning devices. However, they tend to be time consuming and expensive, and their decisions are often compromises that may be ineffectual solutions. Fortunately, abundant guidance is available in the literature on developing effective groups by taking advantage of their positive potential while avoiding the negative.[15]

Communication Networks

Downward, upward, horizontal, and diagonal communication flows can be combined into patterns called communication networks, which are communicators interconnected by communication channels.[16] Figure 9.4 illustrates the five common networks: chain, Y, wheel, circle, and all-channel. The chain network is the standard format for communicating upward and downward; it follows line authority relationships. An example is a staff nurse who reports to a nurse manager, who reports to a nursing supervisor, who reports to the vice president for nursing, who reports to the CEO.

The Y pattern (inverted) shows two people reporting to a superior, who reports to another. An example is two staff pharmacists who report to the pharmacy director, who reports to the vice president for professional affairs, who reports to the chief operating officer. The wheel pattern shows four subordinates reporting to one manager; subordinates do not interact, and all communications are channeled through the manager at the center of the wheel. This pattern is rare in HSOs/HSs, although four vice presidents may report to a president, and the vice presidents have little interaction. Even though this network pattern is not common, it may be used if urgency or secrecy is required. For example, in an organizational emergency, the president might communicate with vice presidents in a wheel pattern because time does not permit using other modes. Similarly, if secrecy is important, such as when investigating possible embezzlement, the president may require that all relevant communication with the vice presidents is confidential.

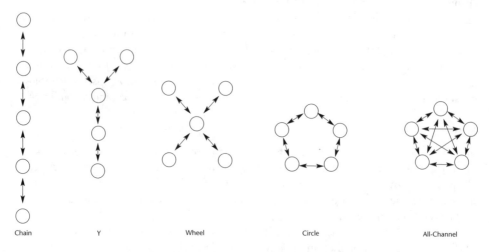

| Chain | Y | Wheel | Circle | All-Channel |

Figure 9.4.   Common communication networks.

The circle pattern allows the first person to communicate with only two persons. Then each of them communicates with others in the network. The effect is that everyone receives the message, which may have become distorted. There is no central authority or leader. The all-channel network is a circle pattern except each person may interact with all others in the network.

Communication networks vary along several dimensions; none is always best. The wheel and all-channel networks fast and accurate compared with the chain or Y-pattern networks. The chain and Y pattern promote clear lines of authority and accountability. The circle and all-channel networks improve morale among those in the networks better than other patterns because everyone is treated equally; but communication is slower. The challenge for HSO/HS managers is choosing the best communication network(s).

Informal Communication

Coexisting with formal communication flows and networks within HSOs/HSs are informal communication flows, which have an infrastructure that results from interpersonal relationships. The common name for informal communication flow is "the grapevine," a term that arose during the American Civil War, when telegraph wires were strung between trees, much like a grapevine.[17] Messages transmitted over those flimsy lines were often garbled. As a result, any rumor was said to have come through the grapevine.

Informal communication flows in an organization are as natural as the patterns of social interaction that develop in all organizations. Informal communication channels are routinely misused in HSOs/HSs. For example, in times of crisis, organizations are rife with rumors; often they consist of false information. Informal communication can be useful, however. Downward flows move through the grapevine much faster than through formal channels. In an HSO/HS, much of the coordination among units occurs through informal give-and-take using horizontal and diagonal flows. In the case of upward flow, informal communication can be a rich source of information about performance, ideas, feelings, and attitudes. Because of the potential usefulness and pervasiveness of informal communication, managers should understand and use it to advantage. Chapter 12 addresses some issues of social media in HSOs/HSs.

Similar in concept to formal communication flows, informal flows follow predictable patterns and identifiable networks. Figure 9.5 illustrates four common patterns that the grapevine takes: single strand, gossip, probability, and cluster.

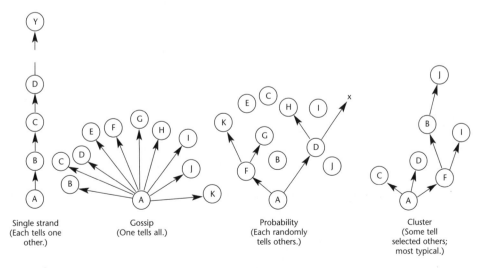

Figure 9.5. Grapevine networks. (From Newstrom, John W. *Organizational Behavior: Human Behavior at Work*, 13th ed., 71. New York: McGraw-Hill/Irwin, 2011. Reproduced with permission of the McGraw-Hill Companies, Inc.)

Managers occasionally get the impression that the grapevine operates like a long chain in which A tells B, who tells C, who then tells D, and the like, until Y receives the information— usually late and incorrect. (See the single-strand network in Figure 9.5.) Sometimes the grapevine operates this way, but generally it follows a different pattern. Employee A tells three or four others, such as C, D, and F. (See the cluster network in Figure 9.5.) Only one or two of the several receivers passes the information along, usually to more than one person. Then, as the information grows older and the proportion of those knowing it increases, it dies out because not all receivers repeat it. This network is a cluster chain because each link in the chain tends to inform a cluster of others instead of one person.

Informal communication present in every organization can either aid or inhibit effectiveness. Managers may be able to achieve certain organizational objectives by paying attention to informal communication (even inaccurate rumors reflect some aspects of employees' feelings and views) and by occasionally and selectively using informal communication, especially when speed is critical.

To summarize, each of the multidirectional communication flows (Figure 9.3 reflects downward, upward, horizontal, and diagonal communication) and the networks they form within HSOs/HSs have a purpose, and each is an important tool for managers. The networks they form in HSOs/HSs have a purpose; each has potential as a tool for managers. These flows are planned and designed into HSO's/HS's formal organizational design. They are the formal communication channels and networks. Informal communication channels and networks arise among people outside the formal design. Information flow through formal or informal channels is as crucial to the life of an organization as the circulation of blood is to human life.

Communicating with External Stakeholders

Typically, HSOs/HSs maintain relationships with numerous external stakeholders. As defined earlier, stakeholders are individuals, groups, or organizations interested in the performance achieved by the organization or system, and they attempt to influence that performance, either negatively or positively. (See the stakeholder map in Figure 9.1 for the range of external stakeholders affecting a small healthcare provider.)

External stakeholders may affect HSOs/HSs dramatically. The relationship and communication among them can be complex. HSOs/HSs are dynamic, open systems in complex and turbulent external environments, as discussed in Chapter 10. In most cases, the sheer number and variety of external stakeholders complicate communicating with them.

Communication with stakeholders is complicated by the nature of the relationship. Communicating with external stakeholders is more effective when the relationship is positive. Figure 9.6 uses a large hospital to illustrate the diverse stakeholders with which relationships must be maintained. Some of the relationships in Figure 9.6 are positive (shown by the plus [+] symbol), some are negative (shown by the minus [–] symbol), and some are neutral (shown by zero [0]). It is important to note that the arrows connecting the hospital with stakeholders go both directions, showing that managers must be concerned about communication both to and from external stakeholders.

Boundary spanning is another name for the process by which managers communicate with external stakeholders. Boundary spanners obtain information from external stakeholders. Strategizing and marketing are examples of boundary spanning. Conversely, boundary spanners represent the entity to its external stakeholders. This includes marketing, and relations with patients, visitors, the community and service area, and government. Because obtaining information is essential, boundary-spanning, communicating is critical.[18]

Listening to External Stakeholders

When HSO/HSs managers listen to external stakeholders, they are good receivers of communication. This allows them to systematically and analytically use stakeholder analysis to increase the chances of acquiring useful or necessary information.[19] Determining the HSO's/HS's

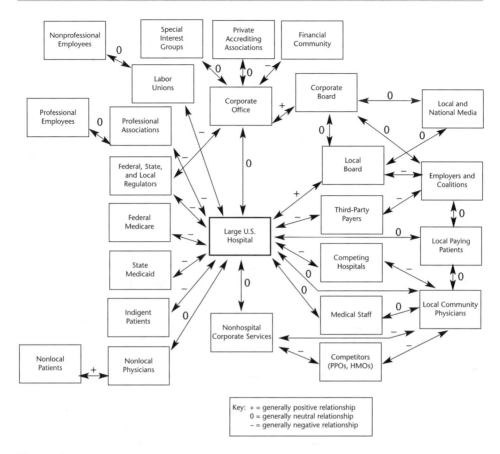

Figure 9.6. Stakeholders in a large hospital. (From Fottler, Myron D., John D. Blair, Carlton J. Whitehead, Michael D. Laus, and Grant T. Savage. "Assessing Key Stakeholders: Who Matters to Hospitals and Why?" *Hospital & Health Services Administration* 34 [Winter 1989]: 530; reprinted by permission. Copyright 1989, Health Administration Press.)

external stakeholders is a matter of judgment. It is helpful to consult ad hoc task forces, committees, or outside consultants. Expert-based techniques to identify stakeholders include the Delphi technique, the Delbecq technique, brainstorming, focus groups, and dialectic inquiry.

- The Delphi technique gathers information from a group of experts with anonymity and limited interaction.

- The Delbecq technique, or nominal group process, gathers information from a group of experts who meet to present, discuss, and defend their ideas.

- Brainstorming is group discussion to generate ideas without judging them.

- Focus groups are group discussions among members selected to represent specific demographic or political attributes.

- Dialectic inquiry is group discussion that focuses on disagreements by using creative conflict to identify and challenge assumptions.

Scanning is followed by monitoring stakeholders' views and positions on matters important to the HSO/HS. Monitoring is critical when views and positions are dynamic, unstructured, or ambiguous as to strategic importance. Monitoring stakeholder views and positions clarifies their degrees of importance or the rates at which they are becoming strategically important. Expert opinions as used in scanning can help managers determine which stakeholders to monitor, while consultants do the actual monitoring.

There are various ways to systematically listen to external stakeholders. Generally, they include interrelated activities, such as the environmental assessments HSOs/HSs make for strategic management (see Chapter 10). In conducting environmental assessments, managers scan the entity's environment to identify strategically important issues, monitor them, forecast trends, assess their importance, and disseminate information obtained to those who need it.[20] In stakeholder analyses, managers in HSOs/HSs scan to identify important stakeholders, forecast or project the trends in stakeholders' views or positions, assess the implications of stakeholder views and positions, and disseminate this information, as needed. In most instances, this is a straightforward task that readily leads to the development of a stakeholder map, such as that shown in Figure 9.6, for a large hospital in the United States.

The views, positions, and perspectives of external stakeholders are dynamic. Even high-quality scanning and monitoring cannot give managers all the information they need. Thus, managers will benefit from forecasting likely changes in stakeholders' views and perceptions. Forecasts allow managers to factor likely changes into their decisions.

Scanning and monitoring views and positions of external stakeholders, and even accurately forecasting trends, do not ensure good stakeholder analysis. Managers must also be concerned about the importance of the information. They must assess and interpret the strategic value of the information. At minimum, this means characterizing stakeholders as positive, negative, or neutral, as shown in Figure 9.6. Determining positive, negative, or neutral positions is easy, but assessing stakeholders' importance is inexact and requires intuition, common sense, and best guess. Beyond the difficulties of collecting and analyzing enough information to make an informed assessment, other problems arise from the prejudices and biases of those judging external stakeholders and their importance. This may result in assessments that fit preconceived notions about which stakeholders are strategically important rather than the realities of a situation.[21]

The final step in conducting stakeholder analyses involves disseminating the results to those in the HSO/HS who need it. This step may be undervalued and sometimes overlooked. Unless results are disseminated effectively, it does not matter how well other steps are performed.

Information about external stakeholders may be disseminated internally in two ways. One relies on the power of senior-level managers to dictate dissemination and use of the information. Alternatively, reason can be used to persuade or educate the decision makers to use the information. Power- and reason-based approaches are most effective when combined.

Dissemination of strategically important information obtained from external stakeholders completes stakeholder analysis. Given the vital linkage between an entity and its external stakeholders, it is unlikely that any organization can succeed without an effective process by which its managers listen to external stakeholders and respond to their communication.

Special Situations of Communicating with External Stakeholders

The purpose of communicating with external stakeholders is to create understanding between sender and receiver. Each stakeholder, however, must be considered in terms of its unique characteristics for communication to be effective. This is especially true of four important sets of external stakeholders of the typical HSO/HS:

1. Those to whom it wants to market its products and services

2. The geographic community in which the organization is located

3. The public sector with which the organization interacts

4. The stakeholder groups that form when something goes wrong in the organization

Communicating with these important external stakeholders is examined next.

Communicating in Marketing

Marketing is discussed in more depth in Chapters 10 and 13. Suffice it to say that the central purpose of marketing is to support the voluntary exchange of something of value between buyer and sellers.[22,23] Successful HSOs/HSs produce and make available services or products that are of value to certain individuals, groups, or organizations (e.g., individual patients or customers, health plans, or government). In turn, individuals, groups, or organizations seek and choose the services or products. Communication is vital to how this process proceeds; indeed, communicating effectively is necessary for the exchanges to occur.

Marketing helps ensure that the number of patients or customers is adequate, their needs are identified and met, and the HSO/HS receives value in return.[24] Major activities in commercial marketing include the following:

- Determining what groups of potential patients or customers (or markets) exist, determining their needs, and identifying which of these groups the HSO/HS wants to serve. These activities determine target markets. If there are competitors, it is also necessary to determine what they are doing or may do regarding the target markets.

- Assessing the current service mix or product line relative to target market needs. This is done to determine what products or services can be provided or developed in response.

- Deciding how to facilitate exchanges among the HSO/HS or its units and its target markets and implement those decisions. Prerequisite to mutually satisfactory exchanges between an entity and its target markets are 1) responding to how and where customers prefer to access and use products and services and 2) developing pricing structures that attract patients or customers and provide the necessary financial resources. Accomplishing both entails communicating effectively with target markets.

- Carrying out activities of commercial marketing. This requires exchanging information through effective communication. Effective communication is essential in the use of social marketing techniques.

When dealing with vulnerable populations, and patients in general, an important distinction must be made in marketing communication. It can be used to create or expand a market for products and services that may not be needed by the patient. For example, direct to consumer advertising, which is illegal in many countries, grew from $2.1 billion in 1997 to $9.6 billion in 2016 in the United States. The second distinction is marketing to clinicians and local institutions that use their expertise to determine which patients might benefit from the product or service.[25] This second distinction depends on trust between patient and clinician that the clinician will order only what the patient needs.[26]

Communicating with Community and Service Areas

Communities and service areas are external stakeholders of HSOs/HSs; their residents must be the focus of communication. Communicating effectively requires an understanding between sender and receiver. That understanding starts by segmenting the community or service area so various receivers receive information important to them, which, in turn, helps the organization to achieve its mission.

Community and service area suggest geographic location. It is more complex, however. *Community* and *service area* may or may not be synonymous. In large metropolitan areas, they are almost certainly not the same because of large populations and many providers. In less populous areas, they are likely synonymous, especially if there is one hospital. Service area may be a function of specialized services (e.g., pediatric or psychiatric) or type of patient (e.g., transplant or physical rehabilitation). The impact of some HSOs/HSs goes beyond geographic location because they attract patients regionally, statewide, or internationally. HSs may have dispersed physical locations and service areas. All HSOs/HSs are concerned with the people and organizations in their immediate geographic area and, historically, the physical location of HSOs is their "community of first loyalty."[27] An HSO's efforts to nurture loyalty from its community and service area require constant attention and effective communication.

In addition to identifying community and service areas, another important aspect of communicating is the nature of the relationship. Perhaps more so with community than with service area, effective communication is the basis for understanding and accepting the expectations each has of the other. Communities expect contributions from HSOs/HSs; this is less true for service areas. Managers must understand their entities' role in the community and what the community provides in terms of customers or patients, employees, infrastructure, or resources. Until such questions are answered, effective communication may be hampered by misunderstanding relationships, responsibilities, and expectations.

Managers' understanding of the relationship their organization has with the community and service area is the foundation for effective communication. HSOs/HSs do much more for their communities than provide healthcare services. In building a relationship with the community, HSO/HS managers are guided by answers to several questions:[28]

- Do our efforts to improve our community's health reflect the determinants of health?

- Do we meet our mission by providing unique benefits to our community?

- Are our economic contributions broadly defined and fully met?

- Are our philanthropic activities established broadly and collaboratively pursued?

- Are we in compliance with legal requirements and obligations?

- Are fiduciary and ethical obligations met?

Communicating with the Public Sector

HSOs/HSs are greatly affected by public policy because they are essential to the nation's health, and they have a major effect on the economy. All levels of government are keenly interested in their performance. This interest is reflected in numerous public policies that directly affect HSOs/HSs, including delivery and financing of healthcare services, as well as production of inputs (e.g., education of health professionals, development of health technology) to those services.[29] The importance of public policy to HSOs/HSs makes effective communication with the public sector a high priority.

Governing body (GB) members and healthcare executives have two important categories of communication responsibilities regarding the public sector.[30] First, they must analyze the public policy environment to acquire information and data to understand the strategic consequences of forces and events in it. Such analyses assess the effects of public policy on the HSO/HS in terms of opportunities and threats, and permit managers to make strategic adjustments that reflect planned responses.

Second, GB members and healthcare executives must influence formulation and implementation of public policy. This responsibility derives from the fact that both groups seek to make the external environment favorable to the HSO/HS. Inherent in this responsibility are requirements to identify public policy objectives consistent with their organization's values, mission, and objectives and meet them appropriately and ethically, such as lobbying and advocating as individuals or through associations and trade groups. Figure 9.7 shows, GB members and executives have many avenues to shape public policy.

Advocacy is influencing public policy using various forms of persuasive communication and is a primary way to influence public policy. All health services leaders must be advocates. Successful advocacy depends on communicating effectively.[31]

Governing body and executive management can influence the formulation or modification of policy by doing the following:

- Helping shape the policy agenda by defining and documenting problems that need to be addressed, developing and evaluating solutions to the problems, and shaping the political circumstances affecting problems and solutions

- Helping develop specific legislation by participating in the drafting of legislation or testifying at legislative hearings

- Documenting the case for modification of policies by sharing operational experiences and formal evaluations of the impact of policies

---

Managers can influence the implementation of policy by doing the following:

- Providing formal comments on draft rules and regulations

- Serving on and providing input to rulemaking advisory bodies

- Interacting with policy implementers

Exerting influence on public policy through each of the means listed previously requires effective and persuasive communication.

Figure 9.7.   Influencing public policy.

Communicating When Things Go Badly

Occasionally, and despite the best efforts, things go badly. Entities in which this happens may face threats of losing accreditation or perhaps their state licensure because of fire code violations, for example. An HSO may have serious financial difficulties, perhaps threatening its continued operation or raising the specter of major layoffs or closure. Serious clinical errors may occur, perhaps causing a patient's death. Based on a 2016 Johns Hopkins study of medical errors mentioned earlier in this chapter,[32] patient safety experts estimated that more than 250,000 deaths annually are due to medical errors in the United States.[33] Figure 9.8 suggests what can go wrong in clinical settings. Table 9.1 lists the eight common root causes of medical errors according to AHRQ. Under fallible human direction, HSOs/HSs use dangerous drugs, devices, and procedures to cure disease and treat injuries. This is complicated by the fact that these technologies are used for people at vulnerable points in their lives and who may have unrealistic expectations of what can be done for them or their loved ones.

For example, a patient being treated in a hospital for complications of diabetes dies unexpectedly, and blood tests taken a few hours before death show insulin levels 200 times normal. There are several possible explanations for the death: a fatal overdose of insulin given accidentally, or intentionally in a criminal act. How should the hospital handle this situation? Whose interests must be protected? What information is to be communicated? To whom? By whom? There are few hard-and-fast rules to guide managers in such circumstances, but ethical guidelines in Chapter 2 help managers communicate internally and externally.

When things go wrong, effective communication is critical. How managers communicate affects resolution of the problem and the internal and external perception of the organization. Action and communication in response to serious problems are a continuum from reactive to proactive. Reactive responses depicted in Figure 9.9 include concealing the problem—do and say nothing. Less extreme, but still reactive, is to admit that a problem may exist but to deny wrongdoing and take no action to find its cause or resolve it. It is not uncommon for organizations to take obstructionist positions.

Diagnostic

Error or delay in diagnosis
Failure to employ indicated test
Use of outmoded tests or therapy
Failure to act on results of monitoring or testing

Treatment

Error in the performance of an operation, procedure, or test
Error in administering the treatment
Error in the dose or method of using a drug
Avoidable delay in treatment or in responding to an abnormal test
Inappropriate (not indicated) care

Preventive

Failure to provide prophylactic treatment
Inadequate monitoring of condition or progress or inadequate follow-up
treatment

Other

Failure of communication
Equipment failure
Other system failure

Figure 9.8.   Types of errors in clinical settings. (Adapted with permission from Leape, Lucian L., Ann G. Lawthers, Troyen A. Brennan, and William G. Johnson, "Preventing Medical Injury," *Quality Review Bulletin,* Vol. 19, No. 5 (May 1993): 144–149. Copyright © Joint Commission Resources.)

A similar reaction to a problem is labeled defensive. The HSO's/HS's managers and spokespeople act and communicate to comply with the letter of the law to minimize legal liability. Some managers, however, take defensive positions with internal and external communications whenever problems arise. They may communicate defensively about layoffs, mergers, closures, or problems in which many stakeholders have a legitimate interest.

Figure 9.9 illustrates reactive responses and two more proactive responses: accommodation and prevention. Accommodation is accepting responsibility for a problem and vigorously resolving it. Communication is characterized by openness and candor about the problem, its causes, and the actions being taken to resolve it. Prevention is farther along the continuum and focuses on actions to prevent future, similar problems.

Table 9.1   Most Common Root Causes of Medical Errors

1. Communication problems (most common cause)
2. Inadequate information flow
3. Human problems relating to how known standards are followed
4. Patient-related problems like patient identification or patient consent
5. Organizational transfer of knowledge like insufficient knowledge by employees
6. Staffing patterns/workflow
7. Technical failures of devices, equipment, and supplies
8. Inadequate policies and procedures

From the Agency for Healthcare Research and Quality. AHRQ's Patient Safety Initiative: Building Foundations, Reducing Risk. Chapter 2. Efforts to Reduce Medical Errors: AHRQ's Response to Senate Committee Appropriations Questions. https://archive.ahrq.gov/research/findings/final-reports/pscongrpt/psini2.html, retrieved on August 8, 2019.

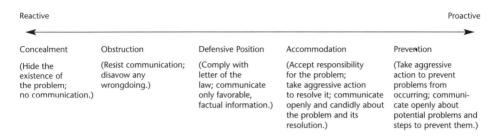

Reactive | Proactive

Concealment	Obstruction	Defensive Position	Accommodation	Prevention
(Hide the existence of the problem; no communication.)	(Resist communication; disavow any wrongdoing.)	(Comply with letter of the law; communicate only favorable, factual information.)	(Accept responsibility for the problem; take aggressive action to resolve it; communicate openly and candidly about the problem and its resolution.)	(Take aggressive action to prevent problems from occurring; communicate openly about potential problems and steps to prevent them.)

Figure 9.9.　Continuum of action and communication to stakeholders in difficult times.

To prevent negative events, managers are turning to integrated sets of activities to ensure that the right things are done, that they are done correctly, and that they are done correctly the first time.[34] These activities have various names. The best is *continuous quality improvement*, or CQI. James[35] suggested that CQI answers three questions: Are we doing the right things? Are we doing things right? How can we be certain that we do things right the first time, every time? Each relies on communication.

HSOs/HSs are best served in managing difficult situations by proactive actions and communications. Reactive responses (concealment, obstruction, and defensive actions) imply crisis management and invite close scrutiny of those the problem affected. Technically, managers who choose accommodation are reacting to a problem, but their response is positive and proactive as they take responsibility, seek to resolve the problem, and communicate openly and candidly about it and their actions. Prevention involves actions to avoid problems. Here, managers communicate to interested parties that problems might occur, but actions have been taken to prevent them or minimize their impact. Problems in HSOs/HSs are inevitable; many can be prevented. Furthermore, the consequences of problems can be managed more effectively if managers have a foundation of understanding and trust with stakeholders by communicating their actions to prevent problems.

Communicating with Internal Stakeholders

While the communication process with all stakeholders is the creation of understanding between sender and receiver, internal stakeholders must be considered in terms of their unique value to the organization. Although effective communication with internal stakeholders sounds simple, it can be more challenging and time consuming than expected. The following are five keys to effective communications with internal stakeholders:[36]

1. Empathy—Attempt to view the organization from the eyes of your internal stakeholders by being accessible and being a good listener.

2. Connection—Each group of associates speaks in a different technical language. For example, the technical language of physicians uses different terminology than the technical language of accountants. Reduce acronyms and jargon in communication. Be aware of the amount of communication with internal stakeholders: Both too much and too little can have negative effects.

3. Comprehension—Provide adequate feedback mechanisms to ensure that messages are understood.

4. Commitment—Credibility through commitment is another important factor in effective communication. Internal stakeholders who lack commitment to the organization or the direction of the organization may not hear the communication as intended.

5. Relationships—Build relationships with internal stakeholders before communicating with them on important matters. Some characterize this as *putting a face with a name*— communication is more effective with those whom you know on a personal level.

Effective communications with internal stakeholders help create a positive attitude within the organization. Effective communication is particularly important in difficult times when communications from external stakeholders might be negative. HSOs and HSs should have a communications spokesperson or communications officer responsible for developing an internal communications plan or strategy that includes the following:[37]

- Organization websites and chat rooms emphasizing pictures and videos

- Information that is interesting, if not entertaining

- Metrics whenever possible

- Messages that do not contradict the mission and vision of the organization

- Opportunities for engagement and feedback

Discussion Questions

1. Draw a model of the communication process. Describe the relationships of its parts.

2. Discuss the importance of feedback in communicating.

3. Discuss various types of communication networks. Describe the advantages and disadvantages of each.

4. Discuss the purpose(s) of downward communication flow in an HSO/HS.

5. Discuss the purpose(s) of upward communication flow in an HSO/ HS.

6. Discuss the role of committees in relation to communication in an HSO/HS.

7. What are barriers to communication? How can they be overcome?

8. Discuss the role of symbols in communication.

9. Think of a situation in which an HSO/HS receives negative media attention. How might the HSO/HS respond along the reactive–proactive continuum? How should it respond to stakeholders?

10. What are the basic differences between formal and informal communication channels?

11. Discuss the impact of the communication process on medical errors. Identify several examples in which problems with communication could result in serious medical errors.

12. An organizational approach to reducing medical errors resulting from communication problems is to develop a positive and safe work culture for physicians and employees. What does this mean?

Case Study 1   How Much Should We Say?

The executive committee of the GB and senior management team of a large midwestern HS met to decide how much information to release to the media about the system's financial condition. After an extensive period of growth and aggressive acquisition of hospitals and physician practices, the HS experienced serious financial difficulties, leading to a bankruptcy filing.

A key decision linked to the bankruptcy filing had been to separate the HSOs in the system into geographic clusters and include only some in the filing. Other HSOs in the system were not included. The stakeholders of the HS and of its various component HSOs were concerned about the financial condition of the HS and its future. Many were interested in exactly how this disastrous situation had come about.

Questions

1. Draw a stakeholder map of this HS.

2. Discuss the options available for how communication with external stakeholders can be undertaken. Which option is best?

3. Consider the relationship this HS had established with its community and discuss the effect it would have on the HS's communication with this important external stakeholder in this situation.

Case Study 2　Getting Help When Needed

Claudia Martinelli, a 79-year-old Bostonian, was hospitalized for congestive heart failure. She needed assistance getting into and out of bed. At 11:15 p.m., Claudia needed the bedside commode and called for help using her nurse call button. The unit clerk did not hear the call because she was away from the nurse station. At 11:30 p.m., Claudia called the station again and reached the clerk. She explained her need for help, using the remote microphone in her room. Claudia could not remember the name of her nurse when asked for it by the clerk. The clerk checked a list for the nurse's name, assuming it was the nurse assigned to Claudia. The clerk placed a call to the nurse at 11:35 p.m. Unaware that she called the wrong nurse, the clerk went about her work.

At 11:40 p.m., Claudia, who was now quite upset by the delay, called the clerk again. Realizing her error and with a sense of urgency, the clerk called Claudia's nurse, who arrived at Claudia's room at 11:45 p.m. The nurse found Claudia sprawled on the floor in great pain. She had stumbled trying to reach the bedside commode.

Claudia suffered a hip fracture and needed hip replacement surgery. Surgery was followed by a month-long stay in a rehabilitation facility. Unable to return home, Claudia was transferred to a nursing facility. Her family filed a malpractice lawsuit against the hospital.

Questions

1. What role did technology have in Claudia's situation? What role did human error have in her situation?

2. How might Claudia's fall have been avoided?

3. What role did communication have in the decision by Claudia's family to sue the hospital?

Case Study 3　Adding Verbal Orders to Written Orders[38]

Sir William Osler (1849–1919), regarded as one of the leading medical educators of the late 19th and early 20th centuries, said, "Look wise, say nothing, and grunt. Speech was given to conceal thought." While perhaps correct 100 years ago, today's physicians, or nurses on their behalf, often use verbal communication to ensure that patients understand written communication, such as discharge instructions. A research team added verbal orders for trans-fer to written discharge instructions for patients who had been hospitalized with respiratory failure. In addition to written discharge orders, the receiving provider on transfer received a phone call from the host provider that allowed two-way communication. Addition of the phone call reduced readmissions to the host provider by one half.

Questions

1. What are the advantages and disadvantages of written communication?

2. What are the advantages of adding verbal communication to written communication?

3. Outline three management scenarios in which adding verbal communication to written communication might be useful.

Notes

1. Freeman, R. Edward. *Strategic Management: A Stakeholder Approach*. New York: Cambridge University Press, 2010; Freeman, R. Edward, Jeffrey S. Harrison, and Stellos Zyglidopoulos. *Stakeholder Theory: Concepts and Strategies*. New York: Cambridge University Press, 2018; Ginter, Peter M., W. Jack Duncan, and Linda E. Swayne. *The Strategic Management of Health Care Organizations*, 8th ed., Hoboken, NJ: John Wiley & Sons, 2018.
2. McAlearney, Ann Scheck, and Anthony R. Kovner. *Health Services Management: A Case Study Approach*, 11th ed. Chicago: Health Administration Press, 2017.
3. U.S. Department of Health & Human Services, Agency for Healthcare Research and Quality. "AHRQ's Patient Safety Initiative: Building Foundations, Reducing Risk." *https://archive.ahrq.gov/research/findings/final-reports/pscongrpt/psini2.html*, retrieved July 17, 2019.
4. Institute of Medicine. *To Err Is Human*. Washington, DC: National Academy Press, 2000. *https://www.ncbi.nlm.nih.gov/pubmed/25077248*, retrieved July 17, 2019.
5. Makary, M., and Michael Daniel. "Medical Error—the Third Leading Cause of Death in the U.S." *British Medical Journal* 2016: 353, i2139. *https://www.bmj.com/content/353/bmj.i2139*, retrieved July 29, 2020.
6. Bernazzani, Sophia. "Costs of Care: Tallying the High Cost of Preventable Harm." *https://costsofcare.org/tallying-the-high-cost-of-preventable-harm/*, retrieved July 17, 2019.
7. Sands, Daniel Z. *Challenges in Healthcare Communications: How Technology Can Increase Efficiency, Safety, and Satisfaction*. San Jose, CA: Cisco Systems, 2008.
8. Longest, Beaufort B., Jr., and Wesley M. Rohrer. "Communications between Public Health Agencies and Their External Stakeholders." *Journal of Health and Human Services Administration* 28, 2 (Fall 2005): 189–217.
9. Newstrom, John W. *Organizational Behavior: Human Behavior at Work*, 14th ed. New York: McGraw-Hill Education, 2019.
10. Kessels, Roy P. "Patients' Memory for Medical Information." *Journal of the Royal Society of Medicine* 96, 5 (May 2003): 219–222. *https://www.ncbi.nlm.nih.gov/pmc/articles/PMC539473/*, retrieved July 22, 2019; Laws, M. Barton, et al. "Factors Associated with Patient Recall of Key Information in Ambulatory Specialty Care Visits: Results of an Innovative Methodology." *PLoS ONE* 13, 2: e0191940. *https://journals.plos.org/plosone/article?id=10.1371/journal.pone.0191940#abstract0*, retrieved July 22, 2019; Makaryuus, A., and Friedman, E. "Patients' Understanding of Their Treatment Plans and Diagnosis at Discharge." *Mayo Clinic Proceedings* 80, 8 (August 2005): 991–994. *https://www.ncbi.nlm.nih.gov/pubmed/16092576*, retrieved July 22, 2019.
11. Olden, Peter C. *Management of Healthcare Organizations: An Introduction*, 3rd ed. Chicago: Health Administration Press, 2019.
12. Porter, Michael E. *Competitive Advantage: Creating and Sustaining Superior Performance*. New York: The Free Press, 1985; Porter, Michael E. *On Competition: Updated and Expanded Edition*. Brighton: Harvard Business Publishing, 2008.
13. Rice, James A. *Leadership Insights*. La Jolla, CA: The International Health Summit, 2003; Bjorseth, Lillian D. "Ten Principles of Communication." *Healthcare Executive* 22, 5 (September/October 2007): 52–55; Ash, E. "Seven Ways to Be a Better Listener." *SmartCompany*. *https://www.smartcompany.com.au/people-human-resources/seven-ways-better-listener/*, retrieved July 22, 2019.
14. Robbins, Stephen P., and Mary Coulter. *Management*, 14th ed. New York: Pearson, 2018.

15. Harris, Thomas E., and John C. Sherblom. *Small Group and Team Communication*, 5th ed. Long Grove, IL: Waveland Press, 2015.

16. Richmond, Virginia Peck, James C. McCroskey, and Larry Powell. *Organizational Communication for Survival*. New York: Pearson, 2013.

17. Newstrom, John W. *Organizational Behavior: Human Behavior at Work*, 14th ed. New York: McGraw-Hill Education, 2019.

18. Longest, Beaufort B., Jr. "Communicating for Understanding." In *Health Program Management: From Development through Evaluation*, 2nd ed., Chapter 6. San Francisco: Jossey-Bass, 2015.

19. Longest. "Communicating for Understanding."

20. Ginter, Peter M., W. Jack Duncan, and Linda E. Swayne. *Strategic Management of Health Care Organizations*, 8th ed. San Francisco: Jossey-Bass, 2018; Longest, Beaufort B., Jr., *Seeking Strategic Advantage through Health Policy Analysis*, 63–79. Chicago: Health Administration Press, 1996.

21. Thomas, James B., and Reuben R. McDaniel, Jr. "Interpreting Strategic Issues: Effects of Strategy and the Information-Processing Structure of Top Management Teams." *Academy of Management Journal* 33 (1990): 288–298.

22. This section is adapted from Longest, Beaufort B., Jr., *Health Program Management: From Development Through Evaluation*, 2nd ed. San Francisco: Jossey-Bass, 2015.

23. Pride, William M., and O. C. Ferrell. *Marketing*, 18th ed. Boston: CENGAGE Learning, 2016.

24. Berkowitz, Eric N. *Essentials of Healthcare Marketing*, 4th ed. Sudbury, MA: Jones & Bartlett Learning, 2017; American Organization of Nurse Executives. *Market-Driven Nursing: Developing and Marketing Patient Care Services*. San Francisco: Jossey-Bass, 1999.

25. Hirsch, Ronald. "The Opioid Epidemic: It's Time to Place Blame Where It Belongs." *Missouri Medicine* 114 (March/April, 2017): 82–83, 90. *https://www.ncbi.nlm.nih.gov/pmc/articles/PMC6140023/*, retrieved on August 7, 2019.

26. Ortiz, Selena E., and Meredith B. Rosenthal. "Medical Marketing, Trust, and the Patient–Physician Relationship." *Journal of the American Medical Association* 321 (January 2019): 40–41. *https:// jamanetwork.com/journals/jama/fullarticle/2720005?guestAccessKey=22c92de4-f52f-44c3-a035 -939b3a93b51b&utm_source=silverchair&utm_campaign=jama_network&utm_content=weekly _highlights&cmp=1&utm_medium=email*, retrieved on August 7, 2019.

27. Friedman, Emily. *The Right Thing: Ten Years of Ethics Columns from the Healthcare Forum Journal*, 228. San Francisco: Jossey-Bass, 1996.

28. Longest, Beaufort B., Jr. "The Civic Roles of Healthcare Organizations." *Health Forum Journal* 41 (September/October 1998): 40–42.

29. Longest, Beaufort B., Jr. *Health Policymaking in the United States*, 5th ed., Chapter 1. Chicago: Health Administration Press, 2010.

30. Longest. *Seeking Strategic Advantage*.

31. Filerman, Gary L., and D. David Persaud. "Advocacy." In *Government Relations in the Healthcare Industry*, edited by Peggy Leatt and Joseph Mapa, 77. Westport, CT: Praeger, 2003.

32. Johns Hopkins Medicine. "Study Suggests Medical Errors Now Third Leading Cause of Death in the U.S." *https://www.hopkinsmedicine.org/news/media/releases/study_suggests_medical_errors_now _third_leading_cause_of_death_in_the_us*, retrieved August 7, 2019.

33. *To Err Is Human: Building a Safer Health System,* edited by Linda T. Kohn, Janet M. Corrigan, and Molla S. Donaldson. Washington, DC: National Academy Press, 2000.

34. White, Kenneth R., and John R. Griffith. *The Well-Managed Healthcare Organization*, 9th ed., Chapter 5. Chicago: Health Administration Press, 2019.

35. James, Brent C. *Quality Management for Healthcare Delivery*. Chicago: The Health Research and Educational Trust of the American Hospital Association, 1989.

36. Spain, Jack. "Effective Communications with Internal Stakeholders." *Fuentek's Tech Transfer Blog*. *https://www.fuentek.com/blog-post/effective-communications-with-internal/*, retrieved January 14, 2020.

37. Adapted from Bovet, Colin. "18 Internal Communication Strategies for 2019." *Enplug Blog*, July 9, 2019. *https://blog.enplug.com/internal-communications-best-practices*, retrieved January 14, 2020.

38. Murphy, Joseph G., and William F. Dunn. "Medical Errors and Poor Communication." *CHEST Journal* 2010; 138(6): 1292–1293. *https://journal.chestnet.org/article/S0012-3692(10)60634-4/fulltext*, retrieved August 8, 2019.

PART III

Application

The third part of this text applies the five management functions—planning, organizing, staffing, directing, and controlling—to HSOs and HSs. Figure III.1 shows them connected by the omnipresent problem solving and decision making. To help understand how managers use the five functions, an open systems model of health services management describes the context of managers' work.

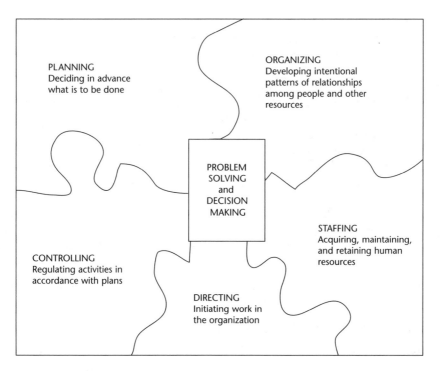

Figure III.1. The management functions are interrelated like the pieces of a puzzle.

Table III.1 Conceptualizing Management Work

Functions	Skills	Roles	NCHL Domains of Competencies[a]
Planning Organizing Staffing Directing Controlling	Technical Human Conceptual	Interpersonal Informational Decisional Designer Strategist Leader	Boundary spanning Execution Relations Transformation Values Health system awareness and business literacy Self-awareness and self-development

[a]An explanation of the National Center for Healthcare Leadership domains and a list of the 28 competencies are at https://www.nchl.org/page?page=272.

Conceptualizing the HSO/HS Management Model

There are various conceptualizations of management. No one offers a comprehensive framework to understand managing and management work in HSOs/HSs. Table III.1 shows four ways to conceptualize management: functions, skills, roles, and domains of competencies. Summed, they are a comprehensive framework. Overarching, of course, is using them well.

The five management functions are the basis for all managers do. Their use enables the organization to achieve its mission. Applying the functions effectively requires that managers use skills and roles shown in Table III.1, which are detailed in Chapter 13. The domains of competencies in Table III.1 have been identified by accreditors and professional associations as needed to manage effectively. They, too, are covered in Chapter 13.

Systems Theory

Systems theory is a framework to conceptualize relationships among organizations and their external environment. A system is a set of interrelated and interdependent parts. A subsystem is part of a system; a suprasystem is a system of systems. Figure III.2 presents an open systems analysis of the healthcare field. An HSO or HS is composed of subsystems such as patient care, ancillary services, staffing, finance, and information technology. An HSO or HS may be described as a subsystem of a larger system of HSOs/HSs in the healthcare environment (8), which is part of the suprasystem called the general environment (9).

Managers interact with the external environment. For example, they affect the flow of supplies by joining a group purchasing cooperative. They influence human resources, such as RNs, by interacting with schools of nursing. They influence potential patients by improving economic conditions or other quality-of-life aspects of their communities.

Figure III.2 conceptualizes managing as an input–conversion–output process in the macro environment. HSOs and HSs interact continuously with their external environments. Managing converts input (human and other resources, and technology) into output (achieving the mission as to services, markets, quality, and other parameters of performance). Figure III.2 shows the following key relationships:

- HSOs and HSs are formal organizations that produce output (achieving mission) using processes (conversion) of input (resources).

- The work of managers is the catalyst that converts input to output.

- HSOs and HSs are open systems that affect and are affected by the external environment.

The input–conversion–output model is incorporated into the comprehensive management model in Figure III.2.

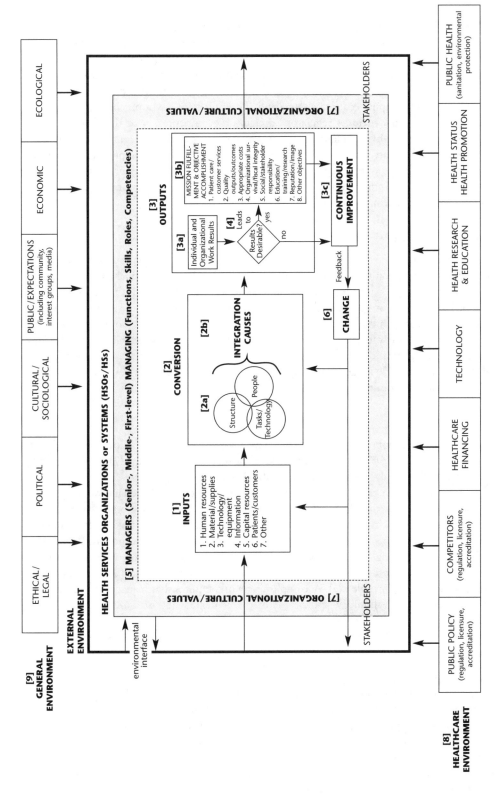

Figure III.2. Management model for HSOs/HSs.

Inputs (Resources)

Inputs (1) in Figure III.2 provide the wherewithal to produce outputs (3). Inputs include human resources, material, technology and equipment, information, financial resources, and patients or customers. Human resources are the organization's staff. Material input (resources) is goods and services. Technology and equipment are machines and devices. Internal information resources are systems, software, and hardware. External information resources are public policy, stakeholder input, economic data, and the immediate environment of the external healthcare system that includes regulators, accreditors, competitors, and third-party payers. Capital resources are physical plant and funds. Patients or customers are sources of input, too.

Diminished resources compromise the organization's effectiveness. Rapid increase in supply costs may affect an output such as service delivery, debt markets may preclude capital expansion, obsolete equipment diminishes quality of care and efficiency, and inadequate human resources prevent offering a service.

Outputs (Mission)

The outputs component (3) in Figure III.2 shows individual and organization outputs (3a) produced by conversion (2) of inputs. Outputs include results of individual and organization work (3a), which (4) helps the organization achieve its mission (3b). HSO and HS mission (3b) includes patient or customer service, quality care, fiscal integrity and survival, meeting stakeholder needs, clinical education and research, and maintaining the organization's reputation. The mission varies by HSO/HS and the services each was established to provide. Typically, the organization with the broadest mission is the general-acute community hospital, which offers a wide range of primary and secondary healthcare services to maintain and improve population health.

Conversion

Conversion (2) of input to output occurs when managers (5) integrate (2b) structure, tasks and technology, and people (2a) within the context of the organization's culture (7) and in response to the needs of internal, interface, and external stakeholders.

The structure element (2a) in Figure III.2 conceptualizes formally designed arrangements such as authority-accountability and superior-subordinate relationships; grouping work activities; and coordination, communication, information, and control. The tasks and technology element (2a) shows specialization of work, as follows: job design; work processes, methods, and procedures; and logistics and workflow. It shows, too, the technology such as equipment, cybernetics, and the information and knowledge that managers and others use in their work. Work occurs through people (2a). Accomplishing work requires that managers integrate (2b) structure, tasks and technology, and people in the context of the organization's values and culture (7) to achieve its mission.

Managers Managing

Managers manage (5) by using skills, roles, and domains of competencies to perform management functions. Doing so requires them to know and integrate the model's components. This is shown in Figure III.2 by the dotted line that surrounds input (1), conversion (2), output (3), continuous improvement (3c), and change (3). By *planning*, managers define individual and organizational outputs that will achieve the mission. When the work to be done is known, human and other input (1) is identified, acquired, and allocated. By *organizing* and *staffing*, managers shape the organizational setting in which conversion (2) occurs—the structure, tasks and technology, and staff relationships. When *directing*, managers initiate and continue efforts to accomplish individual and organizational work (3a). By *controlling*, managers monitor results of individual and organizational work (3a) and compare results with standards and expectations to know how well mission (3b) is being met. If results are less than expectations (4), managers make changes (6) using a feedback loop. If comparisons with best practices show care can be improved, managers change structure, tasks and technology, and people components, and/or change input resources. Even if mission is being achieved (3b), the philosophy of continuous quality improvement (CQI) requires ongoing assessing and improving (3c). CQI states performance can be improved by evaluating, changing (6), and improving (3c) the processes used in conversion (2) and/or input used (1).

Decision-Making and the Management Functions

As Figure III.2 shows, decision making connects all management functions. Managers' decisions result from problem solving. Without problem solving and the decision making that follows, there is no management. Depending on managers' levels in the organization, decisions vary in nature and magnitude and in techniques used. Senior managers make policy or strategic decisions affecting the organization, including resource allocation. Mid- and first-level managers make decisions about allocating and using resources provided by senior management. Chapter 6 addressed problem solving and decision making.

10

Planning

One significant challenge for managers in health services organizations and health systems (HSOs/HSs) is establishing and maintaining relationships with the external environment. This requires assessing internal and external environments and then planning and acting in response, referred to as strategizing or strategic management, which is both a precursor to planning and a continuing activity for senior managers. Strategizing is achieving equilibrium between the organization and its external environment. The activities involved are future oriented and have a large role in how organizations establish and maintain relationships with their external environment. Equilibrium is fleeting because there is constant flux and growing complexity in the environmental forces to which an organization must adapt if it is to succeed.

Strategizing provides the design and justification for the overall focus, direction, and operation of HSOs/HSs. It requires managers "who understand the nature and implications of external change, possess the ability to develop effective strategies to navigate change, and have the will as well as the ability to actively manage the momentum of the organization."[1]

Strategizing is best understood in the context of systems theory and planning, generally. These two aspects are examined here as background.

Strategizing and Systems Theory

Strategizing is consistent with systems theory. The "organization as organism," is a metaphor that organizations, like organisms, interact with their environment and must achieve a relationship with it if they are to survive.[2] The organization as an open system continuously interacts with various forces and entities in its environment even as these environmental factors are dynamically interrelated. See the management model explained as Figure III.2.

Core Concepts of Systems Theory

Systems theory is based on a set of core concepts:

- Input–conversion–output: the system dynamic whereby resources are brought into the organization from its environment to sustain core technologies, which convert inputs into desired outputs (see Figure 14.1)

- Feedback loops: channels that allow the system to monitor outputs, measure them against standards, and adjust inputs and throughput, as needed

- Homeostasis: self-regulation using feedback

- Entropy: the tendency of systems to lose energy and become disorganized

- Negative entropy: the attempt to sustain the system (organism) and counteract entropy

- Differentiation and integration: the system dynamic that reflects the structural relationship of parts to the whole, in which units must be coordinated into subsystems and the latter into a unified whole for the system to be viable

- Requisite variety: the outcome of the organization's mapping its environment to respond to external forces and change accordingly.

The implication of the "requisite variety" attribute of general systems theory for HSOs/HSs is that their internal structures must correspond to the complexity of their environments to achieve a good fit with them. For example, the rapid increase in regulation, including compliance, resulted in hiring in-house legal counsel and risk managers to address compliance with the Employee Retirement Income Security Act (PL 93-406), Health Insurance Portability and Accountability Act (PL 104-191), Americans with Disabilities Act (PL 101-336), Family and Medical Leave Act (PL 103-3), Patient Protection and Affordable Care Act (PL 111-148), Medicare Access and CHIPS Reauthorization Act (PL 114-10), and Tax Cuts and Jobs Act (PL 115-97), as well as changes in requirements and standards of The Joint Commission and Centers for Medicare & Medicaid Services (CMS).

Perhaps the most obvious adaptation of HSOs/HSs to environmental change is the pervasive impact of information technology and systems on business and clinical operations, with the electronic health record becoming the gold standard. Development and implementation of health information systems and information technology have had implications for staffing, training, job design, process engineering, performance evaluation, incentives, and compensation; more are anticipated.

An academic health center exemplifies the dynamics of organizations as an open system. Inputs include staff, expertise, supplies, cash, physical plant and equipment, and the like. Throughput includes core technologies, such as medical, rehabilitative, diagnostic, and related clinical processes, and support processes, such as food service, supply chain, financial management, and legal counsel. Outputs include the following:

- Short-term process and activity measures, such as patient visits, physical therapy treatments, and intensive care unit nursing hours

- Clinical outcomes, such as lower cholesterol levels, increased range of motion, and joint implants

- Impact and long-term effects on population health, or covered lives, such as lower prevalence of obesity, addiction, and decline in breast cancer mortality

Environmental Forces in an Open System

Organizations, as well as organisms, are affected by environmental forces. Figure III.2 illustrates environmental forces for HSOs/HSs. Organizations are influenced and constrained by external forces; concomitantly, they influence them. The extent of influence depends on the organization's size, asset base, financial health, reputation, and strategic direction. For a large, urban HSO, relevant environmental forces include the following:

- Demographic patterns and trends

- Economic conditions (local, regional, and national)

- Technological developments

- State and federal regulation and health policy initiatives

- Labor markets for providers, managers, and support staff

- Professional associations and organized labor

- Public officials and community leaders

- Organized interest groups and advocates

- Media representatives and opinion makers

HSOs/HSs scan their environment to answer questions such as How can we anticipate future demands and adapt to changes in our external environment? Should our mission be reconsidered? How are objectives (desired outputs) determined and what influences them? How do we choose plans to accomplish objectives? Strategizing answers these and similar questions about how an organization establishes and maintains a symbiotic relationship with its external environment and responds to both opportunities and threats from it.

Feedback ensures that the organization receives accurate, timely, and useful intelligence from its environment. Useful feedback for the HSO typically results from its outputs and outcomes. A media report of iatrogenic disease is unwanted, negative feedback as a sentinel indicator of problems with quality management and clinical processes. Similarly, several medical malpractice claims among a group of physicians in a preferred provider organization (PPO) will occasion a review of physician recruitment and selection and its clinical practices. Alternatively, a highly favorable rating on Healthcare Effectiveness Data and Information Set (HEDIS) quality indicators for a health maintenance organization (HMO) could be interpreted as an indication to continue the current approach to customer relationship management.

Strategizing and Planning

Planning includes assessing information about the organization and its environment, making assumptions about the future, evaluating current objectives or developing new ones, and formulating organizational strategies and operational programs to accomplish objectives.

Planning occurs throughout HSOs/HSs. The two distinct but related types of planning are strategic and operational. Strategic planning is performed by the governing body (GB) and senior managers with input from other parts of the organization, including leaders of the professional staff organization (PSO). The GB ensures that effective strategic planning occurs. Strategic planning, or strategizing, determines the intended outputs for an HSO/HS (see the "Strategic Quality Planning: Hoshin Planning" section in Chapter 4). The GB may not originate strategy, although it ensures that strategic proposals brought to it by senior managers are prepared and are consistent with the mission and its responsibilities to stakeholders.

Subsequently, managers use operational planning to determine the means to accomplish the planned outputs. Operational planning is derived from and must be in harmony with strategic planning. Operational planning establishes objectives and operational programs, policies, and procedures in organizational units, such as individual or groups of departments and smaller units and programs. Strategic planning is a multiyear process. Operational planning is short term, with time frames of 1 year or less.

Middle managers undertake operational planning, and they design and implement programs, policies, and procedures for their areas of responsibility. Most often the operational plans include multiple departments. Finally, first-level managers plan specific operations or activities, such as estimating workload, scheduling work activity, and allocating resources.

Planning's Attributes

Planning has three attributes. First, it tries to anticipate the HSO's/HS's future needs. Managers who think systematically about the future, plan its course, and plan for possible contingencies increase the organization's preparedness. Second, planning involves decision making. Determining what to do, when, where, and how requires selecting alternatives and allocating resources. Operational planning clarifies the organization's direction and enhances its effectiveness. Third, planning is dynamic and continuous. The plan is affected by internal and external forces. Thus, environmental surveillance and adaptive change are attributes of planning.

Planning and the Management Model

The management model in Figure III.2 shows the importance of planning. Planning prepares managers to deal with the healthcare environment and the general environment. Planning reduces uncertainty, ambiguity, and risk. The healthcare environment includes public policy (regulation, licensure, and accreditation), competition, public and private healthcare financing, technology, research and education, health status, and public health. The general environment includes ethical and legal, political, cultural and sociological, economic, and ecological forces. For good or ill, these forces affect what managers do and how they do it. By anticipating developments in their environment, and at times proactively influencing environmental variables, such as public policy, managers can respond to myriad forces that affect them. Planning requires managers to focus on outputs. All organizational activity is directed toward accomplishing the mission and objectives, which are the ends to be attained. Desired output determines input.

Planning enables managers to establish priorities and make better decisions about conversion design and allocation of resources. Integration of structure, tasks and technology, and people converts inputs to outputs. By identifying objectives and formulating plans to achieve them, managers can design appropriate conversion processes and systems. These include organizational arrangements discussed in Chapter 11 and initiatives such as continuous quality improvement (CQI) and work process design or redesign described in Chapters 4 and 8. Decision making and its importance to the HSO's/HS's conversion of inputs to outputs are presented in Chapter 6.

As managers initiate organizational activity to accomplish objectives through strategies and operational programs, they do so through people; Chapter 9 addresses communicating; Chapter 13 discusses the management function of directing; both are essential.

Finally, planning is the foundation for resource allocation and control. It enables the HSO/HS to measure progress and determine if expected results are achieved. The management function of controlling discussed in Chapter 14 establishes standards for resource use and monitors organizational activity against them. Criteria for measuring progress are based on objectives identified in the planning function.

HSO/HS Planning Context

The post–World War II (1941–1945) environment was supportive of HSOs/HSs and was an era in which demand for services and capacity to provide them expanded. The environment was stable and predictable. Roles were clear. Risk was low. Efficient HSOs/HSs thrived; even the inefficient survived.

The environment for HSOs/HSs has changed from the mid-1980s. It became turbulent, difficult, even hostile. Most importantly, however, it has become less stable and predictable. The changes wrought by technology are substantial. Societal and third-party payer assertiveness and demands for greater accountability are growing. Power is shifting from providers to purchasers and consumers of healthcare. Public and private sector initiatives to control costs are intensifying; this heightens financial risk. These forces are contributing to intense competition among providers. Some results were the formation of financing and delivery arrangements, including managed care organizations (MCOs) such as HMOs and PPOs; joint ventures; mergers and consolidations; strategic alliances (SAs); and, especially, the formation and increase in HSs. More recently, stimulated by provisions of the Affordable Care Act of 2010, accountable care organizations (ACOs) are emerging as a financing and delivery arrangement. ACOs are doctors, hospitals, and other healthcare providers who organize to coordinate care to Medicare patients.[3] As environmental turbulence has gained momentum and continues unabated in the 21st century, HSOs/HSs are pursuing initiatives to contain the impact of external forces, decrease uncertainty, and lessen financial risk. Recognizing that the rules of the game have changed, senior managers realize their organizations and systems no longer have a guaranteed demand for their services from traditional constituencies, nor are they guaranteed a right to survive. Table 10.1 suggests the complexity and turbulence of the external environment facing HSOs/HSs as they undertake strategic and operational planning.

Strategic responses to environmental forces are 1) embracing the philosophy of continuous quality improvement, 2) increasing the prominence of marketing (see later in this chapter), and 3) undertaking formalized, systematic strategic planning, including strategic issues management, to improve competitive position. Health services marketing is an environmental link to and integral part of strategic planning; strategic issues management is linked to strategic planning to influence public policy issues related to health services.

Products of Planning

Strategic and operational planning yield tangible products, including statements of organization mission, vision, and values for the HSO/HS; organization-level objectives and subobjectives for components; organization-level strategies and substrategies for components; and operational programs, policies, and procedures. Each is described here.

Mission, Vision, and Values

Planning begins with and is grounded in the mission statement, which states the organization's reasons for existence and describes what the organization does.[4] The mission statement answers the following questions: What business(es) are we in and why? Who are our primary constituencies? How do we distinguish ourselves from competitors (other organizations)? Mission statements provide the public with a succinct (and preferably distinctive) statement of purpose.

HSOs/HSs link the mission statement with a vision statement and, often, a set of values. The vision statement is usually shorter, less specific, and more philosophical than the mission statement. It articulates how its leaders want the organization to be perceived by stakeholders and provides a strategic view of direction. A vision statement states what an organization wants to become.

In addition, organizations articulate the core values that serve as guiding principles for the behavior of their members as they reify the organization. Value statements reflect the values

Table 10.1 HSO/HS Environmental Planning Profile for the Early to Mid-21st Century

Factors	Description
Demographics	Growing population. From about 332,639 million in 2020, the U.S. population will grow to a projected 388,922 in 2050. This projection is highly dependent on U.S. immigration policy, with 82% of population growth from 2005 to 2050 attributed to immigrants and their U.S.-born descendants, while the fertility rates for nonimmigrants will reach historic lows.
	Aging population. From about 56,052 million 65 years and over in 2020 (16.9% of the total U.S. population), the U.S. population that is 65 years and over will grow to a projected 85,675 million in 2050 (22.0% of the total U.S. population, peaking at 28.7% in 2030). This projected percentage is highly dependent on U.S. immigration policy: the average age of immigrants arriving in the United States from 2000 to 2017 was 31 years.
	Increasingly diverse population. From 18.7% Latino or Hispanic, 13.8% Black or African American, 6% Asian, 2.9% multiracial, 1.3% American Indian or Alaska Native, 0.2% Native Hawaiian or Other Pacific Islander, in 2020, the U.S. population will grow to a projected 25.7% Latino or Hispanic, 14.6% Black or African American, 8.4% Asian, 5.3% multiracial, 1.4% American Indian or Alaska Native, 0.3% Native Hawaiian or Other Pacific Islander, in 2050.
	Growing prevalence of chronic disease in the population.
Health Policy and Legislation	Funding for Medicare and Medicaid continues to be problematic.
	Partisan battles over the Affordable Care Act.
	Partisan battles over universal healthcare coverage.
	Budget implications of Medicaid expansion at the state level.
	Cost shifting from the uninsured/underinsured to the insured and from employers to employees.
	Navigating technology, cybersecurity, and confidentiality.
	Healthcare's transformation to consumerism.
	Growing prevalence of chronic disease in the population.
	Addressing the opioid epidemic.
	Reducing the cost of pharmaceuticals to the patient.
Scientific and Technological Developments	Research and clinical applications of nanotechnology.
	Developments in animal and human stem cell research.
	New drugs to improve memory recall in Alzheimer patients.
	New treatments for cancer.
	Telemedicine and e-visits to providers.
	New patient-centered monitors for chronic and other disease.
	New medical applications for artificial intelligence.
Economic Trends	Increasing globalization of the economy.
	Growth in private capital funding of new businesses and technology.
	Outsourcing and off-shoring of both manufacturing and service industries, including healthcare.
	Increased privatization of traditional public government functions.
	Nonprofit sector continuing to struggle for funding.
	Decline in numbers and influence of labor unions.

From United States Census Bureau. United States Population Projections: 2000 to 2050 (revised March 19, 2018). https://www.census.gov/library/working-papers/2009/demo/us-pop-proj-2000-2050.html, retrieved September 3, 2019; Pew Research Center. "Key findings about U.S. immigrants." June 17, 2019. https://www.pewresearch.org/fact-tank/2019/06/17/key-findings-about-u-s-immigrants/, retrieved September 4, 2019; Center for Immigration Studies. "Immigrants Are Coming to America at Older Ages: A Look at Age at Arrival among New Immigrants, 2000 to 2017." July 1, 2019. https://cis.org/Report/Immigrants-Are-Coming-America-Older-Ages, retrieved September 4, 2019; Health Administration Press. "Futurescan 2019–2024: Health Care Trends and Implications." Chicago: Author, 2019.

that are the organizational culture and provide guidance for decisions of its staff. In sum, mission, vision, and values constitute a coherent philosophy underlying the organization's work and its role in its environment and the broader society.[5]

Sample mission, vision, and values statements are shown in Table 10.2. Commonly, HSOs/HSs display their statements of mission, vision, and values in their lobbies or other public areas and on their websites.

Objectives and Subobjectives

Objectives are another product of planning and state results to be achieved. In the context of the management model in the Introduction to Part III, objectives are HSO/HS outputs—the ends of organization activity. Most objectives are explicit; some are implicit. Organizational objectives are to be accomplished by the entire organization; subobjectives are those for divisions, departments, and programs.

Organizational objectives are established by the GB. In HSs, subobjectives may be established by senior management with ratification by the GB. Often expressed in broad terms, achieving organizational objectives results in mission fulfillment. Thus, they are derived from and reflect the mission. Examples of HSO/HS objectives, as shown in [3b] of Figure III.2.

Table 10.2 Sample Mission, Vision, and Values Statements of HSOs/HSs[6]

University of Pittsburgh Medical Center (UPMC)	
Mission	UPMC's mission is to serve our community by providing outstanding patient care and to shape tomorrow's health system through clinical and technological innovation, research, and education.
Vision	UPMC will lead the transformation of health care. The UPMC model will be nationally recognized for redefining health care by • Putting our patients, health plan members, employees, and community at the center of everything we do and creating a model that assures that every patient gets the right care, in the right way, at the right time, every time. • Harnessing our integrated capabilities to deliver both superb state-of-the-art care to our patients and high value to our stakeholders. • Employing our partnership with the University of Pittsburgh to advance the understanding of disease, its prevention, treatment and cure. • Serving the underserved and disadvantaged, and advancing excellence and innovation throughout health care. • Fueling the development of new businesses globally that are consistent with our mission as an ongoing catalyst and driver of economic development for the benefit of the residents of the region.
Values	Quality and safety: We create a safe environment where quality is our guiding principle. Dignity and respect: We treat all individuals with dignity and respect. Caring and listening: We listen to and care for our patients, our health plan members, our fellow employees, our physicians, and our community. Responsibility and integrity: We perform our work with the highest levels of responsibility and integrity. Excellence and innovation: We think creatively and build excellence into everything we do.
Florida Department of Health: Miami-Dade County	
Mission	To protect, promote and improve the health of all people in Florida through integrated state, county and community efforts.
Vision	To be the healthiest state in the nation.
Core Values	Innovation: We search for creative solutions and manage resources wisely. Collaboration: We use teamwork to achieve common goals and solve problems. Accountability: We perform with integrity and respect. Responsiveness: We achieve our mission by serving our customers and engaging our partners. Excellence: We promote quality outcomes through learning and continuous performance improvement.

From https://www.upmc.com/about/why-upmc/mission and http://miamidade.floridahealth.gov/about-us/_documents/2017-Annual-Report.pdf.

Objectives evolve but can change dramatically if circumstances become dire. For example, survival is the foremost objective for an HSO/HS with deteriorating market share, declining census and clinical staff, and insolvency.

Subobjectives are ends to be accomplished by an HSO's/HS's unit. They give direction to managers and other staff and are subsidiary to and must conform with organizational objectives. Figure 10.1 shows the hierarchical relationship between organization objectives and subobjectives for an HS and an HSO.

At times, a conscious decision must be made to suboptimize performance of a subsidiary entity or unit if doing so enables the HSO/HS to optimize performance elsewhere. For example, women take the lead in meeting family healthcare needs. An excellent obstetrics experience can initiate a long-term allegiance with the HSO. Thus, it is rational for an HSO to suboptimize financial performance of obstetrics by providing superb accommodations and staffing to win the praise and loyalty of new mothers.

Objectives that state realistic, attainable, and measurable results are important in that they accomplish the following:

- Focus managers' attention on the work to meet specific ends

- Provide prioritizing criteria for decision making about services and programs

- Facilitate efficiency, particularly in allocating and using resources

- Give employees a sense of direction that results in organizational stability

- Provide the knowledge of intended results critical to formulating strategies to accomplish organizational objectives and operational programs to achieve subobjectives.

- Become criteria used in the controlling function to compare actual (outputs) with desired results (objectives).

Organizational Strategies and Operational Plans

Strategy describes how HSO or HS objectives will be accomplished. Strategies are selected by GBs and senior managers. Typically, they are long term and require substantial resources. Examples of strategies include changing the scope of services, perhaps by specializing (e.g., adding a hyperbaric oxygen therapy or gastric bypass surgery), diversification (e.g., establishing a for-profit medical office building subsidiary), and forward or backward integration (e.g., expanding the service area with a satellite family practice center or converting acute care beds to rehabilitation beds).

As shown in Figure 10.1, senior management, with GB oversight, implements organizational strategies. In an HS, senior managers in subsidiary organizations implement strategies to accomplish their objectives. They must, however, support system objectives.

Conversely, operational plans are specific activities that subordinate units, departments, or programs use to implement the organization's strategies. They are less broad and are subordinate to organizational strategies. HSOs/HSs have a hierarchy of objectives and a hierarchy of ways to accomplish them.

- *Organizational culture.* As discussed in Chapter 11, the organizational culture comprises shared beliefs, values, and assumptions acquired by the organization's members over time. Culture is the legacy—what the organization is and what it stands for. Culture shapes the acceptable behavior of members and enables the desired nature of relationships between the HSO/HS and its stakeholders. Objectives must be consistent with the mission and culture.

- *Stakeholders.* Stakeholders are individuals, groups, or organizations affected by the HSO/HS who may seek to influence its objectives and strategies. The GB balances stakeholder

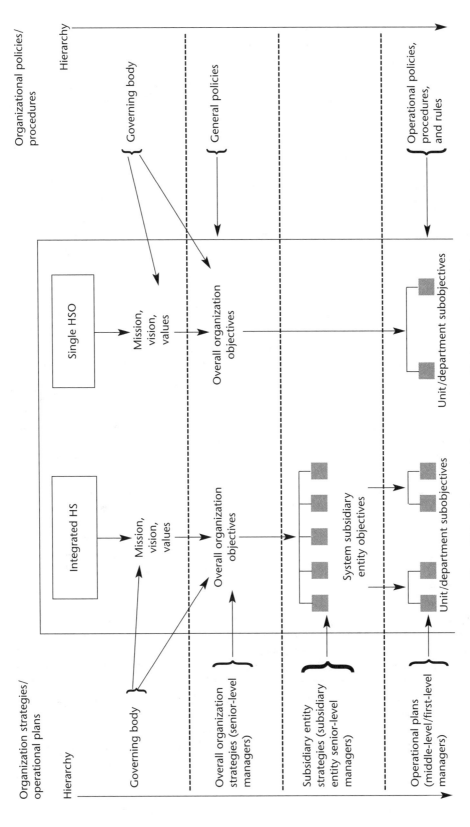

Figure 10.1. Hierarchy of missions, strategies, objectives, and operational plans.

needs and demands and ensures that the mission and vision are compatible with them. Balancing requires maintaining ethical values and social responsibility and preventing inappropriate stakeholder demands from predominating.[7]

- *Values and ethics.* Establishing new objectives or modifying current objectives entails choices. GBs make these choices. Just as culture and stakeholders influence objectives, so do the values and ethics of those who make the choices.

General and Operational Policies and Procedures or Rules

Corporate policies are officially expressed or implied guidelines for the decisions and behavior of the organization's members.[8] Policies are guides to thinking that help organizations attain objectives and thus must be consistent with its objectives and mission. Policies are classified as general and operational.

Familiar general policies governing human resources management are compensation, terms of employment, and on-the-job behavior. Examples are "We are an equal opportunity employer," "Whenever possible, we will promote from within," "Our compensation levels are competitive in the community," and "All patients receive care regardless of ability to pay."

Operational policies (sometimes called procedures or rules) for departments and other units are subsidiary to general policies and must be consistent with them. A human resources department rule might be to continuously update the compensation system's pay grades and rate ranges to remain competitive. A nursing department rule might be to replace licensed practical nurses with registered nurses to improve quality as vacancies occur through attrition.

Procedures and rules are guides for specific situations. Unlike policies, which are guides to thinking, procedures are guides to action; rules prescribe specific actions. In general, they are expressed as steps or tasks necessary to accomplish specific work. For example, there are procedures and rules to admit and discharge patients, requisition supplies, order tests, sterilize equipment, process patient records, and report unsafe conditions or untoward incidents affecting patients.

Good policies and procedures are not easy to develop and implement. To be effective, a policy or procedure must be clear and appropriate. Good policies and procedures have several characteristics.[9] First, their effects must fit with objectives and be well thought out before they are implemented. Policies or procedures whose negative effects were not anticipated can be detrimental. For example, a PSO policy of ordering a full laboratory workup for newly admitted patients may have a noble (or defensive) purpose but may be inconsistent with high-quality care at a reasonable cost.

Second, policies and procedures must be flexible so they can be applied to typical *and* atypical situations. Inflexible policies and procedures diverge from their purpose to guide behavior and decision making. Staff may encounter situations that require judgment. At times, managers appropriately deviate from policy and procedure. For example, not recording an employee's tardiness when the delay was caused by an uncontrollable circumstance, such as severe weather.

Third, policies and procedures must be ethical and legal and reflect the values of the HSO/HS. A policy that permits employees to accept high-value gifts from suppliers may be legal, but it is inconsistent with the ethical value of integrity.

Fourth, to be effective, a policy or procedure must be clear, communicated, understood, and accepted by those to whom it applies. A clear and communicated procedure on reporting sexual harassment informs employees how to act in such a situation. Acceptability means employees consider the policy or procedure to be reasonable, legitimate, and fair. Policies and procedures that display favoritism or that seem arbitrary for no sound purpose will be resisted, even ignored.

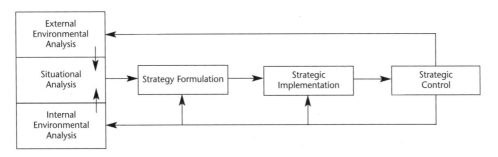

Figure 10.2.   The strategizing process.

Fifth, to serve their purpose, policies, procedures, and rules must be consistent with each other. They should be consistent throughout the organization or system except when special circumstances justify differences. Inconsistently applying guidelines is confusing and causes employee dissatisfaction, frustration, and even litigation, all of which detract from accomplishing objectives. To serve their purpose, policies and procedures must be reevaluated and modified, as necessary.

The Strategizing Process

The prevailing paradigm of strategizing, or strategic management, is that of a multilevel, iterative, and widely participatory process. It is an integrated set of planning, controlling, and decision-making processes looking outward to the HSO's/HS's environment; inward to its strengths, capabilities, and deficiencies; and forward to its future. Figure 10.2 illustrates the strategizing process, which is discussed following here, beginning with situational analysis. This process has several elements of Hoshin planning, as described in Chapter 4.

Situational Analysis

Situational analysis (see Figure 10.2) is the basis for strategizing and involves gathering and evaluating information and making assumptions about the future. It is informed by external and internal environmental analyses. Assessment identifies internal strengths and weaknesses and external opportunities and threats (hence the name *SWOT analysis:* strengths, weaknesses, opportunities, and threats), as well as risks, issues, and deficiencies. Situational analysis is an ongoing review of the strategic position and strategic alternatives. Senior managers are responsible for assessment and presenting results to the GB for consideration, adjustment, and final approval.[10]

Internal Environmental Analysis

An internal environmental analysis (see Figure 10.2) involves cataloging strengths and weaknesses of the HSO/HS. This analysis is an inventory of capability and a resource base to use in strategizing. The analysis focuses on functional areas and results in an organization profile.

Examples of organizational strengths are patient referral patterns, reputation for quality, cost efficiency, technology, qualifications and stature of clinical staff and other professionals, financial and other resources, range and types of services and products provided, a cohesive organizational culture, and proactive management. Weaknesses may include deficiencies such as shortage of capital, outdated physical plant and equipment, hostile labor environment, poor quality or reputation, aging or decreasing numbers of physicians, or reactive management.

Functional Area Analysis

Functional area analysis[11] systematically identifies internal environmental strengths and provides a comprehensive organizational profile. The following are functional areas typically analyzed:

Marketing and service analysis. Includes current patients as to payer type, diagnosis, demographics, source of referral, utilization of services, method of service delivery, and promotional techniques, as well as success rates with each. Marketing and service may include the following about the organization and its PSO: reputation, market share, customer access to the organization as well as barriers to access.

Clinical systems analysis. Includes volume and quality, technology, as well as characteristics of PSO members, such as qualifications, gender, age, and ethnicity.

Production analysis. Includes design of work processes and methods, scheduling and excess capacity, and cost and quality.

Financial analysis. Includes availability and use of capital funds, use of operating funds, use of internal controls, and existence and use of financial systems, such as accounts receivable, inventory, and billing.

Human resources analysis. Includes recruitment and retention as well as staffing levels and skills mix.

Management analysis. Includes organizational structure assessment of roles, competencies, leadership, and effectiveness of managers.

Governing body analysis. Includes selection, composition, orientation, knowledge, commitment, and oversight of the HSO/HS and its mission.

Culture analysis. Includes the organization's philosophy, values and ethics, and the compatibility of the culture with the mission.

Knowing the strengths in functional areas and culture permits conclusions about comparative advantage and the ability to implement strategies. Some conclusions identify the HSO's/HS's competencies; where it excels compared with other, similar organizations; and how it can be differentiated. Is it the low-cost provider? Does it provide the highest-quality service? Does it have the best reputation? Is it committed to CQI and customer satisfaction? Is it on the cutting edge of technology? Comparative advantage is a barrier to market entry that others must overcome to compete with an entity. Information about comparative advantage, strengths, and weaknesses allows consideration of organizational strategies that capitalize on the first two and mitigate the last.

External Environmental Analysis

Environmental scanning identifies *external* opportunities and threats and is essential to effective strategy formulation and choosing from among the alternatives developed. A well-conducted external analysis includes all variables outside boundaries of an HSO/HS that can influence its decisions and actions. Examples include complementary or competitive entities, patients or customers, suppliers, regulators, insurers, and accrediting agencies. Also included are macro-aspects of the external environment that can directly or indirectly affect the organization, such as the general economy, the legal system, the physical environment, and community cultural norms.

Opportunities are favorable circumstances that widen the organization's range of actions. Examples are changed demographics and service patterns; fewer primary care physicians (PCPs) in the service area; and changes in third-party reimbursement. Threats are developments that may have an adverse effect. Examples are new competitors and types and places of service delivery; health status changes in target markets; new technologies; changes in accreditation, regulation, and licensure; and negative economic conditions. Often opportunities and threats are two sides of the same coin.

External environmental analysis has five steps: 1) scanning to identify relevant sources of information for trends, developments, or events that show opportunities or threats; 2) monitoring the sources; 3) forecasting or projecting the future direction of information obtained; 4) analyzing the implications of information; and 5) disseminating analysis to guide decisions and actions.[12] These steps in external environmental analysis are detailed in the sections that follow.[13]

Scanning

Scanning the external environment involves acquiring information about developments that can affect an entity's future. Deciding what to scan based on its strategic importance to an HSO/HS has been described as judgmental, speculative, or conjectural.[14] This nebulousness necessitates both care in selecting what is scanned and the inclusion of several persons in the selection process.

One approach is to use an internal task force or ad hoc committee to provide a group judgment. For example, a CEO might ask several senior and middle managers for advice about what to scan. Another approach uses consultants to provide an expert opinion. Possible, too, is to use formal expert-based techniques.[15]

Determining what to scan is unique to each HSO/HS. Figure 10.3 shows how the complex external environment can be conceptualized. Sector analysis is a model used to organize the decision.

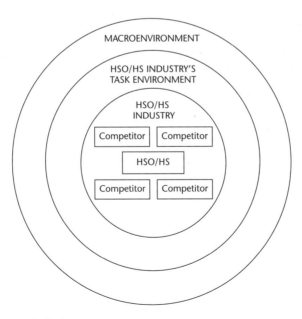

Figure 10.3.   The external environment of an HSO/HS.

Sector Analysis

Sector analysis assesses the condition and future of the healthcare sector and is one way to organize an external environmental assessment. Opportunities and threats are identified, and the competitive position is assessed. Important factors include[16]

Macroenvironment analysis. Major trends and events occurring beyond the healthcare sector, such as the global and national economic trends, including inflation and employment and political trends including regulatory environment.

Economic environment analysis. Major trends and events affecting healthcare, such as inflation rates, employment rates, insurance trends by both private and public third-party payers.

Regulatory environment analysis. Current and proposed regulation that might affect healthcare.

Social environment or culture analysis. Societal practices affecting healthcare, such as diet, substance and alcohol abuse, and cultural attitudes about work, family, and respect for authority.

Political environment assessment. Political mood of the country and potential public policies that could affect healthcare.

Demographics and market analysis. Demographic changes and trends in the marketplace, such as changes in service area composition or target market; age, income, location, and demand for services.

Competitive environment analysis. Competitors and the organization's competitive position, including barriers to entry, threat of new entrants, potential for substitute services and products, strengths and weaknesses of other buyers or sellers, and the organization's strength as a buyer or seller.

Technology environment assessment. Advances in pharmaceuticals, genetics, and high-tech equipment that might affect healthcare sector technology.

External stakeholders' assessment. Stakeholder power and influence, their relative importance to healthcare, and the demands they place on it. Stakeholders include organized medicine, patient advocacy groups, and business coalitions.

Each factor is part of an HSO's/HS's external environment and should be scanned.

Monitoring

Scanning the external environment identifies sources of information about trends, developments, and events that may be opportunities or threats. They should be monitored, which is more than scanning and involves tracking important information.

Monitoring has a narrower focus than scanning because it is used to build a base of information about important or potentially important aspects of the external environment that were identified through scanning or earlier monitoring. Usually, fewer aspects of the external environment are monitored than are scanned. Monitoring is important because it is difficult to determine if information about trends, developments, or events shows opportunities or threats. Under conditions of certainty, managers would understand the information and its consequences for their decisions and actions. As with scanning, techniques that acquire multiple perspectives and expert opinions are helpful. Monitoring provides the background for the next step: forecasting environmental change.

Forecasting

Scanning and monitoring cannot provide managers with all the information they need about the external environment. To use information effectively in strategizing, managers need forecasts, which allow them to adjust strategies and objectives, to revise existing plans, or to formulate new operational plans and implement them in response to new conditions. Some forecasts are made by extending past trends or applying a formula. Or, simulations may be used in forecasting. The worst case is forecasts that are based on conjecture, speculation, and judgment. All methods of forecasting are uncertain. No information exists in a vacuum. Variables change simultaneously, and no forecasting technique or model accounts for this fact.

Trend extrapolation is a common forecasting technique that is simple to use and can be remarkably effective. It tracks information and uses the results to predict future states. It works best predicting general trends, such as the number of patients or customers that will be served by an HSO/HS or Medicare or Medicaid reimbursement rates. For example, if the number of patients or customers increased by 5% for each of the past 5 years, it is reasonable to assume a 5% increase next year. However, trend extrapolation is less effective in a turbulent environment when numbers can change rapidly.

A useful forecasting technique is scenario development.[17] A scenario is a plausible prediction. This technique is appropriate for analyzing environments with many uncertainties, conditions that often characterize the external environment of HSOs/HSs. The essence of scenario development is to define several alternative future states. Each develops contingent strategies from which a choice is made. Alternatively, the scenarios can be used to select what managers consider the most likely future, the one on which strategizing will be based.

Having multiple scenarios allows exploration of various futures, from which the GB and senior managers choose the most likely. A common mistake is to choose a scenario too early in the process. The following is a simple example of three alternate futures for the service area:

1. The numbers of PCPs will increase.

2. The numbers of PCPs will not change.

3. The numbers of PCPs will decline.

Developing multiple scenarios should guide strategic choices.

Assessing

After scanning, monitoring, and forecasting, HSO/HS leadership must assess the strategic importance and implications of the information. Beyond the difficulties of collecting and analyzing enough information of the right kind to inform assessment, problems may be caused by analysts' personal preferences and biases. Accurately determining the relevance and importance of information in predicting the future is not simple. Assessments are inexact because they rely on the judgment of those making them. Prior experience with similar information is useful as are quantification, modeling, and simulation.

At the extreme, assessments may be forced to fit preconceived notions about what is strategically important rather than reflecting a rational assessment of the information. As with other parts of external analysis, multiple judgments about the strategic importance of information help avoid the problem of bias.

Using and Disseminating Information from Analysis

The final step in assessing an HSO's/HS's external environment is to strategize, which starts by giving the information to those whose decisions and actions are affected by it. This step is often undervalued; it may even be overlooked. Information not available to those who need it greatly diminishes the value of the assessment, regardless of the quality in performing it. The managers of HSO/HS components must strategize for their areas of responsibility. The use of strategic information is facilitated in three ways:

1. Require its use in component plans.

2. Persuade others to use it by reasoning with them.

3. Educate as to the importance and usefulness of it in strategizing.

Disseminating and using strategically important information complete the process of analyzing the external environment.

Formulating Strategy

Figure 10.2 shows that strategizing includes formulating strategies using information and insight from situational analysis. Formulating strategies includes identifying strategic options and selecting which to implement.

Various strategies can be identified, evaluated, chosen, and implemented to achieve objectives. Two points are important regarding organizational strategies. First, is the strategy a function of the organization's core services and products? Second, managers rarely implement only one strategy.

Common Strategies

Table 10.3 lists strategies available to HSOs/HSs. There are several different types.[18]

Directional strategies. Articulated in an HSO's/HS's mission, vision, values, and objectives (see Table 10.3). They guide strategic choices in the adaptive, market entry, competitive, and implementation categories.

Adaptive strategies. Delineate how the HSO/HS will expand, contract, or stabilize operations by diversification, vertical integration, or market or product development. Contraction strategies include divestiture, liquidation, and retrenchment.

Table 10.3   Scope and Role of Strategy Types

Strategy	Scope and role
Directional strategies	The broadest strategies set the fundamental direction of the organization by establishing a mission for the organization (Who are we?) and providing a vision for the future (What should we be?). In addition, directional strategies specify the organization's values and the strategic goals.
Adaptive strategies	These strategies are more specific than directional strategies and provide the primary methods for achieving the vision (adapting to the environment). These strategies determine the scope of the organization and specify how the organization will expand, reduce, or maintain scope.
Market entry strategies	These strategies provide the method of carrying out the adaptive strategies (expansion of scope and the maintenance of scope strategies) through purchase, cooperation, or internal development. Market entry strategies are not used for reduction of scope strategies.
Competitive strategies	Two types of strategies, one that determines an organization's strategic posture and one that positions the organization vis-à-vis other organizations within the market. These strategies are market oriented and best articulate competitive advantage.
Implementation strategies	These strategies are the most specific strategies and are directed toward value-added service delivery and value-added support areas. In addition, individual organizational units develop objectives and action plans that carry out the value-added service delivery and value-added support strategies.

From Peter M. Ginter, W. Jack Duncan, and Linda E. Swayne. *Strategic Management of Healthcare Organizations*, 8th ed., 211. Hoboken: John Wiley & Sons, 2018. Used by permission.

Market entry strategies. Support strategies to expand or maintain the scope of an organization, which include acquisition and merger, internal development, alliances, and joint ventures. Market entry strategies are an adaptive strategy.

Competitive strategies. Positioning or generic strategies. Consider how consumers view HSO/HS services and products compared to those of competitors. Include cost leadership, service differentiation, and focus strategies that identify a defined market niche.

Implementation strategies. Implement directional, adaptive, market entry, and competitive strategies. Can apply to entire HSO/HS or functional department(s), such as marketing, finance, and human resources.[19]

In addition to the adaptive strategies in Table 10.3, several adaptive, market entry, and competitive or positioning strategies are used by HSOs/HSs. Several are described next.

Specialization or Niche Strategies

Specialization is a strategy in which HSOs/HSs emphasize selected services or products, often based on disease or acuity of illness. For example, some hospitals are known for oncology, organ transplantation, and cardiac surgery; some nursing facilities (NFs) specialize in rehabilitation; some hospices specialize in memory care. A niche strategy involves focusing on a service area, such as the inner city, or a target market, such as outpatients. An HS specialization strategy might involve its component organizations focusing on rehabilitation or acute care services. Both strategies are usually implemented in tandem—such as a pediatric hospital that specializes by type of care (e.g., neonatal) and has a niche in a specific target market (inner city)—and may involve differentiation based on low-cost, high-technology leadership. Integration and diversification are discussed here as part of strategizing and planning. They are analyzed in Chapter 11 in the context of organizing HSOs/HSs.

Vertical Integration as a Strategy

Vertical integration occurs when an organization controls multiple stages in producing a product or service. It adds upstream or downstream services, which are also called backward or forward integration. Examples of downstream integration for an acute care hospital include involvement in an HS offering ambulatory care, satellite family practice clinics, or wellness promotion. Backward (i.e., upstream) integration includes long-term care and rehabilitation, as well as home health.

Vertical integration may occur in nonservice areas, or factors of production that involve make–buy decisions. Examples are developing or acquiring businesses that provide contract housekeeping or information technology services for the HSO/HS, or that supply or manufacture generic pharmaceuticals, prostheses, or intravenous solutions.

Horizontal Integration as a Strategy

Horizontal integration occurs when an organization acquires or merges with similar organizations. Commonly, horizontal integration enhances core service or product lines and enters new markets with existing services.

Horizontal integration may be achieved using internal development, acquisition, or merger. An acute care hospital that adds robotic surgery to existing core surgical services or builds a suburban acute inpatient hospital is integrating horizontally. Hospital systems or NF chains in which entities offer the same core services are horizontally integrated, and they often use this strategy to reach new markets and achieve economies of scale for support and management services, increase access to capital, and lower overall organizational financial risk.

Horizontally linked HSOs/HSs may be closely coupled through ownership or loosely coupled through affiliations or alliances. An example of a geographically dispersed, horizontally integrated HS is Hospital Corporation of America, with 185 hospitals and 119 freestanding surgery centers located in 21 U.S. states and the United Kingdom.[20]

Diversification as a Strategy

In diversification HSOs/HSs add services or products or enter new markets not directly related to core services or products. Diversification is defined relative to 1) the traditional main line of business or core services, and 2) whether the activity is related or unrelated. For acute care hospitals, diversification includes adding new noninpatient care services or products, such as bariatric surgery and sleep disorder clinics, or nonacute services, such as rehabilitation or substance abuse.

Diversification can be concentric or conglomerate. Concentric diversification occurs when different but related healthcare services or products are added to existing core services. This is done to increase revenue, improve competitive position, or reach new target markets. Concentric diversification may be forward or backward integration. For example, an acute care hospital that diversifies into long-term care by converting acute care beds is also engaging in vertical integration. One way to classify a strategy as vertical integration or diversification is patient flow. If the purpose is to control patient flow, such as by an acute care hospital's acquiring PCP practices, this strategy is vertical integration. If the purpose of acquiring an NF is entering a growth market and not supporting patient flow from the hospital, the strategy is concentric diversification.

The second form of diversification is conglomerate diversification. Here, an HSO/HS produces non–health-related products or services unrelated to its principal business or core services. An example is a hospital's providing laundry or computer services to other HSOs; investing in real estate, such as shopping centers or apartments; or providing food catering services. Concentric diversification is the most common form for HSOs/HSs, but some use conglomerate diversification. Chapter 11 gives further attention to diversification.

Retrenchment or Divestiture as a Strategy

Retrenchment or downsizing involves reducing the scope or intensity of products or services, partially withdrawing from a market area, or decreasing capacity in terms of facilities, equipment, or staff. A divestiture is eliminating services or products, withdrawing from a market area, or closing facilities. If the HSO/HS has no advantage in a market or if demand has decreased, a strategy of retrenchment, or in rare cases, divestiture is used.

Retrenchment is more common. It reduces losses, allows reallocation of resources to more promising activities, and, sometimes, enables survival. Declining birth rates in a service area may cause a hospital to downsize obstetrics, high levels of uncompensated care may cause a hospital to close (retrench) its emergency department, and low inpatient occupancy rates may cause it to reduce the number of acute care beds (retrench) and convert them to long-term or rehabilitative care (both vertical integration and concentric diversification).

Strategic Alliances as a Strategy

SAs are prevalent strategic arrangements in health services. SAs "are loosely coupled arrangements between two or more organizations to achieve some long-term strategic purpose not possible by the organizations separately."[21] SAs arise from mutual need and a willingness among participating HSOs/HSs to share knowledge, risks, and costs; to leverage innovation; and to take advantage of complementary strengths and capabilities. Often, SAs are part of other strategies, such as vertical or horizontal integration.

Selecting Strategies

The range of strategies considered and selected is influenced by the context in which the choice is made. Several aspects of that context are relevant:

- Type of organization

- Strategic decision style

- Managerial philosophy

- Organizational culture and strategic managers' values

- Product and service analysis

- Organization life cycle

- Competitive position

Each of these elements is discussed in this section.

Type of Organization

Type of organization refers to self-image and how the HSO/HS adapts to its external environment, competitors, and customers. Miles and Snow developed the typology of prospector, analyzer, defender, and reactor,[22] which is applicable to HSOs/ HSs.

Prospectors occasionally redefine markets, routinely seek new target markets, seize the initiative, and capitalize on opportunities. They are proactive and tend to be innovative and at the forefront of new technologies. Analyzers are proactive but not as much as prospectors. Analyzers seek to maintain stability in areas of operation, although guided by prospectors they seek new opportunities. A defender maintains the status quo and stability and is not innovative. Defender HSOs/HSs protect their niche, specialized service, or product domain. Reactors are passive and usually stir to action only in a crisis or when external environmental forces cannot be ignored.

Strategic Decision Style

Strategic decision style describes the process by which strategic alternatives are formulated and evaluated and decisions are made. It can be systematic, entrepreneurial, or incremental.[23]

A systematic strategic decision style is proactive. It involves conducting a comprehensive external and internal analysis; understanding relationships of strengths and weaknesses, opportunities and threats, and considering strategic alternatives; and selecting an organizational strategy using rational criteria.

Entrepreneurial strategic decision style is decisions made on "gut" feelings, hunches, or intuition. In general, it does not include full, comprehensive strategic assessment, only selective review. It is a style in which strategic decisions are made quickly. In mature HSOs/HSs, entrepreneurial decision style is usually inappropriate. It may be appropriate, however, for emerging or even mature HSOs/HSs in a turbulent, fast-changing environment, especially if windows of opportunity close rapidly, thus requiring quick decision making.

Incremental strategic decision style is reactive and involves change at the margin. Sometimes it means simply muddling through.[24] Incremental decision styles are piecemeal approaches to strategy choice and do not include a comprehensive, systematic strategic assessment, or reviewing and evaluating a range of strategies.

Managerial Philosophy

Managerial philosophy in the context of choosing strategies is best described as a continuum that ranges from opportunity maximization to cost minimization. The former is proactive, prospector, systematic, or entrepreneurial. It implies that organizational strategies are chosen to take advantage of opportunities and capitalize on strengths.

Cost minimization as a philosophy implies conservatism. It may be seen in a defender but is certainly found in a reactor. It focuses on saving a dollar with no concern for opportunity costs. Organizations are never *only* at one end of the continuum but are closer to one end than the other. Similar descriptive terms are *aggressive–innovative* versus *lethargic–conservative* or *risk taking* versus *risk averse*. HSOs/HSs that are opportunity maximizers, aggressors–innovators, and risk takers usually consider and choose different strategies than those at the other end of the continuum.

Organizational Culture and Strategic Managers' Values

Organizational culture and the values of decision makers who formulate strategies are contextual variables that often affect selection of strategies. Culture is a continuum from harmonious to divisive, and the values of those formulating strategy can be consistent or inconsistent with it. Cultural disarray—perhaps caused by splintered factions, internal hostility, and lack of cohesion, mutual support, and shared beliefs—leads to divisiveness. Under such circumstances, it may be impossible to gain the commitment of participants to implement strategies and weather changes required by the strategy. Mismatching culture and strategy causes implementation problems. This restricts the range of realistic strategies.

HSOs/HSs with strong, cohesive cultures and whose values are shared by GB members and senior managers can prospect, be more opportunistic, and successfully implement a wider range of strategies than those with a divisive culture. Often, what an organization can accomplish is a function of its culture. A strategy is good only if the organization's culture supports it.[25]

Portfolio Analysis

Portfolio analysis is borrowed from marketing and describes and categorizes resource-producing or resource-consuming services and products. The usual metaphor is cows, hogs, and stars.[26] Cows are services or product lines that yield more than they consume, hogs consume more than they yield, and stars, if nurtured, will evolve from embryonic consumers of resources into cows.

Portfolio analysis of services or product lines in an HSO, for example, might determine that pharmacy and radiology are cows, obstetrics is a hog, and sports medicine is a star. Organizations with a preponderance of cows and stars are in a better position to prosper and have greater latitude in strategy formulation than those with a preponderance of hogs. As noted earlier, however, some units may have to suboptimize their financial performance to optimize performance of the whole organization. Portfolio analysis is important to strategy formulation because it allows strategic managers and GBs to recognize the cows, hogs, and stars in their organizations and how alternative strategies may change the ratio of these three categories.[27]

Another variable that affects the context of strategy formulation is strategic business unit analysis, or as applied in HSOs/HSs, strategic service unit (SSU) analysis. This type of segmentation is like portfolio analysis, except that SSUs are identifiable, largely autonomous organizational units with distinct services and product lines offered to distinct target markets. SSUs control their activities, are separate from other SSUs, compete with external groups for market share, and have their own revenues and costs. Each differentiated subsidiary in a vertically integrated HS is a separate SSU. For example, a vertically integrated HS with two hospitals, an HMO, and an NF could segment them into four SSUs. SSUs are important to the context of strategizing because a distinct and even different strategy may be chosen and implemented for each.

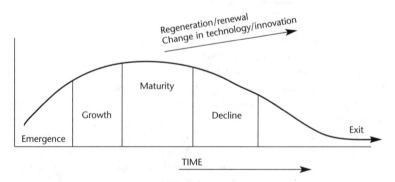

Figure 10.4.   Life cycle of an HSO/HS.

Organization Life Cycle

Organization life cycle refers to the stage of development of an organization. Conceptually, life cycle borrows from theories of aging in human beings and product life cycle in marketing. Organizations, including HSOs/HSs, go through stages of emergence, growth, maturity, decline, and perhaps regeneration, although time spans vary. Figure 10.4 shows the concept.

It is important to note that external or internal events (changing technology, competition) can change the slope of the life cycle curve, lengthen or shorten it, and enable the HSO/HS to regenerate from one stage (maturity) to another (growth) or accelerate from one stage (maturity) to another (decline). Where an HSO/HS is in its life cycle determines the strategic alternatives available and the best choices. In the growth stage, HSOs/HSs may choose aggressive, expansionary-type strategies, such as forward and horizontal integration and concentric diversification. They are likely to be prospectors and opportunity maximizers. Those in decline must retrench, minimize costs, and pursue niche strategies.

A variation on the organization life cycle concept is the service, product, or market life cycle. This concept applies the paradigm of biological development to marketing a product or service. As a biological organism has a cycle of birth to death, so do most services, products, and markets. The service, product, or market life cycle can be described as having at least five stages: birth (entry), growth, maturity, decline, and death. A sixth phase—rebirth or renewal—may be considered. Life cycles of services, products, or markets can be shown as curves plotted against time on the x-axis and growth (sales or revenues) on the y-axis. The market entry phase shows a slow growth in revenues, usually accompanied by a loss because of start-up costs. If the new service or product survives infancy, it enters a phase of rapid growth in revenue and profitability, though profitability will lag until fixed costs are covered by revenues. At maturity, the organization's life cycle curve peaks and flattens; growth stagnates. The life cycle curve then slants downward, reflecting declining sales and profits, heading toward death (market exit or product termination). More resources, product modification, and creative promotion may reverse decline, and the life cycle continues.

Competitive Position

Which strategies are to be considered is a function of an organization's competitive position. Barriers to market entry, threat of new entrants (competitors), availability of substitute products or services, and the HSO's/HS's strength as a seller or buyer describe competitive position. Competitive positioning analysis identifies an entity's position relative to competitors by assessing market share, client perceptions of products and services, and current marketing strategies, prices, and costs.[28] Competitive position can range from dominant to weak and should consider the organization's life cycle.

Strategy Choice

A critical activity in strategy formulation (see Figure 10.2) is choosing organizational strategies. The context variables influencing choice were examined earlier. Choosing among strategic alternatives is influenced by context variables. Choices can be measured against criteria too.

These criteria answer questions such as the following. Will the organizational strategy accomplish objectives? Will the strategy address risk, issues, deficiencies, and gaps? Will the strategy take advantage of opportunities in the environment and optimize strengths and comparative advantage? Will the strategy lessen threats and overcome weaknesses? In addition, attention must be given to the relationship between potential organizational strategies and internal functional areas. That is, considering strengths and weaknesses, is the strategy feasible? Does the organization have the financial resources, managerial systems and human resources, and productivity and conversion processes to implement the strategy successfully? If so, implementing is the next step in strategizing, as depicted in Figure 10.2.

Implementing Strategy

After organization-level strategies are selected, subsidiary organization strategies and operational plans are developed for the HSO/HS and its units. Figure 10.1 shows that subsidiary organization strategies, operational plans, and unit or department subobjectives are derived from strategies and must be consistent with them. It is necessary to allocate resources and design arrangements to support implementation. Challenges to implementing strategies can be significant, including weak strategy, lack of communication, lack of commitment, lack of resources, poor coordination, competing strategies, and uncontrollable environmental factors.[29] No matter how carefully crafted, strategies do not implement themselves.

Inherent in the situational analysis that provides background for selecting strategies is that HSOs/HSs must be capable of implementing the chosen strategy. Senior managers who designed for stability and centralized decision making will have difficulty implementing a corporate growth strategy of unrelated diversification, for example. Similarly, those experienced in implementing growth strategies will have difficulty with divestiture or retrenchment strategies.

Ideally, managers recognize the connection between strategy and implementation capability in the strategy formulation stage, and they factor it into strategy choices. Sometimes, however, they do not or cannot. Divestiture, retrenchment, and other degenerative strategies are often forced on HSOs/HSs by their environment. In such cases it does not matter that the GB and senior managers prefer growth strategies. Consider what strategies have been forced on HSOs/HSs by public policies initiated to slow cost increases in Medicare and Medicaid.

Mismatches between strategies and implementation capabilities cause problems that can be overcome in two ways. Either the strategy can be changed or capabilities to implement it can be changed. If the latter, resources can be redirected, staff can be given additional training and education, or new staff can be hired.

Even a good match between strategies and implementation capabilities requires that those responsible for strategic implementation establish appropriate organizational structures, assemble a workforce, and establish and maintain relationships among organizational units.

Strategic Control

Control is necessary as managers implement strategies. Chapter 14 discusses the management function of controlling. Control is discussed here as necessary to effect strategizing.

Strategic Control Systems

Once implemented, strategic initiatives must be monitored to detect discrepancies between desired and actual performance. Deviation will initiate corrective action. HSOs/HSs use several strategic control systems or devices: budgets, activity reports, exception reports, employee performance appraisal, and consumer or patient satisfaction surveys. Effective strategic control systems can accomplish the following tasks:

• Facilitate coordination in organizations and systems

• Direct effort toward achieving organizational objectives

• Provide early warning that assumptions and conditions about strategies are wrong or changed

• Provide a way for managers to take corrective action

Mechanisms of Strategic Control

If mission and objectives were part of strategy formulation and strategic implementation, strategic control monitors performance by comparing actual with desired results, and correcting deviations or adapting to new strategic realities.

Monitoring Performance

Managers monitor actual performance of their domains and compare it with desired performance. If objectives and standards are clear, monitoring outcomes and comparing them with standards are straightforward. To monitor effectively managers must observe more than operating results, although bottom-line outcomes are always important to judge the success or failure of strategies. One serious problem with using results is that they may be known too late for effective corrective action. In addition, results may not show why deviations occurred. To minimize such problems, effective managers design monitoring systems and techniques carefully.

Management information systems (MISs) can collect, format, store, and retrieve information to monitor strategic initiatives. To monitor and compare actual with desired performance and MIS should have the following characteristics:

- The MIS should match the information it covers to the strategies being managed. The closer the match between information and strategies, the more effectively the control stage in the strategic management process can be carried out.

- Information should identify exceptions at critical points. Effective strategic control requires attention to factors critical to organizational performance. Managers who concentrate on critical points will be more effective. Information in an MIS should be selected judiciously and be worth the cost.

- The information must be understood by those who use it. Some strategic control systems supported by an MIS—especially those based on mathematical formulas, complex statistical analyses, and computer simulations—have elements not always understood by users. Including such elements can be dysfunctional.

- The MIS should report deviations promptly. The ideal MIS for strategic control purposes detects deviations as they occur. Timely information about problems allows managers to take effective corrective action.

- The MIS should be predictive. Perfect control would report instantaneously, but there is usually a lag between deviations and corrective action. Nevertheless, a precursor to effective strategic control is detecting potential or actual deviations early enough to permit corrective action. Thus, managers prefer a forecast of what will likely happen next month, next quarter, or next year—even though there is a margin of error—to information accurate to several decimal points but about which nothing can be done.

- Finally, the MIS should suggest corrective action. A strategic control system that detects deviations from desired results will be only an interesting exercise if it does not include corrective action. Adequate systems disclose where failures are occurring, why they are occurring without blaming staff for process problems, and what corrective action to take.

Taking Corrective Action and Adapting to New Strategic Realities

Based on monitoring and comparisons with desired results, corrective action is taken to bring performance into line with performance objectives. This step is difficult for managers, even if they are guided by good information from control systems. It is often difficult to determine why strategies fail or why implementation falters because many underlying factors can be involved. The strategic management model in Figure 10.2 illustrates that tracing sources of deviation and deciding where to intervene go to each stage of the process where questions such as the following can be answered: Is the information produced in the situational analysis still accurate, complete, and relevant? Are the strategies still appropriate? Are the steps to implement strategies correct? And so on.

Knowing the causes of deviation, managers can take corrective action with hope for good results. Doing so makes managers change agents. They must adapt and adjust prior decisions and activities within the strategizing process. Strategic control and the adaptation and change it triggers brings the strategic management process full circle. The important steps in the process occur when managers determine the continuing relevance of strategies and adapt or change.

Among the most important activities GBs and managers have is to know when adaptations in strategies are needed and how to make them effectively. Adaptations are needed because of discrepancies between desired and actual states. In effect, managers must know when and how to be change agents. Strategic adaptation is defined as discernible, measurable modifications in form, quality, or state in HSO/HS mission, objectives, and strategies. Modifications are ubiquitous; adapting is a constant for managers.

Pressure to add or delete strategies or to adapt existing strategies to new realities comes from internal and external sources. Internally, new technology may offer an opportunity to diversify into new services. The dynamic external environment forces adaptation and change. Growing, declining, or aging populations in the service area or the plans and actions of competitors have significant implications for HSO/HS strategies and usually require adaptation in response. Public policy and regulation exert strong and direct external pressures for strategic adaptation.[30] Changes in Medicare and Medicaid reimbursement cause strategic adaptation in HSOs/HSs.[31]

Mechanisms of Strategic Adaptation

People resist change. Managers must deal with this fact of organizational life in making strategic adaptations. Success requires the use of an approach effective in the circumstances.[32] There are two types of approaches. One uses power—managers coerce or sanction, as needed, to force change. Force-coercion is top down; circumstances may necessitate its use. The need for a rapid response to significant environmental change, such as bankruptcy of a major insurance carrier, requires immediate adaptation. Here, managers inform those affected and explain why change is needed.

The second type of adaptation is participative and uses reason and persuasion. Usually, increasing participation produces better decisions, which lead to higher quality and improved performance. Participative adaptation is bottom-up and works if senior managers facilitate it. Bottom-up participation stimulates creativity and fosters commitment to changes among participants. HSOs/HSs tend to use high-involvement, bottom-up when adaptation involves small parts of the organization, such as one department, or if changes are modest and operational.

Successful implementation of strategic adaptation is never assured, but managers can act in ways to increase its likelihood. Most important is that those affected understand its necessity. Managers should provide information as early as possible, including details about the reasons for change, its nature and timing, and the expected effect. It may be beneficial if major change has a trial period. The familiarity gained and the assurance that it is revocable reduce insecurity and increase the likelihood of acceptance. Allowing time to understand change increases acceptability by those affected.

Managers must minimize disruption of the organization's culture, customs, and informal relationships. Culture and customs help new staff members adjust to the workplace and their roles in it. Informal relationships are a lifeblood of organizations and are interrupted at managers' peril. In minimizing resistance to strategic adaptation, managers must remember that people respond to change in predictable, often negative ways. The history of the work may cause them to react negatively. An HSO/HS with long-term stability will have more difficulty introducing strategic adaptation without resistance. Staff who are part of the status quo and believe it is permanent will see even minor change as disruptive. Conversely, when change is part of the culture, it is more readily accepted.

Being a change agent is never easy. It is most difficult when it involves major strategic adaptations or complex organizational changes. Successfully managing complex adaptation requires that managers have a substantive reason or justification for the change, the skills necessary to make the change, the incentives and resources to make adaptation possible, and a plan for making the change. Lacking any of these factors, adaptation may fail, or it will be more difficult and less successful.

Strategic Marketing

Marketing is a voluntary *exchange* of things of *value*. One party receives something of value (a product, service, or idea) from another party in exchange for something of value. This concept holds that such an exchange requires that sellers or providers create and make available services, products, or ideas, and that buyers or consumers locate and choose services, products, or ideas. Applying this basic concept, the American Marketing Association defines marketing as "the activity, set of institutions, and processes for creating, communicating, delivering, and exchanging offerings that have value for customers, clients, partners, and society at large."[33]

Applying the definition of marketing to healthcare, HSOs/HSs may plan, implement, and evaluate services to patients. For example, HSOs/HSs using a growth strategy, may plan, implement, and evaluate how they provide value to potential new patients, as well as others who may influence patients, such as referring physicians and health plans. Other important target markets for HSOs/HSs include potential employees and staff, donors, and volunteers. Marketing facilitates exchanges between an organization and its target markets, typically by identifying and quantifying the target markets to meet the organization's objectives.

Marketing has various elements. Common elements include the following:

- The perception and expression of an unfulfilled need or want

- An entity (supplier) willing and able to satisfy that need or want with a product or service

- Goods and services that can be valued or priced and made available for exchange now or in the future

- Channels (means or media) for communicating about the terms and conditions of the exchange

- A location, distribution network, or other mechanism to facilitate the transaction (including delivery of the product or service and the payment)

Any activity that includes these components is a marketing transaction regardless of the industry, organizational ownership, private or public sector, or for-profit or not-for-profit nature of the business, including healthcare.

The financial or commercial success of organizations is affected by commercial marketing. In addition, the ability of an HSO/HS to develop and implement clinical programs and activities in its markets may depend on its use of *marketing*. Both marketing and social marketing are useful in HSOs/HSs, although they differ and are distinguished in this chapter.

Social Marketing Defined

The American Marketing Association defines social marketing as "marketing designed to influence the behavior of a target audience in which the benefits of the behavior are intended by the marketer to accrue primarily to the audience or to the society in general and not to the marketer."[34] Social marketing is new thinking about old human endeavors. Since social systems first formed, attempts have been made to inform, persuade, influence, and motivate individuals and groups to gain their acceptance of certain ideas. Social marketing has become an important mechanism in these efforts.

In the United States, social marketing has been and is being used in energy conservation and recycling and in health issues, such as obesity, smoking, safety, drug abuse, drinking and driving, HIV and AIDS, nutrition, physical activity, immunization, breast cancer screening, mental health, and family planning.

What Marketing Is Not

To clarify what marketing is, it is instructive to distinguish between marketing and activities often regarded as equivalent to marketing. The prevailing paradigm states that marketing is not primarily or exclusively any of the following:

- Selling

- Advertising

- Promoting

- Generating revenue

A distinction is made between commercial marketing and *public relations*. Public relations is managing communications between the organization and its stakeholders using public media channels to create, improve, protect, or maintain the desired public image of the organization overall or a perception of an event or activity. Though related to and supportive of marketing, public relations *is not* marketing.

Health promotion is disseminating knowledge and expert judgment using media and other targeted communication channels to prevent disease, illness, and injury and to advocate improved health and wellness. It is like, and may be used in, social marketing. Arguably, public relations, health promotion, and health communications are subsumed within *health communications,* "the study and use of methods to inform and influence individual and community decisions that enhance health."[35] Certainly, the core idea of influencing health-related behavior is relevant to these concepts, directly or indirectly.

HSOs/HSs have engaged in marketing-like activities for decades.[36] Examples include the following:

- Using public relations to influence public perceptions of the organization's overall image and specific events

- Providing health education or health promotion messages to patients and community groups

- Distributing annual reports to key stakeholders and the wider community

- Investing in donor development and fund raising

- Developing new products and services to respond to community needs

- Recruiting and retaining physicians and key staff

- Implementing patient demographic origin studies and patient satisfaction surveys[37]

What Marketing Is

Marketing in HSOs/HSs has changed significantly in the recent past. It is no longer a separate, stand-alone activity to disseminate information about types of services and products and their quality or to gather information about patient or customer satisfaction. Informed people do not construe marketing as only advertising and selling, and they reject the notion that physicians and patients will use HSO/HS facilities only after a substantial promotional effort. Marketing is not the creation of demand for services; instead, marketing is customer focused. Market-oriented HSOs/HSs "are characterized by a concerted effort to collect, share, and respond to [customer] information."[38]

Now, marketing is seen as a designed process, integrated with other activities, in which the organization identifies and satisfies the needs and wants of stakeholders—especially patients or customers and staff, as well as the community—to accomplish its mission and objectives.

In the past, marketing was viewed as advertising and promotional activities of limited relevance to the core business of the HSO/HS. Marketing is essential to strategizing and contributes to achieving short-term financial, clinical, and other operational objectives.

Like most service industries in the 21st century, healthcare marketing is customer focused. For this characterization to be consistent with the current marketing paradigm, more emphasis must be given to developing long-term relationships with stakeholders, incorporating environmental analysis, proceeding through product or service design and delivery, and collecting outcome measures and stakeholder feedback. Rather than a one-time effort, marketing activities are revisited on a periodic if not continual basis to ensure that the HSO/HS evolves with stakeholder needs and wants.

Core Concepts in Marketing

Marketing mix is a core concept in marketing. It is a framework and the logic for marketing by defining essential components of a marketing initiative. These components are the 4 *P*s of marketing: product, place, price, and promotion.[39] Decisions about marketing mix and associated resource commitments define a marketing strategy. Figure 10.5 presents the components of marketing.

Product or Service

Numerous products and services are offered by HSOs/HSs to address real or perceived needs in their markets. For marketing management, this marketing component incorporates product and service development and its design and attributes. Marketing management includes direct healthcare, amenities of the healing environment or experience (aesthetics and comfort), interpersonal encounters with staff, and quality of support services (dietary, chaplaincy, and visiting hours). In the context of CQI, all aspects of the customer's experience with the organization are included in assessing product and service quality.

Relational marketing is customer participation in product development using focus groups, customer satisfaction surveys, customer complaints, and unsolicited feedback. Relational marketing answers the question, What products with which characteristics do we offer to whom?

Based on the managers' identified target markets and satisfaction of present customers,[40] and the extent of competition, managers can continue to ensure that suitable services and products are developed. Such information allows service mix (scope and intensity) and product lines to be expanded, reduced, realigned, or focused. Target markets can be large or small and

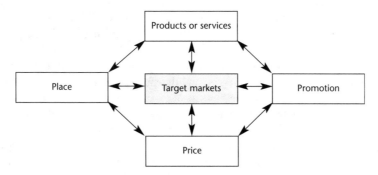

Figure 10.5.   Elements of marketing. (From Longest, Beaufort B., Jr. *Managing Health Programs and Projects*, 250. San Francisco: Jossey-Bass, 2004. Used with permission.)

may be defined geographically or according to other attributes. A general acute care hospital may have a target market (also called the service area) encompassing the community and its environs; a tertiary hospital target market may encompass a region.

Target markets may be classified by type of care (preventive, acute or short term, chronic or long term, rehabilitative), type of service (medical and surgical, obstetrics and gynecology, oncology), age group (gerontology, pediatrics), or type of payer (self-pay, managed care, Medicare, Medicaid). Assessment may reveal gaps in service mix or product line, as well as potential target markets, competitive and other marketplace opportunities, or threats, per SWOT.

Changes in target markets, competition, and technology, as well as customer needs, preferences, and attitudes, require HSOs/HSs to evaluate and realign their mix of services, products, and programs. Such realignment must be consistent with the organization's mission, capabilities, and strengths and may include expansion or elimination of services under conditions of downsizing. For example, a competitor establishing an urgent care center or forming an HMO in the HSO's service area may require reassessment of the target market, plans for how to reach that market, and changes in service. Decline in birth rate means reevaluating obstetrics with a possible aim of redirecting resources elsewhere. Technology may suggest a need to introduce new or expanded services. Identified opportunities may lead to a hospital offering wellness and employee assistance programs to corporations, pharmacy services to NFs, and home health to discharged patients.

Place

The place component of marketing refers to sites or loci to obtain products or services offered. It considers channels for distributing them to customers. Online selling has made "place" more complex. The nature of health services means that timely access, such as affordable transportation to the site, convenient hours of operation, and bilingual staff, are important, perhaps critical.

Establishing satellite ambulatory care and family practice centers and mobile screening units improves access to services and expands market area. Increasingly, family medicine and therapist practices offer evening and weekend hours to accommodate working adults and improve competitive position. This component of marketing mix answers the question, Where do we locate our facilities to ensure effective distribution and convenient access by our customers?

Price

Price refers to what customers pay for products or services. Beyond this, pricing is complex because it must be based on costs of production and delivery, prices for equivalent and substitute products or services in the market, elasticity of demand, number and concentration of competitors, and service or product life cycle. Price for the customer includes nonfinancial costs, such as travel and wait times.[41] In competitive markets, HSOs/HSs must respond to the price sensitivity of large, self-insured employers and insurers that bundle and price services nontraditionally and negotiate effectively.

To the extent that the customer is responsible for payment, it is a barrier to access. When costs are paid by a third party, customers are indifferent to price. Beyond out-of-pocket costs, pricing decisions should reflect intangibles, such as patient anxiety, inconvenience, and opportunity cost of time to obtain treatment. These considerations influence the customer's decisions. In addition, the reputation of HSOs/HSs affects purchase or exchange decisions.

Shifting costs to customers with higher deductibles, copayments for third-party coverage, and medical savings accounts has made customers more price conscious. The fundamental question in pricing is, What should we charge customers, relative to our costs and competitive position in the market?

Promotion

Promotion relies on advertising, defined as "any paid form of non-personal presentation and promotion of ideas, goods or services by an identifiable sponsor that is transmitted via mass media."[42] Promotion includes publicity and personal sales.[43] Customer awareness is especially important and challenging in health services marketing. Customers must know which services (type, scope, quality) are offered, where and when, and at what cost. Such information is provided by promotion. Organizations can project an image analogous to brand identification for products.

Advertising may be broad or may focus on a market segment. Promotion includes incentives to encourage trial use, purchase, and acceptance of the product or service, including point-of-sale samples, discount coupons, rebates, and so on. Promotion should not be viewed as synonymous with marketing (especially not in health services), effective advertising and promotion are critical for a marketing strategy to succeed.

Most criticism of healthcare marketing has been directed at promotion, especially advertising, which some argue generates unnecessary demand for services. This argument is weak, however, given the psychology associated with healthcare decision making. For example, few would choose a colonoscopy unless it were deemed necessary for good health. Furthermore, such criticism is inconsistent with the marketing concept if promotion is properly regarded as the beneficial and necessary dissemination of information about healthcare options, risks, pricing, and access so consumers can make informed purchase decisions.[44] Ethical issues in marketing are considered in Chapter 2.

Examples of Marketing Strategies

Useful typologies of marketing strategies were developed by Miles and Snow[45] and Porter.[46] They are discussed following here, as are other well-known strategies.

Miles and Snow Typology

In the late 20th century, Raymond E. Miles (American [1932–]) and Charles C. Snow (American [1945–]) developed a typology of marketing strategies with continuing relevance.[47] "Specifically, they identified four strategic patterns that differ from one another by the degree to which an organization's leaders are willing to assume risk or take aggressive action in the pursuit of competitive advantage."[48] The Miles and Snow typology is useful to classify or categorize HSOs/HSs into one of four patterns of marketing strategies.

1. *Prospectors:* aggressively search for new market opportunities and often engage in experimentation and innovation

2. *Analyzers:* maintain stability in selected areas of operation but seek new opportunities in other areas (often following the lead of prospector HSOs/HSs)

3. *Defenders:* rely on previously successful strategies and rarely change or even make small adjustments to strategies

4. *Reactors:* slow to perceive threats and opportunities from their external environment and cannot adapt on a consistent and effective basis

Research using Miles and Snow's typology suggests that whether HSOs/HSs fit one (or more) of the categories may be a function of type—acute care hospital, NF, or hospice. In addition, placement in the typology may be linked to forces external to decision making, such as availability of funding for innovation, supply and skills of the healthcare workforce, and demand for healthcare services. Notably, various of an organization's activities may meet criteria for one or several of Miles and Snow's categories: prospecting with one initiative, analyzing with others, and defending or reacting with units elsewhere in the organization.

HSOs/HSs may be able to alter their Miles and Snow classification(s). It is unlikely, however, that defenders or reactors can become prospectors quickly. More likely, the organization will undertake other marketing strategies, a concept known as a strategic comfort zone. Future marketing strategy choices carry the burden of past decisions.

Porter's Competitive Strategies

Another typology of strategic marketing alternatives was developed by Michael Porter (American [1947–]). Positioning strategies relate an HSO/HS to its competitors. Porter's classic analysis of such strategies labels positioning strategies as competitive. He identified three categories of competitive strategies: low-cost leadership strategy, differentiation strategy, and focus strategy.[49]

Low-Cost Leadership

The HSO/HS that pursues a low-cost leadership strategy seeks to reach a broad market of buyers with services or products perceived to be of comparable value (benefit minus cost) to those of competitors but at lower prices. To sustain this strategy, the organization must reduce costs (or shift them elsewhere) while maintaining or improving benefit. This strategy is achieved by economies of scale—producing services or products at higher volume to lower cost. As discussed in Chapter 8, CQI, reengineering, and strategic quality planning—in which quality improvement is central to the strategizing process—lead to increased quality, productivity improvement (i.e., cost effectiveness relative to quality), and improved competitive position. Notably, even if consumers are less sensitive to pricing strategies because they are buffered from costs of services, payers or insurers respond to price differentials. Furthermore, focus on cost increases gross margins, independent of short-term competitive effects.

Product Differentiation

Product differentiation is a strategy in which the HSO/HS distinguishes its products and services from those of competitors on attributes (other than price) important to the customer. In healthcare, examples of product differentiation are providing amenities (e.g., private rooms in acute care and birthing suites), emphasizing state-of-the-art technology (e.g., electronic health records and green facilities), emphasizing prevention and well-being (e.g., offering "silver sneakers" fitness classes), or increasing visibility of the HSO's image (e.g., signs announcing the HSO's national rankings for quality). Promotion is necessary for differentiation to have a competitive effect.

Focused (Niche)

A focused strategy identifies a market segment or niche, to which the HSO directs its marketing effort to attract a customer base. In niche markets, the customer base is smaller, and competitors are fewer. Once established in a niche market, a successful competitor likely has brand loyalty and price-inelastic demand. Given the uniqueness of niche market segments, focused strategies often entail product differentiation and may be compatible with low-cost leadership.[50] Health services examples include cosmetic surgery and corrective eye surgery for more affluent customers and complementary and alternative medicine like acupuncture and Chinese herbal medicine.

Porter's marketing strategies are not mutually exclusive; they may be complementary and used in combination or sequentially. A low-cost strategy may yield different sets of product or service offerings and is attractive in a segmented market. A medical center may use multiple strategies for market segments: bariatric surgery for a more affluent niche, a low-cost strategy for community hospital services and outreach in an economically distressed community, and a range of tertiary clinical services differentiated by world-class quality.

Other Prototypical Marketing Strategies

Marketing strategies must be consistent with the HSO's/HS's mission and vision, core values, strategic direction, objectives, and access to resources. In addition to the marketing strategies already discussed, the following are categories of market *growth* and *contraction*. They are important because an HSO/HS will adopt them in its life cycle.

Growth Strategies

Growth or expansionary strategies include market entry, expansion, and adaptation. Growth of staff, assets, facilities, revenues, and profits is a common indicator of success; anything other than a growth strategy requires justification.

Expansionary strategies include market penetration, market or product development, and diversification.[51] Market penetration means increasing revenues and market share of current products and services in established markets. In a market in which the demand for services is flat or declining, market penetration by one HSO is a zero-sum game; growth in market share for one means less business for another. Assertive advertising, expanding access to services, and negotiated pricing support this strategy. Market development (entry) requires introducing the current product line and services into new markets or to additional segments of an existing market. This may be achieved by geographic expansion, such as establishing a satellite clinic for an academic health center in a rapidly growing suburban community or by attracting new market segments. An example of the latter is an NF opening a wellness center for active, independent-living older adults. Product development is the design and introduction of new or improved products and services in existing markets. Adding a managed care plan to an academic health center is an example of product development closely related to its core business.

Contraction Strategies

Contraction strategies show a declining position in a target market or changes in the perceived attractiveness of a market. Contraction includes divestment, harvesting (or starving), and exit. In divestment, the organization sells assets or otherwise eliminates a product, product line, or service that is underperforming or is no longer a good strategic fit with the core business. This may be necessary to increase liquidity and decrease debt if the HSO/HS has fiscal problems. *Harvesting* is a strategy of milking a product or service for its cash flow but starving it of resources beyond the short term. It might be a precursor to a market exit strategy. Market exit or retrenchment is an organization leaving a market. Such a move may seem wise for strategic reasons. If there is some demand for the services being withdrawn, however, exit costs must include adverse impact on the community and image of the organization. Closing facilities and programs is associated with reorganization, merger, and consolidation and is justified on grounds of optimal resource use.

Strategic Issues Management

This discussion has focused on strategizing to create a more favorable fit of the HSO/HS with its external environment and expands on Figure 10.2. Traditionally, emphasis has been on changing or adapting the organization to meet opportunities and threats from the external environment to improve its competitive position. Strategic issues management (SIM) is a logical extension of strategizing. It is a systematic process that focuses on influencing the external environment to make it more favorable to the organization.[52] That is, SIM involves proactively influencing and affecting strategic issues rather than only reacting and adapting to them. Public policy and its impact on HSOs/HSs provide a good example of strategic issues.

Longest defined policy competency as having the capability to both *analyze and influence* the public policy–making process.[53] Managers must proactively influence public policy affecting their organizations. Otherwise, they are not meeting their responsibilities to defend and further its interests. For HSOs/HSs, survival may depend as much on an ability to anticipate and influence public policy as competitive issues that arise in the marketplace.[54]

The management model in the Part III Introduction shows HSOs/HSs interfacing with the healthcare and general environments. In both, public policy is significant because managers must respond reactively (adapt) when regulations or laws are imposed, or proactively (influence) to help frame the debate about issues and have a part in shaping outcomes. With the latter response, managers seek to affect the external environment so it is favorable or less unfavorable to their entities. Trade associations such as the American Hospital Association, LeadingAge, and America's Health Insurance Plans are effective allies in these efforts.

Discussion Questions

1. Define *planning*.

2. Define *strategizing*.

3. How does systems theory relate to strategizing?

4. All planning, whether strategic or operational, has three distinct attributes. Briefly describe each.

5. Figure 10.2 illustrates the strategizing process and its components. Briefly describe the components.

6. Compare adaptive, market entry, and positioning strategies in HSOs/HSs.

7. Discuss the influence of the context in which strategies are chosen.

8. Discuss the internal and external environmental analysis components identified in Figure 10.2.

9. Discuss strategic control.

10. Resistance is often the human response to strategic changes. What can managers do to minimize resistance?

11. Discuss the differences between marketing and social marketing.

Case Study 1   No Time for Strategizing

Downstate Medical Center is a 400-bed teaching hospital with a GB composed of business and community leaders. Downstate is considered by most in the region it serves to be the key hospital. The GB is devoted to the hospital and meets quarterly. Its executive committee meets monthly and follows financial, quality, and other operational activities at the hospital closely in exercising its oversight duties. The executive committee and the entire board scrutinize the key aspects of the hospital's operation closely and regularly.

It is the custom of Clare Lipton, who chairs the Downstate GB, and Nathan Robertson, president and CEO of the hospital, to have lunch in the hospital's board room weekly. Recently, the conversation has focused on how to get the board more engaged in strategizing.

Lipton made the point that she thinks the board is happy about how things are at the hospital, and about Robertson's performance, but added, "We are sailing along nicely, but we don't know what the future holds for the hospital and where it fits into that future."

Questions

1. What are the appropriate roles of the CEO and the GB in strategizing the future of Downstate Medical Center?

2. If things are going well at Downstate, why should its leaders give more attention to strategizing?

3. What do you recommend to Robertson and to Lipton to begin strategizing for Downstate?

Case Study 2   A Response to Change

As business office manager of Group HMO, Inc., Dana Smith was responsible for the work of approximately 45 employees, of whom 26 were classified as secretarial or clerical. At the direction of the HMO president, a team of outside systems analysis consultants was contracted to make a time study and work method analysis of Smith's area to improve the efficiency and output of the business office.

The consultants began by observing and recording each detail of the work of the secretarial and clerical staff. After 2 days of preliminary observation, the consultants indicated that they were prepared to begin their time study on the next day.

The next morning, five of the business office employees participating in the study were absent. On the following day, 10 employees were absent. Concerned, Smith sought to find reasons for the absenteeism by calling her absent employees. Each related basically the same story. Each was nervous, tense, and physically tired after being a "guinea pig" during the 2 days of preliminary observation. One told Smith that his physician had advised him to ask for a leave of absence if working conditions were not improved.

Shortly after the telephone calls, the head of the study team told Smith that if there were as many absences on the next day, his team would have to delay the study. He stated that a scientific analysis would be impossible with 10 employees absent. Realizing that she would be held responsible for the failure of the study, Smith was very concerned.

Questions

1. What caused the reactions to the study?

2. Could these reactions have been predicted? How?

3. What steps should Smith take to get the study back on track?

Case Study 3   HSO Strategic Assessment

Assume that you are the CEO of an HSO such as a hospital, NF, or HMO. It may be an HSO in your present locale or elsewhere, although you must know some details about it. Use the strategic management model in Figure 10.2 as a guide to determine how you would conduct a strategic assessment, including external environmental analysis and internal environmental analysis.

Questions

1. Compile a list of situational analysis considerations (e.g., factors, items) relevant to the HSO selected.

2. Identify and describe past and present organizational strategies the HSO has implemented or is implementing.

3. Discuss the context in which the HSO made strategic choices. Use the list of aspects of context discussed in this chapter in your response.

Notes

1. Ginter, Peter M., W. Jack Duncan, and Linda E. Swayne. *Strategic Management of Health Care Organizations,* 8th ed., 6. Hoboken: John Wiley & Sons, 2018.

2. Morgan, Gareth. *Images of Organization,* 39. Thousand Oaks, CA: Sage Publications, 2006.

3. Centers for Medicare & Medicaid Services. Accountable Care Organizations. *https://www.cms.gov/ Medicare/Medicare-Fee-for-Service-Payment/ACO/index.htm,* retrieved October 20, 2019.

4. Zuckerman, Alan M. *Healthcare Strategic Planning: Approaches for the 21st Century.* Chicago: Health Administration Press, 1998.

5. Walston, S. L. Strategic Healthcare Management: Planning and Execution, 2nd edition. Chicago: Health Administration Press, 2018.

6. University of Pittsburgh Medical Center. "Our Mission, Vision, and Core Values." *https://www. upmc.com/about/why-upmc/mission,* retrieved September 9, 2019; Florida Department of Health: Miami-Dade County. *2017 Annual Report.* "Vision, Mission, and Core Values." *http://miamidade. floridahealth.gov/about-us/_documents/2017-Annual-Report.pdf,* retrieved October 20, 2019.

7. For an extensive treatment of stakeholder analysis, see Blair, John D., and Myron D. Fottler. *Challenges in Healthcare Management: Strategic Perspectives for Managing Key Stakeholders.* San Francisco: Jossey-Bass, 1990.

8. Dunn, Rose T. *Dunn & Haimann's Healthcare Management,* 10th ed. Chicago: Health Administration Press, 2015.

9. Robbins, Stephen P., David A. DeCenzo, and Mary Coulter. *Fundamentals of Management,* 10th ed. New York: Pearson, 2017.

10. Fallon, L. Fleming, Jr., James W. Begun, and William Riley. *Managing Health Organizations for Quality and Performance,* Chapter 3. Burlington, MA: Jones & Bartlett Learning, 2013; Begun, James, and Kathleen B. Heatwole. "Strategic Cycling: Shaking Complacency in Healthcare Strategic Planning." *Journal of Healthcare Management* 44 (September/October 1999): 339–351.

11. Whyte, E. Gordon, and John D. Blair, "Strategic Planning for Healthcare Providers." In *Healthcare Administration: Principles, Practices, Structure, and Delivery,* 2nd ed., edited by Lawrence F. Wolper, 289-326. Gaithersburg, MD: Aspen Publishers, 1995, adaption reprinted by permission; Manning, Berton. *AcqNotes: Defense Acquisitions Made Easy.* "Functional Area Analysis." *http://acqnotes.com/ acqnote/acquisitions/functional-area-analysis,* retrieved October 20, 2019.

12. The first four steps are adapted from Ginter, Duncan, and Swayne, *Strategic Management of Health Care Organizations.* The fifth step is adapted from Longest, Beaufort B., Jr. *Managing Health Programs and Projects.* San Francisco: Jossey-Bass, 2004.

13. These steps are also discussed in Longest, *Managing Health Programs and Projects,* 42–47; and Longest, Beaufort B., Jr. *Seeking Strategic Advantage through Health Policy Analysis,* 55–82. Chicago: Health Administration Press, 1997.

14. Society of Human Resources Management. *HR Questions and Answers.* "What Are the Basics of Environmental Scanning as Part of the Strategic Planning Process?" *https://www.shrm.org/resourcesandtools/ tools-and-samples/hr-qa/pages/basics-of-environmental-scanning.aspx,* retrieved October 21, 2019.

15. Ginter, Duncan, and Swayne. *Strategic Management of Healthcare Organizations,* 58–63.

16. Adapted from Whyte, E. Gordon, and John D. Blair. "Strategic Planning for Healthcare Providers." In *Healthcare Administration: Principles, Practices, Structure, and Delivery,* 2nd ed., edited by Lawrence F. Wolper, 295. Gaithersburg, MD: Aspen Publishers, 1995; reprinted with permission; Harrison, Jeffrey P. *Essentials of Strategic Planning in Healthcare.* Chicago: Health Administration Press, 2010; Harris, John, ed. *Healthcare Strategic Planning,* 4th ed. Chicago: Health Administration Press, 2018.

17. Chermack, Thomas J. *Foundations of Scenario Planning: The Story of Pierre Wack.* New York: Routledge, 2017. Chermack, Thomas J. *Scenario Planning in Organizations: How to Create, Use, and Assess Scenarios.* San Francisco: Berrett-Koehler Publishers, 2011; Luke, Roice D., Stephen L. Walston, and Patrick M. Plummer. *Healthcare Strategy: In Pursuit of Competitive Advantage,* 54–57. Chicago: Health Administration Press, 2004.

18. Ginter, Duncan, and Swayne. *Strategic Management of Healthcare Organizations,* Chapter 6.

19. Ginter, Duncan, and Swayne. *Strategic Management of Healthcare Organizations,* Chapter 6.

20. HCA. HCA Healthcare At a Glance. "Who We Are." *https://hcahealthcare.com/about/hca-at-a-glance.dot,* retrieved October 21, 2019.

21. Ginter, Duncan, and Swayne. *Strategic Management of Health Care Organizations,* 234.

22. Miles, Raymond E., and Charles C. Snow. *Organizational Strategy, Structure and Process.* New York: McGraw-Hill, 1978; reissued in 2003 by Stanford University Press.

23. Hunger, J. David, and Thomas L. Wheelen. *Essentials of Strategic Management,* 5th ed. Upper Saddle River, NJ: Prentice Hall, 2011.

24. Whyte and Blair. "Strategic Planning for Healthcare Providers," 293.

25. Digman, Lester A. *Strategic Management: Concepts, Decisions, Cases,* 4th ed. Houston, TX: Dame Publications, 1997; Rose, Aanya. *AZCentral.* "The Impact of Organizational Culture on Strategy Implementation." *https://yourbusiness.azcentral.com/impact-organizational-culture-strategy-implementation-17367.html,* retrieved October 21, 2019.

26. Hunger and Wheelen. *Essentials of Strategic Management.*

27. Rutsohn, Phil, and Nabil A. Ibrahim. "Strategically Positioning Tomorrow's Hospital Today: Current Indications for Strategic Marketing." *Journal of Hospital Marketing* 9 (1995): 13–23.

28. Fleisher, Craig S., and Babette E. Bensoussan. *Business and Competitive Analysis: Effective Application of New and Classic Methods,* 2nd ed. Upper Saddle River, NJ: Pearson Education, 2015.

29. Aaltonen, Petri, and Heini Ikavalko. *Implementing Strategies Successfully. https://www.research-gate.net/profile/Heini_Ikaevalko/publication/235284285_Implementing_strategies_successfully/links/5a019cbca6fdcc232e2c6602/Implementing-strategies-successfully.pdf,* retrieved January 12, 2020.

30. Longest, Beaufort B., Jr. *Health Policymaking in the United States,* 5th ed. Chicago: Health Administration Press, 2010.

31. Longest. *Seeking Strategic Advantage through Health Policy Analysis.*

32. Bevan, Richard. *Changemaking: Tactics and Resources for Managing Organizational Change.* Seattle: ChangeStart Press, 2011.

33. American Marketing Association. *Dictionary. http://www.marketingpower.com/_layouts/Dictionary.aspx?dLetter=M,* retrieved January 23, 2013.

34. American Marketing Association. *Dictionary. http://www.marketingpower.com/_layouts/Dictionary.aspx?dLetter=S,* retrieved January 23, 2013.

35. Freimuch, Vickie, Galen Cole, and Susan D. Kirby. "Issues in Evaluating Mass Mediated Health Communication Campaigns." In *Evaluation in Health Promotion: Principles and Perspectives,* edited by Irving Rootman, Michael Goodstadt, Brian Hyndman, David V. McQueen, Louise Potvin, Jane Springet, and Erio Ziglio. Geneva, Switzerland: WHO Regional Publications, 2001. European Series, 92, 475-492.

36. MacStravic, Robin E. "The End of Healthcare Marketing." *Health Marketing Quarterly* 7 (1990): 3.

37. Sturm, Arthur C., Jr. *The New Rules of Marketing: Strategies for Success,* 23. Chicago: Health Administration Press, 1998.

38. Proenca, E. Jose. "Market Orientation and Organizational Culture in Hospitals." *Journal of Hospital Marketing* 11 (1996): 3–18, 6.

39. Keller and Kotler. *Framework for Marketing Management.*

40. Rickert, James. "Measuring Patient Satisfaction: A Bridge between Patient and Physician Perceptions of Care." *Health Affairs Blog. https://www.healthaffairs.org/do/10.1377/hblog20140509.038951/full/,* retrieved October 21, 2019.

41. Berkowitz. *Essentials of Health Care Marketing,* 3rd ed. Sudbury, MA: Jones and Bartlett Learning, 2011.

42. Thomas, Richard K. *Marketing Health Services,* 83. Chicago: Health Administration Press, 2005.

43. Berkowitz. *Essentials of Health Care Marketing.*

44. Kotler, P., Joel Shalowitz, and Robert J. Stevens. *Strategic Marketing for Health Care Organizations: Building a Customer-Driven Health System.* San Francisco: Jossey-Bass, 2008.

45. Miles and Snow. *Organizational Strategy, Structure and Process.*

46. Porter, Michael E. *Competitive Strategy: Techniques for Analyzing Industries and Competitors.* New York: The Free Press, 1980.

47. Miles and Snow. *Organizational Strategy, Structure and Process.*

48. Luke, Walston, and Plummer. *Healthcare Strategy,* 139.

49. Porter, *Competitive Strategy,* 35.

50. McIlwain, Thomas F., and Melody J. McCracken. "Essential Dimensions of a Marketing Strategy in the Hospital Industry." *Journal of Hospital Marketing* 11 (1997): 42; Healthcare Marketing Consultants. *Healthcare Marketing.* "Creating Niche Patient Groups for Precision Target Marketing." *https://healthcaremc.com/creating-niche-patient-groups-for-precision-target-marketing/,* retrieved October 21, 2019.

51. Berkowitz, *Essentials of Healthcare Marketing,* 56–58.

52. Heath, Robert L., and Michael James Palenchar. *Strategic Issues Management: Organizations and Public Policy,* 2nd ed. Thousand Oaks, CA: Sage Publications, 2009; Reeves, Phillip N. "Issues Management: The Other Side of Strategic Planning." *Hospital & Health Services Administration* 38 (Summer 1993): 229–241.

53. Longest, *Health Policymaking in the United States,* 26.

54. Bigelow, Barbara, Margarete Arndt, and Melissa Middleton Stone. "Corporate Political Strategy: Incorporating the Management of Public Policy Issues into Hospital Strategy." *Healthcare Management Review* 22 (Summer 1997): 53–63.

11

Organizing

Managers design and redesign their organizations. Designing or organization design is "the arrangement of responsibility, authority, and flow of information within an organization."[1] The result of designing is the organization structure. Success is much more likely if the organization is designed well. Effective organizing facilitates cooperation and coordination. The complexity of work in health services organizations and health systems (HSOs/HSs) and the wide variety of professional, technical, and support staff require a high degree of cooperation and coordination, a need more prevalent than in almost any other type of organization. Even in units such as imaging or finance, the range of work intersects many skills levels; effective organizing is vital to success.

Designing the Organization

Figure 11.1 shows the relationships among the various aggregations of work that comprise an HSO. Managers at all levels participate in organizational design. Senior managers are concerned with broad aspects of organizing such as authority-accountability relationships, establishing departments and subunits, and developing and maintaining interorganizational relationships (IORs). They must be sure the entity is structured to achieve its mission. Middle managers focus on organizing clusters of workgroups into units with similar activities; nursing is an example. First-level managers organize individual positions into workgroups. This includes job design, process flow, and work methods and procedures. Effective design requires attention to all levels of the organization.

The organizing function is ubiquitous and continuous. Initial design is followed by redesign, as needed. Some events make redesign more likely. For example, problems found during an accreditation site visit may be corrected by redesign. Events in the external environment may stimulate urgent redesign. Reduced reimbursement may cause redesign of individual

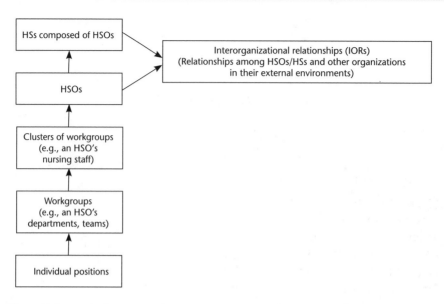

Figure 11.1.   Levels of organization design in HSOs/HSs, including interorganizational relationships (IORs).

positions, groups, departments, or the entire HSO. Developing and implementing a new program, or ending or modifying an existing program, product, or service, requires redesign. A change of senior managers commonly means redesign of the HSO or HS.[2]

Culture and Values

An organization's culture is the shared values that are the context for its work.[3] Cultures can be positive or negative in terms of their effects on patient safety and care. There is no guarantee a culture will be positive and incorporate ethical principles, such as respect for persons, beneficence toward patients, and justice in healthcare delivery. Management must infuse and enhance the values that put patients first. These positive values should be held by staff and guide their behavior and decisions. Positive cultures should be found in both the formal and informal organization. Sometimes, the informal organization is more important. Peer pressure and staff cooperation are key to establishing and maintaining a positive, patient-centered culture. The value system reflects and is reflected by the organization's culture. It is the work context for the staff who bring the organization to life by their interactions with patients, and with one another.

Chapter 10 describes how the planning function produces the HSO's/HS's vision and mission. Vision statements are aspirational—what the organization hopes to achieve. The mission statement is the specific purpose for its existence—its *raison d'être*. By defining values prospectively, the organization clarifies what it stands for and minimizes conflicts with values that diminish its effort. An explicit values system aids in recruiting staff and facilitates socialization of new employees to its modus operandi. These values are the organization's culture. As they are expressed in word and deed, the culture is reinforced. If the values are aspirational, they will move the culture to a higher, more desirable plane.

The sequence of values–vision–mission is the theoretical ideal. More likely, mission is determined first, or it evolves in the context of an implicit, rather than explicit, values system. Use of "visioning" began in the 1980s and continues. It is the rare HSO/HS that has no framed copy of its values, vision, and mission hanging in the lobby.

Mission (and vision) result from location, size, resources, and other aspects of internal and external environments. These elements can be affected over time. Significant change requires reconsidering the mission, which resulted from the values and principles identified by the governing body (GB) and management. That a GB stated the HSO's/HS's value system is no indication that staff comprehend it or agree with it. Likely, staff pay limited attention to such matters. Staff may be unaware or unconcerned about the organization's value system, despite management's best efforts to communicate it. Even were the values known, staff may not be committed to them. Consider how much more effective an organization could be if it were built on a system of shared values and goals. Accepted by staff, a resource-supported goal as simple as "get the caring back into curing" would reap rewards for the organization by improved efficiency, patient-centered care, and improved staff relations. Moving the organization in a direction known in advance and recognized as key will positively affect staff attitude, productivity, and effectiveness.

Theoretical Background

As discussed in Chapter 10, the HSO's/HS's mission is determined by applying the management function of planning. Mission is the organization's reason for being. Managers use the results of planning to design an organization to achieve the mission by establishing patterns of relationships among people and other resources. The result is the organization design. This is the organizing function of management.

Among the most influential classical theorists were a sociologist, Max Weber (German [1864–1920]) and an industrialist, Henri Fayol (French [1841–1925]). The work of Weber[4] and Fayol[5] and their colleagues and contemporary management theorists Luther Gulick (American [1892–1993]), Lyndall Urwick (British [1891–1981]),[6] James Mooney (American [1884–1957]), Alan Reiley (American [1869–1947]),[7] Fritz Roethlisberger (American [1898–1974]), and William Dickson (American [1904–1973])[8] aid contemporary organization design, which makes their work relevant to contemporary HSOs/HSs.

In his treatise on bureaucracy, Weber suggested that organizations must be structured so idiosyncrasies of individuals do not prevent them from accomplishing their work.[9] A bureaucracy does this by assigning each person a place and set of tasks. Figure 11.2 shows a bureaucracy: HSOs are bureaucracies. The relationships of the rectangles in the pyramid suggest that authority and accountability are delegated downward. Figure 11.3 shows an HS bureaucratic structure. Authority relationships among positions (and persons) in bureaucracies are called scalar relationships. They link positions vertically.

Fayol identified five functions as intrinsic to management: planning, organizing, staffing, directing, and controlling. These five organize Part III of this text. In addition, Fayol propounded 14 principles of management, including those discussed below: division of work; authority, responsibility, and accountability; unity of command; degree of centralization; scalar chain; and order.[10]

Division of work is specialization of tasks and the expertise to complete them. Specialization promotes efficiency and increases productivity. The principle of specialization is applicable to managers *and* staff. HSOs are specialized and complex, and various means are used to coordinate and communicate.

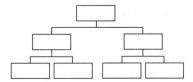

Figure 11.2.   Typical bureaucratic pyramid.

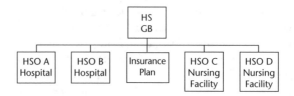

Figure 11.3. Pyramidal organizational structure of HS.

Authority, responsibility, and *accountability* are key concepts in management. Authority is the power to direct others or to cause action to be taken. Responsibility identifies task(s) someone is to perform—something someone is assigned to do. "You are responsible to see that coffee is available each morning." Accountability is being answerable for performing the thing for which someone (or you) is responsible. "Please tell me why coffee wasn't available this morning." Using responsibility and accountability as synonyms is erroneous. Failing to distinguish them causes confusion.

Unity of command had its origins as a principle of military organizing. Fayol defined it as receiving orders from only one supervisor; the staff member is accountable to only one person. Being assigned tasks by more than one manager is confusing; conflicts are likely. Common sense dictates that efficiency is enhanced if a staff member reports in a line of authority to one supervisor.

Degree of centralization is the locus of authority. An organization is "centralized" if authority is kept at the top. That means few, if any, decisions are made lower in the bureaucracy. An organization is decentralized when authority is pushed to lower levels. Commonly, some types of authority are centralized; buying capital (costly) equipment is an example. Some types of authority are decentralized. For example, department heads have authority to hire, retain, and evaluate staff. Similarly, it is common that departments have authority to purchase equipment costing less than a certain amount.

Scalar chain was described by Fayol as relationships in the hierarchy of a bureaucracy. The scalar chain follows a path between an organization's highest and lowest levels. All staff can trace their connection through the bureaucracy to the chief executive officer (CEO). Organization charts of HSOs/HSs show how staff and levels are connected by the scalar chain, which may be called chain of command, a term common in the military.

Order means staff members have a right to resources in amounts sufficient to do their jobs. Management is accountable to provide a safe, clean, and tidy workplace. Required, too, is that the workplace social order allows staff to work effectively. Social order means everyone is respectful, there is no harassment, and all conduct is professional.

The theories of Frederick Winslow Taylor (American [1856–1915]) help in designing and organizing. Taylor studied types of manual labor and developed methods to make them more efficient. His book, *Principles of Scientific Management,* described a type of industrial engineering whose goal was to perform work efficiently. He sought best practices (benchmarking); divided tasks into their components (process redesign); and eliminated those that added no value. He argued that all tasks can be subdivided and performed by unskilled staff. This view put him at odds with craft unions, which asserted that only skilled craftsmen should perform all the steps to make a shoe, for example. Contemporary management theorist, W. Edwards Deming (see Chapter 4), credited Taylor with developing the principles on which his work was based. Taylor emphasized worker input and teamwork less than modern theorists. Regardless, he held workers' interests as high as their employers.[11]

Design

Figure 11.1 shows one sequence of decisions to design an organization. It begins by establishing individual positions determined by how work will be divided. Design proceeds from individual positions to clustering them into workgroups such as units and departments, which are formed into divisions that become the organization. Then, HSOs may be grouped into strategic alliances (SAs) or HSs.

Organizing means assigning authority, which may require several rounds of conceptualizing and clustering. Authority is the power derived from position in the organization. The source of authority is one's superior—the person to whom one reports or is accountable. Accountability is the obligation to perform work for which one is responsible that furthers the organization's mission, whether the work is direct, support, or managerial. Staff members have responsibilities because of their work in the organization. By delegating authority and requiring accountability for performance from subordinates for the work they perform (responsibilities), there is created a relationship based on reciprocal obligations between superior and subordinate. Authority delegated to subordinates must include power to make decisions, use resources, and take actions to do the work for which the subordinates are accountable. Authority and accountability *must* be coequal. Persons can *only* be held accountable if they have authority to control the outcome of work for which they are accountable.

HSO departmentation is based on work being done or to be done. Effective interaction among departments is key. There is a positive, direct correlation between the degree to which an organization's work is divided and specialized and a subsequent need for integration and coordination. Judged by differentiation of work and staff specialization, acute care hospitals are extraordinarily complex. They are characterized by highly technical and specialized work performed by such a variety of staff that significant problems of integration and coordination can arise. Direct, support, and managerial work in hospitals is interdependent.

Functional interdependence makes integration and coordination necessary if organizing is to be effective. A challenge to effective integration and coordination occurs if staff have varying perceptions of the organization's mission and they choose various ways to accomplish it. Integrating and coordinating require managing conflicts among parts of an HSO. Examples include conflict between the professional staff organization (PSO) and senior management, or between nursing and pharmacy. Others involve individuals or conflicts between individuals and the organization. In HSs, relationships between and among components and with headquarters staff are potentially problematic.

Not all conflict is negative, but chronic, low-level conflict, such as "disliking" and "difficulty getting along," reduce organizational effectiveness. Effective integration and coordination prevent or reduce misunderstanding and conflict and are essential managerial activities. This makes organization design that facilitates integration, coordination, and cooperation essential to success.

The organizing function is semifluid. Experience may suggest a need to modify or reorganize to improve effectiveness. Reorganizing means reassigning duties, accountability for them, and the authority to make them a reality. Reorganizing disrupts the organization and should be undertaken only if expected benefits will greatly outweigh costs. Costs to employee morale and discontinuities may be unanticipated; the result is a dysfunctional organization in need of reorganizing.

A leading contemporary theorist, Peter Drucker (American [1909–2005]), suggested that managers selecting an organization design evaluate options against the following criteria:

- Clarity, as opposed to simplicity. The Gothic cathedral is not a simple design, but your position inside it is clear, and you know where to stand and where to go. In contrast, a modern office building may be exceedingly simple in design but very easy to get lost in.

- Economy of effort to maintain control and minimize friction

- Direction of vision toward product rather than process—the result rather than the effort

- Understanding by individuals of their own tasks, as well as that of the organization as a whole

- Decision making that focuses on the right issues, is action oriented, and carried out at the lowest possible level of management

- Stability, as opposed to rigidity, to survive turmoil, and adaptability to learn from it

- Perpetuation and self-renewal, requiring that an organization produce tomorrow's leaders from within, helping each person develop continuously, and that the structure is open to new ideas[12]

Division of Work

The classical theorists—and before them, Adam Smith (Scottish [1723–1790]), author of *The Wealth of Nations* (1776)[13]—recognized the benefits of division of work. For example, Fayol considered division of work to be the most important design concept.[14] He and other classicists saw it—or, as division of work is also known, specialization of work—as an important source of economic benefits. Benefits resulted because specialization increased individuals' proficiency in their work, thereby improving efficiency and effectiveness. For example, the work of a liver transplant team is divided among several persons. Each specializes and becomes proficient. Results are superb because each member's work is excellent; it is efficient because members are proficient and, thus, contribute to team efficiency.

Technically, division of work means dividing work into jobs, each having specific components.[15] Job content is determined by what is to be accomplished: A pharmacist's job is defined by what someone in that position does. The activities differ from those of a nurse, VP for professional affairs, dietitian, or chief information officer (CIO).

Specialization of staff is common in HSOs because licensure and accreditation require employing those who meet special requirements and are credentialed in terms of clinical privileges. Health professionals' work is largely defined and prescribed by regulations. Specialization, including licensure and certification, shows expertise based on education and experience. HSOs/HSs are structured to accommodate the specialties of their staff.

Division of work and specialization has a functional basis.[16] It means organizing into departments or units in which work is similar but between which work is dissimilar. For example, work in dietary is unlike that in admitting. Advantages of specializing include selecting, training, and equipping staff to do work by matching activities with functions. When work is functionally specialized, staff often learns the job more quickly and managers can standardize work to achieve greater control and improve quality.

Contemporary View

Classicists who developed the concept of division of work and specialization saw it as an important, largely untapped source of increased productivity and economic benefit. Division of work has a negative side, however: Staff may find it repetitive, monotonous, and unfulfilling. Benefits of division or specialization of work must be balanced against negative effects. Extreme division of work is likely dysfunctional.

In response, contemporary developments such as cross-training (teaching staff skills and tools to do more than one job), job enlargement (combining tasks to create a new job with more components), and job enrichment (expanding responsibilities so work is more challenging and satisfying) are important. For example, integrated teams formed by job enrichment involve members in decisions and total patient care. Cardiac rehabilitation teams meet patient needs for a course of treatment from diagnosis to extended care.

Many jobs in HSOs are tedious and narrow in scope; patient transportation, food service, and laundry are examples. Such jobs can be enlarged to good effect. Even health professionals with broad duties benefit from job enlargement. Good job enlargement and enrichment programs are consistent with the quality-of-work-life (QWL) movement. Organizations use QWL to make the work environment more compatible with employees' physical, social, and psychological needs.[17] QWL makes work meaningful; people are motivated to perform and derive greater satisfaction from what they do. It is important to recall Deming's admonition that employees will not treat customers (patients) better than they are treated. This is borne out by research that shows improving the employee experience results in increased patient satisfaction.[18]

Authority and Accountability Relationships

A classical design theory important for HSOs/HSs is establishing authority and accountability relationships. Division of work necessitates assigning authority over work and accountability for performing it. Authority is power derived from one's position in an organization. Sometimes called legitimate power, organizational authority enables managers to give orders and expect them to be performed as they engage in the directing function (see Chapter 13). Responsibility is performing duties or achieving objectives and, like authority, comes from one's position in the organization. Those with responsibilities are accountable to meet them.

Classicists viewed authority as a glue that held organizations together. Further, they believed the rights attached to a position were the only important source of power or influence and that managers were all-powerful. Managers may have been all-powerful 100 years ago; now authority is but one element in a larger concept of power in organizations.[19]

Authority is delegated from higher levels to lower levels. This results in scaling or grading levels of authority. The relationships are also known as chain of command. The CEO's authority is different from that of a VP, department head, or staff member. Organizational layers show scalar relationships.

> The scalar chain simply defines the relationships of authority from one level of the organization to another. In the scalar chain, individuals higher up on the chain have more authority than those below them. This is true of all succeeding levels of management from top management to the first-level employee. The scalar chain helps define authority and responsibility and, thus, accountability.[20]

Classical theorists distinguished two forms of authority: line and staff. As concepts of organization design, they are understood best as relationships. In line authority a superior exercises direct control over a subordinate. This is command authority and is shown by the scalar chain (chain of command) in an organization. Chain of command is illustrated by the relationship of staff nurses on a nursing unit to the nurse manager of the unit, to the nurse supervisor, to the VP for nursing, and then to the CEO and GB. If the HSO is part of an HS, then to its top level. Each person in this chain has authority—depending on position—to issue directives to and expect compliance from people lower in the chain.

By contrast, staff authority is advisory. It is advice, guidance, and recommendations. For example, an in-house attorney has staff authority and does not dictate terms of a contract between an HSO and the HS acquiring it. The in-house attorney advises the GB and CEO about contract terms and the law.

Contemporary View

Contemporary views of authority are broader than were the classicists'. Chapter 13 discusses power in the context of the leading function. Power is discussed here to illustrate authority relationships. There are many sources of authority or power and influence in HSOs/HSs, those derived from formal position are but one. Contemporary theory conceptualizes authority or power as having seven bases: legitimate, reward, coercive, expert, referent, information, and ecological. The first three derive from a manager's position in the organization.[21]

Legitimate power or formal authority is intrinsic to managers; it is necessary for them to do their jobs. Managers have legitimate power based on position. Reward power comes from legitimate power and rewards performance with pay increases, promotion, and better work schedules; it buttresses legitimate power. Coercive power is opposite reward power; it punishes employees or prevents them from getting rewards. Sources of power other than that held by managers are important in HSOs/HSs; power and influence are found elsewhere.

Especially important in healthcare is expert power. It derives from having knowledge valued in HSOs/HSs. Expert power is held by a person; legitimate, reward, and coercive power are conferred by the organization. Some staff have authority because of expert power. The power of physicians and other licensed independent practitioners (LIPs),[22] is based on clinical knowledge and skills. LIPs in scarce specialties have more expert power than those with easily replaceable expertise.

Some persons evoke admiration, loyalty, and emulation such that they gain power to influence others. Referent power may be called charismatic power; it is not limited to managers. Like expert power, referent power is not conferred by the organization as are legitimate, reward, and coercive power. Managers who control information and access to it have information power. Developments in artificial intelligence (AI) will enhance information power. Ecological power is held by managers who control a physical environment and its contents.

An important development is the relationship of authority, accountability, and delegation. With rare exceptions, classicists thought decisions should be made at the lowest possible level in the organization and this was compatible with good decision making. This meant higher-level managers should *not* make decisions on matters that could be handled at lower levels. The following is a viewpoint typical of the classicists:

> One of the tragedies of business experience is the frequency with which men [business in 1931 was an almost exclusively male domain], always efficient in anything they personally can do, will finally be crushed and fail under the weight of accumulated duties that they do not know and cannot learn how to delegate.[23]

The importance of delegation was developed by the classicists. It is seen by contemporary managers as integral to centralized or decentralized decision making in HSOs/HSs.[24] Delegation is a common feature of their designs because of the work and skills, expertise, and expectations of many staff, especially clinical professionals.[25] Decentralization is related to delegation, but it, too, is a philosophy that requires more than just handing authority to subordinates. Decentralizing authority means selecting levels at which decisions are made. Also, those given authority must understand its use; this may require education.

Assessing degree of decentralization in an organization is simple: Decentralization increases if important decisions can be made lower in the management hierarchy; a manager's ability to commit to a capital expenditure shows how much authority has been delegated. Another measure of decentralization is the need to check or get clearance for decisions at lower levels. Decentralization is greatest if no review is required; it is less if superiors must be informed of a decision after it has been made. It is even less if superiors must be consulted before a decision is made. The fewer people consulted and the lower they are in the management hierarchy, the greater the decentralization.

AI may drastically change corporate hierarchies. One possible result of AI is that authority becomes more centralized. Conversely, however, because AI performs routine tasks, it is more likely that *decentralization* of authority will occur as the organization's *nonroutine* work is performed by what are called adhocracies. An adhocracy is formed by assembling staff with the skills and knowledge to solve problems.[26] The task force is common to HSOs/HSs; their use as a form of adhocracy will increase with AI. Chapter 12 discusses teams.

Departmentation

All organized human activity, from sandlot baseball to the U.S. Army, has two fundamental, opposing requirements: division of work performed, and integration and coordination of divided work. The classicists recognized that divided work had to be coordinated. They suggested departmentation (sometimes called departmentalization) to address these dual concerns. Departmentation—grouping work and staff into manageable units—heavily influences design of modern organizations.

The classical view of departmentation is a natural consequence of division and specialization of work that also rationally groups similar staff into workgroups, which in turn are grouped into larger and larger clusters until a superstructure is formed (see Figure 11.1). Classicists Gulick and Urwick[27] stated four reasons for departmentation: purpose, process, persons and things, and place. New bases for departmentation have emerged, but the basic concept is largely unchanged. Henry Mintzberg (Canadian [1930–])[28] suggested six bases for grouping staff into units and units into larger units:

1. *Knowledge and skills:* grouping by specialized knowledge or skills (e.g., surgeons in one department and pediatricians in another)

2. *Work process and function:* grouping by processes or functions performed (e.g., departments of marketing or finance or laboratories)

3. *Time:* grouping by when work is done (e.g., day, evening, and night shifts in 24-hour-a-day healthcare organizations)

4. *Output:* grouping by services or products (e.g., production of inpatient or outpatient services)

5. *Client:* grouping by age or gender of clients or patients served (e.g., geriatric and women's health programs)

6. *Physical location:* grouping by where work is done (e.g., operating ambulatory clinics in downtown locations as well as in the city's suburbs)

An HSO/HS may use all six to design an organization. No matter which is/are used, grouping workers establishes the means to coordinate their work within their group and with other workgroups. Mintzberg[29] suggested grouping (departmentation) has four important results for staff and their organizations:

1. Grouping sets up a system of common supervision. Once staff is grouped, a manager can be appointed to coordinate and control the work.

2. Grouping facilitates sharing resources. People in workgroups share a common budget, facilities, and equipment.

3. Grouping leads to common measures of performance. Shared resources on the input side and group-level objectives on the output side permit group members to be evaluated by common performance criteria. Common performance measures encourage group members to coordinate work.

4. Grouping encourages communication. Shared input resources and output objectives and close physical proximity encourage communication, which facilitates coordinating the work of group members.

Classicists favored departmentation by function. Reinforced by the specialized knowledge and skills of staff, departmentation is common in HSOs/HSs—imaging staff in radiology, pharmacists in pharmacy, and so forth. Departmentation also occurs within departments: A large clinical laboratory (departmentation by function) includes specialized workgroups, such as blood bank, chemistry, and hematology.

Contemporary View

One important contemporary development in design of HSOs/HSs is increased focus on patients as a basis for departmentation or grouping. A result of this change is more grouping of staff based on patient needs. As HSOs/HSs build and maintain market share, programs such as geriatric and women's health are common, as are executive health programs for corporate leaders.

Another important development is that rigidly departmented structures, no matter the basis for departmentation, cause significant problems of coordination across departments and with other divisions. The bureaucratic form stresses departmentation and hierarchy but doesn't work well in all circumstances. It is effective in stable situations but is a disadvantage when flexibility is important. Flexible organization designs—more organic designs—are superior in dynamic circumstances.

Organic design responds to a problem managing a large-scale project that requires skills of staff in different departments or when patient care is enhanced by multidisciplinary teams. Project teams use staff from relevant departments to plan programs or engage in quality improvement. They do not replace departments. They are organic complements to mechanistic and bureaucratic structures and eliminate some rigidity. A project team plans home health services for the chronically ill; team members can include staff from nursing, social services, respiratory therapy, occupational therapy, and pharmacy, and physicians specializing in chronic disease. Marketing and finance and reimbursement expertise is provided by administration. A project manager is named. The matrix shown in Figure 11.4 illustrates this design.

Organizing with project teams has several attributes. It is flexible, increases skill development, and enriches jobs for members. There is a negative side, however. Project organization may cause ambiguity for members because they owe allegiance and accountability to their home departments and to the team. Further, working on teams is time consuming because it relies on communication, often in face-to-face meetings. Managers accustomed to departmented structures must use a new approach to manage projects.

A matrix organization is formed by being superimposed on functional departments. This can be done for a program like the home health services example mentioned earlier, or for the whole organization. Figure 11.4 is a matrix design in a psychiatric center. Functional line managers are department heads; program or product line managers head clinical programs or service lines. The staff member shown in Figure 11.4 is a member of nursing service but is assigned to the Alzheimer's program.

Span of Control

An organization design question of fundamental concern to the classicists was how large groups of staff should be: How many people should be in a department? What was the basis for the decision made? In considering these questions, classical theorists developed the concept of span of control. Sometimes called span of management, span of control is defined as the number of subordinates reporting directly to a superior. *Span of authority* or *span of supervision* may be used to describe this concept, as well.

Classical theorists agreed managers must limit the subordinates reporting to them, a pragmatic conclusion based on a need to exercise control. Some theorists specified the optimum span. For Urwick,[30] six was the maximum span for close control. An industrialist, Ralph Davis (American [1894–ca.1960]), divided span of control into two types: executive and operative.[31]

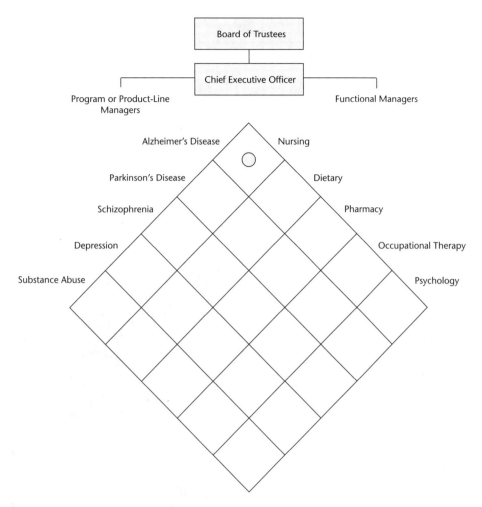

Figure 11.4. A matrix design: a psychiatric center. (From Leatt, Peggy, Ross Baker, and John R. Kimberly, "Organization Design." In *Health Care Management: Organization Design and Behavior*, 5th ed., edited by Stephen M. Shortell and Arnold D. Kaluzny, 332. Clifton Park, NY: Thomson Delmar Learning, 2006. Reprinted with permission of Delmar Learning, a division of Thomson Learning.

Executive span includes senior and middle managers; *operative span* includes first-level managers. Davis asserted that executive spans of control could be three to nine; operative spans might have 30 subordinates reporting to a first-level manager.

How the span-of-control question is answered affects design. Figure 11.5 shows that narrower spans of control produce "tall" organizations; wider spans produce "flat" organizations. The tall (five-level) and flat (three-level) structures in Figure 11.5 have equal numbers of positions.

Complex HSOs tend to have tall structures. An HS's structure depends on whether it is horizontally or vertically integrated. Tall HSOs result from differentiation and specialization of numerous, varied departments (e.g., from dietary to surgery) and consequently a need for narrow spans of control. Less complex HSOs, such as clinics or small nursing facilities (NFs), have flat structures. Large HSOs have flattened their structures by reducing staff to gain efficiency and reduce costs. Often, these cuts have affected middle management.

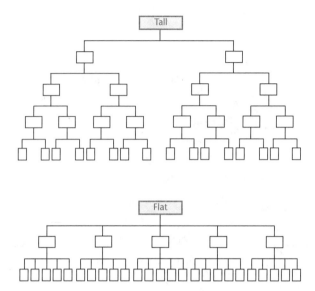

Figure 11.5.   Contrasting spans of control.

Contemporary View

In contemporary thinking, several factors determine spans of control when designing organizations:[32]

- *Level of professionalism and training of subordinates:* Professionalized and highly trained workers (prevalent in healthcare) need less supervision, which allows wider spans of control.

- *Level of uncertainty in the work being done:* Complex and varied work requires closer supervision, compared with simple, repetitive work. Close supervision requires a narrow span of control.

- *Degree of standardization of work:* Standard, routine work—whether professional, as in pharmacy or laboratory, or food preparation—requires less direct supervision; spans of control can be wider.

- *Degree of interaction needed between managers and workers:* Situations needing more interaction between managers and workers require narrower spans of control—effective interaction takes time. Increasing the number of subordinates reporting to a manager exponentially increases the number of possible interactions between managers and subordinates because managers can interact with individuals or groups. The number of possible interactions between a manager and two subordinates, individually or in combination, is six. With five subordinates, possible interactions between manager and subordinates increase to 100; six subordinates mean 222.

- *Degree of task integration required:* If work done in a group is integrated or interdependent, a narrower span of control may be needed.

With caveats, span of control is relevant to contemporary HSO/HS design.[33] Senior levels usually have narrow spans of control (e.g., CEOs may have five or six VPs). If work can be standardized and routinized, wider spans of control are possible. Another factor is type of work. Five file clerks are easier to supervise than five nurses. Also, the ability and availability of managers must be considered. Managers' training and personal qualities may allow them to manage more subordinates. Similarly, better trained subordinates can self-direct and have less need for managers, and span of control can be increased.

Coordination

Chester Barnard (American [1886–1961]) asserted that in most situations, "the quality of coordination is the crucial factor in the survival of the organization."[34] Fayol's concept was representative of how classicists perceived coordination. A well-coordinated organization had distinct characteristics: each department worked harmoniously with other departments, each knew the share of common tasks it must assume, and work schedules were integrated as needed.[35] Classicists saw coordination as consciously assembling and synchronizing work for smooth functioning to attain the organization's objectives. This view remains valid.[36]

Integration has been used to describe coordination: Integration is the process of achieving unity of effort among various parts of an organization.[37] In applied management, however, *coordination* and *integration* are different and are synonyms only in the broadest sense.

Contemporary View

Classicists' view of coordination has an important limitation: an internal focus. Development of HSs and other interorganizational arrangements requires coordination between and among organizations. Elements of classical *intraorganizational* coordination theory apply interorganizationally. Differences are identified later in the chapter. Contemporary coordination facilitates harmony of effort to achieve mission and shared objectives within an HSO or between and among organizations.

The contemporary view of coordination as a design concept is that it is vital to effective HSO/HS operation and performance and that managers can select from a lengthy menu of coordinative mechanisms. Several are described in the next section, including administrative systems; committees; customs; practice guidelines; critical pathways (also known as clinical pathways, care maps, and critical paths); direct supervision; feedback; hierarchy; integrators; linking pins in matrix designs; mutual adjustment; outcome assessment and planning; programming; project management through teams; report cards; standardization of work processes, outputs, or workers' skills; quality improvement teams (QITs); and voluntary action. HSO/HS mangers use them in combination and concurrently. Uses of coordination differ by level. Senior managers coordinate the HSO internally and externally. This latter responsibility is critical for HSOs in an HS. Middle managers coordinate workgroups. First-level managers coordinate their departments or units and with other parts of the HSO. Coordinative mechanisms differ; their use is essential for all managers.

Means of Coordination

Various coordinative means are available within and among HSOs/HSs. Success varies as to when and how they are used. Managers' menus of how to coordinate are *contingent* on when coordination is needed. James G. March (American [1928–2018]) and Herbert A. Simon (American [1916–2001]) identified *programming* and *feedback* as primary types of coordination.[38]

Programming, Feedback, and Relational Coordination

Programming clarifies responsibilities and activities before work is begun and specifies the output, process, and skills needed. It standardizes work to meet requirements. Feedback uses information exchange among staff while work is under way. Communication (discussed in Chapter 9) allows staff to change or modify work in response to unexpected developments.

A newer view of coordination uses programming *and* feedback. Relational coordination "occurs through frequent, high-quality communication, supported by relationships of shared goals, shared knowledge, and mutual respect, [enabling] organizations to better achieve their desired outcomes."[39] Relational coordination is not mechanistic exchange of information, but a process "involving a network of communication and relationship ties among people whose tasks are interdependent."[40]

Hierarchy, Administrative Systems, and Voluntary Activities

Joseph A. Litterer (American [1926–1995]) posited that managers coordinate using the organization's hierarchy or its administrative system, or with voluntary activities.[41] The hierarchy coordinates by putting activities in one line of authority. In a simple HSO, this may be enough. In more complex HSOs, however, hierarchical coordination is more difficult. The CEO is the focal point of authority, but no one person can solve all coordinative problems. Coordination using the hierarchy must be supplemented.

The administrative system can facilitate coordination. As Litterer noted, "A great deal of coordinative effort in organizations is concerned with horizontal flow of routine work. Administrative systems are formal means to carry out this routine coordinative work automatically."[42] Advances in technology have profoundly influenced the means and efficiency of coordination. Staff need not be physically present or available at the same place and time to communicate. Internet access by desktops, laptops, tablets, smartphones, and video conferencing allows creation, distribution, access, and storage of information by anyone, anytime, anywhere.[43] In addition, administrative systems and committees coordinate nonroutine and nonprogrammable matters.

Litterer's third type of coordination is voluntary action. If coordination is needed, individuals or groups find a means. Voluntary coordination requires that individuals know organizational objectives, understand problems requiring coordination, and are motivated to act. Voluntary coordination is motivated by staff professionalism and their values of benefiting to the patient. By communicating objectives and information about problems, managers facilitate voluntary coordination, which occurs easily if coupled with motivation.

Types of Coordination

Mintzberg devised a conceptual framework for types of coordination: mutual adjustment, direct supervision, and standardization of work processes, outputs, and workers' skills.[44] Figure 11.6 shows these coordinative mechanisms.

- *Mutual adjustment:* Coordinates using informal communication among those whose work must be coordinated. Like Litterer's voluntary actions, work is coordinated by those performing it (see Figure 11.6a).

- *Direct supervision:* As with Litterer's hierarchical coordination, someone takes responsibility for others' work, including giving instructions and monitoring actions (see Figure 11.6b).

- *Standardization of work processes:* Programs or specifies work content. HSO establishes standard admission and discharge procedures or standard methods for laboratory tests. Standardization such as patient care protocols (see Figure 11.6c, work processes) is more complex.

- *Standardization of work outputs:* Specifies result or expected output. Staff determine how to perform work (see Figure 11.6c, outputs).

- *Standardization of workers' skills:* Used when neither work processes nor output can be standardized. Results from staff training (see Figure 11.6c, input skills). Useful for HSOs. Complexity may not allow standardized processes or outputs. "When an anesthesiologist and a surgeon meet in the operating room (OR) to remove an appendix, they need hardly communicate; by virtue of their respective training, they know exactly what to expect of each other. Their standardized skills take care of most of the coordination."[45]

Customs

Another framework uses customs as a coordinative mechanism.[46] For example, a custom at an NF may be to invite residents' families for food and social interaction at the holidays. Knowing this custom allows staff to prepare in advance and facilitates coordinating contributions. Customs based on trial and error are a distillation of good practice but are inadequate for coordination in complex HSOs/HSs.

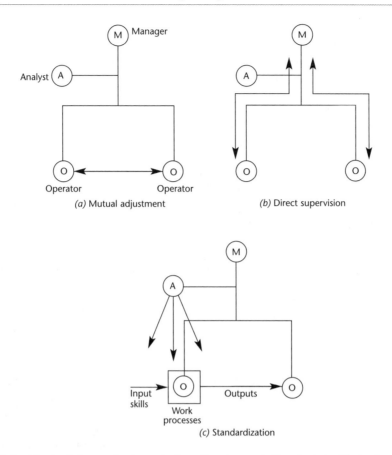

Figure 11.6. Mintzberg's five coordinating mechanisms. (From *Structure in Fives: Designing Effective Organizations*, 2nd edition, 5. Mintzberg, Henry, 1992. Reprinted by permission of Pearson Education, Inc., Upper Saddle River, NJ.)

Committees, Integrators, and Quality Improvement Teams

In addition to coordinative mechanisms identified by March and Simon, Litterer, Mintzberg, and Hage, others are available to HSO/HS managers. Committees of members from departments or functional areas with which there is a need to coordinate may be effective coordinative mechanisms.

One person can be effective in coordination. Paul R. Lawrence (American [1922–2011]) and Jay W. Lorsch (American [1932–]) found well-coordinated organizations rely on individuals, whom they called *integrators*, to achieve coordination. Successful integrators depend more on having relevant expertise than occupying a formal position; integrators are sources of information.[47] Examples are nurses who coordinate departments and subunits for patient care. Those who link to coordinate are *linking pins*.[48]

It is difficult to coordinate large programs, projects using skills from different units, or when multidisciplinary teams provide patient care. Organizational design can aid coordination. The discussion of a matrix design to organize a comprehensive home health program for the chronically ill used the project manager as coordinator for the team and the HSO in which it is imbedded. In the HSO matrix design (Figure 11.4), program and product line managers and staff are integrators.

Cross-functional QITs, also called quality improvement task forces, coordinate.[49] QITs are common in HSOs and in public health.[50] QITs hold small-group, problem-oriented meetings and use data to improve processes. Good communication promotes teamwork and aids coordination. QITs use flow diagrams, nominal group process, multicriterion decision making, cause-and-effect diagrams, and other problem identification and problem-solving tools to improve communication, coordination, and, ultimately, the quality of process output. QITs were described in Chapter 8.

Coordinating Patient Care

Standardization enhances coordination of clinical services, which results in better patient care.[51] Studies of intensive care units show that effective coordination among clinical staff produces more efficient and better care.[52] Similarly, effective coordination of surgical services leads to superior outcomes.[53]

Coordination is part of the standards for accreditors, such as The Joint Commission. Some reference staff coordination specifically.[54] The National Committee for Quality Assurance standards for managed care organizations (MCOs) require staff coordination. "While setting standards obviously cannot ensure good coordination, it does symbolize the growing recognition among accrediting and other oversight bodies that coordination is highly important to the performance of healthcare organizations."[55]

Historically, HSOs were reluctant to improve coordination of care by standardizing. It was thought clinical care could not be standardized.[56] This view came from uncertainty in patient care, professional independence, variation in patient responses to medical intervention, and difficulty defining output of care. Now, efforts to reduce cost and demonstrate the value of patient care are focusing attention on standardizing inputs.[57] Exceptions to guidelines can be made but must be clinically justified.

Standardizing patient care includes practice guidelines (discussed in Chapter 3) and critical pathways, which are "management plans that display goals for patients and provide the corresponding ideal sequence and timing of staff actions to achieve those goals with optimal efficiency."[58] Guidelines specify services for high-volume, high-cost conditions and specify clinical indications for tests or treatments.[59] "Thus, whereas critical pathways standardize the treatment approach for a given clinical condition, clinical [or practice] guidelines standardize the decision process for adopting a treatment approach."[60]

Outcome assessment is another way to standardize patient care. Managers collect, monitor, and report results to standardize outputs of care by focusing on variables such as mortality or complication rates for inpatients and percentage of enrollees in a managed care plan who receive cholesterol screening or other preventive services. Assessments can be made at the population level using outcomes such as health status or incidence of clinical conditions, such as heart disease or diabetes. Some regulatory bodies use outcome assessments called report cards to develop profiles of HSOs/HSs.[61] With these assessments "managers from different organizations or units can detect and attend to undesirable variations in outputs (over time or relative to competitors) by changing or modifying work activities as needed."[62]

Concerns that standardizing patient care may compromise quality and limit provider flexibility[63] have been negated by data showing that patient care is improved by standardizing with feedback. A study of 44 surgical services found that those with standardized care combined with feedback had better outcomes than those that did not.[64] A surgical unit implemented a protocol for nurses to identify patients at high risk for pressure injuries. The staff conference that followed developed prevention strategies for nurses and the surgeon and consulting physician. The protocol standardized practice; the conference provided feedback.

Formal and Informal Organizations

The formal organization is the structure conceived and approved by senior managers and the GB. Figures 11.7 and 11.8 are examples. The formal organization defines relationships; successful managers spend considerable time and effort maintaining them. The design includes accountability relationships, division of work, departmentation, and the hierarchical structure, which are the planned interrelationships among people, activities, and things. Supplementing the formal structure are policies (guides to thinking), procedures (guides to action), and rules (required action). Respective examples are operating policies, work procedures, and salary schedules.

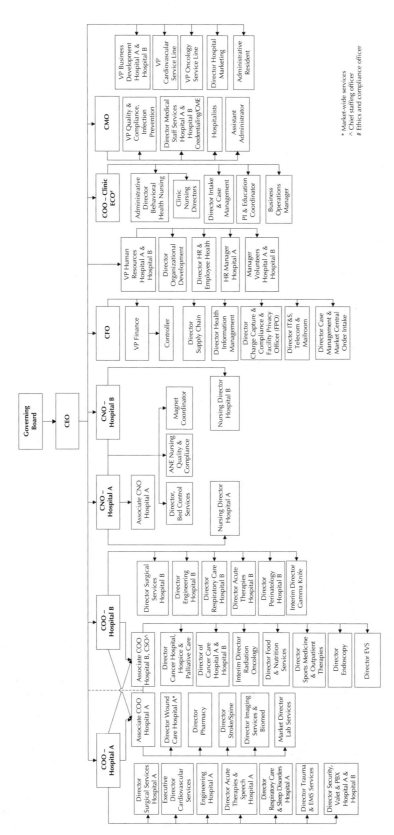

Figure 11.7. Organization chart of a small hospital system.

* Market-wide services
^ Chief staffing officer
# Ethics and compliance officer

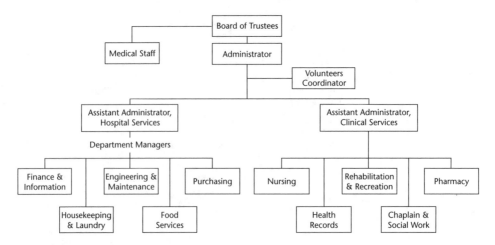

Figure 11.8. Organizational chart of a nursing home. Source: S.M. Shortell and A.D. Kaluzny: *Health Care Management Organization Design and Behavior, Fifth Edition*, 2006, p. 329. Reprinted with permission of Delmar Learning, a division of Thomson Learning.

The informal organization lies within the formal organization and coexists with it. The informal organization results from the spontaneous interactions of persons who work together and establish relationships that could not have been anticipated when designing the formal structure. Every HSO/HS has a formal structure and an informal structure that reflects staff preferences.

The famous Hawthorne studies conducted in the 1930s at the Hawthorne Works of Western Electric, which manufactured telephones, stimulated interest in the informal organization.[65] The research found that an informal organization forms from people's social interactions, and the informal organization can enhance or diminish performance, depending on how managers react. Informal relationships within the formal structure are a fact of organizational life. They occur because people want to protect themselves and make work the best experience it can be. Managers who disrupt or try to suppress informal interactions do so at their peril. The result can be destructive and dysfunctional. Staff members will resist what they see as autocratic management. Resistance in the informal organization will cause negative outcomes, such as work restrictions, insubordination, disloyalty, and similar manifestations of antiorganization or antimanagement attitudes; sabotage may occur.

Both the formal and informal organizations must be considered to optimize performance and meet individual and organizational objectives. Performance is better when the formal organization maintains suitable progress toward its objectives but permits informal relationships. Maintaining a balance between them is difficult; managers can do two things to achieve it. First, they must anticipate informal relationships in their design and show acceptance by minimizing negative effects of decisions. Second, managers can integrate the formal and informal elements of organization design. In doing so, managers should avoid actions by the formal organization that diminish the quality of positive informal relationships. Blending informal relationships with formal design will nurture a strong, positive culture.

Designing Interorganizational Relationships

The top level depicted in Figure 11.1 shows how HSs are formed from HSOs and how HSs form myriad relationships with entities in their external environment. HSOs/HSs establish various interorganizational relationships (IORs). In addition to IORs, HSOs have numerous interdependencies, many of which are shown in Figure 11.9.

Figure 11.9.   Interdependencies among HSOs and other entities.

Types of IORs

The most common IOR is a market transaction. One example secures markets for health services capacity by contracting with insurance companies, employers, or employer groups. A second market transaction is an IOR to purchase supplies directly from a manufacturer or through a purchasing cooperative.

A second type of IOR is the involuntary linkages HSOs/HSs have with government regulators, fiscal intermediaries, bond-rating agencies, utilization management companies, and unions. An example is the IOR between an HSO and the state or local department of health that licenses and regulates hospitals.

The third type is a voluntary IOR formed between and among entities for mutual benefit, such as an enhanced competitive position by improving delivery and coordination of care. HSs result when HSOs form SAs, defined as "loosely coupled arrangements among existing organizations that are designed to achieve some long-term strategic purpose not possible by any single organization."[66]

Central to designing voluntary IORs is integration—joining parts to make a whole.[67] IORs have varying levels of integration. An IOR between an HSO and its PSO has little integration. Conversely, Partners HealthCare is a large, highly integrated HS. Founded by Brigham and Women's Hospital and Massachusetts General Hospital, it includes two academic health centers, community and specialty hospitals, a physician network, community health centers, home health, and other health- and research-related entities.[68]

Design of Voluntary IORs

Voluntary IORs may be as simple as an HSO/HS co-opting parts of interdependent entities by absorbing them.[69] Other than market transactions, co-opting is the most flexible and easiest IOR. Simplicity makes it pervasive. For example, one entity appoints a representative from an interdependent entity to an internal position. An HSO/HS can improve ties to its service area by adding representatives to an advisory panel to guide decision making. Similarly, a health maintenance organization (HMO) concerned about quality may add members of its clinical staff to the HMO's GB.

Also called outsourcing, contract management is more complex than co-opting. Here, an HSO/HS contracts with a firm that has expertise in services such as dialysis, maintaining clinical equipment, waste management, environmental services, laundry, or food service, to manage those departments.[70]

HSs as Voluntary IORs

Voluntary linkages between and among HSOs are pervasive: 100% of community hospitals are in a system *or* network[71]; HSs are IORs that result from mergers (one or more HSOs/HSs is absorbed by another that retains its identity) or consolidations (two or more HSOs/HSs dissolve to form a new legal entity).

Highly integrated HSs are the most complex IORs. They link components of services delivery and financing to meet the healthcare needs of their service area better. Highly integrated HSs "either own or contract with at least three components of healthcare delivery, including at least one acute-care hospital, at least one physician component, and at least one other component of care. Highly integrated HSs have at least one systemwide contract with a payer, such as an HMO."[72]

The forms HSs take are idiosyncratic and have the following objectives:

- Accepting financial risk and able to contract based on a single signature

- Being capable of managing components of risk among different providers

- Developing a strong central GB

- Increasing physician leadership and participation in management

- Creating information systems that integrate financial, operational, clinical, and management data and provide them in an appropriate and timely manner

- Coordinating to ensure a smooth movement of patients along the continuum of care

- Improving outcomes of care and quality of services

Integration can begin with any objective and add the others serially or concurrently. For example, an HS may be well into centralized governance but have made little progress involving physicians in leadership.

Clinical integration may be the most important aspect of integration.[73] Whether vertical or horizontal, clinical integration is defined as "the extent to which patient care services are coordinated across people, functions, activities, processes, and operating units so as to maximize the value of services delivered."[74] At the operational level, clinical integration includes continuity and coordination of care and "disease management, good communication among caregivers, smooth transfer of information and patient records, elimination of duplicate testing and procedures, and efficient use and management of resources."[75]

Mergers can fail if their cultures are incompatible. Cultural tightness and looseness are key. Tight cultures have an efficient orderliness and reassuring predictability. They value consistency and routine, have little tolerance for rebellious behavior, and use strict rules to maintain cultural traditions. Conversely, loose cultures are fluid. They minimize rules, encourage new ideas, value individual discretion, and are more open and creative; they are less organized. Merging organizations can minimize the risk of conflicting cultures by performing a cultural audit to determine if people, practices, and management are tight or loose. To improve chances for success, merging organizations must compromise by becoming looser or tighter, as appropriate.[76]

HSs and Horizontal and Vertical Integration

HSs facilitate horizontal and vertical integration. Horizontal integration forms lateral relationships among like entities performing at the same functional level. It improves efficient resource

(A) Horizontally integrated HS. All HSOs in the HS perform at the same functional level: All are hospitals, nursing facilities, home health agencies, or the like.

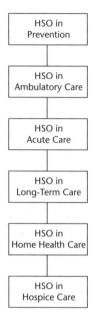

(B) Vertically integrated HS. The HSOs in the HS are performing at different functional levels: prevention, ambulatory care, and so forth.

Figure 11.10.   Horizontally (A) and vertically (B) integrated HSs.

use and improves purchasing power and marketing and management.[77] Examples include two or more community hospitals or NFs joining horizontally (see Figure 11.10A).

Vertical integration is joining dissimilar HSOs (see Figure 11.10B). This type forms relationships among entities at different stages of health services delivery.[78] Vertically integrated HSs provide a range of health services in a coordinated manner.[79]

Strategic Alliances as Voluntary IORs

An SA is a type of voluntary IOR that offers flexibility and responsiveness but retains the basic forms of member organizations.[80] SAs are "arrangements between two or more organizations for purposes of ongoing cooperation and mutual gain/risk sharing."[81] They have characteristics of an organization (shared goals, mutual dependency, task subdivision and specialization, bureaucratic structures, and formal coordination and control mechanisms), but lack an ownership link; contracts establish relationships.

Key to distinguishing HSs and SAs is what binds them. HSs usually involve ownership. Participants coalesce or are loosely coupled[82] into SAs using joint ventures, partnerships, or consortia. Partial pooling of resources is common. Loosely coupled or coalesced SAs link interdependent and mutually responsive HSOs and HSs so their identities and functional autonomy are intact. For example, an SA is formed when an acute care hospital, a multispecialty group practice, an NF, and an insurance carrier contract to create an IOR that designs, produces, and markets a managed care product. These organizations continue operating independently to accomplish other, perhaps mutually exclusive, objectives. Interdependencies among the entities are managed through IORs to avoid the loss of autonomy and identity associated with ownership.

Joint ventures are common to organize loosely coupled SAs. A joint venture is "a legal entity characterized by two or more parties who work on a project together, sharing profits, losses, and control."[83]

Joint ventures may be organized as limited liability partnerships (LLPs) or as limited liability companies (LLCs), which are discussed later in the chapter.

Accountable Care Organizations as SAs

Section 3021 of the Patient Protection and Affordable Health Care Act of 2010 established the Innovation Center in the Centers for Medicare & Medicaid Services (CMS). The center tests delivery models that improve care, lower costs, and align payment systems to support patient-centered practices for Medicare, Medicaid, and the Children's Health Insurance Program. The center evaluates innovative reform efforts in the private sector, develops provider-proposed approaches, and adjusts models in response to feedback from clinicians and patients.[84]

An example was a Medicare pilot program that included bundled payment for inpatient hospital services, physician services, outpatient hospital services, and postacute care services for an episode of care that begins 3 days before a hospitalization and extends 30 days after discharge. CMS used accountable care organizations (ACOs) to test this model. An ACO is a group of providers and suppliers of services (e.g., hospitals, physicians, and others involved in patient care) coordinating care for Medicare fee-for-service beneficiaries.[85] The goal was to deliver seamless, high-quality care for Medicare beneficiaries instead of the fragmented care that so often is part of fee-for-service healthcare.

ACOs may include the following providers of Medicare-covered services:

- ACO professionals in group practice arrangements
- Networks of individual practices of ACO professionals
- Partnerships or joint venture arrangements between hospitals and ACO professionals
- Hospitals employing ACO professionals[86]

ACOs create incentives for providers to cooperate to treat patients across care settings. Medicare rewards the ACOs that reduce growth in healthcare costs while meeting performance standards on quality.

Participants in SAs

SAs are diverse in activity, purpose, and results and can be categorized by their participants. Integrative activities of physicians, HSOs, and HSs forming SAs are discussed next.

Physician–Physician SAs

Physicians integrate when they form a group practice, which may in turn participate in other SAs.[87] Or, they may form an SA such as an independent practice association (IPA), "an association of independent physicians or small groups of physicians formed for the purpose of contracting with one or more managed healthcare organizations."[88] Also, they may organize a physician-owned management services organization (MSO), a "corporation formed to provide practice management services to physicians."[89]

Physician–HSO/HS SAs

SAs are formed when individual physicians or groups are employed by, their practices are owned by, or they contract with HSOs/HSs. The financial success of owned physician practices in highly integrated HSs is mixed. Owned practices must be seen as part of a system. Their financial performance should be suboptimized if doing so optimizes financial performance of the HS.

A fully integrated health system model is often achieved by purchasing physician practices (and subsequent employment of those physicians) or by establishing a staff-model health maintenance organization, or HMO. This model promises the greatest opportunity for hospitals and physicians to respond together to the market, manage outcomes and rationalize resource allocation. While doctors still tend to favor a degree of autonomy over total integration with hospitals, continuing market pressure for effective cost control and the ability to demonstrate quality and performance are moving hospitals and physicians closer together.[90]

This trend began in the 1990s; it shows no evidence of abating.[91] Other types are HSOs/HSs and physicians forming HSO/HS–based MSOs. Services provided to physicians by MSOs include billing, information system management, staffing, staff training and development, managed care contract negotiation, compliance, and other office management functions.[92]

A physician–hospital organization (PHO), is a "legal entity formed by a hospital and a group of (its) physicians to further mutual interests and to achieve market interests."[93] The PHO integrates hospital and physicians to effectively negotiate with health plans, employers, or purchasing coalitions and contract to provide services.[94] The PHO can sponsor surgery or imaging centers, or other business ventures.[95] An SA is established when the PHO contracts with an HMO, for example. MSOs and PHOs involving HSOs/HSs and physicians are usually organized as joint ventures.

HSO–HS SAs

Primarily, HSOs/HSs participate in SAs to reduce costs and enhance revenue. For example, group purchasing organizations (GPOs) are SAs formed to gain purchasing power and reduce supply costs. An example is Intalere, a national GPO. In 2018, its members included 3,795 hospitals, 43,635 clinics, and 13,338 long-term care facilities.[96] It negotiates with suppliers for best prices, terms, and conditions.

HSO–HSO SAs are formed, too, because they increase participants' ability to innovate and adapt to environmental threats, to optimize organizational learning, and to improve quality.[97] For example, SAs such as Harvard Pilgrim Healthcare[98] in Massachusetts, Henry Ford Health System[99] in Michigan, and Lovelace Health System[100] in New Mexico, help SA participants improve quality.[101] Organizations in a negative environment are likely to adapt in an SA that provides information and opportunities for mutual learning.[102]

SAs help achieve stability in an uncertain environment and improve competitive position. Hospital-based SAs compete effectively for managed care contracts; MCOs cannot pit hospitals against each other. The SA can negotiate communitywide contracts, which gives hospitals greater mass and leverage.[103] The same types of SAs are being formed as ACOs, but preliminary results are mixed.[104]

Duration of SAs may be limited or unlimited. Those of limited duration have a specific, short-term reason(s) to exist. SAs with unlimited duration meet a continuing need. Regardless of original intent, however, an SA should be terminated when its mission is complete. Bureaucracies have an uncanny ability to morph into entities (with a new mission) they were never intended to be.

The Triad of Key HSO Components

The use of *triad* (group of three) to describe the GB, CEO, and PSO has a long history in health services—especially as applied to acute care hospitals.

Governing Body

Regardless of ownership, mission, or other characteristics, HSOs/HSs have a GB or its equivalent. GBs range from one person in a sole proprietorship to the GB of an academic health center, to the GB of an HS. GBs are the ultimate authority and decision maker and determine the mission (the "right thing") and evaluate progress toward it. Among a GB's most important tasks is selecting and evaluating the CEO.

Chief Executive Officer

All HSOs/HSs have a CEO. As health services adopted the accoutrements of business enterprise, they began using corporate titles such as *president* and *executive vice president*. The GB selects and delegates authority to a CEO, who is its agent in assembling and organizing inputs (the "right way") to achieve the organization's mission. For many reasons, including legal relationships and financial demands on HSOs/HSs, GBs are being held to a higher standard of ethical and legal accountability. This necessitates an effective working relationship between GB and CEO. That relationship varies greatly and ranges from CEOs with wide latitude in decision making to those with little independence. In the past, the world of business tended to combine the roles and titles of board chair and CEO, with oversight provided by a lead director of the GB.[105] At this writing, board chair and CEO positions are more likely to be separate.[106] Combining them diminishes supervisory and fiduciary accountability that the GB has for a CEO's performance and raises questions as to how well the CEO is monitored and evaluated. The importance of governance in not-for-profit HSOs has limited combining the positions. For-profit HSOs/HSs are an exception.

Professional Staff Organization

The association of clinical staff is likely called the medical staff organization because, historically, it was composed almost exclusively of physicians. Today, the term *professional staff organization* is more accurate because it reflects the broader range of members' clinical preparation and activities. Thus, that term and the acronym, PSO, are used here.

The PSO comprises the clinical staff who control delivery of clinical services in an HSO. The membership and organization of PSOs vary, even within HSOs of the same type. Broadly defined, clinical staff treat or order treatment for patients. Here, *clinical staff* refers to LIPs.[107] Increasingly, HSO clinical staff includes nonphysician LIPs, such as clinical psychologists, podiatrists, nurse midwives, physician assistants, nurse anesthetists, and chiropractors.

It is common that PSOs are separate, unincorporated associations with their own bylaws and rules and regulations. This aspect challenges the usual features of a bureaucracy as defined by Weber. Acute care hospitals have two pyramids—one for the organization, the other for the PSO. The PSO is subordinate to the hospital bylaws, and the PSO's bylaws and rules and regulations must be approved by the GB. The dual pyramid was clearer in the past; regardless, it is common to contemporary acute care hospitals.

PSO members provide clinical services directly or order HSO staff to provide them. Relationships among PSO members depend on setting and services. In HSOs such as a physician group practice there may be more nonphysician LIPs than physicians. Care in NFs is long term and custodial; only intermittent physician contact is needed. NFs have few LIPs; a PSO is unneeded. Care is routine and provided by non-LIPs, such as registered nurses (RNs), licensed practical nurses (LPNs), and certified nursing assistants (CNAs). These caregivers follow standing orders approved by the medical director (chief medical officer [CMO]) of the NF and used for all residents, or as directed by LIP-determined individualized care.

The roles and functions of GBs, CEOs, and PSOs are detailed next. Complex relationships among elements of the triad in HSOs arise from volunteer GB members, not-for-profit HSOs/HSs, lack of employment relationships for most LIPs, and the technical and specialized functions of clinical staff.

Governing Body

As suggested in Chapter 1, the contemporary healthcare environment significantly affects governance of HSOs. Changes include obstacles to financial viability; population shifts; consumerism; physician challenges; quality and patient safety; new medical and information technologies; and public health, community collaborative, and health policy reform.[108] GB members can no longer be chosen to honor them or because they make financial or in-kind contributions. The need for GB effectiveness has increased such that persons who understand health services, are prepared in business, or otherwise have relevant backgrounds are required. GBs involved in monitoring quality contribute to high performance on this metric in their HSO.[109] Desirable personal characteristics include an ability to listen, build consensus, communicate, lead, and think creatively.[110] Members should know finance; strategic and financial planning; quality, performance, and measurement; risk identification and oversight; communication and accountability; CEO selection, performance evaluation, and succession planning; and governance.[111]

Other characteristics include those that reflect community demographics and cultural sensitivity. GBs should comprise persons of different ages, race, ethnicity, religion, and sex. In seeking effective members, consideration is also given to most physical and psychological characteristics and the range of knowledge and capabilities acquired by education and experience relevant to performance on a GB.[112]

Responsibilities and Associated Activities
Table 11.1 shows the responsibilities and associated activities of GBs. The context for what GBs do is ensuring that the organization delivers high-quality healthcare and oversees its continuous improvement. Responsibilities and associated activities are performed in that context.

Composition
GB size ranges from a handful to a hundred; 10–20 is common. Preference is for smaller GBs.[113] The trend to downsize results from the complexity engendered by large size and the demands on boards.[114] GBs of not-for-profit HSOs/HSs tend to be larger than those organized for profit. As noted, GB members able to meet the responsibilities and carry out governance duties need significant skills and knowledge.[115] Likely, potential members self-select and join GBs whose values comport with their own.

An important contemporary change in GB composition is to add LIPs, usually physicians. Historically, not-for-profit hospital GBs excluded them. It was thought that their duality of interests could lead to conflicts of interest regarding resource allocation, capital equipment purchases, and evaluating quality of care (Chapter 2 discusses conflicts of interest). Now, LIP membership is encouraged. It is believed conflicts of interest are avoidable and LIPs bring essential clinical expertise to governance. Involving LIPs in management and governance enhances performance and aligns incentives.[116] Increasingly, they are involved in HSOs/HSs governance.[117]

External GB members are not employed by the HSO/HS. They are business leaders, medical professionals, and community members. Internal GB members are employed by the HSO/HS and include the CEO, chief operating officer (COO), vice president for medical affairs (VP-MA), and chief financial officer (CFO). Internal members will increase as GBs need. more subject matter expertise. This means more members with a duality of interests.

Committees
Committees allow specialized, effective work. Committees, their composition, and function are established in the GB bylaws. Standing committees common to HSO/HS GBs are executive, audit, finance, quality, and nominations. Others may be professional staff, ethics, human resources, strategic planning, public relations and development, investment, capital equipment, and audit. Ad hoc (special) committees are appointed, as needed.

Table 11.1.   HSO/HS GB Responsibilities and Associated Activities

Responsibilities (context is quality care and quality improvement)	Associated activities (context is quality care and quality improvement)
Formulates purposes of the organization	Monitors implementation of mission, vision, and objectives
	Reviews and modifies mission, vision, and objectives
Furthers organizational philosophy	Monitors inculcation and reinforcement of organization values
	Reviews and acts on ethics audit
Ensures quality of care	Monitors LIP credentialing process
	Reviews and approves clinical privileges recommended by PSO
	Monitors assessment processes and clinical outcomes of care
	Makes quality and its improvement the centerpiece of governance
Knows continuous quality improvement (CQI) theory and its application	Understands role of quality improvement
	Ensures CQI is central to efforts to improve quality of care
Ensures performance of chief executive officer (CEO)	Selects, evaluates, and retains (or dismisses) CEO
	Balances relationship with CEO: GB governs/managers manage
Oversees finances and financial performance	Establishes financial objectives
	Approves and monitors operating and capital budgets, and loans
	Reviews investments, retirement program, and similar accounts
Ensures strategic and tactical planning	Reviews/approves strategic plan; monitors implementation
	Monitors and reviews tactical planning by management
Ensures compliance and accreditation status	Monitors all aspects of compliance
	Ensures organization's ability to remain accredited
Assists with development	Contributes time and talent to organization
	Facilitates contributions from community and other donors
Private and public advocacy	Advocates for organization to private and public sectors
	Advocates for healthcare field, generally
Meets and uses stakeholder interests to further mission, vision, and objectives	Identifies and addresses interests of stakeholders
	Understands and works to meet healthcare needs of service area
	Focuses on population health of service area
Governs effectively and efficiently	Ensures GB bylaws, policies, and processes are appropriate
	Ensures members' orientation and self-development
	Monitors members' healthcare and QI knowledge
	Evaluates individual member and GB performance

Author-developed table with supplemental information from the following: Longest, Beaufort B., Jr., and Samuel A. Friede. "The Competent Board: Stitching Together Needed Skills and Knowledge." *Trustee* (February 2002): 16; Center for Healthcare Governance. *The Guide to Good Governance for Hospital Boards*, 2009. Chicago: American Hospital Association. http://trustees.aha.org/boardorientation/09-guide-to-good-governance.pdf, retrieved July 8, 2019; Center for Healthcare Governance. *Transformational Governance: Best Practices for Public and Nonprofit Hospitals and Health Systems*. Chicago: American Hospital Association 2012. http://trustees.aha.org/transforminggovernance/transformational-governance12.pdf, retrieved July 8, 2019; Center for Healthcare Governance. *Transformational Governance: The Challenges Facing Trustees of Nonprofit and Public Hospitals*. Chicago: American Hospital Association, 2012. http://trustees.aha.org/transforminggovernance/12-transformational-governance.pdf, retrieved July 8, 2019.

Two committees are noteworthy. The executive committee is the most important; it monitors GB committees and processes. Its importance is greater if the GB is large or meets infrequently. The executive committee receives reports from other committees, oversees policy implementation, and provides interim (between meetings) decision making. The chair of the GB chairs the executive committee, whose members are chairs of standing committees. Usually, CEOs attend executive committee meetings. Senior executives attend meetings to provide expertise.

The professional staff committee's responsibility for quality of clinical care ranks it second in importance. It reviews PSO recommendations for staff appointments, reappointments, and clinical activities (privileges) and reviews performance of PSO members to determine appropriateness of clinical privileges they are requesting. Both tasks require assistance from the PSO, GB members who are expert, or from consultants. The HSO's ethical and legal duty to protect patients from substandard care is met by thorough GB review of clinical care.

The need for CEO, PSO, and GB to coordinate is met variously. One way, the joint conference committee (JCC), may be a standing committee of the GB or PSO. Typically, it has three members each from the GB and PSO; the CEO is a seventh member. The JCC has no line authority; it analyzes policies and problems. Another way to coordinate GB–PSO–CEO is to have members serve on each other's committees and circulate copies of minutes and reports among committees. Coordination and communication are key to organizational success.

Relationship to CEO

The GB's role in recruiting, selecting, and evaluating the CEO has been noted. CEOs assemble and organize resources and develop systems to implement GB-approved policies and programs to achieve the mission—the right way. The CEO and staff enable the GB to develop policies, monitor implementation, and review results.

The GB should evaluate CEO performance annually and make specific recommendations. Performance should be measured against predetermined objectives mutually identified and accepted by the CEO and GB. GBs must not set objectives for CEOs without giving them the authority and resources to succeed. The American Hospital Association (AHA) has developed a comprehensive CEO evaluation that includes essential CEO accountabilities, personal attributes and leadership qualities, and CEO goals and objectives.[118] It is found at http://trustees.aha.org/execperformance/AHA-Sample-CEO-Performance-Appraisal.pdf. GBs explicitly or implicitly assess CEO performance (and that of other senior managers) by negative developments also.

Employment contracts for CEOs and senior management are common, a pattern similar to business enterprise. Contracts set terms of employment, including severance. CEOs may have incentive-based employment contracts. GBs of not-for-profit HSOs must be mindful that CEO compensation and incentives meet IRS requirements.[119]

CEOs walk a narrow line as they focus GB members' expertise and encourage interest, dedication, and enthusiasm, but simultaneously dissuade them from direct involvement in internal operations. When GB members intervene in operations, CEO and other managers' authority is undercut, and subordinates become frustrated and confused, conditions that diminish effectiveness, efficiency, and morale. GB member interference is forestalled by job descriptions and clarifying roles and activities through GB members' orientation and education.

Commonly, CEOs attend GB meetings; many are voting members. This has the potential for conflicts of interest, just as when PSO members serve on the GB. Evaluating the CEO raises the issue of duality of interests most starkly. CEO views should be considered. As a GB member, however, the CEO has a position of influence that may be at variance with assessing the HSO's/HS's performance and considering its best interests. Recall the earlier discussion of combining roles of CEO and board chair. Problems are lessened if CEOs are absent when matters that affect their self-interest are considered, a practice that reduces but does not eliminate a potential for conflicts of interest. In addition to membership, professional and personal ties between the CEO and GB members may give the CEO excessive influence, as well as lessen objectivity in evaluating and decision making. Conversely, there are major advantages when the CEO is a voting member of the GB: Communication and coordination are enhanced.

GBs should self-evaluate. They must recognize accountability for their actions. Discussions could begin by identifying in what ways the GB adds value to the HSO/HS. Then, members can identify how to use time, skills, and resources better to enhance GB contributions. HSOs and HSs must meet the reform-driven demand to design delivery that focuses on population health, clinical integration, and accountable care across the continuum. This requires a multi-faceted, multiyear approach with cycles of learning.[120]

Chief Executive Officer

Rarely are the complexity and uniqueness of the work of HSO/HS managers matched. They are accountable for organizations that deliver unique personal services to ill, anxious people in complicated settings, often in emotionally charged circumstances. In addition, relationships that HSOs have with professional staff are unparalleled in other industries. CEOs work in competitive, economically demanding environments. Hospitals and HSs are often the largest employers in their states and communities, giving them major opportunities for positive use of economic power.[121]

Historically, various titles applied to an HSO's top manager: *superintendent, administrator, director,* and *president.* This discussion uses *CEO,* a generic title applicable to all HSOs/HSs. There is no standard statement of a CEO's qualifications. The Joint Commission's (www.jcaho.org) definition is helpful: "The chief executive officer is competent and has the education and experience required for the size, complexity, [and] mission of the hospital, and the scope of services it provides."[122] Educational backgrounds of CEOs vary; a master's degree is expected. Doctoral (terminal) degrees for managers are becoming common. Senior managers are encouraged to develop personalized plans of continuing professional education and focused experiences to enhance their abilities and careers;[123] specialized programs are available to assist them.[124]

CEOs of larger HSOs (and HSs, generally) focus on GB and external relations, strategic planning, fundraising, directing capital projects, and sometimes PSO relations. The COO is accountable for operations and reports to the CEO. This division helps meet increasingly complex demands on senior management. The business world is reconsidering the need for a COO.[125] This trend may fit the needs of not-for-profit HSOs/HSs too. Some entities in an HS have no CEO. Rather, a COO manages day-to-day and reports to a senior executive in the HS.

Large HSOs have a CFO and a vice president for medical affairs (VP-MA). The CFO extends the concept of controllership with responsibilities for reimbursement, capital financing, and investment. The VP-MA may be known as the medical director, chief of staff, or chief medical officer. The VP-MA is accountable for PSO relations, credentialing and clinical privileges, and quality of care. The VP-nursing leads nursing service. Large HSOs and HSs have a chief information officer (CIO), chief quality officer (CQO), and chief technology officer (CTO)—who is responsible for IT, quality, and technology, respectively. All these "chiefs" in the executive suite results in it being called the C-suite. Newer additions to C-suites in HSs may include chief innovation officer, chief experience officer, chief transformation officer, chief strategy officer, chief informatics officer, and chief population health management officer.[126]

Having both a CEO and a COO is problematic if their spheres of authority and accountability are ill defined. Confusion is certain if the CEO intervenes directly in matters for which the COO is accountable. Absent emergencies, lines of authority and reporting relationships must be followed. The COO must be cognizant of GB reporting relationships to avoid bypassing and undercutting the CEO. Some subordinates are very clever at probing various executives until they get the answer they want. This cannot be allowed.

Below senior management are managerial levels that ultimately lead to staff who do the day-to-day work. The number of organizational levels—especially middle managers—is declining, a change consistent with recommendations to "flatten" organizations from experts such as Peter Drucker.[127]

CEO Responsibilities, Skills, and Knowledge (Competencies)

The CEO manages the organization and is accountable for designing, changing, and operating a structure to achieve its mission. Doing so requires managing inputs (human resources, material, technology, information, and capital) and the conversion process to produce desired outputs. CEOs delegate authority to subordinate managers, but the accountability to design, change, and operate the management structure cannot be delegated; the GB can and must hold the CEO accountable for organizational performance. To succeed as HSOs/HSs become more complex, CEOs must have broad skills and knowledge. For example, they must be able to build coalitions and negotiate as they establish strategic alliances and partnerships in health services delivery and conduct other business.[128] Effective GBs and CEOs are key to HSO/HS success. As discussed below, members of the PSO admit, diagnose, and treat patients. Without them HSOs would not be needed.

Professional Staff Organization

LIPs who treat and order treatment are the engine that allow an HSO—free-standing or in an HS—to achieve its mission. No treatment can be given without standing orders approved by the PSO, or specific orders of an LIP. HSOs with PSOs have relationships not shown in the typical pyramidal representation of an organization as in Figure 11.2. PSOs in accredited HSOs have bylaws and rules and regulations, officers, committees, and other characteristics that reflect the autonomy of LIPs. LIPs in acute care hospitals are usually independent contractors; they use the hospital as a workshop to treat patients but otherwise have limited involvement with it. Even when salaried, LIPs exhibit a high degree of independence and continue to have more allegiance to their profession and one another than to the HSO. This independence and the technical content of clinical practice meant that, historically, GBs exercised little control over PSOs. GBs and CEOs managed the administrative side; LIPs the clinical. This has changed.

Integrating LIPs into Management

Historically, LIPs had little involvement in management. The spheres of managers and clinicians were considered unique and separate, though both sought the same end of high-quality patient care. The exceptions were clinical managers and officers of the PSO. Since the 1990s, however, the value of broader participation by LIPs has been recognized, and they have become more involved in policy and operational decisions. Such integration is good practice and is recommended by accreditors such as The Joint Commission.

PSO members can be integrated into an HSO's management structure in several ways: They may join PSO management and GB committees; managers may ask their advice, formally and informally; and those who manage clinical departments or units are part of the management team.

Clinical managers are essential to well-managed HSOs. Even small PSOs are divided into departments or sections based on clinical specialty. Medical education and clinical practice teach physicians to think logically, to view problems systematically, and to consider their implications. These attributes are important for managers, but education in management is needed for competence; only competent clinical managers can further the organization's mission. Thus, it is a matter of self-interest that HSOs ensure clinicians' management competence. The presence of full- or part-time salaried clinical managers enables them to be involved in management. When clinicians and managers understand each other's problems, enhanced communication and organizational effectiveness result. This allows managers to align incentives to deliver integrated, coordinated services successfully.[129]

It bears restating that nonclinical managers neither deliver medical services nor judge quality independently. They must have the expert advice and technical assistance of LIPs to make informed judgments about individual and aggregate PSO performance.

Self-Governance

As evidence of a strong tradition of physician independence, PSOs are self-governing. LIPs are part of the PSO whether they are salaried by the HSO or are fee-for-service independent contractors. The PSO's bylaws, which must be approved by the GB, are key to self-governance. Bylaws identify officers, committees and functions, member categories, application process, procedure to amend the bylaws, and the process to review actions adverse to PSO members. In addition, the PSO adopts *rules and regulations* that regulate clinical practice more specifically. These are supplemented with even more detailed rules for clinical departments, specialties, and subspecialties.

Open or Closed

The PSO may be open, closed, or a combination. This concept is most developed in acute care hospitals but may also affect HSOs such as NFs. An open PSO allows any qualified LIP (as defined in the PSO bylaws) to be granted clinical privileges after a credentials review and to admit and treat patients. A closed PSO limits the number of LIPs by applying guidelines developed by the PSO and approved by the GB. The guidelines may include a limit on size of the PSO, limits on numbers in specific specialties, or limits on various types of LIPs. Acute care hospitals have a combination of open and closed departments. Some clinical departments are closed—anesthesia, laboratories, emergency medicine, and radiology—are examples. Medicine, obstetrics and gynecology, and surgery are usually open; any qualified LIP is granted clinical privileges in them. Closing PSOs and clinical departments or sections is justified (and legally defensible) because it improves quality of care and enhances efficiency.

The most common reason for a closed clinical department is because the HSO has an exclusive contract with a provider group known as a concessionaire. Only LIPs in the group as owners or employees may practice in a closed department. Regardless, those LIPs must be granted clinical privileges in the same review process as other LIPs.

Committees

GB and PSO committee structures are similar. The PSO is led by a medical executive committee (MEC). Its members usually include chairs of standing committees. The MEC acts for the PSO, coordinates its activities, provides continuity, and enhances communication between PSO and CEO. Major activities of the MEC are implementing policies, receiving and acting on committee reports and recommendations, making recommendations on membership and clinical privileges, monitoring quality of care, and taking corrective action, including discipline.

The following are other PSO activities that must be managed and for which there may be committees:

- *Credentials:* Reviews qualifications of clinicians for PSO membership and recommends clinical privileges to MEC; reviews continuing appropriateness of privileges

- *Surgical case review:* Reviews justification for surgery; compares pre- and postoperative diagnoses

- *Medical records:* Reviews timely completion of medical records; reviews clinical usefulness and adequacy of records for quality of care

- *Pharmacy and therapeutics:* Develops HSO formulary; reviews drug use and other therapeutics policies; may have special interest in antibiotics use

- *Utilization review:* Reviews use of resources to provide services, with special attention to lengths of inpatient stay and use of ancillary services

- *Quality assessment:* May be used instead of surgical case review and medical records committees; may review pre- and postoperative reports, use of ancillary services such as imaging and laboratories, and condition of patients on discharge to determine appropriateness of treatment

- *Quality improvement:* Monitors and assesses data from PSO to improve clinical processes (Chapters 4 and 8 cover improvement of quality and performance.)

Other common committees are infection control, blood use, risk management and safety, disaster planning, bylaws, and nominating. The CEO or designee should attend PSO meetings, including those of the MEC, as well as related activities.[130] HSOs may have a professional practice evaluation committee (PPEC) that conducts peer review in each clinical department. PPECs may report to the MEC or to a PSO committee with a broader range of responsibilities to improve quality of care.

Clinical Departmentation

Clinical departmentation is a function of an HSO's size and range of services. Nonhospital HSOs, such as MCOs and multispecialty group practices, have clinical departments. NFs and hospice have a medical director but do not need a PSO. Small hospitals have only departments of medicine and surgery. Mid-sized to large hospitals have specialties such as obstetrics and gynecology, pediatrics, and family practice. Departmentation expands as needed to include clinical specialties or subspecialties as separate departments, or sections within departments.

Clinical department heads are elected by department members or appointed by the CEO; regardless, they serve at the pleasure of the GB. Clinical managers may be paid or unpaid, although larger units and greater demands increase the likelihood that clinical managers not already employees will be salaried part time or full time. When specialization or size warrant, divisions and/or sections are established in departments. The upward scalar chain goes to the VP-MA. Larger HSOs salary these positions. Eventually, the scalar chain reaches the GB. The VP-MA reports to the CEO, which is consistent with the accountability that should be asked of the PSO. HSOs/HSs try to enhance managerial skills of clinical managers to develop LIP leaders.[131]

PSO Credentialing: Membership and Clinical Privileges

Credentialing has two parts. The first determines PSO membership and category—if the LIP is eligible for membership as defined in the PSO bylaws. This two-part process applies to both initial appointment and reappointment. PSO bylaws determine the process for each and include due process safeguards. An LIP may be a member of the PSO but has no clinical privileges. Examples include an LIP whose privileges were suspended by disciplinary action. Honorary and emeritus members of the PSO have no clinical privileges.

The second part of credentialing is based on an LIP's demonstrated current competence. It determines what the applicant may do when treating patients in the HSO. This part of credentialing is to delineate and grant clinical privileges.

The process and substance of initial application for PSO membership must be thorough, detailed, and comprehensive. In 1984, The Joint Commission adopted a medical staff standard that allowed acute care hospitals to extend PSO membership to LIPs other than physicians and dentists. This change recognized the roles of nonphysician LIPs such as podiatrists, clinical psychologists, nurse midwives, and chiropractors.

Applicants provide the basic information used in the screening process: demographic data; details on postsecondary, professional, and postgraduate education; certificates of specialty and professional memberships; licenses; information about successful and current challenges to licenses, certifications, registrations, and PSO memberships; voluntary or involuntary limitations, reductions, or losses of clinical privileges, certifications, or registrations; a statement of physical and mental health showing the applicant has no disability inconsistent with the clinical privileges sought; an authorization that allows information to be verified; and references.[132] Federal law requires physicians and LIPs to register with the Drug Enforcement Administration to prescribe or administer controlled substances.[133]

If the applicant meets screening criteria, additional information is required: details of malpractice actions in the previous 5 years and evidence of continuous malpractice insurance policy coverage to a limit set by the HSO/HS; a request for membership and privileges in the department in which the applicant wishes to practice; a signed statement that the PSO bylaws and rules and regulations have been read and will be followed; and a statement that, if appointed, the applicant will provide, or provide for, the continuous care of patients for whom the applicant is accountable.

It is prudent to require government-issued photographs of applicants, so copies can be sent to a reference to verify the applicant's identity. The national practitioner data bank established by the Health Care Quality Improvement Act of 1986 (PL 99-660)[134] (see Chapter 2) must be queried for adverse reports prior to initial appointment *and* reappointment. Problems are investigated and may affect credentialing decisions.

Applicants have the burden of proof and must complete the process to the HSO's satisfaction, which means providing the information and documentation it requires. The applicant may choose character references. The HSO *must* choose the professional references to query; this is the best way to obtain complete, objective information. Again, questions asked of references must be answered to the HSO's satisfaction. LIPs must not begin clinical activities until the application is complete and has been reviewed and approved.

Typically, PSO appointments are made for 2 years. Monitoring of quality is continuous. Reappointment is like initial appointment but has one key difference: During the preceding appointment period, the HSO has monitored and evaluated the LIP's performance. This information is used in decisions about membership category and clinical privileges to be granted, if any, in the next appointment cycle.

Credentialing is crucial to the quality of care and is done by the HSO with the PSO's help. HSs may use central credentials verification, with each HSO reviewing the credentials and granting clinical privileges to LIPs. The credentialing process is organized and monitored by the CEO. Completed files are referred to the clinical department in which the applicant seeks clinical privileges, and then to the PSO credentials committee, which makes a recommendation to the PSO MEC. The next level of review is by the VP-MA and president of the PSO, whose role is yet to be discussed here. Final approval of recommendations for PSO membership and clinical privileges lies with the GB, through its committee structure. Links to guidelines are provided in the endnotes as follows: 1) federal guidelines to document credentials of LIPs, other licensed or certified practitioners, and other clinical staff,[135] and 2) The Joint Commission guidelines on credentialing and granting privileges in accrediting ambulatory care.[136]

PSO Membership

PSOs have several categories of membership, ranging from most involved (active) to least involved (honorary or emeritus). New members, except those in consulting and honorary categories, may be granted provisional appointments. A probationary status allows clinical performance to be monitored, reviewed, and evaluated early in their affiliation with the HSO.

Delineating and Granting Clinical Privileges

Clinical privilege delineation for physicians is critical. Unlike other LIPs, states grant physicians an unlimited license to practice medicine. This means it is legal for them to undertake any clinical action they choose to attempt. Delineating clinical privileges makes their activities in the HSO or HS consistent with demonstrated current competence. By state license, nonphysician LIPs are limited to performing specific clinical activities; podiatrists are licensed to treat the foot and its related or governing structures by medical, surgical, or other means.[137] The clinical activities allowed under the limited licenses of nonphysician LIPs may be narrowed by the HSO or be systemwide in an HS, they may restrict but not expand what a state license allows them to do. The same process of delineating clinical privileges is used for nonphysician LIPs.

Clinical privileges must be delineated (individually or by category) for all LIPs who provide clinical care, regardless of PSO membership category. Clinical activities must be limited to the skills and qualifications the LIP can initially demonstrate and show continued competence to perform. Further, the HSO/HS must be able to support the LIP's clinical activities with staff, equipment, and other resources.

Privilege delineation has two parts. The first is determining the specific clinical privileges an LIP (or group of LIPs) will have. The second is continuing, systematic review of care to determine if changes in privileges are appropriate. Clinical privileges are specific to the HSO or HS. Each procedure or activity may be listed on the application or reapplication form, or there may be a general reference, such as "services intrinsic to internal medicine," with limitations as appropriate for the level of qualification, such as board certification. General terms or categories, such as internal medicine, must be defined in the PSO bylaws or its rules and regulations.

Delineation of clinical privileges for nonphysician LIPs is similar, although privileges are likely granted to a group and listed specifically for each as in the case of physicians. It is common and desirable for special relationships of nonphysician LIPs to physicians to be described in the grant of privileges or referenced in the PSO bylaws or rules and regulations. Examples are nurse midwives, who practice with or are employed by obstetricians, and nurse anesthetists, who practice with or are employed by surgeons or anesthesiologists. Usually, clinical privileges of nonphysician LIPs are granted on a 2-year cycle or as accreditors require.

External sources guide credentialing and privileging. CMS's Conditions of Participation are a general framework. The Joint Commission requires ongoing professional practice evaluation using a documented summary of data to assess an LIP's clinical competence and professional behavior, and a focused professional practice evaluation to gauge privilege-specific competencies of LIPs who want to add privileges or are new to the PSO, or when questions arise as to their ability to provide safe, high-quality patient care.[138] National Association Medical Staff Services (now exclusively NAMSS) lists standards for initial credentialing (https://www.namss.org/Advocacy/Ideal-Credentialing-Standards) and a chart comparing the standards of major accrediting bodies (www.castleworldwide.com/idev/guidelines/CCN Resources/namss_comparison_of_accreditation_standards%20(4).pdf).

Economic Credentialing

Financial issues are causing HSOs/HSs to evaluate economic impact of LIPs as an adjunct to clinical performance. Economic credentialing uses two criteria: volume of referrals and admissions, and practice patterns. Referrals and admissions produce revenue. Practice patterns receive more attention, however. LIPs vary widely in use of resources such as lengths of inpatient stay, diagnostic testing, and types and duration of therapies. Data systems can generate profiles showing each LIP's costs per diagnosis. The criterion should be that patients receive needed services—no more, no less. This is high-quality *and* efficient care. Economic credentialing highlights the value of clinical protocols.

Turf Conflicts

Conflicts as to which LIPs are granted specific clinical privileges arise from professionalism, economics, and technology. Prestige and economics press LIPs to enhance their skills, which may cause them to infringe traditional areas of other LIPs. Reimbursement beckons them toward a procedure-based clinical practice.

New diagnostic and therapeutic technology is usable by various types of LIPs. HSOs/HSs must have a process by which LIPs claiming expertise in new procedures or clinical activities have their proficiency reviewed and receive (or are denied) privileges to perform them. Chapter 5 describes how new technology blurs lines that traditionally separated medicine and surgery, medical and surgical specialties and subspecialties, and the practices of nonphysician LIPs. Blurred lines cause turf conflicts that disrupt referral patterns and professional relationships, with likely negative effects on HSOs/HSs. Economic dimensions of turf conflicts for the organization include duplicate equipment, space, and staff to placate LIPs, as well as disgruntled LIPs severing relationships with the HSO/HS and admitting patients elsewhere.

Impaired LIPs

PSOs (and the profession, as well) have a less-than-enviable record of self-regulation regarding impaired physicians. When a colleague has a problem, PSO members tend to coalesce and prevent or impede internal and external scrutiny. This human tendency may cause HSOs/HSs to be less rigorous in meeting their ethical and legal obligations to patients and staff. HSOs/HSs are morally (and perhaps legally) obliged to try to rehabilitate impaired staff, including LIPs. Regardless, patient and staff safety cannot be compromised.

All states have formal programs to rehabilitate and monitor physicians with psychoactive substance use disorders, as well as mental and physical illnesses.[139] Attention to this issue increased in 1973 when the American Medical Association (AMA) released a policy paper, "The Sick Physician: Impairment by Psychiatric Disorders, Including Alcoholism and Drug Dependence."[140] The AMA recognized impaired physicians as a problem and proposed model legislation for a therapeutic alternative to disciplinary action; alcoholism and other drug addictions were categorized as illnesses. Its Council on Ethical and Judicial Affairs offers guidance as to physicians' health and effects of impairment on professional activities, including patient safety, care, and trust in the profession.[141]

Varied types and subtleties make it hard to detect and document impairment, which may be physical, mental, or both, and be caused by aging, disease, or chemical dependence. Surgeons experience a decline in physical and cognitive abilities from aging, including decrements in sensory function (vision and hearing), visual-spatial ability, inductive reasoning, verbal memory, and other areas of cognition; changes that must be considered in granting clinical privileges.[142] An estimated 12.9% of male physicians and 21.4% of female physicians meet diagnostic criteria for alcohol abuse or dependence. Abuse of prescription drugs and use of illicit drugs are rare.[143] Medical specialties such as surgery have a higher incidence of alcohol abuse or dependence (male surgeons, 13.9%; female surgeons, 25.6%).[144] Major differences by sex warrant investigation. Estimates of impaired nonphysician caregivers are similar: 20% of nurses may be addicted to at least one controlled substance.[145] Another aspect of addiction is physicians' diverting prescription drugs, a significant problem with potentially adverse implications for public health.[146] Such issues must be covered in the PSO bylaws and rules and regulations.[147]

GBs and PSOs have become more attentive to addiction. The authority of CEOs and GBs is clear, as is their accountability. Impairment should be identified by risk management as discussed in Chapter 14.

PSO Disciplinary Action

Disciplinary action against an LIP may become necessary. Often, it results from minor infractions of the PSO bylaws or its rules and regulations. Sometimes, organizational policies are involved. Infrequently is disciplinary action needed because quality of care is deficient. The first ethical duty of the HSO/HS is to protect patients and staff; second is its obligation to improve clinical quality. Absent an emergency, both require PSO action. Depending on the matter, GB review and approval of recommendations may be needed.

A common problem is LIPs do not complete medical records of discharged patients in the time set by the PSO. Such lapses diminish quality of care but likely pose little direct risk to patients. Verbal or written warnings are first steps in discipline. A continuing problem causes temporary suspension of admitting privileges; elective admissions end. Loss of admitting privileges likely gets a prompt, positive response from the LIP.

PSO bylaws include options for disciplinary action. In order of *increasing* severity, they are mandatory continuing or special medical education, letter of admonition, supervision, suspension of admitting or clinical privileges or both, censure, reduction of privileges, and termination of privileges. Underlying such actions is the ethical (and legal) duty to protect patients from harm.

Depending on the disciplinary action, the LIP may be entitled to due process as stated in the PSO bylaws. If so, the PSO recommendation is reviewed by the GB, whose decision is final. If patient harm is imminent, the CEO or designee acts for the GB. The Health Care Quality Improvement Act of 1986 requires that actions adverse to clinical privileges for more than 30 days must be reported to a national practitioner data bank.

Organization of Select HSOs

In various permutations, the triad of GB, CEO, and PSO is found in all HSOs. Following is a discussion of how four types of HSOs are organized: acute care hospitals, NFs, MCOs, and public health departments. The triad is applied to each.

In addition to these examples, myriad other types of organizations provide healthcare. Few are classified as HSOs. Most are small measured by staff and clinical impact. In aggregate, however, they are significant to the health services system. Examples include the following:

Residential care facilities Provide 24-hour social and personal care to children, the elderly, and others with limited ability to care for themselves. Various health professionals care for residents of assisted-living facilities, alcohol and drug rehabilitation centers, group homes, halfway houses, and similar settings.

Offices of physicians In 2016, about half the 713,800 active physicians and surgeons worked in physicians' offices.[148] They may be in solo or group practice. The latter offers backup coverage, lessens overhead costs, and facilitates consultation. Increasingly, physicians are salaried staff of group practices, HSOs, or HSs.

Offices of dentists In 2016, there were about 153,500 dentists. Dentists tend to practice solo; some have a partner or are employed. They employ a few staff to provide dental care, including oral surgery.[149]

Offices of other health practitioners Examples include chiropractors, optometrists, podiatrists, occupational and physical therapists, psychologists, audiologists, speech-language pathologists, dietitians, among others. HSOs may contract for these services. Some practice complementary and alternative medicine: acupuncturists, homeopaths, hypnotherapists, massage therapists, and naturopaths.

Medical and diagnostic laboratories Medical and diagnostic laboratories provide analytic or diagnostic services to the medical profession or directly to patients from a physician's prescription. They analyze blood, take x-rays and scans, and perform other clinical tests. They provide few jobs.

The U.S. Bureau of Labor Statistics (www.bls.gov) reported employment in healthcare and social assistance of 20.3 million in 2019, making it the nation's largest employer. In early 2019 there were 1.6 million healthcare and social assistance establishments in the private sector. Almost 8 million are employed in ambulatory services healthcare.[150]

Legal Status of HSOs/HSs

HSOs/HSs have specific legal status. Nongovernmental (privately owned) HSOs may be sole proprietorships (a form rare today), general and limited liability partnerships, corporations, and limited liability companies. Some HSOs/HSs are owned by state and local (county, city, hospital authority) governments and are organized under state enabling laws. Legal status of federally owned HSOs derives from federal law; other governmental jurisdictions regulate them only with permission. Examples are Department of Veterans Affairs hospitals; U.S. Air Force, Army, and Navy hospitals; and U.S. Public Health Service clinics.

Partnerships are contracts between two or more persons to engage in commerce or business. Partnerships are general or limited. Physicians in a group practice may be general partners. *General* means each partner is liable for the debts and errors of other partners—very undesirable. LLPs require state approval. They have one or more general partners who are jointly and severally liable for the partnership; liability of limited partners is limited to assets they invested. LLPs are common in joint ventures between HSOs/HSs and LIPs. A joint venture results from a contract to establish a legal entity (LLP or LLC) that engages in activities in which costs, revenue, and control are shared. It is used, for example, to establish an imaging center. Here, the HSO/HS is the general partner; LIPs are the limited partners. Usually, the general partner invests most of the capital and is the managing partner. Limited partners invest little capital. That fact has raised questions about not-for-profit HSOs/HSs with the U.S. Internal Revenue Service. The primary reason HSOs/HSs form joint ventures with LIPs is not the capital they bring; it is the close ties and referrals. Or, as with a medical office building near a hospital, LIPs rent space (at fair market value) and practice there. Bonding or tying independent contractor LIPs into joint ventures helps HSOs/HSs improve profitability, market position, and, perhaps, relations with them. Joint ventures may be organized as LLCs too. This hybrid uses partnership and corporate legal principles. LLCs are favored for HSOs and some HS relationships because they offer the same protection from liability as incorporating while treating owners as partners for tax purposes.

Corporation is the universal form for HSOs/HSs. On application and filing articles of incorporation, the state issues a charter to create an artificial person known as a corporation. Corporations may be organized not-for-profit or for-profit. Advantages and disadvantages of each depend on tax laws in the state of incorporation and the purposes for which the corporation is organized. Corporations must have bylaws that detail their organization: GB composition, meetings, elections, committees, officers, and roles of CEO and PSO, if any. Bylaws are the organization's basic law; activities must be consistent with them. States allow physicians and LIPs such as dentists, clinical psychologists, podiatrists, and chiropractors to organize professional corporations, which are designated PCs. A designation Limited (Ltd.) is similar. This status provides protection from personal liability and may offer tax advantages.

Nongovernmental HSOs/HSs are regulated by all levels of government (see Chapter 2). States may delegate authority to local governments, which regulate them as any entity with similar functions (e.g., preparing, storing, and serving food). State and federal regulations apply to activities such as control, storage, use, and disposal of radioactive materials. The three levels of government may cooperate with enforcement.

Acute Care Hospitals

There have been hospitals for millennia. About 5,000 years ago, Greek temples were among the first. Similar entities were part of ancient Egyptian, Hindu, and Roman societies. These "hospitals" evolved from temples of worship and recuperation to almshouses and pest-houses, and, finally, to sites for applied medical technology.

Hospital is derived from the Latin, *hospitalis*. Early hospitals were well regarded. From the Middle Ages until the mid-19th century; however, they served the poor and were not well regarded. Their reputation improved slowly from the mid-1800s with the introduction of antisepsis and asepsis. Well into the 20th century, physicians provided charity care in hospitals but treated private, paying patients in their homes. New medical technology made hospital treatment, especially surgery, efficacious. This focused attention on acute care hospitals, which had the equipment, staff, and facilities for surgical patients. As private-paying patients became inpatients, acute care hospitals gained prestige and acceptance. This evolution was well under way by the 1920s as acute care hospitals became differentiated and specialized to organize and deliver an expanding scope of efficacious medical and surgical services.

Acute care hospitals have four primary functions. Foremost, they diagnose and treat the sick and injured; other functions depend on the mission. Medical condition determines the care a patient receives and the type of hospital in which it is provided, either as an inpatient or outpatient.

A second function is preventing illness and promoting health. Examples include instructing patients about self-care after discharge, providing referrals to services such as home health, conducting disease screening, and offering childbirth education and smoking cessation education.

A third function is training professionals and nonprofessionals to work in healthcare. Physicians in residencies and fellowships are examples, as are nursing assistants, medical social workers, clinical pharmacists, and therapeutic dietitians. Health services management education may require field experience.

A fourth function is research. Examples include clinical trials for drugs and devices, assessing intensive care units, and monitoring the use of standard (universal) precautions in emergency departments. A type of nonclinical research (health services research) is process improvement to enhance quality of care. See Chapters 4 and 8.

Diversification or being in an HS brings acute care hospitals into a broader range of activities. Examples are home health (61%), skilled nursing/long-term care (52%), and hospice (65%).[151]

Hospitals by the Numbers

By common use, *community hospital* refers to an acute care hospital that provides healthcare services to the public. This title applies to not-for-profit and for-profit hospitals. A community hospital has permanent facilities (including inpatient beds) and provides continuous nursing services as well as diagnosis and treatment through an organized PSO for surgical and nonsurgical conditions. "Special" hospitals admit only certain types of patients or those with specific illnesses or conditions.

From a peak of 7,174 hospitals of all types registered with the AHA in 1974, the number declined to 6,649 in 1990 to 5,759 in 2004.[152] The downward trend reversed in 2017 when 6,210 hospitals were registered with the AHA.[153] About half of community hospitals have fewer than 100 beds. Small hospitals tend to be isolated and need linkages through HSs.

Classification

Hospitals are classified by length of stay, type of control, and type of service. Length of stay is short or long term. *Acute* (short duration or episodic) is a synonym for *short term*. *Chronic* (long duration) is a synonym for *long term*. AHA defines short-term hospitals as having an average length-of-stay (ALOS) of less than 30 days, and long-term hospitals as having an ALOS of 30 days or more. Over 90% of hospitals are short term. Community hospitals are acute care (short term). Rehabilitation and chronic disease hospitals are long term. Psychiatric hospitals are usually long term. Some acute care hospitals have long-term care units for psychiatric care or rehabilitation. Hospital-based care may be inpatient (more than 23 hours ALOS) or outpatient. Staffing varies, based on size, location, mission, funding, organization, and management style. In 1999, federal legislation created the long-term care hospital whose patients have ALOS of more than 25 days.

Type of service denotes if the hospital is "general" or "special." General hospitals provide a broad range of medical and surgical services, to which are often added obstetrics and gynecology; pediatrics; orthopedics; and eye, ear, nose, and throat. *General* describes both acute and chronic care hospitals but usually applies to short-term hospitals. *Special* hospitals offer services in one medical or surgical specialty, such as pediatrics, obstetrics and gynecology, rehabilitation medicine, or psychiatry, or a discrete surgical procedure, such as hernia repair. Hospitals may add long-term care and home health to offer a comprehensive range of services.

A third classification method divides hospitals by control or ownership into not for profit, for profit (investor owned), or governmental (operated by federal, state, or local governments, or a hospital authority). Figure 11.11 shows types of hospital ownership. In 2017, there were 6,210 hospitals in the United States. Of these, 5,262 were community hospitals: 56% were

PRIVATE (NONGOVERNMENT) OWNERSHIP

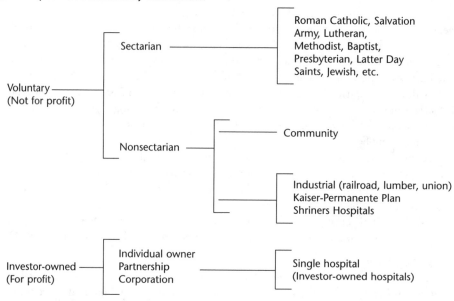

GOVERNMENT OWNERSHIP

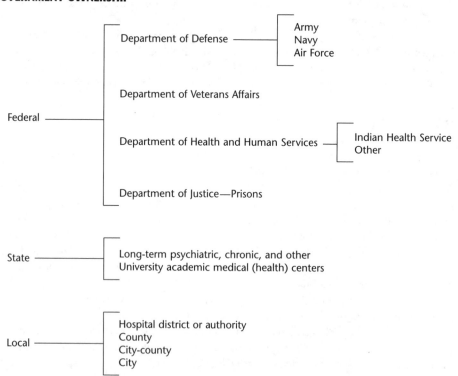

Figure 11.11.   Hospital ownership.

not for profit; 25% were investor owned, and 19% were owned by government. Community hospitals had 798,921 staffed beds and over 34 million inpatients. Total expenses for community hospitals were almost $1 trillion.[154] These data show that the long tradition of voluntarism (not for profit) in the acute care hospital field continues. During the late 19th and early 20th centuries, acute care hospitals became larger, more complex, and costlier. In part, the increase in not-for-profit acute care hospitals resulted from favorable tax treatment; the federal Hill-Burton program (begun in 1946) provided federal funds for hospital construction, expansion, and refurbishment. Prior to passage of Medicare in 1965, investor-owned acute care hospitals had almost disappeared. After Medicare was passed, investor-owned community hospitals increased rapidly (the law guaranteed a rate of return); after stabilizing in the 700–800 range,[155] the number of community hospitals grew to 1,322 by 2017.[156] Investor-owned (for-profit) companies manage many hospitals, including those organized not for profit.

The federal government has given doctor-owned (for-profit) hospitals special, negative attention. The Patient Protection and Affordable Care Act (ACA [PL 111-148 {2010}]) denies Medicare reimbursement to new doctor-owned hospitals and those adding new ORs or in-patient beds. The 275 doctor-owned hospitals responded by extending hours of operation, increasing procedures not restricted by the law, and declining to take Medicare patients—thus avoiding ACA mandates. These hospitals have much higher profit margins than others and higher levels of efficiency and patient satisfaction.[157]

In the 1980s, some states blurred the definition of an acute care hospital by licensing new types of HSOs. Postoperative (postacute) recovery centers, sometimes called medical inns or recovery care centers, are neither traditional hospitals nor ambulatory care centers. They offer a lower-cost option to support patients recovering from outpatient surgery and who need a period of observation. Some states license extended-stay hospitals or long-term care hospitals with a service level between an acute care hospital and an NF.

Organization of Acute Care Hospitals

The acute care hospital would be far less complex if it fit the usual organizational pyramid shown in Figure 11.2. Its structure, however, differs from the usual bureaucratic model. The differences result from the unusual relationships between authority of position in the managerial hierarchy and authority of knowledge of PSO members and other content area experts. Most PSO members do not fit the usual pyramid, as do staff who are paid by the hospital. Except for administrative work, LIPs in acute care hospitals are unlikely to be paid by the hospital. These HSOs have a "dual pyramid," with managerial and PSO hierarchies side by side. Department of Veterans Affairs hospitals and military hospitals integrate the PSO into the organizational structure; their PSO members are salaried. Contemporary hospitals do not emphasize this duality, but it continues. Adding the GB to PSO and managerial hierarchy completes the triad of acute care hospitals.

Figure 11.7 is the organization chart for a small, integrated for-profit healthcare system with two hospitals and a clinic. It shows both a service line (matrix) and traditional functional organization. The hospital GB is atop the organization and has overall accountability for and authority over it. GB members must respond to the external environment, are more scrutinized, and are under pressure to perform. The trend toward smaller, better-qualified, more-active hospital GBs was noted. Competence of GB members can be increased by continuing education. Some hospitals use the business enterprise model, which pays directors.

Acute care hospitals have several management levels, beginning with the CEO. Figure 11.7 suggests the dual hierarchy of administration and PSO common in acute care hospitals. The CMO (VP-MA) reports to the CEO and has numerous duties regarding the PSO. Departments and activities that provide direct patient care, clinical support, and administrative functions can be identified from the position titles in Figure 11.7. In addition, departments and units such as planning and marketing, business development, and human resources perform staff functions. Various departments and units deliver clinical services: nursing, pharmacy, dietary and nutrition services, radiology, and laboratories. Figure 11.7 shows the range of support departments: environmental services, engineering, supply chain, security, health information, and bed control/admitting.

In future, successful hospitals will have to offer new ways to deliver clinical services as they compete for fewer and fewer inpatient days. One strategy is developing centers of excellence to diagnose and treat disease; another is to focus on groups such as women and children or physical fitness and sports enthusiasts. These diagnostic and therapeutic services may be offered both inpatient and outpatient, with financial incentives to use the least costly site. Such initiatives reflect a trend toward market segmentation and boutique medicine. Common, too, are joint risk taking or joint ventures between hospitals and their PSOs and efforts to improve patient convenience and patient-centered care.

Chapter 5 describes technology's increasing portability (use beyond traditional settings) and implications for acute care hospitals; one is PSO members will expand nonhospital portions of their practices at the hospital's expense. Simultaneously cooperating and competing with their PSOs is perilous. Extrapolating the portability trend suggests major changes ahead for inpatient care.[158] Acute care hospitals may become large intensive care units—only very sick patients will be hospitalized. This will change staff-to-patient ratios, greatly increase costs per patient day, and make the work of GBs and managers even more demanding.

Nursing Facilities

Saint Helena (A.D. 250–330) established one of the first homes for older persons *(gerokomion)*. "She was a wealthy, intelligent, Christian convert and mother of Constantine the Great. Like other early Christian 'nurses' who devoted their lives to the sick and needy, she gave direct care herself."[159] In early America many towns operated almshouses—poorhouses, poor farms, or workhouses, were other names—for those "down on their luck" who needed a sheltered environment. In the early 1900s, affluent elderly lived at home or in privately owned boarding houses; church-sponsored homes for older Americans emerged.[160] NFs were rare.

NFs are likely to be freestanding. Some may be hospital based or part of an HS. They are licensed in all states and are highly regulated. They provide inpatient nursing, rehabilitation, and health-related services to residents who need continuous nursing care but not hospitalization.

In 2016, there were 15,600 NFs with 1.7 million licensed beds serving 1.3 million residents. About 69% were for profit, 23% were not for profit, and 7% were government owned. About 57% were part of an HS. In 2016, over 95% of NF beds were certified for both Medicare and Medicaid.[161]

Medicare and Medicaid (1966) covered skilled nursing services in NFs. This caused the average size of NFs to increase. Medicare Part A covers postoperative and posthospitalization care and rehabilitation. The Nursing Home Reform Act, part of the Omnibus Budget Reconciliation Act of 1987 (PL 100-203), included staff training and continuing education, professional and nonprofessional staffing, quality of life, and residents' rights.[162] States provide Medicaid to residents who meet financial and medical criteria. Payment for NF services comes from Medicaid 62%, Medicare 13%, and private pay 25%.[163]

Medicare-certified NFs have a range of staff. Most are in nursing service: RNs, LPNs, and CNAs, who provide most direct care. Federal law requires Medicare-certified NFs to have an activities director and a dietitian. The ideal treatment milieu in an NF is a multidisciplinary team with specialized expertise in gerontology, clinical pharmacology, dental/oral hygiene, medicine, nursing, nutrition support, ophthalmology, podiatry, surgery, psychiatry/psychology, rehabilitation therapy, physical therapy, and occupational therapy. Large NFs have these skills on staff; smaller NFs contract for them.

Organizational Structure of NFs

NFs have departments such as clinical services, physician and dental care, nursing, rehabilitation (occupational therapy [OT] and physical therapy [PT]), and speech-language pathology; clinical support services, such as laboratory, radiology, and pharmacy; and ancillary services such as housekeeping, laundry, and maintenance. Staffing is a challenge, especially for RNs and PTs. Recruiting and retaining CNAs is also problematic. The medical director provides clinical care and coordinates private physicians and PSO committees, if present.

Depending on size, NF organizational structures may be pyramidal (tall)—several levels of management, or flat—few levels. Small NFs have few managers or management levels between the CEO and staff. Large NFs have levels of managers who perform line and staff functions, such as administration and financial and human resources management. Figure 11.8 is an organization chart for a large not-for-profit NF.

Historically, NFs had few beds and were organized as for-profit sole proprietorships or partnerships, forms that are rare today. Most contemporary NFs are for-profit corporations, with few GB members; governance and management may be combined. Larger for-profit or not-for-profit NFs are corporations with a GB called the board of directors or board of trustees, respectively, and are like acute care hospital GBs in this regard. In addition to a CEO, various managers bring special skills, as size and activities require. CEOs of NFs in an HS, especially those organized for profit, likely have little independence. HSs tend to centralize functions, usually financial management and capital expenditures; policies, procedures, and rules are developed centrally and promulgated to the operating units.

All states require that NFs have a licensed administrator of record. Most states use the national licensure examination administered by the National Association of Long Term Care Administrator Boards to test basic competencies of entry-level administrators. The examination has five content domains: customer care, supports, and services; human resources; finance; environment; and management and leadership.[164]

A CMO is required by Medicare and is good practice, regardless. The CMO may be full or part time and ensures that medical services are coordinated and appropriate. The CMO is accountable for activities such as credentialing LIPs, ensuring compliance with regulations and disciplinary procedures, and reviewing and maintaining quality of care.[165] PSOs of NFs receiving federal funds must have written bylaws and rules and regulations, just as in acute care hospitals. PSOs may be open or closed. Unlike acute hospitals, NFs have few LIPs. Standing orders allow treatment without patient-specific orders.

LIPs undergo a credentialing process; a statement of privileges results. Most NF care is chronic and use of technologies is rare. Credentialing may be less demanding since patients are perceived as low risk. NFs should be guided by the rigorous credentialing processes of acute care hospitals. NF residents may be admitted by any licensed physician. Residents whose physicians have clinical privileges at the NF may be treated by them and are paid by the resident or third-party payer. Larger NFs may have salaried physicians who supplement the role of a resident's private physician.

Pessimistic predictions about the future of NFs suggest that inadequate reimbursement, costly federal regulation, and sicker residents may cause an economic crisis. Also, those who entered NFs in the past now have alternatives, including assisted living facilities and aging in place in their homes using supportive services such as home health. An estimated 200–300 NFs close annually. Those remaining have fewer residents, with a decrease from 1.48 million in 2000[166] to 1.30 million in 2015.[167] Demographics support more optimistic predictions, however, and suggest that rising demand for NF beds and more affluent elderly forecast a brighter future. There were 49.2 million adults aged 65 and older in 2016, or 15.2% of the population. Their numbers are projected to be 98 million by 2060. More important in terms of care needs is that the 85 and over population is projected to more than double from 6.4 million in 2016 to 14.6 million in 2040.[168]

Managed Care Organizations

The most significant expression of managed care and MCOs is the HMO, formerly called prepaid group practice plans. *Health maintenance organization* was first used in the early 1970s in the Health Maintenance Organization Act of 1973 (PL 93-222).[169] HMOs' unique philosophy about healthcare stressed a close relationship between patient and physician, as well as a financial arrangement and preventive measures (compared with the acute care focus of traditional insurance) and provided incentives to insureds and providers to minimize hospital services. Prepaid group practice and early HMOs used salaried physicians and were closed-end—all care had to be provided in the HMO. One premium covered all services.

A current manifestation of HMOs is the accountable care organization (ACO). ACOs are groups of doctors, hospitals, and other healthcare providers, who voluntarily join to give coordinated, high-quality care to Medicare patients. Coordinated care helps ensure that patients, especially the chronically ill, receive appropriate care. The goal is to avoid duplication of services and prevent medical errors. ACOs that deliver high-quality care and spend fewer dollars share in the savings.[170]

Early HMOs grouped hospitals, physicians, and other providers and staff into an "organization"—more accurately, an arrangement—that offered comprehensive medical services to an enrolled population for a fixed, prepaid fee. HMOs could be a set of contracts—a virtual HSO—or an actual, vertically integrated HSO. Compared with other arrangements, HMOs were unique because they combined delivery and financing. Contemporary HMOs go well beyond the closed-end model and have become MCOs that offer various plans and products. For example, a point-of-service plan combines HMO and traditional insurance; members may stay within the HMO network or go outside it to receive care using traditional insurance.[171]

In 2016, there were 470 licensed HMOs, a decrease of 17% from 2011. Despite fewer HMOs, the number of enrollees increased.[172] In 2017, HMOs covered 94.8 million; preferred provider organizations (PPOs) covered 165 million.[173]

Types of MCOs

In the early 1900s health insurance was rare and likely to be an indemnity policy; insureds could go to any physician, hospital, or other provider. The insurer paid a fixed amount for the service; the insured paid any difference. Indemnity coverage was predictable and actuarily sound for insurance carriers. Insurance plans that paid for medical services provided to the insured became common in the mid-1900s. Service plans were offered by employers and insured through not-for-profit carriers, such as Blue Cross/Blue Shield plans.

From modest beginnings in the latter part of the 1900s, managed care became the most common delivery mechanism. MCOs are entities that offer HMO, PPO, or PSO plans, or a combination, such as high-deductible health plans (HDHPs). They are owned by national managed care companies, physician groups, hospitals, commercial health insurers, Blue Cross/Blue Shield plans, community cooperatives, private investors, or other organizations, which may be for profit and not for profit. In 2018, three-quarters of Americans were enrolled in an MCO.[174] Types of MCOs are described here.[175]

- *Health maintenance organizations:* Offer comprehensive health services to members for a fixed monthly fee by contracting with hospitals and employing or contracting with physicians and staff to provide services to enrollees. Ownership is a gamut from national MCOs to regional Blue Cross/Blue Shield plans, to independent. There are four basic types of HMOs.

  Staff model: Physicians and other providers are salaried employees who work only for that HMO and care only for its patients. Care is usually delivered at HMO sites.

  Group model: Has an exclusive contract with a physician practice to provide comprehensive services to enrollees. HMO and group practice are separate entities. The HMO pays the group, which pays physicians.

IPA model: Contracts with individual physicians or groups to treat patients in their offices. Physicians are organized as solo practitioners or small group practices. IPA physicians may treat nonplan patients.

Network model: Contracts with several large multispecialty groups or IPAs, rather than individual physicians or small practices. These groups or IPAs may treat nonplan patients.

- *Preferred provider organizations:* PPOs are networks of hospitals, physicians, and other providers that provide services for a negotiated fee. PPOs often sold as an option—a rider—to traditional health insurance. Financial risk is assumed by the sponsoring organization—an insurance company, third-party administrator, or self-insured employer. PPOs do not perform the usual HMO functions of underwriting, utilization management, and review of quality.

- *Provider-sponsored organizations:* PSOs are owned or controlled by providers. Many HMOs are provider controlled. PSO describes provider organizations formed to contract directly with purchasers to deliver services. Unlike IPAs and other providers, PSOs assume financial risk for insureds. PSOs are formed by entities such as IPAs, PHOs, and integrated delivery systems (IDSs).

- *High-deductible health plan:* HDHPs are a hybrid model used in conjunction with a health savings account (HSA). They were also used in the ACA. High deductibles reduce premiums and are favored by employers. HDHPs have had rapid growth.[176;]

No matter the type, all MCOs have six characteristics and functions:[177]

1. Arrange with hospitals and LIPs to provide a defined set of services to members

2. Establish criteria and develop processes for selecting and monitoring performance of LIPs

3. Establish processes to measure utilization, LIP referral patterns, and quality

4. Provide incentives for members to use MCO-associated LIPs and HSOs, or require that they do

5. Provide incentives for associated LIPs and HSOs to encourage appropriate use of services

6. Provide and encourage use of programs and activities to improve health status of members

Despite shared characteristics, MCOs differ widely in paying providers; most use several types of payment, even in the same market. Salaried physicians and other LIPs in staff-model HMOs are the simplest. Hospitals may be paid discounted fee-for-service, per diem, or per-case rates; diagnosis-related groups (DRGs); or capitation. Home health is paid a per-hour or per-visit fee. Payment methods such as discounted fee-for-service may apply to all providers. PPOs use discounted fee-for-service almost exclusively.[178]

Organization of MCOs

MCOs have varied organizational structures. All are corporations organized for profit or not for profit. Their GBs perform the usual governance functions, such as set policy and evaluate performance. Managers include a CEO whose title is usually executive director or president. Commonly, MCO CEOs are physicians prepared in management. Small MCOs have flat organizations; large MCOs have taller structures.

The CMO is an important senior manager responsible for clinical activities, of which review of medical and hospital services utilization is crucial. Other responsibilities include monitoring quality, recruiting and credentialing LIPs, managing disciplinary actions, and developing and implementing policies and procedures. The CMO helps negotiate and manage provider contracts and participates in enrollee relations.

MCOs organize the professional staff variously. Few use the hospital PSO model. The most tightly controlled is the staff-model HMO in which physicians and other LIPs are screened and credentialed as in hospitals. Least controlled are MCOs with IPA characteristics. Historically, HMOs did not credential their LIPs, relying instead on hospital credentialing. Problems with this approach, including legal liability, caused MCOs to begin credentialing LIPs. Further, accreditors such as the National Committee for Quality Assurance (NCQA) (www.ncqa. org) and The Joint Commission began to require credentialing. Using LIP-provided information, the process likely includes primary source verification, such as licensure and specialty board certification, medical training, drug dispensing (U.S. Drug Enforcement Administration) license, hospital clinical privileges, malpractice history and insurance coverage, national practitioner data bank entries, and Medicare and Medicaid sanctions.

Relationships with LIPs are contractual and contrast with their status at hospitals where they have privileges. In the latter, LIPs are unlikely to be employees and have no financial relationship with it. As independent contractors, these LIPs use the hospital as a clinical workshop. The least complex contract is a staff-model HMO, which employs LIPs and staff. Nonphysician LIPs may have employment contracts that specify duties and compensation. Support staff are employees at will and unlikely to have contracts.

MCOs are accredited with NCQA criteria, including quality management and improvement; population health management; network management; utilization management; credentialing and recredentialing; members' rights and responsibilities; member connections; and Medicaid benefits and services.[179] The Health Effectiveness Data and Information Set (HEDIS) evaluates performance on more than 90 measures in six domains of care: effectiveness of care; access/availability of care; experience of care; utilization and risk-adjusted utilization; health plan descriptive information; and measures collected using electronic clinical data systems for use by consumers and purchasers.[180]

Despite an early presence in U.S. healthcare and a major boost from federal law, numbers of HMOs have varied. Contributing factors include consumer hesitance to give up choice of physicians and physician reluctance to relinquish their autonomy and fee-for-service payment. Efforts by employers and, to a lesser extent, enrollees, to control costs have supported and enhanced MCO financing and provision of services. MCOs have shown their importance among providers, payers, and employers trying to control costs. Winners in the continuing managed care drama will be well-managed, diversified MCOs with high levels of patient satisfaction and documented delivery of high-quality, cost-efficient services.

Public Health

The HSOs/HSs already described here deliver personal health services. The broader healthcare system includes public health entities, which are many and varied in organization and specific functions and which emphasize delivery of services to groups or populations. The Centers for Disease Control and Prevention (CDC) has identified 10 functions of public health:

1. Monitor health status to identify and solve community health problems
2. Diagnose and investigate health problems and health hazards in the community
3. Inform, educate, and empower people about health issues
4. Mobilize community partnerships and action to identify and solve health problems
5. Develop policies and plans that support individual and community health efforts
6. Enforce laws and regulations that protect health and ensure safety
7. Link people to needed personal health services and assure the provision of healthcare when otherwise unavailable

8. Assure competent public and personal health care workforce

9. Evaluate effectiveness, accessibility, and quality of personal and population-based health services

10. Research for new insights and innovative solutions to health problems[181]

Public health functions are provided at all three levels of government. Examples at the federal level are the Food and Drug Administration (www.fda.gov) and the CDC (www.cdc.gov). States have health departments. The Virginia Department of Health (VDH) (http://www.vdh.virginia.gov/) is an example. In addition to the 50 states, the District of Columbia, and eight U.S. territories, public health entities in cities, counties, and other local governmental jurisdictions totaled over 3,000 in 2016.[182] Prince William County (VA) Health District (http://www.vdh.virginia.gov/prince-william/) is an example of a local government health entity. The websites include organization charts.

Organization of Public Health

In 2016, 29 state public health entities were freestanding (independent); 21 were part of a larger combined health and human services organization, commonly known as an umbrella organization. About half of public health entities were governed by a board of health or similar body.[183] Governance functions of public health boards mirror those of HSOs/HSs. State boards promulgate rules; advise elected officials on public health polices and concerns; and develop public health policies and legislative agendas. Members include public health professionals, citizens, consumers, business professionals, and educators.[184]

State health entities have a CEO, usually known as the state health secretary or commissioner of health. Most are nominated by the governor and confirmed by the state legislature or a board or commission. In 2015, the income of public health entities was about $28.6 billion. In 2014–2015, the two largest spending categories as a proportion of states' total budgets were clinical services/consumer care and women, infants, and children's services. In 2016, public health entities had about 100,000 employees.[185] State public health governance and management structures and processes tend to be replicated at the local government levels.

Health Systems

Figure 11.10 (A and B) shows horizontal and vertical integration. Figure 11.12 shows a system integrated both horizontally and vertically. Horizontal integration occurs when two or more entities that deliver the same or similar healthcare services form an SA, merge, or are acquired to improve service delivery and market position. In healthcare, vertical integration results from joining in one entity the continuum of health services providers. Both types can use contracts and/or ownership. Contractual relationships are simplest and least capital intensive. In 2016, 626 HSs included 70% of nonfederal general acute care hospitals, which had 91.6% of hospital discharges.[186] See the Agency for Healthcare Research and Quality website (https://www.ahrq.gov/chsp/compendium/index.html). In 2016, the three largest U.S. HSs were for profit, with about 75,000 staffed inpatient beds; the next three largest were not for profit, with about 49,000 staffed inpatient beds.[187] Integration as part of strategizing and planning is considered in Chapter 10.

Highly integrated describes an HS that has by ownership or contract three or more stages of health services delivery, including at least one acute care hospital; one physician component, such as a PHO or group practice; one other stage, such as an HMO, NF, home health agency (HHA), or ambulatory surgery center (ASC); and one systemwide contract with a payer, such as an employer or employer coalition, traditional insurer, MCO, or government entity.[188] The University of Pittsburgh Medical Center (www.upmc.com) is a highly integrated HS that serves western Pennsylvania and has international initiatives. It owns a health plan, insurance

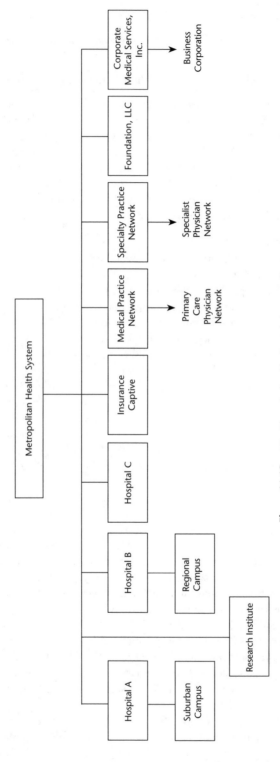

Figure 11.12. HS with vertical and horizontal elements of integration.

436

company, 40 hospitals, and 700 physicians' office and clinics, and employs 4,900 physicians. Other names for highly integrated HSs are integrated delivery system (IDS), organized delivery system (ODS), or integrated delivery network (IDN).

The highly integrated HS "provides or arranges to provide a coordinated continuum of services to a defined population and is willing to be held clinically and fiscally accountable for the outcomes and the health status of the population served."[189] Such entities are difficult to establish; they may be even more difficult to maintain and nurture. A philosophical commitment to integration by HS leadership is crucial. Table 11.2 shows factors key to HS success.

An HS formed by contracts between or among HSOs is a virtual HS; constituent HSOs are not owned. HSs can be distinguished, too, by integration based on ownership or contract. HSs formed by contracts are *health networks;* those formed by ownership are *health systems.* HSOs may be loosely or tightly coupled in an SA depending on if there are multiple contracts (as a health network) or one owner (as an HS). Combinations of these relationships may be found in the same SA.

HSs were highly touted as the best or even the only way to deliver health services. Positive results in terms of quality and costs were expected. Many HSs have not achieved their potential, however.[190] Worse, there is evidence that HSs raise prices and increase costs without observable improvement in quality, despite a plethora of reasons why cost control and improved quality should occur.[191]

By offering a continuum of services, integrated HSs with the characteristics shown in Table 11.2 are more likely to achieve commercial success.

The Triad in HSs

Effective HS governance begins by understanding the whole is the sum of its parts. Synergies will, however, make it much greater than that sum. HS governance involves three areas: 1) governing

Table 11.2.   Characteristics of Successfully Integrated Health Systems

1. Diverse stakeholders committed to a unified vision: quality healthcare requires patient-centered, comprehensive, integrated services
2. Flatter, more responsive integrated organization structure that adds needed services but avoids duplication and contains costs
3. Facilitates strategic alliances and other interorganizational relationships to enhance delivery of integrated services
4. Recruits and appoints effective physician leadership to key system positions
5. Fosters interprofessional collaboration and individual accountability in the context of team-based delivery
6. Takes responsibility to identify and serve healthcare needs of diverse populations
7. Values measurement and uses information systems for continuous quality improvement and staff education
8. Incorporates evidence-based care guidelines and translates new knowledge into clinical practice
9. Blends wellness, health promotion, and social services programs to improve healthcare outcomes and population health
10. Offers market-driven health insurance for service coverage and access at multiple points of care

Author-developed table with supplemental information from the following: Esther Suter, Nelly D. Oelke, Carol E. Adair, Gail D. Armitage. "Ten Key Principles for Successful Health Systems Integration." *Healthcare Quarterly* 13, spec. no. (2009): 16–23. https://www.ncbi.nlm.nih.gov/pmc/articles/PMC3004930/, retrieved July 26, 2019; Marjorie A. Satinsky. *The Foundation of Integrated Care: Facing the Challenges of Change,* 73. Chicago: American Hospital Publishing, 1998.

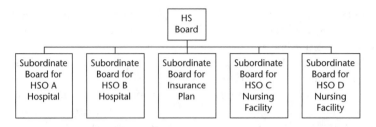

Figure 11.13. Decentralized governance structure.

the whole (the HS); 2) governing the components (HSOs); and 3) resolving problems between the two levels. Governing freestanding HSOs is relatively straightforward. The more complex an HS, the more challenging it will be to govern.

Centralized or Decentralized Governance

Centralized governance, known as the corporate or system board model, places governance in one GB that controls component HSOs. Figure 11.3 shows a centralized structure. Component HSOs may have *advisory* bodies or boards with little authority and limited fiduciary duty. Centralized HSs have one GB.

In decentralized governance, the system GB shares governance functions with GBs of constituent HSOs. An advantage of sharing governance is that it delegates functions that are performed best at the level where the unique circumstances of system components are known. In Figure 11.13, the parent or system GB has authority over subordinate GBs. Authority commonly retained includes controlling capital budgets, selecting and retaining the component CEO, and selling assets. A major task in decentralized governance is to monitor and coordinate subordinate GBs. This is difficult if varying philosophies of GBs cause tension among them. Often, the HS CEO is caught in the middle of these disputes. A parent GB may have a futuristic vision; component GBs may focus on operations and finance. Conflicts occur even if some members of subordinate GBs serve on the parent GB. HS CEOs minimize these conflicts by working with their GBs to develop a shared vision in the strategic plan. Hoshin planning is useful here (see Chapter 4).

Subordinate GBs in decentralized HSs may be organized variously. Figure 11.13 shows subordinate boards responsible for various types of organizations in the HS. Figure 11.14

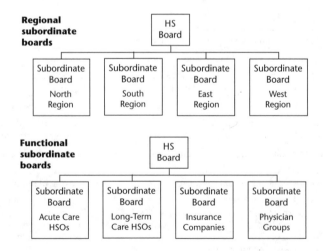

Figure 11.14. Decentralized governance structures with regional or functional subordinate boards.

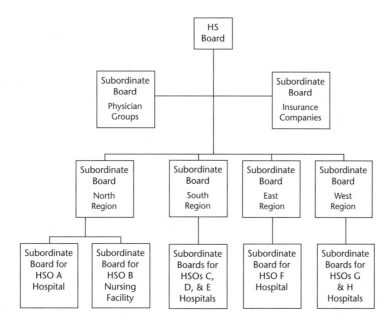

Figure 11.15. Complex governance structure combining organizational, regional, and functional bases of structuring subordinate boards.

shows a decentralized HS with subordinate GBs responsible for regions or functions. Regionalized subordinate GBs are accountable for a service area or geographic region. Functionally organized subordinate GBs govern entities performing similar functions, such as physician groups, hospitals, or insurance companies.

Figure 11.15 shows the organization of a highly integrated HS. Its GB governs physician group and insurance company GBs and the regional GBs to which GBs of operating components report. In this example, 11 GBs report directly or indirectly to the HS GB.

Centralized and decentralized governance have advantages and disadvantages. Centralized governance can make faster decisions; CEOs spend less time on governance; and GBs can focus on strategic issues. Disadvantages are fewer stakeholders with governance roles and the potentially corrupting effect of power.

Decentralized governance allows system GBs to delegate activities to subordinate GBs. Subordinate GBs understand local community and HSO issues better. Decentralization allows more stakeholders to serve in governance. The confusion and conflict as to roles and responsibilities of multiple GBs may lead to gridlock, however. Multiple boards use more CEO time in GB interactions, and the decision-making process may be slower, especially if subordinate GBs focus on local interests and less on the system's.

Composition of the GB

Related to centralized versus decentralized governance is GB composition, which can include representative members, nonrepresentative members, or both.[192] Representative members of a centralized GB are chosen because they have a relationship with a component HSO. Nonrepresentative members are neither directly aligned with, nor represent a component HSO. Representative members of a system-level GB may be CEOs or GB members of component HSOs. As HSs grow, GBs grow—perhaps to a point of unmanageability. Representational HS governance has an important drawback: Members may feel obliged to represent and further the interests of their component HSO. It takes time for them to develop a mindset focused on the greater HS.[193]

Governance Responsibilities

Governance in an HS differs from that in a free-standing HSO. GB members of both must meet five general responsibilities to fulfill their obligations to stakeholders.[194] Table 11.2 identifies 10 specific characteristics linked to governance success of HSs.

First, GBs determine the HS's vision and values (organizational philosophy) from which the mission is derived. When discussing the conceptual competence needed by HS GBs, the mission of a highly integrated HS focuses on enhancing the health status of a defined population, not treating individual patients. HS governance defines health broadly and maximizes advantages of integrated delivery of health services.

Second, GBs ensure the CEO's performance, including selection, defining expectations, and appraising performance. Difficulties of those who organized and managed highly integrated HSs have shown that "the healthcare industry has not been through massive consolidation and restructuring before. Amateurish moves, setbacks, and missed opportunities are commonplace."[195] Historically, hubris has been a problem; it will likely remain a risk for HS GBs and their CEOs.

Third, HS GBs are ethically and legally accountable for quality of care. They organize a framework to monitor LIP credentialing and the processes that measure quality, utilization, risk management, and health at the population level. Integrating providers on a continuum of care enhances use of clinical algorithms, guidelines, and pathways to improve outcomes, and opportunities to improve service quality and customer satisfaction. GBs must ensure data integrity and use a consolidated quality statement and an accountability model to report performance.[196]

The fourth accountability is financial performance. GBs in free-standing HSOs were accountable for meeting financial objectives; maintaining financial controls; and ensuring that financial management, including investments, was successful. These aspects of financial performance are present in HSs, even as GBs add new areas. HSs gain financial advantage by unified selling when service integration allows single-signature contracting and the HS can manage clinical outcomes, develop continua-of-care, and reduce costs per episode of care. HSs garner managed care contracts with insurers and other payers under favorable terms. Mature HSs can undertake risk contracting with third-party payers.

The fifth area of GB accountability is to self. Those who govern must do their job well. Meeting this challenge means adopting and maintaining bylaws to guide governance, selecting capable members for the HS GB (and HSOs in a decentralized HS), and ensuring that GB performance and member development are evaluated. The difference between free-standing HSOs and HSs is scope and complexity. Coordinating GBs of constituent HSOs in a decentralized HS is especially problematic.

CEOs

The CEO of a successful HS does the following:[197]

- Seeks harmony in HS interactions

- Balances analysis (examining parts of the HS) with synthesis (seeing the parts as a whole)

- Focuses on the whole HS with all its parts, large and small

- Emphasizes patterns of change over time rather than snapshots of activity or behavior

- Pursues root causes of performance problems to avoid responses to symptoms

- Focuses on integration, interconnectedness, and interrelationships in the HS

Chapter 13 details the managerial competencies. Summarized here are those relevant to HS CEOs.[198] The importance of conceptual competence to envision the place and role of an

HSO is heightened when applied to an HS. Two aspects are essential. First, the CEO must visualize and understand the entities in the HS and the HS in its environment. Second, compared with HSOs, system CEOs manage more complex organizations; a major part of the complexity results from a need to share more leadership with physicians. "Success in integrated healthcare requires physicians in leadership positions."[199] It is likely that pluralistic approaches will be used, including "combinations of owned physician groups, independent practice associations, physician-hospital organizations, management services organizations, and the like."[200]

HS CEOs need extensive technical managerial/clinical competence and the expertise to understand work occurring throughout the HS. CEOs and senior managers will be much more effective interacting with physicians if they are knowledgeable about clinical medicine. HSs offer a wide range of services; clinical expertise must be more expansive than in freestanding HSOs.

Interpersonal/collaborative competence is necessary to manage an HS. It includes negotiating contracts that form the SAs and IORs intrinsic to HSs, and then managing them. Resolving interorganizational conflicts is part of this competence. HS CEOs must convince executives of component HSOs to judge success using the HS's vision, values, and objectives. This may require them to suboptimize their HSO's performance to optimize performance of the HS.

CEOs of HSs need political/commercial competence, which enables them to assess effects of public policy and influence policy making and policy makers.[201] Commercial competence means understanding markets and positioning the HS for best advantage. Commercially successful HSs contract with health plans and employers to offer comprehensive benefits packages. HS CEOs must have governance competence to assist the GB to perform it functions. Further, HS CEOs must be knowledgeable about strategic management since many are HS GB members, and it is difficult to separate governance from strategic management.

Professional Staff Organization

An HS has no PSO. Only organizations that deliver health services need a PSO. An HS provides the organizational superstructure for horizontal or vertical integration of health services.

There are many ways HSs can encourage system LIPs to work for their own benefit while simultaneously benefiting the HS. For example, the HS may encourage its HSOs to partner with their PSOs to deliver services using HS-developed or HS-determined models. Or, the HS may support establishing group practices or other shared LIP arrangements that benefit the LIPs, and the HSO and HS. LIPs may form an MSO. This benefits LIPs by improving their practices, which in turn benefits LIPs' patients, the HSO, and the HS. CMS allows HSs to have unified, integrated, systemwide PSOs. Constituent PSOs must agree to join by majority vote.[202]

HSs will likely standardize elements of managing PSOs at constituent HSOs. For example, HSs may assist constituent HSOs to develop, implement, and review PSO bylaws and rules and regulations. Primary background checks of PSO applicants may be centralized in the HS. A problem common to PSOs is inadequately prepared clinical managers such as section chiefs and department heads. HSs may help solve that problem by setting qualification minimums and assisting in training. HSs support constituent HSOs by standardizing clinical maps and practice guidelines; establishing policies and procedures for activities such as reporting patient care statistics; and suggesting benchmarks for clinical and financial performance.

Individually or as groups, LIPs may be employed by, contract with, or have their practices owned by the HS or a constituent HSO. Results of HS (and HSO) ownership of physician practices have been mixed.

Currently, about 40 percent of physicians are employed by hospitals, and this trend is accompanied by a corresponding reduction in the proportion of physicians with a practice ownership stake. In some markets, well over half of the physician practices are hospital owned. Furthermore, there appears to be an association between horizontal hospital consolidation and physician employment, which suggests that in consolidated markets, physicians may feel pressure to align with one of the dominant systems out of concern that the systems will bring in other physicians to compete with them.

The trend toward hospital affiliation meets the needs of younger physicians, who seem interested in financial security, work–life balance, and shelter from an increasingly complex and unstable health care marketplace and, thus, are willing to exchange the professional autonomy that comes with independent, entrepreneurial practice for these personal advantages. The hospital-anchored health system can offer the predictable working hours, freedom from administrative demands, management expertise, and capital that small practices lack, while also providing higher incomes.[203]

Other relationship models include MSOs. In contrast to physician-only MSOs, these are in the HSOs/HSs. The types of services provided by HSO/HS-linked MSOs are billing, information system acquisition and installation, staffing, staff training and development, managed care contract negotiation and compliance, and office management.[204] As noted, physicians and a hospital in (or outside) an HS can form a PHO. Grouping physicians and a hospital into one entity eases contracting with health plans, employers, or purchasing coalitions.[205] MSOs and PHOs are commonly organized as joint ventures.

Summary

Much remains to be learned about integrated healthcare delivery. Yet to be identified are system-level factors that result in more efficient service delivery. Research using similar organizations may show how integration improves clinical outcomes and identify key characteristics of successful systems. Communicating outcomes of comparative healthcare systems research disseminates best practices and the benefits of integration for quality, affordability, accessibility, and effectiveness.[206]

Diversification in HSOs and HSs

Several types of HSOs/HSs have been described. None is in a static state; they will evolve in significant ways. Diversification is an important part of these changes. Since the mid-1980s, HSOs/HSs have used diversification to generate revenue from collateral services such as home health. Chapter 10 analyzes diversification in the context of planning.

HSOs/HSs diversify by adding to existing service lines or entering new markets. Diversification provides new revenue streams to supplement traditional sources, such as inpatient services, and enhancing revenue and profitability may be the most important reasons to diversify. Other reasons include meeting service area health needs, offering new services and innovating how existing services are offered, spreading financial risk among several activities and markets, and seeking to improve relations with the professional staff.[207]

Types of Diversification

Diversification can be concentric or conglomerate. Concentric diversification adds different but related and complementary services. Conglomerate diversification adds services unrelated to core activities. Almost all HSO/HS diversification is concentric.

Concentric diversification builds on core competencies and develops or acquires services that complement existing ones, expands sales in current markets, and/or enters new markets.

It is dominant in health services because of unique competencies that are protected by licensure and professional dominance. Rarely are there substitutes. A proclivity for concentric diversification distinguishes HSOs/HSs from other types of organizations for which diversifying within core competencies may be less important.

Conglomerate diversification adds services unrelated to an organization's core services. In the 1970s and 1980s some large acute care hospitals became conglomerates by adding hotels, service stations, and apartment buildings. The nationwide gasoline shortage justified adding service stations; others were justified by needs of patients and clinicians in training. The mindset that "if we can manage something as complex as an acute care hospital, we can manage anything" was pervasive in hospitals that undertook conglomerate diversification. Few of these (ad)ventures succeeded, however; it became apparent that managing a hospital did not prepare one to manage everything.[208] Focusing on core business has proven to be a safer, more effective way to diversify.

Concentric diversification is achieved by internal development or acquisition and is limited only by the related and complementary services an HSO/HS does not offer. Examples include outpatient cancer treatment using chemotherapy and radiation, diagnostic services such as medical imaging, and health promotion services such as health screening and fitness centers. Other acute care hospital examples are inpatient services for rehabilitation, or psychiatric, obstetric, pediatric, or trauma services.

By connecting HSOs/HSs with potential markets and market segments, diversification has important secondary effects. Adding obstetrics opens a new population to other hospital services—women who had a good experience during delivery will continue a relationship with the hospital. Since women take primary responsibility for family health, their goodwill is important. Initiatives for the elderly, such as adult day services, home-delivered meals, home medical equipment, and in-home skilled nursing are other examples.

Diversification that establishes satellite primary care or urgent care centers creates sources of new customers, both for the new center and for referral to existing services. This couples vertical integration with diversification. Diversification may also include establishing new patient referral patterns for existing services. This widely used strategy redefines markets such as patient flow, which in the past was almost exclusively from routine to specialty care. High-cost teaching hospitals were primary beneficiaries. Increased price sensitivity, however, caused consumers and payers to seek referrals for routine care to less-expensive settings. The advantages of a highly integrated HS become apparent. The lowest cost entity able to provide the care needed is where the patient is referred. HSOs/HSs with efficient referral patterns more easily expand markets for their services.

Diversification has been a popular strategy. Reconsidering it reflects a new external environment, confused lines of authority in some arrangements, a management ill-prepared for its demands, differing views of mission among CEOs and GB members, high overhead costs, diversification into activities not supportive of mission, risk to tax-exempt status, and damage to community image. A simpler corporate structure reduces administrative costs, as well.[209]

The HSO/HS Environment

HSOs/HSs are in a complex and dynamic external environment, a fact that will influence how they are organized and affiliated. These pressures continue to include the following:[210]

- Changing demographics of the population served, with increasing numbers of elderly

- Greater sophistication of consumers and their demands on the system

- Increasing range of services provided outside hospitals, including ambulatory care, home health care, long-term care, community health centers, and so on

- Growing involvement with the community to address health issues resulting from teen pregnancy, substance abuse, and violence

- Increasing competition among HSOs/HSs that provide similar services in the same service area

- Increasing attempts by governments to regulate quantity and quality of services

- Changing systems of reimbursement to control costs

- Expanding private-sector involvement to augment services and control costs

- Increasing involvement of trustees, physicians, and other health professionals in planning and managing HSOs

- Increasing efforts by professional associations and accreditors to set standards for professional conduct in HSOs

- Increasing demand for outcome accountability and greater value

- Increasing focus on patient safety and quality of care by insurers and employee groups

- Rapidly developing medical technologies and proliferation of specialized services

- Increasing information demands, real-time information processing for the external environment, and growth of artificial intelligence systems

No challenge for HSOs/HSs is greater than providing quality services with a high degree of patient safety. Two decades ago, the Institute of Medicine (IOM) concluded, "At its best, healthcare in the United States is superb. Unfortunately, it is often not at its best."[211] That observation applies today. IOM identified 10 expectations patients (customers) should have of health services providers. Among them are access, autonomy, safety, transparency, value, and information and cooperation from caregivers. This list suggests the magnitude of the challenge to provide high-quality, safe health services to all.[212] Quality and safety problems are not limited to the United States. A study of the British National Health Service found "the inertia built into established ways of working, and the effort needed to implement new work processes," are among the important difficulties.[213]

A few analytic frameworks guide initiatives to measure quality. Among the most influential is the IOM framework as a complement to the expectations. They include six aims for the healthcare system:[214]

1. Safe: avoiding harm to patients from the care that is intended to help them

2. Effective: providing services based on scientific knowledge to all who could benefit and refraining from providing services to those not likely to benefit (avoiding underuse and misuse, respectively)

3. Patient-centered: providing care that is respectful of and responsive to individual patient preferences, needs, and values and ensuring that patient values guide all clinical decisions

4. Timely: reducing waits and sometimes harmful delays for both those who receive and those who give care

5. Efficient: avoiding waste, including waste of equipment, supplies, ideas, and energy

6. Equitable: providing care that does not vary in quality because of personal characteristics such as gender, ethnicity, geographic location, and socioeconomic status

Discussion Questions

1. Select an HSO or HS. Summarize *and* critique its mission.

2. How does the organizing function connect with the planning function? How does organizing prepare an HSO or HS to undertake its mission?

3. How do roles of HSOs and HSs differ? Discuss the importance of integrating the missions and cultures when an HSO becomes part of an HS. Distinguish ownership from an SA.

4. Define centralization and decentralization of authority. Apply decentralization of authority to the QWL concept of job enrichment.

5. The responsibility to perform duties is delegable. Why is accountability for performing responsibilities nondelegable? How does your explanation comport with the roles of CEOs and GBs?

6. How does span of control guide organizing? Provide two examples of applying it.

7. Choose one of Fayol's principles. How does the classicist's view differ from the contemporary view? Are they complementary?

8. Describe the concept of a matrix organization. How does its use improve an HSO's effectiveness?

9. Identify the typical legal status of various types of HSOs. Why are HSOs organized as corporations? (Review background in Chapter 2.)

10. Describe the LIP credentialing process. How does it differ for an acute care hospital, an NF, and an independent practice association model HMO? Why?

11. Identify why the triad is problematic *and* why it is synergistic.

12. Identify typical internal and external stakeholders of an acute care hospital *and* an HS. For each describe why the stakeholder is 1) important, 2) influential, and 3) a positive influence *or* threat.

13. What are the roles of public health organizations at state *and* local levels?

14. Identify three reasons why HSOs join HSs. Discuss differences between conglomerate and nonconglomerate diversification.

Case Study 1   The Clinical Staff

You are the CEO of Bradley Hospital, a 400-bed voluntary, general acute care hospital. The recently elected president of the PSO has just told you that many members of the PSO, but especially the physicians, are unhappy because they believe you are trying to control their clinical activities. She stated, "We feel that hospital management should take care of the nonmedical areas and leave the practice of medicine where it belongs—in the hands of professionals."

Questions

1. How should you respond to the president of the PSO?

2. What arguments should you use to support your position?

3. Sketch an outline showing the appropriate relationship among the GB, CEO, and PSO.

Case Study 2	State Allocation Decisions—Centralize or Decentralize[216]

The 50 states vary in how much control of operations and funding is delegated to city and county health departments. In Ohio, for instance, the state health department provides very little funding for local health departments and provides little direction as to how they manage public health programs for the state.

In Kentucky, each local health department is generously supported by the state health department and is expected to be its agent in managing programs such as family planning, health education, and well-baby clinics. However, numerous "strings" come with the money in Kentucky. Unlike in Ohio, the Kentucky state health department dictates the local health department's accounting systems, restaurant inspection fee structure, septic tank exception, employee health insurance benefits, and many other decisions that would be left to the local health departments in Ohio.

Still another type of state–local arrangement is that in Virginia. Local health departments in Virginia are staffed solely with state employees and are operated exclusively by policies set in the state capital.

These varied relationships raise a classic management question as to centralization or decentralization of operational authority. Each approach has significant advantages and disadvantages. For example, some managers prefer the clarity and fairness of centralized systems. Others want policy setting to be more flexible and responsive—keeping it as close to the delivery site and its clients as possible.

Questions

1. What risks are present with the Ohio policy that allows local health departments to establish their own bookkeeping systems?

2. Why might some regulated clients, such as home builders and restaurant chains, prefer to have local health department policies and fees determined centrally for the entire state?

3. Why might a decentralized local health department prefer to negotiate its own employees' health insurance package even if it represents a group of smaller size that cannot get as low a premium?

4. Based on considerations of centralization and decentralization, would you prefer to be the *state* health department director in Kentucky, Ohio, or Virginia? Why?

Case Study 3	Physicians' Unprofessional Behavior[217]

The common public perception of physicians is that they are consummate professionals: patient-focused, judicious in words and actions, and respectful of others, regardless of their status. Reports in the medical literature, however, describe an undesirable dimension of physicians' behavior behind closed doors, and sometimes more publicly. Examples include joking about an anesthetized woman's genitalia before vaginal surgery; dancing and singing a common Mexican song after treating an anesthetized Latina; commenting about an anesthetized man's weight and size before bariatric surgery; and making disparaging remarks about a patient during a colonoscopy. Medical students who witnessed these behaviors were very disturbed but pretended to be amused along with other hospital staff.

Surprisingly, rather than unanimous condemnation about these behaviors, several physicians said it is understandable, even excusable, because of the intensity, stress, and pressures of many clinical situations physicians face.

Questions

1. The behavior described here is not defined as "disruptive." It does have adverse consequences on delivery of patient care, as well as staff cohesiveness and morale. Compare disruptive with unprofessional behavior by physicians and other professionals.

2. The values of organized medicine and those of HSOs do not align with the behavior described here. Organized medicine, however, is remote from delivery of services. How does an HSO bring physicians and other clinical professionals into line with its values?

3. The PSO has a disciplinary role. How should it—through the office of the VP-MA—act to discipline physicians in situations such as this?

4. An aphorism states that "a fish rots from the head." Physicians lead the care team. How does their bad behavior affect others on the team?

Case Study 4   CEO Salary versus Patient Care[218]

Located in St. Thomas, United States Virgin Islands, the Schneider Regional Medical Center (SRMC) is a healthcare system with three components: Schneider Hospital, a 169-bed general acute-care facility; a community health center; and the Kimelman Cancer Institute (KCI), which opened in 2006. SRMC is government owned and receives significant public subsidies.

Service availability problems at KCI began in 2007. By 2008, the KCI had sporadic unavailability of chemotherapy agents, and its radiation therapy equipment was inoperative at times because it needed repairs. The problems occurred because SRMC did not pay vendors as billed; eventually, vendors refused to continue extending credit. In mid-2007, KCI staff met with the SRMC CEO, Rodney Miller, Sr., to tell him the hospital's failure to pay its bills was undermining patient care. Later, KCI staff members said they thought some patients died prematurely because scheduled treatments were unavailable.

Even as cancer patients could not continue their treatment regimens at times because of problems at the KCI, the SRMC CEO, Rodney Miller, Sr., was paid what the media described as an exorbitant salary and benefits. In 2008, Miller received over $750,000 in salary and deferred compensation, as well as perquisites and benefits. His compensation package made him the highest-paid public official in the U.S. Virgin Islands. Miller was appointed CEO in 2002.

Questions

1. What is the governing body's (GB) role in this HSO? Why are boundaries between policy decisions (the right thing [GB]) and execution of those policies (the right way [CEO]) important?

2. Identify the types of interactions between GB and CEO that might have 1) prevented failures at KCI and 2) improved its operation. Identify types of reporting or information flow between GB and CEO that are usually present in a small health system such as SRMC.

3. There is no information about SRMC's financial situation. How do the macroenvironment and third-party payments affect HSOs? What internal issues might affect an HSO's timely payments to vendors?

4. State three arguments that CEO compensation is not relevant to accounts payable and the services delivery problems at KCI. Formulate three arguments that it is relevant.

Notes

1. Charns, Martin P., and Gary Young. "Organization Design and Coordination." In *Shortell & Kaluzny's Health Care Management: Organization Design & Behavior,* 6th ed., edited by Lawton Robert Burns, Elizabeth H. Bradley, and Bryan J. Weiner, 66. Clifton Park, NY: Delmar, Cengage Learning, 2012.
2. Leatt, Peggy, Ross Baker, and John R. Kimberly. "Organization Design." In *Healthcare Management: Organization Design and Behavior,* 5th ed., edited by Stephen M. Shortell and Arnold D. Kaluzny, 318. Albany, NY: Thomson Delmar Learning, 2006.
3. This section is adapted from Kurt Darr, *Ethics in Health Services Management,* 6th ed. Chapter 3. Health Professions Press, 2019.
4. Weber, Max. *The Theory of Social and Economic Organization.* Translated by A. M. Henderson and Talcott Parsons. New York: The Free Press, 1947.
5. Fayol, Henri. *General and Industrial Management.* Translated by Constance Storrs. London: Sir Isaac Pitman & Sons, 1949.
6. Luther Gulick and Lyndall Urwick, eds. *Papers on the Science of Administration.* New York: Institute of Public Administration, 1937.
7. Mooney, James D., and Alan C. Reiley. *Onward Industry: The Principles of Organization and Their Significance to Modern Industry.* New York: Harper & Brothers, 1931.
8. Roethlisberger, Fritz J., and William J. Dickson. *Management and the Worker.* Cambridge, MA: Harvard University Press, 1939.
9. Weber. *The Theory of Social and Economic Organizations,* 151–157.
10. *14 Principles of Management (Fayol). https://www.toolshero.com/management/14-principles-of-management/,* retrieved November 27, 2018.
11. Frederick Winslow Taylor (1856–1915). *http://web.ist.utl.pt/ist11038/acad/cq/text/bio.Taylor.pdf,* retrieved November 28, 2018.
12. Drucker, Peter F. "New Templates for Today's Organizations." *Harvard Business Review* 52 (January/February 1974): 51.
13. Smith, Adam. *The Wealth of Nations.* London: Dent, 1910.
14. Fayol, *General and Industrial Management.*
15. Robbins, Stephen P. and Mary Coulter, *Management,* 11th ed. Upper Saddle River, NJ: Prentice-Hall Chapter 10.
16. Fallon, L. Fleming, Jr., James W. Begun, and William Riley. *Managing Health Organizations for Quality and Performance.* Burlington, MA: Jones & Bartlett Learning, 2013; Leatt, Baker, and Kimberly, "Organization Design," 328.
17. Schermerhorn, John R., Jr. *Management,*11th ed., Hoboken, NJ: John Wiley & Sons, 2012 Yeo, Roland K., and Jessica Li. "Working Out the Quality of Work Life: A Career Development Perspective with Insights for Human Resource Management." *Human Resource Management International Digest* 19, 3 (2011): 39–45.
18. "Problems with Patient Surveys: Hospitals Must Keep Track of Patient Satisfaction, but Does Quality of Care Suffer?" *Quality Progress,* May 2019, 9–11.
19. Clegg, Stewart, David Courpasson, and Nelson Philips. *Power and Organizations.* Thousand Oaks, CA: Sage Publications, 2006.
20. Higgins, James M. *The Management Challenge: An Introduction to Management,* 42. New York: Macmillan, 1991.
21. French, John R. P., and Bertram H. Raven. "The Basis of Social Power." In *Studies of Social Power,* edited by Dorwin Cartwright, 150–167. Ann Arbor, MI: Institute for Social Research, 1959.
22. Licensed independent practitioners (LIPs) are allowed by law and regulation to provide services without direction or supervision within the scope of their license and consistent with privileges granted by an HSO. States define LIPs variously.
23. Mooney and Reiley, *Onward Industry,* 39.
24. Charns and Young, "Organization Design and Coordination," 80.
25. Dunn, Rose T. *Dunn & Haimann's Healthcare Management,* 9th ed. Chicago: Health Administration Press, 2010.

26. Malone, Thomas W. "What AI Will Do to Corporate Hierarchies." *Wall Street Journal*, April 2, 2019, R6.
27. Gulick and Urwick, *Papers on the Science,* 15.
28. Mintzberg, Henry. *Structuring of Organizations,* 108–111. Englewood Cliffs, NJ: Prentice Hall, 1979.
29. Mintzberg, *Structuring of Organizations,* 106.
30. Urwick, Lyndall. *The Elements of Administration.* New York: Harper & Row, 1944.
31. Davis, Ralph C. *Fundamentals of Top Management.* New York: Harper & Row, 1951.
32. Barkdull, Charles W. "Span of Control: A Method of Evaluation." *Michigan Business Review* 15 (May 1963): 27–29; Steiglitz, Harry. *Organizational Planning.* New York: National Industrial Conference Board, 1966.
33. Cowen, Mark E., Lakshmi K. Halasyamani, Daniel McMurtrie, Denise Hoffman, Theodore Polley, and Jeffrey A. Alexander. "Organizational Structures for Addressing the Attributes of the Ideal Healthcare Delivery System." *Journal of Healthcare Management* 53, 6 (November/December 2008): 407–418; Mays, Glen P., F. Douglas Scutchfield, Michelyn W. Bhandari, and Sharla A. Smith. "Understanding the Organization of Public Health Delivery Systems: An Empirical Typology." *Milbank Quarterly* 88, 1 (March 2010): 81–111.
34. Barnard, Chester I. *The Functions of the Executive,* 256. Cambridge, MA: Harvard University Press, 1938.
35. Fayol, *General and Industrial Management,* 104.
36. Daft, Richard L. *Management.* Chapter 10. Mason, OH: South-Western, Cengage Learning, 2012.
37. Lawrence, Paul R., and Jay W. Lorsch. "Differentiation and Integration in Complex Organizations." *Administrative Science Quarterly* 11 (June 1967): 1–47.
38. March, James G., and Herbert A. Simon. *Organizations.* New York: John Wiley & Sons, 1958.
39. Gittell, Jody Hoffer, Dana Beth Weinberg, Adrienne L. Bennett, and Joseph A. Miller. "Is the Doctor In? A Relational Approach to Job Design and the Coordination of Work." *Human Resource Management* 47, 4 (Winter 2008): 729–755.
40. Charns and Young, "Organization Design and Coordination," 85.
41. Litterer, Joseph A. *The Analysis of Organizations,* 223–232. New York: John Wiley & Sons, 1965.
42. Litterer, *Analysis of Organizations,* 227.
43. Wallace, P. (2004) *The Internet in the Workplace: How New Technology Is Transforming Work.* New York: Cambridge University Press.
44. Mintzberg, *Structuring of Organizations;* Mintzberg, Henry. *Structure in Fives: Designing Effective Organizations.* Englewood Cliffs, NJ: Prentice Hall, 1983.
45. Mintzberg, *Structuring of Organizations,* 6–7.
46. Hage, Jerald. *Theories of Organizations: Forms, Processes, and Transformations.* New York: Wiley Interscience, 1980.
47. Lawrence and Lorsch, "Differentiation and Integration."
48. Likert, Rensis. *The Human Organization,* 156. New York: McGraw-Hill, 1967.
49. Dunn, *Dunn & Haimann's Healthcare Management,* 302–312.
50. Riley, William J., John W. Moran, Liza C. Corso, Leslie M. Beitsch, Ronald Bialek, and Abbey Cofsky. "Defining Quality Improvement in Public Health." *Journal of Public Health Management and Practice* 16, 1 (January/February 2010): 5–7.
51. Charns and Young, "Organization Design and Coordination," 83.
52. Shortell, Stephen M., Jack E. Zimmerman, Denise M. Rousseau, Robin R. Gillies, Douglas P. Wagner, Elizabeth A. Draper, William A. Knaus, and Joanne Duffy. "The Performance of Intensive Care Units: Does Good Management Make a Difference?" *Medical Care* 32, 5 (1994): 508–525.
53. Young, Gary J., Martin P. Charns, Jennifer Daley, Maureen G. Forbes, William Henderson, and Shukri F. Khuri. "Best Practices for Managing Surgical Services: The Role of Coordination," *Healthcare Management Review* 22, 4 (1997): 72–81; Young, Gary J., Martin P. Charns, Kamal Desai, Shukri F. Khuri, Maureen G. Forbes, William Henderson, and Jennifer Daley. "Patterns of Coordination and Surgical Outcomes: A Study of Surgical Services," *Health Services Research* 33 (December 1998): 1211–1223.
54. The Joint Commission. *Comprehensive Accreditation Manual for Hospitals, Provision of Care, Treatment, and Services.* Oakbrook Terrace, IL: The Joint Commission, 2012.
55. Longest, Beaufort B., Jr., and Gary J. Young, "Coordination and Communication." *In Healthcare Management: Organization Design and Behavior,* 5th ed., edited by Stephen M. Shortell and Arnold D. Kaluzny, p. 241. Albany, NY: Thomson Delmar Learning, 2006.
56. Flood, Anne B. "The Impact of Organizational and Managerial Factors on the Quality of Care in Healthcare Organizations." *Medical Care Review* 51, 4 (1994): 381–428.
57. Katz, Mitchell H. "Decreasing Hospital Costs While Maintaining Quality: Can It Be Done?" *Archives of Internal Medicine* 170, 4 (February 2010): 317–318.

58. Pearson, Steven D., Dorothy Goulart-Fischer, and Thomas H. Lee. "Critical Pathways as a Strategy for Improving Care: Problems and Potential." *Annals of Internal Medicine* 123 (December 1995): 941–948.

59. Pearson, Goulart-Fischer, and Lee, "Critical Pathways as a Strategy for Improving Care."

60. Longest and Young, "Coordination and Communication."

61. General Accounting Office. *Healthcare Reform: Report Cards Are Useful but Significant Issues Need to Be Addressed.* Report to the Chairman, Committee on Labor and Human Resources, U.S. Senate, September 1994. GAO/HEHS-94-219; Kapp, Marshall B. "Cookbook Medicine: A Legal Perspective." *Archives of Internal Medicine* 150 (March 1990): 496–500.

62. Longest and Young, "Coordination and Communication," 246.

63. Kapp, "Cookbook Medicine"; Flood, "The Impact of Organizational and Managerial Factors."

64. Young, Charns, Daley, Forbes, Henderson, and Khuri, "Best Practices for Managing Surgical Services"; Young, Charns, Desai, Khuri, Forbes, Henderson, and Daley, "Patterns of Coordination and Surgical Outcomes."

65. Roethlisberger and Dickson. *Management and the Worker.*

66. Ginter, Peter M., W. Jack Duncan, and Linda E. Swayne. *Strategic Management of Health Care Organizations,* 7th ed., Chapter 6. San Francisco: Jossey-Bass, 2013.

67. Coddington, Dean C., Keith D. Moore, and Elizabeth A. Fischer. *Making Integrated Healthcare Work.* Englewood, CO: Center for Research in Ambulatory Healthcare Administration, 1996.

68. Partners Healthcare. "About Partners." *https://www.partners.org/About/Members.aspx,* retrieved May 20, 2019.

69. Thompson, James D. *Organizations in Action.* New York: McGraw-Hill, 1967.

70. Sunseri, Reid. "Outsourcing Loses Its 'MO.'" *Hospital & Health Networks* 72, 22 (November 20, 1998): 36–40.

71. American Hospital Association. *Fast Facts on U.S. Hospitals. https://www.aha.org/statistics/fast-facts-us-hospitals,* retrieved May 5, 2019.

72. Sanofi, "Hospitals in Multihospital Systems," *Managed Care Digest Series 2012–2013: Hospital Systems Digest,* 7th ed. (2012), p. 63.

73. Shortell, Stephen M., Robin R. Gillies, David A. Anderson, Karen Morgan Erickson, and John B. Mitchell. *Remaking Healthcare in America: The Evolution of Organized Delivery Systems,* 2nd ed., 129. San Francisco: Jossey-Bass, 2000.

74. Shortell, Gillies, Anderson, Erickson, and Mitchell, *Remaking Healthcare in America,* 28.

75. Satinsky, Marjorie A. *The Foundations of Integrated Care: Facing the Challenges of Change,* 15. Chicago: American Hospital Publishing, 1998.

76. Gelfand, Michele, Sarah Gordon, Chengguang Li, Virginia Coi, and Piotr Prokopowicz. "One Reason Mergers Fail: The Two Cultures Are Incompatible." *Harvard Business Review,* October 2, 2018. *https://hbr.org/2018/10/one-reason-mergers-fail-the-two-cultures-arent-compatible,* retrieved September 11, 2019.

77. Conrad, Douglas A., and Stephen M. Shortell. "Integrated Health Systems: Promise and Performance." *Frontiers of Health Services Management* 7 (Fall 1996): 3–40.

78. Dowling, William L. "Strategic Alliances as a Structure for Integrated Delivery Systems." In *Partners for the Dance: Forming Strategic Alliances in Healthcare,* edited by Arnold D. Kaluzny, Howard S. Zuckerman, and Thomas C. Ricketts, III, 141. Chicago: Health Administration Press, 1995; Conrad, Douglas A., and William L. Dowling. "Vertical Integration in Health Services: Theory and Managerial Implications." *Healthcare Management Review* 14 (Fall 1990): 9–22.

79. Ginter, Duncan, and Swayne, *Strategic Management of Health Care Organizations.*

80. Zuckerman, Howard S., Arnold D. Kaluzny, and Thomas C. Ricketts, III. "Alliances in Healthcare: What We Know, What We Think We Know, and What We Should Know." *Healthcare Management Review* 20 (Winter 1995): 54–64, 54.

81. Zajac, Edward J., Thomas A. D'Aunno, and Robert Lawton Burns, "Managing Strategic Alliances," in Burns, Bradley, and Weiner in *Shortell & Kaluzny's Health Care Management,* 323

82. Weick, Kenneth. "Educational Organizations as Loosely Coupled Systems." *Administrative Science Quarterly* 21 (March 1976): 1–19; Zuckerman, Howard S., and Thomas A. D'Aunno. "Hospital Alliances: Cooperative Strategy in a Competitive Environment." *Healthcare Management Review* 15 (1990): 21–30.

83. O'Leary, Margaret R. *Lexikon,* 366. Oakbrook Terrace, IL: The Joint Commission on Accreditation of Healthcare Organizations, 1994.

84. About the CMS Innovation Center. *https://innovation.com.gov/About/,* retrieved May 20, 2019.

85. Centers for Medicare & Medicaid Services. "Summary of Final Rule Provisions for Accountable Care Organizations under the Medicare Shared Savings Program," October 2011. *http://www.cms.gov/Medicare/Medicare-Fee-for-Service-Payment/sharedsavingsprogram/Downloads/ACO_Summary_Factsheet_ICN907404.pdf,* retrieved May 18, 2020.

86. Centers for Medicare & Medicaid Services, "Summary of Final Rule Provisions for Accountable Care Organizations."

87. Coddington, Moore, and Fischer, *Making Integrated Healthcare Work,* 14–21.

88. MediLexicon at *www.medilexicon.com.*

89. Ginter, Duncan, and Swayne, *Strategic Management of Health Care Organizations,* Chapter 6.

90. Orlikoff, James E., and Mary K. Totten. "New Relationships with Physicians: An Overview for Trustees." *Trustee* 50 (July/August 1997 [workbook insert]).

91. Goldsmith, Jeff, Nathan Kaufman, Lawton Burns. The Tangled Hospital-Physician Relationship. *Health Affairs Blog.* May 9, 2016. *https://www.healthaffairs.org/do/10.1377/hblog20160509.054793/full/,* retrieved May 20, 2019.

92. Orlikoff and Totten, "New Relationships."

93. O'Leary. *Lexikon.*

94. Burns, Lawton R., and Darrell P. Thorpe. "Physician–Hospital Organizations: Strategy, Structure, and Conduct." In *Integrating the Practice of Medicine: A Decision Maker's Guide to Organizing and Managing Physician Services,* edited by Ronald B. Connors, Chapter 17. Chicago: AHA Press, 1997.

95. Dowling, "Strategic Alliances as a Structure for Integrated Delivery Systems," 140.

96. 2018 Intalere at a Glance. *http://www.intalere.com/Portals/4/SalesSheets/Intalere-at-a-Glance.pdf?ver=2016-07-14-112641-753,* retrieved May 21, 2019.

97. Kraatz, Matthew S. "Learning by Association? Interorganizational Networks and Adaptation to Environmental Change." *Academy of Management Journal* 41 (December 1998): 621–643; Zajac, Edward J., Brian R. Golden, and Stephen M. Shortell. "New Organizational Forms for Enhancing Innovation: The Case of Internal Corporate Joint Ventures." *Management Science* 37 (1991): 170–184.

98. Harvard Pilgrim Healthcare. "About Harvard Pilgrim Healthcare." *www.harvardpilgrim.org,* retrieved May 21, 2019.

99. Henry Ford Health System. "About Henry Ford Health System." *www.henryford.com,* retrieved May 21, 2019.

100. Lovelace Health System. "About Us." *www.lovelace.com,* retrieved May 21, 2019.

101. Satinsky, *Foundations of Integrated Care.*

102. Ingram, Paul. *Interorganizational Learning,* edited by Joel A.C. Baum. Wiley Online Library. August 11, 2017. *https://doi.org/10.1002/9781405164061.ch28,* retrieved May 22, 2019.

103. Luke, Roice, Peter C. Olden, and James D. Bramble. "Strategic Hospital Alliances: Countervailing Responses to Restructuring Healthcare Markets." In *Handbook of Healthcare Management,* edited by W. Jack Duncan, Peter M. Ginter, and Linda E. Swayne, 86. Malden, MA: Blackwell, 1998.

104. Lewis, Valerie A., Katherine I. Tierney, Carrie H. Colla, and Stephen M. Shortell. "The New Frontier of Strategic Alliances in Health Care: New Partnerships under Accountable Care Organizations." *Social Science & Medicine* 190 (October 2017): 1-10. *https://www.sciencedirect.com/science/article/abs/pii/S0277953617302939,* retrieved May 23, 2019.

105. About 40% of companies in the S&P (Standard and Poor's) 500 keep their CEO and chairman positions separate. Hufford, Austen. "Caterpillar Puts CEO in Charge of Board." *Wall Street Journal,* December 14, 2018, B2.

106. Sun, Mengqi. "More Companies Split Leadership Roles." *Wall Street Journal,* January 25, 2019, B6.

107. The Joint Commission defines licensed independent practitioner (LIP) as "any practitioner permitted by law and by the organization to provide care and services, without direction or supervision, within the scope of the practitioner license and consistent with individually assigned clinical responsibilities." Joint Commission. *2012 Comprehensive Accreditation Manual for Hospitals: The Official Handbook* (CAMH). Oakbrook, IL: Joint Commission Resources, Inc., 2012.

108. Rice, James A. *Environmental Scan: Trends and Responses for Great Governance 2005–2010.* San Diego: The Governance Institute, 2005.

109. Millar, Ross, Russell Mannion, Tim Freeman, and Huw T.O. Davies. "Hospital Board Oversight of Quality and Patient Safety: A Narrative Review and Synthesis of Recent Empirical Research." *Milbank Q* 91, 4 (December 2013): 738–770. Published online 2013. *https://www.milbank.org/quarterly/articles/hospital-board-oversight-of-quality-and-patient-safety-a-narrative-review-and-synthesis-of-recent-empirical-research/,* retrieved May 18, 2020.

110. Bader, Barry S., and Sharon O'Malley. "Putting All the Pieces Together: The Complete Board Needs the Right Mix of Competencies." *Trustee* (March 2000): 7–10.

111. Center for Healthcare Governance. *The Guide to Good Governance for Hospital Boards.* December 2009. *http://trustees.aha.org/boardorientation/09-guide-to-good-governance.pdf,* retrieved May 14, 2019.

112. Longest, Beaufort B., Jr., and Samuel A. Friede. "The Competent Board: Stitching Together Needed Skills and Knowledge." *Trustee* (February 2002): 16–20.

113. White, Kenneth R. and John R. Griffith. *The Well-Managed Healthcare Organization,* 9th ed., 120. Chicago: Health Administration Press, 2019.

114. Gage, Larry S. *Transformational Governance: Best Practices for Public and Nonprofit Hospitals and Health Systems, 2012.* Center for Healthcare Governance. Chicago. *http://trustees.aha.org/transforminggovernance/transformational-governance12.pdf,* retrieved May 24, 2019.

115. Orlikoff, James E., and Mary K. Totten. *The Trustee Handbook for Healthcare Governance.* Chicago: American Hospital Publishing, 1998; Pointer, Dennis D., and James E. Orlikoff. *Board Work: Governing Healthcare Organizations.* San Francisco: Jossey-Bass, 1999.

116. Shortell, Stephen M., Robin R. Gillies, David A. Anderson, Karen Morgan Erickson, and John B. Mitchell. *Remaking Healthcare in America,* 2nd ed.

117. Lister, Eric D. "Physicians in the Boardroom: Essential or Conflicted?" *Healthcare Executive* (July/August 2007): 61.

118. American Hospital Association. Sample chief executive officer performance appraisal process and assessment form. *http://trustees.aha.org/execperformance/AHA-Sample-CEO-Performance-Appraisal.pdf,* retrieved July 5, 2019.

119. Friede, Samuel A. "Paying for Performance: Executive Compensation Should Be Examined from Many Different Angles." *Modern Healthcare* (November 14, 2005): S6–S7; *Nonprofit Hospital Systems: Survey on Executive Compensation Policies and Practices.* Washington, DC: U.S. Government Accountability Office, June 30, 2006. (GAO-06-907R.)

120. Stout, Luanne R. "Board Governance: Reform-Driven Transformation and Reexamination of Fundamentals." *Frontiers of Health Services Management 31, 4* (Summer 2015): 43–49. *https://search-proquest-com.proxygw.wrlc.org/docview/1691164183/EB97BAD8181C4F21PQ/8?accountid=11243,* retrieved May 25, 2019.

121. Haefner, Morgan. "Hospitals Are Largest Employers in 16 States." *Becker's Hospital Review E-Weekly.* April 1, 2019. *https://www.beckershospitalreview.com/rankings-and-ratings/hospitals-largest-employers-in-16-states.html,* retrieved May 25, 2019; Samuelson, Kate. "The Role of Hospitals in Community and Economic Development." Fels Institute of Government, Philadelphia. May 4, 2017. *https://www.fels.upenn.edu/recap/posts/1071,* retrieved May 25, 2019.

122. Joint Commission on Accreditation of Healthcare Organizations. *2012 Comprehensive Accreditation Manual for Hospitals: The Official Handbook (CAMH).* Oakbrook, IL: Joint Commission Resources, 2012.

123. Warden, Gail L., and John R. Griffith. "Ensuring Management Excellence in the Healthcare System." *Journal of Healthcare Management 46, 4* (2001): 228–238.

124. *Shaping the Future of Health Care. https://www.exed.hbs.edu/testimonials/strategy-health-care-delivery-michael-ero,* retrieved May 18, 2020.

125. Neilson, Gary L., and Julie Wulf. "How Many Direct Reports?" *Harvard Business Review* 90, 4 (April 2012): 112–119.

126. Justice, Brian. "Healthcare Changes and New C-Suite Roles." *Healthcare Executive* 33, 6 (November/December 2018): 30–37.

127. Drucker, Peter F. "The Coming of the New Organization." *Harvard Business Review* 66 (January/February 1988): 45–53.

128. Shortell, Stephen M., and Arnold D. Kaluzny. "Creating and Managing the Future." In *Healthcare Management: Organization Design and Behavior,* 5th ed., edited by Stephen M. Shortell and Arnold D. Kaluzny, 488–521. Clifton Park, NY: Thomson Delmar Learning, 2006.

129. Orlikoff, James E., and Mary K. Totten. "New Relationships with Physicians: An Overview for Trustees." *Trustee* 50 (July/August 1997): W1–W4.

130. Lambdin, Morris, and Kurt Darr. *Guidelines for Effectively Organizing the Professional Staff.* Baltimore: Health Professions Press, 1999.

131. Asplund, Jon. "Physician Relations." In *Leadership Report 1998: Key Issues Shaping the Future of Healthcare,* edited by Alden Solovy, 181–184. Chicago: American Hospital Publishing, 1998.

132. Lambdin, Morris, and Kurt Darr. *Guidelines for Effectively Organizing the Professional Staff.* Baltimore: Health Professions Press, 1999.

133. 21 U.S.C. Section 824(g) requires physicians and LIPs to register with the Drug Enforcement Administration to prescribe or administer controlled substances. *https://www.deadiversion.usdoj.gov/21cfr/21usc/index.html,* retrieved May 17, 2019.

134. Health Care Quality Improvement Act of 1986, PL 99-660, 100 Stat. 3784 (1986).

135. Department of Health and Human Services. Health Resources and Services Administration. Bureau of Primary Health Care. Health Center Program Site Visit Protocol: Credentialing and Privileging File Review Resource. *https://bphc.hrsa.gov/sites/default/files/bphc/programrequirements/pdf/c_and_p_file_review_resource.pdf,* retrieved June 9, 2019.

136. The Joint Commission. *Ambulatory Care Program: The Who, What, When, and Where's of Credentialing and Privileging. https://www.jointcommission.org/assets/1/6/AHC_who_what_when_and_where_credentialing_booklet.pdf,* retrieved June 9, 2019.

137. American Podiatric Medical Association. "What Is Podiatry." *www.apma.org,* retrieved July 21, 2006.

138. Larson, Laurie. "Streamlining the Credentialing and Privileging Process: A Standardized Approach Can Align Expectations and Give the Board Peace of Mind." *Trustee Insights. http://trustees.aha.org/quality/articles/streamlining-the-credentialng-and-privilegeing-process.shtml,* retrieved June 12, 2019.

139. American Medical Association. "Federation of State Physician Health Programs, History." *http://www.ama-assn.org/ama/pub/category/5706.html,* retrieved July 22, 2006.

140. Council on Mental Health, American Medical Association. "The Sick Physician: Impairment by Psychiatric Disorders, Including Alcoholism and Drug Dependence." *Journal of the American Medical Association* 223 (1973): 684–687.

141. Council on Ethical and Judicial Affairs, American Medical Association. AMA Code of Medical Ethics' Opinions on Physicians' Health and Conduct. Opinion 9.0305 - Physician Health and Wellness. October 2011. *https://journalofethics.ama-assn.org/article/ama-code-medical-ethics-opinions-physicians-health-and-conduct/2011-10,* retrieved June 13, 2019.

142. Katlic, Mark R., JoAnn Coleman, and Marcia M. Russell. "Assessing the Performance of Aging Surgeons." *JAMA.* Published online January 14, 2019. *https://www.researchgate.net/publication/330379808_Assessing_the_Performance_of_Aging_Surgeon,* retrieved September 8, 2019.

143. Oreskovich, Michael R., Tait Shanafelt, Lotte N. Dyrbye, Litjen Tan, et al. "The Prevalence of Substance Use Disorders in American Physicians." *American Journal of Addictions.* 2015. *https://onlinelibrary.wiley.com/doi/abs/10.1111/ajad.12173,* retrieved July 5, 2019.

144. Oreskovich, Michael R. Krista L. Kaups, Charles M. Balch, John B. Hanks, et al. "Prevalence of Alcohol Use Disorders among American Surgeons." *Archives of Surgery* 147, 2 (February 2012): 168–174. *https://jamanetwork.com/journals/jamasurgery/fullarticle/1107783,* retrieved July 5, 2019.

145. "Don't Ask Don't Tell: Substance Abuse and Addiction among Nurses." *Journal of Clinical Nursing. http://onlinelibrary.wiley.com/doi/10.1111/j.1365-2702.2010.03518.x/full,* retrieved October 1, 2012.

146. Cummings, Simone Marie, Lisa Merlo, and Linda B. Cottler. "Mechanisms of Prescription Drug Diversion among Impaired Physicians." *Journal of Addictive Diseases. http://www.tandfonline.com/doi/full/10.1080/10550887.2011.581962,* retrieved July 5, 2019.

147. Question of the Week: December 21, 2017. HortySpringer. Pittsburgh, PA. *https://www.hortyspringer.com/question-of-the-week/december 21-2017/,* retrieved December 21, 2017.

148. U.S. Department of Labor. Bureau of Labor Statistics. *Occupational Outlook Handbook.* April 12, 2019. *https://www.bls.gov/ooh/healthcare/physicians-and-surgeons.htm,* retrieved June 9, 2019.

149. U.S. Department of Labor. Bureau of Labor Statistics. *Occupational Outlook Handbook.*

150. Bureau of Labor Statistics. Health Care and Social Assistance. *http://www.bls.gov/iag/tgs/iag62.htm,* retrieved July 5, 2019.

151. American Hospital Association. *Chartbook: Trends Affecting Hospitals and Health Systems,* Table 2-6. Percentage of Hospitals Offering "Non-hospital" Services, 2004–2014. *https://www.aha.org/system/files/research/reports/tw/chartbook/2016/table2-6.pdf,* retrieved May 19, 2019.

152. American Hospital Association. *AHA Hospital Statistics.* Chicago: Health Forum LLC (an American Hospital Association Company), various years.

153. American Hospital Association. *Fast Facts on US Hospitals. https://www.aha.org/statistics/fast-facts-us-hospitals,* retrieved May 19, 2019.

154. American Hospital Association. *Fast Facts,* retrieved June 10, 2019.

155. American Hospital Association. *AHA Hospital Statistics.* Chicago: Health Forum LLC (an American Hospital Association Company), 2006.

156. American Hospital Association. *Fast Facts,* retrieved June 10, 2019.

157. Mundy, Alicia. "Doc-Owned Hospitals Prep to Fight." *Wall Street Journal,* May 14, 2013, B1.

158. Berenson, Robert A., Thomas Bodenheimer, and Hongmai H. Pham. "Specialty-Service Lines: Salvos in the New Medical Arms Race." *Health Affairs* 25, 5 (September 2006): w337–w343.

159. Stryker, Ruth. "The History of Care for the Aged." In *Creative Long-Term Care Administration,* 4th ed, edited by George Kenneth Gordon, Leslie A. Grant, and Ruth Stryker, 6. Springfield, IL: Charles C. Thomas, 2004.

160. Stryker, Ruth. "The History of Care for the Aged."

161. Centers for Disease Control and Prevention. National Center for Health Statistics. Nursing Homes *https://www.cdc.gov/nchs/fastats/nursing-home-care.htm,* retrieved May 19, 2019.

162. Marek, Karen Dorman, Marilyn J. Rantz, Claire M. Fagin, and Janet Wessel Krejci. "OBRA '87: Has It Resulted in Positive Change in Nursing Homes?" *Journal of Gerontological Nursing* 22 (December 1996): 32–40.

163. Kaiser Family Foundation. United States: Distribution of Certified Nursing Facility Residents by Primary Payer Source, 2017. *https://www.kff.org/other/state-indicator/distribution-of-certified-nursing-facilities-by-primary-payer-source/,* retrieved July 5, 2019.

164. National Association of Long Term Care Administrator Boards. *https://www.nabweb.org,* retrieved May 30, 2019.

165. AMDA. Medical Director Roles and Responsibilities. *http://www.amda.com/about/roles.cfm#roles,* retrieved November 20, 2012.

166. Span, Paula. "In the Nursing Home, Empty Beds and Quiet Halls." *New York Times,* September 28, 2018. *https://www.nytimes.com/2018/09/28/health/nursing-homes-occupancy.html,* retrieved January 6, 2019.

167. Centers for Disease Control and Prevention. National Center for Health Statistics. Nursing Homes *https://www.cdc.gov/nchs/fastats/nursing-home-care.htm,* retrieved May 19, 2019.

168. 2017 Profile of Older Americans. U.S. Department of Health and Human Services. Administration for Community Living. *https://acl.gov/sites/default/files/Aging%20and%20Disability%20 in%20America/2017OlderAmericansProfile.pdf,* retrieved May 30, 2019.

169. Health Maintenance Organization Act of 1973, PL 93-222, 87 Stat. 914 (1973).

170. Centers for Medicare & Medicaid Services. "Accountable Care Organizations (ACOs): General Information." *https://innovation.cms.gov/initiatives/aco/,* retrieved May 30, 2019.

171. Swayne, Linda M., W. Jack Duncan, and Peter M. Ginter. *Strategic Management of Healthcare Organizations,* 5th ed., 51. Malden, MA: Blackwell, 2006, 52.

172. Kaiser Family Foundation. State Health Facts. January 2016. *https://www.kff.org/state-category/ health-insurance-managed care/,* retrieved May 30, 2019.

173. Sanofi-Aventis. *Managed Care Digest Series,* 2019. Payer Digest. *http://www.managedcaredigest.com/ pdf/PayerDigest.pdf,* retrieved July 6, 2019.

174. Managed Care On-Line. "Managed Care Fact Sheets: Current National Managed Care Enrollment." *http://www.mcol.com/factsheetindex,* retrieved June 1, 2019.

175. Knight, Wendy. *Managed Care: What It Is and How It Works,* 24. Gaithersburg, MD: Aspen Publishers, 1998.

176. Rosato, Donna. "How to Survive a High-Deductible Health Plan." *Consumer Reports,* November 17, 2016. *https://www.consumerreports.org/health-insurance/high-deductible-health-plan/,* retrieved June 1, 2019.

177. Knight. *Managed Care: What It Is and How It Works.*

178. Knight. *Managed Care: What It Is and How It Works,* 99–100.

179. NCQA. Health Plan Accreditation. *https://www.ncqa.org/programs/health-plans/health-plan-accreditation-hpa/,* retrieved May 11, 2019.

180. HEDIS® includes more than 90 measures across 6 domains of care. *https://www.ncqa.org/hedis/,* retrieved May 11, 2019.

181. Centers for Disease Control and Prevention. The Public Health System & the 10 Essential Public Health Services. *https://www.cdc.gov/publichealthgateway/publichealthservices/essentialhealthservices. html,* retrieved June 18, 2019.

182. Association of State and Territorial Health Officers. Profile of State and Territorial Public Health, Volume Four. *http://www.astho.org/Profile/Volume-Four/2016-ASTHO-Profile-of-State-and-Territorial-Public-Health/,* retrieved June 18, 2019.

183. Association of State and Territorial Health Officers. *Profile of State and Territorial Public Health.*

184. Association of State and Territorial Health Officers. *Profile of State and Territorial Public Health.*

185. Association of State and Territorial Health Officers. *Profile of State and Territorial Public Health.*

186. Department of Health and Human Services. Agency for Healthcare Research and Quality. *Compendium of U.S. Health Systems, 2016. https://www.ahrq.gov/chsp/data-resources/compendium.html,* retrieved June 15, 2019.

187. Ellison, Ayla. "15 Largest Health Systems in the U.S." *Becker's Hospital Review,* June 15, 2016. *https://www.beckershospitalreview.com/lists/15-largest-health-systems-in-the-u-s-june15.html,* retrieved July 7, 2019.

188. Sanofi Aventis. *Managed Care Digest Series: eHospitals/Systems Digest for 2006. http://www. managedcaredigest.com/index.jsp,* retrieved July 27, 2006.

189. Shortell, Stephen M., Robin R. Gillies, David A. Anderson, Karen Morgan Erickson, and John B. Mitchell. *Remaking Healthcare in America: Building Organized Delivery Systems,* 7. San Francisco: Jossey-Bass, 1996. Reaffirmed in Shortell, Stephen M., Robin R. Gillies, David A. Anderson, Karen Morgan Erickson, and John B. Mitchell. *Remaking Healthcare in America: The Evolution of Organized Delivery Systems,* 2nd ed. San Francisco: Jossey-Bass, 2000.

190. Shortell, Stephen M. and Rodney K. McCurdy. "Integrated Health Systems." *Information Knowledge Systems Management* 8 (2009): 369–382. *https://content.iospress.com/articles/information-knowledge-systems-management/iks00147,* retrieved June 15, 2019.

191. Berenson, Robert A. "A Physician's Perspective on Vertical Integration." *Health Affairs* 36, 9 (September 2017). *https://doi-org.proxygw.wrlc.org/10.1377/hlthaff.2017.0848,* retrieved June 15, 2019.

192. Pointer, Dennis D., Jeffrey A. Alexander, and Howard S. Zuckerman. "Loosening the Gordian Knot of Governance in Integrated Healthcare Delivery Systems." *Frontiers of Health Services Management* 11 (Spring 1995): 3–37.

193. Jones, Jeff. "A New Health System Means New Governance." *Trustee*, October 10, 2016. *https://www.trusteemag.com/articles/1137-governing-integrated-health-systems,* retrieved September 10, 2019.

194. Ervin, Cathleen O., Amy Yarbrough Landry, Avery C. Livingston, and Ashley Dias. "Effective Governance and Hospital Boards Revisited: Reflections on 25 Years of Research." *Medical Care Research and Review* (January 31, 2018). *https://journals-sagepub-com.proxygw.wrlc.org/doi/abs/10.1177/1077558718754898#,* retrieved June 7, 2019.

195. Ummel, Stephen L. "Pursuing the Elusive Integrated Delivery Network." *Healthcare Forum Journal* 40 (March/April, 1997): 13–19, 13.

196. Pronovost, Peter J. C. Michael Armstrong, Renee Demski, Ronald R. Peterson, Paul B. Rothman. "Next Level of Board Accountability in Health Care Quality." *Journal of Health Organization and Management* 32, 1 (2018). *https://search-proquest-com.proxygw.wrlc.org/docview/2010759,* retrieved June 5, 2019.

197. Orlikoff, James E., and Mary K. Totten. "Systems Thinking in Governance." *Trustee* 52 (January 1999): workbook insert.

198. This discussion is adapted from Longest, Beaufort B., Jr. "Managerial Competence at Senior Levels of Integrated Delivery Systems." *Journal of Healthcare Management* 43 (March/April 1998): 115–135.

199. Coddington, Dean C., Keith D. Moore, and Elizabeth A. Fischer. "Physician Leaders in Integrated Delivery." *Medical Group Management Journal* 44, 5 (September/October 1997): 85–90, 90.

200. Shortell, Stephen M., Robin R. Gillies, David A. Anderson, Karen Morgan Erickson, and John B. Mitchell. *Remaking Healthcare in America,* 2nd ed., 68. San Francisco: Jossey-Bass, 2000.

201. Longest, Beaufort B., Jr. *Health Policymaking in the United States,* 4th ed. Chicago: Health Administration Press, 2006.

202. HortySpringer. Question of the Week, October 10, 2019. *https://www.hortyspringer.com/category/question-of-the-week/page/2/,* retrieved October 10, 2019.

203. Berenson. "A Physician's Perspective on Vertical Integration."

204. Orlikoff and Totten, "New Relationships with Physicians: An Overview for Trustees."

205. Burns, Lawton R., and Darrell P. Thorpe. "Physician-Hospital Organizations: Strategy, Structure, and Conduct." In *Integrating the Practice of Medicine: A Decision Maker's Guide to Organizing and Managing Physician Services,* edited by Ronald B. Connors, Chapter 17. Chicago: AHA Press, 1997.

206. Maeda, Jared Lane K. "Comparative Health Systems Research among Kaiser Permanente and Other Integrated Delivery Systems: A Systematic Literature Review." *Permanent Journal* 18, 3 (Summer 2014): 66–77. *https://www.ncbi.nlm.nih.gov/pmc/articles/PMC4116268/,* retrieved June 17, 2019.

207. Wood, Debra. "Hospital Mergers and Acquisitions Increase, Benefiting Communities." *Healthcare News* June 4, 2013. *https://www.amnhealthcare.com/latest-healthcare-news/hospital-mergers-acquisitions-increase-benefiting-communities/,* retrieved July 7, 2019.

208. Andreoua, Panayiotis C., John A. Doukas, Demetris Koursaros, and Christodoulos Louca. "Valuation Effects of Overconfident CEOs on Corporate Diversification and Refocusing Decisions." *Journal of Banking & Finance* 100 (March 2019): 182–204. *https://www.sciencedirect.com/science/article/pii/S0378426619300159?via%3Dihub,* retrieved July 7, 2019.

209. Johnsson, Julie. "Hospitals Dismantle Elaborate Corporate Restructurings." *Hospitals* 65 (July 5, 1991): 41–45.

210. Leatt, Baker, and Kimberly. "Organization Design," 336–337.

211. National Roundtable on Healthcare Quality. *Statement on Quality of Care,* 11. Washington, DC: Institute of Medicine, 1998.

212. From the Committee on Quality of Health Care in America, Institute of Medicine, *Crossing the Quality Chasm: A New Health System for the 21st Century,* 63. Washington, DC: The National Academies Press, 2001.

213. Ham, Chris, Ruth Kipping, and Hugh McLeod. "Redesigning Work Processes in Health Care: Lessons from the National Health Service." National Center for Biotechnology Information. *Milbank Quarterly,* September 2003. *http://www.ncbi.nlm.nih.gov/pubmed/12941002,* retrieved November 20, 2012.

214. U.S. Department of Health and Human Services. Agency for Healthcare Research and Quality. Six Domains of Health Care Quality. *https://www.ahrq.gov/talkingquality/measures/six-domains.html#_ftnref3,* retrieved July 7, 2019.

215. From *Healthcare Executives' Responsibilities to Their Communities.* Chicago: American College of Healthcare Executives. Reprinted with permission of the American College of Healthcare Executives, November 2016. *https://www.ache.org/about-ache/our-story/our-commitments/policy-statements/healthcare-executives-responsibility-to-their-communities,* retrieved June 19, 2019.

216. Written by Gary E. Crum, Ph.D., M.P.H., District Director of Health (retired), Northern Kentucky Independent District Health Department. Used with permission.

217. Rabin, Roni Caryn. "Doctors Behaving Badly." *New York Times,* August 21, 2015. *https://well. blogs.nytimes.com/2015/08/21/doctors-behaving-badly/,* retrieved September 5, 2018.

218. Blackburn, Joy, and Tim Fields. "Salaries First, Patients Later." *The Virgin Islands Daily News,* July 28, 2008, 1.

12

Staffing

Background

In 2019, the healthcare field, including ambulatory care, hospitals, and nursing and residential facilities, employed over 16 million, an increase of almost 20% since 2009.[1] Healthcare is the largest source of employment in the United States. Health services organizations (HSOs) are labor intensive and have a broad mix of support staff and highly skilled, expensive clinical staff. Labor costs are two thirds or more of operating expenses. The financial aspects and clinical skills used in service delivery show the importance of human resources (HR) in HSOs and health systems (HSs).

Health professions are highly fragmented by skills area. About 200 different types are needed to staff a general acute care community hospital, and more than 300 for a large teaching facility. Skills types are proliferating. This makes acquisition and retention of a qualified workforce a major challenge for HSOs. Artificial scarcity of some health professions occupations is created by associations that accredit educational programs, and those that certify practitioners. Artificial scarcity adds to salaries for those professions; this leads to a ripple effect on salaries for other health professions *and* administrative staff. The result is higher salaries for some and higher national healthcare costs for all. Scarcity is artificial because professional groups and associations control the availability of programs to educate health professionals. The next step in most health professions is field experience—a clerkship, residency, or similar practicum—for applied training. Education and training are followed by the certification and licensure required for almost all health professions. These, too, are controlled by the profession or a surrogate organization, as discussed in Chapter 1. Thus, normal market forces that modulate supply and demand are thwarted, artificial scarcity results, and healthcare costs increase. Those who accredit professional education and training assert that private regulation assures quality. As with certification and to a lesser extent, licensure, proof of that assertion is elusive.[2]

To implement strategies, accomplish objectives, and fulfill their missions, HSOs need qualified staff in the right number. When managers integrate technology and people into formal structures (organizational arrangements), meaningful work occurs. The human element is the catalyst that converts inputs of material, supplies, technology, information, and capital into outputs of individual and organizational work. The management model (Figure 1 in the Part III introduction) shows this process.

The Joint Commission's accreditation standards highlight the importance of the staffing function in HSOs and note that HR's contribution to delivery of safe, quality care cannot be overstated. The staff determine quality of care. Staff quality is assured by education, training, continuing education, and on-the-job training, all of which enable the organization to provide quality care and keep patients safe.[3] As noted in Chapter 4, Donabedian concluded that "good structure, that is, a sufficiency of *resources* and proper system design, is probably the *most* important means of protecting and promoting the quality of care."[4] Staff is an obvious, essential part of the "resources."

HR recruits and screens new employees (acquisition), enhances employees' competencies and helps keep them in the organization (maintenance and retention), facilitates exit (separation) of those who leave, and develops policies, procedures, and rules for employment (coordinating). HR is a staff activity, compared with a line or operating activity. HR supports HSOs and HSs through the staffing function, which provides guidance, expertise, and programs too.

Staffing

Historically, *personnel administration* described the staffing function. The contemporary name for a much more comprehensive concept is human resources management (HRM). Its day-to-day operationalization is performed by an HR department or unit. Other than in small HSOs, the staffing function is centralized in and coordinated by HR, the unit or department responsible for staffing the organization and developing and implementing relevant policies, procedures, and rules. HR takes the lead in managing labor relations, in consultation with legal counsel. Small HSOs may have an HR office and outsource some or all of HRM. Because staff is the organization's most important resource, the HR manager is part of senior management and typically has a title such as vice president of human resources (VP-HR).

Staffing HSOs (and HSs) with competent employees involves widely ranging activities to enable acquisition, retention and maintenance, compensation, and separation. Centralizing HR services does not diminish the need for managers to understand basic HRM. To varying degrees, all managers engage in the staffing function: selecting, training and developing, appraising performance, promoting, compensating, and disciplining and corrective counseling. Managers are accountable for the productivity and quality of their units. This role emphasizes the importance of understanding basic staffing. Better-informed managers deploy human resources effectively and are less likely to make unethical or illegal decisions.

The planning component of HRM determines staffing. Workforce needs must be understood in the context of a dynamic external environment that affects changes in programs, initiatives, and delivery. Staffing needs reflect organizational change and staff turnover. Change results from increased demand for or intensification of services, facility expansion, and new services. Staffing changes if services are eliminated or location of delivery is revised. In addition to turnover and growth, changes in technology require different skills. The HR manager monitors the need for staff to meet service needs. The HR manager meshes HRM with the HSO's/HS's strategic and operating plans.[5]

HSs centralize elements of staffing and issue systemwide policies, procedures, and rules, and provide support for HR and HRM. Large HSOs and HSs undertake strategic human resources management (SHRM), the broadest concept of the staffing function.

HRM Activities

The phases of staffing are shown in Figure 12.1. Acquisition includes HR planning, recruitment, screening, and onboarding/orientation after selection by the manager. Retention and maintenance include placement, training and development, performance appraisal, discipline and corrective counseling, compensation and benefits administration, employee assistance and career counseling, and safety and health. Separation is the third and final phase of the staffing function.

Acquiring Human Resources

HR Planning

Acquisition is the first step in the process model in Figure 12.1. Acquisition highlights the need for HR planning. HSOs/HSs are dynamic; staffing needs change. Work force planning occurs in this context. Staff mix and staffing levels result from modifications in services offered, employee turnover, and changes in technology. HR planning ensures that the HSO/HS has staff with the qualifications and skills to meet care and quality needs.[6] HR and managers predict staffing needs by referencing the strategic profile, estimating, inventorying, forecasting, and planning. The plan identifies recruitment and hiring, transfers, and/or enhancing skills of current staff through training and development.

Step 1: Strategic Profile

Developing a strategic business plan requires managers to profile the HSO/HS as it is expected to be at a future point. This plan is used to estimate numbers and types of jobs (skills) required. The HRM estimates have elements of uncertainty and subjectivity. The organization's strategic business plan, predicted demand for services, changes in professional practice or labor supply, and staffing new technologies, programs, and services are included in projections.

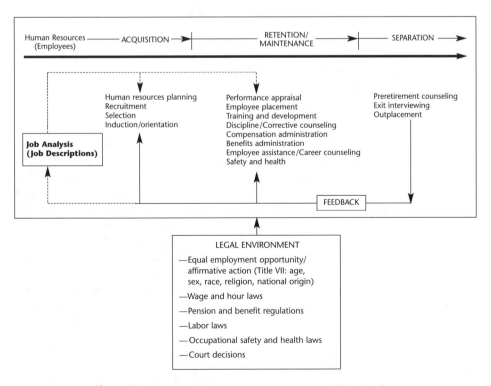

Figure 12.1.   Personnel/Human resources management activities time flow.

The organization HRM profile is necessarily dynamic and ongoing and adjusted as internal and external forces affect it. Planning is addressed in Chapter 10.

Step 2: Estimating

Once the organization's strategic business profile is developed, staffing needs are estimated. If variables can be identified and quantified, this step is straightforward. The healthcare industry has developed staffing ratios for many types of service delivery. For example, knowing the square feet in a new facility allows estimates of environmental services staff needed. Similarly, nurse staffing ratios are available for inpatient beds using estimates of patient acuity and occupancy rates.

Step 3: Inventorying

A skills inventory (sometimes called a talent inventory), assesses skills, abilities, and potential of an organization's human resources and how they are being used.[7] Skills inventories are based on an audit that compiles information about each staff member's job title, experience, length of service, performance, education, special skills, and current placement. The internal audit identifies staff and areas that could benefit from training. It is added to the self-assessed training and educational needs identified by each employee. The inventory enables the organization to determine skills available *now* and those needed for future strategic and tactical plans.[8] It is vital to have *and use* such information.

Step 4: Forecasting

Planners forecast changes in the HSO's/HS's workforce that result from entry, transfer, and exit because of retirement, death, voluntary separation, or discharge. Historical data can be used to forecast staffing. HSOs differ from most other types of organizations in that clinical staff, such as RNs, dietitians, and pharmacists, are credentialed and/or licensed. Such requirements impede upward and lateral movement and prevent transfers to unrelated positions. States may require continuing education for some health services occupations. Likely, professional groups that certify members have similar requirements. Succession planning is needed for senior managers. Workforce forecasting considers all these aspects.

Step 5: Planning

The assumptions and information in steps 1 through 4 support the action plan and help ensure staff with requisite skills are available. HR needs identified by organization-wide or systemwide continuous quality improvement (CQI) efforts are also part of the plan.

Job Analysis and Job Descriptions

HR develops and maintains job descriptions for all positions. This fundamental responsibility is an example of control. The HSO/HS is financially motivated to hire staff at a level and with the minimum qualifications to ensure quality at least cost. Monitoring this aspect of HR management is especially important. Proliferation of job classifications and a propensity of health services workers and their professional associations to limit market entry by educational requirements, licensure and/or accreditation, as well as regularly enhancing credentials and certifications, require continuous monitoring of minimum job qualifications.

HRM requires job descriptions.[9] Though not required by the Americans with Disabilities Act, equal employment opportunity law uses the job description as a basic document. It should reference the status of the job in terms of the federal Fair Labor Standards Act, as well.[10] Good HR management and legal requirements make developing and maintaining job descriptions essential.

Job Analysis

New staff can be recruited only if HR knows what training, skills, and experience are needed. Job analysis provides this information, which is reflected in the job description. The three main elements of job analysis are knowledge, skills, and abilities needed to perform the job.[11]

Usually, the analysis is done by a job analyst from HR. The analyst uses questionnaires and interviews of incumbents, observes the job being done, determines job content (duties and responsibilities), describes physical conditions of performing the job, and identifies relationships with other jobs. In aggregate, this is the basis for a job description.[12]

Job Descriptions

Generally, job descriptions include job title, location, job summary, five to nine general duties and responsibilities, supervision given or received, special working conditions (including equipment or systems used), hazards, and qualifications. The statement of qualifications includes minimum education, training, experience, and skills required.[13] Job descriptions should be concise to ease use and worded to maximize flexibility in work design.

Job descriptions must be updated when job content, performance requirements, or qualifications change. They are used in HRM and by HR to recruit, select, train, appraise performance, counsel, and compensate. They are important, too, as basic documents in grievances, arbitration, and legal disputes. The job description simplifies communication among managers, employees, applicants, and HR. HR is notified if a vacancy occurs or more staff of the same type is needed. The job description has basic information for recruiting.

Recruiting

Sources

Staff can be recruited internally and externally. Filling vacancies internally by transfer or promotion is cost-effective, is usually faster, has lower recruiting and relocation costs, and enhances staff morale. Effective use of current staff requires that the talent inventory noted earlier is complete and includes career path planning, and that employees with potential have been identified and trained for promotion or transfer.

External sources used depend on skills and qualifications needed, supply in the labor market and geographic area, employer's reputation, and teaching affiliations. If no special skills or training are required for a job and supply is ample, external recruiting may require no more than reviewing previous applications. Health professions that are in short supply, however, will require the organization to compete for staff. Internal and external recruiting in healthcare is complex because of job fragmentation and specialization, uneven workforce distribution, demand for the health professions, career alternatives, and unpredictable public support for education.

Methods

Recruiting internally involves job posting, promotion, and transfer of staff. Recruiting externally can include contacting retirees; former employees; applicants not selected; executive search, contingency, and outplacement firms; state employment offices; employment agencies; professional associations; senior centers; retiring military; and attending job fairs. The Internet eases external recruiting by using social media, job boards, and the organization's website.[14] HSOs may pay incentives to staff to recruit specific categories. Recruiting materials and personal interactions with potential candidates *must* include information about the organization's philosophy—its value system—as well as its mission and vision. Likely, this information will cause candidates with incompatible personal values to self-select other employment. Chapter 2 discusses the value system, mission, and vision as an essential context for HSO/HS services delivery. Advertising vacancies or asking current employees to pass the word will generate applications. Using few methods to recruit reduces the candidate pool, however, and limits workplace diversity. For example, using only "word-of-mouth" recruiting has been criticized by the Equal Employment Opportunity Commission as potentially discriminatory.[15]

Electronic Recruiting

Recruiting is increasingly automated and streamlined because of the Internet and social media. Openings can be posted on Internet jobsites easily and inexpensively. Posting on social media may recruit persons not actively looking for jobs (passive jobseekers). Software scans electronic resumes for words and phrases to identify superior candidates. Usefulness of scans may be thwarted, however, as candidates learn how to finesse key words and phrases. Software tests for skills, knowledge, and psychological factors, such as leadership and teamwork traits. Online video conferencing reduces cost and facilitates preliminary or screening interviews. Such changes are producing paperless HR offices and should increase efficiency and speed of recruiting.[16]

Selection

Prospective staff members who have been recruited must be screened to determine if they meet minimum requirements for the job and are suitable in terms of training, experience, and ability. Information for screening is derived from application forms, interviews, and testing. The organization's value system and mission and vision provide essential context for employment and must be included on the application form and reiterated in interviews.

Applications

Written applications are used for initial screening. They must not ask for problematic or prohibited information, such as a photograph, age or birthdate, immigration status, criminal history (including arrest records [which alone do not establish guilt]), compensation history, and whom to contact in an emergency. In addition to the federal Equal Employment Opportunity Commission, state and local governments regulate if (or when) such questions may be asked. Some questions prohibited early in the process may be asked after the initial interview.[17] Information on bona fide occupational qualifications (BFOQ) must and should be asked when it is legal and appropriate to do so.

Screening

Figure 12.1 suggests that health services managers work in a complex legal and regulatory environment. This is especially true for employment. HR ensures that staffing and HRM policies, procedures, and rules comply with the law. Regardless of HR's role, managers must understand basic employment law. HR manages the content of application forms, preemployment interviews, and preemployment testing, which must meet legal requirements. The complexity means managers consult with HR and through HR to legal counsel, as needed.

Interviews

In-person, telephone, electronic, or video interviews are essential to obtain information about candidates. Interviews must be conducted by experienced staff members who use a standard interview form that includes only questions and topics specific to performing the job. Open-ended questions are useful for a better understanding of the candidate, but they must be job related and must not solicit prohibited information.[18] Questions about race, sex, age, national origin, and information elicited must be relevant to the qualifications, competence, and skills needed for the job. BFOQs permit discriminatory practices in employment if religion, sex, or national origin are a BFOQ reasonably necessary to normal operation of the business.[19] A female attendant for a female locker room may be an example. Given the large number of professionals, the clinical staffing of healthcare likely has few BFOQs. Behavioral interviews allow an interviewer to learn a candidate's strengths, areas for development, and fit for the position. They are appropriate for some jobs.[20]

Clinical Credentials Verification

Chapter 11 describes the credentialing process for licensed independent practitioners (LIPs). In credentialing, the HSO reviews the LIP's qualifications to determine whether to grant the LIP clinical privileges to treat patients. The limited HR function for LIPs is managed by the HSO's "medical staff" office. Physicians, for example, are LIPs in all states. Other healthcare clinicians, such as physician assistants, nurse practitioners, nurse anesthetists, and nurse midwives are licensed as LIPs in some states but not others. "For example, nurse practitioners are licensed in 17 states as 'independent practitioners' or, LIPs; for the remaining states, they are licensed as 'practicing under supervision of a[n] LIP.'"[21] HSOs must be mindful of state licensing laws and medical practice acts for the various types of practitioners and credential them accordingly. At this writing, Stanford Health Care credentials 17 different groups of advanced practice providers with varying clinical preparations.[22] The Centers for Medicare & Medicaid Services (CMS) Conditions of Participation (CoPs) allow advanced practice clinicians (APCs) to be appointed to the professional staff organization (PSO) and granted clinical privileges consistent with state-scope-of-practice laws. It is becoming common for a provision to be added to the PSO bylaws addressing APCs, including serving on PSO committees with voice and vote.[23]

Although not licensed to practice independently, many HSO clinical staff have professional qualifications that give them the skills and knowledge to interact with patients in medically significant ways. These dependent clinical staff act on orders or under the supervision of an LIP. Examples are registered nurses, pharmacists, and dietitians. Before such staff begin work, HR must determine they have the qualifications required by verifying their licensure, certification, or registration, as well as obtaining the usual information, such as education, work experience, and the like. The example of clinical pharmacists is instructive. To practice pharmacy, U.S.-educated pharmacists must have an accredited professional pharmacy degree and a state license awarded on successful completion of the national postgraduation examination administered by the National Association of Boards of Pharmacy on behalf of state boards of pharmacy.[24] Added credentials in pharmacy are acquired variously, such as by completing a disease-specific continuing education program or through the examination process required to become board certified by the Board of Pharmaceutical Specialties. Privileging of hospital pharmacists may occur at the organizational level so they can perform patient care services. A university medical center created and implemented a voluntary pharmacist privileging program to allow pharmacists to be providers, document clinical competencies, and be consistent with other healthcare providers.[25]

Nonclinical Credentials Verification

Résumé enhancement and fabricated academic and employment backgrounds are common. Examples include misleading résumés or those with misrepresentations, unearned degrees, falsified employment dates, and employment at nonexistent companies.[26] Most can be discovered with simple checks. Failing to investigate accuracy of résumés and entries on applications poses a potential risk to patients and staff and is a potential legal risk to the organization. At the very least the organization will be embarrassed if a failed check results in employing an unlicensed RN, or a senior manager who does not have a credential that was important to being offered the job.

Reference Checks

Potential legal problems from reference checks cause former employers to provide only dates of employment, title, and salary. This is safe for former employers, but there are social costs—the next employer may be deprived of important information.[27] In a worst-case scenario, a new employee may harm patients, staff, or others, and this risk was known to the former employer. Most egregious are situations in which former employers or colleagues know of serious flaws, such as drug addiction, do not communicate that information, and may even offer a praiseful recommendation. Courts have recognized a duty to warn if there is a likelihood of harm. Regardless, information provided by candidates must be verified to the extent possible. The best check is to have the hiring manager call references in coordination with HR. Creative use of social media will find others at the same organization who know the candidate and can provide insights.[28] A risk is staff may see this as spying or a breach of personal confidentiality.

Background Checks

Reference checks and background checks provide different information about applicants. Employers must have job-related reasons to perform checks on an applicant's criminal or credit background. The U.S. Equal Employment Opportunity Commission (EEOC) administers and enforces civil rights laws against workplace discrimination. The Fair Credit Reporting Act (FCRA [P.L. 91-508]), as amended, requires accuracy, fairness, and privacy of information held by consumer reporting agencies (CRAs). In addition, state laws may apply. Employers may ask CRAs for reports to assess character and general reputation to evaluate, promote, reassign, or retain an applicant or employee. FCRA and state law regulate how background checks are done and how the information is used.[29]

Selecting

Despite myriad techniques, selection of new staff is not a science. Ideally, the decision to hire is made by the manager to whom the new staff member will report, with guidance from HR. This process ensures that credentials are adequate; legal requirements are met; policies, procedures, and rules are followed; and those selected meet quality standards and agree with the HSO's/HS's values. It cannot be overstated that hiring those who are a good fit with the organization's values is critical to minimizing turnover, enhancing morale and job satisfaction, and enabling employees to achieve "joy in work," as Deming termed it. The result will be an environment for delivering high-quality care. HR may make job offers and hire health professionals in short supply, such as registered nurses (RNs), with no involvement of a manager. It is assumed RNs can be placed somewhere in the HSO, and quick action may be necessary to secure this category of employee.

Job Offer

With rare exceptions, the hiring manager should make the verbal job offer, with a written offer to follow from HR. Involving the manager connects the new employee, job, and manager in a very important way. Almost all employees are at-will employees. This means they are not hired for a fixed or definite term. The employee can quit at any time; the employer can fire the employee at any time with or without cause. There are legal exceptions, however, depending on the state.[30] Executives likely have contracts, a written agreement stating length of employment and/or that employment may be terminated only for cause or by following specific procedures.[31]

Onboarding

Onboarding is the process of bringing new employees quickly and with best effect into a comprehensive, positive relationship with the organization. It includes induction and orientation and begins after selection and acceptance by the employee of the job offer.

Induction

For some new employees, getting on the payroll is the most memorable part of joining the staff, but the process is far more extensive. Induction activities are usually performed by HR, with contributions from parts of the organization such as finance, security, and IT. It includes enrolling new staff in the compensation and benefits program, issuing an identification badge, and creating a personal database. Receiving a paper or electronic copy of the employee handbook is an important part of induction. New employees should be asked to acknowledge in writing that they have received and understand the contents of the handbook.[32]

The medical examination HSOs require before new employees begin work screens for communicable disease, ensures new staff can do the job without harming themselves or others, determines workers' compensation risk, and documents existing health issues. Drug testing and vaccination status are a likely part of the process. It must be clear the offer of employment is contingent on passing the medical examination. Care must be taken not to violate the Americans with Disabilities Act.[33]

Orientation

New employee orientation should include information about the physical facility, organizational structure, standard (universal) precautions, fire and safety programs, employee health service, employee assistance program (EAP), and other HR services they may use. Organizational policies and procedures should be described. Some departments orient and train new staff in their specific procedures, work methods, and rules using on-the-job training, preceptors, and classroom instruction. Critical in orienting new staff is instructing them about the organization's mission, vision, and values and explaining its culture. Successful orientation builds new employees' sense of identity with the organization, helps them gain acceptance with staff, and communicates what they need to know. Orientation must enable new employees to understand the entire organization and how their work *and* their unit fit into it. Commonly included are a tour of the facility, learning about supplemental information available on the employee website, and a reception for new employees. An example of an electronic orientation program for Brigham Health's Brigham and Women's Hospital may be found online (https://www.brighamandwomens.org/about-bwh/human-resources/new-employee-checklist).

Done well, onboarding boosts morale and improves long-term retention. In addition, onboarding helps new employees become productive sooner, connects them with the organization's mission and values, helps them fit in more quickly, and strengthens corporate culture by making new staff aware of the history and traditions of the organization.[34]

Turnover is costly in both dollars and lessened quality of patient care. The federal Bureau of Labor Statistics reported a 33% annual turnover rate in 2018 for healthcare and social assistance workers.[35] Stated another way, about 3% of this type of employee leaves *each month*. Direct dollar costs of turnover are tens of thousands of dollars for each employee who is replaced. Replacing one RN is estimated to cost $22,000–64,000.[36] Costs include recruitment, orientation and training, and lower productivity during the first several months of a new employee's tenure. RN turnover is especially high. Indirect effects of turnover affect quality of patient care: communication among RNs and other healthcare professionals is less effective, patient care teams are less effective, and staff left behind experience a sense of rejection and a decrease in morale. Reduction in quality of patient care resulting from turnover is more difficult to measure.[37]

Dress Code

Even into the 1970s RNs wore a heavily starched white uniform and the hat unique to their school of nursing. Those days are history; no longer are RNs easily distinguishable from other nursing staff, or sometimes even other types of staff. There is significant homogeneity of dress among clinical staff in hospitals. Badges identify staff members by first name and title or category. Last names are no longer used because security concerns can arise if a staff member's given and surname are on the name badge.

Employers may impose a dress or grooming code if there is a legitimate business reason for doing so *and* if the dress code does not discriminate by sex, race, religion, or other protected class. In office settings, suit jackets, ties, and appropriate slacks for men and suits, dresses, and skirts and blouses for women are a common unofficial "uniform." If "casual Fridays" or similar concessions are made to less formal dress, the employer should define acceptable and unacceptable casual wear in writing and provide examples.[38] Many clinical staff change from their street clothes and don (surgical) scrubs to wear for their clinical duties. Scrubs are a two-piece garment of lightweight cotton with baggy pants and a loose-fitting top, usually blue or green in color. Some HSOs use color-coded scrubs keyed to a specific clinical area. Scrubs become soiled but are worn nonetheless in public or quasi-public areas, such as the HSO's cafeteria and coffee bar. To maintain public appearances and propriety and minimize the spread of infection, HSOs should impose rules about wearing scrubs outside clinical areas. These rules are more likely to be broken than kept, however, especially by LIPs. The COVID-19 (now

SARS-CoV-2) pandemic of 2020 raised unique issues of monitoring and controlling spread of a highly infectious disease.

Retaining Employees

HRM maintenance and retention activities begin after placement. These include performance appraisal; promotion, demotion, and transfer; disciplinary counseling and separation; compensation and benefits management; employee assistance; career counseling; and ensuring personal safety and a healthy workplace (see Figure 12.1).

Performance Appraisal

HR develops and maintains the performance appraisal process. Appraisal systems compare actual with expected performance. Chapter 4 noted Deming's conclusion that 85%–94% of work results occur because of the *process*. Thus, managers should understand staff's limited role in affecting outcomes of individual work *effort*. The primary purpose of appraising employees should be to focus on their training or other needs, rather than assume they are the source of poor outcomes. In this regard, managers should be mentors and coaches to staff and facilitate their ability(ies) to do their jobs well and achieve the "joy in work" that motivates them to *want* to come to work every day.

Supervisors who perform a policing function do their staff no favors. This master–servant approach diminishes or prevents communication needed for supervisors to assist staff members to do their best. For coaching to work, staff must be willing and able to speak about their needs and how the supervisor can help them improve their job performance. This complements the supervisor's role, which, as a coach, is to instruct and support staff members so they can do well. A willingness to seek help from their supervisors evidences an adult, symbiotic relationship, from which both benefit. The coach-supervisor must initiate and nurture this relationship, which is not a friendship, but one of colleagues who are working toward a shared goal: providing or supporting provision of high-quality services. This cooperative sense of purpose puts everyone on a team moving in the same direction.

Uses of Performance Appraisal

Performance appraisal has several uses, including the following:

- *Determining if individual work results meet expectations:* Appraisal collects information to learn if the results are those expected and, if not, to try to understand the cause for less-then-optimal results. Managers *must* understand how the process affects performance.

- *Providing feedback to employee and supervisor:* The appraisal interview is an opportunity for two-way communication. Less-than-satisfactory performance can be discussed, and reasons and interventions identified—again, understanding the role of the process.

- *Identifying high, marginal, and unsatisfactory performers:* Depending on what is needed to enable employees to perform better, various interventions should be used. Less-than-satisfactory performance often results from variables such as lack of job skills or experience, or poor process or job design. This information allows interventions such as education, skills training, or job redesign. Unsatisfactory performance because of attitude and behavior warrants counseling, discipline, or separation. The goal of performance appraisal should be to monitor and, whenever possible, improve, employees' ability to do their jobs well.

- *Identifying potential and desirable employee movement within the organization:* Performance appraisal affects employees' potential for promotion, as well as transfer and demotion. High performers may be promoted with or without further skills building; low performers may be given additional training or transferred to more suitable jobs.

- *Providing information for compensation:* Organizations whose wage and salary systems use merit increases should be cautious using appraisals to determine pay adjustments. Here, too, the role of processes in determining how well employees perform must be understood.

- *Providing information for employee assistance and counseling:* If, for example, performance is unsatisfactory because of substance abuse or off-the-job personal problems, appraisal may show a need to recommend or require assistance in the organization's EAP program.

Most HRM retention activities are linked to performance appraisal. This makes it an information-gathering system of great importance to healthcare managers.

Benefits of Systematic Appraisal

It is common for written appraisals of all employees to be done annually. They may occur using date of hire, or all appraisals may be done at one time. In addition, good management practice requires frequent, informal feedback, both positive and negative. If an employee has started a new position, formal appraisal within 3 months is advisable. As employees achieve longevity, periodic appraisals enhance morale and reaffirm management's interest in the employee's development.

Traditional performance appraisals are roundly disliked by staff *and* managers. Often, staff see them as arbitrary and only a popularity contest. Managers tend to see them as a distasteful, subjective exercise. Adding ranking, rating, and forced distributions compounds problems with appraisals. In addition, they stimulate competition among staff when, in fact, efforts should be made to reduce competition and encourage cooperation and teamwork. Organizations should *reconsider traditional* employee appraisals or, even better, abandon them entirely.

Evaluations provide a rational basis to promote, discipline, or terminate. The latter two should be rare and avoided, if possible. Sometimes, a 360-degree assessment or multi-rater feedback system is used. Here, evaluations by peers, direct reports, and perhaps outside customers and clients are added to the supervisor's. A 360-degree evaluation program requires careful planning and clear communication as to how and why it is used. Follow-up on results is also necessary lest substantial time is wasted collecting useless or unused data.[39]

Electronic Support for Employees

Performance Appraisal. Real-time performance appraisals have potential in healthcare. Technology allows employee performance to be monitored in real time, which allows supervisors to know if employees can meet the expectations of the job. As noted, traditional performance appraisals are conducted annually and are disliked by supervisors and employees. Technology allows monitoring key performance indicators to know if an employee is doing well or to provide training, as needed. This same technology allows employees to receive ongoing feedback from supervisors to help them do better.[40] Such dialogue is consistent with the mentoring and coaching approach to managing advocated by Deming and others.

Education and Training. Similarly, developments in virtual reality, augmented reality, virtual presence, and machine learning will greatly change not only how new staff members are onboarded and trained but how they are supported in their job. See-what-I-see (augmented) glasses allow employees to share what they are seeing.[41] For example, an RN expert at identifying (hospital-acquired) pressure injuries (decubiti) can confirm with a less-skilled nurse that a patient is developing a pressure injury. Or, a biomedical equipment technician can show and discuss with the manufacturer repair of a piece of equipment. Education and training are covered in more detail in the next section.

Educating and Training

Background

Education, including training, is intrinsic to HRM in maintaining, retaining, and developing human resources. Education describes both general preparation relevant to the job to be done and a broader concept of education as will be described. Education relevant to the job occurs when an RN takes a formal course in pharmacology to learn the uses, incompatibilities, and interactions of drugs. Training occurs when an RN is taught a specific clinical task, such as how to use a new type of catheter. HSOs/HSs support training because it bears directly on doing the job. They are less likely to support educating an RN in pharmacology because direct application to the RN's job is less clear. It is even less likely that HSOs/HSs will support education unrelated to healthcare. This is shortsighted. Learning in unrelated fields provides benefits to the staff member that redound to the organization: 1) staff become more qualified; 2) morale improves because staff see that "they care about us"; 3) insights—some profound—about job-related problems come from seemingly unrelated thinking and stimulation of education in collateral fields. Offering programs in-house or providing educational benefits are relatively inexpensive ways to realize the advantages of education.

Specialized Training

Background
Some training adds to staff knowledge and skills; other training modifies behavior. Both improve job performance and can be provided formally or informally. Training may be offered by HR or a separate unit. Large HSOs may have trainers who provide training unique to a unit. Independent HSOs can share training resources; HSs may centralize training and offer it to system components. Chapter 11 noted the value of cross-training (teaching staff skills and tools to do more than one job), job enlargement (combining tasks to create a new job with more components), and job enrichment (expanding responsibilities so work becomes more challenging and satisfying).

Preparing Supervisors
Many HSO staff promoted to supervisory positions have a technical or clinical background. Members of the PSO who become clinical department heads or are otherwise in a position needing managerial skills need preparation too. Successful HSOs/HSs prepare them to manage. Needed are education in leadership, motivation, communication, and problem solving. Training may be department specific and provided by professional trainers or senior line managers. Training in budgeting and report writing is desirable. Online programs are readily available; enrolling in them should be encouraged and subsidized, if possible. Better-prepared managers result in better managed organizations. Further, they help ensure success in quality and productivity improvement.

Continuous Quality Improvement
Peter Drucker noted, "Quantity without quality is the worst thing and will result in total failure."[42] Every employee should be taught basic CQI theory and its application; those who serve on a quality improvement team need additional preparation. Performance appraisals help monitor quality of care. Data from them allow managers to judge the success of current job design and workflow (processes), progress in achieving objectives, and individual performance to the extent it affects quality because, for example, an employee is inadequately trained. Real-time performance feedback is required to achieve CQI. Criteria for evaluation include using customer satisfaction to identify opportunities for process improvement, individual performance, or both; pre-identifying results or expectations and if they are met or exceeded; and identifying and measuring behavioral skills that improve quality and customer satisfaction (see discussion of CQI in Chapters 4 and 8).[43] The Hospital Consumer Assessment of Healthcare Providers and Systems (HCAPS) survey gives users of hospital services a voice in assessing quality.

Conclusion
Technologies such as mobile devices, webinars, teleseminars, podcasts, videos, online courses, social media, and "gamification" make learning easy, convenient, and, maybe, enjoyable.

Asynchronicity enhances their attractiveness. Supervisors and organization should provide individual coaching for staff with job-related problems and for those with high potential. Education efforts must use adult learning theory. The talent inventory noted earlier must be complete, and needs-assessment data should be added before education initiatives are undertaken. Needs can be identified by employees, peers, direct reports, and customers.[44]

Electronic education and training are best suited to conveying facts and specific information. Even interactive modalities do not capture the human dynamic of face-to-face situations. Some types of education and training needs cannot be met using only electronic means. Basic facts, information, and preparation can be taught using technology-based platforms, but learning and applying the skills require other techniques. Learning team, meeting, and negotiation skills; leadership; public speaking and presentations; and group dynamics do not lend themselves to remote or technologically based education. For them, in-house mentoring, coaching, and tutored practice are essential. Options are to bring faculty into the organization or to support external education and training for employees of high promise.

In 2016, the average U.S. company spent about $1,000 in training per employee, usually delivered in the traditional format of classrooms and seminars. Though touted as avant-garde, online training mimics traditional methods. Machine learning and augmented reality will take traditional approaches to the next level by giving staff the latest, most accurate information as it is needed.[45]

Compensation Administration

Effective compensation administration is needed to maintain and retain a qualified workforce. *Compensation* is a generic term for wages, salaries, and fringe benefits, all of which affect an organization's ability to attract and retain employees. Compensation is key to HR management and requires constant vigilance. Healthcare managers can respond to the challenges by understanding compensation planning and policy and the special compensation needs of LIPs and other healthcare providers.[46]

Equity is key in compensation programs. Depending on size and clinical services, HSOs/HSs may have more than 200 different types of jobs. Determining compensation for each uses three elements: internal equity, external equity, and philosophy of the HSO/HS.

1. *Internal equity:* How does compensation of various jobs compare? What should an RN earn compared with a social worker or dietitian? There are several ways to achieve internal equity. At minimum, job requirements must be identified, and their complexity evaluated. Evaluation is usually reduced to a numerical factor (rating) so jobs can be compared more easily.

2. *External equity:* How does the organization's compensation for jobs compare with competitors? External equity has become important as market forces increasingly affect HSOs/HSs. Shortages of staff such as medical technologists, sonographers, and pharmacists cause compensation wars. That plus union pressures prompt market analysis to remain competitive.

3. *Philosophy:* How well does the HSO's/HS's compensation compare with the market? A mature compensation philosophy succinctly describes how an HSO/HS uses data about internal and external equity to compete for staff. Its philosophy might be "our pay range midpoints will be 10% above the projected median of our market for professional (higher-level) jobs and equal to the projected median of our market for service (lower-level, entry) jobs." There is no "right" philosophy for compensation. Labor supply, market definition, projected human resources needs, type of organization, fiscal constraints, and the like must be considered.

Establishing and Administering a Compensation System

Job evaluation determines the monetary value of jobs in an organization.[47] As noted, information for job evaluation is derived from job descriptions developed from job analysis. Surveys add context to ensure that the compensation system is internally and externally fair and competitive.

Job evaluation may use ranking, job classification, and point and factor comparison systems. The result is a schedule of logically connected hourly wage and salary ranges. Procedures that allow changes in compensation *within* grades use criteria such as performance and experience; a means to move employees to new grades or classifications based on changes such as job enrichment or further education; and a way to maintain internal equity.

Executive and Incentive Compensation

Executive salaries and benefits fall outside the compensation system used for other supervisory and nonsupervisory positions. All executives should have a job description as the basis for the scope and content of their work. Internal candidates are a common source of applicants. Promoting from within facilitates transitions but carries risks, such as inertia and lack of innovation. Often, internal candidates are named "acting" for a position before being appointed permanently. Use of executive search firms is common for senior positions. Such searches are costly but usually bring high-quality candidates. The market determines base compensation. In addition, there are perquisites or benefits executives usually receive: car allowance, club memberships, mobile devices, and equipment for home offices. Cash or incentive bonuses and awards, plus a retirement plan are common.[48]

A need to recruit and retain exceptional managers prompted the healthcare field to join industry in using bonuses that link compensation to performance.[49] Incentive compensation programs are thought to attract talented managers, encourage development of multiple skills, increase tolerance for risk taking, motivate innovative behavior, and reward cost saving.

Benefits Administration

Fringe benefits are an important (and costly) part of employee compensation and are usually one fourth to one third of payroll costs. Common fringe benefits are health insurance (hospital, professional services, dental, and vision care); retirement plan contributions; life and disability insurance; paid holidays; and vacation, sick leave, and bereavement days, which may be combined into paid time off (PTO). PTO is taken as approved, but with no designation as to use. Examples of government-mandated benefits include Social Security withholding, workers' compensation for on-the-job injuries, Family and Medical Leave Act, COBRA (Consolidated Omnibus Budget Reconciliation Act of 1985 [P.L. 99-272]) benefits, and unemployment insurance. These benefits add greatly to employer overhead, or the cost of doing business.

HSOs/HSs may self-insure to control benefits costs. This is done for nonmandated programs by establishing a trust fund or reserve fund to pay claims without involving an insurance carrier. The savings from forgone insurance premiums fund the trust or reserve fund and pay claims. This specialized activity requires involvement of experts. Excess liability coverage (stop-loss insurance) with a high deductible protects the organization from major risks and losses.

Another way to control benefits costs *and* increase employee satisfaction is the cafeteria, or full, flexible benefits plan.[50] Here, the employer allocates a dollar amount to each employee, who designs a benefits package from a menu of options. Empowering employees to choose benefits that fit their needs increases satisfaction. An advantage to employers is that costs are more predictable. Flexible spending accounts for health and childcare expenses are key to cafeteria plans and are frequently offered as freestanding benefits. Employees put pretax dollars into accounts reserved for them to use during the year. Employers do not pay Social Security or withhold income tax on money put into flexible spending accounts. Unused dollars may be lost. These accounts reduce costs and increase take-home pay. A disproportionate number of female and single-parent employees has prompted some HSOs/HSs to provide on-site childcare services, which reduce absenteeism, enhance recruitment, increase morale and retention, and reduce parental stress. Such efforts must be well planned and properly supervised.

Employee Assistance Programs

From a narrow focus—assisting alcoholic employees—the mission of EAPs has been enlarged to help staff solve problems that affect their work negatively: substance abuse; legal, financial, and emotional problems; general health issues; and personal development. Considering only chemical abuse, EAPs have significant potential. It is estimated that 9.1% of full-time employed adults and 10.3% of part-time employed adults abuse alcohol, illicit drugs, or prescription drugs.[51] These employees are three and a half times more likely to be injured on the job than nonabusers, are five times more likely to file a workers' compensation claim, and likely function at about two thirds of their capability.[52] EAPs can reduce employer costs by decreasing absenteeism and use of medical insurance and sick time; improving job performance; and enhancing quality and productivity.[53] In sum, EAPs salvage human resources. HSOs/HSs may provide EAP-type services to other organizations on an outpatient basis. This is ideal because EAP-type services from an outside organization are confidential, and self-referred employees have less fear of retribution or a record of counseling that might negatively affect employment. HSO/HS EAPs may be offered in-house or by a contract third party.

Career counseling is a second area in which HR assists staff. Staff shortages have stimulated HSOs to develop employees' skills. Expenditures for direct skills training, subsidized professional education, and management development invest in staff. Career counseling and needs assessment by HR reduce costs of mismatching staff and jobs and enhance the organization's return on investment in staff.

Health education and health promotion are a third area for EAPs. By educating staff to manage their own health and assist them with stress management, weight reduction, and smoking cessation, employers improve morale and productivity, reduce insurance costs, and contribute to the positive climate needed for employee retention. Such investments in human capital have significant psychic and financial returns for the staff and the organization.

Workplace Health and Safety

Chapter 8 notes HSOs are dangerous places to work. Caustic and toxic chemicals in the laboratory and pharmacy, food processing equipment in dietary, radiation sources in oncology and medical imaging, chemicals and gases used for sterilization, and infectious organisms in patient care areas are but a few of the hazards. Chapter 8 discusses preventing or reducing workplace violence.

The Occupational Safety and Health Act of 1970 (P.L. 91-596) affects organizations, including nongovernmental HSOs, and covers safety and health issues linked to machines, chemicals, pollutants, and environmental dangers in the workplace.[54] As implemented by the Occupational Safety and Health Administration, the law requires three primary activities: 1) promulgating and enforcing safety standards to eliminate or lessen hazards, 2) keeping records, and 3) training and educating.

Acquired immunodeficiency syndrome, now known as stage III HIV infection (stage 3), has posed unique problems for HSOs, especially hospitals. Protecting healthcare staff from patients is compounded by a need to protect patients from healthcare staff. Universal precautions, now standard precautions (SPs), presume every patient is human immunodeficiency virus (HIV) positive. SPs protect staff and patients by reducing risk of cross-infection. The question of mandatory testing of healthcare workers, especially physicians and dentists, is unresolved. SPs make it a nonissue. The COVID-19 (SARS-CoV-2) pandemic in 2020 caused major staffing issues. There were situations of inadequate amounts of effective personal protective equipment and of staff resigning because of alleged unsafe working conditions.

Separation from Employment (Exit)

Discipline (Corrective Counseling)

Disciplinary action should be rare. Given that qualified, carefully selected staff are placed correctly, it is reasonable to assume that employees come to work wanting to do a good job and will do their job as well as the processes in which they work allow. For answers to performance problems, management must look first to the processes in which staff work. This means assessing connected processes: the HR recruitment process may have failed to find someone prepared for the job; orientation or training processes may have been deficient; staff may not understand their role(s) in a process and how their job contributes to the process and its customers; and a staff member may be in the wrong job or wrong part of the process. Everyone involved in processes must understand Juran's description of the worker's triple role: customer, processor, and supplier, a concept shown in Figure 4.1. Managers' first task is to be a mentor and coach and facilitate staff members' ability to do their jobs.

The HSO/HS should have a formal grievance process that allows employees unable to resolve work-related issues with their supervisor to seek redress. Typically, a grievance process includes review by the supervisor and/or a review by the supervisor's supervisor. Formal grievances should be rare because supervisors and employees who communicate effectively will informally resolve issues before a formal review is required. Grievances are a symptom of other problems; the review must focus on underlying issues, such as job placement, training, tools and equipment, and employees' knowledge of the process and their roles in it. Several grievances from one unit or section suggest deeper, perhaps systemic, problems. Other indicators of significant problems in a unit or department are high turnover and poor morale.

Despite best efforts as mentors and coaches, managers may have to use corrective counseling. If corrective counseling is to be positive, policies, procedures, and rules must be reasonable, and employees must understand what is expected of them. Employers have the legal right to a well-ordered, cooperative work force and, if necessary, have the authority to act as the situation requires.

Separation

Employees leave HSOs/HSs for various reasons. HR assists in and monitors separation activities, which include facilitating an employee's exit; collecting employer-provided equipment, keys, and paper and electronic records; completing HR records; processing final pay; and conducting an exit interview. Other activities include preretirement planning and outplacement.

- *Preretirement Planning:* Preretirement counseling prepares employees for the psychological, emotional, and financial changes in retirement. Staff is helped to understand lifestyle changes, emotional and physical needs, financial planning, Social Security benefits, pensions, and legal matters, such as estate planning.

- *Outplacement:* Outplacement occurs most often when jobs are eliminated because services are reduced or abandoned, or facilities close or merge. Outplacement recognizes the employer's social and financial commitment to help employees find other employment. It may include contacting other employers, advertising on an employee's behalf, counseling, retraining, and providing the services of an outplacement firm.

- *Exit interviews:* HR conducts confidential exit interviews to obtain information about the work environment. Goals include confirming reasons for separation, learning job likes and dislikes, and opinions about supervisors, the facility, benefits package, and compensation. HR tries to resolve problems so staff leave on a positive note. Some organizations conduct postseparation surveys 3 to 6 months after separation as a follow-up and to gain additional insight on the employment experience.[55] Despite being retrospective, exit interviews give management important information.

Human Resources and LIPs

The functions and scope of HR have grown significantly, but PSO relations remain the exclusive domain of the HSO/HS governing body and senior management. This is understandable because LIPs are rarely employees. Salaried LIPs have most of the characteristics of employees, including participating in employee benefits. Even then, however, HR is rarely involved in salary administration or maintaining files. HSOs/HSs do not consider LIPs typical employees. As more LIPs are employed, however, HR's involvement will likely increase.

Human Resources in HSs

In a more centralized way HRM activities apply to HSs. HR develops HS-wide policies, procedures, and rules; provides support in acquisition, retention, and separation of staff; and provides support for labor relations with bargaining units, as needed. The role of HSs includes setting overall HR policy, coordinating HRM among affiliated HSOs, and providing support for their delivery of services. Corporate efforts include establishing systemwide guidelines ranging from compensation and benefits, regional training and development, and recruitment and selection to intraorganizational behavior, such as workplace romances and sexual harassment. System assistance can be provided to component HSOs regarding activities such as succession planning and regional training. System support can range from informal consultation on compensation plan design to benefit plan administration. Well-designed HR functions save time and money for HSs and expand the capabilities and usefulness of HR services.

Labor Relations Law and Unionization

Background

Employees unionize when they are dissatisfied with conditions of employment and elements of democracy in the workplace and when they think collective bargaining will give them a better situation. Put simply, unions are a means for redress if employee needs are unmet. A union's primary role is to improve job security and economic circumstances and, possibly, the professional interests of employees. Collective bargaining allows unions to address other terms and conditions of employment and organizational policies, procedures, and rules affecting the employer–employee relationship and, sometimes, occupational status.

Conditions of employment are primarily economic and security issues, and elements of the workplace. Economic concerns are compensation: wages and salaries, and benefits. Wages and salaries are absolute pay rates, relative pay in similar organizations, pay differentials among job classifications, and shift differentials. Examples of benefits are health and life insurance, retirement programs, PTO, and EAPs.

Elements of the workplace include hours of employment, scheduling patterns, break times, physical work environment, and personal security. Job security as affected by the mix of part-time and full-time employees, contracting out (outsourcing) work previously done in-house, and employee reductions and reassignment after mergers, acquisitions, and downsizing are legitimate employee concerns. Collective bargaining subjects these aspects of employment to negotiation.

Democracy in the workplace describes the organization's attitude toward employees and application of HR policies, procedures, and rules. Policies and criteria for promotion, transfer, discipline, termination, job reassignment, performance appraisal, grievances, and compensation are important, as are consistent application and fairness in treating individuals or groups of employees. Unclear policies or inconsistent application cause dissatisfaction and provide an important stimulus to unionize.

The organization's philosophy about human resources is key to the employment relationship's context. Employees want to be treated as individuals, not just another resource, and they want to know the HSO/HS is sincerely concerned about them and their well-being. Employees' perceptions of the organization and policies and attitudes toward them are largely derived from their immediate supervisors—the organization's representatives with whom employees interact most frequently. Supervisors' management practices affect this perception. If supervision is fair, consistent, and concerned, employee dissatisfaction will be lower than the reverse, especially if conditions of employment and democracy in the workplace are positive. Such an atmosphere of employment incorporates meaningfulness of work into job design and involves, when possible, shaping jobs to individual strengths, skills, and interests. It depends on two-way communications, which lessen information vacuums and encourage two-way listening. Risk-free upward communication and downward information flow to be informed are important employee needs. Perceptive, well-qualified first-level managers contribute greatly to fostering this positive atmosphere. Communication and openness as hallmarks of the organization's culture facilitate patient-centered care and a focus on patient safety. Staff should be encouraged to report inappropriate, unprofessional, and questionable behavior without fear of retribution. Their reports should be substantiated, investigated, and action taken as warranted. Unprofessional behavior by surgeons is associated with significantly increased risks of surgical and medical complications among their patients.[56] This suggests that correcting behavioral problems of LIPs (and likely other caregivers) will improve employee morale and reduce patient complication rates. Another aspect of organizational life is that harassment and misconduct may occur. HR should lead responses to such problems, which means staff members must be willing to report them to HR. (Involving HR presumes the problems cannot be resolved by managers.) Staff may be reluctant to report harassment and misconduct because HR is not trusted. Such problems may put HR in a difficult position: it wants to be responsive but must be mindful of organizational interests. Creating a respectful workplace requires fair investigations after reports of harassment and misconduct, as well as proper training and education of staff, work usually done by HR.[57] HSO/HS value systems as reflected in their cultures must be intolerant of harassment, misconduct, and other interactions that treat patients, visitors, or staff disrespectfully. In sum, staff will treat their patients/customers only as well as they are treated by the organization.

Job autonomy and empowerment are important to many employees, especially professionals such as RNs and technical staff. They are concerned with their work roles and how they relate to the task-structure elements of the organization and patient care. Actualization of professional and autonomy needs is important. Staff want expanded responsibilities and involvement in decision making in their areas of competence. Assertiveness among clinical professionals who seek recognition and greater participation in managing patient care is a powerful force. For them, job dissatisfaction stems from unclear roles, conflict with LIPs, and poorly performing and/or insufficient staff. They may see unionization as the preferred alternative to what is perceived to be organizational indifference or unwillingness to deal with professional issues.

Unionization changes the nature of the relationship between employees and the organization in a fundamental way. HSOs/HSs that want to remain union-free must maintain positive relationships with employees, nurture a team attitude, and treat employees with respect. They do so by having well-prepared first-line supervisors and excellent communication with employees. Unions tend to foster an "us vs. them" mentality. Employee opinion surveys, lunches with managers, hotlines for suggestions, and an open-door policy with HR and supervisors facilitate and track employee engagement. Including employees in decision making when possible is also effective. Giving employees multiple ways to communicate directly with managers is effective in facilitating employee engagement and avoiding unionization.[58]

U.S. Department of Labor, Bureau of Labor Statistics (BLS) data do not report healthcare employees as a distinct category. Thus, the precise number of union members in the healthcare field is elusive. It is a relatively low percentage, however. More employees are unionized in HSOs owned by government (public) than private-sector HSOs, whether for profit or not for profit. In 2018, union membership in BLS data ranged from 6.7% for healthcare and social assistance workers to 11.4% for healthcare practitioners and technical occupations. Healthcare support occupations reported 8.1% union membership. Add 1% or 2% to these groups to count employees who are *represented* by a union but are not *members* of the union.[59] This difference results because workers may be represented by a union without joining it: they are part of a collective bargaining contract that doesn't require them to join the union, likely because they are in a "right to work" state as will be described in the next section.

Federal Labor Law

Federal government policy toward unions before the 1930s was "hands-off." State and local governments tended to support employers against employees and union organizing. This changed during the Great Depression, which began at the end of the 1920s and continued for 10 years. The Protestant work ethic, factory systems, and common law employer property rights that had supported employers gave way to a new social ethic. Some states had passed labor legislation earlier. The Depression, however, fueled a view that federal government had a special responsibility for blue collar workers. Numerous federal labor laws were enacted beginning in 1932. Those with special effect on HSOs are discussed briefly.

Prior to passage of the Norris-LaGuardia Act (Anti-injunction Act. [PL 106-73, 1932]) employers sought injunctions in federal court to stop union organizing activity. Norris-LaGuardia prohibited federal courts from issuing nonmeritorious injunctions against union organizing.

The Wagner Act (National Labor Relations Act [NLRA {PL 74-198}1935]) ensured that private-sector employees had a right to organize and bargain collectively. It sought to balance the bargaining power between employers and employees and specified unfair labor practices by employers. The NLRA created the National Labor Relations Board (NLRB) to monitor union recognition and collective bargaining.

The Taft-Hartley Act (Labor-Management Relations Act [PL 80–101, 1947]) amended the NLRA and sought to rebalance the employer–employee relationship that had moved too far toward labor. Taft-Harley changed the structure of the NLRB, protected employee rights not to join a union, and enumerated union unfair labor practices and requirements for collective bargaining.

The Nonprofit Hospital Amendments to the Taft-Hartley Act (PL 93-360, 1974) had a profound effect on health services because all HSOs became subject to federal labor law. Before 1974 the law of collective bargaining in health services varied by type of ownership. The Taft-Hartley Act of 1947 excluded from its definition of employer "any corporation or association operating a hospital, if no part of the net earnings inures to the benefit of any private shareholder or individual" (section 2[3]). This meant that not-for-profit hospitals were excluded from federal labor law. Investor-owned HSOs/HSs were included.

Thus, since 1974, not-for-profit *and* investor-owned HSOs/HSs, as well as unions, have had to comply with the recognition, election, and unfair labor practice provisions of the Wagner and Taft-Hartley acts. The 1974 amendments included provisions unique to HSOs/HSs and recognized their vital role in public health and safety: contract notice, strike notification, conciliation of disputes, and union dues for employees with religious convictions. These provisions are outlined as follows:

- Contract notice requires a 90-day notice that a party wants to modify an existing contract and notice to the Federal Mediation and Conciliation Service (FMCS). This gives the parties more time and involves the FMCS in resolving a dispute.[60]

- Strike notice of at least 10 days must be given if there is a collective bargaining agreement. Striking, picketing, or a concerted refusal to work without properly notifying the HSO/HS or the FMCS is an unfair labor practice.[61]

- Conciliation of labor disputes requires the FMCS to appoint an impartial board of inquiry to help resolve issues if it is determined that "a threatened strike or lockout affecting a healthcare institution . . . will substantially interrupt the delivery of healthcare in the locality concerned." (Section 213[a]).

- Those with religious convictions are exempt from paying union dues, even in a union shop, if the individual "is a member of and adheres to established and traditional tenets or teachings of a *bona fide* religion, body, or sect that has historically held religious conscientious objections to joining or financially supporting labor organizations." The person must donate an equivalent amount to a charitable fund approved by the institution and labor organization.

Unions active in healthcare include SEIU (Service Employees International Union) United Healthcare East, National Nurses United, American Federation of Labor and Congress of Industrial Organizations (AFL-CIO), and The United Food and Commercial Workers International Union.[62] More information regarding federal labor law is available at the U.S. Department of Labor website: https://www.dol.gov. In response to union collective bargaining agreement restrictions on nonunion workers and consistent with provisions of the Taft-Hartley Act, about half the states have enacted "right-to-work" laws that make union security clauses (e.g., closed shop, union shop, and agency shop) in collective bargaining agreements illegal.[63]

Evidence of Union Organizing Activity

Unions commonly use the following tactics for organizing campaigns:[64]

- Telephone solicitation

- Off-site meetings

- Distribution of leaflets

- Indirect influence

- Picketing

- Salting (putting union organizers into organizations as employees)

Likely, these union tactics occur in conjunction with employee involvement, such as the following activities:[65]

- Distributing union fliers

- Wearing union apparel or hat or displaying a pro-union button

- Unusual gatherings of employees

- Previously unconnected employees become involved

- Organization equipment used for personal purposes

- Increase in complaints or grievances

Such developments require the organization to take immediate action to avoid unionization, including the following steps:[66]

- Report suspected union activity to HR and/or senior management

- Seek expert advice from labor consultants and attorneys

- Enforce nonsolicitation rules to prevent union access to the organization's electronic systems

- Brief managers about avoiding unfair labor practices

- Educate managers about what can *and* cannot be said about negative aspects of a union

Despite best efforts, HSOs/HSs may fail to prevent a successful union organizing drive. Presence of a bargaining unit and union representative(s) interceding between employee and employer makes managing more difficult, but not impossible. Management, especially first-line supervisors, must be prepared to avoid missteps that can cause a grievance or a strike. Employees may find that a union provides few benefits and is not worth the dues they pay. If a majority agrees, there is a process to decertify the bargaining unit.

Self-Service HR

Technology makes do-it-yourself or self-service HR a reality. Newer generations of employees are tech savvy and likely more comfortable using an electronic device rather than a printed document for information. Not only are HR materials and publications available electronically, but ease of use and instant access make electronic HR an important adjunct to, or even primary source for HR's work. Such access adds efficiency to the staffing function and involves managers and employees in ways unpredicted even a few years ago.[67]

The following are some transactions with employees that can be performed with little to no direct involvement by HR:

- Managing employee personal data and updates

- Employee onboarding

- Benefits enrollment

- Employee training and e-learning

- Performance management

- Time and attendance records

- Attendance scheduling

- Access to the HR handbook

- Access to HR policies, procedures, and rules

- Information about HSO/HS history, values, and culture

- Wellness surveys and resources

- Department training

Technology can bring several benefits, such as the following, to the staffing function by facilitating HR's work:[68]

- More staff loyalty

- Enhanced employee engagement

- Real-time assessment of performance

- Improved employee experience

- Better skills (talent) management and recruitment

- Less paperwork and more streamlined bureaucratic functions

- Employees empowered to become better decision makers

- Elimination of "silos" and improved intraorganizational communication

- Ability of HR to analyze performance data and offer custom training

- A more strategic role for HR in the organization

New technologies require revisions of organizational policies and materials, especially the employee handbook and similar documents employees use frequently. To be addressed are questions such as employee e-mail received on the employer's system; access to and viewing nonwork-related websites; personal use of employer-issued devices, such as smartphones; telecommuting; instant messaging; personal use of the employer's computers; and monitoring employees' communications. These issues are addressed more fully in the next sections. Suffice it to say here that they are fraught with legal (and ethical) aspects and must be developed carefully and approved by legal counsel to ensure they conform with the law. Social media and blogging are other areas in which employers have legitimate concerns—with special emphasis on guidance that employees must be clear they speak only for themselves, not the organization.[69]

Foreign Workers

Historically, wealthy and powerful countries have attracted talented professions from all fields, including medicine. An example is the famous Greek physician, anatomist, and biological empiricist, Galen of Pergamum (A.D. 130–200), who served the aristocracy in Rome. In addition, he tended the medical needs of its gladiators.[70] Galen is known for diagnosing the discharge of pus from the penis in gladiators afflicted with gonorrhea (discharge of seeds) as a discharge of semen. Contemporary foreign recruitment includes RNs (among the most notable sources was the Republic of the Philippines) after World War II (1941–1945). RNs and physicians emigrate to the United States from Canada and other British Commonwealth countries. Physicians, pharmacists, and dentists come from India and elsewhere in the Near East and Middle East. Medical professionals must meet licensing and certification requirements of the jurisdictions in which they work. Currently, unskilled caregivers from African countries are being recruited for nursing facilities and as private-pay personal care attendants.[71] Though a natural result of economics and human hope and opportunity, international recruitment raises ethical issues, especially if it deprives developing countries of needed medical personnel.

Legal entry of foreign medical professionals is regulated by the U.S. Department of Homeland Security and the Department of State, and to a lesser extent the Department of Labor. It is illegal for employers to hire, recruit, or enlist in a similar manner anyone *ineligible* to work in the United States. *All* new employees must complete Form I-9, which requires employers to verify documentation of the employees' eligibility to work in the United States; both employers and employees must attest to that eligibility.[72] Employers may require employees to be able to speak English.[73] This seems essential in healthcare, even with the possibility of lesser-skilled English speakers working in jobs having little interaction with the public. Even here, coworkers must be able to communicate with them, and poor English skills may become problematic. Similar problems arise when work such as environmental services is outsourced.

Healthcare staff coming to work in the United States from Canada and Mexico have a separate set of requirements under the North American Free Trade Act (NAFTA). NAFTA defines a professional as someone holding a bachelor's degree, and they enter under a TN (Trade NAFTA) protocol.[74] H-1B visas allow a foreign specialty worker (bachelor's degree or equivalent) to be employed in the United States for 3 years, renewable for another 3. The

United States-Mexico-Canada Agreement (USMCA) ratified in early 2020 made no changes to treatment of TN professionals as provided in NAFTA.[75]

The quota of H-1B visas fills quickly. In addition, availability of H-1B visas is subject to change by executive order of the president. This requires employers to be alert to developments at the federal level. Employers initiate recruitment and must follow a multistep process. The foreign worker must be paid prevailing wages and offered the same benefits.[76] Despite being academically qualified the foreign worker will likely require much more orientation and training than someone educated in the United States. These costs can be significant. HSOs/HSs must consider carefully if recruiting from abroad is cost effective compared with providing a work environment attractive to comparably prepared U.S.-trained staff who will be productive more quickly, will understand the culture, and are fluent in English. Improving retention is the most effective way to reduce the need to recruit, and it will enhance the stability and morale of the HSO workplace.

Teams

HSOs/HSs use large numbers of teams for various purposes. These include teams that are cross-functional, project, self-directed (autonomous work group), task force, process improvement (employee involvement group), and virtual.[77] Almost all are established as needed and dissolve when the work is done.

Cross-Functional Team

Functions in HSOs are commonly described as the silos made famous in discussions of communication problems in organizations. Many processes in HSOs cross functional areas. For example, patients admitted to inpatient status from the emergency department (ED) cross several functional areas: ED, admissions, transportation, and nursing. If a problem crosses functional areas, the team assembled to solve it must include staff with expertise in those functional areas so that, for example, a new management information system needed for the process can be selected. Another example is a quality improvement team (QIT) established to improve the process of admitting an ED patient to an inpatient bed. This is a cross-function QIT. It must include staff members with process knowledge—even though that knowledge is limited to one part of the process. The sum of knowledge of those on the QIT is the entire process.

Project Team

These teams are established to complete a specific task, such as designing a new form to collect information in a clinical area, planning a new clinical service line, or developing criteria to determine eligibility to park in a new parking ramp. Task force teams need expertise from several areas. Staff with expertise may volunteer or be appointed. Project work is often time consuming and takes team members from their normal responsibilities. If time needed for the project goes beyond normal work hours, it is only fair to pay additional salary or recognize the work on the team in other, substantive ways.

Self-Directed Team

These teams include highly trained staff who are accountable for a work process.[78] Self-directed teams have several uses. For example, matrix organizations can use a self-directed team to provide the various management skills needed to solve a problem in this more complex organizational arrangement. Or, a self-directed team might be responsible to solve a problem arising from a service line that crosses several functional areas.

Task Force

A task force (team) is established to address and solve a major problem. For example, in the face of a determined union-organizing effort, the CEO may establish a task force composed of the chief operating officer (COO), VP-HR, several senior managers, in-house legal counsel, external legal counsel, and consultants who are expert on union organizing to try to thwart the organizing effort. For internal members, this additional work may take considerable time. If so, they should be assisted in their usual duties. Task forces dissolve when the need for them ends either because the problem is solved or it is overtaken by events.

Process Improvement Team

As noted, one type of QIT is established to improve a cross-functional process. The other type of QIT is internal to a department or function and is known as a functional QIT. For example, nurse staffing or scheduling affects only nursing. Improving nurse scheduling focuses on that process, and the QIT is internal to nursing. Similarly, if pharmacy wants to improve the process that begins when a medication order is received in pharmacy and ends when the medication is delivered to the patient's unit, that process is solely in the hospital pharmacy. Both functional and cross-functional QITs must comprise staff members who have process knowledge. This tends to eliminate from QIT membership managers, unless they manage the department or functional area that includes the process, or a unit affected by a process that crosses functional areas. Those who work in the process are the best choices for a QIT. Most managers think they know how a process works but are likely far removed from its actual functioning. Further, if the process was designed by that manager, there is a vested interest in how the process was established and should function—even if it does not. This preconceived view may interfere with the manager's ability to help improve it. Processes entropy over time and devolve to their least efficient functioning. Those who work in a process are more likely to know that entropy is affecting its efficiency, whereas managers may know only that the process is not working well and must be "fixed."

Virtual Team

A virtual team requires technology to do its work. Technology allows members of a virtual team to be geographically remote from one another. Their presence must be synchronous if the work is to be effective, however. Some aspects of a virtual team's work may be nonsynchronous as, for example, a subcommittee report is reviewed by other team members asynchronously. Audio conferencing and telephone conferencing are other usable technologies and ways to describe the work of a virtual team. In-person interactions may be necessary for final phases of the team's work, however.

Virtual Workforce

Technology allows work to be done remotely. The virtual team already discussed is but one example. Delivery of healthcare is a labor-intensive, hands-on service industry that does not lend itself readily to staff members being physically elsewhere. Nonetheless, some types of work and portions of usual HSO functions can be performed other than in the same location at which healthcare services are delivered. Examples of activities and/or functions that can be performed remotely wholly or in part include financial management (e.g., budgets, accounts receivable and payable, collections), HR, electronic health records (EHRs) (medical records), medical staff office, supply chain, and security. The virtual workforce has positives and negatives.[79] Positives include the following:

- Reduced need for space on site

- Increased productivity—remote staff have fewer distractions

- Reduced sick leave

- Lower healthcare costs—sick staff do not come to the HSO/HS to spread their illness

- Larger labor pool—working remotely widens both the range of, and geographic area for, potential staff

- Zero commuting time and little need for attention to personal grooming and apparel

Negatives include the following:

- Managers may have difficulty managing remote employees

- Technology costs to support remote staff can be high

- Morale may suffer for staff members whose job is not fully compatible with remote work

- Staff may feel disconnected from the organization, despite being connected technologically

- Monitoring productivity may be difficult, especially for nonroutine work

- Fits best with asynchronous jobs that are more support than direct engagement

Establishing a virtual workforce requires careful planning to know it fits with the organization's needs and the roles of staff who perform it. It is prudent to begin with a few small, pilot programs to learn how well a virtual workforce fits the organization's needs. Management must be willing to end all or parts of a virtual workforce if it proves to be less than what is needed to support the organization's mission. And, of course, there is no requirement that a virtual workforce is an all or nothing situation. For example, those working remotely can be available for meeting and face-to-face activities. Perhaps, a day or two a week will be enough—and on-site presence need not be the same each week. On-site presence can be the summative effort for the functions they perform; background and preparatory work is done remotely.

The preceding discussion addressed nonclinical applications of off-site work that was termed virtual. The legal aspects of telemedicine were discussed in Chapter 2; the clinical applications in Chapter 5. It, too, is a type of virtual workforce. Robotic surgery, for example, can be performed by an operator in a distant physical location with an on-site colleague if that level of assistance is needed.

Social Media in the Workplace and in HR

The organization's uses of social media were discussed earlier. Technology-savvy millennials and generation Z employees are at ease with social media and are likely heavy users. HSOs/HSs should have policies to guide employees' actions and use of social media in the workplace. The policies should link to the organization's code of conduct, privacy policy, and employee handbook; describe what is allowed, with examples; describe consequences of violating the policies; update the policies frequently to include new technology; remind employees to write only about what they know; and include contractors and vendors in the policies.[80] The organization has two distinct interests in employee use of social media: legal aspects and employee engagement.

Legal Aspects

The Internet has a wealth of information about prospective and current employees. Among the billions of subscribers to social media are certain to be persons whose postings are of a business interest to the organization. It is clear from media reports that many persons are indiscrete with potentially damning information about their personal and professional lives regarding illegal activity, postings about employers and/or colleagues, political views, and the

like. The challenge for the organization and its managers is to know what information is legitimate for them to obtain and use because it is relevant to the employment relationship. Once
having such information, the employer may face allegations it was used in decision making.
That use may be illegal. States may prohibit employers from considering after-hours activities
when making employment decisions if the activity(ies) are lawful and do not interfere with
job performance. Some states prohibit employers from requesting usernames and passwords
for online accounts. If access to the online account was obtained by circumventing a security
device or guessing the password, the employer may have violated the federal Electronic Communications Privacy Act of 1986 (P.L. 99-508). Employers who use Internet searches in their
application process should have persons not involved in decision making eliminate purely
personal and irrelevant information. This gives ultimate decision makers only job-related information for the hiring decision.[81]

Employee Engagement

Engaging employees is a major challenge for organizations and even more so in healthcare
because of its demanding and stressful work environment. HR can use social media to build
morale; tell success stories; inform about internal and relevant external developments; build
teamwork; share ideas; and bridge the gap among organizational "silos."[82] The organization
can use social media to further its mission, vision, and values. Employees can reinforce what
the organization seeks to do by retweeting messages and commenting favorably on developments and the culture. Conversely, however, employees may do great harm to the organization
if they use social media to defame it and/or their colleagues; reveal proprietary information;
attack competitors; cause disharmony and grievances; spread (malicious) gossip; and generally
sow discontent in the organization.[83] This means the organization must monitor the social
media, either using internal resources or by engaging a vendor. Astute managers may find early
warnings on social media that suggest problems in a nursing unit, for example, perhaps even
before nursing leadership is aware of it. Also, employees may be more forthright on social media than they are with each other and/or their supervisors. Care must be taken, however, that
staff do not perceive management to be conducting an organized spying campaign on them.
Even though there is easy public access to many social media sites, employees may believe that,
when they tweet with each other, no one else should read what is said. Electronic means such
as direct messaging allow private one-on-one conversations. The HSO/HS may have rules,
however, that limit use of electronic devices in the workplace, whether the device is issued by
the organization for employee use or owned by the employee.

The Electronic Monitoring & Surveillance Survey (https://www.amanet.org/articles/the-
latest-on-workplace-monitoring-and-surveillance/) from the American Management Association and The ePolicy Institute shows the pervasiveness of monitoring employees. Employers
are motivated by concerns about litigation and increasing use of electronic evidence in lawsuits
and government investigations. Generally, monitoring of employees is unregulated. Unless
company policy states otherwise, the employer may monitor most workplace activities. Employer guidelines are provided in employee handbooks, memos, and union contracts, and on
the employer website. Courts have ruled that when they are on the job, employees' expectation
of privacy is limited.[84]

Numerous guidelines and limitations affect employees in the workplace. Employers own
the computer network and terminals and, generally, may monitor employee use of workplace
computers and workstations. Some employers notify employees about monitoring. Union
contracts may limit it. A company's email or instant messaging systems are owned by the
employer who may view their contents. Employees should assume that internal and external
e-mail and instant messaging on a company system are not private. Usually, employers may
listen to employee telephone calls at work, such as for quality control. States may have different

rules for *intrastate* calls. Federal law regulates that *interstate* calls and personal calls may not be monitored unless employers prohibit them. Generally, employers may monitor use of employer-provided mobile phones or devices. Monitoring apps can secretly record text messages, e-mail, Internet use, location, contacts, call logs, photos, and videos.

Some employers allow employees to use personal mobile devices for work, either instead of or in addition to employer-provided devices. This is called bring your own device (BYOD). BYOD programs must balance security of employer data and protection of employee privacy; here the law is fluid.[85] BYOD has several risks: lost or stolen devices, employees leaving the HSO/HS with valuable data and information, lack of security updates on the device making it subject to hacking, and using unsecured wi-fi access to the Internet. Policies and processes regarding BYOD should include limits on employer monitoring, guidelines on using devices, and which devices are acceptable. Employers should consider cyber liability insurance to offset the economic consequences of hacking, loss of proprietary information, and, especially important in healthcare, the risk of breaching patient confidentiality and attendant legal liability.[86] HSOs/HSs should consider extending BYOD policies, procedures, and rules to LIPs who are independent contractors.

Video monitoring deters theft, maintains security, and monitors employees. Federal law does not prevent video monitoring even when employees do not know or consent to it. Some courts have upheld employee privacy when monitoring is physically invasive, such as hidden cameras in locker rooms or bathrooms. Generally, employers may use global positioning system (GPS) devices to track employees who use employer-owned vehicles. Few courts have addressed GPS tracking. Most of those have ruled that employers may use GPS tracking devices on company-owned equipment, when the employee has no reasonable expectation of privacy. Employers may open mail addressed to employees and delivered to their workplace. Federal law prohibits mail obstruction, but mail is considered delivered when it reaches the workplace. Many companies have social media policies limiting what employees may and may not post on social networking sites about their employer. Some state laws prohibit employers from disciplining employees for off-duty activity on social networking sites unless the activity damages the company. Generally, however, work-related posts are potentially damaging to the company.[87]

Personality Testing

Organizational success depends on the quality of human capital; selection must produce high-performance employees. The "good fit" theory is widely used for hiring decisions in HSOs/HSs and other organizations.[88] As the name suggests, good fit focuses on how well an applicant's credentials fit the job, *and* how well the applicant's personality fits the organizational culture. An example of fit analysis is knowing an applicant thrives as part of a team but loses motivation when working alone. This applicant would be a poor fit in an organization that values workers with an independent style.

The good fit approach is a workplace application of the general psychological model of human behavior that asserts behavior is a function of person and environment.[89] A body of research asserts that measures of personality are correlated with a wide range of human activities, including job performance. That research has methodological limitations, however, including consistent use of terms and definitions, poor design of some studies, and limited data to support the relationship between personality and job performance.[90] Given the high cost of bad hires, however, tools that promise predictive value for hiring have obvious appeal.[91]

The interview is the traditional method used to evaluate candidates as persons. The hiring manager and other staff interact with candidates, observe their behavior, and decide if they are a good fit. Interviews and similar interactions have limitations that diminish their reliability, however. For example, interviews are often short, candidates are observed under stressful and artificial conditions, and interviewers may be positively or negatively biased. Some candidates are skilled at impression management and can manipulate interviewers into providing positive assessments.

Could the good fit strategy be improved by using another method instead of or in addition to the interview for assessing personality? Unfortunately, the good fit strategy has a serious impediment. Personality cannot be measured *objectively*. Psychologists created the theory of personality to explain observable differences in how individuals think, feel, and behave.[92] Nevertheless, because predicting behavior has strong practical appeal for managers and decision makers, a multitude of personality tests have been designed and are available. Some personality tests are tailored to unique jobs, such as police officers[93] and firefighters.[94] Others focus on measuring empathy and the ability to handle stress, traits relevant to healthcare workers. Most personality tests are simple, self-reported questionnaires that produce a rating or score associated with a qualitative description of a personality type. Assessing certain desirable and undesirable personal qualities in potential health professionals during the selection process could have considerable long-term benefits.[95] Here, the specific application was to medical students.

The "Big Five" or "Five Factor Model (FFM)" is an indirect method for measuring personality that many psychologists accept.[96] The "five" refers to five behavioral "traits" consolidated by statistical factor analysis from large data sets describing individual behavior traits considered close approximations of personality. All human beings are presumed to possess these five traits. Significantly, however, in predicting behavior, research has shown human beings vary widely in "how much" of each trait they have. The FFM traits are agreeableness, conscientiousness, extraversion, emotional stability (originally called neuroticism), and openness. There are several versions of the FFM questionnaire. A common version has 50 items that ask respondents to rate how well the item describes them. Responses range from agree strongly to disagree strongly and have a value of 1 to 5, corresponding to the level of agreement with the statement. Each statement measures one FFM trait. Ratings are summed and averaged for each trait. For example, a measure of conscientiousness is, "I see myself as someone who does a thorough job." This item illustrates another serious limitation of FFM and all self-reported measures. How is it known if the respondent answers truthfully? What is the likelihood that respondents who see themselves as manifestly *not* thorough are going to reveal that on an employment screening questionnaire?

Finally, using personality tests in the workplace raises legal issues.[97] For example, personality tests claiming to diagnose mental disorders have been challenged in court when used for employment purposes. Applicants may claim such medical testing violates their right to privacy of medical information. Furthermore, test scores revealing mental disabilities may be grounds for an unlawful discrimination claim. Personality tests have been challenged as discriminatory if data show individual scores correlate with membership in protected groups.

At this writing, personality tests with greater reliability and validity are needed. However, HR should continue seeking ways to bring the power of data analytics to hiring decisions.[98] Given scientific interest and practical demand, efforts to improve and apply tools such as the FFM will likely continue. Organizations considering psychological testing should consult psychologists who specialize in them and legal counsel to assess benefits and risks of their use. Employers must have substantial and convincing evidence the personality tests they use are job related, are consistently applied, and have a business purpose. Employers have the burden of proving the need for their use to skeptical regulators.[99]

Outsourcing Some HRM

An increasingly complex environment and the resulting higher workload augur the outsourcing of some traditional HR activities. Outsourcing means the activity is performed outside the HSO/HS by contract vendors. Complexity arises from the plethora of laws and regulations affecting HR. Added to legal complexity is administering a wide range of employee benefits. Likely,

HSs have systemwide contracts for services that are required or optional for constituent entities. HSOs affiliated in an SA or other cooperative arrangement may contract as a group to outsource services. HSOs/HSs may purchase services through an organization, such as a purchasing group.

Frequently outsourced HR functions include the following:[100]

- Administration of 401(k) (retirement) plans

- Pre-employment testing and assessment

- Background screening

- Administration of flexible spending accounts

- Employee assistance programs (EAPs)

- Administration of healthcare benefits and COBRA conversions

- Temporary staffing

- Administering pension and retirement benefits

- Relocation for eligible staff

- Payroll

- Retirement planning

Outsourcing some HR activities has advantages: HR staff can work on strategy and other activities of more direct benefit to the organization; vendors performing the activities have expertise that makes them less likely to stumble in meeting legal requirements; the vendor is more efficient in performing the work so costs may be lower; and legal liability for errors is largely transferred outside the HSO. Likely disadvantages include a need to disclose proprietary information; employees feeling less connected with the organization if HR activities are performed by vendors; and the vendor lacking sensitivity to the culture and unique circumstances of the HSO and its employees.[101]

Discussion Questions

1. Outline the relationships between the planning and organizing functions performed by an HSO at the macro level and the staffing function at the macro level. How does the staffing function at the macro level connect with the directing function discussed in Chapter 13?

2. Outline the relationship between HR and the work of managers. Distinguish that relationship in terms of the concepts of staff and line roles/activities in an HSO.

3. Identify and discuss briefly five reasons why HRM in HSOs such as hospitals is more complex than similar activities in a typical business enterprise.

4. There is a planning function within HRM. Identify the components of planning done in HR.

5. Outline the process of recruiting in an HSO. Identify the roles of HR and managers.

6. Interview an HR manager at a local HSO. Summarize several problems that manager identifies. In your summary of the interview, suggest how each problem can be prevented or minimized.

7. Identify five reasons unionization of HSOs is considered by GBs and managers to be undesirable.

8. Electronic devices are ubiquitous in everyday life and in work settings. Use your personal experience to identify positive *and* negative aspects of the ready availability and use of personal electronic devices in the workplace.

9. Employing clinicians who are non-U.S. citizens has a long history in HSOs. Identify five positive aspects *and* five negative aspects of such employment.

10. The COVID-19 pandemic of 2020 highlighted the value and use of teleworking. Discuss use of teleworking in HSOs *and* HSs. Identify several effects for morale and compensation when some staff can telework, but those who must interact with patients cannot.

Case Study 1   Today's Workforce

The population from which HSOs/HSs draw their workforces is composed of four generations: Baby Boomers, Generation X, Millennials (Generation Y), and Generation Z. There is variation, but each has distinct characteristics, as suggested in the following table:

Generation	Years	Population	Values and Characteristics
Baby Boomers	1946–1964	76 million	Individuality; goal driven for success; measure work ethic in hours worked and financial rewards; embrace teamwork; emphasize relationships; expect loyalty from colleagues; career equals identity; want work/life balance
Generation X	1965–1978	60 million	Self-reliant; well educated; questioning; risk averse; loyal employees; want open communications; respect productivity over tenure; want control of their time; invest loyalty in persons, not organizations
Generation Y (Millennials)	1979–1995	88 million	Image conscious; need feedback and reinforcement; value instant gratification; idealist; team oriented; want open communications; seek someone to help them achieve their goals; want job for personal fulfillment; want to shed stress in their lives; race and ethnicity of reduced importance
Generation Z	1996–present	86 million	Realistic, not idealistic; somewhat jaded; know life requires hard work; private, avoid tracking on social media; entrepreneurial, interested in starting a business; multitaskers; hyper-aware, especially of surroundings; 4D thinking; technology reliant (technology is as important as air and water)

Adapted from the American Hospital Association. *Workforce 2015: Strategy Trumps Shortage*, 13. Chicago: American Hospital Association, 2010; and Tim Elmore, "On Leading the Next Generation: Six Defining Characteristics of Generation Z." https://growingleaders.com/blog/six-defining-characteristics-of-generation-z/, retrieved August 22, 2019.

Questions

1. Identify three management implications of having multiple generations work in HSOs/HSs.

2. Which management functions are most affected by having multiple generations in a workplace?

3. What effect does the presence of four generations in the workforce have on the HSO's culture and workforce?

| Case Study 2 | The Photographer Who Posed as a Gynecologist[102] |

In July 2014, world-renowned Johns Hopkins Hospital in Baltimore, Maryland, settled a class action lawsuit against it by agreeing to pay $190 million to women secretly photographed by a gynecologist-obstetrician it employed. Dr. Nikita Levy used tiny cameras to secretly make hundreds of videos and photographs showing the genitals of more than 7,000 women and girls during gynecological examinations. The settlement was one of the largest in the United States that involved physician sexual misconduct.

Dr. Levy had worked for the Johns Hopkins Health System more than 25 years. In February 2013, a female coworker told authorities about a pen-like camera he wore around his neck. He was fired after an investigation uncovered his misdeeds. Dr. Levy committed suicide soon after being fired and before criminal charges could be brought.

Baltimore police and the Federal Bureau of Investigation found 1,200 videos and 140 images stored on Dr. Levy's home computers. Plaintiffs' lawyers said thousands of women were traumatized, though faces were not visible in the images and it was impossible to know which patients—or how many—had been photographed. Investigators concluded the images had not been shared. This, lawyers for the hospital stated, would help "those affected achieve a measure of closure." Some women, however, alleged verbal abuse and inappropriate touching by Dr. Levy. Others said they were regularly summoned to his office for unnecessary pelvic examinations.

Plaintiffs argued Hopkins knew or should have known what Dr. Levy was doing. Specifically, he violated hospital protocol by sending chaperones out of the room when he examined patients. Hopkins took the position that Dr. Levy "went rogue" and it "had no inkling" of what was happening when he examined patients.

A Hopkins spokesman stated the settlement was covered by insurance.

Questions

1. Identify process failures at Hopkins that enabled Dr. Levy's actions. What changes should be made to prevent similar problems? What is the role of HR?

2. Identify and discuss briefly the legal relationship(s) between Hopkins and Dr. Levy that resulted in Hopkins's liability. What is the role of insurance carriers in these types of cases? How might insurance diminish an HSO's interest in effective prevention of such actions? Chapter 2 discusses legal aspects.

3. From the facts provided, refute the statement by Hopkins's attorneys that it "had no inkling" about Dr. Levy's behavior. What should staff members have done when Dr. Levy violated protocol by sending chaperones from the examining room? What is the role of HR?

4. Staff members knew Dr. Levy sent chaperones from the examining room in contravention of hospital rules. Identify several problems with the culture at Hopkins that facilitated Dr. Levy's actions. What should HR do to help prevent future similar lapses?

| Case Study 3 | Doctor of Death[103] |

By all accounts Michael Swango was fascinated by death. A cavalier attitude toward death and his mishandling of cadavers caused fellow medical students to give him the nickname "Double-O Swango, Licensed to Kill," an obvious parody on the 007 moniker for the James Bond series so popular in the 1980s. He took special interest in dying patients—studying their charts, lingering at their bedsides, and asking questions about their pain and how it was affecting them. Dr. Swango's killing of patients continued for 12 years. It is unknown how many he killed.

After finishing medical school at Southern Illinois University where he was considered a brilliant student—despite falsifying a patient report and receiving an evaluation of "poor"—Dr. Swango began a neurosurgery residency at Ohio State University Medical Center (OSUMC). There, a nurse found him injecting something into a patient who later became ill. Other nurses reported that healthy patients died unexpectedly after Dr. Swango saw them. Nurses urged hospital administration to act. After a brief investigation the nurses were told they were being paranoid. Other nurses contacted the local prosecutor, whose investigation was blocked by the hospital.

As his initial residency at OSUMC was ending in June 1984, Dr. Swango provided take-out chicken for colleagues. Soon after eating it they became violently ill with vomiting and diarrhea. Following the incident, OSUMC withdrew its offer for Dr. Swango to continue training there. Regardless of his history at OSUMC, its glowing recommendation allowed him to become licensed.

Unable to find a residency in neurosurgery, Dr. Swango worked as an emergency medical technician—a job well below his level of training—in Quincy, Illinois. There, co-workers suspected he had brought them poisoned donuts. They set a trap and found he had laced iced tea they were expected to drink with ant poison (arsenic). Dr. Swango was arrested, pled guilty to aggravated battery, and was sentenced to 5 years in prison.

Dr. Swango served only 2 years and was released for good behavior. In 1992, he was appointed to a residency at the University of South Dakota Sanford School of Medicine after presenting forged documents that showed his prison time had been only 6 months as punishment for a barroom brawl. Neither OSUMC nor law enforcement in Quincy, Illinois, was contacted by Sanford to verify his application. A year later he was offered a residency at the Health Science School for Medicine at Stony Brook University in New York; again, with no thorough background check. Part of his residency included training at Northport Veterans Administration Medical Center (VAMC).

About this time the television news magazine, *20-20*, rebroadcast an interview Dr. Swango had given while in prison in Illinois. This caused Dr. Swango to be dismissed from his residency. At about the same time a psychiatrist at the Northport VAMC reported to the VA office of the inspector general that he suspected a physician there was killing patients.

At that point, Dr. Swango went to Africa for 3 years, during which time it is estimated he killed 60 patients. Part of the time he worked in Zimbabwe, whose government later charged him in absentia with poisoning seven patients, killing five. Dr. Swango was arrested on his return to the United States on charges of fraud for presenting false credentials to Stony Brook and for illegally distributing controlled substances. He pled guilty and began serving 3 1/2 years in prison. In the meantime, the VA's office of the inspector general exhumed five bodies of patients believed to have been Dr. Swango's victims. Three showed traces of epinephrine, which speeds up the heart and in excess can cause death, and succinylcholine, which causes paralysis. Based on this evidence, Dr. Swango was charged with three counts of murder. In a plea bargain, he agreed to serve three consecutive life sentences in exchange for not being extradited to Zimbabwe.

Dr. Swango was able to continue his medical career (and killing patients)—even after time in prison—because of deficient background checks by hospitals at which he was hired. It was also apparent that some hospital executives refused to believe a physician could be a serial killer.

Because his crimes were secretive and hard to prove, it took Department of Veterans Affairs investigators 5 years to prepare its case against Dr. Swango. Even then it was impossible to know how many patients he had killed. Five bodies were exhumed in an investigation of Dr. Swango's time at OSUMC; autopsies were inconclusive.

Questions

1. This case is like situations in which nursing or other clinical staff kill patients in hospitals and NFs. What is HR's role in preventing situations involving nurses who might harm patients?

2. What obligation does staff in healthcare settings have to observe, report, and take action when situations such as those described in this case occur?

3. Nurses acted when they suspected problems with Dr. Swango's patients. Management investigated but took no action and told the nurses they were being paranoid. What message does management send to staff when it responds as described in the case?

4. Describe the role of HR in promoting a culture of openness, communication, and concern for quality of care and patient safety. In your description identify specific points and means of promoting such a positive culture.

Case Study 4   Let the Punishment Fit the Crime[104]

The newspaper headline seemed to say it all: "VA Pharmacists Escape Punishment for Mistakes." The article's first line described how pharmacists at a Veterans Administration hospital in New Jersey not only kept their jobs after they made serious dispensing errors but were not even severely disciplined. In one case, a pharmacist dispensed an overdose of a chemotherapy agent that was five times the prescribed amount; the patient died within weeks. A root cause analysis of the error (which is mandated by The Joint Commission) found that death was hastened by the overdose. In another case, a pharmacist dispensed a potentially fatal dose of a medication, but neither the pharmacist nor his supervisor, who also had a history of making dispensing errors, was disciplined. Instead, they were ordered to undergo counseling.

The problem at the New Jersey VA hospital became public knowledge because, in an unrelated appeal hearing, a pharmacist claimed his firing was discriminatory. He asserted he was fired for an error, but pharmacists who made even worse mistakes were not fired. The attorney for the pharmacist whose firing was being appealed suggested fault lay with the hospital when she stated that after previous dispensing errors no systems had been instituted to prevent errors, track errors, or determine their extent. At the appeals hearing another pharmacist testified that when he worked at a VA nursing facility he was expected to fill over 240 prescriptions during an 8-hour shift. He called such a workload dangerous and one that should never be allowed.

Questions

1. Describe HR's role in verifying credentials of staff members such as pharmacists. What should HR's response have been *after* this case arose?

2. How does HR participate if there are disciplinary problems with staff in a clinical department? Should it? Outline an example of a situation such as that described in the case *and* identify HR's involvement.

3. As described in Chapter 1, the U.S. Department of Veterans Affairs, Veterans Health Administration, has scores of hospitals and other sites at which healthcare professionals such as pharmacists work. How can its HRM function assist in equitable application of its HR policies, procedures, and rules?

4. Assume the pharmacist alleging inequitable application of disciplinary rules is a member of a union. Outline the effects the presence of a union will have on HR at the site, its efforts to discipline following a significant dispensing error, and the process(es) involved.

Notes

1. U.S. Department of Labor, Bureau of Labor Statistics. "Employment by Industry. Seasonally Adjusted." *https://www.bls.gov/charts/employment-situation/employment-levels-by-industry.htm*, retrieved August 19, 2019.

2. Bessen, James. "Everything You Need to Know about Occupational Licensing." *Vox.* November 18, 2014. *https://www.vox.com/2014/11/18/18089272/occupational-licensing*, retrieved September 8, 2019,

3. The Joint Commission. *2013 Hospital Accreditation Standards.* Oak Brook Terrace, IL: Joint Commission Resources, Inc., 2013.

4. Donabedian, Avedis. *Explorations in Quality Assessment and Monitoring. Vol. I. The Definition of Quality and Approaches to Its Assessment,* 81. Ann Arbor, MI: Health Administration Press, 1980.

5. Armstrong, Sharon, and Barbara Mitchell. *The Essential HR Handbook,* 5–11. Newburyport, MA: Career Press, 2019.

6. Armstrong and Mitchell. *The Essential HR Handbook,* 5–11.

7. Cascio, Wayne F. *Managing Human Resources: Productivity, Quality of Work Life, Profits,* 5th ed., 148. Boston: Irwin/McGraw-Hill, 1998.

8. Roberts, Gary, Gary Seldon, and Carlotta Roberts. *Human Resources Management,* n.d. U.S. Small Business Administration. *http://sdcc.vn/template/3043_eb-humanrsmanagement.pdf,* retrieved August 20, 2019.

9. Armstrong and Mitchell. *The Essential HR Handbook,* 10.

10. Mitchell, Barbara, and Cornelia Gamlem. *The Big Book of HR,* 49, 51. Wayne, NJ: Career Press, 2017.

11. Mitchell and Gamlem. *The Big Book of HR,* 47–48.

12. Mitchell and Gamlem. *The Big Book of HR,* 48–49.

13. Mitchell and Gamlem. *The Big Book of HR,* 48–51.

14. Mitchell and Gamlem. *The Big Book of HR,* 61–65.

15. Fleischer, Charles H. *The SHRM Essential Guide to Employment Law,* 25. Alexandria, VA: Society for Human Resource Management, 2018.

16. Armstrong and Mitchell. *The Essential HR Handbook,* 151–152.

17. Fleischer. *The SHRM Essential Guide,* 26–27.

18. Fleischer. *The SHRM Essential Guide,* 27–28.

19. Mitchell and Gamlem. *The Big Book of HR,* 80–81.

20. Armstrong and Mitchell. *The Essential HR Handbook,* 20. Pages 21–24 show examples of behavioral interview questions.

21. The Joint Commission. "Ambulatory Care Program: The Who, What, When, and Where's of Credentialing and Privileging," n.d. *https://www.jointcommission.org/assets/1/6/AHC_who_what_when _and_where_credentialing_booklet.pdf,* retrieved August 21, 2019.

22. Stanford Health Care. "Medical Staff: Credentialing and Privileging." *https://stanfordhealthcare.org /health-care-professionals/medical-staff/credentialing-and-privileging.html,* retrieved August 21, 2019.

23. "Question of the Week." May 30, 2019. Horty Springer, Pittsburgh, PA. *https://www.hortyspringer. com/question-of-the-week/may-30-2019,* retrieved May 30, 2019.

24. Council on Credentialing in Pharmacy. "Credentialing and Privileging of Pharmacists: A Resource Paper from the Council on Credentialing in Pharmacy." *American Journal of Health-System Pharmacy* 71 (2014): 1891–1900.

25. ACCP White Paper. "Future Clinical Pharmacy Practitioners Should Be Board-Certified Specialists." American College of Clinical Pharmacy. *Pharmacotherapy* 26, 12 (2006). *https://accpjournals .onlinelibrary.wiley.com/doi/epdf/10.1592/phco.26.12.1816,* retrieved August 21, 2019.

26. Mitchell and Gamlem. *The Big Book of HR,* 83.

27. Fleischer. *The SHRM Essential Guide,* 77–78.

28. Mitchell and Gamlem. *The Big Book of HR,* 83–84.

29. Fleischer. *The SHRM Essential Guide,* 29.

30. Fleischer. *The SHRM Essential Guide,* 450.

31. Fleischer. *The SHRM Essential Guide,* 454.

32. Armstrong and Mitchell. *The Essential HR Handbook,* 229.

33. Armstrong and Mitchell. *The Essential HR Handbook,* 33.

34. Armstrong and Mitchell. *The Essential HR Handbook,* 30.

35. U.S., Department of Labor. Bureau of Labor Statistics. *Economic News Release.* Table 16. Annual total separation rates by industry and region, not seasonally adjusted. *https://www.bls.gov/news .release/jolts.t16.htm,* retrieved June 23, 2019.

36. Hegwer, Laura Ramos. "Retaining Your Most Valued Resource: Appreciated High-Value Staff Improve Patient Care." *Healthcare Executive* 34,1 (January/February 2019): 21.

37. Fried, Bruce J., and Michael Gates. "Recruitment, Selection, and Retention." In *Human Resources in Healthcare: Managing for Success,* 4th ed., edited by Bruce J. Fried and Myron D. Fottler, 220–221. Chicago: Health Administration Press, 2019.

38. Fleischer. *The SHRM Essential Guide,* 47–48.

39. Fleischer. *The SHRM Essential Guide,* 42.

40. Armstrong and Mitchell. *The Essential HR Handbook,* 155–156.

41. Samit, Jay. "4 Ways Augmented Reality Could Change Corporate Training Forever." *Fortune*, July 22, 2017. *https://fortune.com/2017/07/22/augmented-reality-corporate-training/*, retrieved July 23, 2019.
42. Drucker, Peter F. *Managing the Non-Profit Organization,* 62. New York: HarperCollins, 1990.
43. Cascio, *Managing Human Resources,* 321, 148.
44. Armstrong and Mitchell. *The Essential HR Handbook,* 39–43.
45. Samit. "4 Ways Augmented Reality."
46. Fried, Bruce J., and Howard L. Smith. "Compensation Practices, Planning, and Challenges." In *Human Resources in Healthcare: Managing for Success,* 4th ed., edited by Bruce J. Fried and Myron D. Fottler, 277. Chicago: Health Administration Press, 2019.
47. Fried and Smith. "Compensation Practices, Planning, and Challenges," 287.
48. Clement, Dolores G., Maria A. Curran, and Sharon L. Jahn. "Employee benefits." In *Human Resources in Healthcare: Managing for Success,* 4th ed., edited by Bruce J. Fried and Myron D. Fottler, 343. Chicago: Health Administration Press, 2019.
49. Hofrichter, David A., and Gordon W. Hawthorne. "Governing Performance: Examining the Board's Role in Executive Compensation." *Trustee* 50 (June 1997): 7; Keefe, Thomas J., George R. French, and James L. Altman. "Incentive Plans Can Link Employee and Company Goals." *Journal of Compensation and Benefits* 9, 4 (January/February 1994): 27.
50. Armstrong and Mitchell. *The Essential HR Handbook,* 83.
51. Substance Abuse and Mental Health Services Administration. *Results from the 2012 National Survey on Drug Use and Health: Summary of National Findings.* NSDUH Series H-46, HHS Publication No. (SMA) 13-4795. Rockville, MD: Substance Abuse and Mental Health Services Administration, 2013.
52. National Business Group on Health. "An Employer's Guide to Workplace Substance Abuse: Strategies and Treatment." *http://www.businessgrouphealth.org/pub/f3151957-2354-d714-5191-c11a80a07294,* retrieved September 8, 2013.
53. Armstrong and Mitchell. *The Essential HR Handbook,* 81.
54. Occupational Safety and Health Act of 1970, PL 91-596, 29 U.S.C. sect 651 et seq.; Twomey, David P. *A Concise Guide to Employment Law, EEO & OSHA,* 109. Cincinnati, OH: South-Western Publishing, 1986.
55. Mitchell and Gamlem. *The Big Book of HR,* 266.
56. Cooper, William O., David A. Spain, Oscar Guillamondegui, et al. "Association of Coworker Reports about Unprofessional Behavior by Surgeons with Surgical Complications in Their Patients. *JAMA Surgery.* Published online June 19, 2019. *https://jamanetwork.com/journals/jamasurgery/article-abstract/2736337,* retrieved August 28, 2019.
57. Cutter, Chip. "Going to HR Is Tough Decision." *Wall Street Journal,* October 18, 2019, B6.
58. *Becker's Hospital Review.* "How Hospitals and Unions Can Bridge Their Gaps." July 3, 2013. *https://www.beckershospitalreview.com/human-capital-and-risk/how-hospitals-and-unions-can-bridge-their-gaps.html,* retrieved July 16, 2019.
59. U.S. Department of Labor, Bureau of Labor Statistics. *Union Members–2018. https://www.bls.gov/news.release/pdf/union2.pdf,* retrieved August 22, 2019.
60. Office of the General Counsel, National Labor Relations Board. *A Guide to Basic Law,* Government Printing Office, 1991, p. 8.
61. Office of the General Counsel, National Labor Relations Board. *A Guide to Basic Law,* 22.
62. *Becker's Hospital Review.* "4 of the Most Powerful National Healthcare Unions." July 11, 2014. *https://www.beckershospitalreview.com/human-capital-and-risk/5-of-the-most-powerful-national-healthcare-unions.html,* retrieved July 16, 2019.
63. Fleischer. *The SHRM Essential Guide,* 438–439.
64. Mitchell and Gamlem. *The Big Book of HR,* 237.
65. Mitchell and Gamlem. *The Big Book of HR,* 237.
66. Mitchell and Gamlem. *The Big Book of HR,* 237.
67. Armstrong and Mitchell. *The Essential HR Handbook,* 154–155.
68. Armstrong and Mitchell. *The Essential HR Handbook,* 158.
69. Armstrong and Mitchell. *The Essential HR Handbook,* 159.
70. *Internet Encyclopedia of Philosophy. https://www.iep.utm.edu/galen/,* retrieved July 24, 2019.
71. Batalova, Jeanne. "Immigrant Health-Care Workers in the United States in 2018," May 14, 2020. *https://www.migrationpolicy.org/article/immigrant-health-care-workers-united-states-2018#Region and Country of Birth,* retrieved August 7, 2020.
72. Fleischer. *The SHRM Essential Guide,* 382.
73. Fleischer. *The SHRM Essential Guide,* 390.
74. Fleischer. *The SHRM Essential Guide,* 387–388.

75. Succar, Suzanne (Dickinson Wright). "USMCA: Immigration Chapter and TN Visas Unaffected by New Law," February 3, 2020. *https://www.jdsupra.com/legalnews/usmca-immigration-chapter-and-tn-visas-92274/*, retrieved August 7, 2020.

76. Fleischer. *The SHRM Essential Guide,* 387–388.

77. Fleischer. *The SHRM Essential Guide,* 386–387.

78. Fottler, Myron D. "Job Analysis and Job Design." In *Human Resources in Healthcare: Managing for Success,* 4th ed., edited by Bruce J. Fried and Myron D. Fottler, 164. Chicago: Health Administration Press, 2019.

79. Fottler. "Job Analysis and Job Design."

80. Armstrong and Mitchell. *The Essential HR Handbook,* 175–177.

81. Mitchell and Gamlem. *The Big Book of HR,* 69–70.

82. Fleischer. *The SHRM Essential Guide,* 347–348.

83. Armstrong and Mitchell. *The Essential HR Handbook,* 157.

84. Armstrong and Mitchell. *The Essential HR Handbook,* 157.

85. American Management Association. "The Latest on Workplace Monitoring and Surveillance." April 8, 2019. *https://www.amanet.org/articles/the-latest-on-workplace-monitoring-and-surveillance/*, retrieved August 24, 2019.

86. American Management Association. "The Latest on Workplace Monitoring and Surveillance."

87. Pochepan, Jeff. "Employees Working on Their Personal Devices? Here's How You Can Protect Your Business Data." *Inc.com.* Apr 27, 2018. *https://www.inc.com/jeff-pochepan/employees-working-on-their-personal-devices-heres-how-you-can-protect-your-business-data.html,* retrieved August 28, 2019.

88. American Management Association. "The Latest on Workplace Monitoring."

89. Piotrowski, Chris, and Terry Armstrong. "Current Recruitment and Selection Practices: A National Survey of *Fortune* 1,000 Firms." *North American Journal of Psychology* 8, 3 (2006): 489–496. *https://www.researchgate.net/publication/285661081_Current_recruitment_and_selection_practices_A_national_survey_of_Fortune_1000_firms,* retrieved September 3, 2019.

90. McCormick, Brian. W., Russell P. Guay, Amy E. Colbert, and Greg L. Stewart. "Proactive Personality and Proactive Behaviour: Perspectives on Person–Situation Interactions." *Journal of Occupational and Organizational Psychology* 92, 1 (March 2019): 30–51.

91. Barrick, Murray R., Michael K. Mount, and Timothy A. Judge. "Personality and Performance at the Beginning of the New Millennium: What Do We Know and Where Do We Go Next?" *Personality and Performance* 9, 1 (2001): 9-30.

92. Frye, Lisa. "The Cost of a Bad Hire Can Be Astronomical." May 9, 2017. *https://www.shrm.org/resourcesandtools/hr-topics/employee-relations/pages/cost-of-bad-hires.aspx,* retrieved September 1, 2019.

93. Friedman, Howard S. and Miriam W. Schustack. *Personality: Classic Theories and Modern Research,* 6th ed. New York: Pearson Education, 2016.

94. Barrett, Gerald V., Rosanna F. Miguel, and Jennifer M. Hurd. "Practical Issues in the Use of Personality Tests in Police Selection." *Public Personnel Management,* published online December, 1, 2003. *https://journals.sagepub.com/doi/10.1177/009102600303200403,* retrieved September 1, 2019.

95. Firefighters Lifestyle. *The Firefighter Psych Test. http://www.firefighterslifestyle.com/firefighter-psych-test/,* retrieved September 1, 2019.

96. Powis, David. "Personality Testing in the Context of Selecting Health Professionals." *Medical Teacher* 31, 12 (2009): 1045–1046.

97. McCrae, Robert R., and Paul T. Costa, Jr. *Personality in Adulthood: A Five-Factor Theory Perspective.* New York: Guilford Press, 2003.

98. Stabile, Susan T. "The Use of Personality Tests as a Hiring Tool: Is the Benefit Worth the Cost? *University of Pennsylvania Journal of Labor and Employment Law* 4, 2 (2002): 279–313.

99. Gupta, Manual, and Joey F. George. "Toward the Development of a Big Data Analytics Capability." *Information & Management* 53, 8 (2016): 1049–1064; *https://heidrick.com/Knowledge-Center/Publication/future-of-data-analytics-in-human-resources,* retrieved September 5, 2019.

100. "Question of the Week." November 15, 2018. Horty Springer, Pittsburgh, PA. *https://www.hortyspringer.com/question-of-the-week/november-15-2018/*, retrieved November 16, 2018.

101. Armstrong and Mitchell. *The Essential HR Handbook,* 177.

102. Armstrong and Mitchell. *The Essential HR Handbook,* 178.

103. Sources for this case were Gabriel, Trip. "Hospital to Pay $190 Million over Recording of Pelvic Exams." *New York Times*, July 22, 2014, A13; Linderman, Juliet. "Paging Dr. Sicko: Hosp Will Pay $190M over Perv Gyno's Pix." *New York Post*, July 22, 2014, 22.

104. Getlen, Larry. "Doctor of Doom." *New York Post,* September 9, 2018, 42.

105. McElhatton, Ian. "VA Pharmacists Escape Punishment for Mistakes." *Washington Times,* January 13, 2015, A1.

13

Directing

More than a century ago, Henri Fayol (France [1841–1925]) identified directing as the fourth management function. The word's root, *direct*, is used in *director*, a title often used in healthcare to refer to various managers. The contemporary literature, however, eschews the use of *directing* in favor of *leading*, which is used almost exclusively. This shift may have occurred because *directing* suggests a degree of prescriptiveness and top-down management incompatible with the prevailing view that management should be collegial, cooperative, and team oriented. Or, perhaps the use of *leading* rather than *directing* results from an evolution of management concepts and the associated language. This section uses *leading* as more-or-less synonymous with *directing*. There are technical differences between them, but they are close enough to be used interchangeably in the following discussion. The almost exclusive use of *leading* to the exclusion of *directing* is a regrettable mischaracterization of the word and the concept of directing.

Managers are met with challenges from many forces: remarkable scientific and technological advances in medicine (see Chapter 5), new organizational forms and relationships for providing health services (see Chapter 11), and new policies and programs for financing services (see Chapters 1 and 7), to name some of the most important. Managers in health services organizations and health systems (HSOs/HSs) are accustomed to challenges. They face high expectations from consumers and patients, clinicians, and service payers and are scrutinized as to the cost and quality of what they do. These managers are familiar with the challenges of demands for greater efficiency and effectiveness. All of this redounds to the importance of the directing function.

Managing HSOs/HSs will become more challenging. Managers must improve quality, reduce costs, and meet the needs of their service area. They are expected to deliver *value*, "defined as the quotient of quality divided by cost."[1] This means that their organizations must "deliver a higher level of quality at the same cost, the same level of quality at a lower cost, or higher quality at a lower cost."[2]

Directing as Leading: Defined and Modeled

Definitions of *leading* (as *directing*) are varied.[3] A comprehensive definition is that *leading* is the process of *influencing* others to understand and agree about what needs to be done to achieve the mission and vision of the organization by facilitating individual and group contributions to achieve the desired results. Influencing is critical and central to success because it is how leaders persuade others to follow their advice, suggestions, or orders.[4] The definition facilitates understanding of this complex, multidimensional activity. The definition applies to transformational-, organizational-, or system-level leading and transactional leading by managers. Figure 13.1 shows a simplified model of the process.

Transactional and transformational leading differ. Managers leading individuals and groups tend to work with staff whose work is homogeneous, whereas transformational leadership likely has staff diversity and heterogeneity. Leadership of whatever type requires ethical behavior. As discussed in this chapter, meeting this responsibility is central to effective directing as leading.

Work of Managers

Managers perform one of three distinct but interrelated types of work in HSOs/HSs.[5] Examples of *direct work* are patient care, research, education, and providing products or services. A second type, *support work*, is a facilitative adjunct to direct work. Examples of support work are fundraising and development, marketing, public relations, finance, and human resources management. The third type of work, *management*, is the focus of Part III. It involves developing a mission and objectives consistent with the organization's capacity relative to the external environment. Management work involves assembling and effectively using resources—human, material and supplies, technology and equipment, information, capital, and patients or customers. This allows direct work aided by support work to meet the organization's mission by accomplishing objectives.

This chapter identifies ways to assess, understand, and study management work. It can be analyzed in terms of the *functions* managers perform, the *skills* they use in doing their work, their *roles* in performing work, and the *competencies* they need to do the work well. Each of these factors is considered and used to illustrate important aspects of management work.

Managers

Managers are formally appointed to positions of authority in organizations. They enable others to do direct or support work, have responsibility for resource use, and are accountable for work results. As stated in the American College of Healthcare Executives (ACHE) *Code of Ethics,* "The fundamental objectives of the healthcare management profession are to maintain or enhance the overall quality of life, dignity and well-being of every individual needing healthcare services and to create an equitable, accessible, effective and efficient healthcare system."[6]

In HSOs/HSs, managers include persons with titles such as nurse team manager; maintenance director; dietary, surgery, or medical records director or supervisor; pharmacy, laboratory, outpatient clinic, social services, or business office director; medical director; chief medical officer (CMO); chief nursing officer (CNO); chief financial officer (CFO); chief information officer (CIO); vice president (VP); and chief compliance officer (CCO) or president or chief

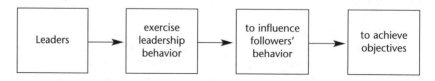

Figure 13.1.   The process of leadership.

executive officer (CEO). The variety of managers in these settings can be identified in part by their managerial level in the organization.

Classification methods typically identify managers as senior, middle, and supervisory or first-level managers. Regardless of title or level, managers have several common attributes: They are formally appointed to positions of authority, they are charged with directing and enabling others to do their work, they are responsible for using resources, and they are accountable to superiors for results.

The primary differences among levels of managers are degree of authority and scope of responsibility. For example, CEOs and other senior managers in the executive suite have authority over and are responsible for entire HSOs/HSs—all staff, resources, and individual and organizational results—because governing bodies (GBs) grant authority to them and demand accountability in return. Reporting to senior managers are numerous middle managers, each of whom is responsible for smaller units of the organization. Middle managers, such as department heads and heads of services, have authority over and are responsible for specific parts of the HSO/HS. Finally, first-level managers, who generally report to middle managers, have authority over and are responsible for overseeing the work of specific groups of staff. Managers at each level are responsible for various activities and accountable for results. All these activities are important, and no HSO/HS is successful unless management work at each level is done well and unless work is carefully coordinated and integrated within and across levels.

Management

No matter their level, all managers engage in the process of management. *Management* is defined as the process composed of interrelated social and technical functions and activities, occurring within a formal organizational setting for the purpose of helping establish objectives and accomplishing the predetermined objectives through the use of human and other resources. All managing has four elements:

1. It is a process, a set of interactive and interrelated ongoing functions and activities.

2. It involves establishing and accomplishing organizational objectives.

3. It involves achieving these objectives through people and the use of other resources.

4. It occurs in a formal organizational setting, which invariably exists in the context of larger external environments.

Managers focus on establishing and achieving organizational mission, goals, and objectives. The scope of managerial work includes providing the context in which direct and support work can be performed effectively. Managerial work includes preparing organizations and systems to deal with threats and opportunities from their external environments. In effect, managers help shape the culture and philosophy of the entities they manage in important ways; more than anyone, they determine their organization's overall performance.

Management Functions, Skills, Roles, and Competencies

What managers do can be grouped into one or more functions.[7] The social and technical functions of the management process (see the earlier definition of *management*) include planning, organizing, staffing, directing (leading, motivating, and communicating), and controlling. Figure 13.2 illustrates the interdependence of the management functions. Problem solving and decision making imbue the five functions and are integral to each.

The management functions are the logical grouping of generic management activities. All managers perform them to some degree regardless of hierarchical (scalar) level. In considering the management functions, it is convenient to separate them so that each can be discussed

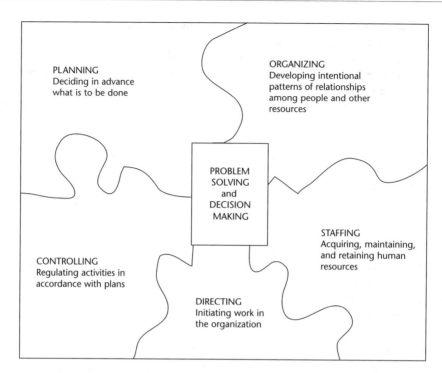

Figure 13.2.   The management functions are interrelated like the pieces of a puzzle.

independently, but the process of managing is not a series of separate functions. In practice, a manager performs these functions at the same time—the interdependent mosaic of functions, as shown in Figure 13.2.

Management Skills

The process of management is understood through the functions of planning, organizing, staffing, directing, and controlling, and the connective role of decision making. The functions, however, say little about the skills needed to execute them. Thus, another way to analyze management work is to examine the skills needed to do them.[8]

A classic article on management skills has stood the test of time and remains the prototypical discussion of skills required of managers.[9] Based on this article, and as shown in Table III.1 in the Introduction to Part III, effective managers use three distinct types of skills. Technical skills include the ability to use the methods, processes, and techniques of managing. It is easy to visualize the technical skills of a surgeon or a physical therapist, but counseling a subordinate or developing a departmental budget also require specific technical skills. Human, or interpersonal, skills enable managers to work successfully with others, understand them, and motivate and lead them in the workplace. Conceptual skills enable managers to visualize complex interrelationships—relationships among people, departments or units, organizations in a system, and between an organization or system and its external environment. Managers use conceptual skills to understand how various factors fit together and interact.

All managers rely on the three types of skills, though they are unlikely to use them to the same degree or in the same combination. For example, a hospital nursing service has different levels of management and requires different combinations of technical, human, and conceptual skills. The CNO (a senior manager) is concerned with how nursing service is organized and fits into hospital operation. The CNO relies on nursing service staff to accomplish technical work. By contrast, a shift supervisor (a middle manager), whose primary responsibility is to

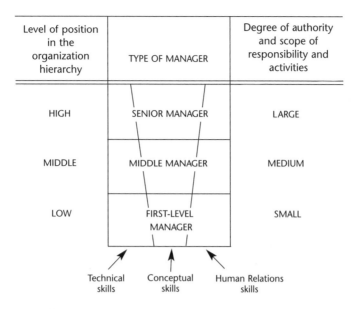

Level of position in the organization hierarchy	TYPE OF MANAGER	Degree of authority and scope of responsibility and activities
HIGH	SENIOR MANAGER	LARGE
MIDDLE	MIDDLE MANAGER	MEDIUM
LOW	FIRST-LEVEL MANAGER	SMALL

Technical skills   Conceptual skills   Human Relations skills

Figure 13.3.   Skills used by different types of HSO/HS managers.

"troubleshoot" the nursing staff on a shift, makes decisions on the basis of a technical knowledge of nursing, with little time spent (or interest in) thinking about relationships between nursing service and other departments. A nurse in charge of a nursing unit (charge nurse) uses technical skills because, in addition to being a manager, a charge nurse practices nursing. As can be seen by these examples, almost all first-level manager's work involves direct contact with people and requires human or interpersonal skills.

The extent to which each management skill is used varies with the manager's position in the organization, degree of authority, and scope of responsibility, and the number, types, and skills of subordinates. Senior managers typically use more conceptual skills than middle- or first-level managers. Conceptual demands include recognizing and evaluating multiple, complex issues and understanding their relationships, engaging in planning and problem solving, and thinking globally about the organization or system and its environment. By contrast, first-level managers use more job-related technical skills and skills that involve specialized knowledge than either middle- or senior-level managers. Figure 13.3 shows the relationship of these skills, degree of authority, and scope of responsibility and activities for each management level.

Management Roles in Directing

All managers engage in the management functions of planning, organizing, staffing, directing, and controlling; all managers use some mix of technical, conceptual, and human relations skills; and all managers engage in decision making. This does not, however, capture all that managers do. For example, a hospital CEO or other senior manager may serve on an areawide mental health task force, the president of a health maintenance organization may testify before a legislative body, the administrator of a nursing facility may serve on a state licensing board, the CNO at an academic medical center may lecture in a nursing education program, and a Department of Veterans Affairs senior official may testify before Congress to justify budget increases. Such activities are not fully encompassed in traditional descriptions of management functions or skills.

Mintzberg's Interpersonal, Informational, and Decisional Roles

In a seminal study of management work, Henry Mintzberg (Canadian/American [1939–]) observed a sample of managers over time and recorded what they did.[10] He concluded that

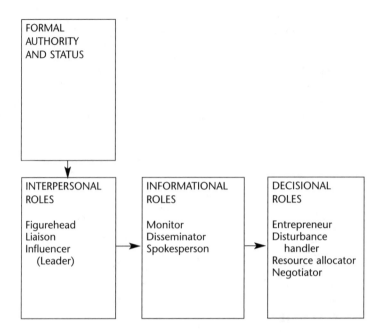

Figure 13.4. The manager's roles. (Reprinted by permission of *Harvard Business Review* from Mintzberg, Henry. The Manager's Job: Folklore and Fact. 53 [July–August 1975]. Copyright © 1975 by the Harvard Business School Publishing Corporation; all rights reserved.)

management work can be described meaningfully in terms of roles that all managers play. Roles in organizations are the typical or customary sets of behavior that are part of an organizational position. Mintzberg compared the roles of managers with those of actors on a stage and concluded that, just as actors play roles, managers, because they are managers, adopt certain patterns of behavior, as needed. He viewed the work of managers as a series of three broad categories of roles—interpersonal, informational, and decisional—with each category comprising several distinct but interrelated roles. Figure 13.4 summarizes Mintzberg's view of management roles. Thus, a third way to examine the work of managers is to consider the different roles they play (see Table III.1, page 350).

Interpersonal Roles
In Mintzberg's schema, all managers are granted formal authority over the organizations, systems, or organizational units they manage, and this leads to their interpersonal roles as figurehead, leader, and liaison. All managers, but especially senior managers, play the figurehead role when engaging in ceremonial and symbolic activities, such as presiding over the opening of a new physical plant or giving a speech about healthcare to a local civic club. Managers play the role of an influencer, or leader, when they seek to motivate, inspire, and set examples with their personal behavior. The liaison role allows managers to establish formal and informal relationships that will help them advance organizational performance and achieve its mission and objectives. Playing interpersonal roles gives managers opportunities to gather and use information, which generate a second set of roles.

Informational Roles
Managers' informational roles include monitor, disseminator, and spokesperson roles. As monitors, managers gather information from their contacts (including those established in their liaison roles), filter and evaluate the information, and decide whether to act on the information. The disseminator role results from managers' access to information and choosing what to do with it. In dissemination, managers choose whom should receive information in- and

outside the organization. The third informational role, spokesperson, is related to managers' figurehead role and involves communicating their entities' positions to internal and external stakeholders in their areas of responsibility.

Decisional Roles

Managers' decisional roles include entrepreneur, disturbance handler, resource allocator, and negotiator. Their authority, supported by their interpersonal and informational roles, permits managers to play decisional roles. As entrepreneurs, managers are initiators and designers of changes intended to improve performance in their domains. In this role, managers are change agents. As disturbance handlers, managers decide how to respond to various problems or issues arising in their work. For example, senior managers may face disturbances created by their professional staff organizations, by regulatory agencies, or by competitors' actions. First-level managers face disturbances ranging from a heavy snowfall that keeps away necessary staff, to conflicts between subordinates and budget cuts. Making good decisions when handling disturbances is key to managerial success.

As resource allocators, managers assign human, physical, and technological resources to various uses. Decisions about resource allocation become more difficult and more important, when resources are constrained. As negotiators, managers interact and bargain with employees, suppliers, regulators, customers and clients, and others. Negotiating includes deciding what objectives or outcomes to seek through negotiation and how to conduct the negotiation.

Competencies Needed by Senior Managers

The National Center for Healthcare Leadership (NCHL) model of managerial competencies (knowledge, skills, and roles that have been mastered) applies to all levels of managers even though the model was designed for senior managers.[11] Successful senior managers have six competencies. The clusters of knowledge and skills are 1) conceptual, 2) technical managerial and clinical, 3) interpersonal or collaborative, 4) political, 5) commercial, and 6) governance. In part, this categorization of managerial competencies builds on the work of Robert L. Katz (American [1933–2010]), who developed a model of the conceptual, technical, and interpersonal skills used by managers.[12] The competencies include conceptual competence, albeit more expansive than that envisioned by Katz. The set also includes a technical managerial and clinical cluster of knowledge and skills and an interpersonal or collaborative cluster, each of which extends elements in Katz's model. The political, commercial, and governance clusters are important additional competencies increasingly required of senior managers in HSOs/HSs.

Conceptual Competence

In all organizations, having a cluster of conceptual knowledge and skills permits senior managers to envision the places and roles of their organization in society. This competency allows them to visualize complex interrelationships within their organizations—relationships between staff and other resources, among units of an HSO, and among various organizations in an HS. In short, conceptual competence allows senior managers to identify, understand, and interact with the organization's myriad external and internal stakeholders. Conceptual competence improves their ability to comprehend the organization's culture and values and to visualize the organization's future.

HSOs/HSs are works in progress. Their structures and operations change often. Each change expands the notion of an adequate level of conceptual competence. Apart from organizational and operational complexities, senior managers face new or expanded conceptualizations of mission. When the mission changes, everything about an organization, including its culture, may change. The missions of HSs differ from those of component HSOs, although they are interrelated. Furthermore, as HSOs join other organizations in HSs, senior managers face new and more complex conceptualizations of their own managerial roles and the roles of managers with whom they work. CEOs are more likely to share their managerial roles with physicians. Physician managers are at the heart of designing better ways to coordinate care among entities and across the care continuum.[13]

In HSs, CEOs and senior managers must shift their concept of managerial success from advancing individual HSOs to integrating sets of HSOs and likely other entities. As integration continues, conceptual competence for managers becomes more important. To achieve success, senior managers in HSs and other strategic alliances (SAs) must be creative and synthesize the new forms and patterns. They must adapt their domains to evolving circumstances by relying on information from disparate sources to build frameworks, concepts, and hypotheses about the future. These managers must identify and evaluate options for solving complex challenges and select from among them.

Technical Managerial and Clinical Competence

The cluster of knowledge and associated skills that constitute technical competence for senior managers covers a broad range of managerial activities: planning for a new service or facility, devising and operating an incentive-based compensation program, arranging financing of long-term debt, and so on. CEOs and senior managers in HSOs/HSs must understand clinical work to support its effective delivery, and they rely on experts to ensure quality. Effective senior managers rely on clinically *and* managerially based technical knowledge.

As with conceptual competence, the technical managerial and clinical competence required of senior managers in complex HSs is more extensive than that needed for an independent HSO. The degree of clinical and management expertise must increase significantly in highly integrated HSs

In highly integrated HSs, for example, managers lead their systems in developing and implementing continua of health services. To do so, they must acquire and use competencies to assess the health needs in populations they serve and measure performance as improvement in population health. They must use population-based data to determine appropriate system size and configuration of primary and specialty providers, acute care and nursing facility beds, home health, hospice, and related components of the continuum of service. Highly integrated HSs assume financial risk for services.

Interpersonal or Collaborative Competence

An important ingredient of managerial success is the cluster of human interaction knowledge and related skills and relationships by which managers direct or lead others to achieve the organizational mission and objectives. A survey of executives to identify competencies most important to success in managing ambulatory health services found that interpersonal skills was rated highest.[14]

Interpersonal competence incorporates knowledge and skills for interacting with others, including the knowledge and related skills that permit a senior manager to develop and instill a common vision and stimulate a determination in others to pursue the vision and fulfill the objectives related to it. The essence of the interpersonal competence of managers is knowing how to motivate people, communicate their visions and preferences, negotiate, and manage conflict.

The core elements of interpersonal competence expand when HSOs establish and maintain SAs, particularly in forming and managing HSs. This expansion results from the differences between interpersonal relationships within organizations and those that occur between and among organizations in an SA. Achieving and managing interorganizational integration and coordination require knowledge and skills that facilitate synergistic interaction.

Two sets of knowledge and skills make up collaborative competence. The first element of collaborative competence is the ability to partner—to create and maintain multiparty organizational arrangements, negotiate complex agreements and contracts that sustain these arrangements, and produce mutually beneficial outcomes through such arrangements.[15] The second element, closely related to but distinct from partnering ability, is the ability to manage in the context of an HS. This context is unlike that of an independent HSO and requires different decisions and actions by CEOs and senior managers.

A partnering skill crucial to success in establishing and maintaining effective HSs is developing a common culture. In this context, culture is the pattern of shared values and beliefs that become ingrained in HS participants over time and influence collaborative behavior and decisions. A senior manager in one HS noted, "Nothing is more important to the long-term success of integrated systems than developing a culture. We have to do it or we won't survive. Without it, we won't be able to stand the pressures and develop the team approach we need."[16]

Collaborative competence means not only establishing a new mission statement and organizational objectives but modifying mission and objectives to fit HS needs. In independent HSOs, organizational objectives typically pertain to success in meeting volume, revenue, and market share, as well as quality targets. Objectives at the system level are added and pertain to enhancing the health status of a defined population and integrating functionally diverse organizations.

The core interpersonal or collaborative challenge is to convince CEOs and senior managers of the system's component organizations to avoid thinking of success in terms of advancing individual organizational priorities and instead to think of the system's broader mission and objectives. They may have to suboptimize performance of some components to optimize performance of the whole system. Suboptimization is addressed in Chapter 4. Managers throughout an HS's component HSOs are challenged to adjust their thinking about success and to help subordinates do the same by changing perceptions and ingrained habits.

In the context of independent HSOs, conflict management responsibilities primarily involve managers in resolving issues of intrapersonal conflict (within a person), interpersonal conflict (between persons), intragroup conflict (within a group), or intergroup conflict (between or among groups). Increased levels of integration in HSOs as they form larger and more complex HSs mean that CEOs and other senior managers must add conflict management and resolution between and among system entities to the list of management responsibilities.

As integration increases through formation of HSs or other types of SAs, senior managers are involved in interorganizational conflict. Integration of providers at different points in the patient service continuum brings into proximity disparate organizations, particularly when HSs are linked with insurers or health plans. Conflicts are unavoidable, and the knowledge and skills used to manage them are imperative. Interpersonal or collaborative competence is required of senior managers in all HSOs, but it is even more complex and important in HSs.

Political Competence
Political competence, defined as the dual abilities to accurately assess impact of public policy on performance of the senior managers domain of responsibility and to influence public policy making is very important.[17] Managers can use position, reward, and expert power to influence policy making at all levels of government.

CEOs and other senior managers can influence the public policy environment of their organizations at many levels. For example, they can help define problems that policies address, design solutions, or create the political circumstances necessary to advance solutions through the policy-making process.[18] Their central vantage points in the health industry enable senior managers to understand healthcare and related problems, such as Medicare and Medicaid coverage and financing that must be addressed by public policy. HSOs/HSs that are demonstration sites for innovative delivery of health services, for example, can participate in the policy debate and contribute to solving access and quality issues.

Furthermore, individually and through interest groups, senior managers can participate in drafting legislative proposals, and testifying at legislative and regulatory hearings. They can influence implementation of policy making by focusing on regulatory rulemaking. Rulemaking precedes and guides implementation of public policy and allows input from those affected by the regulations.

Commercial Competence

Commercial competence is the ability of managers to establish and facilitate value-creating situations in which economic exchanges occur. As noted, *value* in health services has specific meaning. It requires that buyers and providers think about quality *and* price. Value is quality divided by cost.[19] Value in health services is created when services have more quality attributes desired by buyers than competitors offer. Value is also created when an HSO/HS sells a set of quality attributes desired by buyers at a lower cost than competitors. Determining value in health services is not as straightforward as these relationships might suggest, however.

The quality of a single health service, such as hernia repair, is difficult to assess. Even more difficult is determining the value of a large and diverse bundle of services. Similarly, comparing price is difficult because bundles of services are purchased. Fair price comparisons must compare the same benefits or services in various bundles, including copayments or deductibles. Despite these difficulties, however, commercial success of HSOs/HSs increasingly requires them to compete on value.

Commercial competence uses knowledge and associated skills to identify markets and positions in markets and establish product or service strategies that increase the ability to compete effectively. Increasingly, commercial success for HSOs/HSs is determined by their ability to contract with health plans to provide a comprehensive bundle of services and, in some cases, to contract with employers to provide services directly to employees. Indeed, the ability to enter such contracts is a principal motive in forming many HSs.

Governance Competence

Each HSO/HS relies on its GB, CEO, and senior managers working in concert at its "strategic apex"[20] to establish a clear vision for the HSO/HS, to foster a culture that supports realization of the vision, to assemble and effectively allocate resources to realize the vision, to lead the organization through various challenges, and to ensure accountability to stakeholders.[21] In the context of governance, *accountability* means "taking into account and responding to political, commercial, community, and clinical/patient interests and expectations."[22] Although the boundaries between governance and management are not always clear, governance "holds management and the organization accountable for its actions and helps provide management with overall strategic direction in guiding the organization's activities."[23]

The knowledge and associated skills incorporated in governance competence are important for senior managers for three reasons. First, CEOs often participate directly in the governance function as members of GBs.[24] Other senior managers, such as CFOs and CMOs with specific expertise, are often either members or ex officio members of the GB.

A second reason for senior managers to have governance competence is that, at the strategic apex, it is difficult to separate what occurs under the rubric of governance from what is strategic management. Consequently, effective senior managers must be knowledgeable about management *and* governance. Governance competence enables CEOs and other managers to help GBs meet occasionally overlapping governance and management responsibilities. The third reason senior managers must have governance competence is that it enables them to assist GB members to do a better job. This includes providing development programs for GB members.

The extent to which senior managers have conceptual, technical managerial or clinical, interpersonal or collaborative, political, commercial, and governance competencies will largely determine their contribution to their HSO's/HS's performance.

Managers and Leaders: Are They Different?

Leadership theorist Abraham Zaleznik (American [1924–2011]) asked about that difference in 1977, and he and others researched the question for decades. Zaleznik, a clinical psychoanalyst, believed the difference was the conceptions of chaos and order that managers or leaders held in their psyches.[25] Managers believe in process, stability, and control, and seek to resolve problems quickly; leaders tolerate chaos and lack of structure and delay problem solving until they understand the problem. A precursor to Zaleznik's work was research published in the 1950s and 1960s identifying basic assumptions about what motivates people: Abraham Maslow (American [1908–1970]), Frederick Herzberg (American [1923–2000]), Victor H. Vroom (American [1932–]), Lyman W. Porter (American [1930–2015]), and Edward E. Lawler, III (American [1938–]).[26]

During the 1960s, Rensis Likert (American [1903–1981]) and his University of Michigan colleagues studied the effects of a manager's *employee orientation* or a manager's *production orientation* on employee productivity.[27] In the 1970s, Ralph Stogdill (American [1904–1978]) and his Ohio State University colleagues published research showing that the differences between managers and leaders were based on psychological and physical traits.[28] The Michigan studies and the Ohio State studies helped move the discussion from theories that successful managers had one trait or dimension toward theories that traits or dimensions occurred on a continuum.

Warren Bennis (American [1925–2014]) and Burt Nanus (American [1936–]) suggested that managers do things right and leaders do the right things. Managers are problem solvers; leaders are problem finders. Managers are past oriented; leaders are future oriented. Managers are efficient; leaders are effective. In 1989, Bennis addressed how leaders and managers developed: Management skills are learned in the classroom, and leadership is based at least partly on character and vision.[29] In *Where Have All the Leaders Gone?* Bennis argued that managers are safe, but leaders are endangered. He maintained that institutional autonomy no longer exists and has been replaced by a fragmentation of not only community but also a sense of shared values and any real possibility of consensus.[30] John P. Kotter (American [1947–]) argued that managers produce predictability and order; leaders produce change.[31] Kotter asserted that both management and leadership are necessary in successful organizations and can be present in the same individual (but rarely are), and organizations should develop and promote for both management and leadership excellence.[32] Table 13.1 summarizes the differences between managers and leaders.

Table 13.1   Summarizing Management and Leadership Differences

	Management	**Leadership**
Position	Formal	Formal and/or informal
Power	Legitimate/functional, transactional	Expert, referent, charismatic, transformational
Communication	Messages	Symbols
Focus/purpose	Problem solvers	Vision developers
Time orientation	Focused on past/present	Focused on past, present, and future
Internal rewards/motivation	Efficiency	Effectiveness
Vision	Predictability	Change
Measurement	Counting value	Creating value
Sense of followers	Policies, procedures, orders	Influence
Perceptions of risk	Risk adverse	Risk taking
Goal making	Short-term	Long-term
Interaction style	Direct	Coach
Perception of others	Employees	Colleagues, associates
View of errors	Precision/outcomes	Learning/process improvement

Developed with the assistance of Kimberly Lee, PhD, Assistant Professor of Health Administration, Texas State University

As defined earlier, management is a process, composed of interrelated social and technical functions and activities, occurring within a formal organizational setting for the purpose of helping establish objectives and accomplishing the predetermined objectives using human and other resources. Leadership is a broader concept than management. "Leading is the process of influencing others to understand and agree about what needs to be done to achieve the mission and vision of the leader by facilitating the individual and collective contributions of others to achieve these desired results."[33]

The quality of leading in HSOs/HSs affects the work accomplished by individuals and groups, as well as the performance of organizations and systems in pursuing their mission and objectives.[34] In a classic work, James M. Burns (American [1918–2014]) argued that leading an organization has two distinct parts: transactional and transformational.[35] Transactional leading occurs when managers value order and structure. Transactional leadership depends on self-motivated followers who work well in directed environments; leaders and followers undertake transactions from which each receives something of value. Good leadership skills and techniques facilitate transactions that are essential if followers are to perform well in organizations and systems.

In the second type of leading—more likely to be practiced in organizations and systems by senior managers—the purpose is change in the status quo. In practicing transformational leadership, managers focus on creating change, not on exchanges, as in transactional leadership. In transformational leadership roles, managers focus on changes that are organization- or systemwide and affect aspects such the following:

- Vision, values, mission, and objectives

- Attaining or modifying the level of support for the mission among internal and external stakeholders

- Allocating responsibility for the HSO's/HS's operation and performance

- Developing new strategies or implementing existing ones differently

- Altering the balance among economic, professional, and social interests of the HSO/HS and those who work in it

- Establishing new, or discarding existing, relationships with other organizations or systems with which interdependencies are shared

Rosabeth Moss Kanter (American [1943–]) has posited that transformational managers must be aware of the reasons for which people resist change: loss of control, uncertainty, fear of surprises, fear of difference, loss of status, concerns about competence, concerns about more work, ripple effect of the status quo, past resentments, and sometimes the change (threat) is real.[36]

In contrast to the transactional leading between managers and others, a transformational leader must have a vision for the entity and must lead both inside and outside followers if the vision is to be realized.[37] Some contemporary authors argue for an overt extension of transformational leadership into meta-leadership. Louis Rowitz (American [1935–]), for example, suggests that leaders in public health "need to move outside their organizational positions and utilize their talents, knowledge, and transactional and transformational skills to create new models for collaboration with partners."[38]

"Leadership" is often seen as synonymous with transformational leadership. When an organization's perceived success is attributed to effective leadership, it generally means leaders have made good decisions about mission, objectives, structure, service mix, quality, and new technologies, not that its leaders (managers) have only been good transactional leaders. Noel Tichy (American [1945–]) believed transactional leadership, through which better performance from people is achieved as leaders help them plan tasks, coordinate work, or learn new skills, is important but is not the only determinant of senior managers' success in transformational leader roles.[39]

Wesley M. Rohrer (American [1922–2000]) proposed a third type of leadership, translational leadership, which is a mediating linkage between the first-level or supervisors and senior managers.[40] Translational leadership is associated with middle managers because they are key communication channels between managers at senior and first levels. Those in the middle operationalize the mission, vision, and strategic direction articulated by the GB and senior managers: action plans, staffing requirements, schedules, budgets, performance targets and incentives, and so on. The corporate downsizing movement of the 1990s eliminated many middle managers. The result was short-term cost reduction but possible adverse consequences for long-term performance. Although transformational and transactional leadership functions are not limited to senior and lower management levels, translational leadership best fits the role of middle managers. Translational leadership has been applied to team development.[41]

Senior managers lead in part by managing organizational culture, which focuses on decisions and activities that affect the entire organization, including those that ensure its survival and overall health.[42] They lead by providing strategic direction and vision to the entity, ensuring that its mission and objectives are achieved. Effective organization- or system-level leaders inculcate desirable values, build intraorganizational and interorganizational coalitions, and interpret and respond to challenges and opportunities from the external environment, which includes trying to alter that environment.

After discussing the research and theories about transactional and transformational leadership, it is necessary to define *leading* and model it as a process, consider ethical responsibilities of leaders, discuss power and influence as central to leading, and consider the role of motivation in leading effectively.

Ethical Responsibilities of Leaders

Ethics undergirds effective leadership. Without clear core values consistent with those acknowledged to be central to healthcare practice (i.e., respect for persons, beneficence, nonmaleficence, and justice), the healthcare leader's actions and decisions are not adequately grounded, and the leader's strategic compass becomes unreliable. Kurt Darr (American [1940–]) expresses this consideration clearly: "For the health services managers, a personal ethic is a moral framework for relationships with patients, staff members, their organization, and their community. In these relationships, the manager morally affects and is morally affected by what is done or not done. This gives special meaning to misfeasance, malfeasance, and nonfeasance. Management's decisions are not value-free; in a moral sense, they affect the organization's environment, and that environment affects future decisions."[43] The moral compasses of healthcare managers profoundly affect the credibility and viability of the HSOs/HSs they lead.

The Preamble of the ACHE *Code of Ethics* describes the role of ethics as follows:

> The purpose of the Code of Ethics of the American College of Healthcare Executives is to serve as a standard of conduct for members. It contains standards of ethical behavior for healthcare executives in their professional relationships. These relationships include colleagues, patients or others served; members of the healthcare executive's organization and other organizations; the community; and society as a whole. The Code of Ethics also incorporates standards of ethical behavior governing individual behavior, particularly when that conduct directly relates to the role and identity of the healthcare executive.

> The fundamental objectives of the healthcare management profession are to maintain or enhance the overall quality of life, dignity and well-being of every individual needing healthcare service and to create a more equitable, accessible, effective and efficient healthcare system.

Healthcare executives have an obligation to act in ways that will merit the trust, confidence, and respect of healthcare professionals and the general public. Therefore, healthcare executives should lead lives that embody an exemplary system of values and ethics.

In fulfilling their commitments and obligations to patients or others served, healthcare executives' function as moral advocates and models. Since every management decision affects the health and well-being of both individuals and communities, healthcare executives must carefully evaluate the possible outcomes of their decisions. In organizations that deliver healthcare services, they must work to safeguard and foster the rights, interests and prerogatives of patients or others served.

The role of moral advocate requires that healthcare executives take actions necessary to promote such rights, interests, and prerogatives.

Being a model means that decisions and actions will reflect personal integrity and ethical leadership that others will seek to emulate.[44]

Among the more notable themes of these guidelines is associating the ethical conduct of healthcare managers with the broad mission of HSOs/HSs. Another is the expectation that healthcare managers are exemplars of the professional values and ethics that result from personal integrity and ethical leadership.

The ethical dimension of leadership is central to Burns's theory of transformational leadership rooted in the value commitments of leaders to their organizations and systems and the communities they serve. The primacy of value-based decision making is readily seen in the professions of healthcare management and public health. Burns contends that "transforming leaders 'raise' their followers up through the levels of morality."[45]

Managers' decisions reflect their ethical values. At the very least, healthcare leaders are expected to be as considerate of and responsive to ethical issues as their healthcare providers. As discussed in Chapter 2, and noted earlier in this chapter, the ethical principles of respect for persons, beneficence, nonmaleficence, and justice should be part of managers' (and leaders') ethic and guide their decision making.

Beyond these principles, which are applicable in healthcare and beyond, other ethical considerations are unique to healthcare. Some were addressed in Chapter 2. Three relevant to leaders in HSOs/HSs are discussed here.

Peter G. Northouse endorses community building as an ethical commitment in health services leadership. He contends that "transformational leaders and followers begin to reach out to wider social collectivities and seek to establish higher and broader moral purposes. An ethical leader is concerned with the common good."[46] This characterization may be seen as having special application to leaders in HSOs/HSs and in the broader public health domain because building coalitions of agencies, interest groups, advocates, and community leaders is increasingly important in both.

Another ethical consideration important to leaders in some HSOs/HSs is the concept of servant leadership. For example, Robert K. Greenleaf (American [1904–1990]) posits a model of altruistic leadership that is not only explicitly ethical but has a spiritual dimension.[47] Servant leadership is based on the premise that leaders are most effective if they act as would a servant by enabling, resourcing, supporting, and empowering their followers. Subordinating the usual symbols, status differentials, and behavior associated with power wielding and authority hierarchies allows the leader to become most effective because followers are capable and engaged. The importance of trust as an organizational cultural value is consistent with the values underlying servant leadership. The leader with "a servant's heart" can win the trust and acceptance of followers and peers. The danger here may be dissembling and inauthentic leadership where a superficial "I'm on your side, trust me" posture is a cover for cynical manipulation. The ethical leader is not required to adopt this style of leadership, nor is the servant leader guaranteed to be effective in all situations. The servant leadership model makes values explicit and challenges the impersonal command-and-control model of leadership.

A third ethical consideration important to leaders in HSOs/HSs is the use and abuse of power. In healthcare, all direct care providers have expert and referent power that should be used to benefit patients. Abuses have occurred, however, and were so egregious that patient rights and protections were encoded. Equivalent checks on managerial use of institutional power are less visible. John A. Worthley (American [1945–]) links power and its use with values and controls. Use of power by leaders is usually checked by internal controls to ensure that core values of an HSO's/HS's mission and strategic direction are well served and protected. Unethical leaders may, however, substitute and act on renegade values and distort or evade controls that would otherwise limit an abuse of power. Regardless, power is never value free or neutral, and controls on power are necessary for both society at large and organizations dedicated to the public welfare.[48]

Potential for abuse aside, understanding power in HSOs/HSs is crucial for leaders because it inextricably links to their ability to exert influence. Ability to influence is essential to ability to lead, a relationship discussed next.

Power and Influence in Leading

The essence of leading is influencing followers; therefore, influence is central to the leading process and success in the leader role. To have influence, however, one must have power, which is the potential to exert influence. More power means more potential to influence others and events. To understand influence, one must understand interpersonal power and its sources.

Sources of Power

Those who want to exert influence must first acquire power by using various sources available to them. The classic scheme for categorizing bases of position power identified by John R. P. French (American [1913–1995]) and Bertram Raven (American [1926–])[49] includes legitimate, reward, coercive, expert, and referent power. Building on this earlier work, Gary Yukl (American [1940–])[50] extended understanding of sources of position power to include information power and ecological power, and he moved expert power and referent power to a category called personal power (Figure 13.5).

Legitimate power is derived from a person's position in an organization. It is also called formal power or authority. Formal power or authority is needed so persons in organizations can do their jobs. Based on their position, all managers have some degree of legitimate power or authority, which fluctuates with level in the organization.

Reward power is based on the ability to reward behavior. Reward power stems partly from legitimate power granted by the organization. In other words, by virtue of their position

---

POSITION POWER

Legitimate Power
Reward Power
Coercive Power
Information Power
Ecological Power

PERSONAL POWER

Referent Power
Expert Power

Figure 13.5. Different types of power.

managers control certain rewards, which buttress legitimate or positional power. Rewards include pay increases, promotions, work schedules, recognition of accomplishments, and status symbols, such as office size and location, and parking.

Coercive power is opposite reward power and is based on the ability to punish people or prevent them from obtaining rewards. As described later in this chapter, reward and punishment are powerful motivational tools, although managers as leaders are generally better served by reward power than by coercive power.

Information power depends on access to information and control of its distribution. Ecological power stems from control over the physical environment in the workplace, as well as control over technology and organization designs used there.

Expert power derives from having knowledge valued by the organization, such as expertise in problem solving, medicine, or technology. Expert power is specific to the person who possesses the expertise. Thus, it is different from legitimate, reward, and coercive power, which are delegated by the organization, even though people may be granted these forms of power because they have expert power. For example, health professionals enter management positions because of their expertise. This change gives them legitimate, reward, and coercive power in addition to expert power. It is noteworthy that when work is technical or professional, expert power alone makes people powerful. For example, the power of the professional staff is based on clinical knowledge and skills. Physicians with scarce expertise, such as neurosurgeons, have more power than physicians with easily replaceable expertise. Expert power is not reserved for clinicians or technicians. The ability to effectively manage complex HSOs/HSs is a source of power too.

Referent power results when people engender admiration, loyalty, and emulation to the extent that they can influence others. This is sometimes called charismatic power. Charismatic leaders have a vision for the groups or organizations they lead, strong convictions about the integrity of the vision, and self-confidence in their ability to realize the vision. Their followers perceive them as agents of change.[51] Rarely do transactional or transformational leaders gain enough power to influence followers using referent or charismatic power. As with expert power, referent power cannot be given by the organization as are legitimate, reward, and coercive power.

Effective Use of Power

The seven sources of interpersonal power considered in the previous section are not necessarily separate; they can be complementary. Leaders who use reward power wisely strengthen their referent power. Conversely, leaders who abuse coercive power will weaken or lose referent power. Effective leaders can translate power into influence, understand the sources of their power, and act accordingly. Effective interpersonal and political skills distinguish those who effectively use power to influence others. Politics in organizations and systems can be thought of as activities to help individuals or groups acquire, develop, and use power and other resources to obtain preferred outcomes.[52] Mintzberg attributes successful use of power in organizations to leaders' political skills, which he defined as follows:

> The ability to use the bases of power effectively—to convince those to whom one has access, to use one's resources, information, and technical skills to their fullest in bargaining, to exercise formal power with a sensitivity to the feelings of others, to know where to concentrate one's energies, to sense what is possible, and to organize the necessary alliances.[53]

As noted, people in organizations derive power, in part, from their positions. Position or legitimate power (see Figure 13.5) includes the authority granted to managers by the organization and control over resources, processes, and information. However, power in organizations also depends on interpersonal relationships between leaders and followers. Personal power includes task expertise, friendship and the loyalty some people engender in others, and, sometimes, the leader's charisma. Finally, power depends on political processes and skills. Political power is derived from a leader's legitimate power: control of key decisions, and the ability to form coalitions, to co-opt or diffuse and weaken the influence of rivals in the organization, and to institutionalize the leader's power by exploiting ambiguity to interpret events in a manner favorable to the leader.[54]

Depending on circumstances, power from sources shown in Figure 13.5 is available in various degrees to leaders in HSOs/HSs. For example, at the departmental level, where leadership is primarily transactional, first-level managers have the power to influence or lead because they have formal authority. First-level managers control some resources, rewards, punishments, and information (position power), and they may have more expertise in the work than others in the unit (expert power). Such managers may have little political power.

In contrast, senior managers derive power from the same menu of sources but in a different mix. For example, CEOs have political power derived from the legitimate power to make decisions, form coalitions of decision makers, or co-opt opponents. The CEO may have charisma, loyal assistants, and friendships with key physicians and GB members, all of which give the CEO personal power. The CEO's position power can be great in control of resources and information. Finally, the CEO may be in a strong position to control access to the sources of power in the organization.[55] This is an important source of power.

What is known about power and influence is pertinent to understanding leadership. Leadership involves one person influencing others, and power is the ability to influence others. Power and influence do not explain leader effectiveness or the success or failure of leaders, however. Motivating others to perform well is also key to leading successfully.

Motivation Defined and Modeled

Motivation is a crucial concept in effective managing and leading. Understanding the motivation or behavior of people working in HSOs/HSs is important because the organization benefits from several types of behavior. First, however, people must be motivated to enter the workforce. Then, they must be motivated to continue their employment relationship, and motivated to attend work regularly and punctually. This is motivated behavior. People must be motivated to perform their work with acceptable quantity and quality. Finally, organizations need good citizenship behavior from those working in them.[56] People can be motivated to exhibit behavior such as cooperation, altruism, protecting other staff and property, and going above and beyond the call of duty, as needed. Good citizenship behavior makes the manager's job easier and contributes to organizational performance. Leaders must motivate people to practice these behaviors.

The concept of motivation is at once simple and complex. Motivation is simple because behavior is goal directed and induced by well-understood forces, some internal to the individual, others external. Motivation is complex because mechanisms that induce behavior include complex and individualized needs, wants, and desires shaped, affected, and satisfied in different ways.

For example, at a simple level, human needs are physiological. A hungry person needs food, is driven by hunger, and is motivated to satisfy that need or, stated another way, to overcome that deficiency. Other needs are more complex; some are psychological (e.g., the need for self-esteem) and some are sociological (e.g., the need for social interaction). In short, unmet needs trigger and energize human behavior. This fact is the basis for a model of the motivation process.

Figure 13.6 shows that the motivation process is cyclical. It begins with an unmet need and cycles through the person's assessment of efforts to satisfy the need, which may confirm the continuation of an unmet need or identify a new one. Meanwhile, the person searches for ways to satisfy the unmet need and exhibits goal-directed behavior intended to satisfy it. The process is simplified but contains the main elements by which human motivation occurs. Motivation is driven by unsatisfied needs and results in goal-directed behavior, even though it can be influenced by external factors.

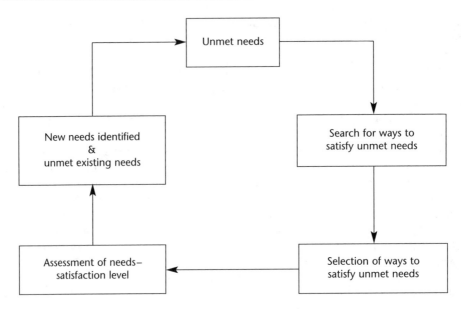

Figure 13.6. The motivation process. (From Longest, Beaufort B., Jr. *Health Professionals in Management*, 247. Stamford, CT: Appleton & Lange, 1996; reprinted by permission.)

Motivation is key to work performance. Motivation alone does not explain performance, however; it is one of many variables. Intelligence, physical and mental abilities, previous experience, and the nature of the work environment also affect performance. Good equipment and pleasant surroundings facilitate higher performance levels. Variables affecting performance can be conceptualized as follows:

$$Performance = Ability,\ Talent,\ and\ Experience \times Environment \times Motivation$$

This equation shows performance as a function of, or resulting from, interaction of variables, an interaction that goes beyond being merely additive.[57] Without motivation, no amount of ability or talent and no environmental conditions can produce acceptable performance.

These attributes and qualities must be understood in the context of processes as discussed in Chapters 4 and 8. In brief, the theories of W. Edwards Deming state that those who work in a process are constrained by that process—what it allows them to do. Thus, regardless of how motivated, talented, experienced, and the like someone is, the limiting factor of their efforts is largely the process(es) in which they work. Since processes are designed and implemented by managers it is they who indirectly constrain performance.

How Motivation Occurs

Understanding motivation and how it occurs is critical to effective leading. Therefore, much attention is given to determining the mechanisms of human motivation. To motivate participants, managers must know answers to questions such as the following: What energizes or causes participants to behave in contributory ways? What variables help direct their energies into acceptable behavior? Can the energized state be intensified or made to last longer?

Research has yet to develop a comprehensive theory about motivation or how leaders and managers affect it. Theories can be grouped into two broad categories: *content* and *process* (Table 13.2). Each contributes to understanding motivation and its implications for leading.

The content category focuses on the internal needs and desires that initiate, sustain, and eventually end behavior. The focus is *what* motivates. In contrast, the process category explains *how* behavior is initiated, sustained, and ended. Combined, they define variables that explain

Table 13.2 Comparison of Content and Process Perspectives on Motivation

Content Perspective	
Focus	Identifying factors within individuals that initiate, sustain, or terminate behaviors
Key studies	Maslow's five levels of human needs in hierarchy
	Alderfer's three levels of human needs in hierarchy
	Herzberg's two sets of factors
	McClelland's three learned needs
Implication for managers in leading	Managers must pay attention to the unique and varied needs, desires, and goals of participants
Process Perspective	
Focus	Explaining how behaviors are initiated, sustained, and terminated
Key studies	Vroom's expectancy theory of choices
	Adams's equity theory
	Locke's goal-setting theory
Implication for managers in leading	Managers must understand how the unique and varied needs, desires, and goals of participants interact with their preferences, and with rewards and accomplishments to affect their behavioral choices

From Beaufort B. Longest, Jr. *Health Program Management: From Development through Evaluation,* 2nd ed., 127. San Francisco: Jossey-Bass, 2015. Reprinted by permission.

motivation and show how they interact and influence one another to produce patterns of behavior. Studies and theories that underpin contemporary thought about motivation in the workplace are noted in Table 13.2 and are briefly described here, beginning with four theories that fall within the content perspective.

Maslow's Hierarchy of Needs

Perhaps the most widely recognized theory about what motivates human behavior—certainly the one with the most enduring impact—was advanced by psychologist Abraham Maslow (American [1908–1970]) in the 1940s. Maslow's theory of motivation stressed two premises.[58] In the first, he argued that human beings have various needs; *unmet* needs influence behavior, whereas fulfilled needs are not motivators. His second premise placed needs in a hierarchy, in which "higher" needs become dominant only after "lower" needs are satisfied. Figure 13.7 shows Maslow's needs hierarchy, with an example for each type and how it can be met in an HSO/HS.

From lowest to highest order, the five categories of needs in Maslow's hierarchy begin with basic physiological needs, such as air, water, food, shelter, and sex, which are necessary for survival. Participants can satisfy these needs using the resources that paychecks provide. Once survival needs are met, attention is turned toward continued survival by protecting oneself from physical harm and deprivation. Safety and security needs are met by ensuring job security and having health insurance and other benefits. The third level of needs relates to people's social and gregarious nature and includes their need for belonging, friendship, affection, and love.

It is notable that third-level needs are a breaking point in the hierarchy because they are removed from the physical or quasi-physical needs of the first two levels. This level reflects the need for association or companionship, belonging to groups, and giving and receiving friendship and affection.

The fourth level includes two types of ego needs: the need for a positive self-image and self-respect and recognition and respect from others. Examples of ego needs include independence, achievement, recognition from others, self-esteem, and status. Opportunities for advancement in a unit, or the larger organization, help meet these needs.

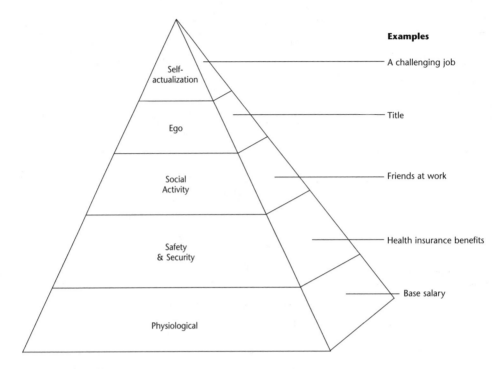

Figure 13.7. Maslow's needs hierarchy. (From Longest, Beaufort B., Jr. *Health Professionals in Management*, 251. Stamford, CT: Appleton & Lange, 1996; reprinted by permission.)

The top level of Maslow's hierarchy is self-actualization. It includes realizing one's potential for continued growth and development, which is the need to become everything someone is capable of becoming. Self-actualization is shown by creativity and opportunities for self-expression and self-fulfillment. A challenging and satisfying job is a primary pathway to satisfying such needs.

Managerial Implications of Maslow's Model
Because of its intuitive appeal, Maslow's concept of motivation is widely accepted. In a remarkable bit of candor, however, he wrote that the theory was "being swallowed whole by all sorts of enthusiastic people, who really should be a little more tentative."[59] Although his view has limitations, it makes a valid point; people have numerous needs that they seek to fulfill. In this way, Maslow contributed important insight to the nature of motivation and especially how unmet needs influence behavior. His theories on motivation are a conceptual framework within which to build and test more sophisticated theories about needs and how they affect behavior. Two are described next.

Alderfer's ERG Theory
Clayton Alderfer (American [1940–2015])[60] theorized that the needs hierarchy is more accurately conceptualized with only three categories, not five as in Maslow's formulation.[61] The ERG theory has three categories of needs: existence, relatedness, and growth. Existence includes material and physical needs that can be satisfied by air, water, money, and working conditions, for example. Relatedness includes needs that involve other people and are satisfied by social and interpersonal relationships. Growth needs involve creative efforts satisfied by creative or productive contributions.

Alderfer's existence needs conform with Maslow's physiological and safety needs, relatedness parallels Maslow's affection and social activity needs, and growth is similar to Maslow's ego and self-actualization needs. The important difference is how needs influence behavior.

Maslow theorized that unmet, lower-level needs are predominant, and the next higher level of needs is not activated until predominant (unmet lower-level) needs are satisfied. He called this the satisfaction–progression process. In contrast, Alderfer argued that the three categories of needs form a hierarchy only in the sense of increasing abstractness or decreasing concreteness: As a person moves from existence to relatedness to growth needs, the means to satisfy them become increasingly less concrete.

In Alderfer's ERG, people focus first on needs satisfied in more concrete ways; then on needs satisfied more abstractly. This is reminiscent of Maslow's idea of satisfaction–progression. Alderfer asserted, however, that a "frustration–regression process" is also present in determining which category of needs predominates at any time. By this he meant that someone unable to satisfy growth needs may regress and focus on satisfying more concrete relatedness or even more concrete existence needs. In Alderfer's view, coexistence of the satisfaction–progression and the frustration–regression processes leads to *cycling* among categories of needs.

Managerial Implications of Alderfer's Theory

A case example will clarify Alderfer's concept of cycling. Jennifer Smith, a 32-year-old registered nurse works in a women's health program sponsored by a major hospital. Smith is a single parent of two young children. She finds social interactions with co-workers rewarding but is concerned about the security of her position and the pay and benefits. Smith is an excellent nurse who enjoys her work.

When a vacancy occurred in a nurse manager position, Smith considered the opportunities this presented for professional growth and development, as well as a higher salary. She applied for the position and looked forward to the challenges of the job.

A more experienced and equally qualified nurse was promoted, however. Smith's disappointment showed, and she became quite concerned about her future in the women's health program. Several colleagues saw her reaction and tried to ease her disappointment. They said there would be other opportunities and with more experience she would be selected.

The new nurse manager was sensitive to this situation and made a point of telling Smith what a valuable contribution she was making to the success of the women's health program. After a few weeks, Smith returned to her earlier level of enjoyment in her work. In terms of predominant needs, she had *cycled* from existence and relatedness needs to growth needs represented by the promotion and then back to relatedness needs, all in a few weeks. In other words, Smith had experienced a satisfaction–progression process and a frustration–regression process.

An important difference between ERG and Maslow's hierarchy is that in ERG, when people satisfy existence and relatedness needs, they become less important. The opposite is true for growth needs, however. In Alderfer's view, as growth needs are satisfied, they become more important. As people become more creative and productive, their growth goals increase and are not satisfied until the new goals are achieved. In the case of Jennifer Smith, this means that when she becomes a nurse manager, her goals will change to include further growth and development in her career.

Important for managers is ERG's assumption that all employees have the potential for continued growth and development. Recognizing this fact leads to the "desirability of offering ongoing opportunities for training and development, transfer, promotion, and career planning to all employees."[62]

Herzberg's Two-Factor Theory

Herzberg took a different approach to study what motivates workplace behavior. He began with questions about what satisfies or dissatisfies people at work and assumed that the answers would contribute to understanding what motivates people.[63]

Herzberg and associates found one set of factors associated with satisfaction and high levels of motivation and a different set of factors associated with dissatisfaction and low levels of motivation. The two-factor theory of motivation asserts that "satisfiers" or "motivators" result in satisfaction and high motivation when they are present at adequate levels. These factors are achievement, recognition, advancement, the work itself, the possibility for growth, and responsibility. The other set of factors, "dissatisfiers" or "hygiene factors," cause dissatisfaction and low motivation when they are not present at adequate levels. These factors include organizational policy and administration, supervision, interpersonal relations, and working conditions.

Managerial Implications of Herzberg's Theory

Importantly, Herzberg's formulation caused managers to consider factors that contribute to motivation and what they can do to enhance satisfaction from work. To motivate employees managers must be concerned with one set of factors to minimize dissatisfaction *and* another to help employees achieve satisfaction and be motivated in their work.

McClelland's Learned Needs Theory

Another important contributor to the content perspective of motivation was David McClelland (American [1917–1998]), who developed the learned needs theory.[64] McClelland posited that people learn their needs from life experiences; they are not born with them. This theory builds on the earlier work of Henry A. Murray (American [1893–1988]),[65] who theorized that people acquire individual profiles of needs by interacting with their environment. McClelland was influenced by the work of John William Atkinson (American [1923–2003])[66] and Atkinson and Joel O. Raynor (American [1942–]).[67]

McClelland and Atkinson argued that people have three sets of needs: 1) the need for achievement, including the need to excel, achieve in relation to standards, accomplish complex tasks, and resolve problems; 2) the need for power, including the need to control or influence how others behave and to exercise authority over others; and 3) the need for affiliation (affiliation motive), including the need to associate with others, form and sustain friendly and close interpersonal relationships, and avoid conflict.

McClelland hypothesized that people are not born with these needs. Instead, they are *learned* or acquired as they mature. For example, children learn the need to achieve through encouragement and reinforcement of autonomy and self-reliance from adults.

McClelland posited that people typically have the three sets of needs, although one predominates and most strongly affects behavior. This is important because it relates to how well people fit a work situation. In fact, the most useful aspect of McClelland's formulation is the importance of matching people, considering their dominant needs. Done well, participants will be more motivated; performance will reflect this motivation.

Transition from Content to Process Theories and Models of Motivation

The content perspective of motivation—as reflected in the four theories or models just discussed—emphasizes that human motivation originates from the needs of people and their efforts to satisfy them. Each theory defines needs differently, but all support the concept that managers can motivate employees by helping them identify their needs and can, in part, meet those needs in the workplace.

The models emphasize managers' roles in helping participants understand their needs and the complex task of satisfying these unique and changing needs in the workplace. Managers can help participants identify and meet their needs by empathizing with them. Combining empathy with effective two-way communication (discussed in Chapter 9) about needs and the potential to satisfy them in the workplace usually results in progress in meeting them.

The content perspective of motivation, with its focus on *what* motivates behavior, provides insights for managers. Other models provide insight into the *process* of motivation. The process perspective focuses on *how* a person's performance is influenced by expectations and preferences for outcomes. A central element in the process perspective is that people as decision makers weigh the personal advantages and disadvantages of their behavior.

Table 13.2 outlines three models of the process perspective of motivation: Victor H. Vroom's (Canadian/American [1932–]) expectancy model, John Stacey Adams's (Belgian/American [1925–]) equity model, and Edwin Locke's (American [1938–]) goal-setting model. Each seeks to explain *how* motivation occurs.

Vroom's Expectancy Model

Vroom's model of motivation agrees that people are driven by unmet needs, and they make decisions about how they will behave as they attempt to fulfill them. Three conditions affect decisions: 1) people must believe that their own efforts will achieve the desired performance, 2) people must believe that achieving the desired performance will lead to some concrete outcome or reward, and 3) people must value the outcome.[68] Figure 13.8 shows the three central components and relationships of expectancy theory.

In this model, *expectancy* is what people perceive to be the probability that their efforts will lead to the desired performance. If a person believes that more effort will lead to improved performance, expectancy will be high. If, however, the person believes that trying harder will not improve performance, expectancy will be low.

Instrumentality is the probability perceived by individuals that their performance will lead to the desired outcomes or rewards. If a person believes that better performance will be rewarded, the instrumentality of performance to reward is high. Conversely, if the person believes that improved performance will not be rewarded, the instrumentality of improved performance is low.

Outcomes are listed only once in Figure 13.8, but they have two important roles in the expectancy model. Level of performance (in the center of Figure 13.8) represents an outcome of the "individual effort to perform" component of the figure. This is a first-order outcome, examples of which are productivity, creativity, absenteeism, quality of work, and other behavior that results from a person's performance. The outcome component on the right side of Figure 13.8 is a second-order outcome that results from attaining first-order outcomes, examples of which include merit pay increase, esteem of co-workers, approval of managers, promotion, and flexible work schedules.

Crucial to Vroom's expectancy model is that people have preferences for outcomes. According to Vroom, the value that a person attaches to an outcome is its *valence*. When a person has a strong preference for an outcome, it has a high valence; similarly, a lower preference for an outcome has a lower valence. People have valences for both first- and second-order

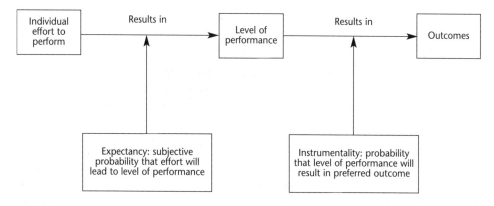

Figure 13.8. Simplified model of expectancy theory.

outcomes. For example, one person might prefer a merit pay increase to a flexible work schedule; another might prefer the flexibility (second-order outcomes). Someone might prefer to produce high-quality work (a first-order outcome) because it is believed that this will lead to a merit pay increase (a second-order outcome).

The three components of the expectancy theory (expectancy, instrumentality, and valence for outcomes) can be combined into an equation to express the motivation to work:

$$Motivation = Expectancy \times Instrumentality \times Valence$$

or

$$M = E \times I \times V$$

Notably, the equation is multiplicative; a low value assigned to any variable will yield a low result. For example, if a person is certain that effort will lead to performance (an expectancy value of 1.0 is assigned), is certain that performance will lead to reward (an instrumentality value of 1.0 is assigned), but does not have a very high preference for the reward involved (a valence value of 0.5 is assigned), when the components are multiplied ($1.0 \times 1.0 \times 0.5 = 0.5$), the result is low, indicating that motivation is low. For motivation to be high, expectancy, instrumentality, and valence values must all be high.

Adams's Equity Model

Equity is an extension of expectancy theory. In addition to preferences for outcomes or rewards associated with performance, people assess if potential rewards will be distributed fairly. Equity theory posits that people calculate the ratios of their efforts to the rewards they receive and compare them to ratios they believe exist for others in similar situations. They do this because they want to be treated fairly. Adams argues that people judge equity with the following equation:[69]

$$\frac{O_P}{I_P} = \frac{O_O}{I_O}$$

where

O_P is the person's perception of the outcomes received.

I_P is the person's perception of personal inputs.

O_O is the person's perception of the outcomes that a comparison person (or comparison other) is receiving.

I_O is the person's perception of the inputs of the comparison person (or comparison other).

This formula suggests that participants perceive there is equity when the ratio of inputs (efforts) to outcomes received (rewards) is equivalent to that of some "comparison other" or "referent." Conversely, inequity exists when the ratios are not equivalent.

Notably, perception, not reality, is used in the equation. Furthermore, there are options for the "comparison others" or "referents" in the equation. These options include people in similar circumstances (e.g., co-workers or those thought to be similar), a group of people in similar circumstances (e.g., all registered nurses working in the organization), or the perceiving person under different circumstances (e.g., in the present or previous position). Choice of referent is a function of information available and perceived relevance. Finally, the equation may have numerous inputs and outcomes. Inputs are what people believe they contribute to their job—such as experience, time, effort, dedication, and intelligence. Outcomes are what they believe they get from their job, such as pay, promotion, status, esteem, monotony, fatigue, and danger.

Equity theory recognizes that people are concerned with both absolute rewards received for their efforts and the relationship of rewards to what others receive. Staff in programs and projects make judgments about the relationship between their inputs and outcomes and inputs and outcomes of others.

When faced with situations they perceive to be inequitable, people try to restore equity in various ways. For example, people who feel an inequity about their pay (i.e., they feel it is too low or they work harder than others with the same pay) may decrease their input by reducing effort to compensate for this perceived inequity. Alternatively, they may seek to change their total compensation to reduce the perceived pay inequity. They may seek to modify their comparisons or referents. For example, they may try to persuade low performers who are receiving equal pay to increase their effort, or they may try to discourage high performers from exerting so much effort.

Others, perhaps in desperation, may distort reality and rationalize that perceived inequities are somehow justified. Finally, people may choose to leave an inequitable situation. This action usually occurs only when people cannot resolve the inequities and conclude that they will not be resolved. Thus, participants can attempt to restore equity by changing the reality or the perception of the inputs and outcomes in the equity equation, which can create serious problems for managers.

Managerial Implications of the Equity Model

Equity theory's important contribution to understanding human motivation shows that motivation is significantly influenced by absolute *and* relative rewards. It shows, too, that when people perceive inequity, they act to reduce it. Thus, managers should minimize inequities— real and perceived. This means helping participants understand differences among jobs and rewards and making certain rewards reflect performance requirements.

The bottom line of equity theory is that people who feel treated fairly are more satisfied. Satisfaction does not ensure high-level performance. Dissatisfaction, especially when many participants feel it, has negative consequences, including higher absenteeism and turnover, less citizenship behavior, more work-related grievances and lawsuits, stealing, sabotage, vandalism, more job stress, and other costly, negative consequences. Equity theory emphasizes the importance of managers' fair treatment of those they manage and lead.

Locke's Goal-Setting Theory

A third model of process perspective of motivation is derived from the work of Edwin A. Locke.[70] Building on the goal directedness of human behavior, Locke viewed goal setting as a cognitive process through which conscious goals and intentions about pursuing them are developed and become primary determinants of behavior.[71] Locke's central premise is that people focus on tasks related to attaining their goals, and they persist until the goals are achieved.[72]

In general, studies confirm the importance of goals in motivation.[73] Locke's original theory that goal specificity (the quantitative precision of the goal) and goal difficulty (the performance needed to reach the goal) are important to motivation is supported by other research.[74] It is well established that specific goals lead to improvement in individuals' performance because they understand what is to be done.[75] Finally, research has increased the understanding of goals in motivation by showing a positive relationship between goal acceptance by a person and that person's performance.[76] Other studies show more acceptance of goals (other than goals they set for themselves), especially difficult goals, when they participate in setting them.[77]

Goals that motivate desirable behavior in the workplace have characteristics for managers to keep in mind as they set goals or encourage those in their areas of responsibility to set goals for themselves. Most important is that they are acceptable. Acceptability is increased when work-related goals do not conflict with personal values and when people have clear reasons to pursue them. It is also important that goals are challenging but attainable, specific, quantifiable, and measurable.[78] In addition, managers must provide participants with timely, specific feedback on their progress toward achieving the goals.

Managerial Implications of Goal-Setting Theory

Locke's studies have important implications for managers. Significant challenges of motivating arise because managers do not specify desired results—outputs, outcomes, and impacts. Timely and specific feedback on progress toward goal achievement is important. The most widely adopted method of goal setting is management by objectives (MBO). MBO involves developing specific, attainable, and measurable personal objectives (goals), which mesh with and support attainment of organizational objectives.[79] Figure 13.9 shows MBO applied in HSOs/HSs.

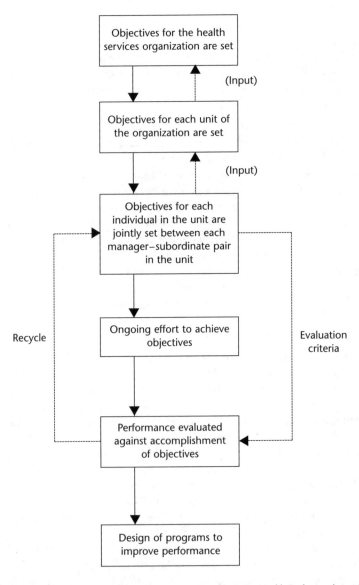

Figure 13.9. The MBO process in HSOs/HSs. (From Longest, Beaufort B., Jr. *Health Professionals in Management*, 226. Stamford, CT: Appleton & Lange, 1996; reprinted by permission.)

Conclusions About Power, Influence, and Motivation in Leading

Motivation is as essential to leading as are power and influence. Leading is defined as influencing others to understand and agree about what needs to be done to achieve the HSO/HS mission and objectives *and* facilitating individual and group contributions to achieve them. Influencing is central to the leading process and success in the leadership role. To have influence, however, one must also have power, which is the potential to exert influence. Motivation, defined earlier as "a state of feeling or thinking in which one is energized or aroused to perform a task or engage in a particular behavior,"[80] is important to leading successfully. The content and process perspectives on motivation presented in Table 13.2 guide researchers looking for answers to what motivates human behavior and how motivation occurs. Understanding motivation supports a manager's core activity of leading effectively and therefore means influencing participants to contribute to achieving the desired results established for the organization. Motivation is a means to lead (influence) people to make contributions that help accomplish desired results. In combination with effectively using power to influence, motivating others contributes significantly to leading them. Additional variables explain leadership effectiveness and success or failure of leaders. The three broad approaches to effective leadership help build an integrative framework for understanding leading.

Approaches to Understanding Leadership

There is no definitive theory of effective leadership. Generally, the research fits three constructs. One is that functions, skills, roles, or competencies explain why some are better leaders. Functions, skills, roles, and competencies do not fully explain leadership effectiveness, however, and two other theories have been posited. One asserts that certain behavior is associated with successful leaders. Another is integrative and focuses on the results of interactions among leaders, followers, and situations in which they find themselves.

Trait, behavior, and situational conceptualizations are basic to understanding successful leadership. Figure 13.10 shows their evolutionary relationships. Leading is best understood by integrating them.

Trait Theories of Leadership

The link between interpersonal and political skills and personal characteristics, such as expertise and charisma, as important bases of power suggest that certain skills, roles, and competencies are associated with effective leaders. Most studies of leadership in the first half of the 20th century looked for distinguishing traits in physical characteristics and personality.

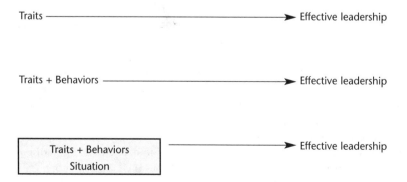

Figure 13.10.   Comparing three approaches to leadership.

Researchers theorized that identifiable traits distinguished leaders and followers, or success-ful and unsuccessful leaders. The studies focused on traits associated with effective leaders in business, but they also looked at government, military, and religious leaders. To prove that traits explained leadership, it was necessary to find traits common to all leaders. Traits studied included physical characteristics, such as height, weight, appearance, and personality, and traits such as alertness, originality, integrity, self-confidence, and intelligence or cleverness.

No study seeking universal leader traits was successful. A metanalysis by Ralph M. Stogdill (American [1904–1978]), reviewed major studies of leader traits and concluded that "a person does not become a leader by virtue of the possession of some combination of traits. . . . The pattern of personal characteristics of the leader must bear some relevant relationship to the characteristics, activities, and goals of the followers."[81] This conclusion was used in later research that studied leadership in the context of specific situations.

The search for traits associated with successful leaders continued. Research used improved methods and added administrative and technical abilities to traits of intelligence and personal-ity studied earlier. Many studies found associations between certain traits and leader effective-ness. In a review of the new studies, Stogdill confirmed his original negative assessment of efforts to identify universal leader traits, as did other researchers.[82] He concluded, however, that it is possible to develop a trait profile for successful leaders:

> The leader is characterized by a strong drive for responsibility and task completion, vigor and persistence in pursuit of goals, venturesomeness, and originality in problem solving, drive to exercise initiative in social situations, self-confidence and sense of personal identity, willingness to accept consequences of decision and action, readiness to absorb interpersonal stress, willingness to tolerate frustration and delay, ability to influence other persons' behav-ior, and capacity to structure social interaction systems to the purpose at hand.[83]

There is no longer a search for universal leader traits, but traits associated with leader effective-ness continue to be refined.[84]

Emotional Intelligence (Goleman)

A variant of the traits approach to leadership is Daniel Goleman's (American [1946–]) focus on emotional intelligence as essential to leader effectiveness.[85] Based on research of executive man-agers Goleman contends emotional intelligence is the essential characteristic that complements other cognitive, analytic, and technical skills.[86] Goleman's construct of emotional intelligence includes the following characteristics: self-awareness, self-regulation, motivation, empathy, and social skill. They are defined in Table 13.3, and hallmarks of their presence are provided.

Goleman defines self-awareness as understanding one's emotions, strengths, weaknesses, needs, and drives.[87] This is equivalent to the ancient Greek injunction to "know thyself." Al-though Goleman defines self-regulation as primarily controlling one's emotions and impulses, it might be viewed more broadly as living (and modeling) a disciplined life. Goleman links this characteristic to personal and organizational integrity. Motivation, or the leader's influence on followers, is framed as the leader's intrinsic need or desire to achieve for its own sake. Empathy is the leader's ability to recognize and respond to the feelings (emotional signals) displayed by followers, at least to the extent they affect individual performance and fulfillment of mission and objectives. Goleman characterizes social skill as "friendliness with a purpose" to direct team performance toward desired goals. He views social skill as the behavioral manifestation of other components and the one critical for effective leadership.

Because the search for universal leader traits was unsuccessful, researchers expanded their view of leader traits in leadership effectiveness. They came to define traits as predispositions to behavior, that "a particular trait, or set of them, tends to predispose (although does not cause) an individual to engage in certain behavior that may or may not result in leadership effectiveness."[88] They began to appreciate that traits had an impact, but not as in the earlier

Table 13.3 The Five Components of Emotional Intelligence at Work

Component	Definition	Hallmarks
Self-awareness	The ability to recognize and understand your moods, emotions, and drives, as well as their effect on others	Self-confidence Realistic self-assessment Self-deprecating sense of humor
Self-regulation	The ability to control or redirect disruptive impulses and moods The propensity to suspend judgment—to think before acting	Trustworthiness and integrity Comfort with ambiguity Openness to change
Motivation	A passion to work for reasons that go beyond money or status A propensity to pursue goals with energy and persistence	Strong drive to achieve Optimism, even in the face of failure Organizational commitment
Empathy	The ability to understand the emotional makeup of other people Skill in treating people according to their emotional reactions	Expertise in building and retaining talent Cross-cultural sensitivity Service to clients and customers
Social skill	Proficiency in managing relationships and building networks An ability to find common ground and build rapport	Effectiveness in leading change Persuasiveness Expertise in building and leading teams

search for universal traits of leaders. Researchers began to understand that a particular set of traits is not as important as how the traits are expressed in the behavior and styles of leaders.[89]

Behavior Theories of Leadership

The premise of studies to identify relationships between behavior or styles of leaders and their effectiveness was that it would allow leadership to be taught. Leaders would not have to be born with certain traits. Studies focused on describing leader behavior, developing concepts and models of styles of leading (styles were defined as combinations of behavior), and examining the relationships between styles and leader effectiveness.

One contribution of these studies has been to define leadership behavior. Gary Yukl (American [1940–]) posits that agreement as to behavior associated with successful leading includes the following elements:[90]

- *Planning:* develops short-term plans for the work, determines how to schedule and coordinate activities to use people and resources efficiently, determines the steps and resources needed to complete a project or activity

- *Clarifying:* explains task assignments and member responsibilities, sets specific goals and deadlines for important aspects of the work, explains priorities for different objectives, explains rules, policies, and standard procedures

- *Monitoring:* checks progress and quality of work, examines sources of information to determine how well important tasks are being performed, evaluates performance of members systematically

- *Problem solving:* identifies work-related problems that can disrupt operations, makes systematic, rapid diagnosis and takes action to resolve the problems in decisively and confidently

- *Supporting:* shows concern for needs and feelings of individual members, provides support and encouragement for a difficult or stressful task, and expresses confidence that members can successfully complete it

- *Recognizing:* praises effective performance by members, provides recognition for member achievements and contributions to the organization, recommends appropriate rewards for members with high performance

- *Developing:* provides feedback and coaching for members who need it, provides career advice, encourages members to take advantage of opportunities for skill development

- *Empowering:* involves members in making important work-related decisions and considers their suggestions and concerns, delegates responsibility and authority to members for important tasks, and allows them to resolve work-related problems without prior approval

- *Advocating change:* identifies an emerging threat or opportunity, explains why a policy or procedure is no longer appropriate and should be changed, proposes desirable changes, takes personal risks to push for approval of essential but difficult changes

- *Envisioning change:* communicates a clear, appealing vision of what could be accomplished, links the vision to member values and ideals, describes a proposed change or new initiative with enthusiasm and optimism

- *Encouraging innovation:* talks about the importance of innovation and flexibility, encourages innovative thinking and new approaches for solving problems, encourages and supports efforts to develop innovative new products, services, or processes

- *Facilitating collective learning:* uses systematic procedures to learn how to improve work unit performance, helps members understand causes of work unit performance, encourages members to share new knowledge with each other

- *Networking:* attends meetings or events, joins professional associations or social clubs, uses social networks to build and maintain favorable relationships with peers, superiors, and outsiders who can provide useful information or assistance

- *External monitoring:* analyzes information about events, trends, and changes in the external environment to identify threats, opportunities, and other implications for the work unit

- *Representing:* lobbies for funding or resources, promotes and defends the reputation of the work unit or organization, negotiates agreements and coordinates related activities with other parts of the organization or with outsiders

Studies of leadership behavior add an important dimension to understanding leading and new insight into effectiveness in directing as leading. It should be noted that leader behavior studies do not fully explain successful leadership. As Yukl concluded, "Extensive research on leadership behavior during the past half century has yielded many different behavior taxonomies and a lack of clear results about effective behavior."[91] Despite this conclusion, leadership behavior studies add to our understanding of leading or directing by managers.

Studies of Leadership Styles

Behavioral studies provided the intellectual foundation to identify effective styles of leading (i.e., combinations of behavior) by finding the optimal mix of leader behavior. Robert R. Blake (American [1918–2004]) and Jane Mouton (American [1930–1987])[92] identified variation in leadership styles. The work was expanded by Blake and Anne Adams McCanse.[93] Their model used two variables—concern for people and concern for production—as the axes of a diagram that plots styles.

A concern-for-people orientation focuses on the leader's relationships with followers. The concern-for-production orientation focuses on tasks and objectives in performing work. The two are used in a diagram to show variation in styles of leading. For example, using a scale from 1 (minimum concern) to 10 (maximum concern), a style characterized by minimum concern for both people and production would be located at the bottom left side of the diagram. Similarly, maximum concern for both people and production would be located at the top right of the diagram. Different levels of concern for the two variables permit plotting various styles of leading.

A Turning Point in the Study of Leaders' Behavior or Styles

Robert Tannenbaum (American [1915–2003]) and Warren H. Schmidt (American [1920–2016])[94] developed a model in which alternative styles of leading are arrayed on a continuum (Figure 13.11) based on the degree of participation that leaders permit in their decision making. The resulting styles of leading are as follows:

- *Autocratic leaders* make decisions and announce them to participants. The role of participants is to carry out orders without an opportunity to materially alter decisions already made by the manager.

- *Consultative leaders* convince participants of the correctness of the decision by explaining the rationale for the decision and its effect on participants and the program or project. A second consultative style is practiced when managers permit slightly more involvement by participants; the manager presents decisions to participants but invites questions to increase understanding and acceptance.

- *Participative leaders* present tentative decisions that will be changed if participants can make a convincing case. A second participative style is practiced when a manager presents a problem to participants, seeks their advice and suggestions, and makes the decision. This style of leading makes greater use of participation and less use of authority than do autocratic and consultative styles.

- *Democratic leaders* define limits of the situation and problem to be solved and permit participants as a group to make the decision.

- *Laissez-faire leaders* permit participants to make their own decisions with the least amount of interference from the leader.

Tannenbaum and Schmidt concluded the best style of leading depends on circumstances. Style should consider forces internal to the manager (e.g., value system, confidence in other participants, and tolerance for ambiguity and uncertainty), forces within participants (e.g., expectations, need for independence, ability, knowledge, and experience), and forces in the situation (e.g., type of organization, nature of problem to be solved, or work to be done, and time pressure).

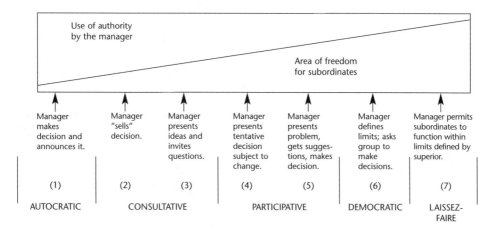

Figure 13.11. Continuum of leader decision-making authority. (Tannenbaum, Robert, and Warren H. Schmidt. "How To Choose a Leadership Pattern." *Harvard Business Review* 51 (May–June 1973): 162–180; reprinted by permission of *Harvard Business Review*. Copyright 1973 by the Harvard Business School Publishing Corporation; all rights reserved.)

Leaders must change styles to fit the situation. An autocratic style is appropriate in clinical situations when work is urgent, such as a medical emergency. This style could be disastrous in other situations (e.g., routine supervision of professionals in which a more laissez-faire style is appropriate).[95] The Tannenbaum and Schmidt model is a turning point between the early trait and behavioral studies of leading and the contemporary—and more sophisticated—situational or contingency models of leading described next.

Situation or Contingency Theories of Leadership

Because traits, behavior, or styles could not fully explain effectiveness in leading, researchers began incorporating situational influences, or contingencies, into models of leading. From the many models that seek to explain how situational variables determine relative effectiveness of leading styles, three are described briefly here.

Fiedler's Contingency Model

Fred Fiedler (Austrian/American [1922–2017]) identified situations in which certain leader styles are effective. He hypothesized that effective leading depends on whether the elements in a situation fit the specific style of the leader. Complex theories have room for criticism, but research supports Fiedler's model.[96] Fiedler identified leader styles that fit situations and could improve leader effectiveness if leader styles were changed to fit situations, leaders whose styles fit situations were selected, leaders were moved to situations that fit their styles, or situations were changed to fit leader styles.[97]

Fiedler's model is complex, but the underlying theory can be understood by knowing the leader styles he examined and how he assessed situations. He was interested in whether a leader was more task or relations motivated. The task-motivated leader is concerned about task success and task-related problems and is not motivated to establish good relationships with followers unless the work is going well and there are no serious task-related problems.

The relations-motivated leader is more concerned with good leader–follower relations, is motivated to have close interpersonal relationships, and will act in a considerate, supportive manner when relationships must be improved. For such leaders, achieving task objectives is important only if the primary affiliation motive is satisfied by good personal relationships with followers.

Fiedler considered the two orientations to be polar. He measured them in leaders by using the least preferred co-worker (LPC) score. The LPC questionnaire asked leaders to think of the present or past co-worker with whom they least liked to work. The LPC questionnaire uses attribute sets such as pleasant–unpleasant, with an eight-point rating scale. The LPC score is the sum of the ratings for the attribute sets. It reflects the degree of regard a leader has for the LPC. Leaders with low LPC scores, interpreted as reflecting disregard for the LPC, have a task-motivated leadership style. Leaders with high LPC scores, interpreted as reflecting favorable assessments of the LPC, have a relations-motivated leadership style.

According to Fiedler, the relationship between a leader's LPC score and leadership effectiveness depends on a complex variable he called situational favorability (sometimes called situational control). Favorability is determined by three aspects of a situation:

1. Leader–follower relations can be good or poor (good leader–follower relations imply the leader is able to obtain compliance with minimum effort, whereas poor relations imply compliance with reservation and reluctance, if at all).

2. Tasks can be structured (specific instructions and standard procedures provide for task completion) or unstructured (the task has only vague, inexplicit procedures without step-by-step guidelines).

3. Leader position power can be strong or weak and refers to the extent the leader has authority (including reward, coercive, and legitimate power) to evaluate the performance of followers (workgroup members) and reward or punish them.

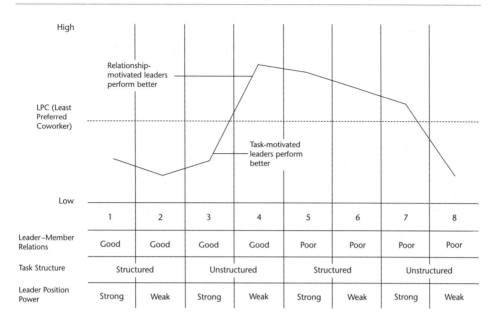

Figure 13.12. How the style of effective leadership varies with the situation. (Adapted from Fiedler, Fred E. "Engineer the Job to Fit the Manager." *Harvard Business Review* 51 [Sept/Oct 1965]: 118. Reprinted by permission of *Harvard Business Review*. Copyright 1974 by the Harvard Business School Publishing Corporation; all rights reserved.)

Figure 13.12 shows that the style of effective leadership varies with the situation and illustrates information relevant to Fiedler's contingency theory. The bottom portion shows combinations of the three situational favorability aspects just described. The result is eight unique combinations, which Fiedler referred to as octants.

Octant 1 shows good leader–follower relations, a structured task, and a leader with strong position power. Octant 8 shows poor leader–follower relations, an unstructured task, and a leader with weak position power. An intermediate octant, Octant 4, shows good leader–follower relations, an unstructured task, and a leader with weak position power. Octant 1 is the most favorable and Octant 8 the least favorable in Fiedler's schema to measure the favorability of situations for leaders.

Fiedler tested relationships using his method. The upper portion of Figure 13.12 shows that relationship-motivated leaders (with high LPC scores) do well (relative to task-motivated leaders) in moderately favorable situations. Conversely, task-motivated leaders (with low LPC scores) do relatively well in situations that are either very favorable or very unfavorable.

Fiedler[98] attributed success of relationship-motivated leaders in situations with intermediate favorability to the leader's nondirective, permissive approach; a more directive approach could cause anxiety in followers, conflict in the workgroup, and lack of cooperation. He attributed success of the task-motivated leader in very favorable situations to the leader's power, formal backing, and a well-structured task, which makes followers ready to be directed in their tasks. Success of the task-motivated leader in very unfavorable situations is attributed to the fact that without the leader's active and aggressive intervention and control, the group might become less cohesive.

Fiedler's work was the first comprehensive attempt to incorporate situational variables into a model of leading. This new dimension was refined in subsequent studies. The contingency model is useful in practice. It emphasizes managers systematically assessing their relationships with participants and the organization designs and processes used in relationship to their leading styles and, in turn, how these factors determine their effectiveness as leaders.

Hersey and Blanchard's Situational Model

Paul Hersey (American [1931–2012]) and Ken Blanchard (American [1939–]) developed a leadership model that explains effective leadership as interplay among three factors: 1) the leader's relationship behavior, defined as the extent to which the leader maintains personal relationships with followers through open communication and supportive behavior and actions toward them; 2) the leader's task behavior, or the extent to which the leader organizes, defines roles, and guides and directs followers; and 3) the followers' readiness level, defined as readiness to perform a task or function or to pursue an objective.[99] This model focuses on followers' readiness to perform as the key situational variable. The premise is that the most effective leadership style is determined by the readiness level of the people whom the leader is attempting to influence. Their model focuses on only one variable, the situational leadership model.

Appreciation of the situational leadership model requires understanding how it incorporates leadership styles, as well as a concept called follower readiness. Hersey and Blanchard assume that the relative presence (high–low) of task and relationship behavior identifies four leadership styles (S1–S4):

S1. Telling (high task, low relationship): The leader makes the decision. The leader defines roles and tells followers what, how, when, and where to do various tasks, emphasizing directive behavior.

S2. Selling (high task, high relationship): The leader makes the decision and then explains it to followers. The leader provides both directive behavior and supportive behavior.

S3. Participating (low task, high relationship): The leader and followers share decision making. The main role of the leader is to encourage and assist followers in contributing to sound decisions.

S4. Delegating (low task, low relationship): The followers make the decision. The leader provides little direction or support.

Follower readiness in the situational leadership model is readiness to perform a task. Readiness is assessed by ability and willingness. Ability is the knowledge, experience, and skill of an individual or group. Willingness is the extent of individual or group motivation, confidence, and commitment to accomplish a task.[100]

Hersey and Blanchard used followers' abilities and their willingness (divided into commitment–motivation and confidence) to develop a four-stage continuum of follower readiness, from low (R1) to high (R4):

R1. Followers are unable and unwilling to take responsibility for performing a task (i.e., they do not have the ability, and they feel insecure about taking responsibility).

R2. Followers are unable but willing to do job tasks (i.e., they do not have the ability, but they are motivated and feel confident if the leader provides guidance).

R3. Followers are able but unwilling to do what the leader wants (i.e., they have the ability, but they feel insecure about doing what the leader wants).

R4. Followers are able and willing to do what is asked of them (i.e., they have the ability, and they feel confident that they can do what is asked of them).

In the Hersey and Blanchard model, the leadership styles of telling, selling, participating, and delegating are used best with specific levels of follower readiness. Leadership effectiveness results when the leader's style matches followers' readiness. The model suggests that as followers reach high levels of readiness (R4), the leader should respond by decreasing task and relationship behavior. At R4, the leader does very little because followers are willing and able to take responsibility. At the lowest level of follower readiness (R1), followers need explicit direction because they are unable and unwilling to take responsibility. At moderate or intermediate levels (R2 and R3), different leadership styles are needed. At R2, the followers are unable but willing, and the leader must exhibit high levels of task and relationship behavior. High-level task behavior compensates for followers' lack of ability, and high-level relationship behavior may help them buy into the leader's wishes. At R3, followers are able but unwilling or insecure; therefore, a leadership style that incorporates high levels of relationship behaviors may help overcome unwillingness or insecurity among followers.

Despite limited research confirming the relationships theorized in the situational leadership model, it is widely used by managers because it is intuitively appealing.[101] The model illustrates important aspects of leader behavior. Leaders must be concerned about their followers' readiness to be led, and they must recognize that their actions can affect the level of readiness. This model reminds leaders to treat followers as individuals and that individuals' readiness changes over time.[102]

House's Path–Goal Model of Leading

Like the situational or contingency models of leading described previously, the path–goal model predicts leader behavior that is effective in various situations. In the original model, Robert J. House (American [1932–2011] posited that the leader's role is to increase personal payoffs to followers for attaining their work-related goals and to smooth the path to these payoffs.[103] As House and Terence Mitchell, noted,

> According to this theory, leaders are effective because of their impact on subordinates' motivation, ability to perform effectively, and satisfaction. The theory is called path–goal because its major concern is how the leader influences the subordinates' perceptions of their work goals, personal goals, and paths to goal attainment. The theory suggests that a leader's behavior is motivating or satisfying to the degree that the behavior increases subordinate goal attainment and clarifies the paths to these goals.[104]

This model of leading relies on the results of Ohio State University and the University of Michigan management studies and on the expectancy theory of motivation, described previously. Expectancy is the perceived probability that effort will affect performance, instrumentality is the perceived probability that performance will lead to outcomes, and the valence is the value that a person attaches to an outcome. The expectancy model of motivation describes relationships between expectancy, instrumentality, and valence. The path–goal model focuses on factors that affect expectancy, instrumentality, and valence. Leaders can increase valences associated with work goal attainment, instrumentalities of work goal attainment, and expectancy that effort will result in work goal attainment.

The path–goal model is situational. Its basic premise is that the effect of leader behavior on follower performance and satisfaction depends on the situation, specifically the characteristics of followers *and* the work to be performed. Restated: Different leader behavior works better for different situations. House and Mitchell identified four categories of leader behavior.[105] Each is best suited to a given situation:

1. *Directive leading:* The leader tells followers what they must do and how to do it, requires that they follow rules and procedures, and schedules and coordinates the work.

2. *Supportive leading:* The leader is friendly and approachable and exhibits consideration for the well-being and needs of followers.

3. *Participative leading:* The leader consults with followers, asks for opinions and suggestions, and considers them.

4. *Achievement-oriented leading:* The leader establishes challenging goals for followers, expects excellent performance, and exhibits confidence that they will meet expectations.

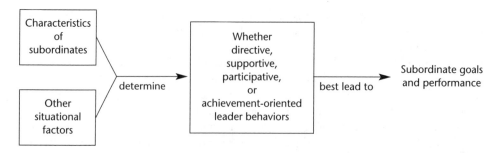

Figure 13.13.   Path–goal model of leadership. (From Longest, Beaufort B., Jr. *Health Professionals in Management*, 236. Stamford, CT: Appleton & Lange, 1996; reprinted by permission.)

The four styles of leader behavior should be used as the situation dictates; effective leaders match styles to situations, which vary along two dimensions. One is the people being led. Followers may or may not have the ability to do the job. They differ, too, in their perceived degree of control that they have over their work. The second dimension is the nature of the task, which may be routine, and followers may have prior experience with it, or it may be new, and help is needed for followers to perform well.

Figure 13.13 illustrates how leaders can match behavior styles with subordinate characteristics and the nature of the task. For example, directive leadership is used when followers are not well trained and the work they do is partly routine and partly ambiguous. Supportive or participative leadership is appropriate if followers do routine work and have experience. Achievement-oriented leadership is most effective if followers do innovative and ambiguous work and have a high level of related knowledge and skill.

The path–goal model suggests that functions of effective leaders include 1) making the path to achieving work goals easier by providing coaching and direction as needed, 2) removing or minimizing frustrating barriers that interfere with followers' abilities to achieve work goals, and 3) increasing payoffs for followers when they achieve work-related goals.

House and Mitchell intend the path–goal theory to be a partial explanation of the motivational effects of leader behavior, and they do not include all relevant variables. Despite limited validation of the path–goal theory, it is a useful construct because it merges leadership and motivation theories. It also provides a valuable pragmatic framework for managers who try to match their leader behavior to the follower and the task.

Path–goal theory suggests substitutes for leadership. For example, if being an effective leader means clarifying the path to a follower's goal, clear organizational rules and plans that clarify the path partially substitute for leadership. Substitutes for leader behavior include actions that clarify role expectations and motivate or satisfy employees. Because of their professional workforce and many standardized activities, this method is significant for HSOs/HSs.

Toward an Integrative Approach to Effective Leading

Managers' leader effectiveness contributes to the performance of participants, teams and work groups, departments, and larger units, and the entire HSO/HS.

Each of the three approaches to understanding leading—traits, behaviors, and situational or contingency approaches (see Figure 13.9) helps to understand leaders and their effectiveness. Studies using these approaches produced numerous models, each seeking to explain effective leading. Individually, however, none fully explains how a leader is effective. Samuel Levey (South African/American [1932–2015]) stated, "We will probably never be able to achieve a truly elegant and rigorous general theory of leadership."[106] This view reflects the complexity and variety of variables involved in leading. Leading is a dynamic process "that does not reside solely within a given person or a given situation; rather, situations create an interplay of needs, and effective leaders work to continually identify and meet them."[107]

It is possible, however, to integrate parts of different models into a comprehensive statement about leading effectively. Leading effectiveness results from interactions among variables, including leader traits and behaviors selected to fit situations that are mediated or influenced by intervening variables, such as participants' efforts and abilities, organizational design features, and the availability of appropriate inputs or resources. In HSOs/HSs, participative styles of leading usually work best.

Above all, managers must realize that leading is influencing participants to contribute to achieving the results wanted by an organization, and they must motivate participants to contribute. The simplest advice is to select motivated participants to fill positions. Previous high performers are motivated and will likely continue performing well under favorable conditions. The most significant challenges of leading and motivating participants arise because managers do not clearly specify the results wanted. Effective leaders begin with clear statements of desired results. These statements are especially useful when those who are affected by them have participated in their formulation.

Models of motivation show direct connections between participants' efforts, performance, and rewards. Critical to motivating people is rewarding desired performance while bearing in mind that rewards can be intrinsic to the work or extrinsic. A contemporary approach to rewarding performance is pay-for-performance, or P4P. It pays bonuses to individuals or groups for outstanding performance.[108] "Payers, consumers, and other stakeholders believe that health care organizations are not providing services at a satisfactory level of quality or cost, and that strengthening the link between performance and financial rewards will produce better results."[109]

People have different valences or preferences about rewards. Some want challenging assignments, or more vacation time, instead of money. The reward must be important to the person receiving it if it is to be an effective motivator. Often, valences can be determined by discussing them with participants. Viewed broadly, managers' authority over rewards can lead them to job redesign and job enrichment, changes in leading styles, changes in how they permit others to participate in decisions, and changes in pay and benefits.

Motivation only partially explains participants' performance or contribution to results. Performance is determined, too, by a person's abilities and constraints in the work situation, such as uncoordinated workflow or inadequate budgets for technology or training. As discussed in Chapters 4 and 8, it is important to remember the significant role of process(es) in how well persons working in them can perform. Managers must remove or minimize barriers to performance and provide additional resources, as needed. Performance can be addressed by process improvement, by education and training, or by carefully matching people and positions. Environmental constraints, such as inadequate resources or organization and process designs that impede performance, must be remedied.

Leading effectively, includes attention to the quality of work life (QWL). QWL includes several dimensions: 1) adequate and fair compensation; 2) safe and healthful work environment; 3) commitment to developing participants; 4) social environment or organizational culture that fosters personal identity, freedom from prejudice, appreciation for diversity, and a sense of community; 5) careful attention to personal privacy, dissent, and due process; 6) work role minimizing infringement on leisure and family needs; and 7) commitment to socially responsible organizational actions.[110]

Health Leadership Competency Model

The NCHL is a not-for-profit organization, "that works to ensure that high-quality, relevant, and accountable leadership is available to meet the needs of 21st century healthcare."[111] The NCHL competency model contains 28 leadership competencies organized into four action domains: boundary spanning, execution, relations, and transformation; and three enabling domains: values, health system awareness and business literacy, and self-awareness self-development.[112]

Action domains describe the work of leaders:

1. *Boundary spanning:* Optimizing relationships between a leader's span of control and the departments, organizations, communities, and/or broader networks within which it operates

2. *Execution:* Translating vision and strategy into actions supporting optimal organizational performance

3. *Relations:* Leading, through example and actions, to create an organizational climate that values employees from all backgrounds, provides a healthy and energizing environment in which to work, and encourages everyone's ongoing development

4. *Transformation:* Creating and implementing compelling and inclusive change processes in support of improving health quality, efficiency, and access

Enabling domains describe preparation and development activities that leaders need to lead effectively:

1. *Values:* Understanding and utilizing personal, professional, and organizational values to guide decision-making

2. *Health system awareness and business literacy:* Understanding the health system's current business and operating frameworks as well as the dynamic context within which they operate (e.g., community, competitive, human resources, financial, legal, policy, and environmental)

3. *Self-awareness and self-development:* Ongoing habits and actions taken to continuously improve self-knowledge, interpersonal effectiveness, and well-being

Graduate healthcare management programs accredited by the Commission on Accreditation of Healthcare Management Education "must adopt a set of competencies that align with the Program's mission and types of jobs graduates enter. The Program will use these competencies as the basis of its curriculum, course content, learning objectives, and teaching and assessment methods."[113] The aforementioned NCHL domains and associated competencies are one such set of competencies. Other sources of healthcare leadership competencies are the Healthcare Leadership Alliance[114] and the Saint Louis University Master of Health Administration Competencies.[115]

Discussion Questions

1. Define *management* and include the basic ingredients of the definition. Why is management a process?

2. How are managers at various levels in HSOs/HSs classified and differentiated?

3. Figure 13.3 shows various managerial roles. Relate these roles to the management functions and to management competencies.

4. Examine Figure III.2 in the Part III Introduction. Describe and discuss its components, how they flow and link, and the way management functions, skills, roles, and competencies interrelate with the components.

5. Figure III.2 shows two external environments and forces that affect HSOs/HSs. How do these forces affect HSOs/HSs? Are there others?

6. Distinguish the roles of leaders in transactional and transformational leadership.

7. Describe the relationships between influence and leadership and between power and influence.

8. Compare the three basic conceptual approaches to the study of leadership (traits skills, leader behavior, and situational or contingency approaches) and explain why different approaches to the study of leadership have been taken.

9. How do process theories of motivation differ from content theories of motivation?

10. Draw a general model of expectancy theory. Use the model to discuss how expectations relate to performance.

11. Define *equity theory*. How are people in the workplace likely to react to perceived inequities?

12. Briefly describe three situational theories of leadership presented in this chapter.

Case Study 1   Healthcare Executives' Responsibility to Their Communities[116]

Statement of the Issue

The healthcare executive's responsibility to the community is multifaceted. It encompasses a commitment to increasing access to needed care, improving community health status, and addressing the societal issues that contribute to poor health and health disparities as well as personally working for the betterment of the community at large. Taking a leadership role in serving the community is the responsibility of all healthcare executives regardless of occupational setting or ownership structure. When providers, individuals, and communities work toward common goals, the results can be significant: healthier children, healthier adults, reduced healthcare costs, appropriate use of limited healthcare resources and, ultimately, a healthier community.

Policy Position

The American College of Healthcare Executives (ACHE) believes all healthcare executives have a professional obligation to serve their communities through support of organizational initiatives and personal involvement in community and civic affairs. In addition, ACHE believes that healthcare executives should take a proactive role in individual and community health improvement efforts. ACHE recognizes that communities vary widely in demographic characteristics, resources, traditions and needs. Therefore, each community may identify different priorities and approaches.

Healthcare executives can lead or participate in community and organizational initiatives through the following actions:

• Actively engage in collaborative efforts with public health and other government agencies, businesses, associations, educational groups, religious organizations, elected officials, financing entities, foundations, and others to measure and assess the community's health status, including the most prevalent health problems and concerns, underlying causes, associated risk factors, and the diversity of available resources that may be applied to improve the community's well-being.

- Support efforts to eliminate health disparities for vulnerable populations, including reducing barriers to access; increasing the supply of health workers and other resources in underserved communities; systematically collecting race, ethnicity, and language preference data of your patients; and training to help healthcare providers deliver culturally competent care.

- Support the dissemination of accurate information about community health status, the services provided, and the programs available to prevent and treat illness, and patients' responsibility for their own health.

- Participate in efforts to communicate organizational effectiveness in matching healthcare resources with community needs, improved clinical outcomes and community health status, and their organization's volunteerism roles.

- Incorporate community service responsibilities into policies and programs over which they have authority.

- Demonstrate that their commitment to the community is multifaceted and may include support of medical research, training of healthcare professionals, charity care, and civic contributions as well as a host of other activities that contribute to the community's well-being beyond that of their own organization.

- Offer health promotion and illness prevention programs to their employees, positively benefiting staff as well as sending an important message to the community.

Questions

1. What aspects of organizational culture and values should CEOs of HSOs/HSs address in their organizations and systems as they seek to address their responsibilities to their communities?

2. Give two examples of how senior-level managers in HSOs/HSs can seek to meet their responsibilities to their communities.

3. Discuss how fulfilling their responsibilities to their communities is part of the environmental activity shown in Figure III.2.

Case Study 2 — The Young Associate's Dilemma

Jane O'Hara faced a serious choice. Five years after receiving her master's degree in health services administration from a prestigious midwestern university, she was advancing quickly in a large consulting firm. She was receiving assignments with some of the firm's most important clients, and her salary had increased steadily. She was certain that she made at least $15,000 more per year than classmates working in hospitals. The only thing that bothered her about her position, besides the travel, was a nagging feeling that she wanted to become the CEO of a large hospital. One of O'Hara's clients is a large eastern teaching hospital that has a vice president for finance who is about 5 years from retiring. He is set in his ways; O'Hara judges him to be about a decade behind the sophisticated financial management techniques in her "bag of tools." She was surprised when he offered her a position as his assistant—with a strong hint that he wanted to groom a replacement. The salary is about what she makes with the consulting firm, and the hospital position has slightly better fringe benefits.

When she discussed the offer with her managing partner, he showed a resigned interest in learning what it would take to retain her. Over the next several weeks, the firm developed a counteroffer that included an $8,000 salary increase and a clear indication that she was pegged for a partnership position in a few years.

O'Hara took a long weekend to consider her choice.

Questions

1. Identify and describe the motivation variables present in this case.

2. Would these two positions permit O'Hara to fulfill different needs? If so, what are they?

3. What would you do if you were O'Hara? Why?

Case Study 3   Ethical Aspects of Leadership[117]

Diana Diligent, assistant director of nursing services at Bottom Line Hospital, was asked to attend a department chairs' meeting for her boss, Mike Murky, director of nursing services, 1 hour before the meeting was scheduled. Murky said he had just received a text message requiring him to attend to a family situation immediately and that Diligent must represent him at the meeting. In response to Diligent asking what she should do to prepare for the meeting, Murky suggested that she might be asked about the delay in submitting the department's budget request for the next fiscal year. Murky advised Diligent that if questioned about this, she should suggest that a chronic problem with the fiscal planning software was a major obstacle that was compounded by the extended medical leave of a senior member of the staff. Furthermore, preparation for the upcoming Joint Commission accreditation site visit contributed to an administrative backlog that had delayed completion of the department's budget package.

Diligent did not know about any software problem but recognized that one of the recently hired nurse supervisors had been on sick leave for the past week, and a recent bout of influenza had resulted in uncertain staffing. Murky had been on a 3-week leave to attend a national conference and vacation. Although The Joint Commission's site visit was projected for later in the year, Diligent knew that no formal planning process had been initiated in the department.

It was true the unit had been short staffed for at least the past 12 months, which put pressure on all staff nurses and unit supervisors. The resulting overload and stress led to increased turnover and loss of productivity in training new staff. However, Diligent was not convinced that the staffing situation had any direct effect on preparing the budget projections. In fact, Murky had asked Diligent to prepare a draft budget plan, and she had submitted it to him more than a month ago but had yet to receive feedback. Diligent expressed her concerns about her role in the meeting, but Murky advised her to relax and just wing it if asked any specific questions.

As the first agenda item, the vice president for fiscal and support services, Ron Requisite, announced that, as indicated in an earlier e-mail to department heads, all managers were expected to make a short presentation on this unit's budget proposal. The head of radiology, who was asked to begin the process, made a polished presentation using PowerPoint slides and handouts. After some tough questions about the budget assumptions and projections, Requisite turned to Diligent and asked her to make the presentation for the nursing services department.

Questions

1. If you were in Diligent's position, how would you have responded given the circumstances?

2. What ethical issues are relevant to this situation and to Diligent's response?

3. What actions should Diligent take after the department heads' meeting?

4. Who has ethical accountability in this situation, Diligent, Murky, or both?

5. What other supervisory–managerial issues are suggested in this case?

Case Study 4 | Reluctant Leader[118]

It has been reported that Dwight D. Eisenhower was entered in a Republican party presidential primary in 1952 without his permission. In fact, at the time few Americans knew Eisenhower's political party affiliation. Based on his success as Supreme Allied Commander during WWII, Americans wanted a leader to navigate the post-WWII era. Eisenhower announced that he was happy to serve, but reluctant to lead—now known as the Eisenhower Code.

Questions

1. What other leaders had a duty to serve but were reluctant to do so?

2. Under what conditions do followers want a manager? A leader?

3. Are followers willing to cede more power to a reluctant leader? Why or why not?

Notes

1. Burns, Lawton Robert, Elizabeth H. Bradley, and Byran J. Weiner. *Shortell & Kaluzny's Health Care Management: Organization Design & Behavior,* 6th ed., 4. Clifton Park, NY: Delmar, Cengage Learning, 2012.
2. Burns, Bradley, and Weiner. *Shortell & Kaluzny's Health Care Management,* 4.
3. Robbins, Stephen P., and Timothy A. Judge. *Organizational Behavior,* 15th ed. Upper Saddle River, NJ: Prentice Hall, 2012; Yukl, Gary A. *Leadership in Organizations,* 8th ed. Upper Saddle River, NJ: Prentice Hall, 2012; Banaszak-Holl, Jane, Ingrid Nembhard, Lauren Taylor, and Elizabeth H. Bradley. "Leadership and Management: A Framework for Action." In *Shortell and Kaluzny's Health Care Management: Organization Design and Behavior,* 6th ed., edited by Lawton Robert Burns, Elizabeth H. Bradley, and Bryan J. Weiner, 33–62. Clifton Park, NY: Delmar, Cengage Learning, 2012; Northouse, Peter G. *Leadership: Theory and Practice,* 6th ed. Thousand Oaks, CA: Sage Publications, 2013.
4. Frisina, Michael E. *Influential Leadership: Change Your Behavior, Change Your Organization, Change Healthcare.* Chicago: Health Administration Press, 2014.
5. Charns, Martin P., and Jody Hoffer Gittell. "Work Design." In *Healthcare Management: Organization Design and Behavior,* 5th ed., edited by Stephen M. Shortell and Arnold D. Kaluzny, 212–236. Clifton Park, NY: Thomson Delmar Learning, 2006.
6. American College of Healthcare Executives. *ACHE Code of Ethics.* Chicago: American College of Healthcare Executives. *https://www.ache.org/about-ache/our-story/our-commitments/ethics/ache-code-of-ethics,* retrieved November 5, 2019.
7. Daft, Richard L. *Management,* 10th ed. Mason, OH: South-Western Cengage Learning, 2012; Carroll, Stephen J., and Dennis J. Gillen. "Are the Classical Management Functions Useful in Describing Managerial Work?" *Academy of Management Review* 12 (January 1987): 38–51; Marquis, Bessie L., and Carol J. Huston. *Leadership Roles and Management Functions in Nursing: Theory and Application,* 7th ed. Philadelphia: Lippincott Williams & Wilkins, 2011; Dunn, Rose T. *Dunn & Haimann's Healthcare Management,* 10th ed., Chapter 1. Chicago: Health Administration Press, 2020.
8. Certo, Samuel C., and S. Trevis Certo. *Modern Management: Concepts and Skills,* 12th ed. Saddle River, NJ: Prentice Hall, 2012.
9. Katz, Robert L. "Skills of an Effective Administrator." *Harvard Business Review* 52 (September/October 1974): 90–102.
10. Mintzberg, Henry. *The Nature of Managerial Work.* New York: Harper & Row, 1973; Mintzberg, Henry. "The Manager's Job: Folklore and Fact." *Harvard Business Review* 53 (July/August 1975): 49–61, reprinted as a Harvard Business Review Classic in 1990.
11. Adapted from Longest, Beaufort B., Jr. "Managerial Competence at Senior Levels of Integrated Delivery Systems." *Journal of Healthcare Management* 43 (March/April 1998): 115–135.
12. Katz, Robert L. "Skills of an Effective Administrator." *Harvard Business Review* 52 (September/October 1974): 90–102.
13. Witt Kieffer. *Physician Leaders Transforming Strategy into Performance Excellence. https://www.wittkieffer.com/practices/healthcare/physician-integration-and-leadership/,* retrieved November 4, 2019.
14. Hudak, Ronald P., Paul P. Brooke, Jr., Kenn Finstuen, and James Trounson. "Management Competencies for Medical Practice Executives: Skills, Knowledge and Abilities Required for the Future." *Journal of Health Administration Education* 15 (Fall 1997): 219–239.

15. Gilbert, Douglas J. "Collaborative Competence: Redefining Management Education Through Social Construction." *Journal of Psychological Issues in Organizational Culture* 4, 3 (2013): 26–42. *https://onlinelibrary.wiley.com/doi/pdf/10.1002/jpoc.21116,* retrieved November 6, 2019.

16. Coddington, Dean C., Keith D. Moore, and Elizabeth A. Fischer. *Making Integrated Healthcare Work,* 119. Englewood, CO: Center for Research in Ambulatory Healthcare Administration, 1996.

17. Longest, Beaufort B., Jr. *Health Policymaking in the United States,* 5th ed. Chicago: Health Administration Press, 2010.

18. Kingdon, John W. *Agendas, Alternatives, and Public Policies,* Update Edition. New York: Pearson, 2011.

19. Aluko, Yele. "The Delicate Balance between Cost and Quality in Value-Based Healthcare." *Beckers Hospital CFO Report,* February 20, 2017. *https://www.beckershospitalreview.com/finance/the-delicate-balance-between-cost-and-quality-in-value-based-healthcare.html,* retrieved November 6, 2017.

20. Mintzberg, Henry. *Power In and Around Organizations.* Englewood Cliffs, NJ: Prentice Hall, 1983.

21. White, Kenneth R., and John R. Griffith. *The Well-Managed Healthcare Organization,* Chapter 4. Chicago: Health Administration Press, 2019.

22. Gamm, Larry D. "Dimensions of Accountability for Not-for-Profit Hospitals and Health Systems." *Healthcare Management Review* 21 (Spring 1996): 74–75.

23. Shortell, Stephen M., and Arnold D. Kaluzny. "Organization Theory and Health Services Management." In *Healthcare Management: Organization Design and Behavior,* 5th ed., edited by Stephen M. Shortell and Arnold D. Kaluzny, 5–41. Clifton Park, NY: Thomson Delmar Learning, 2006.

24. *Raising the Bar: Increased Accountability, Transparency, and Board Performance: 2005 Biennial Survey of Hospitals and Healthcare Systems.* San Diego, CA: The Governance Institute, 2006.

25. Zaleznik, Abraham. "Managers and Leaders: Are They Different?" *Harvard Business Review* 55 (1977): 67–78.

26. Maslow, Abraham H. *Motivation and Personality.* New York: Harper & Brothers, 1954; Herzberg, Frederick, Bernard Mausner, and Barbara Block Snyderman. *The Motivation to Work,* 2nd ed. New York: John Wiley & Sons, 1959; Vroom, Victor H. *Work and Motivation.* New York: John Wiley & Sons, 1964; Porter, Lyman W., and Edward E. Lawler, III. *Managerial Attitudes and Performance.* Homewood, IL: Richard D. Irwin, 1968.

27. Likert, Rensis. *New Patterns of Management.* New York: McGraw-Hill Book Company, 1961.

28. Stogdill, Ralph. *Handbook of Leadership: A Survey of Theory and Research.* New York: The Free Press, 1974.

29. Bennis, Warren. *On Becoming a Leader.* Reading: Addison-Wesley, 1989.

30. Bennis, Warren. "Where Have All the Leaders Gone?" *Technology Review* 75 (1977): 3–12.

31. Kotter, John P. *A Force for Change: How Leadership Differs from Management.* New York: The Free Press, 1990.

32. Kotter, John P. "What Leaders Really Do." *Harvard Business Review,* 68, May/June 1990, 103–111.

33. Keys, Bernard, and Thomas Case. "How to Become an Influential Manager." *Executive,* 4, November 1990, 38.

34. *Contemporary Issues in Leadership,* 7th ed., edited by William E. Rosenbach, Robert L. Taylor, and Mark A. Youndt. New York: Routledge, 2018.

35. Burns, James M. *Leadership.* New York: Harper & Row, 1978.

36. Kanter, Rosabeth Moss. "Ten Reasons People Resist Change." *Harvard Business Review,* September 25, 2012. *https://hbr.org/2012/09/ten-reasons-people-resist-chang,* retrieved November 12, 2019.

37. Longest, Beaufort B., Jr., Kurt Darr, and Jonathon S. Rakich. "Organizational Leadership in Hospitals." *Hospital Topics* 71 (1993): 11–15.

38. Rowitz, Louis. *Public Health Leadership: Putting Principles into Practice,* 2nd ed., 58. Sudbury, MA: Jones & Bartlett Publishers, 2009.

39. Tichy, Noel M., and Mary A. Devanna. *The Transformational Leader,* 2nd ed., New York: John Wiley & Sons, 1997.

40. Rohrer, Wesley M., III. "The Three Ts of Leadership: Leadership Theory Revisited." *Topics in Health Records Management* 9, 3 (1989): 14–25.

41. Harrigan, Rosanne C., and L. M. Emery. "Translational Leadership: New Approaches to Team Development." *Ethnicity and Disease* 2010 (Winter): 141–145.

42. Deal, Terrence E. "Healthcare Executives as Symbolic Leaders." *Healthcare Executive* 5 (March/April 1990): 24–27; Nutt, Paul C. "How Top Managers in Health Organizations Set Directions That Guide Decision Making." *Hospital & Health Services Administration* 36 (Spring 1991): 57–75.

43. Darr, Kurt. *Ethics in Health Services Management,* 6th ed. 1. Baltimore: Health Professions Press, 2019.

44. American College of Healthcare Executives. *Code of Ethics, Preamble,* as amended by the Board of Governors on November 13, 2017. *https://www.ache.org/about-ache/our-story/our-commitments/ethics/ache-code-of-ethics,* retrieved November 10, 2019.

45. Burns. *Leadership,* 426.

46. Northouse. *Leadership,* Chapter 9.

47. Greenleaf, Robert K. *The Servant as Leader.* Westfield, IN: The Greenleaf Center for Servant Leadership, 2008.

48. Worthley, John A. *The Ethics of the Ordinary in Healthcare: Concepts and Cases.* Chicago: Health Administration Press, 1997.

49. French, John R. P., and Bertram H. Raven. "The Bases of Social Power." In *Studies of Social Power,* edited by Dorwin Cartwright, 150–167. Ann Arbor, MI: Institute for Social Research, 1959.

50. Yukl. *Leadership in Organizations.*

51. Longest, Beaufort B., Jr. *Managing Health Programs and Projects,* 129. San Francisco: Jossey-Bass, 2004.

52. Hoff, Timothy, and Kevin W. Rockmann. "Power, Politics, and Conflict Management." In *Shortell and Kaluzny's Health Care Management: Organization Design and Behavior,* 6th ed., edited by Lawton Robert Burns, Elizabeth H. Bradley, and Bryan J. Weiner, 188–220. Clifton Park, NY: Delmar, Cengage Learning, 2012; Pfeffer, Jeffrey. *Managing with Power: Politics and Influence in Organizations.* Boston: Harvard Business School Press, 1992; Alexander, Jeffrey A., Thomas G. Rundall, Thomas J. Hoff, and Laura L. Morlock. "Power and Politics in Health Services Organizations." In *Healthcare Management: Organization Design and Behavior,* 5th ed., edited by Stephen M. Shortell and Arnold D. Kaluzny, 276–310. Clifton Park, NY: Thomson Delmar Learning, 2006.

53. Mintzberg, Henry. *Power In and Around Organizations,* 26.

54. Yukl. *Leadership in Organizations.*

55. Mintzberg. *Power In and Around Organizations.*

56. Sun, Li-Yun, Samuel Aryee, and Kenneth S. Law. "High-Performance Human Resource Practices, Citizenship Behavior, and Organizational Performance: A Relational Perspective." *Academy of Management Journal* 50, 3 (2007): 558–577.

57. O'Connor, Stephen. "Motivating Effective Performance," 438, in W. Jack Duncan, Peter M. Ginter, and Linda E. Swayne (eds.), *Handbook of Health Care Management.* Malden, MA: Blackwell Publishers, 431-470; Colquitt, Jason, Jeffrey LePine, and Michael Wesson. *Organizational Behavior: Improving Performance and Commitment in the Workplace,* 3rd ed. New York: McGraw-Hill/Irwin, 2012.

58. Maslow, Abraham H. "A Theory of Human Motivation." *Psychological Review* 50 (July 1943): 370–396; Maslow, Abraham H. *Motivation and Personality,* 2nd ed. New York: Harper & Row, 1970.

59. Maslow, Abraham H. *Eupsychian Management,* 56. Homewood, IL: Dorsey-Irwin, 1965.

60. Alderfer, Clayton P. "A New Theory of Human Needs." *Organizational Behavior and Human Performance* 4 (May 1969): 142–175.

61. Alderfer, Clayton P. *Existence, Relatedness, and Growth: Human Needs in Organizational Settings.* New York: Free Press, 1972.

62. Fottler, Myron D., Stephen J. O'Connor, Mattia J. Gilmartin, and Thomas A. D'Aunno. "Motivating People." In *Healthcare Management: Organization Design and Behavior,* 5th ed., edited by Stephen M. Shortell and Arnold D. Kaluzny, 89. Clifton Park, NY: Thomson Delmar Learning, 2006.

63. Herzberg, Frederick. "One More Time: How Do You Motivate Employees?" *Harvard Business Review* 87 (September/October 1987): 109–117; Herzberg, Frederick, Bernard Mausner, and Barbara Snyderman. *The Motivation to Work.* New York: John Wiley & Sons, 1959.

64. McClelland, David C. *The Achieving Society.* Princeton, NJ: Van Nostrand, 1961; McClelland, David C. *Power: The Inner Experience.* New York: Irvington Publishers, 1975; McClelland, David C. *Human Motivation.* Glenview, IL: Scott Foresman, 1985.

65. Murray, Henry A. *Explorations in Personality.* New York: Oxford University Press, 1938.

66. Atkinson, John W. *An Introduction to Motivation.* New York: Van Nostrand, 1961.

67. Atkinson, John W., and Joel O. Raynor. *Motivation and Achievement.* Washington, DC: Winston, 1974.

68. Vroom, Victor H. *Work and Motivation.* New York: Wiley, 1964.

69. Adams, J. Stacy. "Toward an Understanding of Inequity." *Journal of Abnormal and Social Psychology* 67 (November 1963): 422–436; Adams, J. Stacy. "Inequity in Social Exchanges." In *Advances in Experimental Social Psychology:* 267-299, edited by Leonard Berkowitz, vol. 2. New York: Academic Press, 1965.

70. Locke, Edwin A. "Toward a Theory of Task Motivation and Incentives." *Organizational Behavior and Performance* 3 (May 1968): 157–189; Locke, Edwin A. "Purpose without Consciousness: A Contradiction." *Psychological Reports* 24 (June 1969): 991–1009; Locke, Edwin A. "The Ubiquity of the Technique of Goal Setting in Theories of and Approaches to Employee Motivation." In *Motivation and Work Behavior,* edited by Richard M. Steers and Lyman W. Porter, 4th ed., 111–120. New York: McGraw-Hill, 1987.

71. Locke, Edwin A., and Gary P. Latham. *A Theory of Goal Setting and Task Performance.* Englewood Cliffs, NJ: Prentice Hall, 1990; Wood, Robert E., and Edwin A. Locke. "Goal Setting and Strategy Effects on Complex Tasks." In *A Theory of Goal Setting and Task Performance,* edited by Edwin A. Locke and Gary P. Latham, 293–319. Englewood Cliffs, NJ: Prentice Hall, 1990.

72. Latham, Gary P., and Edwin A. Locke. "Goal-Setting: A Motivational Technique That Works." In *Motivation and Work Behavior,* 4th ed., edited by Richard M. Steers and Lyman W. Porter, 120–134. New York: McGraw-Hill Book Company, 1987; Locke and Latham, *A Theory of Goal Setting and Task Performance;* Muchinsky, Paul M. *People at Work: The New Millennium.* Pacific Grove, CA: Brooks/Cole Publishing Company, 2000; Locke, Edwin A., and Gary P. Latham. "What Should We Do about Motivation Theory? Six Recommendations for the Twenty-First Century," *Academy of Management Review* 29, 3 (July 2004): 388–403.

73. Mento, Anthony J., Robert P. Steel, and Ronald J. Karren. "A Meta-Analytic Study of the Effects of Goal Setting on Task Performance: 1966–1984." *Organizational Behavior and Human Decision Processes* 39 (February 1987): 52–83.

74. Naylor, James C., and Daniel R. Ilgen. "Goal Setting: A Theoretical Analysis of a Motivational Technique." In *Research in Organizational Behavior,* edited by Barry M. Staw and Larry L. Cummings, vol. 6, 95–140. Greenwich, CT: JAI Press, 1984.

75. Latham, Gary P., and J. James Baldes. "The Practical Significance of Locke's Theory of Goal Setting." *Journal of Applied Psychology* 60 (February 1975): 122–124.

76. Erez, Miriam, and Frederick H. Kanfer. "The Role of Goal Acceptance in Goal Setting and Task Performance." *Academy of Management Review* 8 (July 1983): 454–463.

77. Erez, Miriam, P. Christopher Earley, and Charles L. Hulin. "The Impact of Participation on Goal Acceptance and Performance: A Two-Step Model." *Academy of Management Journal* 28 (March 1985): 50–66; Schwartz, Robert H. "Coping with Unbalanced Information about Decision-Making Influence for Nurses." *Hospital & Health Services Administration* 35 (Winter 1990): 547–559.

78. Bateman, Thomas S., and Carl P. Zeithaml. *Management: Function and Strategy,* 2nd ed. Burr Ridge, IL: McGraw-Hill Higher Education, 1993.

79. Drucker, Peter F. *The Practice of Management.* New York: Harper & Brothers, 1954; Duncan, W. Jack. *Great Ideas in Management.* San Francisco: Jossey-Bass, 1989.

80. Fottler, Myron, D., Stephen J. O'Connor, Mattia J. Gilmartin, and Thomas A. D'Aunno, "Motivating People," 93.

81. Stogdill, Ralph M. "Personal Factors Associated with Leadership." *Journal of Psychology* 25 (January 1948): 35–71.

82. Bass, Bernard M., and Ruth Bass. *The Bass Handbook of Leadership: Theory, Research, and Managerial Applications,* 4th ed. New York: The Free Press, 2008.

83. Stogdill. *Handbook of Leadership.*

84. Ledlow, Gerald R., and M. Nicholas Coppola. "Leadership Theory and Influence," 167-190. In *Health Organizations: Theory, Behavior, and Development,* edited by James A. Johnson. Sudbury, MA: Jones & Bartlett, 2009.

85. Goleman, Daniel. *Emotional Intelligence.* New York: Bantam Books, 1995; Goleman, Daniel. "What Makes a Leader?" *Harvard Business Review,* November–December 1998, 93–102.

86. Goleman, "What Makes a Leader?"

87. Goleman, "What Makes a Leader?" 94.

88. Pointer, Dennis D. "Leadership: A Framework for Thinking and Acting." In *Healthcare Management: Organization Design and Behavior,* 5th ed., edited by Stephen M. Shortell and Arnold D. Kaluzny, 132. Clifton Park, NY: Thomson Delmar Learning, 2006.

89. Van Fleet, David D., and Gary A. Yukl. "A Century of Leadership Research." In *Contemporary Issues in Leadership,* 2nd ed., edited by William E. Rosenbach and Robert L. Taylor, 65–90. Boulder, CO: Westview Press, 1989.

90. Yukl, Gary. "Effective Leadership Behavior: What We Know and What Questions Need More Attention." *Academy of Management Perspectives* 26 (November 2012): 66–85, 84–85.

91. Yukl, Gary. "Effective Leadership Behavior," 66.

92. Blake, Robert R., and Jane S. Mouton. *The Managerial Grid III: The Key to Leadership Excellence.* Houston, TX: Gulf Publishing Company, 1985.

93. Blake, Robert R., and Anne Adams McCanse. *Leadership Dilemmas—Grid Solutions.* Houston, TX: Gulf Publishing Company, 1991.

94. Tannenbaum, Robert, and Warren H. Schmidt. "How to Choose a Leadership Pattern." *Harvard Business Review* 51 (May/June 1973): 162–180.

95. Sutton, Robert I. "Bosses, Get Out of Your Employees' Way." *Wall Street Journal,* October 27, 2019. *https://www.wsj.com/articles/bosses-get-out-of-your-employees-way-11572228361,* retrieved May 26, 2020.

96. Peters, Lawrence H., Darnell D. Hartke, and John T. Pohlman. "Fiedler's Contingency Theory of Leadership: An Application of the Meta-Analysis Procedures of Schmidt and Hunter." *Psychological Bulletin* 97 (March 1985): 274–285.

97. Fiedler, Fred E. "A Contingency Model of Leadership Effectiveness." In *Advances in Experimental Social Psychology,* edited by Leonard Berkowitz. New York: Academic Press, 1964; Fiedler, Fred E. *A Theory of Leadership Effectiveness.* New York: McGraw-Hill, 1967.

98. Fiedler. *A Theory of Leadership Effectiveness.*

99. Hersey, Paul, Kenneth H. Blanchard, and Dewey E. Johnson. *Management of Organizational Behavior: Leading Human Resources,* 10th ed. Upper Saddle River, NJ: Prentice Hall, 2012.

100. Hersey, Blanchard, and Johnson. *Management of Organizational Behavior.*

101. Yukl. *Leadership in Organizations.*

102. Bateman and Zeithaml. *Management;* Bateman and Snell. *Management.*

103. House, Robert J. "A Path–Goal Theory of Leader Effectiveness." *Administrative Science Quarterly* 16 (September 1971): 321–339.

104. House, Robert J., and Terence R. Mitchell. "Path–Goal Theory of Leadership." *Journal of Contemporary Business* 3 (Autumn 1974): 81–98.

105. House and Mitchell, "Path–Goal Theory of Leadership."

106. Levey, Samuel. "The Leadership Mystique." *Hospital & Health Services Administration* 35 (Winter 1990): 479–480.

107. Druskat, Vanessa Urch, and Jane V. Wheeler. "Managing from the Boundary: The Effective Leadership of Self-Managing Work Teams." *Academy of Management Journal* 46, 4 (August 2003): 435–457.

108. Dunn, Rose T. *Dunn and Haimann's Healthcare Management,* 9th ed. Chicago: Health Administration Press, 2010.

109. Fottler, Myron, D., Stephen J. O'Connor, Mattia J. Gilmartin, and Thomas A. D'Aunno, "Motivating People," 109.

110. Bateman and Zeithaml. *Management;* Bateman and Snell. *Management.*

111. National Center for Healthcare Leadership. "About Us." *https://www.nchl.org/page?page=45,* retrieved November 12, 2019.

112. The material in this section is largely from National Center for Healthcare Leadership, *NCHL Healthcare Leadership Competency Model, version 3.0.* Chicago: Author, 2018.

113. Commission on the Accreditation of Health Management Education. *Self-Study Handbook for Graduate Programs in Healthcare Management Education, Criteria for Accreditation, Revised May, 2018,* 3. *https://cahme.org/files/resources/CAHME_Self_Study_Handbook_Fall2017_Revised May2018.pdf,* retrieved November 12, 2019.

114. Healthcare Leadership Alliance. *HLA Competency Directory, version 2.0.* Chicago: Author, 2017. *http://www.healthcareleadershipalliance.org/,* retrieved November 12, 2019.

115. Saint Louis University, College for Public Health and Social Justice, Department of Health Management and Policy. *Master of Health Administration Competencies.* St. Louis: Author, 2016. *https://www.slu.edu/public-health-social-justice/pdfs/slu_mha_competencymodel_reviewedfall2016.pdf,* retrieved November 12, 2019.

116. American College of Healthcare Executives. "Healthcare Executives' Responsibility to Their Communities," revised 2016. *Policy Statements. https://www.ache.org/about-ache/our-story/our-commitments /policy-statements/healthcare-executives-responsibility-to-their-communities,* retrieved November 12, 2019, used by permission.

117. Written by Wesley M. Rohrer, III, and used with his permission.

118. Walker, Sam. "The Eisenhower Code: Happy to Serve, Reluctant to Lead." *Wall Street Journal,* December 7, 2018. *https://www.wsj.com/articles/the-eisenhower-code-happy-to-serve-reluctant-to-lead -1544191201,* retrieved November 12, 2019.

14

Controlling

Control is last in the list of Fayol's management functions. It follows planning, organizing, staffing, and directing. Management control is the systematic comparison of performance with predetermined standards to determine if it meets standards, and to act if performance does not meet them.[1] Arguably, controlling is the most important, but it cannot occur until the first four have been implemented. Managers' control ensures that expected results occur after a structure or task is integrated with technology or people. Control depends on information provided to managers, who monitor sensors to ensure that work results are effective and desirable and organizational objectives are accomplished within resource constraints. The management model in Figure III.2 (page 349) reflects these relationships.

Control allows managers to know if services provided by an HSO or HS are high quality. Control enables managers to determine effectiveness of processes. Control measures the quality of input, if inputs are properly allocated, and if use of inputs is appropriate. Control allows a determination that organization objectives are being achieved. Control or control-like activities include quality control, infection control, performance improvement (PI), risk management, cost control, utilization review, narcotics control, budgets, position control of staffing, and clinical credentials review.

Chapter 13 describes the control function as gathering information about and monitoring activities and performance, comparing actual results with expected or desired results, and, as

The section on Healthcare and Public Health Emergency Preparedness was written by Knox Walk, Director, Emergency Preparedness, and William M. Smith, Consultant, both at the University of Pittsburgh Medical Center.

The section on Project Management was written by Neal McKelvey, M.Sc., MA-HCA, a retired senior hospital executive, with updating by the authors.

The section on Compliance was written by Vidya R. Battu, JD, MHA, CHC, Consultant.

appropriate, taking corrective action by changing inputs or processes. Control and planning are closely linked; the standards and desired results used in control are derived from strategic and operational plans of HSOs and HSs.

Monitoring (Control) and Intervention Points

Control systems are information based. The generic control system in Figure 14.1 identifies monitoring (control) and intervention points.[2] Control systems collect and monitor information at three points: input utilization, functioning of conversion processes, and outputs. Results inconsistent with expectations or standards should cause intervention and change, which can occur at input point (A), process point (B), or both.

Output Control

Feedback control is the best-known type of output control. It is retrospective and measures quantitative and qualitative output of persons, processes, departments, and organizations. Whether measured qualitatively or quantitatively, output or results are usually expressed numerically.

Job performance is a type of individual measure. Quantitative measures for departments include the numbers or units of output, such as laboratory tests performed, images taken, surgical procedures performed, meals served, patients admitted, medication orders filled, and pounds of laundry processed. Qualitative measures used by departments include accuracy, timeliness, and customer satisfaction. Organization-wide quantitative measures include average length of stay (ALOS), occupancy rate, market share, and financial integrity. Organization-wide qualitative measures include quality of care based on clinical outcomes, range of services, and stakeholder satisfaction. Output standards and expectations are derived from, and reflect, unit and departmental subobjectives and overall organizational objectives.

Process Control

Converting inputs into outputs requires processes. Quality of outputs is determined by the effectiveness of processes that produce them and the amount and appropriateness of inputs. Usually, the controlling function directs attention at outputs (quantity and quality of service), but it is equally important in monitoring myriad integrative conversion processes whose total effort generates outputs. A foundational principle of continuous quality improvement (CQI)

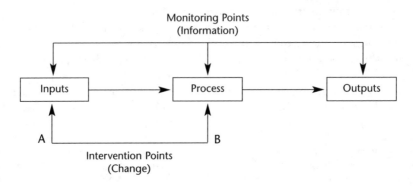

Figure 14.1.   Generic control system.

is that processes can be improved. This can occur only if there is a monitoring system to identify how well processes are functioning. The following are examples of integrative conversion processes in HSOs/HSs:

- Work systems such as patient admitting and discharge, transportation, materials handling and distribution, direct patient care, and ancillary services

- Specific job design and staff, and machine, technology, and facility relationships

- Financial record keeping and information collection, storage, retrieval, and dissemination systems

- Decision and resource allocation and planning processes

- Managerial methods, practices, and styles, along with organizational structuring, coordination, and communication methods and flow

Because a process (in combination with inputs) yields outputs, concurrent process control is important. Process control focuses on what happens between input and output. Furthermore, the process is one of two points at which intervention can occur if outputs are inconsistent with expectations (see point B in Figure 14.1). Standards and expectations are easier to develop for processes that produce tangibles, are consistent, and are simple to document and understand. Developing standards and expectations is more difficult for less tangible processes. For example, what are the effects on conversion (and, ultimately, on output) of different managerial methods of problem solving and decision making, leadership and supervisory styles, approaches to motivation, or methods of communication? This may help explain why control has historically focused on outputs generated and inputs consumed rather than on processes. CQI focuses the control function on processes and their improvement.

Input Control

As noted, resource consumption in creating outputs is a major focus of control. Input controls are prospective. Effective HSOs/HSs control inputs by developing standards and expectations about resource consumption. Examples include nursing hours per patient day, materials and supplies consumed, and the ratio of various types of staff to beds. Often called feed forward control, input control ensures that the right instructions and amount of resources are available before work begins. The philosophy of CQI suggests that choosing the best inputs before conversion will diminish the potential for problems with outputs. For example, the quality of human resources inputs can be controlled by licensure and credentialing, which help ensure that clinical staff has acceptable levels of training and skills. Input control, however, cannot substitute for process and output control.

Control Model

Thus far, control has been described as a process through which to collect information about results and performance at the monitoring (control) points of inputs, process, and outputs. Comparing actual results with standards and expectations, appraising comparisons, and making changes at either the input or process points or both are the remaining components of control. Figure 14.2 incorporates these components in an expanded control process model to show actual results measured and compared with standards and expectations. Depending on results, the control process follows one of four loops, each of which may indicate a need to intervene.

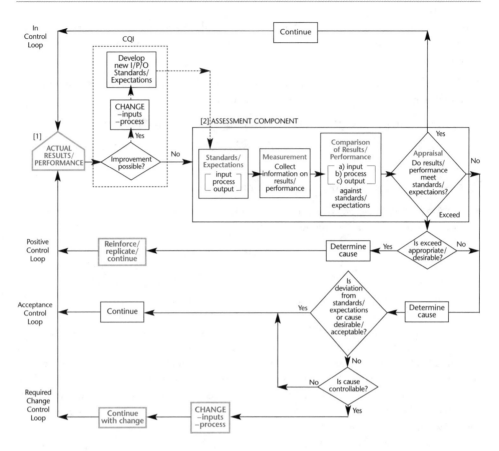

Figure 14.2. Expanded control model under the condition of deviation (retrospective).

In Control Loop

The *in control loop* in Figure 14.2 is the simplest. When evaluation of information from the three monitoring points—inputs, process, and outputs—indicates standards and expectations are being met, intervention is unnecessary, and activity continues.

Acceptance Control Loop

When monitoring indicates performance does not meet expectations, managers investigate to determine the cause(s) of deviation. If deviation is desirable or acceptable, or its cause is uncontrollable, there is no intervention. For example, overtime hours higher than budgeted (standard) may be acceptable if the census is proportionately higher. If the deviation is undesirable but the cause is uncontrollable, actual performance must be accepted. For example, a number of registered nurse (RN) hours per patient that is less than the desired number of hours, but more than the minimum needed for good patient care may result from an inadequate number of RNs available to the organization.

Required Change Control Loop

Intervention should occur when information shows that deviation is unacceptable and the cause is controllable. For example, if the ALOS is substantially longer than the standard, intervention is required. This deviation may occur if physicians (input point) do not write patient discharge orders in a timely manner or if ineffective work systems (process point) cause delays in reporting test results. Another example is higher-than-normal staff turnover that results from a negative organizational climate, inadequate compensation, or poor supervision. Here, too, input or process point intervention is required.

Positive Control Loop

Control can also be positive. For example, the cause of performance that exceeds standards should be identified, reinforced, integrated into the process, and replicated elsewhere when possible. Effective managerial style, positive employee attitude and commitment, and well-designed processes will likely result in a work unit that is consistently under budget, produces high-quality results, and has satisfied customers. Positive control that recognizes and emphasizes the positive must be a focus.

There are instances when it is undesirable for actual performance to be better than standards. For example, it may seem desirable that nursing service hours per patient day are below budget (i.e., standard), but evaluation may show that this is unacceptable if quality of care is at risk. Expenditures to maintain the physical plant may be less than budget, but this is undesirable if preventive maintenance is postponed. If actual results and performance are better than standards and expectations but are undesirable or inappropriate, the cause should be determined, and either the *acceptance* or *required change* control loops should be used to intervene.

Levels of Control

Managers use three basic levels of control: strategic, operational, and functional. *Strategic* control focuses on attaining overall HSO/HS objectives, including financial performance. Senior managers monitor organizational performance to determine if strategies being used are accomplishing strategic objectives and whether a change in the external environment requires reevaluation. Figures 10.2 and 10.3 depict the role of the external environment in strategizing. *Operational* control monitors day-to-day unit or department activities (operational plans). This control is the responsibility of middle- and first-level managers who are concerned with their unit or department work schedules, budgets, and resource use. *Functional* control focuses on logically grouped functional areas, such as clinical services, billing, information systems, and marketing. Senior functional area managers, as well as middle- and first-level managers, are responsible for control in operational and functional areas.[3]

Control Considerations

Several managerial and design considerations are important in managing control systems.

Managerial Considerations

Questions managers must answer when a control system is implemented or modified include the following:

- *Where is control focused?* Control may focus on input (resource use), process or conversion (efficiency of work systems that convert inputs to outputs), or output (individual process, aggregations of processes, or organization-wide results).

- *What types of measures are used for standards and monitoring results?* Measures used in control depend on focus, quantifiability of results, and extent to which measures convey accurate, usable, and meaningful information.

- *Who has the authority to establish standards?* A principle of control is that those whose activities are monitored have input, but do not have sole authority to establish standards and monitor results. Checks are universal in accounting systems; for example, persons who handle cash do no final audits or reconciliations. Similarly, review of clinical services is not performed by those who provide the service.

- *How flexible should standards be?* Blind and inflexible use of numerical measures for control purposes can cause distortions. Changes and unforeseen circumstances require that control systems use judgment, common sense, and flexibility.

- *Who has access to control system information?* Controlling requires disseminating information, but some information is restricted to certain levels of management or specific managers.

- *Who is responsible for intervention?* Just as organizations have a defined authority-account-ability hierarchy, managerial considerations in control include identifying who is responsible and who intervenes.

Design Considerations

Sometimes, control systems cause unintended or undesirable consequences, cost more than they save, measure the wrong things correctly, or measure the right things incorrectly. Control systems should include the following to decrease the potential for dysfunctional outcomes:

- *When possible, control should be prospective.* Control cannot always be forward looking or predictive. Usually, data flow or organizational constraints limit information to that which is concurrent or retrospective. If available, however, feed forward control provides information to managers to enable them to anticipate deviation and become more effective.

- *Control should be organizationally realistic and understandable to users.* Control systems must be harmonious with the organization, fit realistically, and be understandable. A system that creates barriers or artificial constraints is dysfunctional. For example, inventory data are best controlled by supply chain. Centralizing access to and control of printers in one location may be unrealistic and inefficient.

- *Control should be accurate, timely, and reliable.* When control systems are designed, the standards and measurements must be accurate and reliable. Corrections that use inaccurate or unreliable information defeat the purpose of control, as does using data unreflective of the current situation.

- *Control should be significant, have economic benefit, or both.* *Significant* refers to the importance of what is being controlled. *Economic benefit* refers to the cost of control relative to the value of what is controlled. There is little economic benefit to monitoring disposal (destruction) of used syringes. Its benefits result from preventing use by drug addicts and protecting those who handle medical waste. Narcotics control has significant clinical and economic benefits and is required by law. Conversely, control of disposable surgical gowns—except as they are biohazards—has little economic value, and control costs will exceed benefits.

Important indicators can be lost if there is too much information. Too little information prevents managers from finding critical elements. Control systems must give managers enough, discriminating information in a timely, usable manner.

Control and CQI

Meeting standards does not end the control process. The philosophy of CQI uses continuous inquiry to improve inputs and processes so that outputs are enhanced. Figure 14.2 shows CQI in the rectangle outlined by dashes. If no improvement of inputs or processes is possible, the control loop flows from actual results/performance [1] through to the assessment component [2]. If improvement is possible, change is made to either inputs or processes, or both, and new standards and expectations are developed to replace those used previously in the assessment component [2].

Control and Problem Solving

As noted in Chapter 6, problem solving is based on information from the control function. The four conditions that begin problem solving are opportunity/threat, crisis, deviation, and improvement. *Opportunity* is prospective and anticipatory and results from favorable internal or external circumstances that enable the HSO/HS to achieve or enhance desired results. *Threat* is also prospective and anticipatory, but it is the converse of opportunity, and problem solving seeks to minimize potential internal and external threats. *Crisis* problem solving occurs when failing to act promptly will cause untoward results. *Deviation* problem solving is the most common and occurs when work results are inconsistent with those desired. Problem solving under the condition of *improvement* improves inputs or processes to affect outputs positively.

Control and Information Systems

Managers require information. Effective planning, problem solving, and control occur only when managers receive appropriate, accurate, and timely information based on reliable data presented in a usable format. "The organization that can successfully and efficiently manage information will produce better quality healthcare because it will be able to measure, monitor, and improve the care it delivers."[4] By improving access to information and facilitating communication among providers and team members, the information system (IS) is important in addressing the forces for change in healthcare, including concerns about costs, medical errors and poor quality, access to care and health disparities, and growth in the use of evidence-based medicine and management.[5] Chapter 5 considers the applications of IS technology to the clinical aspects of health services delivery.

Management IS is a generic concept that refers to the use of electronic systems to gather, format, process, store, and report data that are converted to information retrievable by managers for use in planning, executing, and controlling organizational activities. Traditional IS is applications driven; data are retrieved from discrete files created by organizational units. In IS design, users specify type and extent of data. IS applications in HSOs began in the 1960s with systems developed by in-house analysts and programmers. In the 1980s, commercial vendors began providing software for administrative and clinical functions.

Generally, IS in HSOs/HSs falls into two broad categories. First, administrative and financial systems provide information supporting administrative operations and managerial planning, resource allocation, and control activities. Second, clinical and medical systems provide information to support patient care. Other uses include cost accounting, resource utilization and productivity analysis, and market intelligence.

The senior manager responsible for IS is the chief information officer (CIO). The CIO should be 1) technically competent, including in managing internal systems, knowledge about developments in IS, and awareness of technology used by competitors; 2) attuned to organizational objectives, the organization's stage of evolution in information technology, and its clientele; 3) business savvy to understand the importance of information in a competitive market and technology's high cost; and 4) a leader, especially as a change agent, team builder, and communicator.[6]

Networks

The sophistication of IS ranges from applications reporting systems to database management systems to decision support systems. Applications reporting is the most familiar to HSO/HS managers and consists of tailored reports about organizational operations or areas of activity, such as payroll, inventory, budgets, admissions, census, and scheduling.

Advances in computer hardware and software make database IS ubiquitous in HSOs/HSs. Data from throughout the organization are integrated and consolidated in a single database or multiple databases accessible to authorized users, rather than segregated for specific applications. Often, these systems are inquiry based. Local area networks (LANs) allow communication among computers and peripherals within an HSO or among HSOs/HSs in a limited area. Extended into large geographic areas, LANs become wide area networks (WANs), which allow long-distance input and inquiry information access. WANs enable geographically distant operating units to exchange information, create computer-based patient records, and develop integrated outcome measures and statistics. Networks can be hard wired or wireless.[7] Chapter 5 provides additional information on LANs and WANs.

Management and Clinical IS

MDSS

A management decision support system (MDSS) is a type of specialized IS application. The MDSS merges external databases, financial databases, clinical systems, and other data sources into a decision support systems database from which users obtain data that can become the information for decision making. MDSSs are model based and can perform statistical analyses and simulations. An interactive capability allows managers to make hypothetical queries, such as, What would be the effect on net margins if Medicare days were to increase by 20%?

Management Expert Systems

Management expert systems go beyond data storage, retrieval, modeling, and reporting capabilities of a decision support system. They seek to replicate human reasoning. Expert systems are an artificial intelligence program with expert-level knowledge. Expert systems complement and may even substitute for a human expert.[8]

CSS

Patient care applications of IS are widely used in HSO clinical support systems (CSSs). CSSs use IS for managing internal processes and for communicating with other departments or processes. For example, the laboratory uses IS to automate and control processes and to report results. Medical imaging and radiology use IS for both clinical and management purposes. Medical imaging systems use technology to process and enhance digital images, and radiology uses IS to schedule procedures, record and report test results, report charges, and prepare management reports. A clinical application is computer-aided detection (CAD) used in interpreting mammograms. CAD can find microcalcifications in breast tissue that are highly correlated with disease.[9] IS applications are found in pharmacy, physical and respiratory therapy, nursing services, critical care units, and emergency services.

CDSS

Like MDSS, the clinical decision support system (CDSS) is a leap in technology application. CDSSs are expert systems used to assist licensed independent practitioners (LIPs) and other clinicians in diagnosis and treatment. CDSSs consist of evidence-based modeling routines driven by automated clinical knowledge (natural language processing can extract and encode massive amounts of text data in literature and medical reports in a short time). Using artificial intelligence (AI), CDSS outputs consist of quantitative comparisons of clinical outcomes associated with alternate medical decisions. The Acute Physiology and Chronic Health Evaluation

(APACHE), development of which began at The George Washington University Hospital in the early 1980s, is an example. APACHE uses physiological variables, age, and chronic health status to predict severity of illness. It is especially useful as a CDSS in intensive care units.[10]

Electronic Health Records

The electronic health record (EHR) allows easy access to the medical record and, if accessible throughout an HSO/HS, offers major technological advantages. Chapter 5 introduced the advantages and disadvantages of EHRs. For purposes of control, several advantages and disadvantages are summarized here.

The advantages of using EHRs include but are not limited to the following:

• Facilitate use of medical and health information

• Reduce offline storage and retrieval costs

• Improve quality and coherence of the care process

• Automate (potentially) clinical practice guidelines

• Support research and quality improvement

• Ease reporting requirements with readily available data

There are also disadvantages of using EHRs, including the following:

• The large number of data sources internal and external to the organization, often with their own system

• The need for interfaces among various systems

• The need to maintain confidentiality, privacy, and consent for access to private health information

• Cost savings that may be elusive

• Patient perceptions of caregivers who use computers during treatment

Most EHRs have CDSS capabilities in that they can generate alerts and reminders, such as checking for drug–drug and drug–food adverse effects. More advanced CDSS capabilities include evidence-based medicine protocols that have the best possible outcomes for patients.[11]

Responding to the Institute of Medicine's finding that between 44,000 and 98,000 patients die each year from medical error,[12] the federal government provided financial incentives through the American Recovery and Reinvestment Act of 2009 (PL 111-5) for physicians and hospitals to adopt EHR and published compliance stages for adoption known as meaningful use: Stage 1 promoted basic EHR adoption and data gathering, Stage 2 emphasized care coordination and exchange of patient information, and Stage 3 improved health outcomes. In 2018, the Centers for Medicare & Medicaid Services (CMS) renamed the incentive programs as "promoting interoperability programs." For LIPs, meaningful use criteria (called advancing care information under Medicare Access and the Children's Health Insurance (CHIP) Reauthorization Act of 2015 (MACRA [PL 114-10]) and additional criteria related to public health and clinical data exchange have been folded into the quality payment program established by MACRA.[13]

IS Issues

Advances in IS technology in the past several decades have been profound. They have enhanced resource utilization through better managerial control and improved patient care through better clinical decision making. The advances have been costly, however. Hardware and software are expensive, as is IS support staff. In addition, issues have been raised regarding patient care and clinical IS use. For example, applications such as CDSS typically build on IS designed for administrative and claims/transactions processing. Often, such systems lack standardization and create problems of compatibility.

> As part of the HIT (health information technology) strategic planning process, the (HIT) steering committee should study requirements for data interchange, including HIPAA (Health Insurance Portability and Accountability Act of 1996 [PL 104-191]) mandates and should develop a policy on data standardization for the organization. For example, many hospitals and integrated delivery systems are specifying that all software purchased from vendors must meet an industry standard protocol such as HL7 (Health Level Seven, or HL7, refers to a set of international standards for the transfer of data).[14]

IS Uses

Quality and control depend on information. Austin and Boxerman delineated several areas in which IS supports managers and clinicians (Table 14.1).[15]

In terms of controlling, IS should provide information that meets the needs of managers. It should allow them to 1) monitor input, process, and output; 2) provide for each level of management and area of responsibility reports that contain accurate, relevant, and timely information to improve decisions on control (intervention); and 3) extract and pinpoint critical and high-priority items requiring management analysis and, perhaps, intervention. Clinical IS that incorporates practice parameters for use by LIPs improves quality and achieves a level of control. Also known as clinical guidelines, practice guidelines, and critical paths, practice

Table 14.1   Healthcare Applications

Applications	Examples
Clinical information systems	• Laboratory automation and laboratory information systems
	• Pharmacy information systems
	• Medical imaging and radiology information systems
	• Other service department systems: PT, pulmonary, ED, and the like
	• Order entry and results reporting
	• Nursing information systems
Management/administrative and financial systems	• Financial information systems
	• Human resources information systems
	• Resource utilization and scheduling systems
	• Materials management systems
	• Facilities and project management systems
	• Office automation systems
Information systems for nonhospital healthcare organizations	• Ambulatory care information systems
	• Long-term care information systems
	• Home health information systems
Other information system applications in healthcare	• Clinical decision support systems
	• Executive information systems
	• Evidence-based medicine and disease management systems
	• Computer-assisted medical instrumentation
	• Telemedicine
	• Computer applications in medical research and education

From Glandon, Gerald L., Detlev H. Smaltz, and Donna J. Slovensky. *Austin and Boxerman's Information Systems for Healthcare Management*, 7th ed., Part III. Chicago: Health Administration Press, 2008.

parameters guide clinical decision making. Clinical IS allows comparisons of clinical outcomes and resource use internally and with other HSOs and benchmarks, and it can be used to profile LIP practice patterns. Practice guidelines are discussed in Chapter 8. The potential for clinical IS has yet to be realized, however. Measuring LIP compliance with practice parameters is largely retrospective, not concurrent. Usable clinical IS must provide guidance to clinicians while the patient is being treated. Typically, IS systems "are not set up to feed that information back quickly to the clinicians producing the results, to analyze the problems that the measures turn up, and to facilitate actions that improve quality and safety."[16]

Risk Management and Quality Improvement

Historically, safety programs and efforts to measure the quality of clinical services were separate control activities, usually limited to acute care hospitals. In the early 1970s, safety programs began evolving into the broader concept of risk management (RM) and included managing risk proactively. RM includes activities in HSOs/HSs that conserve financial resources. Those functions include a range of administrative activities to reduce losses from patient, employee, or visitor injuries; property loss or damage; and other sources of potential organizational liability.[17]

A comprehensive RM program includes identifying, controlling, and financing risks of all types. Inherent in RM is preventing risk and minimizing the effects of untoward events, should they occur. RM programs are common in HSOs/HSs and are required in a number of states.[18] Part of RM, patient safety programs, are required in a number of Joint Commission standards and patient safety goals.[19] While not required by The Joint Commission, HSOs/HSs typically have a safety committee and a safety officer to show that environment of care activities are effectively coordinated.[20] Patient safety is an initiative of the American College of Healthcare Executives.[21] Patient and staff safety is addressed in more detail in Chapter 8. Not to be forgotten are the nonfinancial losses HSOs/HSs suffer from the negative effects of bad publicity and loss of reputation resulting from clinical errors and administrative failures.

Internal and external factors caused a broadening of RM. Internally, HSO/HS managers increasingly recognized their ethical duty to provide a safe environment for patients, staff, and visitors and to deliver high-quality clinical services. External stimuli included increasing litigiousness and court decisions putting greater legal liability on HSOs/HSs; 2) state laws mandating RM programs; 3) federal laws such as the Occupational Safety and Health Act of 1970[22] that mandated the study of hazards in acute care hospitals so national standards could be set; and 4) requirements of private and public organizations such as The Joint Commission and U.S. Department of Health and Human Services (DHHS), respectively, and their state counterparts, increasingly emphasized quality of services and managing risk. Better RM programs followed as it became apparent HSOs/HSs had to manage the costs of risk.

In the 1990s, improving clinical quality (quality assessment and improvement [QA/I]) for patients was an important part of this expanded concept of RM. In 1992, The Joint Commission moved away from the terms and methodology of quality assurance and mandated QA/I as a more proactive and effective focus to evaluate and improve quality. Those standards linked, but did not integrate, QA/I and RM activities. The evolution continued, and by the late 1990s, QA/I and RM were integrated into PI.[23] By 2013, RM activities were a source of "important information" and were integrated into PI.[24] Integrating quality improvement (QI) and RM is prudent and enhances the effectiveness of both. HSOs/HSs must never suggest, however, that they are more concerned with reducing economic risk than with providing high-quality clinical services, despite their connection.

RM and efforts to improve clinical quality are similar. The Venn diagram in Figure 14.3 shows the overlap between RM and QI, most of which is found in PI. Risk financing, employee benefits, and general liability issues have been unique to RM and are likely to remain so. Patient

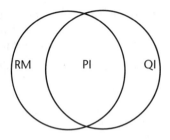

- Patient/customer focus
- Data-driven, complementary databases
- Includes clinical *and* administrative areas
- Process improvement orientation
- Staff involvement at all levels
- Loss(es) viewed as process failure
- Leadership from the top
- Ongoing education of staff
- QI viewed as step to managing risk
- Problem identification
- Culturally embedded

Figure 14.3.   Relationship and integration of RM and QI.

satisfaction, employee empowerment, and PI are largely linked to QI, even though they may affect risk. The evolution of QA to PI expands the historical focus of QA beyond clinical activities to include improvement of the processes that support them. This change further diminishes the distinctions between RM and clinical activities and increases their linkages and the need for integration. Opportunities to benefit from cooperation will increase. In the meantime,

> for some professionals on both sides, integration means that one function envelops and subsumes the other—a circumstance that would not be in the best interests of either function. Operational linkages is a term that is vague enough to allow for a variety of organizational models, reporting relationships, and data flow.[25]

Risk Management

As late as the 1970s, it was even common for larger HSOs to assign the director of maintenance collateral duties in facility safety. Directors of maintenance were unlikely to have formal preparation in RM and patient safety, however. RM was underappreciated as part of controlling, and the various risks facing HSOs/HSs were neither integrated nor managed comprehensively. Insurance was the typical means of protecting organizations from monetary loss; proactive RM was supported by insurance companies seeking to decrease their exposure. Figure 14.4 shows a risk control (management) system with four quadrants: consequential loss, property loss, liability loss, and bodily injury. It illustrates relationships that arise among governance, senior management, and the HSO's/HS's organization, staff, and activities.

Link to Senior Management

Regardless of the integration of RM and QI, encouragement and commitment by senior management are necessary for a successful RM program. Governing board (GB) support is shown by allocating resources to the chief executive officer (CEO) for RM activities, support that should be readily available given the positive economics of prevention. RM has a staff, rather than a line, relationship to the CEO. A committee develops policy and provides general oversight. To the extent RM and QI are integrated, this committee includes members of professional staff organization (PSO) committees and is more clinically oriented.

The Risk Manager

Traditional preparation for health services risk managers includes education in RM, nursing, management, insurance, and law. Larger HSOs and all HSs need full-time RM expertise. Integrating RM and QI suggests the need for more academic preparation, perhaps as an adjunct to a clinical background. RM in an HS is likely to be managed by someone with significant operational experience, perhaps complemented with a legal or clinical background. Traditional risk management has been silo driven; problems were identified in certain areas but were seldom connected. Enterprise RM looks at multiple categories of risk to determine the effect on the whole organization.[26]

Risk managers have become increasingly important in HSOs/HSs. As risk managers' role matured, duties began to include identifying and evaluating risks, loss prevention and reduction,

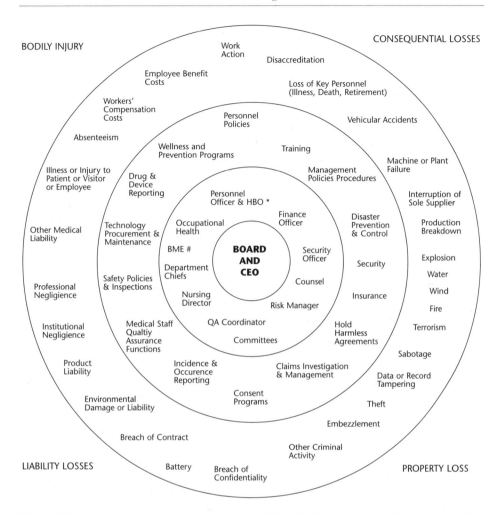

BODILY INJURY   CONSEQUENTIAL LOSSES

LIABILITY LOSSES   PROPERTY LOSS

Figure 14.4.   Risk control (management) system (*HBO, health benefits officer; #BME, biomedical equipment). (From Kavaler, Florence, and Allen D. Spiegel. *Risk Management in Health Care Institutions: A Strategic Approach*, 6. Sudbury, MA: Jones & Bartlett, 1997. www.jbpub.com. Reprinted by permission.)

managing the insurance program, safety and security administration, litigation management and claims handling, assisting in adjusting losses, RM consultation, and QI and related activities. Reviewing business relationships (including contracts) is a necessary function for risk managers; examples include clinical and educational affiliations, vendor relationships, interorganizational relationships (in an HS and among HSOs), contracts with clinicians, management services, employment contracts, equipment purchase and lease agreements, and joint ventures.[27] A background in law or involvement of house counsel is suggested by greater participation of risk managers in legal matters.

Risk managers hold staff positions. This requires them to depend on and cooperate and coordinate with HSO/HS units and departments. Working effectively with persons over whom the risk manager has no line authority requires good interpersonal skills and an ability to coordinate and integrate resources and sources of information. The risk manager may have the effect of exerting de facto line authority by providing information that is the basis for senior management decision making, and by persuading senior management to act. Nevertheless, the risk manager's influence is indirect.

Principles of Managing Risk

The steps in managing risk include identifying, evaluating, eliminating, reducing, and transferring risk. There are several ways to *identify* risk to the HSO/HS. The most common is to collect and analyze data about problems or potential problems. Examples are workers' compensation claims, patient infections, injuries to staff from "sharps," unexpected patient deaths, patient falls, and injuries to visitors. Contributing to these data are the written occurrence, or incidence reports completed by staff with knowledge about the event. Patient and staff safety are discussed in Chapter 8.

Finding patterns in these data is important. Safety inspections and audits of various activities and functions, ranging from financial (e.g., contracts) to fire protection, are ways to identify potential problem areas. Managing risk must be more than reactive, however. It should concentrate on evaluating, eliminating, reducing, and transferring risk.

Evaluating risk means reviewing and categorizing information about problems over time. This allows the risk manager to focus on areas with the greatest potential for loss. Evaluating risk should be prospective, too, because it can be predicted actuarially that certain types of problems will occur or have a probability of occurring. Prospective, retrospective, and concurrent efforts can use evaluative techniques, such as cost–benefit and cost-effectiveness analyses, to select the best course of action. Evaluation assists in identifying strategies to eliminate, reduce, or transfer risk.

Eliminating or *reducing* risk (or both) can be achieved variously. Examples include offering education and awareness programs for staff, modifying the physical plant and structure, enhancing the PSO credentialing process and reviewing clinical staff activities, improving processes, initiating material management systems, improving patient and staff relations, and hiring qualified staff in appropriate categories. Eliminating risk is preferred, but this may be impossible for many types of risk. In such cases, the emphasis must be on minimization of risk.

Corporate reorganization (restructuring) can eliminate certain economic risks. For example, assets of a separately incorporated operating HSO may be leased from the HS, which likely makes the HSO immune from recovery by successful plaintiffs. Establishing trusts and foundations in a corporate reorganization, which is common when HSs are established or when restructuring occurs, has the same effect. Putting HSO assets beyond the legal reach of successful plaintiffs has its place and is a legitimate business strategy. Failing to provide fair compensation for persons who have been clinically or financially injured because of interacting with an HSO or HS, however, is socially irresponsible and unethical.

Some risks can be *transferred* to others. A common method of doing this is the "hold harmless" agreement, which requires a party doing business with an HSO/HS to indemnify it for liability incurred because of that party's negligence. Equipment purchase contracts commonly include such clauses. As permitted by law, transfer of risk clauses should be used in all agreements with subcontractors. Insurance is the most common way to transfer risk.[28] Entering a risk pool—joining those with similar exposure to risk—allows risk to be shared. Actuarial methods determine the potential for loss, and a premium can be assigned. This allows individual exposure to loss to be minimized.

Financing Risk

Some risks, such as casualty (e.g., damage from fire, water, or wind storm), general liability (e.g., injury to visitors or suppliers), business interruption (e.g., equipment failure, strike, vandalism, or acts of nature), theft (e.g., embezzlement), and medical and administrative malpractice can be minimized but cannot be eliminated or transferred. The financial viability of the HSO/HS must be protected from them. Insurance is the most common means of doing so. Commercial insurance requires that the insured pay a premium. Coverage under the contract of insurance provides specified protection against certain losses for a fixed period. The contract between the HSO/HS (the insured) and the insurer (carrier) places obligations on the insured as well. Examples include staff training, providing inspection reports to insurance carriers, promptly reporting potentially compensable events, and cooperating in the carrier's investigation and defense of claims. In addition to commercial insurance, HSOs/HSs may participate in insurance programs through captive insurance companies that have been established by the state, a trade association, a consortium of HSOs/HSs, or a large HSO/HS. "Off-shore" insurance companies are an example. Recurring malpractice "crises" resulting from rapid increases in malpractice insurance premiums made non-U.S.-based, captive insurers popular. Some commercial insurance carriers stopped writing medical malpractice liability insurance. This made availability a factor too.

Prior to the 1980s, medical malpractice liability insurance was written on an "occurrence" basis—the insured had coverage if a policy was in effect at the time of the event (occurrence). Occurrence coverage protected the insured if the claim was filed within the statute of limitations, regardless of how long that was after the injury. This resulted in a "long tail," meaning claims could be brought years or even decades after the event that caused a claim to be filed. The statute of limitations begins to run only after the event is, or should have been, discovered, and this adds more length to the "tail." For example, a newborn infant can bring suit for 21 years plus the statute of limitations for negligent medical treatment. Insurance carriers argued this degree of uncertainty made it almost impossible to actuarially determine their risk (exposure). In turn, an inability to predict exposure made it impossible to calculate an appropriate premium. To avoid this problem, insurers began writing policies with "claims-made" coverage. Claims-made coverage "eliminated the 'long tail' of occurrence coverage because the insurer knows at the expiration of a given policy all of the claims that will be reported against that policy. The insurer need not be concerned with unknown claims that may be made in future years at inflated costs."[29] This change meant that the insured must have a policy in effect when the claim is brought rather than when the insured event occurs, as with occurrence coverage. This shift helped reduce the rate of increase in medical malpractice liability insurance premiums.

Larger HSOs/HSs can self-insure. Self-insurance programs are usually broader than medical malpractice liability and may include financial protection against risks such as business interruption, fire, and other casualty losses and bonding for employees with financial responsibilities. Establishing a self-insurance program involves much more than stating the HSO/HS is self-insured. There must be actuarial studies to determine the potential for various types of losses, including special attention to the specific risk from clinical services offered or contemplated by the organization. Using these data, the HSO/HS must establish dedicated financial reserves to meet expected claims. Usually it takes several years to accumulate the reserves needed for a self-insurance program to be financially viable. In the interim, commercial coverage is necessary. In addition, after the program is established, vigilance is needed to ensure that the fund is both adequate to meet expected claims and not raided for other purposes. Underfunding or stripping reserves for self-insurance protection can have disastrous consequences for the organization's economic viability should a major need for cash arise.

Even when the self-insurance program is mature, prudent HSOs/HSs will carry excess liability and casualty coverage against very large claims. For example, an HSO/HS might self-insure for losses to $3 million; beyond that it has a policy with a commercial carrier to a total coverage of $20 million, or more. Even if an HSO/HS has only commercial insurance, the policy likely has a deductible, which is a form of self-insurance. Deductibles must be met from reserves.

Good business practice demands HSOs/HSs protect themselves against the full range of financial risks. In addition, it is socially responsible and ethical that they do so. "Going bare" in terms of medical malpractice claims means the HSO/HS neither self-insures nor carries commercial insurance. This practice is not uncommon among LIPs, especially those with poor medical malpractice liability histories. Their assets are in a spouse's name or otherwise beyond the reach of plaintiffs. This, too, is socially irresponsible. It is prudent for HSOs/HSs to require that members of their PSOs provide evidence of insurance coverage as a condition of clinical privileges. This is standard in acute care hospitals and required by accreditors.

Non-LIP caregivers and managers should carry personal liability insurance to protect themselves as individuals from legal actions for alleged negligence. Individual malpractice policies have become common among RNs, and there are significant legal and professional reasons to purchase such coverage, even if the employer has an umbrella policy that covers employees.[30] Managers must remember that they, too, are liable for errors and omissions (malpractice) committed in their professional activities. Despite an umbrella liability policy, litigation has many nuances for employers and employees. Soon after litigation begins, it becomes apparent that defendants have substantially different interests. Umbrella policies of the type common to HSOs/HSs do not include employees as named insureds. This means that, legally, an individual employee has no voice in a decision to settle a lawsuit. Although not a legal determination, settling a lawsuit suggests an admission of fault. This may be adverse to employees' interests in terms of professional reputation, licensure, certification, and references. Conversely, a personal policy gives one a much stronger position. The Health Care Quality Improvement Act of 1986[31] requires that payments made for the benefit of physicians and LIPs must be reported to the national practitioner data bank. This greatly increases the effects of settling a malpractice claim and makes it important for affected parties to have maximum control. Members of HSO/HS GBs are not employees. They should be protected against legal actions for errors and omissions under a directors' and officers' liability policy, a policy provided by the HSO/HS. They, too, should consider having a personal errors and omissions liability insurance policy.

Process of RM

The RM program must systematically report circumstances that put HSOs/HSs at risk. These can be fire and safety problems, accidents, or any type of negligence. Data collection for analysis of actual and potential loss may be done with a sophisticated RM software program or a simple manual entry system. Establishing databases for incident reports, claims, insurance coverage, hazardous materials, and other sources of information may be accomplished by using both internal and external sources. The use of data in RM continues to evolve.[32]

Common to internal control systems is a written statement, usually called an incident report or an occurrence report. Incident reports alert risk managers to specific problems, and aggregating the data will show problem areas and patterns. Because clinical incidence reporting and associated activities are used to improve the quality of care, laws in most states prevent plaintiffs' attorneys from obtaining (discovering) them. Shield laws were passed because access to such information could have a chilling effect on the willingness of LIPs to engage in peer review. A collateral result of limiting access to documents is that the plaintiff (injured party) is less likely to prevail. On balance, however, society's interests are served by promoting activities that improve quality of care, even given the potential for abuse of a shield law.

Analysis of data from reporting systems is used in the feedback loop—it informs the risk manager about problems and suggests steps to correct them. For example, data about falls resulting from patients' excessive waits for assistance with toileting can be used to support a nursing service request for more staff. Data about postsurgical wound infections can be used to improve staff training in sterile processing, or to teach correct hand hygiene techniques to staff with direct patient contact. Data about injuries to staff who move obese patients justify a training program for good lifting techniques and the purchase of specialized equipment.

Legal counsel review of the RM program is essential. If counsel is available on-site (in-house counsel), it is likely that the person is more involved in RM than is external or retainer counsel. Some HSOs/HSs use in-house counsel as risk managers. Regardless, legal counsel must participate to provide the legal perspective for RM.

After injury to a patient has occurred, the risk manager can minimize loss by immediately taking the following four steps:

1. If the patient has been discharged, the medical record (including radiographs) must be secured and absolute custody retained by the risk manager.

2. If the patient continues under treatment and the EHR is active, the risk manager must obtain a copy of the original, with real-time access to new entries. This procedure should be known throughout the HSO.

3. Meetings should be held with the patient, the family, or both to determine their interest in settling a potential claim. Once an injured patient retains legal counsel, the case becomes more complex, costly, and less likely to be settled early.

4. The HSO should do whatever it can to retain the patient's goodwill.

Above all, insult should not be added to injury: an injured patient who needs additional services should not be billed for them. Angry patients are more likely to sue than those who believe the HSO did the best it could under the circumstances and acted responsibly. To reduce anger, the HSO's staff must communicate honestly with the patient and family. Injured parties who believe they are being misled or kept from the truth will react with anger and a strong desire to learn what happened. Expressing concern, providing information, and apologizing reduce the likelihood an injured party will take legal action.[33] Chapter 9 discusses communicating about clinical errors.

Efforts at early settlement raise a duality of interests that can cause a conflict of interest. Patients and their relatives should understand that the risk manager is an employee of the HSO. Risk managers must never allow patients or family members to believe they are advocates for the patient or are acting as legal counsel for the patient. Honesty and forthrightness succeed better than other tactics. At a minimum, fraud or misrepresentation by the risk manager is unethical. Further, it will cause a court to set aside an agreement; it could result in criminal charges or punitive civil damages against the HSO/HS.

Summary

The process of RM has an important place in the control function shown in Figure 14.2. Change is difficult in HSOs/HSs because much that is done is a personal service rendered by clinical staff who sometimes have no employment relationship with the organization. For managers, this requires attention to interpersonal skills and an ability to work with and through people. Maintaining and improving the quality of care for patients and protecting employees and visitors depend largely on these skills. It is platitudinous, but true nevertheless, to say that managers must be part of the solution or they will remain part of the problem. Managers should be unwilling to accept an attitude anywhere in the HSO/HS that what is being done is "good enough."

Healthcare and Public Health Emergency Preparedness

Emergency preparedness in healthcare and public health has received expanded emphasis in the recent past.[34] Natural disasters have shown the importance of hospital and public health emergency preparedness and their shared mission to support the community and preserve health and well-being.[35]

In 2005, Hurricane Katrina struck New Orleans. Memorial Medical Center was devastated by the storm surge that followed. The hospital lost basic services, including water and electricity, but still had to care for patients in ambient temperatures over 100 degrees. In 2009, a pandemic of H1N1 influenza challenged the capabilities of public health departments and hospitals. The September 2010 shooting of a surgeon by a disgruntled family member of a patient at The Johns Hopkins Hospital, Baltimore, Maryland, resulted in evacuations of part of the facility and disrupted the hospital for hours. In May 2011, St. John's Hospital in Joplin, Missouri, was rendered uninhabitable by a tornado that killed five patients and required evacuation of 183 others. In November 2012, Bellevue Hospital and other HSOs in New York City had to be evacuated because of Superstorm Sandy and the associated flooding that compromised operation of their emergency power capabilities. In 2014–2015 an outbreak of Ebola in West Africa caused a worldwide alert affecting every healthcare facility. In 2017,

Hurricane Irma caused evacuation of several healthcare facilities in Florida, and Hurricane Harvey caused significant damage to three hospitals in Texas. In 2020, the COVID-19 pandemic once again challenged the preparedness of hospitals and public health departments. By the end of 2020, COVID-19 was responsible for over 1,270,000 deaths worldwide, 240,000 deaths in the United States, and the slowdown of the world's economy. 29 percent of nurses surveyed in the United States during the pandemic reported their hospitals had plans in place for isolating COVID-19 patients.[36]

These situations created conditions beyond what can normally be expected in hospital operations. In each case, emergency operations plans were implemented (some ad hoc) to try to prevent loss of life and maintain an environment of care. The situations affirmed the saying that "all disasters are local," meaning the first impact, and, therefore, the need for first response, occurs at the immediate, local level.

Organizing for Emergency Preparedness

The first step in HSO/HS preparedness planning should be development of a comprehensive hazard vulnerability analysis (HVA). The HVA identifies situations that may have an emergent impact on the organization. "The HVA provides a systematic approach to recognizing hazards that may affect demand for the hospital's services or its ability to provide them. Risks associated with each hazard are analyzed to prioritize planning, mitigation, response, and recovery activities."[37]

The HVA is the basis for all emergency preparedness (EP) because it identifies the nature and severity of potential disasters that could affect an individual HSO or an HS. Involvement of local emergency management agencies (EMAs) is also essential to creating the HVA. There are numerous tools and models for the HVA, but the most effective is a realistic summary of possible events and their associated effects. Typically, they use a numeric ranking to reflect severity. Events with higher scores receive priority. EP professionals recommend that organizations should plan and prepare for any event that has occurred in the past 5–10 years, even if it did not directly affect the facility. As an example, if the HVA lists tornado risk as low but the community has had a tornado within 8 years, the facility's plan should include response to a tornado.

Concurrent with creation of the HVA is the need for an emergency preparedness management structure. The makeup of this structure in an HSO depends on type of facility. The management structure for emergency preparedness need not be a separate committee or team. The work can be done by an existing multidisciplinary group if those involved understand the principles of emergency preparedness and organizational operations. The Joint Commission requires that the manager of emergency management activities be appointed by the leadership of the organization.

Typically, the emergency preparedness group or committee has representatives with medical, administrative, and operations backgrounds. This is important because these areas will be affected by a disaster and must be able to respond. Table 14.2 shows an example of an emergency management committee. Regulators recommend that participants undergo annual training in emergency management principles.

At minimum, the coordinator of an emergency preparedness program should be someone trained and/or experienced in the principles of emergency preparedness, organizational operations, team leadership, and communications. The coordinator will have significant contact with internal staff—including administration, LIPs, and various committees, and external contacts such as local, state, and federal public safety officials, as well as public health and other healthcare representatives. Minimally, the person responsible for the emergency preparedness program has a bachelor's degree in one of the following: environmental health and safety, security, nursing, facilities management, information technology, or prehospital care. Many community colleges and universities provide certificate, undergraduate, and graduate programs

Table 14.2 Recommended Composition of an Emergency Management Committee

Team leader	Person familiar with the principles of emergency management, disaster operations, and hospital functions
Administration	Need not be team leader, but is part of hospital leadership; provides input and communication with senior management
Medical staff	Involving PSO in planning is crucial; mandated by some regulators
Safety officer	Person responsible for hospital environmental health and safety
Nursing	Chief nursing officer (CNO) or designee
Supply chain/materials management	Person familiar with HSO logistics
Human resources	Person versed in HSO HR policies, procedures, and pay practices
Infection prevention and control	Important for input on pandemic and bioterrorism-related occurrences
Security	Security team leader
Information technology/ communications	Person(s) versed in operating and maintaining HSO's telecommunication and IT infrastructures and redundant communications processes
Media relations	Person who knows HSO policies and procedures on media interaction

in emergency management. Additional training can be obtained through the Federal Emergency Management Agency. Although not required by many organizations, certification as a disaster recovery planner, business continuity planner, or safety professional may be preferred. Two of the oldest and most respected certifications are certified business continuity professional offered by the Disaster Recovery Institute International (DRII) (http://www.drii.org), and certified emergency manager, offered by the International Association of Emergency Managers (http://www.iaem.com). These and other organizations offer various certifications (e.g., associate, certified, and advanced, or master's level). DRII has a healthcare certification track (https://drii.org/certification/certification.php).

Involvement of LIP leadership is an often overlooked but critical element of emergency planning. Frequently, operational planners develop disaster procedures that repurpose areas of the hospital during an emergency. Chiefs of clinical services should not learn that their departments (with risk to patients [and their livelihoods]) are being subordinated to a disaster plan after an emergency occurs. Thoughtful planning with the PSO will avoid this problem and ensure an effective response.

An important element of an emergency preparedness program is participation and support of the organization's leadership. Sometimes, emergency preparedness is seen as a necessary evil to avoid the liability of being unprepared or in violation of accreditation standards or government regulations. An engaged, knowledgeable leader will recognize and support the importance of emergency preparedness to patient safety, business continuity, and, ultimately, revenue protection. Healthcare leaders should be involved in and visibly support development of emergency operations plans and participate in disaster exercises, and post-event critiques. This level of participation by organizational leaders lends credence to the importance of this effort to the HSO.

When an event necessitates implementation of the emergency plan, it is vital that senior leaders know their roles and responsibilities. Assigning someone as the incident commander does not necessarily follow the established administrative hierarchy, and in many cases it should not. Often, operational personnel are better suited to manage the response, but this depends on the nature of the emergency and level of involvement by senior leaders in planning. Leadership systems should be implemented for smaller or planned events to allow participants to train to manage emergencies.

An additional external entity that should be involved in HSO emergency planning is the local EMA. It is crucial that the EMA and HSO understand the capabilities and limitations of the HSO and what support and assistance the EMA can provide. It is also advantageous if those in charge of the emergency preparedness program are personally acquainted with members of the EMA before an emergency occurs. This makes communication and coordination smoother and more efficient.

Emergency Operations Plans

Once the HVA is complete, development of emergency operations plans (EOPs) is begun. EOPs are typically developed in several sections utilizing an "All Hazards" approach. This means certain parts of the plan are performed without change regardless of the emergency. Examples are the structure of the incident command system (ICS), activation and deactivation protocols, communication processes, succession planning, defining span of authority (how many people can be managed), supply management, and coordination with local authorities.

Remaining sections of the EOP are divided into "external" and "internal" disaster response plans and are usually shown as appendices to the basic document. External disasters are events that occur outside the HSO but will affect HSO operations either by creating a surge in demand for medical treatment or by interrupting services such as electricity or water.

Examples of external disasters include mass casualty situations, earthquakes, or severe weather. Internal disasters affect the facility but not the external environment. Examples include fire, loss of utilities, criminal activity, bomb or terrorist threats, chemical spills, and contingencies for labor disruptions.

The additional sections of the EOP (unlike the all hazards sections) should deal with specific operational and response plans for emergencies identified via the HVA. For example, operational mobilization in response to an Ebola outbreak will differ from interruption of electrical power.

All emergency plans should be based on the four phases of emergency responses:

1. Planning/mitigation

2. Preparedness

3. Response

4. Recovery

Planning/mitigation includes organizational activities to avert or lessen the effect of the types of emergencies prioritized in its HVA. The best example of mitigation is installation of emergency power generators. HSOs identify loss of normal electrical power as a high-priority emergency because of their heavy reliance on electricity for patient care. *Preparedness* is the pre-event actions taken by the HSO to have an appropriate response to a disaster. Development of emergency operations plans, stockpiling critical supplies, and conducting employee training are examples of preparedness activities. *Response* is implementation of operations plans and efforts during an emergency. The most overlooked element of emergency preparedness is recovery. *Recovery* is the process of returning the facility to normal or near-normal operations. It is crucial that this be identified prior to disasters for several reasons: reestablishing the HSO as a community resource, continuing critical medical treatments suspended during the emergency, determining when the event is sufficiently resolved that the HSO can return to a safe operational condition, and restoring financial viability.

Planning Scenarios

What key plans should HSOs have in place? It is neither likely, nor necessarily prudent, that a facility has a detailed response plan for every possible type of disaster. The likelihood that the event will occur exactly as the plan projects is slim. Therefore, a flexible plan is crucial.

The EOP must also consider the varying nature and dimensions of different types of disasters that may occur. Emergencies follow two scales: time and impact. They are shown in Figure 14.5.

Direct Impact on the Facility

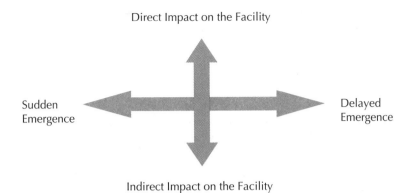

Sudden
Emergence

Delayed
Emergence

Indirect Impact on the Facility

Figure 14.5. Direct and indirect effects of a disaster on an HSO. (From William M. Smith, Senior Director, Emergency Preparedness, and Kathleen Criss, CBCP, Director, Preparedness Operations, both of the University of Pittsburgh Medical Center. Used with permission.)

Events such as earthquakes will have an immediate or sudden impact and will have a direct effect on the facility in damage to buildings or interruption of utilities. Other emergent events may include a mass influx of injured persons (e.g., major transportation accident). Mass casualty situations cause a rapid increase in numbers of patients, but this usually has little direct effect on the HSO's ability to continue its mission. Events such as pandemics of infectious disease may have a limited effect on the facility (depending on how many staff members are affected) and tend to develop more slowly. Environmental events such as hurricanes may progress slowly but have a significant effect on the facility. The quadrants of Table 14.3 take these factors into account in development and execution of response plans.

The emergency preparedness process is summarized in Figure 14.6. Each of the four stages in Figure 14.6 includes actions to be taken. In *Plan* and *Prepare*, emergency management efforts focus on the following:

• Identifying potential risks (hazard vulnerability analysis)

• Developing plan frameworks based on risks identified in the HVA

Table 14.3 Factors in Development and Execution of Response Plans

Sudden emergence/direct impact	Delayed emergence/direct impact
Tornado	Hurricane
Earthquake	Severe heat or cold
Utility interruption	Supply chain interruption
Tsunami	Work stoppage (internal)
Terrorist activity (internal)	IT interruption
Internal hazmat incident	
Active shooter	
IT interruption	
Sudden emergence/indirect impact	**Delayed emergence/indirect impact**
Transportation accident	Bioterrorism event
Terrorist activity (external)	Pandemic of infectious disease
External hazmat incident	Work stoppage (external)
Bioterrorism event	
V.I.P. event	
Other media event	

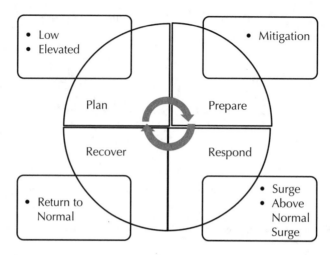

Figure 14.6. Emergency preparedness process. (From the Federal National Disaster Medical System [http://www.phe.gov/preparedness/responders/ndms/Pages/default.aspx].)

- Informing and training staff involved in command and operations aspects of the emergency operations plan

- Identifying and acquiring supplies and equipment needed in an emergency

- Developing and maintaining communication and collaboration with local emergency management authorities, healthcare cooperative organizations, and other local and regional resources (such as the National Disaster Medical System, https://www.phe.gov/Preparedness/responders/ndms/Pages/default.aspx)

In the *Prepare* stage an emerging threat has been identified (e.g., a pandemic), requiring specific responses.

The *Response* phase implements plans developed previously and addresses other issues that arise. Key elements are as follows:

- Communicating plan implementation and expectations to employees and physicians

- Establishing operational "command and control" centers as dictated by the nature and scope of the emergency

- Managing disaster victims, as well as routine patients. (Persons with acute and nonacute conditions [unrelated to the emergency] will come to the HSO.)

- Maintaining facility security

- Managing and credentialing volunteers and physicians

- Establishing and managing media briefings

- Ensuring appropriate staffing levels during the emergency

- Monitoring inventories of critical supplies and pharmaceuticals and maintaining communication with prime vendors for restocking

- Communicating and coordinating with local emergency management authorities

- Reporting plan implementation to state health officials and regulatory agencies, as appropriate

Proper management of the *Recovery* phase is essential for two reasons: returning an important health infrastructure asset to support the community and reestablishing the normal revenue stream for the HSO. Recovery includes the following:

- Alerting local and public health authorities interrupted services are restarting

- Completing an "after-action" report that summarizes accomplishments during the emergency and opportunities for improvement

- Establishing contact with and rescheduling appointments for patients whose treatment was canceled

- Inventorying supplies and pharmaceuticals for replenishment

- Establishing critical incident stress management debriefing for employees and victims affected by the emergency

- Establishing staffing schedules that consider hours already worked during the emergency

- Completing an analysis and summary of costs incurred as part of the response for potential reimbursement from state and federal agencies

- Issuing media releases and conducting briefings on the status of the facility

Incident Command

A key element of emergency operations is establishing an incident command and an ICS. Basically, incident command is identifying who is in charge and providing the terminology, operational infrastructure, and management tools to meet the response objectives of the plan. The most common ICS is the National Incident Management System (NIMS).[38] The federal government uses NIMS to coordinate responses to large-scale emergencies.

A healthcare version of ICS is the hospital incident command system (HICS). This model mirrors the NIMS ICS and was developed in the 1980s by a national group of subject matter experts to enable hospitals to prepare for, and respond to, disasters.[39]

The HICS establishes precise, standardized spans of control and reporting structures for responding to emergencies. Among the advantages of this system are that it establishes a clear chain of command, uses a common terminology across multiple organizations, facilitates accurate and efficient communication, allows better interface with local emergency management personnel, arranges tasks and responsibilities in a standardized, comprehensive fashion, and is scalable to the nature and size of the event.

It is unlikely that a typical hospital will staff all or even most HICS positions. Regardless of the event, however, there is always an incident commander. The nature and scope of the emergency and number of staff needed will dictate which other positions are filled and when.

Regulatory Requirements of Emergency Preparedness

In addition to the moral imperative that HSOs prepare for disasters, there are numerous local and national requirements for emergency preparedness. Table 14.4 details several.

Table 14.4 shows that the consequences of a noncompliant emergency preparedness program are significant. Occupational Safety and Health Administration fines have increased significantly. As of 2020, maximum fines were $13,494 for the initial violation, $13,494 per day for failure to abate, and $134,937 for willful or repeated violations.[40]

In 2016, CMS published *Emergency Preparedness Requirements for Medicare and Medicaid Participating Providers and Suppliers.*[41] This regulation has sweeping requirements for 17 provider types, including hospitals and long-term care and ambulatory surgery facilities.

Table 14.4   Regulatory Requirements Related to Emergency Preparedness

Authority	Standard(s)	Requirements	Effect of noncompliance
The Joint Commission	Emergency management standards	HVA Emergency operations plans Drills Leadership involvement Community involvement	Potential loss of accreditation
Centers for Medicare and Medicaid Service (CMS)	Hospital and long-term care federal conditions of participation (COP)	Written plans Drills Follow-up Leadership involvement	Potential loss of Medicare/Medicaid payments
Occupational Safety and Health Administration (OSHA)	Emergency organization standard	Emergency plans Employee training	Citations, fines, and potential imprisonment
	Hazardous waste operations and hazard communications	Plan for dealing with hazardous materials Employee training Selection and use of personal protective equipment	
	General duty clause	Furnish to each employee employment and a place of employment that are free from recognized hazards that are causing or are likely to cause death or serious physical harm	
State regulations		Typically follow closely the CMS requirements	Citations
Office of the Assistant Secretary for Preparedness and Response	Hospital preparedness program	Compliance with 8 healthcare preparedness capabilities to qualify for HPP grant funding	Loss of grant funding

Source: Department of Health and Human Services, Office of the Assistant Secretary for Preparedness and Response, Hospital Preparedness Program: National Guidance for Healthcare System Preparedness, January 2012.

Previously, these providers had few, if any, emergency preparedness regulatory requirements. States have emergency management requirements like CMS's, and compliance will require significant effort.

Control Methods

Managers use numerous methods and techniques to monitor and control inputs, processes, and/or outputs. RM and PI are examples of structured, programmatic control methods. Others are credentialing, compliance, budgeting, and financial statement analysis.

Credentialing[42,43]

An important example of control is the credentialing process covered in Chapter 11. When hospital malpractice cases involve LIPs, the credentialing process (obtaining, verifying, and assessing qualifications) and privileging process (determining the scope and content of what an LIP can do in the HSO) becomes an important element of the discovery process. Both lawyers for plaintiff patients and lawyers for defendant LIPs have vested interests in tying the physician's negligence to the hospital's credentialing process. Lawyers for plaintiff patients see the HSO as "deep pockets" in a possible recovery of damages; lawyers for defendant LIPs are quite willing to redirect culpability from the LIP to the organization. Under the legal doctrine of corporate negligence, organizations can be held liable for an LIP's actions by breaching a duty the organization owes to the patient—the duty to properly select and supervise physicians and other members of the PSO. Case law in corporate negligence is well established as to the organization's duty to select competent physicians as in *Johnson v. Misericordia Community Hospital* 294 NW.2d 501 (1980) and the duty to supervise physicians as in *Darling v. Charleston Community Memorial Hospital*, 383 U.S. 946 (1966).

Johnson provided the following credentialing criteria for HSOs for meeting their legal duty in selecting competent physicians.

- Require completion of the PSO application and verify accuracy of applicant's statements. The application should be procedure specific.

- Solicit information from applicant's peers, including those not referenced in the application, who are knowledgeable about applicant's education, training, experience, health, competence, and ethical behavior.

- Determine if applicant is currently licensed to practice in the state and if the license has been or is being challenged.

- Inquire if applicant has been involved in malpractice claim and if applicant has experienced a loss of PSO membership or privileges at other providers.

- Inquire and verify information from secondary sources such as Drug Enforcement Administration, National Practitioner Data Bank, American Medical Association Masterfile, and Federation of State Medical Boards.

When the credentialing and privileging process is complete, the PSO makes a recommendation to the GB, which appoints the applicant to the PSO.

Compliance

There is no statutory or standard definition of compliance in healthcare.[44] Put simply, it consists of conformity with federal, state, and local laws affecting HSOs and HSs. For staff, compliance is knowing and following these laws, as well as internal policies and procedures. An HSO's/HS's compliance program should promote conformity with the laws governing HSOs/HSs to avoid fines, civil monetary penalties, criminal penalties, and possible exclusion from federal programs, such as Medicare, Medicaid, Tricare, and CHIP.

Healthcare compliance has its roots in the Defense Industry Initiative (DII). The 1980s had numerous bribery and corruption scandals involving federal defense contractors.[45] A common scheme was for a government employee to approve an inflated invoice for goods or services from a defense contractor. The defense contractor would give the government employee a portion of the overpayment and keep the rest. In 1986, influenced by the Packard Commission[46] and the inspector general (IG) of the U.S. Department of Defense, defense contractors agreed to self-regulate and voluntarily adopted a code of conduct to minimize fraud and waste known as the DII.[47] The office of the inspector general (OIG) of the DHHS acted similarly in the 1990s. HSOs/HSs were encouraged to self-regulate. In addition, HHS increased antifraud activity.[48] In 1996, the Health Insurance Portability and Accountability Act (HIPAA [PL 104-191]) established a national Healthcare Fraud and Abuse Control Program jointly directed by the U.S. attorney general and secretary of HHS, to coordinate federal, state, and local law enforcement to prevent fraud, waste, and abuse in the healthcare system.[49] The Patient Protection and Affordable Care Act (ACA [PL 111-148]) included a provision authorizing the secretary of HHS to mandate that healthcare providers establish a compliance plan as a condition for participating in Medicare, Medicaid, and CHIP.[50]

In 2018, U.S. healthcare spending increased 4.6% from the prior year to a total of $3.6 trillion, or roughly $11,172 per person.[51] This amount was 17.7% of the 2018 gross domestic product.[52] Also in 2018, the federal government recovered over $2.3 billion in penalties and fines from fraud, waste, and abuse in federal healthcare programs.[53] The National Health Care Anti-Fraud Association estimates monetary losses due to healthcare fraud are tens of billions of dollars annually.[54] The estimate ranges from a low of 3% of U.S. healthcare expenditures to some government and law enforcements estimates as high as 10%.[55] The costs of healthcare fraud, waste, and abuse are not, however, only monetary. Often, they result in patient exposure to unnecessary or unsafe medical procedures, intentional misdiagnoses, and privacy breaches from compromised medical information.

Compliance Programs and Plans

An effective compliance program is more than a piece of paper or a handbook. It is an ongoing process that HSOs/HSs *must* undertake. The OIG of HHS enumerated seven elements of an effective compliance program for HSOs and HSs.[56]

1. Implementing written policies, procedures, and standards of conduct, which include items such as a code of conduct for HSO/HS employees, a record retention policy, and appropriate privacy policies to ensure confidentiality and privacy of patient information.

2. Designating a compliance officer and compliance committee. HSOs/HSs should have an independent chief compliance officer who should *not* report to the general counsel. HSOs/HSs should have an active GB that meets regularly with a set agenda.

3. Conducting appropriate training and education to ensure that HSO/HS employees can carry out their duties in compliance with applicable laws, rules, and regulations. Training and education may be live, by video, or online. The training and education should address areas such as patient privacy and confidentiality, patient safety, and patient rights.

4. Developing effective lines of communication to respond quickly and appropriately to compliance problems. Examples of effective lines of communication are an anonymous, well-publicized, 24-hours per day, 7 days per week, compliance hotline; locked suggestion boxes located accessibly throughout the HSO/HS; and, a well-publicized policy clearly stating that there will be no retribution for reporting misconduct.

5. Conducting internal monitoring and auditing to help avoid submitting incorrect claims to federal and private insurance payers. Monitoring and auditing practices should be reviewed annually.

6. Enforcing standards through well-publicized disciplinary guidelines, which should be clearly written, describe consequences for noncompliance, and include sanctions for noncompliance and failure to report noncompliance.

7. Responding promptly to detect offenses and taking corrective action. Corrective action may include the HSO/HS reporting its noncompliant activities to the OIG or HHS's office of civil rights within a statutorily defined time, depending on the nature and extent of the offense.

Sample Compliance Plan

Compliance plans should be based on OIG Compliance Program Guidance. Each HSO/HS should modify its plan, as appropriate, but plans should include the following 10 sections:

1. *Introduction:* The introduction should include the purpose of a compliance plan, which is to ensure conformity of all staff actions with federal, state, and local laws. The HSO's/HS's mission, vision, and values statements should also be included here.

2. *Code of Conduct:* The HSO/HS should include in its plan a written code of conduct as adopted by the GB.

3. *Fraud, Waste, Abuse, Anti-Kickback (AKS), and Self-Referral Laws:* HSOs/HSs are subject to several federal and state laws regulating their practices. The HSO/HS should explain the federal Anti-Kickback Statute, Stark Law, HIPAA, and the Emergency Medical Treatment and Labor Act (EMTALA). The HSO/HS should also identify and explain state laws that apply to it.

4. *Claims Billing Guidance:* The HSO/HS should state its commitment to diligent and accurate billing according to CMS guidelines for services provided. This section should include a statement expressing the HSO's/HS's policy to avoid duplicate billing, upcoding, and inappropriate unbundling. This section should state that the HSO/HS submits only medically necessary claims that have been ordered by a physician or other licensed staff member.

5. *Auditing Policy:* The HSO/HS should include its annually reviewed auditing policy that outlines its process for auditing to measure compliance and assist in process improvement.

6. *Documentation and Record Retention Policy:* This policy explains steps each HSO/HS staff member takes to maintain records, as appropriate. In general, medical records are kept for 5–10 years after patient discharge.

7. *Compliance Office:* The HSO/HS should identify the chief compliance officer, location of the compliance office, and telephone number of the compliance hotline.

8. *Nonretaliation Policy:* The HSO/HS should express the importance of staff to report noncompliant activities and clearly state that employees will not face retaliatory action for reporting.

9. *Training:* The HSO should state which training must be completed by hospital staff, such as annual HIPAA training.

10. *Statement of Receipt:* A form should be included that requires each staff member to acknowledge by signature and date receipt and review of the compliance plan.

Laws and Cases

Several federal laws are important in healthcare compliance, including

- HIPAA,[57]

- False Claims Act[58] (FCA [PL 104-410]),

- Anti-Kickback Statute[59] (AKS [PL 99-634]),

- Stark Laws[60] (Stark [PL 92-603, PL 95-142, PL 96-499, PL 98-369, PL 99-500, PL 100-93, PL 100-517, PL 101-239, PL 101-508, PL 103-66, PL 103-432, PL 104-316, PL 105-33, PL 106-113, PL 108-173, PL 110-275, PL 111-148, and PL 111-152]), and

- EMTALA[61] (EMTALA [PL 99-272]).

As noted, violations carry significant penalties.

HIPAA is among the most widely recognized. It includes the HIPAA Privacy Rule[62] and the HIPAA Security Rule.[63] The Privacy Rule safeguards protected health information (PHI) by limiting what an HSO/HS may disclose without patient consent. PHI includes test results, medical histories, demographic information, and other information obtained from a patient that may be used to identify the individual patient. Under the Privacy Rule, covered entities (healthcare providers such as HSOs/HSs, health plans, and healthcare clearinghouses) may only disclose PHI without a patient's authorization if disclosure is to the patient; for the covered entities' treatment, payment, and operation activities; and, for public benefit and public interest activities. The HIPAA Security Rule deals with electronic PHI (ePHI) and mandates that covered entities implement administrative, physical, and technical safeguards to protect individual ePHI. Safeguards include locking computers containing ePHI to desks to prevent theft and requiring passwords to access ePHI.

A case illustrative of a HIPAA violation is *United States v. Huping Zhou*.[64] Zhou was a research assistant at the University of California Los Angeles Health System (UHS). After UHS fired Zhou for performance-related reasons, he accessed patient records 323 times over 3 weeks without authorization. The information contained ePHI. Zhou did not improperly use or attempt to sell the information. He claimed he did not know that what he was doing was illegal. Nonetheless, a federal court found him guilty of violating HIPAA because HIPAA provides that it is a misdemeanor to access confidential records without a valid reason or authorization.[65] Zhou was sentenced to 4 days in jail and fined $2,000.[66]

The False Claims Act (known as the Lincoln law because it was originally passed during the U.S. Civil War), imposes liability on persons or entities who defraud government programs, including Medicare, Medicaid, CHIP, and Tricare. The act makes it a crime for a person or organization to knowingly make a false record or file a false claim, or cause another to knowingly make a false record or file a false claim, regarding a federal healthcare program to get a false claim paid by the government.[67] In *United States of America et al. v. BlueWave Healthcare Consultants, Inc.*, defendants Dent, Johnson, and Mallory conspired to pay kickbacks to physicians nationwide to encourage them to order medically unnecessary blood tests from Health Diagnostics Laboratory, Inc., and Singulex, Inc.[68] Defendants arranged for "processing and handling fees" of $17 to be paid to a physician per referral, and waived patient co-pays and deductibles. As a result of the kickback payments, physicians sent patients' blood samples to Health Diagnostics Laboratory and Singulex for medically unnecessary blood tests. Health Diagnostics Laboratory and Singulex submitted claims to Medicare and Tricare for payment. The court found the defendants guilty of violating the False Claims Act and assessed damages of $51.2 million against them.[69]

The Anti-Kickback Statute prohibits offering, paying, soliciting, or receiving anything of value to induce or reward referrals to generate federal healthcare program business.[70] The law prohibits physicians from knowingly and willfully accepting kickbacks, bribes, gifts above a nominal value, and other forms of remuneration in exchange for generating business from federal healthcare programs. There are, however, several "safe harbors" that are exceptions to payment and business practices that otherwise may have resulted in civil and criminal prosecution under the Anti-Kickback Statute.[71] Safe harbors include certain warranties, discounts, and space rental agreements. In 2017, Dr. Jerrold Rosenberg pleaded guilty to healthcare fraud and conspiracy to receive kickbacks in federal district court.[72] Rosenberg prescribed the highly addictive drug Subsys. He made false claims to federal programs and private insurers that patients met the insurance criterion of having breakthrough cancer pain when they did not in order to obtain insurance payment. Insys, the manufacturer of the drug, paid Rosenberg over $188,000 in "speaker's fees" to promote the drug. Rosenberg admitted that the speaker's fees were a significant factor in his decision to prescribe Subsys. Rosenberg was sentenced to 51 months in prison.[73] Insys signed a global resolution agreement with the U.S. Department of Justice (DOJ) for $225 million to settle civil and criminal investigations. In addition, the CEO of Insys was sentenced to 66 months in prison, and several other Insys employees were sentenced in this far-reaching scheme.[74]

The physician self-referral law, commonly known as the Stark law (Stark), prohibits HSOs/HSs and physicians from referring patients to an entity that provides designated healthcare services (DHSs) if the HSO/HS or physician (or an immediate family member) has a financial relationship with that entity.[75] Examples of DHSs include clinical laboratory, physical therapy, and certain radiology and imaging services.[76] Like the Anti-Kickback Statute, Stark has numerous exceptions. In general, they require that financial relationships are commercially reasonable, do not take into account the volume or value of referrals, and do not exceed fair market value.[77] In 2017, Tri-City Medical Center (Tri-City) in Oceanside, California, paid DOJ fines of over $3.2 million for violating Stark and the False Claims Act.[78] DOJ alleged that Tri-City had five arrangements with its chief of staff that did not comply with Stark because they were not commercially reasonable and were not at fair market value. DOJ identified 92 financial arrangements with community-based physicians and practice groups employing Tri-City physicians that did not satisfy a Stark exception because the written agreements could not be located, were expired, or were missing signatures. This case shows Stark's intent to prevent fraud, waste, and abuse by ensuring patient referrals result from patient's medical needs, not on a physician's financial interests.[79]

EMTALA[80] was enacted in 1986 to prevent patient dumping or refusing to treat patients in the emergency department (ED) for financial or other reasons. EMTALA requires that any patient presenting to an ED with an emergency medical condition must receive an appropriate medical screening exam.[81] The hospital must provide the treatment required (within the hospital's capability) to be stabilized, regardless of the patient's ability to pay or insurance coverage, before the patient is discharged or transferred to another facility. In 2019, the HHS OIG alleged Rockdale Medical Center (RMC), Conyers, Georgia, violated EMTALA by not providing an appropriate medical screening or stabilizing treatment before transferring a 79-year-old woman.[82] The patient had been involved in a motor vehicle accident and presented at RMC's ED via ambulance with several injuries. The ED physician directed the ambulance to take the patient to a trauma center; she was transported to the trauma center without receiving an appropriate medical screening exam. The patient's condition worsened during transport, and she died at the receiving hospital. RMC settled with the HHS OIG for $70,000 to resolve the EMTALA violation.[83]

Creating a Culture and Environment of Compliance

To avoid the risk of fraud, waste, and abuse, HSOs/HSs must create a culture and environment of compliance. Establishing such a culture goes beyond annual training or occasional review of the organization's policies and procedures. A culture of compliance must be acknowledged and enforced in daily operations and with employees. The chief compliance officer and compliance office must be open and accessible in their behavior and broadly visible in their actions. While everyone in the HSO/HS is responsible for compliance, it is imperative that the organization's executives express and show a commitment to compliance to shape a culture committed to it. An HSO's/HS's management and GB must understand compliance if they are to be an example for everyone to follow and to show that the rules apply everywhere, including the C-suite. Employees should be proactive in their actions. Only reacting after compliance infractions will result in civil monetary penalties and fines, criminal charges, damage to reputation, and poor patient outcomes. In the future, healthcare compliance will evolve due to the ever-changing landscape of the U.S. healthcare system and new laws and regulations. Since its inception, compliance has become more complex, and HSOs/HSs face greater regulation. This trend will likely continue given the increasing use of telemedicine and digital care. Such technologies pose a higher likelihood of cyberattacks on HSOs/HSs and will stimulate more regulation to protect patient privacy and treatment. States may take a larger role in healthcare compliance too. After passage of the Health Information Technology for Economic and Clinical Health Act of 2009, state attorneys general, as well as the HHS IG, have authority to bring civil actions on behalf of state residents for HIPAA violations.[84] As regulation increases, GBs, executives, and staff must be attentive to healthcare compliance requirements and make them integral to their activities.

Budgeting

Budgets are among the most common methods of control. They are the control standard against which results are compared and managers are evaluated. Budgets are considered extensively in Chapter 7.

Project Management[85]

Introduction

The Project Management Institute defines project management as one-time, ad hoc work performed by a team to achieve a unique product, process, or outcome.[86] For a project to be judged a success, its deliverables must consistently meet critical, predefined performance requirements relating to scope, stakeholder, and quality expectations. These outcomes must be achieved on schedule and within budget. Success relies on relationship building, accurate and timely information, effective communication, teamwork, and executive-level commitment. Project management can be used to guide the implementation of a wide array of tasks, including selection and installation of an EHR system, improvement of door-to-balloon time for patients with acute myocardial infarction, initiation of a hospital handwashing program, introduction of proton therapy to an oncology service line, as well as renovating, expanding, or replacing facilities. Emphasis here is on the application of project management to construction. Its wider application should be borne in mind, however.

The project management process, as adapted from the Deming Plan-Do-Check-Act model,[87] is shown in Figure 14.7. It comprises five major groups of activities,[88] each of which can be influenced by the topic, complexity, and pace of the project.

History

Current project management practice emerged primarily in two stages. The earliest technical advances, such as the program evaluation and review technique (PERT), critical path method and electronic computing came from military weapons development (e.g., Manhattan atomic bomb project and Polaris submarine–launched ballistic missiles). Subsequent management advances, such as work processes, team activity, performance metrics, and desktop microprocessing emerged later from academia and consulting. Cleland and Ireland provide an overview that traces development of project management.[89] In addition, Rhoades describes the most remarkable and readable examination of a process in *The Making of the Atomic Bomb*.[90]

Application in Healthcare

Like leaders in other sectors, health services executives have found that project management is an effective way to take advantage of training investment and engage staff to implement major organizational change. Equally important, project management is an effective way of responding to competitive threats and emerging opportunities.

Project Organization and Initiation

Preparation of documents that describe a potential project's scope and a preliminary work plan along with their review and approval by senior management are the major activities in this important initial planning stage. It is unlikely, however, that these documents will be produced and acted upon unless a senior management–directed decision-making process is in place and support staff is assigned to develop the necessary foundational material.

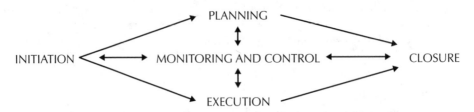

Figure 14.7. Project management process, Deming Plan-Do-Check-Act model. (Adapted from *A Guide to the Project Management Body of Knowledge* (PMBOK Guide), 5th ed. Newtown Square, PA: PMI Publications, 2013, p. 50.)

Senior Management Role

At the outset, senior management's role includes the following tasks:

- Ensure that a program improvement analysis has been done and it supports the project's rationale and general approach.[91]

- Examine the project's alignment with organizational strategies, goals, and capabilities.

- Identify possible conflicts with previously approved projects.

- Prioritize the organization's overall project portfolio.

- Secure and evaluate feedback from key stakeholders.

- Appreciate the magnitude of subsequent time, financial, and staffing commitments.

- Recognize the likelihood of risk and the need for both schedule and budget contingencies.

This review and approval role is often assigned to an ongoing, core oversight/steering group made up of senior managers. For approved projects, this group serves as a change control board to review and act on proposed changes to the approved scope, schedule, and resource allocations. It is also important for a member of this steering group to serve as a sponsor or champion for each potential project. In the sponsor role, this senior manager provides guidance to staff preparing the scope and preliminary work plan, assists in critical communication tasks, and provides a recommended course of action to the steering group. For an approved project the sponsor selects the project manager and ensures adherence to the project's approved scope and work plan.

Support and Functional Staff Roles

The need to comply with a growing number of external performance requirements and the increasing reliance on producing project-induced organizational change have led organizations to develop a well-trained, highly specialized outcome management staff. These staff entities are spread throughout the organization and are made up of specialized, well-trained, tenured members of the organization's medical, clinical, and administrative staff. They reside in departments such as quality and process improvement, infection control, care management, revenue cycle management, and clinical informatics. They can provide technical and analytical advice to help managers prepare documentation for senior management review and approval. The outcome management staff is invaluable in preparing templates to guide future project development and, when a project is approved, for providing advice to project leaders and members.

Initiating the Process

Potential project topics can emerge from the organization's formal strategic planning process, or, increasingly, from a quality improvement team or a department or service line manager. The project decision-making process relies on two documents: the project scope, which provides a detailed definition of the desired product, process, or outcome, and the preliminary work statement, which addresses how the project scope will be achieved.

The project scope establishes the basic business case for the project. It details potential goals and objectives, key assumptions and constraints, major deliverables, project boundaries, and performance expectations with associated metrics. The scope also identifies key stakeholders, anticipated organizational change effects, alignment with ongoing projects, and potential conflicts.

The preliminary work statement outlines how the project scope will be implemented. Previously developed templates for various projects are particularly helpful to identify appropriate procedures for each of the five stages in the project life cycle. Top-down estimating techniques that draw on prior projects and accepted standards make it possible to provide preliminary information on specific tasks and their duration and staged resource requirements.

If the project is approved, attention shifts to developing and obtaining the sponsor's approval of a project manager position description. This is followed by recruitment, interviews, and the sponsor's project manager selection. The sponsor and project manager then interview and select members of the project team.

Project Manager

The attributes for a successful project manager include organizational tenure, established evidence of leadership skills, and the recognition and respect of members throughout the organization. The importance of these attributes explains why selection of an outside consultant for routine project work is often a poor choice. It is also helpful if the individual can identify and attract talented staff from within the organization and build an effective team. Other key attributes include dependability and a calm and confident demeanor.

Project Team Members

Success in executing the project rests largely on the work of a multidisciplinary team whose members have the requisite knowledge, interest, and commitment to the project. At the outset, team members rarely have all the necessary attributes, but with time and on-the-job training they can become proficient. Including department managers in the initial development of the project scope helps secure a commitment to free up their staff members to serve on project teams.

It is a challenge to select an effective project manager and assemble a productive team in today's busy hospital operational environment. In recruiting talent, it is useful to emphasize that involvement in projects enables members to come into contact with organizational strategy, systems, processes, and infrastructure, as well as with a cross section of staff throughout the organization. In recruiting project managers, it is important to emphasize that the role offers a distinct opportunity to develop and employ a wide range of skills, behaviors, attitudes, and credentials that are highly regarded. The Project Management Institute offers globally recognized, multilevel practitioner certification that is valuable early in the career of a healthcare executive.

Specific Construction Applications

Projects that require limited renovation can often be supported by a department's operating budget and by the HSO's facility department. Projects that entail more extensive renovation, expansion, or facility replacement require comprehensive foundational documents and several important early decisions. Examples of these decisions include determining the extent of construction needed to support the proposed program and whether to use newer project delivery methods, such as integrated project delivery (IPD), rather than traditional individual participant contracts and a bid-based approach. IPD is based on ideas developed by the Toyota Production System; it uses a collaborative approach that operates with a joint contractual agreement among the design and construction participants and the owner.[92] Another decision is whether the owner should hire an independent commissioning engineer. The practice of commissioning was initiated by the U.S. Navy to test the actual design and capability of new vessels. In HSO construction the commissioning engineer determines that the facility can do what it is intended to do. A hospital construction agent oversees the design and operation of infrastructure systems to ensure that multiple components and systems are designed properly and the facility is operating efficiently and as intended.[93] These decisions are made more easily in organizations with a strong planning emphasis. Such HSOs have a current master facility plan, appropriate land acquisition policy, full compliance with The Joint Commission's environment of care standards, and advanced process improvement and change management capability.

Expansion or replacement projects also require early discussions with community members and local and state government officials. A properly prepared project scope and work statement are necessary for the multiple reviews and to secure approval from the organization's GB (and HS) and the state certificate of need agency, if applicable. They are also necessary to receive zoning approval from local authorities. Project scope and work documents and their use by design and construction team members allow for examining basic project assumptions and initial schedule and budget estimates. This is also the point at which additional decisions must be made. One decision is whether to use the evidence-based patient and environment-centered design concepts developed by groups such as the Center for Health Design, Texas A&M's Center for Health Systems & Design, and the Planetree Alliance.[94] Another decision is linked to sustainability. Leadership in Energy & Environmental Design (LEED) developed by the U.S. Green Building Council sets the global standard for building sustainability. It operates at increasingly demanding levels—certified, silver, gold, and platinum—in which up to 100 points are awarded based on owner submissions as to five major categories (sustainable sites, water efficiency, energy and atmosphere, building material and resources, and indoor environmental quality).

If major construction is envisioned, it is helpful to begin preparation for the following:

- Recruiting a clinical construction coordinator from nursing to coordinate the design, construction, and equipment selection activity with clinical staff

- Securing involvement of supply chain or procurement, information technology or information systems, and facility and security managers

- Engaging equipment, transition, food service, and other specialty consultants

- Identifying appropriate technical staff from key infrastructure and equipment vendors

Project Planning

To this point in the project development process, attention has focused on the opportunity, initial actions to be taken, and those who will be involved. Important deliverables, such as a detailed project scope and initial estimates of project time (schedule), cost (budget), and resources required, have been produced, evaluated, and approved. A project manager and a multidisciplinary team are in place and have begun to experience the challenges and satisfaction of group leadership and work. The project approval process that has involved senior managers as well as key stakeholders provides the basis for subsequent communication and project control in later project segments.

Currently, pressure to begin project execution with a launch meeting is understandable but premature. To prepare for the critical design, execution, and monitoring activities that follow, it is necessary to extend the planning segment and revisit and refine key components of the project scope. As Deming noted, failure to effectively complete the planning stage (0th Stage) invariably leads to subsequent changes that disrupt and delay the work schedule and result in greatly increased expense.[95]

This advanced planning effort should begin with senior managers, team members, and key stakeholders reviewing and validating important elements and assumptions in the project scope with emphasis on the explicit purpose and desired outcomes of the project. Then the project team begins to delineate specific tasks to be accomplished and work products to be produced. It is also necessary to complete remaining work on the project's organization and its operating protocol and to provide additional training required by the project team members and project consultants.

The major initial team effort is development of the work breakdown structure (WBS), which is a logical, organized, and detailed project work and responsibility statement. In the WBS, individual tasks are identified and sequenced by members of the project team in collaboration with stakeholders. Individual tasks are assigned durations and resource requirements and are grouped into small work packages and aggregated into major work elements. Developing the larger grouping of work elements makes it possible to focus on the progress of each major work element rather than on individual tasks.

In addition to detailing required tasks and durations, the WBS reflects important issues relating to task sequences and interdependencies. It establishes the basis for estimating and illustrating the project schedule that is created using tools such as Gantt charting or, in more complex projects, network or critical path scheduling. Figure 14.8 shows the elements of a clinical WBS and a Gantt chart depicting the schedule for completing the work.

Figure 14.9 highlights a milestone schedule of major work elements in a construction project using a Gantt chart. Figure 14.10 shows a network schedule showing interdependencies in the rough-in portion of a construction project. An excellent description of the overall estimation process and network scheduling was developed by Gould in *Managing the Construction Process.*[96]

Likewise, the WBS and its schedule permit accurate delineation of key staffing, resource, and logistical requirements, which encompass labor, material, space, license and other fees, training, and travel. Careful analysis of work packages by the project team will identify potential problem areas and determine how workflow and staffing adjustment can be used to overcome disruptions in schedule or budget. This information permits development of a time-phased, bottom-up project budget and establishes the basis for an accurate financial draw schedule. The draw schedule is a document that enables the chief financial officer to anticipate the timing and amount of funds required. Figure 14.11 shows the budget for a proposed medical office building. It uses the major work elements or construction divisions to depict the cost of building a 75,000-square-foot structure over 10 months. Careful delineation of tasks and resources needed enables more accurate bottom-up assessments compared to the more general estimates produced earlier.

Construction Application

Hospital construction entails unique challenges and risks that must be anticipated and addressed in the planning stage. Recognizing and mitigating risks to patients, staff, and visitors are covered in The Joint Commission's environment of care standard, which requires assessing air quality, infection control, noise and vibration, work area access, and utility operation.[97] As construction proceeds, the hospital must continually review the assessment and document actions that mitigate risk. Likewise, situations such as excavation, material shortages or price escalation, and temporary relocation of patients or parking require ongoing assessment with appropriate adjustments of both schedule and budget.

Major construction introduces a greater level of complexity and makes it more difficult to secure necessary internal and external approvals and government permits quickly. It also adds significant numbers of people to the initial project team and creates increased coordination and communication challenges for the project manager.

From the hospital perspective, it makes little sense to design around inadequate processes, existing facility limitations, and inefficient locations of clinical or support departments. Thus, before beginning space programming, thought must be given to certain factors, including desired changes in the flow of patients and visitors, the most effective way to deliver various types of care efficiently, and modifications needed so key processes can provide safe care. All improvements to patient flow, for example, should be completed prior to starting space programming and design for any renovation.

Activity/Task	Responsibility	Due Date	Status
A. Define Phase			
1) Write the problem statement		31-Dec	Complete
2) Identify project statement		31-Dec	Complete
3) Write the objective statement		31-Dec	Complete
4) Determine high-level financial forecast		31-Dec	Complete
5) Choose team members		31-Dec	Complete
6) Develop macro map		31-Dec	Complete
7) Champion meeting			
B. Measure Phase			
1) Conduct team kick-off meeting		15-Nov	Complete
2) Submit preliminary data request		30-Nov	Complete
3) Receive data from preliminary data request		30-Nov	Complete
4) Review/analyze preliminary data		30-Nov	Complete
5) Conduct measurement systems analysis			n/a
6) Conduct initial capability analysis		05-Dec	Complete
7) Develop "as-is" process flow diagram		05-Dec	Complete
8) Identify trends, barriers, bottlenecks		19-Dec	In-progress
9) Collect additional measurements as identified		26-Dec	In-progress
10) Develop detailed financial forecast		16-Jan	
11) Validate financial forecast		23-Jan	
12) Team meeting			
C. Analyze Phase			
1) Graphical techniques		31-Dec	Complete
2) Statistical analysis		31-Dec	Complete
3) Team meetings			
D. Improve Phase			
1) Finalize list of root causes		30-Jan	
2) Define recommendations		13-Feb	
3) Implement/evaluate (DOE, Pilot)		27-Feb	
4) Team meetings			
E. Control Phase			
1) Initiate control plans		13-Mar	
2) Develop metric measurement plan		13-Mar	
3) Transition to process owner		20-Mar	
4) Complete final report		27-Mar	
5) Team meetings			

Timing (week of): 11/3/08, 11/10/08, 11/17/08, 11/24/08, 12/1/08, 12/8/08, 12/15/08, 12/22/08, 12/29/08, 1/5/09, 1/12/09, 1/19/09, 1/26/09, 2/2/09, 2/9/09, 2/16/09, 2/23/09, 3/2/09, 3/9/09, 3/16/09, 3/23/09

Figure 14.8. Work breakdown structure with Gantt chart. (From Neal McKelvey. Used with permission.)

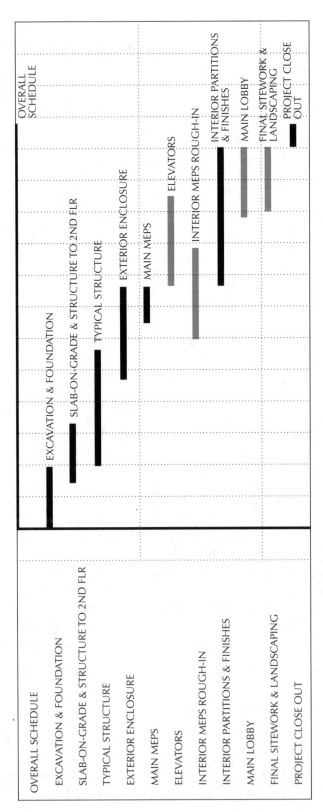

Figure 14.9. Milestone schedule for major construction elements. (From Neal McKelvey. Used with permission.)

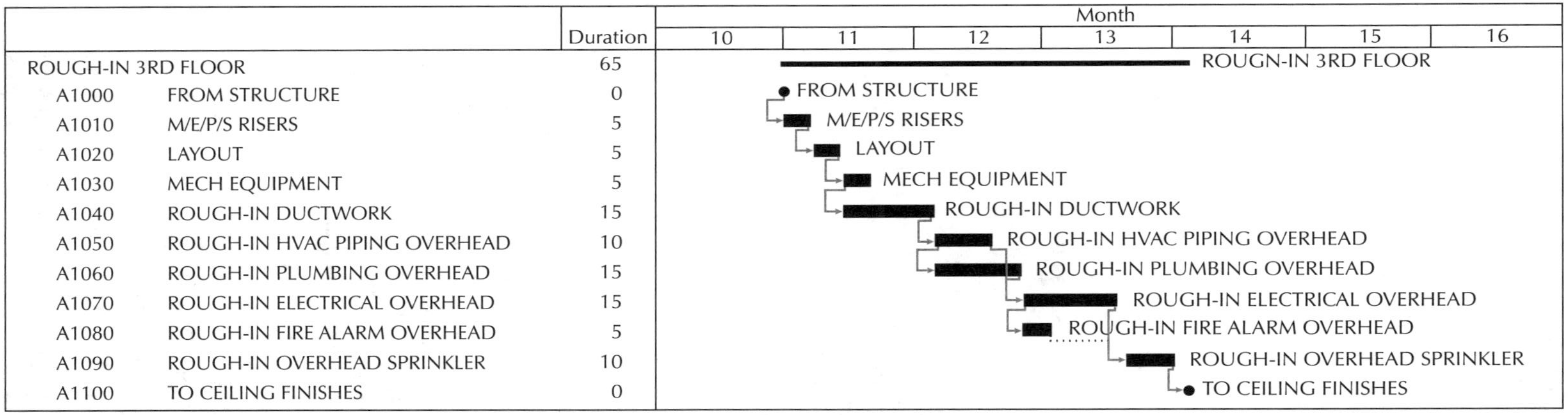
Duration
Month
10
11
12
13
14
15
16
ROUGH-IN 3RD FLOOR 65
A1000 FROM STRUCTURE 0
A1010 M/E/P/S RISERS 5
A1020 LAYOUT 5
A1030 MECH EQUIPMENT 5
A1040 ROUGH-IN DUCTWORK 15
A1050 ROUGH-IN HVAC PIPING OVERHEAD 10
A1060 ROUGH-IN PLUMBING OVERHEAD 15
A1070 ROUGH-IN ELECTRICAL OVERHEAD 15
A1080 ROUGH-IN FIRE ALARM OVERHEAD 5
A1090 ROUGH-IN OVERHEAD SPRINKLER 10
A1100 TO CEILING FINISHES 0
ROUGN-IN 3RD FLOOR
FROM STRUCTURE
M/E/P/S RISERS
LAYOUT
MECH EQUIPMENT
ROUGH-IN DUCTWORK
ROUGH-IN HVAC PIPING OVERHEAD
ROUGH-IN PLUMBING OVERHEAD
ROUGH-IN ELECTRICAL OVERHEAD
ROUGH-IN FIRE ALARM OVERHEAD
ROUGH-IN OVERHEAD SPRINKLER
TO CEILING FINISHES

Figure 14.10. Network schedule for interior rough-in activities. (From Neal McKelvey. Used with permission.)

Cost Model

PROJECT:	Medical Office Building		DPR JOB NO:	TBD
LOCATION:	▮▮▮▮▮▮		ESTIMATE NO:	TBD
CLIENT:	Confidential		DATE:	
ARCHITECT:	TBD		ESTIMATOR:	▮▮▮▮▮▮

TOTAL GROSS AREA	75,000 SF
DURATION	10 MO
BUILDING TYPE	Ground Up-MOB

SYSTEMS NUMBER	DESCRIPTION	TOTAL	COST/SF
1	Div 2 Sitework	995,250	13.27
2	Div 3 Concrete	609,750	8.13
3	Div 4 Masonry	792,750	10.57
4	Div 5 Metals	1,379,220	18.39
5	Div 6 Wood	175,485	2.34
6	Div 7 Thermal and Moisture Protection	627.000	8.36
7	Div 8 Openings	979,590	13.06
8	Div 9 Interiors	640,855	8.54
9	Div 10 Specialties	29,700	0.40
10	Division 12 Special Construction	145,500	1.94
11	Division 14 Conveying	160,000	2.13
12	Division 15 Mechanical	1,870,500	24.94
13	Division 16 Electrical	900,000	12.00
15	JOBSITE MANAGEMENT	431,420	5.75
16	PROJECT REQUIREMENTS	79,480	1.06
	SUBTOTAL	$ 9,816,500	$130.89
	Construction Contingency	294,495	3.93
	Subcontractor Default Insurance/Subguard	117,798	1.57
	Contractors Insurance	115,216	1.54
	Fee	245,413	3.27
	PROJECTED CONSTRUCTION COSTS	$10,589,422	$141.19

Figure 14.11. Detailed proposed project budget for medical office building. (From John Anania, DPR Construction. Used with permission.)

Given the likelihood that significant changes will continue to occur and pressure to conserve resources will increase, it is reasonable to anticipate the most important of the expected changes and to provide for the most flexible and sustainable facility and engineering design that can be supported financially.

Design is an iterative process reflecting increased levels of detail:

- Program and space design

- Conceptual design

- Schematic design—30% of drawings complete

- Design development—60% of drawings complete

- Construction-level documents (CDs) including technical specifications and general conditions

Figure 14.12 shows the work performed in each of the five project development steps and illustrates at each step the progression of work to include imaging capability within an emergency department (ED).

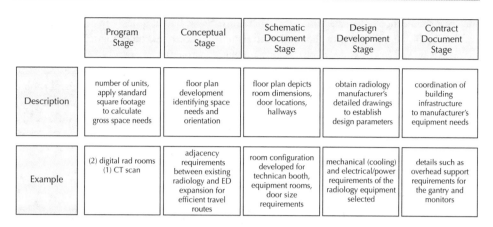

Program Stage	Conceptual Stage	Schematic Document Stage	Design Development Stage	Contract Document Stage
Description number of units, apply standard square footage to calculate gross space needs	floor plan development identifying space needs and orientation	floor plan depicts room dimensions, door locations, hallways	obtain radiology manufacturer's detailed drawings to establish design parameters	coordination of building infrastructure to manufacturer's equipment needs
Example (2) digital rad rooms (1) CT scan	adjacency requirements between existing radiology and ED expansion for efficient travel routes	room configuration developed for technican booth, equipment rooms, door size requirements	mechanical (cooling) and electrical/power requirements of the radiology equipment selected	details such as overhead support requirements for the gantry and monitors

Figure 14.12. Design stages for radiology installation in ED. (From John Anania, DPR Construction. Used with permission.)

The CDs are circulated to the building trades. In the traditional project delivery approach, these provide the basis for selecting and contracting after interviews and a review of proposed schedules and costs identify the preferred organizations. CDs are the foundation for a set of documents used to secure building permits and, subsequently, to guide field inspections and award final building occupancy permits.

Increasingly, preparation of project documents is aided by use of multidimensional design and documentation software (i.e., building information modeling [BIM]) to digitally represent the physical and functional features of a new structure. In addition to supporting the IPD method discussed previously, BIM is a platform that enhances a construction project's overall life cycle (i.e., plan, design, construct, and operate). It enables fully informed design coordination of architects as well as structural, site, and building infrastructure engineers. For the construction team, BIM encourages technical collaboration and makes schedule, labor, and material estimates more accurate. It enables important logistical decisions by mechanical and millwork contractors to prefabricate and preassemble systems offsite, which eliminates the need for onsite space and allows faster installation. In addition to providing the owner with fully documented and accessible as-built design documents, BIM permits facility staff to more quickly troubleshoot and correct the inevitable operating problems (e.g., water leaks).

Project Executive and Control

Projects are developed to address the distinct business need expressed in the project scope. This is accomplished by developing and introducing change in the form of a new or revised process, service, product, or facility modification. At this point in development of the project, successful achievement of project objectives relies on both effective execution and carefully monitoring progress.

The execution stage, which almost always consumes the largest portion of a project's schedule, draws on all previous planning to efficiently accomplish individual tasks and work packages that show the work breakdown. Success involves multiple factors, but it is primarily a reflection of thorough planning, effective leadership, team member cohesion and hard work, timely training, and a comprehensive work program. It requires competent communication with senior managers and key stakeholders coupled with regular, carefully structured, and highly participative status meetings with all the members of the project team.

Assessing progress is a continuous effort and compares implementation with critical scope, schedule, budget, and resource targets. It requires effective action in responding to inevitable variances that emerge during execution. Change requests in the form of project revisions and change orders are always made during project work. Senior managers try to ban these requests, but they should not be rejected outright. They must be evaluated quickly by the change control board. Some will improve the result and should be accepted, incorporated into the task list, and reflected in schedule, resource, and budget adjustments.

Risks arise during the course of any project. Some result from the project's size and complexity, shifts in the business environment, or negative effects on existing practice and should be anticipated during the planning stage. Others, such as departure of the project manager or key senior managers and problems with team member performance or availability, need a rapid response.

Recent Developments in Project Management

The following developments[98] are changing project management:

- Artificial intelligence—Complex projects will benefit from AI prioritizing projects, allocating resources, and producing real-time schedules.

- Soft skills—Opposite of AI, and perhaps because of it, soft skills such as emotional intelligence and coordinating, communicating, and teaching are increasingly ranked highly by employers. Social skills ranked second only to problem-solving skills desired by employers in the future.[99]

- Method melding—Project methodologies like Lean (streamlining and eliminating waste to increase value) or Waterfall (planning projects fully, then executing in phases) or even Agile (collaborating constantly to deliver whatever works) are morphing into hybrids.

- Global, gig economy—Project team members can be in remote locations and may be involved in several different projects simultaneously.

- Competition—Increasing competition from traditional noncompetitors like the retail industry are causing specialization in project management.

- Customer (patient)-centered—In response to project methodologies like Lean and Agile, which tend to emphasize efficiency over people, a refocus on the customer is often necessary.

- Data—Data-driven decisions (evidence-based medicine, for example) demand that data become an important part of any project.

- Team diversity—Project teams will become increasingly diverse in traditional ways, such as age, but also in more subtle ways, such as employment status (part-time, contract, remote).

Conclusion

Project work is an increasingly important mechanism for examining operational and performance issues and introducing group-directed change into contemporary HSOs. A major challenge for senior managers is balancing demands of projects with ongoing work and performance requirements of daily operations. Leadership must evaluate each project's workload, potential for success, and likely level of contribution to organizational success before undertaking it. Experts who have evaluated results of the project management process have developed several factors associated with success:[100]

- Alignment with important organizational goals and strategies and elimination of overlapping projects

- Securing and retaining senior management involvement, support, and resources

- Nurturing continuing stakeholder involvement and support with ongoing communication of project status coupled with agreement on project results

- A thorough planning process that includes the project purpose, approach, and deliverables, as well as reliable estimates of effort, time, staffing resources, and budget. (These project attributes are achieved best if tested project templates are developed and used.)

- Recruitment and selection of an effective project manager and selecting a project team with clear roles and responsibilities

- Routine formal and informal assessments by the project sponsor of the project manager's performance, as well as direct observation of team member participation, morale, and performance

- Selection of external project team members through a competitive, participative process that emphasizes topic familiarity and full-team capability (e.g., the combined talents of the aggregate of team members)

- Regular assessment of project progress and accomplishments against baseline expectations. Communication of results in briefings with GB and key stakeholders, including members of the PSO, foundation, and community. Procedures to review proposed changes to project scope and result parameters that are available and rapidly employed. Necessary changes, which are reflected as revisions to project work plans, schedules, and budgets.

- Recognition of and solutions for disruptive effects that project implementation often has on staff and existing processes

Discussion Questions

1. Define *control*. What are the major elements of control?

2. What are the three monitoring and two intervention points for control? Why are management information systems (MISs) important to control?

3. Review the control model in Figure 14.2 and give examples of situations for each control loop. identify similarities between the control model (Figure 14.2) and the problem-solving model in Figure 6.4?

4. How does CQI relate to control? Specifically, what control point is its focus, and how does this affect the control model (see Figure 14.2)?

5. Describe the purpose, structure, and process of RM and QI. From the perspective of control, why are both important to HSOs/HSs?

6. What are the duties of risk managers? How do they fit into the organization of HSOs? HSs?

7. Discuss the concept of insurance. What is the role of insurance in HSO/HS management? How does insurance fit into an RM program?

8. Explain the media's role during a disaster and how coordinating information between the evacuating organization and the media can improve communications to the public.

9. Describe the differences between a planned, voluntary hospital evacuation—such as the move to a new facility—and an emergency evacuation. Which actions within the plan, prepare, respond, and recover cycle are effective during either situation?

10. Discuss the role of the chief compliance officer in an HSO or HS.

11. What factors explain the increase in use of project management in healthcare? What are the challenges to continued growth?

12. What unique features are involved in applying project management to healthcare construction?

13. Why is hands-on experience in project management important for early-career managers? Why is the project management credential valuable?

14. What key factors contribute to a successful project?

Case Study 1   Centralized Printers

Carey Snook saw Ted Rath drinking coffee in the cafeteria. "I thought you guys in management services were up to your eyeballs in productivity improvement projects," Snook said as he walked over to sit down with Rath.

"We are," Rath said. "In fact, we have so much work and so many project deadlines coming up that we've had to work Saturdays." Snook responded, "Then how come you're goofing off by wasting time and drinking coffee?" "I'm not wasting time," said Rath. "I'm waiting." "For what?" asked Snook. "For some layout prints to be printed. We're in the middle of a systems analysis project. We're redesigning the outpatient department layout and work process flow. I can't continue with the project until I get the template layout drawings printed in central printing. Our secretary took them over there 20 minutes ago, and they won't be ready for another 20 minutes. So, I'm waiting. This happens about three times a week to each of the three of us in my department."

Rath continued, "We used to have a printer in our department. Well, some people were caught printing personal documents. This probably cost the hospital about $10 a week, so they centralized all printing equipment to save money on use and have fewer machines. Now we have to walk our materials way over there to the central building and wait until it's our turn to have them printed.

"I guess the biggest gripe I have is with Smith, head of centralized printing. Sometimes it takes 10 minutes to convince Smith that a printing job is hospital business and is important. Smith really seems to like the authority. Anyway, take this isometric drawing I have here; I bet Smith will think it's my 6-year-old daughter's homework assignment. I wonder how long it will take me to convince Smith it is job related."

"Want some more coffee?" asked Snook.

Questions

1. What is the focus of control in this situation?

2. What dysfunctional results have occurred from centralizing printing?

Case Study 2   Healthcare Emergency Preparedness[101]

In addition to being ill, hospital patients are frail, in pain, and bed bound. Thus, hospital evacuations are a last resort and occur only when the physical plant and its support systems fail or are likely to do so. The difficulties of moving hospitalized patients make it impossible to practice an evacuation.

An exercise was conducted in southwestern Pennsylvania to simulate evacuation of a hospital because of structural damage sustained during a natural disaster. In addition to an ED and adult intensive care unit, the hospital has one of the largest neonatal intensive care units (NICUs) in the eastern United States and a large labor and delivery program. The exercise required the simulated evacuation of 309 patients requiring various levels of care. The exercise scenario involved a powerful micro-burst windstorm that struck near the hospital. The storm propelled an SUV through the five-story glass atrium of the building and into load-bearing support columns. The damage made the facility unsafe for continued use. Hospital ED staff began treating the injured and communicated the need for additional assistance to local command officials.

The hospital implemented its emergency operations plan and activated the Incident Command System to assess building damage, continue provision of care, and evaluate next steps. In consultation with the local Emergency Management Authorities the decision was made to evacuate the facility.

The municipal emergency operations center (MEOC) was activated, and key command positions were assigned. Movement of patients from the stricken hospital to other healthcare facilities was coordinated by health and medical services (emergency support function 8) located in the MEOC.[102]

Several issues were identified:

- Some hospitals that were to receive healthy mothers and babies lacked the appropriate staff (nurses, obstetricians, and pediatricians) and supplies (diapers and formula) to care for infants.

- Local hospitals that were expected to provide neonatology services did not have enough staff or beds to "surge" their NICUs. These hospitals requested that the evacuating hospital send its clinicians, beds, pharmaceuticals, and supplies with the infants.

- Due to the limited number of NICU beds in the region, 38 infants would have to be transported to hospitals in neighboring regions and states.

Questions

1. What types of preparedness activities would be needed to successfully evacuate a hospital?

2. How is the decision to evacuate a hospital made?

3. What internal and external communications are essential during a hospital evacuation?

Case Study 3   Placing Imaging Services to Support ED Operations[103]

Hospital EDs are the primary entry point for unscheduled hospital admissions. EDs are the best place to get complex, time-efficient, diagnostic workups, and decisions from skilled generalist physicians. Because they are vital for inpatients and outpatients, c linical support services such as medical imaging are typically provided in locations away from the ED.

After a careful examination of ED operations, Hospital "A" determined that almost 40% of surgical admissions and 86% of medical admissions came through its ED. Imaging studies are performed on 30%–40% of the 300 patients seen in the ED each day. As part of their diagnostic workups, many ED patients receive two imaging studies while being seen in the ED. The process improvement study revealed that factors such as transportation delays (imaging is one floor above the ED and must use hospital-wide transportation services) and competition for access to key imaging equipment resulted in significant ED delays. The study showed patient and staff dissatisfaction, poor collaboration between ED and imaging staff, and unacceptable turnaround times for imaging studies. A decision to expand the ED was made several months ago.

To maintain this important portal of access to the hospital, senior management decided to provide diagnostic, computed tomography, and ultrasonography imaging either within or adjacent to the ED.

Questions

1. You have been asked to serve on a group to recommend a location for imaging after identifying and evaluating the positives and negatives of the two locations: within ED or adjacent to ED. Prepare your analysis.

Monitoring (Control) and Intervention Points

Notes

1. Schermerhorn, Jr., John R. "9—Control Processes and Systems." *Management*, 12th ed. New York: Wiley, 2012.
2. The information in the "Monitoring (Control) and Intervention Points" section is largely from Schermerhorn, "9—Control Processes and Systems." *Management*, 12th ed. New York: Wiley, 2012.
3. Griffin, Ricky W. "14—Controlling." *Fundamentals of Management*, 8th ed. Boston: Cengage Learning, 2016. *https://shamsfoe.files.wordpress.com/2019/01/fundamentalsofmanagement8thedition rickygriffin978-1285849041.pdf*, retrieved November 17, 2019.
4. Enthoven, Alain C., and Carol B. Vorhaus. "A Vision of Quality in Health Care Delivery." *Health Affairs* 16 (May/June 1997): 48.
5. Glandon, Gerald L., Donna J. Slovensky, and Detiev H. Smaltz. *Information Systems for Healthcare Management*, 8th ed. Chicago: Health Administration Press, 2014.
6. Glandon, Slovensky, and Smaltz. *Information Systems*, 81–112.
7. Glandon, Slovensky, and Smaltz. *Information Systems*, 161–204.
8. Robin. "Expert Systems." *Artificial Intelligence*, 2010. *http://intelligence.worldofcomputing.net/ai-branches/expert-systems.html#*, retrieved November 19, 2019.
9. Zhang, Ziaoyong, Noriyasu Homma, Shotaro Goto, Ysuke Kawasumi, Tadashi Ishibashi, Makoto Abe, Norihiro Sugita, and Makoto Yoshizawa. "A Hybrid Image Filtering Method for Computer-Aided Detection of Microcalcification Clusters in Mammograms." *Journal of Medical Engineering*, 2013. *https://www.ncbi.nlm.nih.gov/pmc/articles/PMC4782620/*, retrieved December 2, 2019.
10. Mangarano, L., and M. Stark. "APACHEFoundations." 2010. *https://apachefoundations.cerner works.com/apachefoundations/resources/APACHE%20Foundations%20User%20Guide.pdf*, retrieved May 27, 2020.
11. Glandon, Slovensky, and Smaltz. *Information Systems*, 257–284.
12. Institute of Medicine. *To Err Is Human: Building a Safer Health System*. Washington, DC: The National Academies Press, 2000.
13. Centers for Disease Control and Prevention. *Public Health and Promoting Interoperability Programs* (formerly known as *Electronic Health Records Meaningful Use*). *https://www.cdc.gov/ehrmeaningfuluse/introduction.html*, retrieved November 20, 2019.
14. Glandon, Slovensky, and Smaltz, *Information Systems*, 123.
15. Glandon, G. L., D. H. Smaltz, and D. J. Slovensky. "Applications." In *Austin and Boxerman's Information Systems for Healthcare Management*, 7th ed., Chapter 8, 201–231. Chicago, IL: Health Administration Press, 2008.
16. John Morrissey. "The Quality Disconnect." *Hospitals & Health Networks* 86, 10 (October 2012): 25.
17. Blake, I. A. "Risk Manager Responsibilities in a Hospital Setting." *Houston Chronicle*. *http://work.chron.com/risk-manager-responsibilities-hospital-setting-17331.html*, retrieved May 27, 2020.
18. Kavaler, Florence, and Allen D. Spiegel. *Risk Management in Health Care Institutions: Limiting Liability and Enhancing Care*, 3rd ed. Sudbury, MA: Jones & Bartlett, 2014.
19. The Joint Commission. *Facts about Patient Safety*. *https://www.jointcommission.org/facts_about_patient_safety/*, retrieved November 22, 2019.
20. Joint Commission. *Standards FAQ Details*. *https://www.jointcommission.org/standards_information/jcfaqdetails.aspx?StandardsFAQId=1297*, retrieved on November 24, 2019.

21. American College of Healthcare Executives. *Leading a Culture of Safety: A Blueprint for Success.* *http://safety.ache.org/blueprint/,* retrieved November 22, 2019.

22. Occupational Safety and Health Act of 1970, PL 91-596, 84 Stat. 1590 (1970).

23. Productivity improvement and performance improvement are similar concepts, though not synonymous. The quality improvement literature uses *productivity improvement,* The Joint Commission uses *performance improvement.*

24. The Joint Commission. *2013 Hospital Accreditation Standards.* Oak Brook Terrace, IL: Joint Commission Resources.

25. Harpster, Linda Marie, and Margaret S. Veach, eds. *Risk Management Handbook for Health Care Facilities,* 107. Chicago: American Hospital Publishing, 1990.

26. Carroll, Roberta L., Gisele A. Norris, and Michael Zuckerman. "Basics of Enterprise Risk Management in Healthcare." In *Risk Management Handbook for Healthcare Organizations, Volume 1,* 6th ed., edited by Roberta Carroll, 1–18. San Francisco: Jossey-Bass, 2011.

27. Lynch, Krishna. "The Healthcare Risk Management Professional." In *Risk Management Handbook for Healthcare Organizations, Volume 1,* 6th ed., edited by Roberta Carroll, 125–168. San Francisco: Jossey-Bass, 2011.

28. *Black's Law Dictionary* defines *insurance* as "a contract whereby one undertakes to indemnify another against loss, damage, or liability arising from an unknown or contingent event and is applicable only to some contingency or act to occur in the future." Black, Henry Campbell. *Black's Law Dictionary,* 5th ed., 721. St. Paul, MN: West Publishing Company, 1979.

29. Mahaffey, Paul F. "Lawyers' Professional Liability Insurance." *Lawyers' Liability Review Quarterly Journal* (April 1989): 1–3.

30. Pohlman, Katherine J. "Why You Need Your Own Malpractice Insurance." *American Nurse Today,* November 10, 2015. *https://www.americannursetoday.com/need-malpractice-insurance/,* retrieved November 24, 2019.

31. Health Care Quality Improvement Act of 1986, PL 99-660, 100 Stat. 3784 (1986).

32. Hoppes, Michelle, Jeanie Taylor, and Keith Higdon. "Using Data as a Risk Management Tool." In *Risk Management Handbook for Healthcare Organizations, Volume 1,* 6th ed., edited by Roberta Carroll, 301–330. San Francisco: Jossey-Bass, 2011.

33. Kellogg, Sarah. "The Art and Power of the Apology." *Washington Lawyer* 21, 10 (June 2007): 20–26.

34. The section on Healthcare and Public Health Emergency Preparedness was written by Knox Walk. Director, Emergency Preparedness, and William M. Smith, Consultant, both of the University of Pittsburgh Medical Center.

35. Centers for Disease Control and Prevention, Office of Public Health Preparedness and Response, Public Health Emergency Preparedness (PHEP) Cooperative Agreements. *https://www.cdc.gov/cpr/readiness/phep.htm,* retrieved June 5, 2019.

36. Johnson, Steven Ross. "COVID-19 outbreak exposes weaknesses in infection prevention." *Modern Healthcare,* 50, 10 (March 9, 2020): 8.

37. California Hospital Association. "Hazards Vulnerability Analysis." *http://www.calhospitalprepare.org/hazard-vulnerability-analysis,* retrieved May 27, 2020.

38. Federal Emergency Management Agency "National Incident Management System" *https://www.fema.gov/national-incident-management-system,* retrieved June 5, 2019.

39. California Emergency Medical Services Authority. Hospital Incident Command System. *https://emsa.ca.gov/disaster-medical-services-division-hospital-incident-command-system-resources/,* retrieved June 5, 2019.

40. United States Department of Labor, Occupational Safety and Health Administration. *OSHA Penalties* as of January 10, 2020. *https://www.osha.gov/penalties,* retrieved May 27, 2020.

41. Centers for Medicare and Medicaid Services. *Emergency Preparedness Requirements for Medicare and Medicaid Participating Providers and Suppliers, 2016. https://www.cms.gov/Medicare/Provider-Enrollment-and-Certification/SurveyCertEmergPrep/Emergency-Prep-Rule* Retrieved May 27, 2020.

42. Nowicki, Michael. "Reducing Your Credentialing Liability—an Expert's View." *Synergy,* November/December 2000, 1–2.

43. The Joint Commission. *Ambulatory Care Program: The Who, What, When, and Where's of Credentialing and Privileging. https://www.jointcommission.org/assets/1/6/AHC_who_what_when_and_where_credentialing_booklet.pdf,* retrieved on December 2, 2019.

44. The section on compliance was written by Vidya R. Battu, JD, MHA, CHC, Consultant.

45. Kurland, Nancy. "The Defense Industry Initiative: Ethics, Self Regulation, and Accountability." *Journal of Business Ethics* 12 (February 1993): 137. *https://www.researchgate.net/publication/226434933_The_Defense_Industry_Initiative_Ethics_self-regulation_and_accountability,* retrieved January 2, 2020.

46. The Packard Commission was a blue-ribbon commission created by President Reagan to investigate defense contracting procurement fraud. The Packard Commission's recommendation was for defense contractors to voluntarily adopt an ethics program. Kurland. "The Defense Industry Initiative," 137.

47. Kurland, "The Defense Industry Initiative," 137–138.

48. Bartrum, Thomas E., and L. Edward Bryant, Jr. "The Brave New World of Healthcare Compliance Programs." *Annals of Health Law* 6, 1 (1997): 51–56. *https://pdfs.semanticscholar.org/c773/db44b60f5ed953d29e61793810308aa533f1.pdf*, retrieved January 2, 2020.

49. "The Department of Health and Human Services [DHHS] and the Department of Justice Health Care Fraud and Abuse Control Program [HCFAC] Annual Report for Fiscal Year 2018," 5. *https://oig.hhs.gov/publications/docs/hcfac/FY2018-hcfac.pdf*, retrieved May 27, 2020.

50. Patient Protection and Affordable Care Act §6102(b).

51. CMS. "National Health Expenditures 2018 Highlights." *https://www.cms.gov/files/document/highlights.pdf*, retrieved January 12, 2020.

52. CMS. "National Health Expenditures 2018 Highlights."

53. DHHS and HCFAC Annual Report, 7.

54. NHCAA. *The Challenge of Health Care Fraud. https://www.nhcaa.org/resources/health-care-anti-fraud-resources/the-challenge-of-health-care-fraud.aspx*, retrieved January 12, 2020.

55. NHCAA. *The Challenge of Health Care Fraud.*

56. HHS. *OIG Supplemental Compliance Guidance for Hospitals.* 70 FR 4858 (pp. 4874-4876). *https://www.govinfo.gov/content/pkg/FR-2005-01-31/pdf/05-1620.pdf*, retrieved December 29, 2019.

57. 45 CFR, Part 164.

58. 31 U.S.C. §§3729-3733.

59. 42 U.S.C. §§1320(a)-7b.

60. 42 U.S.C. §§1395nn.

61. 42 U.S.C §§1395dd.

62. 45 C.F.R. Subpart E.

63. 45 C.F.R. Part 160, and Subparts A and C of Part 164.

64. *United States v. Huping Zhou,* 678 F.3d 1110 (9th Cir. 2012) at 1113.

65. HIPAA § 1320d-6.

66. 678 F.3d 1110 (9th Cir. 2012) at 1113.

67. 31 U.S.C. §§ 3729–3733.

68. *United States of America, et al. v. BlueWave Healthcare Consultants, Inc., et al.* (9:14-cv-00230-RMG).

69. *United States of America, et al. v. BlueWave Healthcare Consultants, Inc., et al.*

70. See generally 31 U.S.C. §§ 3729–3733.

71. 42 C.F.R. § 1001.952.

72. DOJ press release number 17-126, *https://www.justice.gov/usao-ri/pr/ri-doctor-admits-healthcare-fraud-accepting-kickbacks-prescribing-highly-addictive*, retrieved May 27, 2020.

73. DOJ press release number 17-126.

74. DOJ press release number 19-11. *https://www.justice.gov/usao-cdca/pr/opioid-manufacturer-insys-therapeutics-agrees-enter-225-million-global-resolution*, retrieved January 25, 2020.

75. See 42 U.S.C. § 1395nn.

76. CMS maintains an annually updated list of CPT and HCPCS codes that are considered DHS services at *https://www.cms.gov/Medicare/Fraud-and- Abuse/PhysicianSelfReferral/List_of_Codes.*

77. See 42 C.F.R. §411.357.

78. DOJ press release number 16-057.

79. DOJ press release number 16-057.

80. 42 U.S.C. § 1395dd.

81. See 42 U.S.C § 135dd.

82. *Georgia Hospital Settles Case Involving Patient Dumping Allegation.* U.S. Department of Health and Human Services Office of Inspector General Civil Monetary Penalties and Affirmative Exclusions Fraud Alert. November 22, 2019. *https://oig.hhs.gov/fraud/enforcement/cmp/cmp-ae.asp*, retrieved January 14, 2020.

83. *Georgia Hospital Settles Case Involving Patient Dumping Allegation.*

84. 42 U.S.C. 17951 § 13421.

85. This section was written by Neal McKelvey, M.Sc., MA-HCA, a retired senior hospital executive, who led several large teams on hospital replacement and expansion projects. Mr. McKelvey lectured at The George Washington University.

86. Project Management Institute. *A Guide to the Project Management Body of Knowledge (PMBOK Guide)*, 5th ed. Newtown Square, PA: PMI Publications, 2013, 3.

87. Richardson, Gary L. *Project Management Theory and Practice,* 272, 273. Boca Raton, FL: Auerbach Publications (Taylor and Francis Group), 2010.

88. Figure 14.7 is adapted from *PMBOK Guide,* 50.

89. Cleland, David, and Lewis Ireland. *Project Management: Strategic Design and Implementation,* 5th ed., 3–20. New York, NY: McGraw-Hill, 2007.

90. Rhodes, Richard. *The Making of the Atomic Bomb.* New York: Simon and Schuster, 1986.

91. To be considered, the program analysis should examine the following: 1) the problem/opportunity has been clearly identified and its magnitude quantified, 2) the current process has been detailed in a flow chart and subjected to root cause analysis, and 3) alternative solutions have been identified.

92. Kemper, John E. *Launching a Capital Facility Project: A Guide for Healthcare Leaders.* 2nd ed. Chicago: Health Administration Press, 2010. An article describing experience with the use of IPD in the new Temecula (CA) Valley Hospital appears in Robeznicks, Andis. "Built-In Efficiencies." *Modern Healthcare* (May 21, 2012): 32, 33.

93. This information was gathered through a phone conversation with and written documentation from James T. Morrissey, director for Commissioning Agents, Inc., Indianapolis, IN.

94. An interesting article can be found in Sadler, Blair, L., Leonard L. Berry, et al., "Fable Hospital 2.0: The Business Case for Building Better Healthcare Facilities." *Hastings Center Report* (January–February 2011): 13–23. A basic text in the field is Cama, R. *Evidence Based Healthcare Design.* Hoboken, NJ: John Wiley and Sons, 2009.

95. Deming, W. Edwards. *The New Economics for Industry, Government, Education,* 2nd ed., 136–139. Cambridge, MA: MIT-CAES, 1994.

96. Gould, Frederick. *Managing the Construction Process: Estimating, Scheduling and Project Control.* 4th ed., 55–150, 162–196. Upper Saddle River, NJ: Prentice-Hall, 2012.

97. The Joint Commission. "Environment of Care." *Evidence-Based Care Sheet—2018. http:// eds.a.ebscohost.com/eds/pdfviewer/pdfviewer?vid=1&sid=8f3149ba-9763-419e-8d71-5d2c64962 cee%40sessionmgr4006,* retrieved November 24, 2019.

98. Aston, Ben. "Prepare for These 7 Project Management Trends Transforming the PM Role." *Digital Project Manager,* 2019. *https://www.thedigitalprojectmanager.com/project-management-trends-2019/,* retrieved December 9, 2019; Brownlee, Dana. "4 Project Management Trends on the Horizon . . . Are You Ready?" *Forbes.* 2019. *https://www.forbes.com/sites/danabrownlee/2019/07/21/4-project -management-trends-on-the-horizonare-you-ready/#8657b3d67692,* retrieved December 9, 2019.

99. World Economic Forum. *The Future of Jobs Report 2018.* Geneva: Author. *http://www3.weforum .org/docs/WEF_Future_of_Jobs_2018.pdf,* retrieved December 9, 2019.

100. The success factors list is drawn from multiple sources, including Horine, Gregory M. *Absolute Beginner's Guide to Project Management,* 32, 33. Indianapolis, IN: Que Publishing, 2005; Richardson, Gary L. *Project Management Theory,* 331; and Cleland, David I., and Lewis R. Ireland, *Project Management,* 334–336; as well as personal experience and discussions with multiple project management practitioners.

101. Written by William M. Smith, Senior Director, Emergency Preparedness, and Kathleen Criss, CBCP, Director, Preparedness Operations, both of the University of Pittsburgh Medical Center. Used with permission.

102. The federal National Response Framework (NRF) contains the guiding principles that enable all response partners to prepare for and provide a unified national response to disasters and emergencies from the smallest incident to the largest catastrophe. As part of the NRF, emergency support functions (ESFs) are primary mechanisms at the operational level to organize and assist. Of the 15 ESFs, health and medical services are designated number 8.

103. Written by Neal McKelvey, M.Sc., MA-HCA, a retired senior hospital executive. Used with permission.

Index

Page numbers followed by "f" and "t" indicate figures and tables.